Proceed

MW01273393

Fourth IEEE International Conference on Data Mining

ICDM 2004

Proceedings

Fourth IEEE International Conference on Data Mining

ICDM 2004

1-4 November 2004 • Brighton, United Kingdom

Editors
Rajeev Rastogi, *Bell Laboratories, Lucent, USA*
Katharina Morik, *University of Dortmund, Germany*
Max Bramer, *University of Portsmouth, UK*
Xindong Wu, *University of Vermont, USA*

Sponsored by
IEEE Computer Society Technical Committee on Computational Intelligence (TCCI)
IEEE Computer Society Technical Committee on Pattern Analysis and Machine Intelligence (TCPAMI)

Los Alamitos, California

Washington   •   Brussels   •   Tokyo

IEEE Computer Society Order Number P2142
ISBN 0-7695-2142-8
Library of Congress Number 2004103507

Additional copies may be ordered from:

IEEE Computer Society	IEEE Service Center	IEEE Computer Society
Customer Service Center	445 Hoes Lane	Asia/Pacific Office
10662 Los Vaqueros Circle	P.O. Box 1331	Watanabe Bldg., 1-4-2
P.O. Box 3014	Piscataway, NJ 08855-1331	Minami-Aoyama
Los Alamitos, CA 90720-1314	Tel: + 1-732-981-0060	Minato-ku, Tokyo 107-0062
Tel: + 1-714-821-8380	Fax: + 1-732-981-9667	JAPAN
Fax: + 1-714-821-4641	http://shop.ieee.org/store/	Tel: + 81-3-3408-3118
E-mail: cs.books@computer.org	customer-service@ieee.org	Fax: + 81-3-3408-3553
		tokyo.ofc@computer.org

Editorial production by Stephanie Kawada
Cover art production by Joe Daigle/Studio Productions
Printed in the United States of America by The Printing House

ICDM 2004 Proceedings

Fourth IEEE International Conference on Data Mining

Table of Contents

Regular Papers

Short Papers

xi

Welcome to ICDM 2004

Welcome to the Fourth IEEE International Conference on Data Mining (ICDM 2004)! We hope that you enjoy your visit to Brighton, UK, and that you have fond memories of the technical and social programs of the conference, including the excursion to the Historic Dockyard in Portsmouth.

Previously we have had several successful conferences: ICDM '01 in San Jose, California, USA; ICDM '02 in Maebashi City, Japan; and ICDM '03 in Melbourne, Florida. This year's conference convenes international researchers and practitioners who have an opportunity to collaborate and share their original research and practical development experiences in Data Mining technology. Attendees come from many related data-mining areas such as machine learning, automated scientific discovery, statistics, pattern recognition, knowledge acquisition, databases, data warehousing, data visualization, and knowledge-based systems.

Data mining is a highly interdisciplinary field. The ICDM '04 conference and workshop proceedings will cover a diverse range of topics related to data-mining theory, systems, and applications. These include, but are not limited to, the following areas:

- Foundations of data mining
- Data mining and machine learning algorithms and methods in the traditional areas (such as classification, regression, clustering, probabilistic modeling, and association analysis), as well as new areas
- Mining text and semistructured data, and mining temporal, spatial and multimedia data
- Mining data streams
- Pattern recognition and trend analysis
- Collaborative filtering/personalization
- Data and knowledge representation for data mining
- Query languages and user interfaces for mining
- Complexity, efficiency, and scalability issues in data mining
- Data preprocessing, data reduction, feature selection, and feature transformation
- Postprocessing of data mining results
- Statistics and probability in large-scale data mining
- Soft computing (including neural networks, fuzzy logic, evolutionary computation, and rough sets) and uncertainty management for data mining
- Integration of data warehousing, OLAP, and data mining
- Human-machine interaction and visual data mining
- High performance and parallel/distributed data mining
- Quality assessment and interestingness metrics of data mining results
- Security, privacy, and social impact of data mining
- Data mining applications in bioinformatics, electronic commerce, Web, intrusion detection, finance, marketing, healthcare, telecommunications, and other fields

Thanks to the support, contributions, and participation of world-renowned experts and new researchers from the international data-mining community, ICDM has received an overwhelming response every year since its establishment in 2001. ICDM has become one of the premier conferences in Data Mining. This year, we received 451 paper submissions from 47 different countries, including Australia, Austria, Bangladesh, Belgium, Brazil, Canada, China, Czech Republic, Egypt, Finland, France, Germany, Greece, Hong Kong, India, Iran, Ireland, Israel, Italy, Japan, Korea, New Zealand, Pakistan, Poland, Portugal, Romania, Russia, Singapore, Slovak Republic, Slovenia, Spain, Switzerland, Taiwan, Thailand, Turkey, Tunisia, UK, USA, and Vietnam.

The 451 submissions underwent a rigorous review process. Each paper was sent to at least three Program Committee members for reviews. We ensured that every paper received at least two reviews with a majority of the papers receiving three or more reviews. The Vice Chairs provided in-depth critiques to the Program Committee

Chairs. Based on the reviews, the Vice Chairs' feedback, and additional discussions, the Program Committee reached their final acceptance decisions at their July 26, 2004 meeting.

Out of the 451 submissions, 39 regular papers and 66 short papers were selected for presentation at the conference and for publication in the proceedings. Extremely selective this year, the Program Committee accepted less than 25% of the total papers submitted, with fewer than 1 out of 10 papers being chosen for the regular track. Overall, we are pleased with the high-quality papers that will generate stimulating discussions and a strong technical program. In addition to association analysis and clustering which are still the topics with the most contributions, analyzing streams of data and temporal data mining have received increasing attention. Also, the area of preprocessing—including feature selection and outlier detection—is increasingly becoming a hot topic. Text classification and Web mining keep their important positions in data mining as does quality assessments.

The workshops and tutorials reflect these main trends, but also complement the conference by presenting new areas. A panel discusses the state of the art and the future of the field.

We would like to express our special appreciation to our world-class invited speakers: Wray Buntine (Helsinki Institute of Information Technology), David Hand (Imperial College), Thorsten Joachims (Cornell University), and Ming Li (University of Waterloo).

A large conference like ICDM always requires a tremendous effort by many individuals. We would like to thank the Vice Chairs, Industry Chair, Workshops Chair, Tutorials Chair, Panels Chair, Publicity Chair, members of the Program Committee, and additional reviewers, for the countless hours they devoted to various conference activities (their names all appear elsewhere in the proceedings). This year, the Program Committee members have worked hard reviewing the large number of submissions. Some of them as well as additional reviewers were asked to provide last-minute reviews on a very short notice. Ning Zhong and his Web development staff deserve recognition for the invaluable support that the Cyberchair system provided for paper and registration management. We would also like to express our special thanks to Jianfeng Feng for his great work in local arrangements. The Steering Committee provided valuable feedback and discussions on important aspects of the conference during the course of the year.

We are grateful to the ICDM '04 corporate sponsors for their support: IBM Research, StatSoft LTD, Web Intelligence Consortium, and the *Knowledge and Information Systems Journal*.

Last but not least, we thank all of the authors who submitted papers and all conference attendees who contributed toward the success of this conference. ICDM '04 maintains the important ICDM traditions of (a) being truly international, (b) having exciting social programs as well as impressive technical programs, and (c) being designed and organized by a broad collection of people.

We look forward to seeing you again at ICDM '05 in New Orleans!

Katharina Morik and **Rajeev Rastogi**
ICDM '04 Program Chairs

Max Bramer
ICDM '04 Conference Chair

Conference Organization

Conference Chair
Max Bramer, *University of Portsmouth, UK (Max.Bramer@port.ac.uk)*

Program Committee Chairs
Katharina Morik, *University of Dortmund, Germany (morik@ls8.cs.uni-dortmund.de)*
Rajeev Rastogi, *Bell Laboratories, USA (rastogi@research.bell-labs.com)*

Vice Chairs
Jean-Francois Boulicaut, *University of Lyon, France*
Johannes Fuernkranz, *University of Vienna, Austria*
Minos Garofalakis, *Bell Labs, USA*
Thomas Hofmann, *Brown University, USA*
H.V. Jagadish, *University of Michigan, USA*
Eamonn Keogh, *University of California, Riverside, USA*
Xiaohui Liu, *Brunel University, UK*
Ramakrishnan Srikant, *IBM Research, USA*
Jaideep Srivastava, *University of Minnesota, USA*
Einoshin Suzuki, *Yokohama National University, Japan*

Industry Chair
Gholamreza Nakhaeizadeh, *Daimler Research, Germany (gholamreza.nakhaeizadeh@daimlerchrysler.com)*

Panels Chair
Fosca Giannotti, *University of Pisa, Italy (fosca.giannotti@isti.cnr.it)*

Workshops Chair
Stan Matwin, *University of Ottawa (Canada) (stan@site.uottawa.ca)*

Tutorials Chair
Kyuseok Shim, *Seoul National University, South Korea (shim@ee.snu.ac.kr)*

Publicity Chair/Web Master
Ning Zhong, *Maebashi Institute of Technology, Japan (zhong@maebashi-it.ac.jp)*

Local Arrangements Chair
Jianfeng Feng, *Sussex University, UK (jianfeng@cogs.susx.ac.uk)*

Proceedings Chair
Xindong Wu, *University of Vermont, USA (xwu@emba.uvm.edu)*

Sponsorship Chair
Naoki Abe, *IBM Research, USA (nabe@us.ibm.com)*

Steering Committee

Max Bramer, *University of Portsmouth, UK*
Nick Cercone, *Dalhousie University, Canada*
Ramamohanarao Kotagiri, *University of Melbourne, Australia*
Vipin Kumar, *University of Minnesota, USA*
Katharina Morik, *University of Dortmund, Germany*
Gregory Piatetsky-Shapiro, *KDnuggets, USA*
Benjamin W. Wah, *University of Illinois, Urbana-Champaign, USA*
Xindong Wu (Chair), *University of Vermont, USA*
Philip S. Yu, *IBM T. J. Watson Research Center, USA*
Ning Zhong, *Maebashi Institute of Technology, Japan*

Program Committee

Program Chairs

Katharina Morik, *University of Dortmund, Germany*
Rajeev Rastogi, *Bell Laboratories, USA*

Program Committee

Gedas Adomavicius, *University of Minnesota, USA*
Charu Aggarwal, *IBM T. J. Watson Research, USA*
Aijun An, *York University, Canada*
Hiroki Arimura, *Kyushu University, Japan*
Daniel Barbara, *George Mason University, USA*
Rohan Baxter, *CSIRO, Australia*
Roberto Bayardo, *IBM Almaden, USA*
Abraham Bernstein, *University of Zurich, Switzerland*
Phil Bohannon, *Bell Labs, USA*
Paul Bradley, *Apollo Data Technologies, USA*
Yuri Breitbart, *Kent State University, USA*
Kaushik Chakrabarti, *Microsoft, USA*
Chee-Yong Chan, *National University of Singapore, Singapore*
Phil Chan, *Florida Institute of Technology, USA*
Kevin Chang, *University of Illinois Urbana Champaign, USA*
Ming-Syan Chen, *National Taiwan University, Taiwan*
Ken Church, *Microsoft, USA*
Chris Clifton, *Purdue University, USA*
Graham Cormode, *Rutgers University, USA*
Susan Craw, *Robert Gordon University, UK*
Honghua Dai, *Deakin University, Australia*
Gautam Das, *Microsoft Research, USA*
Tamraparni Dasu, *AT&T Research, USA*
Inderjit Dhillon, *University of Texas, USA*
Chris Ding, *Computational Research Division, USA*
AnHai Doan, *University of Illinois, Urbana Champaign, USA*
Alin Dobra, *University of Florida, USA*
Guozhu Dong, *Wright State University, USA*
Tina Eliassi-Rad, *Lawrence Livermore National Laboratory, USA*
Martin Ester, *Simon Fraser University, Canada*
Wei Fan, *IBM T. J. Watson, USA*
Usamma Fayyad, *DMX Group, USA*
Ronen Feldmann, *University Bar-Illan, Israel*
Jianfeng Feng, *Sussex University, UK*
Peter A. Flach, *University of Bristol, UK*
Ada Fu, *Chinese University of Hong Kong, China*
Matjaz Gams, *Jozef Stefan Institute, Slovenia*
Venkatesh Ganti, *Microsoft Research, USA*
Lee Giles, *Pennsylvania State University, USA*
Aristides Gionis, *University of Helsinki, Finland*
Bart Goethals, *University Helsinki, Finland*

Non-PC Reviewers

Helena Ahonen-Myka
Luiza Antonie
Ines Arana
Dmitri Asonov
Dipti Aswath
Kaan Ataman
Sanghamitra Bandyopadhyay
Arindam Banerjee
Sugato Basu
Alina Beygelzimer
Kanishka Bhaduri
Axel Blumenstock
Shannon Bradshaw
Nicolas Bredeche
Justin Brickell
Mark Brodie
Chris Bryant
Yixin Chen
Gong Chen
Jie Chen
Lijun Chen
Stella Chen
Wei Chen
Yun Chi
I-Jen Chiang
Krishna P Chitrapura
Hyuk Cho
Kun-Ta Chuang
Darya Chudova
Antoine Cornuejols
J. P. Costa
Vasa Curcin
Agnieszka Dardzinska
Mahesh Datt
Jason Davis
Fan Deng
Kevin DeRonne
Mukund Deshpande
Anca Doloc-Mihu
Magdalini Eirinaki
Mohammad El-Hajj
Roberto Esposito
Zhe Feng
Thomas Finley
Andrew Foss
Arianna Gallo

Byron Gao
Like Gao
Minos Garofalakis
Floris Geerts
Liqiang Geng
Moustafa Ghanem
Amol Ghoting
Aris Gkoulalas
Guruditta Golani
Hector Gonzalez
Yuqiang Guan
Rahul Gupta
Maria Halkidi
Hao He
Hongxing He
Lu Hong
Tamas Horvath
Patrik Hoyer
Cheng Hu
Faliang Huang
Jun Huan
Jimmy Huang
Jin Huang
Seung-won Hwang
Mohmaed Ali Jafri
Ravi Jamalla
Ravi Janga
Chris Jermaine
Chunyu Jiang
Mingfei Jiang
Yuelong Jiang
Huidong Jin
Juyong Jin
Wen Jin
Sachindra Joshi
Dmitri Kalashnikov
Murat Kantarcioglu
Kamran Karimi
Martin Kelin
Steffen Kempe
Chulyun Kim
Ivan Koychev
Mehmet Koyuturk
Brian Kulis
Krishna Kummamuru
Pavani Kuntala

Michihiro Kuramochi
Kay Kussmann
Matti Kääriäinen
Leo Lau
Aleksander Lazarevic
Iosif Lazaridis
Byung S. Lee
Jia Li
Jin Li
Xiaolei Li
Xiaoli Li
Yifan Li
Wei-qiang Lin
Xiaodong Lin
C. J. Liau
Jinze Liu
Kun Liu
Meiling Liu
Rohit Lotlikar
Yiming Ma
Hiroshi Mamitsuka
Shihong Mao
Dragos Margineantu
Keith Marsolo
Ujjwal Maulik
S.M. McConnell
Leonard McMillan
Sameep Mehta
Prem Melville
Srujana Merugu
Gabriela Moise
Sougata Mukherjea
Alexandros Nanopoulos
Gulisong Nasierding
Samer Nassar
Jennifer Neville
Phu Chien Nguyen
Ryan Nicoletti
Stephen North
Irene Ntoutsi
Kouzou Ohara
Michael Ortega-Binderberger
Michelle Osmond
Mourad Ouzzani
Themis Palpanas
Spiros Papadimitriou

Hyoungmin Park
Nikos Pelekis
Xinzhou Qin
Filip Radlinski
Huzefa Rangwala
Ari Rantanen
Ralf Rantzau
Shourya Roy
Apkar Salatian
Dawit Seid
Jouni Seppanen
Biren Shah
Zheng Shao
Shengli Sheng
Reza Sherkat
Hyunjin Shin
Thorsten Schnier
Ashwin Shriram
Javed Siddique
Gyorgy Simon
Sohraab Soltani
Suvrit Sra
Ying Sun
Injae Sung
Madhukar Suryaprakash
Deborah Swayne

Ankur Teredesai
Alexandre Termier
Evimaria Terzi
Keith Thompson
Yiqing Tu
Matt Vagnoni
Vassilios Verykios
Huy Vu
Matt Walker
Chao Wang
Jun Wang
Jianyong Wang
Min Wang
Qian Wan
Xin Wang
Gary Weiss
Dietrich Wettschereck
Chi-Wing Wong
Raymond C.W. Wong
Rebecca Wright
Yonghua Wu
Yi Xia
Chong Xie
Ying Xie
Dong Xin
Hui Xiong

Wanhong Xu
Yong Xu
Bojun Yan
Xifeng Yan
Yirong Yang
Hui Yang
Ying Yang
Hong Yao
Qingsong Yao
Jieping Ye
Jeonghee Yi
Yunfei Yin
Hang Yu
Jeffrey Xu Yu
Lei Yu
Ding Yuan
Bianca Zadrozny
Jilian Zhang
Pusheng Zhang
Xiang Zhang
Yi Zhang
Yong Zhang
Ying Zhao
Qi Zhong
Ling Zhuang

Corporate Sponsors

IBM Research

Knowledge and Information Systems

StatSoft Ltd., UK

Web Intelligence Consortium

Regular Papers

Detection of Significant Sets of Episodes in Event Sequences

Mikhail Atallah *
Purdue University
Department of Computer Sciences
mja@cs.purdue.edu

Robert Gwadera [†]
Purdue University
Department of Computer Sciences
gwadera@cs.purdue.edu

Wojciech Szpankowski [‡]
Purdue University
Department of Computer Sciences
spa@cs.purdue.edu

Abstract

We present a method for a reliable detection of "unusual" sets of episodes in the form of many pattern sequences, scanned simultaneously for an occurrence as a subsequence in a large event stream within a window of size w. We also investigate the important special case of all permutations of the same sequence, which models the situation where the order of events in an episode does not matter, e.g., when events correspond to purchased market basket items. In order to build a reliable monitoring system we compare obtained measurements to a reference model which in our case is a probabilistic model (Bernoulli or Markov). We first present a precise analysis that leads to a construction of a threshold. The difficulties of carrying out a probabilistic analysis for an arbitrary set of patterns, stems from the possible simultaneous occurrence of many members of the set as subsequences in the same window, the fact that the different patterns typically do have common symbols or common subsequences or possibly common prefixes, and that they may have different lengths. We also report on extensive experimental results, carried out on the Wal-Mart transactions database, that show a remarkable agreement with our theoretical analysis. This paper is an extension of our previous work in [8] where we laid out foundation for the problem of the reliable detection of an "unusual" episodes,

but did not consider more than one episode scanned simultaneously for an occurrence.

1 Introduction

Detecting subsequence patterns in event sequences is important in many applications, including intrusion detection, monitoring for suspicious activities, and molecular biology. Whether an observed pattern of activity is significant or not (i.e., whether it should be a cause for alarm) depends on how likely it is to occur fortuitously. A long enough sequence of observed events will almost certainly contain any subsequence, and setting thresholds for detecting significant patterns of activity is an important issue in a monitoring system.

In order to decide whether a particular sequence of events in the monitored event sequence is significant one must compare it to a reference model. In our work the reference model is a probabilistic model either generated by a memoryless (Bernoulli) source or a Markov source. The question is *when is a certain number of occurrences of a particular subsequence in a monitored even sequence unlikely to be generated by the reference model (i.e., indicative of suspicious activity or statistically significant event)?* A quantitative analysis of this question allows one to compute a *threshold* on-line while monitoring the event sequence in order to detect significant patterns. By knowing the most likely number of occurrences and the probability of deviating from it, we can compute a threshold such that the probability of missing real unusual activities is small. Such a quantitative analysis can also help to choose the size of the sliding window of observation. Finally even in a court case one cannot consider certain observed "bad" activity as a convincing evidence against somebody if that activity is

---

*Portions of this author's work were supported by Grants EIA-9903545, IIS-0219560, IIS-0312357, and IIS-0242421 from the National Science Foundation, Contract N00014-02-1-0364 from the Office of Naval Research, by sponsors of the Center for Education and Research in Information Assurance and Security, and by Purdue Discovery Park's e-enterprise Center.

[†]The work of this author was supported by the NSF Grant CCR-0208709, and NIH grant R01 GM068959-01.

[‡]The work of this author was supported by the NSF Grant CCR-0208709, and AFOSR Grant FA 8655-04-1-3074.

3

quite likely to occur under the given circumstances. Therefore it is very important to quantify such probabilities and present a universal and reliable framework for analyzing a variety of event sources.

In [10] Mannila et al. introduced the problem of finding frequent episodes in event sequences, subject to observation-window constraint, where an episode was defined as a partially ordered collection of events, that can be represented as a directed acyclic graph. The paper [10] defined the frequency $fr(\alpha, s, win)$ of an episode α as the fraction of windows of length win in which the episode occurs in an event sequence s. Given a frequency threshold min_fr, [10] considered an episode to be frequent if $fr(\alpha, s, win) \geq min\_fr$. In the framework of [10], our problem can be stated as follows. Given an episode α, what window size win and what frequency threshold min_fr should we choose to ensure that the discovered frequent episode is meaningful? Observe that for an appropriately low frequency min_fr and large window size win the episode will certainly occur in the reference model. Our problem can also be stated as follows. Given a collection of frequent episodes $\mathcal{C}(w)$, discovered using the algorithm given in [10], what is the rank of the episodes with respect to their significance?

In our paper [8] the problem of the reliable detection of unusual episodes was investigated, where we considered an episode in the form of a single sequence occurring as an ordered subsequence of a large event stream *within a window of a given fixed size*. This kind of episode is called a "serial episode" in the terminology of [10], and we henceforth adopt this terminology. In [8] we proposed a method for reliable detection of significant episodes, where as a measure of significance we used $\Omega^{\exists}(n, w, m)$ the number of windows of length w which contain at least one occurrence of serial episode S of length m as a subsequence in event sequence T after n shifts of the window. We proved that appropriately normalized $\Omega^{\exists}(n, w, m)$ has the Gaussian distribution, where the expected value $\mathbf{E}[\Omega^{\exists}(n, w, m)] = nP^{\exists}(w, m)$ and $P^{\exists}(w, m)$ is the probability that a serial episode S of length m occurs at least once in a window of length w in an event sequence T over an alphabet $\mathcal{A}$. We also showed that the variance $\mathbf{Var}[\Omega^{\exists}(n, w, m)] \leq cn \left[P^{\exists}(w, m) - (P^{\exists}(w, m))^2\right]$ for $c > 0$. Given a reference model (Bernoulli or Markov), and for a given probability $\beta(b)$, we presented the upper threshold for detecting significant episodes $\tau_u(w) = P^{\exists}(w, m) + \frac{b\sqrt{\mathbf{Var}[\Omega^{\exists}(n, w, m)]}}{n}$, where $P^{\exists}(w, m)$ and $\mathbf{Var}[\Omega^{\exists}(n, w, m)]$ depend on the probabilistic model and episode type. For a given probability $\beta(b)$ of the cumulative normal probability distribution function, we select b such that $P\left(\frac{\Omega^{\exists}(n,w,m)}{n} > \tau_u(w)\right) \leq \beta(b)$. That is, if one *observes* more than $\tau_u(w) \cdot n$ occurrences of windows with certain episodes, it is highly

unlikely that such a number is generated by the reference source (i.e., its probability is smaller than $\beta(b)$). The quantity $\frac{\Omega^{\exists}(n,w,m)}{n}$ corresponds to the frequency $fr(S, T, w)$ [10] and is an estimator of $P^{\exists}(w, m)$ denoted $P_e^{\exists}(w, m)$.

While developing the formula for $P^{\exists}(w, m)$ we found a formula for the set of all distinct windows $\mathcal{W}^{\exists}(w, m)$ of length w containing a serial episode S of length m at least once as a subsequence. The importance of $\mathcal{W}^{\exists}(w, m)$ stems from the fact that $P^{\exists}(w, m) = \sum_{x \in \mathcal{W}^{\exists}(w,m)} P(x)$ for the Markov model of an arbitrary order including 0-th order (Bernoulli), where $P(x)$ is the probability of x as a string of symbols of length w in a given model. The advantage of the Bernoulli model versus the first order Markov or higher is that for the Bernoulli model $P^{\exists}(w, m)$ can be computed efficiently exploiting the structure of $\mathcal{W}^{\exists}(w, m)$ and the fact that the model requires only $|\mathcal{A}|$ probabilities of symbols of the alphabet $\mathcal{A}$. Therefore in [8] we focused on the Bernoulli model for which we gave an efficient dynamic programming method for computing $P^{\exists}(w, m)$. Using generating functions and complex asymptotics we presented an asymptotic approximation of $P^{\exists}(w, m)$, which is of the form $P^{\exists}(w, m) = 1 - \Theta(\rho^w)$ for large w and $0 < \rho < 1$. In experiments, we chose two apparently nonmemoryless sources (the English alphabet and the web access data) and showed that, even for these cases, $P^{\exists}(w, m)$ closely approximated the actual $P_e^{\exists}(w, m)$, which proved that the memoryless assumption did not limit the practical usefulness of the formula. We tested $\tau_u(w)$ by artificially injecting "bad" episodes into the monitored event sequence and observed that $\tau_u(w)$ did indeed provide a sharp detection of intentional (bad) episodes. Our paper [8] laid out foundations, but did not consider the case of detecting more than one serial episode simultaneously.

This paper builds on [8] by extending it to the case of an arbitrary number of serial episodes, monitored simultaneously for an occurrence, including the important special case of all permutations of the same serial episode, called a "parallel episode" in the terminology of [10]. The parallel episode case captures situations where the ordering of the events within the window of observation does not matter, e.g., the events correspond to basket items scanned by cashier. More formally, we analyze episodes in one of the following forms:

1. An arbitrary set of episodes $\mathbf{S} = \{S_1, S_2, \ldots, S_{|\mathbf{S}|}\}$ where every S_i of length m_i is a serial episode for $1 \leq i \leq |\mathbf{S}|$ and by an occurrence of the set $\mathbf{S}$ we mean a logical OR of occurrences of members of $\mathbf{S}$ within a window of size w.

2. Set of all distinct permutations of an episode $S = S[1]S[2], \ldots S[m]$ of length m (parallel episode), where by an occurrence we mean a logical OR of occurrences of permutations of S.

The reason we distinguish the parallel episode case is because we will take advantage of the structure of permutations of S to design an efficient algorithm instead of representing the parallel episode as a set of serial episodes. Thus, the goal of the current paper is to quantify $\Omega^{\exists}(n, w, m_1, m_2, \ldots, m_{|\mathbf{S}|})$ the number of windows containing at least one occurrence of $\mathbf{S} = \{S_1, S_2, \ldots, S_{|\mathbf{S}|}\}$ as a subsequence within a window of size w in a event sequence T over an alphabet $\mathcal{A}$. This analysis leads to a formula for the threshold for detecting significant sets of episodes. In the full version of this paper [3] we prove that $\Omega^{\exists}(n, w, m_1, m_2, \ldots, m_{|\mathbf{S}|})$ is Gaussian. In order to compute $P^{\exists}(w, m_1, m_2, \ldots, m_{|\mathbf{S}|})$ the probability that a window of length w contains an occurrence of $\mathbf{S}$ we need a formula for $\mathcal{W}^{\exists}(w, m_1, m_2, \ldots, m_{|\mathbf{S}|})$ the set of all windows of length w containing an occurrence of $\mathbf{S}$ as a subsequence. However a considerable source of difficulty is the fact that $\mathcal{W}^{\exists}(w, m_1, m_2, \ldots, m_{|\mathbf{S}|})$ for $|\mathbf{S}| > 1$ is not equal to the enumeration of sets of $\mathcal{W}^{\exists}(w, m_i)$ for each $S_i \in \mathbf{S}$ because in general $\mathcal{W}^{\exists}(w, m_i) \cap \mathcal{W}^{\exists}(w, m_j) \neq \emptyset$ for $i \neq j$ where $i, j \leq |\mathbf{S}|$ and considering $\mathcal{W}^{\exists}(w, m_i)$ and $\mathcal{W}^{\exists}(w, m_j)$ independently would lead to a failure of the probabilistic analysis of $P^{\exists}(w, m_1, m_2, \ldots, m_{|\mathbf{S}|})$ due to double counting of respective probabilistic events. To appreciate the difficulty of this extension, consider the much-simplified case when there are only two pattern sequences ($\mathbf{S} = \{S_1, S_2\}$) and no symbol is common to S_1 and S_2. Even in this case the set of windows of length w containing S_1 as a subsequence and the set of windows of length w containing S_2 as a subsequence do have some elements in common, i.e., $\mathcal{W}^{\exists}(w, m_1) \cap \mathcal{W}^{\exists}(w, m_2) \neq \emptyset$ for appropriately large w. Add to this the fact that the different patterns typically do have common symbols or common subsequences or possibly common prefixes, that they may have different lengths, and the problem becomes fraught with nasty interactions that prevent any straightforward analytical solution to the case $|\mathbf{S}| > 1$.

The main contribution of the current paper is a computational formula for $P^{\exists}(w, m_1, m_2, \ldots, m_{|\mathbf{S}|})$ for and arbitrary set of episodes including the special case of the parallel episode. We provide a recurrence system for constructing $\mathcal{W}^{\exists}(w, m_1, m_2, \ldots, m_{|\mathbf{S}|})$. Because the recurrence contains conditional statements representing interactions of symbols of members of $\mathbf{S}$ we cannot find a practical analytical solution to the recurrence. Therefore we propose an efficient algorithmic method for enumerating $\mathcal{W}^{\exists}(w, m_1, m_2, \ldots, m_{|\mathbf{S}|})$ using recursion graphs, which leads to a formula for $P^{\exists}(w, m_1, m_2, \ldots, m_{|\mathbf{S}|})$ for an arbitrary order of Markov model. However, we focus on Bernoulli model in this paper because of its compactness and efficiency. Our current work builds on [8] and provides the first probabilistic analysis that quantifies $\Omega^{\exists}(n, w, m_1, m_2, \ldots, m_{|\mathbf{S}|})$ the number of windows

of length w containing at least one occurrence of $\mathbf{S} = \{S_1, S_2, \ldots, S_{|\mathbf{S}|}\}$ as a subsequence. This analysis allows to compute the threshold for detecting significant sets of episodes scanned simultaneously for an occurrence. We also proposed a new $O(n \log(m))$ tree based algorithm for discovering parallel episodes, presented in the full version of the paper [3]. We applied our theoretical results by running an extensive series of experiments on real data. We used a part of *Wal-Mart* sales data for the years 1999 and 2000. We first show that our formulas for the probability closely approximate the experimental data. Then we demonstrate an application of the upper threshold by keeping inserting a given episode into random positions in the event sequence, until the episode gets detected as significant through our threshold mechanism (cf. Fig. 9).

The paper is organized as follows. In section 2 we present our main results containing theoretical foundation. Section 3 contains experimental results demonstrating applicability of the derived formulas. Proofs were omitted because of space limitations and are included in the full version of the paper in [3]. Interested readers can visit our on-line threshold calculator at `http://www-cgi.cs. purdue.edu/cgi-bin/gwadera/demo.cgi` for a demonstration of the reliable threshold computation.

2 Main Results

Given an alphabet $\mathcal{A} = \{a_1, a_2, \ldots, a_{|\mathcal{A}|}\}$ and a set of patterns $\mathbf{S} = \{S_1, S_2, \ldots S_{|\mathbf{S}|}\}$ where $S_i = S_i[1]S_i[2] \ldots S_i[m_i]$ and $S_i[j] \in \mathcal{A}$ for $1 \leq i \leq |\mathbf{S}|$, we are interested in occurrences of members of $\mathbf{S}$ as a *subsequence* within a window of size w in another sequence known as the event sequence $T = T[1]T[2] \ldots$.

We analyze the number of windows of length w containing *at least one* occurrence of $\mathbf{S}$ when sliding the window along n consecutive events in the event sequence T, where by an occurrence of $\mathbf{S}$ we mean a logical *OR* of occurrences of $S_1, S_2, \ldots, S_{|\mathbf{S}|}$. We use $\Omega^{\exists}(n, w, m_1, m_2, \ldots, m_{|\mathbf{S}|}, \mathbf{S}, \mathcal{A})$ to denote this number, that can range from 0 to n.

Notation: Throughout the paper, whenever $\mathcal{A}$, $\mathbf{S}$ or $m_1, m_2, \ldots, m_{|\mathbf{S}|}$ are implied and we do not reference them in our notations, we simplify our notations by dropping them accordingly using $\Omega^{\exists}(n, w)$, $\mathcal{W}^{\exists}(w)$ and $P^{\exists}(w)$ instead. We also occasionally use index $m_i - k$ to mean "dropping the last k symbols of S_i", e.g., $P^{\exists}(w, m_1 - k, m_2)$ implies a pattern that is the prefix of S_1 of length $m_1 - k$ and that the second pattern is all of S_2.

Given a probabilistic model of the reference source (in this paper we use Bernoulli model with probabilities $P(a_i)$ for $a_i \in \mathcal{A}, i = 1, 2, \ldots, |\mathcal{A}|$), a frequent episode $\mathbf{S}$, $\Omega^{\exists}(n, w)$ and a probability $\beta(b)$ (e.g., $\beta(b) = 10^{-5}$) we compute the upper threshold $\tau_u(w)$ for

$P\left(\frac{\Omega^\exists(n,w)}{n} \geq \tau_u(w)\right) \leq \beta(b)$, using the equation system as follows

$$\begin{cases} \tau_u(w) &= P^\exists(w) + \frac{b\sqrt{\mathbf{Var}[\Omega^\exists(n,w)]}}{n} \\ \beta(b) &= \frac{1}{\sqrt{2\pi}} \int_\infty^b e^{\frac{-t^2}{2}} dt \end{cases}$$

which follows from the fact that $\Omega^\exists(n,w)$ is Gaussian as we proved in [3]. Also, $P^\exists(w)$ and $\mathbf{Var}[\Omega^\exists(n,w)]$ depend on the episode type and the probabilistic model (Bernoulli or Markov). Once the threshold $\tau_u(w)$ is computed if $\frac{\Omega^\exists(n,w)}{n} \geq \tau_u(w)$ then the probability that the episode $\mathbf{S}$ is not significant is less than $\beta(b)$, i.e., the probability of an false alarm is less than $\beta(b)$. Given a collection of frequent episodes $\mathcal{C}(w)$ we can rank their significance using $\beta(b)$.

For the sake of the presentation we focus throughout the paper on the case where either $\mathbf{S} = \{S_1, S_2\}$, or $\mathbf{S}$ is the set corresponding to a parallel episode S but our derivations will easily be seen to generalize to an arbitrary set of episodes $\mathbf{S}$.

2.1 Analysis of $P^\exists(w)$

Let $\mathcal{W}^\exists(w, m_1, m_2)$ be the *set* of all possible distinct windows of length w containing S_1 or S_2 at least once as a subsequence then $P^\exists(w, m_1, m_2) = \sum_{x \in \mathcal{W}^\exists(w,m_1,m_2)} P(x)$.

Because in the memoryless model $P(x)$ is a product of individual probabilities of symbols, to any recursive formula for $\mathcal{W}^\exists(w, m_1, m_2)$ there corresponds a similar formula for $P^\exists(w, m_1, m_2)$ (and vice-versa). We now show that $P^\exists(w, m_1, m_2)$ for the set $\mathcal{A} = \{S_1, S_2\}$ satisfies the following recurrence

$$\begin{cases} \mathbf{if} \quad S_1[m_1] \neq S_2[m_2] \quad \mathbf{then} \\ P^\exists(w, m_1, m_2) = \\ P(S_1[m_1])P^\exists(w-1, m_1-1, m_2)+ \\ P(S_2[m_2])P^\exists(w-1, m_1, m_2-1)+ \\ (1 - P(S_1[m_1]) - P(S_2[m_2]))P^\exists(w-1, m_1, m_2) \\ \mathbf{for} \quad w > 0, m_1, m_2 > 0 \\[1em] \mathbf{if} \quad S_1[m_1] = S_2[m_2] \quad \mathbf{then} \\ P^\exists(w, m_1, m_2) = \\ P(S_1[m_1])P^\exists(w-1, m_1-1, m_2-1)+ \\ (1 - P(S_1[m_1]))P^\exists(w-1, m_1, m_2) \\ \mathbf{for} \quad w > 0, m_1, m_2 > 0 \\[1em] P^\exists(w, 0, 0) = 1 \quad \mathbf{for} \quad w > 0 \\ P^\exists(0, m_1, m_2) = 0 \quad \mathbf{for} \quad m_1, m_2 > 0 \\ P^\exists(1, m_1, 0) = 1 \quad \mathbf{for} \quad m_1 > 0 \\ P^\exists(1, 0, m_2) = 1 \quad \mathbf{for} \quad m_2 > 0 \\ P^\exists(0, 0, 0) = 1 \end{cases}$$

Indeed, consider a window of size w containing S_1 or S_2 as a subsequence. Then depending on whether the last sym-

bols of S_1 and S_2 are equal or not there are two cases. If $S_1[m_1] \neq S_2[m_2]$ then there are three cases: either $S_1[m_1]$ is the last symbol in the window giving the term $P(S_1[m_1])P^\exists(w-1, m_1-1, m_2)$, or $S_2[m_2]$ is the last symbol in the window giving the term $P(S_2[m_2])P^\exists(w-1, m_1, m_2-1)$, or none of the above which leads to the term $(1 - P(S_1[m_1]) - P(S_2[m_2]))P^\exists(w-1, m_1, m_2)$. If $S_1[m_1] = S_2[m_2]$ then there are two cases depending on whether the last symbol of the window is equal to $S_1[m_1]$ or not. From the above discussion it is clear that the shape of the "recursion graph" is determined by interactions between symbols in S_1 and S_2, i.e., whether their symbols at pairs of positions are equal or not. Therefore in order to find a solution to $P^\exists(w, m_1, m_2)$ we have to enumerate all pairs of indices (i, j) such that $P^\exists(k, i, j)$ appears in the recursion tree (not all such pairs of indices qualify). This recursion graph is now described more formally (as stated earlier, in addition to depicting the recurrence, the graph also describes all elements of $\mathcal{W}^\exists(w, m_1, m_2)$).

Let $G(\mathbf{S}) = (V, E)$ be an edge-labeled directed graph defined as follows. The vertex set V is a subset of all the pairs (i, j), $0 \leq i \leq m_1$, $0 \leq j \leq m_2$. That subset, as well as E, are defined inductively as follows.

- $(0, 0)$ is in V.

- If (i, j) is in V, $i < m_1$, and $S_1[i+1] \neq S_2[j+1]$ then $(i+1, j)$ is also in V, and an edge from from (i, j) to $(i+1, j)$ labeled $S_1[i+1]$ exists in E.

- If (i, j) is in V, $j < m_2$, and $S_1[i+1] \neq S_2[j+1]$ then $(i, j+1)$ is also in V, and an edge from (i, j) to $(i, j+1)$ labeled $S_2[j+1]$ exists in E.

- If (i, j) is in V, $i < m_1$ and $j < m_2$, and $S_1[i+1] = S_2[j+1]$ then $(i+1, j+1)$ is also in V, and an edge from (i, j) to $(i+1, j+1)$ labeled $S_1[i+1] (= S_2[j+1])$ exists in E.

- A self-loop from vertex (i, j) to itself exists and has label equal to (i) $\mathcal{A}$ if $i = m_1$ or $j = m_2$, (ii) $\mathcal{A} - \{S_1[i+1]\} - \{S_2[j+1]\}$ if $i < m_1$ and $j < m_2$.

The following observations, in which we do not count self-loops towards the in-degree and out-degree of a vertex, follow from the above definition of $G(\mathbf{S})$.

- The in-degree of vertex $(0, 0)$ (start vertex) equals zero, the out-degree of vertices $(m_1, j), (i, m_2)$ for $i \leq m_1, j \leq m_2$ (end-vertices) equals zero.

- The in-degree and out-degree of every vertex (i, j) is at most three; if $\mathbf{S}$ consisted of $|\mathbf{S}| > 2$ serial episodes then the in-degree and out-degree of any vertex would be at most $|\mathbf{S}| + 1$.

- $|V| = O(m_1 m_2)$ and $|E| = O(|\mathbf{S}|m_1 m_2)$.

Let $Edges(path)$ and $Vertices(path)$ denote the sequence of consecutive edges and (respectively) vertices in any *path*, except that $Vertices(path)$ does not include the last vertex on *path* (why this is so will become apparent below). In what follows, if vertex (i, j) is in $Vertices(path)$, then we use $n_{i,j}(path)$ to denote the number of times the self-loop at (i, j) is used; if *path* is understood and there is no ambiguity, then we simply use $n_{i,j}$ rather than $n_{i,j}(path)$. Let $\mathcal{R}$ be the set of all distinct simple paths (i.e., without self-loops) from the start-vertex to any end-vertex. Now let $\mathcal{L}_w$ be the set of all distinct paths of length w, *including self-loops*, from the start-vertex to all end-vertices (that is, self-loops do count towards path length). Then we have

$$\mathcal{W}^{\exists}(w, m_1, m_2) = \{Edges(path) : path \in \mathcal{L}_w\}.$$

Examples of $G(\mathbf{S})$ are shown in Figure 1 and in Figure 2.

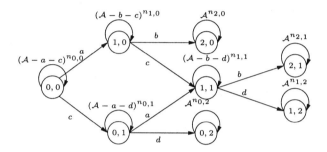

Figure 1. $G(\mathbf{S})$ for $\mathbf{S} = \{ab, cd\}$

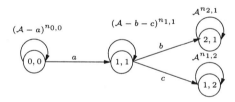

Figure 2. $G(\mathbf{S})$ for $\mathbf{S} = \{ab, ac\}$

Theorem 1 *Consider a memoryless source with $P(S_i[k])$ being the probability of generating the k-th symbol of $S_i \in \mathbf{S} = \{S_1, S_2\}$. Let also*

$$P(Edges(path)) = \prod_{edge \in Edges(path)} P(label(edge)).$$

Then for m_1, m_2 and $w \geq m_i$ we have

$$P^{\exists}(w, m_1, m_2) = \sum_{path \in \mathcal{R}} P(Edges(path)) \sum_{g=0}^{w - |Edges(path)|} \cdot$$
$$\sum_{\sum n_{i,j}(path) = g} \prod_{(i,j) \in Vertices(path)}$$
$$(1 - P(\{S_1[i+1]\} \cup \{S_2[j+1]\}))^{n_{i,j}(path)}.$$

In our experiments, we implemented an efficient dynamic programming algorithm based on Theorem 1. In section 3.1.2 we present evidence how Theorem 1 works well on real data by comparing it to the estimate $P_e^{\exists}(w) = \frac{\Omega^{\exists}(n,w)}{n}$ given the actual $\Omega^{\exists}(n, w)$. We also solved $P^{\exists}(w)$ for an important special case when $\mathbf{S}$ consist of all permutations of one pattern S, which is the case of a parallel episode. Using Theorem 1 directly to design an algorithm in such an unordered case would be inefficient because we would then need to consider a graph having a disastrous $|V| = O(m^{m!})$.

In order to simplify the graph $G(\mathbf{S})$ that would result from all permutations, and bring its number of vertices down to a manageable size (quantified below), we exploit the structure of a set of all permutations to design a different graph. Notice that, for a parallel episode, every path in $\mathcal{R}$ is a permutation of symbols in S. In addition, the out-degree of a vertex is at most m if all symbols of S are different. Furthermore a transition from from $P^{\exists}(k, i, j, \ldots)$ to $P^{\exists}(k+1, i', j', \ldots)$ takes place for any symbol of S not seen so far since the order of symbols does not matter. This observations allow us to introduce a variant of $G(\mathbf{S})$ called $G_{\parallel}(\mathbf{S})$.

Let $G_{\parallel}(\mathbf{S}) = (V, E)$ be a directed edge-labeled graph defined as follows. The vertex set V consist of submultisets of size $i = 0, 1, \ldots, m$ of the multiset of sorted symbols in S denoted as $\{S[1], S[2], \ldots, S[m]\}$. We represent the submultisets equivalently as binary vectors of the form $(i_1, i_2, \ldots, i_m)$, where $i_j = 1$ if the vertex contains symbol $S[i_j]$ in its submultiset or $i_j = 0$ otherwise. V and E can be defined inductively as follows.

- $(0, 0, \ldots, 0)$ and $(1, 1, \ldots, 1)$ are in V.

- If $(i_1, i_2, \ldots, i_m)$ is V and $\sum_{j=1}^{m} i_j < m$ then $(i'_1, i'_2, \ldots, i'_m)$ is in V if $\sum_{j=1}^{m} i'_j = \sum_{j=1}^{m} i_j + 1$ and an edge with label equal to $\{i'_1 \cdot S[1], i'_2 \cdot S[2], \ldots, i'_m \cdot S[m]\} - \{i_1 \cdot S[1], i_2 \cdot S[2], \ldots, i_m \cdot S[m]\}$ exists in E.

- A self-loop from vertex $(i_1, i_2, \ldots, i_m)$ to itself exists and has label equal to (i) $\mathcal{A}$ for $(1, 1, \ldots, 1)$, (ii) $\mathcal{A} - \bigcup_{i_j = 0} \{S[i_j]\}$ otherwise.

The following observations, in which we do not count self-loops towards the in-degree and out-degree of a vertex, follow from the above definition of $G_{\parallel}(\mathbf{S})$.

- The in-degree of the start-vertex $(0, 0, \ldots, 0)$ equals zero, the out-degree of the end-vertex $(1, 1, \ldots, 1)$ equals zero. The in-degree and out-degree of every vertex is at most m.

- $|V| = O(2^m)$ and $|E| = O(|V|m)$.

Examples of $G_{\parallel}(S)$ are shown in Figure 3 and in Figure 4. The next theorem is an adoption of Theorem 1 to the case of a parallel episode.

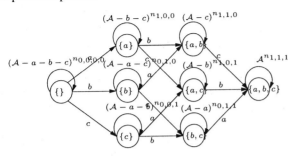

Figure 3. $G_{\parallel}(S)$ for $S = abc$ and $\mathcal{A} = \{a, b, c, d\}$

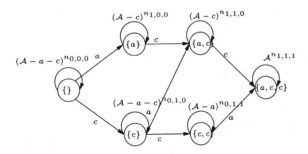

Figure 4. $G_{\parallel}(S)$ for $S = acc$ and $\mathcal{A} = \{a, b, c, d\}$

Theorem 2 *Consider a memoryless source with $P(S[k])$ being the probability of generating the k-th symbol of S where S is a parallel episode with*

$$P(S) = \prod_{i=1}^{m} P(S[i])$$

then for all m and $w \geq m$ we have

$$P^{\exists}(w) = \sum_{path \in \mathcal{R}} P(S) \sum_{g=0}^{w-m}$$
$$\sum_{\sum n_{i_1, i_2, \ldots, i_m}(path) = g} \prod_{(i_1, i_2, \ldots, i_m) \in Vertices(path)}$$
$$\left(1 - P\left(\bigcup_{i_j=0}\{S[i_j]\}\right)\right)^{n_{i_1, i_2, \ldots, i_m}(path)} .$$

In our experiments we implemented an efficient dynamic programming algorithm based on Theorem 2 for computing $P^{\exists}(w)$. In section 3.1.1 we presented how Theorem 2 works well on real data where the formula for $P^{\exists}(w)$ agrees with $P_e^{\exists}(w)$ on the Wal-Mart transactions.

3 Experiments

The purpose of our experiments was to test applicability of the analytical results for real sources. Therefore we

selected *Wal-Mart* data available on the departmental Oracle server in the Department of Computer Sciences, Purdue University. The database contains part of *Wal-Mart* sales data for the years 1999 and 2000 in 135 stores. We selected one of the stores, one category of items of cardinality 35 ($|\mathcal{A}| = 35$) and extracted 9.66 million records from table $Item\_Scan$, sorted by scan time. We divided our sources into training sets and testing sets. Training sets are data sets, which we consider to constitute the reference source. We used the first 9.56 million records as a training set to compute $P(a_i)$ for $a_i \in \mathcal{A}, i = 1, 2, \ldots, |\mathcal{A}|$ for the Bernoulli reference source. Once the probability model of the reference source has been built, we can start monitoring unknown data called testing data. In section 3.1 we tested how well the formulas for $P^{\exists}(w)$ worked on the *Wal-Mart* data by comparing $P_e^{\exists}(w) = \frac{\Omega^{\exists}(n,w)}{n}$ to the computed $P^{\exists}(w)$ for different values of w. We used the following error metric $d = \left[\frac{1}{r}\sum_{i=1}^{r} \frac{|P_e^{\exists}(w_i) - P^{\exists}(w_i)|}{P_e^{\exists}(w_i)}\right] 100\%$ where $w_1 < w_2 < \ldots w_r$ are the tested window sizes. In section 3.2 we tested the detection properties of the threshold $\tau_u(w)$ as a function of the window length w. All our algorithms have been implemented in C++ and run under Linux operating system.

3.1 Estimation of $P^{\exists}(w)$

In all experiments in this section we used the same testing source of length $n = 10^5$ events.

3.1.1 The case of a parallel episode S

We set $S = \{it_0, it_4, it_5, it_6, it_9, it_{10}, it_{17}\}$ and then ran the tree based detection algorithm [3] for finding $\Omega(10^5, w)$ for $w \in [10, 180]$ and compared $P_e(w)$ to the analytically computed $P^{\exists}(w)$ using our algorithm based on Theorem 2. The results are shown in Figure 5, which indicate an exceptionally close fit between $P^{\exists}(w)$ and $P_e^{\exists}(w)$ with the difference d of order 2%. The results confirm our expectations that the Bernoulli model and parallel episode models well sources as the *Wal-Mart* item scans where the source seems to generate events independently.

3.1.2 The case of a set of two serial episodes

We set $S_1 = \{it_0, it_4, it_5, it_6, it_9, it_{10}, it_{17}\}$ and $S_2 = \{it_0, it_6, it_5, it_4, it_{10}, it_9, it_{17}\}$ where S_2 is a permuted version of S_1. This case reflects a situation when a pattern of interest is only partially restricted and the serial case is too restrictive but the parallel case too relaxed. We ran an algorithm for finding $\Omega(10^5, w)$ for $\mathbf{S}$ for $w \in [10, 180]$. Then compared $P_e(w)$ to the analytically computed $P^{\exists}(w)$ using our algorithm based on Theorem 1. The results are shown in Figure 6, which indicate a very close fit between $P^{\exists}(w)$

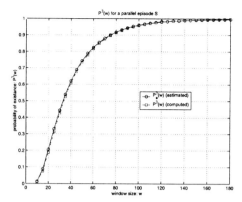

Figure 5. $P_e^\exists(w) = \frac{\Omega^\exists(n,w)}{n}$ and $P^\exists(w)$ **for a parallel episode** S**, using Wal-Mart data**

and $P_e^\exists(w)$ with d of order 13% but not so close as in the parallel case ($d = 2\%$). The reason may be the fact that this set of episodes is too restricted comparing to the parallel episode given the unordered nature of the item scans.

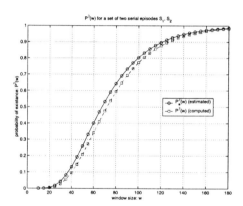

Figure 6. $P_e^\exists(w) = \frac{\Omega^\exists(n,w)}{n}$ and $P^\exists(w)$ **for a set** $S = \{S_1, S_2\}$ **of serial episodes, using** *Wal-Mart* **data**

3.1.3 Comparison of the three cases: parallel, two serial and one serial

In this experiment we investigate the relationship between the formulas for $P(w)$ and the experimental $P_e(w)$ for the episode S in the three cases: parallel, partially ordered (S_2 is a permutation of S_1) and serial (investigated in [8]). For the first two cases we use the results obtained in the previous experiments. For the third case we ran an algorithm for discovering a serial episode in the event sequence for $w \in [10, 180]$ as in the previous experiment to create $\Omega(10^5, w)$ at the same points. The results for $P^\exists(w)$ are shown in Figures 7 and the corresponding estimates are

shown in Figure 8. The figures clearly indicate that the serial and parallel cases of an episode S establish the lower and upper bound on the probability of existence of S in window of size w.

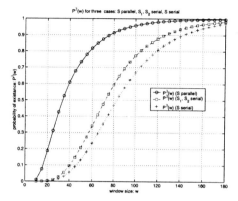

Figure 7. $P^\exists(w)$ **for three cases:** S **parallel,** $\{S_1, S_2\}$ **serial and** S **serial, using Wal-Mart data**

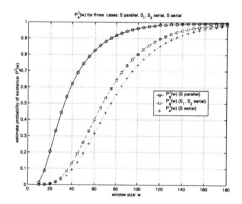

Figure 8. $P_e^\exists(w) = \frac{\Omega^\exists(n,w)}{n}$ **for three cases:** S **parallel,** $\{S_1, S_2\}$ **serial and** S **serial, using Wal-Mart data**

3.2 Threshold $\tau_u(w)$

This experiment demonstrates an application of the upper threshold $\tau_u(w)$ for detecting a significant number of occurrences of a parallel episodes S. It also shows the relationship between $\tau_u(w)$ and w in detecting unusual episodes. We set $S = \{it_8, it_{12}, it_{14}, it_{15}, it_{19}, it_{20}, it_{26}\}$ and consider the parallel case of S. We selected a part of the scans of length $n = 50000$ as the test source. We compute the threshold $\tau_u(w) = P^\exists(w) + b\frac{\sqrt{\text{Var}[\Omega^\exists(n,w)]}}{n}$ for

$\beta(b) = 10^{-6}$ for which we obtained $b = 4.26$ using an algorithm for computing the inverse of $\beta(b)$. We repeated the threshold computation for three values of $w = 40, 30, 25$ for the same episode S. We simulated an attack by keeping inserting the episode S as a string into the testing source until we exceeded the threshold. We normalized the number of insertion by n. Figure 9 presents results. We conclude that the if w increases then the number of attacks causing $\frac{\Omega^{\exists}(n,w)}{n}$ to rise above the $\tau_u(w)$ increases exponentially which is caused by the exponential growth of $P^{\exists}(w)$ in the formula for $\tau_u(w)$.

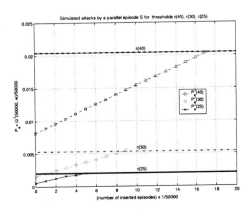

Figure 9. The upper threshold $\tau_u(w)$ as a function of w for a parallel episode S, using the Wal-Mart database

4 Conclusions

We presented the exact formulas for the probability of existence $P^{\exists}(w)$, for an arbitrary set of serial episodes **S** including the case of a parallel episode S. Using the formulas we showed how to compute the upper threshold $\tau_u(w)$ to measure significance of **S**. Since we adopted a computational probability approach it is valid for the Markov model of any order. The choice of the 0-the order (Bernoulli) was dictated only by its compactness and suitability to implementation through efficient dynamic programming algorithms. However in experiments on *Wal-Mart* transactions we showed that formulas for the Bernoulli model very closely approximated the real life data. Realization of Markov model of order higher then 0 would require computation of $P^{\exists}(w)$ using conditional probabilities of the respective order.

Acknowledgment

The authors are very grateful to Prof. Chris Clifton for many valuable remarks and encouragements.

References

[1] A. Aho and M. Corasick (1975), Efficient String Matching: An Aid to Bibliographic Search *Programming Techniques*.

[2] A. Apostolico and M. Atallah (2002), Compact Recognizers of Episode Sequences, *Information and Computation*, 174, 180-192.

[3] M. Atallah, R. Gwadera and W. Szpankowski. Detection of significant sets of episodes in event sequences. http://www.cs.purdue.edu/homes/gwadera/icdm2full.ps.

[4] P. Billingsley (1986), *Probability and measure*, John Wiley, New York.

[5] L. Boasson, P. Sequels, I. Guessarian, and Y. Matiyasevich (1999), Window-Accumulated Subsequence Matching Problem is Linear, *Proc. PODS*, 327-336.

[6] G. Das, R. Fleischer, L. Gasieniec, D. Gunopulos, and J. Kärkkäinen (1997), Episode Matching, In *Combinatorial Pattern Matching, 8th Annual Symposium, Lecture Notes in Computer Science* vol. 1264, 12–27.

[7] P. Flajolet, Y. Guivarc'h, W. Szpankowski, and B. Vallée (2001), Hidden Pattern Statistics, ICALP 2001, Crete, Greece, LNCS 2076, 152-165.

[8] R. Gwadera, M. Atallah, and W. Szpankowski. Reliable detection of episodes in event sequences. In *Third IEEE International Conference on Data Mining*, pages 67-74, Melbourne, Florida.

[9] J. Han, J. Pei, Y. Yin, R. Mao, Mining Frequent Patterns without Candidate Generation: A Frequent-Pattern Tree Approach, *Data Mining and Knowledge Discovery*, 8, 53-87, 2004

[10] H. Mannila, H. Toivonen, and A. Verkamo (1997), Discovery of frequent episodes in event sequences *Data Mining and Knowledge Discovery*, 1(3), 241-258.

[11] M. Régnier and W. Szpankowski (1998), On pattern frequency occurrences in a Markovian sequence *Algorithmica*, 22, 631-649.

[12] W. Szpankowski (2001), *Average Case Analysis of Algorithms on Sequence*, John Wiley, New York.

Subspace Selection for Clustering High-Dimensional Data

Christian Baumgartner, Claudia Plant
University for Health Sciences, Medical Informatics and Technology, Innsbruck, Austria
{christian.baumgartner,claudia.plant}@umit.at

Karin Kailing, Hans-Peter Kriegel, Peer Kröger
Institute for Computer Science, University of Munich, Germany
{kailing,kriegel,kroegerp}@dbs.ifi.lmu.de

Abstract

In high-dimensional feature spaces traditional clustering algorithms tend to break down in terms of efficiency and quality. Nevertheless, the data sets often contain clusters which are hidden in various subspaces of the original feature space. In this paper, we present a feature selection technique called SURFING (SUbspaces Relevant For clusterING) that finds all subspaces interesting for clustering and sorts them by relevance. The sorting is based on a quality criterion for the interestingness of a subspace using the k-nearest neighbor distances of the objects. As our method is more or less parameterless, it addresses the unsupervised notion of the data mining task "clustering" in a best possible way. A broad evaluation based on synthetic and real-world data sets demonstrates that SURFING is suitable to find all relevant subspaces in high dimensional, sparse data sets and produces better results than comparative methods.

1. Introduction

One of the primary data mining tasks is clustering which is intended to help a user discovering and understanding the natural structure or grouping in a data set. In particular, clustering aims at partitioning the data objects into distinct groups (clusters) while minimizing the intra-cluster similarity and maximizing the inter-cluster similarity. A lot of work has been done in the area of clustering (see e.g. [8] for an overview). However, many real-world data sets consist of very high dimensional feature spaces. In such high dimensional feature spaces, most of the common algorithms tend to break down in terms of efficiency and accuracy because usually many features are irrelevant and or correlated. In addition, different subgroups of features may be irrelevant or correlated according to varying subgroups of data objects. Thus, objects can often be clustered differently in varying subspaces. Usually, global dimensionality reduction techniques such as PCA cannot be applied to these data sets because they cannot account for local trends in the data.

To cope with these problems, the procedure of feature selection has to be combined with the clustering process more closely. In recent years, the task of subspace clustering was introduced to address these demands. In general, subspace clustering is the task of automatically detecting all clusters in all subspaces of the original feature space, either by directly computing the subspace clusters (e.g. in [3]) or by selecting interesting subspaces for clustering (e.g. in [9]).

In this paper, we propose an advanced feature selection method preserving the information of objects clustered differently in varying subspaces. Our method called SURFING (*SU*bspaces *R*elevant *F*or cluster*ING*) computes all relevant subspaces and ranks them according to the interestingness of the hierarchical clustering structure they exhibit.

The remainder of this paper is organized as follows. We discuss related work and point out our contributions in Section 2. A quality criterion for ranking the interestingness of subspaces is developed in Section 3. In Section 4 the algorithm SURFING is presented. An experimental evaluation of SURFING in the context of comparative subspace clustering methods is presented in Section 5. Section 6 concludes the paper.

2. Related Work

2.1. Subspace Clustering

The pioneering approach to subspace clustering is CLIQUE [3], using an *Apriori*-like method to navigate through the set of possible subspaces. The data space is partitioned by an axis-parallel grid into equi-sized units of width ξ. Only units whose densities exceed a threshold τ are retained. A cluster is defined as a maximal set of connected dense units. The performance of CLIQUE heavily depend on the positioning of the grid. Objects that naturally belong to a cluster may be missed or objects that are naturally noise may be assigned to a cluster due to an unfavorable grid position.

Another recent approach called DOC [10] proposes a mathematical formulation for the notion of an optimal projected cluster, regarding the density of points in subspaces. DOC is not grid-based but as the density of subspaces is measured using hypercubes of fixed width w, it has similar problems like CLIQUE.

In [2] the method PROCLUS to compute projected clusters is presented. However, PROCLUS misses out the information of objects clustered differently in varying subspaces. The same holds for ORCLUS [1].

2.2. Feature Selection for Clustering

In [9] a method called RIS is proposed that ranks the subspaces according to their clustering structure. The ranking is based on a quality criterion using the density-based clustering notion of DBSCAN [7]. An *Apriori*-like navigation through the set of possible subspaces in a bottom-up way is performed to find all interesting subspaces. Aggregated information is accumulated for each subspace to rank its interestingness.

In [6] a quality criterion for subspaces based on the entropy of point-to-point distances is introduced. However, there is no algorithm presented to compute the interesting subspaces. The authors propose to use a forward search strategy which most likely will miss interesting subspaces, or an exhaustive search strategy which is obviously not efficient in higher dimensions.

2.3. Our Contributions

Recent density-based approaches to subspace clustering or subspace selection methods (RIS) use a global density threshold for the definition of clusters due to efficiency reasons. However, the application of a global density threshold to subspaces of different dimensionality and to all clusters in one subspace is rather unacceptable. The data space naturally increases exponentially with each dimension added to a subspace and clusters in the same subspace may exceed different density parameters or exhibit a nested hierarchical clustering structure. Therefore, for subspace clustering, it would be highly desirable to adapt the density threshold to the dimensionality of the subspaces or even better to rely on a hierarchical clustering notion that is independent from a globally fixed threshold.

In this paper, we introduce SURFING, a feature selection method for clustering which does not rely on a global density parameter. Our approach explores all subspaces exhibiting an *interesting* hierarchical clustering structure and ranks them according to a quality criterion. SURFING is more or less parameterless, i.e. it does not require the user to specify parameters that are hard to anticipate such as the number of clusters, the (average) dimensionality of subspace clusters, or a global density threshold. Thus, our algorithm addresses the *unsupervised* notion of the data mining task "clustering" in a best possible way.

3. Subspaces Relevant for Clustering

Let DB be a set of N feature vectors with dimensionality d, i.e. $DB \subseteq \mathbb{R}^d$. Let $\mathcal{A} = \{a_1, \ldots, a_d\}$ be the set of all attributes a_i of DB. Any subset $S \subset \mathcal{A}$, is called a *subspace*. T is a *superspace* of S if $S \subset T$. The projection of an object o onto a subspace $S \subseteq \mathcal{A}$ is denoted by o_S. We assume that $d : DB \times DB \to \mathbb{R}$ is a metric distance function.

3.1. General Idea

The main idea of SURFING is to measure the "interestingness" of a subspace w.r.t. to its hierarchical clustering structure, independent from its dimensionality. Like most previous approaches to subspace clustering, we base our measurement on a density-based clustering notion. Since we do not want to rely on a global density parameter, we developed a quality criterion for relevant subspaces built on the k-nearest neighbor distances (k-nn-distances) of the objects in DB.

For a user-specified $k \in \mathbb{N}$ ($k \le N$) and a subspace $S \subseteq \mathcal{A}$ let $NN_k^S(o)$ be the set of k-nearest neighbors of an object $o \in DB$ in a subspace S. The k-nn-distance of o in a subspace S, denoted by $nn\text{-}Dist_k^S(o)$, is the distance between o and its k-nearest neighbor, formally:

$$nn\text{-}Dist_k^S(o) = \max\{d(o_S, p_S) \mid p \in NN_k^S(o)\}.$$

The k-nn-distance of an object o indicates how densely the data space is populated around o in S. The smaller the value of $nn\text{-}Dist_k^S(o)$, the more dense the objects are packed around o, and *vice versa*. If a subspace contains a recognizable hierarchical clustering structure, i.e. clusters with different densities and noise objects, the k-nn-distances of objects should differ significantly. On the other hand, if all points are uniformly distributed, the k-nn-distances can be assumed

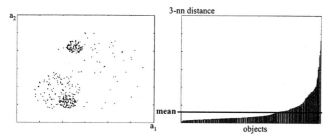

(a) Hierarchical clustering structure in a 2D subspace(left); according sorted 3-nn graph (right)

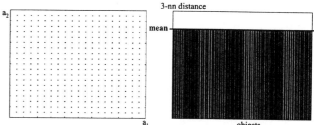

(b) Uniform distribution in a 2D subspace (left); according sorted 3-nn graph (right)

Figure 1: Usefulness of the k-nn distance to rate the interestingness of subspaces.

to be almost equal. Figure 1 illustrates these considerations using a sample 2D subspace $S = \{a_1, a_2\}$ and $k = 3$. Consequently, we are interested in subspaces where the k-nn-distances of the objects differ significantly from each other, because the hierarchical clustering structure in such subspaces will be considerably clearer than in subspaces where the k-nn-distances are rather similar to each other.

3.2. A Quality Criterion for Subspaces

As mentioned above we want to measure how much the k-nn-distances in S differ from each other. To achieve comparability between subspaces of different dimensionality, we scale all k-nn-distances in a subspace S into the range $[0, 1]$. Thus, we assume that $nn\text{-}Dist_k^S(o) \in [0, 1]$ for all $o \in DB$ throughout the rest of the paper.

Two well-known statistical measures for our purpose are the mean value μ_S of all k-nn-distances in subspace $S$and the variance. However, the variance is not appropriate for our purpose because it measures the squared differences of each k-nn-distance to μ_S and thus, high differences are weighted stronger than low differences. For our quality criterion we want to measure the non-weighted differences of each k-nn-distance to μ_S. Since the sum of the differences of all objects *above* μ_S is equal to the sum of the differences of all objects *below* μ_S, we only take half of the sum of all differences to the mean value, denoted by $diff_{\mu_S}$, which can be computed by

$$diff_{\mu_S} = \frac{1}{2} \sum_{o \in DB} |\mu_S - nn\text{-}Dist_k^S(o)|.$$

In fact, $diff_{\mu_S}$ is already a good measure for rating the interestingness of a subspace. We can further scale this value by μ_S times the number of objects having

a smaller k-nn-distance in S than μ_S, i.e. the objects contained in the following set:

$$Below_S := \{o \in DB \mid nn\text{-}Dist_k^S(o) < \mu_S\}.$$

Obviously, if $Below_S$ is empty, the subspace contains uniformly distributed noise.

Definition 1 (quality of a subspace) *Let $S \subseteq \mathcal{A}$. The quality of S, denoted by $quality(S)$, is defined as follows:*

$$quality(S) = \begin{cases} 0 & if\, Below_S = \emptyset \\ \frac{diff_{\mu_S}}{|Below_S| \cdot \mu_S} & else. \end{cases}$$

The quality values are in the range between 0 and 1. A subspace where all objects are uniformly distributed (e.g. as depicted in Figure 1(b)) has a quality value of approximately 0, indicating a less interesting clustering structure. On the other hand, the clearer the hierarchical clustering structure in a subspace S is, the higher is the value of $quality(S)$. For example, the sample 2D subspace in which the data is highly structured as depicted in Figure 1(a) will have a significantly higher quality value. Let us note that in the synthetic case where all objects in $Below_S$ have a k-nn-distance of 0 and all other objects have a k-nn-distance of $2 \cdot \mu_S$, the quality value $quality(S)$ is 1.

In almost all cases, we can detect the relevant subspaces with this quality criterion, but there are two artificial cases rarely found in natural data sets which nevertheless cannot be ignored.

First, there might be a subspace containing some clusters, each of the same density, and without noise (e.g. data set A in Figure 2). If the number of data objects in the clusters exceeds k, such subspaces cannot be distinguished from subspaces containing uniformly distributed data objects spread over the whole attribute range (e.g. data set B in Figure 2) because in both

13

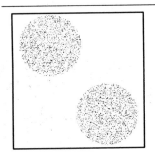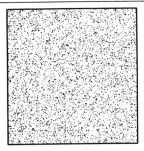

| data set A | data set B |

% of inserted points	$quality(A)$	$quality(B)$
0	0.13	0.15
0.1	0.15	0.15
0.2	0.19	0.15
0.5	0.31	0.15
1	0.38	0.15
5	0.57	0.15
10	0.57	0.15

Figure 2: Benefit of inserted points.

cases, the k-nn-distances of the objects will marginally differ from the mean value.

Second, subspaces containing data of one Gaussian distribution spread over the whole attribute range are not really interesting. However, the k-nn-distances of the objects will scatter significantly around the mean value. Thus, such subspaces cannot be distinguished from subspaces containing two or more Gaussian clusters without noise.

To overcome these two artificial cases, we can virtually insert some randomly generated points before computing the quality value of a subspace. In cases of uniform or Gaussian distribution over the whole attribute range, the insertion of a few randomly generated additional objects does not significantly affect the quality value. The k-nn-distances of these objects are similar to the k-nn-distances of all the other data objects. However, if there are dense and empty areas in a subspace, the insertion of some additional points very likely increases the quality value, because these additional objects have large k-nn-distances compared to those of the other objects. The table in Figure 2 shows the quality value of the 2D data set A depicted in Figure 2 w.r.t. the percentage of virtually inserted random objects. Data set B in Figure 2 has no visible cluster structure and therefore the virtually inserted points do not affect the quality value. For example, 0.2 % additionally inserted points means that for $n = 5,000$ 10 random objects have been virtually inserted before calculating the quality value.

Thus, inserting randomly generated points is a proper strategy to distinguish (good) subspaces containing several uniformly distributed clusters of equal density or several Gaussian clusters without noise from (bad) subspaces containing only one uniform or Gaussian distribution. In fact, it empirically turned out that 1% of additional points is sufficient to achieve the desired results. Let us note that this strategy is only required, if the subspaces contain a clear clustering structure without noise. In most real-world data sets the subspaces do not show a clear cluster structure and often have much more than 10% noise. In addition, the number of noise objects is usually growing with increasing dimensionality. In such data sets, virtually inserting additional points is not required. Since our quality criterion is very sensible to areas of different density, it is suitable to detect relevant subspaces in data sets with high percentages of noise, e. g. in gene expression data sets or in synthetic data sets containing up to 90% noise.

4. Algorithm

The pseudocode of the algorithm SURFING is given in Figure 3. Since lower dimensional subspaces are more likely to contain an interesting clustering, SURFING generates all relevant subspaces in a bottom-up way, i.e. it starts with all 1-dimensional subspaces S_1 and discards as many irrelevant subspaces as early as possible. Therefore, we need a criterion to decide whether it is interesting to generate and examine a certain subspace or not. Our above described quality measure can only be used to decide about the interestingness of an already given subspace. An important information we have gathered while proceeding to dimension l is the quality of all $(l-1)$-dimensional subspaces. We can use this information to compute a quality threshold which enables us to rate all l-dimensional candidate subspaces S_l. We use the lowest quality value of any $(l-1)$-dimensional subspace as threshold. If the quality values of the $(l-1)$-dimensional subspaces do not differ enough (it empirically turned out that a difference of at least $1/3$ is a reasonable reference difference), we take half of the best quality value instead. Using this quality threshold, we can divide all l-dimensional subspaces into three different categories:

Interesting subspace: the quality value increases or stays the same w.r.t. its $(l-1)$-dimensional subspaces.
Neutral subspaces: the quality decreases w.r.t. its $(l-1)$-dimensional subspaces, but lies above the threshold and thus might indicate a higher dimensional interesting subspace.
Irrelevant subspaces: the quality decreases w.r.t its

$(l-1)$-dimensional subspace below the threshold. We use this classification to discard all irrelevant l-dimensional subspaces from further consideration. We know that these subspaces are not interesting itself and, as our quality value is comparable over different dimensions, we further know that no superspace of such a subspace will obtain a high quality value compared to interesting subspaces of dimensionality l. Even if through adding a "good" dimension, the quality value would slightly increase it will not be getting better than already existing ones.

However, before we discard an irrelevant subspace S of dimensionality l, we have to test whether its clustering structure exhibits one of the artificial cases mentioned in the previous section. For that purpose, if the quality of S is lower than the quality of a subspace containing an l-dimensional Gaussian distribution, we insert 1% random points and recompute the quality of S. Otherwise, the clustering structure of S cannot get better through the insertion of additional points. In case of a clean cluster structure without noise in S, the quality value improves significantly after the insertion. At least it will be better than the quality of the l-dimensional Gaussian distribution, and, in this case, S is not discarded.

If, due to the threshold, there are only irrelevant l-dimensional subspaces, we don't use the threshold, but keep all l-dimensional subspaces. In this case, the information we have so far, is not enough to decide about the interestingness.

Finally, the remaining l-dimensional subspaces in $\mathcal{S}_l$ are joined if they share any $(l-1)$-dimensions to generate the set of $(l+1)$-dimensional candidate subspaces $\mathcal{S}_{l+1}$. SURFING terminates if the resulting candidate set is empty.

SURFING needs only one input parameter k, the choice of which is rather simple. If k is too small, the k-nn-distances are not meaningful, since objects within dense regions might have similar k-nn-distance values as objects in sparse regions. If k is too high, the same phenomenon may occur. Obviously, k must somehow correspond to the minimum cluster size, i.e. the minimal number of objects regarded as a cluster.

5. Evaluation

We tested SURFING on several synthetic and real-world data sets and evaluated its accuracy in comparison to CLIQUE, RIS and the subspace selection proposed in [6] (in the following called Entropy). All experiments were run on a PC with a 2.79 GHz CPU and 504 MB RAM. We combined SURFING, RIS and Entropy with the hierarchical clustering algorithm OP-

---

```
algorithm SURFING(Database DB, Integer k)
// 1-dimensional subspaces
    𝒮₁ := {{a₁}, ..., {a_d}};
    compute quality of all subspaces S ∈ 𝒮₁;
    S_l := S ∈ 𝒮₁ with lowest quality;
    S_h := S ∈ 𝒮₁ with highest quality;
    if quality(S_l) > 2/3 · quality(S_h) then
        τ := quality(S_h)/2;
    else
        τ := quality(S_l);
        𝒮₁ = 𝒮₁ − {S_l};
    end if
// k-dimensional-subspaces
    k := 2;
    create 𝒮₂ from 𝒮₁;
    while not 𝒮_k = ∅ do
        compute quality of all subspaces S in 𝒮_k;
        Interesting := {S ∈ 𝒮_k | quality(S) ↑};
        Neutral := {S ∈ 𝒮_k | quality(s) ↓ ∧ quality(S) > τ};
        Irrelevant := {S ∈ 𝒮_k | quality(S) ≤ τ};
        S_l := S ∈ 𝒮_k with lowest quality;
        S_h := S ∈ 𝒮_k − Interesting with highest quality;
        if quality(S_l) > 2/3 · quality(S_h) then
            τ := quality(S_h)/2;
        else
            τ := quality(s_l);
        end if
        if not all subspaces irrelevant then
            𝒮_k := 𝒮_k − Irrelevant;
        end if
        create 𝒮_{k+1} from 𝒮_k;
        k := k + 1;
    end while
end
```

Figure 3: Algorithm SURFING.

TICS [4] to compute the hierarchical clustering structure in the detected subspaces.

Synthetic Data. The synthetic data sets were generated by a self-implemented data generator. It permits to specify the number and dimensionality of subspace clusters, dimensionality of the feature space and density parameters for the whole data set as well as for each cluster. In a subspace that contains a cluster, the average density within that cluster is much larger than the density of noise. In addition, it is ensured that none of the synthetically generated data sets can be clustered in the full dimensional space.

Gene Expression Data. We tested SURFING on a real-world gene expression data set studying the yeast mitotic cell cycle [11]. We used only the data set of the CDC15 mutant and eliminated those genes from our test data set having missing attribute values. The re-

Table 1: Results on synthetic data sets.

data set	d	cluster dim.	N	# subspaces		time (s)
				m	%	
02	10	4	4936	107	10.45	351
03	10	4	18999	52	5.08	2069
04	10	4	27704	52	5.08	4401
05	15	2	4045	119	0.36	194
06	15	5	3802	391	1.19	807
07	15	3,5,7	4325	285	0.87	715
08	15	5	4057	197	0.60	391
09	15	7	3967	1046	3.19	3031
10	15	12	3907	4124	12.59	15321
11	10	5	3700	231	22.56	442
12	20	5	3700	572	0.05	1130
13	30	5	3700	1077	0.0001	2049
14	40	5	3700	1682	$1.5 \cdot 10^{-7}$	3145
15	50	5	3700	2387	$2.1 \cdot 10^{-10}$	4255
16	15	4,6,7,10	2671	912	2.8	4479

sulting data set contains around 4000 genes measured at 24 different time slots. The task is to find functionally related genes using cluster analysis.

Metabolome Data. In addition we tested SURFING on high-dimensional metabolic data provided from the newborn screening program in Bavaria, Germany. Our experimental data sets were generated from modern tandem mass spectrometry. In particular we focused on a dimensionality of 14 metabolites in order to mine single and promising combinations of key markers in the abnormal metabolism of phenylketonuria (PKU), a severe amino acid disorder. The resulting database contains 319 cases designated as PKU and 1322 control individuals expressed as 14 amino acids and intermediate metabolic products. The task is to extract a subset of metabolites that correspond well to the abnormal metabolism of PKU.

5.1. Efficiency

The runtimes of SURFING applied to the synthetic data sets are summarized in Table 1. In all experiments, we set $k = 10$.

For each subspace, SURFING needs $O(N^2)$ time to compute for each of the N points in DB the k-nn-distance, since there is no index structure which could support the partial k-nn-queries in arbitrary subspaces in logarithmic time. If SURFING analyzes m different subspaces the overall runtime complexity is $O(m \cdot N^2)$. Of course in the worst case m can be 2^d, but in practice we are only examining a very small percentage of all possible subspaces. Indeed, our experiments show, that the heuristic generation of subspace candidates

used by SURFING ensures a small value for m (cf. Table 1). For most complex data sets, SURFING computes less than 5% of the total number of possible subspaces. In most cases, this ratio is even significantly less than 1%. For data set 10 in Table 1 where the cluster is hidden in a 12-dimensional subspace of a 15-dimensional feature space, SURFING only computes 12.5% of the possible subspaces. Finally, for both the real world data sets, SURFING computes even significantly less than 0.1% of the possible subspaces (not shown in Table 1). The worst ever observed percentage was around 20%. This empirically demonstrates that SURFING is a highly efficient solution for the complex subspace selection problem.

5.2. Effectivity

Results on Synthetic Data. We applied SURFING to several synthetic data sets (cf. Table 1). In all but one case, SURFING detected the correct subspaces containing the relevant clusters and ranked them first. Even for data set 16, SURFING was able to detect 4 out of 5 subspaces containing clusters, although the clustering structure of the subspaces containing clusters was rather weak, e.g. one of the 4-dimensional subspaces contained a cluster with only 20 objects having an average k-nn-distance of 2.5 (the average k-nn-distance for all objects in all dimensions was 15.0). SURFING only missed a 10-dimensional subspace which contained a cluster with 17 objects having an average k-nn-distance of 9.0.

Results on Gene Expression Data. We tested SURFING on the gene expression data set and retrieved a hierarchical clustering by applying OPTICS [4] to the top-ranked subspaces. We found many biologically interesting and significant clusters in several subspaces. The functional relationships of the genes in the resulting clusters were validated using the public Saccharomyces Genome Database[1]. Some excerpts from sample clusters in varying subspaces found by SURFING applied to the gene expression data are depicted in Table 2. Cluster 1 contains several cell cycle genes. In addition, the two gene products are part of a common protein complex. Cluster 2 contains the gene STE12, an important regulatory factor for the mitotic cycle [11] and the genes CDC27 and EMP47 which are most likely co-expressed with STE12. Cluster 3 consists of the genes CDC25 (starting point for mitosis), MYO3 and NUD1 (known for an active role dur-

---

1 http://www.yeastgenome.org/

16

Table 2: Results on gene expression data.

Gene Name	Function
Cluster 1 (subspace 90, 110, 130, 190)	
RPC40	builds complex with CDC60
CDC60	tRNA synthetase
FRS1	tRNA synthetase
DOM34	protein synthesis, mitotic cell cycle
CKA1	mitotic cell cycle control
MIP6	RNA binding activity, mitotic cell cycle
Cluster 2 (subspace 90, 110, 130, 190)	
STE12	transcription factor (cell cycle)
CDC27	possible STE12-site
EMP47	possible STE12-site
XBP1	transcription factor
Cluster 3 (subspace 90, 110, 130, 190)	
CDC25	starting control factor for mitosis
MYO3	control/regulation factor for mitosis
NUD1	control/regulation factor for mitosis
Cluster 4 (subspace 190, 270, 290)	
RPT6	protein catabolism; complex with RPN10
RPN10	protein catabolism; complex with RPT6
UBC1	protein catabolism; part of 26S protease
UBC4	protein catabolism; part of 26S protease
Cluster 5 (subspace 70, 90, 110, 130)	
SOF1	part of small ribosomal subunit
NAN1	part of small ribosomal subunit
RPS1A	structural constituent of ribosome
MIP6	RNA binding activity, mitotic cell cycle
Cluster 6 (subspace 70, 90, 110, 130)	
RIB1	participate in riboflavin biosynthesis
RIB4	participate in riboflavin biosynthesis
RIB5	participate in riboflavin biosynthesis

Table 3: Comparative tests on synthetic data.

data set	# clusters/ subspaces	correct clusters/subspaces found by			
		CLIQUE	RIS	E	SURFING
06	2	1	2	0	2
07	3	1	2	0	2
08	3	1	3	0	3
16	5	0	3	0	4

ing PCA. Only components with eigen value > 1 were extracted. Varimax rotation was applied. PCA findings showed 4 components (eigen values of components 1-4 are 4.039, 2.612, 1.137 and 1.033) that retain 63% of total variation. However, SURFING's best ranked single metabolites ArgSuc, Glu, Cit and Arg are not highly loaded (> 0.6) on one of four extracted components. Moreover, combinations of promising metabolites (higher dimensional subspaces) are not able to be considered in PCA. Particularly in abnormal metabolism, not only alterations of single metabolites but more interactions of several markers are often involved. As our results demonstrate, SURFING is more usable on metabolic data taking higher dimensional subspaces into account.

Influence of Parameter k. We re-ran our experiments on the synthetic data sets with $k = 3, 5, 10, 15, 20$. We observed that if $k = 3$, SURFING did find the correct subspaces but did not rank the subspaces first (i.e. subspaces with a less clear hierarchical clustering structure got a higher quality value). In the range of $5 \leq k \leq 20$, SURFING produced similar results for all synthetic data sets. This indicates that SURFING is quite robust against the choice of k within this range.

Comparison with CLIQUE. The results of CLIQUE applied to the synthetic data sets confirmed the suggestions that its accuracy heavily depends on the choice of the input parameters which is a nontrivial task. In some cases, CLIQUE failed to detect the subspace clusters hidden in the data but computed some dubious clusters. In addition, CLIQUE is not able to detect clusters of different density. Applied to our data sets which exhibit several clusters with varying density (e.g. data set 16), CLIQUE was not able to detect all clusters correctly but could only detect (parts of) one cluster (cf. Table 3) — even though we used a broad parameter setting. A similar result can be reported when we applied CLIQUE to the gene expression data set. CLIQUE was not able to obtain any useful clusters for a broad range of parameter settings. In sum-

ing mitosis) and various other transcription factors required during the cell cycle. Cluster 4 contains several genes related to the protein catabolism. Cluster 5 contains several structural parts of the ribosomes and related genes. Let us note, that MPI6 is clustered differently in varying subspaces (cf. Cluster 1 and Cluster 5). Cluster 6 contains the genes that code for proteins participating in a common pathway.

Results on Metabolome Data. Applying SURFING to metabolic data, we identified 13 subspaces considering quality values > 0.8. In detail, we extracted 5 one-dimensional spaces (the metabolites ArgSuc, Phe, Glu, Cit and Arg), 6 two- dimensional spaces (e.g. Phe-ArgSuc, Phe-Glu) and 3 three-dimensional spaces (e.g. Phe-Glu-ArgSuc). Alterations of our best ranked single metabolites correspond well to the abnormal metabolism of PKU [5]. We compared SURFING findings with results us-

mary, SURFING does not only outperform CLIQUE by means of quality, but also saves the user from finding a suitable parameter setting.

Comparison with RIS. Using RIS causes similar problems as observed when using CLIQUE. The quality of the results computed by RIS also depends, with slightly less impact, on the input parameters. Like CLIQUE, in some cases RIS failed to detect the correct subspaces due to the utilization of a global density parameter (cf. Table 3). For example, applied to data set 16, RIS was able to compute the lower dimensional subspaces, but could not detect the higher dimensional one. The application of RIS to the gene expression data set is described in [9]. SURFING confirmed these results but found several other interesting subspaces with important clusters, e.g. clusters 5 and 6 in subspace 70, 90, 110, 130 (cf. Figure 2). Applying RIS to the metabolome data set the best ranked subspace contains 12 attributes which represent nearly the full feature space and are biologically not interpretable. The application of RIS to all data sets, was limited by the choice of the right parameter setting. Again, SURFING does not only outperform RIS by means of quality, but also saves the user from finding a suitable parameter setting.

Comparison with Entropy. Using the quality criterion Entropy (E) in conjunction with the proposed forward search algorithm in [6], none of the correct subspaces were found. In all cases, the subspace selection method stops at a dimensionality of 2. Possibly, an exhaustive search examining all possible subspaces could produce better results. However, this approach obviously yields unacceptable run times. Applied to the metabolome data, the biologically relevant 1D subspaces are ranked low.

6. Conclusion

In this paper, we introduced a new method to subspace clustering called SURFING which is more or less parameterless and — in contrast to most recent approaches — does not rely on a global density threshold. SURFING ranks subspaces of high dimensional data according to their interestingness for clustering. We empirically showed that the only input parameter of SURFING is stable in a broad range of settings and that SURFING does not favor subspaces of a certain dimensionality. A comparative experimental evaluation shows that SURFING is an efficient and accurate solution to the complex subspace clustering problem. It outperforms recent subspace clustering methods in terms of effectivity.

Acknowledgment

Parts of this work is supported by the German Ministry for Education, Science, Research and Technology (BMBF) (grant no. 031U112F) and by the Austrian Industrial Research Promotion Fund FFF (grand no. HITT-10 UMIT).

References

[1] C. Aggarwal and P. Yu. "Finding Generalized Projected Clusters in High Dimensional Space". In *Proc. ACM SIGMOD Int. Conf. on Management of Data (SIGMOD'00)*, 2000.

[2] C. C. Aggarwal and C. Procopiuc. "Fast Algorithms for Projected Clustering". In *Proc. ACM SIGMOD Int. Conf. on Management of Data (SIGMOD'99)*, 1999.

[3] R. Agrawal, J. Gehrke, D. Gunopulos, and P. Raghavan. "Automatic Subspace Clustering of High Dimensional Data for Data Mining Applications". In *Proc. ACM SIGMOD Int. Conf. on Management of Data (SIGMOD'98)*, 1998.

[4] M. Ankerst, M. M. Breunig, H.-P. Kriegel, and J. Sander. "OPTICS: Ordering Points to Identify the Clustering Structure". In *Proc. ACM SIGMOD Int. Conf. on Management of Data (SIGMOD'99)*, 1999.

[5] C. Baumgartner, C. Böhm, D. Baumgartner, G. Marini, K. Weinberger, B. Olgemöller, B. Liebl, and A. A. Roscher. "Supervised machine learning techniques for the classification of metabolic disorders in newborns". *Bioinformatics*, 2004. in press.

[6] M. Dash, K. Choi, P. Scheuermann, and H. Liu. "Feature Selection for Clustering – A Filter Solution". In *Proc. IEEE Int. Conf. on Data Mining (ICDM'02)*, 2002.

[7] M. Ester, H.-P. Kriegel, J. Sander, and X. Xu. "A Density-Based Algorithm for Discovering Clusters in Large Spatial Databases with Noise". In *Proc. 2nd Int. Conf. on Knowledge Discovery and Data Mining (KDD'96)*, 1996.

[8] J. Han and M. Kamber. *Data Mining: Concepts and Techniques*. Academic Press, 2001.

[9] K. Kailing, H.-P. Kriegel, P. Kröger, and S. Wanka. "Ranking Interesting Subspaces for Clustering High Dimensional Data". In *Proc. 7th European Conf. on Principles and Practice of Knowledge Discovery in Databases (PKDD'03)*, 2003.

[10] C. M. Procopiuc, M. Jones, P. K. Agarwal, and T. M. Murali. "A Monte Carlo Algorithm for Fast Projective Clustering". In *Proc. ACM SIGMOD Int. Conf. on Management of Data (SIGMOD'02)*, 2002.

[11] P. Spellman, G. Sherlock, M. Zhang, V. Iyer, K. Anders, M. Eisen, P. Brown, D. Botstein, and B. Futcher. "Comprehensive Identification of Cell Cycle-Regulated Genes of the Yeast Saccharomyces Cerevisiae by Microarray Hybridization.". *Molecular Biolology of the Cell*, 9:3273–3297, 1998.

Multi-View Clustering

Steffen Bickel and Tobias Scheffer
Humboldt-Universität zu Berlin
Department of Computer Science
Unter den Linden 6, 10099 Berlin, Germany
{bickel, scheffer}@informatik.hu-berlin.de

Abstract

We consider clustering problems in which the available attributes can be split into two independent subsets, such that either subset suffices for learning. Example applications of this multi-view *setting include clustering of web pages which have an intrinsic view (the pages themselves) and an extrinsic view (e.g., anchor texts of inbound hyperlinks); multi-view learning has so far been studied in the context of classification. We develop and study partitioning and agglomerative, hierarchical multi-view clustering algorithms for text data. We find empirically that the multiview versions of k-Means and EM greatly improve on their single-view counterparts. By contrast, we obtain negative results for agglomerative hierarchical multi-view clustering. Our analysis explains this surprising phenomenon.*

1. Introduction

In some interesting application domains, instances are represented by attributes that can naturally be split into two subsets, either of which suffices for learning. A prominent example are web pages, which can be classified based on their content as well as based on the anchor texts of inbound hyperlinks; other examples include collections of research papers. If few labeled examples and, in addition, unlabeled data are available, then the co-training algorithm [4] and other multi-view classification algorithms [15, 5] improve the classification accuracy often substantially.

Multi-view algorithms train two independent hypotheses which bootstrap by providing each other with labels for the unlabeled data. The training algorithms tend to maximize the agreement between the two independent hypotheses. Dasgupta et al. [7] have shown that the disagreement between two independent hypotheses is an upper bound on the error rate of one hypothesis; this observation explains at least some of the often remarkable success of multiview learning. It also gives rise to the question whether the multi-view approach can be used to improve clustering algorithms.

Partitioning methods – such as k-Means, k-Medoids, and EM – and hierarchical, agglomerative methods [11] are among the clustering approaches most frequently used in data mining. We study multi-view versions of these families of algorithms for document clustering.

The rest of this paper is organized as follows. We review related work in Section 2, the problem setting and evaluation issues in Section 3. We discuss partitioning multiview clustering algorithms in Section 4 and hierarchical algorithms in Section 5. Section 6 concludes.

2. Related Work

Research on multi-view learning in the semi-supervised setting has been introduced by two papers, Yarowsky [18] and Blum and Mitchell [4]. Yarowsky describes an algorithm for word sense disambiguation. It uses a classifier based on the local context of a word (view one) and a second classifier using the senses of other occurrences of that word in the same document (view two), where both classifiers iteratively bootstrap each other.

Blum and Mitchell introduce the term co-training as a general term for bootstrapping procedures in which two hypotheses are trained on distinct views. They describe a cotraining algorithm which augments the training set of two classifiers with the n_p positive and n_n negative highest confidence examples from the unlabeled data in each iteration for each view. The two classifiers work on different views and a new training example is exclusively based on the decision of one classifier.

Blum and Mitchell require a conditional independence assumption of the views and give an intuitive explanation on why their algorithm works, in terms of maximizing agreement on unlabeled data. They also state that the Yarowsky algorithm falls under the co-training setting. The co-EM algorithm [16, 10, 5] is a multi-view version of the Expectation Maximization algorithm for semi-supervised learning.

Collins and Singer [6] suggest a modification of the co-training algorithm which explicitly optimizes an objective function that measures the degree of agreement between the rules in different views. They also describe an extension to the AdaBoost algorithm that boosts this objective function.

Dasgupta et al. [7] give PAC bounds for the generalization error of co-training in terms of the agreement rate of hypotheses in two independent views. This also justifies the Collins and Singer approach of directly optimizing the agreement rate of classifiers over the different views.

Clustering algorithms can be divided into two categories [3]: generative (or model-based) approaches and discriminative (or similarity-based) approaches.

Model-based approaches attempt to learn generative models from the documents, with each model representing one cluster. Usually generative clustering approaches are based on the Expectation Maximization (EM) [8] algorithm. The EM algorithm is an iterative statistical technique for maximum likelihood estimation in settings with incomplete data. Given a model of data generation, and data with some missing values, EM will locally maximize the likelihood of the model parameters and give estimates for the missing values.

Similarity-based clustering approaches optimize an objective function that involve the pairwise document similarities, aiming at maximizing the average similarities within clusters and minimize the average similarities between clusters. Most of the similarity based clustering algorithms follow the hierarchical agglomerative approach [11], where a dendrogram is build up by iteratively merging closest examples/clusters.

Related clustering algorithms that work in a multi-view setting include reinforcement clustering [17] and a multi-view version of DBSCAN [12].

3. Problem Setting and Evaluation

We consider the problem that data is generated by a mixture model. Without knowing the true parameters of the mixture model, we want to estimate parameters of mixture components and thereby cluster the data into subsets so that with high probability two examples that are generated by the same mixture component get assigned to the same cluster, and examples generated by different components get assigned to different clusters. We consider the special case of a multi-view setting, where the available attributes V of examples are split into disjoint sets $V^{(1)}$ and $V^{(2)}$. An instance x is decomposed and viewed as $(x^{(1)}, x^{(2)})$, where $x^{(1)}$ and $x^{(2)}$ are vectors over the attributes $V^{(1)}$ and $V^{(2)}$, respectively. These views have to satisfy the *conditional independence* assumption.

Definition 1 *Views $V^{(1)}$ and $V^{(2)}$ are conditionally independent given a mixture component y, when $\forall x^{(1)} \in$*

$V^{(1)}, x^{(2)} \in V^{(2)} : p(x^{(1)}, x^{(2)}|y) = p(x^{(1)}|y)p(x^{(2)}|y)$.

To measure the quality of a clustering, we use the average entropy over all clusters (Equation 1). It is based on the impurity of a cluster given the true mixture components of the data. p_{ij} is the proportion of the mixture component j in cluster i. m_i is the size of cluster i, k is the number of clusters, and m the total number of examples.

$$E = \sum_{i=1}^{k} \frac{m_i \left(-\sum_{j} p_{ij} log(p_{ij}) \right)}{m} \qquad (1)$$

In order to evaluate the clustering algorithms presented in the next sections we will use several data sets. One popular data set for evaluating multi-view classifiers is the WebKB data set [4, 15].

Based on its content ($V^{(1)}$) as well as on the anchor texts of inbound links ($V^{(2)}$) a web page can be classified into six different types of university web pages (course, department, faculty, project, staff, student). We select all pages from the data set for which links with anchor text exist. This results in a data set with 2316 examples distributed over six classes having the two-views property. We generate tfidf-vectors without stemming.

For the WebKB data set the conditional independence assumption might be slightly violated. To construct an artificial data set that has the conditional independence property, we adapt an experimental setting of [16]. We use 10 of the 20 classes of the well known 20 newsgroups data set. After building tfidf vectors, for each of the five classes, we generate examples by concatenating vectors $x^{(1)}$ from one group with randomly drawn vectors $x^{(2)}$ from a second group to construct multi-view examples $(x^{(1)}, x^{(2)})$. This procedure generates views which are perfectly independent (peers are selected randomly). The resulting classes are based on the following five pairs of the original 20 newsgroup classes: (comp.graphics, rec.autos), (rec.motorcycles, sci.med), (sci.space, misc.forsale), (rec.sport.hockey, soc.religion.christian), (comp.sys.ibm.pc.hardware, comp.os.ms-windows.misc).

We randomly select 200 examples for each of the 10 newsgroups, which results in 1000 concatenated examples uniformly distributed over the five classes.

In order to find out how our algorithms perform when there is no natural feature split in the data, we use document data sets and randomly split the available attributes into two subsets and average the performance over 10 distinct attribute splits. We choose six data sets that come with the CLUTO clustering toolkit: re0 (Reuters-21578), fbis (TREC-5), la1 (Los Angeles Times), hitech (San Jose Mercury), tr11 (TREC) and wap (WebACE project). For a detailed description of the data sets see [19].

For all experiments with partitioning clustering algorithms the diagrams are based on averaging over ten clustering runs to compensate for the randomized initialization. Error bars indicate standard errors.

4. Multi-View EM Clustering

In this section we want to analyze whether we can extend EM based cluster algorithms, so that they incorporate the multi-view setting with independent views. Different EM applications differ in specific models. We focus on models that are suitable for document clustering. Gaussian models could be used for multi-view EM as well, but are not applicable for document clustering. We firstly describe the general EM algorithm extended for two views, then we describe two instances of this algorithm and present and analyze empirical results.

4.1. General Multi-View EM Algorithm

In the field of semi-supervised learning, co-EM based methods Positive results on the co-EM algorithm for the problem of semi-supervised learning [16, 5] lead to the question whether co-EM can improve on EM for unsupervised learning setting as well. The co-EM algorithm is shown in Table 1. In each iteration i, each view v finds the model parameters $\Theta_i^{(v)}$ which maximize the likelihood given the expected values for the hidden variables of the other view. In turns M, E steps in view one and M, E steps in view two are executed. The single expectation and maximization steps are equivalent to the the E and M steps of the original EM algorithm [8].

The algorithm is not guaranteed to converge. Our experiments show that the algorithm often does not converge. As displayed in Table 1, we do not run the algorithm until convergence but until a special stopping criterion is met.

4.2. Mixture of Multinomials EM Algorithm

We now instantiate the general multi-view EM definition of Table 1 by a multi-view version of mixture-of-multinomials EM. The mixture-of-multinomials model for document clustering is based on the idea that generating a document of length n from mixture component j can be modeled as a process in which n words are drawn at random from the dictionary. There is an individual probability for each word in the dictionary and words are drawn with replacement; hence, the number of occurrences of a specific word in the document is governed by a multinomial distribution. Since there is a distinct distribution of words in each mixture component, the resulting distribution which governs the document collection is a mixture of multinomials. Like all other tractable models, this model assumes in-

Table 1. Multi-View EM.

Input: Unlabeled data $D = \{(x_1^{(1)}, x_1^{(2)}), \ldots, (x_n^{(1)}, x_n^{(2)})\}$.

1. Initialize $\Theta_0^{(2)}, T, t = 0$.
2. E step view 2: compute expectation for hidden variables given the model parameters $\Theta_0^{(2)}$
3. Do until stopping criterion is met:
   (a) For $v = 1 \ldots 2$:
      i. $t = t + 1$
      ii. M step view v: Find model parameters $\Theta_t^{(v)}$ that maximize the likelihood for the data given the expected values for the hidden variables of view $\bar{v}$ of iteration $t - 1$
      iii. E step view v: compute expectation for hidden variables given the model parameters $\Theta_t^{(v)}$
   (b) End For v.
4. return combined $\hat{\Theta} = \Theta_{t-1}^{(1)} \cup \Theta_t^{(2)}$

dependence of the word occurrences given the mixture components – any model that does not make this assumption has to deal with a number of covariances which is quadratic in the number of dictionary entries.

For the estimation of mixture-of-multinomials model parameters we use an expectation maximization approach. We adopt the definition of EM for mixture-of-multinomials from [20]. The expectation step is shown in Equations 2 (likelihood) and 3 (posterior). The maximization step is shown in Equations 4 (word probabilities) and 5 (prior), where $n_{il}^{(v)}$ is the number of word w_l's occurrences in document $x_i^{(v)}$ in view v. $\Theta^{(v)}$ denotes the combined set of parameters $\theta_j^{(v)}$ and $\alpha_{ij}^{(v)}$.

$$P(x_i^{(v)}|\theta_j^{(v)}) = \prod_l P_j^{(v)}(w_l)^{n_{il}^{(v)}} \tag{2}$$

$$P(j|x_i^{(v)}, \Theta^{(v)}) = \frac{\alpha_{ij}^{(v)} P(x_i^{(v)}|\theta_j^{(v)})}{\sum_{j'} \alpha_{ij'}^{(v)} P(x_i^{(v)}|\theta_{j'}^{(v)})} \tag{3}$$

$$P_j^{(v)}(w_l) = \frac{1 + \sum_i P(j|x_i^{(v)}, \Theta^{(v)}) n_{il}^{(v)}}{\sum_l (1 + \sum_i P(j|x_i^{(v)}, \Theta^{(v)}) n_{il}^{(v)})} \tag{4}$$

$$\alpha_j^{(v)} = \frac{1}{m} \sum_i P(j|x_i^{(v)}, \Theta^{(v)}) \tag{5}$$

According to Table 1, running the mixture-of-multinomials EM as multi-view EM means running M-step and E-step in the respective view and interchanging the posteriors $P(j|x_i^{(v)}, \Theta^{(v)})$. After each iteration we compute the log-likelihood of the data (Equation 6) for each view. We terminate the optimization process, if the log-likelihood of the data did not reach a new maximum for a fixed number of iterations in each view.

$$\log P(X^{(v)}|\Theta^{(v)}) = \sum_{i=1}^{m} \log \left(\sum_{j=1}^{k} \alpha_{ij}^{(v)} P(x_i^{(v)}|\theta_j^{(v)}) \right) \quad (6)$$

The final assignment of examples to partitions π_j, $j = 1, \ldots, k$ after termination is shown in Equation 7. We assign an example to the cluster that has the largest averaged posterior over both views.

$$\pi_j = \{x_i \in X : j = \text{argmax}_{j'}(P(j'|x_i^{(1)}, \Theta^{(1)}) +$$
$$P(j'|x_i^{(2)}, \Theta^{(2)}))\} \quad (7)$$

In our experiments we often encountered empty clusters for the mixture-of-multinomials EM. To prevent prior estimations of zero, we set the prior to a constant value $\alpha_j^{(v)} = \frac{1}{k}$.

4.3. Multi-View Spherical k-Means

A drawback of mixture-of-multinomials, described in the preceding section, is that documents with equal composition of words but with different word counts yield different posteriors $P(j|x_i^{(v)}, \Theta^{(v)})$. We can overcome this problem by normalizing each document vector to unit length. A clustering algorithm that deals with this type of normalized document vectors is spherical k-Means [9], which is the regular k-Means algorithm with cosine similarity as distance (similarity) measure.

In order to describe the multi-view version of spherical k-Means, we simply need to describe the single expectation and maximization steps, the sequence of those steps in the multi-view setting again follows Table 1. The parameter Θ_v consists of the concept vectors $c_j^{(v)}$; $j = 1, \ldots, k$; $v = 1, 2$; that have unit length $\|c_j^{(v)}\| = 1$. k is the desired number of clusters. All example vectors also have unit length $\|x_i^{(v)}\| = 1$. We start with randomly initialized concept vectors $c_j^{(2)}$, $j = 1, \ldots, k$. An expectation step assigns the documents that are closest to its concept vector $c_j^{(v)}$ to the corresponding partition $\pi_j^{(v)}$ (Equation 8).

$$\pi_j^{(v)} = \{x_i^{(v)} \in X^{(v)} : \langle x_i^{(v)}, c_j^{(v)} \rangle > \langle x_i^{(v)}, c_\ell^{(v)} \rangle, \ell \neq j\} \quad (8)$$

A maximization step computes new concept vectors (model parameters) according to Equation 9.

$$c_j^{(v)} = \frac{\sum\limits_{x^{(v)} \in \pi_j^{(v)}} x^{(v)}}{\left\| \sum\limits_{x^{(v)} \in \pi_j^{(v)}} x^{(v)} \right\|} \quad (9)$$

According to Table 1, after a maximization and an expectation step in one view, the partitions $\pi_j^{(v)}$ get interchanged for

a maximization and an expectation step in the other view, and so on.

After each iteration we compute the objective function for each view (Equation 10). We terminate the optimization process, if the objective function did not reach a new minimum for a fixed number of iterations in each view.

$$\sum_{j=1}^{k} \sum_{x^{(v)} \in \pi_j^{(v)}} \langle x^{(v)}, c_j^{(v)} \rangle \quad (10)$$

After termination, the corresponding cluster partitions $\pi_j^{(1)}$ and $\pi_j^{(2)}$ do not necessarily contain exactly the same examples. In order to obtain a combined clustering result we want to assign each example to one distinct cluster that is determined through the closest concept vector. In order to do this we compute a consensus mean for each cluster and view. Only those examples are included that both views agree on (Equation 11).

$$m_j^{(v)} = \frac{\sum\limits_{x_i^{(1)} \in \pi_j^{(1)} \wedge x_i^{(2)} \in \pi_j^{(2)}} x_i^{(v)}}{\left\| \sum\limits_{x_i^{(1)} \in \pi_j^{(1)} \wedge x_i^{(2)} \in \pi_j^{(2)}} x_i^{(v)} \right\|} \quad (11)$$

We assign each example to the final cluster that provides the most similar consensus vector, determined by averaging over the arcus cosine values in both views (Equation 12).

$$\pi_j = \{x_i \in X : \quad (12)$$
$$\arccos(\langle m_j^{(1)}, x_i^{(1)} \rangle) + \arccos(\langle m_j^{(2)}, x_i^{(2)} \rangle) <$$
$$\arccos(\langle m_\ell^{(1)}, x_i^{(1)} \rangle) + \arccos(\langle m_\ell^{(2)}, x_i^{(2)} \rangle), j \neq \ell\}$$

4.4. Empirical Results

The comparison of multi-view mixture-of-multinomials EM and spherical k-Means with their single-view counterparts for the WebKB data set is shown in Figure 1. The number of clusters is set to $k = 6$. Figure 2 displays the same setting, but with different number of desired clusters k. We notice a tremendous improvement of cluster quality with the multi-view algorithms.

Figure 3 displays results for the artificial data set built from the 20 newsgroup data set, as described in Section 3. On this data set the multi-view algorithms improve the entropy even more than for the WebKB data set. The total independence property of the artificial data set seems to support the success of multi-view EM.

Figure 4 shows the results for the six document data sets without natural multi-view property, where we randomly split the available attribute sets into two subsets. In ten of twelve cases the multi-view outperform the single-view algorithms significantly.

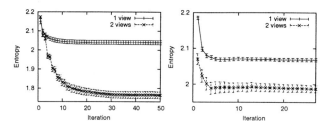

Figure 1. Single and multi-view mixture-of-multinomials EM (left) and spherical k-Means (right) for the WebKB data set.

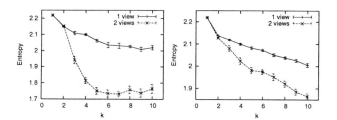

Figure 2. Single and multi-view mixture-of-multinomials EM (left) and spherical k-Means (right) for the WebKB data set and different k.

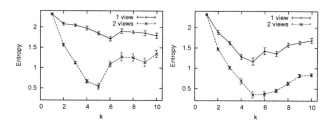

Figure 3. Single and multi-view mixture-of-multinomials EM (left) and spherical k-Means (right) for the artificial data set and different k.

4.5. Analysis

We now want to investigate why the multi-view algorithms obtain such dramatic improvemtents in terms of cluster entropy over their single-view counterparts.

Dasgupta et al. [7] and Abney [1] have made the important observation that the disagreement between two independent hypotheses is an upper bound on the error risk of either hypothesis. Let us briefly sketch why this is indeed always the case. Consider a clustering problem with two mixture components; let x be an instance with true mixture component y, and let $\pi^{(1)}(x)$ and $\pi^{(2)}(x)$ be two independent clustering hypotheses which assign x to a cluster. Let furthermore both hypotheses $\pi^{(1)}$ and $\pi^{(2)}$ have a risk of assigning an instance to a wrong mixture component of at most 50%.

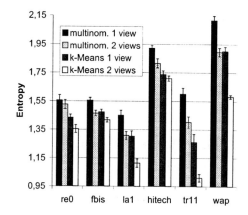

Figure 4. Single and multi-view clustering for six document data sets with random feature splits.

In Equation 13 we distinguish between the two possible cases of disagreement (either hypothesis may be wrong), utilizing the independence assumption. In Equation 14 we exploit the assumed error rate of at most 50%: both hypotheses are less likely to be wrong than just one hypothesis. Exploiting the independence assumption again takes us to Equation 15.

$$
\begin{aligned}
& P(\pi^{(1)}(x) \neq \pi^{(2)}(x)) \\
& = P(\pi^{(1)}(x) = y, \pi^{(2)}(x) = \bar{y}) \\
& \quad + P(\pi^{(1)}(x) = \bar{y}, \pi^{(2)}(x) = y) \qquad (13) \\
& \geq \max_i P(\pi^{(i)}(x) = \bar{y}, \pi^{(\bar{i})}(x) = \bar{y}) \\
& \quad + P(\pi^{(i)}(x) = \bar{y}, \pi^{(\bar{i})}(x) = y) \qquad (14) \\
& = \max_i P(\pi^{(i)}(x) \neq y) \qquad (15)
\end{aligned}
$$

In unsupervised learning, the risk of assigning instances to wrong mixture components cannot be minimized immediately. However, the above argument says that by minimizing the disagreement between two independent hypotheses, we can minimize an upper bound on the probability of an assignment of an instance to a wrong mixture component.

In order to find out whether the multi-view EM algorithm does in fact maximize the agreement between the views, we determine the agreement rate of the mixture-of-multinomials multi-view EM as shown in Equation 16. It is the number of examples the views agree on the assignment to components, divided by the total number of examples m.

$$
\frac{\#\left(\operatorname*{argmax}_{j} P(j|x_i^{(1)}, \Theta^{(1)}) = \operatorname*{argmax}_{j'} P(j'|x_i^{(1)}, \Theta^{(2)})\right)}{m} \quad (16)
$$

For each iteration step the entropy and the corresponding agreement rate are shown in Figure 5. With increasing entropy the agreement of the views increases as well. This

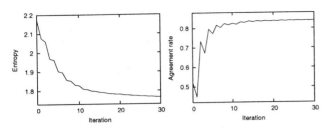

Figure 5. Entropy and agreement rate.

means our algorithm optimizes an objective function where the agreement rate is part of the optimization criterion.

Additionally we want to analyze the relationship between the results of multi-view and single-view EM regarding the single-view objective function. We run the mixture-of-multinomials multi-view EM until termination, concatenate the resulting word probability vectors $P_j^{(v)}(w_l)$ and use the resulting vector as initialization for a single-view clustering run in the concatenated space. Figure 6 shows the log-likelihood and entropy of the multi-view run, the following single-view run and the single-view run with regular random initialization. We calculate the log-likelihood of the multi-view algorithm by computing the regular single-view log-likelihood but replacing $P(x_i|\theta_j)$ with $P(x_i^{(1)}|\theta_j)P(x_i^{(2)}|\theta_j)$ (Equation 17).

$$\log(P(X|\Theta)) = \sum_{i=1}^{n} \log \left(\sum_{j=1}^{k} \alpha_{ij} P(x_i^{(1)}|\theta_j) P(x_i^{(2)}|\theta_j) \right) \quad (17)$$

The single-view algorithm yields a higher likelihood – which is not surprising because only the single-view algorithm directly optimizes the likelihood. Surprisingly, however, we observe an even greater log-likelihood at the end of the single-view run initialized with the multi-view result. This means we find better local optima by running co-EM and transferring the resulting model-parameter into the single-view setting compared to running single-view EM with random initialization. We notice that the single-view clustering which follows multi-view clustering does not affect the entropy – hence, running a single-view algorithm after a multi-view algorithm is not beneficial.

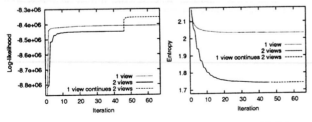

Figure 6. Log-likelihoods (left) and entropy (right) of multi-view, continued single-view and regular single-view EM (left).

In Section 4.1 we mentioned that the multi-view EM al-

gorithm is not guaranteed to converge. We consider the following simple example. We assume that we are clustering with the multi-view k-Means algorithm with $k = 2$. There is one specific example whose attribute vector in view one equals the concept vector of component one and in view two equals the concept vector of component two.

By running the multi-view k-Means algorithm this example will be in turns assigned to component one and component two. The algorithm will not converge because the assignment of the specific example alternates.

5. Multi-View Agglomerative Clustering

Agglomerative clustering algorithms are based on iteratively merging nearest clusters. A natural extension of this procedure for the multi-view setting is splitting up the iterative merging procedure so that one iteration executes one merging step in one view and the next iteration step in the other view and so on. We want to find out if this approach has advantages compared to clustering with a single view. We will now describe this algorithm, present empirical results and analyze its behavior.

5.1. Algorithm

The general idea of our agglomerative multi-view clustering is inspired by the co-training algorithm [4]. Co-training greedily augments the training set with the n_p positive and n_n negative highest confidence examples from the unlabeled data in each iteration for each view. Each new training example is exclusively based on the decision of one classifier in its view.

Agglomerative clustering is based on a distance measure between clusters. In the multi-view setting we have two attribute sets $V^{(1)}$ and $V^{(2)}$ and two distance measures $d^{(1)}(C_i, C_j)$ and $d^{(2)}(C_i, C_j)$. Agglomerative clustering starts with each example having its own cluster. Then iteratively merging the closest clusters builds up a dendrogram. The multi-view agglomerative clustering is similar but merges in turns the closest clusters in view one and view two. All merging operations work on a combined dendrogram for both views, this results in one final dendrogram. The algorithm is shown in Table 2.

By following this procedure, we assume that with low dependence between the views we get a better quality clustering than on the concatenated views. If a cluster pair has a low distance in one view but a medium distance in the other view, then our algorithm would probably merge this pair in an earlier iteration than the clustering on concatenated views would do. The clustering dendrogram gets built up on high confidence decisions made in the separate views and one view might benefit from

Table 2. Multi-view agglomerative clustering.

Input: Unlabeled data $D = \{(x_1^{(1)}, x_1^{(2)}), \ldots, (x_n^{(1)}, x_n^{(2)})\}$, distance measures $d^1(C_i, C_j)$ and $d^2(C_i, C_j)$.

1. Initialize $C_i = x_i$, $i = 1 \ldots n$.

2. For $t = 1 \ldots n$: For $v = 1 \ldots 2$:

   (a) Find pair of closest clusters $(C_i, C_j) = \underset{(C_i, C_j)}{\text{argmin}} \ d^v(C_i, C_j)$, for $i, j = 1 \ldots (n - t + 1)$.

   (b) Merge C_i and C_j.

3. Return dendrogram.

---

high confidence decision made in the other view. As distance measure $d(C_i, C_j)$, we use cosine similarity with $d_{min}(C_i, C_j)$ (single-linkage), $d_{max}(C_i, C_j)$ (complete-linkage) and $d_{avg}(C_i, C_j)$ (average-linkage) according to [13].

5.2. Empirical Results

We compare the cluster quality of multi-view agglomerative clustering with the regular single-view clustering on the concatenated views. Figure 7 shows the entropy values for different values of k (number of clusters) by starting from the root node and expanding the first $k - 1$ clusters in reversed order as they were merged.

We notice that the multi-view agglomerative clustering does not achieve lower entropy values compared to the corresponding single-view clustering. In some cases, especially for the WebKB data set with average-linkage, the entropy of single-view clustering is much lower.

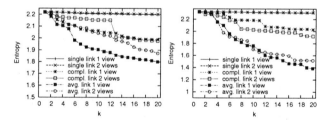

Figure 7. Single and multi-view agglomerative clustering for WebKB (left) and artificial data set (right).

5.3. Analysis

The question is, why does agglomerative multi-view clustering deteriorate cluster quality in most cases, even if our views are perfectly independent, as with the artificial data set?

If we assume that our data is actually generated by a set of mixture components, the the goal in agglomerative clus-

tering is to avoid merges of instances that belong to different mixture components. We want to analyze the risk for those cross-component merges for agglomerative multi-view and single-view clustering.

We use cosine similarity in our agglomerative clustering, so we are clustering in a space of directional data. We assume a von Mises-Fisher (vMF) distribution for the real distribution of our mixture components ([2]). The von Mises-Fisher distribution, for directional data, is the analog to the Gaussian distribution for Euclidean data in the sense that it is the unique distribution of L_2-normalized data that maximizes the entropy given the first and second moments of the distribution ([14]).

According to this assumption, the vMF probability density of one component in one view is shown in Equation 18. $\mu^{(v)}$ is the mean vector, $\kappa^{(v)}$ the variance of the distribution and $c(\kappa^{(v)})$ a normalization term.

$$f(x^{(v)}|\mu^{(v)}, \kappa^{(v)}) = c(\kappa^{(v)})e^{\frac{cos(x^{(v)} \triangleleft \mu^{(v)})}{\kappa^{(v)}}}$$
$$= c(\kappa^{(v)})e^{\frac{\langle \mu^{(v)}, x^{(v)} \rangle}{\kappa^{(v)}\|\mu^{(v)}\|\|x^{(v)}\|}} \quad (18)$$

Before we proceed, we show that the cosine similarity between two example vectors x and y in the concatenated space can be written as the average over the cosine similarities of the subspace vectors (Equation 20), if we assume that $\|x^{(1)}\| = \|x^{(2)}\|$ and $\|y^{(1)}\| = \|y^{(2)}\|$.

$$cos(x \triangleleft y) = \frac{\begin{pmatrix} x^{(1)} \\ x^{(2)} \end{pmatrix}}{\sqrt{\|x^{(1)}\|^2 + \|x^{(2)}\|^2}} \frac{\begin{pmatrix} y^{(1)} \\ y^{(2)} \end{pmatrix}}{\sqrt{\|y^{(1)}\|^2 + \|y^{(2)}\|^2}}$$
$$= \frac{\langle x^{(1)}, y^{(1)} \rangle + \langle x^{(2)} y^{(2)} \rangle}{2\|x^{(1)}\| \cdot \|y^{(1)})\|} \quad (19)$$
$$= \frac{cos(x^{(1)} \triangleleft y^{(1)}) + cos(x^{(2)} \triangleleft y^{(2)})}{2} \quad (20)$$

If the two views are independent we can write the probability density of the concatenated views as a product of the single densities as shown in Equation 21.

$$f(x|\mu, \kappa) = f(x^{(1)}|\mu^{(1)}, \kappa^{(1)})f(x^{(2)}|\mu^{(2)}, \kappa^{(2)}) \quad (21)$$
$$= c(\kappa^{(1)})e^{\frac{\langle \mu^{(1)}, x^{(1)} \rangle}{\kappa^{(1)}\|\mu^{(1)}\| \cdot \|x^{(1)}\|}} c(\kappa^{(2)})e^{\frac{\langle \mu^{(2)}, x^{(2)} \rangle}{\kappa^{(2)}\|\mu^{(2)}\| \cdot \|x^{(2)}\|}}$$

For reasons of a simplified presentation we assume that $\kappa^{(1)} = \kappa^{(2)}$, $\|x^{(1)}\| = \|x^{(2)}\|$ and $\|\mu^{(1)}\| = \|\mu^{(2)}\|$. With this assumption we get Equation 22 and applying Equation 20 leads to Equation 23.

$$f(x|\mu, \kappa) = c^2(\kappa^{(1)})e^{\frac{\langle \mu^{(1)}, x^{(1)} \rangle + \langle \mu^{(2)}, x^{(1)} \rangle}{\kappa^{(1)}\|\mu^{(1)}\| \cdot \|x^{(1)}\|}} \quad (22)$$
$$= c^2(\kappa^{(1)})e^{\frac{cos(x \triangleleft \mu)}{2\kappa^{(1)}}} \quad (23)$$

We see that the resulting distribution is again vMF distributed with variance $\kappa = \frac{1}{2}\kappa^{(1)}$. If we consider the case with only two mixture components, the distribution densities in the concatenated space have a smaller overlap, because the the variance is halved compared to the separate views. We might assume that the similarity of the means of the components in the concatenated views are doubled (as the variance is halved), but this is not the case according to Equation 20. The similarity of the means in the concatenated space is just the averaged similarity over the mean similarities in the separate views. If distributions have a smaller overlap, then the probability for cross-component merges is smaller.

6. Conclusion

We presented the problem setting of clustering in a multi-view environment and described two algorithm types that work in this setting in terms of incorporating the conditional independence property of the views.

The EM-based multi-view algorithms significantly outperform the single-view counterparts for several data sets. Even when no natural feature split is available, and we randomly split the available features into two subsets, we gain significantly better results than the single-view variants in almost all cases.

In our analysis we discovered that the multi-view EM algorithm optimizes agreement between the views. Because the disagreement is an upper bound on the error rate of one view, the good performance of multi-view EM can be explained through this property.

The agglomerative multi-view algorithm yields equal or worse results than the single-view version in most cases. We identified that the reason for this behavior is that the mixture components have a smaller overlap when the views are concatenated. This means in the single-view setting the probability for cross-component merges is lower, which directly improves cluster quality.

Acknowledgment

This work has been supported by the German Science Foundation DFG under grant SCHE540/10-1.

References

[1] S. Abney. Bootstrapping. In *Proc. of the 40th Annual Meeting of the Association for Comp. Linguistics*, 2002.

[2] A. Banerjee, I. Dhillon, J. Ghosh, and S. Sra. A comparative study of generative models for document clustering. In *Proceedings of The Ninth ACM SIGKDD Conference on Knowledge Discovery and Data Mining*, 2003.

[3] P. Berkhin. Survey of clustering data mining techniques. *Unpublished manuscript, available from accrue.com*, 2002.

[4] A. Blum and T. Mitchell. Combining labeled and unlabeled data with co-training. In *Proceedings of the Conference on Computational Learning Theory*, pages 92–100, 1998.

[5] U. Brefeld and T. Scheffer. Co-EM support vector learning. In *Proc. of the Int. Conf. on Machine Learning*, 2004.

[6] M. Collins and Y. Singer. Unsupervised models for named entity classification. In *EMNLP*, 1999.

[7] S. Dasgupta, M. Littman, and D. McAllester. PAC generalization bounds for co-training. In *Proceedings of Neural Information Processing Systems (NIPS)*, 2001.

[8] A. Dempster, N. Laird, and D. Rubin. Maximum likelihood from incomplete data via the EM algorithm. *Journal of the Royal Statistical Society, Series B*, 39, 1977.

[9] I. S. Dhillon and D. S. Modha. Concept decompositions for large sparse text data using clustering. *Machine Learning*, 42-1:143–175, 2001.

[10] R. Ghani. Combining labeled and unlabeled data for multi-class text categorization. In *Proceedings of the International Conference on Machine Learning*, 2002.

[11] A. Griffiths, L. Robinson, and P. Willett. Hierarchical agglomerative clustering methods for automatic document classification. *Journal of Doc.*, 40(3):175–205, 1984.

[12] K. Kailing, H. Kriegel, A. Pryakhin, and M. Schubert. Clustering multi-represented objects with noise. In *Proc. of the Pacific-Asia Conf. on Knowl. Disc. and Data Mining*, 2004.

[13] G. N. Lance and W. T. Williams. A general theory of classificatory sorting strategies. i. hierarchical systems. *Computer Journal*, 9:373–380, 1966.

[14] K. V. Mardia. Statistics of directional data. *Journal of the Royal Statistical Society, Series B*, 37:349–393, 1975.

[15] I. Muslea, C. Kloblock, and S. Minton. Active + semi-supervised learning = robust multi-view learning. In *Proceedings of the International Conference on Machine Learning*, pages 435–442, 2002.

[16] K. Nigam and R. Ghani. Analyzing the effectiveness and applicability of co-training. In *Proceedings of Information and Knowledge Management*, 2000.

[17] J. Wang, H. Zeng, Z. Chen, H. Lu, L. Tao, and W. Ma. Recom: Reinforcement clustering of multi-type interrelated data objects. In *Proceedings of the ACM SIGIR Conference on Information Retrieval*, 2003.

[18] D. Yarowsky. Unsupervised word sense disambiguation rivaling supervised methods. In *Proc. of the 33rd Annual Meeting of the Association for Comp. Linguistics*, 1995.

[19] Y. Zhao and G. Karypis. Criterion functions for document clustering: Experiments and analysis. Technical Report TR 01-40, Department of Computer Science, University of Minnesota, Minneapolis, MN, 2001, 2001.

[20] S. Zhong and J. Ghosh. Generative model-based clustering of directional data. In *SDM Workshop on Clustering High-Dimensional Data and Its Applications*, 2003.

Density Connected Clustering with Local Subspace Preferences

Christian Böhm, Karin Kailing, Hans-Peter Kriegel, Peer Kröger
Institute for Computer Science, University of Munich, Germany
{boehm,kailing,kriegel,kroegerp}@dbs.ifi.lmu.de

Abstract

Many clustering algorithms tend to break down in high-dimensional feature spaces, because the clusters often exist only in specific subspaces (attribute subsets) of the original feature space. Therefore, the task of projected clustering (or subspace clustering) has been defined recently. As a novel solution to tackle this problem, we propose the concept of local subspace preferences, which captures the main directions of high point density. Using this concept we adopt density-based clustering to cope with high-dimensional data. In particular, we achieve the following advantages over existing approaches: Our proposed method has a determinate result, does not depend on the order of processing, is robust against noise, performs only one single scan over the database, and is linear in the number of dimensions. A broad experimental evaluation shows that our approach yields results of significantly better quality than recent work on clustering high-dimensional data.

1. Introduction

Clustering is one of the major data mining tasks. Many useful clustering methods proposed in the last decade (see e.g. [6] for an overview) compute flat or hierarchical partitions of the data points in a complete feature space, i.e. each dimension is equally weighted when computing the distance between points. These approaches are successful for low-dimensional data sets. However, in higher dimensional feature spaces, their accuracy and efficiency deteriorates significantly. The major reason for this behavior is the so-called curse of dimensionality: In high dimensional feature spaces, a full-dimensional distance is often no longer meaningful, since the nearest neighbor of a point is expected to be almost as far as its farthest neighbor [7].

A common approach to cope with high dimensional feature spaces is the application of a global dimensionality reduction technique such as Principal Component Analysis (PCA). A standard clustering method can then be used to compute clusters in this subspace. But if different subsets of the points cluster well on different subspaces of the feature space, a global dimensionality reduction will fail.

To overcome these problems of global dimensionality reduction, recent research proposed to compute *subspace clusters*. Subspace clustering aims at computing pairs (C, S) where C is a set of objects representing a cluster and S is a set of attributes spanning the subspace in which C exists. Mapping each cluster to an associated subspace allows more flexibility than global methods projecting the entire data set onto a single subspace. In the example given in Figure 1, a subspace clustering algorithm will find the two clusters (C_1, A_1) and (C_2, A_2) (see Figure 1(a)). As a d-dimensional data set has 2^d subspaces which may contain clusters, the output of subspace clustering algorithms is usually very large. However, a lot of application domains require that the data set is divided into one single partitioning, where each point belongs exclusively to one cluster. For this case, projected clustering algorithms have been introduced, where each point is assigned to a unique cluster. One of the problems of this approach is shown in Figure 1(a): the points in the black circle can only be assigned to one of the two clusters. In this case, it is not clear to which cluster they should be assigned.

In this paper, we introduce the concept of *subspace preferences* to avoid this ambiguity. Our new approach PreDeCon is founded on the concept of density connected sets proposed in density-based clustering (DBSCAN) [5]. In the example it will generate the two clusters (C_1, A_1) and (C_2, A_2) visualized in Figure 1(b). Of course, in this example DBSCAN itself could have found the two clusters. But in high-dimensional spaces the parameter ε specifying the density threshold must be chosen very large, because a lot of dimensions contribute to the distance values. Thus, using the Euclidian distance measure and a large ε will result in large and unspecific clusters, while a small ε will yield only noise. To ensure the quality of the clusters in high-

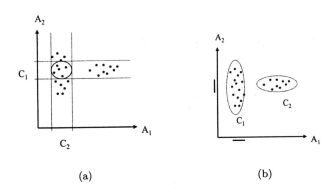

Figure 1: Clusters according to projected/subspace clustering (a) and according to subspace preference clustering (b).

dimensional spaces we suggest to use a weighted Euclidean distance measure to compute smaller but more specific clusters instead of trying to cluster all available points, resulting in large and unspecific clusters. Thus, we build for each point a so-called subspace preference vector based on the variance in each attribute and use a weighted Euclidean distance measure based on this subspace preference vector. Using this more flexible model, we propose the algorithm *PreDeCon* (subspace PREference weighted DEnsity CONnected clustering) to efficiently compute exact solutions of the subspace preference clustering problem. PreDeCon performs a single scan over the database, and is linear in the number of dimensions. The user can select a parameter λ indicating the dimensionality threshold of the searched clusters. Only those clusters with a subspace dimensionality of no more than λ are determined.

The remainder of the paper is organized as follows: In Section 2, we discuss related work and point out our contributions. In Section 3, we formalize our notion of subspace preference clusters. We present the algorithm PreDeCon to efficiently compute such subspace preference clusters in Section 4. Section 5 contains an extensive experimental evaluation and Section 6 concludes the paper.

2. Related Work and Contributions

2.1. Density-Based Clustering

The density-based notion is a common approach for clustering used by various clustering algorithms such as DBSCAN [5], DENCLUE [8], and OPTICS [4]. All these methods search for regions of high density in a feature space that are separated by regions of lower density. A typical density-based clustering algorithm needs two parameters to define the notion of density: First, a parameter μ specifying the minimum number of points, and second, a parameter ε specifying a volume. These two parameters determine a density threshold for clustering. Our approach follows the formal definitions of density connected clusters underlying the algorithm DBSCAN [5]. In this model, a cluster is defined as a maximal set of density connected points.

2.2. Projected and Subspace Clustering

The pioneering approach to subspace clustering is CLIQUE [3], a grid-based algorithm using an *Apriori*-like method to recursively navigate through the set of possible subspaces in a bottom-up way. A density connected version of subspace clustering is SUBCLU [9]. As the number of subspaces which possibly contain clusters is 2^d, the output of those clustering algorithms is usually very large, because points may be assigned to multiple clusters. However, for a lot of application domains a single partitioning of the data is mandatory. Thus, we focus on projected clustering algorithms.

PROCLUS (PROjected CLUStering) [2] is a projected clustering algorithm, which picks up the concepts of k-medoid clustering. The number of clusters k and the average subspace dimension l are input parameters. PROCLUS iteratively computes good medoids for each cluster. The Manhattan Distance divided by the subspace dimension is used as normalized metric for trading between subspaces of different dimensionality. For performance reasons, the iterative medoid-searching phase is performed on a sample using a greedy hill-climbing technique. After this iterative search, an additional pass over the data is performed for refinement of clusters, medoids and associated subspaces. An extension to PROCLUS is the algorithm ORCLUS [1] which computes arbitrarily oriented (i.e. not axis-parallel) projected clusters which are usually hard to interpret and thus, are not suitable for many applications.

In [11] a mathematical definition of an "optimal projected cluster" is presented along with a Monte Carlo algorithm called DOC to compute approximations of such optimal projected clusters. Using the user-specified input parameters w and α, an optimal projected cluster is defined as a set of points C associated with a subspace of dimensions D such that C contains more than $\alpha\%$ points of the database and the projection of C onto the subspace spanned by D must be contained in a hyper-cube of width w whereas in all other dimensions $d \notin D$ the points in C are not contained in a hyper-cube of width w. The proposed algorithm DOC only finds approximations because it generates projected clusters of width $2w$. In addition, no assumption on the distribution of points inside such a hyper-cube is made. The reported projected clusters may contain additional noise objects (especially when the size of the projected cluster is considerably smaller than $2w$) and/or may miss some points that naturally belong to the projected cluster (especially when the size of the projected cluster is considerably larger than $2w$).

Both methods are limited to computing approximations using sampling techniques and therefore, the assignment of points to clusters is no longer determinate and may vary for different runs of the algorithm.

2.3. Our Contributions

In this paper, we make the following contributions: Analogously to projected clustering which was introduced to enhance the quality of k-means like clustering algorithms in high-dimensional space, we extend the well-founded notion of density connected clusters to ensure high quality results even in high-dimensional spaces. We do not use any sampling or approximation techniques, thus the result of our clustering algorithm is determinate. We propose an efficient method called PreDeCon which is able to compute all subspace preference clusters of a certain dimensionality in a single scan over the database and is linear in the number of dimensions. And finally, we successfully apply our algorithm PreDeCon to several real-world data sets, showing its superior performance over existing approaches.

3. The Notion of Subspace Preference Clusters

In this section, we formalize the notion of subspace preference clusters. Let $\mathcal{D}$ be a database of d-dimensional points ($\mathcal{D} \subseteq \mathbb{R}^d$), where the set of attributes is denoted by $\mathcal{A} = \{A_1, \ldots A_d\}$. The projection of a point p onto an attribute $A_i \in \mathcal{A}$ is denoted by $\pi_{A_i}(p)$. Let $dist : \mathbb{R}^d \times \mathbb{R}^d \to \mathbb{R}$ be a metric distance function between points in $\mathcal{D}$, e.g. one of the L_p-norms. Let $\mathcal{N}_\varepsilon(p)$ denote the ε-neighborhood of $p \in \mathcal{D}$, i.e. $\mathcal{N}_\varepsilon(p)$ contains all points q where $dist(p,q) \leq \varepsilon$.

Intuitively, a subspace preference cluster is a density connected set of points associated with a certain subspace preference vector. In order to identify subspace preference clusters, we are interested in all sets of points having a small variance along one or more attributes, i.e. a variance smaller than a given $\delta \in \mathbb{R}$.

Definition 1 (variance along an attribute)
Let $p \in \mathcal{D}$ and $\varepsilon \in \mathbb{R}$. The variance of $\mathcal{N}_\varepsilon(p)$ *along an attribute $A_i \in \mathcal{A}$, denoted by $\mathrm{VAR}_{A_i}(\mathcal{N}_\varepsilon(p))$, is defined as follows:*

$$\mathrm{VAR}_{A_i}(\mathcal{N}_\varepsilon(p)) = \frac{\sum_{q \in \mathcal{N}_\varepsilon(p)}(dist(\pi_{A_i}(p), \pi_{A_i}(q)))^2}{|\mathcal{N}_\varepsilon(p)|}$$

Definition 2 (subspace preference dimensionality)

Let $p \in \mathcal{D}$ and $\delta \in \mathbb{R}$. The number of attributes A_i with $\mathrm{VAR}_{A_i} \leq \delta$ is called the subspace preference dimensionality *of $\mathcal{N}_\varepsilon(p)$, denoted by $\mathrm{PDIM}(\mathcal{N}_\varepsilon(p))$.*

The intuition of our formalization is to consider those points as core points of a cluster which have enough dimensions with a low variance in their neighborhood. Therefore, we associate each point p with a subspace preference vector $\bar{\mathbf{w}}_p$ which reflects the variance of the points in the ε-neighborhood of p along each attribute in $\mathcal{A}$.

Definition 3 (preference weighted similarity measure)

Let $p \in \mathcal{D}$, $\delta \in \mathbb{R}$ and $\kappa \in \mathbb{R}$ be a constant with $\kappa \gg 1$. Let $\bar{\mathbf{w}}_p = (w_1, w_2, \ldots w_d)$ be the so-called subspace preference vector of p, where

$$w_i = \begin{cases} 1 & if \quad \mathrm{VAR}_{A_i}(\mathcal{N}_\varepsilon(p)) > \delta \\ \kappa & if \quad \mathrm{VAR}_{A_i}(\mathcal{N}_\varepsilon(p)) \leq \delta \end{cases}$$

The preference weighted similarity measure *associated with a point p is denoted by*

$$dist_p(p,q) = \sqrt{\sum_{i=1}^{d} w_i \cdot (\pi_{A_i}(p) - \pi_{A_i}(q))^2}$$

where w_i is the i-th component of $\bar{\mathbf{w}}_p$.

Let us note, that the preference weighted similarity measure $dist_p(p,q)$ is simply a weighted Euclidean distance. The parameter δ specifies the threshold for a low variance. As we are only interested in distinguishing between dimensions with low variance and all other dimensions, weighting the dimensions inversely proportional to their variance is not useful. Thus, our weight vector has only two possible values.

The preference weighted similarity measure is visualized in Figure 2. The ε-neighborhood of a 2-dimensional point p exhibits low variance along attribute A_1 and high variance along attribute A_2. The similarity measure $dist_p$ weights attributes with low variance considerably lower (by the factor κ) than attributes with a high variance. However, we face the problem that the similarity measure in Definition 3 is not symmetric, because $dist_p(p,q) = dist_q(q,p)$

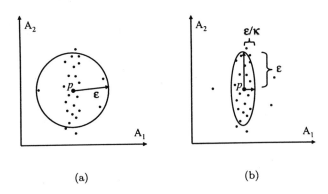

(a)   (b)

Figure 2: ε-neighborhood of p according to (a) simple Euclidean and (b) preference weighted Euclidean distance.

does obviously not hold in general. If an asymmetric similarity measure is used in DBSCAN, a different clustering result can be obtained depending on the order of processing (e.g. which point is selected as the starting point). Although the result is typically not seriously affected by this ambiguity effect, we avoid this problem easily by an extension of our similarity measure which makes it symmetric. We simply combine both similarity measures $dist_p(p,q)$ and $dist_q(p,q)$ by a suitable arithmetic operation such as the maximum of the two.

Definition 4 (general preference weighted similarity)

The general preference weighted similarity of two arbitrary points $p, q \in \mathcal{D}$, denoted by $dist_{pref}(p,q)$, is defined as the maximum of the corresponding preference weighted similarity measures of p ($dist_p$) and q ($dist_q$), formally:

$$dist_{pref}(p,q) = \max\{dist_p(p,q), dist_q(q,p)\}.$$

Based on these considerations, we define the preference weighted ε-neighborhood as a symmetric concept:

Definition 5 (preference weighted ε-neighborhood)

Let $\varepsilon \in \mathbb{R}$. The preference weighted ε-neighborhood of a point $o \in \mathcal{D}$, denoted by $\mathcal{N}_\varepsilon^{\bar{\mathbf{W}}_o}(o)$, is defined by:

$$\mathcal{N}_\varepsilon^{\bar{\mathbf{W}}_o}(o) = \{x \in \mathcal{D} \mid dist_{pref}(o,x) \leq \varepsilon\}.$$

Preference weighted core points can now be defined as follows.

Definition 6 (preference weighted core point)
Let $\varepsilon, \delta \in \mathbb{R}$ and $\mu, \lambda \in \mathbb{N}$. A point $o \in DB$ is called preference weighted core point w.r.t. ε, μ, δ, and λ (denoted

by $\text{CORE}_{\text{den}}^{\text{pref}}(o)$), if the preference dimensionality of its ε-neighborhood is at most λ and its preference weighted ε-neighborhood contains at least μ points, formally:

$$\text{CORE}_{\text{den}}^{\text{pref}}(o) \Leftrightarrow \text{PDIM}(\mathcal{N}_\varepsilon(o)) \leq \lambda \wedge |\mathcal{N}_\varepsilon^{\bar{\mathbf{W}}_o}(o)| \geq \mu.$$

Let us note that in $\text{CORE}_{\text{den}}^{\text{pref}}$ the acronym "pref" refers to the parameters δ and λ which are responsible for preference weighting. In the following, we omit the parameters ε, μ, δ, and λ wherever the context is clear and use "den" and "pref" instead.

Definition 7 (direct preference weighted reachability)

Let $\varepsilon, \delta \in \mathbb{R}$ and $\mu, \lambda \in \mathbb{N}$. A point $p \in \mathcal{D}$ is directly preference weighted reachable from a point $q \in \mathcal{D}$ w.r.t. ε, μ, δ, and λ (denoted by $\text{DIRREACH}_{\text{den}}^{\text{pref}}(q,p)$), if q is a preference weighted core point, the subspace preference dimensionality of $\mathcal{N}_\varepsilon(p)$ is at most λ, and $p \in \mathcal{N}_\varepsilon^{\bar{\mathbf{W}}_q}(q)$, formally:

$\text{DIRREACH}_{\text{den}}^{\text{pref}}(q,p) \Leftrightarrow$
(1) $\text{CORE}_{\text{den}}^{\text{pref}}(q)$
(2) $\text{PDIM}(\mathcal{N}_\varepsilon(p)) \leq \lambda$
(3) $p \in \mathcal{N}_\varepsilon^{\bar{\mathbf{W}}_q}(q).$

Direct preference weighted reachability is symmetric for preference weighted core points. Both $dist_p(p,q) \leq \varepsilon$ and $dist_q(q,p) \leq \varepsilon$ must hold.

Definition 8 (preference weighted reachability)

Let $\varepsilon, \delta \in \mathbb{R}$ and $\mu, \lambda \in \mathbb{N}$. A point $p \in \mathcal{D}$ is preference weighted reachable from a point $q \in \mathcal{D}$ w.r.t. ε, μ, δ, and λ (denoted by $\text{REACH}_{\text{den}}^{\text{pref}}(q,p)$), if there is a chain of points $p_1, \cdots p_n$ such that $p_1 = q, p_n = p$ and p_{i+1} is directly preference weighted reachable from p_i, formally:

$\text{REACH}_{\text{den}}^{\text{pref}}(q,p) \Leftrightarrow$
$\exists p_1, \ldots, p_n \in \mathcal{D} : p_1 = q \wedge p_n = p \wedge$
$\forall i \in \{1, \ldots, n-1\} : \text{DIRREACH}_{\text{den}}^{\text{pref}}(p_i, p_{i+1}).$

It is easy to see, that preference weighted reachability is the transitive closure of direct preference weighted reachability.

Definition 9 (preference weighted connectivity)

Let $\varepsilon, \delta \in \mathbb{R}$ and $\mu, \lambda \in \mathbb{N}$. A point $p \in \mathcal{D}$ is preference weighted connected to a point $q \in \mathcal{D}$, if there is a point $o \in \mathcal{D}$ such that both p and q are preference weighted reachable from o, formally:

$\text{CONNECT}_{\text{den}}^{\text{pref}}(q,p) \Leftrightarrow$
$\exists o \in \mathcal{D} : \text{REACH}_{\text{den}}^{\text{pref}}(o,q) \wedge \text{REACH}_{\text{den}}^{\text{pref}}(o,p).$

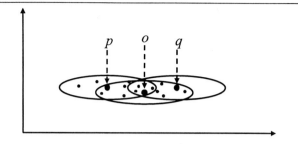

Figure 3: p and q are preference weighted connected via o.

Preference weighted connectivity is a symmetric relation. The concept is visualized in Figure 3. A subspace preference cluster can now be defined as a maximal preference weighted connected set:

Definition 10 (subspace preference cluster)
Let $\varepsilon, \delta \in \mathbb{R}$ and $\mu, \lambda \in \mathbb{N}$. A non-empty subset $\mathcal{C} \subseteq \mathcal{D}$ is called a subspace preference cluster w.r.t. ε, μ, δ, and λ, if all points in $\mathcal{C}$ are preference weighted connected and $\mathcal{C}$ is maximal w.r.t. preference weighted reachability, formally:
$$\text{CONSET}_{\text{den}}^{\text{pref}}(\mathcal{C}) \Leftrightarrow$$
Connectivity: $\forall o, q \in \mathcal{C} : \text{CONNECT}_{\text{den}}^{\text{pref}}(o, q)$
Maximality: $\forall p, q \in \mathcal{D} : q \in \mathcal{C} \wedge \text{REACH}_{\text{den}}^{\text{pref}}(q, p) \Rightarrow p \in \mathcal{C}$.

The following two lemmata are important for validating the correctness of our clustering algorithm. Intuitively, they state that we can discover a subspace preference cluster for a given parameter setting in a two-step approach: First, choose an arbitrary preference weighted core point o from the database. Second, retrieve all points that are preference weighted reachable from o. This approach yields the subspace preference cluster containing o.

Lemma 1
Let $p \in \mathcal{D}$. If p is a preference weighted core point, then the set of points, which are preference weighted reachable from p is a subspace preference cluster, formally:
$$\text{CORE}_{\text{den}}^{\text{pref}}(p) \wedge \mathcal{C} = \{o \in \mathcal{D} \mid \text{REACH}_{\text{den}}^{\text{pref}}(p, o)\}$$
$$\Rightarrow \text{CONSET}_{\text{den}}^{\text{pref}}(\mathcal{C}).$$

Proof.
(1) $\mathcal{C} \neq \emptyset$:
By assumption, $\text{CORE}_{\text{den}}^{\text{pref}}(p)$ and thus, $\text{PDIM}(\mathcal{N}_\varepsilon(p)) \leq \lambda$
$\Rightarrow \text{DIRREACH}_{\text{den}}^{\text{pref}}(p, p)$
$\Rightarrow \text{REACH}_{\text{den}}^{\text{pref}}(p, p)$
$\Rightarrow p \in \mathcal{C}$.
(2) Maximality:

Let $x \in \mathcal{C}$ and $y \in \mathcal{D}$ and $\text{REACH}_{\text{den}}^{\text{pref}}(x, y)$
$\Rightarrow \text{REACH}_{\text{den}}^{\text{pref}}(p, x) \wedge \text{REACH}_{\text{den}}^{\text{pref}}(x, y)$
$\Rightarrow \text{REACH}_{\text{den}}^{\text{pref}}(p, y)$ (since preference weighted reachability is a transitive relation)
$\Rightarrow y \in \mathcal{C}$.

(3) Connectivity:
$\forall x, y \in \mathcal{C} : \text{REACH}_{\text{den}}^{\text{pref}}(p, x) \wedge \text{REACH}_{\text{den}}^{\text{pref}}(p, y)$
$\Rightarrow \text{CONNECT}_{\text{den}}^{\text{pref}}(x, y)$ (via p). $\square$

Lemma 2
Let $\mathcal{C} \subseteq \mathcal{D}$ be a subspace preference cluster. Let $p \in \mathcal{C}$ be a preference weighted core point. Then $\mathcal{C}$ equals the set of points which are preference weighted reachable from p, formally:
$$\text{CONSET}_{\text{den}}^{\text{pref}}(\mathcal{C}) \wedge p \in \mathcal{C} \wedge \text{CORE}_{\text{den}}^{\text{pref}}(p)$$
$$\Rightarrow \mathcal{C} = \{o \in \mathcal{D} \mid \text{REACH}_{\text{den}}^{\text{pref}}(p, o)\}.$$

Proof. Let $\bar{\mathcal{C}} = \{o \in \mathcal{D} \mid \text{REACH}_{\text{den}}^{\text{pref}}(p, o)\}$. We have to show that $\bar{\mathcal{C}} = \mathcal{C}$:

(1) $\bar{\mathcal{C}} \subseteq \mathcal{C}$: obvious from the definition of $\bar{\mathcal{C}}$.

(2) $\mathcal{C} \subseteq \bar{\mathcal{C}}$: Let $q \in \mathcal{C}$. By assumption, $p \in \mathcal{C}$ and $\text{CONSET}_{\text{den}}^{\text{pref}}(\mathcal{C})$
$\Rightarrow \exists o \in \mathcal{C} : \text{REACH}_{\text{den}}^{\text{pref}}(o, p) \wedge \text{REACH}_{\text{den}}^{\text{pref}}(o, q)$
$\Rightarrow \text{REACH}_{\text{den}}^{\text{pref}}(p, o)$ (since both o and p are preference weighted core points and preference weighted reachability is symmetric for preference weighted core points.
$\Rightarrow \text{REACH}_{\text{den}}^{\text{pref}}(p, q)$ (transitivity of preference weighted reachability)
$\Rightarrow q \in \bar{\mathcal{C}}$. $\square$

4. Efficiently Computing Subspace Preference Clusters

4.1. Algorithm PreDeCon

PreDeCon performs one pass over the database to find all subspace preference clusters for a given parameter setting. The pseudo code of the algorithm is given in Figure 4. At the beginning each point is marked as unclassified. During the run of PreDeCon all points are either assigned a certain cluster identifier or marked as noise. For each point which is not yet classified, PreDeCon checks whether this point is a preference weighted core point. If so, the algorithm expands the cluster belonging to this point. Otherwise the point is marked as noise. To find a new cluster, PreDeCon starts with an arbitrary preference weighted core point o and searches for all points that are preference weighted reachable from o. This is sufficient to find the whole cluster containing the point o, due to Lemma 2. When PreDeCon

```
algorithm PreDeCon(𝒟, ε, μ, λ, δ)
    // assumption: each point in 𝒟 is marked as unclassified
    for each unclassified o ∈ 𝒟 do
        if COREᵖʳᵉᶠ_den(o) then        // expand a new cluster
            generate new clusterID;
            insert all x ∈ 𝒩ε^w̄ₒ(o) into queue Φ;
            while Φ ≠ ∅ do
                q = first point in Φ;
                compute ℛ = {x ∈ 𝒟 | DIRREACHᵖʳᵉᶠ_den(q, x)};
                for each x ∈ ℛ do
                    if x is unclassified then
                        insert x into Φ;
                    if x is unclassified or noise then
                        assign current clusterID to x
                remove q from Φ;
        else        // o is noise
            mark o as noise;
end.
```

Figure 4: Pseudo code of the PreDeCon algorithm.

has found a preference weighted core point, a new cluster identifier "clusterID" is generated which will be assigned to all points found in the generation of the subspace preference cluster. PreDeCon begins by inserting all points in the preference weighted ε-neighborhood of point o into a queue. For each point in the queue, it computes all directly preference weighted reachable points and inserts those points into the queue which are still unclassified. This is repeated until the queue is empty and the entire cluster is computed.

As mentioned above, the results of PreDeCon do not depend on the order of processing, i.e. the resulting clustering (number of clusters and association of core points to clusters) is determinate.

4.2. Complexity Analysis

As the performance of most index structures deteriorates in high-dimensional spaces, we base our complexity analysis of PreDeCon on the assumption of no index structure.

Lemma 3 *The overall worst-case time complexity of our algorithm based on the sequential scan of the data set is $O(d \cdot n^2)$.*

Proof. *Our algorithm has to associate each point of the data set with a preference weighted similarity weight vector that is used for searching neighbors (cf. Definition 3). The corresponding vector must be computed once for each point. The computation of the preference weighted similarity weight vector $\bar{\mathbf{w}}$ is based on the result of a Euclidean range query which can be evaluated in $O(d \cdot n)$*

time. Then the vector is built by checking the variance of the points in the Euclidean ε-neighborhood along each dimension which requires $O(d \cdot n)$ time. For all points together, this sums up to $O(d \cdot n^2)$.

Checking the preference weighted core point property according to Definition 6, and expanding a preference weighted cluster, requires for each point in the Euclidean ε-neighborhood the evaluation of a weighted Euclidean distance which can be done in $O(d \cdot n)$ time. For all points together (including the above cost for the determination of the preference weighted similarity weight vector), we obtain a worst-case time complexity of $O(d \cdot n^2)$. □

Let us note, that the runtime of our algorithm does not depend on the dimensionality of the subspace preference clusters.

4.3. Input Parameters

PreDeCon has four input parameters, two density parameters ε and μ and two preference parameters λ and δ.

The parameter $\lambda \in \mathbb{N}$ specifies the preference dimension of the subspace preference clusters to be computed, i.e. the maximum number of attributes that have a low variance (cf. Definition 2). In our experiments, it turns out that the clusters computed by PreDeCon need not to have a preference dimension of λ. In fact, λ rather specifies a upper bound for the preference dimensions of the computed clusters. The parameter $\delta \in \mathbb{R}$ specifies the upper bound for the variance in an attribute. If the variance along an attribute is less than δ, this attribute is considered to yield a dense projection. The choice of δ depends on the maximum value MAX_{A_i} in each attribute A_i. It empirically turned out that PreDeCon is rather robust against different choices for δ. Our experiments showed that $\delta \leq 5$ is usually a good choice for data sets with $MAX_{A_i} = 100$. We suggest to normalize data sets that contain attributes not scaled within $[0, 100]$ accordingly.

The parameters $\varepsilon \in \mathbb{R}$ and $\mu \in \mathbb{N}$ specify the density threshold which clusters must exceed. They should be chosen as suggested in [5].

5. Evaluation

In this section, we present a broad evaluation of PreDeCon. We implemented PreDeCon as well as the three comparative methods DBSCAN, PROCLUS, and DOC in JAVA. All experiments were run on a Linux workstation with a 2.0 GHz CPU and 2.0 GB RAM.

We evaluated PreDeCon using several synthetic data sets generated using a self-implemented data generator.

We varied the dimension of the data sets from 2 to 50, the number of clusters from 2 to 5, the subspace dimensionality of the clusters from 2 to 10 and the amount of noise from 50% to 75%. The density of the clusters was chosen randomly. In all experiments, PreDeCon separated the generated clusters hidden in the data from each other and from noise.

Due to space limitations we focus on the following experiments using two different real world data sets: The first data set is derived from a gene expression experiment studying the yeast cell cycle by extracting the expression level of approximately 2800 genes at 17 time spots [12]. Since the genes have no class label, we have to judge the accuracy of the clustering by looking at the results. The aim is to find clusters of co-expressed genes that share similar functions. Biological criteria for similar functions of genes are direct interactions of genes, common complexes of gene products, or gene products participating in common pathways. We analyzed the clustering results according to these criteria using the publicly available Saccharomyces Genome Database (SGD) [1]. The second data set [10] is derived by a newborn screening and contains the concentrations of 43 metabolites in 2000 newborns. Each newborn has a class label attached indicating its genetic disease. All attribute values were normalized between 0 and 100.

Gene Expression Data. The clusters in the gene expression data set were generated using the following parameter setting: $\varepsilon = 80.0$, $\mu = 7$, $\delta = 4.0$, and $\lambda = 12$. PreDeCon found several clusters with varying size of around 10 to 40 genes. Each cluster contains functionally related genes according to the biological criteria mentioned above. For example, one cluster contains several genes that are involved in chromatin modelling and maintenance (NHP10, DPB4, IES3, and TAF9) where IES3 and NHP10 are even direct interaction partners. A second cluster contains more than 30 genes coding for structural components of the ribosome and 4 genes that are localized in the ribosome and build a larger complex (CDC33, TEF4, EFB1, and NHP2). A third cluster contains several genes involved in the glycolysis pathway (CDC19, TPI1, TDH2, FBA1, and GPM1). Let us note, that each cluster also contains a few genes of different or unknown function, which is no wonder since gene expression data is very noisy due to experimental impacts during data generation. Summing up, the clusters found by PreDeCon contained genes that interact with each other, build complexes with each other or participate in common pathways, and thus are functionally related. The detected groups

---

1 http://www.yeastgenome.org/

Table 1: Confusion matrix of clustering results on metabolome data.

cluster id	size	class labels				
		control	PKU	LCHAD	MCAD	others
1	269	264	3	2	0	0
2	29	0	29	0	0	0
3	38	0	38	0	0	0
4	10	0	10	0	0	0

of co-expressed genes are therefore biologically relevant and meaningful.

Metabolome Data. The clusters in the metabolome data set were generated using the following parameter setting: $\varepsilon = 150.0$, $\mu = 10$, $\delta = 3.0$, and $\lambda = 4$. PreDeCon found 4 clusters. The contents of these clusters are visualized as confusion matrix in Table 1. As it can be seen, more than 98% of the points in the first cluster are healthy newborns (label "control"). The other three clusters contain 100% newborns suffering from the PKU (phenylketonuria), one of the prevalent inborn metabolic diseases. Newborns suffering from one of the other diseases were classified as noise, i.e. they were not separated by PreDeCon. However, a significant majority of healthy newborns and newborns suffering from PKU were separated by PreDeCon. In addition, the list of attributes (metabolites) exhibiting low variance in each cluster give useful hints for further medical research.

Comparison with DBSCAN. DBSCAN is a full-dimensional clustering algorithm, i.e. it computes clusters giving each dimension equal weights. For each run of DBSCAN on the biological data sets, we chose the parameters according to [5] using a k-nn-distance graph. Applied to the gene expression data, DBSCAN found 6 relatively large clusters where the fraction of genes with functional relationships was rather small. We made similar observations when we applied DBSCAN to the metabolome data: the computed clusters contained newborns with all sorts of class labels.

Comparison with PROCLUS. We implemented PROCLUS [2] as an axis-parallel version of ORCLUS [1] as the authors of ORCLUS state that this version is slightly more stable and accurate than the original PROCLUS implementation. We tested PROCLUS on the metabolome data set using different values of k (from 5 to 13) and l (from 3 to 15). But in all cases, we did not get any cluster containing objects of less than 4 different classes. In all larger clusters almost all class labels appear. The clusters obtained for the gene expression data set seem equally unspecific — independent of the chosen parameters.

Comparison with DOC. DOC is a projected clustering algorithm proposed recently. Since the suggestions on how to choose the parameters for DOC presented in [11] are rather misleading, we had to choose valid parameters to run DOC on the biological data sets. In particular, we chose the following parameter settings for both data sets: the number m of random sets generated for each seed was set to 10 and the size r of these random sets was set to 20. In addition, we tested two density thresholds of the clusters, $\alpha = 0.05$ and $\alpha = 0.005$, where as the width w of the hypercubes was set to 30. The fraction of the cluster points that must be conserved, when an attribute is added to the cluster, was set to $\beta = 0.9$. Thus, for the computation of one cluster, DOC generated $\lfloor \frac{2}{\alpha} \rfloor = 40$ random points as seeds. We performed multiple runs of DOC on both biological data sets. The results of the runs on each data set were rather different. Applied to the gene expression data set, DOC found 2 to 7 clusters with varying dimensionality (ranging from 1 to 14 dimensions) in 10 runs. In all cases, the clusters contained more than 200 members. Each detected functional relationship was statistically meaningless. Applied to the metabolome data set, DOC found 4 to 24 clusters of a dimensionality varying from 26 to 38. In most clusters, the instances from different classes (newborns with different diseases) were rather equally distributed.

6. Conclusions

In this paper, we proposed PreDeCon, an algorithm for computing clusters of subspace preference weighted connected points. This algorithm searches for local subgroups of a set of feature vectors having a low variance along one or more (but not all) attributes. The attributes with low variance may vary between different clusters. PreDeCon is designed to find clusters in moderate-to-high dimensional feature spaces where traditional, "full-dimensional" clustering algorithms tend to break down. PreDeCon is determinate, robust against noise, and efficient with a worst case time complexity of $O(d \cdot n^2)$. Our extensive experimental evaluation shows a superior clustering accuracy of PreDeCon over relevant methods like DBSCAN, CLIQUE, ORCLUS, and DOC.

Acknowledgements

Parts of this work is supported by the German Ministry for Education, Science, Research and Technology (BMBF) (grant no. 031U112F).

References

[1] C. Aggarwal and P. Yu. "Finding Generalized Projected Clusters in High Dimensional Space". In *Proc. ACM SIGMOD Int. Conf. on Management of Data (SIGMOD'00), Dallas, TX*, 2000.

[2] C. C. Aggarwal and C. Procopiuc. "Fast Algorithms for Projected Clustering". In *Proc. ACM SIGMOD Int. Conf. on Management of Data (SIGMOD'99), Philadelphia, PA*, 1999.

[3] R. Agrawal, J. Gehrke, D. Gunopulos, and P. Raghavan. "Automatic Subspace Clustering of High Dimensional Data for Data Mining Applications". In *Proc. ACM SIGMOD Int. Conf. on Management of Data (SIGMOD'98), Seattle, WA*, 1998.

[4] M. Ankerst, M. M. Breunig, H.-P. Kriegel, and J. Sander. "OPTICS: Ordering Points to Identify the Clustering Structure". In *Proc. ACM SIGMOD Int. Conf. on Management of Data (SIGMOD'99), Philadelphia, PA*, pages 49–60, 1999.

[5] M. Ester, H.-P. Kriegel, J. Sander, and X. Xu. "A Density-Based Algorithm for Discovering Clusters in Large Spatial Databases with Noise". In *Proc. 2nd Int. Conf. on Knowledge Discovery and Data Mining (KDD'96), Portland, OR*, pages 291–316. AAAI Press, 1996.

[6] J. Han and M. Kamber. *"Data Mining: Concepts and Techniques"*. Morgan Kaufman, 2001.

[7] A. Hinneburg, C. C. Aggarwal, and D. A. Keim. "What is the Nearest Neighbor in High Dimensional Spaces". In *Proc. 26th Int. Conf. on Very Large Databases (VLDB'00), Cairo, Egypt*, 2000.

[8] A. Hinneburg and D. A. Keim. "An Efficient Approach to Clustering in Large Multimedia Databases with Noise". In *Proc. 4th Int. Conf. on Knowledge Discovery and Data Mining (KDD'98), New York, NY*, pages 224–228. AAAI Press, 1998.

[9] K. Kailing, H.-P. Kriegel, and P. Kröger. "Density-Connected Subspace Clustering for High-Dimensional Data". In *Proc. SIAM Int. Conf. on Data Mining (SDM'04), Lake Buena Vista, FL*, 2004.

[10] B. Liebl, U. Nennstiel-Ratzel, R. von Kries, R. Fingerhut, B. Olgemöller, A. Zapf, and A. A. Roscher. "Very High Compliance in an Expanded MS-MS-Based Newborn Screening Program Despite Written Parental Consent". *Preventive Medicine*, 34(2):127–131, 2002.

[11] C. M. Procopiuc, M. Jones, P. K. Agarwal, and T. M. Murali. "A Monte Carlo Algorithm for Fast Projective Clustering". In *Proc. ACM SIGMOD Int. Conf. on Management of Data (SIGMOD'02), Madison, Wisconsin*, pages 418–427, 2002.

[12] S. Tavazoie, J. D. Hughes, M. J. Campbell, R. J. Cho, and G. M. Church. "Systematic Determination of Genetic Network Architecture". *Nature Genetics*, 22:281–285, 1999.

On Closed Constrained Frequent Pattern Mining

Francesco Bonchi
Pisa KDD Laboratory
ISTI - CNR, Area della Ricerca di Pisa
Via Giuseppe Moruzzi, 1 - 56124 Pisa, Italy
e-mail: francesco.bonchi@isti.cnr.it

Claudio Lucchese
Pisa HPC Laboratory
ISTI - CNR, Area della Ricerca di Pisa
Via Giuseppe Moruzzi, 1 - 56124 Pisa, Italy
e-mail: claudio.lucchese@isti.cnr.it

Abstract

Constrained frequent patterns and closed frequent patterns are two paradigms aimed at reducing the set of extracted patterns to a smaller, more interesting, subset. Although a lot of work has been done with both these paradigms, there is still confusion around the mining problem obtained by joining closed and constrained frequent patterns in a unique framework. In this paper we shed light on this problem by providing a formal definition and a thorough characterization. We also study computational issues and show how to combine the most recent results in both paradigms, providing a very efficient algorithm which exploits the two requirements (satisfying constraints and being closed) together at mining time in order to reduce the computation as much as possible.

1. Introduction

Frequent itemsets play an essential role in many data mining tasks that try to find interesting patterns from databases, such as association rules, correlations, sequences, episodes, classifiers, clusters. Although the collection of all frequent itemsets is typically very large, the subset that is really interesting for the user usually contains only a small number of itemsets. Therefore, the paradigm of *constraint-based mining* was introduced. Constraints provide focus on the interesting knowledge, thus reducing the number of patterns extracted to those of potential interest. Additionally, they can be pushed deep inside the mining algorithm in order to achieve better performance. For these reasons the problem of how to push different types of constraints into the frequent itemsets computation has been extensively studied [13, 15, 19].

Extracting too many uninteresting frequent patterns, with large requirements both in terms of time and space, is an even harder problem when mining dense datasets containing strongly related transactions. Such datasets are much harder to mine since only a few itemsets can be pruned by the anti-monotonicity of frequency, and the number of frequent itemsets

grows very quickly while the minimum support threshold decreases. As a consequence, the mining task becomes rapidly intractable by traditional mining algorithms, which try to extract all the frequent itemsets. *Closed itemsets mining* is a solution to this problem. Closed itemsets are a small subset of frequent itemsets, but they represent exactly the same knowledge in a more succinct way. From the set of closed itemsets it is straightforward to derive both the identities and supports of all frequent itemsets. Mining the closed itemsets is thus semantically equivalent to mining all frequent itemsets, but with the great advantage that closed itemsets are orders of magnitude fewer than frequent ones.

How to integrate the two paradigms of constrained frequent itemsets and closed frequent itemsets is clearly an interesting issue.

Following the constraints framework, one could wrongly express the property of being closed as just another constraint $\mathcal{C}_{close}$. Consider the following inductive query:

$$\mathcal{Q} : \mathcal{C}_{freq}(X) \wedge \mathcal{C}_{close}(X) \wedge sum(X.price) \leq 22$$

which requires to mine itemsets which are frequent, are closed and have a sum of prices less than 22. Such a query has ambiguous semantics. In fact there are two possible different interpretations for query $\mathcal{Q}$:

- I_1 : mine all frequent closed itemsets which have the additional property of having sum of prices less than 22;

- I_2 : mine all frequent itemsets having sum of prices less than 22 and which have the additional property of being closed (w.r.t. the other two constraints).

In this paper we shed light on this problem showing that these two possible interpretations produce different solution sets: this is due to the fact that being closed is not a property which an itemset satisfies or not for its own characteristics, but it is a property of an itemset in the context of a collection of itemsets. Then we show that the interpretation I_2 is the meaningful one and, according to it, we define the *closed constrained frequent itemset mining problem.* Finally, we study computational issues and we provide a very efficient algorithm which exploits the two requirements (satisfying constraints and being closed) at mining time in order to reduce the computation as much as possible.

1.1. Problem Definition and Notation

Let $\mathcal{I} = \{x_1, ..., x_n\}$ be a set of distinct literals, called *items*, where an item is an object with some attributes (e.g., price, type, etc.). An *itemset* X is a non-empty subset of $\mathcal{I}$. If $|X| = k$ then X is called a *k-itemset*. A constraint on itemsets is a function $\mathcal{C} : 2^{\mathcal{I}} \rightarrow \{true, false\}$. We say that an itemset I satisfies a constraint if and only if $\mathcal{C}(I) = true$. We define the *theory* of a constraint as the set of itemsets which satisfy the constraint: $Th(\mathcal{C}) = \{X \in 2^{\mathcal{I}} \mid \mathcal{C}(X)\}$.

A *transaction database* $\mathcal{D}$ is a bag of itemsets $t \in 2^{\mathcal{I}}$, called *transactions*. The *support* of an itemset X in database $\mathcal{D}$, denoted $sup_{\mathcal{D}}(X)$, is the cardinality of the set of transactions in $\mathcal{D}$ which are superset of X. Given a user-defined *minimum support* σ, an itemset X is called *frequent* in $\mathcal{D}$ if $sup_{\mathcal{D}}(X) \geq \sigma$. This defines the minimum frequency constraint: $\mathcal{C}_{freq[\mathcal{D},\sigma]}(X) \Leftrightarrow sup_{\mathcal{D}}(X) \geq \sigma$. When the dataset and the minimum support threshold are clear from the context, we address the frequency constraint simply $\mathcal{C}_{freq}$. Thus with this notation, the set of frequent itemsets can be denoted $Th(\mathcal{C}_{freq})$.

Since we are usually interested in mining problems which requires to output the support of each solution itemset, we define a special *frequency-theory* which is a set of couples *itemset-support*.

Definition 1 (F-Theory) *Given a non-empty conjunction of constraints $\mathcal{C}$ and a transaction database $\mathcal{D}$, we define:* $FTh_{\mathcal{D}}(\mathcal{C}) = \{\langle X, sup_{\mathcal{D}}(X) \rangle \mid X \in Th(\mathcal{C})\}.$

In the following, we define the concepts of *closures* and *borders* of theories, which will be useful to characterize the solutions spaces of our mining problems.

Definition 2 (Closure of a F-Theory) *The closure of a F-Theory is a function $Cl : FTh_{\mathcal{D}} \rightarrow FTh_{\mathcal{D}}$ which restricts the F-Theory to those itemsets which do not have a superset in the F-theory with the same support:*

$$Cl(FTh_{\mathcal{D}}(\mathcal{C})) = \{\langle X, sup_{\mathcal{D}}(X) \rangle \in FTh_{\mathcal{D}}(\mathcal{C}) \mid \nexists Y \supset X :$$
$$\langle Y, sup_{\mathcal{D}}(Y) \rangle \in FTh_{\mathcal{D}}(\mathcal{C}) \wedge sup_{\mathcal{D}}(Y) = sup_{\mathcal{D}}(X)\}$$

Definition 3 ($\mathcal{C}_{AM}$ and $\mathcal{C}_M$ constraints) *Let X be an itemset, a constraint $\mathcal{C}_{AM}$ is anti-monotone if $\forall Y \subseteq X : \mathcal{C}_{AM}(X) \Rightarrow \mathcal{C}_{AM}(Y)$.*
A constraint $\mathcal{C}_M$ is monotone if $\forall Y \supseteq X : \mathcal{C}_M(X) \Rightarrow \mathcal{C}_M(Y)$.

Definition 4 (Borders of theories) *Given a $\mathcal{C}_{AM}$ constraint and a $\mathcal{C}_M$ constraint we define the borders of their theories respectively as:*

$$\mathcal{B}(Th(\mathcal{C}_{AM})) = \{X \mid \forall Y \subset X. \mathcal{C}_{AM}(Y) \wedge \forall Z \supset X. \neg \mathcal{C}_{AM}(Z)\}$$

$$\mathcal{B}(Th(\mathcal{C}_M)) = \{X \mid \forall Y \supset X. \mathcal{C}_M(Y) \wedge \forall Z \subset X. \neg \mathcal{C}_M(Z)\}$$

Moreover, we distinguish between positive and negative borders. Given a general constraint $\mathcal{C}$ we define:

$$\mathcal{B}^+(Th(\mathcal{C})) = \mathcal{B}(Th(\mathcal{C})) \cap Th(\mathcal{C})$$

$$\mathcal{B}^-(Th(\mathcal{C})) = \mathcal{B}(Th(\mathcal{C})) \setminus Th(\mathcal{C})$$

Analogously we can define the borders of a F-Theory.

With this notation, given a transaction database $\mathcal{D}$, a minimum support threshold σ and a general conjunction of constraints $\mathcal{C}$ we have the following classical mining problems:

- $\mathcal{MP}_1$: the *frequent itemset mining problem* requires to compute $FTh_{\mathcal{D}}(\mathcal{C}_{freq[\mathcal{D},\sigma]})$ [1];

- $\mathcal{MP}_2$: the *maximal frequent itemset mining problem* requires to compute $\mathcal{B}^+(FTh_{\mathcal{D}}(\mathcal{C}_{freq[\mathcal{D},\sigma]}))$ [3];

- $\mathcal{MP}_3$: the *constrained frequent itemsets mining problem* requires to compute $FTh_{\mathcal{D}}(\mathcal{C}_{freq[\mathcal{D},\sigma]} \wedge \mathcal{C})$ [13];

- $\mathcal{MP}_4$: the *closed frequent itemset mining problem* requires to compute $Cl(FTh_{\mathcal{D}}(\mathcal{C}_{freq[\mathcal{D},\sigma]}))$ [14].

The problem which we address in this paper is the conjunction of problems $\mathcal{MP}_3$ and $\mathcal{MP}_4$. According to the interpretation I_2, discussed in the Introduction, we provide the following definition.

- $\mathcal{MP}_5$: the *closed constrained frequent itemset mining problem* requires to compute:

$$Cl(FTh_{\mathcal{D}}(\mathcal{C}_{freq[\mathcal{D},\sigma]} \wedge \mathcal{C}))$$

This definition will be proven to be the only reasonable in Section 3.

1.2. Related Work

Even if a lot of work has been done with closed itemsets and with constrained itemsets, there are only a few approaches analyzing the conjunction of these two frameworks. The first approach is [8] where instead of mining closed itemsets, it is proposed to mine *free* itemsets, i.e. the minimal elements of each equivalence class of frequency (closed itemsets are the maximal elements of such classes). The output of the algorithm is made with all the free itemsets satisfying a given set of monotone and anti-monotone constraints. The authors propose a variation of the A-CLOSE [14] algorithm, with constraints pushed into the computation. Free itemsets representation is concise, though the number of

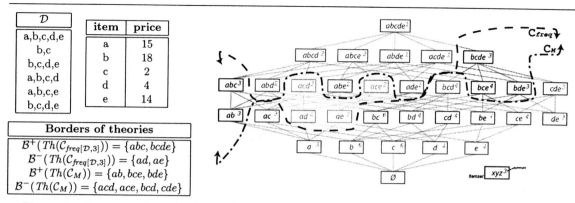

Figure 1. A transaction database $\mathcal{D}$, **an item-price table, the borders of theories of** $\mathcal{C}_{freq[\mathcal{D},3]}$, **and** $\mathcal{C}_M \equiv sum(X.prices) \geq 33$. **In this case we have that** $FTh_{\mathcal{D}}(\mathcal{C}_{freq[\mathcal{D},3]} \wedge \mathcal{C}_M) = \{\langle ab, 3 \rangle, \langle abc, 3 \rangle, \langle bcde, 3 \rangle, \langle bce, 4 \rangle, \langle bde, 3 \rangle\}$.

free sets is greater than the number of closed ones, but it is not lossless. In fact, it is not possible to reconstruct the whole $Th(\mathcal{C}_{freq})$ unless additional scans through the dataset are performed. Moreover we will see how this representation retains the same ambiguity in mining constrained free sets. Since this kind of representation is itself problematic (i.e. it is not lossless), and since it does not bring any advantage in mining the constrained solution space, we will focus on closed itemsets in this paper instead of free itemsets.

In [11], hard constraints are pushed into the frequent closed itemsets mining process. The output of the algorithm is the same of a post-processing one, i.e. first closed itemsets are discovered and then they are tested against a given set of constraints. Both these works exploit the interpretation I_1, without addressing the problem of the information loss it produces. This choice is explicitly made in order to simplify the mining process. In this paper we quantify such information loss given by the post-processing approach and give a new accurate definition of the problem of constrained closed itemset mining, which provides a concise and lossless condensed representation of the solution space.

2. Preliminaries

In this Section we review and deeply characterize the constrained frequent itemsets mining problem $\mathcal{MP}3$ and the closed frequent itemset mining problem $\mathcal{MP}4$. The provided characterization will then be useful to characterize the new problem $\mathcal{MP}5$.

2.1. Constrained Frequent Itemsets

A naïve solution to the constrained frequent itemset mining problem ($\mathcal{MP}_3$), is to first find all frequent itemsets and then test them for constraints satisfac-

tion. However more efficient solutions can be found by analyzing the property of constraints comprehensively, and exploiting such properties in order to push constraints in the frequent pattern computation. Following this methodology, some classes of constraints which exhibit nice properties (and the relative computational strategies) have been defined in literature (e.g. anti-monotonicity, monotonicity, succinctness, convertibility) [13, 15, 6]. In this paper we focus on the two basic classes of constraints: *anti-monotone* and *monotone* constraints (see Definition 3).

The most studied anti-monotone constraint is the frequency one. The anti-monotonicity of $\mathcal{C}_{freq}$ is used by the Apriori [2] algorithm with the following heuristic: if an itemset X does not satisfy $\mathcal{C}_{freq}$, then no superset of X can satisfy $\mathcal{C}_{freq}$, and hence they can be pruned. Another typical example of $\mathcal{C}_{AM}$ constraint is $sum(X.price) \leq m$, while, symmetrically, $sum(X.price) \geq m$ is a $\mathcal{C}_M$ constraint. In the rest of this paper we will consider these two constraints as prototypical $\mathcal{C}_{AM}$ and $\mathcal{C}_M$ constraints without loss of generality.

We now characterize the solutions spaces of the two problems $Th(\mathcal{C}_{freq} \wedge \mathcal{C}_{AM})$ and $Th(\mathcal{C}_{freq} \wedge \mathcal{C}_M)$.

Since any conjunction of $\mathcal{C}_{AM}$ constraints is still a $\mathcal{C}_{AM}$ constraint, and since $\mathcal{C}_{freq}$ is a $\mathcal{C}_{AM}$ constraint, the solutions space $Th(\mathcal{C}_{freq} \wedge \mathcal{C}_{AM})$ is a downward closed theory, i.e. if an itemset X is a solution, all subsets of X will be solutions as well. In other words, solution itemsets are those one that lie under both borders (the border of frequency and the border of $\mathcal{C}_{AM}$).

Proposition 1

$$X \in Th(\mathcal{C}_{freq} \wedge \mathcal{C}_{AM}) \Leftrightarrow \exists Y \in \mathcal{B}^+(Th(\mathcal{C}_{freq})),$$
$$\exists Z \in \mathcal{B}^+(Th(\mathcal{C}_{AM})) : X \subseteq Y \wedge X \subseteq Z$$

In order to characterize the other problem $Th(\mathcal{C}_{freq} \wedge \mathcal{C}_M)$ we use a graphical example. In Figure 1 we have a transaction database $\mathcal{D}$ and a item-price table, and we show the borders of theories of the frequency constraint $\mathcal{C}_{freq[\mathcal{D},3]}$, and of the monotone constraint $\mathcal{C}_M \equiv sum(X.prices) \geq 33$. The solutions to the problem $Th(\mathcal{C}_{freq[\mathcal{D},3]} \wedge \mathcal{C}_M)$ are the itemsets that lie in between the two borders: under the border of frequency and over the monotone border. The next Proposition states algebraically what we have just seen graphically.

Proposition 2

$$X \in Th(\mathcal{C}_{freq} \wedge \mathcal{C}_M) \Leftrightarrow \exists Y \in \mathcal{B}^+(Th(\mathcal{C}_{freq})),$$
$$\exists Z \in \mathcal{B}^+(Th(\mathcal{C}_M)) : Z \subseteq X \subseteq Y$$

2.2. Closed Frequent Itemsets

The set of frequent closed itemsets is a *condensed representation* of frequent itemsets. Condensed representation is a term first introduced in [12], which we use to indicate a representation of a theory, which is both:

concise: the size of the representation is significantly smaller than the original theory;

lossless: from the representation it should be possible to reconstruct all the information present in the original theory without mining the database again.

According to this definition, the set of *maximal frequent itemsets*, $\mathcal{B}^+(Th(\mathcal{C}_{freq}))$, is a condensed representation (concise and lossless) of $Th(\mathcal{C}_{freq})$, while for $FTh_{\mathcal{D}}(\mathcal{C}_{freq})$ is just concise but not lossless: in fact from maximal frequent itemsets we can reconstruct the full set of frequent itemsets but not their supports.

On the other hand the set of closed itemsets $Cl(FTh_{\mathcal{D}}(\mathcal{C}_{freq}))$ is a condensed representation of $FTh_{\mathcal{D}}(\mathcal{C}_{freq})$, since closed itemsets are orders of magnitude fewer than the frequent ones and from them is possible to reconstruct all frequent itemsets and their supports without accessing the transaction database any more. Moreover, association rules extracted from closed sets have been proved to be more concise and meaningful, because all redundancies are discarded.

The problem of mining closed frequent itemsets ($\mathcal{MP}_4$) was first introduced in [14] and since then it has received a great deal of attention especially by an algorithmic point of view [16, 20, 17].

Formally, given the functions: $f(T) = \{i \in \mathcal{I} \mid \forall t \in T, i \in t\}$, which returns all the items included in the set of transactions T, and $g(X) = \{t \in \mathcal{D} \mid \forall i \in X, i \in t\}$ which returns the set of transactions supporting a given itemset X, the composite function $f \circ g$ is called *Galois operator* or *closure operator*. We have the following definition:

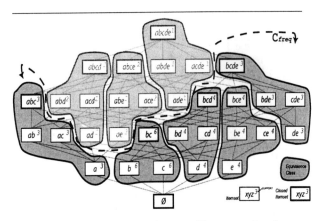

Figure 2. Equivalence classes of itemsets for the dataset $\mathcal{D}$ defined in Figure 1.

Definition 5 *An itemset I is said to be closed if and only if* $c(I) = f(g(I)) = f \circ g(I) = I$

Now we can define a set of equivalence classes over the lattice of frequent itemsets, where two itemsets X, Y belong to the same class if and only if $c(X) = c(Y)$, i.e. they have the same closure. Closed itemsets are exactly the maximal elements of these equivalence classes. Figure 2 shows the lattice of frequent itemsets derived from the same simple dataset of Figure 1. Each equivalence class contains elements sharing the same supporting transactions, and closed itemsets are their maximal elements. In this situation we have that $Cl(FTh_{\mathcal{D}}(\mathcal{C}_{freq[\mathcal{D},3]})) = \{\langle abc, 3\rangle, \langle bc, 6\rangle, \langle bcd, 4\rangle, \langle bcde, 3\rangle, \langle bce, 4\rangle\}$. Note that the number of closed frequent itemsets (5) is much less than the number of frequent itemsets (19).

It trivially holds that these equivalence classes of frequency are never cut by the border of frequency (as shown in Figure 2); but what happens to these equivalence classes when they are cut by some $\mathcal{C}_{AM}$ or $\mathcal{C}_M$ constraints? In the next Section by giving an answer to this question, we provide a characterization of $\mathcal{MP}_5$.

3. Closing Theories of Constraints

Recall the mining query discussed in the Introduction:

$$\mathcal{Q} : \mathcal{C}_{freq}(X) \wedge \mathcal{C}_{close}(X) \wedge sum(X.price) \leq 22$$

The two different interpretations of $\mathcal{Q}$ are as follows (where $\mathcal{C}_{AM} \equiv sum(X.price) \leq 22$):

- $I_1:$ $Cl(FTh_{\mathcal{D}}(\mathcal{C}_{freq[\mathcal{D},\sigma]})) \cap FTh_{\mathcal{D}}(\mathcal{C}_{AM})$
- $I_2:$ $Cl(FTh_{\mathcal{D}}(\mathcal{C}_{freq[\mathcal{D},\sigma]} \wedge \mathcal{C}_{AM}))$

We now prove that these two different interpretations lead to different results sets.

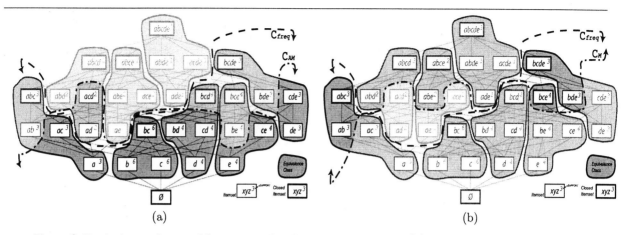

Figure 3. Equivalence classes of frequency when intersected by a $\mathcal{C}_{AM}$ (a), and by a $\mathcal{C}_M$ (b) constraint.

Example 1 *In Figure 3(a) we show the usual itemsets lattice with the frequency equivalence classes and the border of the theory of $\mathcal{C}_{AM} \equiv sum(X.price) \leq 22$. In this situation we have that $I_1 = \{\langle bc, 6 \rangle\}$ while on the other hand $I_2 = \{\langle ac, 3 \rangle, \langle bc, 6 \rangle, \langle bd, 4 \rangle, \langle cd, 4 \rangle, \langle ce, 4 \rangle \langle cde, 3 \rangle\}$.*

What has happened is that some equivalence classes have been cut by the $\mathcal{C}_{AM}$ constraint. With interpretation I_1 we mine closed frequent itemsets and then we remove those ones which do not satisfy the $\mathcal{C}_{AM}$ constraint: this way we lose the whole information contained in those equivalence classes cut by the $\mathcal{C}_{AM}$ constraint. On the other hand, according to interpretation I_2, we mine the set of itemsets which satisfy the $\mathcal{C}_{AM}$ constraint and then we compute the closure of such itemsets collection: thus, by definition, the itemsets bd and cd are solutions because they satisfy $\mathcal{C}_{AM}$ and they have not a superset in the result set with the same support and satisfying the constraint.

Which one of the two different interpretations is the most reasonable? It is straightforward to see that interpretation I_1 is not a condensed representation since it loses a lot of information. In extreme cases it could output an empty solutions set even if there are many frequent itemsets which satisfy the given set of user-defined constraints. On the other hand, interpretation I_2, which corresponds to the definition $Cl(FTh_{\mathcal{D}}(\mathcal{C}_{freq[\mathcal{D},\sigma]} \wedge \mathcal{C}_{AM}))$, is a concise and lossless representation of $FTh_{\mathcal{D}}(\mathcal{C}_{freq[\mathcal{D},\sigma]} \wedge \mathcal{C}_{AM})$.

Observe that I_2 is a superset of I_1: it contains all closed itemsets which are under the $\mathcal{C}_{AM}$ border (as I_1), plus those itemsets which arise in equivalence classes which are cut by the $\mathcal{C}_{AM}$ border (such as for instance ce and cde in Figure 3(a)).

Proposition 3

$Cl(FTh_{\mathcal{D}}(\mathcal{C}_{freq} \wedge \mathcal{C}_{AM})) \supseteq Cl(FTh_{\mathcal{D}}(\mathcal{C}_{freq})) \cap FTh_{\mathcal{D}}(\mathcal{C}_{AM})$

Let us move to the dual problem. In Figure 3(b) we show the usual equivalence classes and how they are cut by $\mathcal{C}_M \equiv sum(X.prices) \geq 33$. Since $\mathcal{C}_M$ constraints are upward closed, we have no problems with classes which are cut: the maximal element of the equivalence class will be in the alive part of the class. In other words when we have a $\mathcal{C}_M$ constraint, the two interpretations I_1 and I_2 correspond.

Proposition 4

$Cl(FTh_{\mathcal{D}}(\mathcal{C}_{freq} \wedge \mathcal{C}_M)) = Cl(FTh_{\mathcal{D}}(\mathcal{C}_{freq})) \cap FTh_{\mathcal{D}}(\mathcal{C}_M)$

The unique problem that we have with this condensed representation, is that, when reconstructing $FTh_{\mathcal{D}}(\mathcal{C}_{freq[\mathcal{D},\sigma]} \wedge \mathcal{C}_M)$ from it we must take care of testing itemsets which are subsets of elements in $Cl(FTh_{\mathcal{D}}(\mathcal{C}_{freq} \wedge \mathcal{C}_M))$ against $\mathcal{C}_M$, in order not to produce itemsets which are below the monotone border $\mathcal{B}^+(Th(\mathcal{C}_M))$. Note that, however, we do not need to access the transaction dataset $\mathcal{D}$ anymore.

Since we mine maximal itemsets of the equivalence classes it is impossible to avoid this problem, unless we store, together with our condensed representation, the border $\mathcal{B}^+(Th(\mathcal{C}_M))$ even if it does not contain any closed itemset. This could be an alternative. However, since closed itemsets provide a much more meaningful set of association rules, we consider a good trade-off among performance, conciseness and meaningfulness the use of $Cl(FTh_{\mathcal{D}}(\mathcal{C}_{freq} \wedge \mathcal{C}_M))$ as condensed representation.

Finally, if we use free sets instead of closed, we only shift the problem leading to a symmetric situation. Using free sets interpretations I_1 and I_2 coincide when dealing with anti-monotone constraints because minimal elements are not cut off by the constraint (e.g. de in Fig. 3(a)), but I_1 is lossy when dealing with monotone constraints (e.g. no free solution itemsets in Fig. 3(b)).

4. Algorithms

In this Section we study algorithms for the computation of $\mathcal{MP}_5$. We first discuss separately how monotone and anti-monotone constraints can be pushed in the computation, then we show how they can be exploited together by introducing the *CCIMiner* algorithm.

4.1. Pushing Monotone Constraints

Pushing $\mathcal{C}_{AM}$ constraints deep into the frequent itemset mining algorithm (attacking the problem $FTh_{\mathcal{D}}(\mathcal{C}_{freq[\mathcal{D},\sigma]} \wedge \mathcal{C}_{AM}))$ is easy and effective [13], since they behave exactly as $\mathcal{C}_{freq}$. The case is different for $\mathcal{C}_M$ constraints, since they behave exactly the opposite of frequency. Indeed, $\mathcal{C}_{AM}$ constraints can be used to effectively prune the search space to a small downward closed collection, while the upward closed collection of the search space satisfying the $\mathcal{C}_M$ constraints cannot be exploited at the same time. This tradeoff holding on the search space of the computational problem $FTh_{\mathcal{D}}(\mathcal{C}_{freq[\mathcal{D},\sigma]} \wedge \mathcal{C}_M)$ has been extensively studied [18, 9, 4], but all these studies have failed to find the real synergy of these two opposite types of constraints, until the recent proposal of ExAnte [6]. In that work it has been shown that a real synergy of the two opposites exists and can be exploited by reasoning on both the itemset search space and the transactions input database *together*.

According to this approach each transaction can be analyzed to understand whether it can support any solution itemset, and if it is not the case, it can be pruned. In this way we prune the dataset, and we get the fruitful side effect to lower the support of many useless itemsets, that in this way will be pruned because of the frequency constraint, strongly reducing the search space. Such approach is performed with two successive reductions: μ-reduction (based on monotonicity) and α-reduction (based on anti-monotonicity). According to μ-reduction we can delete transactions which do not satisfy $\mathcal{C}_M$, in fact no subset of such transactions satisfies $\mathcal{C}_M$ and therefore such transactions cannot support any solution itemsets. After such reduction, a singleton item may happen to become infrequent in the pruned dataset, an thus it can be deleted by the α-reductions. Of course, these two step can be repeated until a fixed point is reached, i.e. no more pruning is possible. This simple yet very effective idea has been generalized in an Apriori-like breadth-first computation in *ExAMiner* [5], and in a FP-growth [10] based depth-first computation in *FP-Bonsai* [7].

Since in general depth-first approaches are much more efficient when mining closed itemsets, and since FP-Bonsai has proven to be more efficient than ExAMiner, we decide here to use a FP-growth based depth-first strategy for the mining problem $\mathcal{MP}_5$. Thus we combine *Closet* [16], which is the FP-growth based algorithm for mining closed frequent itemset, with FP-Bonsai, which is the FP-growth based algorithm for mining frequent itemset with $\mathcal{C}_M$ constraints.

4.2. Pushing Anti-monotone Constraints

Anti-monotone constraints $\mathcal{C}_{AM}$ can be easily pushed in a Closet computation by using them in the exact same way as the frequency constraint, exploiting the downward closure property of anti-monotone constraints. During the computation, as soon as a closed itemset X s.t. $\neg \mathcal{C}_{AM}(X)$ is discovered, we can prune X and all its supersets by halting the depth first visit. But whenever, such closed itemset X s.t. $\neg \mathcal{C}_{AM}(X)$ is met (e.g. *bcd* in Figure 3(a)), some itemsets $Y \subset X$ belonging to the same equivalence class and satisfying the constraint may exist (e.g. *bd* and *cd* in Figure 3(a)). For this reason we store every such X in a separate list, named $\mathcal{E}dge$, and after the mining we can reconstruct such itemsets Y by means of a simple top-down process, named *Backward-Mining*, described in Algorithm 1.

Algorithm 1 Backward-Mining

Input: $\mathcal{E}dge, C, \mathcal{C}_{AM}, \mathcal{C}_M$
    // C is the set of frequent closed itemsets
    // $\mathcal{C}_{AM}$ is the antimonotone constraint
    // $\mathcal{C}_M$ is a monotone constraint (if present)
Output: $\mathcal{MP}_5$
1: $\mathcal{MP}_5 = C$;
    // split $\mathcal{E}dge$ by cardinality
2: k = 0;
3: **for all** $c \in \mathcal{E}dge$ s.t. $\mathcal{C}_M(c)$ **do**
4:     $\mathcal{E}_{|c|} = \mathcal{E}_{|c|} \cup \{c\}$;
5:     **if** $(k < |c|)$ **then**
6:        k=c;
    // generate and test subsets
7: **for** $(i = k; i > 1; i - -)$ **do**
8:     **for all** $c \in \mathcal{E}_{|i|}$ s.t. $\mathcal{C}_M(c)$ **do**
9:        **for all** $(i - 1)$-subset s of c **do**
10:           **if** $(\neg \exists Y \in \mathcal{MP}_5 \mid s \subseteq Y)$ **then**
11:              **if** $\mathcal{C}_{AM}(s)$ **then**
12:                 $\mathcal{MP}_5 = \mathcal{MP}_5 \cup s$;
13:              **else**
14:                 $\mathcal{E}_{|i-1|} = \mathcal{E}_{|i-1|} \cup s$;

The backward process in Algorithm 1, generates level-wise every possible subset starting from the border defined by $\mathcal{E}dge$ without getting into equivalence classes which have been already mined (Line 10). If such subset satisfies the constraint then it can be added to the output (Line 12), otherwise, it will be reused later to generate new subsets (Line 14). If we have a monotone constraint in conjunction, the backward process is stopped whenever the monotone border $\mathcal{B}^+(Th(\mathcal{C}_M))$ is reached (Lines 3 and 8).

4.3. Closed Constrained Itemsets Miner

The two techniques which have been discussed above are independent. We push monotone constraints working on the dataset, and anti-monotone constraints working on the search space. It's clear that these two can coexist consistently. In Algorithm 2 we merge them in a Closet-like computation obtaining *CCIMiner*.

Algorithm 2 CCIMiner
Input: $X, \mathcal{D}\mid_X, C, \mathcal{E}dge, \mathcal{MP}_5, \mathcal{C}_{AM}, \mathcal{C}_M$
    // X is a closed itemset
    // $\mathcal{D}\mid_X$ is the conditional dataset
    // C is the set of closed itemsets visited so far
    // $\mathcal{E}dge$ set of itemsets to be used in the Backward-Mining
    // $\mathcal{MP}_5$ solution itemsets discovered so far
    // $\mathcal{C}_{AM}, \mathcal{C}_M$ constraints
Output: $\mathcal{MP}_5$
1:   $C = C \cup X$
2:   **if** $\neg\mathcal{C}_{AM}(X)$ **then**
3:      $\mathcal{E}dge = \mathcal{E}dge \cup X$
4:   **else**
5:      **if** $\mathcal{C}_M(X)$ **then**
6:         $\mathcal{MP}_5 = \mathcal{MP}_5 \cup X$
7:      **for all** $i \in f_{list}(\mathcal{D}\mid_X)$ **do**
8:         $I = X \cup \{i\}$ // new itemset
          // avoid duplicates
9:         **if** $\neg\exists Y \in C \mid I \subseteq Y \wedge supp(I) = supp(Y)$ **then**
10:          $\mathcal{D}\mid_I = \emptyset$ // create conditional fp-tree
11:          **for all** $t \in \mathcal{D}\mid_X$ **do**
12:            **if** $\mathcal{C}_M(X \cup t)$ **then**
13:             $\mathcal{D}\mid_I = \mathcal{D}\mid_I \cup \{t\mid_I\}$ // μ-reduction
14:          **for all** items i occurring in $\mathcal{D}\mid_I$ **do**
15:            **if** $i \notin f_{list}(\mathcal{D}\mid_I)$ **then**
16:             $\mathcal{D}\mid_I = \mathcal{D}\mid_I \setminus i$ // α-reduction
17:          **for all** $j \in f_{list}(\mathcal{D}\mid_I)$ **do**
18:            **if** $sup_{\mathcal{D}\mid_I}(j) = sup(I)$ **then**
19:             $I = I \cup \{j\}$ // accumulate closure
20:             $\mathcal{D}\mid_I = \mathcal{D}\mid_I \setminus \{j\}$
21:          $CCIMiner(I, \mathcal{D}\mid_I, C, B, \mathcal{MP}_5, \mathcal{C}_{AM}, \mathcal{C}_M)$
22:   $\mathcal{MP}_5 = Backward\text{-}Mining(\mathcal{E}dge, \mathcal{MP}_5, \mathcal{C}_{AM}, \mathcal{C}_M)$

For the details about FP-Growth and Closet see [10, 16]. Here we want to outline three basic steps:

1. the recursion is stopped whenever an itemset is found to violate the anti-monotone constraint $\mathcal{C}_{AM}$ (Line 2);

2. μ and α reductions are merged in to the computation by pruning every projected conditional FP-Tree (as done in FP-Bonsai [7]) (Lines 11-16);

3. the Backward-Mining has to be performed to retrieve closed itemsets of those equivalence classes which have been cut by $\mathcal{C}_{AM}$ (Line 22).

5. Experimental Results

The aim of our experimentation is to measure performance benefits given by our framework, and to quantify the information gained w.r.t. the other lossy approaches.

All the tests were conducted on a Windows XP PC equipped with a 2.8GHz Pentium IV and 512MB of RAM memory, within the *cygwin* environment. The datasets used in our tests are those ones of the FIMI repository[1], and the constraints were applied on attribute values (e.g. *price*) randomly generated with a gaussian distribution within the range [0, 150000].

In order to asses the information loss of the post-processing approach followed by previous works, in Figure 4(a) we plot the difference in cardinality of the solution sets given by two interpretations, i.e. $|I_2 \setminus I_1|$. On both datasets PUMBS and CHESS this difference rises up to 10^5 itemsets, which means about the 30% of the solution space cardinality. It is interesting to observe that the difference is larger for medium selective constraints. This seems quite natural since such constraints probably cut a larger number of equivalence classes of frequency.

In Figure 4(b) the number of FP-tree data structures built during the mining is reported. On every dataset tested, the number of FP-trees decrease of about four orders of magnitude with the increasing of the selectivity of the constraint. This means that the technique is quite effective independently of the dataset.

Finally, in Figure 4(c) we plot run-time comparison of our algorithm CCIMiner w.r.t. Closet at different selectivity of the constraint. Since the post-processing approach must first compute all closed frequent itemsets, we can consider Closet execution-time as a lower-bound on the post-processing approach performance. Recall that CCIMiner exploits both requirements (satisfying constraints and being closed) together at mining time. This exploitation can give a speed up of about to two orders of magnitude, i.e. from a factor 6 with the dataset CONNECT, to a factor of 500 with the dataset CHESS. Obviously the performance improvements become stronger as the constraint become more selective.

---

1   http://fimi.cs.helsinki.fi/data/

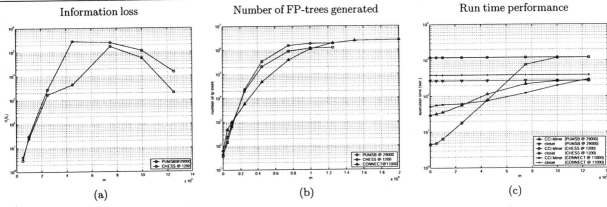

Information loss	Number of FP-trees generated	Run time performance
(a)	(b)	(c)

Figure 4. Experimental results with $\mathcal{C}_{AM} \equiv sum(X.price) \leq m$.

6. Conclusions

In this paper we have addressed the problem of mining frequent constrained closed patterns from a *qualitative* point of view. We have shown how previous works in literature overlooked this problem by using a postprocessing approach which is not lossless, in the sense that the whole set of constrained frequent patterns cannot be derived. Thus we have provided an accurate definition of constrained closed itemsets w.r.t the conciseness and losslessness of this constrained representation, and we have deeply characterized the computational problem. Finally we have shown how it is possible to *quantitative* push deep both requirements (satisfying constraints and being closed) into the mining process gaining performance benefits with the increasing of the constraint selectivity.

References

[1] R. Agrawal, T. Imielinski, and A. N. Swami. Mining association rules between sets of items in large databases. In *Proceedings ACM SIGMOD*, 1993.

[2] R. Agrawal and R. Srikant. Fast Algorithms for Mining Association Rules in Large Databases. In *Proceedings of the 20th VLDB*, 1994.

[3] R. J. Bayardo. Efficiently mining long patterns from databases. In *Proceedings of ACM SIGMOD*, 1998.

[4] F. Bonchi, F. Giannotti, A. Mazzanti, and D. Pedreschi. Adaptive Constraint Pushing in frequent pattern mining. In *Proceedings of 7th PKDD*, 2003.

[5] F. Bonchi, F. Giannotti, A. Mazzanti, and D. Pedreschi. ExAMiner: Optimized level-wise frequent pattern mining with monotone constraints. In *Proc. of ICDM*, 2003.

[6] F. Bonchi, F. Giannotti, A. Mazzanti, and D. Pedreschi. Exante: Anticipated data reduction in constrained pattern mining. In *Proceedings of the 7th PKDD*, 2003.

[7] F. Bonchi and B. Goethals. FP-Bonsai: the art of growing and pruning small fp-trees. In *Proc. of the Eighth PAKDD*, 2004.

[8] J. Boulicaut and B. Jeudy. Mining free itemsets under constraints. In *International Database Engineering and Applications Symposium (IDEAS)*, 2001.

[9] C. Bucila, J. Gehrke, D. Kifer, and W. White. DualMiner: A dual-pruning algorithm for itemsets with constraints. In *Proc. of the 8th ACM SIGKDD*, 2002.

[10] J. Han, J. Pei, and Y. Yin. Mining frequent patterns without candidate generation. In *Proceedings of ACM SIGMOD*, 2000.

[11] L.Jia, R. Pei, and D. Pei. Tough constraint-based frequent closed itemsets mining. In *Proc.of the ACM Symposium on Applied computing*, 2003.

[12] H. Mannila and H. Toivonen. Multiple uses of frequent sets and condensed representations: Extended abstract. In *Proceedings of the 2th ACM KDD*, page 189, 1996.

[13] R. T. Ng, L. V. S. Lakshmanan, J. Han, and A. Pang. Exploratory mining and pruning optimizations of constrained associations rules. In *Proc. of SIGMOD*, 1998.

[14] N. Pasquier, Y. Bastide, R. Taouil, and L. Lakhal. Discovering frequent closed itemsets for association rules. In *Proceedings of 7th ICDT*, 1999.

[15] J. Pei, J. Han, and L. V. S. Lakshmanan. Mining frequent item sets with convertible constraints. In *(ICDE'01)*, pages 433–442, 2001.

[16] J. Pei, J. Han, and R. Mao. CLOSET: An efficient algorithm for mining frequent closed itemsets. In *ACM SIGMOD Workshop on Research Issues in Data Mining and Knowledge Discovery*, 2000.

[17] J. Pei, J. Han, and J. Wang. Closet+: Searching for the best strategies for mining frequent closed itemsets. In *SIGKDD '03*, August 2003.

[18] L. D. Raedt and S. Kramer. The levelwise version space algorithm and its application to molecular fragment finding. In *Proc. IJCAI*, 2001.

[19] R. Srikant, Q. Vu, and R. Agrawal. Mining association rules with item constraints. In *Proceedings ACM SIGKDD*, 1997.

[20] M. J. Zaki and C.-J. Hsiao. Charm: An efficient algorithm for closed itemsets mining. In *2nd SIAM International Conference on Data Mining*, April 2002.

Efficient Density-Based Clustering of Complex Objects

Stefan Brecheisen, Hans-Peter Kriegel, Martin Pfeifle
Institute for Computer Science, University of Munich, Germany
{brecheisen, kriegel, pfeifle}@dbs.informatik.uni-muenchen.de

Abstract

Nowadays data mining in large databases of complex objects from scientific, engineering or multimedia applications is getting more and more important. In many different application domains complex object representations along with complex distance functions are used for measuring the similarity between objects. Often not only these complex distance measures are available but also simpler distance functions which can be computed much more efficiently. Traditionally, the well known concept of multi-step query processing which is based on exact and lower-bounding approximative distance functions is used independently of data mining algorithms. In this paper, we will demonstrate how the paradigm of multi-step query processing can be integrated into the two density-based clustering algorithms DBSCAN and OPTICS resulting in a considerable efficiency boost. Our approach tries to confine itself to ε-range queries on the simple distance functions and carries out complex distance computations only at that stage of the clustering algorithm where they are compulsory to compute the correct clustering result. In a broad experimental evaluation based on real-world test data sets, we demonstrate that our approach accelerates the generation of flat and hierarchical density-based clusterings by more than one order of magnitude.

1. Introduction

Effective data mining in large databases of complex objects, e.g. chemical compounds, CAD drawings, XML data, web sites or images, is a very challenging task, but often cannot be performed due to efficiency problems. An important area where this complexity problem is a strong handicap is that of density-based clustering. Density-based clustering algorithms like DBSCAN [7] and OPTICS [1] are based on ε-range queries for each database object. Each range query requires a lot of exact distance calculations, especially when high ε-values are used. Therefore, these algorithms are only applicable to large collections of complex objects, if those range queries are supported efficiently. When working with complex objects, the necessary distance calculations are the time-limiting factor. Thus, the ultimate goal is to save as many as possible of these complex distance calculations.

The core idea of our approach is to integrate the multi-step query processing paradigm directly into the clustering algo-

rithm rather than using it "only" for accelerating the single range queries. Our clustering approach itself exploits the information provided by simple distance measures lower-bounding complex and expensive exact distance functions. Expensive exact distance computations are only used when the information provided by simple distance computations, which are often based on simple object representations, is not enough to compute the exact clustering.

The remainder of this paper is organized as follows: In Section 2, we first introduce the basics of density-based clustering before discussing the flat density-based clustering algorithm DBSCAN [7] and the hierarchical density-based clustering algorithm OPTICS [1]. Then, we will present the related work on efficient density-based clustering and describe its limitations. Thereafter, we present our new approach which integrates the multi-step query processing paradigm directly into the clustering algorithms rather than using it independently. Finally, in Section 3, we present a detailed experimental evaluation showing that the presented approach can accelerate the generation of density-based clusterings on complex objects by more than one order of magnitude. We close this paper, in Section 4, with a short summary and a few remarks on future work.

2. Efficient Density-Based Clustering

In this section, we will discuss in detail how we can efficiently compute a flat (DBSCAN) and a hierarchical (OPTICS) density-based clustering. First, in Section 2.1, we present the basic concepts of density-based clustering along with the two algorithms DBSCAN and OPTICS. Then we look in Section 2.2 at different approaches presented in the literature for efficiently computing these algorithms. We will explain why the presented algorithms are not suitable for expensive distance computations if we are interested in the exact clustering structure. In Section 2.3, we will present our new approach which tries to use lower-bounding distance functions before computing the expensive exact distances.

2.1. Density-based Clustering

The key idea of density-based clustering is that for each object of a cluster the neighborhood of a given radius ε has to contain at least a minimum number of *MinPts* objects, i.e. the cardinality of the neighborhood has to exceed a given threshold. In the following, we will present the basic definitions of density-based clustering.

Definition 1 (directly density-reachable)

Object p is *directly density-reachable* from object q w.r.t. ε and *MinPts* in a set of objects D, if $p \in N_\varepsilon(q)$ and $|N_\varepsilon(q)| \geq MinPts$, where $N_\varepsilon(q)$ denotes the subset of D contained in the ε-neighborhood of q.

The condition $|N_\varepsilon(q)| \geq MinPts$ is called the *core object* condition. If this condition holds for an object q, then we call q a *core object*. Other objects can be directly density-reachable only from core objects.

Definition 2 (density-reachable and density-connected)

An object p is *density-reachable* from an object q w.r.t. ε and *MinPts* in the set of objects D, if there is a chain of objects $p_1, ..., p_n, p_1 = q, p_n = p$ such that $p_i \in D$ and p_{i+1} is directly density-reachable from p_i w.r.t. ε and *MinPts*. Object p is *density-connected* to object q w.r.t. ε and *MinPts* in the set of objects D, if there is an object $o \in D$ such that both p and q are density-reachable from o w.r.t. ε and *MinPts* in D.

Density-reachability is the transitive closure of direct density-reachability and does not have to be symmetric. On the other hand, density-connectivity is a symmetric relation.

2.1.1. DBSCAN. A flat density-based cluster is defined as a set of density-connected objects which is maximal w.r.t. density-reachability. Then the noise is the set of objects not contained in any cluster. Thus a cluster contains not only core objects but also objects that do not satisfy the core object condition. These border objects are directly density-reachable from at least one core object of the cluster.

The algorithm DBSCAN [7], which discovers the clusters and the noise in a database, is based on the fact that a cluster is equivalent to the set of all objects in O which are density-reachable from an arbitrary core object in the cluster (cf. lemma 1 and 2 in [7]). The retrieval of density-reachable objects is performed by iteratively collecting directly density-reachable objects. DBSCAN checks the ε-neighborhood of each point in the database. If the ε-neighborhood $N_\varepsilon(q)$ of a point q has more than *MinPts* elements, q is a so-called *core point*, and a new cluster C containing the objects in $N_\varepsilon(q)$ is created. Then, the ε-neighborhood of all points p in C which have not yet been processed is checked. If $N_\varepsilon(p)$ contains more than *MinPts* points, the neighbors of p which are not already contained in C are added to the cluster and their ε-neighborhood is checked in the next step. This procedure is repeated until no new point can be added to the current cluster C. Then the algorithm continues with a point which has not yet been processed trying to expand a new cluster.

2.1.2. OPTICS. While the partitioning density-based clustering algorithm DBSCAN [7] can only identify a "flat" clustering, the newer algorithm OPTICS [1] computes an ordering of the points augmented by additional information, i.e. the *reachability-distance*, representing the intrinsic hierarchical

```
Algorithm OPTICS:
  repeat {
      if the seedlist is empty {
          if all points are marked "done", terminate;
          choose "not-done" point q;
          add (q, infinity) to the seedlist;
      }
      (o₁,r) = seedlist entry with smallest reachability value;
      remove (o₁, r) from seedlist;
      mark o₁ as "done";
      output (o₁, r);
      update-seedlist(o₁);
  }
```

Figure 1. The OPTICS algorithm.

(nested) cluster structure. The result of OPTICS, the cluster-ordering, is displayed by the so-called reachability plot. Thus, it is possible to explore interactively the clustering structure, offering additional insights into the distribution and correlation of the data.

In the following, we will shortly introduce the definitions underlying the OPTICS algorithm, the *core-distance* of an object p and the *reachability-distance* of an object p w.r.t. a predecessor object o.

Definition 3 (core-distance)

Let p be an object from a database D, let ε be a distance value, let $N_\varepsilon(p)$ be the ε-neighborhood of p, let *MinPts* be a natural number and let *MinPts-dist(p)* be the distance of p to its *MinPts*-th neighbor. Then, the *core-distance* of p, denoted as $core\text{-}dist_{\varepsilon,MinPts}(p)$ is defined as *MinPts-dist(p)* if $|N_\varepsilon(p)| \geq MinPts$ and *UNDEFINED* otherwise.

Definition 4 (reachability-distance)

Let p and o be objects from a database D, let $N_\varepsilon(o)$ be the ε-neighborhood of o, let *dist(o,p)* be the distance between o and p, and let *MinPts* be a natural number. Then, the *reachability-distance* of p w.r.t. o denoted as $reachability\text{-}dist_{\varepsilon,MinPts}(p, o)$ is defined as $max(core\text{-}dist_{\varepsilon,MinPts}(o), dist(o,p))$ if $|N_\varepsilon(o)| \geq MinPts$ and *UNDEFINED* otherwise.

The OPTICS algorithm (cf. Figure 1) creates an ordering of a database, along with a reachability-value for each object. Its main data structure is a *seedlist*, containing tuples of points and reachability-distances. The seedlist is organized w.r.t. ascending reachability-distances. Initially the seedlist is empty and all points are marked as *not-done*.

The procedure update-seedlist (o_1) executes an ε-range query around the point o_1, i.e. the first object of the sorted seedlist, at the beginning of each cycle. For every point p in $N_\varepsilon(o_1)$ it computes $r = reachability\text{-}dist_{\varepsilon,MinPts}(p, o_1)$. If the seedlist already contains an entry (p, s), it is updated to $(p, min(r, s))$, otherwise (p, r) is added to the seedlist. Finally, the order of the seedlist is reestablished.

2.2. Related Work

DBSCAN and OPTICS determine the local densities by repeated range queries. In this section, we will sketch different approaches from the literature to accelerate these density-based clustering algorithms and discuss their unsuitability for complex object representations.

Multi-Dimensional Index Structures. The most common approach to accelerate each of the required single range queries is to use multi-dimensional index structures. For objects modelled by low-, medium-, or high-dimensional feature vectors there exist several specific R-tree [10] variants. For more detail we refer the interested reader to [9].

Metric Index Structures. Besides feature vectors, there exist quite a few other promising and approved modelling approaches for complex objects, e.g. trees, graphs, and vector sets, which cannot be managed by the index structures mentioned in the last paragraph. Nevertheless, we can use index structures, such as the M-tree [6] for efficiently carrying out range queries as long as we have a metric distance function for measuring the similarity between two complex objects. For a detailed survey on metric access methods we refer the reader to [5].

Multi-Step Query Processing. The main goal of multi-step query processing is to reduce the number of complex and, therefore, time consuming distance calculations in the query process. In order to guarantee that there occur no false drops, the used filter distances have to fulfill a lower-bounding distance criterion. For any two objects p and q, a lower-bounding distance function d_f in the filter step has to return a value that is not greater than the exact object distance d_o of p and q, i.e. $d_f(p, q) \leq d_o(p, q)$. With a lower-bounding distance function it is possible to safely filter out all database objects which have a filter distance greater than the current query range because the exact object distance of those objects cannot be less than the query range. Using a multi-step query architecture requires efficient algorithms which actually make use of the filter step. Agrawal, Faloutsos and Swami proposed such an algorithm for range queries [2] which form the foundation of density-based clustering. For efficiency reasons, it is crucial that $d_f(p, q)$ is considerably faster to evaluate than $d_o(p, q)$, and, furthermore, in order to achieve a high selectivity $d_f(p, q)$ should be only marginally smaller than $d_o(p, q)$.

Using Multiple Similarity Queries. In [3] a schema was presented which transforms query intensive KDD algorithms into a representation using the similarity join as a basic operation without affecting the correctness of the result of the considered algorithm. The approach was applied to accelerate the clustering algorithm DBSCAN and the hierarchical cluster structure analysis method OPTICS by using an R-tree like index structure. In [4] an approach was introduced for efficiently supporting multiple similarity queries for mining in metric databases.

It was shown that many different data mining algorithms can be accelerated by multiplexing different similarity queries.

Summary. Multi-dimensional index structures based on R-tree variants and clustering based on the similarity join are restricted to vector set data. Furthermore, the main problem of all approaches mentioned above is that distance computations can only be avoided for objects located outside the ε-range of the actual query object. In order to create, for instance, a reachability plot without loss of information, the authors in [1] propose to use a very high ε-value. Therefore, all of the above mentioned approaches lead to $O(|DB|^2)$ exact distance computations for OPTICS.

Furthermore, there exist other approaches which do not aim at producing the exact density-based clustering structure, but try to compute efficiently an approximated on. In this paper, we will propose an approach which computes an exact density-based clustering trying to confine itself to simple distance computations lower-bounding the exact distances. Basically, we do not carry out ε-range queries on the exact object distances but *MinPts*-nearest-neighbor queries on the exact object distances which are based on ε-range queries on the filter information. Further expensive exact distance computations are postponed as long as possible, and are only carried out at that stage of the algorithm where they are compulsory to compute the exact clustering.

2.3. Accelerated Density-Based Clustering

In this section, we will demonstrate how to integrate the multi-step query processing paradigm into the two density-based clustering algorithms DBSCAN and OPTICS. We discuss in detail our approach for OPTICS and sketch how a simplified version of this extended OPTICS approach can be used for DBSCAN.

2.3.1. Basic Idea. DBSCAN and OPTICS are both based on numerous ε-range queries. None of the approaches discussed in literature can avoid that we have to compute the exact distance to a given query object q for all objects contained in $N_\varepsilon(q)$. Especially for OPTICS, where ε has to be chosen very high in order to create reachability plots without loss of information, we have to compute $|DB|$ exact distance computations for each single range query, even when one of the methods discussed in Section 2.2 is used. In the case of DBSCAN, typically, the ε-values are much smaller. Nevertheless, if we apply the traditional multi-step query processing paradigm with non-selective filters, we also have to compute up to $|DB|$ many exact distance computations.

In our approach, the number of exact distance computations does not primarily depend on the size of the database and the chosen ε-value but rather on the value of *MinPts*, which is typically only a small fraction of $|DB|$, e.g. *MinPts* = 5 is a suitable value even for large databases [1, 7]. Basically, we use

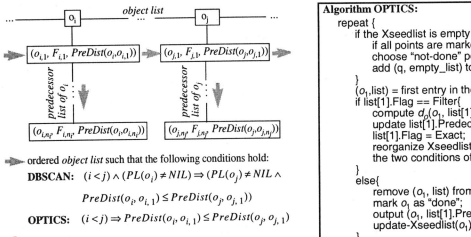

ordered *object list* such that the following conditions hold:

DBSCAN: $(i < j) \wedge (PL(o_i) \neq NIL) \Rightarrow (PL(o_j) \neq NIL \wedge$

$$PreDist(o_i, o_{i,1}) \leq PreDist(o_j, o_{j,1}))$$

OPTICS: $(i < j) \Rightarrow PreDist(o_i, o_{i,1}) \leq PreDist(o_j, o_{j,1})$

ordered *predecessor lists* such that the following conditions hold:

DBSCAN: $\forall i: (l < k) \Rightarrow PreDist(o_i, o_l) \leq PreDist(o_i, o_k)$

OPTICS: $\forall i: (l < k) \Rightarrow PreDist(o_i, o_l) \leq PreDist(o_i, o_k)$

Figure 2. Data structure *Xseedlist*.

MinPts-nearest neighbor queries instead of ε-range queries on the exact object representations in order to determine the "core-properties" of the objects. Further exact complex distance computations are only carried out at that stage of the algorithms where they are compulsory to compute the correct clustering result.

2.3.2. Extended OPTICS. The main idea of our approach is to carry out the range queries based on the lower-bounding filter distances instead of using the expensive exact distances. In order to put our approach into practice, we have to slightly extend the data structure underlying the OPTICS algorithm, i.e. we have to add additional information to the elements stored in the seedlist.

The Extended Seedlist. We do not any longer use a single seedlist as in the original OPTICS algorithm (cf. Figure 1) where each list entry consists of a pair (*ObjectId, ReachabilityValue*). Instead, we use a list of lists, called *Xseedlist*, as shown in Figure 2. The *Xseedlist* consists of an ordered list of objects, called *object list*, quite similar to the original seedlist but without any reachability information. The order of this object list, cf. the horizontal arrow in Figure 2, is determined by the first element of the second list anchored at each object of the first list. This second list is called *predecessor list PL*, cf. the vertical arrows in Figure 2.

An entry located at position l of the *predecessor list PL(o_i)* belonging to object o_i consists of the following information:

- **Predecessor ID.** An object $o_{i,l}$ which was already reported throughout the OPTICS run, i.e. $o_{i,l}$ was already added to the reachability plot, which is computed from left to right.

```
Algorithm OPTICS:
    repeat {
        if the Xseedlist is empty {
            if all points are marked "done", terminate;
            choose "not-done" point q;
            add (q, empty_list) to the seedlist;
        }
        (o₁,list) = first entry in the Xseedlist;
        if list[1].Flag == Filter{
            compute dₒ(o₁, list[1].PredecessorID);      (*)
            update list[1].PredecessorDistance;
            list[1].Flag = Exact;
            reorganize Xseedlist according to
            the two conditions of Figure 2;
        }
        else{
            remove (o₁, list) from Xseedlist;
            mark o₁ as "done";
            output (o₁, list[1].PredecessorDistance);
            update-Xseedlist(o₁);
        }
    }
```

Figure 3. The extended OPTICS algorithm.

- **Filter Flag.** A flag F indicating whether we already computed the exact object distance between o_i and $o_{i,l}$, i.e. $d_o(o_i, o_{i,l})$, or whether we only computed the distance of these two objects based on the lower-bounding filter information, i.e. $d_f(o_i, o_{i,l})$.
- **Predecessor Distance.** $PreDist(o_i, o_{i,l})$ is equal to either $max(core\text{-}dist_{\varepsilon,MinPts}(o_{i,l}), d_o(o_i,o_{i,l}))$ or to $d_f(o_i,o_{i,l})$ dependent on the fact whether we already computed the exact object distance $d_o(o_i,o_{i,l})$ or only the filter distance $d_f(o_i,o_{i,l})$.

Throughout our new algorithm, the conditions depicted in Figure 2 belonging to this extended OPTICS algorithm are maintained. In the following, we will describe the extended OPTICS algorithm trying to minimize the number of exact distance computations.

Algorithm. The extended OPTICS algorithm exploiting the filter information is depicted in Figure 3. The algorithm always takes the first element o_1 from the sorted *object list*. If it is at the first position due to a filter computation, we compute the exact distance $d_o(o_1, o_{1,1})$ and reorganize the *Xseedlist*. The reorganization might displace $o_{1,1}$ from the first position of $PL(o_1)$. Furthermore, object o_1 might be removed from the first position of the *object list*. On the other hand, if the filter flag $F_{1,1}$ indicates that an exact distance computation was already carried out, we add object o_1 to the reachability plot with a reachability-value equal to $PreDist(o_1, o_{1,1})$. Furthermore, we carry out the procedure *update-Xseedlist(o_1)*.

Update-Xseedlist. This is the core function of our extended OPTICS algorithm. First, we carry out a range query around object o_1 based on the filter information. Then we compute the core-level of the current query object o_1 by computing the *MinPts*-nearest neighbors of o_1 as follows:

- We carry out an ε-range query around o_1 based on the filter information, yielding the result set $N_\varepsilon^{filter}(o_1)$.
- We order all elements in $N_\varepsilon^{filter}(o_1)$ in ascending order according to their filter distance to o_1 yielding a $SortList_\varepsilon(o_1)$.
- We walk through $SortList_\varepsilon(o_1)$ starting at the first element. For the first element we compute the exact distance and reorder the $SortList_\varepsilon(o_1)$ which might move o_1 upward in this sorted list. This step is repeated until the first $MinPts$ elements of $SortList_\varepsilon(o_1)$ are at their final position due to an exact distance computation. The core-level of our current query object o_1 is equal to the distance between o_1 and the object stored at the $MinPts$-th position of the final $SortList_\varepsilon(o_1)$.

Some of the elements $o_j \in N_\varepsilon^{filter}(o_1)$ along with their actual reachability values w.r.t. o_1 are inserted into the *Xseedlist*.

- Elements o_j for which we already computed the exact distance to o_1 and for which $o_j \in N_\varepsilon(o_1)$ holds, are inserted as follows: If there exists no entry in the *object list* for o_j, $(o_j, <(o_1, Exact, max(d_o(o_j, o_1), core\text{-}dist_{\varepsilon,MinPts}(o_1)))>)$ is inserted into the *object list*. If there already exists an entry in the *object list* belonging to o_j, $(o_1, Exact, max(d_o(o_j, o_1), core\text{-}dist_{\varepsilon,MinPts}(o_1)))$ is inserted into $PL(o_j)$. Note that in both cases the ordering of Figure 2 has to be maintained. On the other hand, if $o_j \notin N_\varepsilon(o_1)$, o_j is not inserted into the *Xseedlist*.
- If we have not yet computed $d_o(o_j, o_1)$, o_j is inserted into the *Xseedlist*. If there exists no entry in the *object list* belonging to o_j, $(o_j, (o_1, Filter, d_f(o_j, o_1))>)$ is inserted into the *object list*. If there already exists an entry in the *object list* for o_j, $(o_1, Filter, d_f(o_j, o_1))$ is inserted into $PL(o_j)$. Again, the ordering of Figure 2 has to be maintained.

Note that this approach carries out exact distance computations only for those objects o which are very close to the actual query object q according to the filter information. On the other hand, the traditional multi-step query approach would compute exact distance computations for all objects $o \in N_\varepsilon^{filter}(q)$. As ε has to be chosen very high in order to create reachability plots without loss of information [1], the traditional approach has to compute $|DB|$ exact distance computations, even when one of the approaches discussed in Section 2.2 is used. On the other hand, the number of exact distance computations in our approach does not depend on the size of the database but rather on the value of $MinPts$, which is only a small fraction of the cardinality of the database. Note that our approach only has to compute $|DB| \cdot MinPts$, i.e. $O(|DB|)$, exact distance computations if we assume an optimal filter, in contrast to the $O(|DB|^2)$ distance computations carried out by the original OPTICS run. Only if necessary, we carry out further additional exact distance computations (cf. line (*) in Figure 3).

2.3.3. Extended DBSCAN.
Our extended DBSCAN algorithm is a simplified version of the extended OPTICS algorithm using also the *Xseedlist* as the main data structure. Again, we carry out an ε-range query for each database object q on the lower-bounding filter distances yielding a result set $N_\varepsilon^{filter}(q)$. Due to the lower-bounding properties of the filters, $N_\varepsilon(q) \subseteq N_\varepsilon^{filter}(q)$ holds. Therefore, if $|N_\varepsilon^{filter}(q)| < MinPts$ holds, q is certainly no core-point. Otherwise, we test whether q is a core-point as follows.

We organize all $o \in N_\varepsilon^{filter}(q)$ in ascending order according to their filter distance $d_f(o, q)$ yielding a $SortList_\varepsilon(q)$. We walk through this sorted list, and compute for each visited object o_i the exact distance $d_o(o_i, q)$ until for $MinPts$ elements $d_o(o_i, q) \leq$ ε holds or until we reach the end. If we reached the end, we certainly know that q is no core point. Otherwise q is a core point and in the case of DBSCAN this information is enough. The main difference to the extended OPTICS algorithm is that we do not have to reorder $SortList_\varepsilon(q)$, as we do not have to compute the core-level of q.

If our current object q is a core object, some of the objects $o_i \in N_\varepsilon^{filter}(q)$ are inserted into the *Xseedlist* (cf. Figure 2). All objects for which we have already computed $d_o(o_i, q)$, and for which $d_o(o_i, q) \leq$ ε holds, certainly belong to the same cluster as the core-object q. At the beginning of the *object list*, we add the entry (o_i, NIL), where $PL(o_i) = NIL$ indicates that o_i certainly belongs to the same cluster as q. Objects o_i for which $d_o(o_i, q) >$ ε holds are discarded. All objects $o \in N_\varepsilon^{filter}(q)$ for which we did not yet compute $d_o(o_i, q)$ are handled as follows:

- If there exists no entry in the *object list* belonging to o_i, $(o_i, < (q, Filter, d_f(o_i, q)>)$ is inserted into the *object list* in such a way that the ordering conditions of Figure 2 still hold.
- If there already exists an entry in the *object list* for o_i and, furthermore, $PL(o_i) = NIL$ holds, nothing is done.
- If there already exists an entry in the *object list* for o_i and, furthermore, $PL(o_i) \neq NIL$ holds, $(q, Filter, d_f(o_i, q))$ is inserted into $PL(o_i)$ in such a way that the ordering conditions of Figure 2 still hold.

DBSCAN expands a cluster C as follows. We take the first element o_1 from the object list and, if $PL(o_1) = NIL$ holds, we add o_1 to the current cluster, delete o_1 from the *object list*, carry out a range query around o_1, and try to expand the cluster C. If $PL(o_1) \neq NIL$ holds, we compute $d_o(o_1, o_{1,1})$. If $d_o(o_1, o_{1,1}) \leq$ ε, we process similar to the case where $PL(o_1) = NIL$ holds. If $d_o(o_1, o_{1,1}) >$ ε holds and length of $PL(o_1) > 1$, we delete $(o_{1,1}, F_{1,1}, PreDist(o_1, o_{1,1}))$ from $PL(o_1)$. If $d_o(o_1, o_{1,1}) >$ ε holds and length of $PL(o_1) = 1$, we delete o_1 from the *object list*. Iteratively, we try to expand the current cluster by examining the first entry of $PL(o_1)$ until the current *object list* is empty.

2.3.4. Length-Limitation of the Predecessor Lists. In this section, we introduce an approach for limiting the size of the predecessor lists to a constant l_{max} trying to keep the main memory footprint as small as possible.

OPTICS. For each object o_i in the *object list*, we store all potential predecessor objects $o_{i,p}$ along with *PreDist* $(o_i, o_{i,p})$ in $PL(o_i)$. Due to the lower-bounding property of d_f, we can delete all entries in $PL(o_i)$ which are located at positions $l' > l$, if we have already computed the exact distance between o_i and the predecessor object $o_{i,l}$ located at position l. So each exact distance computation might possibly lead to several delete operations in the corresponding predecessor list. In order to limit the main memory footprint, we introduce a parameter l_{max} which restricts the allowed number of elements stored in a predecessor list. If more than l_{max} elements are contained in the list, we compute the exact distance for the predecessor $o_{i,1}$ located at the first position. Such an exact distance computation between o_i and $o_{i,1}$ usually causes $o_{i,1}$ to be moved upward in the list. All elements located behind its new position l are deleted. So if $l \leq l_{max}$ holds, the *predecessor list* is limited to at most l_{max} entries. Otherwise, we repeat the above procedure.

DBSCAN. If the predecessor list of o_i is not NIL, we can limit its length by starting to compute $d_o(o_i, o_{i,1})$, i.e. the exact distance between o_i and the first element of $PL(o_i)$. If $d_o(o_i, o_{i,1}) \leq \varepsilon$ holds, we set $PL(o_i) =$ NIL indicating that o_i certainly belongs to the current cluster. Otherwise, we delete $(o_{i,1}, F_{i,1}, PreDist(o_i, o_{i,1}))$ and if the length of $PL(o_i)$ is still larger than l_{max}, we iteratively repeat this limitation procedure.

3. Evaluation

In this section, we present a detailed experimental evaluation which demonstrates the characteristics and benefits of our new approach.

3.1. Settings

Test Data Sets. As test data, we used real-world CAD data represented by 81-dimensional feature vectors [13] and vector sets consisting of 7 6D points [12]. Furthermore, we used graphs [14] to represent real-world image data. If not otherwise stated, we used 1,000 complex objects from each data set. The used filter and exact object distance functions can be characterized as follows:

- The exact distance computations on the graphs are very expensive. On the other hand, the used filter is rather selective and can efficiently be computed [14].

- The exact distance computations on the feature vectors and vector sets are also very expensive as normalization aspects for the CAD objects are taken into account. We compute 48 times the distance between two 81-dimensional feature vectors, and between two vector sets, in order to determine a normalized distance between two CAD objects [12, 13]. The filter used for the feature vectors is not very selective, but can be computed very efficiently as we only have to compute once the distance between two numerical values. The filter used for the vector sets is more selective than the filter for the feature vectors but also computationally more expensive.

Implementation. The original OPTICS and DBSCAN algorithms, along with their extensions introduced in this paper and the used filter and exact object distances were implemented in Java 1.4. The experiments were run on a workstation with a Xeon 2.4 GHz processor and 2 GB main memory under Linux.

Parameter Setting. As suggested in [1], we used for an OPTICS run a maximum ε-parameter in order to create reachability plots containing the complete hierarchical clustering information. For DBSCAN, we chose an ε-parameter yielding as many flat clusters as possible. Furthermore, if not otherwise stated, the *MinPts*-parameter is set to 5, the length of the predecessor lists is not limited, and the used filters are the ones sketched above.

Comparison Partners. As a comparison partner for extended OPTICS, we chose the full table scan based on the exact distances, because any other approach would include an unnecessary overhead and is not able to reduce the number of the required $|DB|^2$ exact distance computations. Furthermore, we compared our extended DBSCAN algorithm to the original DBSCAN algorithm based on a full table scan on the exact object distances, and we compared it to a version of DBSCAN which is based on ε-range queries efficiently carried out according to the multi-step query processing paradigm [2]. According to all our tests, this second comparison partner outperforms a DBSCAN algorithm using ε-range queries based on an M-tree [6] and the DBSCAN algorithm according to [4].

3.2. Experiments

In this section, we first investigate the dependency of our approach on the filter quality, the *MinPts*-parameter, and the maximum allowed length of the predecessor lists. For these tests, we concentrate on the discussion of the overall number of distance computations. Furthermore, we investigate the influence of the ε-value in the case of DBSCAN, and, finally, we present the absolute runtimes, in order to show that the required overhead of our approach is negligible compared to the saved exact distance computations.

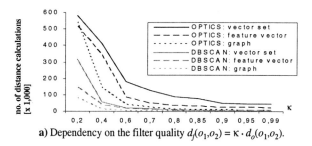

a) Dependency on the filter quality $d_f(o_1,o_2) = \kappa \cdot d_o(o_1,o_2)$.

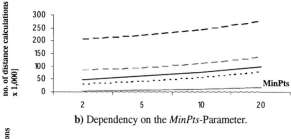

b) Dependency on the *MinPts*-Parameter.

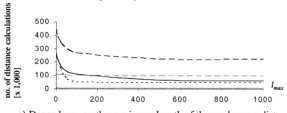

c) Dependency on the maximum length of the predecessor lists.

Figure 4. Dependency on various parameters.

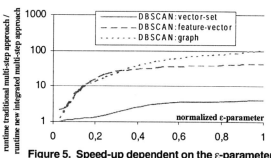

Figure 5. Speed-up dependent on the ε-parameter.

Dependency on the Filter Quality. In order to demonstrate the dependency of our approach on the quality of the filters, we utilized in a first experiment artificial filter distances d_f lower bounding the exact object distances d_o, i.e. $d_f(o_1, o_2) = \kappa \cdot d_o(o_1, o_2)$ where κ is between 0 and 1. Figure 4a depicts the number of distance computations n_{dist} w.r.t. κ. In the case of DBSCAN, even rather bad filters, i.e. small values of κ, help to reduce the number of required distance computations considerably, indicating a possible high speed up compared to both comparison partners of DBSCAN. For good filters, i.e. values of κ close to 1, n_{dist} is very small for DBSCAN and OPTICS indicating a possible high speed up compared to a full table scan based on the exact distances d_o.

Dependency on the MinPts-Parameter. Figure 4b demonstrates the dependency of our approach for a varying *MinPts*-parameter while using the filters introduced in [12, 13, 14]. As our approach is based on *MinPts*-nearest neighbor queries, obviously, the efficiency of our approach is the better the smaller the *MinPts*-parameter. Note that even for rather high *MinPts*-values around 10 = 1%·|DB|, our approach saves up to one order of magnitude of exact

distance computations compared to a full table scan based on d_o, if selective filters are used, e.g. the filters for the vector sets and the graphs. Furthermore, even for the filter of rather low selectivity used by the feature vectors, our approach needs only 1/9 of the maximum number of distance computations in the case of DBSCAN and about 1/4 in the case of OPTICS.

Dependency on the Maximum Allowed Length of the Predecessor Lists. Figure 4c depicts how the number of distance computations n_{dist} depends on the available main memory, i.e. the maximum allowed length l_{max} of the predecessor lists. Obviously, the higher the value for l_{max}, the less exact distance computations are required. The figure shows that for OPTICS we have an exponential decrease of n_{dist} w.r.t. l_{max}, and for DBSCAN n_{dist} is almost constant w.r.t. changing l_{max} parameters indicating that small values of l_{max} are sufficient to reach the best possible runtimes.

Dependency on the ε-parameter. Figure 5 shows how the speed-up for DBSCAN between our integrated multi-step query processing approach and the traditional multi-step query processing approach depends on the chosen ε-parameter. The higher the chosen ε-parameter, the more our new approach outperforms the traditional one which has to compute the exact distances between o and q for all $o \in N_\varepsilon^{filter}(q)$. In contrast, our approach confines itself to *MinPts*-nearest neighbor queries on the exact distances and computes further distances only if compulsory to compute the exact clustering result.

Absolute Runtimes. Figure 6 presents the absolute runtimes of the new extended DBSCAN and OPTICS algorithms which integrate the multi-step query processing paradigm compared to the full-table scan on the exact object representations. Furthermore, we compare our extended DBSCAN also to a DBSCAN variant using ε-range queries based on the traditional multi-step query processing paradigm. Note, that this comparison partner would induce an unnecessary overhead in the case of OPTICS where we have to use very high ε-parameters in order to detect the complete hierarchical clustering order. In all experiments, our approach was always the most efficient one. For instance, for DBSCAN on the feature vectors, our approach

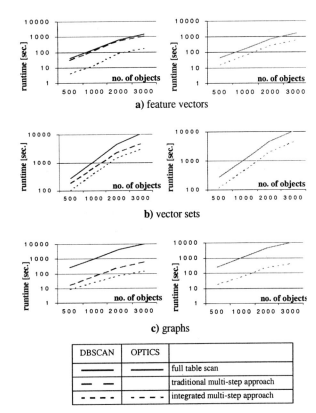

a) feature vectors

b) vector sets

c) graphs

DBSCAN	OPTICS	
——————	——————	full table scan
— —	— —	traditional multi-step approach
- - - -	- - - -	integrated multi-step approach

Figure 6. Absolute runtimes w.r.t. varying database sizes. (left: DBSCAN, right: OPTICS)

outperforms both comparison partners by an order of magnitude indicating that already rather bad filters are useful for our new extended DBSCAN algorithm. Note that the traditional multi-step query processing approach does not benefit much from non-selective filters even when small ε-values are used. In the case of OPTICS, the performance of our approach improves with increasing filter quality. For instance, for the graphs we achieve a speed-up of more than 30 indicating as well the suitability of our extended OPTICS algorithm.

4. Conclusion

In many different application areas, density-based clustering is an effective approach for mining complex data. Unfortunately, the runtime of these data-mining algorithms is very high, as the distance functions between complex object representations are often very expensive. In this paper, we showed how to integrate the well-known multi-step query processing paradigm directly into the two density-based clustering algorithms DBSCAN and OPTICS. We replaced the expensive exact ε-range queries by *MinPts*-nearest neighbor queries which themselves are based on ε-range queries on the

lower-bounding filter distances. Further exact complex distance computations are only carried out at that stage of the algorithms where they are compulsory to compute the correct clustering result.

In a broad experimental evaluation based on real-world test data sets we demonstrated that our new approach leads to a significant speed-up compared to a full-table scan on the exact object representations as well as compared to an approach, where the ε-range queries are accelerated by means of the traditional multi-step query processing concept.

In our future work, we will demonstrate that other data mining algorithms dealing with complex object representations also benefit from a direct integration of the multi-step query processing paradigm.

References

[1] Ankerst M., Breunig M., Kriegel H.-P., Sander J.: *OPTICS: Ordering Points To Identify the Clustering Structure.* SIGMOD'99, pp. 49-60.

[2] Agrawal R., Faloutsos C., Swami A. *Efficient Similarity Search in Sequence Databases.* FODO'93, pp. 69-84.

[3] Böhm C., Braunmüller B., Breunig M., Kriegel H.-P.: *High Performance Clustering Based on the Similarity Join.* CIKM'00, pp. 298-313.

[4] Braunmüller B., Ester M., Kriegel H.-P., Sander J.: *Efficiently Supporting Multiple Similarity Queries for Mining in Metric Databases.* ICDE'00, pp. 256-267.

[5] Chávez E., Navarro G., Baeza-Yates R., Marroquín J.: *Searching in Metric Spaces.* ACM Computing Surveys 33(3): pp. 273-321, 2001.

[6] Ciaccia P., Patella M., Zezula P.: *M-tree: An Efficient Access Method for Similarity Search in Metric Spaces.* VLDB'97, pp. 426-435.

[7] Ester M., Kriegel H.-P., Sander J., Xu X.: *A Density-Based Algorithm for Discovering Clusters in Large Spatial Databases with Noise.* KDD'96, pp. 226-231.

[8] Fonseca M. J., Jorge J. A.: *Indexing High-Dimensional Data for Content-Based Retrieval in Large Databases.* DASFAA'03, pp. 267-274.

[9] Gaede V., Günther O.: *Multidimensional Access Methods.* ACM Computing Surveys 30(2), pp. 170-231, 1998.

[10] Guttman A.: *R-trees: A Dynamic Index Structure for Spatial Searching.* SIGMOD'84, pp. 47-57.

[11] Jain A. K., Dubes R. C.: *Algorithms for Clustering Data,* Prentice-Hall, 1988.

[12] Kriegel H.-P., Brecheisen S., Kröger P., Pfeifle M., Schubert M.: *Using Sets of Feature Vectors for Similarity Search on Voxelized CAD Objects.* SIGMOD'03, pp. 587-598.

[13] Kriegel H.-P., Kröger P., Mashael Z., Pfeifle M., Pötke M., Seidl T.: *Effective Similarity Search on Voxelized CAD Objects.* DASFAA'03, pp. 27-36.

[14] Kriegel H.-P., S. Schönauer S.: *Similarity search in structured data.* DAWAK'03, pp. 309-319.

Test-Cost Sensitive Naive Bayes Classification

Xiaoyong Chai, Lin Deng and Qiang Yang
Department of Computer Science
Hong Kong University of Science and Technology
Clearwater Bay, Kowloon, Hong Kong, China
{carnamel, ldeng, qyang}@cs.ust.hk

Charles X. Ling
Department of Computer Science
The University of Western Ontario
London, Ontario N6A 5B7, Canada
cling@csd.wuo.ca

Abstract

Inductive learning techniques such as the naive Bayes and decision tree algorithms have been extended in the past to handle different types of costs mainly by distinguishing different costs of classification errors. However, it is an equally important issue to consider how to handle the test costs associated with querying the missing values in a test case. When the value of an attribute is missing in a test case, it may or may not be worthwhile to take the effort to obtain its missing value, depending on how much the value will result in a potential gain in the classification accuracy. In this paper, we show how to obtain a test-cost sensitive naive Bayes classifier (csNB) by including a test strategy which determines how unknown attributes are selected to perform test on in order to minimize the sum of the misclassification costs and test costs. We propose and evaluate several potential test strategies including one that allows several tests to be done at once. We empirically evaluate the csNB method, and show that it compares favorably with its decision tree counterpart.

1. Introduction

Inductive learning techniques such as the naive Bayes and decision tree algorithms, have met great success in building classification models with the aim to minimize the classification errors [9][12]. As an extension, much previous inductive learning research has also considered how to minimize the costs of classification errors, such as the cost of false positive (FP) and the cost of false negative (FN) in binary classification tasks. The misclassification costs are useful in deciding whether a learned model tends to make correct decisions on assigning class labels for new cases, but they are not the only costs to consider in practice. When performing classification on a new case, we often consider the "test costs" when missing values must be obtained through physical "tests" which incur costs themselves. These costs are often as important as the misclassification costs.

As an example, consider the task of a medical practice that examines incoming patients for a certain illness. Suppose that the doctors' previous experience has been compiled into a classification model such as a naive Bayes classifier. When diagnosing a new patient, it is often the case that certain information for this patent may not yet be known; for example, the blood test or the X-ray test may not have been done yet. Performing these tests will incur certain extra costs, but different tests may provide different informational values towards minimizing the misclassification costs. It is the balancing act of the two types of costs – namely the misclassification costs and the test costs – that determines which tests will be done.

Tasks that incur both misclassification and test costs abound in practice ranging from medical diagnosis to scientific research to drug design. One possible approach is to use the strategy in naive Bayes classification in dealing with missing values. That is, when a test case is classified by a naive Bayes classifier, and an attribute is found to have a missing value, no test will be performed to obtain its value; instead, the attribute is simply ignored in the posterior computation. The problem with this approach is that it ignores the possibility of obtaining the missing value with a cost, and thus reducing the misclassification cost and the total cost.

Inductive learning methods that consider a variety of costs are often referred to as *cost-sensitive learning* [15][5]. In this paper, we refer to cost-sensitive learning that specifically considers test costs as *test-cost sensitive learning*. We propose a test-cost sensitive naive Bayes algorithm (*csNB* for short) to minimize the sum of the misclassification costs and the test costs. The naive Bayes algorithm can be extended straightforwardly to incorporate the concept of "costs" by minimizing the risk instead of the classification error [4]. However, we observe that so far, few extensions have been made to consider naive Bayes classification with associated test costs for obtaining the missing values. In addition, different test strategies will result in different decisions on how the tests are performed. In this paper we consider two types of test strategies: the sequential test strategy and the batch test strategy. The former takes tests for missing values sequentially. Decisions on whether an additional test is needed or which unknown attribute should be tested next are made sequentially based on the outcome of the previous tests. The latter, the batch test strategy, requires several tests to be done at once rather than in a sequential manner. This scenario is more practical. For example, it is often the case that doctors need to have a number of test results all at once before making a diagnosis.

The novelty of our work can be seen as follows:

1. Previous work on naive Bayes classification has mostly considered how to reduce the misclassification costs by considering different classification risks. In our *csNB* framework, we additionally consider the test costs and aims to minimize the sum of them.

2. Previous work on test-cost sensitive learning has considered how to use decision trees, coupled with a sequential test strategy, to decide which attributes to perform test on one by one. In contrast, we consider a natural extension in *csNB* by which a batch test strategy can be easily derived and performed effectively.

2. Related Work

Much work has been done in machine learning on minimizing the classification errors. This is equivalent to assigning the same cost to each type of classification errors, and then minimizing the total misclassification costs. In Turney's survey article [15], a whole variety of costs in machine learning are analyzed, and the test cost is singled out as one of the least considered. In particular, two types of costs are considered:

- Misclassification costs: these are the costs incurred by classification errors. Works such as [2][5][7] considered classification problems with non-uniform misclassification costs.

- Test costs: these are the costs incurred for obtaining attribute values. Previous work such as [10][13] considered the test costs alone without incorporating misclassification cost. As pointed out in [15], it is obviously an oversight.

As far as we know, the only works that considered both misclassification and test costs include [8][16][6][14]. Of these works, [8] proposed a decision tree based method that explicitly considers how to directly incorporate both types of costs in decision tree building processes and in determining the next attribute to test, should the attributes contain

missing values. Their method naturally extends the decision tree construction algorithm by using *minimal cost* as the splitting criterion and builds a sequential test strategy in a local search framework. Through experimentation with this method, however, we have also found some shortcomings. Because a decision tree places different levels of importance on the attributes by the natural organization of the tree, it cannot be easily fitted to make flexible decisions on selecting unknown attributes for tests. Furthermore, a decision tree is not well-suited for performing batch tests that involve a number of tests to be done together, since it is aimed at serializing attribute tests along its paths. In contrast, the naive Bayes based algorithms overcome these difficulties more naturally. As we will see, the performance offered by the test-cost sensitive naive Bayes is significant over its decision-tree counterpart.

In [16], the cost-sensitive learning problem is cast as a Markov Decision Process (MDP), and solutions are given as searches in a state space for optimal policies. For a given new case, depending on the values obtained so far, the resulting policy can suggest a best action to perform in order to minimize both the misclassification and test costs. However, it may take very high computational cost to conduct the search process. In contrast, we adopt the local search algorithm using the concepts of utility and gain, which is more efficient and also offers high quality solutions.

Similar in the interest in constructing an optimal learner, [6] studied the theoretical aspects of active learning with test costs using a PAC learning framework. [14] presented a system called ICET, which uses a genetic algorithm to build a decision tree to minimize the sum of both costs. In contrast, because our algorithm essentially adopts the conditional probability based framework, which requires only a linear scan through the dataset, our algorithm is expected to be more efficient than Turney's genetic algorithm based approach.

3. Test-cost sensitive naive Bayes

Naive Bayes classifier is shown to perform very well in practice to minimize classification errors, even in many domains containing clear attribute dependences [3]. For classification, the standard naive Bayes algorithm computes the posterior probability $P(c_j|x)$ of sample x belonging to class c_j according to the Bayes' rule:

$$P(c_j|x) = \frac{P(x|c_j)P(c_j)}{P(x)}.$$

x is predicted to belong to the class c_{j^*} where $j^* = \arg\max_j P(c_j|x)$. When there exist missing values in sample x, the corresponding attributes are simply left out in likelihood computation and the posterior probability is computed only based on the known attributes.

However, classification errors are not the only criteria in evaluating a learned model. In practice, costs involved during classification are even more important in deciding whether the model is effective in making correct decisions. Therefore, a naive Bayes classifier should be extended to be cost-sensitive.

3.1. Costs in Naive Bayes Classification

In this paper, we consider two types of costs in naive Bayes classification: the misclassification cost and the test cost.

The misclassification cost is considered when there are different types of classification errors, and the costs they bring are different. The standard naive Bayes algorithm (NB) can be extended to take the misclassification cost into account. Suppose that C_{ij} is the cost of predicting a sample of class c_i as belonging to class c_j. The expected misclassification cost of predicting sample x as class c_j is also known as the *conditional risk* [4], which is defined as: $R(c_j|x) = \sum_i C_{ij} \times P(c_i|x)$, where $P(c_i|x)$ is the posterior probability given by a NB classifier. Sample x is then predicted to belong to class c_{j*} which has the minimal conditional risk $R(c_{j*}|x) = \min_j R(c_j|x)$.

To consider the test cost, take medical diagnosis as an example. Suppose that in diagnosing the disease of hepatitis, 21% of patients are positive (have hepatitis, c_1) and 79% are negative (healthy, c_2). Therefore, the priors are $P(c_1) = 21\%$ and $P(c_2) = 79\%$, respectively. The costs of different classification errors can be specified by setting the corresponding C_{ij}. Assume that the costs (conditional risk) are $C_{12} = 450$, $C_{21} = 150$, and $C_{11} = C_{22} = 0$.

Suppose there are four attributes to characterize a patient, and testing the value (*positive* or *negative*) of each attribute brings a certain amount of cost. The test costs of the four attributes and their likelihoods are listed in Table 1 below.

| Attri- | Test | Hepatitis (c_1) | | healthy (c_2) | |
butes	Cost	Pos	Neg	Pos	Neg
liver firm	18	51.7%	48.3%	61.8%	38.2%
spleen	24	56.9%	43.1%	81.9%	18.1%
spiders	26	29.0%	71.0%	75.6%	24.4%
ascites	32	54.8%	45.2%	95.0%	5.0%

Table 1. Likelihoods of attributes

When a patient first comes, values of these four attributes are unknown. To diagnose whether the patient has hepatitis or not, a doctor must decide whether a medical test is worthwhile to perform and if so, which one. Each test has its own discriminating power on disease and meanwhile, brings a certain amount of cost. Therefore, decisions must be made by considering both factors. After a test is selected and performed, based on its outcome, similar decisions are made subsequently on the unknown attributes left. As a consequence, during the process of diagnosis, the doctor adopts a sequential test strategy with the aim to minimize the sum of the misclassification cost and test costs.

In practice, the situation is even more complicated when more attributes are involved and some tests are with delayed results. For example, the blood tests are usually shipped to a laboratory and the results are sent back to doctors the next day. In these cases, for the sake of patients, doctors often ask for a batch of tests simultaneously. Therefore, a batch test strategy must consider the costs of the several tests done in one shot.

3.2. Problem Formulation

The classification problem of Test-Cost Sensitive Naive Bayes is formulated as follows:

Given: (D, C, T), where

- D is a training dataset consisting of N samples $(x_1, x_2, \cdots, x_N)$ from P classes $(c_1, c_2, \cdots, c_P)$. Each sample x_i is described by M attributes $(A_1, A_2, \cdots, A_M)$ among whom there can be missing values.

- C is a misclassification cost matrix. Each entry $C_{ij} \triangleq C(i, j)$ specifies the cost of classifying a sample from class c_i as belonging to class c_j $(1 \leq i, j \leq P)$. Usually, $C_{ii} = 0$.

- T is a test-cost vector. Each entry $T_k \triangleq T(k)$ specifies the cost of taking a test on attribute A_k $(1 \leq k \leq M)$;

Build: a test-cost sensitive naive Bayes classifier *csNB* and for every test case, a test strategy (see Section 4) with the aim to minimize the sum of the misclassification cost C_{mc} and test cost C_{test}.

The above formulation provides a more general framework than the traditional naive Bayes does. Actually, the latter is just a special case of *csNB* where the test costs T_k are sufficiently large so that no test will be performed. Also, the conditional risk [4] can be equivalently implemented by setting the misclassification cost matrix C.

csNB classification consists of two procedures: First, a *csNB* classifier is learned from the training dataset D. Second, for each test case, a test strategy is designed to minimize the total cost based on the *csNB* obtained.

Learning a *csNB* classifier is basically the process of estimating the distribution parameters as in traditional NB. Let $c_j \in \{c_1, c_2, \cdots, c_P\}$ be the jth predefined class and $v_{m,k} \in \{v_{m,1}, v_{m,2}, \cdots, v_{m,|A_m|}\}$ be one of the possible values attribute A_m can take. The learning procedure is exactly the estimation of prior probabilities $\hat{P}(c_j)$ and likelihoods $\hat{P}(A_m = v_{m,k}|c_j)$ from the training dataset D. In addition, when there are missing values in the training examples, the corresponding attributes are just ignored in the likelihood computation.

The real intriguing problem is how to design a test strategy for each test case with the aim to minimize the sum of the misclassification cost C_{mc} and test cost C_{test}. It is essentially an optimization problem that minimizes the total cost. However, to find an optimal test strategy given a test case is computationally difficult, since the problem can also be equivalently formulated as a MDP as in [16] which is shown to be NP-hard [11]. The problem is more complicated when different types of test strategies are demanded, such as the sequential test strategy (Section 4) and batch test strategy (Section 5). In this paper, we are interested in finding approximation solutions.

4. Prediction with Sequential Test Strategy

When a new test case with missing values comes, a *csNB* classifier need to design a test strategy as to how and which unknown attributes are selected to test. In this section, we consider sequential test strategies and leave batch test strategies to Section 5.

A sequential test strategy is as follows. During the process of classification, based on the results of previous tests, decisions are made sequentially on whether a further test on an unknown attribute should be performed, and if so, which attribute to select. More specifically, the selection of a next unknown attribute to test is not only dependent on all the values of initially known attributes, but also dependent on the values of those unknown attributes previously tested.

Suppose that $x = (a_1, a_2, \cdots, a_M)$ is a test example. Each attribute a_i can be either known or unknown. Let $\widetilde{A}$ denote the set of known attributes among all the attributes A and $\overline{A}$ the unknown attributes. The expected misclassification cost of classifying x as class c_j based on $\widetilde{A}$ is:

$$R(c_j|x) = R(c_j|\widetilde{A}) = \sum_{i=1}^{P} C_{ij} \times P(c_i|\widetilde{A}), 1 \le j \le P \quad (1)$$

where $P(c_j|\widetilde{A}) = \frac{P(\widetilde{A}|c_j)P(c_j)}{P(\widetilde{A})}$ is the posterior probability obtained using Bayes' rule.

Prediction can be made based on $\widetilde{A}$. c_{j*} with the minimum expected cost is predicted as the class label. Finally, the misclassification cost C_{mc} is C_{ij*} if c_i is the actual class label of x. The test cost C_{test} is 0, since no test is performed. However, a sequence of tests on some unknown attributes may be more preferable to reduce the misclassification cost and thus to minimize the total cost. To decide

whether a test is needed and if so, which attribute $\overline{A}_i \in \overline{A}$ to select, we introduce the *utility* of testing an unknown attribute $\overline{A}_i$ as follows:

$$Util(\overline{A}_i) = Gain(\widetilde{A}, \overline{A}_i) - C_{test}(\overline{A}_i) \quad (2)$$

$C_{test}(\overline{A}_i)$ is the test cost of $\overline{A}_i$ given by T_i. $Gain(\widetilde{A}, \overline{A}_i)$ is the reduction in the expected misclassification cost obtained from knowing $\overline{A}_i$'s true value, which is given by:

$$Gain(\widetilde{A}, \overline{A}_i) = C_{mc}(\widetilde{A}) - C_{mc}(\widetilde{A} \cup \overline{A}_i) \quad (3)$$

$C_{mc}(\widetilde{A}) = \min_j R(c_j|\widetilde{A})$ is easily obtained using (1). What is not trivial is the calculation of $C_{mc}(\widetilde{A} \cup \overline{A}_i)$, since the value of $\overline{A}_i$ is not revealed until the test is performed. We calculate it by taking expectation over all possible values of $\overline{A}_i$ as follows:

$$C_{mc}(\widetilde{A} \cup \overline{A}_i) = E_{\overline{A}_i} \left[\min_j \left(R(c_j|\widetilde{A} \cup \overline{A}_i) \right) \right] \quad (4)$$

$$= \sum_{k=1}^{\|\overline{A}_i\|} P(\overline{A}_i = v_{i,k}|\widetilde{A}) \times \min_j R(c_j|\widetilde{A}, \overline{A}_i = v_{i,k}) \quad (5)$$

In Equation (4), the expected minimum misclassification cost is conditional on the values of attributes $\widetilde{A}$ known so far. In the expended form (5), the minimum misclassification cost given $\overline{A}_i = v_{i,k}$ is weighted by the conditional probability $P(\overline{A}_i = v_{i,k}|\widetilde{A})$ which can be obtained using Bayes' rule.

Overall, an attribute $\overline{A}_i$ is worth testing on if testing it offers more gain than the cost it brings. Therefore, by using Equation (2) to calculate all the utilities of testing unknown attributes in $\overline{A}$, we can decide whether a test is needed ($\exists_i Util(\overline{A}_i) > 0$) and which attribute $\overline{A}_{i*}$ to test ($i^* = \arg\max_i Util(\overline{A}_i)$).

After the attribute $\overline{A}_{i*}$ is tested, its true value is revealed. The set of known attributes $\widetilde{A}$ is expanded to $\widetilde{A} \cup \{\overline{A}_{i*}\}$ and correspondingly, $\overline{A}$ is reduced to $\overline{A}/\{\overline{A}_{i*}\}$. Such a selection process is repeated until the utility of testing any unknown attribute is non-positive or there is no unknown attribute left. A class label is then predicted based on the expanded known attribute set $\widetilde{A}$.

Finally, the misclassification cost C_{mc} is C_{ij} if example x predicted as class c_j is actually from class c_i. All the costs brought by the attribute tests comprise the test cost C_{test}. Consequently, the total cost $C_{total} = C_{mc} + C_{test}$. The details of the csNB-sequential prediction are given in Algorithm 1. As the output, the algorithm gives the prediction of a test example x as well as the test cost C_{test} included.

Back to the example in Section 3.1, initially $\widetilde{A} = \phi$ and $\overline{A} = A$ since all the four attributes are unknown. At step 5, the utilities of the four attributes are calculated, which are -6.5, 8.6, 22.2 and 24.1, respectively. Consequently, at step 10, the attribute "ascites" with the maximum utility 24.1 is selected to test and its true value is revealed. "ascites" is then removed from $\overline{A}$ to $\widetilde{A}$. Attribute selection for testing in the next round will be different depending on the outcome of the test on "ascites". If it is *positive*, the attribute "spleen" is chosen for testing; otherwise, the attribute "spiders" is selected. The same process continues and finally a sequential test strategy can be obtained during classification.

Algorithm 1 csNB-sequential-predict(x, cl)

Input: x — a test example, cl — a *csNB* classifier;
Output: Label — the predicted class, C_{test} — the test cost;
Steps:
1: Let $\widetilde{A}$ and $\overline{A}$ denote the set of known attributes and the set of unknown attributes of x.
2: Set $C_{test} = 0$.
3: **while** $\overline{A}$ is not empty **do**
4:     **for all** $\overline{A}_i \in \overline{A}$ **do**
5:        Calculate $Util(\overline{A}_i)$ using Equation (2);
6:     **end for**
7:     **if** not $\exists_i Util(\overline{A}_i) > 0$ **then**
8:        break;
9:     **end if**
10:     $\overline{A}_{i*} = \max_i Util(\overline{A}_i)$
11:     Reveal $\overline{A}_{i*}$'s missing value v.
12:     $C_{test} = C_{test} + T_{\overline{A}_{i*}}$
13:     $\widetilde{A} \leftarrow \widetilde{A} \cup \{\overline{A}_{i*} = v\}$
14:     $\overline{A} \leftarrow \overline{A}/\{\overline{A}_{i*}\}$
15: **end while**
16: Calculate the expected misclassification costs $R(c_j|\widetilde{A})$ by Equation (1).
17: Label $= \arg\min_j R(c_j|\widetilde{A})$.

A desirable property is that even when all the test costs are zero, *csNB* may not do tests for all the missing attributes. One reason is that the gain from knowing the missing value of an attribute $\overline{A}_i$ is not always positive. According to Equation (3), if the expected misclassification cost $C_{mc}(\widetilde{A} \cup \overline{A}_i)$ is equal to or even larger than the original cost $C_{mc}(\widetilde{A})$, the gain is non-positive. This creates a paradox: adding new features (especially unrelated features) to a naive Bayes classifier may actually lead to more misclassification cost. The basic source can be traced back to the wrong independent assumption of naive Bayes [4]. For the same reason, adding these features to *csNB* can increase the misclassification cost and is therefore not preferred. Another possible reason is that the characteristics of the misclassification cost matrix C can affect the test strategy. As an example, suppose the entries $C_{.j_0}$ in the j_0th column of matrix C is much smaller than other entries in C, so that the minimizing functions, $\arg\min_j R(c_j|\widetilde{A})$ and $\arg\min_j R(c_j|\widetilde{A}\cup\overline{A}_i)$, always have j_0 returned. In this case, the gain from any unknown

attribute $\overline{A}_i$ may be zero and *csNB* will not do any test even if no cost is brought.

5. Prediction with Batch Test Strategy

A sequential test strategy is optimal in the sense that (1) it takes expectation over all possible outcomes of attribute tests, and (2) decisions are made in a sequential manner such that the next selection is dependent on the test results of the previous ones. However, in many situations, tests are required to be done all at once due to some practical constraints, such as time. In these situations, several unknown attributes are tested simultaneously and a batch test strategy is needed instead.

Specifically, while both batch test strategies and sequential test strategies aim to minimize the total cost, they are different in that: In batch test, tests on unknown attributes must be determined in advance before any one of them is carried out; therefore, strategies are designed beforehand. In sequential test, as discussed in Section 4, strategies are designed on the fly during prediction.

To find an optimal batch test strategy for a new test example, one possible way is to examine all possible subsets of unknown attributes $\overline{A}$ by calculating the utilities, and choose the one with the maximum utility. Let $\overline{A}'$ denote a subset of $\overline{A}$ ($\overline{A}' \subseteq \overline{A}$). $C_{mc}(\widetilde{A} \cup \overline{A}')$, the expected minimum misclassification cost is calculated to obtain its utility. To achieve it, expectation is taken over all possible value combinations of the unknown attributes in $\overline{A}'$. However, it is computationally difficult to do so.

By assuming the conditional independence among attributes, we can extend the sequential test algorithm using a greedy method. The idea is that in each round, after the best unknown attribute is selected (the one with maximum utility), its test cost is counted. However, its true value is not revealed. After that, this attribute is removed from $\overline{A}$ to $\widetilde{A}$ and the selection process continues. Equivalently, all unknown attributes with non-negative utility are selected.

Again, let $\overline{A}'$ denote the batch of attributes selected and C_{test} the test cost. They are computed as follows:

$$\overline{A}' = \{\overline{A}_i | Util(\overline{A}_i) > 0, \overline{A}_i \in \overline{A}\} \qquad (6)$$

$$C_{test} = C_{test}(\overline{A}') = \sum_{\overline{A}_i \in \overline{A}'} C_{test}(\overline{A}_i) \qquad (7)$$

In the above equations, the utility of an unknown attribute $\overline{A}_i$ is calculated as in Section 4, and the costs of testing the attributes in $\overline{A}'$ comprise the overall test cost C_{test}. The batch tests on $\overline{A}'$ are then taken, and the values of attributes in $\overline{A}'$ are revealed and added into $\widetilde{A}$. Finally, the class label is predicted as in the *csNB*-sequential prediction algorithm (Step 16-17).

Back to the example in Section 3.1, $\overline{A}' = \{$"spleen", "spiders", "ascites"$\}$, since these three unknown attributes have non-negative utilities. The test cost C_{test} is $24 + 26 + 32 = 82$ and the batch test strategy is to perform tests on these three attributes in one shot.

6. Experiments

In order to evaluate the performance of *csNB* with both sequential and batch test strategies, experiments were carried out on eight datasets from the UCI ML repository [1]. For comparison, two variations of traditional naive Bayes classifiers were used as the baselines. The first one is the naive Bayes classifier augmented to minimize the misclassification cost (conditional risk) as given in [4]. This classifier is termed Lazy Naive Bayes (LNB) since it simply predicts class labels based on the known attributes and requires no further tests to be done on any unknown one. The second variation is the naive Bayes classifier extended further from LNB. It requires all the missing values to be made up before prediction. Since this classifier allows no missing values, it is termed Exacting Naive Bayes (ENB).

Comparisons were also made between *csNB* and the Cost-Sensitive Decision Tree (csDT) proposed in [8]. The latter is a novel and effective method for building and testing decision trees that also aims to minimize the sum of the misclassification cost and the test costs. The algorithm was shown to significantly outperform C4.5 and its variations.

In summary, four methods were examined: (1) Lazy Naive Bayes (LNB), (2) Exacting Naive Bayes (ENB), (3) Test-Cost Sensitive Naive Bayes (*csNB*), and (4) Cost-Sensitive Decision Trees (csDT).

The eight datasets used are listed in Table 2. These datasets were chosen because they have discrete attributes, binary class, and a sufficient number of examples. We only consider binary class problems in the following experiments to be consistent with the csDT algorithm, although our *csNB* algorithm can be used in multiple class problems naturally. Also, the numerical attributes in datasets were discretized using minimal entropy method as in [8].

Name of datasets	No. of attributes	Name of datasets	No. of attributes
Ecoli	6	Breast	9
Heart	8	Thyroid	24
Australia	15	Cars	6
Voting	16	Mushroom	22

Table 2. Datasets used in the experiments

We ran a 3-fold cross validation on these data sets. In the experiments, no missing value is assigned in the training examples and for the testing examples, a certain percentage (missing rate) of attributes are randomly selected and marked as unknown. If during classification, an algorithm decides to perform a test on an unknown attribute, its true value is revealed and the test cost is accumulated. Finally, the misclassification cost C_{mc} can be obtained by comparing the predicted label with the true class label, and C_{test} is the accumulated test cost. The performance of the algorithms is then measured in terms of the total cost $C_{total} = C_{mc} + C_{test}$. To the binary class problems, let c_1 be the positive class and c_2 the negative class. The misclassification matrix was set as $C_{12} = C_{21} = 600$ and $C_{11} = C_{22} = 0$, where C_{12} can be interpreted as false negative and C_{21} false positive. The test cost of each attribute is set randomly between 0 and 100.

6.1. Sequential Test Strategy

Figures 1 and 2 show the results of different algorithms with sequential test strategy on all the eight datasets. In these experiments, the percentage of unknown attributes is 40%. Each group of four bars represents the runs of four algorithms on one particular dataset. The height of a bar represents the average total cost, and therefore the lower the better. Each bar consists of two parts: the lower dark portion standing for the average misclassification cost and the upper light portion standing for the average test costs.

There are several interesting observations from these experiments. First, although the misclassification costs of ENB are almost always the lowest among the four methods, the average total costs of it are the highest. This is because the low misclassification costs are achieved at the cost of testing all unknown attributes, which is costly when the missing rate is high.

Second, despite of its lazy nature, LNB performs well, even better than csDT. This can be explained by the fact that, while csDT uses the splitting criterion of minimal costs for attribute selection in tree building, whenever trees are built, the test sequences are fixed. Only the attributes along a tree path are examined and the others are ignored. However, those attributes not examined can still be informative in classification. LNB, on the other hand, is capable of making use of these attributes.

Third, our *csNB* method performs the best overall because of its ability in selecting unknown attributes for testing. As we can see from the figures, *csNB* not only lowers the misclassification costs compared with LNB, but also maintains a low level of test costs compared with ENB.

To investigate the impact of the percentage of unknown attributes on the average total costs, experiments were carried out on the performance with the increasing percentage of unknown attributes. Figure 3 shows the results on the Mushroom dataset (other figures are spared for space). As we can see, when the percentage increases ($> 40\%$), the

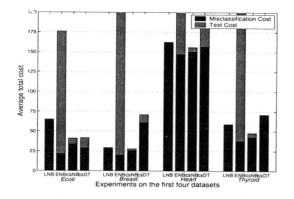

Figure 1. Average total cost comparisons of four methods on datasets: Ecoli, Breast, Heart and Thyroid.

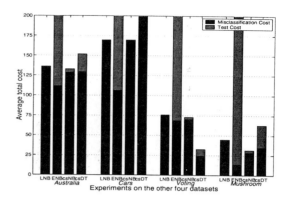

Figure 2. Average total cost comparisons of four methods on datasets: Australia, Cars, Voting and Mushroom.

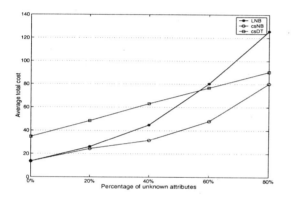

Figure 3. Comparisons with varying missing rates.

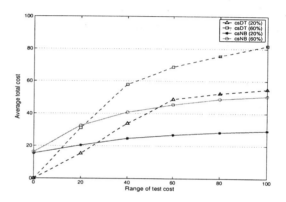

Figure 4. Comparisons with varying test costs.

average total cost of LNB increases significantly and surpasses that of csDT. Again, *csNB* is the best overall.

Another set of experiments was conducted to compare two cost-sensitive algorithms csDT and *csNB* in terms of varying test costs. Figure 4 shows the results on the Mushroom dataset with both the missing rates 20% and 60%. Still, *csNB* outperforms csDT overall. Also, as we can see, *csNB* is less sensitive to the test costs than csDT as the increasing of test costs. This reveals that the *csNB* method is effective at balancing the misclassification and test costs.

6.2. Batch Test Strategy

Batch test is another important scenario we want to investigate. In order to compare *csNB* with csDT in terms of their abilities with batch test strategy, we extended the csDT algorithm as suggested in [8]. The basic idea is that during classification, when a test case is stopped at the first

attribute whose value is unknown, this attribute, together with all unknown attributes in the sub-tree will be tested.

The results of average total cost on the 8 datasets with 40% missing rate are shown in Figure 5. Again, the test cost of each attribute is set randomly between 0 and 100, and $C_{12} = C_{21} = 400$ while $C_{11} = C_{22} = 0$. Overall, *csNB* outperforms csDT greatly. On average, *csNB* incurs 29.6% less total cost than csDT. This reveals that although both algorithms aim to minimize the total cost, *csNB* trades off the misclassification cost and the test costs much better than csDT. Besides the same reasons as explained in sequential test (Section 6.1), in batch test, the advantage of *csNB* over csDT can also be explained as follows. By the nature of decision trees in tree-building, attributes are considered sequentially and conditionally one by one. Therefore, csDT is inflexible to derive batch test strategies. On the other hand, *csNB* has no such constraint and all the attributes can be evaluated at the same level.

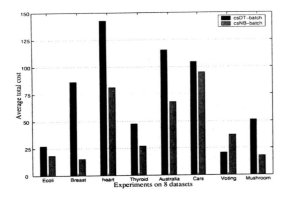

Figure 5. Comparisons in batch test on all the 8 datasets.

Figure 6 shows the two runs on the Breast and Mushroom datasets with the variation of percentage of unknown attributes. As we can see, *csNB* exhibits less sensitivity to the missing rate and performs mush better than csDT.

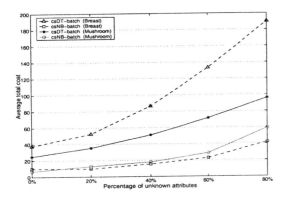

Figure 6. Comparisons in batch test with varying missing rates.

7. Conclusions and future work

In this paper, we proposed a test-cost sensitive naive Bayes algorithm for designing classifiers that minimize the sum of the misclassification cost and the test costs. In the framework of *csNB* , attributes are intelligently selected for testing to get both sequential test strategies and batch test strategies. Experiments show that our method outperforms other competing algorithms, including the cost-sensitive decision tree algorithm.

In the future, we plan to consider several extensions of our work. One direction to generalize the ideas to design testing strategies for other classifiers, such as Neural Nets, SVMs. It is also interesting to consider the cost of finding the missing values for training data. Another direction is to develop more effective algorithms for batch test strategies. In addition, it is worth considering the conditional test costs [15] in which the cost of a certain test is conditional on the other attributes. For example, in medical diagnosis, the cost of an exercise stress test on a patient may be conditional on whether the patient has heart disease or not.

8 Acknowledgments

This work is supported by Hong Kong Research Grant Committee (RGC) and Innovation and Technology Fund (ITF).

References

[1] C. L. Blake and C. J. Merz. UCI repository of machine learning databases, 1998.

[2] P. Domingos. Metacost: A general method for making classifiers cost-sensitive. In *KDD99*, pages 155–164, 1999.

[3] P. Domingos and M. Pazzani. On the optimality of the simple bayesian classifier under zero-one loss. *Machine Learning*, 29:103–130, 1997.

[4] R. O. Duda, P. E. Hart, and D. G. Stork. *Pattern Classification*. Willey and Sons, Inc., New York, 2nd edition, 2001.

[5] C. Elkan. The foundations of cost-sensitive learning. In *Proc. of the IJCAI01*, pages 973–978, 2001.

[6] R. Greiner, A. Grove, and D. Roth. Learning cost-sensitive active classifiers. *Artificial Intelligence Journal*, 139(2):137–174, 2002.

[7] M. T. Kai. Inducing cost-sensitive trees via instance weighting. In Springer-Verlag, editor, *Principles of Data Mining and Knowledge Discovery, Second European Symposium*, pages 139–147, 1998.

[8] C. Ling, Q. Yang, J. Wang, and S. Zhang. Decision trees with minimal costs. In *Proc. of ICML04*, 2004.

[9] T. M. Mitchell. *Machine Learning*. McGraw Hill, 1997.

[10] M. Nunez. The use of background knowledge in decision tree induction. *Machine Learning*, 6:231–250, 1991.

[11] C. H. Papadimitriou and J. N. Tsitsiklis. The complexity of markov decision processes. *Mathematics of operations research*, 12(3):441–450, 1987.

[12] J. R. Quinlan. *C4.5: Programs for Machine Learning*. Morgan Kaufmann Publishers, 1993.

[13] M. Tan. Cost-sensitive learning of classification knowledge and its applications in robotics. *Machine. Learning Journal*, 13:7–33, 1993.

[14] P. D. Turney. Cost-sensitive classification: Empirical evaluation of a hybrid genetic decision tree induction algorithm. *Journal of Artificial Intelligence Research*, 1995.

[15] P. D. Turney. Types of cost in inductive concept learning. In *Workshop on Cost-Sensitive Learning at the 17th International Conference on Machine Learning*, 2000.

[16] V. B. Zubek and T. G. Dieterich. Pruning improves heuristic search for cost-sensitive learning. In *Proc. of ICML02*, pages 27–34, Sydney, Australia, 2002.

Moment: Maintaining Closed Frequent Itemsets over a Stream Sliding Window

Yun Chi,* Haixun Wang†, Philip S. Yu†, Richard R. Muntz*
*Department of Computer Science, University of California, Los Angeles, CA 90095
†IBM Thomas J. Watson Research Center, Hawthorne, NY 10532
ychi@cs.ucla.edu, {haixun,psyu}@us.ibm.com, muntz@cs.ucla.edu

Abstract

This paper considers the problem of mining closed frequent itemsets over a sliding window using limited memory space. We design a synopsis data structure to monitor transactions in the sliding window so that we can output the current closed frequent itemsets at any time. Due to time and memory constraints, the synopsis data structure cannot monitor all possible itemsets. However, monitoring only frequent itemsets will make it impossible to detect new itemsets when they become frequent. In this paper, we introduce a compact data structure, the closed enumeration tree (CET), to maintain a dynamically selected set of itemsets over a sliding-window. The selected itemsets consist of a boundary between closed frequent itemsets and the rest of the itemsets. Concept drifts in a data stream are reflected by boundary movements in the CET. In other words, a status change of any itemset (e.g., from non-frequent to frequent) must occur through the boundary. Because the boundary is relatively stable, the cost of mining closed frequent itemsets over a sliding window is dramatically reduced to that of mining transactions that can possibly cause boundary movements in the CET. Our experiments show that our algorithm performs much better than previous approaches.

1 Introduction

Mining data streams for knowledge discovery is important to many applications, such as fraud detection, intrusion detection, trend learning, etc. In this paper, we consider the problem of mining closed frequent itemsets on data streams.

Mining frequent itemset on static datasets has been studied extensively. However, data streams have posed new challenges. First, data streams are continuous, high-speed, and unbounded. It is impossible to mine association rules from them using algorithms that require multiple scans. Second, the data distribution in streams are usually changing with time, and very often people are interested in the most recent patterns.

It is thus of great interest to mine itemsets that are *currently* frequent. One approach is to always focus on frequent itemsets in the most recent window. A similar effect can be achieved by exponentially discounting old itemsets.

For the window-based approach, we can come up with two naive methods:

1. Regenerate frequent itemsets from the entire window whenever a new transaction comes into or an old transaction leaves the window.

2. Store every itemset, frequent or not, in a traditional data structure such as the prefix tree, and update its support whenever a new transaction comes into or an old transaction leaves the window.

Clearly, method 1 is not efficient. In fact, as long as the window size is reasonable, and the concept drifts in the stream is not too dramatic, most itemsets do not change their status (from frequent to non-frequent or from non-frequent to frequent) often. Thus, instead of regenerating all frequent itemsets every time from the entire window, we shall adopt an *incremental* approach.

Method 2 is incremental. However, its space requirement makes it infeasible in practice. The prefix tree [1] is often used for mining association rules on static data sets. In a prefix tree, each node n_I represents an itemset I and each child node of n_I represents an itemset obtained by adding a new item to I. The total number of nodes is exponential. Due to memory constraints, we cannot keep a prefix tree in memory, and disk-based structures will make real time update costly.

In view of these challenges, we focus on a *dynamically selected* set of itemsets that are i) informative enough to answer at any time queries such as "what are the (closed) frequent itemsets in the current window", and at the same time, ii) small enough so that they can be easily maintained in memory and updated in real time.

The problem is, of course, what itemsets shall we select for this purpose? To reduce memory usage, we are tempted to select, for example, nothing but frequent (or even closed frequent) itemsets. However, if the frequency of a non-frequent itemset is not monitored, we will never know when it becomes frequent. A naive approach is to monitor all itemsets whose support is above a reduced threshold $minsup - \epsilon$, so that we will not miss itemsets whose current support is within ϵ of $minsup$ when they become frequent. This approach is apparently not general enough.

In this paper, we design a synopsis data structure to keep track of the boundary between closed frequent itemsets and the rest of the itemsets. Concept drifts in a data stream are reflected by boundary movements in the data structure. In

*The work of these two authors was partly supported by NSF under Grant Nos. 0086116, 0085773, and 9817773.

other words, a status change of any itemset (e.g., from non-frequent to frequent) must occur through the boundary. The problem of mining an infinite amount of data is thus converted to mine data that can potentially change the boundary in the current model. Because most of the itemsets do not often change status, which means the boundary is stable, and even if some does, the boundary movement is local, the cost of mining closed frequent itemsets is dramatically reduced.

Our Contribution This paper makes the following contributions: (1) We introduce a novel algorithm, Moment[1], to mine closed frequent itemsets over data stream sliding windows. To the best of our knowledge, our algorithm is the first one for mining *closed* frequent itemsets in data streams. (2) We present an in-memory data structure, the *closed enumeration tree* (CET), which monitors closed frequent itemsets as well as itemsets that form the boundary between the closed frequent itemsets and the rest of the itemsets. We show that i) a status change of any itemset (e.g., from non-frequent to frequent) must come through the boundary itemsets, which means we do not have to monitor itemsets beyond the boundary, and ii) the boundary is relatively stable, which means the update cost is minimum. (3) We introduce a novel algorithm to maintain the CET in an efficient way. Experiments show Moment has significant performance advantage over state-of-the-art approaches for mining frequent itemsets in data streams.

Related Work Mining frequent itemsets from data streams has been investigated by many researchers. Manku et al [14] proposed an approximate algorithm that for a given time t, mines frequent itemsets over the *entire* data streams up to t. Charikar et al [6] presented a 1-pass algorithm that returns most frequent *items* whose frequencies satisfy a threshold with high probabilities. Teng et al [15] presented an algorithms, FTP-DS, that mines frequent temporal patterns from data streams of itemsets. Chang et al [5] presented an algorithm, *estDec*, that mines recent frequent itemsets where the frequency is defined by an aging function. Giannella et al [10] proposed an approximate algorithm for mining frequent itemsets in data streams during arbitrary time intervals. An in-memory data structure, *FP-stream*, is used to store and update historic information about frequent itemsets and their frequency over time and an aging function is used to update the entries so that more recent entries are weighted more. Asai et al [3] presented an online algorithm, *StreamT*, for mining frequent rooted ordered trees. To reduce the number of subtrees to be maintained, an update policy that is similar to that in online association rule mining [12] was used and therefore the results are inexact. In all these studies, approximate algorithms were adopted. In contrast, our algorithm is an exact one because we assume that the approximation step has been implemented through the sampling scheme and our algorithm works on a sliding window containing the random samples (which are a synopsis of the data stream).

In addition, closely related to our work, Cheung et al [7, 8] and Lee et al [13] proposed algorithms to maintain discovered frequent itemsets through incremental updates. Although these algorithms are exact, they focused on mining *all* frequent itemsets (as do the above approximate algorithms). The large number of frequent itemsets makes it impractical to maintain information about all frequent itemsets using in-memory data structures. In contrast, our algorithm maintains only closed frequent itemsets. As demonstrated by extensive experimental studies, e.g., [17], there are usually much fewer closed frequent itemsets compared to the total number of frequent itemsets.

2 Problem Statement

Preliminaries Given a set of items Σ, a database $\mathcal{D}$ wherein each transaction is a subset of Σ, and a threshold s called the *minimum support* (*minsup*), $0 < s \leq 1$, the frequent itemset mining problem is to find all itemsets that occur in at least $s|\mathcal{D}|$ transactions.

We assume that there is a lexicographical order among the items in Σ and we use $X \prec Y$ to denote that item X is lexicographically smaller than item Y. Furthermore, an itemset can be represented by a sequence, wherein items are lexicographically ordered. For instance, $\{A, B, C\}$ is represented by ABC, given $A \prec B \prec C$. We also abuse notation by using $\prec$ to denote the lexicographical order between two itemsets. For instance, $AB \prec ABC \prec CD$.

As an example, let $\Sigma = \{A, B, C, D\}$, $\mathcal{D} = \{CD, AB, ABC, ABC\}$, and $s = \frac{1}{2}$, then the frequent itemsets are

$$\mathcal{F} = \{(A, 3), (B, 3), (C, 3), (AB, 3), (AC, 2), (BC, 2), (ABC, 2)\}$$

In $\mathcal{F}$, each frequent itemset is associated with its support in database $\mathcal{D}$.

Combinatorial Explosion According to the *a priori* property, any subset of a frequent itemset is also frequent. Thus, algorithms that mine *all* frequent itemsets often suffer from the problem of combinatorial explosion.

Two solutions have been proposed to alleviate this problem. In the first solution (e.g., [4], [11]), only *maximal* frequent itemsets are discovered. A frequent itemset is *maximal* if none of its proper supersets is frequent. The total number of maximal frequent itemsets $\mathcal{M}$ is much smaller than that of frequent itemsets $\mathcal{F}$, and we can derive each frequent itemset from $\mathcal{M}$. However, $\mathcal{M}$ does not contain information of the support of each frequent itemset unless it is a maximal frequent itemset. Thus, mining only maximal frequent itemsets loses information.

In the second solution (e.g., [16], [17]), only *closed* frequent itemsets are discovered. An itemset is closed if none of its proper supersets has the same support as it has. The total number of closed frequent itemsets $\mathcal{C}$ is still much smaller than that of frequent itemsets $\mathcal{F}$. Furthermore, we can derive $\mathcal{F}$ from $\mathcal{C}$, because a frequent itemset I must be a subset of one (or more) closed frequent itemset, and I's support is equal to the maximal support of those closed itemsets that contain I.

In summary, the relation among $\mathcal{F}$, $\mathcal{C}$, and $\mathcal{M}$ is $\mathcal{M} \subseteq \mathcal{C} \subseteq \mathcal{F}$. The closed and maximal frequent itemsets for the above examples are

$$\mathcal{C} = \{(C, 3), (AB, 3), (ABC, 2)\}$$
$$\mathcal{M} = \{(ABC, 2)\}$$

---

[1]Maintaining Closed Frequent Itemsets by Incremental Updates

Since $\mathcal{C}$ is smaller than $\mathcal{F}$, and $\mathcal{C}$ does not lose information about any frequent itemsets, in this paper, we focus on mining the closed frequent itemsets because they maintain sufficient information to determine all the frequent itemsets as well as their support.

Problem Statement The problem is to mine closed frequent itemsets in the most recent N transactions in a data stream. Each transaction has a time stamp, which is used as the *tid* (transaction id) of the transaction. Figure 1 is an example with $\Sigma = \{A, B, C, D\}$ and window size $N = 4$. We use this example throughout the paper with minimum support $s = \frac{1}{2}$.

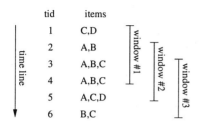

Figure 1: A Running Example

To find frequent itemsets on a data stream, we maintain a data structure that models the current frequent itemsets. We update the data structure incrementally. The combinatorial explosion problem of mining frequent itemsets becomes even more serious in the streaming environment. As a result, on the one hand, we cannot afford keeping track of all itemsets or even frequent itemsets, because of time and space constraints. On the other hand, any omission (for instance, maintaining only $\mathcal{M}$, $\mathcal{C}$, or $\mathcal{F}$ instead of all itemsets) may prevent us from discovering future frequent itemsets. Thus, the challenge lies in designing a compact data structure which does not lose information of any frequent itemset over a sliding window.

3 The Moment Algorithm

We propose the Moment algorithm and an in-memory data structure, the *closed enumeration tree*, to monitor a dynamically selected small set of itemsets that enable us to answer the query "what are the current closed frequent itemsets?" at any time.

3.1 The Closed Enumeration Tree

Similar to a prefix tree, each node n_I in a *closed enumeration tree* (CET) represents an itemset I. A child node, n_J, is obtained by adding a new item to I such that $I \prec J$. However, unlike a prefix tree, which maintains *all* itemsets, a CET only maintains a *dynamically selected* set of itemsets, which include i) closed frequent itemsets, and ii) itemsets that form a *boundary* between closed frequent itemsets and the rest of the itemsets.

As long as the window is reasonably large, and the concept drifts in the stream are not too dramatic, most itemsets do not change their status (from frequent to non-frequent or from non-frequent to frequent). In other words, the effects

of transactions moving in and out of a window offset each other and usually do not cause change of status of many involved nodes.

If an itemset does not change its status, nothing needs to be done except for increasing or decreasing the counts of the involved itemsets. If it does change its status, then, as we will show, the change must come through the boundary nodes, which means the changes to the entire tree structure is still limited.

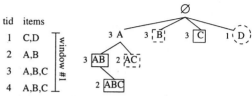

Figure 2: The Closed Enumeration Tree Corresponding to Window #1 (each node is labeled with its *support*)

We further divide itemsets on the boundary into two categories, which correspond to the boundary between frequent and non-frequent itemsets, and the boundary between closed and non-closed itemsets, respectively. Itemsets within the boundary also have two categories, namely the closed nodes, and other intermediary nodes that have closed nodes as descendants. For each category, we define specific actions to be taken in order to maintain a shifting boundary when there are concept drifts in data streams (Section 3.3). The four types of itemsets are listed below.

infrequent gateway nodes A node n_I is an infrequent gateway node if i) I is an infrequent itemset, ii) n_I'parent, n_J, is frequent, and iii) I is the result of joining I's parent, J, with one of J's frequent siblings. In Figure 2, D is an infrequent gateway node (represented by dashed circle). In contrast, AD is not an infrequent gateway node (hence it does not appear in the CET), because D is infrequent.

unpromising gateway nodes A node n_I is an unpromising gateway node if i) I is a frequent itemset, and ii) there exists a closed frequent itemset J such that $J \prec I$, $J \supset I$, and J has the same support as I does. In Figure 2, B is an unpromising gateway node because AB has the same support as it does. So is AC because of ABC. In Figure 2, unpromising gateway nodes are represented by dashed rectangles. For convenience of discussion, when a node in the CET is neither an infrequent gateway node nor an unpromising gateway node, we call it a *promising* node.

intermediate nodes A node n_I is an intermediate node if i) I is a frequent itemset, ii) n_I has a child node n_J such that J has the same support as I does, and iii) n_I is not an unpromising gateway node. In Figure 2, A is an intermediate node because its child AB has the same support as A does.

closed nodes These nodes represent closed frequent itemsets in the current sliding-window. A closed node can be an internal node or a leaf node. In Figure 2, C, AB, and ABC are closed nodes, which are represented by solid rectangles.

3.2 Node Properties

We prove the following properties for the nodes in the CET. Properties 1 and 2 enable us to prune a large amount of itemsets from the CET, while Property 3 makes sure certain itemsets are not pruned. Together, they enable us to mine closed frequent itemsets over a sliding window using an efficient and compact synopsis data structure.

Property 1. *If n_I is an infrequent gateway node, then any node n_J where $J \supset I$ represents an infrequent itemset.*

Proof. Property 1 is derived from the *a priori* property. □

A CET achieves its compactness by pruning a large amount of the itemsets. It prunes the descendants of n_I and the descendants of n_I's siblings nodes that subsume I. However, it 'remembers' the boundary where such pruning occurs, so that it knows where to start exploring when n_I is no longer an infrequent gateway node. An infrequent gateway node marks such a boundary. In particular, infrequent gateway nodes are leaf nodes in a CET. For example, in Figure 2, after knowing that D is infrequent, we do not explore the subtree under D. Furthermore, we do not join A with D to generate A's child nodes. As a result, a large amount of the itemsets are pruned.

Property 2. *If n_I is an unpromising gateway node, then n_I is not closed, and none of n_I's descendents is closed.*

Proof. Based on the definition of unpromising gateway nodes, there exists an itemset J such that i) $J \prec I$, and ii) $J \supset I$ and $support(J) = support(I)$. From ii), we know n_I is not closed. Let i_{max} be the lexicographically largest item in I. Since $J \prec I$ and $J \supset I$, there must exist an item $j \in J \backslash I$ such that $j \prec i_{max}$. Thus, for any descendant $n_{I'}$ of n_I, we have $j \notin I'$. Furthermore, because $support(J) = support(I)$, itemset $J \backslash I$ must appear in every transaction I appears, which means $support(n_{I'}) = support(n_{\{j\} \cup I'})$, so I' is not closed. □

Descendants of an unpromising gateway node are pruned because no closed nodes can be found there, and it 'remembers' the boundary where such pruning occurs.

Property 3. *If n_I is an intermediate node, then n_I is not closed and n_I has closed descendants.*

Proof. Based on the definition of intermediate nodes, n_I is not closed. Thus, there must exists a closed node n_J such that $J \supset I$ and $support(J) = support(I)$. If $I \prec J$, then n_J is n_I's descendant since $J \supset I$. If $J \prec I$, then n_I is an unpromising gateway node, which means n_I is not an intermediate node. □

Property 3 shows that we cannot prune intermediate nodes.

3.3 Building the Closed Enumeration Tree

In a CET, we store the following information for each node n_I: i) the itemset I itself, ii) the node type of n_I, iii) *support*: the number of transactions in which I occurs, and iv) *tid_sum*: the *sum* of the tids of the transactions in which I occurs. The purpose of having *tid_sum* is because we use a hash table to maintain closed itemsets.

The Hash Table We frequently check whether or not a certain node is an unpromising gateway node, which means we need to know whether there is a closed frequent node that has the same support as the current node.

We use a hash table to store all the closed frequent itemsets. To check if n_I is an unpromising gateway node, by definition, we check if there is a closed frequent itemset J such that $J \prec I$, $J \supset I$, and $support(J) = support(I)$.

We can thus use *support* as the key to the hash table. However, it may create frequent hash collisions. We know if $support(I) = support(J)$ and $I \subset J$, then I and J must occur in the same set of transactions. Thus, a better choice is the set of *tids*. However, the set of *tids* take too much space, so we instead use $(support, tid\_sum)$ as the key. Note that tid_sum of an itemset can be incrementally updated. To check if n_I is an unpromising gateway node, we hash on the $(support, tid\_sum)$ of n_I, fetch the list of closed frequent itemsets in the corresponding entry of the hash table, and check if there is a J in the list such that $J \prec I$, $J \supset I$, and $support(J) = support(I)$.

Tree Construction To build a CET, first we create a root node $n_\emptyset$. Second, we create $|\Sigma|$ child nodes for $n_\emptyset$ (i.e., each $i \in \Sigma$ corresponds to a child node $n_{\{i\}}$), and then we call *Explore* on each child node $n_{\{i\}}$. Pseudo code for the *Explore* algorithm is given in Figure 3.

Explore $(n_I, \mathcal{D}, minsup)$
1:   **if** $support(n_I) < minsup \cdot |\mathcal{D}|$ **then**
2:      mark n_I an infrequent gateway node;
3:   **else if** $leftcheck(n_I) = true$ **then**
4:      mark n_I an unpromising gateway node;
5:   **else**
6:      **foreach** frequent right sibling n_K of n_I **do**
7:         create a new child $n_{I \cup K}$ for n_I;
8:         compute $support$ and tid_sum for $n_{I \cup K}$;
9:      **foreach** child $n_{I'}$ of n_I **do**
10:      Explore$(n_{I'}, \mathcal{D}, minsup)$;
11:      **if** $\exists$ a child $n_{I'}$ of n_I such that $support(n_{I'}) = support(n_I)$ **then**
12:      mark n_I an intermediate node;
13:      **else**
14:      mark n_I a closed node;
15:      insert n_I into the hash table;

Figure 3: The *Explore* Algorithm

Explore is a depth-first procedure that visits itemsets in lexicographical order. In lines 1-2 of Figure 3, if a node is found to be infrequent, then it is marked as an infrequent gateway node, and we do not explore it further (Property 1). However, the *support* and *tid_sum* of an infrequent gateway node have to be stored because they will provide important information during a CET update when an infrequent itemset can potentially become frequent.

In lines 3-4, when an itemset I is found to be non-closed because of another lexicographically smaller itemset, then n_I is an unpromising gateway node. Based on Property 2, we do not explore n_I's descendants, which does not contain any closed frequent itemsets. However, n_I's *support* and

tid_sum must be stored, because during a CET update, n_I may become promising.

In *Explore*, $leftcheck(n_I)$ checks if n_I is an unpromising gateway node. It looks up the hash table to see if there exists a previously discovered closed itemset that has the same support as n_I and which also subsumes I, and if so, it returns *true* (in this case n_I is an unpromising gateway node); otherwise, it returns *false* (in this case n_I is a promising node).

If a node n_I is found to be neither infrequent nor unpromising, then we explore its descendants (lines 6-10). After that, we can determine if n_I is an intermediate node or a closed node (lines 11-15) according to Property 3.

Complexity The time complexity of the *Explore* algorithm depends on the size of the sliding-window N, the minimum support, and the number of nodes in the CET. However, because *Explore* only visits those nodes that are necessary for discovering closed frequent itemsets, so *Explore* should have the same asymptotic time complexity as any closed frequent itemset mining algorithm that is based on traversing the enumeration tree.

3.4 Updating the CET

New transactions are inserted into the window, as old transactions are deleted from the window. We discuss the maintenance of the CET for the two operations: addition and deletion.

Adding a Transaction

In Figure 4, a new transaction T (*tid* 5) is added to the sliding-window. We traverse the parts of the CET that are related to transaction T. For each related node n_I, we update its $support$, tid_sum, and possibly its node type.

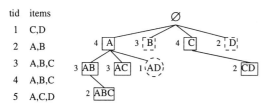

Figure 4: Adding a Transaction

Most likely, n_I's node type will not change, in which case, we simply update n_I's $support$ and tid_sum, and the cost is minimum. In the following, we discuss cases where the new transaction T causes n_I to change its node type.

n_I **was an infrequent gateway node.** If n_I becomes frequent (e.g., from node D in Figure 2 to node D in Figure 4), two types of updates must be made. First, for each of n_I's left siblings it must be checked if new children should be created. Second, the originally pruned branch (under n_I) must be re-explored by calling *Explore*.

For example, in Figure 4, after D changes from an infrequent gateway node to a frequent node, node A and C must be updated by adding new children (AD and CD, respectively). Some of these new children will become new infrequent gateway nodes (e.g., node AD), and others may be-

come other types of nodes (e.g., node CD becomes a closed node). In addition, this update may propagate down more than one level.

n_I **was an unpromising gateway node.** Node n_I may become promising (e.g., from node AC in Figure 2 to node AC in Figure 4) for the following reason. Originally, $\exists (j \prec i_{max}$ and $j \notin I)$ s.t. j occurs in each transaction that I occurs. However, if the new transaction T contains I but not any of such j's, then the above condition does not hold anymore. If this happens, the originally pruned branch (under n_I) must be explored by calling *Explore*.

n_I **was a closed node.** Based on the following property, n_I will remain a closed node.

Property 4. *Adding a new transaction will not change a node from closed to non-closed, and therefore it will not decrease the number of closed itemsets in the sliding-window.*

Proof. Originally, $\forall J \supset I, support(J) < support(I)$; after adding the new transaction T, $\forall J \supset I$, if $J \subset T$ then $I \subset T$. Therefore if J's support is increased by one because of T, so is I's support. As a result, $\forall J \supset I, support(J) < support(I)$ still holds after adding the new transaction T. However, if a closed node n_I is visited during an addition, its entry in the hash table will be updated. Its $support$ is increased by 1 and its tid_sum is increased by adding the tid of the new transaction. $\square$

n_I **was an intermediate node.** An intermediate node, such as node A in Figure 2, can possibly become a closed node after adding a new transaction T. Originally, n_I was an intermediate node because one of n_I's children has the same support as n_I does; if T contains I but none of n_I's children who have the same support as n_I had before the addition, then n_I becomes a closed node because its new support is higher than the support of any of its children. However, n_I cannot change to an infrequent gateway node or an unpromising gateway node. First, n_I's support will not decrease because of adding T, so it cannot become infrequent. Second, if before adding T, $leftcheck(n_I) = false$, then $\nexists (j \prec i_{max}$ and $j \notin I)$ s.t. j occurs in each transaction that I occurs; this statement will not change after we add T. Therefore, $leftcheck(n_I) = false$ after the addition.

Figure 5 gives a high-level description of the addition operation. Adding a new transaction to the sliding-window will trigger a call of *Addition* on $n_\emptyset$, the root of the CET.

Deleting a Transaction

In Figure 6, an old transaction T (*tid* 1) is deleted from the sliding-window. To delete a transaction, we also traverse the parts of the CET that is related to the deleted transaction. Most likely, n_I's node type will not change, in which case, we simply update n_I's $support$ and tid_sum, and the cost is minimum. In the following, we discuss the impact of deletion in detail.

If n_I was an infrequent gateway node, obviously deletion does not change n_I's node type. If n_I was an unpromising gateway node, deletion may change n_I to infrequent but will not change n_I to promising, for the following reason. For an unpromising gateway node n_I, if before deletion,

63

Figure 5: The *Addition* Algorithm

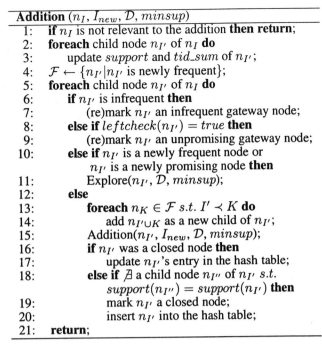

Figure 6: Deleting a Transaction

$leftcheck(n_I) = true$, then $\exists (j \prec i_{max}\ and\ j \notin I)$ s.t. j occurs in each transaction that I occurs; this statement remains true when we delete a transaction.

If n_I was a frequent node, it may become infrequent because of a decrement of its support, in which case, all n_I's descendants are pruned and n_I becomes an infrequent gateway node. In addition, all of n_I's left siblings are updated by removing children obtained from joining with n_I. For example in Figure 6, when transaction T (*tid* 1) is removed from the window, node D becomes infrequent. We prune all descendants of node D, as well as AD and CD, which were obtained by joining A and C with D, respectively.

If n_I was a promising node, it may become unpromising because of the deletion, for the following reason. If before the deletion, $\exists (j \prec i_{max}\ and\ j \notin I)$ s.t. j occurs in each transaction that I occurs, except only for the transaction to be deleted, then after deleting the transaction, I becomes unpromising. This happens to node C in Figure 6. Therefore, if originally n_I was neither infrequent nor unpromising, then we have to do the *leftcheck* on n_I. For a node n_I to change to unpromising because of a deletion, n_I must be contained in the deleted transaction. Therefore n_I will be visited by the traversal and we will not miss it.

If n_I was a closed node, it may become non-closed. To demonstrate this, we delete another transaction T (*tid* 2) from the sliding-window. Figure 7 shows this example

where previously closed node n_I (e.g. A and AB) become non-closed because of the deletion. This can be determined by looking at the supports of the children of n_I after visiting them. If a previously closed node that is included in the deleted transaction remains closed after the deletion, we still need to update its entry in the hash table: its *support* is decreased by 1 and its *tid_sum* is decreased by subtracting the *tid* of the deleted transaction.

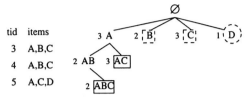

Figure 7: Another Deletion

From the above discussion we derive the following property for the deletion operation on a CET.

Property 5. *Deleting an old transaction will not change a node in the CET from non-closed to closed, and therefore it will not increase the number of closed itemsets in the sliding-window.*

Proof. If an itemset I was originally non-closed, then before the deletion, $\exists j \notin I$ s.t. j occurs in each transaction that I occurs. Obviously, this fact will not be changed due to deleting a transaction. So I will still be non-closed after the deletion. □

Figure 8 gives a high-level description of the deletion operation. Some details are skipped in the description. For example, when pruning a branch from the CET, all the closed frequent itemsets in the branch should be removed from the hash table.

Discussion

In the addition algorithm, *Explore* is the most time consuming operation, because it scans the transactions in the sliding-window. However, as will be demonstrated in the experiments, the number of such invocations is very small, as most insertions will not change node types. In addition, the new branches grown by calling *Explore* are usually very small subsets of the whole CET, therefore such incremental growing takes much less time than regenerating the whole CET. On the other hand, deletion only involves related nodes in the CET, and does not scan transactions in the sliding-window. Therefore, its time complexity is at most linear to the number of nodes. Usually it is faster to perform a deletion than an addition.

It is easy to show that if a node n_I changes node type (frequent/infrequent and promising/unpromising), then I is in the added or deleted transaction and therefore n_I is guaranteed to be visited during the update. Consequently, our algorithm will correctly maintain the current close frequent itemsets after any of the two operations. Furthermore, if n_I remains closed after an addition or a deletion and I is contained in the added/deleted transaction, then its position in the hash table is changed because its *support* and *tid_sum* are changed. To make the update, we delete the itemset

```
Deletion (n_I, I_old, minsup)
─────────────────────────────────────────────
 1:  if n_I is not relevant to the deletion then return;
 2:  foreach child node n_{I'} of n_I do
 3:      update support and tid_sum of n_{I'};
 4:  F ← {n_{I'}|n_{I'} is newly infrequent};
 5:  foreach child node n_{I'} of n_I do
 6:      if n_{I'} was infrequent or unpromising then
 7:          continue;
 8:      else if n_{I'} is newly infrequent then
 9:          prune n_{I'}'s descendants from CET;
10:          mark n_{I'} an infrequent gateway node;
11:      else if leftcheck(n_{I'}) = true then
12:          prune n_{I'}'s descendants from CET;
13:          mark n_{I'} an unpromising gateway node;
14:      else
15:          foreach n_K ∈ F s.t. I' ≺ K do
16:              prune n_{I'∪K} from the children of n_{I'};
17:          Deletion(n_{I'}, I_old, minsup);
18:          if n_{I'} was closed and ∃ a child n_{I''} of n_{I'}
                  s.t. support(n_{I''}) = support(n_{I'}) then
19:              mark n_{I'} an intermediate node;
20:              remove n_{I'} from the hash table;
21:          else if n_{I'} was a closed node then
22:              update n_{I'}'s entry in the hash table;
23:  return;
```

Figure 8: The *Deletion* Algorithm

from the hash table and re-insert it back to the hash table based on the new key value. However, such an update has amortized constant time complexity.

In our discussion so far, we used sliding-windows of fixed size. However, the two operations–*addition* and *deletion*–are independent of each other. Therefore, if needed, the size for the sliding-window can grow or shrink without affecting the correctness of our algorithm. In addition, our algorithm does not restrict a deletion to happen at the end of the window: at a given time, any transaction in the sliding-window can be removed. For example, if when removing a transaction, the transaction to be removed is picked following a random scheme: e.g., the newer transactions have lower probability of being removed than the older ones, then our algorithm can implement a sliding-window with *soft* boundary, i.e., the more recent the transaction, the higher chance it will remain in the sliding-window.

4 Experimental Results

We performed extensive experiments to evaluate the performance of Moment and we present some of them in this section. For more results, we refer readers to the full version of this paper [9]. We use Charm, a state-of-the-art algorithm proposed by Zaki et al [17], as the baseline algorithm to generate closed frequent itemsets without using incremental updates. All experiments were done on a 2GHz Intel Pentium IV PC with 2GB main memory, running Red-Hat Linux 7.3 operating system. All algorithms are implemented in C++ and compiled using the g++ 2.96 compiler.

T20I4D100K The first dataset is generated using the synthetic data generator described by Agrawal et al in [2]. Data from this generator mimics transactions from retail stores.

We have adopted the commonly used parameters: the number of transactions D is 100,100, the average size of transactions T is 20, the average size of the maximal potentially frequent itemsets I is 4. We call this dataset $T20I4D100K$. We report the average performance over 100 consecutive sliding windows (each with size $N = 100,000$).

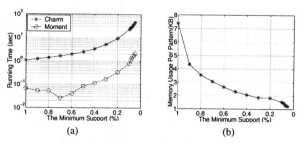

Figure 9: Running Time and Memory Usage for $T20I4D100K$

Figure 9 gives the result on $T20I4D100K$. Figure 9(a) shows the average running time for Moment and for Charm over the 100 sliding windows under different minimum supports. As can be seen from the figure, as minimum support decreases, because the number of closed frequent itemsets increases, the running time for both algorithms grows. However, the response time of Moment is faster than that of Charm by more than an order of magnitude under all the minimum supports.

minsup (in %)	closed itemset #	CET node #	CET node # per closed	changed node #	new node #
1.0	4097	148450	36.2	0.14	6.28
0.9	5341	168834	31.6	0.06	0.92
0.8	6581	187076	28.4	0.13	0.64
0.7	8220	212774	25.9	0.09	0.35
0.6	10270	249549	24.3	0.08	1.30
0.5	12655	309575	24.5	0.10	2.58
0.4	16683	433595	26.0	0.18	4.20
0.3	24907	722645	29.0	0.26	9.52
0.2	45353	1614726	35.6	0.67	27.23
0.1	172396	5955425	34.5	3.41	88.69
0.05	722261	19691999	27.3	14.75	286.34
0.03	1704558	45246906	26.5	41.07	646.84

Table 1: Data Characteristics for $T20I4D100K$

Table 1 shows the characteristics of the data and the mining results. All reported data are average values taken over the 100 sliding windows. The first three columns show the minimum support, the number of closed itemsets, and the number of nodes in the CET. From the table we can see that as the minimum support decreases, the number of closed itemsets grows rapidly. So does the number of nodes in the CET. However, the ratio between the number of nodes in the CET and the number of closed itemsets (which is reported in column 4) remains approximately the same. This implies that the sizes of the CET is linear in the number of closed frequent itemsets.

Because an addition may trigger a call for *Explore()* which is expensive, we study how many nodes change their status from infrequent/unpromising to frequent/promising (column 5) and how many new nodes are created due to the addition (column 6). From the data we can see that during an addition, the average number of nodes that change from infrequent to frequent or from unpromising to promising in the CET is very small relative to the total number of nodes in the CET. Similarly, the number of new nodes created due to an addition is also very small. These results verify the postulation behind our algorithm: that an update usually only affects the status of a very small portion of the CET and the new branches grown because of an update is usually a very small subset of the CET.

We also studied the memory usage for Moment. As shown in Figure 9(b), the average memory usage per closed frequent itemset actually decreases as the minimum support decreases. This suggests that as the CET becomes larger, it becomes more memory-efficient in terms of memory usage per closed frequent itemset.

BMS-WebView-1 The second dataset we used is BMS-WebView-1, which is a real dataset that contains a few months of clickstream data from an e-commerce web sites. This dataset was used in KDDCUP 2000 [18]. There are 59,602 transactions in the dataset. We set the sliding window size N to be 50,000 and do experiment on 100 consecutive sliding windows. Other parameters are: the number of distinct items is 497, the maximal transaction size is 267, and the average transaction size is 2.5.

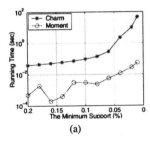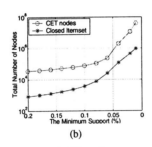

(a)　　　　　　　(b)

Figure 10: Performance for BMS-WebView-1

Figure 10(a) shows the running time for Moment and Charm. From the figure we can see that because the average transaction size of this data set (2.5) is smaller than that of the previous synthetic dataset (20), the relative performance of Moment is even better–it outperforms Charm by 1 to 2 orders of magnitudes. Figure 10(b) shows the total number of nodes in the CET and the total number of closed itemsets. As can be seen, although both grow exponentially as the minimum support decreases, the relative ratio between the two remains approximately the same, which suggests that for real data, the CET size is also linear in the number of closed frequent itemsets.

5　Conclusion

In this paper we propose a novel algorithm, Moment, to discover and maintain all closed frequent itemsets in a sliding window that contains the most recent samples in a data stream. In the Moment algorithm, an efficient in-memory data structure, the closed enumeration tree (CET), is used to record all closed frequent itemsets in the current sliding window. In addition, CET also monitors the itemsets that form the boundary between closed frequent itemsets and the rest of the itemsets. We have also developed efficient algorithms to incrementally update the CET when newly-arrived transactions change the content of the sliding window. Experimental studies show that the Moment algorithm outperforms a state-of-the-art algorithm that mines closed frequent itemsets without using incremental updates. In addition, the memory usage of the Moment algorithm is shown to be linear in the number of closed frequent itemsets in the sliding window.

Acknowledgement We thank Professor Mohammed J. Zaki at the Rensselaer Polytechnic Institute for providing us the Charm source code.

References

[1] R. C. Agarwal, C. C. Aggarwal, and V. V. V. Prasad. A tree projection algorithm for generation of frequent item sets. *Journal of Parallel and Distributed Computing*, 61(3):350–371, 2001.

[2] R. Agrawal and R. Srikant. Fast algorithms for mining association rules. In *Proc. of the 20th Intl. Conf. on Very Large Databases (VLDB'94)*, 1994.

[3] T. Asai, H. Arimura, K. Abe, S. Kawasoe, and S. Arikawa. Online algorithms for mining semi-structured data stream. In *Proc. 2002 Int. Conf. on Data Mining (ICDM'02)*, 2002.

[4] R. J. Bayardo, Jr. Efficiently mining long patterns from databases. In *Proceedings of the ACM SIGMOD*, 1998.

[5] J. H. Chang and W. S. Lee. Finding recent frequent itemsets adaptively over online data streams. In *Proc. of the 2003 Int. Conf. Knowledge Discovery and Data Mining (SIGKDD'03)*, 2003.

[6] M. Charikar, K. Chen, and M. Farach-Colton. Finding frequent items in data streams. In *Proc. of the 29th Int'l Colloquium on Automata, Languages and Programming*, 2002.

[7] D. W. Cheung, J. Han, V. Ng, and C. Y. Wong. Maintenance of discovered association rules in large databases: An incremental updating technique. In *Proceedings of the Twelfth International Conference on Data Engineering*, 1996.

[8] D. W. Cheung, S. D. Lee, and B. Kao. A general incremental technique for maintaining discovered association rules. In *Proceedings of the Fifth International Conference on Database Systems for Advanced Applications (DASFAA)*, 1997.

[9] Y. Chi, H. Wang, P. S. Yu, and R. R. Muntz. Catch the moment: Maintaining closed frequent itemsets over a data stream sliding window. Technical Report, IBM, 2004.

[10] C. Giannella, J. Han, E. Robertson, and C. Liu. Mining frequent itemsets over arbitrary time intervals in data streams. Technical Report tr587, Indiana University, 2003.

[11] K. Gouda and M. J. Zaki. Efficiently mining maximal frequent itemsets. In *Proceedings of the 2001 IEEE Int'l Conf. on Data Mining*, 2001.

[12] C. Hidber. Online association rule mining. In *Proc. of the ACM SIGMOD int'l conf. on Management of data*, 1999.

[13] C. Lee, C. Lin, and M. Chen. Sliding-window filtering: an efficient algorithm for incremental mining. In *Proc. of the int'l conf. on Info. and knowledge management*, 2001.

[14] G. Manku and R. Motwani. Approximate frequency counts over data streams. In *Proceedings of the 28th International Conference on Very Large Data Bases*, 2002.

[15] W.-G. Teng, M.-S. Chen, and P. S. Yu. A regression-based temporal pattern mining scheme for data streams. In *Proceedings of 29th International Conference on Very Large Data Bases (VLDB'03)*, 2003.

[16] J. Wang, J. Han, and J. Pei. Closet+: searching for the best strategies for mining frequent closed itemsets. In *Proc. of the 2003 Int. Conf. Knowledge Discovery and Data Mining (SIGKDD'03)*, 2003.

[17] M. J. Zaki and C. Hsiao. Charm: An efficient algorithm for closed itemset mining. In *2nd SIAM Int'l Conf. on Data Mining*, 2002.

[18] Z. Zheng, R. Kohavi, and L. Mason. Real world performance of association rule algorithms. In *Proc. of the 2001 Int. Conf. Knowledge Discovery and Data Mining (SIGKDD'01)*, 2001.

Communication Efficient Construction of Decision Trees Over Heterogeneously Distributed Data

Chris Giannella   Kun Liu   Todd Olsen
Hillol Kargupta
Department of Computer Science and Electrical Engineering
University of Maryland Baltimore County, Baltimore, MD 21250 USA
{cgiannel,kunliu1,tolsen1,hillol}@cs.umbc.edu
(H. Kargupta is also affiliated with AGNIK, LLC, USA.)

Abstract

We present an algorithm designed to efficiently construct a decision tree over heterogeneously distributed data without centralizing. We compare our algorithm against a standard centralized decision tree implementation in terms of accuracy as well as the communication complexity. Our experimental results show that by using only 20% of the communication cost necessary to centralize the data we can achieve trees with accuracy at least 80% of the trees produced by the centralized version.

Key words: Decision Trees, Distributed Data Mining, Random Projection

1 Introduction

Much of the world's data is distributed over a multitude of systems connected by communications channels of varying capacity. In such an environment, efficient use of available communications resources can be very important for practical data mining algorithms. In this paper, we introduce an algorithm for constructing decision trees in a distributed environment where communications resources are limited and efficient use of the available resources is needed. At the heart of this approach is the use of random projections to estimate the dot product between two binary vectors and some message optimization techniques. Before defining the problem and discussing our approach, we briefly discuss distributed data mining to provide context.

1.1 Distributed Data Mining (DDM)

Overview: Bluntly put, DDM is data mining where the data and computation are spread over many independent sites. For some applications, the distributed setting is more natural than the centralized one because the data is inherently distributed. The bulk of DDM methods in the literature operate over an abstract architecture where each site has a private memory containing its own portion of the data. The sites can operate independently and communicate by message passing over an asynchronous network. Typically communication is a bottleneck. Since communication is assumed to be carried out exclusively by message passing, a primary goal of many methods in the literature is to minimize the number of messages sent. Similarly, our goal is to minimize the number of messages sent. For more information about DDM, the reader is referred to two recent surveys [8], [10]. These provide a broad overview of DDM touching on issues such as: association rule mining, clustering, basic statistics computation, Bayesian network learning, classification, and the historical roots of DDM.

Data format: It is commonly assumed in the DDM literature that each site stores its data in tables. Due to the ubiquitous nature of relational databases, this assumption covers a lot of ground. One of two additional assumptions are commonly made regarding how the data is distributed across sites: homogeneously (horizontally partitioned) or heterogeneously (vertically partitioned). Both assumptions adopt the conceptual viewpoint that the tables at each site are partitions of a single global table.[1] In the homogeneous case, the global table is horizontally partitioned. The tables at each site are subsets of the global table; they have exactly the same attributes. In the heterogeneous case, the table is vertically partitioned, each site contains a collection of columns (sites do not have the same attributes). However, each tuple at each site is assumed to contain a unique identifier to facilitate matching across sites (matched tuples contain the same identifier).

---

[1] It is not assumed that the global table has been or ever was physically realized.

Note that the definition of "heterogeneous" in our paper differs from that used in other research fields such as the Semantic Web and Data Integration. In particular we are not addressing the problem of schema matching.

1.2 Problem Definition and Results Summary

We consider the problem of building a decision tree over heterogeneously distributed data. We assume that each site has the same number of tuples (records) and they are ordered to facilitate matching, *i.e.*, the ith tuple on each site matches. This assumption is equivalent to the commonly made assumptions regarding heterogeneously distributed data described earlier. We also assume that the ith tuple on each site has the same class label. Our approach can be applied to an arbitrary number of sites, but for simplicity, we restrict ourselves to the case of only two parties: Adam and Betty. However, in section 4.3 we describe the communication complexity for an arbitrary number of sites. At the end, Adam and Betty are to each have the decision tree in its entirety. Our primary objective is to minimize the number of messages transmitted.

One way to solve this problem is to transmit all of the data from Adam's site to Betty. She then applies a standard centralized decision tree builder and finally, transmits the final tree back to Adam. We call this method the *centralized approach (CA)*. While straightforward, the CA may require excessive communication in low communication bandwidth environments. To address this problem, we have adapted a standard decision tree building algorithm to the heterogeneous environment. The main problem in doing so is computing the information gain offered by attributes in making splitting decisions. To reduce communication, we approximate information gain using a random projection based technique. The technique converges on the correct information gain as the number of messages transmitted increases. We call this approach to building a decision tree the *distributed approach (DA)*.

The tree produced by DA may not be the same as that produced by CA. However, by increasing the number of messages transmitted, the DA tree can be made arbitrarily close. We conducted several experiments to measure the trade-off between accuracy and communication. Specifically, we built a tree using CA (with the standard Weka tree builder implementation) and others using DA while varying the number of messages used in information gain approximation and the depth of the tree. We observed that by using only 20% of the communication cost necessary to centralize the data we can achieve trees with accuracy at least 80% of the CA. Henceforth, when we discuss communication cost or communication complexity, we mean the total number of messages required. A message is a four byte number *e.g.* a standard floating point number.

1.3 Paper Layout

In Section 2 we cite some related work. In Section 3 we describe the basic algorithm for building a decision tree over heterogeneously distributed data using a distributed dot product as the primary distributed operation. Then we propose a method for approximating a distributed dot product using a random projection. In Section 4 we describe the complete algorithm and give the communication complexity. In Section 5 we discuss how different message optimization techniques are employed to further reduce the communication. In Sections 6 we present the results of our experiments. Finally, in Section 7 we describe several directions for future work and conclusions.

2 Related Work

Most algorithms for learning from homogeneously distributed data (horizontally partitioned) are directly related to ensemble learning [9, 3], meta-learning [12] and rule-based [5] combination techniques. In the heterogeneous case, each site observes only partial attributes (features) of the data set. Traditional ensemble-based approaches usually generate high variance local models and fail to detect the interaction between features observed at different sites. This makes the problem fundamentally challenging. The work addressed in [11] develops a framework to learn decision tree from heterogeneous data using a scalable evolutionary technique. In order to detect global patterns, they first make use of boosting technique to identify a subset of the data that none of the local classifiers can classify with high confidence. This subset of the data is merged at the central site and another new classifier is constructed from it. When a combination of local classifiers cannot classify a new record with a high confidence, the central classifier is used instead. This approach exhibits a better accuracy than a simple aggregation of the models. However, its performance is sensitive to the confidence threshold. Furthermore, to reduce the complexity of the models, this algorithm applies a Fourier Spectrum-based technique to aggregate all the local and central classifiers. However, the cost of computing the Fourier Coefficient grows exponentially with the number of attributes. On the other hand, our algorithm generates a single decision tree for all the data sites and does not need to aggregate at all. The work in [2] presents a general strategy of distributed decision tree learning by exchanging among different sites the indices and counts of the records that satisfy specified constraints on the values of particular attributes. The resulting algorithm is provably exact compared with the decision tree constructed on the centralized data. The communication complexity is given by $O((M + |L|NV)ST)$ where M is the total number of records, $|L|$ is the number of classes, N is the total number of attributes, V is the maximum number of possible values per attribute, S is the number of sites and T is the number of nodes of the tree. However, instead of repeatedly sending the whole indices vectors to the other site, our algorithm applies a random projection-based strategy to compute distributed dot product as the building blocks of tree induction. This kind of dimension reduction technique, together with some other message reusing and message sharing schemas reduce as many unnecessary messages as possible. The number of messages for one dot product is bounded by $O(k)$ ($k << M$), and the total communication cost of our algorithm is $O((LT + kIT)(S - 1))$ (LT is the number of leaf node and IT is the number of non-leaf node), which is less than that in [2]. The work presented in [4] deals with a privacy preserving two-party decision tree learning problem where no party is willing to divulge their data to the other. The basic tree induction procedure is similar with ours. However, a *secure* dot product protocol is proposed here as the building block such that only the information gain of the testing attribute is disclosed to both parties and nothing else. The communication complexity of only one dot product protocol is $O(4M)$, the total communication cost is higher than ours.

3 Building a Distributed Decision Tree: the Basic Algorithm

For simplicity of exposition, we only discuss discrete data and assume that each node of the tree has a corresponding attribute and a child branch for each distinct value. Our algorithm, however, generalizes to other cases (*e.g. continuous attributes*) without any conceptual difficulties.

3.1 Notation

Both sites have M tuples ordered in such a way that tuple i on Adam's site corresponds to tuple i on Betty's site. Tuples on both sites have an associated class label drawn from a set L. The tuples are labeled consistently across sites *i.e.* the ith tuple on Adam and Betty's site has the same class label. Let N denote the total number of attributes from all sites.

Let $\mathcal{A}$ denote the union of attributes over both sites and $\mathbb{D}$ denote the data set formed by joining the data from both sites (Adam's i^{th} tuple is concatenated with Betty's to form the ith tuple in $\mathbb{D}$). Given attribute $A \in \mathcal{A}$, let $\Pi(A)$ denote the set of distinct values that appear in the A column. Given set of attributes $X \subseteq \mathcal{A}$ and list of values $\vec{x} \in \times_{A \in X}\Pi(A)$, let $\mathbb{D}(X = \vec{x})$ denote the set of tuples t in $\mathbb{D}$ such that the X columns of t agree with $\vec{x}$ *i.e.* for all $A \in X, t[A] = \vec{x}[A]$.

Given $\hat{\mathbb{D}} \subseteq \mathbb{D}$, attribute $A \in \mathcal{A}$ and value $a \in \Pi(A)$, let $\#_{A=a}(\hat{\mathbb{D}})$ denote the number of tuples t in $\hat{\mathbb{D}}$ such that

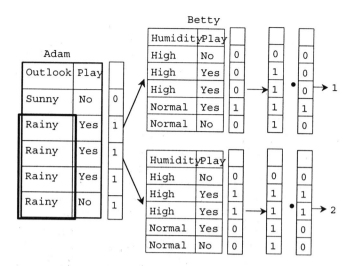

Figure 1. Calculating information gain using the dot product. ("Play" is the class name, and · denotes the dot product.)

$t[A] = a$. Given class label $\ell \in L$, let $\#_\ell(\hat{\mathbb{D}})$ denote the number of tuples in $\hat{\mathbb{D}}$ with label ℓ. Let $\#_{\ell, A=a}(\hat{\mathbb{D}})$ denote the number of tuples t in $\hat{\mathbb{D}}$ with $t[A] = a$ and label ℓ. The *class entropy* of A over $\hat{\mathbb{D}}$ is denoted $E_A(\hat{\mathbb{D}})$ and defined as[2]

$$-\sum_{a \in \Pi(A)} \frac{\#_{A=a}(\hat{\mathbb{D}})}{|\hat{\mathbb{D}}|} \sum_{\ell \in L} \frac{\#_{\ell, A=a}(\hat{\mathbb{D}})}{|\hat{\mathbb{D}}|} log_2(\frac{\#_{\ell, A=a}(\hat{\mathbb{D}})}{|\hat{\mathbb{D}}|}).$$

The *information gain* of A over $\hat{\mathbb{D}}$ is denoted $G_A(\hat{\mathbb{D}})$ and defined as

$$-\sum_{\ell \in L} \frac{\#_\ell(\hat{\mathbb{D}})}{|\hat{\mathbb{D}}|} log_2(\frac{\#_\ell(\hat{\mathbb{D}})}{|\hat{\mathbb{D}}|}) - E_A(\hat{\mathbb{D}}).$$

Our distributed decision tree building approach can be applied without change to other forms of information gain such as the Gini index. For ease of discussion, we stick with entropy based information gain.

3.2 Distributed Decision Tree Building Using a Dot Product

We adapt the following version of the standard, depth-first decision tree building algorithm (on discrete data). Initially the tree is empty and the first call is made to determine the root node. The call chooses the attribute A_1 from $\mathcal{A}$ with the largest information gain over $\mathbb{D}$ to become the root. For each $a \in \Pi(A_1)$, a recursive call is made with list $\{(A_1, a)\}$. Each of these recursive calls will determine the children of the root (with branches labeled with the values in $\Pi(A_1)$).

At any call passed list $(A_1, a_1), \ldots (A_k, a_k)$, the tuples in $\mathbb{D}(X = \vec{x})$ where $X = \{A_1, \ldots, A_k\}$ and $\vec{x} = (a_1, \ldots, a_k)$ are examined to determine the next splitting attribute. The attribute from $\mathcal{A} - X$ with the largest information gain over $\mathbb{D}(X = \vec{x})$ is chosen.

---

[2]We assume $0log_2(0)$ equals zero.

69

Since the attributes are not all on one site, computing the information gain may not be possible. For example, assume at least one of the attributes from X were on Adam's site and consider D an attribute on Betty's site and not in X. To compute the information gain, Betty must compute $\#_\ell(\mathbb{D}(X = \vec{x}))$ and $\#_{\ell, D=d}(\mathbb{D}(X = \vec{x}))$ for all $d \in \Pi(D)$ and $\ell \in L$. These values cannot be computed directly since Betty does not have $\mathbb{D}(X = \vec{x})$. Adam must send Betty information to carry out this computation. To reduce the amount of messages we approximate the values using a technique based on random projections.

Each of the values can be modeled as a dot product computation (similar to [2] and [4]). Let X_A denote the attributes from X on Adam's site and $\vec{x}_A$ their associated values from the passed list; likewise define X_B and $\vec{x}_B$. Let $\vec{V}(X_A = \vec{x}_A)$ be a length M vector of zeros and ones. The ith entry is one if the ith tuple t_i in $\mathbb{D}$ satisfies $t_i[X_A] = \vec{x}_A$. All other entries are zero. Likewise, let $\vec{V}(D = d, X_B = \vec{x}_B, \ell)$ be the 0/1 vector whose i^{th} entry is one if $t_i[D] = d$, $t_i[X_B] = \vec{x}_B$ and t_i has label ℓ. It can be easily seen that the dot product of $\vec{V}(X_A = \vec{x}_A)$ and $\vec{V}(D = d, X_B = \vec{x}_B, \ell)$ equals $\#_{\ell, D=d}(\mathbb{D}(X = \vec{x}))$. Moreover, the dot product of $\vec{V}(X_A = \vec{x}_A)$ and $\vec{V}(X_b = \vec{x}_B, \ell)$ equals $\#_\ell(\mathbb{D}(X = \vec{x}))$. Figure 1 illustrates this concept. Adam sends Betty a binary vector representing the tuples with "Outlook = Rainy". Betty constructs two vectors representing "Humidity = Normal && Play = Yes" and "Humidity = High && Play = Yes", respectively. The dot products gives the number of tuples in the whole database that satisfy the constrains "Outlook = Rainy && Humidity = Normal && Play = Yes" and "Outlook = Rainy && Humidity = High && Play = Yes". Note that the notation above deals with the case where Betty computes the information gain of her attributes. However, our algorithm will also require the reverse case: Adam computes the information gain of all his attributes. The notation is analogous. Actually, in our algorithm, instead of sending the original binary vectors directly to the other site, we project the vectors into a lower dimensional space first and transmitting the new vectors to all other sites. This leads to the distributed dot product computation in the next section.

3.3 Distributed Dot Product

In the previous section, we observed that distributed dot product of boolean vectors is the building block of decision tree induction. In this section, we propose a random projection-based distributed dot product technique that can greatly reduce the dimensionality of the vector, thereby reducing the cost of building the tree. Similar form of this algorithm appears elsewhere in a different context [7].

Given vectors $\vec{a} = (a_1, \ldots, a_m)^T$ and $\vec{b} = (b_1, \ldots, b_m)^T$ at two distributed site A and B, respectively, we want to approximate $\vec{a}^T\vec{b}$ using a small number of mes-

sages between A and B. Algorithm 3.3.1 gives the detailed procedure.

Algorithm 3.3.1 Distributed Dot Product Algorithm($\vec{a}, \vec{b}$)

---
1. A sends B a random number generator seed. **[1 message]**
2. A and B cooperatively generate $k \times m$ random matrix R where $k \ll m$. Each entry is generated independently and identically from any distribution with zero mean and unit variance. A and B compute $\hat{a} = R\vec{a}$, $\hat{b} = R\vec{b}$, respectively.
3. A sends $\hat{a}$ to B. B computes $\hat{a}^T\hat{b} = \vec{a}^T R^T R\vec{b}$. **[k messages]**
4. B computes $D = \frac{\hat{a}^T\hat{b}}{k}$.

So instead of sending a m-dimensional vector to the other site, we only need to send a k-dimensional vector where $k \ll m$ and the dot product can still be estimated.

The above algorithm is based on the following fact:

Lemma 3.1 *Let R be a $p \times q$ dimensional random matrix such that each entry $r_{i,j}$ of R is independently and chosen from some distribution with zero mean and unit variance. Then,*

$$E[R^T R] = pI, \text{ and } E[RR^T] = qI.$$

Proof Sketch: The (i, j) entry of $R^T R$ is the dot product of the ith and j^{th} columns of R. If $i = j$, then the expected value of the dot product equals the p times the variance plus the square of the mean, hence, p. If $i \neq j$, then the expected value of the dot product equals p times the square of the mean, hence zero. The second part of the lemma is proven analogously. $\square$

Intuitively, this result echoes the observation made elsewhere [6] that in a high-dimensional space vectors with random directions are almost orthogonal. A similar result was proved elsewhere [1].

3.4 Accuracy Analysis

We give a Chernoff-like bound to quantify the accuracy of our distributed dot product for decision tree induction as follows:

Lemma 3.2 *Let $\vec{a}$ and $\vec{b}$ be any two boolean vectors. Let $\hat{a}$ and $\hat{b}$ be the projections of $\vec{a}$ and $\vec{b}$ to $\Re^k$ through a random matrix R whose entries are identically, independently chosen from $N(0,1)$ such that $\hat{a} = R\vec{a}$ and $\hat{b} = R\vec{b}$, then for any $\epsilon > 0$, we have*

$$Pr\{\vec{a}^T\vec{b} - \epsilon m \leq \frac{\hat{a}^T\hat{b}}{k} \leq \vec{a}^T\vec{b} + \epsilon m\} \geq$$
$$1 - 3\left(((1+\epsilon)e^{-\epsilon})^{\frac{k}{2}} + ((1-\epsilon)e^{\epsilon})^{\frac{k}{2}}\right)$$

k	Mean	Var	Min	Max
100(1%)	0.1483	0.0098	0.0042	0.3837
500(5%)	0.0795	0.0035	0.0067	0.2686
1000(10%)	0.0430	0.0008	0.0033	0.1357
2000(20%)	0.0299	0.0007	0.0012	0.0902
3000(30%)	0.0262	0.0005	0.0002	0.0732

Table 1. Relative errors in computing the dot product.

Proof: Omitted due to space constraints.

This bound shows that the error goes to 0 exponentially fast as k increases. Note that although the lemma is based on normal distribution with zero mean and unit variance, it is also true for other distributions that are symmetric about the origin with unit variance. Table 1 depicts the relative error of the distributed dot product between two synthetically generated binary vectors of size 10000. k is the number of randomized iterations (represented as the percentage of the size of the original vectors). Each entry of the random matrix is chosen independently and uniformly from $\{1, -1\}$. In practice, this bound can be used to find the suitable k.

4 Algorithm Details

4.1 Main Procedure

At the commencement of the algorithm, each site determines which local attribute offers the largest information gain. No communication is required to accomplish this. The best attribute from each site is then compared and the attribute with the globally largest information gain, A_G, is selected to define the split at the root node of the tree. For each distinct value $a \in \Pi(A_G)$, a new branch leading down from the root is created. For each these branches, the site containing A_G constructs a binary vector representing which tuples correspond to this new branch, $\vec{V}(A_G = a)$, and sends the projection of it to the other site. Upon receiving each vector, the other site indexes it according to it's path and stores it in a *vector cache* for later use.

At each non-root node Z, each party, P attempts to find the nearest closest ancestor of Z that splits on an attribute *not* local to P (one may not exist). Consider Figure 2 with $P = Adam$. When considering node $Z1$, path (1), the nearest non-local ancestor would be the grandparent of $Z1$. For node $Z2$, path (2), the nearest non-local ancestor would be the parent of $Z2$. For node $Z3$ no non-local ancestor exists.

If P fails to find a non-local ancestor for Z (*i.e.*. the search terminated at *root*)then P does not require any information from the other party to compute the information gain of it's attributes. In this case the evaluation of the information gain proceeds as it does at *root* and can be calculated

exactly. Otherwise, P retrieves the appropriate entry from it's *vector cache* and uses it to approximate the information gain of it's local attributes using the distributed dot product. Note that,in either case, no communication is required.

As before, once each site determines the local attribute with the largest information gain, the attribute with the globally largest information gain, A_G, is selected to define the split at Z. Following this, each party now executes one of the following actions

- If A_G is local to P then, for each $a \in \Pi(A_G)$, a new branch leading down from the root is created. For each branch, P constructs a binary vector representing which tuples corresponding to this new path and sends the projection of it the other party.

- If A_G is non-local then P waits until it receives the projection vector from the other party, indexes it according to it's respective path, and stores it in the local *vector cache*.

The total number of messages required the above actions is k (the number of columns of R).

In order to reduce the memory signature of the algorithm each site will occasionally check the contents of it's *vector cache* and delete any invalid entries. A vector becomes *invalid* when (1) every path associated with that vector terminates in a leaf node, or (2) the node which generated the vector is no longer the nearest non-local ancestor to any of it's descendants.

We made one minor change to the algorithm presented above. When the number of ones/zeros in a binary vector is less than the number of iterations k, we can just transmit the list of indices directly. Not only does this reduce the communication cost of the algorithm even further, it allows the calculation of information gain further down the tree to be made in an exact, rather than approximate, manner.

4.2 Leaf Nodes Determination

The construction of a path down the decision tree continues until a *leaf node* is reached, which meets at least one of the following criteria: (1) All of the tuples for the node belong to one class. The node is then labeled by that class. (2) If any child of a node is empty, label that child as a leaf representing the most frequent class in this node. (3) There are less than *minNumObj* (4 in our experiments) tuples for the node, regardless of class. The node is then labeled by the most frequent class of all the tuples in this node. Note here that the calculations used to determine this may be approximations based on the distributed dot product.

From the above criteria, we can see that the determination of a leaf node can actually be made by its parent since information gain computation enables the parent to get the

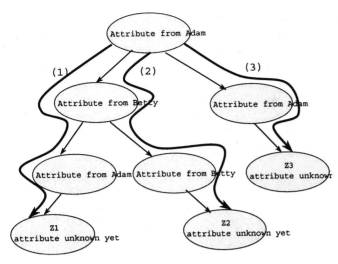

Figure 2. Sample distributed tree structure.

total number tuples for each child, together with the number of tuples belonging to different classes in its child. After a node is split, and if the leaf node is determined, the site who owns the splitting attribute can just send the other site(s) the tree branch name, total number of tuples covered by the leaf and the number of misclassified ones (No projected vector is transmitted). This information will be later used for tree pruning.

4.3 Communication Complexity

For each non-leaf node (except the root where only 2 messages are required to find the best split), to find the best split, only one party needs to send a projected vector to the other (k messages). After each party evaluating its local attributes, they exchange the name and information gain value of their best attribute and decide the split (2 messages). Note that, the leaf node can be decided right away by its parent, then one parent needs to send the other site the branch name, total number of tuples covered by the leaf and total number of misclassified ones (3 message). The total number of messages is bounded by $O(LT + kIT)$ where IT denotes the number of non-leaf node (except root) and LT is the number of leaf nodes. This can be generalized to S sites as $O((LT + kIT)(S - 1))$.

Note that the communication complexity does not depend on the number of distinct values of any attribute. As a result, continuous attributes do not directly increase the communication complexity. However, if continuous attributes are split using the standard single threshold method, they may create deeper trees thus indirectly increasing communication complexity.

4.4 Tree Pruning

Pessimistic post-pruning approach can be applied. From the discussion in the previous section, we know that each leaf node has the information about total number of records it covers and the number of misclassified ones. We can therefore compute the predicted error rate over the entire population of the records covered by this leaf from the confidence limits. Furthermore, because both parties will have a copy of the tree, and no validation data are required, they can prune the tree independently. Since this procedure requires no message communication and is totally the same for both centralized and distributed models, in our experiment we only compared the performance without pruning.

5 Optimizations

The algorithm described in Section 4.1 implicitly applies two important communication optimization strategies: *message sharing* and *message reusing*.

Message Sharing: *Messages associate with a projected vector from one site can be used to compute the information gains of all the attributes owned by the other site.* As a concrete illustration, consider the tree in Figure 2. To find the best split for node $Z1$ on path (1), Betty needs to evaluate her local attributes. Since the parent node is split by Adam's attribute, Adam will send Betty one projected vector which contains the information about tuples that satisfy the constrains induced by Adam's attributes along path (1). On receiving this information, Betty can approximate the information gain of all her attributes without any other communications.

Message Reusing: *Previously sent messages can also be reused as we descend down the tree.* This property is realized by the cache employed for each active path as we discussed in Section 4.1. As an example, consider again node $Z1$ on path (1) in Figure 2. In order for Adam to evaluate his attributes on node $Z1$, he needs to know the information about tuples that satisfy the constrains specified by Betty's attributes along the path. However, in this case no message are required because Adam has cached this information before when evaluating the parent node of $Z1$. Further more, this cached information can be continuously used if all the nodes along the path starting from N are split on Adam's local attributes. The cache will not be updated until a node on the path is split by Betty's attribute.

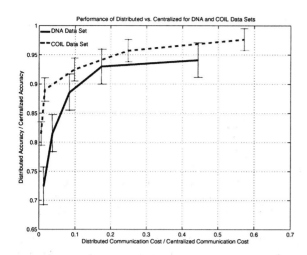

Figure 3. Accuracy vs. Cost of distributed decision tree over DNA and COIL data sets using 10-fold cross validation.

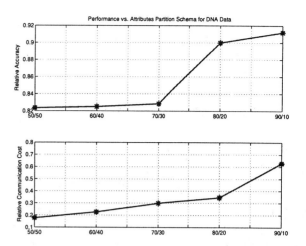

Figure 4. Performance of distributed decision tree with regard to different attributes partition schema for DNA data.

6 Experiments

We conducted experiments on two public domain data sets to evaluate the performance of our algorithm. The first one is StatLog DNA data set [3] which is a processed version of Molecular Biology Databases from UCI Machine Learning Repository. This data set consists of 2000 DNA nucleotide sequences, each with 180 binary attributes and 1 three-valued class label. The second one comes from COIL 2000 Challenge [4]. It contains information on customers of an insurance company and consists of 5822 samples with 86 nominal valued attributes. We vertically partitioned each data set into two separate subsets with alternative sampling of the attribute. The implementation is based on J48 from Weka-3-4.

Figure 3 illustrates the results of our experiments. The X-axis indicates the ratio of the communication cost induced by the distributed algorithm to the cost of centralizing data which is simply half of the size of the original data, *i.e,* $0.5MN$. The Y-axis corresponds to the ratio of the accuracy of the distributed model to the centralized model. We computed the 95% confidence interval of the accuracy of centralized model, together with the confidence interval of distributed model for different communication cost. Then a best case optimistic bound (confidence upper bound of the accuracy of distributed model divided by the lower bound of the centralized model) and worst case pessimistic bound (confidence lower bound of the accuracy of distributed model divided by the upper bound of the centralized model) are calculated and plotted as the error bar.

[3] http://www.liacc.up.pt/ML/statlog/datasets/dna/dna.doc.html
[4] http://kdd.ics.uci.edu/databases/tic/tic.html

In both cases, the figure shows that by using only 20% of the communication cost necessary to centralize the data we can achieve trees at least 80% as accurate as the centralized version. Although we didn't carry out experiments for more than two sites, our analysis shows that the communication complexity scales linearly with the number of sites.

To investigate the effect of the way that attributes are partitioned among different sites on the performance of distributed decision tree, we fixed the random seed and length of the projected vectors, then tested the algorithm while changing the number of attributes present on each site (50 vs.50, 60 vs.40, ..., 90 vs.10). Figure 4 gives the result. Generally, the accuracy increases as the attributes are partitioned more and more unequally among different sites. We believe that this is due to the increasing likelihood, as the attributes become more and more unbalanced, that the entire paths through the tree, from *root* to *leaf*, will split on attributes mostly located on the same site. Thus the information gain for the corresponding splits can be computed locally and will not suffer from the randomization inherent in the distributed dot product. In the meantime, we also noticed a corresponding increase of the relative communication cost as the partition becomes more unequally. Although we are still looking into this behavior, we do have an intuitive explanation. Since when centralizing the data, we will always send the data from the site with fewer attributes to the site with more. Therefore, the cost of centralized algorithm decreases linearly with the number of attributes on the smaller site. On the other hand the communication cost of our distributed algorithm depends primarily on the number of interior nodes of the resulting tree, which in turn depends on characteristics of the dataset itself and not on the way the data is partitioned. With regard to the *cost-benefit ratio,* our algorithm might perform at it's best when the attributes are partioned in a balanced fashion. The results shown in Figure 3, which were obtained with attributes evenly distributed between two sites, support this hypothesis.

7 Conclusions and Future Work

We have presented an algorithm that allows the efficient construction of a decision tree over heterogeneously distributed data. The key of our approach is a random projection-based dot product estimation and message sharing strategy. The experimental results are very promising and show that this technique reduces the communication by a factor of five while still retaining 80% of the original accuracy.

A primary set of directions for future work is motivated by the fact that our distributed algorithm requires more computation (local) than the centralized algorithm. One of the fundamental reasons is that our algorithm must compute a matrix, vector product for each frequency count. The overall benefit of our algorithm hinges on a trade-off: increased local computation, reduced communication. In settings where total computation time is the most important factor, the overall benefit depends on communication delay. One direction for future work involves carrying out a careful timing study to compare the total algorithm times (distributed vs. centralized) taking into account communication delays. The goal would be to determine how large the communication delay need be to offset the extra local computation time.

In settings where factors other than time cannot be ignored (*e.g.* energy consumption, privacy), the reduced communication could offer benefits in spite of an increased total computation time. For example, in energy constrained environments, communication typically requires more energy that computation. Also, if maintaining the privacy of each party's data is a high priority, increased computation time is reasonable sacrifice for reduced communication since this means less information need be protected. The reduced communication offered by our algorithm makes it a decent starting point for developing a more efficient privacy-preserving distributed decision tree induction algorithm than currently reported in the literature. Indeed, another direction for future work involves incorporating secure multi-party computation (SMC) based protocols to address privacy constrains while retaining low communication complexity.

Acknowledgments

The authors acknowledge supports from the United States National Science Foundation (NSF) CAREER award IIS-0093353, NSF Grant IIS-0329143, and NASA (NRA) NAS2-37143.

References

[1] R. I. Arriaga and S. Vempala. An algorithmic theory of learning: Robust concepts and random projection. In *Proceedings of the 40th Foundations of Computer Science*, New York, NY, October 1999.

[2] D. Caragea, A. Silvescu, and V. Honavar. Learning decision trees from distributed heterogeneous autonomous data sources. In *Proceedings of the Conference on Intelligent Systems Design and Applications (ISDA'03)*, Tulsa, Oklahoma, 2003.

[3] T. Dietterich. An experimental comparison of three methods for constructing ensembles of decision trees: Bagging, boosting and randomization. *Machine Learning*, 40(2):139–158, 2000.

[4] W. Du and Z. Zhan. Building decision tree classifier on private data. In *Workshop on Privacy, Security, and Data Mining at the 2002 IEEE International Conference on Data Mining (ICDM'02)*, Maebashi, Japan, December 2002.

[5] L. O. Hall, N. Chawla, K. W. Bowyer, and W. P. Kegelmeyer. Learning rules from distributed data. In M. J. Zaki and C.-T. Ho, editors, *Large-Scale Parallel Data Mining*, volume 1759 of *Lecture Notes in Computer Science*. Springer-Verlag, 2000.

[6] R. Hecht-Nielsen. Context vectors: General purpose approximate meaning representations self-organized from raw data. In *Computational Intelligence: Imitating Life*, pages 43–56. IEEE Press, 1994.

[7] H. Kargupta and V. Puttagunta. An efficient randomized algorithm for distributed principal component analysis from heterogeneous data. In *Agnik L.L.C. Technical Report 2004-002*, 1450 S. Rolling Road, Baltimore, MD 21227, USA, 2004.

[8] H. Kargupta and K. Sivakumar. Existential pleasures of distributed data mining. In H. Kargupta, A. Joshi, K. Sivakumar, and Y. Yesha, editors, *Data Mining: Next Generation Challenges and Future Directions*. MIT/AAAI press, 2004.

[9] D. Opitz and R. Maclin. Popular ensemble methods: An empirical study. *Journal of Artificial Intelligence Research*, 11:169–198, 1999.

[10] B. Park and H. Kargupta. Distributed data mining: Algorithms, systems, and applications. In N. Ye, editor, *The Handbook of Data Mining*, pages 341–358. Lawrence Erlbaum Associates, Mahwah, N.J., 2003.

[11] B. Park, H. Kargupta, E. Johnson, E. Sanseverino, D. Hershberger, and L. Silvestre. Distributed, collaborative data analysis from heterogeneous sites using a scalable evolutionary technique. *Applied Intelligence*, 16, January 2002.

[12] A. Prodromidis and P. Chan. Meta-learning in distributed data mining systems: Issues and approaches. In H. Kargupta and P. Chan, editors, *Advances of Distributed Data Mining*. AAAI Press, 2000.

Non-Redundant Data Clustering

David Gondek   Thomas Hofmann
Department of Computer Science, Brown University
Providence, RI 02912 USA
{dcg,th}@cs.brown.edu

Abstract

Data clustering is a popular approach for automatically finding classes, concepts, or groups of patterns. In practice this discovery process should avoid redundancies with existing knowledge about class structures or groupings, and reveal novel, previously unknown aspects of the data. In order to deal with this problem, we present an extension of the information bottleneck framework, called coordinated conditional information bottleneck, which takes negative relevance information into account by maximizing a conditional mutual information score subject to constraints. Algorithmically, one can apply an alternating optimization scheme that can be used in conjunction with different types of numeric and non-numeric attributes. We present experimental results for applications in text mining and computer vision.

1 Introduction

Data mining and knowledge discovery aim at finding concepts, patterns, relationships, regularities, and structures of interest in a given data set. However, in practice it is rather atypical to be faced with data about which nothing is known already. More typically, some knowledge has already been acquired in the past, possibly through precedent knowledge discovery processes. The goal then is more precisely to mine for concepts, relationships, etc. that will augment the existing knowledge and that are in some sense non-redundant and novel, relative to the available background knowledge. This leads to the general problem of how to *subtract* or *factor out* the background knowledge in a principled way, in order to *augment* it through additional data mining and exploration.

We address this problem in an information-theoretic framework that makes use of the concept of *conditional mutual information* as its cornerstone. We propose to quantify the information or knowledge gained by a data mining process in terms of how much *new information* it adds about relevant aspect of our data, conditioned on the already available knowledge. It is this conditioning that will provide a well-founded basis for the subtraction process we alluded to.

In this paper, we investigate the important problem of non-redundant data clustering, which deals with finding classes that are in some sense orthogonal to existing knowledge. As far as the form of this knowledge is concerned, our focus is on problems that involve conditioning on one or more attributes or properties of instances. This includes conditioning on known classification schemes as a special case of particular relevance. There are many applications and problems that can be subsumed under this general setting, of which we enumerate a few here to provide some further motivation.

(i) Clustering a set of documents in a way that does not overlap with or recover known classification schemes, but rather discovers new ways in which to group documents. For instance, news stories may be clustered by geographic region as well as by topic. Assuming that documents are annotated by region, conditioning on this information may be valuable to enforce a clustering by topic. (ii) Clustering documents such that the found clusters are not correlated with the occurrence of certain terms. Using the above news story example, one may want to condition on the occurrence of certain geographic terms such as country and city names to introduce a bias that favors document clusters that are not based on geography. (iii) Grouping users for which transactional data has been collected in a way that is not based on certain demographic attributes. For instance, one may want to group users in ways that are not correlated with stratifications based on gender or income. (iv) Finding non-dominant clustering solutions in arbitrary data sets. By first finding the dominant grouping structure and by then conditioning on the latter, non-dominant clustering alternatives can be discovered.

While our method can be applied to these and many similar problems, our emphasis is on a common modeling framework and on the derivation of a general data mining methodology. We will only investigate specific instantiations in an exemplary manner in the experiment section.

2 Related work

Our contribution is in line with a number of recent papers that have argued in favor of data mining techniques that are exploratory, and allow for user interaction and control (e.g. [8]): Techniques should allow users to interactively refine or modify queries based on the results of previous queries. They should furthermore allow users to specify prior knowledge and provide feedback in order to guide the search, both towards desired solutions and away from undesired solutions. Techniques have been presented for tasks ranging from constrained itemset mining [1] to constrained association rule mining [8].

For the clustering problem a variety of constrained clustering techniques exist. Constraints may take the form of *cluster aggregate constraints* [12, 15], e.g. by constraining clustering solutions to equally-sized clusters. Another line of work has focused on *instance-level constraints* [13, 6, 14]. As described in [13], these constraints are informed by prior knowledge of the desired clustering and typically take the form of relations such as *must-link* and *cannot-link* which are enforced between pairs of instances. This approach is extended by [6, 14] which infer from instance-level constraints proximity matrices and formal distance metrics respectively. The common trait of these approaches is the assumption that prior knowledge takes the form of *positive* information about certain characteristics of a desired clustering solution.

Constrained clustering techniques which take *negative* information in the form of information about undesired solutions were first formulated in [2]. Another conceptually related framework has been presented in [4]. We will postpone a detailed discussion of these methods until the end of the following section.

3 Coordinated Conditional Information Bottleneck

3.1 Preliminaries

The mutual information $I(A; B)$ between two (discrete) random variables A, B is defined as

$$I(A; B) \equiv \sum_a \sum_b P_{AB}(a, b) \log \frac{P_{AB}(a, b)}{P_A(a) P_B(b)}, \quad (1)$$

where the sums are over the respective sample spaces for A and B. We have utilized a generic notation for probability mass functions using subscripts involving random variables. Alternatively and equivalently one may define mutual information via conditional entropies as $I(A; B) = H(A) - H(A|B)$.

The conditional mutual information $I(A; B|C)$ between random variables A, B given a random variable C can be defined as

$$\begin{aligned} I(A; B|C) &\equiv H(A|C) - H(A|B, C) \quad (2) \\ &= I(A; B, C) - I(A; C). \end{aligned}$$

3.2 Setting and notation

We use the following notation: x refers to objects or items, such as documents, that should be clustered, y to features that are considered relevant, e.g. word occurrences in documents, c to clusters of objects, and z to available background knowledge. Uppercase letters X, Y, C, Z are used to denote the corresponding random variables. To simplify the presentation, we assume that background knowledge and features depend deterministically on the object, i.e. $Y = Y(X)$ and $Z = Z(X)$.

We work in a probabilistic setting, where objects are probabilistically assigned to clusters. The goal of data clustering is thus to find a stochastic mapping $P_{C|X}$ of objects x to clusters $c \in \{1, \ldots, k\}$, where the number of clusters k is assumed to be given. Here $P_{C|X}$ refers to the conditional distribution of C given X, i.e. $P_{C|X}(c|x)$ – or $P(c|x)$ for short – denotes the probability of assigning object x to cluster c.

3.3 Conditional Information Bottleneck

Given a particular choice for $P_{C|X}$, we would like to quantify the amount of information preserved in the clustering about the relevant features Y. However, we also need to take into account that we assume to have access to the background knowledge Z. A natural quantity to consider is the conditional mutual information $I(C; Y|Z)$. It describes how much information C, Z convey jointly about relevant features Y compared to the information provided by Z alone. Finding an optimal clustering solution should involve maximizing $I(C; Y|Z)$.

In addition, we would like to avoid over-confidence in grouping objects together. Cluster assignment probabilities should reflect the uncertainty with which objects are assigned to clusters. One way to accomplish this is to explicitly control the fuzziness of the stochastic mapping $P_{C|X}$. The latter can be measured by the mutual information $I(C; X)$ between cluster and object identities. Here $I(C; X) = 0$, if objects are assigned to clusters completely at random, whereas $I(C; X)$ becomes maximal for non-stochastic mappings $P_{C|X}$. $I(C; X)$ also can be given a well-known interpretation in terms of the channel capacity required for transmitting probabilistic cluster assignments over a communication channel [11].

Combining both aspects, we define the optimal clustering as the solution to the following constrained optimization problem, the Conditional Information Bottleneck (CIB), first introduced in [5]:

$$\text{(CIB)} \quad P^*_{C|X} = \operatorname*{argmax}_{P_{C|X} \in \mathcal{P}} I(C;Y|Z), \quad \text{where} \quad \text{(3a)}$$

$$\mathcal{P} \equiv \{P_{C|X} : I(C;X) \leq C_{\max}\}. \quad \text{(3b)}$$

Stated in plain English, we are looking for probabilistic cluster assignments with a minimal fuzziness such that the relevant information jointly encoded in C, Z is maximal.

3.4 Coordinated CIB

While the conditional information reflects much of the intuition behind non-redundant data mining, there still is a potential caveat in using Eq. (3): the definition of C may lack global coordination. That is, clustering solutions obtained for different values z may not be in correspondence. For instance, if Z can take a finite number of possible values, then the meaning of each cluster c is relative to a particular value z. The reason for this is that $I(C;Y|Z)$ only measures the information conveyed by C and Z in conjunction, but does not reflect how much relevant information C provides on its own, i.e. without knowing Z. We call this problem the *cluster coordination problem*.

One way to formally illustrate that the CIB does not address the coordination problem is via the following proposition which we state here without proof.

Proposition 1. *Suppose Z and C are finite random variables and define pre-image sets of Z by $\mathcal{X}_z = \{x : Z(x) = z\}$. Assume that $P^*_{C|X}$ has been obtained according to Eq. (3). Then one can chose arbitrary permutations π^z over C, one for every value z of Z, and define permuted cluster assignments $P^\pi_{C|X}(c|x) \equiv P^*_{C|X}(\pi^{Z(x)}(c)|x)$ such that $P^\pi_{C|X}$ is also optimal for CIB.*

Intuitively this proposition states that by independently renumbering (i.e. permuting) cluster labels within each set $\mathcal{X}_z$, the optimality of the solution is not affected. A solution to the CIB problem will effectively correspond to a subcategorization or a *local* refinement of the partition induced by Z. Generally, however, one is more interested in concepts or annotations C that are consistent across the whole domain of objects. We propose to address this problem by introducing an additional constraint involving $I(C;Y)$. This yields the following *Coordinated Conditional Information Bottleneck (CCIB)* formulation:

$$\text{(CCIB)} \quad P^*_{C|X} = \operatorname*{argmax}_{P_{C|X} \in \mathcal{P}} I(C;Y|Z), \quad \text{where} \quad \text{(4a)}$$

$$\mathcal{P} \equiv \{P_{C|X} : I(C;X) \leq C_{\max}, I(C;Y) \geq I_{\min}\}. \quad \text{(4b)}$$

With $I_{min} > 0$ the CCIB favors clustering solutions that obey some global consistency across the sets $\mathcal{X}_z$.

3.5 Alternating optimization

The formal derivation of an alternation scheme to compute an approximate solution for the CCIB is somewhat involved, but leads to very intuitive re-estimation equations. As shown in the appendix, one can compute probabilistic cluster assignments according to the following formula:

$$P(c|x) \propto P(c) \exp\left[\frac{\lambda}{\rho} \sum_y P(y|x) \log P(y|c)\right] \quad \text{(5)}$$

$$\times \exp\left[\frac{1}{\rho} \sum_z P(z|x) \sum_y P(y|x,z) \log P(y|c,z)\right],$$

where we have dropped all subscripts, since the meaning of the probability mass functions is clear from the naming convention for the arguments. The scalars $\rho \geq 0$ and $\lambda \geq 0$ are Lagrange multipliers enforcing the two inequality constraints; their values depend on $C_{\max}$ and $I_{\min}$. Notice that $P(y|c)$ and $P(y|c,z)$ appearing on the right-hand side of Eq. (5) implicitly depend on $P(c|x)$. However iterating this equation is guaranteed to reach a fixed point corresponding to a local maximum of the CCIB criterion.

3.6 Relation to related work

The CCIB formulation is an extension of the seminal work by Tishby et al. [11] on the information bottleneck (IB) framework. Among the different generalizations of IB proposed so far, our approach is most closely related to the IB with side information [2]. One way to formulate the latter is as the problem of minimizing $I(C;Z)$ subject to constraints on $I(C;Y)$ and $I(C;X)$. The main disadvantage that we see in this procedure is the difficulty in adjusting the trade-off between minimizing redundancy between C and Z expressed by $I(C;Z)$, and maximizing relevant information as expressed by the lower bound on $I(C;Y)$. Notice that the latter is problematic, since $I(C;Y)$ and $I(C;Z)$ may live on very different scales, e.g. $I(C;Y)$ may scale with the number of relevant features, while $I(C;Z)$ may scale with the cardinality of the state space of Z. In the CCIB formulation, this is taken into account by conditioning on the side information Z in $I(C;Y|Z)$, which enforces non-redundancy without the need for an explicit term $I(C;Z)$ to penalize redundancy.

The CIB method from [5] is less general than CCIB as it requires a seed set of labeled data in order to address the coordination problem. The CIB objective in Eq. (3a) may also be justified using the multivariate information bottleneck (MIB) framework [4]. Using the so-called $\mathcal{L}^{(1)}$ principle, one may directly derive (3a). The derivation follows that of the parallel information bottleneck, only using the assumption that Z is known a priori. However, the coordination problem is not addressed in [4]. In fact the MIB formulation has a distinctly different goal from the one pursued with the CCIB method.

4 Finite sample considerations

So far we have tacitly assumed that the joint distribution P_{XYZ} is given. However, since this will rarely be the case in practice, it is crucial to be able to effectively deal with the finite sample case. Let us denote a sample set drawn i.i.d. by $\mathcal{X}_n = \{(x_i, y_i, z_i) : i = 1, \ldots, n\}$. We will first clarify the relationship between CCIB and likelihood maximization and then investigate particular parametric forms for the approximating distribution, leading to specific instantiations of the general scheme presented in the previous section.

4.1 Likelihood maximization

A natural measure for the predictive performance of a model is the average conditional log-likelihood function

$$L(\mathcal{X}_n) = \frac{1}{n} \sum_{i=1}^{n} \sum_c P_{C|X}(c|x_i) \log \hat{P}_{Y|C,Z}(y_i|c_i, z_i). \quad (6)$$

Here $\hat{P}_{Y|C,Z}$ is some approximation to the true distribution. This amounts to a two-stage prediction process, where x_i is first assigned to one of the clusters according to $P_{C|X}(c|x_i)$ and then features are predicted using the distribution $\hat{P}_{Y|C,Z}(y_i|c, z_i)$. Asymptotically one gets

$$L(\mathcal{X}_n) \xrightarrow{n \to \infty} \sum_{y,z} P_{C,Y,Z}(c, y, z) \log \hat{P}_{Y|C,Z}(y|c, z)$$

$$= -H(Y|C, Z) - \mathbf{E}_{C,Z} \left[KL(P_{Y|C,Z} \| \hat{P}_{Y|C,Z}) \right]. \quad (7)$$

Provided that the estimation error (represented by the expected Kullback-Leibler divergence) vanishes as $n \to \infty$, maximizing the log-likelihood with respect to $P_{C|X}$ will thus asymptotically be equivalent to minimizing $H(Y|C, Z)$ and thus to maximizing the conditional information $I(C; Y|Z)$.

The practical relevance of the above considerations is that one can use the likelihood function Eq. (6) as the basis for computing a suitable approximation $\hat{P}_{Y|C,Z}$. For instance, if the latter is parameterized by some parameter θ, then one may compute the optimal parameter θ^* as the one that maximizes $L(\mathcal{X}_n)$.

4.2 Categorical background knowledge

Let us focus on the simplest case first, where Z is finite and its cardinality is small enough to allow estimating separate conditional feature distributions $P_{Y|C,Z}$ and $P_{Y|Z}$ for

every combination c, z and every z, respectively. As discussed before, we can estimate the above probabilities by conditional maximum likelihood estimation. For concreteness, we present and discuss the resulting update equations and algorithm for the special case of a multinomial sampling model for Y, which is of some importance, for example, in the context of text mining application. It is simple to derive similar algorithms for other sampling models such as Bernoulli, normal, or Poisson.

Denote by n_{ij} observed feature frequencies for the i-th object and the j-th possible Y-value and by n_i the total number of observations for x_i. For instance, n_{ij} may denote the number of times the j-th term occurs in the i-th document in the context of text mining. Then we can define the relevant empirical distributions by

$$P(y_j|x_i) = P(y_j|x_i, z_i) \equiv \frac{n_{ij}}{n_i}, \ P(z|x_i) \equiv \delta(z, z_i). \quad (8)$$

The maximum likelihood estimates for given probabilistic cluster assignments can be computed according to

$$P(y_j|c) = \frac{\sum_{i=1}^{n} P(c|x_i) n_{ij}}{\sum_{i=1}^{n} P(c|x_i) n_i}, \quad (9a)$$

$$P(y_j|c, z) = \frac{\sum_{i=1}^{n} P(z|x_i) P(c|x_i) n_{ij}}{\sum_{i=1}^{n} P(z|x_i) P(c|x_i) n_i}, \quad (9b)$$

$$P(c) = \frac{1}{n} \sum_{i=1}^{n} P(c|x_i). \quad (9c)$$

These equations need to be iterated in alternation with the re-estimation equation in Eq. (5), where the sum over y is replaced by a sum over the feature index j.

4.3 Continuous-valued background knowledge

A more general case involves background knowledge consisting of a vector $z \in \mathbb{R}^d$. This includes situations where Z might be a function of Y or might consists of a subset of the features (cf. Section 1). In order to obtain an estimate for $P(y|c, z)$ one has to fit a regression model that predicts the relevant features Y from the background knowledge Z for every cluster. If the response variable Y is itself vector-valued, then we propose to fit regression models for every feature dimension separately.

The parametric form of the parametric regression function depends on the type and sampling model of the feature variable Y. For instance, Y may be a multivariate normal, a multinomial variable, or a vector of Bernoulli variables. In order to cover most cases of interest in a generic way, we propose to use of the framework of *generalized linear models* (GLMs) [7]. Since a detailed presentation of GLMs is beyond the scope of this paper, we only provide a brief outline of what is involved in this process: We assume that the conditional mean of Y can be written as a function of C and Z in the following way $\mathbf{E}[Y|C,Z] = \mu(C,Z) = h(\langle \theta, \phi(C,Z) \rangle)$, where h is the inverse link function and ϕ is a vector of predictor variables. Taking $h = \text{id}$ results in standard linear regression based on the independent variables $\phi(C,Z)$, but a variety of other (inverse) link functions can be used dependent on the application.

In this general case, computing the quantities $P(y|c) = P(y|c;\eta)$ and $P(y|c,z) = P(y|c,z;\theta)$ requires to estimate η and θ by maximizing the log-likelihood criterion in Eq. (6). The latter can be accomplished by standard model fitting algorithms for GLMs, which may themselves be iterative in nature.

4.4 Deterministic annealing

We now address the issue of how to deal with the free parameters $C_{\max}$ and $I_{\min}$ of the CCIB or – equivalently – the Lagrange multipliers ρ and λ. Notice that the constraint $I(C;Y) \geq I_{\min}$ leads to a Lagrangian function that additively combines two (conditional) mutual informations $I(C;Y|Z) + \lambda I(C;Y)$. It is often more natural to directly set λ which controls the trade-off between conditional and unconditional information maximization. Since the $I(C;Y)$ term has been added to address the coordination problem, we will in practice typically chose $\lambda \leq 1$.

The ρ parameter in Eq. (5) on the other hand directly controls the fuzziness of the assignments such that hard clusterings are computed in the limit of $\rho \to 0$. We propose to adjust ρ using a well-known continuation method called deterministic annealing [10]. This has two advantages: Conceptually, non-zero values for ρ avoid over-confidence in assigning objects to clusters and thus addresses the crucial problem of overfitting in learning from finite data. For instance, we may chose to select a value for ρ that maximizes the predictive performance on some held-out data set.

The second advantage is algorithmic in nature. The proposed alternating scheme is sensitive with respect to the choice of initial values. As a result of that, convergence to poor local optima may be a nuisance in practice, a problem that plagues many similar alternating schemes such as k-means and mixture modeling. However, a simple control strategy that starts with high entropy cluster assignments and then successively lowers the entropy of the assignments has proven to be a simple, yet effective tool in practice to improve the quality of the solutions obtained (cf. [10, 11]). In analogy of a physical system, one may think of ρ in terms of a *computational temperature*.

We thus propose the following scheme: Starting with a large enough value for $\rho = \rho_0$, one alternates the update equations until convergence. Then one lowers ρ according to some schedule, for instance an exponential schedule

Algorithm	mean		opt	
	$Prec_B$	$Prec_C$	$Prec_B$	$Prec_C$
CIB	0.540	0.773	0.540	0.773
CCIB1	0.566	0.970	0.566	0.970
CCIB2	0.562	0.919	0.590	0.939

Table 1. Synthetic data results with 50 sample sets and 10 random initializations on each.

$\rho \leftarrow b\rho$ with $b < 1$. The process terminates, if the chosen ρ leads to a value for $I(C;X)$ that is close to the desired bound $I_{\max}$ or if cluster assignments numerically reach hard assignments.

5 Experimental results

5.1 Synthetic data

We have generated test data sets with binary features $y \in \{0,1\}^m$ where $m = 12$. Two independent partitionings B and C with $k = 2$ are embedded in the data by associating B with 8 of the features and C with 4 of the features, making B the dominant partitioning. Noise is introduced by randomly flipping each binary feature with probability $p_{noise} = 0.1$.

In the experiments on synthetic data, we investigate two types of background knowledge Z: the dominant classification itself $Z = B$ (CCIB1) and the features associated with the dominant classification (CCIB2). For comparison, we also consider $Z = B$ when the coordination term is not used (CIB). In all cases, a Bernoulli distribution is assumed for the features Y. The results are summarized in Table 1. Here 'mean' denotes the average precision of individual runs, whereas 'opt' is the precision obtained by selecting the best out of 10 solutions based on the CCIB criterion. Discovered and target clustering have been aligned using an optimal matching.

Both algorithms, CCIB1 and CCIB2, recover the target clustering with high accuracy, significantly outperforming CIB. The CCIB1 version using categorical side information slightly outperforms the GLM version CCIB2, which is due to the feature noise.

5.2 Face database

We consider a set of 369 face images with 40×40 grayscale pixels and gender annotations. We performed clustering with $k = 2$ clusters and a Gaussian noise model for the features. Initially, no background knowledge was used. All of 20 trials converged to the same clustering, suggesting that this clustering is the dominant structure in

 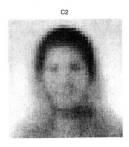

Figure 1. Centroids from initial clustering with no side information.

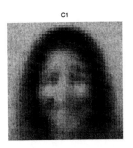 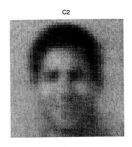

Figure 2. Centroids from second clustering using initial clustering as side information.

the data set. The precision score between the discovered clustering and the gender classification was 0.5122, i.e. the overlap is close to random. Examining the centroids of each cluster in Figure 1 shows the clustering which was obtained partitions the data into face-and-shoulder views and face-only views.

We then introduce the clustering generated from the first attempt as background knowledge and perform a second attempt. The resulting precision score is substantially higher, at 0.7805. Confusion matrices for both clusterings are in Table 2. Centroids for this clustering are in Figure 2 and confirm that the dominant structure found in the previous attempt has been avoided, revealing lower-order structure that is more informative with respect to gender.

initial clustering		
	female	male
c_1	140	144
c_2	45	40
Precision = 0.5122		

second clustering		
	female	male
c_1	105	1
c_2	80	183
Precision = 0.7805		

Table 2. Confusion matrices for face data.

5.3 Text mining

We evaluate performance on several real-world text data sets. Each may be partitioned according to either one of two independent classification schemes. Experiments are performed using either one of these classification schemes as background knowledge. An algorithm is considered successful if it finds a clustering not associated with the background knowledge, that is similar to the other classification scheme. Documents are represented by term frequency vectors that are assumed to follow a multinomial distribution. For all experiments described, $\lambda = 0.3$ is used and k is set to the cardinality of the target categorization.

We use the CMU 4 Universities WebKB data set as described in [3] which consists of webpages collected from computer science departments and has a classification scheme based on page type: ('course', 'faculty', 'project', 'staff', 'student') as well source university: ('Cornell', 'Texas', 'Washington', 'Wisconsin'). Documents belonging to the 'misc' and 'other' categories, as well as the 'department' category which contained only 4 members, were removed, leaving 1087 pages remaining. Stopwords were removed, numbers were tokenized, and only terms appearing in more than one document were retained, leaving 5650 terms.

Additional data sets were derived from the Reuters RCV-1 news corpus which contains multiple labels for each document. We first select a number of topic labels *Topic* and region labels *Region* and then sample documents from the set of documents having labels $\{Topic \times Region\}$. We take up to n documents from each combination of labels. For ease of evaluation, those documents which contain multiple labels from *Topic* or multiple labels from *Region* were excluded. We selected labels which would produce high numbers of eligible documents and generated the following sets: (i) *RCV1-gmcat2x2*: *Topic* = { MCAT (Markets), GCAT (Government/Social) } and *Region* = {UK, INDIA}: 1600 documents and 3295 terms. (ii) *RCV1-ec5x6*: 5 of the most frequent subcategories of the ECAT (Economics) and 6 of the most frequent country codes were chosen: 5362 documents and 4052 terms. (iii) *RCV1-top7x9*: ECAT (Economics), MCAT (Markets) and the 5 most frequent subcategories of the GCAT (General) topic and the 9 most frequent country codes were chosen: 4345 documents and 4178 terms. As with the WebKB set, stopwords were removed, numbers were tokenized and a term frequency cutoff was used to remove low-frequency terms.

Results of the CCIB method on the text data sets are shown in Table 3. It is interesting to note that results improve as sets with more categories are considered. In all cases, the solutions found are more similar to the target classification than the known classification although the task appears to be more difficult for the RCV1-ec5x6 set.

Data set	$Z = \text{L1}$				$Z = \text{L2}$			
	$Prec_{L2}$	$I(C, L1)$	$I(C, L2)$	time(s)	$Prec_{L1}$	$I(C, L1)$	$I(C, L2)$	time (s)
WebKB	0.2917	0.0067	0.0189	54.3	0.4735	0.2342	0.0085	61.5
RCV1-gmcat2x2	0.5516	0.0015	0.0107	12.5	0.9781	0.8548	0.0001	9.1
RCV1-ec5x6	0.1970	0.0792	0.3027	389.8	0.4189	0.2801	0.2296	519.6
RCV1-top7x9	0.2758	0.0224	0.1383	333.6	0.6076	0.4781	0.0074	183.2

Table 3. Results on text data sets averaged over 10 initializations for $L1$ = Topic/page type, $L2$ = Region/university.

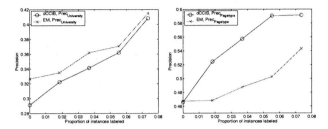

Figure 3. WebKB results: adding labeled data

5.4 Semi-supervised learning

Up to this point, all experiments have been performed subject to the assumption that no positive supervised information is available. We now address the question of whether semi-supervised learning may be enhanced by avoiding redundancy with background knowledge. We assume a small set of examples is labeled according to a desired classification. Performance is compared against EM augmented with a Naive Bayes model for labeled data, as described in [9]. Labeled data is incorporated into the CCIB framework by fixing the corresponding $C(x_i)$ for each labeled instance x_i. Results for varying amounts of labeled data per class are shown in Figure 3. The results show that for the considered regime, using side information about undesired clusterings can significantly improve the classification performance. In the first case, where C = 'page type', for proportions of labeled instances greater than 0.04, the CCIB method has performance slightly less than that of EM in finding solutions similar to the target clustering. In the second case, where C = 'university', the CCIB method substantially outperforms EM over the entire range considered.

5.5 Parameter sensitivity

We have conducted a series of experiments to investigate the sensitivity of the results on the parameters, most crucially the relative weight λ ensuring cluster coordination. Due to lack of space, we can only report the main observations. On synthetic data as well as on the text data sets, we have found the procedure to be highly robust with respect to

variations of λ in a typical range of $[0.2; 1.0]$. As expected, too small values for λ lead to solutions that lack global coordination and for values that are too large, the $I(C; Y)$ tends to dominate. In comparison, we have verified that the side information bottleneck of [2] is much more sensitive with respect to the corresponding tuning parameter, with the optimal range varying significantly across different data sets.

6 Conclusion

We have presented a general information-theoretic framework for non-redundant clustering based on the idea of maximizing conditional mutual information relative to given background knowledge. We have pointed out the cluster coordination problem and provided a way to deal with it in the Coordinated Conditional Information Bottleneck. A generic alternating optimization and special instantiations thereof have been derived and discussed, emphasizing the principled nature of our approach as well as its broad applicability. Experiments on synthetic and real-world data sets have underpinned that claim.

Acknowledgment

D.G. has been supported by an NSF IGERT Ph.D. fellowship. Part of this work was completed while T.H. was at the Max-Planck Institute for Biological Cybernetics in Tübingen, Germany.

Appendix

The Lagrangian of the CCIB problem is given by

$$F = I(C; Y|Z) - \rho I(C; X) + \lambda I(C; Y).$$

We rewrite mutual informations as (conditional) entropy differences and after dropping constant terms, we arrive at

$$F' = -H(Y|C, Z) - \rho H(C) + \rho H(C|X) - \lambda H(Y|C).$$

We introduce cross entropies with auxiliary parameters Q_C, $Q_{Y|C}$, and $Q_{Y|C,Z}$, non-negative and normalized. Now we define

$$\tilde{H}(C) = -\sum_c P_C(c) \log Q_C(c),$$

$$\tilde{H}(Y|C) = -\sum_{c,y} P_{CY}(c,y) \log Q_{Y|C}(y|c),$$

$$\tilde{H}(Y|C,Z) = -\sum_{c,y,z} P_{CYZ}(c,y,z) \log Q_{Y|CZ}(y|c,z),$$

and a new objective

$$\tilde{F} = -\tilde{H}(Y|Z,C) - \rho\tilde{H}(C) + \rho H(C|X) - \lambda\tilde{H}(Y|C).$$

The advantage of $\tilde{F}$ is that it is concave in $P_{C|X}$ for given Q, since $H(C|X)$ is concave and the $\tilde{H}$ terms are linear in $P_{C|X}$. Moreover, $\tilde{F}$ is also concave in the Q parameters for given $P_{C|X}$, since the logarithm function is concave.

More precisely the solutions over Q can be obtained as follows: First observe that the only $\tilde{H}(C)$ depends on Q_C, only $\tilde{H}(Y|C)$ depends on $Q_{Y|C}$, and $H(Y|C,Z)$ on $Q_{Y|C,Z}$. Differentiating $\tilde{F}$ with respect to the Q parameters and setting to zero results in $Q_C = P_C$, $Q_{Y|C} = P_{Y|C}$, and $Q_{Y|C,Z} = P_{Y|C,Z}$, as is straightforward to prove (cf. [11], Lemma 2). These correspond to maxima of the function $\tilde{F}$ for given clustering probabilities $P_{C|X}$.

Finally, in order to optimize $\tilde{F}$ explicitly over the clustering probabilities $P_{C|X}$ one makes use of the relation

$$\frac{\partial \sum_x P_{CXYZ}(c,x,y,z)}{\partial P_{C|X}(c|x)} = P_{XYZ}(x,y,z).$$

Setting to zero and accounting for the normalization of $P_{C|X}$ one gets

$$P(c|x) \propto Q(c) \exp\left[\frac{\lambda}{\rho} \sum_y P(y|x) \log Q(y|c)\right]$$

$$\times \exp\left[\frac{1}{\rho} \sum_z P(z|x) \sum_y P(y|x,z) \log Q(y|c,z)\right],$$

where subscripts of P and Q have been dropped for better readability.

At a stationary point (corresponding to a maximum or saddle-point of $\tilde{F}$) this can again be rewritten more suggestively as a characterization of the resulting joint distribution, since there Q probabilities agree with their P counterparts. The asymptotic convergence of this scheme is a simple consequence of the fact that $\tilde{F}$ is reduced in every update iteration and that is bounded from below. This may not correspond to a global maximum, but it will fulfill the optimality conditions over the $P_{C|X}$ and Q subspaces separately.

References

[1] C. Bucila, J. Gehrke, D. Kifer, and W. White. Dualminer: A dual-pruning algorithm for itemsets with constraints. In *Proc. 8th SIGKDD Intl. Conf. on Knowledge Discovery and Data Mining*, 2002.

[2] G. Chechik and N. Tishby. Extracting relevant structures with side information. In *Advances in Neural Information Processing Systems 15 (NIPS '02)*, 2002.

[3] M. Craven, D. DiPasquo, D. Freitag, A. K. McCallum, T. M. Mitchell, K. Nigam, and S. Slattery. Learning to extract symbolic knowledge from the World Wide Web. In *Proc. of the 15th Conf. of the American Association for Artificial Intelligence*, pages 509–516, 1998.

[4] N. Friedman, O. Mosenzon, N. Slonim, and N. Tishby. Multivariate information bottleneck. In *Proceedings of the 17th Conference on Uncertainty in Artificial Intelligence*, 2001.

[5] D. Gondek and T. Hofmann. Conditional information bottleneck clustering. In *3rd IEEE International Conference on Data Mining, Workshop on Clustering Large Data Sets*, 2003.

[6] D. Klein, S. D. Kamvar, and C. D. Manning. From instance-level constraints to space-level constraints: Making the most of prior knowledge in data clustering. In *Proceedings of the Nineteenth International Conference on Machine Learning*, 2002.

[7] P. McCullagh and J. Nelder. *Generalized Linear Models*. Chapman & Hall, London, U.K., 1989.

[8] R. T. Ng, L. V. Lakshmanan, J. Han, and A. Pang. Exploratory mining and pruning optimizations of constrained association rule. In *Proceedings of ACM SIGMOND*, pages 13–24, 1998.

[9] K. Nigam, A. K. McCallum, S. Thrun, and T. M. Mitchell. Text classification from labeled and unlabeled documents using EM. *Machine Learning*, 39(2/3):103–134, 2000.

[10] K. Rose. Deterministic annealing for clustering, compression, classification, regression, and related optimization problems, 1998.

[11] N. Tishby, F. C. Pereira, and W. Bialek. The information bottleneck method. In *Proceedings of the 37-th Annual Allerton Conference on Communication, Control and Computing*, pages 368–377, 1999.

[12] A. Tung, R. Ng, J. Han, and L. Lakshmanan. Constraint-based clustering in large databases. In *Proceedings 2001 International Conference on Database Theory*, pages 405–419, 2001.

[13] K. Wagstaff and C. Cardie. Clustering with instance-level constraints. In *Proc. of the Seventeenth International Conference on Machine Learning*, pages 1103–1110, 2000.

[14] E. P. Xing, A. Y. Ng, M. I. Jordan, and S. Russell. Distance metric learning, with application to clustering with side-information. In *Advances in Neural Information Processing Systems*, 2003.

[15] S. Zhong and J. Ghosh. Model-based clustering with soft balancing. In *Proc. 3rd IEEE Int. Conf. Data Mining*, pages 459–466, 2003.

Fast and Exact Out-of-Core K-Means Clustering

Anjan Goswami   Ruoming Jin   Gagan Agrawal

Department of Computer Science and Engineering
Ohio State University
{goswamia,jinr,agrawal}@cse.ohio-state.edu

Abstract

Clustering has been one of the most widely studied topics in data mining and k-means clustering has been one of the popular clustering algorithms. K-means requires several passes on the entire dataset, which can make it very expensive for large disk-resident datasets. In view of this, a lot of work has been done on various approximate versions of k-means, which require only one or a small number of passes on the entire dataset.

In this paper, we present a new algorithm which typically requires only one or a small number of passes on the entire dataset, and provably produces the same cluster centers as reported by the original k-means algorithm. The algorithm uses sampling to create initial cluster centers, and then takes one or more passes over the entire dataset to adjust these cluster centers. We provide theoretical analysis to show that the cluster centers thus reported are the same as the ones computed by the original k-means algorithm. Experimental results from a number of real and synthetic datasets show speedup between a factor of 2 and 4.5, as compared to k-means.

1. Introduction

Clustering has been one of the most widely studied topics in data mining. Clustering refers to techniques for grouping similar objects in clusters. Formally, given a set of d dimensional points and a function $f : \Re^d \times \Re^d \mapsto \Re$ that gives the *distance* between two points in $\Re^d$, we are required to compute k cluster centers, such that the points falling in the same cluster are similar and points that are in different cluster are dissimilar.

Most of the initial clustering techniques were developed by statistics or pattern recognition communities, where the goal was to cluster a modest number of data instances. However, within the data mining community, the focus has been on clustering large datasets. Developing clustering algorithms to effectively and efficiently cluster rapidly growing datasets has been identified as an important challenge. For example, Ghosh states *"The holy grail of scalable clustering can be to find near linear algorithm that involve only a small number of passes through the database"* [9].

In this paper, we address the problem of *fast data clustering* on a very large and out-of-core datasets, using one or a small number of passes over the data, *without compromising on its result*. Our work is in the context of k-means clustering. K-means clustering algorithm was developed by MacQueen [14] in 1967 and later improved by Hartigan [12]. Bottou and Bengio [3] proved the convergence properties of the k-means algorithm. It has been shown to be very useful for a corpus of practical applications. The original k-means algorithm works with memory resident data, but can be easily extended for disk-resident datasets.

The main problem with the k-means algorithm is that it makes one scan over the entire dataset for every iteration, and it needs many such iterations before converging to a quality solution. This makes it potentially very expensive to use, particularly for large disk-resident datasets. A number of algorithms or approaches focus on reducing the number of passes required for k-means [4, 5, 7, 10]. However, these approaches only provide approximate solutions, possibly with deterministic or probabilistic bounds on the quality of the solutions. A key advantage of k-means has been that it converges to a local minimum [11], which does not hold true for the approximate versions.

Therefore, an interesting question is, *"Can we have an algorithm which requires fewer passes on the entire dataset, and can produce the same results as the original k-means algorithm?"*. In this paper, we present an algorithm that makes one or a few passes over the data and produces the exact cluster centers as would be generated by the original k-means algorithm. We refer this algorithm as Fast and Exact K-Means algorithm, denoted by FEKM.

The main idea in the algorithm is as follows. We initially sample the data and run the original k-means algorithm. We store the centers computed after each iteration of the run of the k-means on the sampled data. We now use this information and take one pass over the entire dataset. We identify and store the points which are more likely to shift from one cluster to another, as the cluster centers could move. These points are now used to try and adjust the cluster centers.

We provide theoretical analysis to show that the algorithm produces the same cluster centers. In the worst case, the algorithm can require the same number of passes as the original k-means. However, our detailed experimental analysis on several synthetic and real datasets shows that it requires at most 3 passes, whereas, the average number of passes required is less than 1.5. This results in speedups between 2 and 4.5 as compared to the original k-means.

The outline of the rest of the paper is as follows. In section 2, we discuss the related work. In section 3, we present the main ideas of the FEKM algorithm and explain the details of the pseudo code of the algorithm. In section 4, we provide the theoretical framework for the algorithm. The experimental results are provided in section 5. We conclude in Section 6.

2. Related Work

There has been an extensive study on clustering algorithms in the literature. Comprehensive survey on this subject can be obtained from the book [13] and papers [2, 9]. In this discussion, we limit ourselves to the improvements over k-means.

Moore and Pelleg [17] proposed a variant of k-means using a k-d tree based data structure to store distance information, which can make each iteration of k-means significantly faster. This algorithm focuses on the in-core datasets.

Bradley and Fayyad [4] have developed a single pass approximation of multi-pass k-means. This algorithm summarizes the input points based on their likely-hood to belong to different centers. Farnstorm and his colleagues [8] have further refined this idea.

Domingos and Hulten [7] proposed a faster version (sublinear) of k-means using sampling based on Hoeffding or similar statistical bound. The algorithm consists of a number of runs of k-means with sample where in every iteration sample size is increased to maintain the loss bound from the multi-pass k-means. The goal here is to converge to a solution which is close to that of a multi-pass k-means by a predefined bound with good probability. Motwani, Charikar, and their colleagues [6, 1, 16, 10, 5] proposed a series of constant factor approximation algorithms for one pass k-center and k-median problems.

More recently, Nittel *et. al.* [15] propose to apply k-means algorithm to cluster massive datasets, scanning the dataset only once. Their algorithm splits the entire dataset into chunks, and each chunk can fit into the main memory. Then, it applies k-means on each chunk of data, and merge the clustering results by another k-means type algorithm. Good results are shown for a real dataset, however, no theoretical bounds on the results are established.

All of the above efforts on reducing the number of passes on the data involve algorithms that cannot maintain the exact result which will be obtained using a multi-pass k-means algorithm. Developing an algorithm with this goal is the focus of our work.

3. Algorithm Description

This section describes new algorithm, Fast and Exact K-means (FEKM) that we have developed. Initially, we describe the main ideas behind the algorithm. Then, we give some formal definitions, present and explain the pseudocode, and explain some of the choices we have made in our current implementation.

3.1. Main Ideas

The basic idea behind our algorithm is as follows. We believe that approximate cluster centers computed using sampling can be corrected and moved to *exact* cluster centers using only one or a small number of passes on the entire data. By exact cluster centers, we mean the cluster centers that are computed by the original k-means algorithm. Thus, we can use sampling to speedup the computation of exact clusters.

There are three key questions to be addressed. First, when approximate cluster centers are computed using sampling, what information need to be stored. Second, how can this information be used to avoid a large number of passes on the entire dataset. Third, how do we know that we have computed the same cluster centers as in the original k-means algorithm.

We initially run the k-means algorithm on a sample, using the same convergence criteria and same initial points as we would use for the k-means. The following information is stored for future use. After every iteration of k-means on the sampled data, we store the k centers that have been computed. In addition, we compute and store another value, referred to as the *Confidence Radius* of each cluster, whose computation will be described later. This information can be stored in a table with k columns, and the number of rows equaling the number of iterations for which k-means was run on the sampled data. Each entry of the table contains a tuple (center, radius) for each cluster.

Next, we take one pass through the entire dataset. For every point and each row of the table, we compute the cluster to which this point will be assigned at this iteration, assuming that executing the algorithm on the entire dataset produces the same cluster centers as the initial run on sampled data. Next, we try to estimate how likely it is that this point will be assigned to a different cluster when the algorithm is executed on the entire dataset.

Our goal is to identify and store the points which could be assigned to a different cluster during any of the iterations. These points are refereed to as *boundary points*, because intuitively, they fall at the boundary of the clusters. If these points could be identified and stored in memory, we can eliminate any need for any further passes on the entire dataset. However, we can only estimate these points, which means that we could require additional passes if our estimate is not correct.

Thus, for a given point and row of the table, we determine if this point is a boundary point. If it is, it is stored in a buffer. Otherwise, we update the *sufficient statistics tuple*, which has the number and sum of the data points for the cluster.

After the pass through the dataset and storing the boundary point, we do the following processing. Starting from the first row of the table, we recompute centers using the boundary points and sufficient statistics tuple. If any of the new computed centers fall outside the pre-estimated confidence radius which means that our computation of boundary points is not valid, we need to take another pass through the data. We use the new centers as new initialization points and again repeat all the steps. However, if the new computed centers are within the confidence radius, we use these centers for the next iteration and continue. The key observation is that using cluster centers from sampling, boundary points, and sufficient statistics, we are able to compute the same cluster centers that we would have gotten through one pass on the entire dataset. Finally, the algorithm terminates by checking for the same termination condition that one would use in the original algorithm.

3.2 Formal Definitions

This subsection formalizes some of the ideas on which the algorithm is based.

Suppose we execute the original k-means algorithm on the complete dataset At i^{th} iteration, the k centers are denoted by $c_1^i, c_2^i, \ldots, c_k^i$, respectively. In the new algorithm, FEKM, initially the k-means algorithm is executed on the sampled dataset with the same initialization. At i^{th} iteration, let the k centers be denoted as $s_1^i {}_2 s^i \ldots, s_k^i$, respectively. For convenience, the first k centers are called as the *k-means centers*, and the later k centers are called as the *sampling centers*.

Further, for each sampling center s_j^i, FEKM associates a *confidence radius*, δ_j^i with it. The confidence radius δ_j^i is based upon an estimate of the upper-bound of the distance between the sampling center s_j^i and the corresponding k-means center c_j^i. Ideally, the confidence radius δ_j^i should be small, but should still satisfy the condition $d(c_j^i, s_j^i) \le \delta_j^i$, where d is the distance function.

Now, consider the scan of the complete dataset taken by FEKM. As we discussed before, the sampling centers are stored in a table with k columns, where the ith row represents the ith iteration. To facilitate our discussion, we call the closest center among a set of k centers for a point as the *owner* of this point.

Definition 1 *For any point p in the complete dataset, assuming s_j^i to be the owner of point p with respect to the sampling centers at the i-th iteration, if there exists $l, l \ne j$, such that*

$$0 \le d(s_l^i, p) - d(s_j^i, p) \le \delta_j^i + \delta_l^i$$

*then, p is a **boundary point** for the i-th iteration.*

The complete set of boundary points is the union of boundary points for all iterations. Thus, the complete set of boundary points includes the points in the entire dataset whose owners with respect to the k-means centers are quite likely to be different from the owners with respect to the sampling centers, for one or more of the iterations.

For a given iteration i, the **stable points** are the points in the complete dataset that are not boundary points for the ith iteration. Usually, for any stable point, the difference between its distance to its owner with respect to the sampling centers and its distance to other sampling centers is quite large. Mathematically, assuming s_j^i to be owner of the point p with respect to the sampling centers at the i-th iteration, for any $l, l \ne j$, we have

$$d(s_l^i, p) - d(s_j^i, p) > \delta_j^i + \delta_l^i$$

3.3 Detailed Description

The detailed algorithm is shown in Figure 3.2. We now explain the algorithm.

The main data structure in FEKM is the table containing the summary of k-means run on sample data. We call this table as the *cluster abstract table* or the *CAtable*. Our algorithm starts with building a CAtable from a sample of the original dataset. Initially, each entry of the CAtable contains the two tuple, the center and the confidence radius of each cluster in that iteration. This is done through the function *BuildCATable*. After this, we take one scan over the complete dataset and find out the likely *boundary points* for each iteration or for each row of the table. The function *IsBndrPoint* checks for each data point if it meets the conditions of being a boundary point.

If one point becomes a boundary point for one particular row, it is possible that the same point also be a boundary point for the next rows or next iterations of the CAtable. We define two lists, one to store the points and another to store the indexes of the rows where these points are found as boundary point. The first list is named as *Buffer* and the second list is named as *Index*. The second list is two dimensional where each row signifies one specific point and each column has ν bits, where ν is the number of iterations or rows in CAtable. If the specific point is found as a boundary point in the j-th row of the CAtable, then the j-th bit of the corresponding column of the *Index* list is set to 1. We also store the number and sum of the non-boundary points with each CAtable entry. The function *UpdateSufficientStats* accomplishes this.

Next, we recompute centers for each row of the CAtable from the boundary points corresponding to that row and from the sufficient statistics. In the Figure 3.2, it has been done by the function *RecomputeCtrs*. We then verify if the new centers are located within the pre-estimated confidence radius to maintain the correctness. The function *IsCtrsWithinRadii* is responsible for this verification. If we find that the new centers are located within the confidence radius of corresponding clusters, we update the centers of the CAtable in the next

```
Input: D_i (Data Points), S_i (Sample Data Points),
    InitCtrs (Initial Centers), ε (Stopping criteria
    in kmeans algorithm)
Output: k Cluster Centers
begin
    flag ⟵ 1 ;
    while flag do
        List Buffer ⟵ NULL ;
        Index[] ⟵ NULL ;
        Table CAtable ⟵ NULL;
        NumRow ⟵ BuildCATable (InitCtrs,
        S_i, CAtable, ε) ;
        for each D_i do
            for each row_j ∈ NumRow do
                if (ClosestCenter ⟵ IsBndrPoint (D_i))
                then
                    BufferInsert (D_i) ;
                    Index[BndCnt][j] ⟵ 1 ;
                    BndCnt + + ;

                else
                    UpdateSufficientStats (
                    ClosestCtr, CAtable, D_i, row_j)
                    ;
                end
            end
        end
        for each row_j ∈ NumRow do
            NewCtrs ⟵ RecomputeCtrs (CAtable,
            Buffer, Index, row_j) ;
            if    (IsCtrsWithinRadii (NewCtrs,
            CAtable, row_{j+1}) then
                UpdateCATableCtrs (NewCtrs,
                CAtable, row_{j+1}) ;
                flag ⟵ 0 ;

            else
                InitCtrs ⟵ NewCtrs;
                flag ⟵ 1;
            end
        end
    end
    OutputCATableCtrs (CAtable, row_{NumRow})
    ;
end
```

Algorithm 1: Pseudo Code of Fast and Exact Out of Core KMeans (FEKM).

row using the function *UpdateCAtableCtrs*. If any of the new centers is found outside the confidence radius of the corresponding cluster, the initial centers are replaced by those new centers and the algorithm repeats from the creation of CAtable.

3.4. Computation of Confidence Radius

The computation of confidence radius for each cluster and each iteration is an important aspect of the algorithm. Large radius values are likely to result in a large number of boundary points, which cannot be stored in memory. At the same time, very small confidence radius values could mean that the difference between corresponding sampling centers and k-means centers could be greater than this value, and therefore, an additional pass on the entire dataset may be required.

In our implementation, we use the following method for computing the confidence radius. Recall that at the iteration i, the confidence radius for the cluster j is denoted by δ_j^i. We use

$$\delta_j^i = f \times \left(\frac{\sum_{p=1}^{N} (X_p - X_c)}{N} \right)^{\frac{1}{2}}$$

where, X_p denotes a d dimensional point assigned to the cluster j at the iteration i, X_c is the center of the cluster j at iteration i, N is the number of points assigned to the cluster j, and f is a factor that is chosen experimentally. For a fixed f, the above expression will choose confidence radius value that is proportional to the average distance of a point in the cluster to the cluster center. This ensures small confidence radius values for a dense cluster, and larger radius values otherwise.

Clearly, a problem that can arise is that number of boundary points can be huge and in the worst case, can also exceed memory size. Thus, in our implementation, we have two conditions on the number of boundary points. First, they should not exceed 20% of all points in the complete dataset. Second, they should not exceed the available memory. If during an execution, the number of boundary points violate either of the above two conditions, we reduce all the confidence radii by choosing a lower value of f, and repeat the computation of boundary points. For our experiments, the value of f was always fixed at 0.05.

4 Theoretical Analysis

In this section, we initially present a proof of correctness for the FEKM algorithm. Then, we also analyze the execution time of this algorithm.

4.1 Proof of Correctness

We now show how FEKM computes the same cluster centers as k-means. Our description here builds on the definitions of k-means centers, sampling centers, owners, boundary points, and stable points given in the previous section. We further add the definition of changing points.

Definition 2 *For the ith iteration, the **changing points** are defined as the points in the dataset that have different owners with respect to the sampling centers and the k-means centers.*

Lemma 1 *Suppose at i^{th} iteration, the following condition holds for each center j, $1 \leq j \leq k$,*

$$d(s_j^i, c_j^i) \leq \delta_j^i$$

Then, the stable points will have the same owners with respect to the sampling centers and the k-means centers, and the set of changing point is a subset of the set of boundary points.

Proof: Consider any point p in the complete dataset, and let s_j^i be the owner of p with respect to the sampling centers at the ith iteration. For any $l, l \neq j$, from the *triangle inequality*, we have

$$d(s_j^i, p) - d(s_j^i, c_j^i) \leq d(c_j^i, p) \leq d(s_j^i, p) + d(s_j^i, c_j^i)$$

$$d(s_l^i, p) - d(s_l^i, c_l^i) \leq d(c_l^i, p) \leq d(s_l^i, p) + d(s_l^i, c_l^i)$$

Further, applying the condition that is assumed, we can have the following inequalities

$$d(s_j^i, p) - \delta_j^i \leq d(c_j^i, p) \leq d(s_j^i, p) + \delta_j^i$$

$$d(s_l^i, p) - \delta_l^i \leq d(c_l^i, p) \leq d(s_l^i, p) + \delta_l^i$$

Therefore,

$$d(s_l^i, p) - d(s_j^i, p) - \delta_l^i - \delta_j^i \leq d(c_l^i, p) - d(c_j^i, p)$$

Case 1: If p is a stable point,

$$d(s_l^i, p) - d(s_j^i, p) > \delta_l^i + \delta_j^i$$

Therefore, we have the inequality

$$0 < d(c_l^i, p) - d(c_j^i, p)$$

This suggests that the center j is still the owner of the point p.

Case 2: If the point p changes its owner in the complete dataset, there exists a center l, such that

$$d(c_l^i, p) - d(c_j^i, p) < 0$$

Therefore, we have

$$d(s_l^i, p) - d(s_j^i, p) \leq \delta_l^i + \delta_j^i$$

This suggests that the point p is a boundary point. Combining both cases, we prove the lemma.

Lemma 2 *If FEKM has computed the k-means correctly at the ith iteration, and at the ith iteration, the condition*

$$d(s_j^i, c_j^i) \leq \delta_j^i \ \forall j, 1 \leq j \leq k$$

holds, then FEKM will compute the k-means centers for the iteration $i + 1$ correctly.

Proof: This follows the result of Lemma 1. The stable points will have the same owners with respect to sampling centers and the k-means centers at the ith iteration. Therefore, in the ith row in the $CAtable$, we maintain the correct and sufficient statistics to summarize the stable points. Further, after the ith iteration, each boundary point can be assigned to the correct owner since we have the correct k-means centers for the ith iteration. Therefore, each center in the ith iteration owns the correct partition of the complete dataset, and the k-means centers of the iteration $i + 1$ can be computed correctly.

Theorem 1 *Suppose that for each iteration $i, 0 \leq i \leq m$, the condition*

$$d(s_j^i, c_j^i) \ \leq \ \delta_j^i \ \forall j, 1 \leq j \leq k$$

holds, and at the iteration $m + 1$, this condition does not hold. Then, for each iteration $i, 0 \leq i \leq m+1$, the k-means centers of the ith iteration can be computed correctly by FEKM.

Proof: This can be proved inductively. For the base case, we use the fact that at iteration 0, the same initialization centers are used by k-means and FEKM. For the induction step, we use the Lemma 2.

Theorem 2 *Assuming the same termination condition, FEKM will iterate the same number of times for the centers as the k-means algorithm, and at each iteration, will generate the same centers as the k-means algorithm.*

Proof: Recall that once the FEKM algorithm finds that the distance between sampling centers and k-means centers is greater than the confidence radius, it will sample again and take the k-means centers at that iteration as the initialization centers. Using this, and the Theorem 1, we have the above result.

4.2   Analysis of Performance

We now analyze the execution time for our algorithm, and compare it with that of original k-means.

Let the number of iterations that k-means takes on entire dataset be n. Let the I/O cost for reading the dataset once be C_I, and let the computing cost (besides the I/O cost) associated with each pass on the complete dataset be C_c. Therefore, the total running time of k-means algorithm $T_{k-means}$ can be expressed as

$$T_{KM} = n \times (C_I + C_c)$$

Now, let us consider our algorithm. Let P denote the number of times we need to sample the dataset. Also, let the size of each sample be a fraction SS of the entire dataset. Further, let the execution of k-means on the sampled dataset require an average of m iterations. This suggests that the total number of rows that are maintained in FEKM is $m \times P$. Therefore, the total running time of FEKM algorithm T_{KEKM} can be expressed as

$$T_{FEKM} = P \times (SS \times (C_I + C_c) + C_I + m \times C_c)$$
$$= P \times (SS + 1) \times C_I + P \times (SS + m) \times C_c$$

From the expression above, we can see that in most cases, FEKM has higher computing cost than the k-means algorithm, since usually, FEKM has to compute more rows ($P \times m$) than the number for k-means (n). For execution on disk-resident datasets, the computing cost of k-means is typically much smaller than the I/O cost. Also, if we have the ability to overlap computation and I/O, the overall execution time reduces to the maximum of the I/O and computational costs, which is likely to be the I/O cost. In either case, we can see that if P is small, FEKM will be much faster than the k-means algorithm.

Our experiments have shown that P is 1 in most cases, and at most 2 or 3. Furthermore, a sampling fraction of 5% or 10% is usually sufficient. For such cases, the above expressions suggest a clear advantage for the FEKM algorithm. The next section further demonstrates this through experimental results.

5. Experimental Results

$cxdy$	dataset with x clusters and y dimensions
I_{KM}	No. of iterations in k-means.
Init "g"	good initialization
Init "b"	bad initialization
T_{KM}	Running Time of k-means (Sec.)
T_{FEKM}	Running Time of FEKM (Sec.)
SS	Sample Size (%)
P	Number of Passes by FEKM
se	Squared Error between final centers and the centers after sampling

Table 1. Explanation of the notations used in the result tables.

This section reports on a number of experiments we conducted to evaluate the FEKM algorithm. Our experiments were conducted using a number of synthetic and real datasets. Our main goal was to compare the execution time of our algorithm with that of the k-means algorithm. Additionally, we were interested in seeing how many passes over the entire dataset were required by the FEKM algorithm. All our experiments were conducted on 700 MHz Pentium machines with 1 GB memory.

In all the experiments, the initial center points and the stopping criteria for this algorithm are kept same as those of the k-means algorithm. As the performance of k-means

is very sensitive to the initialization, we considered different initializations. We used two different initialization techniques. In the first technique, which could only be applied for the synthetic datasets, we perturbed each dimension in the original center points of the Gaussians which were used to generate the data sets. Two different initializations, referred to as *good* and *bad*, were obtained by varying the range of perturbation. In the second technique, we randomly selected the initial center points from a sample of the dataset, such that distance between any two points chosen is greater than a *threshold*. In this case, the *good* and the *bad* initializations corresponded to a *large* and *small* value of this threshold, respectively.

Data	I_{KM}	Init	T_{KM}	T_{FEKM}	SS	P
c5d200	3	g	1452.83	644.66	10	1
c5d200	3	g	1452.83	571.22	5	1
c5d100	6	b	2688.65	902.81	10	1
c5d100	6	b	2688.65	762.47	5	1
c5d50	8	b	3602.31	1114.62	10	2
c5d50	8	b	3602.31	987.43	5	2
c5d20	8	b	3313.84	1098.41	10	1
c5d20	8	b	3313.84	940.47	5	1
c5d20	2	g	829.29	507.94	10	1
c5d20	2	g	829.29	412.53	5	1
c5d10	8	g	3833.44	1633.39	10	1
c5d10	8	g	3833.44	1302.52	5	1
c5d5	6	b	3116.89	1387.13	10	1
c5d5	6	b	3116.89	1236.51	5	1

Table 2. Performance of k-means and FEKM Algorithms on Synthetic Datasets, 5 Clusters

We used two convergence criteria. The algorithm stops when (1) the new centers are not sufficiently different from those generated in the previous iteration, or (2) it has run for a specified maximum number of iterations. The second criteria is useful with bad initializations, where the algorithm could run for a large number of iterations. The notation used in the tables containing the results of the experiments are explained in the Table 1.

5.1 Evaluation with Synthetic Datasets

The evaluation with synthetic datasets was done using 18 1.1 GB datasets and 2 4.4 GB datasets. The datasets involve different number of clusters and dimensions. For generating each synthetic dataset, points are drawn from a mixture of fixed number of Gaussian distributions. Each Gaussian is assigned a random weight which determines the size of each cluster. For each dimension, we kept the mean and variance of each Gaussian in the interval $[-5, 5]$ and $[0.7, 1.5]$, respectively, to retain the flavor of the datasets used in the experiments by Bradley *et al.* [4] and in the experiments by Farnstorm *et al.* [8]. We did the experiments using 5, 10 and 20

Data	I_{KM}	Init	T_{KM}	T_{FEKM}	SS	P
c10d200	10	b	4808.48	1559.70	10	2
c10d200	10	b	4808.48	1324.38	5	2
c10d200	2	g	954.33	577.22	10	1
c10d200	2	g	954.33	459.52	5	1
c10d100	3	g	1081.45	435.25	10	1
c10d100	3	g	1081.45	386.49	5	1
c10d50	100	b	49144.98	11267.28	10	2
c10d50	3	g	1462.43	725.22	10	1
c10d50	3	g	1462.43	649.60	5	1
c10d20	10	b	4570.63	1708.57	10	2
c10d20	10	b	4570.63	1408.57	5	2
c10d10	3	g	1623.10	867.50	10	1
c10d10	3	g	1623.10	773.64	5	1
c10d5	100	b	60310.89	26491.76	10	2
c10d5	100	b	60310.89	19349.28	5	2

Table 3. Performance of k-means and FEKM **Algorithms on Synthetic Datasets, 10 Clusters**

Data	I_{KM}	Init	T_{KM}	T_{FEKM}	SS	P
c20d200	100	b	54862.33	27388.85	10	2
c20d200	3	g	1898.65	746.51	10	1
c20d200	3	g	1898.65	584.88	5	1
c20d100	100	b	41029.15	18106.51	10	2
c20d100	3	g	1233.12	646.75	10	1
c20d100	3	g	1233.12	585.63	5	1
c20d50	3	g	1796.30	938.90	10	1
c20d50	3	g	1796.30	882.36	5	1
c20d20	10	b	5335.15	2528.11	10	2
c20d20	10	b	5335.15	2112.42	5	2
c20d10	6	g	3919.08	1814.73	10	1
c20d10	6	g	3919.08	1643.75	5	1
c20d5	6	b	4619.95	2899.76	10	1
c20d5	6	b	4619.95	2353.41	5	1

Table 4. Performance of k-means and FEKM **Algorithms on Synthetic Datasets, 20 Clusters**

Data	I_{KM}	Init	T_{KM}	T_{FEKM}	SS	P
c20d100	2	g	4393.02	2931.53	10	1
c20d100	2	g	4393.02	2204.42	5	1
c20d100	10	b	21985.62	8194.07	10	1
c20d100	10	b	21985.62	7467.53	5	1
c5d20	10	b	43254.34	10341.42	10	2
c5d20	10	b	43254.34	9632.71	5	2

Table 5. Performance of k-means and FEKM **Algorithms with 4.4 GB Synthetic Datasets**

clusters and with 5, 10, 20, 50, 100, and 200 dimensions.

We first consider the results from the 1.1 GB datasets. Tables 2, 3, and 4 show the execution times for FEKM and original k-means with 5, 10, and 20 clusters, respectively. As these tables show, FEKM requires one or at most two passes on the entire dataset. FEKM is faster by a factor between 2 and 4 in almost all cases. The relative speedup of FEKM is higher with bad initializations, where a larger number of iterations are required. We have considered sample sizes that are 5% and 10% of the entire dataset. FEKM is always faster with 5% sample size, because it reduces the execution time for the k-means, and did not require any additional passes on the entire dataset. The number of clusters or dimensions do not make a significant difference to the relative performance of the two algorithms.

Next, we consider the results from the 2 4.4 GB that we generated. Table 5 shows these results. The first set has 20 clusters and 100 dimensions. The second dataset has 5 clusters and 20 dimensions. The relative speedup of FEKM is between 2 and 4.5.

5.2. Evaluation with Real Data Set

We evaluated our algorithm with three publicly available real datasets. These datasets are KDDCup99, Corel image database, and the Reuters-21578. All these datasets are available from University of Irvine's KDD archive[1]. We preprocessed each of these datasets and generated feature vectors using standard techniques, briefly described below. We then applied k-means and the FEKM algorithm. To be able to experiment with out-of-core datasets, we increased the size of the datasets by random sampling.

---
[1]http://kdd.ics.uci.edu

It should be noticed that the running time of both the algorithms can vary depending on particular preprocessing of the real dataset. In our experiments, we used simple preprocessing techniques which can be improved upon. We used Euclidean distance function to compute distance between two points. Different distance metrics may help in obtaining better quality clusters and it can also reduce number of iterations, particularly for the datasets with categorical attributes.

The KDD Cup 99 data consists of feature vectors generated from network connection. This dataset is used for evaluating network intrusion detection techniques. The size of this dataset is about 743 MB. We enumerated different symbols of each type of categorical attributes. Each attribute is normalized by dividing with the maximum value of that attribute. After the preprocessing step, we obtained normalized continuous-valued feature vectors of 38 dimensions. The number of clusters specified in our experiments was 5. By supersampling the data, we created 5 million feature vectors for a resulting dataset size of 1.8 GB.

Corel image database has 68,040 images of different categories. We used the 32 dimensions color histogram feature

Data	I_{KM}	Init	T_{KM}	T_{FEKM}	SS	P	se
kdd99	19	g	7151	2317	10	2	4.0
kdd99	19	g	7151	2529	15	2	3.5
kdd99	19	g	7151	2136	5	2	4.2
Corel	43	g	28442	10503	10	3	2.2
Corel	43	g	28442	12603	15	3	2.15
Corel	43	g	28442	9342	5	3	3.24
Reuter	20	b	41290	10311	10	2	10.1
Reuter	20	b	41290	11204	15	2	8.6
Reuter	20	b	41290	9214	5	2	14.9

Table 6. Performance of k-means and FEKM **Algorithms, Real Datasets**

vectors of these images which is available from UCI KDD archive. This dataset is about 20 MB. We thus increased the size of the dataset by randomly selecting vectors from the dataset and created a 1.9 GB dataset containing 6,804,000 continuous-valued feature vectors. We kept the number of clusters at 16. All attribute values are normalized between zero to one.

Reuters text database is extensively used for text categorization. We created integer-valued feature vectors of 258 dimensions by counting the frequency of most frequent words in 135 different categories. Following Fayyad, Bradley and Reina [4], we kept the number of clusters at 25 for our experiments. We then increased the size of the dataset by supersampling and created 4.3 million records of 258 dimensions. The size of the resulting dataset was approximately 2 GB.

Table 6 presents the experimental results from these three real datasets. Similar to what we observed from synthetic datasets, the speedup from FEKM is between 2 and 4.5. The number of passes required by FEKM is either 2 or 3.

Clearly, FEKM produces the same cluster centers as the ones from the original k-means. One question is, how do they compare with the results from clustering the sampled data. We report some data in this regard from the real datasets. The column labeled se shows the squared difference between the final centers and the centers obtained from running k-means on sampled data. The values of all attributes were normalized to be between 0 and 1 for the real datasets. In view of this, we consider the reported squared errors to be significant. Further, it should be noted that all datasets were super-sampled, which favors sampling. Thus, we believe that using an accurate algorithm like FEKM is required for getting high-quality cluster centers.

6. Conclusions

We have presented, analyzed, and evaluated an algorithm that provably produces the same cluster centers as the k-means clustering algorithm, and typically requires one or a small number of passes on the entire dataset. This can sig-

nificantly reduce the execution times for clustering on large or disk-resident datasets, with no compromise on the quality of the results. While a number of approaches existed for approximating k-means or similar algorithms with sampling or using a small number of passes, none of these approaches could provably produce the same cluster centers as the original k-means algorithm. The basic idea in our algorithm is to use sampling to create approximate cluster centers, and use these approximate cluster centers for speeding up the computation of correct or exact cluster centers. Our experimental evaluation on a number of synthetic and real datasets have shown a speedup between 2 and 4.5.

References

[1] Mihai Badoiu, Sariel Har-Pelad, and Piotr Indyk. Approximate clustering via core-sets. In *Proceedings of the Annual ACM Symposium on Theory of Computing*, 2002.

[2] Pavel Berkhin. Survey of clustering data mining techniques. Technical report, Accrue Software, 2002.

[3] Leon Bottou and Yoshua Bengio. Convergence properties of the K-means algorithms. In G. Tesauro, D. Touretzky, and T. Leen, editors, *Advances in Neural Information Processing Systems*, volume 7, pages 585–592. The MIT Press, 1995.

[4] P. S. Bradley, Usama Fayyad, and Cory Reina. Scaling clustering algorithms to large databases. In *Proceedings of the Fourth International Conference on Knowledge Discovery and Data Mining*, August 1998.

[5] Moses Charikar, Liadan O'Callaghan, and Rina Panigrahi. Better streaming algorithms for clustering problems. In *Proceedings of the 35th Annual ACM Symposium on Theory of Computing*, 2003.

[6] Moses Cherikar, Chandra Chekuri, Tomas Feder, and Rajeev Motwani. Incremental clustering and dynamic information retrieval. In *Proceedings of Symposium of Theory of Computing*, 1997.

[7] Pedro Domingos and Geoff Hulten. A general method for scaling up machine learning algorithms and its application to clustering. In *Proceedings of the Eighteenth International Conference on Machine Learning*, 2001.

[8] Fredrik Farnstrom, James Lewis, and Charles Elkan. Scalability for clustering algorithms revisited. *SIGKDD Explorations*, 2(1):51–57, 2000.

[9] Joydeep Ghosh. Scalable clustering methods for data mining. In Nong Ye, editor, *Handbook of Data Mining*, chapter 10, pages 247–277. Lawrence Ealbaum Assoc, 2003.

[10] Sudipto Guha, Adam Meyerson, Nina Mishra, Rajeev Motwani, and Liadan O'Callaghan. Clustering data streams: Theory and practice. *IEEE Transactions on Knowledge and Data Engineering*, 15(3):515–528, May 2003.

[11] Jiawei Han and Micheline Kamber. *Data Mining: Concepts and Techniques*. Morgan Kaufmann Publishers, 2000.

[12] J. A. Hartigan and M. A. Wong. A k-means clustering algorithm. *Applied Statistics*, (28):100–108, 1979.

[13] Anil K. Jain and Richard C. Dubes. *Algorithms for Clustering Data*. Prentice-Hall International, 1988.

[14] J. MacQueen. Some methods for classification and analysis of multivariate observations. In *Proceedings of the Fifth Berkeley Symposium on Mathematical Statistics and Probability*, volume 1, pages 281–297, 1967.

[15] Silvia Nittel, Kelvin T. Leung, and Amy Braverman. Scaling clustering algorithms for massive data sets using data stream. In Umeshwar Dayal, Krithi Ramamritham, and T. M. Vijayaraman, editors, *Proceedings of the 19th International Conference on Data Engineering, March 5-8, 2003, Bangalore, India*. IEEE Computer Society, 2003.

[16] Liadan OCallaghan, Nina Mishra, Adam Meyerson, Sudipto Guha, and Rajeev Motwani. Streaming-data algorithms for high-quality clustering. In *Proceedings of International Conference of Data Engineering*, 2002.

[17] Dan Pelleg and Andrew Moore. Accelerating exact k-means algorithms with geometric reasoning. In *In Proceedings of Fifth International Conference of Knowledge Discovery and Data Mining*, pages 277–281, 1999.

Mining Frequent Itemsets from Secondary Memory

Gösta Grahne and Jianfei Zhu
Concordia University, Montreal, Canada
{grahne, j_zhu}@cs.concordia.ca

Abstract

Mining frequent itemsets is at the core of mining association rules, and is by now quite well understood algorithmically for main memory databases. In this paper, we investigate approaches to mining frequent itemsets when the database or the data structures used in the mining are too large to fit in main memory. Experimental results show that our techniques reduce the required disk accesses by orders of magnitude, and enable truly scalable data mining.

1 Introduction

Mining frequent itemsets is a fundamental problem for mining association rules [2, 3, 5]. It also plays an important role in many other data mining tasks such as sequential patterns, episodes, multi-dimensional patterns and so on [4, 9, 8]. In addition, frequent itemsets are one of the key abstractions in data mining.

The description of the problem is as follows. Let $I = \{i_1, i_2, \ldots, i_n\}$, be a set of *items*. Items will sometimes also be denoted by $a, b, c, \ldots$. An *I-transaction* τ is a subset of I. An *I*-transactional *database* $\mathcal{D}$ is a finite bag of *I*-transactions. The *support* of an itemset $S \subseteq I$ is the proportion of transactions in $\mathcal{D}$ that contain S. The task of mining frequent itemsets is to find all S such that the support of S is greater than some given *minimum support* ξ, where ξ either is a fraction in $[0, 1]$, or an absolute count.

Most of the algorithms, such as Apriori [3], DepthProject [1], and dEclat [12] work well when the main memory is big enough to fit the whole database or/and the data structures (candidate sets, FP-trees, etc). When a database is very large or when the minimum support is very low, either the data structures used by the algorithms may not be accommodated in main memory, or the algorithms spend too much time on multiple passes over the database. In the *First IEEE ICDM Workshop on Frequent Itemset Mining Implementations, FIMI '03* [5], many well known algorithms were implemented and independently tested. The results show that "*none* of the algorithms is able to gracefully scale-up to very large datasets, with millions of transactions" [5].

At the same time very large databases do exist in real life. In a medium sized business or in a company big as Walmart, it's very easy to collect a few gigabytes of data. Terabytes of raw data are ubiquitously being recorded in commerce, science and government. The question of how to handle these databases is still one of the most difficult problems in data mining.

In this paper we consider the problem of mining frequent itemsets from *very* large databases. We adopt a divide-and-conquer approach. First we give three algorithms, the general divide-and-conquer algorithm, then an algorithm using basic projection (division), and an algorithm using aggressive projection. We also analyze the disk I/O's required by these algorithms.

In a detailed divide-and-conquer algorithm, called *Diskmine*, we use the highly efficient *FPgrowth** method [6] to mine frequent itemsets from an FP-tree for the main memory part of data mining. We describe several novel techniques useful in mining frequent itemsets from disks, such as the *FP-array* technique, and the *item-grouping* technique.

We also present experimental results that demonstrate the fact that our *Diskmine*-algorithm can outperform previous algorithms by orders of magnitude, and scales up to terabytes of data.

2 Mining from disk

How should one go about when mining frequent itemsets from very large databases residing in a secondary memory storage, such as disks? Here "very large" means that the data structures constructed from the database for mining frequent itemsets can not fit in the available main memory.

One approach is *sampling* [11]. Unfortunately, the results of sampling are probabilistic, some critical frequent itemsets could be missing. Besides the sampling, there are basically two strategies for mining frequent itemsets, the datastructures approach, and the divide-and-conquer approach.

The *datastructures* approach consists of reading the database buffer by buffer, and generate datastructures (i.e. candidate sets or FP-trees). Since the datastructure do not fit into main memory, additional disk I/O's are required. The number of passes and disk I/O's required by the approach depend on the algorithm and its datastructures. For examples, if the algorithm is Apriori [3] using a hash-tree for candidate itemsets, disk based hash-trees have to be used. If the algorithm is FP-growth method, as suggested in [7], FP-trees have to be written to the disk. Then the number of disk I/O's for the trees depends on the size of the trees on disk. Note that the size of the trees could be the same as or even bigger than the size of the database.

The basic strategy for the *divide-and-conquer* approach is shown in the procedure *diskmine*. In the approach, $|\mathcal{D}|$ denotes the size of the data structures used by the mining algorithm, and M is the size of available main memory. Function *mainmine* is called if candidate frequent itemsets (not necessary all) can be mined without writing the data structures used by a mining algorithm to disks. In *diskmine*, a very large database is decomposed into a number of smaller databases. If a "small" database is still too large, i.e, the data structures are still too big to fit in main memory, the decomposition is recursively continued until the data structures fit in main memory. After all small databases are processed, all candidate frequent itemsets are combined in some way (obviously depending on the way the decomposition was done) to get all frequent itemsets for the original database.

Procedure *diskmine*$(\mathcal{D}, M)$
if $|\mathcal{D}| \leq M$ **then return** *mainmine*$(\mathcal{D})$
else decompose $\mathcal{D}$ into $\mathcal{D}_1, \ldots \mathcal{D}_k$.
    return *combine diskmine*$(\mathcal{D}_1, M)$,
                     .... ,
                diskmine$(\mathcal{D}_k, M)$.

The efficiency of *diskmine* depends on the method used for mining frequent itemsets in main memory and on the number of disk I/O's needed in the decomposition and combination phases. Sometimes the disk I/O is the main factor. Since the decomposition step involves I/O, ideally the number of recursive calls should be kept small. The faster we can obtain small decomposed databases, the fewer recursive call we will need. On the other hand, if a decomposition cuts down the size of the projected databases drastically, the trade-off might be that the combination step becomes more complicated and might involve heavy disk I/O.

In the following we discuss two decomposition strategies, namely decomposition by partition, and decomposition by projection.

Partitioning [10] is an approach in which a large database is decomposed into cells of small non-overlapping databases. The cell-size is chosen so that all frequent itemsets in a cell can be mined without having to store any data structures in secondary memory. However, since a cell only contains partial frequency information of the original database, all frequent itemsets from the cell are local to that cell of the partition, and could only be *candidate* frequent itemsets for the whole database. Thus the candidate frequent itemsets mined from a cell have to be verified later to filter out false hits. Consequently, those candidate sets have to be written to disk in order to leave space for

processing the next cell of the partition. After generating candidate frequent itemsets from all cells, another database scan is needed to filter out all infrequent itemsets. The partition approach therefore needs only two passes over the database, but writing and reading candidate frequent itemsets will involve a significant number of disk I/O's, depending on the size of the set of candidate frequent itemsets.

We can conclude that the partition approach to decomposition keeps the recursive levels down to one, but the penalty is that the combination phase becomes expensive.

To get an easier combination phase, we adopt another decomposition strategy, which we call *projection*. This approach projects the original database on several databases, each determined by one or more frequent item(s). One advantage of this approach is that any frequent itemset mined from a projected database is a frequent itemset in the original database. To get *all* frequent itemsets, we only need to take the union of the frequent itemsets discovered in the small projected databases. The biggest problem of the projection approach is that the total size of the projected databases could be too large, and there could be too many disk I/O's for the projected databases. Thus, there is a tradeoff between the easier combination phase and possible too many disk I/O's.

To analyze the recurrence and required disk I/O's of the general divide-and-conquer algorithm when the decomposition strategy is projection, let us suppose that:

- The original database size is D bytes.
- The data structure is an FP-tree.
- The FP-tree constructed from original database $\mathcal{D}$ is T, and its size is $|T|$ bytes.
- If a conditional FP-tree T' is constructed from an FP-tree T, then $|T'| \leq c \cdot |T|$, for some constant $c < 1$.
- The main memory mining method is the *FP-growth* method [7]. Two database scans are needed for constructing an FP-tree from a database.
- The block size is B bytes.
- The main memory available is M bytes.

In the first line of the algorithm *diskmine*, if T can not fit in memory, then projected databases will be generated. We assumed that the size of the FP-tree for a projected database is $c \cdot |T|$. If $c \cdot |T| \leq M$, function *mainmine* can be called for the projected database, otherwise, the decomposition goes on. At pass m, the size of the FP-tree constructed from a projected database is $c^m \cdot |T|$. Thus, the number of passes needed by the divide-and-conquer projection algorithm is $1 + \lceil \log_c M/T \rceil$. Based on our experience and the analysis in [7], we can say that for all practical purposes the number of passes will be at most two. For example, Let $D = 100$ gigabytes, $T = 10$ gigabytes, $M = 1$ gigabytes, and $c = 10\%$. Then the number of passes is $1 + \lceil \log_{0.1} 2^{30}/(10 \times 2^{30}) \rceil = 2$. In five passes we can handle databases up to 100 Terabytes. Namely, we get $1 + \lceil \log_{0.1} 2^{30}/(10 \times 2^{40}) \rceil = 5$.

Assume that there are two passes, and that the sum of the sizes of all projected databases is D'. After the first database scan for finding all frequent single items, the second database scan attempts to construct an FP-tree from the database. If the main memory is not big enough, the scan will be aborted. We assume on average half of $\mathcal{D}$ is read at this stage, which means $1/2 \cdot D/B$ disk I/O's. The third scan is for decomposition. Totally, there are $5/2 \times D/B$ disk I/O's. The projected databases have to be written to the disks first, then later each scanned twice for building the FP-tree. This step needs $3 \times D'/B$ disk I/O's. Thus, the total disk number of disk I/O's for the general divide-and-conquer projection algorithm is at least

$$5/2 \cdot D/B + 3 \cdot D'/B. \qquad (1)$$

Obviously, the smaller D', the better the performance.

One of the simplest projection strategies is to project the database on each frequent item, which we call *basic projection*. First we need some formal definitions.

Definition 1 Let I be a set of items. By I^* we will denote *strings* over I, such that each symbol occurs at most once in the string. If α, β are strings, then $\alpha.\beta$ denotes the concatenation of the string α with the string β.

Let $\mathcal{D}$ be an I-database. Then $freqstring(\mathcal{D})$ is the string over I, such that each frequent item in $\mathcal{D}$ occurs in it exactly once, and the items are in decreasing order of frequency in $\mathcal{D}$. ∎

As an example, consider the $\{a, b, c, d, e\}$-database $\mathcal{D} = \{\{a, c, d\}, \{b, c, d, e\}, \{a, b\}, \{a, c\}\}$. If the minimum support is 50%, then $freqstring(\mathcal{D}) = acbd$.

Definition 2 Let $\mathcal{D}$ be an I-database, and let $freqstring(\mathcal{D}) = i_1 i_2 \cdots i_k$. For $j \in \{1, \ldots, k\}$ we define $\mathcal{D}_{i_j} = \{\tau \cap \{i_1, \ldots, i_j\} : i_j \in \tau, \tau \in \mathcal{D}\}$.

Let $\alpha \in I^*$. We define $\mathcal{D}_\alpha$ inductively: $\mathcal{D}_\epsilon = \mathcal{D}$, and let $freqstring(\mathcal{D}_\alpha) = i_1 i_2 \cdots i_k$. Then, for $j \in \{1, \ldots, k\}$, $\mathcal{D}_{\alpha.i_j} = \{\tau \cap \{i_1, \ldots, i_j\} : i_j \in \tau, \tau \in \mathcal{D}_\alpha\}$. ∎

Obviously, $\mathcal{D}_{\alpha.i_j}$ is an $\{i_1, \ldots, i_j\}$-database. The decomposition of $\mathcal{D}_\alpha$ into $\mathcal{D}_{\alpha.i_1}, \ldots, \mathcal{D}_{\alpha.i_k}$ is called the *basic projection*.

To illustrate the basic projection, let's consider the above example, starting from the least frequent item in the *freqstring*, we obtain $\mathcal{D}_d = \{\{a, c, d\}, \{b, c, d\}\}$, $\mathcal{D}_b = \{\{c, b\}, \{a, b\}\}$, $\mathcal{D}_c = \{\{a, c\}, \{c\}, \{a, c\}\}$, and $\mathcal{D}_a = \{\{a\}, \{a\}, \{a\}\}$.

Definition 3 Let $\alpha \in I^*$, $i_j \in I$, and let $\mathcal{D}_{\alpha.i_j}$ be an I-database. Then $freqsets(\xi, \mathcal{D}_{\alpha.i_j})$ denotes the subsets of I that contain i_j and are frequent in $\mathcal{D}_{\alpha.i_j}$ when the minimum support is ξ. Usually, we shall abstract ξ away, and write just $freqsets(\mathcal{D}_{\alpha.i_j})$. ∎

Lemma 1 Let $\mathcal{D}_\alpha$ be an I-database, and $freqstring(\mathcal{D}_\alpha) = i_1 i_2 \cdots i_k$. Then

$$freqsets(\mathcal{D}_\alpha) = \bigcup_{j \in \{1, \ldots, k\}} freqsets(\mathcal{D}_{\alpha.i_j}) \qquad ∎$$

In the previous example, for $\mathcal{D}_d$, $freqsets(\mathcal{D}_d) = \{\{d\}, \{c, d\}\}$. Note though $\{c\}$ is also frequent in $\mathcal{D}_d$, it is not listed since it does not contain d. It will be listed in $freqsets(\mathcal{D}_c)$. Similarly, $freqsets(\mathcal{D}_b) = \{\{b\}\}$, $freqsets(\mathcal{D}_c) = \{\{c\}, \{a, c\}\}$ and $freqsets(\mathcal{D}_a) = \{\{a\}\}$. We also can notice that $\mathcal{D}_d$ and $\mathcal{D}_c$ are not that much smaller than the original database. The upside is though that the set of all frequent itemsets in $\mathcal{D}$ now simply is the union of $freqsets(\mathcal{D}_d)$, $freqsets(\mathcal{D}_b)$, $freqsets(\mathcal{D}_c)$ and $freqsets(\mathcal{D}_d)$. This means that the combination phase is a simple union.

The following procedure *basicdiskmine* gives a divide-and-conquer algorithm that uses basic projection. A transaction τ in $\mathcal{D}_\alpha$ will be partly inserted into $\mathcal{D}_{\alpha.i_j}$ if and only if τ contains i_j. The parallel projection algorithm introduced in [7] is an algorithm of this kind.

Procedure *basicdiskmine*$(\mathcal{D}_\alpha, M)$
if $|\mathcal{D}_\alpha| \leq M$ **then return** *mainmine*$(\mathcal{D}_\alpha)$
else let $freqstring(\mathcal{D}_\alpha) = i_1 i_2 \cdots i_n$,
    return *basicdiskmine*$(\mathcal{D}_{\alpha.i_1}, M) \cup$
        $\cdots \cup$
      basicdiskmine$(\mathcal{D}_{\alpha.i_n}, M)$.

Let's analyze the disk I/O's of the algorithm *basicdiskmine*. As before, we assume that there are two passes, that the data structure is an FP-tree, and that the main memory mining method is *FP-growth*. If in $\mathcal{D}_\epsilon$, each transaction contains on the average n frequent items, each transaction will be written to n projected databases. Thus the total length of the associated transactions in the projected databases is $n + (n-1) + \cdots + 1 = n(n+1)/2$, the total size of all projected databases is $(n+1)/2 \cdot D \approx n/2 \cdot D$.

Still there are two full database scans and a incomplete database scan for $\mathcal{D}_\epsilon$, as explained for formula (1). The number of total disk I/O's is $5/2 \cdot D/B$. The projected databases have to be written to the disks first, then later scanned twice each for building an FP-tree. This step needs at least $3 \cdot n/2 \times D/B$. Thus, the total disk I/O's for the divide-and-conquer algorithm with basic projection is

$$5/2 \cdot D/B + n \cdot 3/2 \cdot D/B \qquad (2)$$

The recurrence structure of *basicdiskmine* is shown in Figure 1. The reader should ignore nodes in the shaded area at this point, they represent processing in main memory.

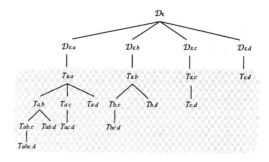

Figure 1. Recurrence of Basic Projection

In a typical application n, the average number of frequent items could be hundreds, or thousands. It therefore makes sense to devise a smarter projection strategy. Before we go further, we introduce some definitions and a lemma.

Definition 4 Let $\mathcal{D}_\alpha$ be an I-database, and let $freqstring(\mathcal{D}_\alpha) = \beta_1.\beta_2.\cdots.\beta_k$, where each β_j is a string in I^*. We call $\beta_1.\beta_2.\cdots.\beta_k$ a *grouping* of $freqstring(\mathcal{D}_\alpha)$. Let $\beta_j = i_{j_1}.\cdots.i_{j_m}$, for $j \in \{1, \ldots, k\}$. We now define $\mathcal{D}_{\alpha.\beta_j} =$

$$\{\tau \cap \{i_{1_1}, \ldots, i_{j_m}\}, \tau \in \mathcal{D}_\alpha, \tau \cap \{i_{j_1}, \ldots, i_{j_m}\} \neq \emptyset\}.$$

In $\mathcal{D}_{\alpha.\beta_j}$, items in β_j are called *master items*, items in $\beta_1, \ldots, \beta_{j-1}$ are called *slave items*. ∎

For the previous example, $freqstring(\mathcal{D}_\alpha) = acbd$, $\beta_1 = ac$, $\beta_2 = bd$ gives the grouping $ac.bd$ of $acbd$. Now $\mathcal{D}_{bd} = \{\{a, c, d\}, \{b, c, d\}, \{a, b\}\}$ and $\mathcal{D}_{ac} = \{\{a, c\}, \{c\}, \{a\}, \{a, c\}\}$.

Definition 5 Let $\{\alpha, \beta\} \subset I^*$, and let $\mathcal{D}_{\alpha.\beta}$ be an I-database. Then $freqsets(\mathcal{D}_{\alpha.\beta})$ denotes the subsets of I that contain at least one item in β and are frequent in $\mathcal{D}_{\alpha.\beta}$. ∎

Lemma 2 Let $\alpha \in I^*$, $\mathcal{D}_\alpha$ be an I-database, and $freqstring(\mathcal{D}_\alpha) = \beta_1\beta_2 \cdots \beta_k$. Then

$$freqsets(\mathcal{D}_\alpha) = \bigcup_{j \in \{1, \ldots, k\}} freqsets(\mathcal{D}_{\alpha.\beta_j}) \qquad ∎$$

By following the above example, we can get $freqsets(\mathcal{D}_{bd}) = \{\{d\}, \{b\}, \{c, d\}\}$, and $freqsets(\mathcal{D}_{ac}) = \{\{c\}, \{a\}, \{a, c\}\}$.

Based on Lemma 2, we can obtain a more aggressive divide-and-conquer algorithm for mining from disks. The following shows the algorithm *aggressivediskmine*. Here, $freqstring(\mathcal{D}_\alpha)$ is decomposed into several substrings β_j, each of which could have more than one item. Each substring corresponds to a projected database. A transaction τ in $\mathcal{D}_\alpha$ will be partly inserted into $\mathcal{D}_{\alpha.\beta_j}$ if and only if τ contains at least one item a in β_j. Since there will be fewer projected databases, there will be fewer disk I/O's. Compared with the algorithm *basicdiskmine*, we can expect that a large amount of disk I/O will be saved by the algorithm *aggressivediskmine*.

Procedure *aggressivediskmine*$(\mathcal{D}_\alpha, M)$

    if $|\mathcal{D}_\alpha| \leq M$ **then return** *mainmine*($\mathcal{D}_\alpha$)
    else let $freqstring(\mathcal{D}_\alpha) = \beta_1\beta_2 \cdots \beta_k$,
        return *aggressivediskmine*$(\mathcal{D}_{\alpha.\beta_1}, M) \cup$
                 $\ldots \cup$
        aggressivediskmine$(\mathcal{D}_{\alpha.\beta_k}, M)$.

Let's analyze the recurrence and disk I/O's of the aggressive divide-and-conquer algorithm. The number of passes needed is still $1 + \lceil \log_c M/T \rceil \approx 2$, since grouping items does not change the size of an FP-tree for a projected

database. However, for disk I/O, suppose in $\mathcal{D}_\epsilon$, each transaction contains on average n frequent items, and that we can group them into k groups of equal size. Then the n items will be written to the projected databases with total length $n/k + 2 \cdot n/k + \ldots + k \cdot n/k = (k+1)/2 \cdot n$. Total size of all projected databases is $(k+1)/2 \cdot D \approx k/2 \cdot D$. The total disk I/O's for the aggressive divide-and-conquer algorithm is then

$$5/2 \cdot D/B + k \cdot 3/2 \cdot D/B \qquad (3)$$

The recurrence structure of algorithm *aggressivediskmine* is shown in Figure 2. Compared to Figure 1, we can see that the part of the tree that corresponds to decomposition (the nonshaded part) is much smaller in Figure 2. Although the example is very small, it exhibits the general structure of the two trees.

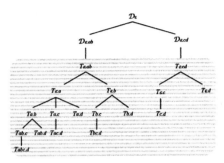

Figure 2. Recurrence of Aggressive Projection

If $k \ll n$, we can expect the aggressive divide-and-conquer algorithm will significantly outperform the basic one.

3 Algorithm Diskmine

The algorithm *Diskmine* is shown below. In the algorithm, $\mathcal{D}_\alpha$ is the original database or a projected database, and M is the maximal size of main memory that can be used by *Diskmine*.

Procedure *Diskmine*$(\mathcal{D}_\alpha, M)$

scan $\mathcal{D}_\alpha$ and compute *freqstring*$(\mathcal{D}_\alpha)$
call *trialmainmine*$(\mathcal{D}_\alpha, M)$
if *trialmainmine*$(\mathcal{D}_\alpha, M)$ aborted **then**
    compute a grouping $\beta_1\beta_2 \cdots \beta_k$ of *freqstring*$(\mathcal{D}_\alpha)$
    Decompose $\mathcal{D}_\alpha$ into $\mathcal{D}_{\alpha.\beta_1}, \ldots, \mathcal{D}_{\alpha.\beta_k}$
    for j = 1 **to** k **do begin**
        if β_j is a singleton **then** *Diskmine*$(\mathcal{D}_{\alpha.\beta_j}, M)$
        else *mainmine*$(\mathcal{D}_{\alpha.\beta_j})$
    end
else return *freqsets*$(\mathcal{D}_\alpha)$

Diskmine uses the FP-tree [7] as data structure and *FP-growth** [6] as main memory mining algorithm. Since the FP-tree encodes all frequency information of the database, we can shift into main memory mining as soon as the FP-tree fits into main memory.

Since an FP-tree usually is a significant compression of the database, our *Diskmine* algorithm begins optimistically, by calling *trialmainmine*, which starts scanning the database and constructing the FP-tree. If the tree can be successfully completed and stored in main memory, we have reached the bottom level of the recursion, and can obtain the frequent itemsets of the database by running *FP-growth** on the FP-tree in main memory.

Procedure *trialmainmine*($\mathcal{D}_\alpha, M$)
start scanning $\mathcal{D}_\alpha$ and building the FP-tree
$\quad T_\alpha$ in main memory.
if $|T_\alpha|$ exceeds M **then return** the incomplete T_α
else call *FPgrowth**(T_α) and **return** *freqsets*($\mathcal{D}_\alpha$).

If, at any time during *trialmainmine* we run out of main memory, we abort and return the partially constructed FP-tree, and a pointer to where we stopped scanning the database. We then resume processing *Diskmine*($\mathcal{D}_\alpha, M$) by computing a grouping $\beta_1, \ldots, \beta_k$ of *freqstring*($\mathcal{D}_\alpha$), and then decomposing $\mathcal{D}_\alpha$ into $\mathcal{D}_{\alpha.\beta_1}, \ldots, \mathcal{D}_{\alpha.\beta_k}$. We recursively process each decomposed database $\mathcal{D}_{\alpha.\beta_j}$. During the first level of the recursion, some groups β_j will consist of a single item only. If β_j is a singleton, we call *Diskmine*, otherwise we call *mainmine* directly, since we put several items in a group only when we estimate that the corresponding FP-tree will fit into main memory.

In computing the grouping $\beta_1, \ldots, \beta_k$ we assume that transactions in a very large database are evenly distributed, i.e., if the size of the FP-tree is n for $p\%$ of the database, then the size of the FP-tree for whole database is $n/p \cdot 100$. Most of the time, this gives an overestimation, since an FP-tree increases fast only at the beginning stage, when items are encountered for the first time and inserted into the tree. In the later stages, the changes to the FP-tree will be mostly counter updates.

Procedure *mainmine*($\mathcal{D}_{\alpha.\beta}$)
build a modified FP-tree $T_{\alpha.\beta}$ for $\mathcal{D}_{\alpha.\beta}$
for each i in β **do begin**
$\quad$ construct the FP-tree $T_{\alpha.i}$ for $\mathcal{D}_{\alpha.i}$ from $T_{\alpha.\beta}$
$\quad$ call *FPgrowth**($T_{\alpha.i}$) and **return** *freqsets*($\mathcal{D}_{\alpha.i}$).
end

In *basicdiskmine*, since there is only one master item in each projected database (for $\mathcal{D}_\epsilon$, no master item at all), an FP-tree can be constructed without considering the master item. In procedure *mainmine*, since $\mathcal{D}_{\alpha.\beta}$ is for multiple master items, the FP-tree constructed from $\mathcal{D}_{\alpha.\beta}$ has to contain those master items. However, the item order is a problem for the FP-tree, because we only want to mine all frequent itemsets that contain master items. To solve this problem, we simply use the item order in the partial FP-tree returned by the aborted *trialmainmine*($\mathcal{D}_\alpha$). This is what we mean by a "modified FP-tree" on the first line in the algorithm *mainmine*.

The entire recurrence structure of *Diskmine* can be seen in Figure 2. Compared to the basic projection in Figure 1

we see that since the aggressive projection uses main memory more effective, and that the decomposition phase is shorter, resulting in fewer disk I/O's.

In Figure 2, the shaded area shows the recursive structure of FP-growth*. Comparing with the shaded area in Figure 1 which shows the recursive structure of the FP-growth method, we can see that the main difference is the extra shaded level in Figure 2. This level is for the FP-trees of groups. For each group, since the total size of all FP-trees for its master items may be greater than the size of main memory, a "modified FP-tree" is constructed. This FP-tree will fit in main memory. From the FP-tree, smaller FP-trees can be constructed one by one, as shown in both figures. As an example, in Figure 1, *basicdiskmine* enters the main memory phase for instance for the conditional database $\mathcal{D}_{\epsilon.a}$. Then FP-growth first constructs the FP-tree $T_{\epsilon.a}$ from $\mathcal{D}_{\epsilon.a}$ (in Figure 2, $T_{\epsilon.a}$ is constructed from $T_{\epsilon.ab}$). The tree rooted at $T_{\epsilon.a}$ shows the recursive structure of FP-growth, assuming for simplicity that the relative frequency remains the same in all conditional pattern bases.

Theorem 1 *Diskmine*($\mathcal{D}$) returns *freqsets*($\mathcal{D}$) ∎.

Applying the FP-array Technique. In *Diskmine*, the Frequent Pairs Array (FP-array) technique developed for FP-growth* [6] is also applied to save one tree traversal for each recursive call. Furthermore, when projected databases are generated, the FP-array technique can save a great number of disk I/O's.

Recall that in *trialmainmine*, if an FP-tree can not be accommodated in main memory, the construction stops. Suppose now we decided to stop scanning the database. Then later, after generating all projected databases, two database scans are required to construct an FP-tree from a projected database. To save one scan, in *Diskmine* we calculate an FP-array for each FP-tree. When constructing the FP-tree from $\mathcal{D}_\alpha$, if it is found that the tree can not fit in main memory, the construction of the FP-tree T_α stops, but the scan of the database $\mathcal{D}_\alpha$ continues so that we finish filling the cells of the array A_α. Later, only one database scan is needed to construct an FP-tree from a projected database because of the existence of the array A_α.

Grouping items. In *Diskmine*, the fourth line computes a grouping $\beta_1\beta_2 \cdots \beta_k$ of *freqstring*($\mathcal{D}_\alpha$). For each β, a new projected database $\mathcal{D}_{\alpha.\beta}$ will be computed from $\mathcal{D}_\alpha$, then written to disk and read from disk later. Therefore, the more groups, the more disk I/O's. In other words, there should be as many items in each β as possible. To group items, two questions have to be answered.

1. If β currently only has one item i_j, after projection, is the main memory big enough for accommodating $T_{\alpha.i_j}$ constructed from $\mathcal{D}_{\alpha.i_j}$ and running the *FP-growth** method on $T_{\alpha.i_j}$?

2. If more items are put in β, after projection, is the main memory big enough for accommodating $T_{\alpha.\beta}$ constructed from $\mathcal{D}_{\alpha.\beta}$ and running *FPgrowth** on $T_{\alpha.\beta}$ only for items in β?

To answer the questions, algorithm *Diskmine* collects statistics on the partial FP-tree T_α and the rest of database $\mathcal{D}_\alpha$.

For the first question, for each item i_j, by counting the number of nodes in the FP-tree $T_{\alpha.i_j}$ constructed from the partial FP-tree T_α, we can use the number to estimate the size of FP-tree $T_{\alpha.i_j}$ constructed from $\mathcal{D}_\alpha$. We write the number as $\mu[j](T_\alpha)$ for each i_j, and suppose the number of transactions in $\mathcal{D}_\alpha$ is $t(\mathcal{D}_\alpha)$ and the number of transactions used for constructing the partial FP-tree T_α is $t(T_\alpha)$. By the assumption that the transactions in $\mathcal{D}_\alpha$ are evenly distributed and that the partial T_α represents the whole FP-tree for $\mathcal{D}_\alpha$, the estimated size of FP-tree $T_{\alpha.i_j}$ is $\mu[j](T_\alpha) \cdot t(\mathcal{D}_\alpha)/t(T_\alpha)$.

Before answering the second question, we introduce the *cut point* from which the first group can be easily found.

Finding the cut point. Notice that in *FPgrowth**, when mining frequent itemsets for i_k, all frequency information about $i_{k+1}, \ldots, i_n$ is useless. Thus, though a complete FP-tree T_α constructed from $\mathcal{D}_\alpha$ could not fit in main memory, we can find many k's such that the trimmed FP-tree containing only nodes for items $i_k, \ldots, i_1$ will fit into main memory. All frequent itemsets for $i_k, \ldots, i_1$ can be then mined from one trimmed tree. We call the biggest of such k's the *cut point*. At this point, main memory is big enough for storing the FP-tree containing only $i_k, \ldots, i_1$, and there is also enough main memory for running *FPgrowth** on the tree. Obviously, if the cut point k can be found, items $i_k, \ldots, i_1$ can be grouped together. Only one projected database is needed for $i_k, \ldots, i_1$.

There are two ways to estimate the cut point. One way is to get cut point from the value of $t(\mathcal{D}_\alpha)$ and $t(T_\alpha)$. Figure 3 illustrates the intuition behind the cut point. In the figure, $l = t(T_\alpha)$, and $m = t(\mathcal{D}_\alpha)$. Since the partial FP-tree for $t(T_\alpha)$ of $t(\mathcal{D}_\alpha)$ transactions can be accommodate in main memory, we can expect that the FP-tree containing $i_k, \ldots, i_1$, where $k = \lfloor n \cdot t(T_\alpha)/t(\mathcal{D}_\alpha) \rfloor$, also will fit in main memory.

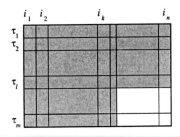

Figure 3. Cut Point

The above method works well for many databases, especially for those databases whose corresponding FP-trees have plenty of sharing of prefixes for items from i_1 to the cut point. However, if the FP-tree constructed from a database does not share prefixes that much, the estimation could fail, since now the FP-tree for items from i_1 to the cut point could be too big. Thus, we have to consider

another method. Let $\nu[j](T_\alpha)$ be the size of the FP-tree after the partial FP-tree T_α is trimmed and only contains items $i_1, \ldots, i_j$. Based on $\nu[j](T_\alpha)$ the number of nodes in the complete FP-tree for item i_j can be estimated as $\nu[j](T_\alpha) \cdot t(\mathcal{D}_\alpha)/t(T_\alpha)$. Now, suppose $\nu(T_\alpha)$ is the number of nodes in T_α, finding the cut point becomes finding the biggest k such that $\nu[k](T_\alpha) \cdot t(\mathcal{D}_\alpha)/t(T_\alpha) \leq \nu(T_\alpha)$, and $\nu[k+1](T_\alpha) \cdot t(\mathcal{D}_\alpha)/t(T_\alpha) > \nu(T_\alpha)$.

Sometimes the above estimation only guarantees that the main memory is big enough for the FP-tree which contains all items between i_1 and the cut point, while it does not guarantee that the descendant trees from that FP-tree can fit in main memory. This is because the estimation does not consider the size of descendant trees correctly. Actually, from $\mu[j](T_\alpha)$ we can get a more accurate estimation of the size of the biggest descendant tree. To find the cut point, we need to find the biggest k, such that $(\nu[k](T_\alpha) + \mu[j](T_\alpha)) \cdot t(\mathcal{D}_\alpha)/t(T_\alpha) \leq \nu(T_\alpha)$, and $(\nu[k+1](T_\alpha) + \mu[m](T_\alpha)) > \nu(T_\alpha)$, where $j \leq k$, $\mu[j](T_\alpha) = max_{j \in \{1,\ldots,k\}}\mu[j](T_\alpha)$, and $m \leq k+1$, $\mu[m](T_\alpha) = max_{m \in \{1,\ldots,k+1\}}\mu[m](T_\alpha)$.

Grouping the rest of the items. Now we answer the second question, how to put more items into a group? Here we still need $\mu[j](T_\alpha)$. Starting with $\mu[cutpoint + 1](T_\alpha)$, we test if $\mu[cutpoint + 1](T_\alpha) \cdot t(\mathcal{D}_\alpha)/t(T_\alpha) > \nu(T_\alpha)$. If not, we put next item cutpoint+2 into the group, and test if $(\mu[cutpoint + 1](T_\alpha) + \mu[cutpoint + 2](T_\alpha)) \cdot t(\mathcal{D}_\alpha)/t(T_\alpha) > \nu(T_\alpha)$. We repeatedly put next item in $freqstring(\mathcal{D})$ into the group until we reach an item i_j, such that

$$\sum_{m=cutpoint+1}^{j} \mu[m](T_\alpha) \cdot t(\mathcal{D}_\alpha)/t(T_\alpha) > \nu(T_\alpha).$$

Then starting from i_j, we put items into next group, until all items find its group.

Why can we put items $i_j, \ldots, i_k$ together into group β? This is because even if we construct $T_{\alpha.i_j}, \ldots, T_{\alpha.i_k}$ from the projected databases $\mathcal{D}_{\alpha.i_j}, \ldots, \mathcal{D}_{\alpha.i_k}$ and put all of them into main memory, the main memory is big enough according to the grouping condition. At this stage, $T_{\alpha.i_j}, \ldots, T_{\alpha.i_k}$ all can be constructed by scanning $\mathcal{D}_\alpha$ once. Then we mine frequent itemsets from the FP-trees. However, we can do better. Obviously $T_{\alpha.i_j}, \ldots, T_{\alpha.i_k}$ overlap a lot, and the total size of the trees is definitely greater than the size of $T_{\alpha.\beta}$. It also means that we can put more items into each β, only if the size of $T_{\alpha.\beta}$ is estimated to fit in main memory. To estimate the size of $T_{\alpha.\beta}$, part of T_α has to be traversed by following the links for the master items in T_α.

The disk I/O's. Let's re-count the disk I/O's used in *Diskmine*. The first scan is still for obtaining all frequent items in $\mathcal{D}_\epsilon$, and it needs D/B disk I/O's. In the second scan we construct a partial FP-tree T_ϵ, then continue scanning the rest database for statistics. The second scan is a full scan, which needs another D/B disk I/O's.

Suppose then that k projected databases have to be computed. According to Section 2, the total size of the projected databases is approximately $k/2 \cdot D$. For computing the projected databases, the frequency information in T_ϵ is reused, so only part of $\mathcal{D}_\epsilon$ is read. We assume on average half of $\mathcal{D}_\epsilon$ is read at this stage, which means $1/2 \cdot D/B$ disk I/O's. By using of the FP-array technique [6], writing and later reading k projected databases now only take $2 \cdot k/2 \cdot D/B = k \cdot D/B$ disk I/O's. Suppose all frequent itemsets can be mined from the projected databases without going to the third level. Then the total disk I/O's is

$$5/2 \cdot D/B + k \cdot D/B \qquad (4)$$

Compared with formula 3, *Diskmine* saves at least $k/2 \cdot D/B$ disk I/O's, thanks to the various techniques used in the algorithm.

4 Performance Study

In this section, we present the results from a performance comparison of *Diskmine* with the *Parallel Projection* algorithm in [7] and the *Partitioning* algorithm in [10]. The scalability of *Diskmine* is also analyzed, and the accurateness of our memory size estimations are validated.

As mentioned in Section 2, the *Parallel Projection* algorithm is a basic divide-and-conquer algorithm, since for each item a projected database is created. For performance comparison, we implemented *Parallel Projection* algorithm, by using *FP-growth* as main memory method, as introduced in [7]. The Partitioning algorithm is also a divide-and-conquer algorithm. We implemented the partitioning algorithm by using the Apriori implementation [1]. We chose this implementation, since it was well written and easy to adapt for our purposes.

We ran the three algorithms on both synthetic datasets and real datasets. Some synthetic datasets have millions of transactions, and the size of the datasets ranges from several megabytes to several hundreds gigabytes. Due to lack of space, only the results for some synthetic datasets and a real dataset are shown here.

All experiments were performed on a 2.0Ghz Pentium 4 with 256 MB of memory under Windows XP. For *Diskmine* and the *Parallel Projection* algorithm, the size of the main memory is given as an input. For the Partitioning algorithm, since it only has two database scans and each main-memory-sized partition and all data structures for Apriori are stored into main memory, the size of main memory is not controlled, and only the running time is recorded.

We first compared the performance of three algorithms on synthetic dataset. Dataset *T100I20D100K* was generated from the benchmark application of IBM research center [2]. The dataset has 100,000 transactions and 1000 items, and occupies about 40 megabytes of memory. The average transaction length is 100, and the average pattern length is

[1] www.cs.helsinki.fi/u/goethals/software
[2] www.almaden.ibm.com/software/quest/Resources

20. The dataset is very sparse and FP-tree constructed from the dataset is bushy. For Apriori, a large number of candidate frequent itemsets will be generated from the dataset.

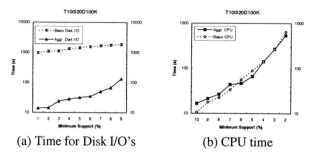

(a) Time for Disk I/O's   (b) CPU time

Figure 4. Experiments on synthetic dataset

When running the algorithms, the main memory size was given as 128 megabytes. Figure 4 shows the experimental results. In the figure, "Basic" represents the *Parallel Projection* algorithm, and "Aggressive" represents the *Diskmine* algorithm. Since the Partitioning algorithm is the slowest in the group, its total running time is always an order of magnitude greater than the *Basic* algorithm and the *Aggressive* algorithm, we didn't separate its CPU time and the time for disk I/O's. Consequently the lines for Partitioning algorithm are not shown in the figures. From Figure 4 (a), as expected, we can see that the disk I/O time of the *Aggressive* algorithm is orders of magnitude smaller than that of the *Basic* algorithm. On the other hand, in Figure 4 (b) we can see that the *Basic* algorithm, however, is not slower than the *Aggressive* algorithm if we only compare their CPU time. In [6], where we were concerned with main memory mining, we found that if a dataset is sparse the boosted *FPgrowth** method has a much better performance than the original *FP-growth*. The reason here the CPU time of the *Aggressive* algorithm is not always less than that of *Basic* algorithm is that the *Aggressive* algorithm has to spend CPU time on calculating statistics. However, from Figure 4, we also can see that the CPU overhead used by the *Aggressive* algorithm now become insignificant compared to the savings in disk I/O.

We then ran the algorithms on a real dataset *Kosarak*, which is used as a test dataset in [5]. The dataset is about 40 megabytes. Since it is a dense dataset and its FP-tree is fairly small, we set the main memory size as 16 megabytes for the experiments. Results are shown in Figure 5.

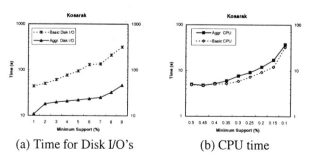

(a) Time for Disk I/O's   (b) CPU time

Figure 5. Experiments on real dataset

In Figure 5, for the same reason as above, results for the Partitioning algorithm is not shown. It is still the slowest comparing the total running time. This is because it generates too many candidate frequent itemsets from the dense dataset. Together with the data structures, the candidate sets use up main memory and virtual memory was used. In Figure 5 (a), the time used for disk I/O's of the *Aggressive* algorithm is still remarkably less than the time used for disk I/O's of the Basic Algorithm. We can again notice that the CPU time of the Basic Algorithm is less than that of the *Aggressive* algorithm. This is because *Kosarak* is a dense dataset so the FP-array technique does not help a lot. In addition, calculating the statistics takes an amount of time.

To test the effectiveness of the techniques for grouping items, we run *Diskmine* on *T100I20D100K* and see how close the estimation of the FP-tree size for each group is to its real size. We still set the main memory size as 128 megabytes, the minimum support is 2%. When generating the projected databases, items were grouped into 7 groups (the total number of frequent items is 826). As we can see from Figure 6 (a), in all groups, the estimated size is always slightly larger than the real size. Compared with the Basic Algorithm, which constructs an FP-tree for each item from its projected database, the *Aggressive* algorithm almost fully uses the main memory for each group to construct an FP-tree.

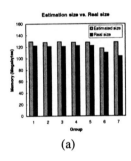
(a)

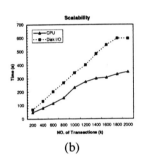
(b)

Figure 6. Estimation Accuracy and Scalability of Diskmine

As a divide-and-conquer algorithm, one of the most important properties of *Diskmine* is its good scalability. We ran *Diskmine* on a set of synthetic datasets. In all datasets, the item number was set as 10000 items, the average transaction length as 100, and the average pattern length as 20. The number of the transactions in the datasets varied from 200,000 to 2,000,000. Datasets size ranges from 100 megabytes to 1 gigabyte. Minimum support was set as 1.5%, and the available main memory was 128 megabytes. Figure 6 (b) shows the results. In the figure, the CPU and the disk I/O time is always kept in a small range of acceptable values. Even for the datasets with 2 million transactions, the total running time is less than 1000 seconds. Extrapolating from these figures using formula (4), we can conclude that a dataset the size of the Library of Congress collection (25 Terabytes) could be mined in around 18 hours with current technology.

5 Conclusions

We have investigated several divide-and-conquer algorithms for mining frequent itemset from secondary memory. We also analyzed the recurrences and disk I/O's of all algorithms. We then gave a detailed divide-and-conquer algorithm which almost fully uses the limited main memory and saves a numerous number of disk I/O's. We introduced many novel techniques used in our algorithm.

Our experimental results show that our algorithm successfully reduces the number of disk access, sometimes by orders of magnitude, and that our algorithm scales up to terabytes of data. The experiments also validate that the estimation techniques used in our algorithm are accurate.

Future extensions of this work will include mining maximal and closed frequent itemsets, as well as exploring disk layout for various datastructures, for instance for candidate sets, since there are some situations where Apriori indeed outperforms the FP-tree based methods.

References

[1] R. C. Agarwal, C. C. Aggarwal, and V. V. V. Prasad. Depth first generation of long patterns. In *KDD'00*, pages 108–118, 2000.

[2] R. Agrawal, T. Imielinski, and A. N. Swami. Mining association rules between sets of items in large databases. In *ACM SIGMOD'93*, pages 207–216, Washington, D.C., 1993.

[3] R. Agrawal and R. Srikant. Fast algorithms for mining association rules. In *VLDB'94*, pages 487–499, 1994.

[4] R. Agrawal and R. Srikant. Mining sequential patterns. In *ICDE'95*, pages 3–14, 1995.

[5] B. Goethals and M. J. Zaki. Advances in frequent itemset mining implementations: Introduction to fimi03. In *Prodeeding of the 1st IEEE ICDM Workshop on Frequent Itemset Mining Implementations (FIMI'03)*, Nov 2003.

[6] G. Grahne and J. Zhu. Efficiently using prefix-trees in mining frequent itemsets. In *1st IEEE ICDM Workshop on Frequent Itemset Mining Implementations (FIMI'03)*, Nov 2003.

[7] J. Han, J. Pei, Y. Yin, and R. Mao. Mining frequent patterns without candidate generation: A frequent-pattern tree approach. *Data Mining and Knowledge Discovery*, 8:53–87, 2004.

[8] M. Kamber, J. Han, and J. Chiang. Metarule-guided mining of multi-dimensional association rules using data cubes. In *Knowledge Discovery and Data Mining*, pages 207–210, 1997.

[9] H. Mannila, H. Toivonen, and A. I. Verkamo. Discovery of frequent episodes in event sequences. *Data Mining and Knowledge Discovery*, 1(3):259–289, 1997.

[10] A. Savasere, E. Omiecinski, and S. B. Navathe. An efficient algorithm for mining association rules in large databases. In *VLDB'95*, pages 432–444, 1995.

[11] H. Toivonen. Sampling large databases for association rules. In *VLDB'96*, pages 134–145, Sep. 1996.

[12] M. Zaki and K. Gouda. Fast vertical mining using diffsets. In *ACM SIGKDD'03*, Washington, DC, Aug. 2003.

A Bayesian Framework for Regularized SVM Parameter Estimation

Jens Gregor and Zhenqiu Liu
University of Tennessee
Department of Computer Science
Knoxville, TN 37996-3450, USA
jgregor@cs.utk.edu, zliu@utk.edu

Abstract

The support vector machine (SVM) is considered here in the context of pattern classification. The emphasis is on the soft margin classifier which uses regularization to handle non-separable learning samples. We present an SVM parameter estimation algorithm that first identifies a subset of the learning samples that we call the support set and then determines not only the weights of the classifier but also the hyperparameter that controls the influence of the regularizing penalty term on basis thereof. We provide numerical results using several data sets from the public domain.

1. Introduction

A general two-class pattern classification problem can be described as follows. Given a set of N learning samples, $D = \{(\mathbf{x}_1, y_1), \ldots, (\mathbf{x}_N, y_N)\}$, find a classifier for which the discriminant function satisfies $y_i = f(\mathbf{x}_i)$ where $\mathbf{x}_i$ is a multi-dimensional feature vector and $y_i = \{-1, +1\}$ denotes the class label. In practice, it is often necessary to allow some learning samples to be misclassified, as it may be impossible to achieve perfect separation of the two classes. A more realistic goal is instead to find a classifier that minimizes an error criterion associated with these misclassifications. The emphasis of this paper is on how to achieve this goal for the support vector machine (SVM) introduced by Vapnik [15], a framework which embodies both linear and non-linear classifiers.

A typical SVM application maps the feature vector to a high-dimensional feature space and then computes a linear classifier for that space. Non-separable learning samples are handled by introducing so-called slack variables, leading to a regularized optimization problem. The hyperparameter that controls the influence of the slack variables on the solution must be chosen carefully. Too low a value may result in more misclassifications being allowed than desirable.

Conversely, too high a value may lead to the cost of misclassifications being too great. Choosing the wrong value could potentially yield a classifier that fails to generalize the true nature of the class separation. Complicating matters further is the fact that the optimal choice depends both on the application and the data.

Several authors have proposed algorithms that allow the value of the hyperparameter to be adjusted during the SVM parameter estimation process. For example, Kwok [9] and Lin [10] considered the case of least absolute value based regularization while Graepel et al. [6] and van Gestel et al. [14] addressed the problem from a least squares point of view. These algorithms all reformulate the original regularized optimization problem, which is constrained as described below, so that it becomes unconstrained. We propose an algorithm for regularized SVM parameter estimation that leaves the constraints intact while refining an initial user-supplied estimate of the hyperparameter.

We give a brief SVM overview in Section 2 for the benefit of the reader unfamiliar with this relatively new approach to pattern classification. Section 3 introduces the concept of support set and outlines the computational steps of our algorithm which is based thereon. In Section 4, we provide numerical results based on several data sets from the public domain.

We note that an alternative hyperparameter estimation approach exists based on minimization of some generalized SVM classification error rate. Chapelle et al. [2] give a general introduction to this idea while Keerthi [8] and Chung et al. [3] address the special case of minimizing the radius/margin error bound. A comparison between our Bayesian method and this alternative is beyond the scope of the present paper.

2. Support Vector Machine (SVM) Basics

Let Φ denote a function that maps feature vector $\mathbf{x}$ into an N_w-dimensional space. The mapping function could simply be the identity function or it could be any one of a number of linear or non-linear functions. The general SVM discriminant function is then of the form:

$$f(\mathbf{x}) = \mathbf{w}^T \Phi(\mathbf{x}) + w_0 \qquad (1)$$

Classification is based on the sign of $f(\mathbf{x})$.

When the learning samples are separable, $\mathbf{w}$ and w_0 can be found by solving a quadratic programming problem [15]:

$$\mathbf{w} = \operatorname{argmin} \frac{1}{2} \sum_{i=1}^{N_w} w_i^2 \qquad (2)$$
$$\text{s.t. } y_i f(\mathbf{x}_i) \geq 1$$
$$w_0 = -\frac{1}{2} \mathbf{w}^T (\Phi(\mathbf{x}_m) + \Phi(\mathbf{x}_p)) \qquad (3)$$

where $\mathbf{x}_m$ and $\mathbf{x}_p$ are any two so-called support vectors with one from each of the two classes. A support vector is a learning sample for which $y_i f(\mathbf{x}_i) = 1$. These are the only learning samples that need to be considered since the SVM parameters would not change if all the the other learning samples had been left out. The resulting classifier is called a maximum margin classifier because the associated hyperplane is as far away from the closest learning sample as it can possibly be.

While (2) adequately describes the optimization problem that must be solved, it is computationally convenient to solve the equivalent dual problem:

$$\mathbf{w} = \sum_{i=1}^{N} \alpha_i y_i \Phi(\mathbf{x}_i) \qquad (4)$$

where

$$\alpha = \operatorname{argmin} \frac{1}{2} \sum_{i=1}^{N} \sum_{j=1}^{N} \alpha_i \alpha_j y_i y_j \Phi(\mathbf{x}_i)^T \Phi(\mathbf{x}_j) - \sum_{i=1}^{N} \alpha_i$$
$$\text{s.t. } \sum_{i=1}^{N} \alpha_i y_i = 0 \text{ and } 0 \leq \alpha_i \qquad (5)$$

The Lagrange multipliers, $\alpha_1, \ldots, \alpha_N$, divide the learning samples into two sets: those for which α_i equals zero and those for which α_i is strictly greater than zero. The former can be discarded from further consideration. The latter are the support vectors which define the classifier.

When the learning samples are non-separable, misclassifications are accounted for using slack variables $\xi_i = |1 - y_i f(\mathbf{x}_i)|_+$ where $|\varepsilon|_+ = \varepsilon$ if ε is positive and zero otherwise. The slack variables are folded into the optimization problem by means of a regularization penalty term [4]:

$$\mathbf{w} = \operatorname{argmin} \frac{1}{2} \sum_{i=1}^{N_w} w_i^2 + \beta p^{-1} \sum_{i=1}^{N} \xi_i^p \qquad (6)$$
$$\text{s.t. } y_i f(\mathbf{x}_i) \geq 1 - \xi_i$$

Normally, $p = 1$ or 2 which ensures that the programming problem remains quadratic. Hyperparameter β balances the

desire to have a maximum margin classifier with the desire to reduce the classification error. The resulting classifier is called a soft margin classifier.

Computationally, β acts as an upper bound on the Lagrange multipliers of the dual problem. That is:

$$\mathbf{w} = \sum_{i=1}^{N} \alpha_i y_i \Phi(\mathbf{x}_i) \qquad (7)$$

where

$$\alpha = \operatorname{argmin} \frac{1}{2} \sum_{i=1}^{N} \sum_{j=1}^{N} \alpha_i \alpha_j y_i y_j \Phi(\mathbf{x}_i)^T \Phi(\mathbf{x}_j) - \sum_{i=1}^{N} \alpha_i$$
$$\text{s.t. } \sum_{i=1}^{N} \alpha_i y_i = 0 \text{ and } 0 \leq \alpha_i \leq \beta \qquad (8)$$

The learning samples for which α_i equals zero can once again be discarded. The support vectors are those learning samples for which α_i is both strictly greater than zero and strictly less than β. The learning samples for which $\alpha_i = \beta$ are misclassified samples that lie within the support region.

Often it is convenient to give an implicit definition of Φ in terms of a kernel function that substitutes for the above inner product. That is, $K(\mathbf{x}_i, \mathbf{x}_j) \equiv \Phi(\mathbf{x}_i)^T \Phi(\mathbf{x}_j)$. Typical examples of kernel functions include $(\mathbf{x}_i^T \mathbf{x}_j + 1)^q$ which implements a polynomial classifier, $\exp(-||\mathbf{x}_i - \mathbf{x}_j||^2 / 2\sigma^2)$ which produces a Gaussian radial basis function (RBF) classifier, and $\tanh(\mathbf{x}_i^T \mathbf{x}_j - \theta)$ which is commonly used in multilayer perceptrons. Parameters q, σ, and θ are predefined. Note that the kernel function approach may preclude $\mathbf{w}$ from being precomputed which leads to the following redefinition of the discriminant function:

$$f(\mathbf{x}) = \sum_{i=1}^{N} \alpha_i y_i K(\mathbf{x}_i, \mathbf{x}) + w_0 \qquad (9)$$

where

$$w_0 = -\frac{1}{2} \sum_{i=1}^{N} \alpha_i y_i (K(\mathbf{x}_i, \mathbf{x}_m) + K(\mathbf{x}_i, \mathbf{x}_p)) \qquad (10)$$

Having to re-compute the kernel function for each support vector can, of course, be computationally costly if there are many of them. But without an explicit definition of mapping function Φ, this cannot be avoided. Many public domain software packages exist that can solve (7) in the context of kernel functions, e.g., Gunn's Matlab SVM toolbox [7].

3. Least Squares Bayesian Regularization

In order to derive an algorithm for estimating not only $\mathbf{w}$ and w_0 but also β, we would like to reformulate the error function being minimized in a way that eliminates the discontinuity introduced by the $|\varepsilon|_+$ operator. The following lemma by Lin [10] provides a means toward reaching this goal.

Lemma 1 *For $y \in \{-1, +1\}$ and $f \in [-1; +1]$, it holds that $|1 - yf(\mathbf{x})|_+^p = |y - f(\mathbf{x})|^p$.*

Proof: *From $|yf(\mathbf{x})| \leq 1$, $|1 - yf(\mathbf{x})|_+^p = (1 - yf(\mathbf{x}))^p$. Furthermore, $y \in \{-1, +1\}$ implies that $(1 - yf(\mathbf{x}))^p = |y(1 - yf(\mathbf{x}))|^p = |y - y^2 f(\mathbf{x})|^p = |y - f(\mathbf{x})|^p$.* $\square$

Next we note that by choosing a value for β and solving the regularized SVM optimization problem described in the previous section, we can divide the learning samples into those for which $y_i f(\mathbf{x}_i) > 1$ (or, equivalently, $\alpha_i = 0$) and those for which $y_i f(\mathbf{x}_i) \leq 1$ (or, equivalently, $0 < \alpha_i \leq \beta$). The former are either well on the safe side of the decision boundary or grossly misclassified. These learning samples would either not affect a re-design of the classifier or possibly affect it negatively. The latter are samples that lie within the initial estimate of the support region which makes them good candiates for fine-tuning of the SVM parameters. Furthermore, this subset of the learning samples, which we henceforth shall refer to as the *support set*, satisfy the premise of the lemma and thus allow a differentiable error function to be introduced.

We therefore propose the following two-step algorithm for regularized SVM parameter estimation. In step one, an initial, predefined value of β is used to compute the first estimate of $\mathbf{w}$. The learning samples that belong in the corresponding support set are identified. All other learning samples are discarded from further consideration. In step two, the support set learning samples, of which we assume there are N_s, are used to iteratively re-estimate first β and then $\mathbf{w}$ through minimization of a least squares error function, namely:

$$E(\mathbf{w}, \beta) = E_W(\mathbf{w}) + \beta E_D(\mathbf{w}) \qquad (11)$$

where

$$E_W(\mathbf{w}) = \frac{1}{2} \sum_{i=1}^{N_w} w_i^2 \qquad (12)$$

$$E_D(\mathbf{w}) = \frac{1}{2} \sum_{i=1}^{N_s} (y_i - f(\mathbf{x}_i))^2 \qquad (13)$$

The algorithm terminates when the difference between two successive β estimates is sufficiently small. In our work, we set the threshold to one tenth of a percent of the initial value.

An added benefit of dealing only with support set learning samples in step two is that we can compute $\mathbf{w}$ indirectly in terms of the Lagrange multipliers that solve a simple Karush-Kuhn-Tucker system of equations. Specifically, let matrix $\mathbf{A}$ denote the Hessian of the least squares error function with respect to $\mathbf{w}$. That is:

$$\mathbf{A} = \nabla^2 E(\mathbf{w}, \beta) = \mathbf{I} + \beta \mathbf{K} \qquad (14)$$

where $\mathbf{I}$ is the identity matrix and $\mathbf{K} = [K(\mathbf{x}_i, \mathbf{x}_j)]$ is the so-called kernel matrix. Also, let class label vector $\mathbf{y} = [y_i]$. Then [14]:

$$\begin{bmatrix} \alpha \\ w_0 \end{bmatrix} = \begin{bmatrix} \mathbf{A} & 1 \\ 1^T & 0 \end{bmatrix}^{-1} \begin{bmatrix} \beta \mathbf{y} \\ 0 \end{bmatrix} \qquad (15)$$

where 1 is a column vector of ones. Discriminant function f is then computed either in terms of (1) and (7) or (9) depending on whether mapping function Φ or kernel function K is known.

An update scheme for β can be derived from a Bayesian point of view [11, 12, 13]. Let the model priors for β and $\mathbf{w}$ respectively be a uniform distribution, i.e., $P(\beta) = 1/\beta$, and a zero mean Gaussian with unit variance:

$$P(\mathbf{w}) = (2\pi)^{-N_w/2} \exp\{-E_W(\mathbf{w})\} \qquad (16)$$

Furthermore, let the data likelihood be a zero mean Gaussian for which β represents the inverse variance of the distribution:

$$P(D|\mathbf{w}, \beta) = (2\pi/\beta)^{-N_s/2} \exp\{-\beta E_D(\mathbf{w})\} \qquad (17)$$

Let $\hat{\beta}$ be our current β estimate. Computing $\mathbf{w}$ through minimization of $E(\mathbf{w}, \hat{\beta})$ is equivalent to maximization of $P(\mathbf{w}|\hat{\beta}, D)$. The question is how to choose $\hat{\beta}$. Under the assumption that $P(\beta|D)$ peaks sharply around this value, we have that:

$$P(\mathbf{w}|\hat{\beta}, D) \approx \int P(\mathbf{w}|\beta, D) P(\beta|D) d\beta \qquad (18)$$

With $P(\beta)$ being a constant, $P(\beta|D) \propto P(D|\beta)$. Thus, a reasonable choice for $\hat{\beta}$ would be the maximizer of the latter. This leads to:

$$\left. \frac{\partial}{\partial \beta} \log P(D|\beta) \right|_{\beta = \hat{\beta}} = 0. \qquad (19)$$

As a first step toward solving this equation, we integrate the data likelihood over all possible weights:

$$\int P(D|\mathbf{w}, \beta) P(\mathbf{w}) d\mathbf{w} = \qquad (20)$$
$$(2\pi)^{-N_w/2} (2\pi/\beta)^{-N_s/2} \int \exp\{-E(\mathbf{w}, \beta)\} d\mathbf{w}$$

By applying a second-order Taylor series expansion to $E(\mathbf{w}, \beta)$ centered at $\hat{\mathbf{w}}$, the current estimate for $\mathbf{w}$, we see that:

$$\int \exp\{-E(\mathbf{w}, \beta)\} d\mathbf{w} \approx \qquad (21)$$
$$(2\pi)^{N_w/2} (\det \mathbf{A})^{-1/2} \exp\{-E(\hat{\mathbf{w}}, \beta)\}$$

Eliminating irrelevant constants, we obtain:

$$\log P(D|\beta) = N_s \log \beta - \log(\det \mathbf{A}) - 2E(\hat{\mathbf{w}}, \beta) \qquad (22)$$

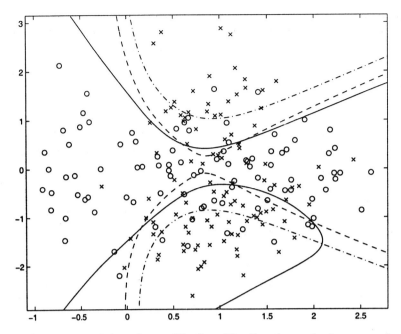

Figure 1. Gaussian training data with classification boundaries superimposed.

Finally, solving (19) while keeping in mind that the determinant of a matrix is equal to the product of its eigenvalues, we can write:

$$\hat{\beta} = \frac{1}{2E_D(\hat{\mathbf{w}})} \sum_{i=1}^{N_s} \frac{1}{1+\mu_i} \qquad (23)$$

where $\mu_1, \ldots, \mu_{N_s}$ are the eigenvalues of $\beta\mathbf{K}$. A more efficient update expression can be obtained by noting that $\mu_i = \beta\lambda_i$ where $\lambda_1, \ldots, \lambda_{N_s}$ are the eigenvalues of $\mathbf{K}$:

$$\hat{\beta}_{\text{new}} = \frac{1}{2E_D(\hat{\mathbf{w}})} \sum_{i=1}^{N_s} \frac{1}{1+\beta_{\text{old}}\lambda_i}. \qquad (24)$$

Computationally, the advantage of this recursive approach is that the kernel matrix eigenvalues can be precomputed since they do not change from iteration to iteration.

With respect to the initial choice for β, a low value is preferable since it produces a larger support set than does a high value which means that it imposes less of a restriction on the solution. The caveat is that too low a value may lead to the support set being so large that the matrix inverse and the eigenvalues needed when updating respectively $\mathbf{w}$ and β become difficult to compute.

4. Numerical Results

We first consider a two-dimensional 'toy' problem that allows us to illustrate the classification boundaries. Data for class one consists of two Gaussians with means $\mu_{11} =$

$(0, -0.2)$ and $\mu_{12} = (1.6, 0)$, and covariance matrices

$$\Sigma_{11} = \begin{pmatrix} 0.64 & \text{-0.22} \\ \text{-0.22} & 0.88 \end{pmatrix}, \ \Sigma_{12} = \begin{pmatrix} 0.25 & 0.00 \\ 0.00 & 0.25 \end{pmatrix}.$$

Data for class two similarly consists of two Gaussians with means $\mu_{21} = (1, 1)$ and $\mu_{22} = (1, -1)$, and covariance matrices

$$\Sigma_{21} = \begin{pmatrix} 0.22 & \text{-0.14} \\ \text{-0.14} & 0.98 \end{pmatrix}, \ \Sigma_{22} = \begin{pmatrix} 0.24 & 0.13 \\ \text{-0.13} & 0.41 \end{pmatrix}.$$

The covariance matrices are defined to ensure a reasonable degree of class overlap. A total of 200 data points were generated. Figure 3 shows the decision boundaries obtained for the optimal classifier computed directly from the known distributions (solid lines) and the two SVM classifiers based respectively on a user-supplied hyperparameter estimate of $\beta_{\text{init}} = 0.1$ (dash-dotted lines) and the one produced by the proposed method, namely, $\beta_{\text{final}} = 3.68$ (dashed lines). We see that there is good agreement between the optimal and the estimated decision boundaries for the final beta value while the one derived from the initial beta value causes more learning samples to be misclassified. An RBF (Gaussian) kernel function with $\sigma = 0.75$ was used for all SVM computations. The support set contained 139 vectors. Figure 3 provides per iteration plots of the training error in the form of E_D and hyperparameter β. The monotonic behavior seen for both is typical. In order to further illustrate the "correctness" of the computed beta value, an additional 400 data points were generated and subsequently classified using a wide range of beta values. Figure 3 shows the result

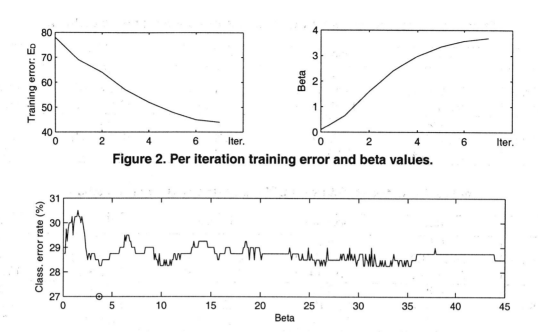

Figure 2. Per iteration training error and beta values.

Figure 3. Classification error rates as a function of beta for Gaussian test data. The dot-circle marker indicates the computed beta value.

of this experiment. We note that the classification error rate achieved for the computed β_{final} value coincides with the overall minimum classification error rate for the number of test samples and the range of beta values considered here.

We now turn the attention to multi-dimensional 'real-world' problems. This work is based on five data sets from the UCI repository of machine learning databases [1]. One of these data sets represents a credit screening problem. The task is to predict whether or not an applicant will default. The database contains case histories for 690 applicants, each described by 15 features and a class label which indicates whether or not a default ultimately occurred. Some entries are incomplete. We chose 6 features that allowed us to extract complete information for 666 applicants. The other four data sets are the Johns Hopkins University Ionosphere data which consists of 351 samples and 34 variables, the Pima Indians data which consists of 768 samples and 8 variables, the Cleveland Heart data which consists of 297 samples and 13 variables, and the Galaxy Dim data which consists of 4192 samples and 14 variables.

Our experiments are based on ten-fold cross-validation. That is, each data set was divided into ten subsets of approximately the same size, and each subset was then used as test data with the other nine subsets used for estimating the classifier parameters. We report average results for these ten experiments based on $\beta_{\text{init}} = 0.1$ and RBF kernel functions with the following sigmas for the five data sets: 0.5, 1.2, 100.0, 7.5, and 21.5. The sigmas were determined empirically using trial-and-error.

Table 1 lists the classification error rates obtained for both the training data and the independent test data using an initial user-supplied beta value and the computed beta value, respectively. Better classifiers are obtained for all five data sets when using the latter. A person would have had great difficulty guessing the same hyperparameter values which, as it can be seen, vary significantly from data set to data set.

For comparison purposes, Tables 2 and 3 list the beta values and classification error rates obtained using two methods that we mentioned in the introduction, namely, the least absolute value based method by Kwok [9] and the least squares method by Gestel et al. [14]. These results are nearly identical to those listed in Table 1, the main difference being that the proposed method shows a significant improvement over these other two methods for three of the training data sets. We also note that Kwok's and Gestel's methods require about 500, 316, 691, 267, 3773 samples to be processed at each iteration. In contrast, our method identifies and discards the learning samples that are easy to classify correctly as well as those that tend to be grossly misclassified leaving 283, 164, 386, 99, and 2001 samples to be processed at each iteration. For larger data sets than the relatively small ones considered here, this built-in data reduction could potentially translate into important computational savings, especially with respect to the computing of the kernel matrix eigenvalues which is required by all three methods.

Table 4 lists the best published SVM classification error rates for the five data sets. The Ionosphere and Cleveland Heart numbers are from Fung and Mangasarian [5] while the Credit Screening, Pima Indians, and Galaxy Dim num-

Table 1. Classifier statistics for UCI data sets using the proposed method.

	Credit	Ionosphere	Indians	Heart	Galaxy
β_{init}	0.1	0.1	0.1	0.1	0.1
Training Error	24.6% (1.1)	17.6% (0.8)	23.8% (0.8)	15.1% (0.6)	13.4% (0.4)
Test Error	28.5% (5.4)	16.5% (4.7)	24.3% (5.2)	17.1% (6.2)	13.7% (2.7)
β_{final}	4.90	2.95	1.26	0.41	126.50
Training Error	6.3% (0.5)	4.3% (0.4)	22.1% (0.6)	10.2% (1.2)	4.5% (1.1)
Test Error	23.1% (5.4)	5.9% (3.1)	22.7% (2.6)	13.2% (3.4)	5.3% (3.8)

Table 2. Classifier statistics for UCI data sets using Kwok's method.

	Credit	Ionosphere	Indians	Heart	Galaxy
β_{init}	0.1	0.1	0.1	0.1	0.1
Training Error	24.6% (1.0)	17.7% (0.7)	23.7% (0.8)	16.4% (0.6)	13.3% (0.8)
Test Error	29.1% (5.1)	16.8% (4.2)	24.3% (5.3)	17.5% (6.3)	13.5% (5.4)
β_{final}	4.70	3.12	1.23	0.38	128.56
Training Error	9.6% (1.0)	4.0% (0.4)	23.2% (0.6)	12.8% (1.3)	5.3% (0.8)
Test Error	23.7% (5.1)	6.1% (4.3)	22.9% (2.4)	13.4% (3.1)	5.3% (4.7)

Table 3. Classifier statistics for UCI data sets using Gestel et al.'s method.

	Credit	Ionosphere	Indians	Heart	Galaxy
β_{init}	0.1	0.1	0.1	0.1	0.1
Training Error	25.2% (1.3)	17.2% (7.3)	24.1% (0.8)	14.9% (0.7)	13.6% (0.6)
Test Error	28.7% (2.1)	16.7% (4.6)	24.4% (4.9)	17.2% (5.1)	13.7% (3.4)
β_{final}	5.10	3.43	1.11	0.44	121.32
Training Error	10.2% (1.3)	4.6% (0.4)	22.3% (0.8)	11.3% (1.2)	5.6% (1.3)
Test Error	23.7% (3.7)	6.1% (2.8)	22.8% (3.3)	13.2% (5.5)	5.4% (3.7)

Table 4. Best published classifier statistics for UCI data sets.

	Credit	Ionosphere	Indians	Heart	Galaxy
Test Error	23.7%	5.5%	22.0%	12.9%	5.3%

bers are from Gestel et al. [14]. We note that our classification error rates are in close agreement with these results.

To illustrate the "correctness" of the β_{final} values listed in Table 1, we evaluated the five test data classification error rates using a wide range of beta values. Figure 4 shows the result of this experiment. Like before, we find the computed β_{final} values to coincide with the overall minimum classification error rates. Thus, while the proposed method is heuristic and does not guarantee optimality, it does seem to perform quite well in practice.

5. Conclusion

We have presented a simple two-step algorithm for regularized SVM parameter estimation. By solving the standard constrained SVM quadratic programming problem given an initial estimate of the hyperparameter, we identify a subset of the learning samples. This so-called support set allows the SVM parameters to be re-estimated using an unconstrained least squares algorithm. The approach is easy to implement and was shown to work well on several data sets from the public domain.

References

[1] C. Blake and C. Merz. UCI Repository of machine learning databases. Technical Report http://www.ics.uci.edu/~mlearn/MLRepository.html, Department of Information and Computer Sciences, University of California, Irvine, 1998.

[2] O. Chapelle, V. Vapnik, O. Bousquet, and S. Mukherjee. Choosing multiple parameters for support vector machines. *Machine Learning*, 46:131–159, 2002.

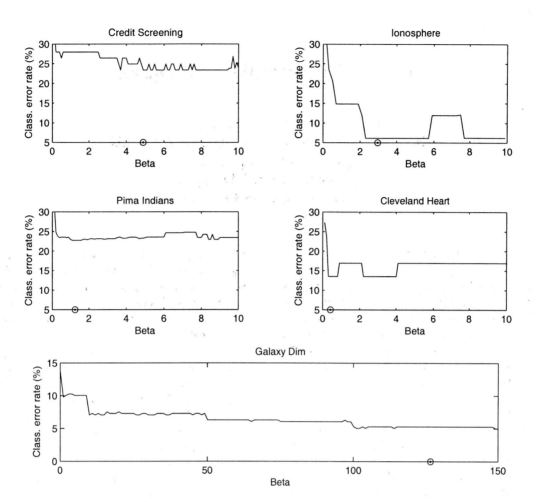

Figure 4. Classification error rates as a function of beta for UCI datasets. The dot-circle marker indicates the computed beta value.

[3] K.-M. Chung, W.-C. Kao, C.-L. Sun, L.-L. Wang, and C.-J. Lin. Radius margin bounds for support vector machines with the RBF kernel. *Neural Computation*, 15:2643–2681, 2003.

[4] C. Cortes and V. Vapnik. Support vector networks. *Machine Learning*, 20:273–297, 1995.

[5] G. Fung and O. Mangasarian. A feature selection Newton method for support vector machine classification. Technical Report DMI-02-03, Data Mining Institute, University of Wisconsin, 2002.

[6] T. Graepel, R. Herbrich, and K. Obermayer. Bayesian transduction. *Advances in Neural Information System Processing*, 12:456–462, 2000.

[7] S. Gunn. Support vector machines for classification and regression. Technical Report ISIS-1-98, Image, Speech and Intelligent Systems Research Group, University of Southampton, 1998.

[8] S. Keerthi. Efficient tuning of SVM hyperparameters using radius/margin bound and iterative algorithms. *IEEE Trans. Neural Networks*, 13:1225–1229, 2002.

[9] J. Kwok. Integrating the evidence framework and the support vector machine. *Proc. European Symp. Artificial Neu-*

ral Networks, ESANN'99 (Bruges, Belgium), pages 177–182, 1999.

[10] Y. Lin. Support vector machines and the Bayes rule in classification. *Data Mining and Knowledge Discovery*, 6:259–275, 2002.

[11] D. MacKay. Bayesian interpolation. *Neural Computation*, 4:415–447, 1992.

[12] I. Nabney. *Netlab: Algorithms for Pattern Recognition*. Springer, 2001.

[13] P. Sollich. Probabilistic interpretation and Bayesian methods for support vector machines. *Proc. Intl. Conf. Artificial Neural Networks (ICANN'99)*, pages 177–182, 1999.

[14] T. van Gestel, J. Suykens, G. Lanckriet, A. Lambrechts, B. de Moor, and J. Vandewalle. Bayesian framework for least squares support vector machine classifiers, Gaussian processes and kernel Fisher discriminant analysis. *Neural Computation*, 14:1115–1147, 2002.

[15] V. Vapnik. *The Nature of Statistical Learning Theory*. Springer, 1995.

Unimodal Segmentation of Sequences

Niina Haiminen and Aristides Gionis
Helsinki Institute for Information Technology, BRU
Department of Computer Science
University of Helsinki, Finland
first.lastname@cs.helsinki.fi

Abstract

We study the problem of segmenting a sequence into k pieces so that the resulting segmentation satisfies monotonicity or unimodality constraints. Unimodal functions can be used to model phenomena in which a measured variable first increases to a certain level and then decreases. We combine a well-known unimodal regression algorithm with a simple dynamic-programming approach to obtain an optimal quadratic-time algorithm for the problem of unimodal k-segmentation. In addition, we describe a more efficient greedy-merging heuristic that is experimentally shown to give solutions very close to the optimal. As a concrete application of our algorithms, we describe two methods for testing if a sequence behaves unimodally or not. Our experimental evaluation shows that our algorithms and the proposed unimodality tests give very intuitive results.

1 Introduction

The problem of regression, which deals with fitting curves or functions to a set of points, is among the most well-studied problems in statistics and data mining. Regression functions represent data models that can be used for knowledge extraction, understanding of the data, and prediction [6]. In many cases, the data are assumed to come from an a priori known class of distributions and the task is to find the parameters of the distribution that best fits the data. In this paper we focus on the case where the regression functions are required to be *monotonic* or *unimodal*. The problem of computing monotonic and unimodal regression functions has drawn attention in statistics [10, 14, 15] and computer science [11, 12], because it arises in a wide range of applications, such as statistical modeling [14], operations research [8], medicine and drug design [7], and image processing [13].

Unimodal functions can be used to model phenomena in which a measured variable shows a single-mode behav-ior: its expected value first rises to a certain level and then drops. Examples of data that exhibit unimodal behavior include (*i*) the size of a population of a species over time, (*ii*) daily volumes of network traffic, (*iii*) stock-market quotes in quarterly or annual periods, when small fluctuations are ignored, etc.

Monotonicity is a special case of unimodality. A monotonic regression function for a real-valued sequence can be computed in linear time by variants of the classic "pool adjacent violators" (PAV) algorithm [1]. Recently, Stout [15] has shown how to cleverly organize the PAV operations to achieve a linear-time algorithm for the seemingly more complex problem of unimodal regression. However, one of the drawbacks of the above methods is that they do not restrict the size of the resulting regression and they can potentially report models with very high complexity.

In this paper we address the issue of compact representation of unimodal regression functions by studying the following problem: Given a univariate sequence and an integer k, partition the sequence into k segments and represent each segment by a constant value, so that the segment values satisfy unimodality (or monotonicity) constraints and the total representation error is minimized. We call this problem unimodal (or monotonic) k-segmentation. The problem is polynomial, but naive dynamic programming algorithms have running times of the order of high-degree polynomials.

In this paper we show that the unimodal k-segmentation problem can be solved in $O(n^2k)$ time, which is the same as the time required to solve the unrestricted k-segmentation problem, i.e., segmenting without the unimodality constraints. Our algorithm is a simple combination of the PAV algorithm and dynamic programming techniques. However, the proof for its optimality is somewhat non-trivial. The algorithm can be extended to handle higher-mode segmentations, e.g., bimodal, and the optimality proof holds with minor changes to it. In addition to the optimal algorithm, we describe a fast greedy heuristic, which runs in time $O(n \log n)$ and in practice gives solutions very close to optimal.

106

In our experimental evaluation we show that the proposed algorithms provide intuitive segmentations. Additionally, we discuss how to apply our algorithms in order to devise unimodality tests for sequences. We explore two alternatives: comparison with unrestricted segmentations and a permutation test. We found that both tests are able to separate the sequences that exhibit unimodal behavior from the ones that do not.

This paper is organized as follows. In Section 2 we introduce the notation and define the problem of unimodal k-segmentation. In Section 3 we describe our algorithms, while the optimality proofs are given in Section 4. In Section 5 we discuss our experiments, and Section 6 contains a short conclusion.

2 Preliminaries

A real-valued sequence X consists of n values (also referred to as points), i.e., $X = \langle x_1, \ldots, x_n \rangle$. The problems of *regression* and *segmentation* seek for representing the sequence X in a way that satisfies certain constraints. For the *monotonic-* and *unimodal*-regression problems, monotonicity constraints are imposed on the regression values of the sequence. For the segmentation problem, the representation of the sequence is constrained to a small number of piecewise constant segments.

Monotonic regression: The goal of *increasing monotonic regression* is to map each point x_i of the sequence X to a point $\hat{x}_i$, so that

$$\hat{x}_1 \leq \hat{x}_2 \leq \ldots \leq \hat{x}_n,$$

and the regression error

$$E_R = \sum_{i=1}^{n} (x_i - \hat{x}_i)^2 \qquad (1)$$

is minimized. *Decreasing monotonic regression* is defined in a similar fashion. Equation (1) defines the regression error with respect to the L_2 norm. In general, any L_p norm, $1 \leq p \leq \infty$, can be used; the norms L_1 (sum of absolute values) and L_∞ (max) are also commonly used in statistics.

Unimodal regression: Similarly to monotonic regression, a unimodal regression maps each value x_i of the sequence X to a value $\hat{x}_i$. However, in this case it is required that the regression values increase up to some point $\hat{x}_t$ and then decrease for the rest of the points. In other words, the goal is to minimize the regression error E_R defined by Equation (1), subject to the unimodality constraints

$$\hat{x}_1 \leq \ldots \leq \hat{x}_{t-1} \leq \hat{x}_t \geq \hat{x}_{t+1} \geq \ldots \geq \hat{x}_n.$$

Note that only one point of the sequence (or multiple points with the same value) is mapped to the value $\hat{x}_t$, called the *top* of the unimodal regression. If this was not the case, the regression error could be reduced by making a point mapped to the top, with a value higher than $\hat{x}_t$, a new top of the regression.

We can also define unimodal regression that is first decreasing and then increasing. In the rest of the paper, without loss of generality, we refer by "unimodal" to regressions whose values are first increasing and then decreasing. Since monotonicity is a special case of unimodality, all our results hold also for monotonic segmentations.

Let us denote by r_j, $j = 1, \ldots, m$, a set of consecutive points $x_i \in X$ that are represented by the same value $\hat{x}$ in the regression. The value $\hat{x}$, common for all the points in r_j, is denoted by $\hat{r}_j$. The subsequence r_j can be represented by the indices of its first and last points, denoted here by f_j and l_j, respectively. Thus the regression U can be written as $\langle (f_1, l_1, \hat{r}_1), \ldots, (f_m, l_m, \hat{r}_m) \rangle$, with $f_j \leq l_j$, $f_1 = 1$, $l_m = n$, and $f_j = l_{j-1} + 1$, for $j = 2, \ldots, m$. By definition, the values $\hat{r}_j$ are strictly increasing up to $\hat{x}_t$ and then strictly decreasing. The set of points within the closed interval $[f_j, l_j]$, for $j = 1, \ldots, m$, will be referred to as *regression segment* r_j. The value of m is not specified as input to the regression problem; any solution that satisfies the regression constraints is a feasible one, and the optimal solution is defined over all feasible solutions. The solutions improve as m increases, up to some sequence-dependent value, after which the error does not decrease anymore when increasing the number of regression segments.

k-segmentation: The task of k-segmentation is to represent the sequence with k piecewise constant segments with as small an error as possible. A segmentation of the original sequence X is a sequence S of k segments s_j, $j = 1, \ldots, k$, with $s_j = (f_j, l_j, \bar{s}_j)$. Thus each segment s_j is specified by two boundary points f_j, l_j and a value $\bar{s}_j$. Naturally we have $f_j \leq l_j$, $f_1 = 1$, $l_k = n$, and $f_j = l_{j-1} + 1$, for $j = 2, \ldots, k$. A point x_i in the original sequence is represented by the value of the segment s_j to which the point x_i belongs, that is, $\bar{x}_i = \bar{s}_j$ where $f_j \leq i \leq l_j$. Given a value for k, the goal is to find the segmentation that minimizes the total error, defined as

$$E_S = \sum_{i=1}^{n} (x_i - \bar{x}_i)^2. \qquad (2)$$

Unimodal segmentation: We now define the problem of unimodal segmentation, which is the focus of this paper. Unimodal segmentation combines the two previous problems in a natural way: we seek to represent a sequence by a small number of segments and subject to the unimodality constraints.

Problem 1 (UNIMODAL SEGMENTATION)
Given a sequence $X = \langle x_1, \ldots, x_n \rangle$, and an integer $k \leq n$, find the k-segmentation S of X that minimizes the error of the segmentation E_S as defined by Equation (2), and satisfies the unimodality constraints $\bar{s}_1 \leq \ldots \leq \bar{s}_p \geq \ldots \geq \bar{s}_k$.

The unimodal regression and segmentation problems can also be considered in higher dimensions with appropriately defined error metrics, but the algorithms and results presented in this paper apply only to univariate sequences. We are not aware of any algorithms for monotonic or unimodal regression for higher-dimensional data.

3 Algorithms

In this section we describe our main algorithm for the problem of unimodal segmentation. The algorithm combines in a natural way two previously known algorithms: (*i*) the PAV algorithm for unimodal regression, and (*ii*) the dynamic-programming algorithm for k-segmentation. In fact, the algorithm is quite simple: it first applies PAV on the original sequence, and then uses dynamic programming on the resulting unimodal sequence to obtain a k-segmentation. Our algorithm runs in time $O(n^2 k)$ for a sequence of n points. In the next section we prove that this simple algorithm produces the optimal unimodal k-segmentation.

To provide relevant background, in Sections 3.1 and 3.2 we describe in slightly more detail the PAV and the dynamic-programming algorithms. In addition to the optimal algorithm, we describe in Section 3.4 a more efficient greedy-merging heuristic that is experimentally shown to give solutions very close to optimal. In Section 3.5 we also briefly discuss a naive algorithm that can easily be shown to produce the optimal result, but with a prohibitively expensive running time.

3.1 Regression algorithms

Computing a monotonic regression of a sequence can be done in linear time by the classic algorithm of "pool-adjacent violators" (PAV) by Ayer et al. [1]. The PAV algorithm is surprisingly simple: it starts by considering each point of the sequence as a separate regression value, and as long as two adjacent values violate the monotonicity constraint they are merged and replaced by their weighted average. The process continues until no violators remain. It can be shown that this process computes the optimal regression regardless of the order in which the pairs are merged [14].

Based on the PAV algorithm, the unimodal regression can be easily computed in $O(n^2)$ time [3, 4]: just try all the points in the sequence as candidate top points, find the optimal monotonic regression left and right of the top point, and select the best solution from among all the candidates.

However, Stout [15] was able to devise a linear-time algorithm for the problem of unimodal regression. He realized that in the above quadratic-time algorithm some information is recomputed due to independent calls to monotonic regression, and he showed how to cleverly organize these calls to achieve linear-time computation of the regression.

3.2 Segmentation algorithm

From the classic result by Bellman [2], the problem of k-segmentation can be solved by dynamic programming in time $O(n^2 k)$. The solution is based on computing in incremental fashion an $(n \times k)$-size table E_S, where the entry $E_S[i, p]$ denotes the error of segmenting the sequence $\langle x_1, \ldots, x_i \rangle$ using p segments. The computation is based on the equation

$$E_S[i, p] = \min_{1 \leq j \leq i} (E_S[j-1, p-1]) + E[j, i]), \quad (3)$$

where $E[j, i]$ is the error of representing the subsequence $\langle x_j, \ldots, x_i \rangle$ with one segment.

3.3 The OPT algorithm

In this section we discuss our main algorithm, which we call OPT. Given a sequence X, OPT first finds the unimodal regression U of X, resulting in m regression segments r_j. The values of the regression segments are then segmented to reduce the number of segments from m to k. Pseudocode is given in Figure 1.

If the number of regression segments is smaller than k, i.e., $m \leq k$, the m unimodal segments in U are taken to be the output of the algorithm. One can see that the m segments of U form the best k-segmentation. The reason is that, since using more segments can only help, the error of the optimal k-segmentation can not be greater than the error of the m-segmentation U. On the other hand, U is the optimal over *all* possible segmentations, and in particular its error can not be greater than of the optimal k-segmentation, therefore the two have to be equal. If it is required that the final segmentation has *exactly* k segments, then we can insert "artificial" segment boundaries and increase the number of segments from m to k without changing the error of the solution.

More interesting is the situation in which the number of required segments k is smaller than the number of the regression segments, i.e., $m > k$. In this case, OPT views the m segments of U as weighted points, and it applies the dynamic-programming segmentation algorithm on those points. In the next section we will show that the resulting segmentation is unimodal, and in fact it is the optimal unimodal k-segmentation. In other words, the optimal k-segmentation will never need to split any regression seg-

108

Opt

Input: $X = \langle x_1, \ldots, x_n \rangle$
Output: Unimodal segmentation $S = s_1, s_2, \ldots, s_k$
$U \leftarrow$ Unimodal-regression(X)
% U has m regression sets
if $m \leq k$ **then**
  $S \leftarrow U$
else
  $S \leftarrow k$-segmentation(U)
end if

Figure 1. Opt **algorithm.**

ment r_j into two segments r_j^p and r_j^s; it will only need to combine regression segments into larger segments.

As far as the running time of the algorithm is concerned, the unimodal regression algorithm runs in $O(n)$ time, and the dynamic programming algorithm for producing k segments on a sequence of m points runs in time $O(m^2k)$. Since $m = O(n)$, the overall complexity of Opt is $O(n^2k)$. In all of our experiments m was much smaller than n, so in practice the actual running time of $O(n + m^2k)$ might be significantly less than the worst case of $O(n^2k)$. Note that one can also apply the *approximate segmentation* technique of Guha et al. [5] and obtain a $(1 + \epsilon)$-approximation to the optimal unimodal k-segmentation in time $O(\frac{1}{\epsilon}k^2n \log n)$.

3.4 The Greedy algorithm

For large sequences the quadratic running time of Opt can be a bottleneck. In this section we describe a more efficient algorithm, called Greedy. The Greedy algorithm consists of the same two steps as Opt: unimodal regression and segmentation. The difference is that in the segmentation step, instead of applying the expensive dynamic-programming algorithm, a greedy merging process is performed: starting with m regression segments, we iteratively merge the two consecutive segments that yield the least error, until reaching k segments.

Since the error of a segment $s = (f, l, \bar{s})$ can be computed by the formula $E(s) = \sum_{i=f}^{l}(x_i - \bar{s})^2 = \frac{1}{l-f+1}\sum_{i=f}^{l}x_i^2 - (\frac{1}{l-f+1}\sum_{i=f}^{l}x_i)^2$, the error of each potential merging can be computed in constant time by keeping two precomputed arrays of the sequence: the sum and the sum of squares of the values of all prefixes in the sequence. We can store the error values of merging each two consecutive segments in a priority queue. Initially, each point is a segment on its own, and the queue contains the errors associated with merging any two consecutive points. As segments are merged, the entries of the segments adjacent to the newly merged segments are also updated. This structure yields the overall running time of $O(n \log n)$ for

the algorithm Greedy.

As we have already mentioned, this greedy-merging algorithm does not produce optimal solutions. Consider a simple example of $m = 4$ monotone regression points with values $\langle 1, 2 + \epsilon, 3 - \epsilon, 4 \rangle$, for vanishingly small ϵ, and segmentations with $k = 2$. The algorithm Greedy will generate segmentation $\langle 1, 2, 3 \rangle \langle 4 \rangle$ or $\langle 1 \rangle \langle 2, 3, 4 \rangle$ with error $E_S = (1-2)^2 + (2+\epsilon-2)^2 + (3-\epsilon-2)^2 + (4-4)^2 \approx 2$, while the optimal solution is the segmentation $\langle 1, 2 \rangle \langle 3, 4 \rangle$ with error $E_S = 2(\frac{1+\epsilon}{2})^2 + 2(\frac{1-\epsilon}{2})^2 \approx 1$. In fact, we have not been able to find a counterexample with an error ratio worse than 2, even when looking at much more complicated situations. Furthermore, in all of our experiments the ratio of the two errors was smaller than 1.2. An interesting open problem is to examine if there exists some guarantee for the quality of the results produced by Greedy.

3.5 A dynamic programming alternative

For comparison with our main algorithm we briefly sketch an alternative "brute force" algorithm. We first explain how this algorithm works for the monotonic segmentation. The idea is to extend the dynamic programming solution of Equation (3), by considering that each segment takes a value from a finite set $L = \{l_1, \ldots, l_N\}$, where $l_i \leq l_j$ for $i < j$. If we denote by $E_S[i, p, h]$ the segmentation error for the sequence $\langle x_1, \ldots, x_i \rangle$, with exactly p segments, and where no segment exceeds the h-th value of the set L, we have the equation

$$E_S[i, p, h] = \min_{1 \leq j \leq i}(E_S[j-1, p-1, h-1]) + E[j, i, l_h]),$$

where $E[j, i, l_h]$ is the error of the sequence $\langle x_j, \ldots, x_i \rangle$ using at maximum the value l_h as its level. The crucial observation is that the admissible values for the set L are only the averages of subsequences of the original sequence, and thus $|L| = O(n^2)$. Computing the above equation by dynamic programming gives the optimal monotonic k-segmentation, but it requires time $O(n^4k)$, which is prohibitively expensive in practice.

The unimodal k-segmentation can be computed by performing two monotonic k-segmentations, one increasing from left to right and one decreasing from right to left. In fact, the computation can be done with no additional overhead by utilizing information stored in the dynamic-programming tables (we omit the details).

4 Analysis of the algorithms

In this section we prove some properties of our algorithms, namely that they always produce unimodal segmentations, and that the Opt algorithm is indeed optimal. Our first lemma is quite intuitive and it shows that the algorithms Opt and Greedy both produce unimodal segmentations.

Lemma 1 *Let X be a sequence and U a unimodal regression of X. Any possible way of combining consecutive segments of U into larger segments yields a unimodal segmentation for X.*

Proof: We prove the Lemma by induction, by showing that combining any two segments of a unimodal k-segmentation gives a unimodal $(k-1)$-segmentation. Consider merging segments s_j and s_{j+1}. By our assumption, the subsequences $s_1 \ldots s_{j-1}$ and $s_{j+2} \ldots s_k$ are unimodal. There are three possible cases of merging, with respect to the top of the regression r_t:

1. Neither s_{j-1}, s_j, s_{j+1} nor s_{j+2} contain r_t. All the values in s_j and s_{j+1} are then in between the levels of their neighboring segments, and merging does not violate unimodality.

2. The top r_t is contained in either s_{j+2} or s_{j-1}. In the first case, the average of the points in $s_j s_{j+1}$ is $\geq \hat{s}_{j-1}$, in the second it is $\geq \hat{s}_{j+2}$. Thus $\hat{s}_{j+2}$, or $\hat{s}_{j-1}$, can be arbitrary without violating unimodality.

3. The top is contained in s_j or s_{j+1}. All the points in $s_j s_{j+1}$ are either $\geq \hat{s}_{j-1}$ or $\geq \hat{s}_{j+2}$ (or both). Thus the level of the new segment can not be both $< \hat{s}_{j-1}$ and $< \hat{s}_{j+2}$, so again merging does not violate unimodality.

Thus, merging any two consecutive segments of a unimodal k-segmentation guarantees a unimodal $(k-1)$-segmentation. □

Next we show that the OPT algorithm indeed gives the optimal solution.

Lemma 2 *Let X be a sequence and R be an optimal increasing monotonic regression of X. For any regression segment r_j of R, and any split of r_j into a prefix segment r_j^p and a suffix segment r_j^s, we have $\bar{r}_j^p \geq \bar{r}_j^s$.*

Proof: The Lemma follows from the definition of increasing monotonic regression.

Let us assume that the points in some prefix r_j^p of $r_j \in R$ has an average a_j^p that is smaller than the average a_j^s of the points in the suffix r_j^s.

Now the error associated with the regression can be decreased by assigning the points in r_j^s to any level between $\hat{r}_j$ and a_j^s. If the new level satisfies $d_j^s < \hat{r}_{j+1}$, then we can simply separate r_j^s into a new regression segment and assign it level a_j^s. If $a_j^s \geq \hat{r}_{j+1}$, we can separate r_j^s into a new segment with level $\hat{r}_{j+1}$.

Both of these operations clearly preserve the monotonicity of R by adding one regression segment r_j^s in between r_j and r_{j+1}, whose level $\hat{r}_j^s$ is in the interval $(\hat{r}_j, \min\{a_j^s, \hat{r}_{j+1}\}]$. The resulting regression R' has error $E_{R'} < E_R$, which contradicts the optimality of R. □

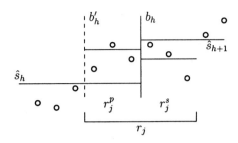

Figure 2. Second case in Theorem 1.

Theorem 1 *Given a sequence X and an integer k, the algorithm described in Section 3.3 yields the optimal unimodal k-segmentation.*

Proof: Let R be the unimodal regression computed by PAV and S be the optimal unimodal k-segmentation. We prove the optimality of the algorithm by showing that the segment boundaries in S never split any regression segment $r_j \in R$.

First consider the increasing monotonic regression. Let us assume that there exists a segment boundary b_h, such that for some regression segment r_j its prefix r_j^p and suffix r_j^s belong to two different segments s_h and s_{h+1}. Let the levels of the segments be $\hat{s}_h$ and $\hat{s}_{h+1}$. There are now two possible cases. Either $\bar{r}_j^s$ is closer to $\hat{s}_h$ or it is closer to $\hat{s}_{h+1}$ (when $\hat{s}_h$ and $\hat{s}_{h+1}$ are equally close, we can choose either one).

In the first case, the error of the segmentation is reduced when the points in r_j^s are assigned to segment s_h instead of segment s_{h+1} (level values $\hat{s}_h$ and $\hat{s}_{h+1}$ can remain unchanged). In the second case, the error is reduced when the points in r_j^p are assigned to segment s_{h+1}. This holds, because if the average of the suffix $\bar{r}_j^s$ is closer to $\hat{s}_{h+1}$ than to $\hat{s}_h$, then also $\bar{r}_j^p$ is closer to that level, since $\bar{r}_j^p \geq \bar{r}_j^s$ by Lemma 2, and $\hat{s}_{h+1} \geq \hat{s}_h$. This case is demonstrated in Figure 2, with b_h' marking the new segment boundary yielding a smaller error than the boundary b_h.

The argumentation goes similarly for the decreasing case. The top regression segment r_t does not cause any difficulties, as it will always consist of a single point, and can therefore not be divided between segments. If r_t contained more than one point, the error of the regression could be reduced by making the highest point into a new regression segment (this would not violate the unimodality constraint).

In each case, the error of the segmentation S can be reduced by moving a segment boundary that occurs within a regression segment, which means that S was not an optimal segmentation. Thus the segment boundaries can never split any regression segment. □

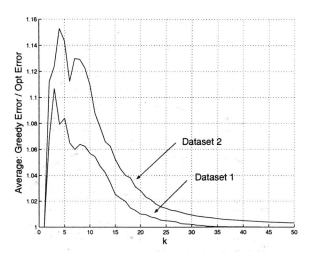

Figure 3. Averages of the error ratio GREEDY/OPT for two datasets. Dataset 1: 11 unimodal sequences of 750 points, Dataset 2: 20 non-unimodal sequences of 2000 points.

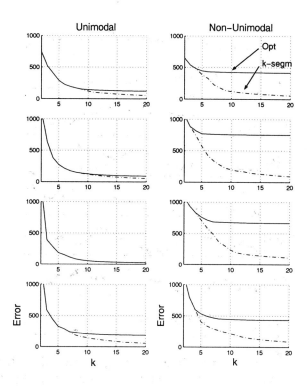

Figure 5. Error for unrestricted segmentation and OPT with $k = 2, \ldots, 20$.

5 Experiments

We conducted experiments to demonstrate the performance of the algorithm GREEDY compared to OPT, and to validate two methods for measuring the unimodality of a sequence. First we ran both GREEDY and OPT on two different datasets, and measured the average ratio of the errors they produced. Dataset 1 consisted of 11 unimodally-behaving sequences of 750 points, extracted from water-level measurements [9], and Dataset 2 from 20 generated random walk sequences of 2000 points. We observed that the algorithms give results very close to each other, both for the unimodal and non-unimodal datasets. The error ratios are displayed in Figure 3. For $k = 1$, the ratio is 1; as k increases up to some small value, the ratio increases, as well, and then it starts to decrease and approach 1 again. This shows that the greedy algorithm gives very good results in practice.

The aim of the second set of experiments was to test methods for measuring unimodality of the data, by applying unimodal k-segmentation. We developed two methods for deciding if a given sequence is unimodal or not, and we applied them on 8 sequences of about 2000 points, extracted from exchange-rate data [9]. The idea was to compare the results of our methods between sequences that seemed unimodal by visual inspection and sequences that did not seem to exhibit unimodal behavior. The dataset that we experimented on consisted of four sequences that seemed roughly unimodal, and four sequences that did not seem to display unimodal behavior (see Figure 4).

The first approach was to compare the error of an optimal unimodal k-segmentation to the error of an optimal unrestricted k-segmentation, i.e., a segmentation with no unimodality constraints. The idea is that if the sequence exhibits unimodal behaviour, then the error of its unimodal segmentation does not differ very much from the error of its unrestricted segmentation. The errors for k-segmentation and OPT can be found in Figure 5.

The results differ clearly between the sequences that seem to display unimodal behaviour, and the ones that do not seem to behave unimodally. For $k = 1$, both algorithms give the same result (with average of the sequence as the only level). When k increases, the unrestricted error starts to deviate from the unimodal error. When k reaches the number of the regression segments in the sequence, unimodal error does not decrease anymore, while the unrestricted error decreases up to $k = n$. With non-unimodal sequences, the unimodal error stays at a level clearly higher than the unrestricted error. For, say, $k = 20$ the difference between the two types of sequences is already clear (as well as for a wide range of other values of k).

For being able to distinguish between the unimodal and non-unimodal sequences, some kind of concrete measure of unimodality is needed, based on which sequences can then be classified. One such measure could be a simple ratio: the error of unrestricted k-segmentation divided by the error

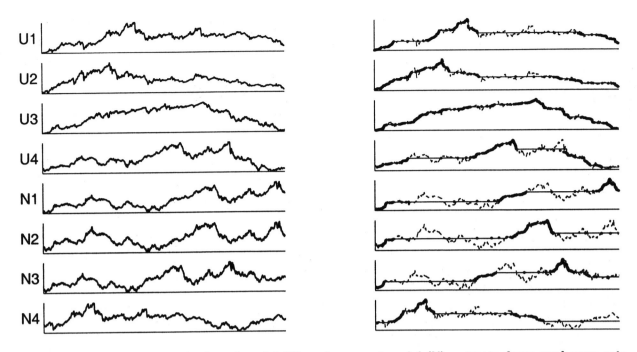

Figure 4. Left: Four seemingly unimodal (U) and non-unimodal (N) extracts from exchange-rate data [9]. Right: Sequence (dashed line), regression segments (points), and segmentation by OPT (horizontal lines) with $k = 20$.

	m	E_k	E_O	E_G	$\frac{E_k}{E_O}$	$\frac{E_O}{E_P}$	t-test
U_1	151	51.3	121.7	129.0	0.42	0.18	4.374
U_2	158	53.9	91.7	101.3	0.59	0.09	4.929
U_3	262	26.3	27.5	36.9	0.96	0.02	4.478
U_4	176	57.9	186.1	192.7	0.31	0.17	4.507
N_1	124	57.2	417.3	419.8	0.14	0.50	2.215
N_2	91	92.3	750.6	751.5	0.12	0.76	1.143
N_3	117	111.5	663.2	668.8	0.17	0.59	2.080
N_4	110	87.2	433.0	437.3	0.20	0.40	2.301

Figure 6. Unimodality measures. m: **number of regression segments,** E_k: **error of unrestricted k-segmentation,** E_O: **error of OPT, E_G: error of GREEDY, E_P: average error of OPT for randomly permuted sequences.**

of unimodal k-segmentation. We can set k to be a value large enough to demonstrate the different behavior of the two types of sequences (we chose $k = 20$) and calculate the error ratios for each sequence. The results are shown in Figure 6. For this data, a simple threshold of e.g. 0.3 can be used to classify the sequences: values higher than the threshold imply unimodality of the sequence.

The second experiment was to randomly permute the

unimodal segments in the data, and to see if the error of unimodal k-segmentation on the permuted sequence was comparable to the error on the original sequence. First, we applied OPT on the sequence and permuted the discovered segments to obtain sequences consisting of a concatenation of the k segments in a random order. Then we applied OPT on the permuted sequences. If the original sequence was indeed unimodal, then the error of the permutations should be larger in a statistically significant way. On the other hand, if the data did not behave unimodally, then the random permutations would be expected to have an error relatively close to the error of the original sequence. The idea is that a random permutation is going to completely destroy the unimodal structure of the sequence, if such exists.

We chose k to be 20, and performed 100 iterations for each sequence. A histogram of the errors is presented in Figure 7. It seems clear that the errors for the unimodal sequences deviate more from the permutation errors than those for the non-unimodal sequences. To get a similar statistic than for the previous experiment, we measured the ratio of the segmentation error of the original sequence to the average error for the permutations. The results are shown in Figure 6. It seems that this ratio also separates unimodal and non-unimodal sequences, and we can set a threshold at e.g., 0.2. Values smaller than the threshold imply unimodal behavior of the sequence.

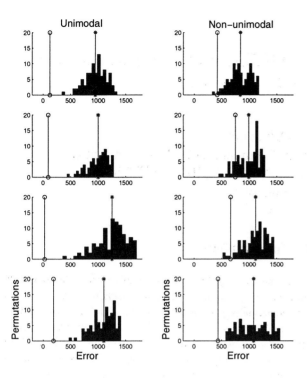

Figure 7. Errors in 100 permutations for $k = 20$, with error for the original sequence (o) and average error of the permutations (*).

To obtain an alternative statistical measure of unimodality, we performed a standard t-test to see if the error of the original sequence seems to stem from the same distribution as the permutation errors. Those results are also shown in Figure 6. The larger results for the unimodal sequences indicate that they differ significantly from the error distribution of the random permutations. Again, a threshold value can be used to distinguish between the two types of sequences.

6   Conclusions

We have presented two algorithms for the problem of segmenting a sequence into k pieces with monotonicity or unimodality constraints. We proved the optimality of our first algorithm, OPT, which is based on a well-known regression algorithm and on dynamic programming. The second algorithm, GREEDY, is not optimal, but it is more efficient and we experimentally verified that it gives very good results. Additionally, we described two tests for distinguishing if a sequence behaves unimodally or not. Our experiments with real datasets provided evidence that the suggested algorithms and the unimodality tests perform very well in practice. An interesting open problem is to examine

if there exists some guarantee for the quality of the results produced by GREEDY. Another remaining problem is to devise unimodal segmentation algorithms for other norms, in particular L_1 and L_∞, for which Theorem 1 does not hold.

Acknowledgments We thank Heikki Mannila, Kari Laasonen and Evimaria Terzi for many useful discussions and suggestions.

References

[1] M. Ayer, H. D. Brunk, G. M. Ewing, and W. T. Reid. An empirical distribution function for sampling with incomplete information. *The annals of mathematical statistics*, 26(4):641–647, 1955.

[2] R. Bellman. On the approximation of curves by line segments using dynamic programming. *Communications of the ACM*, 4(6), 1961.

[3] M. Frisén. Unimodal regression. *The Statistician*, 35:304–307, 1980.

[4] Z. Geng and N. Shi. Isotonic regression for umbrella orderings. *Applied Statistics*, 39, 1990.

[5] S. Guha, N. Koudas, and K. Shim. Data-streams and histograms. In *ACM Symposium on Theory of Computing*, pages 471–475, 2001.

[6] D. Hand, H. Mannila, and P. Smyth. *Principles of Data Mining*. MIT Press, 2001.

[7] J. P. Hardwick and Q. F. Stout. Optimizing a unimodal response function for binary variables. In *Optimum Design*, pages 195–208, 2000.

[8] Y. Kaufman and A. Tamir. Locating service centers with precedence constraints. *Discrete Applied Mathematics*, 47:251–261, 1993.

[9] E. Keogh. UCR Time Series Data Mining Archive, http://www.cs.ucr.edu/ eamonn/TSDMA/.

[10] C. I. C. Lee. The min-max algorithm and isotonic regression. *Annal of statistics*, 11:467–477, 1983.

[11] P. M. Pardalos and G. Xue. Algorithms for a class of isotonic regression problems. *Algorithmica*, 23(3):211–222, 1999.

[12] P. M. Pardalos, G. Xue, and L. Yong. Efficient computation of the isotonic median regression. *Applied Mathematics Letters*, 8(2):67–70, 1995.

[13] A. Restrepo and A. C. Bovik. Locally monotonic-regression. *IEEE Transactions on Signal Processing*, 41:2796–2780, 1994.

[14] T. Robertson, F. T. Wright, and R. L. Dykstra. *Order Restricted Statistical Inference*. 1988.

[15] Q. F. Stout. Optimal algorithms for unimodal regression. In *Computing science and statistics 32*, 2000.

Dependencies between transcription factor binding sites: comparison between ICA, NMF, PLSA and frequent sets

Heli Hiisilä and Ella Bingham
Neural Networks Research Centre, Laboratory of Computer and Information Science
Helsinki University of Technology, P.O. Box 5400, FIN-02015 HUT, Finland
heli.hiisila@hut.fi, ella@iki.fi

Abstract

Gene expression of eucaryotes is regulated through transcription factors, which are molecules able to attach to the binding sites in the DNA sequence. These binding sites are small pieces of DNA usually found upstream from the gene they regulate. As the binding sites play an important role in the gene expression, it is of interest to find out their characteristics.

In this paper we look for dependencies and independencies between these binding sites using independent component analysis (ICA), non-negative matrix factorization (NMF), probabilistic latent semantic analysis (PLSA) and the method of frequent sets. The data used are human gene upstream regions and possible binding sites listed in a biological database. Also, results on the baker's yeast (S.Cerevisiae) upstream regions are briefly discussed for comparison.

ICA, NMF and PLSA are latent variable methods that decompose the observed data into smaller components. Of these, ICA and NMF were originally aimed for continuous data. We show that these methods can be successfully used on discrete DNA data as well. PLSA and the method of frequent sets were created for discrete data sets.

The above methods reveal partially overlapping sets of possible binding sites such that the binding sites within a set are dependent of each other. The methods of frequent sets and NMF give a good overview of the most common data structures, whereas using ICA and PLSA we find large sets that are surprisingly frequent. That is, sets of very frequently occurring possible binding sites can be found near hundreds or thousands of genes; also interesting but less frequent ones co-occur surprisingly often.

1 Introduction

In the eucaryotic cells such as yeast or human, certain proteins, which are called *transcription factors* (TF), influence the transcription of a gene and thus participate in the gene expression. Factors bind to short pieces of DNA strand found mostly at the promoter regions upstream from the gene. These pieces of DNA are called as transcription factor binding sites, or in short, motifs.

The detection of these relatively small pieces of DNA that may regulate the gene expression has been under study in the past few years. Computational, probabilistic and statistical approaches [1][2][7][20] have been used, as well as methods utilizing gene expression data [3][14] to find possible DNA binding sites from the DNA sequence. The TRANSFAC [19] database contains a large amount of known transcription factor binding sites. In this study, we aim at characterizing the co-occurrences of these binding sites.

We are not able to detect online how the transcription happens with different genes, but as the DNA sequence includes the information of how this process is done, we may use it to get new knowledge of these processes. Two biologically interesting questions are: Are there common motifs, possible binding sites, near many genes? If there are, are there groups of these motifs co-occurring near many genes? These dependencies are looked for using four different kinds of algorithms: frequent sets, ICA, NMF and PLSA.

The idea of frequent sets is intuitive because we get the most frequently occurring patterns of the data as an output of the algorithm. The latent variable methods ICA and NMF have originally been developed to decompose a continuous data set into smaller parts, components. Here we use these methods to find components from a discrete data matrix. PLSA is a latent variable model that has a probabilistic point of view.

The aim in this paper is to find interesting patterns that characterize the dependencies of the motifs in the data set

114

well or patterns that are surprising, and to provide a comparison between the methods used. We will introduce the methods briefly in section 2. Experimental results are given in section 3. Also baker's yeast upstream regions were used as a comparison, and the results are briefly discussed in section 4. Section 5 gives a conclusion.

2 Methods

The starting point of our study is an observation matrix X of attributes and observations. Each column of X is an upstream region of a gene (that is, an observation). The rows of X correspond to different motifs (attributes). If an upstream region contains a motif, the corresponding entry of X has a value 1; otherwise the value is 0. To find dependencies between the attributes, the method of frequent sets [18], independent component analysis (ICA) [12], nonnegative matrix factorization (NMF) [16] and probabilistic latent semantic analysis (PLSA) [10] are used.

2.1 Frequent sets

Advanced algorithms for finding frequent collections of events from databases are introduced by Mannila et al. [18]. The basic idea is to find sets of events that co-occur frequently. In the case of matrices built of the occurrences of motifs in the gene upstream regions, frequent sets are groups of DNA motifs occurring together in many upstream regions.

The algorithm used for finding frequent sets uses the Apriori candidate generation. The search for frequent sets begins from the sets of only one attribute, and frequent sets of size n are used when creating the candidates of sets of size $n + 1$. The iterations end when no more frequent sets can be found.

The frequency threshold percentage parameter gives the limit of how many times must a set occur in the data set so that it is called frequent. With low values of the parameter, the amount of frequent sets tends to grow very large, and the results are not easy to analyze. With large parameter values only very common patterns in the data are revealed.

2.2 Independent component analysis (ICA)

Independent Component Analysis (ICA) [5][12][13] is a sophisticated method for finding latent variables s, that are statistically independent of each other, from the observed data. It is assumed that the observed data can be represented as a linear mixture: $x_j = a_{j1}s_1 + a_{j2}s_2 + \ldots + a_{jn}s_n$ for all j, where a_{ji} are mixing coefficients, all s_i are latent variables and x_j is an entry of a vector x.

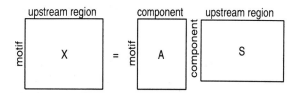

Figure 1. ICA mixing model. X **matrix is the data matrix,** A **matrix explains which motifs (attributes) belong to which components and the** S **matrix lists the upstream regions (observations) where each component is found.**

This mixing model may be written using vector-matrix notation:

$$x = As \qquad (1)$$

where A is a matrix that has elements a_{ji}. The matrix A is unknown and constant for all observations x. Figure 1 illustrates the matrices of the mixing model of equation 1. The matrix X has observation vectors x as its columns. The columns of the A matrix explain to which degree each attribute is present in each component. The matrix S contains the vectors s as its rows.

Independent components can be estimated from the observed data with an assumption of the component independence and non-Gaussian distribution and assuming A is of full column rank [5].

The equation 1 may be written in a form $s = A^{-1}x = Wx$ when A^{-1} is a denoted by W. The ICA problem is solved by finding W such that the resulting s are statistically independent. Algorithms for ICA are given e.g. in [12]. In this paper we use the FastICA [13] [9] and we choose to maximize the skewness of s.

ICA was originally developed for continuous data in signal processing. Lately it has been discovered that it is a promising method for discrete data as well, for example text documents [4].

2.3 Non-negative matrix factorization (NMF)

The basic idea of Non-negative matrix factorization (NMF) is to search for matrices A and S such that $X = AS$, using iterative update rules given in [16] [17].

The setting is similar to Figure 1. But in contrast to ICA, in NMF one does not assume anything about the nature of A and S, except for nonnegativity. Again a column of the A matrix gives the attributes belonging to a latent component. In this paper we use an algorithm that minimizes the Euclidean distance $\|X - AS\|$, presented in [17].

2.4 Probabilistic Latent Semantic Analysis (PLSA)

Thomas Hofmann [10] [11] has created a method called probabilistic latent semantic analysis (PLSA) for factor analysis of count data. PLSA is influenced by latent semantic analysis (LSA), but has a probabilistic point of view.

The idea of PLSA is as follows. The observations (d) consist of occurrences of attributes (w). The prior probability for observation d is $P(d)$. $P(z|d)$ is the probability to pick a latent variable z in observation d and $P(w|z)$ is the probability to generate an attribute w, given latent variable z. Observations d and attributes w are assumed to be conditionally independent given z. An occurrence of attribute w in observation d is represented as a pair (d, w).

Data generation process may be written as [10] $P(d, w) = P(d)P(w|d)$, where $P(w|d) = \sum_z P(w|z)P(z|d)$, giving $P(d, w) = P(d) \sum_z P(w|z)P(z|d)$.

The goal is to identify the conditional probabilities $P(w|z)$ and $P(z|d)$ by maximizing the log-likelihood function using the EM algorithm. In the expectation (E) step, posterior probabilities will be computed for the latent variables and in the M-step the expected complete data log-likelihood should be maximized. Each component or latent variable z can be characterized by listing the attributes w which give the largest values for $P(w|z)$. This is analogous to listing the attributes having a high value in a column of the of the A matrix in ICA and NMF.

2.5 Selecting the relevant sets

In the sequel, we will use the term "component" to refer to a set of motifs (transcription factor binding sites). Such a set is identified either as a frequent set, or as attributes having a large value in a column of the A matrix in ICA or NMF or as attributes w having a large value of $P(w|z)$ in PLSA.

One problem with all the methods described in this section is that it is not easy to select the parameters defining the amount of components to be looked for. A fair selection of these parameters is especially important when comparing the results produced by different methods.

When the data matrix is large, as in the case of human gene upstream regions, it may also contain a large amount of components. The solution selected here is to first look for a relatively large amount of components, and then select the best components based on certain criteria. With the smaller yeast data of section 4 this is unnecessary as we are able to analyze all the components found.

A good method finds components explaining the observations well. Also the components should not be trivial, but rather reveal some underlying structure in the data set, and be surprisingly frequent.

With each method described above in this section, the component selection used here goes as follows. First we find a large set of components. Then we choose, one by one, the components that cover the observations best. At each step the best component explains a larger amount of observations than any other component. When the best component is found, the 1's explained by this component are removed from the data matrix, and the remaining ones may still be explained by other components. A certain amount of the best components are then reported. This procedure is used with each method described in this section.

Another desired feature of a component is that it is surprising. Surprisingness here is defined based on the amount of component occurrences $F(C)$ in the data and the expected frequency $E(C)$ of the component C. The expected frequency of the component is calculated based on the frequencies of the attributes of the component:

$$E(C) = N \prod_{i \ s.t. \ w_i \in C} f(w_i) \qquad (2)$$

where C is the component, N is the total number of upstream regions in the matrix X, w_i is a transcription factor binding site belonging to the component C, and $f(w_i)$ is the frequency of the factor w_i in the binary matrix X. $F(C)$ is the amount of upstream regions where an occurrence of component C can be found. The ratio $F(C)/E(C)$ describes how surprising the component C is based on the frequencies of the attribute w_i belonging to the component C.

3 Experimental results

3.1 Data used

The upstream regions of 18406 human genes were downloaded from [6], and the areas of 1000 bp upstream from the genes were selected. Also a large collection of transcription factor (TF) binding site sequences (motifs) was downloaded from the TRANSFAC database [19]. Very long and very short motifs were left out as well as ones including an other motif as a subsequence. After removing these uninteresting motifs, a total of 216 motifs were selected.

When starting to analyze this problem, we have only little knowledge of the TF binding sites in the upstream regions. The aim is to discover both common and more rare but surprising structures from the data using different methods. A binary matrix, like the X matrix of figure 1, was created by searching for motif occurrences in each upstream region. The X matrix of size 216×18406 contains approximately 6.8% ones and 93.2% zeros, and X is thus quite sparse. There are many motifs, binding sites, that occur very frequently, and the 10 most common ones are introduced in Table 1. Each of these motifs may be found in as many as 37-50% of all upstream regions.

Table 1. Most common motifs and their frequencies in the observation matrix.

Motif	$F(w)$
GGCGGG	9304
CCGCCC	8947
GGGCGG	8872
GGTGGG	8544
GGGAAG	8266
GGGGCC	7869
AGGCGG	7178
TTCCTT	6925
AAGGAA	6849
GAGGCG	6737

3.2 Results

The amount of components looked for with ICA, NMF and PLSA methods was 200, and the frequency threshold percentage for finding about 200 frequent sets was 10%. Components with only one motif were left out, as they do not include information about the relationships of the motifs. For each method ten components giving the best coverage of the data are reported here.

The results given by different methods are shown in Tables 2, 3, 4, 5 and 6. Some comparison between the methods can be found in the section 3.3 and discussion about the biological relevance of the results in the section 3.4.

3.2.1 Frequent sets

First the frequent sets were searched for and the sets giving the best coverage of the data are reported in Table 2. For comparison, maximal frequent sets were also extracted, and the sets covering the observations are available in Table 3. The frequency threshold parameter in both experiments was 10%, that is, each frequent set can be found in at least 10% of gene upstream regions.

The frequent sets of Table 2 include groups of motifs that appear very frequently in the gene upstream regions. These 10 components cover 25% of all observations, and thus give a good overview of the most common structures in the data matrix. The components are short, as they only include two motifs. Three of the first components include overlapping motifs and are not thus very interesting, even though consensus motifs GGGCGGG, CCCCGCCC, GAGGCGG must be very important motifs, as they can be found so frequently in the data. The other sets 4 to 10 are nontrivial, although not very surprising, and found in more than 1200 gene upstream regions.

Table 2. Frequent sets giving the best coverage of the data.

	Frequent set C	$F(C)$	$\frac{F(C)}{E(C)}$
1	GGGCGG GGCGGG	7437	1.7
2	CCGCCC CCCCGCC	5215	1.8
3	GAGGCG AGGCGG	5123	1.9
4	GGGGCC GGTGGG	4442	1.2
5	GGGAAG AAGGAA	3208	1.0
6	TTCCTT TTTCCA	2708	1.1
7	CACCTG TGTGGG	2125	1.0
8	GGGAAG CCCCTCC	1763	1.2
9	AAGGAA GGAAAT	1280	1.3
10	TTCCTT AAGTGA	1237	1.1

Table 3. Maximal frequent sets giving the best coverage of the data.

	Maximal frequent set C	$F(C)$	$\frac{F(C)}{E(C)}$
1	GGGCGG GGCGGG CCGCCC GAGGCG AGGCGG	2194	7.0
2	GGGCGG GGCGGG GGGGCC GGGAAG	1628	3.3
3	AAGGAA GGTGGG	3001	0.94
4	TTCCTT TTTCCA	2708	1.1
5	CCCCTCC CCGCCC CCCCGCC	1758	2.7
6	GGGAAG CACCTG	2418	1.0
7	GGGGCC TGTGGG	2092	1.1
8	GGTGGG GACCCT	1537	1.1
9	CCGCCC ACGCCC	1446	1.3
10	TGTCCT GGCGGG	1413	0.97

The maximal frequent sets with best coverage of observations shown in Table 3 explain 19% of all 1's of the data matrix. Component 1 includes components 1 and 2 of Table 2, and can still be found in many upstream regions. Also component 2 includes component 1 of Table 2 and component 5 includes component 2 of Table 2. Other components of Tables 2 and 3 seems to also have some common motifs, but with other pairs.

3.2.2 ICA components

The FastICA algorithm was run and 200 independent components were estimated. For each component i we picked those motifs j for which the entry a_{ij} in A was significantly larger than zero. Components with only one motif were left out as was done in the case of frequent sets, too. Ten components giving the best coverage of the data were selected, and represented in Table 4.

Components of Table 4 cover only about 7% of the observations, but there are some longer and more surprising components also included. For example, component 4 of Table 4 can be found in 211 gene upstream regions, though

Table 4. ICA giving the best coverage of the data.

	ICA component C	$F(C)$	$\frac{F(C)}{E(C)}$
1	GGGAAG GGGGCC GGTGGG TGTGGG	1002	2.0
2	TTTCCA TGTCCT	1817	1.0
3	TTGGCA GATTGG	856	1.3
4	GGGCGG GAGGCG GGGGCC GGCGGG CCCCTCC CCGCCC CCCCGCC ACGCCC	211	33
5	TTCCTT CTTTGCT	794	1.2
6	CTATCT TTTCCA	697	1.1
7	CAAAAGG AAGGAA	681	1.4
8	GGGAAG TGCAAAG	650	1.1
9	CACCTG CATCTG TGTCCT	372	1.4
10	GGGCGG GGGAAG CACCTG GGTGGG GACCCT	202	1.9

it has as many as 8 motifs. Component 8 shares common motifs with maximal frequent sets 2 and 5 of Table 3. One may consider these long independent components as a kind of summary components, as the subsets of these components are very frequent.

3.2.3 NMF components

The NMF algorithm was run and 200 components were searched. As in the case of ICA, we picked those motifs j whose entry a_{ij} in A was significantly larger than zero. Again, components with only one motif were left out and the components giving the best coverage can be found in Table 5.

Table 5. NMF components giving the best coverage of the data.

	NMF component C	$F(C)$	$\frac{F(C)}{E(C)}$
1	GGGCGG GGCGGG	7437	1.7
2	CCGCCC CCCCGCC	5215	1.8
3	GAGGCG AGGCGG	5123	1.9
4	GGGAAG GGGGCC	4122	1.2
5	AAGGAA GGTGGG	3001	0.94
6	TTCCTT TTTCCA	2708	1.1
7	CCCCTCC CTGCCCC	1678	1.5
8	TGGGTC GGTGGG	1455	1.2
9	GGTGGG CCGCCC	915	1.1
10	GGGGCC CCGCCC	621	1.1

The NMF components of Table 5 give a nice coverage of 24% of the data, but contain only two motifs each. The motifs in the NMF components are also very common. NMF algorithm has also found many components where the motifs are overlapping. This kind of components are 1 (with consensus sequence GGGCGGG), 2 (CCCCGCCC) and 3

(GAGGCGG). These components are a result of a longer consensus motif, not of two different motifs, like other NMF components found. There are several common components found by NMF (Table 5) and frequent sets (Table 2).

3.2.4 PLSA components

Instead of decomposing X into A and S, PLSA gives the probabilities of motifs in latent components. For each component z we pick the motifs w whose probability $P(w|z)$ is significantly larger than zero. The PLSA algorithm was used to estimate 200 components from the data set, and the components giving the best coverage of the data are shown in Table 6. Again, components consisting of one motif only were discarded.

Table 6. PLSA components giving the best coverage of the data.

	PLSA component C	$F(C)$	$\frac{F(C)}{E(C)}$
1	AAGGAA TCGCGG	2068	1.4
2	TAGCGGGTG GAGGCG	1617	100
3	TTCCGA CACCTG	1614	2.0
4	ACCTGTT TTCCTT	1613	3.2
5	CACAGGAA CCTTATATGG GGGGCC	760	3200
6	TTCCGA TCGCGG	235	1.8
7	GGTTAG GAGGATGT	200	4.5
8	TATGGTAAT TTCCTT	104	8.4
9	CACAGGAA CCTTATATGG ATTGAA	63	1300
10	CACAGGAA CCCCACCTC	65	3.5

Though PLSA components of Table 6 cover only 4% of the data, they are quite interesting. There are many longer and less frequent motifs in the components, which makes components like 5 and 9 quite surprising.

3.3 Comparison of methods

When analyzing biological data sets, one should always keep in mind to use more than one computational method. Also the selection of parameters may be tricky, as they may have a major impact to the results. When selecting the method to be used, one also needs to decide whether to concentrate to the big picture or to details.

Components found using frequent sets naturally include most common and thus quite short motifs. Components with longer and more frequent motifs are not found using the method of frequent sets. If details are wanted, a very small frequency threshold parameter must be used, and the amount of frequent sets found grows very high, which makes finding interesting sets gets even more difficult. The strength of the frequent sets method is to get exact knowledge of the common structures of data. Other complimentary methods may be used when details is what we are looking for. Maximal frequent sets is a more compact way of presenting components and rules of the data structure as well. However, frequent sets did give a better coverage of data, as the found components were shorter and matched with more observations.

In general, ICA finds relatively long components that are not very frequent. However, the subsets of these long components are very frequent. It seems that ICA is able to create summary components of the data and thus find underlying structures. As ICA is able to extract these surprising long components, it is also a good method for extracting interesting details from the data set. Most of the independent components found in different runs are similar.

NMF components found are similar to frequent sets: they are short, and contain very common motifs. NMF gives a very good coverage of data set, but the components found are only pairs of motifs. The selection of parameter values seems to have more effect to NMF than to other methods, and longer components may be found with different amount of components to be estimated.

PLSA found components with rare and long motifs. These motifs co-occur together very often. PLSA is most suitable for count data instead of binary data, which may be one of the reasons why PLSA did not cover the data well. Also, in PLSA it is assumed that all attributes (motifs) belonging to a component might not appear in the same observation (upstream region). However, PLSA found most surprising components: components containing motifs that have strong dependencies.

The data coverage of the components found by each of the methods may seem poor, but one must remember that we have discarded components consisting of one motif only. The data could be nicely covered with these motifs that are very common, but in this study we aim at finding relationships between the motifs.

One of the advantages of latent variable methods such as ICA, NMF and PLSA is that they give a parsimonious representation of the data. We may present the data as a set of latent variables, and these latent variables can be described either as lists of representative attributes (here, motifs) or as lists of representative observations (here, upstream regions). This can be seen as multi-way clustering, where the clusters are allowed to overlap.

3.4 Biological relevance

There are still much unknown issues when it comes to transcription and gene expression in general. There are transcription factors and there are sites where they bind, but we are not able to detect how this all really happens. Because of

this, we must use the data we have: DNA sequence, which includes the binding sites.

Based on the experiments with frequent sets and NMF, one may conclude that there is a group of very common motifs occurring in the upstream regions of genes. As all of these motifs have been listed in biological databases as transcription factor binding sites of certain genes, it is quite interesting that they can be found near thousands of other genes also. This common vocabulary might suggest that if certain genes have similar regulatory patterns, their gene expressions have common functionalities. ICA and PLSA algorithms found less frequent components, but the motifs of these components have strong dependencies. So there are also less frequent binding sites that co-occur together very often.

An interesting application of the structures found would be to cluster genes based on these binding site profiles. This kind of clustering would certainly give us new knowledge of the genes based on their regulatory regions. Also interesting topics are to compare transcription profiles of gene families or genes of different chromosomes.

The structures found and introduced in this study are characteristic to a large amount of gene upstream regions. This knowledge of the sequences before the genes could be used to improve gene prediction. As the known genes have groups of motifs shown in this paper, similar groups may probably be found in the upstream regions of new genes also. If some of the components introduced previously are found in the DNA, a gene may very well be near by.

4 Yeast data

As a comparison to human upstream regions, the same experiments were done with the upstream regions of baker's yeast, Saccharomyces Cerevisiae. The data set is much smaller, as there were 6349 gene upstream regions and 48 motifs. Similar binary matrix was created based on this data, and the methods introduced previously were used. A short summary of the results is given in section 4.1 and human and yeast results are briefly discussed in section 4.2.

The yeast data included 9 very common motifs: ATTTTT (4474 upstream regions include at least one occurrence), TTATC (4383), GATAA (4343), TGAAAA (3647), ATATAA (3235), GAGGA (3079), TATAAA (3030), TCTCC (3005), CATCC (2761). All of these motifs can be found in more than 43% of all upstream sequences and they all co-occur in 32 different upstream regions. When comparing to the most common human motifs of Table 1, there are no matches.

4.1 Yeast results

Due to the limited space, we cannot present all components found by different methods here. Let us just list a few interesting examples of the results on yeast.

About 20 components were looked for using the four algorithms, and because of the smaller size of the data set, they were all analyzed. Component selection such as what was described in Section 2.5 was not needed here.

Maximal frequent sets found give the most common pairs of motifs and cover 56% of the data, but the sets are not surprising. In that sense, there is no special intelligence in the method: the most common components are selected based on the frequencies and the chosen frequency threshold parameter. An interesting example of the frequent sets found is a component containing motifs ATTTTT, GATAA and TTATC. Motifs GATAA and TTATC are complements and reversed versions of each other and the component can be found in 2225 yeast gene upstream regions.

Independent components found were surprising, as the components occur in average 1.6 times more often than one could expect based on the motif frequencies. Also the components were larger and contain a larger amount of different motifs than components found with other methods. The data coverage of 32% is also fairly good. One of the most interesting ICA components was found in 73 gene upstream regions and had 6 motifs: ATATAA, ATTATCAA, GAGGA, GATAA, TATAAA and TTATC, and thus includes at least binding sites of well-known transcription factors TBP/TATA, MATalpha2 and GATA.

The NMF components found cover approximately 41% of the data. The components found were in average longer and more diverse than the ones found by the basic method of frequent sets. However, NMF components were not as surprising as the ICA components.

PLSA algorithm did a poor job in finding components of motifs from the yeast gene upstream regions. The components were quite rare and short and not really surprising. The PLSA components covered only 6.8% of the ones in the data matrix. Also the amount of components to be estimated has a major effect to the components found by the PLSA algorithm.

4.2 Comparison of human and yeast results

The analysis of yeast data is very different from the analysis of human data as the sizes of the data sets differ a lot. In the yeast data we were able to study all components exhaustively whereas in the case of human data we must select a subset of the components for display.

Human and yeast transcription factor binding sites are dissimilar, and thus it is not relevant to compare the exact components found. However, there is a certain group of very common motifs in the upstream regions of both species. Both organisms have also larger groups of motifs that are less common. Yeast motifs include more A's and T's whereas human motifs have much G's and C's.

The results of frequent sets on human and yeast data are quite similar in nature: simple components consisting of very common motifs are found. ICA may find several motifs, such that subsets of these motif sets are very common, meaning that an ICA component gives a summary of common patterns in the data. NMF found larger groups of yeast motifs than human motifs. PLSA did a poor job with the smaller yeast data, whereas PLSA results with human data are quite interesting.

5 Conclusions

What we have learned by doing this study is that there are many common structures of possible binding sites in the upstream regions of genes. Some are very frequent, occurring before thousands of genes; some other structures include many motifs which co-occur surprisingly often. Without going to details, one may conclude that the upstream regions have a common vocabulary, which may be a key to understanding the gene expression better. If certain genes have similar regulatory patterns, their gene expression may have common functionalities. Similar results were obtained with both human and yeast data sets.

Different kinds of approaches may be taken when decomposing a data matrix into smaller parts. In addition to methods discussed in this paper — frequent sets, ICA, NMF and PLSA — there are others suitable for binary observations. To mention a few, the Proximus method [15] decomposes the data matrix recursively by rank-one approximations consisting of binary feature vectors and their binary occurrence vectors. However, there is no latent variable interpretation in their model. Single-cause Bernoulli mixtures [8] are a common method but are restricted to assuming one latent cause per observation vector, whereas we wish to allow the appearance of several latent variables in an observation vector.

In our experiments, frequent sets and NMF give components with very common motifs, independent components are more rare but form kind of summary components and the PLSA algorithm finds surprising components with long and rare motifs. The 10 components giving the best coverage of motif occurrences in the human upstream regions found by each method have been presented here. With the smaller yeast data PLSA did not do very well, but ICA and NMF found interesting longer components and maximal frequent sets gave a good coverage of data.

We have shown that the observations can be decomposed into meaningful components using the frequent sets and latent variable methods. Also other similar kinds of biological data sets may be analyzed using the solutions given in this paper. If a quick overview of the most common patterns in the data matrix is needed, maximal frequent sets or NMF might be good methods to use. However, if interesting longer patterns should be looked for, ICA and PLSA might be a suitable choice. Or better still, to discover both frequent and surprising components, use all of the methods.

A possible future direction would be to find the most common and often simple data patterns by the method of frequent sets. After that, the "residual" (the part of data not covered by frequent sets) could be analyzed with ICA, PLSA or NMF, giving insight into the detailed structure of the data. Also the clustering of the genes based on their upstream region structures is something to consider. Finding groups of genes with similar patterns in their regulatory regions would give us new insights of the gene expression.

6 Acknowledgments

The authors would like to thank Professor Heikki Mannila for his insights into the topic. We would also like to thank Teemu Hirsimäki for the use of his PLSA algorithm implementation.

References

[1] A. Brazma, I. Jonassen, J. Vilo, and E. Ukkonen. Predicting gene regulatory elements in silico on a genomic scale. *Genome Research*, 8(11):1202–1215, November 1998.

[2] H. J. Bussemaker, H. Li, and E. D. Siggia. Building a dictionary for genomes: Identification of presumptive regulatory sites by statistical analysis. *PNAS*, 97(18):10096–10100, August 2000.

[3] H. J. Bussemaker, H. Li, and E. D. Siggia. Regulatory element detection using correlation with expression. *Nature Genetics*, 27:167–171, February 2001.

[4] J. Charles Lee Isbell and P. Viola. Restructuring sparse high dimensional data for effective retrieval. In *NIPS*, pages 480–486, 1998.

[5] P. Comon. Independent component analysis, a new concept? *Signal Processing*, 36:287–314, 1994.

[6] A. Derti. Upstream sequences for human and mouse Refseq mRNAs. http://arep.med.harvard.edu/labgc/adnan/hsmmupstream/.

[7] E. Eskin and P. A. Pevzner. Finding composite regulatory patterns in DNA sequences. *Bioinformatics*, 18(1):354–363, 2002.

[8] M. Gyllenberg, T. Koski, E. Reilink, and M. Verlaan. Nonuniqueness in probabilistic numerical identification of bacteria. *Journal of Applied Probability*, 31:542–548, 1994.

[9] Helsinki University of Technology: Neural Networks Research Centre. The FastICA Matlab package. http://www.cis.hut.fi/projects/ica/fastica/.

[10] T. Hofmann. Probabilistic latent semantic indexing. In *SIGIR '99*, pages 50–57, Berkeley, CA, 1999.

[11] T. Hofmann. Unsupervised learning by probabilistic latent semantic analysis. *Machine Learning*, 42:177–196, 2001.

[12] A. Hyvärinen, J. Karhunen, and E. Oja. *Independent Component Analysis*. John Wiley & Sons, 2001.

[13] A. Hyvärinen and E. Oja. A fast fixed-point algorithm for independent component analysis. *Neural Computation*, 9:1483–1492, 1997.

[14] S. Keles, M. van der Laan, and M. B. Eisen. Identification of regulatory elements using a feature selection method. *Bioinformatics*, 18(9):1167–1175, 2002.

[15] M. Koyutürk and A. Grama. PROXIMUS: A framework for analyzing very high-dimensional discrete attributed datasets. In *Proc. Ninth ACM SIGKDD Intl. Conf. on Knowledge Discovery and Data Mining (KDD 2003)*, pages 147–156, 2003.

[16] D. D. Lee and H. S. Seung. Learning the parts of objects by non-negative matrix factorization. *Nature*, 401:788–791, October 1999.

[17] D. D. Lee and H. S. Seung. Algorithms for non-negative matrix factorization. In *NIPS*, pages 556–562, 2000.

[18] H. Mannila, H. Toivonen, and I. Verkamo. Discovery of frequent episodes in event sequences. *Data Mining and Knowledge Discovery*, 1(3):259–289, 1997.

[19] V. Matys, E. Fricke, R. Geffers, E. G. ling, M. Heubrock, R. Hehl, K. Hornischer, D. Karas, A. Kel, O. V. Kel-Margoulis, D.-U. Kloos, S. Land, B. Lewicki-Potapov, H. Michael, R. Münch, I. Reuter, S. Rotert, H. Saxel, M. Scheer, S. Thiele, and E. Wingender. TRANSFAC: transcriptional regulation, from patterns to profiles. *Nucleic Acids Research*, 31(1):374–378, 2003.

[20] J. van Helden, B. André, and J. Collado-Vides. Extracting regulatory sites from the upstream region of yeast genes by computational analysis of oligonucleotide frequencies. *Journal of Molecular Biology*, 281:827–842, 1998.

Mass Spectrum Labeling: Theory and Practice

Z. Huang, L. Chen, J-Y. Cai, D. Gross*, D. Musicant*, R. Ramakrishnan, J. Schauer*, S.J. Wright

Abstract

*We introduce the problem of **labeling a particle's mass spectrum** with the substances it contains, and develop several formal representations of the problem, taking into account practical complications such as unknown compounds and noise. This task is currently a bottle-neck in analyzing data from a new generation of instruments for real-time environmental monitoring.*

1. Introduction

Mass spectrometry is widely used for the identification and quantification of elements, chemicals and biological materials. Historically, the specificity of mass spectrometry has been aided by upstream separation to remove mass spectral interference between different species. However, in the past decade, a wide range of real-time mass spectrometry instruments have been employed, and the nature of these instruments often precludes separation and clean-up steps. The mass spectrum produced for a particle in real-time by one of these instruments, e.g., the Aerosol Time-of-Flight Mass Spectrometer (ATOFMS) [12,9,14,16], is therefore comprised of overlaid mass spectra from several substances, and the overlap between these spectra makes it difficult to identify the underlying substances. The commercially available ATOFMS instrument can obtain mass spectra for up to about 250 particles per minute, producing a time-series with unusual complexity. The data analysis challenges we describe are equally applicable to other real-time instruments that utilize mass spectrometry, such as the Aerosol Mass Spectrometer (AMS).

Unlabeled Spectrum: Labeled Spectrum:

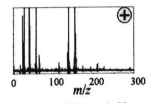 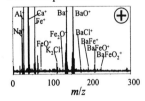

Figure 1: Mass spectrum labeling

Mass spectrum labeling consists of "translating" the raw plot of intensity versus mass-to-charge (m/z) value to a list of chemical substances or ions and their rough quantities (the quantities omitted in Figure 1) present in the particle. Labeling spectra allows us to think of a stream of mass spectra as a time-series of observations, one per collected particle, where each observation is a set of ion-quantity pairs. This is similar to a time-series of transactions, each recording the items purchased by a customer in a single visit to a store [1,4,13]. This analogy makes a wide range of association rule [3] and sequential pattern algorithms [2] applicable to the analysis of labeled mass spectrometry data.

The contributions of this paper include the following: In this and a companion paper [7], we introduce an important class of data mining problems involving mass spectra. The focus in this paper is on the labeling of individual spectra (Section 2), which is the foundation of a class of group-oriented labeling tasks discussed in [7]. We introduce a rigorous framework for labeling and present a theoretical characterization of *ambiguity*, which arises due to overlapped spectra (Section 3). We account for practical complexities such as noise, errors, and the presence of unknown substances (Section 4), and present algorithms together with several optimizations and theoretical results (Section 5). We then present a detailed synthetic data generator that is based on real mass spectra, conforms to realistic problem scenarios, and allows us to produce labeled spectra while controlling several fundamental parameters such as ambiguity and noise (Section 6). Finally, we introduce a metric for measuring the quality of labeling, and evaluate our labeling algorithms, showing that although slower than some machine learning approaches, they achieve uniformly superior accuracy *without the need for training datasets* (Section 7). In many real settings, it is unrealistic to expect labeled training sets (e.g., when deploying an instrument in a new location, or when the ambient conditions change significantly). We also apply our algorithms to a collection of real spectra and compare our results with hand-labeling by domain scientists; they are effective enough (achieving 93% accuracy in detecting true labels) to be immediately useful.

2. Problem formalization

A **mass spectrum** (or spectrum) is a vector $\vec{b} = [b_1, \cdots b_r]$, where $b_i \in R$ is the signal intensity at mass-to-charge (m/z) value i. For simplicity, we assume all spectra have the same 'range' and 'granularity' over the m/z axis; i.e., they have the same dimension r and the ith element of a spectrum always corresponds to the same m/z value i. Intuitively, each m/z ratio corresponds to a particular isotope of some chemical element. The **signature** of an ion is a vector $\vec{s} = [I_1, I_2 \cdots I_r]$, $I_i \in R$ and $\sum I_i = 1$, representing the distribution of isotopes. I_i is the proportion of the isotope with m/z value i. A **signature library** is a set of known signatures $S = \{\vec{s}_1, \vec{s}_2 \cdots \vec{s}_n\}$, in which $\vec{s}_j$ is the signature of ion j. Additionally, there may be ions that appear on particles, and are therefore reflected in mass spectra, but that for which signatures are not included in the signature library.

The spectrum $\vec{b}$ of a particle is a linear combination of the signatures of ions that it contains. $\vec{b} = \sum_j w_j \vec{s}_j$, where w_j is the quantity of ion j in the particle. The task of **mass spectrum labeling** is to find all ions present in the particle as well as their quantities w_i, given an input spectrum. Formally, a **label** for an ion with respect to a given spectrum is an $<ion, quantity>$ pair;

---

* Profs. Gross and Musicant are at Carleton College, and the remaining authors are at University of Wisconsin-Madison. The contact email is raghu@cs.wisc.edu. Work supported by NSF ITR grant IIS-0326328.

a **label** for the spectrum is the collection of labels for all ions in the signature library. The task of labeling an input spectrum can be viewed as a search for a linear combination of ions that best approximates the spectrum, and the success that is achievable depends on the extent of unknown ions. In Sections 3 to 5, for simplicity we assume that the signature library is complete, i.e., there are no unknown ions. We evaluate the impact of unknowns in Sections 6 and 7.

3. When is labeling hard?

In this section, we formulate the labeling task as solving a set of linear equations, and then discuss the fundamental challenge involved: the interference between different combinations of signatures and the consequent ambiguity in labeling.

3.1. Linear system abstraction

We can represent the signature library $S = \{\vec{s}_1, \vec{s}_2 \cdots \vec{s}_n\}$ as a matrix $A = [\vec{s}_1, \vec{s}_2, ..., \vec{s}_n]$, where $\vec{s}_k$, the kth column of A, is the signature of ion k. A spectrum label is an n-dimensional vector $\vec{x}$ whose j^{th} component $\vec{x}[j]$ indicates the quantity of ion j in the particle. Labeling consists of solving the linear system $A\vec{x} = \vec{b}, \vec{x} \geq 0$. Noticing that $A\vec{x} = \vec{b} \Rightarrow A(c\vec{x}) = c\vec{b}$ for any constant c, we can assume without loss of generality that $\vec{b}$ is normalized (i.e., $\sum_i \vec{b}[i] = 1$). By definition of signatures, each column of A also sums to 1. It follows immediately from this fact and $\sum_i \vec{b}[i] = 1$ that $\sum_i \vec{x}[i] = 1$. The exact quantities of all ions can be easily calculated by multiplying the quantity distribution vector $\vec{x}$ by the overall quantity of the particle, which is simply the sum of signal intensities over all m/z values in the original spectrum before normalization.

3.2. Uniqueness

Definition 1: An input spectrum $\vec{b}$ is said to have the **unique labeling** property with respect to signature library A if there exists a unique solution $\vec{x}_0$ to the system $A\vec{x} = \vec{b}, \vec{x} \geq 0$.

In general, given library A and input spectrum $\vec{b}$, neither existence nor uniqueness of solutions is guaranteed for the above equation. Our first result identifies a class of libraries for which every input spectrum is guaranteed to have a unique label.

Theorem 1: Consider signature library $A = [\vec{s}_1, \vec{s}_2, ..., \vec{s}_n]$ and a spectrum $\vec{b}$ where $\vec{s}_1, \vec{s}_2, ..., \vec{s}_n$ are linearly independent (i.e., there is no vector $\vec{a} = [a_1, a_2, ..., a_n]$ such that $\sum_{i=1}^{n} a_i \vec{s}_i$ and at least one $a_i \neq 0$). Then, either $\vec{b}$ has the unique labeling property w.r.t. A, or the system of equations (1) has no solution. □

Even if a signature library does not satisfy the conditions of Theorem 1, there may still be input spectra $\vec{b}$ for which the solution of (1) is unique, e.g. when

$$A = \begin{pmatrix} 0 & 1 & 1/2 \\ 1 & 0 & 1/2 \end{pmatrix} \quad \vec{b} = \begin{pmatrix} 1 \\ 0 \end{pmatrix},$$

there is a unique solution $\vec{x}^T = [0, 1, 0]$.

Conversely, for a given spectrum, there will typically be infinitely many solutions when the signature library does not satisfy the conditions of Theorem 1. Theorem 2 shows an important case with infinite solutions.

Theorem 2: Consider the signature library $A = [\vec{s}_1, \vec{s}_2, ..., \vec{s}_n]$ and a spectrum $\vec{b}$ where $\vec{s}_1, \vec{s}_2, ..., \vec{s}_n$ are *not* linearly independent. If there is a solution $\vec{x} = [x_1, x_2, ..., x_n]$ to $A\vec{x} = \vec{b}, \vec{x} \geq 0$ such that $min_{i=1,2,...,n} x_i > 0$, then $\vec{b}$ has infinitely many labels. □

3.3. Spectra with unique labeling

We now present our main theoretical result, which is an elegant characterization of the complete set of spectra that have the unique labeling property with respect to a given signature library. We explain the concept through an example and state a theorem that describes this set.

Suppose the signature library has only four signatures $\vec{s}_1, \vec{s}_2, \vec{s}_3, \vec{s}_4$. Figure 2(a) shows the case in which $\vec{s}_1, \vec{s}_2, \vec{s}_4$ are linearly dependent. All normalized spectra that can be represented as a conic combination (that is, a linear combination of the vectors $\vec{s}_1, \vec{s}_2, \vec{s}_3, \vec{s}_4$ in which the coefficients are nonnegative) form the triangle $\triangle s_1 s_2 s_3$ in this example. The ambiguity of the labeling comes from the linear dependency among $\vec{s}_1, \vec{s}_2, \vec{s}_4$, since $\vec{s}_4$ is itself a conic combination of $\vec{s}_1$ and $\vec{s}_2$. However, any point lying on the line $s_1 s_3$ can be uniquely represented as a conic combination of s_1 and s_3. The intuitive reason for this is clear: Any involvement of a positive fraction of $\vec{s}_2$ or $\vec{s}_4$ (or both) will lift the point out of the line $s_1 s_3$. Similarly, the points on the line $s_2 s_3$ can be uniquely represented as a conic combination of $\vec{s}_2$ and $\vec{s}_4$. The case in which $\vec{s}_4$ combines all three vectors, $\vec{s}_1, \vec{s}_2, \vec{s}_3$ is shown in Figure 2(b). In this case, any point lying on the boundary of triangle $\triangle s_1 s_2 s_3$ can be uniquely represented as a conic combination of two signatures among $\vec{s}_1, \vec{s}_2, \vec{s}_3$.

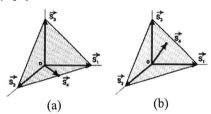

| (a) | (b) |

Figure 2: Vector space spanned by signatures

Definition 2: Given a signature library $S = \{\vec{s}_1, \vec{s}_2 \cdots \vec{s}_n\}$, the **convex hull** generated by S is defined as:

$$ch(S) = \{\sum_{i=1}^{n} w_i \vec{s}_i \mid n \geq 1, \sum_{i=1}^{n} w_i = 1, w_i \geq 0, \vec{s}_i \in S, 1 \leq i \leq n\}$$

The following theorem is a necessary and sufficient condition for an input spectrum to have a unique label with respect to a given signature library. The full proof is involved, and is included in an appendix; we provide a proof outline below.

Theorem 3: The set of spectra with the unique labeling property w.r.t. library S is the set of points in $ch(S)$ that do not lie in the interior of the convex span of some affine dependent subset of S. Further, there is a polynomial time algorithm to test whether a given spectrum has a unique spectrum w.r.t. a library S.□

4. Handling ambiguity and errors

In practice, signal intensities are not precisely calibrated, and the background noise causes measurement errors and introduces uncertainty. We therefore introduce an error bound E and a distance function D, and recast the labeling problem in terms of mathematical programming, as an "exhaustive" feasibility task:

Seek all $\vec{a}$ such that $D(A\vec{a},\vec{b}) \leq E, \vec{a} \geq 0$.　　(1)

Given a library A with n signatures and input spectrum $\vec{b}$, the search space for problem (1) is an n-dimensional space. The **solution space** for input spectrum $\vec{b}$ is defined as follows:

Definition 3 : Given a signature library A, an input spectrum $\vec{b}$ and an error bound E with respect to distance function D, the **solution space** of spectrum $\vec{b}$ is $L_{\vec{b}} = \{\vec{a} \mid D(A\vec{a},\vec{b}) \leq E, \vec{a} \geq 0\}$.

It is worth noting that the choice of the distance function D may affect the complexity of the problem significantly. We use *Manhattan Distance* (also known as ℓ_1 norm) as our distance measurement. The Manhattan distance between two vectors is defined as $\ell_1(\vec{\alpha}, \vec{\beta}) = \sum_i |\alpha_i - \beta_i|$. With Manhattan distance, the solution set for (2) can be found using the following linear programming (LP) model:

$$min \sum_i s_i \quad s.t.$$
$$A\vec{\alpha} - \vec{b} \leq s, \quad A\vec{\alpha} - \vec{b} \geq -s \quad (2)$$
$$\alpha_i \geq 0, s_i \geq 0, i = 1,2,3,...$$

We observe that if the distance function is convex, the solution space of an input spectrum $\vec{b}$ is convex (see below). We will explore this property further in Section 5; for now, we note that *Manhattan Distance* is a convex distance function.

Theorem 4:　If the distance function D has the form $D(u,v) = d(u - v)$, where d is a *convex function*, then the solution space of the search described by Equation (1) is convex. □

4.1. Discretization

Even if an input spectrum has an infinite number of labels (for a given signature library) due to the ambiguity, in practice, we do not need to distinguish between solutions that are very similar. A natural approach to deal with a continuous space is to discretize it into grids, so that the number of possible solutions becomes finite.

Formally, a **threshold vector** $\vec{t} = [t_0, t_1,...,t_d]$ divides each dimension of the search space into d ranges, where t_i and t_{i+1} are the lower bound and upper bound of range i. Given a threshold vector, we introduce the notion of **index vector** to represent a continuous subspace.

Definition 4: Given a threshold vector $\vec{t} = [t_0, t_1,...,t_d]$, an **index vector** $I = [(l_1, h_1) ...,(l_n, h_n)]$, $l_i < h_i, l_i, h_i \in Z$　represents a continuous subspace,

$$S_I = \{\vec{a} \mid \forall i, \vec{t}[l_i] < \vec{a}[i] \leq \vec{t}[h_i], \vec{a}[i] \in R\} \quad (4)$$

Since an index vector represents a unique subspace, we will refer to a subspace simply by its corresponding index vector when the context is clear. Using the index vector representation, we in turn define the notion of cell.

Definition 5: A subspace $[(l_1,h_1),(l_2,h_2),...,(l_n,h_n)]$ is a **cell** if $\forall j, l_j + 1 = h_j$.

The cell is the finest granularity of the discretization, which reflects the degree of detail which users care about. A threshold vector $\vec{t} = [t_0, t_1,...,t_d]$ divides the whole search space into d^n cells, where n is the number of dimensions (which is equivalent to the total number of signatures). Each cell also corresponds to a distinct n-dimensional integer vector

$$\vec{y} = [y_1, y_2,...,y_n], 1 \leq y_i \leq d, y_i \in Z$$

which defines a subspace Y corresponding to the index vector $[(y_1, y_1 + 1),(y_2, y_2 + 1),...,(y_n, y_n + 1)]$.

4.2. Optimization model

We now redefine the task of **spectrum labeling** as follows: *Find all the cells that intersect the solution space of the input spectrum.* A **label** of spectrum $\vec{b}$ is then simply an integer vector $\vec{x}$ representing a cell that intersects the solution space of $\vec{b}$. All such integer vectors form the **label set** of spectrum $\vec{b}$. Formally,

Definition 6:　A vector $\vec{x} = (x_1, x_2,...,x_n)$, $x_i \in [0...d-1]$ is a **label** of spectrum $\vec{b}$　if the subspace defined by the index vector $X = [(x_1, x_1 + 1),(x_2, x_2 + 1),...,(x_n, x_n + 1)]$ intersects the solution space of spectrum $\vec{b}$. In the other word, $\vec{x}$ is the label if $\exists \vec{\alpha}$, s.t $D(A\vec{\alpha},\vec{b}) \leq E$, $\vec{t}[x_i] < \alpha_i \leq \vec{t}[x_i + 1]$.　$\vec{b}$'s **label set** is $L = \{\vec{x} \mid \vec{x} \text{ is a label of } \vec{b}\}$.

To simplify the discussions in the following sections, we also introduce the notion of **feasible space** to describe a subspace that intersects the solution space of the input spectrum. A feasible space is a collection of one or more cells. If the *feasible space* is a cell, it is also called a *label*. Table 1 summarizes our notations and model.

Figure **Error! Bookmark not defined.** illustrates the concepts discussed in this section. Suppose there are only two signatures in the signature library. The whole search space is a two dimensional space *ABCD* within which $S_1 S_2 S_3 S_4$ forms the solution space of an input spectrum. It intersects the *cells LFGM* and *MGHA*, each of which corresponds to a *label*. Subspace *ALFH* intersects with the solution space, so it is a *feasible space*. *MBEG* is also a *feasible space*.

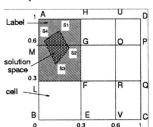

Figure 3: Illustration of concepts
Table 1: Operational definitions of labeling

Notations	$\vec{x}$	An n-dimensional integer vector, $0 \leq x_i < d$
	$\vec{b}$	Normalized input mass spectrum
	$\vec{t}$	Threshold vector for discretization
	d	Number of ranges per dimension
	L	Label set of input spectrum
	A	Signature library with n signatures
	D	Distance function
	E	Error bound
$L \leftarrow \varnothing$		
for each possible x, *Seek* $\vec{a}$ s.t.		
$D(A\vec{\alpha},\vec{b}) \leq E$		
$\vec{t}[j] < \vec{a}[i] \leq \vec{t}[j+1], j = \vec{x}_i$		
if exists such $\vec{\alpha}$, $L = L \cup \{\vec{x}\}$		

5. Labeling Algorithms

In Section 4, we showed that given n signatures and discretization granularity d, the search space contains d^n cells. A brute force approach that tests the feasibility of each cell is not practical, considering that there are hundreds of signatures. In this section, we propose two algorithms: DFS is a general algorithm which works for any distance function, and Crawling algorithm exploits convexity property of distance functions.

5.1. Feasibility test

Given a subspace S, we use the algorithm shown in Table **Error! Bookmark not defined.** to test the feasibility of the subspace; this module is the building block of the later algorithms. Notice that for each test; exactly one LP call is invoked.

Table 2: Test the feasibility of a subspace

Input:	$\bar{b}$	Input mass spectrum
	E	Error bound
	$\bar{t}$	Threshold vector
Output:	TRUE if the subspace is feasible, FALSE otherwise	

Is_feasible(subspace S)

Seek $\bar{a}$ s.t.

$\quad D(A\bar{a},\bar{b}) \le E$ (*)

$\quad \bar{t}[l_j] < \bar{a}[j] \le \bar{t}[h_j]$, for $j = 1,2,...,n$

$\quad [(l_1,h_1),(l_2,h_2),...,(l_n,h_n)]$ is the index vector of subspace S

if (*) succeeds, return TRUE, otherwise return FALSE

5.2. Depth-First Search (DFS) algorithm

We first state an important property of subspace feasibility which guarantees the correctness of the DFS algorithm. The proof is straightforward and is omitted.

Table 3: DFS Algorithm

Input:	$\bar{b}$	Input mass spectrum
	E	Error bound
	$\bar{t}$	Threshold vector
Output:	Label set $L(\bar{b})$	

Depth_First_Search(subspace S)
$\quad L \leftarrow \varnothing$
$\quad$ if not *Is_feasible*(S) then
$\quad\quad$ return $\varnothing$
$\quad$ else
$\quad\quad$ if S is a cell then
$\quad\quad\quad L \leftarrow$ label corresponding to S;
$\quad\quad\quad$ return L;
$\quad\quad$ else
$\quad\quad\quad$ *pick_dimension(j)*
$\quad\quad\quad \{S_i\} = split\_subspace(S, j)$
$\quad\quad\quad$ for each S_i
$\quad\quad\quad\quad L \leftarrow L \bigcup Depth\_First\_Search(S_i)$
$\quad\quad\quad$ return L;

Main : *Depth_First_Search(whole search space W)*

Theorem 5: Let a spectrum $\bar{b}$ and a signature library A with n signatures be given. If subspace S is feasible, then any subspace T, with $S \subset T$ is also feasible.□

The DFS labeling algorithm explores a search tree in which each node is associated with a particular subspace, and the subtree rooted at that node corresponds to the subsets of that subspace. At each node, the algorithm first tests the feasibility of the subspace for that node. If not feasible, that node and its subtree are pruned. Otherwise, we select a dimension j that has not been subdivided to the finest possible granularity in the subspace of that node, and divide the subspace further along dimension j. Each smaller space created thus corresponds to a child of the current node.

In Table **3**, the *pick_dimension* method chooses a dimension (which is not already at the finest granularity possible) to split the current subspace and *split_subspace* divides the current subspace into smaller pieces along the chosen dimension. Details of these two methods are discussed in [10].

The correctness of DFS algorithm is proved in [10]. In [7] we show that the complexity of the DFS algorithm is $O(knd)$

5.3. Crawling algorithm

DFS is a general algorithm in which we can use any distance function D, even one that is non-convex. The Crawling algorithm requires the distance function to be convex and exploits the *connectivity property*[1] derived from the convexity of solution spaces, as described in Theorem 4.

Connectivity Property: Given two labels l_1 and l_n, there exists a path of connecting labels ($l_1,...,l_{i-1},l_i,...l_n$) in which l_{i-1}, l_i are adjacent, i.e., differ only in one dimension by 1.

The Crawling algorithm first finds a solution to the linear system $D(A\bar{a},\bar{b}) \le E, \bar{a}[i] \ge 0$ by invoking one LP call. The cell that contains solution is a label and is used as the start point to explore other connected cells in a breath-first fashion. If the cell discovered has not been visited before and is a label, its neighbors will be explored subsequently. Otherwise, it is discarded and no further exploration will be incurred by it. The algorithm stops when all labels and their neighbors are visited. The connectivity property guarantees that all labels are connected to the first label we found and can be discovered by "crawling" from that start point. Due to lack of space, we omit details of the algorithm; see [10], which also contains a correctness proof and shows that the time and space complexity are $O(kn)$.

Let's take Figure 3 in Section 4 again as an example. The input spectrum's label set contains two labels which are the cells in shade. The crawling algorithm first finds a solution point. Suppose it falls in cell *LFGM*. It then starts from *LFGM* and explores its neighbors *LBEF*, *FROG* and *MGHA*. Among the three, only cell *MGHA* is a label and will incur further exploration. It has only two adjacent cells. One is already visited and the other is not a label. Thereby the algorithm terminates and outputs *LFGM* and *MGHA* as the input spectrum's label set.

Theorem 6 Given an input spectrum $\bar{b}$, a signature database $A = [\bar{S}_1, \bar{S}_2,..., \bar{S}_n]$ and a threshold vector $\bar{t} = [t_1, t_2,..., t_{d+1}]$, suppose the number of labels for $\bar{b}$ is k, the Crawling algorithm will find the complete set of the labels for input spectrum. □

---

[1] Convexity is actually stronger than the connectivity property.

Theorem 7: Given an input spectrum $\vec{b}$, a signature library $A = [\vec{s}_1, \vec{s}_2, ..., \vec{s}_n]$ and a threshold vector $\vec{t} = [t_0, t_1, ..., t_d]$, suppose the number of labels for $\vec{b}$ is k, then the number of LP calls invoked by the Crawling algorithm is $O(kn)$. The number of index vectors stored in the queue is $O(kn)$. □

6. Data generation

There is a fundamental difficulty in evaluating algorithms for labeling mass spectra: manual labeling of spectra (to create training sets) is laborious, and must additionally be cross-validated by other kinds of co-located measurements, such as traditional filter-based or "wet chemistry" techniques. For any given application, rigorously establishing appropriate "ground truth" datasets can take months of field-work. In this section, we describe a detailed approach to synthetic data generation that allows us to use domain knowledge to create signature libraries and input particle spectra that reflect specific applications and instrument characteristics.

Our generator has two parts: generation of the signature library, and generation of input spectra. We begin with a collection of real ion signatures, and select a set of n linearly independent signatures to serve as "seeds". New signatures are generated using a non-negative weighted average of seed signatures. The set of all generated signatures is partitioned into two sets: the *signature library*, and the *unknowns*.

The generation of new signatures for the signature library is done in "groups" as follows, in order to control the degree of (non-)uniqueness, or ambiguity. Each group consists of two "base" signatures from the seeds (chosen such that no seed appears in multiple groups) plus several "pseudo-signatures" obtained using non-negative weighted averages of these two signatures. The generated signatures in each group are effectively treated as denoting new ions in the signature library. Of course, they do not correspond to real ions at all; rather, they represent ambiguity in that it is impossible to distinguish them from the weighted average of base signatures used to generate them when labeling an input spectrum that contains ions from this group. Intuitively, the larger the size of a group, the greater the ambiguity in input spectra that contain ions from the group; observe that interference can only occur within groups. We create a total of k groups with $i+1$ pseudo-signatures in group i.

The set of n original signatures plus the $(k+3) \cdot k / 2$ pseudo-signatures generated as above constitute our "universe" of all signatures. Next, we select some of these signatures to be unknowns, as follows: We randomly select one signature from each of the k groups; these k signatures are "interfering unknowns". We also randomly select u-k seed signatures that were not used in group generation; these u-k signatures are "non-interfering unknowns", giving us a total of u unknowns.

The second part of our generator is the generation of input spectra. An input spectrum is generated by selecting m signatures from the universe of signatures and adding them according to a weighting vector $\vec{w}$. Ambiguity and unknowns are controlled by the careful selection of signatures that contribute to the spectrum, and the input weighting vector controls the composition of the spectrum as well as the contribution of unknowns. We observe that the effect of many unknowns contributing to an input spectrum can be simulated by aggregating them into a single unknown signature with an appropriate weighting vector; accordingly, we use at most a single unknown signature. Table 4 summarizes the parameters for spectrum generation.

Table 4: Parameters used for spectrum generation

m	number of signatures
q	number of groups
$\vec{w}$	vector for the weight of the signatures
o	whether the unknown signature is used
g	average amount of noise

We begin by randomly selecting two signatures from group q. Then, if unknowns are desired in the generated spectrum ($o=1$), we choose either the qth unknown signature, or a randomly selected non-interfering unknown signature, depending on whether or not the unknown is desired to interfere with known ions in the spectrum ($v = 1$ or 0). The contribution of unknowns is controlled by the last component of the weighting vector. Next, we randomly select signatures from the signature library that do not belong to any of the k "groups" to get a total of m signatures. These signatures are linearly independent seeds, and thus the ambiguity of the generated spectrum will depend solely on the first 2 (or 3, if an interfering unknown is chosen) signatures.

Finally, we select values for m random variables following a normal distribution whose means are given by the weighting vector of arity m. The values for these variables are used as the weights w_i to combine the m signatures: $\sum_{j-1}^{m} w_j s_j$. (We note that when an unknown signature is used in the generation, the last element of the weighting vector is reset to be the relative quantity of the unknown signature and the whole weighting vector is normalized to sum up to 1.)

We account for noise by simply adding a noise value (a random variable following a normal distribution) to each component (i.e., m/z position) of the generated spectrum.

7. Experimental results

We now describe experiments to evaluate our labeling algorithms with respect to both quality and labeling speed. To give the reader an idea of the speed, we observed an average processing rate of about one spectrum per second when we ran our algorithms on over 10,000 real mass spectra collected using an ATOFMS instrument in Colorado and Minnesota; this is adequate for some settings, but not all, and further work is required. Speed and scalability are not the focus of this paper, but are addressed in [7], and extensive experiments are reported. We also tested the accuracy of our labeling algorithm against a small set of manually labeled spectra; all were correctly labeled by the algorithm. Admittedly, this is not an extensive test, but we are limited by the fact that manual labeling is a tedious and costly process. (This underscores the importance of not requiring training datasets.)

In this section, we therefore evaluate our algorithms using the data generator from Section 6; this approach also allows us to study the effect of ambiguity, unknown signatures and noise levels in a controlled fashion. For comparison, we also evaluated machine learning (ML) algorithms. However, the reader should note that our algorithms can label input spectra *given only the signature library,* whereas the ML approaches require extensive training datasets, which is unrealistic with manual labeling. In addition, the ML algorithm ignores equivalent alternatives and only generates one label. Nonetheless, we propose two different quality measures and include the comparison for completeness, and to motivate a promising direction for future work, namely the development of hybrid algorithms that combine the strengths of these approaches.

7.1. Machine learning approach

Our ML algorithm builds upon WEKA classifiers [18]. For each signature in the signature library, we train a classifier to take a given input spectrum and output a presence category (*absent, uncertain* or *present*), i.e., to detect whether or not the ion represented by the signature is present in the particle represented by the spectrum. The predictive attributes are the (fixed set of) m/z locations, taking on as values the signal intensities at these locations in the input spectrum. To label a spectrum, we simply classify it using the classifiers for all signatures in the library. When we are only interested in the presence of a subset of ions, of course, we need only train and run the classifiers for the corresponding signatures. We evaluated four types of classifiers: Decision Trees (J48), Naïve Bayes, Decision Stumps, and Neural Networks. Decision Trees consistently and clearly outperformed the other three, and we therefore only compare our algorithms against this approach in the rest of this section.

7.2. Datasets

The (common) dimension of all signatures and spectra is set to be 255. We used n=78 base signatures of real ions, and generated k=5 groups containing 2 to 6 pseudo-signatures respectively. Including the original 78, we thus obtained 98 signatures, 15 of which were withheld as unknown; the remaining 83 comprised the signature library. For generating input spectra, we set the number of signatures used for spectrum generation to be m=10. The relative proportion of these m signatures was controlled by the weighting vector [0.225, 0.2, 0.2, 0.1, 0.1, 0.06, 0.06, 0.03, 0.01, 0.01].

We generated five testing datasets with controlled ambiguity, unknown signature and noise levels. Each dataset contains several files, each of which contains 1,000 spectra generated by using the same set of parameter values. Dataset 1 is designed to test the effect of noise. It consists of 10 files. Each file corresponds to a distinct noise level from 0% to 360% of a preset error bound, which is 0.01 of the total intensity. No ambiguity or unknown signature is involved in this dataset. Dataset 2 tests the effect of ambiguity. It consists of 5 files corresponding to 5 ambiguity levels. Dataset 3 has no noise or ambiguity, but contains some non-interfering unknown signatures. This dataset contains ten files, with the weight on the unknown signature varying from 0% to 180% of the preset error bound. Dataset 4 is identical to Dataset 3 except that the unknown signatures selected are interfering unknowns. Dataset 5 is designed to test the combined effect of noise and ambiguity. Five ambiguity degrees used in Dataset 2 and five noise levels selected from the 10 noise levels used in Dataset 1 result in 25 different combinations of noise and ambiguity, and 25 files are generated for each such combination. The discretization criteria used for all the datasets above is controlled by a threshold vector [0, 0.08, 0.18, 1], which indicates *absent, uncertain* and *present* respectively.

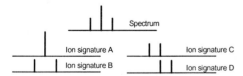

Figure 4: Indistinguishable spectrum labels

7.3. Labeling quality

Given a particle, consider the "*ideal*" version of its spectrum obtained by eliminating noise and unknowns, and is therefore strictly the weighted sum of known ion signatures present in the particle. Even such an ideal mass spectrum might not have unique labels. The spectrum shown in Figure 4 might represent a particle that contains ions A and B, or a particle that contains C and D. Given only the input spectrum, the combinations AB and CD are mathematically indistinguishable, and should be presented to domain experts for further study. The complete set of such "*indistinguishable spectrum labels*" for the "*ideal*" version of an input spectrum is the best result we can expect from labeling; we call each label in this set a **correct** label. Intuitively, it is the set of all feasible combinations of ions in the particle. This is exactly the *label set* of the ideal spectrum defined in Section 4 (with the error bound set to 0). By Theorem 7, our algorithms generate this label set when no unknown or noise is present, i.e., the ideal version is the given input spectrum itself. However, as noise and unknowns are added, the labels found by our algorithm will no longer be the same as the desired set of all correct labels.

Our first proposed metric comparing the result of a labeling algorithm with the set of all correct labels. This metric consists of two ratios: the *hit ratio* and *false ratio*. The *hit ratio* is the percentage of correct labels in the result set of the labeling algorithm. The *false ratio* is the proportion of labels in the result set that are not correct labels. Formally, let the *label set* of a particle's *ideal spectrum* be L_T and let the set of labels found by a labeling algorithm for the particle's real spectrum under the presence of noise and unknowns be L_O:

Hit Ratio $= |L_T \cap L_O| / |L_T|$ *False Ratio* $= |L_O - L_T| / |L_O|$

Experiments under this metric will be called *full labeling tests,* and are presented in Section 7.3.1.

Our second metric relaxes the requirement of finding the correct combinations of ions, and focuses on the proportion of individual ions whose presence or absence is correctly classified. Given a collection of *interesting ions*, we aggregate the set of correct spectrum labels to obtain a set of ion labels IL_T as follows: An ion of interest is marked *present* if all correct labels mark it as *present*, *absent* if all correct labels mark it as *absent*, and marked *uncertain* in all other cases. Similarly, we can obtain a set of ion labels IL_O from the result set of the labeling algorithm. Our second metric consists of two ratios based on these ion labels:

Partial Hit Ratio $= |IL_T \cap IL_O| / |IL_T|$

Partial False Ratio $= |IL_O - IL_T| / |IL_O|$

Partial hit ratio is similar to *hit ratio*, and describes the percentage of ions that are correctly labeled, while *partial false ratio* is the proportion of ions that are incorrectly labeled. Experiments under this second metric will be called *partial labeling tests,* and are presented in Section 7.3.2.

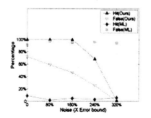 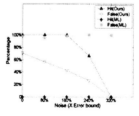

Figure 5: Effect of noise w/o ambiguity   **Figure 6: Effect of noise with ambiguity**

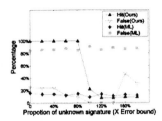
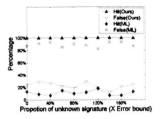

Figure 7: Effect of non-interfering unknown

Figure 8: Effect of interfering unknown

It is worth noting that for any given spectrum, our algorithms will generate exactly the same result. Therefore, for quality evaluation, we simply refer to them as "our algorithm" or the "LP" algorithm, since they both build upon linear programming.

7.3.1. Full labeling tests In the following graphs, each data point for our algorithm is the average of results on 1000 spectra, while each data point for the ML algorithm is the result of 5-fold cross validation on the same dataset. Figure **5** shows the result on Dataset 1, which contains no ambiguity or unknowns. Even in this simple case, the ML algorithm performs poorly. Its hit ratio is close to zero while the false ratio is close to one. In contrast, our algorithm shows great strength in identifying a possible combination of ions to explain the spectrum. The hit ratio remains almost perfect when the noise is within 180% of error bound, but drops sharply when noise grows above that threshold. This shows a limitation of our algorithm: *the error bound is the only component that accounts for noise, and our results are sensitive to the choice of the error bound relative to noise levels.* While the error bound helps in accounting for noise, it also introduces a degree of freedom that allows incorrect labels to be included. Surprisingly, the *false ratio*, which measures the percentage of incorrect labels in the result, actually goes down as the noise level increases; the noise intuitively takes up the slack introduced by error bound. This observation suggests that we might be able to automatically tune the error bound by estimating the noise level. Figure **6** shows the results on Dataset 5, which contains both ambiguity and noise. As we can see, the already low hit ratio of the ML algorithm drops further, essentially to zero, and the false ratio goes over 95%. Our algorithm performs consistently well in Figure **6**, demonstrating its ability to handle ambiguity even in the presence of noise. Figures **7** and **8** summarize the experimental results on Datasets 3 and 4, which show the effect of unknowns. Intuitively, if the unknown ion is non-interfering, it acts like additional noise at some m/z positions, which makes it harder to compensate for. The hit ratio of our algorithm drops sharply when the non-interfering unknown proportion exceeds the error bound. The spike in the *false ratio* at the very end is an artifact caused by the fact that the number of labels found is reduced to one essentially, and that one is incorrect. The effect of interfering unknowns is more interesting. While it raises the false ratio as more and more unknowns are added, as expected, surprisingly, it also helps the hit ratio (because it can be interpreted as some linear combination of known signatures that effectively increases the quantity of the known signatures).

7.3.2 Partial labeling tests We run the exact same set of experiments as for the Full Labeling Test, but apply the second metric. The ten signatures of interest are set to be those used to generate the spectrum, so that ambiguity w.r.t. the signatures of interest is still under control. Figures **9** and **10** illustrate the effect

of noise and unknowns combined with ambiguity. The figures only show *hit ratio*, since in our setting the *false ratio is just 1-hit ratio*. In both graphs, the triangle series show the hit ratio of our algorithm and the square/diamond series represent the ML algorithm. Solid lines represent the results on datasets with no ambiguity while dotted lines represent a dataset with ambiguity. The first observation is that the ML algorithm achieves decent performance under this metric, although it is still uniformly dominated by the LP algorithm. The performance degradation of the ML algorithm from diamond curves to square curves in both graphs again shows the weakness of the ML approach, namely its *inability to handle ambiguity*. Both noise and unknowns have a similar effect on our algorithm as in the full labeling tests. On the other hand, the almost horizontal *hit ratio* curves for the ML algorithm illustrate an interesting point: *the ML algorithm tends to be less sensitive to unknowns than our algorithm.* This is because our algorithm assumes complete knowledge of ion signatures and tries to combine all signatures simultaneously, whereas the ML algorithm simply looks at one ion at a time.

Overall, our algorithm clearly beats the ML algorithm in terms of labeling quality, even in partial labeling tests. In addition, the ML algorithm needs substantial training data. This is not realistic to get at all. However, the ML algorithm does show promise in partial labeling, which suggests a promising research direction, namely a hybrid algorithm that combines the speed of ML and the ambiguity-handling ability of our LP-based approach.

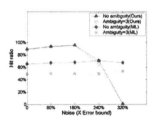
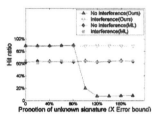

Figure 9: Effect of noise

Figure 10: Effect of unknowns

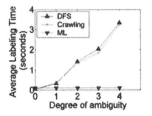
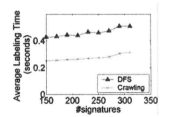

Figure 11: Effect of ambiguity on label time

Figure 12: Scalability w.r.t #signatures

7.3.3 Labeling speed We ran efficiency tests on the five datasets described in Section 7.2. Results show that the presence of noise and unknown signature does not affect the performance of our algorithms much, unless the noise or weight on the non-interfering unknown signature is significantly larger than the error bound. When no ambiguity is present, labeling takes about one second for both DFS and Crawling algorithms. However, as more ambiguity is included and the label set size increases sharply, the performance of our algorithms degrades significantly. Figure **11** shows the running time of our algorithms on Dataset 2, which contains five files of spectra with five different degrees of ambiguity. Series 1 and 2 show the performance of DFS and Crawling algorithms. The Crawling algorithm exploits the convexity of the distance function and runs slightly faster than DFS, but both become much slower as ambiguity is increased. This is mainly due to the dramatic increase in the number of correct labels. The ML algorithm is much faster than our algorithms, but it is worth noting that when no ambiguity is involved and the number of correct labels is small, the running time of our algorithm is almost the same as for ML. In addition, the training time of the ML approach is not reflected at all in these graphs. Further, when we are only interested in detecting a small number of signatures, we can revise our DFS algorithm to only pick the signatures of interest and do partial labeling. This optimization greatly speeds up DFS, to about 100 spectra per second. Figure **12** summarizes the results of algorithm scalability with respect to the number of signatures in the signature library.

7.4. Labeling spectra from a real application

We now present results on data from a real application, comparing our labeling results with manual labeling by a domain expert. The spectra in our experiment come from particles collected in a diesel engine test. Most of the ions in our library are inorganic or simple organic. The signatures of most of ions have a single major peak, i.e., for signature $\bar{s} = \{ I_1, I_2, ... \}$, there exist I_i such that $I_i \gg I_j$, for all $j \neq i$. Hence, most of the ambiguity in the signature library comes from ions which have their major peaks at the same m/z value, although some of the signatures, such as Hg and $TEANO_3$, do have multiple peaks.

We used both our algorithms to label a set of 85 input spectra, with identical results. The labels were evaluated by a chemist who is studying the spectra. In this specific application, the goal is to detect all present ions rather than to quantify their abundance. Our algorithms performed remarkably well, correctly detecting the ions in 93% of the spectra.

When our labeling algorithms failed, it was due to one of three reasons. First, there are ions which exist in the spectra but whose signatures are not included in the signature library. Our algorithms can tolerate some degree of "unknown" ions, in that unknown and "uninteresting" ions do not (usually) prevent us from identifying ions of interest (i.e., in the library). However, if these ions are of interest to the scientist and must be identified when present, we require that they be included in the signature library. Overcoming this limitation requires us to detect certain "missing" signatures by comparing labels from multiple spectra, and is a direction for future work; such a step is currently not included in our model. Even when we do include the correct label as an alternative, it is important to be able to identify the correct label and to distinguish it from the alternatives that arise due to ambiguity. Again, further work is needed in this area.

The second problem is related to the ambiguity of the signature library. Some ions in the library have exact the same signature. It is impossible to distinguish these ions without integrating domain knowledge. This is another important direction for improvement.

The third problem with our labeling result is peak "drifting". Due to the interaction between different ions in the chamber of the mass spectrometer, the peak in the spectrum is actually not a spike that stands on one unique m/z value. Instead, it is a curve that is distributed over multiple m/z values. Our current model is sensitive to this type of error, and additional work is needed.

8. Related work and conclusion

Methods of categorizing aerosol particles using clustering and neural networks have been proposed [1,12,9,16], but none of them deals with the labeling problem directly. The linear programming method used in this paper is standard, see, e.g.,

[13]. Related nonlinear or integer programming tasks arising from the use of Euclidean distance or discretization are also well studied in the optimization community [6,13,19]. Recent work on knowledge-based optimization and machine learning [8,17] are promising extensions to the framework we propose. Machine learning methods such as clustering [5,20] can be applied to our basic linear programming approach by helping identify better initial points and optimization constraints.

Our future work includes finding better labeling algorithms, utilizing domain knowledge in the labeling process, discovering unknown signatures and validating our algorithm on real data. Interested readers can check the technical report [10] for detailed discussion.

9. References

[1] Agrawal, R., Imielinski, T., Swami, A., Mining Associations between Sets of Items in Massive Databases, *Proc. ACM-SIGMOD*, 1993.
[2] Agrawal, R., Faloutsos, C. and Swami, A. Efficient Similarity Search in Sequence Databases. *FODO*, 1993
[3] Agrawal, R., Mannila, H., et. al., Fast Discovery of Association Rules, *Advances in Knowledge Discovery and Data Mining*, 1995.
[4] Agrawal, R. and Srikant R.: Fast Algorithms for Mining Association Rules, *Proc. VLDB*, 1994
[5] Basu, Sugato, Banerjee, Arindam and Mooney, Raymond J., Semi-supervised Clustering by Seeding. *Proc. ICML*, 2002.
[6] Benson, Steven J., More, Jorge J, A Limited Memory Variable Metric Method, in *Subspaces and Bound Constrained Optimization Problems*, 2001.
[7] Chen, L., Huang, Z. and Ramakrishnan, R., Cost-Based Labeling of Groups of Spectra, *Proc. ACM-SIGMOD*, 2004.
[8] Fung, G., Mangasarian, O.L. and Shavlik, J., Knowledge-Based Support Vector Machine Classifiers. *Proc. NIPS 2002*.
[9] Gard, E., Mayer J.E., et. al., Real-Time Analysis of Individual Atmospheric Aerosol Particles: Design and Performance of a Portable ATOFMS, *Anal. Chem.* 1997, 69, 4083-4091.
[10] Huang, Z., Chen, L., et. al., Spectrum Labeling: Theory and Practice, 2004, Technical Report, UW-Madison.
[11a] Jayne, J.T., D.C. Leard, X. Zhang, et. al., Development of an aerosol mass spectrometer for size and composition analysis of submicron particles, *Aerosol Sci. Tech..*, 2000, 33, 49-70.
[11] McCarthy, J., Phenomenal data mining, *In Communications of the ACM 43 (8)*, 2003
[12] Noble, C.A. and Prather K.A., Real-time Measurement of Correlated Size and Composition Profiles of Individual Atmospheric Aerosol Particles. *Environ. Sci. Technol*, 1996
[13] Nocedal, J. and Wright, S.J., Numerical Optimization, *Springer*, 1st edition, 1999.
[14] Prather, K.A., Nordmeyer, T., and Salt, K. Real-time Characterization of Individual Aerosol Particles Using ATOFMS. *Anal. Chem.*, 1994; 66, 1403-1407.
[15] Srikant, R. and Agrawal, R., Mining Quantitative Association Rules in Large Relational Tables, *Proc ACM-SIGMOD*, 1996.
[16] Suess, D.T. and Prather K.A., Mass Spectrometry of Aerosols, *Chemical Reviews*, 1999, 99, 3007-3035.
[17] Towell, G.G. and Shavlik J., Knowledge-Based Artificial Neural Networks. *Artificial Intelligence*, 1994.
[18] Witten, Ian H. and Frank, Eibe, Practical Machine Learning Tools and Techniques with Java Implementation, *Morgan Kaufmann*, 1999.
[19] Wolsey, L., Integer Programming, John Wiley, 1998.
[20] Zhang, T., Ramakrishnan, R. and Livny M., BIRCH: An Efficient Data Clustering Method for Very Large Databases, *Proc. ACM-SIGMOD*, 1996.

Generation of Attribute Value Taxonomies from Data for Data-Driven Construction of Accurate and Compact Classifiers

Dae-Ki Kang, Adrian Silvescu, Jun Zhang, and Vasant Honavar
Artificial Intelligence Research Laboratory
Department of Computer Science
Iowa State University, Ames, IA 50011 USA
{dkkang, silvescu, junzhang, honavar}@iastate.edu

Abstract

Attribute Value Taxonomies (AVT) have been shown to be useful in constructing compact, robust, and comprehensible classifiers. However, in many application domains, human-designed AVTs are unavailable. We introduce AVT-Learner, an algorithm for automated construction of attribute value taxonomies from data. AVT-Learner uses Hierarchical Agglomerative Clustering (HAC) to cluster attribute values based on the distribution of classes that co-occur with the values. We describe experiments on UCI data sets that compare the performance of AVT-NBL (an AVT-guided Naive Bayes Learner) with that of the standard Naive Bayes Learner (NBL) applied to the original data set. Our results show that the AVTs generated by AVT-Learner are competitive with human-generated AVTs (in cases where such AVTs are available). AVT-NBL using AVTs generated by AVT-Learner achieves classification accuracies that are comparable to or higher than those obtained by NBL; and the resulting classifiers are significantly more compact than those generated by NBL.

1. Introduction

An important goal of inductive learning is to generate accurate and compact classifiers from data. In a typical inductive learning scenario, instances to be classified are represented as ordered tuples of attribute values. However, attribute values can be grouped together to reflect assumed or actual similarities among the values in a domain of interest or in the context of a specific application. Such a hierarchical grouping of attribute values yields an attribute value taxonomy (AVT). For example, Figure 1 shows a human-made taxonomy associated with the nominal attribute *'Odor'* of the UC Irvine AGARICUS-LEPIOTA mushroom data set [5].

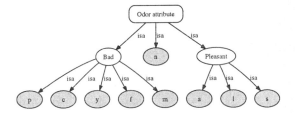

Figure 1. Human-made AVT from 'odor' attribute of UCI AGARICUS-LEPIOTA mushroom data set.

Hierarchical groupings of attribute values (AVT) are quite common in biological sciences. For example, the Gene Ontology Consortium is developing hierarchical taxonomies for describing many aspects of macromolecular sequence, structure, and function [1]. Undercoffer et al. [24] have developed a hierarchical taxonomy which captures the features that are observable or measurable by the target of an attack or by a system of sensors acting on behalf of the target. Several ontologies being developed as part of the Semantic Web related efforts [4] also capture hierarchical groupings of attribute values. Kohavi and Provost [15] have noted the need to be able to incorporate background knowledge in the form of hierarchies over data attributes in electronic commerce applications of data mining.

There are several reasons for exploiting AVT in learning classifiers from data, perhaps the most important being a preference for comprehensible and simple, yet accurate and robust classifiers [18] in many practical applications of data mining. The availability of AVT presents the opportunity to learn classification rules that are expressed in terms of *abstract* attribute values leading to simpler, easier-to-comprehend rules that are expressed in terms of hierarchically related values. Thus, the rule $(odor = pleasant) \rightarrow (class = edible)$ is likely to be preferred over $((odor =$

130

$a) \wedge (color = brown)) \vee ((odor = l) \wedge (color = brown)) \vee$ $((odor = s) \wedge (color = brown)) \rightarrow (class = edible)$ by a user who is familiar with the odor taxonomy shown in Figure 1.

Another reason for exploiting AVTs in learning classifiers from data arises from the necessity, in many application domains, for learning from small data sets where there is a greater chance of generating classifiers that over-fit the training data. A common approach used by statisticians when estimating from small samples involves *shrinkage* [7] or grouping attribute values (or more commonly class labels) into bins, when there are too few instances that match any specific attribute value or class label, to estimate the relevant statistics with adequate confidence. Learning algorithms that exploit AVT can potentially perform *shrinkage* automatically thereby yielding robust classifiers. In other words, exploiting information provided by an AVT can be an effective approach to performing regularization to minimize over-fitting [28].

Consequently, several algorithms for learning classifiers from AVTs and data have been proposed in the literature. This work has shown that AVTs can be exploited to improve the accuracy of classification and in many instances, to reduce the complexity and increase the comprehensibility of the resulting classifiers [6, 11, 14, 23, 28, 30]. Most of these algorithms exploit AVTs to represent the information needed for classification at different levels of abstraction.

However, in many domains, AVTs specified by human experts are unavailable. Even when a human-supplied AVT is available, it is interesting to explore whether alternative groupings of attribute values into an AVT might yield more accurate or more compact classifiers. Against this background, we explore the problem of automated construction of AVTs from data. In particular, we are interested in AVTs that are useful for generating accurate and compact classifiers.

2. Learning attribute value taxonomies from data

2.1. Learning AVT from data

We describe AVT-Learner, an algorithm for automated construction of AVT from a data set of instances wherein each instance is described by an ordered tuple of N nominal attribute values and a class label.

Let $A = \{A_1, A_2, \ldots, A_n\}$ be a set of nominal attributes. Let $V_i = \{v_i^1, v_i^2, \ldots, v_i^{m_i}\}$ be a finite domain of mutually exclusive values associated with attribute A_i where v_i^j is the jth attribute value of A_i and m_i is the number possible number of values of A_i, that is, $|V_i|$. We say that V_i is the set of primitive values of attribute A_i. Let

$C = \{C_1, C_2, \ldots, C_k\}$ be a set of mutually disjoint class labels. A data set is $D \subseteq V_1 \times V_2 \times \ldots \times V_n \times C$.

Let $T = \{T_1, T_2, \ldots, T_n\}$ denote a set of AVT such that T_i is an AVT associated with the attribute A_i, and $Leaves(T_i)$ denote a set of all leaf nodes in T_i. We define a cut δ_i of an AVT T_i to be a subset of nodes in T_i satisfying the following two properties: (1) For any leaf $l \in Leaves(T_i)$, either $l \in \delta_i$ or l is a descendant of a node $n \in \delta_i$; and (2) for any two nodes $f, g \in \delta_i$, f is neither a descendant nor an ancestor of g [12]. For example, $\{Bad, a, l, s, n\}$ is a cut through the AVT for *odor* shown in Figure 1. Note that a cut through T_i corresponds to a partition of the values in V_i. Let $\Delta = \{\delta_1, \delta_2, \ldots \delta_n\}$ be a set of cuts associated with AVTs in $T = \{T_1, T_2, \ldots T_n\}$.

The problem of learning AVTs from data can be stated as follows: given a data set $D \subseteq V_1 \times V_2 \times \ldots \times V_n \times C$ and a measure of dissimilarity (or equivalently similarity) between any pair of values of an attribute, output a set of AVTs $T = \{T_1, T_2, \ldots, T_n\}$ such that each T_i (AVT associated with the attribute A_i) corresponds to a hierarchical grouping of values in V_i based on the specified similarity measure.

We use hierarchical agglomerative clustering (HAC) of the attribute values according to the distribution of classes that co-occur with them. Let $DM(P(x) \| P(y))$ denote a measure of pairwise divergence between two probability distributions $P(x)$ and $P(y)$ where the random variables x and y take values from the same domain. We use the pairwise divergence between the distributions of class labels associated with the corresponding attribute values as a measure of the dissimilarity between the attribute values. The lower the divergence between the class distributions associated with two attributes, the greater is their their similarity. The choice of this measure of dissimilarity between attribute values is motivated by the intended use of the AVT, namely, the construction of accurate, compact, and robust classifiers. If two values of an attribute are indistinguishable from each other with respect to their class distributions, they provide statistically similar information for classification of instances.

The algorithm for learning AVT for a nominal attribute is shown in Figure 2. The basic idea behind AVT-Learner is to construct an AVT T_i for each attribute A_i by starting with the primitive values in V_i as the leaves of T_i and recursively add nodes to T_i one at a time by merging two existing nodes. To aid this process, the algorithm maintains a cut δ_i through the AVT T_i, updating the cut δ_i as new nodes are added to T_i. At each step, the two attribute values to be grouped together to obtain an abstract attribute value to be added to T_i are selected from δ_i based on the divergence between the class distributions associated with the corresponding values. That is, a pair of attribute values in δ_i are merged if they have more similar class distributions than any other pair of

```
AVT-Learner:
begin
1. Input : data set D
2. For each attribute $A_i$:
3.    For each attribute value $v_i^j$ :
4.       For each class label $c_k$: estimate the probability
$p\left(c_k|v_i^j\right)$
5.       Let $P\left(C|v_i^j\right) = \left\{p\left(c_1|v_i^j\right),...,p\left(c_k|v_i^j\right)\right\}$ be
the class distribution associated with value .
6.       Set $\delta_i \leftarrow V_i$; Initialize $T_i$ with nodes in $\delta_i$.
7.    Iterate until $|\delta_i| = 1$:
8.          In $\delta_i$, find $(x,y) =$
$argmin\left\{DM\left(P\left(C|v_i^x\right)||P\left(C|v_i^y\right)\right)\right\}$
9.       Merge $v_i^x$ and $v_i^y$ $(x \neq y)$ to create a new value $v_i^{xy}$.
10.      Calculate probability distribution $P\left(C|v_i^{xy}\right)$.
11.      $\lambda_i \leftarrow \delta_i \cup \{v_i^{xy}\} \setminus \{v_i^x, v_i^y\}$.
12.      Update $T_i$ by adding nodes $v_i^{xy}$ as a parent of $v_i^x$
and $v_i^y$.
13.      $\delta_i \leftarrow \lambda_i$.
14. Output : $T = \{T_1, T_2, ..., T_n\}$
end.
```

Figure 2. Pseudo-code of AVT-Learner

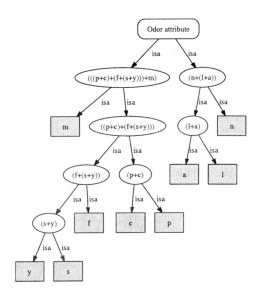

Figure 3. AVT of 'odor' attribute of UCI AGARICUS-LEPIOTA mushroom data set generated by AVT-Learner using Jensen-Shannon divergence (binary clustering)

attribute values in δ_i. This process terminates when the cut δ_i contains a single value which corresponds to the root of T_i. If $|V_i| = m_i$, the resulting T_i will have $(2m_i - 1)$ nodes when the algorithm terminates.

In the case of continuous-valued attributes, we define intervals based on observed values for the attribute in the data set. We then generate a hierarchical grouping of adjacent intervals, selecting at each step two adjacent intervals to merge using the pairwise divergence measure. A cut through the resulting AVT corresponds to a discretization of the continuous-valued attribute. A similar approach can be used to generate AVT from ordinal attribute values.

2.2. Pairwise divergence measures

There are several ways to measure similarity between two probability distributions. We have tested thirteen divergence measures for probability distributions P and Q. In this paper, we limit the discussion to Jensen-Shannon divergence measure.

Jensen-Shannon divergence [21] is weighted information gain, also called Jensen difference divergence, information radius, Jensen difference divergence, and Sibson-Burbea-Rao Jensen Shannon divergence. It is given by:

$$I\left(P||Q\right) = \frac{1}{2}\left[\sum p_i log\left(\frac{2p_i}{p_i+q_i}\right) + \sum q_i log\left(\frac{2q_i}{p_i+q_i}\right)\right]$$

Jensen-Shannon divergence is reflexive, symmetric and bounded. Figure 3 shows an AVT of 'odor' attribute generated by AVT-Learner (with binary clustering).

3. Evaluation of AVT-Learner

The intuition behind our approach to evaluating the AVT generated by AVT-Learner is the following: an AVT that captures relevant relationships among attribute values can result in the generation of simple and accurate classifiers from data, just as an appropriate choice of axioms in a mathematical domain can simplify proofs of theorems. Thus, the simplicity and predictive accuracy of the learned classifiers based on alternative choices of AVT can be used to evaluate the utility of the corresponding AVT in specific contexts.

3.1. AVT guided variants of standard learning algorithms

It is possible to extend standard learning algorithms in principled ways so as to exploit the information provided by AVT. AVT-DTL [26, 30, 28] and the AVT-NBL [29] which extend the decision tree learning algorithm [20] and the Naive Bayes learning algorithm [16] respectively are examples such algorithms.

The basic idea behind AVT-NBL is to start with the Naive Bayes Classifier that is based on the most abstract at-

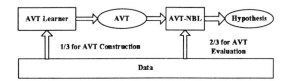

Figure 4. Evaluation of AVT using AVT-NBL

tribute values in AVTs and successively refine the classifier by a scoring function - a Conditional Minimum Description Length (CMDL) score suggested by Friedman et al. [8] to capture trade-off between the accuracy of classification and the complexity of the resulting Naive Bayes classifier.

The experiments reported by Zhang and Honavar [29] using several benchmark data sets show that AVT-NBL is able to learn, using human generated AVT, substantially more accurate classifiers than those produced by Naive Bayes Learner (NBL) applied directly to the data sets as well as NBL applied to data sets represented using a set of binary features that correspond to the nodes of the AVT (PROP-NBL). The classifiers generated by AVT-NBL are substantially more compact than those generated by NBL and PROP-NBL. These results hold across a wide range of missing attribute values in the data sets. Hence, the performance of Naive Bayes classifiers generated by AVT-NBL when supplied with AVT generated by the AVT-Learner provide useful measures of the effectiveness of AVT-Learner in discovering hierarchical groupings of attribute values that are useful in constructing compact and accurate classifiers from data.

4. Experiments

4.1. Experimental setup

Figure 4 shows the experimental setup. The AVT generated by the AVT-Learner are evaluated by comparing the performance of the Naive Bayes Classifiers produced by applying

- NBL to the original data set

- AVT-NBL to the original data set (See Figure 4).

For the benchmark data sets, we chose 37 data sets from UCI data repository [5].

Among the data sets we have chosen, AGARICUS-LEPIOTA data set and NURSERY data set have AVT supplied by human experts. AVT for AGARICUS-LEPIOTA data was prepared by a botanist, and AVT for NURSERY data was based on our understanding of the domain. We are not aware of any expert-generated AVTs for other data sets.

In each experiment, we randomly divided each data set into 3 equal parts and used 1/3 of the data for AVT construction using AVT-Learner. The remaining 2/3 of the data were used for generating and evaluating the classifier. Each set of AVTs generated by the AVT-Learner was evaluated in terms of the error rate and the size of the resulting classifiers (as measured by the number of entries in conditional probability tables). The error rate and size estimates were obtained using 10-fold cross-validation on the part of the data set (2/3) that was set aside for evaluating the classifier. The results reported correspond to averages of the 10-fold cross-validation estimates obtained from the three choices of the AVT-construction and AVT-evaluation. This process ensures that there is no information leakage between the data used for AVT construction, and the data used for classifier construction and evaluation.

10-fold cross-validation experiments were performed to evaluate human expert-supplied AVT on the AVT evaluation data sets used in the experiments described above for the AGARICUS-LEPIOTA data set and the NURSERY data set.

We also evaluated the robustness of the AVT generated by the AVT-Learner by using them to construct classifiers from data sets with varying percentages of missing attribute values. The data sets with different percentages of missing values were generated by uniformly sampling from instances and attributes to introduce the desired percentage of missing values.

4.2. Results

AVT generated by AVT-Learner are competitive with human-generated AVT when used by AVT-NBL.

The results of our experiments shown in Figure 5 indicate that AVT-Learner is effective in constructing AVTs that are competitive with human expert-supplied AVTs for use in classification tasks with respect to the error rates and the size of the resulting classifiers.

AVT-Learner can generate useful AVT when no human-generated AVT are available.

For most of the data sets, there are no human-supplied AVT's available. Figure 6 shows the error rate estimates for Naive Bayes classifiers generated by AVT-NBL using AVT generated by the AVT-Learner and the classifiers generated by NBL applied to the DERMATOLOGY data set. The results shown suggest that AVT-Learner, using Jensen-Shannon divergence, is able to generate AVTs that when used by AVT-NBL, result in classifiers that are more accurate than those generated by NBL.

Additional experiments with other data sets produced similar results. Table 1 shows the classifier's accuracy on original UCI data sets for NBL and AVT-NBL that uses

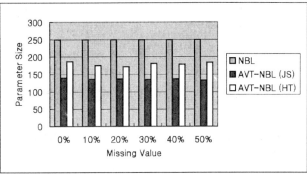

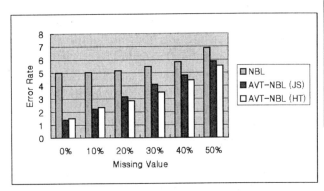

Figure 5. The estimated error rates of classifiers generated by NBL and AVT-NBL on AGARICUS-LEPIOTA data with different percentages of missing values. HT stands for human-supplied AVT. JS denotes AVT constructed by AVT-Learner using Jensen-Shannon divergence.

Figure 7. The size (as measured by the number of parameters) of the Standard Naive Bayes Learner (NBL) compared with that of AVT-NBL on AGARICUS-LEPIOTA data. HT stands for human-supplied AVT. JS denotes AVT constructed by AVT-Learner using Jensen-Shannon divergence.

AVTs generated by AVT-Learner. 10-fold cross-validation is used for evaluation, and Jensen-Shannon divergence is used for AVT generation. The user-specified number for discretization is 10.

Thus, AVT-Learner is able to generate AVTs that are useful for constructing compact and accurate classifiers from data.

AVT generated by AVT-Learner, when used by AVT-NBL, yield substantially more compact Naive Bayes Classifiers than those produced by NBL

Naive Bayes classifiers constructed by AVT-NBL generally have smaller number of parameters than those from NBL (See Figures 7 for representative results). Table 2 shows the classifier size measured by the number of parameters on selected UCI data sets for NBL and AVT-NBL that uses AVTs generated by AVT-Learner.

These results suggest that AVT-Learner is able to group attribute values into AVT in such a way that the resulting AVT, when used by AVT-NBL, result in compact yet accurate classifiers.

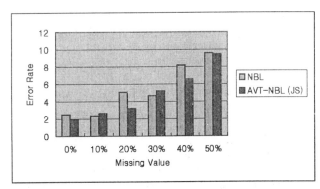

Figure 6. The error rate estimates of the Standard Naive Bayes Learner (NBL) compared with that of AVT-NBL on DERMATOLOGY data. JS denotes AVT constructed by AVT-Learner using Jensen-Shannon divergence.

5. Summary and discussion

5.1. Summary

In many applications of data mining, there is a strong preference for classifiers that are both accurate and compact [15, 18]. Previous work has shown that attribute value taxonomies can be exploited to generate such classifiers from data [28, 29]. However, human-generated AVTs are

Table 1. Accuracy of NBL and AVT-NBL on UCI data sets

Data	NBL	AVT-NBL
Anneal	86.3029	98.9978
Audiology	73.4513	76.9912
Autos	56.0976	86.8293
Balance-scale	90.4	91.36
Breast-cancer	71.6783	72.3776
Breast-w	95.9943	97.2818
Car	85.5324	86.169
Colic	77.9891	83.4239
Credit-a	77.6812	86.5217
Credit-g	75.4	75.4
Dermatology	97.8142	98.0874
Diabetes	76.3021	77.9948
Glass	48.5981	80.8411
Heart-c	83.4983	87.1287
Heart-h	83.6735	86.3946
Heart-statlog	83.7037	86.6667
Hepatitis	84.5161	92.9032
Hypothyroid	95.281	95.7847
Ionosphere	82.6211	94.5869
Iris	96	94.6667
Kr-vs-kp	87.8911	87.9224
Labor	89.4737	89.4737
Letter	64.115	70.535
Lymph	83.1081	84.4595
Mushroom	95.8272	99.5938
Nursery	90.3241	90.3241
Primary-tumor	50.1475	47.7876
Segment	80.2165	90
Sick	92.6829	97.8261
Sonar	67.7885	99.5192
Soybean	92.9722	94.5827
Splice	95.3605	95.768
Vehicle	44.7991	67.8487
Vote	90.1149	90.1149
Vowel	63.7374	42.4242
Waveform-5000	80	65.08
Zoo	93.0693	96.0396

Table 2. Parameter size of NBL and AVT-NBL on selected UCI data sets

Data	NBL	AVT-NBL
Audiology	3720	3600
Breast-cancer	104	62
Car	88	80
Dermatology	906	540
Kr-vs-kp	150	146
Mushroom	252	124
Nursery	140	125
Primary-tumor	836	814
Soybean	1919	1653
Splice	864	723
Vote	66	66
Zoo	259	238

unavailable in many application domains. Manual construction of AVTs requires a great deal of domain expertise, and in case of large data sets with many attributes and many values for each attribute, manual generation of AVTs is extremely tedious and hence not feasible in practice. Against this background, we have described in this paper, AVT-Learner, a simple algorithm for automated construction of AVT from data. AVT-Learner recursively groups values of attributes based on a suitable measure of divergence between the class distributions associated with the attribute values to construct an AVT. AVT-Learner is able to generate hierarchical taxonomies of nominal, ordinal, and continuous valued attributes. The experiments reported in this paper show that:

- AVT-Learner is effective in generating AVTs that when used by AVT-NBL, a principled extension of the standard algorithm for learning Naive Bayes classifiers, result in classifiers that are substantially more compact (and often more accurate) than those obtained by the standard Naive Bayes Learner (that does not use AVTs).

- The AVTs generated by AVT-Learner are competitive with human supplied AVTs (in the case of benchmark data sets where human-generated AVTs were available) in terms of both the error rate and size of the resulting classifiers.

5.2. Discussion

The AVTs generated by AVT-Learner are binary trees. Hence, one might wonder if k-ary AVTs yield better results when used with AVT-NBL. Figure 8 shows an AVT of 'odor' attribute generated by AVT-Learner (with quaternary

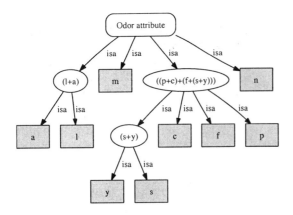

Figure 8. AVT of 'odor' attribute of UCI AGARICUS-LEPIOTA mushroom data set generated by AVT-Learner using Jensen-Shannon divergence (with quaternary clustering)

Table 3. Accuracy of NBL and AVT-NBL for k-ary AVT-Learner

Data	2-ary	3-ary	4-ary
Nursery	90.3241	90.3241	90.3241
Audiology	76.9912	76.5487	76.9912
Car	86.169	86.169	86.169
Dermatology	98.0874	97.541	97.541
Mushroom	99.5938	99.7292	99.7538
Soybean	94.5827	94.4363	94.4363

clustering). Table 3 shows the accuracy of AVT-NBL when k-ary clustering is used by AVT-Learner. It can be seen that AVT-NBL generally works best when binary AVTs are used. It is because reducing internal nodes in AVT-Learner will eventually reduce the search space for possible cuts in AVT-NBL, which leads to generating a less compact classifier.

5.3. Related work

Gibson and Kleinberg [10] introduced STIRR, an iterative algorithm based on non-linear dynamic systems for clustering categorical attributes. Ganti et. al. [9] designed CACTUS, an algorithm that uses intra-attribute summaries to cluster attribute values. However, both of them did not make taxonomies and use the generated for improving classification tasks. Pereira et. al. [19] described distributional clustering for grouping words based on class distributions associated with the words in text classification. Yamazaki et al., [26] described an algorithm for extracting hierar-

chical groupings from rules learned by FOCL (an inductive learning algorithm) [17] and reported improved performance on learning translation rules from examples in a natural language processing task. Slonim and Tishby [21, 22] described a technique (called the agglomerative information bottleneck method) which extended the distributional clustering approach described by Pereira et al. [19], using Jensen-Shannon divergence for measuring distance between document class distributions associated with words and applied it to a text classification task. Baker and McCallum [3] reported improved performance on text classification using a technique similar to distributional clustering and a distance measure, which upon closer examination, can be shown to be equivalent to Jensen-Shannon divergence [21].

To the best of our knowledge, there has been little work on the evaluation of techniques for generating hierarchical groupings of attribute values (AVTs) on classification tasks using a broad range of benchmark data sets using algorithms such as AVT-DTL or AVT-NBL that are capable of exploiting AVTs in learning classifiers from data.

5.4. Future work

Some directions for future work include:

- Extending AVT-Learner described in this paper to learn AVTs that correspond to tangled hierarchies (which can be represented by directed acyclic graphs (DAG) instead of trees).

- Learning AVT from data for a broad range of real world applications such as census data analysis, text classification, intrusion detection from system log data [13], learning classifiers from relational data [2], and protein function classification [25] and identification of protein-protein interfaces [27].

- Developing algorithms for learning hierarchical ontologies based on part-whole and other relations as opposed to ISA relations captured by an AVT.

- Developing algorithms for learning hierarchical groupings of values associated with more than one attribute.

6. Acknowledgments

This research was supported in part by grants from the National Science Foundation (IIS 0219699) and the National Institutes of Health (GM 066387). The authors wish to thank members of the Iowa State University Artificial Intelligence Laboratory and anonymous referees for their helpful comments on earlier drafts of this paper.

References

[1] M. Ashburner, C. Ball, J. Blake, D. Botstein, H. Butler, J. Cherry, A. Davis, K. Dolinski, S. Dwight, J. Eppig, M. Harris, D. Hill, L. Issel-Tarver, A. Kasarskis, S. Lewis, J. Matese, J. Richardson, M. Ringwald, G. Rubin, and G. Sherlock. Gene ontology: tool for the unification of biology. the gene ontology consortium. *Nature Genetics*, 25(1):25–29, 2000.

[2] A. Atramentov, H. Leiva, and V. Honavar. A multi-relational decision tree learning algorithm - implementation and experiments. In T. Horváth and A. Yamamoto, editors, *Proceedings of the 13th International Conference on Inductive Logic Programming (ILP 2003). Vol. 2835 of Lecture Notes in Artificial Intelligence : Springer-Verlag*, pages 38–56, 2003.

[3] L. D. Baker and A. K. McCallum. Distributional clustering of words for text classification. In *Proceedings of the 21st annual international ACM SIGIR conference on Research and development in information retrieval*, pages 96–103. ACM Press, 1998.

[4] T. Berners-Lee, J. Hendler, and O. Lassila. The semantic web. *Scientific American*, May 2001.

[5] C. Blake and C. Merz. UCI repository of machine learning databases, 1998.

[6] V. Dhar and A. Tuzhilin. Abstract-driven pattern discovery in databases. *IEEE Transactions on Knowledge and Data Engineering*, 5(6):926–938, 1993.

[7] R. O. Duda, P. E. Hart, and D. G. Stork. *Pattern Classification (2nd Edition)*. Wiley-Interscience, 2000.

[8] N. Friedman, D. Geiger, and M. Goldszmidt. Bayesian network classifiers. *Mach. Learn.*, 29(2-3):131–163, 1997.

[9] V. Ganti, J. Gehrke, and R. Ramakrishnan. Cactus - clustering categorical data using summaries. In *Proceedings of the fifth ACM SIGKDD international conference on Knowledge discovery and data mining*, pages 73–83. ACM Press, 1999.

[10] D. Gibson, J. M. Kleinberg, and P. Raghavan. Clustering categorical data: An approach based on dynamical systems. *VLDB Journal: Very Large Data Bases*, 8(3–4):222–236, 2000.

[11] J. Han and Y. Fu. Exploration of the power of attribute-oriented induction in data mining. In U. M. Fayyad, G. Piatetsky-Shapiro, P. Smyth, and R. Uthurusamy, editors, *Advances in Knowledge Discovery and Data Mining*. AIII Press/MIT Press, 1996.

[12] D. Haussler. Quantifying inductive bias: AI learning algorithms and Valiant's learning framework. *Artificial intelligence*, 36:177 – 221, 1988.

[13] G. Helmer, J. S. K. Wong, V. G. Honavar, and L. Miller. Automated discovery of concise predictive rules for intrusion detection. *J. Syst. Softw.*, 60(3):165–175, 2002.

[14] J. Hendler, K. Stoffel, and M. Taylor. Advances in high performance knowledge representation. Technical Report CS-TR-3672, University of Maryland Institute for Advanced Computer Studies Dept. of Computer Science, 1996.

[15] R. Kohavi and F. Provost. Applications of data mining to electronic commerce. *Data Min. Knowl. Discov.*, 5(1-2):5–10, 2001.

[16] P. Langley, W. Iba, and K. Thompson. An analysis of bayesian classifiers. In *National Conference on Artificial Intelligence*, pages 223–228, 1992.

[17] M. Pazzani and D. Kibler. The role of prior knowledge in inductive learning. *Machine Learning*, 9:54–97, 1992.

[18] M. J. Pazzani, S. Mani, and W. R. Shankle. Beyond concise and colorful: Learning intelligible rules. In *Knowledge Discovery and Data Mining*, pages 235–238, 1997.

[19] F. Pereira, N. Tishby, and L. Lee. Distributional clustering of English words. In *31st Annual Meeting of the ACL*, pages 183–190, 1993.

[20] J. R. Quinlan. *C4.5: programs for machine learning*. Morgan Kaufmann Publishers Inc., 1993.

[21] N. Slonim and N. Tishby. Agglomerative information bottleneck. In *Proceedings of the 13th Neural Information Processing Systems (NIPS 1999)*, 1999.

[22] N. Slonim and N. Tishby. Document clustering using word clusters via the information bottleneck method. In *Proceedings of the 23rd annual international ACM SIGIR conference on Research and development in information retrieval*, pages 208–215. ACM Press, 2000.

[23] M. Taylor, K. Stoffel, , and J. Hendler. Ontology based induction of high level classification rules. In *SIGMOD Workshop on Research Issues on Data Mining and Knowledge Discovery*, 1997.

[24] J. L. Undercoffer, A. Joshi, T. Finin, and J. Pinkston. A Target Centric Ontology for Intrusion Detection: Using DAML+OIL to Classify Intrusive Behaviors. *Knowledge Engineering Review*, January 2004.

[25] X. Wang, D. Schroeder, D. Dobbs, and V. G. Honavar. Automated data-driven discovery of motif-based protein function classifiers. *Inf. Sci.*, 155(1-2):1–18, 2003.

[26] T. Yamazaki, M. J. Pazzani, and C. J. Merz. Learning hierarchies from ambiguous natural language data. In *International Conference on Machine Learning*, pages 575–583, 1995.

[27] C. Yan, D. Dobbs, and V. Honavar. Identification of surface residues involved in protein-protein interaction – a support vector machine approach. In A. Abraham, K. Franke, and M. Koppen, editors, *Intelligent Systems Design and Applications (ISDA-03)*, pages 53–62, 2003.

[28] J. Zhang and V. Honavar. Learning decision tree classifiers from attribute value taxonomies and partially specified data. In *the Twentieth International Conference on Machine Learning (ICML 2003)*, Washington, DC, 2003.

[29] J. Zhang and V. Honavar. AVT-NBL: An algorithm for learning compact and accurate naive bayes classifiers from attribute value taxonomies and data. In *International Conference on Data Mining (ICDM 2004)*, 2004. To appear.

[30] J. Zhang, A. Silvescu, and V. Honavar. Ontology-driven induction of decision trees at multiple levels of abstraction. In *Proceedings of Symposium on Abstraction, Reformulation, and Approximation 2002. Vol. 2371 of Lecture Notes in Artificial Intelligence : Springer-Verlag*, 2002.

Semi-Supervised Mixture-of-Experts Classification

Grigoris Karakoulas
Department of Computer Science
University of Toronto
Toronto, Ontario, Canada M5S 1A4
grigoris@cs.toronto.edu

Ruslan Salakhutdinov
Department of Computer Science
University of Toronto
Toronto, Ontario, Canada M5S 1A4
rsalakhu@cs.toronto.edu

Abstract

We introduce a mixture-of-experts technique that is a generalization of mixture modeling techniques previously suggested for semi-supervised learning. We apply the bias-variance decomposition to semi-supervised classification and use the decomposition to study the effects from adding unlabeled data when learning a mixture model. Our empirical results indicate that the biggest gain from adding unlabeled data comes from the reduction of the model variance, whereas the behavior of the bias error term heavily depends on the correctness of the underlying model assumptions.

1. Introduction

In many application domains, such as information filtering, credit scoring, customer marketing and drug design, the cost of assigning labels to the input data can be very expensive. The machine learning challenge in this scenario is to build a learning algorithm that can make effective use of unlabeled data by improving classification accuracy. For this reason, researchers have used the idea of applying mixture modeling and EM-based learning for combining labeled and unlabeled data [12, 13, 14]. However, the resulting techniques seem to be disparate as their formulation is intertwined with specific application contexts.

At the same time, due to some reports of degradation in classification performance from the addition of unlabeled data, researchers have tried to analyze the performance of semi-supervised learning with mixture models. Zhang and Oles [15] and Cozman et al. [3] have studied this using asymptotic analysis that offers limited practical guidance in real-world applications.

Thus, the purpose of this paper is two-fold: (i) to develop a semi-supervised mixture modeling technique that is more robust than existing mixture modeling techniques when adding unlabeled data; and (ii) to study the effect of unlabeled data on learning mixture models. As part of our work for (i) we introduce a unifying mixture-model framework for semi-supervised learning. Under this framework we study several variations for modeling a probabilistic classifier and draw connections

with existing work. For (ii) we apply the analysis of bias-variance decomposition to semi-supervised learning. Using this analysis we aim to provide finite sample results for answering the question of when and why unlabeled data can help or hurt performance, particularly with respect to bias and variance.

In Section 2 we provide the framework of mixture modeling. In Section 3 we define the different mechanisms that can explain labels being missing and show how unlabeled data can be incorporated into this modeling framework. In Section 4 we present the mixture model variants for semi-supervised learning, including the mixture-of-experts (MoE) model that we propose. In Section 5 we describe EM-based learning for MoE. In Section 6 we present a procedure for estimating the bias-variance decomposition in semi-supervised classification. In Section 7 we analyze the empirical results from studying the effects of unlabeled data on the mixture model variants. The paper concludes with a discussion.

2. Mixture modeling background

Consider a classification problem with K classes y_k, $k = 1, 2, ..., K$. In our general framework of learning with labeled and unlabeled data, we assume that the training set consists of two subsets: $X = \{X_l, X_u\}$, where $X_l = \{(x_1, y_1), (x_2, y_2), ..., (x_L, y_L)\}$ is the labeled subset, and $X_u = \{x_{L+1}, x_{L+2}, ..., x_{L+U}\}$ is the unlabeled subset. We define x_i, $i = 1, 2, ..., L+U$, to be a d-dimensional feature vector. We also note that in many application domains, the labeled set X_l is very small and the unlabeled set X_u is generally much larger.

Suppose that the data was generated by M components, and that these components can be well approximated by the densities $p(x \mid j, \theta_j)$, $j = 1, 2, ..., M$, with θ_j being the corresponding parameter vector. The feature vectors are then generated according to the density:

$$p(x \mid \theta) = \sum_{j=1}^{M} \pi_j p(x \mid j, \theta_j) \qquad (1)$$

where $\pi_j = p(j)$ are the mixing proportions of the components that have to sum to one. Thus, we can express the generation process of a pair (x_i, y_i) that is fully observed by obtaining the joint distribution of x_i and y_i:

$$p(x_i, y_i \mid \Theta) = \sum_{j=1}^{M} p(j, x_i, y_i \mid \Theta)$$

$$= \sum_{j=1}^{M} \pi_j p(x_i \mid j, \theta_j) p(y_i \mid j, x_i, \xi_j) \quad (2)$$

where Θ denotes the whole set of model parameters.

To apply this mixture model to solving a supervised classification problem, we need to compute the posterior probability of the class label given a feature vector:

$$p(y_i \mid x_i, \Theta) = \sum_{j=1}^{M} p(j \mid x_i, \Theta) p(y_i \mid x_i, j, \xi_j)$$

$$= \sum_{j=1}^{M} \left[\frac{\pi_j p(x_i \mid j, \theta_j)}{\sum_{l=1}^{M} \pi_l p(x_i \mid l, \theta_l)} p(y_i \mid x_i, j, \xi_j) \right] \quad (3)$$

Equation (3) shows that the posterior probabilities of the model have a mixture of expert structure, originally introduced in [9]. In such structure, several local experts model the input-dependent distribution of the output in small regions of the input space. The output of the mixture model is computed via a gating network. The latter probabilistically combines the estimates of each local expert. In our case, the units of the gating network correspond to component probabilities $p(j \mid x_i, \theta_j)$, and the local experts are represented by $p(y_i \mid x_i, j, \xi_j)$. Each of the local experts is parameterized by vector ξ_j, $j = 1, 2, \dots, M$. In general, a local expert could be trained with any parametric or non-parametric probabilistic classification algorithm, i.e. logistic regression, Naive Bayes, etc. In this work we will focus on using Naive Bayes for each local expert.

The above mixture-of-experts model applies to the case of supervised classification. In Sections 3 and 4 we show how this modeling framework can be extended to handle unlabeled data for semi-supervised learning.

3. Incorporating unlabeled data into mixture models

The key idea is to estimate a mixture model from labeled and unlabeled data by modeling the missing labels through a hidden variable, in addition to the hidden variable that is used for modeling the components in the standard supervised setting. To pursue this idea, we first need to define the three different missing label mechanisms that can explain why data may occur as unlabeled.

Under the first mechanism, the class label is missing *completely at random* (MCAR) if the probability that y is labeled does not depend on the value of y or x, i.e. *P(labeled=1|x,y)=P(labeled=1)*. In this case one does not need to explicitly model the missing label mechanism within the mixture. Under the second mechanism, the class label is *missing at random* (MAR) if labeling depends on x but it does not depend on y given x, i.e. *P(labeled=1|x,y)=P(labeled=1|x)*. However, the conditional distribution of x given y is not the same in the labeled and unlabeled data, i.e. there is a bias in the labeled set compared to the data distribution in the population. In generative modeling techniques that aim to learn such conditional distributions one needs to correct for this bias by incorporating unlabeled data. Under the third mechanism, the class label is *missing not at random* (MNAR) if labeling depends on y, even when conditioned on x, i.e. *P(labeled=1|x,y)≠P(labeled=0|x,y)*. This introduces a sample-selection bias [7] for any modeling technique. The bias has to be corrected by modeling the underlying missing mechanism. This is the most difficult case of unlabeled data amongst the three. Correcting for this bias remains an open research issue. In the following we assume that unlabeled data are of MAR type.

To estimate a semi-supervised mixture model for MAR data we define the joint data likelihood that incorporates both labeled and unlabeled data [15], i.e.

$$P(D \mid \Theta) = \prod_{(x_i, y_i) \in X_l} \sum_{j=1}^{M} \pi_j p(x_i \mid j, \theta_j) p(y_i \mid x_i, j, \xi_j)$$

$$+ \prod_{x_i \in X_u} \sum_{j=1}^{M} \pi_j p(x_i \mid j, \theta_j) \quad (4)$$

Instead of maximizing the above quantity, we will work with the joint data log-likelihood function $L(\Theta \mid D) \equiv \log P(\Theta \mid D)$. Thus, we obtain from (4):

$$L(\Theta \mid D) = \sum_{(x_i, y_i) \in X_l} \log \sum_{j=1}^{M} \pi_j p(x_i \mid j, \theta_j) p(y_i \mid x_i, j, \xi_j)$$

$$+ \sum_{x_i \in X_u} \log \sum_{j=1}^{M} \pi_j p(x_i \mid j, \theta_j) \quad (5)$$

In equation (5) the likelihood function contains a "supervised" term, which is derived from X_l labeled data, and an "unsupervised" term, which is based on X_u unlabeled data.

4. Semi-supervised mixture variations

In this section we present three different variations for modeling the probabilistic classifier in the mixture of experts framework. The variations differ in terms of how they model the conditional probability $p(y_i \mid x_i, j, \xi_j)$.

4.1. Common components mixture

Consider applying the following simplistic assumption: the posterior probability of the class label is conditionally independent of the feature vector given the mixture component, in other words $p(y_i \mid x_i, j, \xi_j) = p(y_i \mid j)$ in equation (5). This model essentially makes the assumption that class conditional densities are modeled via a mixture having common components for the classes [6,12].

4.2. Separate components mixture

Another approach to modeling $p(y_i \mid x_i, j, \xi_j)$ is through the separate component (SC) mixture model: each class conditional density is modeled by its own mixture components [14]. In our setting this amounts to constraining in advance the conditional probability table (CPT), $p(y_i \mid j) \in \{0,1\}$. This establishes a deterministic mapping between mixture components and classes by restricting components to modeling only one pre-specified class. As an example, consider modeling class k with $M_k \in M$ number of components. Then we can constrain the conditional probability table by setting $p(y_i = k \mid j) = 1$ for $j \in M_k$, and $p(y_i = k \mid j) = 0$ for $j \notin M_k$. Clearly this restricts the mixture components $M_k \in M$ to focus on modeling input feature vectors of class k only.

It is worth pointing out that a well-known EM-based technique for text classification using labeled and unlabeled documents is actually using the SC model, although the technique was approached from a different perspective [13]. In that work, the complete set of model parameters is a set of mixture components for estimating $p(x \mid j, \theta_j)$, parameterized by multinomials, and prior probabilities π_j over those multinomials. Furthermore, the conditional probability table $p(y_i \mid j) \in \{0,1\}$ represents a predetermined, deterministic mapping between mixture components and classes.

4.3. Mixture of experts with Naïve Bayes as a local expert

In the previous sections we made a simplistic assumption with respect to the local experts: $p(y_i \mid x_i, j, \xi_j) = p(y_i \mid j)$. In this section we abandon this assumption and consider modeling each local expert via a more powerful model, Naive Bayes, that models the class y as conditionally dependent on the input feature vector x_i.

For the sake of simplicity and without restricting generality, let us assume that feature vectors are discrete. Consider each attribute taking on $v = 1,2,...,V$ values. We make the standard Naive Bayes assumption that each feature of the input feature vector is conditionally independent of all the other features:

$$p(x, y \mid \xi) = p(y \mid \xi) \prod_{d=1}^{D} p(x^d \mid y, \xi) \qquad (6)$$

We define conditional probability table $\xi_{cdp} = p(x^d = v \mid y = c)$, which is the probability that a feature x^d takes on value v given value c for the class. The idea is that each local, Naïve Bayes expert will specialize in the region of the input space defined by the mixture components. The probability of a class label given the input feature vector and a mixture component takes the form:

$$p(y_i \mid x_i, j, \xi^*) \approx p(y_i \mid \xi^*) \prod_{d=1}^{D} p(x_i^d \mid y_i, j, \xi^*) \qquad (7)$$

The conjugate prior of the multinomial distribution of features is the Dirichlet distribution, $p(\xi) \sim \prod_{v=1}^{V} (\xi_p)^{\gamma_v - 1}$, where the hyper-parameter, γ, affects the strength of the prior. For the experiments reported in this paper, we set $\gamma = 2$. This essentially amounts to Laplace smoothing.

5. Semi-supervised training using EM

To perform maximum likelihood estimation of the joint data log-likelihood (equation (5)), we apply the EM algorithm. The latter alternates between estimating missing information (hidden) variables given the current model and refitting the model given the estimated, complete data.

In our problem there is missing information regarding the class labels as well as the mixture components. Thus, for each feature vector $x \in \{X_l, X_u\}$ we consider an M dimensional binary vector $z(x)$ that indicates which component generated x. Also, for each unlabeled feature vector $x \in \{X_u\}$ we introduce a K dimensional binary vector $y(x)$, a second hidden variable, which indicates the class label of x. The complete data log-likelihood is:

$$L(\Theta \mid D) = \sum_{(x_i, y_i) \in X_l} \sum_{j=1}^{M} z_j(x_i) \qquad (8)$$
$$\log(\pi_j p(x_i \mid j, \theta_j) p(y_i \mid x_i, j, \xi_j))$$
$$+ \sum_{x_i \in X_u} \sum_{j=1}^{M} \sum_{c=1}^{K} z_j(x_i) y_c(x_i)$$
$$\log(\pi_j p(x_i \mid j, \theta_j) p(y_i = c \mid x_i, j, \xi_j))$$

Since each introduced variable $z(x)$ and $y(x)$ is unobserved (missing), we can only employ an approximation to these variables via their expected values, and then proceed by maximizing the resulting "expected" complete data likelihood. More specifically, the EM algorithm iterates through two steps, i.e.

- **E-Step:** $(\bar{z},\bar{y})^{t+1} = E[(z,y) \mid D,\Theta^t]$
- **M-Step:** Set $\Theta^{t+1} = \arg\max_\Theta P(\Theta \mid D,(\bar{z},\bar{y})^{t+1})$

In the E-step the algorithm estimates probabilistic component labels for the entire datasets as well as probabilistic class labels for the unlabeled data vectors. In the M-step it maximizes the expected complete log-likelihood defined in equation (8). This iterative process is repeated until some stopping criterion is met. Under certain regularity conditions the EM algorithm is guaranteed to find a local optimum. Due to space constraints, the specifics of the EM-based training of the three model variants with real-valued or discrete data are given in a longer version of this paper [10].

6. Bias-variance decomposition and the value of unlabeled data

The question of whether unlabeled data can help generalization performance has received growing interest in specific application contexts. For example, the authors in [12,13] have empirically shown that in text classification unlabeled data can result to better model posterior class probabilities by improving estimation of the mixture density. At the same time, a few researchers [3,15] have studied this question by analyzing the asymptotic behavior of maximum likelihood estimators in semi-supervised learning. In [15], Zhang and Oles use the Cramér-Rao bound estimated from the Fisher information matrix to show that under the assumption of unbiased estimators unlabeled data always help. In [3], Cozman et al., have also used analysis of asymptotic behavior in order to explain the phenomenon of performance degradation from unlabeled data in terms of asymptotic bias in the estimators. However, this asymptotic analysis provides limited practical guidance in real-world applications, as the labeled set X_l tends to be small.

Therefore, to analyze the value of unlabeled data across different application contexts we introduce the bias plus variance decomposition in semi-supervised learning. In general, the bias-variance decomposition forms a powerful tool for analyzing the performance of supervised learning algorithms [5]. There are a few approaches proposed in the literature for the bias-variance decomposition in supervised classification. We use the decomposition in [11] for the zero-one (misclassification) loss function, and apply this decomposition to semi-

supervised classification as explained below. Since we use the mixture models for classification, we analyze the behavior of the models with respect to the zero-one loss function. We leave for future work the bias-variance decomposition of the log-likelihood loss as in [8].

Let Y_H be the random variable that represents the label of the observed feature vector in the hypothesis space, and Y_F be the random variable that represents the label in the target function. Then:

$$Error = \sum_x P(x)(\sigma_x^2 + bias_x^2 + \text{var}_x) \qquad (9)$$

$$\sigma_x^2 \equiv \frac{1}{2}(1 - \sum_{y \in Y} P(Y_F = y \mid x)^2)$$

$$bias_x^2 \equiv \frac{1}{2}\sum_{y \in Y}[P(Y_F = y \mid x) - P(Y_H = y \mid x)]^2$$

$$\text{var}_x \equiv \frac{1}{2}(1 - \sum_{y \in Y} P(Y_H = y \mid x)^2)$$

where σ^2 is the intrinsic "target noise", which is the expected error of the Bayes-optimal classifier.

We apply the two-stage sampling procedure described in [11] to the semi-supervised setting. This procedure can help us in studying the effect of the unlabeled data on the learning algorithm. Note that in practice, it is impossible to estimate the intrinsic noise. However, this procedure estimates the bias term that includes the intrinsic noise.

First, the data is split into the test and training sets. From the training set D, we sample a small labeled set L. This labeled set remains fixed throughout the procedure. The remaining set constitutes the relatively large unlabeled set U. To empirically generate the bias and variance terms:

- Uniformly sample repeatedly without replacement m examples from the unlabeled set U, holding the labeled set L fixed. To get better error estimates, we repeat this process N times, forming N training sets (L,U_n), $n=1,2,...,N$. We set $N=20$.
- Apply the semi-supervised learning algorithm on each of the training sets and estimate the terms in equation (9), by applying each resulting classifier to the test set.

In many real-world applications, one would typically have small, fixed amount of labeled data, and great abundance of unlabeled data. Thus, to estimate the effect of the unlabeled data on the bias-variance decomposition, we increase the size of the sampled unlabeled set, while holding the labeled set fixed. If we increased the labeled and unlabeled data at the same time then we would not be able to distinguish the effects of the unlabeled data from that of the labeled data. This is different from the original method for supervised learning in [11] where the size of the labeled set is increased.

141

7. Empirical analysis

Our experiments aim to address the following two questions. Given a small labeled set:

(i) Are unlabeled data useful for the MoE learner compared to the CC and SC learners?

(ii) Do they help in reducing the variance of each learner, or do they introduce additional bias?

To find answers to these questions we conducted a series of experiments across four well-known datasets: *Adult, Satimage* and *SpamBase* from the UCI repository [1], and the web categorization dataset, *WebKB*, [4]. We also used two synthetic *Artificial* datasets to study the effect of incorrect model assumptions on the bias and variance terms.

7.1. Dataset description

The details of the datasets are provided in Table 1. For the Satimage dataset we transformed the original dataset from 6 classes to a binary classification problem by merging the first 5 classes into a single class. The WebKB dataset consists of web-pages gathered from university computer science departments, where each web-page represents one of four categories: *course, student, faculty,* and *project*. The original dataset contains more categories, however these four are the most populated ones. We then transformed the dataset into "course" and "non-course" target values. For our experiments we used preprocessed WebKB dataset[1]. We formed the feature set by selecting the 200 most informative features (word counts) as measured by information gain.

Table 1. Description of the datasets

Name	Training Set	Test Set	Nom/Cont Attrs
Adult	32561	16281	8/6
SpamBase	3101	1500	0/57
Satimage	4435	2000	0/36
WebKB	3199	1000	0/200
Artificial I,II	8000	4000	0/30

We built two artificial datasets by controlling the degree of independence and relevance amongst features. These two characteristics can affect the bias of the mixture models and Naïve Bayes. More specifically, the Artificial I and II datasets consist of 30 continuous features, out of which in Artificial I 30% (=9) are independent with 80% (=7) of those being relevant, whereas in Artificial II 80% (=24) are independent with

80% (=19) of those being relevant. All independent features are drawn from $N(0,1)$. Random noise is added to all the features from $N(0,.1)$, and then the features are rescaled and shifted randomly. The relevant features are centered and rescaled to a standard deviation of 1. The binary class labels are assigned according to a random weight vector using only the relevant features. The class ratio in these two datasets is 80/20.

Depending on the value type of the features in a given dataset we used mixtures of gaussians or mixtures of multinomials. To apply Naïve Bayes in the MoE model we pre-descretized the continuous features of each dataset into 20th-percentiles. In general one could use cross-validation to tune the number of components. However, given the number of experiments reported here it would not have been practical to do such fine-tuning. Furthermore, our goal in this paper is to provide insight into learning from labeled and unlabeled data with mixture models, rather than to find out which technique performs the best. Thus, for each mixture technique we trained models with 10 and 30 components in order to also analyze the effects of model complexity. We initialized each mixture model with k-means then trained five mixture models with different random seeds and selected the model with the highest log-likelihood in the training data.

7.2. Results

Table 2 presents the summary of the results across the four real-world datasets, as we increase the pool of unlabeled data and the complexity of the mixture models, i.e. number of mixture components, from 10 to 30. The first column of the results shows the error from supervised learning, i.e. no unlabeled data, $|X_u|=0$. For the latter type of learning we also report performance of the Naive Bayes model for benchmarking purspuses.

In three out of the four datasets, Adult being the exception, unlabeled data helped across all mixture models. For those three datasets more unlabeled data help, with the biggest improvement noticed for the semi-supervised MoE model over its supervised counterpart. This is because the MoE model has higher complexity than the other two mixture models and the unlabeled data act as a regularizer to prevent MoE from overfitting by reducing the variance term of the error. In fact in those three datasets unlabeled data always help the MoE model.

The SC model seems to be more sensitive to the amount of unlabeled data than MoE. In the Satimage dataset more unlabeled data hurt SC's performance. Even in the Adult dataset where all mixture models show deterioration with unlabeled data MoE shows the least deterioration. The CC model is not so sensitive as the SC model. It is, however, lagging performance compared to the other two models across all four datasets.

[1] The preprocessed dataset is available at
http://www.cs.technion.ac.il/~ronb/thesis.html

Table 2. Bias-variance decomposition of the semi-supervised mixture models as the size of the unlabeled data increases across various datasets. Best performances per dataset and number of components are shown in bold.

|X$_l$|=100	|X$_u$|=0 Err	|X$_u$|=50 Err	Bias	Var	|X$_u$|=200 Err	Bias	Var	|X$_u$|=800 Err	Bias	Var	|X$_u$|=2000 Err	Bias	Var
ADULT, M=10, Mixture of Multinomials													
NB	0.21												
CC	0.22	0.22	0.12	0.10	0.22	0.11	0.11	0.23	0.12	0.11	0.24	0.12	0.12
SC	**0.20**	0.20	0.13	0.08	0.21	0.13	0.08	0.24	0.17	0.07	0.26	0.20	0.06
MoE	**0.20**	0.20	0.13	0.07	0.20	0.15	0.06	0.21	0.16	0.05	0.21	0.17	0.04
M=30													
CC	0.21	0.21	0.12	0.10	0.22	0.12	0.10	0.21	0.12	0.09	0.22	0.12	0.10
SC	0.21	0.21	0.13	0.08	0.21	0.14	0.08	0.23	0.15	0.07	0.26	0.21	0.05
MoE	**0.20**	0.20	0.13	0.07	0.20	0.15	0.06	0.21	0.16	0.05	0.21	0.18	0.04
SPAMBASE, M=10, Mixture of Multinomials													
NB	0.13												
CC	0.17	0.17	0.07	0.09	0.15	0.07	0.08	0.14	0.06	0.07	0.12	0.06	0.06
SC	0.10	0.10	0.07	0.03	0.10	0.07	0.03	0.10	0.07	0.03	0.09	0.07	0.02
MoE	0.14	0.12	0.09	0.04	0.11	0.06	0.05	0.08	0.06	0.02	**0.08**	0.07	0.01
M=30													
CC	0.16	0.16	0.08	0.08	0.14	0.07	0.08	0.14	0.06	0.07	0.12	0.06	0.06
SC	0.11	0.11	0.07	0.04	0.10	0.07	0.04	0.11	0.07	0.04	0.09	0.07	0.03
MoE	0.14	0.13	0.08	0.05	0.12	0.06	0.06	0.11	0.07	0.04	**0.09**	0.06	0.03
SATIMAGE, M=10, Mixture of Multinomials													
NB	0.14												
CC	0.12	0.13	0.07	0.06	0.13	0.07	0.07	0.13	0.07	0.06	0.13	0.07	0.06
SC	0.10	**0.10**	0.06	0.04	0.15	0.09	0.06	0.16	0.09	0.06	0.21	0.13	0.07
MoE	0.12	0.12	0.08	0.04	0.11	0.08	0.03	0.11	0.08	0.02	0.10	0.09	0.01
M=30													
CC	0.12	0.10	0.07	0.04	0.11	0.07	0.04	0.11	0.07	0.04	0.11	0.07	0.03
SC	0.11	**0.10**	0.07	0.04	0.16	0.11	0.05	0.17	0.12	0.05	0.18	0.14	0.05
MoE	0.12	0.12	0.07	0.05	0.11	0.07	0.04	0.12	0.08	0.04	0.11	0.09	0.02
WebKB, M=10, Mixture of Multinomials													
NB	0.30												
CC	0.31	0.27	0.15	0.12	0.26	0.15	0.11	0.26	0.15	0.11			
SC	0.22	0.22	0.16	0.06	0.22	0.17	0.04	**0.22**	0.18	0.03			
MoE	0.27	0.25	0.14	0.11	0.23	0.13	0.10	**0.22**	0.13	0.09			
M=30													
CC	0.28	0.25	0.14	0.11	0.24	0.14	0.10	0.22	0.13	0.09			
SC	0.23	0.21	0.15	0.06	0.20	0.15	0.04	**0.20**	0.16	0.03			
MoE	0.28	0.23	0.14	0.09	0.21	0.14	0.07	**0.21**	0.16	0.05			

In the SpamBase and WebKB datasets unlabeled data significantly help across all variants of the mixture models, especially the MoE model. This is consistent with the literature on using unlabeled data in text classification.

To understand the reason for the overall positive impact of unlabeled data on MoE we examined the bias-variance decomposition of error in the WebKB and Adult datasets, two markedly different datasets in terms of MoE performance. In addition, we applied MoE to Artificial I and II. As mentioned above, Artificial I represents the type of dataset where the Naive-Bayes model assumptions within each local expert are incorrect. Such dataset could help us explain the relatively poor performance of MoE with unlabeled data in Adult.

Figure 1 shows the results of this comparison. For each dataset there are three graphs. The first two are the bias-variance decomposition bar charts for 10 and 30 components. The first bar in each chart shows the error from supervised learning of MoE. The third graph depicts the feature correlation matrix of the respective dataset; the less the correlation the darker the pixel. In the case of Adult we computed the mutual information matrix. In WebKB and Artificial II unlabeled data reduce the error of MoE because they cause the variance term of error to decrease while keeping the bias term almost constant. The higher the complexity of MoE is, the bigger the variance reduction and, hence, the error reduction. In contrast, in Adult and Artificial I the bias term increases as more unlabeled data are added even though variance decreases.

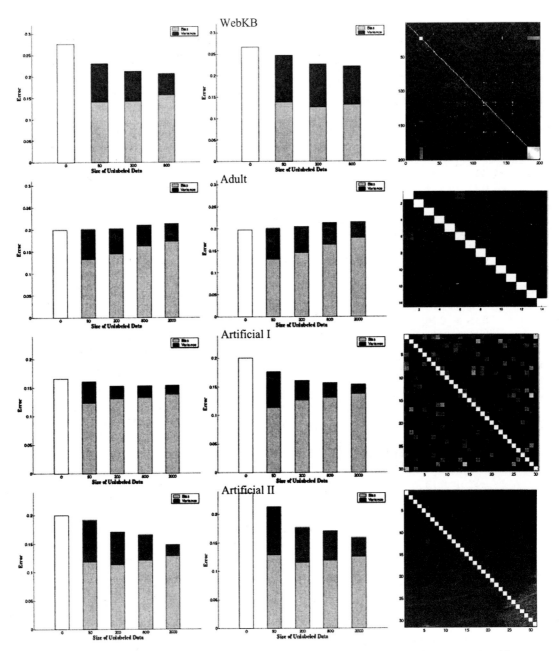

Figure 1. Bias-variance decomposition of the semi-supervised mixture-of-experts classifier for 10 mixture components (left column) and 30 mixture components (middle column), as the size of the unlabeled set increases, for four datasets: WebKB, Adult, Artificial I and Artificial II. The plots on the right column show correlation matrices of the feature vectors conditioned on class 1.

In the case of Adult the variance decrease is not enough to fully offset the increase in the bias term and this leads to a slight increase in error. This increase in the bias term can be attributed to incorrect model assumptions for the local experts as implied by the similar structure of the correlation matrix in these two datasets. Cozman et al. [3] have used asymptotic analysis to also argue that bias may be adversely affected by unlabeled data. In this regard our analysis has provided finite sample results. In WebKB and

Artificial II the model assumptions do not seem to be violated as much since the corresponding correlation matrices have far less structure.

9. Conclusions

In this paper we have introduced a semi-supervised mixture-of-experts technique, and provided EM-based learning using both labeled and unlabeled data. We showed that many popular EM-based approaches to semi-supervised learning can be seen as variants of one underlying model – mixture of experts.

Our empirical findings suggest that unlabeled data can help the MoE learner the most compared to the other two mixture-model learners, CC and SC. At the same time in cases where addition of unlabeled data can degrade performance of the mixture learners, particularly that of SC, MoE seems to be the most robust of the three learners as its performance degrades the least.

We used the bias-variance decomposition to explain the effects of unlabeled data on semi-supervised learning. We showed that when unlabeled data help they do so by reducing the variance more than increasing the bias error term. This particularly applies to the MoE learner that exhibits the largest benefit from unlabeled data. It is worth pointing out that although increasing the complexity (number of components) of the supervised MoE learner causes the learner to overfit, the addition of unlabeled data counteracts this overfitting and improves performance of the more complex semi-supervised MoE model, even relative to the less complex supervised MoE model. Thus, unlabeled data seem to be acting as a regularizer by preventing MoE to overfit.

We also showed that the behavior of the bias error term heavily depends on the correctness of model assumptions: due to incorrect model assumptions, unlabeled data can potentially introduce additional bias by inferring missing class labels and thus degrade the performance of the model.

There is work underway to extend the empirical evaluation of semi-supervised MoE to more datasets, including multi-class ones. There are also two streams of future work. The first one is to apply the bias-variance decomposition for analyzing the performance of other semi-supervised learning techniques. The second one is to take advantage of the regularization effect of unlabeled data by deciding which area of the example space to select unlabeled data from and by how much depending on the variance of the learner in that area.

10. References

[1] C.L. Blake and C.J. Merz, *UCI repository of machine learning databases*, URL http://www.ics.uci.edu/mlearn/MLRepository.html, 1998.

[2] A. Blum and T. Mitchell, "Combining labeled and unlabeled data with co-training", *Proceedings of the 11th Annual Conference on Computational Learning Theory (COLT-98)*, ACM Press, New York, 1998, pp. 92-100.

[3] F. G. Cozman, I. Cohen, and M. Cirelo, "Semi-supervised learning of mixture models and bayesian networks", *Proceedings of 20th International Conference on Machine Learning*, Morgan Kaufmann, Washington DC, 2003, pp. 99-106.

[4] M. Craven, D. DiPasquo, D. Freitag, A.K. McCallum, T. Mitchell, K. Nigam, and S. Slattery. "Learning to extract symbolic knowledge from the World Wide Web", *Proceedings of AAAI-98, 15th Conference of the American Association for Artificial Intelligence*, AAAI Press, Madison, 1998, pp. 509-516.

[5] S. Geman, E. Bienenstock and R. Doursat, "Neural networks and the bias/variance dilemma", *Neural Computation*, 1992, pp. 1-48.

[6] Ghahramani, Z. and M.I. Jordan, *Learning from incomplete data*, Technical Report 108, MIT Center for Biological and Computational Learning, December 1994.

[7] J. Heckman, "Sample selection bias as a specification error", *Econometrica*, 1979, pp. 153-161.

[8] T. Heskes, "Bias/variance decompositions for likelihood-based estimators", *Neural Computation*, 1998, pp. 1425-1433.

[9] R. A. Jacobs, M. I. Jordan, S. J. Nowlan, and G. E. Hinton, "Adaptive mixtures of local experts", *Neural Computation*, 1991, pp. 79-87.

[10] Karakoulas, G and R. Salakhutdinov, *Mixture models for classification using both labeled and unlabeled data*, Technical Report, Customer Behaviour Analytics, CIBC, Toronto, Canada, 2003.

[11] R. Kohavi and D. Wolpert, "Bias plus variance decomposition for zero-one loss functions", *Proceedings of 13th International Conference on Machine Learning*, 1996, pp. 275-283.

[12] D. Miller and S. Uyar. "A mixture of experts classifier with learning based on both labelled and unlabelled data", *Advances in Neural Information Processing Systems 9*, MIT Press, 1997, pp. 571-578.

[13] K. Nigam, A.K. McCallum, S. Thrun, and T.M. Mitchell, "Text classification from labeled and unlabeled documents using EM", *Machine Learning*, 2000, pp. 103-134.

[14] B. Shahshahani and D. Landgrebe, "The effect of unlabeled samples in reducing the small sample size problem and mitigating the Hughes phenomenon", *IEEE Transactions on Geoscience and Remote Sensing*, 1994, pp. 1087-1095.

[15] T. Zhang and F.J. Oles, "A probability analysis on the value of unlabeled data for classi- fication problems", *Proceedings of 17th International Conference on Machine Learning*, Morgan Kaufmann, 2000, pp. 1191-1198.

Transduction and typicalness for quality assessment of individual classifications in machine learning and data mining

Matjaž Kukar
University of Ljubljana,
Faculty of Computer and Information Science,
Tržaška 25, SI-1001 Ljubljana, Slovenia
matjaz.kukar@fri.uni-lj.si

Abstract

In the past machine learning algorithms have been successfully used in many problems, and are emerging as valuable data analysis tools. However, their serious practical use is affected by the fact, that more often than not, they cannot produce reliable and unbiased assessments of their predictions' quality. In last years, several approaches for estimating reliability or confidence of individual classifiers have emerged, many of them building upon the algorithmic theory of randomness, such as (historically ordered) transduction-based confidence estimation, typicalness-based confidence estimation, and transductive reliability estimation. Unfortunately, they all have weaknesses: either they are tightly bound with particular learning algorithms, or the interpretation of reliability estimations is not always consistent with statistical confidence levels. In the paper we propose a joint approach that compensates the mentioned weaknesses by integrating typicalness-based confidence estimation and transductive reliability estimation into joint confidence machine. The resulting confidence machine produces confidence values in the statistical sense (e.g., a confidence level of 95% means that in 95% the predicted class is also a true class), as well as provides us with a general principle that is independent of to the particular underlying classifier We perform a series of tests with several different machine learning algorithms in several problem domains. We compare our results with that of a proprietary TCM-NN method as well as with kernel density estimation. We show that the proposed method significantly outperforms density estimation methods, and how it may be used to improve their performance.

Keywords: machine learning, confidence estimation, typicalness, transduction, quality assessment.

1. Introduction

Usually machine learning algorithms output only bare predictions (classifications) for the new unclassified examples. While there are ways for almost all machine learning algorithms to at least partially provide quantitative assessment of the particular classification, so far there is no general method to assess the quality (confidence, reliability) of a single classification. We are interested in the assessment of classifier's performance on a *single example* and not in average performance on an independent dataset. Such assessments are very useful, especially in risk-sensitive applications (medical diagnosis, financial and critical control applications) because there it often matters, how much one can rely upon a given prediction. In such cases an overall quality measure of a classifier (e.g. classification accuracy, mean squared error, ...) with respect to the whole input distribution would not provide the desired value. Another possible use of quality assessment of single classifications is in ensembles of machine learning algorithms for selecting or combining answers from different classifiers [10].

There have been numerous attempts to assign probabilities to machine learning classifiers' (decision trees and rules, Bayesian classifiers, neural networks, nearest neighbour classifiers, ...) in order to interpret their decision as a probability distribution over all possible classes. In fact, we can trivially convert every machine learning classifier's output to a probability distribution by assigning the predicted class the probability 1, and 0 to all other possible classes. The posterior probability of the predicted class can be viewed as a classifier's confidence (reliability) of its prediction. However, such estimations may in general not be good due to inherent applied algorithm's biases.[1] Reliability estimation of a classification ($\widehat{y}$) of a single example (x),

---

[1]An extreme case of inherent bias can be found in a trivial constant classifier that blindly labels any example with a predetermined class with self-proclaimed confidence 1.

given its true class (y) should have the following property:

$$\text{Rel}(\tilde{y}\,|\,x) = t \;\Rightarrow\; P(\tilde{y} \neq y) \leq 1 - t \qquad (1)$$

If Eq. 1 holds, or even better, if it approaches equality, a reliability measure can be treated as a confidence value [11].

1.1. Related work

Several methods for inducing probabilistic descriptions from training data, figuring the use of density estimation algorithms, are emerging as an alternative to more established approaches for machine learning. Frequently kernel density estimation [22] is used for density estimation of input data using diverse machine learning paradigm such as neural networks [20, 5], Bayesian networks and classifiers [6], decision trees [19]. By this approach a chosen paradigm, coupled with kernel density estimation, is used for modelling the probability distribution of input data. Alternatively, stochastically changing class labels in the training dataset is proposed [3] in order to estimate conditionally class probability.

There is some ongoing work for constructing classifiers that divide the data space into reliable and unreliable regions [1]. Such meta-learning approaches have also been used for picking the most reliable prediction from the outputs of an ensemble of classifiers [18].

Meta learning community is partially dealing with predicting the right machine learning algorithm for a particular problem [13] based on performance and characteristics of other, simpler learning algorithms. In our problem of confidence estimation such an approach would result in learning to predict confidence value based on characteristics of single examples.

A lot of work has been done in applications of the transduction methodology [16], in connection with algorithmic theory of randomness. Here, approximations of randomness deficiency for different methods (SVMs, ridge regression) have been constructed in order to estimate confidence of single predictions. The drawback of this approach is that confidence estimations need to be specifically designed for each particular method and cannot be applied to other methods.

Another approach to reliability estimation, similarly based on the transduction principle, has been proposed in [10]. While it is general and independent of the underlying classifier, interpretation of its results isn't always possible in the statistical sense of confidence levels.

A few years ago typicalness has emerged as a complementary approach to transduction [11, 14]. By this approach, a "strangeness" measure of a single example is used to calculate its typicalness, and consequently a confidence in classifier's prediction. The main drawback of this approach is that for each machine learning algorithm it needs an appropriately constructed strangeness measure.

In the paper we present a further development of the latter two approaches where transductive reliability estimation serves as a generic strangeness measure in the typicalness framework. We compare the experimental results to that of kernel density estimation and show that the proposed method significantly outperforms it. We also suggest how basic transduction principle can be used to significantly improve results of kernel density estimation so it almost reaches results of transductive typicalness.

The paper is organized as follows. In Sec. 2 we describe the basic ideas of typicalness and transduction, outline the process of their integration, and review kernel density estimation methods used for comparison. In Sec. 3 we evaluate how our methodology compares to other approaches in 15 domains with 6 machine learning algorithms. In Sec. 4 we present some conclusions and directions for future work.

2. Methods and materials

The produced confidence values should be valid in the following sense. Given some possible label space $\mathcal{Y}$, if an algorithm predicts some set of labels $Y \subseteq \mathcal{Y}$ with confidence t for a new example which is truly labelled by $y \in \mathcal{Y}$, then we would expect the following to hold over randomization of the training set and the new example:

$$P(y \notin Y) \leq 1 - t \qquad (2)$$

Note that Eq. 2 is very general and valid for both classification (Y is predicted set of classes) and regression problems (Y is a predicted interval). As we deal only with single predictions in this paper, Eq. 2 can be simplified to a single predicted class value ($Y = \{\tilde{y}\}$):

$$P(y \neq \tilde{y}) \leq 1 - t \qquad (3)$$

2.1. Typicalness

In the typicalness framework [11, 12, 16] we consider a sequence of examples $(z_1, \ldots, z_n) = ((x_1, y_1), \ldots, (x_n, y_n))$, together with a new example x_{n+1} with unknown label $\tilde{y}_{n+1}$, all drawn independently from the same distribution over $\mathcal{Z} = \mathcal{X} \times \mathcal{Y}$ where $\mathcal{X}$ is an attribute space and $\mathcal{Y}$ is a label space. Our only assumption is therefore that the training as well as new (unlabelled) examples are independently and identically distributed (iid assumption).

We can use the typicalness framework to gain confidence information for each possible labelling for a new example x_{n+1}. We postulate some labels $\tilde{y}_{n+1}$ and for each one we examine how likely (typical) it is that all elements of the extended sequence $((x_1, y_1), \ldots, (x_{n+1}, \tilde{y}_{n+1}))$ might have been drawn independently from the same distribution or how typically *iid* the sequence is. The more typical the sequence, the more confident we are in $\tilde{y}_{n+1}$. To measure the typicalness of sequences, we define, for every $n \in \mathbb{N}$, a typicalness function $t : \mathscr{Z}^n \to [0,1]$ which, for any $r \in [0,1]$ has the property

$$P((z_1,\ldots,z_n) : t(z_1,\ldots,z_n) \le r) \le r \qquad (4)$$

If a typicalness function returns 0.05 for a given sequence, we know that the sequence is unusual because it will be produced at most 5% of the time by any *iid* process. It has been shown [11] that we can construct such functions by considering the "strangeness" of individual examples. If we have some family of functions $f : \mathscr{Z}^n \times \{1,2,\ldots,n\} \to \mathbb{R}$, $n \in \mathbb{N} \ldots$, then we can associate a strangeness value $\alpha(z_i) = f(\{z_1,\ldots,z_n\}; i)$, $i = 1,2,\ldots n$ with each example and define the following typicalness function

$$t((z_1,\ldots,z_n)) = \frac{\#\{\alpha(z_i) : \alpha(z_i) \ge \alpha(z_n)\}}{n} \qquad (5)$$

We group individual strangeness functions α_i into a family of functions $A_n : n \in \mathbb{N}$, where $A_n : \mathscr{Z}^n \to \mathbb{R}^n$ for all n. This is called an individual strangeness measure if, for any n, any permutation $\pi : \{1,\ldots,n\} \to \{1,\ldots,n\}$, any sequence $(z_1,\ldots,z_n) \in \mathscr{Z}^n$, and any $(\alpha_{\pi(1)},\ldots,\alpha_{\pi(n)}) \in \mathbb{R}^n)$ it satisfies the following criterion [11]:

$$\begin{aligned}
(\alpha_1,\ldots,\alpha_n) &= A_n(z_1,\ldots,z_n) \quad \Rightarrow \\
(\alpha_{\pi(1)},\ldots,\alpha_{\pi(n)}) &= A_n(z_{\pi(1)},\ldots,z_{\pi(n)}) \qquad (6)
\end{aligned}$$

The meaning of this criterion is that the same value should be produced for each individual element in sequence, regardless of the order in which their individual strangeness values are calculated. This is a very important criterion, because it can be proven [11] that the constructed typicalness function (5) satisfies the condition from (4), provided that the individual strangeness measure satisfies the criterion (6).

From a practical point of view it is advisable [11] to use positive strangeness measures, ranging between 0 for most typical examples, and some positive upper bound, (up to $+\infty$), for most untypical examples.

2.2. Typicalness in machine learning

In the machine learning setup, for calculating the typicalness of a new example $z_{n+1} = (x_{n+1}, \tilde{y}_{n+1})$ described with attribute values x_{n+1} and labelled with $\tilde{y}_{n+1}$, given the training set $(z_1,\ldots,z_n)$, Eq. 5 changes to

$$t((z_1,\ldots,z_{n+1})) = \frac{\#\{\alpha(z_i) : \alpha(z_i) \ge \alpha(z_{n+1})\}}{n+1} \qquad (7)$$

Note that on the right-hand side of Eq. 7, z_i belongs to the extended sequence, i.e. $z_i \in \{z_1,\ldots,z_{n+1}\}$. For a given

machine learning algorithm, first we need to construct an appropriate strangeness measure and modify the algorithm accordingly.[2] Then, for each new unlabelled example x, all possible labels $\tilde{y} \in Y$ are considered. For each label $\tilde{y}$ a typicalness of labelled example $t((x,\tilde{y})) = t((z_1,\ldots,z_n,(x,\tilde{y})))$ is calculated. Finally, the example is labelled with "most typical" class, that is the one that maximizes $\{t((x,\tilde{y}))\}$. By Eq. 5 the second largest typicalness is an upper bound on the probability that the excluded classifications are correct [14]. Consequently, the confidence is calculated as follows:

$$\text{confidence}((x,\tilde{y})) = 1 - \text{typicalness of second most typical label.} \qquad (8)$$

2.3. Transductive reliability estimation

The transductive reliability estimation process and its theoretical foundations originating from algorithmic theory of randomness are described in more detail in [10]. Briefly sketched, an unlabelled example x is predicted a class $\tilde{y}$ and respective class probability distribution P by the given machine learning classifier. The example x is then labelled with the class $\tilde{y}$, the newly labelled example $((x,\tilde{y}))$ is temporarily inserted into the training set, and then its class and class probability distribution Q are newly predicted. Reliability of the predicted class is estimated as a similarity between the two condition class probability estimations.[3] As a dissimilarity measure between probability distributions P and Q, symmetric Kullback-Leibler divergence [2], normalized to the interval $[0,1]$ was used as $J_N(P,Q)$. Reliability is calculated as an inverted normalized dissimilarity, that is $\text{Rel}((x,\tilde{y})) = 1 - J_N(P,Q)$. While this approach provides a measure that separates correct and incorrect classifications quite well, its numerical values usually cannot be interpreted as confidence levels, and ranges of their values are very much domain- and algorithm- dependent [9].

2.4. Merging the typicalness and transduction frameworks

There is a very good reason for merging typicalness and transductive reliability estimation frameworks together. While transduction gives good reliability estimations, they are often hard to interpret in the statistical sense. On the other hand, the typicalness framework gives clear confidence values, however in order to achieve this a good strangeness measure $\alpha(z_i)$ needs to be constructed.

Of course, there is a trivial solution to it, namely a uniform strangeness measure $\alpha_i = C$, where C is some constant

---

[2]This is the main problem of the typicalness approach, as the algorithms need do be considerably changed.

[3]In the transductive reliability estimation framework it does not matter very much if the original probability estimations are biased.

value. Unfortunately, this does us no good, since it treats all examples as equally strange and can be considered as most conservative strangeness measure. It is therefore necessary to construct a sensible strangeness measure. In [11, 17, 14] some ideas on how to construct strangeness measures for different machine learning algorithms are presented.

On the other hand, as we shall see later, for a strangeness measure we can always use transductive reliability estimation. We may speculate that most reliable examples are also least strange. Therefore we define the strangeness measure for a new example $z_{n+1} = (x_{n+1}, \widetilde{y}_{n+1})$, described with attribute values x_{n+1} and labelled with $\widetilde{y}_{n+1}$, given the training set $(z_1, \ldots, z_n)$ as follows:

$$\alpha(z_{n+1}) = f(z_1, \ldots, z_{n+1}; n+1) = 1 - \text{Rel}(z_{n+1}) \in [0,1] \tag{9}$$

It can be shown that such a strangeness function satisfies the criterion from Eq. 6 and therefore has the property required by Eq. 5.

Theorem 1. *The strangeness measure* $\alpha(z_i) = 1 - \text{Rel}((x_i, \widetilde{y}_i))$ *is independent of the order in which the examples' strangeness values are calculated.*

Proof. The training set is only temporarily changed by including a suitably labelled new example in a transductive step (Sec. 2.3). It is restored back to the initial training set as soon as the reliability estimation is calculated. Therefore the training set remains invariant for all new examples for which the reliability estimation needs to be calculated. It follows that it is irrelevant in which order the examples are presented and the criterion for Eq. 6 is therefore satisfied. Note that Eq. 6 does not require that examples are ordered in any particular way, but only that any permutation of the order of their evaluations produces the same result for each example. □

Consequently we can, for any machine learning classifier, universally use a strangeness measure $\alpha((x, \widetilde{y})) = 1 - Rel((x, \widetilde{y}))$. It is positive, and the "more strange" examples have higher strangeness values, as suggested in [11].

An implementation of transductive reliability estimation in typicalness framework is straightforward. For all training examples, reliability estimation is calculated by leave-one-out testing, and they are labelled as correctly or incorrectly classified. For each new example x with classification $\widetilde{y}$ its confidence $\text{conf}((x, \widetilde{y}))$ is calculated as in Sec. 2.1, Eq. 8. Regardless of the number of classes in original problem, there are only two possibilities (meta-classes) for each classification. It is either correct or incorrect. Therefore only that we always deal with exacly two meta-classes that represent correct classifications and incorrect classifications. As we want the confidence to reflect the probability of a correct classification, we need to invert the confidence values

for incorrect meta-class:

$$\text{confidence}((x, \widetilde{y})) = \begin{cases} \text{conf}((x, \widetilde{y})) & \text{``correct'' meta-class,} \\ 1 - \text{conf}((x, \widetilde{y})) & \text{``incorrect'' meta-class.} \end{cases} \tag{10}$$

2.5. Meta learning and kernel density estimation

The problem of estimating a confidence value can also be viewed as a meta learning problem where the original class value is replaced by correctness of its prediction. Let $\widehat{y}$ be a meta-class for training examples obtained with internal leave-one-out testing (i.e. $\widehat{y} = 1$ for correct and $\widehat{y} = 0$ for incorrect classifications). We can calculate the confidence in a given prediction of a new, previously unseen example x by estimating the function $\widehat{y}(x)$ with a nearest neighbour classifier:

$$\widehat{y}(x) = \frac{1}{K} \sum_{x_i \in N_K(x)} \widehat{y}_i(x_i) \tag{11}$$

Here $N_K(x)$ is the set of K points nearest to x according to some distance measure. However, such simple estimations may be problematic when the attribute space is large (lots of multi-valued, possibly correlated, attributes), and sparsely populated (relatively small number of training examples). Our experimental results (Tab. 2) also shows this problem, as using a nearest neighbour meta-learner results in lowest performance of all methods[4]. Therefore, a transformation of input space is necessary to reduce the dimensionality of input space. We have chosen the principal component analysis (PCA) methodology on the training data, and two components with largest variances were selected as data descriptors. On average, the sum of the two components' relative variances is about 0.7. This means, that the two principal components describe about 70% of data variability.

Rather than giving the nearest neighbours equal weights, we can assign them weights that decrease smoothly with distance from the target point. This leads us to kernel density estimation [21] in reduced and uncorrelated data space. It can be estimated by using the Nadaraya-Watson kernel weighted average:

$$\widehat{y}(x) = \frac{\sum_{i=i}^{N} K_\lambda(x, x_i) \widehat{y}_i(x_i)}{\sum_{i=i}^{N} K_\lambda(x, x_i)} \tag{12}$$

where $\lambda = [\lambda_1, \lambda_2]$ is a vector of kernel parameters (bandwidths), and $K_\lambda(x, x_i)$ is a simplified (uncorrelated) bivariate gaussian kernel:

$$K_{\lambda_1, \lambda_2}(x, x_i) = \frac{1}{2\pi \lambda_1 \lambda_2} e^{-\frac{1}{2} \left(\frac{(x[1] - x_i[1])^2}{\lambda_1^2} + \frac{(x[2] - x_i[2])^2}{\lambda_1^2} \right)} \tag{13}$$

---

[4] To be fair, one must say that other more advanced meta-learners could have been used. However, this was not the aim of the paper.

As the principal component analysis involves a numerical procedure that transforms a number of possibly correlated input variables (attributes) into a (smaller) number of uncorrelated variables (principal components), it is therefore perfectly justified to use a simplified bivariate gaussian kernel for density estimation on uncorrelated variables. Our experiments have shown, that indeed in all cases the correlation between the largest two principal components was less than 10^{-14}, also negligible. For the bivariate gaussian kernels, appropriate bandwidths were calculated from training data according to the rule of thumb as described by Wand [22, p. 98].

For each dataset and algorithm the following procedure was performed. For each training example, a correctness of its classification was determined by the leave-one-out testing methodology. Training examples were partitioned in sets of correctly and incorrectly classified examples, and used for kernel density estimations of correct and incorrect classifications. For each new examples, principal components were calculated and used to calculate the density of correct classifications (cd) as well as the density of incorrect classifications (id) at respective coordinates. The confidence value of a new example was calculated as $cd/(cd+id)$ [4].

2.6. Improving kernel density estimation by transduction principle

The procedure described in Sec. 2.5 is computationally fast when applying to new examples as it involves only calculating the principal components (scaling and one matrix multiplication), and two fast uncorrelated density estimations. Unfortunately, its performance (Tab. 2) compared to transductive confidence estimation is rather uninspiring. The performance, however, can be easily improved by using some ideas from meta learning and transduction frameworks. Namely, we can easily extend the original data description by including the predicted class as well as class probability distributions. They may be obtained with internal leave-one-out testing on the training set.

On extended data the principal components are calculated. A new example's class and class distribution is predicted by the original classifier, and the example's description is enhanced by the classifier's prediction. An enhanced example description is then used in density estimation procedure as described in Sec. 2.5.

2.7. Testing methodology

To validate the proposed methodology we performed extensive experiments with 6 different machine learning algorithms – naive and semi naive Bayesian classifier [8], backpropagation neural network [15], K-nearest neighbour,

locally naive Bayesian classifier (a combination KNN of and naive Bayesian classifier) [10], two kinds of Assistant (ID3-like decision trees) [7] on 14 well-known benchmark datasets from the UCI repository (Mesh, Breast cancer, Diabetes, Heart, Hepatitis, Iris, Chess endgame (king-rook vs. king), LED, Lymphography, Primary tumor, Rheumatology, Soybean, Voting), and on a real-life problem of nuclear cardiology diagnostics (Nuclear).

For each dataset and algorithm we determined for each training example by internal leave-one-out testing its correctness – whether it was correctly (1) or incorrectly (0) classified. For reliability estimations, confidence values and density estimations, we calculated their correlation with correctness. In an ideal case (each correct example has value 1, each incorrect 0), the result would be 1.

We also measured how well a method discriminates between correctly and incorrectly classified examples. For each method (reliability estimations, confidence values, and density estimations) we calculated the boundary b that maximizes purity (information gain) of the discriminated examples. The boundary b is calculated by maximizing Eq. 14.

$$
\begin{aligned}
H(S) &= -\frac{|S_1|}{|S|}\log_2\frac{|S_1|}{|S|} - \frac{|S_2|}{|S|}\log_2\frac{|S_2|}{|S|} \\
H(S;b) &= \frac{|S_1|}{|S|}H(S_1) + \frac{|S_2|}{|S|}H(S_2) \\
&\quad \text{(entropy after split)} \\
\text{Gain}(S,b) &= H(S) - H(S;b) \quad\quad (14)
\end{aligned}
$$

Here, S is the set consisting of all examples, in the set S_1 there are unreliable examples $\{z_i : \text{Rel}(z_i) < b\}$ whereas in the set S_2 there are reliable examples $\{z_i : \text{Rel}(z_i) \geq b\}$. In an ideal case when both splits are pure, the result would be equal to the entropy of classifications $H(S)$.

All experiments were performed by leave-one-out testing. In this setup, one example was reserved, while learning and preparatory calculations were performed on the rest, in many cases two nested leave-one-out testings were carried out.

Final results are averages of leave-one-out experiments on all examples from the dataset.

3. Results

Results of confidence estimation on KNN (nearest neighbour) algorithm are compared with the TCM-NN nearest neighbour confidence machine [14], where a tailor-made strangeness measure for confidence estimation in typicalness framework was constructed. In Tab. 1 experimental results in 15 domains are shown. Results of TCM-NN are slightly better, as could be expected from the tailor-made method, though the differences are not significant with two-tailed, paired t-test).

Table 1. Comparison of confidence estimation on KNN with the algorithm-specific TCM-NN, both with 10 nearest neighbours. Accurracy was obtained with standard 10-NN algorithm.

	Accuracy	Correlation with correctness		Information gain	
	KNN	TCM-NN	KNN	TCM-NN	KNN
Mesh	64.7%	0.49	0.40	0.26	0.19
Brest cancer	80.2%	0.09	0.14	0.02	0.03
Nuclear	81.0%	0.35	0.28	0.12	0.07
Diabetes	73.7%	0.26	0.19	0.06	0.05
Heart	79.3%	0.34	0.18	0.11	0.09
Hepatitis	85.2%	0.28	0.25	0.07	0.07
Iris	94.7%	0.23	0.36	0.12	0.12
Chess end.	92.0%	0.43	0.33	0.21	0.12
LED	73.2%	0.20	0.19	0.04	0.05
Lymphography	83.1%	0.50	0.22	0.32	0.18
Primary tumor	41.3%	0.10	0.37	0.00	0.19
Rheumatology	61.3%	0.42	0.42	0.17	0.16
Soybean	92.1%	0.32	0.38	0.12	0.12
Voting	94.0%	0.42	0.26	0.18	0.09
Average	78.3%	0.32	0.28	0.13	0.11

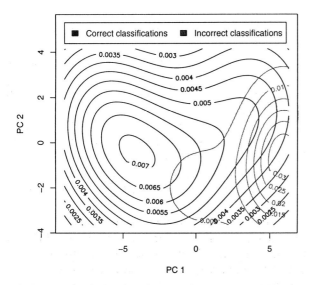

Figure 1. Densities of correct and incorrect classification in Soybean dataset using neural networks.

3.1. Reliability, confidence and density estimation

The obtained confidence values are compared with transductive reliability estimations and density estimations. Our first goal was to evaluate the performance of confidence values in terms of correlation with correctness, and its ability to separate correct and incorrect classifications in terms of information gain. Our second goal was to see whether confidence values are more easily interpretable than transductive reliability estimations.

Figures 2(a) and 2(b) depict how reliability estimations in are transformed to confidence levels. This is a typical example and probably the most important result of our work, as it makes them easily statistically interpretable. On average, the best decision boundary for reliability estimations is 0.74, on the other hand, for confidence it is about 0.45. Also, the mass of correct and incorrect classification has shifted towards 1 and 0, respectively.

In Tab. 2 experimental results are presented. We see that confidence values significantly ($p < 0.05$ with two-tailed, paired t-test) outperform reliability estimations in terms of correlation with correctness. From Fig. 2 it is clear that this is because of the shift towards 1 and 0. Information gains do not differ significantly.

Comparing confidence values and density estimations shows a slightly different picture. Here, in terms of correlation with correctness as well as for for information gain criterion, the differences are significant ($p < 0.01$ with two-tailed, paired t-test). Fig. 1 depicts typical density estimations for both correct and incorrect classifications. On average, the best decision boundary for density estimations is 0.52.

In Tab. 2 we can also see that meta-learning with 10 nearest neighbours (10-NN) performed worst (although 10 was a tuned parameter). This was expected, since it was used in the whole – sparsely populated – attribute space. Density estimations (Den.) performed on a reduced attribute space significantly better ($p < 0.01$ with two-tailed,

Table 2. Experimental results with confidence values, reliability and density estimations with 6 machine learning algorithm in 15 datasets. Accuracy was calculated as an average of all 6 base classifiers.

Domain	Accuracy	Correlation with correctness			Information gain (in bit)		
		Reliability	Confidence	Density	Reliability	Confidence	Density
Mesh	65.7%	0.51	0.46	0.10	0.25	0.25	0.12
Brest cancer	77.4%	0.28	0.22	0.09	0.10	0.10	0.07
Nuclear	88.0%	0.21	0.21	0.09	0.07	0.08	0.07
Diabetes	74.3%	0.26	0.33	0.08	0.18	0.18	0.05
Heart	80.7%	0.26	0.27	0.08	0.11	0.11	0.11
Hepatitis	86.6%	0.25	0.30	0.12	0.12	0.11	0.14
Iris	93.8%	0.23	0.42	0.08	0.13	0.13	0.09
Chess endgame	95.5%	0.09	0.27	0.08	0.11	0.11	0.05
Chess endgame	71.1%	0.11	0.12	0.07	0.10	0.10	0.05
LED	73.0%	0.16	0.18	0.04	0.05	0.05	0.03
Lymphography	81.9%	0.20	0.27	0.13	0.13	0.13	0.17
Primary tumor	44.8%	0.39	0.38	0.07	0.16	0.16	0.07
Rheumatology	58.0%	0.47	0.48	0.10	0.22	0.22	0.10
Soybean	89.4%	0.35	0.37	0.08	0.14	0.13	0.09
Voting	94.0%	0.17	0.22	0.09	0.08	0.08	0.07
Average	78.3%	0.26	0.30	0.09	0.13	0.13	0.08

paired t-test). We can also see that transductive attributes improve the performance of density estimation (Tr. den.) quite significantly ($p < 0.05$ with two-tailed, paired t-test). While it does not reach performance of transductive reliability or confidence estimations, it is much easier to compute as it does not require re-learning of a classifier.

4. Discussion

We propose an approach that compensates the weaknesses of typicalness-based confidence estimation and transductive reliability estimation by integrating them into a joint confidence machine.

The resulting values are true confidence levels, and this makes them much easier to interpret. Contrary to the basic typicalness and transductive confidence estimation, the described approach is not bound to the particular underlying classifier. This is an important improvement since this makes possible to calculate confidence values for almost any classifier, no matter how complex it is.

Experimental comparison on comparable unmodified and modified algorithms (confidence estimation on k-nearest neighbour algorithm and TCM-NN nearest neighbour confidence machine) show that the proposed approach performs similarly to the specially modified algorithm. There is no significant reduction in performance while there is a huge gain in generality.

Comparisons with kernel density estimation show that the computed confidence values significantly outperform density estimations. However, this does not mean that density estimations should not be used as they are much eas-

ier to compute and do not require re-learning of a classifier. Their performance can also be significantly improved by using additional transductive attributes.

Experimental results performed with different machine learning algorithms in several problem domains show that there is no reduction of discrimination performance with respect to transductive reliability estimation. More important than this, statistical interpretability of confidence values makes possible for applications in risk-sensitive problems with strict confidence limits.

The main drawback of our approach is computational complexity, as it needs to perform the leave-one-out testing in advance, and requires temporary re-learning of a classifier for each new example. However, this may not be a problem if incremental learners (such as naive Bayesian classifier) are used. In other cases, density estimation with included transductive attributes may also be used.

In the near future we are planning several experiments in risk-sensitive problems mostly in medical diagnostics and prognostics.

Acknowledgements

This work was supported by the Slovenian Ministry of Education and Science.

References

[1] S. D. Bay and M. J. Pazzani. Characterizing model errors and differences. In *Proc. 17th International Conf. on Machine*

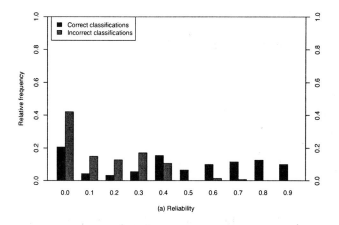

(a) Reliability

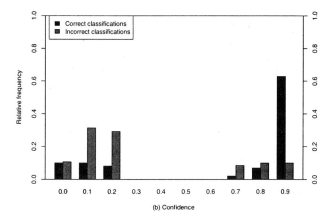

(b) Confidence

Figure 2. Relative frequencies of reliability estimations and confidence levels in Soybean dataset using neural networks.

Learning, pages 49–56. Morgan Kaufmann, San Francisco, CA, 2000.

[2] A. L. Gibbs and F. E. Su. On choosing and bounding probability metrics. *International Statistical Review*, 70(3):419–435, 2002.

[3] O. M. Halck. Using hard classifiers to estimate conditional class probabilities. In T. Elomaa, H. Mannila, and H. Toivonen, editors, *Proceedings of the Thirteenth European Conference on Machine Learning*, pages 124–134. Springer-Verlag, Berlin, 2002.

[4] T. Hastie, R. Tibisharani, and J. Friedman. *The Elements of Statistical Learning*. Springer-Verlag, 2001.

[5] S. S. Ho and H. Wechsler. Transductive confidence machine for active learning. In *Proc. Int. Joint Conf. on Neural Networks 2003*, Portland, OR., USA, 2003.

[6] G. H. John and P. Langley. Estimating continuous distributions in Bayesian classifiers. In P. Besnard and S. Hanks, editors, *Proceedings of the Eleventh Conference on Uncertainty in Artificial Intelligence*. Morgan Kaufmann, San Francisco, USA, 1995.

[7] I. Kononenko, E. Šimec, and M. Robnik-Šikonja. Overcoming the myopia of inductive learning algorithms with ReliefF. *Applied Intelligence*, 7:39–55, 1997.

[8] I. Kononenko. Semi-naive Bayesian classifier. In Y. Kodratoff, editor, *Proc. European Working Session on Learning-91*, pages 206–219, Porto, Potrugal, 1991. Springer-Verlag, Berlin-Heidelberg-New York.

[9] M. Kukar. Transductive reliability estimation for medical diagnosis. *Artif. intell. med.*, pages 81–106, 2003.

[10] M. Kukar and I. Kononenko. Reliable classifications with Machine Learning. In T. Elomaa, H. Mannila, and H. Toivonen, editors, *Proceedings of 13th European Conference on Machine Learning, ECML 2002*, pages 219–231. Springer-Verlag, Berlin, 2002.

[11] T. Melluish, C. Saunders, I. Nouretdinov, and V. Vovk. Comparing the Bayes and typicalness frameworks. In *Proc. ECML 2001*, volume 2167, pages 350–357, 2001.

[12] I. Nouretdinov, T. Melluish, and V. Vovk. Ridge regressioon confidence machine. In *Proc. 18th International Conf. on Machine Learning*, pages 385–392. Morgan Kaufmann, San Francisco, CA, 2001.

[13] B. Pfahringer, H. Bensuasan, and C. Giraud-Carrier. Meta-learning by landmarking various learning algorithms. In *Proc. 17th International Conf. on Machine Learning*. Morgan Kaufmann, San Francisco, CA, 2000.

[14] K. Proedrou, I. Nouretdinov, V. Vovk, and A. Gammerman. Transductive confidence machines for pattern recognition. In *Proc. ECML 2002*, pages 381–390. Springer, Berlin, 2002.

[15] D. Rumelhart and J. L. McClelland. *Parallel Distributed Processing*, volume 1: Foundations. MIT Press, Cambridge, 1986.

[16] C. Saunders, A. Gammerman, and V. Vovk. Transduction with confidence and credibility. In T. Dean, editor, *Proceedings of the International Joint Conference on Artificial Intelligence*, Stockholm, Sweden, 1999. Morgan Kaufmann, San Francisco, USA.

[17] C. Saunders, A. Gammerman, and V. Vovk. Computationally efficient transductive machines. In *Algorithmic Learning Theory, 11th International Conference, ALT 2000, Sydney, Australia, December 2000, Proceedings*, volume 1968, pages 325–333. Springer, Berlin, 2000.

[18] A. Seewald and J. Furnkranz. An evaluation of grading classifiers. In *Proc. 4th International Symposium on Advances in Intelligent Data Analysis*, pages 115–124, 2001.

[19] P. Smyth, A. Gray, and U. Fayyad. Retrofitting decision tree classifiers using kernel density estimation. In A. Prieditis and S. J. Russell, editors, *Proceedings of the Twelvth International Conference on Machine Learning*, pages 506–514, Tahoe City, California, USA, 1995. Morgan Kaufmann, San Francisco, USA.

[20] D. F. Specht and H. Romsdahl. Experience with adaptive pobabilistic neural networks and adaptive general regression neural networks. In S. K. Rogers, editor, *Proceedings of IEEE International Conference on Neural Networks*, Orlando, USA, 1994. IEEE Press, Piscataway, USA.

[21] W. N. Venables and B. D. Ripley. *Modern Applied Statistics with S-PLUS. Fourth edition*. Springer-Verlag, 2002.

[22] M. P. Wand and M. C. Jones. *Kernel Smoothing*. Chapman and Hall, London, 1995.

Mining Associations by Linear Inequalities

Tsay Young ('T. Y.') Lin
Department of Computer Science
San Jose State University
San Jose, CA 95192, USA
tylin@cs.sjsu.edu

Abstract

The main theorem is: Generalized associations of a relational table can be found by a finite set of linear inequalities within polynomial time. It is derived from the following three results, which were established in ICDM0'02 and are re-developed here. They are (1) Isomorphic Theorem: Isomorphic relations have isomorphic patterns. Such an isomorphism classifies relational tables into isomorphic classes. (2) A variant of the classical bitmaps indexes uniquely exists in each isomorphic class. We take it as the canonical model of the class. (3) All possible attributes/features can be generated by a generalized procedure of the classical AOG (attribute oriented generalization). Then, (4) the main theorem for canonical model is established. By isomorphism theorem, we had the final result (5).

Keywords: association, deduction, feature, granules, bitmaps

1 Introduction

Though there is no formal definition of data mining, but its informal version of [?] is rather universal:

- Drawing useful high level information (patterns, knowledge and etc.) from data.

In this paper we will attempt to analyze such a informal notion critically on one of the core techniques, namely, association rule mining [4]. As a byproduct of the analysis, we have the results stated in the abstract.

Our methodology is very rigorous, but we take the informal style to explain the rigorous method. We use illustrations, if formal proofs do not give good insight. The main goal is to get the idea cross.

1.1 Basics Terms in Association Mining (AM)

In AM, two measures, support and confidence, are the criteria. It is well-known among researchers, support is the essential one. In other words, high frequency are more important than the confidence of implications. We call them undirected association rules, associations, or high frequency patterns.

Association mining is originated from the market basket data [1]. However, in many software systems, the data mining tools are applied to *relational tables*. For definitive, we have the following translations of terms and will use them interchangeably:

1. an item is an attribute value,

2. a q-itemset is a subtuple of length q,

3. A q-subtuple is a high frequency q-pattern or a q-association, if its occurrences are greater than or equal to a given threshold.

2 Anatomy of Association Mining(AM)

In order to fully understand the mathematical mechanics of AM, we need to understand how the information are developed. First we set up a convention:

- A symbol is a string of "bit and bytes;" it has no real world meaning. A symbol is termed a word, if the intended real world meaning *participates* in the formal reasoning.

In summary a word is an interpreted symbol and its interpretation is part of reasoning processes. Notations of word and symbol appear to be the same, but their meanings are very different.

154

2.1 Information Flows of AM

1. Representation phase: real world → a relational table of words. Each symbol (column names and attribute values) in the table represents some real world facts; so we refer to them as words. The representations are incomplete. The semantics of words are not implemented and relied on human support (traditional data processing professionals).

2. Data Mining Phase: a table of symbols → patterns of symbols. In this phase, table of words is used as a table of symbols, because data mining algorithms do not consult human for the semantics of symbols; they are treated as "bits and bytes" in AM algorithm. Patterns, which are algebraic or logic expressions of symbols, are derived mathematically. Briefly, the table of symbols is the only "axioms," and the patterns are the "theorems."

3. Interpretation Phase: patterns of symbols → patterns of words. Patterns are discovered as expressions of symbols in the previous phase. In this phase, those individual symbols are regarded as words again(using the meaning acquired in representation Phase).

4. Realizations Phase: patterns of words → real world phenomena. Do patterns of words represent some real world phenomena?

2.2 Axiomatic Approach to Data Mining

To examine the foundation of each data mining technique, we take the axiomatic approach. We require each technique explicitly specified the following items:

1. Input data: Any information utilized by data mining algorithms are considered the input. In AM, the input is a table of symbols. However, in clustering techniques the input is the given set of points plus the background knowledge - the geometry of the ambient space of the given points.

2. The logic/reasoning system: AM uses mathematical deduction (Counting is a very simple deduction).

3. The output patterns: The model of output patterns needs to be specified. The model of the traditional AM is the set of associations. They are "conjunctions" of input symbols. We will generalize it to the set of algebraic or logic expressions of symbols.

Such an approach has been called Deductive Data Mining [8].

2.3 Interpretations of Patterns

In representation phase, each word, to human, does correspond to a real world phenomenon; we express it by saying the meaning of the word is the real world phenomenon. Again such meaning is known only to human, not to the system. For systems words are symbols. The patterns are discovered in the form of expressions of symbols. To interpreting them, we convert the expression of symbols to expression of words based on the *interpretations* established in the *representation phase*. Any pattern (expression of symbols) is said to be an un-interpreted pattern, if the transformation of the expression of symbols to the expression of words has not been done. A pattern is un-interpretable, if such a transformation cannot be done.

2.4 Realization of Patterns

A pattern is un-realizable, if the pattern (= expression of symbol) does not correspond to a real world phenomenon. Note that an expression of words is, of course, interpretable, but may not be realizable; we refer to.

3 Tables of Symbols - Understand the input

First, we will examine how the real world is represented:

1 Select a set of attributes, called relational schema.

2 Represent a set of real world entities by a table of words. These words, called attribute values, are meaningful words to human, but their meaning are *not* implemented in the system.

In traditional data processing (**TDP**) environment, for example, the attribute name, COLOR, means exactly what human thinks. Therefore its possible values are yellow, blue, and etc. More importantly,

- DBMS processes these data under *human commands*, and carries out the human-perceived semantics.

To stress such view, we call it

3 Computing with words

At the same time, it is equally important to stress that

4 the human views or interpretations of those words are **not** implemented in the system. They are merely symbols in the system.

In the system, COLOR, yellow, blue, and etc are "bits and bytes" without any meaning; they are pure symbols. Using AI's terminology [3], those attribute names and values

V	$\rightarrow$	F	G	V	$\rightarrow$	F'	G'
e_1	$\rightarrow$	30	foo	e_1	$\rightarrow$	$30'$	foo'
e_2	$\rightarrow$	30	bar	e_2	$\rightarrow$	$30'$	bar'
e_3	$\rightarrow$	40	baz	e_3	$\rightarrow$	$40'$	baz'
e_4	$\rightarrow$	50	foo	e_4	$\rightarrow$	$50'$	foo'
e_5	$\rightarrow$	40	bar	e_5	$\rightarrow$	$40'$	bar'
e_6	$\rightarrow$	40	bar	e_6	$\rightarrow$	$40'$	bar'
e_7	$\rightarrow$	30	bar	e_7	$\rightarrow$	$30'$	bar'
e_8	$\rightarrow$	40	baz	e_8	$\rightarrow$	$40'$	baz'

Table 1. A Relational Table K and its Isomorphic Copy K'

F-Value	F'-Value	=Bit-Vectors	=Granules
30	$30'$	= 11000110	=($\{e1, e2, e6, e7\}$)
40	$40'$	= 00101001	=($\{e3, e5, e8\}$)
50	$50'$	= 00010000	=($\{e4\}$)
G-Value	G-Value	=Bit-Vectors	=Granules
Foo	Foo'	= 10010000	=($\{e1, e4\}$)
Bar	Bar'	= 01001010	=($\{e2, e5, e7\}$)
Baz	Baz'	= 00100101	=($\{e3, e6, e8\}$)

Table 2. Words in K and K' have the same bitmaps and granules

(column names, and elements in the tables) are the semantic primitives. They are primitives, because they are undefined terms inside the system, yet the symbols do represent (*unimplemented*) human-perceived semantics.

3.1 Isomorphic Tables and Patterns

Let us start this section with obvious, but somewhat a surprise observation. Intuitively, data is a table of symbols(Section 2.2), so if we change some or all of the symbols, the mathematical structure of the table will not be changed. So its patterns, e.g., association rules, will be preserved. Formally, we have the following theorem [9]:

Theorem 3.1. Isomorphic relations have isomorphic patterns.

We will illustrate the idea by an example. The following example is adopted from ([6], pp 702):

Example 3.2. Suppose a relation consists of two attributes, F and G, of type integer and string respectively. The current instance has eight tuples. These tuples are knowledge representations of entities. Table 1 illustrates the representations and isomorphism. To illustrate *Theorem* 3.1., let us assume the support is "two tuples" and count the items. It is easy to see we have:

1. 1-assoication in K: 30, 40, *bar*, *baz*,

2. 1-assoication in K': $30'$, $40'$, *bar'*, *baz'*,

3. 2-assoication in K: (30, *bar*) and (40, *baz*),

4. 2-assoication in K': ($30'$, *bar'*) and ($40'$, *baz'*).

q-association rules (q=1,2) are isomorphic in the sense that adding prime ' to associations in K become associations in K'; this illustrate the theorem.

3.2 The Canonical Models

In this section, we will introduce tables of Bitmaps (TOB), Granules(TOG), and Granular Data Model(GDM). We will illustrate the idea by examples. Let us consider the bitmap indexes for K (see Table 1) the first attributes, F, would have three bit-vectors. The first, for value 30, is 11000110, because the first, second, sixth, and seventh tuple have F=30; see Table 2.

Using Table 2 as the translation table, Table 1 is transformed into bitmap table, Table 3. It should be obvious that we will have the exact same bitmap table for K'.

Next, we note that a bit vector can be interpreted as a granule (subset) of V. For example, the bit vector, 11000110, of F= 30 represents the subset $\{e_1, e_2, e_6, e_7\}$, similarly, 00101001, of $F = 40$ represents the subset $\{e_3, e_5, e_8\}$. As in the bitmap case, Table 1 is transformed into granular table, Table 4.

Note that F-granules forms a partition, and hence induces an equivalence relation, denoted by Q_F; similarly, we have Q_G. Pawlak called the the pair $(V, \{Q_F, Q_G\})$ knowledge base and note that it is equivalent to table of granule. Since knowledge base often means something else, we have called it granular data model(GDM). Now we can summarize these observations in:

Theorem 3.3.

1. Isomorphic tables have the same canonical model.

2. The canonical model has three forms, table of granules (TOG), bitmaps (TOB), and granular data model(GDM). TOB, TOG, and GDM are isomorphic and regarded as synonyms.

Theorem 3.4. It is adequate to do AM in one of the canonical model.

V	F	G	F-bit	G-bit
e_1	30	foo	11000110	10010000
e_2	30	bar	11000110	01001010
e_3	40	baz	00101001	00100101
e_4	50	foo	00010000	10010000
e_5	40	bar	00101001	01001010
e_6	30	baz	11000110	00100101
e_7	30	bar	11000110	01001010
e_8	40	baz	00101001	00100101

Table 3. Tables of Words and Bitmaps)

U	F	G	F-granule	G-granule
$v1$	30	foo	$\{e1, e2, e6, e7\}$	$\{e1, e4\}$
$v2$	30	bar	$\{e1, e2, e6, e7\}$	$\{e2, e5, e7\}$
$v3$	40	baz	$\{e3, e5, e8\}$	$\{e3, e6, e8\}$
$v4$	50	foo	$\{e4\}$	$\{e1, e4\}$
$v5$	40	bar	$\{e3, e5, e8\}$	$\{e2, e5, e7\}$
$v6$	30	baz	$\{e1, e2, e6, e7\}$	$\{e3, e6, e8\}$
e_7	30	bar	$\{e1, e2, e6, e7\}$	$\{e2, e5, e7\}$
e_8	40	baz	$\{e3, e5, e8\}$	$\{e3, e6, e8\}$

Table 4. Tables of Words, and Granules: For each attribute, the collection of granules forms a partition on V

This follows immediately from the isomorphism theorem; see *Theorem* 3.1.

4 The Theory of Features in GDM

The notion of generalizations of features/attributes has not been formally defined; we will examine the classical case and reach our definition; see *Definition*4.1.

Let us first examine the well accepted case. Then we will take an obvious extension.

4.1 Attribute Oriented Generalizations(AOG)

Let K be the given relational table. In the traditional attribute oriented generalization (AOG), concept hierarchy is introduced by recursively defining a sequence of named equivalence relations on a given single attribute of K:

1. A level zero concept is a base concept(distinct attribute values).

2. A level one concept is a named (or interpreted) equivalence class of base concept;

V	$\rightarrow$	F	GF	G
e_1	$\rightarrow$	30	odd	foo
e_2	$\rightarrow$	30	odd	bar
e_3	$\rightarrow$	40	$even$	baz
e_4	$\rightarrow$	50	odd	foo
e_5	$\rightarrow$	40	$even$	bar
e_6	$\rightarrow$	40	$even$	bar
e_7	$\rightarrow$	30	odd	bar
e_8	$\rightarrow$	40	$even$	baz

Table 5. A Generalized Table GK with a new named attribute

3. A level two concept is a named (or interpreted) equivalence class of first level concepts, in general, are the second innermost relation, and etc.

4. A n level two concept is a named (or interpreted) equivalence class of $(n-1)$ level concepts.

5. These concept hierarchy groups the base concepts into a nested sequence of named partitions of based concepts. For each named partition (that is, the partition and each equivalence class has a name), a new attribute is introduced into the given table.

In this example, F-attribute values are the base concepts. A named partition is defined: The equivalence class $\{30, 50\}$ is named *odd*, another equivalence class $\{40\}$ *even*, and the partition GF. This generalization introduces a new named attribute GF (column) into the given table (Table 5.)

4.2 AOG on GDM

In traditional concept hierarchy, all partitions are named. To be uniform, we will consider the unnamed case. We will take the following

- Convention: unnamed partition will be regarded as canonically named, that is, the partition and equivalence classes themselves are their own names.

To illustrate the idea. The newly named GF in K, will be "unnamed" in its GDM. Let us use GDM $(V, \{Q_F, Q_G\})$ of K: the partition $\{\{30, 50\}, \{40\}\}$ of F-attribute induces a new partition on V as follows: From Table 2, 30 defines a granule $\{e1, e2, e6, e7\}$, 50 defines $\{e4\}$, and 40 defines $\{e3, e5, e8\}$. The new granule is $\{e1, e2, e6, e7\} \cup \{e4\}$ $=\{e1, e2, e4, e6, e7\}$, and $\{e3, e5, e8\}$. These two new granules define a new partition Table 6.

The GDM of new $GK =$

$(V, \{Q_F, Q_G, \{\{e1, e2, e4, e6, e7\}, \{e3, e5, e8\}\}\})$:

V	$\rightarrow$	F	$\{\{30, 50\}, \{40\}\}$	G
e_1	$\rightarrow$	30	$\{30, 50\}$	foo
e_2	$\rightarrow$	30	$\{30, 50\}$	bar
e_3	$\rightarrow$	40	$\{40\}$	baz
e_4	$\rightarrow$	50	$\{30, 50\}$	foo
e_5	$\rightarrow$	40	$\{40\}$	bar
e_6	$\rightarrow$	40	$\{40\}$	bar
e_7	$\rightarrow$	30	$\{30, 50\}$	bar
e_8	$\rightarrow$	40	$\{40\}$	baz

Table 6. A Generalized Table GK with a un-interpreted attribute

By the convention, a canonically named partition or equivalence class will be referred to as an un-interpreted attribute or attribute value. Following the same spirit, a TOG, TOB or GDM is called a **un-interpreted** table or data model.

4.3 The Feature Completion on GDM

Traditional AOG focuses on one attribute. There are no reasons to stop at considering one attribute, here we will consider a concept hierarchy on a set $B = \{B^1, B^2, \ldots B^q\}$ of attributes. As we have observed in *Theorem* 3.4., it is adequate to do AM in GDM is (V, Q). In this case, B is a subset of Q; we will denote it bu Q_B.

Definition 4.1. A generalization over Q_B in a GDM is a coarser partition of $Q_{B^1} \cap Q_{D^2} \ldots \cap Q_{B^q}$, where $Q_B = \{Q_{B^1}, Q_{B^2}, \ldots Q_{B^q}\}$ is a non-empty subset of Q.

If we let Q_B varies through all non-empty subsets of Q, we have all possible generalizations of Q_B in GDM. We will denote the set of all generalizations by $AG(Q_B)$. Observe that the intersection of generalizations is still a generalization. For any given finite set of generalizations, there is the smallest generalization. So $AG(Q_B)$ is closed under meet (=the intersection) and join (=the smallest generalization). So $AG(Q_B)$ is a lattice. More importantly, the meet and join are the meet and join in the lattice $\Delta(V)$ of partitions on V. Let $L^*(Q)$ be the smallest sublattice of $\Delta(V)$ that contains Q, and $L^*(Q)$ be the smallest sublattice of $\Delta(V)$ that contains all coarsening of Q. Now we have

Theorem 4.2. $L^*(Q)=AG(Q)$.

Based on this observation, we define

Definition 4.3. GDM $(V, L^*(Q))$ is called Universal Model of (V, Q) in the sense it contains all its generalizations. $L^*(Q)$ is the feature completion of Q.

4.4 Intuitive Discussions on Features/attributes

We often hear such an informal statement "a new feature (attribute) F is selected, extracted, or constructed from a subset $B = \{B^1, B^2, \ldots B^q\}$ of attributes in the table K." What does such a statement mean?

First we observe that feature and attribute have been used interchangeably. In the classical data model, an attribute or a feature is a representation of property, characteristic, and etc.; see e.g., [15]. A feature represents a human perception about the data; each perception is represented by a symbol, and has been called attribute and the set of attributes a schema. Based on our convention, they are words in TDP (Section 3), but are symbols in AM.

Let us assume a new feature F has bee selected, extracted, or constructed. Let us insert it into the table K. The new table is denoted by $(K + F)$. The informal statement probably means in the new table, F is an attribute. As it is derived from B, it is functionally depended on B; as extraction and construction are informal words, we can use the functional dependency as formal definition of feature selection, extraction and constructions. Formally we define

Definition 4.4.1.
F is a feature derived (selected, extracted and constructed feature) from B, if F is functional dependent on B in the new table $(K + F)$.

In *Theorem* 4.2, we have shown that $L^*(Q)$ is feature completion of Q. By the convention in Section 4.2, $L^*(Q)$ is uninterpreted feature completeion of K.

This theorem is rather anti-intuitive. Taking human's view there are infinitely many features. But the theorem says there are only finitely many features (as $L^*(Q)$ is a finite set). How one can reconcile the contradiction? Where did the finite-ness slip in? Our analysis says it comes in at the representation phase. We represent the universe by finite words. However, in phase two, suddenly these words are reduced to symbols. Thus the infinite world now is encoded by a finite set of symbols. In particular, features can only be encoded in a finite distinct ways. A common confusing most likely comes from the confusing of data mining and "facts" mining.

5 Generalized Associations in GDM

As we have observed that it is adequate to conduct AM in the canonical model, such as GDM.

Main Theorem 5.1. Let $(V, L^*(Q))$ be the universal model, Let g be a granule in a partition $P \in L^*(Q)$ such that $\|g\| \geq s$. Then g is an un-interpreted generalized associations.

Let us define an operation of binary number x and a set S. We write S*x to be defined by The two equations

$$S * x = S, \text{ if } x = 1 \text{ and } S \neq$$

$$S * x = 0, \text{ if } x = 0 \text{ or } X =.$$

Main Theorem 5.2.
Let $C = Q^1 \cap Q^2 \cap \ldots \cap Q^n$ be the smallest element in $L^*(Q)$. Let $c_1, c_2, \ldots c_m$ be the granules in C. Then the union

$$c_1 * x_1 \cup \ldots \cup c_m * x_m.$$

is a granule that represents a un-interpreted generalized association rule, if its cardinality

$$(**) \qquad \sum \|c_i\| * x_i \geq s,$$

where s is the threshold.

Remark: The cardinal number of $L^*(Q)$ is bounded by the Bell number [2] of $m = \|C\|$, the cardinal number of $C = Q^1 \cap Q^2 \cap \ldots \cap Q^n$. The total number of derived attributes is bounded by Bell number B_m. However the complexity of (**) is not too high. Let s be the then the possible "minimal solutions" is bounded by the combination mCs. We will report the calculation on real world data in future report soon.

5.1 Find Generalized Association Rule by Linear Inequalities - an example

We will illustrate the idea of the procedure of finding generalized association rules in Table 7 by linear inequality (support: ≥ 3). The association can be expressed as granules:

1. Associations of length one:

   (a) TEN = $\{e_2, e_3, e_4, e_5, e_6\}$
   (b) SJ = $\{e_2, e_3, e_4, e_5, e_6\}$
   (c) LA = $\{e_7, e_8, e_9\}$

2. Associations of length two:

   (a) (TEN,SJ) = TEN $\cap$ SJ = $\{e_2, e_3, e_4, e_5, e_6\}$; where (TEN,SJ) = $(\{e_2, e_3, e_4, e_5, e_6\}, \{e_2, e_3, e_4, e_5, e_6\})$ is in table format, that is equivalent to GDM format: TEN $\cap$ SJ.

3. No associations of length $q \leq 3$.

Now let us examine the universal model in Table **??**. The column C in Table **??** is the smallest element in the complete relation lattice $L^*(Q)$. So every element of $L^*(Q)$ is a coarsening of C. In other words, every granule in $L^*(Q)$

is a union of some granules from the partition C (by the expression *"a granule in $L^*(Q)$"* we mean a granule belonging to one of its partitions).

In this example, the granules in C are

$$c_1 = \text{TWENTY} \cap \text{NY} = \{e_1\},$$

$$c_2 = \text{TEN} \cap \text{SJ} = \{e_2, e_3, e_4, e_5, e_6\},$$

$$c_3 = \text{TWENTY} \cap \text{LA} = \{e_7\},$$

$$c_4 = \text{THIRTY} \cap \text{LA} = \{e_8, e_9\}$$

Let $| \bullet |$ be the cardinality of $\bullet$. The following expression represents the cardinality of granules in $L^*(Q)$, which is a union of some granules from the partition C.

$$\|\text{TWENTY} \cap \text{NY}\| * x_1 + \|\text{TEN} \cap \text{SJ}\| * x_2 + \|\text{TWENTY} \cap \text{LA}\| * x_3 + \|\text{THIRTY} \cap \text{LA}\| * x_4 \geq 3.$$

By taking the actual value of the cardinalities of the granules, we have,

$$\|c_1\| * x_1 + \|c_2\| * x_2 + \|c_3\| * x_3 + \|c_4\| * x_4 \geq 3.$$

$$1 * x_1 + 5 * x_2 + 1 * x_3 + 2 * x_4 \geq 3.$$

We will express the solutions in vector form, (x_1, x_2, x_3, x_4). It is an "integral convex set" in 4-dimensional space:
The "boundary solutions" are:

1 $(0, 1, 0, 0)$; this solution means $TEN \cap SJ$'s cardinality by itself already meets the threshold (≥ 3).

2 $(0, 0, 1, 1)$; this solution means we need the union of two granules,

TWENTY $\cap$ LA and THIRTY $\cap$ LA,

to meet the threshold. In other words, we need a generalized concept that covers both the sub-tuple

(TWENTY, LA)= TWENTY $\cap$ LA and

(THIRTY, LA)= THIRTY $\cap$ LA.

For this particular case, since

LA = (TWENTY, LA) $\cup$ (THIRTY, LA),

hence LA is the desirable generalized concept.

3 $(1, 0, 0, 1)$; this solution means we need the union of two granules,

TWENTY $\cap$ NY $\cup$ THIRTY $\cap$ LA,

Table of Granules					Table of Symbols K		
V		$(Q^0$	Q^2	$Q^3)$		$(S\#$	$STATUS$	$CITY)$
v_1		$(\{v_1\}$	$\{v_1, v_7\}$	$\{v_1\})$		$(S_1$	$TWENTY$	NY)
v_2		$(\{v_2\}$	$\{v_2, v_3, v_4, v_5, v_6\}$	$\{v_2, v_3, v_4, v_5, v_6\})$		$(S_2$	TEN	SJ)
v_3		$(\{v_3\}$	$\{v_2, v_3, v_4, v_5, v_6\}$	$\{v_2, v_3, v_4, v_5, v_6\})$		$(S_3$	TEN	SJ)
v_4	$\rightarrow$	$(\{v_4\}$	$\{v_2, v_3, v_4, v_5, v_6\}$	$\{v_2, v_3, v_4, v_5, v_6\})$	$\rightarrow$	$(S_4$	TEN	SJ)
v_5		$(\{v_5\}$	$\{v_2, v_3, v_4, v_5, v_6\}$	$\{v_2, v_3, v_4, v_5, v_6\})$		$(S_5$	TEN	SJ)
v_6		$(\{v_6\}$	$\{v_2, v_3, v_4, v_5, v_6\}$	$\{v_2, v_3, v_4, v_5, v_6\})$		$(S_6$	TEN	SJ)
v_7		$(\{v_7\}$	$\{v_1, v_7\}$	$\{v_7, v_8, v_9\})$		$(S_7$	$TWENTY$	LA)
v_8		$(\{v_8\}$	$\{v_8, v_9\}$	$\{v_7, v_8, v_9\})$		$(S_8$	$THIRTY$	LA)
v_9		$(\{v_9\}$	$\{v_8, v_9\}$	$\{v_7, v_8, v_9\})$		$(S_9$	$THIRTY$	LA)

Table 7. Table of Granules at left-hand-side is isomorphic to K at right- hand-side: By *Theorem* **3.1. one can find patterns in either table**

as a single generalized concept.

"Internal points" are:[4](1, 1, 0, 0); we skip the interpretations; [5](0, 1, 1, 0) ;[6](0, 1, 0, 1); [7](0, 1, 1, 1); [8](1, 1, 1, 0);[9](1, 1, 0, 1); [10](1, 0, 1, 1)

; [11](1, 1, 1, 1) We re-express these formulas in granular form and simplify them into disjoint normal forms .

1 TEN $\cap$ SJ = TEN = SJ

2 TWENTY $\cap$ LA $\cup$ THIRTY $\cap$ LA =LA

3 TWENTY $\cap$ NY $\cup$ THIRTY $\cap$ LA

4 TWENTY $\cap$ NY $\cup$ TEN $\cap$ SJ = $\neg$ LA

5 TEN $\cap$ SJ $\cup$ TWENTY $\cap$ LA = TEN $\cup$ TWENTY $\cap$ LA = SJ $\cup$ TWENTY $\cap$ LA

6 TEN $\cap$ SJ $\cup$ THIRTY $\cap$ LA = $\neg$ TWENTY

7 TEN $\cap$ SJ $\cup$ TWENTY $\cap$ LA $\cup$ THIRTY $\cap$LA = TEN $\cup$ LA = S J $\cup$ LA

8 TWENTY $\cap$ NY $\cup$ TEN $\cap$ SJ $\cup$ TWENTY $\cap$ LA = TEN $\cup$ TWENTY = $\neg$ THIRTY

9 TWENTY $\cap$ NY $\cup$ TEN $\cap$ SJ $\cup$ THIRTY $\cap$ LA = $\neg$ (TWENTY $\cap$ LA)

10 TWENTY $\cap$ NY $\cup$ TWENTY $\cap$ LA $\cup$ THIRTY $\cap$ LA = $\neg$ SJ

11 TWENTY $\cap$ NY $\cup$ TEN $\cap$ SJ $\cup$ TWENTY $\cap$ LA $\cup$ THIRTY $\cap$ LA = all

If the simplified expression is a single clause (in the original symbols), it is the (non-generalized) associations. We have the following associations

1. TEN (= SJ = TEN $\cap$ SJ)

2. SJ

3. TEN $\cap$ SJ

4. LA (=TWENTY $\cap$ LA $\cup$ THIRTY $\cap$ LA))

6 Conclusions

Data, patterns, method of derivations, and useful-ness are key ingredients in AM. In this paper, we formalize the current state of AM: Data are a table of symbols. The patterns are the formulas of input symbols that repeat. The method of derivations is the most conservative and reliable one, namely, mathematical deductions. The results are somewhat surprising:

1. Patterns are properties of the isomorphic class, not an individual relation - This implies that the notion of patterns may not mature yet and explains why there are so many extracted association rules.

2. Un-interpreted attributes (features)are partitions; they can be enumerated.

3. Generalized associations can be found by solving integral linear inequalities. Unfortunately, the number is enormous. This signifies the current notion of data and patterns (implied by the algorithms) are too primitive.

4. Real world modeling may be needed to create a much more meaningful notion of patterns. In the current state of AM, a pattern is simply a repeated data that may have no real world meaning. So we may need to introduce some semantics into the data model [12],[10],[11].

References

[1] R. Agrawal, T. Imielinski, and A. Swami, "Mining Association Rules Between Sets of Items in Large Databases," in Proceeding of ACM-SIGMOD international Conference on Management of Data, pp. 207-216, Washington, DC, June, 1993

[2] Richard A. Brualdi, Introductory Combinatorics, Prentice Hall, 1992.

[3] A. Barr and E.A. Feigenbaum, The handbook of Artificial Intelligence, Willam Kaufmann 1981

[4] Margaret H. Dunham, Data Mining Introduction and Advanced Topics Prentice Hall, 2003, ISBN 0-13-088892-3

[5] Fayad U. M., Piatetsky-Sjapiro, G. Smyth, P. (1996) From Data Mining to Knowledge Discovery: An overview. In Fayard, Piatetsky-Sjapiro, Smyth, and Uthurusamy eds., Knowledge Discovery in Databases, AAAI/MIT Press, 1996.

[6] H Gracia-Molina, J. Ullman. & J. Windin, J, Database Systems The Complete Book, Prentice Hall, 2002.

[7] T. T. Lee, "Algebraic Theory of Relational Databases," The Bell System Technical Journal Vol 62, No 10, December, 1983, pp.3159-3204.

[8] T. Y. Lin, "Deductive Data Mining: Mathematical Foundation of Database Mining," in: the Proceedings of 9th International Conference, RSFDGrC 2003, Chongqing, China, May 2003, Lecture Notes on Artificial Intelligence LNAI 2639, Springer-Verlag, 403-405

[9] T. Y. Lin, "Attribute (Feature) Completion – The Theory of Attributes from Data Mining Prospect," in: Proceeding of IEEE international Conference on Data Mining, Maebashi, Japan, Dec 9-12, 2002, pp. pp.282-289.

[10] T. Y. Lin, "Data Mining and Machine Oriented Modeling: A Granular Computing Approach," Journal of Applied Intelligence, Kluwer, Vol. 13, No 2, September/October,2000, pp.113-124.

[11] T. Y. Lin, N. Zhong, J. Duong, S. Ohsuga, "Frameworks for Mining Binary Relations in Data." In: Rough sets and Current Trends in Computing, Lecture Notes on Artificial Intelligence 1424, A. Skoworn and L. Polkowski (eds), Springer-Verlag, 1998, 387-393.

[12] E. Louie,T. Y. Lin, "Semantics Oriented Association Rules," In: 2002 World Congress of Computational Intelligence, Honolulu, Hawaii, May 12-17, 2002, 956-961 (paper # 5702)

[13] "The Power and Limit of Neural Networks," Proceedings of the 1996 Engineering Systems Design and Analysis Conference, Montpellier, France, July 1-4, 1996, Vol. 7, 49-53.

[14] Morel, Jean-Michel and Sergio Solimini, Variational methods in image segmentation : with seven image processing experiments Boston : Birkhuser, 1995.

[15] H. Liu and H. Motoda, "Feature Transformation and Subset Selection," IEEE Intelligent Systems, Vol. 13, No. 2, March/April, pp.26-28 (1998)

[16] Z. Pawlak, Rough sets. Theoretical Aspects of Reasoning about Data, Kluwer Academic Publishers, 1991

Improving Text Classification using Local Latent Semantic Indexing

Tao Liu   Zheng Chen*   Benyu Zhang*   Wei-ying Ma*   Gongyi Wu
*Nankai University, China   * Microsoft Research Asia   Nankai University, China*
*liut@office.nankai.edu.cn   *{zhengc,byzhang,wyma}@microsoft.com   wgy@nankai.edu.cn*

Abstract

Latent Semantic Indexing (LSI) has been shown to be extremely useful in information retrieval, but it is not an optimal representation for text classification. It always drops the text classification performance when being applied to the whole training set (global LSI) because this completely unsupervised method ignores class discrimination while only concentrating on representation. Some local LSI methods have been proposed to improve the classification by utilizing class discrimination information. However, their performance improvements over original term vectors are still very limited. In this paper, we propose a new local LSI method called "Local Relevancy Weighted LSI" to improve text classification by performing a separate Single Value Decomposition (SVD) on the transformed local region of each class. Experimental results show that our method is much better than global LSI and traditional local LSI methods on classification within a much smaller LSI dimension.

1. Introduction

Text classification is one of the core problems in Text Mining. Its task is to automatically assign predefined classes or categories to text documents [19]. There have been a lot of research done on text classification and SVM has been proved to be the best algorithm for text classification [6]. However, we found that the performance of a text classifier is strongly biased by the underlying feature representation. First, the inherent high dimension with tens of thousands of terms even for a moderate-sized text collection is prohibitively computational expensive for many learning algorithms [19]and easily raises the over fitting problem [11]. Secondly, polysemy (one word can have different meanings) and synonym (different words are used to describe the same concept) interfere with forming appropriate classification functions and make this task very difficult. [7,22].

There are typically two types of algorithms to represent the feature space used in classification. One type is the so-called "feature selection" algorithms, i.e. to select a subset of most representative features from the original feature space [8,20]. Another type is called "feature extraction",

i.e. to transform the original feature space to a smaller feature space to reduce the dimension. Compared with feature selection, feature extraction can not only reduce the dimensions of the feature space greatly, but also succeed in solving the polysemy and synonym problem in a certain degree.

The most representative feature extraction algorithm is the Latent Semantic Indexing (LSI) which is an automatic method that transforms the original textual data to a smaller semantic space by taking advantage of some of the implicit higher-order structure in associations of words with text objects [1,2]. The transformation is computed by applying truncated singular value decomposition (SVD) to the term-by-document matrix. After SVD, terms which are used in similar contexts will be merged together. Thus, documents using different terminology to talk about the same concept can be positioned near each other in the new space [17].

Although LSI was originally proposed as an information retrieval method, it has also been widely used in text classification as well. For example, [19] used LSI to cut off noise during training process, [22] performed SVD on an expanded term-by-document matrix that includes both the training examples and background knowledge to improve text classification, [18] performed SVD on the term-by-document matrix whose terms include both single-word terms and phrase terms.

While LSI is applied to text classification, there are two common methods. The first one is called "Global LSI", which performs SVD directly on the entire training document collection to generate the new feature space. This method is completely unsupervised, that is, it pays no attention to the class label of the existing training data. It has no help to improve the discrimination power of document classes, so it always yields no better, sometimes even worse performance than original term vector on classification [15]. The other one is called "Local LSI", which performs a separate SVD on the local region of each topic [4,5,12,17]. Compared with global LSI, this method utilizes the class information effectively, so it improves the performance of global LSI greatly. However, due to the same weighting problem, the improvements over original term vector are still very limited.

It is noticed that in local LSI, all documents in the local region are equally considered in the SVD computation. But intuitively, different documents should play different roles to the final feature space and it is expected that more relevant documents to the topic can contributes more to the local semantic space than those non-relevant ones. So based on this idea, we propose a new local LSI method - "Local Relevancy Weighted LSI (LRW-LSI)", which selects documents to the local region in a smooth way. In other words, LRW-LSI gives different weight to each document in the local region according to its relevance before performing SVD so that the local semantic space can be extracted more accurately. Experimental results shown later prove this idea and it is found LRW-LSI is much better than global LSI and ordinary local LSI methods on classification performance within a much smaller LSI dimension.

The rest of this paper is organized as the followings. In Section 2, we give a brief introduction to global LSI and different local LSI methods. In Section 3, we propose our new Local Relevancy Weighted LSI method. Then, several experiments are done to evaluate different LSI methods for text classification and their results are discussed in Section 4. Section 5 concludes this paper.

2. Related Works

The most straightforward method of applying LSI for text classification is the global LSI method, which performs SVD directly on the entire training set and then testing documents are transformed by simply projecting them onto the left singular matrix produced in the original decomposition for evaluation. [15,18,19,22]. Global LSI is completely unsupervised, and it makes no use of class label, word order, syntactic relations or other existing information. It aims at deriving an optimal representation of the original data in a lower dimensional space in the mean squared error sense but this representation does no help the optimal discrimination of classes. This is especially true when there are some original terms that are particularly good at discriminating a category/class. That discrimination power may be lost in the new semantic space. Hence, global LSI performs not as good as expected and even drops the classification performance. Furthermore, Wiener, Pedersen and Weigend [17] also found that global LSI performed increasingly worse as topic frequency decreased due to the fact that infrequent topics are usually represented by infrequent terms, and infrequent terms may be projected out of LSI representations as noise.

To integrate the class information, Hull [4] first proposed the concept of local LSI, which performed SVD on a local region of a topic so that the most important local structure, which is crucial in separating relevant documents from non-relevant documents, can be captured. A drawback of Hull's solution is that the local region is defined by only relevant/positive documents which

contain no discriminative information, which makes the improvement of classification performance very limited. Therefore, it is very necessary to add some of other documents to balance the local region. [5,12,17] did this work and they extended the local region by introducing some non-relevant documents which are most difficult to be distinguished from the relevant documents. The introduction of the most nearby non-relevant documents provides the most valuable discrimination information and is found to be more effective than using relevant documents alone.

Compared to global LSI whose cost of SVD computing is incurred only once, local LSI has an increased cost because a separate SVD has to be computed for each class. However, the SVD is only applied to the local region, which means that the matrix is far smaller than the one used in global LSI so the computation can be extremely fast.

In the following sub-sections, a brief introduction on local LSI methods is given. All local LSI methods are similar in the generation processes of local region. That is, each document in the training set is first assigned with a relevancy score related to a topic, and those documents whose scores are higher than a predefined threshold value are picked to generate the local region.

2.1. Relevant Documents Selecting Method (RDS)

RDS defines the local region for a topic as the relevant documents only [4]. It is the simplest method but the local region contains no discrimination information, so it is very limited to improve the classification performance.

On the other hand, the frequency of topic occurrence varies greatly from topic to topic. For example, in Reuters-21578 data, the biggest topic "earn" has roughly 30% of the documents while only five training documents belong to topic "platinum". So it is very difficult to select a different optimal LSI dimension for different topic. Hence, RDS is not a recommended local LSI method.

2.2. Query-specific Screening Method (QS)

QS is the most widely used local LSI method which defines the local region of a topic as the n most similar documents, where similarity is measured using the inner product score to the query vector which can be generated by Rocchio-expansion or the m most predictive terms of the topic.

2.2.1. Query by Rocchio-expansion. Rocchio-expansion is the simplest method to combine relevant documents and non-relevant documents [10]. It has been widely used to define the query of a topic as the mean of relevant documents in the training set [3,12,13].

2.2.2. Query by predictive terms. Wiener et al. [17] used another method to define the query as the 100 most predictive terms of the topic where the predictive score of a term was measured by Relevancy Score (RS).

Many other measures can be used to rank terms for a topic, such as Information Gain (IG), x^2 statistic (CHI) and Mutual Information (MI) [8,20]. While there is no big difference in selecting a small set of terms between RS, IG and CHI [17], in this paper, we only consider two representative measures: CHI and MI. CHI is defined as equation (1) which measures the association between the term and the topic. MI is defined as equation (2) which only measures how important a term to a topic by the presence of a term occurs in the documents.

$$\chi^2(t,c) = \frac{N \times (p(t,c) \times p(\overline{t},\overline{c}) - p(t,\overline{c}) \times p(\overline{t},c))^2}{p(t) \times p(\overline{t}) \times p(c) \times p(\overline{c})} \quad (1)$$

$$MI(t,c) = \log \frac{p(t,c)}{p(t) \times p(c)} = \log p(t \mid c) - \log p(t) \quad (2)$$

2.3. SVM Screening Method (SS)

Both RDS and QS actually can be viewed as a classification process to generate the local region. So similar with them, for each class, a SVM classifier can be trained using training documents and then be used to classify each training document to get its confidence value. Finally, the n most confident documents are picked as the local region of that class. This method is called the SVM Screening method.

3. Local Relevancy Weighted LSI

As introduced above, in local LSI, each document in the training set is first assigned with a relevancy score related to a topic, and then the documents whose scores are larger than a predefined threshold value are selected to generate the local region. Then SVD is performed on the local region to produce a local semantic space. This process can be simply described as the jump curve in Figure 1. That is 0/1 weighting method is used to generate the local region where documents whose scores are larger than the predefined threshold value are weighted with 1 and others are weighted with 0.

The 0/1 weighting method is a simple but crude way to generate local region. It assumes that the selected documents are equally important in the SVD computation. However, it is obvious that each document plays a different role in the local semantic space and the more relevant documents should contribute more to the local semantic space, and vice versa. Furthermore, in real application, the size of local region is very difficult to tune. When the size is too big, non-relevant documents may be much more than relevant documents so that SVD

may pay more attention to the semantic structure of non-relevant documents and the local semantic space may be very biased. On the other hand, when the size is too small, the local region may contain no enough discriminative information so that the local semantic space may also be limited. Based on these problems, an intuitive idea which can be described as the smooth curve in Figure 1 comes up. That is to introduce documents into the local region in a smooth way. In other words, the relevancy value of each document to a class is further used to weight the document so that more relevant documents can be introduced with higher weights and then they will do more contribution to SVD computation. Hence, the better local semantic space which results in better classification performance can be extracted to separate positive documents from negative documents.

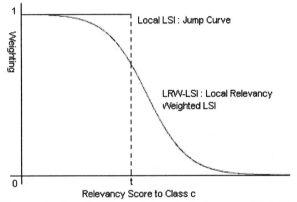

Figure 1. Local LSI and Local Relevancy Weighted LSI

This new method is named "Local Relevancy Weighted LSI (LRW-LSI)".

For each class, assume an initial classifier IC has been trained using training documents in term vector representation which can be can Rocchio classifier, Term Query classifier or SVM classifier as introduced in last Section. Then the training process of LRW-LSI contains the following six steps. At the first step, the initial classifier IC of topic c is used to assign initial relevancy score (rs) to each training document. Then at step two, each training document is weighted according to equation (3). The weighting function is a Sigmoid function which has two parameters a and b to shape the curve. At step three, the top n documents are selected to generate the local term-by-document matrix of the topic c. Then at step four, a truncated SVD is performed to generate the local semantic space. At step five, all other weighted training documents are folded into the new space. Then at the final step, all training documents in local LSI vector are used to train a real classifier RC of topic c.

$$\vec{d}_i' = \vec{d}_i * f(rs_i), \text{ where } f(rs_i) = \frac{1}{1 + e^{-a(rs_i + b)}} \quad (3)$$

In testing process, when a testing document comes in, it is first classified by the initial classifier IC to get its initial relevancy score. Then it is weighted according to the equation (3) and then folded into the local semantic space to get its local LSI vector. Then the local LSI vector is finally used to be classified by the classifier RC to decide whether it belongs to topic c or not.

Note that the parameters a and b of the Sigmoid function define how smoothly to introduce the documents. It is obvious that when the parameters a and b is suitable, for example, when a equals 0 or a and b are large enough, LRW-LSI is actually the same as local LSI, so local LSI is just a special case of LRW-LSI.

4. Experiments

In this Section, we first evaluate four Local LSI methods including QS-Roc, QS-CHI, QS-MI and QS-SS, and compare them with Term Vector and Global LSI. Then we evaluate Local Relevancy Weighted LSI method. SVM light [1] is chosen as the classification algorithm, SVDPAKC/sis [2] is used to perform SVD and F-Measure is used to evaluate the classification results. Two common data sets are used, including Reuters-21578 and Industry Sector.

Before performing classification, a standard stop-word list is used to remove common stop words and stemming technology is used to convert variations of the same words into its base form. Then those terms that appear in less than 3 documents are removed. Finally tf*idf (with "ltc" option) is used to assign the weight of each term in each document.

4.1. Data Sets

Text classification performance varies greatly on different dataset, so we choose two text collections, including Reuters-21578 [3] and Industry Sector [4].

Reuters-21578 (Reuters) is the most widely used text collection for text classification. There are total 21578 documents and 135 categories in this corpus. The frequency of topic occurrence varies greatly from topic to topic. For example, the most frequent topic "earn" appears in more than 30% of the documents while "platinum" is a topic mentioned in only five training documents. In our experiments, we only chose the most frequent 25 topics and used "Lewis" split which results in 6314 training examples and 2451 testing examples.

Industry Sector (IS) is a collection of web pages belonging to companies from various economic sectors. There are 105 topics and total 9652 web pages in this dataset. Compared to Reuters, the topics are averagely distributed in documents. Also, a subset of the 14 categories whose size are bigger than 130 is selected for the experiments. Then a random split of 70% training examples and 30% testing examples is produced which results in 2030 training examples and 911 testing examples.

4.2. Classification Algorithm

Support Vector Machine (SVM) is chosen in our experiment which is very popular and proved to be one of the best classification algorithms for text classification [18,21]. SVM is originally introduced by Vapnic in 1995 for solving two-class pattern recognition problem [16]. It is based on the Structural Risk Minimization principle from the computational learning theory. The idea is to find a hypothesis h to separate positive examples from negative examples with maximum margin. In linear SVM, we use $w*x - b = 0$ to represent the hyper-plane, where the normal vector w and constant b are defined by the distance from the hyper-plane to the nearest positive and negative examples.

4.3. Performance Measures

For evaluating the effectiveness of classification, we use the standard recall, precision and F1 measure. Recall is defined to be the ratio of correct assignments by the system divided by the total number of correct assignments. Precision is the ratio of correct assignments by the system divided by the total number of the system's assignments. The F1 measure, initially introduced by van Rijsbergen [9], combines recall (r) and precision (p) with an equal weight in the following form:

$$F1 = \frac{2rp}{r + p}$$

(4)

There are two ways to measure the average F1 of a binary classifier over multi categories, namely, the macro-averaging and micro-averaging. The former way is to first compute F1 for each category and then average them, while the later way is to first computer precision and recall for all categories and use them to calculate F1. It is clear that macro-averaging gives an equal weight to the performance on every category, regardless how rare or how common a category is, but micro-averaging favors the performance on common categories. Both of them are calculated in our experiments.

---

[1] http://svmlight.joachims.org/

[2] http://www.netlib.org/svdpack/

[3] http://www.daviddlewis.com/resources/testcollections

[4] http://www-2.cs.cmu.edu/afs/cs.cmu.edu

4.4. Experimental Results and Discussion

4.4.1. Global LSI and Local LSI. The first experiment we conduct is to compare four local LSI methods with original term vector and global LSI, including QS-Roc, QS-CHI, QS-MI and SS where QS-Roc means the query is defined as Rocchio-expansion, QS-CHI and QS-MI means the query is defined as the top 100 predictive terms selected by CHI and MI measure. For Reuters-21578, local region is defined as five times the number of positive documents but no less than 350 and no more than 1500 which is similar with [17]. For Industry Sector, local region is defined as five times the number of positive documents.

Table 1. Classification results on Reuters

Method	Dimension	Micro-F1	Macro-F1
Term	>5000	94.02	81.50
Global LSI	250	92.64	73.26
QS-Roc	200	92.90	84.12
QS-CHI	200	93.78	84.79
QS-MI	200	93.99	85.60
SS	200	91.69	83.49

The classification results of Reuters-21578 using different methods are shown in Table 1. As can be seen from this table, term vector is the best representation for SVM classifier. Compared to term vector, global LSI degrades the performance markedly especially on Macro-averaging F1 (relatively 10.1% reduction). There is no remarkable difference between Local LSI methods whose micro-averaging F1 is slightly dropped while macro-averaging F1 is slightly improved.

While micro-averaging favors performance on common topic but macro-averaging gives an equal weight to all topics, we separate the 25 topics of Reuters-21578 averagely into three levels including high, medium and low to conduct a further analysis as in [17]. Table 2 shows the results. As can be seen, global LSI performs increasingly worse as topic frequency decreases which is due to the fact that the signal of infrequent topics is so weak that it is usually treated as noise and projected out of the new semantic space. Contrary to the global LSI, local LSI focuses on the local structure and performs increasingly better as topic frequency decreased. For example, compared to term vector for low frequent topics, both F1 are dropped nearly 29% by global LSI but improved nearly 13% by local LSI.

Similar results can be found on Industry Sector data as shown in Table 3. The best performance is produced by term vector. While all topics have similar frequency which can be viewed as medium frequency, both F1 measures were greatly dropped by global LSI and slightly dropped by local LSI.

Table 2. Classification results on Reuters over three topic frequency ranges

Method	Micro-F1			Macro-F1		
	High	Med	Low	High	Med	Low
Term	95.3	88.3	71.3	85.3	87.8	71.1
Global LSI	94.6	83.1	50.7	83.8	81.7	50.7
Local LSI	94.6	89.6	80.4	85.1	89.3	80.1

Table 3. Classification results on Industry Sector

Method	Dimension	Micro-F1	Macro-F1
Term	>5000	80.91	80.61
Global LSI	250	63.95	63.99
QS-Roc	200	75.08	76.03
QS-CHI	200	76.55	77.81
QS-MI	200	75.56	76.07
SS	200	75.81	77.11

4.4.2. Local Relevancy Weighted LSI. For local relevancy weighted LSI, we use SVM classifier as the initial classifier *IC* to generate each document's initial relevancy score. And the parameters a and b of Sigmoid function are initially set with 5.0 and 0.2.

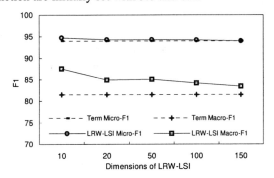

Figure 2. LRW-LSI results on Reuters

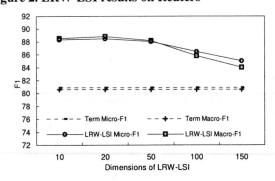

Figure 3. LRW-LSI results on Industry Sector

Figure 2 and Figure 3 displays the classification results on Reuters-21578 and Industry Sector. The dotted lines of term vector are displayed only as the reference points in terms of performance comparison. From these figures, the following observations can be made:

First, compared to term vector, LRW-LSI improves the both F1 performances greatly on both data. For example, using 10 dimensions on Reuters-21578, the micro-averaging F1 is improved by 0.8% and the macro-averaging F1 is improved by 7.4%; using 20 dimensions on Industry Sector, the micro-averaging F1 is improved by 9.4% and the macro-averaging F1 is improved by 10.2%.

Second, the optimal dimension of LRW-LSI is much smaller than that of global LSI and local LSI method. For example, on Reuters-21578, the optimal dimension of LRW-LSI is only 10 while that of the global LSI is 250 and local LSI is 200. Such small dimension also means that the computation is much faster than the computation of the global LSI and local LSI method. Table 4 shows the run time of different LSI methods on a PC with Pentium III 500MHz and 256M memory. The runtime includes both training procedure and testing procedure. As can be seen, term vector is the fastest and it needs only hundred seconds. Global LSI needs much more time than term vector due to the costly SVD computation on entire training set. Although SVD computation on local region is very fast, the overall computation on all topics is extremely high, so local LSI is not expected to be used in practice. Similar with local LSI, LRW-LSI has to perform a separate SVD on local region of each topic, but such a low LSI dimension makes LRW-LSI be extremely rapid. It needs only less than 3 times of runtime of term vector, so it can be widely used in practice.

Table 4. Run Time of Different Methods (Seconds).

Method	Reuters-21578	Industry Sector
Term	372	291
Global LSI	4702	1905
Local LSI	6508	5210
LRW-LSI	1080	752

Third, with the LSI dimension increases, the performances decrease slowly. But even in a relatively high dimension, the performances are still equal or above the performances of term vector. Using 150 dimensions, for example, on Reuters-21578 the micro-averaging F1 is equal and the macro-averaging F1 is still improved by 2.4%; on Industry Sector, the micro-averaging F1 is still improved by 5.1% and the macro-averaging F1 is still improved by 4.2%.

Forth, while local LSI has similar performance with term vector and LRW-LSI is much better than term vector, LRW-LSI is much better than local LSI not only in performance but also in much smaller LSI dimension. It means that LRW-LSI is more effective in separating relevant documents and nearby non-relevant documents. In order to find out the reason, we project the documents into coordinate plane using the first and the second local LSI factors as in [4,5].

Figure 6 shows the local LSI projection and Figure 7 shows the LRW-LSI projection for "interest" topic of Reuters-21578 where the red asterisks represent relevant documents and blue circles represent non-relevant documents. As can be seen from these figures, relevant documents and non-relevant documents are separated by Local LSI only to a certain degree, that is, there are still a big chunk of documents mixed together. Comparatively, LRW-LSI is much more successful in class separation, that is, non-relevant documents are almost clustered around the origin while relevant documents are widely distributed.

In the previous experiment, we set the parameters of Sigmoid function by experience. So in order to learn the influence of the parameters setting, we conduct two testing experiments using different tuning strategies. The first one is to fix the parameter a to 5.0 and change the parameter b from 0~1.0 and the second one is to fix the parameter b to 0.0 and change the parameter a from 0.0 to 6.0. In both tests, 10 dimensions are used for classification.

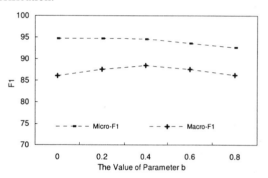

Figure 4 Parameter b Tuning on Reuters

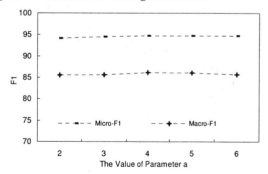

Figure 5 Parameter a tuning on Reuters

Figure 4 and Figure 5 show the testing results on Reuters-21578. We don't display the results on Industry Sector because its results are similar with Reuters-21578. As can be seen from these figures, LRW-LSI is more easily influenced by parameter b than by parameter a. But the performance influences of both parameters are very small, so in general, LRW-LSI is insensitive to both parameters.

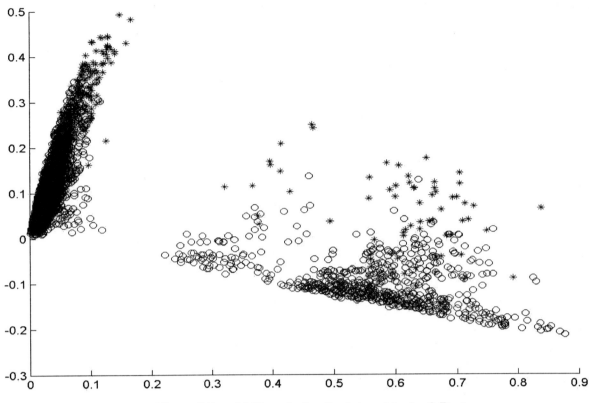

Figure 6. Local LSI projection for interest topic of Reuters

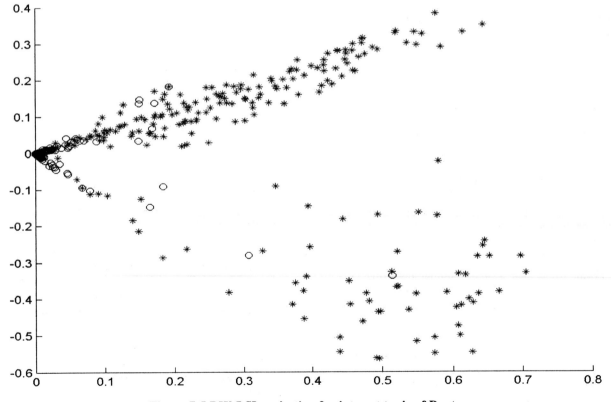

Figure 7. LRW-LSI projection for interest topic of Reuters

5. Conclusion

In this paper, we propose a new Local Relevancy Weighted LSI (LRW-LSI) method to help improve the text classification performance. This method is developed from Local LSI, but different from Local LSI in that the documents in the local region are introduced using a smooth descending curve so that more relevant documents to the topic are assigned higher weights. Therefore, the local SVD can concentrate on modeling the semantic information that is actually most important for the classification task. The experimental results verify this idea and show that LRW-LSI is quite effective. It can improve the classification performance greatly using a much smaller dimension compared to the global LSI and local LSI methods.

Another work we have done is a comparative study on global LSI and several local LSI methods for text classification. It is found that local space is more suitable for LSI than the global space. Global LSI can optimize representation of the whole original data in a low dimensional space but gives no help to optimizing the discrimination of the topic, so it always drops the classification performance. Local LSI captures the important local structure which is crucial in separating relevant documents from nearby non-relevant documents, so it succeeds in keeping or improving slightly the classification performance in a low dimension.

Acknowledgments

The authors would like to thank Weiguo Fan and Wensi Xi from Virginia Polytechnic Institute and State University for fruitful discussions.

References

[1] Berry, M. W., Dumais, S. T., & O'Brien, G. W, Using Linear Algebra for Intelligent Information Retrieval, *SIAM Review*, 37:573-595, 1995

[2] Deerwester, S., Dumais, S. T., Landauer, T. K., Furnas, G. W. & Harshman, R. A, Indexing by latent semantic analysis, *Journal of the Society for Information Science*, 41(6):391-407, 1990

[3] Hearst, M., Pedersen, J., Pirolli, P. & Schutze, H, Xerox Site Report: Four TREC-4 Tracks, *In D. Harman (Ed.) TREC-4*, pp. 97-119, 1996

[4] Hull, D, Improving Text Retrieval for the Routing Problem using Latent Semantic Indexing, *Proc. of SIGIR'94*, pp. 282-289, 1994

[5] Hull, D.A, *Information Retrieval using Statistical Classifcation*. PhD thesis, Stanford University, 1995

[6] Joachims, T, Text Categorization with Support Vector Meachines: Learning with Many Relevant Features, *Proc. of ECML'98*, pp. 137-142, 1998

[7] Lewis, D.D. & Ringuette, M, A Comparison of Two Learning Algorithms for Text Categorization, *Proc. of SDAIR'94*, pp. 81-93, 1995

[8] Liu, T., Liu, S., Chen, Z., & Ma, W, An Evaluation on Feature Selection for Text Clustering, *Proc. of ICML'03*, pp. 488~495, 2003

[9] Rijsbergen, C.J, *Information Retrieval*. Butterworths, 2nd Edition, 1979

[10] Rocchio, J.J, Relevance Feedback in Information Retrieval, *In Gerard Salton, (Ed.)*, The Smart retrieval systeml experiments in automatic document processing, pp. 313~323, 1971

[11] Sebastiani, F, Machine Learning in Automated Text Categorization, *ACM Computing Surveys*, 34(1):1-47, 2002

[12] Schutze, H., Hull, D.A. & Pedersen, J.O, A Comparison of Classifiers and Document Representations for the Routing Problem, *Proc. of SIGIR'95*, pp. 229-237, 1995

[13] Schutze, H., Pedersen, J.O. & Hearst, M. A, Xerox TREC3 Report: Combining Exact and Fuzzy Predictors, *In D. Harman (Ed.) TREC-3*, 1995

[14] Schutze, H. & Silverstein, C, Projections for Efficient Document Clustering, *Proc. of SIGIR'97*, pp. 74~81, 1997

[15] Torkkola, K, Linear Discriminant Analysis in Document Classification, 2002

[16] Vapnic, V, *The Nature of Statistical Learning Theory*, Springer, 1995

[17] Wiener, E., Pedersen, J.O. & Weigend, A.S, A Neural Network Approach to Topic Spotting, *Proc. Of SDAIR'95*, pp. 317-332, 1995

[18] Wu, H. & Gunopulos, D, Evaluating the Utility of Statistical Phrases and Latent Semantic Indexing for Text Classification, *Proc. of ICDM'02*, pp. 713-716, 2002

[19] Yang, Y, Noise Reduction in a Statistical Approach to Text Categorization, *Proc. of SIGIR'95*, pp. 256-263, 1995

[20] Yang, Y. & Pedersen, J. O, A comparative study on feature selection in text categorization, *Proc. of ICML'97*, pp. 412-420, 1997

[21] Yang, Y. & Liu, X, A Re-examination of Text Categorization Methods,. *Proc. of SIGIR'99*, pp. 42-49, 1999

[22] Zelikovitz, S. & Hirsh, H, Using LSI for Text Classification in the Presence of Background Text. *Proc. of CIKM01*, pp. 113-118, 2001

Dependency Networks for Relational Data

Jennifer Neville, David Jensen
Computer Science Department
University of Massachusetts Amherst
Amherst, MA 01003
{jneville|jensen}@cs.umass.edu

Abstract

Instance independence is a critical assumption of traditional machine learning methods contradicted by many relational datasets. For example, in scientific literature datasets there are dependencies among the references of a paper. Recent work on graphical models for relational data has demonstrated significant performance gains for models that exploit the dependencies among instances. In this paper, we present relational dependency networks (RDNs), a new form of graphical model capable of reasoning with such dependencies in a relational setting. We describe the details of RDN models and outline their strengths, most notably the ability to learn and reason with cyclic relational dependencies. We present RDN models learned on a number of real-world datasets, and evaluate the models in a classification context, showing significant performance improvements. In addition, we use synthetic data to evaluate the quality of model learning and inference procedures.

1. Introduction

Relational data pose a number of challenges for model learning and inference. The data have complex dependencies, both as a result of direct relations (e.g., research paper references) and through chaining multiple relations together (e.g., papers published in the same journal). The data also have varying structure (e.g., papers have different numbers of authors, references and citations). Traditional graphical models such as Bayesian networks and Markov networks assume that data consist of independent and identically distributed instances, which makes it difficult to use these techniques to model relational data that consist of non-independent and heterogeneous instances. Recent research in relational learning has produced several novel types of graphical models to address this issue. Probabilistic relational models (PRMs)[1] (e.g. [5, 15, 14]) estimate joint prob-

ability distributions of relational data and have been evaluated successfully in several domains, including the World Wide Web, genomic structures, and scientific literature.

In this paper, we present relational dependency networks (RDNs), an extension of dependency networks [6] for relational data[2]. RDN models are a new form of PRM that offer several advantages over the comparable joint models—relational Bayesian networks (RBNs) [5] and relational Markov networks (RMNs) [15]. Specifically, the strengths of RDNs include: (1) an interpretable representation that facilitates knowledge discovery in relational data, (2) the ability to represent arbitrary cyclic dependencies, including relational autocorrelation, and (3) simple and efficient methods for learning both model structure and parameters.

Graphical models are an attractive modeling tool for knowledge discovery because they are a compact representation of the joint distribution of a set of variables, which allows key dependencies to be expressed and irrelevancies to be ignored [2]. The qualitative properties of the model are encoded in the *structure* of the graph, while the quantitative properties are specified by the *parameters* of the associated probability distributions. The models are often easy to interpret because the graph structure can be used to infer dependencies among variables of interest. PRMs maintain this property as they extend conventional graphical models to relational settings. A compact representation is even more desirable for modeling relational data, because the enormous space of possible dependencies can overwhelm efforts to identify novel, and interesting patterns.

The ability to represent, and reason with, arbitrary cyclic dependencies is another important characteristic of relational models. Relational autocorrelation, a statistical dependency among values of the same variable on related entities [7], is a nearly ubiquitous phenomenon in relational datasets. For example, hyperlinked web pages are more

---

[1]Several previous papers (e.g., [5]) use the term PRM to refer to a specific type of model that the originators now call a relational Bayesian net-

work (Koller, personal communication). In this paper, we use PRM in its more recent and general sense.

[2]This work generalizes our previous work on simple RDNs for classification [12].

likely to share the same topic than randomly selected pages, and proteins located in the same place in a cell are more likely to share the same function than randomly selected proteins. Recent work has shown that autocorrelation dependencies can be exploited to improve classification accuracy, if inferences about related data instances are made simultaneously (e.g., [3, 15, 12]). However, these relational autocorrelation dependencies are often cyclic in nature, making it difficult to encode these dependencies with directed graphical models such as RBNs unless the autocorrelation can be structured to be acyclic (e.g., with temporal constraints) [5]. In contrast, undirected graphical models such as RMNs, and RDNs, can represent arbitrary forms of relational autocorrelation.

During learning, relational models consider a large number of features, thus simple and efficient learning techniques are advantageous, particularly for joint models. The RDN learning algorithm is based on pseudolikelihood techniques [1], which estimate a set of conditional distributions independently. This approach avoids the complexities of estimating a full joint distribution and can incorporate existing techniques for learning conditional probability distributions of relational data. Relatively efficient techniques exist for learning both the structure and parameters of RBN models but the acyclicity constraints of the model precludes the learning of arbitrary autocorrelation dependencies. On the other hand, while in principle it is possible for RMN techniques to learn cyclic autocorrelation dependencies, inefficiencies due to modeling the full joint distribution make this difficult in practice. The current implementation of RMNs is not capable of learning model structure automatically, nor can it automatically identify which features are most relevant to the task; research has focused primarily on parameter estimation and inference procedures. To our knowledge, RDNs are the first PRM capable of *learning* cyclic autocorrelation dependencies.

We begin by reviewing the details of dependency networks for propositional data and then describe how to extend them to a relational setting. Next, we present RDN models learned from four real-world datasets and evaluate the models in a classification context, demonstrating equivalent, or better, performance in comparison to conditional models. Finally, we report experiments on synthetic data that show model learning and inference is robust to varying levels of autocorrelation and that accurate models can be learned from small training set sizes.

2. Dependency Networks

Graphical models represent a joint distribution over a set of variables. The primary distinction between Bayesian networks, Markov networks and dependency networks (DNs) [6] is that dependency networks are an approximate representation. DNs approximate the joint distribution with

a set of conditional probability distributions (CPDs), which are learned independently. This approach to learning is a relatively simple technique for parameter estimation and structure learning that results in significant efficiency gains over exact models. However, because the CPDs are learned independently, DN models are not guaranteed to specify a *consistent* joint distribution. This precludes DNs from being used to infer causal relationships and limits the applicability of exact inference techniques. Nevertheless, DNs can encode predictive relationships (i.e. dependence and independence) and Gibbs sampling (e.g. [11]) inference techniques can be used to recover a full joint distribution, regardless of the consistency of the local CPDs.

DN Representation. A DN encodes probabilistic relationships among a set of variables in a similar manner to Bayesian and Markov networks, combining characteristics of both undirected and directed models. DN models consists of a graph G, which encodes the *structure* of the model, and a set of probability distributions P, which encode the *parameters* of the model. Dependencies among variables are represented with a bidirected graph $G = (V, E)$, where conditional independence is interpreted using graph separation, as with undirected models. However, as with directed models, dependencies are quantified with a set of conditional probability distributions P. Consider the set of variables $\mathbf{X} = (X_1, ..., X_n)$ over which we'd like to model the joint distribution $p(\mathbf{x}) = p(x_1, ..., x_n)$. Each node $v_i \in V$ corresponds to an $X_i \in \mathbf{X}$ and is associated with a probability distribution conditioned on the other variables, $P(v_i) = p(x_i | \mathbf{x} - \{x_i\})$. The parents, pa_i, of node i are the set of variables that render X_i conditionally independent of the other variables ($p(x_i | pa_i) = p(x_i | \mathbf{x} - \{x_i\})$) and G contains a directed edge from each parent node v_j to each child node v_i ($e(v_j, v_i) \in E$ iff $x_j \in pa_i$).

DN Learning. Both the structure and parameters of DN models are determined through learning a set of local conditional probability distributions (CPDs). The DN learning algorithm learns a separate CPD for each variable X_i, conditioned on the other variables in the data ($\mathbf{X} - \{X_i\}$). Any conditional learner can be used for this task (e.g. logistic regression, decision trees). The learned CPD is included in the model as $P(v_i)$, and the variables selected by the conditional learner (e.g., $x_i = \alpha x_j + \beta x_k$) form the parents of X_i (e.g., $pa_i = \{x_j, x_k\}$), which is then reflected in the edges of G appropriately. If the conditional learner is not selective, the DN model will be fully connected (i.e., $pa_i = \mathbf{x} - \{x_i\}$). In order to build understandable DNs, it is desirable to use a selective learner that will learn CPDs that use a subset of all variables.

DN Inference. Although the DN approach to structure learning is simple and efficient, it can result in an inconsistent network, both structurally and numerically. In other words, there may be no joint distribution from which each of the CPDs can be obtained using the rules of probability. For example, a network that contains a directed edge from X_i to X_j, but not from X_j to X_i, is inconsistent— X_i and X_j are dependent but X_j is not represented in the CPD for X_i. A DN is consistent if the conditional distributions in P factor the joint distribution—in this case we can compute the joint probability for a set of values $\mathbf{x}$ directly. In practice, [6] show that DNs will be nearly consistent if learned from large data sets, since the data serve a coordinating function that ensures consistency among the CPDs. If a DN is inconsistent, approximate inference techniques can be used to estimate the full joint distribution and extract probabilities of interest. Gibbs sampling (e.g., [11]) can be used to recover a full joint distribution for $\mathbf{X}$, regardless of the consistency of the local CPDs, provided that each X_i is discrete and each local CPD is positive [6].

3. Relational Dependency Networks

RDNs extend dependency networks to a relational setting. DNs have been shown to perform comparably to BNs for a number of propositional tasks [6], thus we expect they will achieve similar performance levels in relational settings. Also, several characteristics of DNs are particularly desirable for modeling relational data. First, learning a collection of conditional models offers significant efficiency gains over learning a full joint model—this is generally true, but is even more pertinent to relational settings where the feature space is very large. Second, networks that are easy to interpret and understand aid analysts' assessment of the utility of the relational information. Third, the ability to represent cycles in a network facilitates reasoning with relational autocorrelation, a common characteristic of relational data. Finally, while the need for approximate inference is a disadvantage of DNs for propositional data, due to the complexity of relational model graphs in practice, all PRMs use approximate inference.

RDNs extend DNs for relational data in the same way that RBNs [5] extend Bayesian networks and RMNs [15] extend Markov networks. We describe the general characteristics of PRMs and then discuss the details of RDNs.

3.1. Probabilistic Relational Models

PRMs represent a joint probability distribution over a relational dataset. When modeling attribute-value data with graphical models, there is a single graph G that is associated with the model M. In contrast, there are three graphs associated with models of relational data: the *data graph* G_D, the *model graph* G_M, and the *inference graph* G_I.

First, the relational dataset is represented as a typed, attributed graph $G_D = (V_D, E_D)$. For example, consider the data graph in figure 1a. The nodes V_D represent objects in the data (e.g., authors, papers) and the edges E_D represent relations among the objects (e.g., author-of, cites). We use rectangles to represent objects, circles to represent random variables, dashed lines to represent relations, and solid lines to represent probabilistic dependencies. Each node $v_i \in V_D$ is associated with a type $T(v_i) = t_{v_i}$ (e.g., *paper*). Each object type $t \in T$ has a number of associated attributes $\mathbf{X}^t = (X_1^t, ..., X_n^t)$ (e.g., topic, year). Consequently, each object v_i is associated with a set of attribute values determined by its type $\mathbf{X}_{\mathbf{v_i}}^{\mathbf{t_{v_i}}} = (X_{v_i 1}^{t_{v_i}}, ..., X_{v_i n}^{t_{v_i}})$. A PRM model represents a joint distribution over the values of the attributes throughout the data graph, $\mathbf{x} = \{\mathbf{x}_{\mathbf{v_i}}^{\mathbf{t_{v_i}}} : v_i \in V, t_{v_i} = T(v_i)\}$.

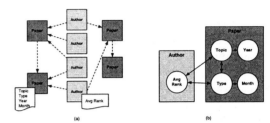

Figure 1. PRM (a) data, and (b) model graph.

The dependencies among attributes are represented in the model graph $G_M = (V_M, E_M)$. Attributes of an object can depend probabilistically on other attributes of the same object, as well as on attributes of other related objects in G_D. For example, the topic of a paper may be influenced by attributes of the authors that wrote the paper. Instead of defining the dependency structure over attributes of specific objects $\mathbf{X}_\mathbf{v}$, PRMs define a generic dependency structure at the level of object types. The set of attributes $\mathbf{X}_\mathbf{k}^\mathbf{t} = (X_{v_i k}^t : v_i \in V, T(v_i) = t)$ is tied together and modeled as a single variable. Each node $v_i \in V_M$ corresponds to an $X_k^t, t \in T \wedge X_k^t \in \mathbf{X^t}$. As in conventional graphical models, each node is associated with a probability distribution conditioned on the other variables. Parents of X_k^t are either: (1) other attributes associated with type t_k (e.g., paper *topic* depends on paper *type*), or (2) attributes associated with objects of type t_j where objects t_j are related to objects t_k in G_D (e.g., paper *topic* depends on author *rank*). For the latter type of dependency, if the relation between t_k and t_j is one-to-many, the parent consists of a set of attribute values (e.g., author ranks). In this situation, PRMs use aggregation functions, either to map sets of values into single values, or to combine a set of probability distributions into a single distribution.

For example, consider the model graph in figure 1b. It models the data in figure 1a, which has two object types: paper and author. In G_M, each object type is represented by a plate, and each attribute of each object type is represented as a node. The edges of G_M characterize the dependencies among the attributes at the type level.

During inference, a PRM uses the G_M and G_D to instantiate an inference graph $G_I = (V_I, V_E)$ in a process sometimes called "rollout". The rollout procedure used by PRMs to produce the G_I is nearly identical to the process used to instantiate models such as hidden Markov models (HMMs), and conditional random fields (CRFs) [9]. G_I represents the probabilistic dependencies among all the object variables in a single test set (here G_D is different from the G_D' used for training). The structure of G_I is determined by both G_D and G_M—each object-attribute pair in G_D gets a separate, local copy of the appropriate CPD from G_M. The relations in G_D constrain the way that G_M is rolled out to form G_I. PRMs can produce inference graphs with wide variation in overall and local structure, because the structure of G_I is determined by the specific data graph, which typically has non-uniform structure. For example, figure 2 shows the PRM from figure 1b rolled out over a data set of three authors and three papers, where P_1 is authored by A_1 and A_2, P_2 is authored by A_2 and A_3, and P_3 is authored by A_3. Notice that there is a variable number of authors per paper. This illustrates why PRM CPDs must aggregate—for example, the CPD for paper-type must be able to deal with a variable number of author ranks.

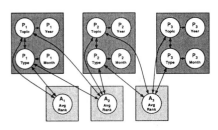

Figure 2. Example PRM inference graph.

3.2. RDN Models

An RDN model encodes probabilistic relationships in a similar manner to DN models, extending the representation to a relational setting. RDNs use a bidirected model graph G_M with a set of conditional probability distributions P. Each node $v_i \in V_M$ corresponds to an $X_k^t \in \mathbf{X^t}, t \in T$ and is associated with a conditional distribution $p(x_k^t \mid pa_{x_k^t})$. Figure 1b illustrates an example RDN model graph for the data graph in figure 1a. The graphical representation illustrates the qualitative component (G_D) of the RDN—it does not depict the quantitative component (P) of the model, which includes aggregation functions. The representation uses a modified plate notation; dependencies among attributes of the same object are contained inside the rectangle and arcs that cross the boundary of the rectangle represent dependencies among attributes of related objects. For example, $month_i$ depends on $type_i$, while $avgrank_j$ depends on the $type_k$ and $topic_k$ for all papers k related to author j in G_D. Although conditional independence is infered using an undirected view of the graph, bidirected edges are useful

for representing the set of variables in each CPD. For example, in figure 1b, the CPD for *year* contains *topic* but the CPD for *topic* does not contain *type*. This shows inconsistencies that may result from the RDN learning technique.

Learning. The RDN learning algorithm is much like the DN learning algorithm, except we use a selective relational classification algorithm to learn a set of conditional models. The algorithm input consists of: (1) a data graph G_D, with a set of types T and attributes X, (2) a conditional relational learner R, and (3) a search limit c, which limits the length of paths in G_D that are considered in R. For each $t \in T$, and each $X_k^t \in \mathbf{X^t}$, the algorithm uses R to learn a CPD for X_k^t given the set of attributes $\{X_{k' \neq k}^t\} \cup \mathbf{X^{t' \neq t}}$, where t' is up to c links away from t in G_D. The resulting CPDs are included in P and are used to form G_M.

We use relational probability trees (RPTs) [13] for the CPD components of the RDN. The RPT learning algorithm adjusts for biases towards particular features due to degree disparity and autocorrelation in relational data [7, 8]. We have shown that RPTs build significantly smaller trees than other conditional models and achieve equivalent, or better, performance. This characteristic of the RPTs is crucial for learning understandable RDN models. The collection of RPTs will be used during inference so the size of the models also has a direct impact on efficiency. We expect that the general properties of RDNs would be retained if other approaches to learning conditional probability distributions were used instead, given that those approaches are both selective and accurate.

RPTs extend probability estimation trees to a relational setting. RPT models estimate probability distributions over class label values in the same manner as conventional classification trees, but the algorithm looks beyond the attributes of the item for which the class label is defined and considers the effects of attributes in the local relational neighborhood ($\leq c$ links away) on the probability distribution. The RPT algorithm automatically constructs and searches over aggregated relational features to model the distribution of the target variable—for example, to predict the value of an attribute (e.g., paper topic) based on the attributes of related objects (e.g., characteristics of the paper's references), a relational feature may ask whether the oldest reference was written before 1980.

Inference. The RDN inference graph G_I is potentially much larger than the original data graph. To model the full joint distribution there must be a separate node (and CPD) for each attribute value in G_D. To construct G_I, the set of template CPDs in P is rolled-out over the data graph. Each object-attribute pair gets a separate, local copy of the appropriate CPD. Consequently, the total number of nodes in the inference graph will be $\sum_{v \in V_D} |\mathbf{X^{T(v)}}|$. Rollout facilitates generalization across data graphs of varying size—we can learn the CPD templates from one data graph and apply the model to a second data graph with a different number of objects by rolling out more CPD copies.

We use Gibbs sampling (e.g. [11]) for inference in RDN models. To estimate a joint distribution, the inference graph consists of a rolled-out network with unobserved variables. The values of all unobserved variables are initialized to values drawn from their prior distributions. Gibbs sampling then iteratively relabels each unobserved variable by drawing from its local conditional distribution, given the current state of the rest of the graph. After a sufficient number of iterations, the values will be drawn from a stationary distribution and we can use the samples to estimate probabilities of interest. For the experiments reported in this paper we use a fixed-length chain of 2000 samples (each iteration relabels every value sequentially), with a burn-in of 200.

4. Experiments

The experiments in this section are intended to demonstrate the utility of RDNs as a joint model of relational data. We learn RDN models of four real world datasets to illustrate the types of domain knowledge that can be garnered. In addition, we evaluate the models in a classification context, where only a single attribute is unobserved in the test set, and report significant performance gains compared to a conditional model. Finally, we use synthetic data to assess the impact of training set size and autocorrelation on RDN learning and inference, showing that accurate models can be learned at small data set sizes and that the model is robust to all but extreme levels of autocorrelation. For these experiments, we used the parameters $R = RPT$ and $c = 2$. The RPT algorithm used *MODE*, *COUNT* and *PROPORTION* features with 10 thresholds per attribute.

The RDN models in figures 3-5 continue with the RDN representation introduced in figure 1. Each object type is represented in a separate plate, arcs inside a plate indicate dependencies among the attributes of a single object and arcs crossing the boundaries of plates indicate dependencies among attributes of related objects. An arc from x to y indicates the presence of one or more features of x in the RPT learned for y.

When the dependency is on attributes of objects more than a single link away, the arc is labeled with small rectangle to indicate the intervening object type. For example, movie genre is influenced by the genres of other movies made by the movie's director, so the arc would be labeled with a small D rectangle.

In addition to dependencies among attribute values, RPTs also learn dependencies between the structure of the relations (edges in G_D) and the attribute values. This *degree* relationship is represented by a small black circle in the corner of each plate, arcs from this circle indicate a dependency between the number of related objects and an attribute value

of a related object. For example, movie receipts is influenced by the number of actors in the movie.

4.1. RDN Models

The first data set is drawn from the Internet Movie Database (www.imdb.com). We collected a sample of 1,382 movies released in the United States between 1996 and 2001. In addition to movies, the data set contains objects representing actors, directors, and studios. In total, this sample contains approximately 42,000 objects and 61,000 links. We learned a RDN model for ten discrete attributes including actor gender and movie opening weekend receipts ($>\$2million$). Figure 3 shows the resulting RDN model. Four of the attributes, movie receipts, movie genre, actor birth year, and director 1st movie year, exhibit autocorrelation dependencies. Exploiting this type of dependency has been shown to significantly improve classification accuracy of RMNs compared to RBNs which cannot model cyclic dependencies [15]. However, to exploit autocorrelation the RMN must be instantiated with a corresponding clique template—the dependency must be pre-specified by the user. To our knowledge, RDNs are the first PRM capable of *learning* this type of autocorrelation dependency.

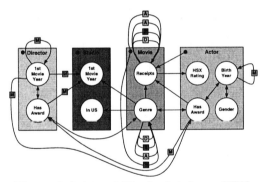

Figure 3. Internet Movie database RDN.

The second data set is drawn from Cora, a database of computer science research papers extracted automatically from the web using machine learning techniques [10]. We selected the set of 4,330 machine-learning papers along with associated authors, cited papers, and journals. The resulting collection contains approximately 13,000 objects and 26,000 links. We learned an RDN model for seven attributes including paper topic (e.g., neural networks) and journal name prefix (e.g., IEEE). Figure 4 shows the resulting RDN model. Again we see that four of the attributes exhibit autocorrelation. In particular, notice that the topic of a paper depends not only on the topics of other papers that it cites, but also on the topics of other papers written by the authors. This model is a good reflection of our domain knowledge about machine learning papers.

The third data set was collected by the WebKB Project [4]. The data consist of a set of 3,877 web pages from four computer science departments. The web pages have been manually labeled with the categories: course, faculty, staff, student, research project, or other. The collection contains approximately 4,000 web pages and 8,000 hyperlinks among those pages. We learned an RDN model for four attributes of the web pages including school and page label. Figure 5a shows the resulting RDN model.

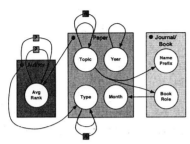

Figure 4. Cora machine-learning papers RDN.

The fourth data set is a relational data set containing information about the yeast genome at the gene and the protein level (www.cs.wisc.edu/~dpage/kddcup2001/). The data set contains information about 1,243 genes and 1,734 interactions among their associated proteins. We learned an RDN model for seven attributes. The attributes of the genes included protein localization and function, and the attributes on the interactions included type and level of expression. Figure 5b shows the resulting RDN model.

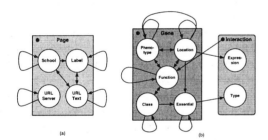

Figure 5. (a) WebKB, and (b) gene data RDNs.

4.2. Classification Experiments

We evaluate the learned models on classification tasks in order to assess (1) whether autocorrelation dependencies among instances can be used to improve model accuracy, and (2) whether the RDN models, using Gibbs sampling, can effectively infer labels for a network of instances. To do this, we compare three models. The first model is a conventional RPT model—an individual classification model that reasons about each instance independently from other instances and thus does not use the class labels of related instances. The second model is a RDN model that exploits additional information available in labels of related instances and reasons about networks of instances collectively. The third model is a probabilistic ceiling for the RDN model.

We use the RDN model but allow the true labels of related instances to be used during inference. This model shows the level of performance possible if the RDN model could infer the true labels of related instances with perfect accuracy.

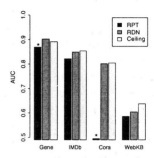

Figure 6. AUC results for classification tasks.

Figure 6 shows area under the ROC curve (AUC) results for each of the three models on four classification tasks. We used the following prediction tasks: IMDb: movie receipts, Cora: paper topic, WebKB: page label, Gene: gene location. The graph shows AUC for the most prevalent class, averaged over a number of training/test splits. For IMDb and Cora, we used 4-5 temporal samples where we learned models on one year of data and applied the model to the subsequent year. For WebKB, we used cross-validation by department, learning on three departments and testing on pages from the fourth held out department. For Gene there was no clear sampling choice, so we used ten-fold cross validation on random samples of the genes. We used two-tailed, paired t-tests to assess the significance of the AUC results obtained from the trials. The t-tests compare the RDN results to each of the other two models. The null hypothesis is that there is no difference in the AUC results of the two models; the alternative is that there is a difference. The differences in performance that are significant at a $p < 0.05$ level are reported in the graph with asterisks.

On three of the tasks, the RDNs models achieve comparable performance to the ceiling models and on the fourth (WebKB) the difference is not statistically significant. This indicates that the RDN model realized its full potential, reaching the same level of performance as if it had access to the true labels of related movies. On the Gene data, the RDN surpasses the performance of the ceiling model, but is only a probabilistic ceiling—the RDN may perform better if an incorrect prediction for one object improves the classification of related objects. Also, the performance of the RDN models is superior to RPT models on all four tasks. This indicates that autocorrelation is both present in the data and identified by the RDN models. The performance improvement over RPTs is due to successful exploitation of this autocorrelation. On the Cora data, the RPT model performance is no better than random because autocorrelation is the only predictor of paper topic (see figure 4).

4.3. Synthetic Data Experiments

To explore the effects of training set size and autocorrelation on RDN learning and inference, we generated homogeneous data graphs with a regular square lattice structure. With the exception of objects along the outer boundary, each object in the lattice links to four immediate neighbors positioned above, below, left, and right. The first and last row and column make up the *frame* of the lattice. In order to control for effects of varying structure, objects in the frame are not used during learning and inference, although their attribute values are available to objects in the core for learning and inference. Thus, training or test sets of size N correspond to a lattice of $(\sqrt{N} + 2)^2$ objects, and models are trained or evaluated on the N objects in the core of the lattice. Each object has four boolean attributes X_1, X_2, X_3 and X_4. We use a simple RDN where X_1 is autocorrelated (through objects one link away), X_2 depends on X_1, and the other two attribute have no dependencies.

We generated the values of attributes using the RDN in the following way. We begin by assigning each object in the lattice an initial value for X_1 with $P(x_1 = 1) = 0.5$. We then perform Gibbs sampling over the entire lattice to estimate the values of X_1 conditioned on neighboring values. The values assigned to each object after 200 iterations are used as the final labels. We use a manually specified RPT that assigns X_1 values to each object based on the X_1 values of objects one link away in G_D. The parameters of this model are varied to produce different levels of autocorrelation in X_1. Once X_1 values are assigned, values for X_2 are randomly drawn from a distribution conditioned on objects' X_1 values. We used the parameters $p(x_2 = 1) = 0.3$ and $p(x_1 = 1|x_2 = 1) = 1 - p(x_1 = 0|x_2 = 1) = 0.9$. Finally, random values are assigned to the two other attributes with $p(x_3 = 1) = p(x_4 = 1) = 0.5$. Once a dataset is generated, we measure the proportion of objects with $X_1 = 1$, and any dataset with a value outside the range $[0.4, 0.6]$ is discarded and replaced by a new dataset. This ensures consistency in the distribution of X_1 across datasets and reduces variance in estimated model performance.

The first set of synthetic experiments examines the effectiveness of the RDN learning algorithm. Figure 7a graphs the log-likelihood of learned models as a function of training set size. Training set size was varied at the following levels $\{25, 49, 100, 225, 484, 1024, 5041\}$. Figure 7b graphs log-likelihood as a function of autocorrelation. Autocorrelation was varied to approximate the following levels $\{0.0, 0.25, 0.50, 0.75, 1.0\}$. (We graph the average autocorrelation for each set of trials, which is within 0.02 of these numbers.) At each data set size (autocorrelation level), we generated 25 training sets and learned RDNs. Using each learned model, we measured the average log-likelihood of another 25 test sets (size 225). Figure 7 plots these measurements as well as the log-likelihood of the test data from

the RDN used for data generation. These experiments show that the learned models are a good approximation to the true model by training set size 1000, and that RDN learning is robust with respect to varying levels of autocorrelation.

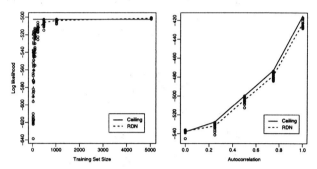

Figure 7. Evaluation of RDN learning.

The second set of synthetic experiments evaluates the RDN inference procedure in a classification context, where only a single attribute is unobserved in the test set. We generated data in the manner described above, learned an RDN for X_1, used the learned models to infer the class labels of unseen test sets, and measured AUC to evaluate the predictions. These experiments compared the same three models as section 4.2, and used the same training set sizes and autocorrelation levels outlined above. At each data set size (autocorrelation level), we generated 25 training and test set pairs, learned the model on the training set, and inferred labels for the test set.

Figure 8a graphs AUC as a function of training set size for RDNs compared to RPTs and the ceiling, plotting the average AUC for each model type. Even at small data set sizes the RDN performance is close to optimal and significantly higher than the performance of the RPTs. Surprisingly, the RPTs are able to achieve moderately good results even without the class labels of related instances. This is because the RPTs are able to use the attribute values of related instances as a surrogate for autocorrelation.

Figure 8b plots average AUC as a function of autocorrelation for RDNs compared to RPTs and the ceiling. When there is no autocorrelation, the RPT models perform optimally. In this case, the RDNs are slightly biased due to excess structure. However, as soon as there is minimal autocorrelation, the RDN models start to outperform the RPTs. At the other extreme, when autocorrelation is almost perfect the RDNs experience a large drop in performance. At this level of autocorrelation, the Gibbs sampling procedure can easily converge to a labeling that is "correctly" autocorrelated but with opposite labels. Although all 25 trials appeared to converge, half performed optimally and the other half performed randomly (AUC ≈ 0.50). Future work will explore ways to offset this drop in performance. However, the utility of RDNs for classification is clear in the range of autocorrelations that have been observed empirically [0.25,0.75].

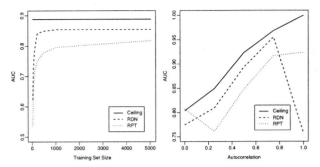

Figure 8. Evaluation of RDN inference.

5. Discussion and Conclusions

In this paper we presented RDNs, a new form of PRM. The primary advantage of RDN models is the ability to learn and reason with relational autocorrelation. We showed the RDN learning algorithm to be a relatively simple method for learning the structure and parameters of a probabilistic graphical model. In addition, RDNs allow us to exploit existing techniques for learning conditional probability distributions. Here we have chosen to exploit our prior work on RPTs, which constructs parsimonious models of relational data, but we expect that the general properties of RDNs would be retained if other approaches to learning conditional probability distributions were used, given that those approaches are both selective and accurate.

The results of the real and synthetic data experiments indicate that collective classification with RDNs can offer significant improvement over conditional approaches to classification when autocorrelation is present in the data—a nearly ubiquitous characteristic of relational datasets. The performance of RDNs also approaches the performance that would be possible if all the class labels of related instances were known. Future work will compare RDN models to RMN models in order to better assess the quality of the pseudolikelihood approximation of the joint distribution. In addition, we are exploring improved inference procedures that consider the autocorrelation dependencies in the data in order to improve inference accuracy and efficiency.

Acknowledgments

The authors acknowledge the invaluable assistance of M. Cornell, A. Shapira, M. Rattigan, M. Hay, B. Gallagher, and helpful comments from A. McGovern, A. Fast, C. Loiselle, and S. Macskassy. This research is supported under a AT&T Labs Graduate Research Fellowship and by NSF and AFRL under contract numbers F30602-00-2-0597, EIA9983215 and F30602-01-2-0566.

References

[1] J. Besag. Statistical analysis of non-lattice data. *The Statistician*, 24:3:179–195, 1975.

[2] W. Buntine. Graphical models for discovering knowledge. In *Advances In Knowledge Discovery And Data Mining*. AAAI Press/The MIT Press, 1996.

[3] S. Chakrabarti, B. Dom, and P. Indyk. Enhanced hypertext categorization using hyperlinks. In *Proceedings of the ACM SIGMOD International Conference on Management of Data*, pages 307–318, 1998.

[4] M. Craven, D. DiPasquo, D. Freitag, A. McCallum, T. Mitchell, K. Nigam, and S. Slattery. Learning to extract symbolic knowledge from the world wide web. In *Proceedings of the 15th National Conference on Artificial Intelligence*, pages 509–516, 1998.

[5] L. Getoor, N. Friedman, D. Koller, and A. Pfeffer. Learning probabilistic relational models. In *Relational Data Mining*. Springer-Verlag, 2001.

[6] D. Heckerman, D. Chickering, C. Meek, R. Rounthwaite, and C. Kadie. Dependency networks for inference, collaborative filtering and data visualization. *Journal of Machine Learning Research*, 1:49–75, 2000.

[7] D. Jensen and J. Neville. Linkage and autocorrelation cause feature selection bias in relational learning. In *Proceedings of the 19th International Conference on Machine Learning*, pages 259–266, 2002.

[8] D. Jensen and J. Neville. Avoiding bias when aggregating relational data with degree disparity. In *Proceedings of the 20th International Conference on Machine Learning*, pages 274–281, 2003.

[9] J. Lafferty, A. McCallum, and F. Pereira. Conditional random fields: Probabilistic models for segmenting and labeling sequence data. In *Proceedings of the 18th International Conference on Machine Learning*, pages 282–289, 2001.

[10] A. McCallum, K. Nigam, J. Rennie, and K. Seymore. A machine learning approach to building domain-specific search engines. In *Proceedings of the 16th International Joint Conference on Artificial Intelligence*, pages 662–667, 1999.

[11] R. Neal. Probabilistic inference using markov chain monte carlo methods. Technical Report CRG-TR-93-1, Dept of Computer Science, University of Toronto, 1993.

[12] J. Neville and D. Jensen. Collective classification with relational dependency networks. In *Proceedings of the 2nd Multi-Relational Data Mining Workshop, KDD2003*, pages 77–91, 2003.

[13] J. Neville, D. Jensen, L. Friedland, and M. Hay. Learning relational probability trees. In *Proceedings of the 9th ACM SIGKDD International Conference on Knowledge Discovery and Data Mining*, pages 625–630, 2003.

[14] S. Sanghai, P. Domingos, and D. Weld. Dynamic probabilistic relational models. In *Proceedings of the 18th International Joint Conference on Artificial Intelligence*, pages 992–1002, 2003.

[15] B. Taskar, P. Abbeel, and D. Koller. Discriminative probabilistic models for relational data. In *Proceedings of the 18th Conference on Uncertainty in Artificial Intelligence*, pages 485–492, 2002.

Hybrid pre-query term expansion using Latent Semantic Analysis

Laurence A. F. Park   Kotagiri Ramamohanarao
ARC Centre for Perceptive and Intelligent Machines
Department of Computer Science
The University of Melbourne
{lapark,rao}@cs.mu.oz.au

Abstract

Latent semantic retrieval methods (unlike vector space methods) take the document and query vectors and map them into a topic space to cluster related terms and documents. This produces a more precise retrieval but also a long query time. We present a new method of document retrieval which allows us to process the latent semantic information into a hybrid Latent Semantic-Vector Space query mapping. This mapping automatically expands the users query based on the latent semantic information in the document set. This expanded query is processed using a fast vector space method. Since we have the latent semantic data in a mapping, we are able to store and retrieve vector information in the same fast manner that the vector space method offers. Multiple mappings are combined to produce hybrid latent semantic retrieval which provide precision results 5% greater than the vector space method and fast query times.

1 Introduction

The recent growth of latent semantic text retrieval methods [5, 1] has generated much excitement in the information retrieval field. These methods use the content of the document sets to generate term topics by use of linear algebraic and probabilistic methods. The topics can then be used to query the documents, rather than the traditional set of key terms, to obtain high precision results. The problems found in these methods is in the query speed and the storage. Once we obtain the document and query vectors in terms of topics, we no longer can exploit the methods we have obtained based on the sparse term-document index. This results in methods which scan through the whole topic-document index to obtain a list of document scores.

In this paper we will be examining a new method of information retrieval that is fast, requires little storage space that is not dependent on the document count and allows

us to utilise the intermediate topic space that the vector space methods ignore. By following this process, we are able to provide results of greater precision to the user. Section 2 introduces our query mapping concept and explains how we can use it in modern information retrieval systems. We follow this with experiments in section 3 displaying the increase in precision when using the query mapping for various document sets. In section 4, we show how the query mappings can be successfully implemented while using vector space fast ranking techniques. Finally, we examine the computational complexity in section 5.

2 Query Mappings

Vector space models (VSM) in document retrieval perform retrieval by comparing the query term set to each document term set. If there are terms in common, the document is ranked accordingly. This retrieval model assumes that a document is a sequence of words $d = \{w_1, w_2, w_3, \ldots, w_n\}$ where each word is drawn independently from the pool of words $\mathbb{W}$. This can be seen in figure 1. In general this is not a valid assumption [5, 3]. When writing a document, an author will have a certain set of topics in mind and write words according to those topics. This is where we include the intermediate topic selection stage for document creation. A document d consists of a set of topics $d_n = \{T_{n_1}, T_{n_2}, T_{n_3}, \ldots, T_{n_x}\}$ where each topic is selected from an existing topic set. $T_m \in \mathbb{T}$ where $\mathbb{T} = \{T_1, T_2, T_3, \ldots, T_l\}$ The mth topic T_m is explained by a function of the set of words relevant to the topic $T_m = f_m(w_{m_1}, w_{m_2}, w_{m_3}, \ldots, w_{m_y})$ where the function f_m describes the relationship of the terms to the topic, $w_m \subset \mathbb{W}$, and $\mathbb{W} = \{w_1, w_2, w_3, \ldots, w_n\}$. This method of document creation builds the document from the selected set of topics. Therefore the words found in the document are not a set of randomly selected words, they are related through the topic they represent. This is shown in figure 2.

To overcome the problem of assumed term independence in the vector space model, Latent Semantic Analysis (LSA)

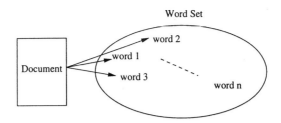

Figure 1. The assumed document creation process based on the current vector space methods. Each of the document words are randomly selected from a pool of words, where each word is independent of each other.

has been used to provide mappings for the documents and queries into a reduced dimensional space. In this reduced space, we are able to find similarity of terms and documents by comparing the directions of each, similar directions imply that they are related to a similar topic. Hence this reduced dimensional space has been labeled the topic space, where each dimension in the space suggests a topic. If the mappings to the topic space are performed correctly we are able to retrieve document at a higher precision than the vector space method. These mapping methods are not widely used because they are not as efficient as the VSM. The VSM deals with sparse matrices, so it can perform very fast retrieval. Once we have mapped our data into the topic space, we are left with dense matrices containing positive and negative real numbers. When given a query, the whole document index must be processed to calculate the document scores.

Instead of mapping the query and documents into the topic space and calculating the document scores within the topic space, we can map the query in and back out of the topic space and calculate the document scores with the sparse document index in the term space. The advantages of this being:

- the document index is kept sparse as in the VSM.

- the mapping is based on the terms (not documents) and does not grow with the document set.

- once we have the query terms from the topic space, we can deal with them as we wish. E.g. only consider a subset of the new terms.

We will now show how LSA is as an extension to the VSM, by using this query mapping. To calculate the document score for document d_i, the vector space method applies the following equation:

$$s_{d_i,q} = \sum_{t \in T} \frac{w_{d_i,t} w_{q,t}}{W_{d_i} W_q} \qquad (1)$$

where $s_{d_i,q}$ is the document score of document d_i with respect to query q, $w_{d_i,t}$ is the weight of term t in document

d_i, $w_{q,t}$ is the weight of term t in query q, W_{d_i} and W_q are the document and query normalisation weights respectively, and T is the set of terms. If we represent the calculation of all document scores as a vector $\tilde{s}$, where:

$$\tilde{s} = \begin{bmatrix} s_{d_1,q} & s_{d_2,q} & \cdots & s_{d_{N-1},q} & s_{d_N,q} \end{bmatrix} \qquad (2)$$

and the set of document vectors as the matrix A, we obtain an equivalent matrix multiplication:

$$\tilde{s} = A\tilde{q}' \qquad (3)$$

where s is the vector containing the resulting document scores, $\tilde{q}'$ is the transposed query vector where each element is $w_{q,t_j}/W_q$, A is the document index matrix consisting of elements $A_{ij} = w_{d_i,t_j}/W_{d_i}$, where w_{d_i,t_j} is the weighted frequency of term t_j in document d_i and W_{d_i} is the document normalisation weight. Note that we have used a tilde (˜) over a variable to represent a vector and a capital letter to represent a matrix. We will adhere to this notation throughout the paper.

To remove the assumption of term independence, we must map the query into the topic space using T and then back to the term space with T'. The documents are then ranked according to the new query. Our document score calculations now take the form:

$$\tilde{s} = ATT'\tilde{q}' \qquad (4)$$

where T is the mapping from the word space to the topic space and therefore T' (the transpose of T) is the mapping from the topic space back to the term space. We can observe from this equation that $T'\tilde{q}'$ is the query vector mapped into the topic space and that AT is the matrix of document vectors mapped into the topic space (as done in LSA). Therefore, our query mapping is given by $M = TT'$ is $\tau \times \tau$ sized matrix, where τ is the number of terms.

2.1 Examining the Query Mapping

The relationship between the topic space and the term space cannot be shown by a simple expression. The cardinality of the term space is limited by the size of the lexicon,

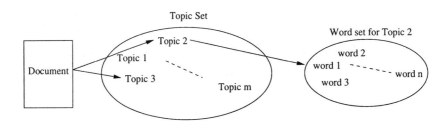

Figure 2. The document creation process including topic selection. First the topics are selected, then the words related to each topic fill in the document.

but the cardinality of the topic space (being a latent variable) is unknown.

We can apply a simplification to the topic-term mapping by assuming a linear relationship. This allows us to express the mapping in terms of a simple matrix multiplication. The mapping is given by the matrix shown in equation 5.

$$T = \begin{bmatrix} \tau_{w_1,t_1} & \tau_{w_1,t_2} & \cdots & \tau_{w_1,t_m} \\ \tau_{w_2,t_1} & \tau_{w_2,t_2} & \cdots & \tau_{w_2,t_m} \\ \vdots & \vdots & \ddots & \vdots \\ \tau_{w_n,t_1} & \tau_{w_n,t_2} & \cdots & \tau_{w_n,t_m} \end{bmatrix} \quad (5)$$

The matrix consists of real valued elements ($\tau_{d,t}$), where each element represents the relevance of the term to the topic. A positive value represents that the term and the topic are related, a negative value represents that the term and the topic oppose each other. A zero value implies that the term and topic have no relationship.

The cardinality of the topic set must be chosen prior to constructing the mapping matrix. This value should be less than the number of terms, so that each topic can consist of many terms. The query process using the mapping $M = TT'$ proceeds as follows:

1. the rows corresponding to the query terms are extracted from the mapping matrix and multiplied with the query terms to obtain our modified query vector

2. the rows corresponding to the terms found in the new query vector are extracted from the index and multiplied to provide the document scores.

This process is illustrated in figure 3. We can see that each step is identical if we disregard the matrix involved. The modified query can be thought of as the set of word scores for the query, which is then given to the document index to obtain the set of document scores. This implies that we can store our query mapping in exactly the same way as we store our document index to obtain the speed and compression benefits that are offered.

2.2 Query Map Construction

To construct the query map we will have to extract the word-topic relationships from the document set in order to derive the word-topic matrix. Many methods of automatically extracting these semantic properties exist in the literature. These include Principle Component Analysis (PCA), Independent Component Analysis (ICA) [6], Singular Value Decomposition (SVD) [3] and Maximum Likelihood methods [5, 1]. We will focus on the SVD method. The concepts shown using the SVD can be easily applied to each of the other methods.

2.2.1 Vector Space Method

As we have shown, the vector space method document scores are calculated by $A\tilde{q}'$. This implies that if we were to build a mapping to obtain the same results, we would simply use an Identity mapping ($M = I$).

2.2.2 Latent Semantic Indexing

In Latent Semantic Indexing (LSI), the topic space is found by calculating the Singular Value Decomposition (SVD) of the document index. For a real matrix A of rank s, the SVD is of the form:

$$A = U\Sigma V' \quad (6)$$

where $U'U = V'V = I$, the identity matrix, and Σ is a square matrix of the form $\text{diag}(\sigma_1, \sigma_2, \ldots, \sigma_s)$. This decomposition provides us with the documents in the topic space ($U\Sigma$) and the terms in the topic space ($V\Sigma$), where U and V and the document and term basis vector respectively.

The SVD orders the document and term basis vectors according to their variance in A, where the most varying dimension of the original A matrix has the corresponding largest singular value found in the Σ matrix. The decomposition also has the feature that if we choose to reduce the dimension of the document and term basis by removing the elements corresponding to the smallest singular values, we obtain the least squares approximation of the A matrix in the new lower dimensional space.

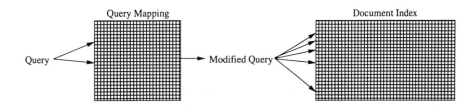

Figure 3. To use the query map, the query selects the rows from the map corresponding to its query terms and combines these to obtain a modified query term set. This modified query is then applied to the document collection index in the usual fashion.

By labeling these new reduced dimensional matrices as $\hat{U}$, $\hat{V}$ and $\hat{\Sigma}$, we obtain the following:

$$\hat{A} = \hat{U}\hat{\Sigma}\hat{V}' \qquad (7)$$

If we treat the A matrix as a set of document vectors, we can see that the SVD provides us with a mapping from the original space to the reduced space:

$$\hat{A} = \left(\hat{U}\hat{\Sigma}\right)\hat{V}' = \hat{D}\hat{V}' \qquad (8)$$

where $\hat{V}'$ is the mapping and $\left(\hat{U}\hat{\Sigma}\right)$ is the new set of document vectors. The same applies for the term vectors found in the columns of A:

$$\hat{A} = \hat{U}\left(\hat{\Sigma}\hat{V}'\right) = \hat{U}\hat{W}' \qquad (9)$$

where $\hat{U}$ is the mapping and $\left(\hat{\Sigma}\hat{V}'\right)$ is the new set of term vectors. To query a latent semantic index, we must map the documents in to the latent topic space ($A\hat{V}$), map the query into the same space ($\tilde{q}\hat{V}$) and apply the inner product to obtain the document scores:

$$\tilde{s} = \left(A\hat{V}\right)\left(\hat{V}'\tilde{q}'\right) \qquad (10)$$

If we let $\hat{V}$ be our word-topic mapping matrix, we obtain equation 4. Therefore, we can represent the LSI process by use of a query map attached to the vector space method. Instead of calculating the document scores in the latent topic space, we can use the mapping to extract related query terms from the topic space and use an inverted index to calculate the document scores in a faster time. This is just one method of generating a query map, if we look further at types of mappings, we will realise that the possibilities are endless. In the next section, we show how we can generate an efficient retrieval system that may employ multiple query mappings.

2.2.3 Information Retrieval Hybrids

Ensemble methods for machine learning obtain results from multiple machine learning methods and chooses as the answer the class that obtains the most votes. If we apply this idea to information retrieval, we would give our query to multiple retrieval systems and choose the documents that appear in most of the relevant document lists. To make the process simpler, we could obtain the document scores from each of the retrieval systems and simply add them. The documents that obtain high scores from all of the retrieval systems will have higher scores, while the ones which vary across the retrieval systems will not have such high scores. To perform this task in the usual manner, we would have to run multiple retrieval systems to obtain the hybrid results. Due to the linear nature of our retrieval methods, we can generate the hybrid results from a single query. If we can express our retrieval systems in terms of a query mapping and a document index, we achieve the following:

$$\tilde{s} = \sum_i AM_i\tilde{q}' = A\left(\sum_i M_i\right)\tilde{q}' \qquad (11)$$

Therefore, for any set of retrieval systems in which we can represent as a query mapping and a document index, we are able to obtain hybrid document scores by simply summing the query mappings and performing the query as usual.

2.3 LSI Problems

In using a query map, we are able to eliminate some of the problems found in the LSI method.

2.3.1 LSI Sampling Problem

We have shown that LSI produces document feature vectors based on the frequency of the terms in each document, therefore, the resulting feature vectors will only be as effective as the data given in the initial set. The SVD organises the content of the document feature vectors based on the appearance of terms in the document in question and the rest of the document set. So, if each of the terms found in the original documents occur in many documents, the SVD will be able to organise the document feature vectors more effectively. If there are terms that have little occurrence in the document set, the SVD will not have enough information about them to make effective use in the feature space. This implies that we should remove all of the terms that appear in a small number of documents, since they would only complicate the SVD calculations and add noise to the feature space.

By removing the under represented terms, we are removing terms that might define certain documents. For instance, if term y appeared in two documents and was removed from the SVD calculation, any search for term y would not provide any results. Therefore, we want to remove uncommon terms to increase the effectiveness of the SVD, but we also want to keep the uncommon terms to use directly. The solution we propose is to merge the LSI and VSM methods to obtain the best of both worlds.

1. Index of all documents and terms A as in the VSM.

2. Extract term vectors that have $> C$ non-zero elements into B.

3. Perform SVD on B to obtain $B = U\Sigma V'$

4. Calculate $M_{SVD} = VV'$

5. Build $M = M_{VSM} \oplus M_{SVD}$, where $M_{VSM} = \alpha I$.

By removing the under represented terms from the SVD calculation, we should obtain better relationships between terms. The rare terms are included in the mapping through a merge ($\oplus$) with the VSM mapping.

In this method, $\oplus$ implies a matrix addition where the elements related to the same term are matched. If there is no related element, we add zero. I is the identity matrix and α is a predefined mixture constant. This operation gives us a hybrid LSA-VSM retrieval method.

2.3.2 Pruning the query vector

After we perform the mapping, we obtain a query vector which consists of many non-zero elements. Most of the elements being close to zero, with some positive values and some negative values. For each additional term that appears in the query, we must extract and add the elements of the corresponding inverted list. Therefore, it is not in our best interests to use such a populated query vector. To reduce the number of non-zero elements, we simply chose to keep the T most significant valued elements and set the rest to zero.

3 Experimental Results

To test and verify our query mapping methods, we experimented with a set of small documents labeled CRAN (1398 abstracts from the Cranfield Institute of Technology), CACM (3204 abstracts from the Communications of the ACM journal), CISI (1460 abstracts from the Institute for Scientific Information), and MED (1033 abstracts from the National Library of Medicine) and ADI (82 abstracts)[1]. We also experimented on the larger AP2 document set (79,919 newspaper articles from the Associated Press)[2]. We chose to use the titles of the queries as the query terms to emulate Web style queries. The results found in this paper show the results from the AP2 set. We structured our initial experiments to determine the impact on the precision of our methods to the adjustment of the mapping file sizes. Therefore, the variables of our experiments were the number of terms included in the SVD mapping and the mixture of the VSM and SVD mapping. In each experiment, we used the Lnu.ltu weighting scheme from SMART [2]. Our experimental mappings were generated using the $M = M_{SVD} \oplus M_{VSM}$ matrix where $M_{SVD} = VV'$ is generated from the SVD of our index and $M_{VSM} = \alpha I$ (representing the combination of the VSM) is the identity matrix of size $T \times T$ multiplied by a mixing factor and $\oplus$ is the merging operator. The results are displayed in sets of two graphs, showing precision after 10 documents and average precision respectively. To successfully encode the floating point values during the SVD calculation, we used 6 bit left geometric quantisation [8]. To sustain the symmetric nature of the matrix during the SVD, we chose to use the same quantisation table for the entire matrix (rather than on a row by row basis). This provides us with a faster quantisation stage, but with larger error in our quantised values.

The number of terms included in the mapping were chosen by selecting terms that appeared in N or more documents. This allows us to choose the terms that are well represented in the document set. We experimented with this value of N using values of $10, 20, 50, 100, 200, 300, 500, 800$ and 1000. We also experimented by varying the α mixing parameter from 0 (pure LSI) to 2. A value of $\alpha = 0.2$ was chosen for the AP2 document set.

Our initial interest was in the precision of the results over the precision of both the LSI and VSM document retrieval methods. The results we obtained from these experiments are found in the left of figure 4. The mapped query vector was built by taking the top 50 and 1000 terms ordered by magnitude. Therefore, negative values were included. As expected, the precision decreases as the number terms in the mapping decreases.

We compared our method to both the VSM and LSI methods but have shown only the VSM method in the graphs. This was due to the VSM precision results being superior to LSI for all of the document sets we tested, except for the MED document set . The low precision LSI results we produced were not in agreement with previous reports which show improvements over the VSM. The previous re-

---

[1]Available from from `ftp://ftp.cs.cornell.edu/pub/smart/`
[2]Available on disk 2 of the TREC collection [4]

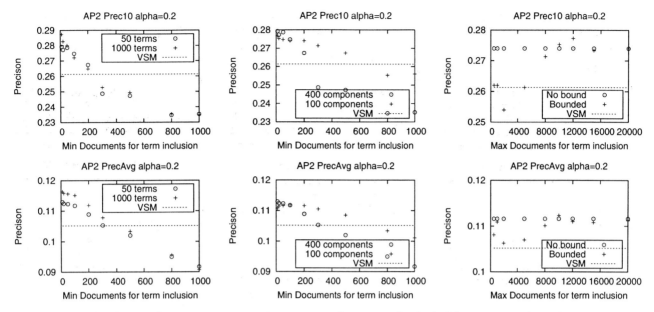

Figure 4. Precision using a query mapping versus the terms included in the mapping. The top and bottom rows show Precision after 10 documents and Average Precision respectively. Min and Max documents for term inclusion are the minimum and maximum number of documents a term must appear in to be included in the mapping. The left plots compare the number of expanded query terms chosen, the centre plot compares the number of SVD components chosen for the mapping, and the right plot compares the inclusion of common terms in the mapping. The dashed line is our precision benchmark using the VSM.

ports used inferior weighting schemes (such as simple tfIdf weights) to weight both the LSI elements and VSM. By using these weights, the LSI displayed higher precision over the VSM, but when using the Lnu.ltu weights (as in our experiments) the VSM surpasses LSI most of the time.

The results show that the precision decreases with a decrease in mapping terms (increase in documents for term inclusion). We also observed that an increase in query terms (choosing 1000 instead of 50) provides us with an increase in precision of the large document set (AP2), and small increases of precision for the smaller document sets. For each term selected for the query (after the mapping is performed), we increase the query time. So this small increase in precision by choosing more query terms comes at a price.

To examine the impact of the number of singular values chosen, we devised an experiment on the AP2 document set. We compared the effect on the precision by selecting 100 and 400 singular values. The results are shown in the centre of figure 4. We can see from these plots that the increase in the number of singular values chosen increase the precision when many terms are included in the mapping, but as the number of terms decrease (Documents for term inclusion increases) the precision drops off rapidly. For the case where we have chosen a smaller number of singular

values, the precision slowly drops off with a decrease in mapping terms.

Our first experiment examined the response of precision to the number of terms included in the query mapping. Terms were removed by ignoring those which were found in less than N documents (rare terms). We will now extend the experiment by observing the response of precision by ignoring those that occur in more than M documents (common terms). The right of figure 4 shows the results of using a mapping that includes terms found in at least 200 document and at most M documents, where M is the x-axis. This shows a peak at about 10000 documents for both precision after 10 documents and average precision. This implies that by including too little or too many terms in the mapping will degrade the precision.

4 Query and Score Accumulation

In order it achieve fast query times, the VSM has adopted an accumulation process to obtain the top D documents related to the query. The accumulation process estimates the top N by selecting the documents with the greatest individual document term weights which are related to the greatest query term weight. Two methods of achieving this are

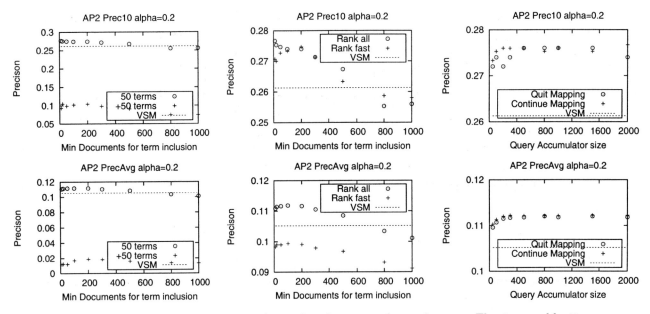

Figure 5. Precision using a query mapping using fast querying schemes. The top and bottom rows show Precision after 10 documents and Average Precision respectively. Min and Max documents for term inclusion are the minimum and maximum number of documents a term must appear in to be included in the mapping. The left plots compare choosing only positive weighted query terms and all query terms, the centre plot compares using an accumulator during the document ranking, and the right plot compares using an accumulator during the term expansion. The dashed line is our precision benchmark using the VSM.

through the *Quit* accumulation method and the more refined *Continue* accumulation method [7]. Throughout our experimentation, we used Continue for our document rank accumulation. As we mentioned earlier, the mapping process is almost identical to the ranking process, therefore we are able to implement an accumulator for the mapping process as well. The mapping accumulator will store the expanded query term weights, therefore the size of the accumulator is set to the number of terms we wish to obtain from the mapping.

4.1 Score Accumulation

The accumulation methods allow us to estimate the top ranking documents by making the assumption that most of the document term weights will be small values and all the values are positive. The document weights are mostly small values close to zero. By taking the greatest weights first, we will be selecting rare weights that will most probably identify with the top ranked documents. The smaller weights will probably be not enough to introduce new documents into the top ranked set.

If we expand the space spanned by the query weights to cover the real domain, the fast ranking method mentioned

above fails. A simple example of failure would be a one term query where the weight of the term is negative. Any document with a large positive weight will be chosen for the accumulator, but once multiplied by the negative query weight, the result is a large negative value for the accumulator. During the initial accumulation phase where we are building the list of relevant documents, the list will be populated by large negative values, and hence return documents which are not relevant to the query. To overcome this, we elected to choose only the positively weighted query terms. Using a document accumulator of size 1000, the left of figure 5 shows a large degradation in choosing only the positive weighted terms from the mapping. This implies that we must base our accumulator weight selection policy on the query term weight and not the document term weights alone.

To investigate this fast ranking method, we ran experiments on the AP2 document with the same parameters as before. The resulting plots can be seen in the centre of figure 5. We can see that by including the query weight in the accumulator element selection process, we achieve results similar to the slower full ranking method. The precision after 10 document shows a greater precision when terms that appear in 200 documents are placed in the mapping matrix, when compared to the full ranking method. If we look at the average precision, we can see that the fast ranking method follows the same path as the full ranking method, but it has a negative offset. From this we can deduce that the fast ranking method is able to organise the top few documents into their correct ranks. But as the document scores become lower it becomes harder to determine their position.

4.2 Query term Accumulation

During our previous experiments, we chose to select the top Q terms from the set of expanded terms based on their weight. To do this, we would calculate the weights of every term, sort the weights and choose the top set. From this process, many of the calculations are wasted, since we want only the top Q term weights. To speed up this process, we can use the fast document ranking methods (*Quit* and *Continue*) on our mapping to produce an estimate of the top Q terms. By storing the mapped query weights in order of magnitude, we are able to use an accumulator to establish an expanded query vector. We have experimented on the effect of changing the accumulation scheme (from Quit to Continue). The results are shown in the right of figure 5. The experiment compared the resulting precision from varying the accumulator size when using the Quit and Continue accumulation methods. We can see in each of the methods, the precision begin low and ascends to a stable precision for both precision after 10 documents and average precision. This implies that we only need an accumulator of size of about 300 terms to obtain a good approximate.

5 Computational Complexity

To obtain an idea of the query time differences between a text retrieval system using an inverted index compared to our system with a query mapping, we will examine the complexity due to the different accumulation methods that we have chosen. Since our retrieval method is simply a mapping to expand the users query attached to a traditional text index, we can split the complexity calculations into two stages. The first stage is retrieving the terms associated to the query terms from the term mapping. If we wish to expand our query from u to v terms, and we use Quit accumulation, we will examine at most $(u(v-1)+1)$ mapping entries. The Continue method will process at most $u\tau$ terms, where τ is the number of terms in the document set. The second stage is simply retrieving the documents from the index using the Continue accumulation method. The number of index elements examined will be at most $v\delta$ where δ is the number of documents in the set. If we combine these two steps we achieve $O(u(v-1)+1+v\delta)$ when using the Quit mapping and $O(u\tau + v\delta)$ when using the Continue mapping. These are compared to $O(u\delta)$ for the vector space method. Experimental results on a Pentium 4 with an average load of 0.15 have shown an average query time of 0.03 seconds for the mapping and 0.35 seconds for the ranking when mapping to 300 terms.

6 Conclusion

We have introduced the concept of a query map which takes the users query and maps it to an expanded query. We have shown a method of building a query map using Singular Value Decomposition which also incorporates the vector space method. We performed experiments using this mapping and we found that 1) we don't have to include all of the terms in the mapping to produce high precision results, 2) the resulting mapped query vector can be pruned to keep only the significant values and still maintain high precision results, 3) more singular values does not mean greater precision, and 4) we can apply fast ranking methods to the mapped query results and receive the same high precision results in a fraction of the time of ranking using all of the documents. Based on these findings, we are able to construct the retrieval system using the query map and obtain all of the benefits of the vector space method (including fast querying) while producing the high precision results from using the query map.

References

[1] D. M. Blei, A. Y. Ng, and M. I. Jordan. Latent dirichlet allocation. *Journal of Machine Learning Research*, 3:993–1022, January 2003.

[2] C. Buckley, A. Singhal, M. Mitra, and G. Salton. New retrieval approaches using smart : TREC 4. In D. Harman, editor, *The Fourth Text REtrieval Conference (TREC-4)*, pages 25–48, Gaithersburg, Md. 20899, November 1995. National Institute of Standards and Technology Special Publication 500-236.

[3] S. T. Dumais. Improving the retrieval of information from external sources. *Behaviour Research Methods, Instruments & Computers*, 23(2):229–236, 1991.

[4] D. Harman, editor. *The Third Text REtrieval Conference (TREC-3)*, Gaithersburg, Md. 20899, March 1994. National Institute of Standards and Technology Special Publication 500-226.

[5] T. Hofmann. Probabilistic latent semantic indexing. In *Proceedings of the 22nd annual international ACM SIGIR conference on Research and development in information retrieval*, pages 50–57. ACM Press, 1999.

[6] A. Hyvarinen, J. Karhunen, and E. Oja. *Independent component analysis*. Wiley-Interscience, 2001.

[7] A. Moffat and J. Zobel. Self-indexing inverted files for fast text retrieval. *ACM Transactions on Information Systems (TOIS)*, 14(4):349–379, 1996.

[8] A. Moffat, J. Zobel, and R. Sacks-Davis. Memory efficient ranking. *Information Processing and Management*, 30(6):733–744, November 1994.

SCHISM: A New Approach for Interesting Subspace Mining [*]

Karlton Sequeira and Mohammed Zaki

Department of Computer Science, Rensselaer Polytechnic Institute, Troy, New York 12180

{sequek,zaki}@cs.rpi.edu

Abstract

High-dimensional data pose challenges to traditional clustering algorithms due to their inherent sparsity and data tend to cluster in different and possibly overlapping subspaces of the entire feature space. Finding such subspaces is called subspace mining. We present SCHISM, a new algorithm for mining interesting subspaces, using the notions of support and Chernoff-Hoeffding bounds. We use a vertical representation of the dataset, and use a depth-first search with backtracking to find maximal interesting subspaces. We test our algorithm on a number of high-dimensional synthetic and real datasets to test its effectiveness.

1. Introduction

Clustering is an unsupervised learning process, in which a multidimensional space is partitioned into disjoint regions, such that all points within any such region/cluster are similar to each other, but dissimilar with respect to points in other clusters. If the clustering is done using all available features, it is called a *full-dimensional* clustering. Many such algorithms like BIRCH, DBSCAN, CURE [14] have been proposed for this task. While they show acceptable performance on lower dimensional datasets, a large number of dimensions poses problems [15]. One of the main reasons is that data is generally very sparse in high dimensional datasets. Also, most of the full dimensional algorithms use distance metrics, which treat every dimension with equal importance. For high dimensional spaces, it has been argued that under certain reasonable assumptions on the data distribution, the ratio of the distances of the nearest and farthest neighbors to a given target is almost 1 for a variety of distance functions and data distributions [7]. In such a scenario, many full dimensional clustering algorithms have little meaning, as the pairwise distances between the points in distinct clusters need not provide an acceptable contrast.

Solutions proposed include, designing new distance metrics [1] and dimension reduction [12]. Dimension reduction techniques, such as the Karhunen-Loeve transformation (KLT) or singular value decomposition (SVD), project the dataset from the original d to a k dimensional space, where $k \ll d$, and each new dimension is a linear combination of the original dimensions; after this clustering is done using only the k dimensions. Such a strategy may be inappropriate since clusters in the transformed feature space may be hard to interpret. Also, data is only clustered in a single k-dimensional space. [4, 20] cite examples in which KLT does not reduce the dimensionality without trading off considerable information, as the dataset contains subsets of points which lie in different and sometimes overlapping lower dimensional subspaces. Another method of dimension reduction is feature selection, in which some of the dimensions are selected heuristically without transformation [8]. This removes the problem of interpretability, but still only a fixed subspace is used for clustering. These challenges have caused the focus of much recent work in clustering to shift towards finding the interesting subspaces within a high-dimensional space[4, 20, 10, 19, 17, 2, 3, 9]. Other challenges encountered in subspace mining are that subspaces may share dimensions as well as objects, etc. The subspace mining problem has wide applications, especially with datasets having ordinal/nominal values, e.g., datasets found in bioinformatics, intrusion detection, etc.

In this paper, we tackle the problem of finding statistically 'interesting' subspaces in a high dimensional dataset using an algorithm called SCHISM (Support and Chernoff-Hoeffding bound-based Interesting Subspace Miner). We use the Chernoff-Hoeffding bound to prune the search for interesting subspaces, as a nonlinear function of the number of dimensions in which the subspace is constrained. We use a vertical representation of the dataset and capitalize on various advances made in itemset mining. We use a depth-first search with backtracking to find maximal interesting subspaces. We finally test our algorithm on a wide array of high-dimensional datasets.

2. Related work

Subspace clustering methods may be classified into two main categories: density-based and projected clustering.

Density-based clustering Agrawal et al. [4], proposed CLIQUE, which discretizes the domain of each of the d dimensions into a user-specified number, ξ, of equal-width intervals. They use *support* (the fraction of points that lie in a subspace) to denote the density of a subspace; only those subspaces above a minimum density threshold are mined. Using a bottom-up Apriori-like [5] approach, higher-dimensional 'dense' maximal, hyper-rectangular subspaces are mined. To prune their search at a faster rate, they use the minimum-description length (MDL) principle as a heuristic, thereby making it an approximate search. They then merge 'dense' subspaces sharing common faces, and use covering algorithms to mine the minimal descriptions of the subspaces.

Instead of support, Cheng [10], proposed using entropy as a measure of subspace interestingness. Subspaces satisfying an entropy threshold are mined. Nagesh et al. in MAFIA[19], partition each dimension into variable width intervals, based on the distribution of points. An interval is 'dense' if the number of points in it exceeds the threshold $(\alpha a n)/D_i$, where n is the number of points in the dataset

---

[*]This work was supported by NSF Grant EIA-0103708 under the KD-D program, NSF CAREER Award IIS-0092978, and DOE Early Career PI Award DE-FG02-02ER25538.

and α is a user-specified parameter, called the *cluster dominance factor*. Here, $(an)/D_i$ corresponds to the number of points expected to lie inside an interval of width a in the i-th dimension, which has range D_i. Using adaptive width intervals reduces rigidity imposed by the grid in CLIQUE.

Kailing et al [18] suggest using a sample of the points in the dataset. They generate dense subspaces enclosing each point of the sample if it is a *core object*, i.e., if it has more than $MinPts$, a user-specified threshold, points within a threshold radius ϵ. The subspaces are then assigned a quality rating, which takes into account the number of dimensions in which the subspace is constrained and this rating is used to prune lower quality subspaces. By providing a rating, it is only possible for the user to determine the relative and not absolute interestingness of a subspace w.r.t. another subspace.

Projected Clustering Aggarwal [2, 3] uses projective clustering to partition the dataset into clusters occurring in possibly different subsets of dimensions in a high dimensional dataset. PROCLUS [2] seeks to find axis-aligned subspaces by partitioning the set of points and then uses a hill-climbing technique to refine the partitions. ORCLUS [3], finds arbitrarily oriented clusters by using ideas related to singular value decomposition. Both the algorithms require the number of clusters and the expected number of dimensions for each cluster to be input.

In DOC [20], Procopiuc et al. devise a Monte Carlo algorithm for finding projective clusters. They propose a mathematical formulation for the notion of optimal projective cluster based on the density of the points in the subspaces. In LDR [9], Chakrabarti et al. search for local correlations in the data and perform dimensionality reduction on the locally correlated clusters of data individually.

3. Interestingness measure

Let $A = \{A_1, A_2, \ldots, A_d\}$ be the set of dimensions. Each dimension A_i has a totally ordered and bounded domain. Then, $S = A_1 \times A_2 \times \ldots \times A_d$ is the high-dimensional space. The input DB, is a set of n points, $DB = \{p_i | i \in [1, n], p_i \in S\}\}$. We partition S into non-overlapping rectangular units, obtained by partitioning each dimension into ξ intervals of equal width.

Definition 1: *A subspace is an axis-aligned hyper-rectangle, $[l_1, h_1] \times [l_2, h_2] \times \ldots \times [l_d, h_d]$, where $l_i = (aD_i)/\xi$, and $h_i = (bD_i)/\xi$, a, b are positive integers, and $a < b \leq \xi$*

If $h_i - l_i = D_i$, the subspace is unconstrained in dimension i whose range is given as D_i. A m-subspace is a subspace constrained in m dimensions, denoted as S_m.

Let X_p be the random variable(RV) denoting the number of points in S_p. If the probability of finding n_p points in S_p, is bounded by a reasonably low, user-specified threshold probability τ, S_p is considered to be interesting [1], i.e., $Pr(X_p \geq n_p) \leq \tau$ implies that S_p is an interesting subspace. Accordingly, we have

Definition 2: *A subspace is* **interesting** *if the number of points it contains is statistically significantly higher than that expected under the assumption that all dimensions are independent and uniformly distributed.*

It is obvious that a dataset that is scattered uniformly and independently, spanning the entire S, is of least interest from a clustering view-point, as the entropy is maximized.

---

[1] Typically τ is set to $O(\frac{1}{n}) \ll 0.05$, which is statistically significant

If a subspace deviates significantly from the uniform distribution, then it is potentially interesting [2]. If n_p points are found in S_p, CLIQUE considers S_p to be 'dense' if $n_p/n \geq s$, where s is the user-specified support threshold. MAFIA considers the subspace 'dense' if $n_p/n \geq (\alpha a)/D_i$ where α is the cluster dominance factor.

In general, all density-based subspace finding algorithms, use a threshold function $thresh : Z^+ \to \Re$ where Z^+ is the set of positive integers, and denotes the number of constrained dimensions in a *candidate* subspace. The value of $thresh \in \Re$ corresponds to the density threshold that must be exceeded for the candidate subspace to be called 'dense'. For example, support based pruning in CLIQUE, $thresh_{CLIQUE}(p) = s, \forall p \in [1, d]$, i.e., no matter what the number of constrained dimensions of a subspace, the pruning threshold is a constant. The $thresh$ function can intuitively be either constant (as in CLIQUE) or monotonically increasing or monotonically decreasing.

Lemma 1 (Effect of monotonicity on $thresh$):
If any subspace $S_{p+1} \subset S$ is interesting, then every p-subspace S_p, which encloses S_{p+1} and is unconstrained in one of the $(p+1)$ constrained dimensions of S_{p+1}, is always interesting if $thresh(p+1) \geq thresh(p), 1 \leq p \leq d-1$, for density function thresh.

Proof: If S_{p+1} is interesting, $\frac{n_{p+1}}{n} \geq thresh(p+1)$. But, $n_p \geq n_{p+1}$ because $S_{p+1} \subset S_p$. Thus, $\frac{n_p}{n} \geq \frac{n_{p+1}}{n} \geq thresh(p+1)$. If, $thresh(p+1) \geq thresh(p)$, then $\frac{n_p}{n} \geq thresh(p)$ and monotonicity is guaranteed.■

Lemma 2 *For $p=1\ldots d$, let thresh be monotonically non-decreasing and let $thresh_2(p) = thresh(r)$, where r is the number of dimensions constrained in S_r, a maximally interesting subspace under thresh. If $S_r \subseteq S_p$, then S_p is also interesting under $thresh_2$.*

Proof: Since S_r is interesting, then $\frac{n_r}{n} \geq thresh(r)$. Also, as $S_r \subseteq S_p, 1 \leq p \leq r-1, n_p \geq n_r$. Hence, $\frac{n_p}{n} \geq \frac{n_r}{n} \geq thresh(r) = thresh_2(p)$. Thus, S_p is also interesting under $thresh_2$.■

A consequence of the above lemmas is that it in order to find all the maximal interesting subspaces found by $thresh_2$, one must set $thresh(1)$ to a very low value so that it converges to $thresh_2$. This causes generation of a number of candidate subspaces which do not yield maximal interesting subspaces but add to computation time. Hence, it makes little sense to have a monotonically increasing threshold function. The $thresh$ function must be either constant or monotonically decreasing. However, it has been observed, that in order to find small subspaces, the constant support threshold function has to be set very low,which makes subspace mining very slow. Hence, we propose a non-linear monotonically decreasing threshold function, which does not guarantee mining all interesting subspaces,[3] but does mine in a more reasonable time. The intuition behind why this might work, is that as p increases, the subspace becomes constrained in more and more dimensions, making its volume smaller and smaller. Hence the threshold too, must decrease for the enclosed (S_{p+1}) and enclosing (S_p) subspaces to have comparable interestingness.

---

[2] See Eq. 3 and following comment

[3] For monotonically decreasing $thresh$, the Apriori principle may not be applicable. Consider, $\frac{n_p}{n} = \frac{n_{p+1}}{n} = thresh(p+1)$. If $thresh(p+1) < thresh(p)$, then $\frac{n_p}{n} < thresh(p)$ and S_p is not interesting although S_{p+1} is.

3.1. Chernoff-Hoeffding bound

We use the Chernoff-Hoeffding bound [11, 16] to bound the tail of the distribution of X_p and measure the level of interestingness. If Y_i, $i = 1 \ldots n$, are independently distributed RV, with $0 \leq Y_i \leq 1$ and $Var[Y_i] < \infty$, then for $Y = \sum_{i=1}^{n} Y_i, t > 0$,

$$Pr[Y \geq E[Y] + nt] \leq e^{-2nt^2} \quad (1)$$

where $E[Y] = \sum_{i=1}^{n} E[Y_i]$ by linearity of expectation.

Given a p-subspace S_p, let Y_i correspond to the RV that the ith point in DB, when projected onto the set of p constrained dimensions of S_p, lies within S_p. Then $Y = X_p$. Using Eq. (1) and for some real $t_p > 0$, S_p is interesting if,

$$Pr[X_p \geq n_p] \leq e^{-2nt_p^2} \leq \tau \quad (2)$$

where $E[X_p] + nt_p = n_p$, which implies that $t_p = \frac{n_p}{n} - \frac{E[X_p]}{n}$. Substituting t_p in the right hand term of (2), we have $e^{-2n\left(\frac{n_p}{n} - \frac{E[X_p]}{n}\right)^2} \leq \tau$ which on simplification gives,

$$\frac{n_p}{n} \geq \frac{E[X_p]}{n} + \sqrt{\frac{1}{2n} ln(\frac{1}{\tau})} \quad (3)$$

Thus, for a p-subspace to be interesting, (3) must hold. (3) makes no assumption, other than independence, about the comparative distribution and hence can be extended to find subspaces interesting w.r.t. distributions, other than that having uniformly distributed dimensions.

Note that the interestingness measure, $thresh(p) = \frac{E[X_p]}{n} + \sqrt{\frac{1}{2n} ln(\frac{1}{\tau})}$ is a non-linear monotonically decreasing function in the number of dimensions p, in which S_p is constrained. Also, note that $thresh$ is analogous to the support and density threshold measures used to prune search in the CLIQUE [4] and MAFIA [19] algorithms respectively. In comparison with CLIQUE, the term $\sqrt{\frac{1}{2n} ln(\frac{1}{\tau})}$ corresponds to minimum density s set by the user. The interestingness threshold probability (τ) seems intuitively easier to set than s. The chief difference is the term $\frac{E[X_p]}{n}$, which makes pruning conscious of the volume of the subspace and hence conscious of the number of constrained dimensions of the subspace on which it is being carried out. Unlike earlier proposed interestingness measures [18], this one gives the user a sense of absolute interestingness.

If we assume that each dimension in the d-dimensional space is independent and uniformly distributed and discretized into ξ levels, then the probability that a point lies in a specific interval of any dimension is $\frac{1}{\xi}$. Hence, the probability that a point lies in a specific p-subspace (assuming it is constrained to a single interval in each of the p constrained dimensions) is $(\frac{1}{\xi})^p$. Thus, the probability of finding n_p points in any subspace S_p, is distributed as per the binomial distribution with mean $E[X_p] = n(\frac{1}{\xi})^p$. Thus, S_p is interesting if, $\frac{n_p}{n} \geq \frac{1}{\xi^p} + \sqrt{\frac{1}{2n} ln(\frac{1}{\tau})}$.

Note that for $p \geq \lceil \frac{log(n)}{log(\xi)} \rceil = v$, we have $\frac{n}{\xi^p} \leq 1$, and thus $\frac{1}{\xi^p} + \sqrt{\frac{1}{2n} ln(\frac{1}{\tau})} \approx \sqrt{\frac{1}{2n} ln(\frac{1}{\tau})}$. The threshold function thus converges to a constant when the number of constrained dimensions $p \geq v$; analogous to minimum threshold s in CLIQUE. To summarize,

$$thresh_{SCHISM}(d \geq p \geq v) = \sqrt{\frac{1}{2n} ln(\frac{1}{\tau})}$$

From Lemma 1, for $p \geq v$, S_{p+1} is interesting implies that S_p is interesting, as SCHISM is similar to CLIQUE and uses support-based pruning for a large part of the subspace mining process. Note that this constant $\sqrt{\frac{1}{2n} ln\left(\frac{1}{\tau}\right)}$ varies inversely as $\sqrt{n}$ and hence $thresh_{SCHISM}$ converges to a higher threshold for smaller datasets, implying more pruning while yielding subspaces of equal interestingness.

While $thresh_{SCHISM}$ is constant for $p \geq v$, we can gain some improvements in empirical results by changing the rate of change in $thresh_{SCHISM}(p < v)$ to increase the likelihood of monotonic search. We do so by trading off some tightness of the bound by using a penalty term. If $f(p)$ is the penalty term, such that $\forall p \in [1, d]$, $f(p) \leq 1$, then $e^{-2nt_p^2} \leq e^{-2nf(p)t_p^2}$. Using this in 2, $Pr(X_p \geq n_p) \leq e^{-2nf(p)t_p^2} \leq \tau$. After simplification,

$$thresh_{SCHISM}(0 < p < v) = \min \left\{ u, \frac{1}{\xi^p} + \sqrt{\frac{1}{2nf(p)} ln\left(\frac{1}{\tau}\right)} \right\}$$

The term u is used to upper bound $thresh_{SCHISM}(1)$, which is empirically too large for typical values of ξ. Typical values of $f(p)$ are $\frac{p}{a} (a \geq v \implies f(p) \leq 1)$, $\frac{1}{(c-bp^2)}$. The last penalty term provides a parabolic as opposed to exponential drop in the threshold as p increases. Typically, $u = 0.05$. In summary, we have

$$thresh_{SCHISM}(p) = \begin{cases} \min \left\{ u, \frac{1}{\xi^p} + \sqrt{\frac{1}{2nf(p)} ln\left(\frac{1}{\tau}\right)} \right\} & \textit{if } p < v \\ \sqrt{\frac{1}{2n} ln\left(\frac{1}{\tau}\right)} & \textit{if } p \geq v \end{cases}$$

$$(4)$$

4. SCHISM algorithm

A number of the subspace mining algorithms [4, 10, 19] use a bottom-up, breadth-first search. In contrast, SCHISM, which is based on the GenMax algorithm that mines maximal itemsets [13], uses a depth-first search with backtracking to mine the maximal interesting subspaces. The main steps in SCHISM are shown in Figure 1; we first discretize the dataset and convert it to a vertical format. Then we mine the maximal interesting subspaces. Finally, we assign each point to its cluster, or label it as an outlier.

Discretization In SCHISM, we first discretize all points (figure 1, line 1). Given the original dataset DB, we divide each dimension into ξ bins, and give each interval a unique id (for example, the intervals in dimension d_0 are labeled from 0 to $\xi - 1$, those for d_1 are labeled from ξ to $2\xi - 1$, etc.). Consider the example dataset DB shown in Table 1

```
SCHISM (DB, s, ξ, τ):
//s is the minimum support threshold
//ξ is the number of intervals per dimension
//τ is the user-specified interestingness threshold
1.   DDB = Discretize(DB, ξ)
2.   VDB=HorizontalToVertical(DDB)
3.   MIS = MineSubspaces(VDB, s, ξ, τ)
4.   AssignPoints (DB, MIS)
```

Figure 1. The SCHISM algorithm

Table 1. Example DB: real & discretized

DB	d_1	d_2	d_3	d_4	d_5	d_6	d_7	d_8
p_1	755	689	306	482	838	657	743	980
p_2	818	166	494	302	378	439	633	805
p_3	418	159	499	260	139	921	986	780
p_4	833	173	484	236	948	17	647	781
p_5	264	960	465	985	70	209	782	309
p_6	991	972	118	986	72	209	804	341
p_7	921	963	910	976	71	220	818	317
p_8	686	965	623	993	68	202	800	287
p_9	448	146	605	205	984	423	654	983

(a) Original DB

DDB	d_1	d_2	d_3	d_4	d_5	d_6	d_7	d_8
p_1	7	16	23	34	48	56	67	79
p_2	8	11	24	33	43	54	66	78
p_3	4	11	24	32	41	59	69	77
p_4	8	11	24	32	49	50	66	77
p_5	2	19	24	39	40	52	67	73
p_6	9	19	21	39	40	52	68	73
p_7	9	19	29	39	40	52	68	73
p_8	6	19	26	39	40	52	68	72
p_9	4	11	26	32	49	54	66	79

(b) Discretized DB

Table 2. Seed subspaces: real & discretized

	d_1	d_2	d_3	d_4	d_5	d_6	d_7	d_8
I_1	-1	-1	-1	478	-1	673	774	-1
I_2	-1	163	475	260	-1	-1	-1	786
I_3	-1	949	-1	985	72	204	806	317

(a) Original Subspaces

	d_1	d_2	d_3	d_4	d_5	d_6	d_7	d_8
I_1	-1	-1	-1	34	-1	56	67	-1
I_2	-1	11	24	32	-1	-1	-1	77
I_3	-1	19	-1	39	40	52	68	73

(b) Discretized Subspaces

(a), generated by our synthetic data generator (see Section 5.1), with $n = 9, \xi = 10$ and $d = 8$. The seed subspaces used to generate DB are shown in Table 2 (a). Here -1 implies that the subspaces are unconstrained in that dimension. Thus, p_1 is generated from subspace I_1, points p_2, p_3, p_4 are generated from I_2, points p_5, p_6, p_7, p_8 are generated from I_3 and p_9 is an outlier. Table 1 (b) shows the discretized dataset DDB obtained from DB; the corresponding discretized subspaces are shown in Table 2 (b).

Data transformation The next step in SCHISM (figure 1, line 2) is to convert the dataset into a vertical tidset format [13], which records for each subspace (initially a single interval), the list of points that belong to it. Using a vertical format dataset gives us a number of advantages. Firstly, better memory utilization results from having only the relevant subspaces in memory at a time, as opposed to the horizontal format in which the entire dataset is scanned. Secondly, computing support of subspaces to be merged via tidset intersections is very fast. Figure 3 (for $p = 1$) shows the tidsets for the initial 'interesting' intervals. For example,

for interval 11, its tidset is given as $t(11) = \{2, 3, 4, 9\}$.

```
MineSubspaces (VDB, ξ, τ):
1.   Find IS₁ and IS₂ //sort IS₁ as optimization
2.   MIS-backtrack(φ, IS₁, MIS, 0, ξ, τ)
3.   return MIS

MIS-backtrack(Sₚ, Cₚ, MIS, l, ξ, τ)
4.   ∀Sₓ ∈ Cₚ
5.      Sₚ₊₁ = Sₚ ∪ Sₓ
6.      Pₚ₊₁ = {Sᵧ ∈ Cₚ | Sᵧ > Sₓ}
7.      If MergeSubspaces(MIS, (Sₚ₊₁ ∪ Pₚ₊₁)) return
8.      Cₚ₊₁ = IS-candidate(Sₚ₊₁, Pₚ₊₁, l, ξ, τ)
9.      If Cₚ₊₁ is empty
10.        If Sₚ₊₁ has enclosed no subspace in MIS,
11.           MIS = MIS ∪ Sₚ₊₁
12.     else MIS-backtrack(Sₚ₊₁, Cₚ₊₁, MIS, p + 1, ξ, τ)

MergeSubspaces(MIS, Zₚ₊₁)
13.  If min_{S_f ∈ MIS} Sim(Zₚ₊₁, S_f) > ρ × min(f, |Zₚ₊₁|)
14.     MIS = MIS − S_f
15.     MIS = MIS ∪ (S_f ∪ (Zₚ₊₁))
16.     return true
17.  return false

IS-candidate(Sₚ₊₁, Pₚ₊₁, l, ξ, τ)
18.  Cₚ₊₁ = φ
19.  ∀Sᵧ ∈ Pₚ₊₁
20.     t(S'ᵧ) = t(Sₚ₊₁) ∩ t(Sᵧ)
21.     If |t(S'ᵧ)|/n ≥ thresh(|S'ᵧ|)
22.        Cₚ₊₁ = Cₚ₊₁ ∪ Sᵧ
23.  return Cₚ₊₁
```

Figure 2. Mining interesting subspaces

Mining Interesting Subspaces In SCHISM, interesting subspaces are mined (figure 1, line 3), using a depth-first search with backtracking, allowing us to prune a considerable portion of the search space. The pseudo-code for MineSubspaces is shown in Figure 2. The method first finds all interesting subspaces in one (IS_1) and two dimensions (IS_2). We next call the recursive MIS-backtrack procedure to mine the set of maximal interesting subspaces (MIS).

MIS-backtrack accepts as input, a single p-subspace S_p, and a set C_p of candidate p-subspaces that can be used to constrain (or extend) S_p in an interval of another dimension. Each $S_x \in C_p$ results in a potential new $p + 1$-subspace $S_{p+1} = S_p \cup S_x$ (line 5), for which we have to calculate the new candidate set C_{p+1} (line 8). We do this by using a *possible* set P_{p+1} (line 6) of potential candidate subspaces, which are all the unprocessed subspaces in $S_y > S_x$ in C_p. If C_{p+1} is empty (line 9), then S_{p+1} is potentially maximal; it will be added to MIS if there is no maximal subspace that encompasses it (lines 10-11). If C_{p+1} is nonempty, then we recursively call MIS-backtrack.

The call to IS-Candidate (line 8) constructs the new candidate set C_{p+1} for S_{p+1} for the next level. The basic idea is to intersect tidset of S_{p+1} with every possible subspace in P_{p+1} (line 20). We keep only those subspace extensions that pass the $thresh()$ function (lines 21-22).

Typically, a depth-first search with backtracking produces a number of subspaces, which may overlap considerably, leading to redundant subspaces. To avoid this behavior, we prune the search tree by using MergeSubspaces (line 7). If the subspace $Z_{p+1} = S_{p+1} \cup P_{p+1}$, resulting from constraining S_{p+1} with all its remaining possible intervals in P_{p+1}, is significantly similar (typically, we set the merging threshold $\rho = 0.8$) to some known $S_f \in MIS$ (line 13), we replace S_f with a typically more constrained subspace (lines 14-15), $S_f \cup Z_{p+1}$. As $\rho < 1$, we may merge subspaces, which are constrained to adjacent intervals in a few dimensions, thus compensating for uniform width intervals in each dimension. The Sim function (line 13) used to calculate the similarity of two subspaces A and B is given as $Sim(A,B) = \sum_{i=1}^{d} JaccardSimilarity(A_i, B_i)$, where A_i, B_i are the sets of interesting intervals spanned by A, B in the i-th dimension and $JaccardSimilarity(X,Y) = \frac{|X \cap Y|}{|X \cup Y|}$. For example for point $p_1 \in DDB$ and seed subspace I_2 (discretized) (see Tables 1 and 2), $Sim(p_1, I_2) = 2$, as they are identically constrained in the second (11) and third (24) dimensions.

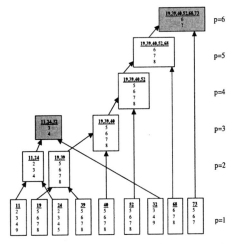

Figure 3. Lattice of running example

Example Let's consider how SCHISM works on our example dataset DB. Let $u = 0.25, \tau = 4/n = 0.44$. Then, $IS_1 = \{11, 19, 24, 32, 39, 40, 52, 68, 73\}$. Likewise we compute IS_2. The initial call to MIS-backtrack is with $S_p = \emptyset$, and $C_p = IS_1$, which results in a recursive call of MIS-backtrack for each interval, with a new candidate set C_{p+1}. For example, the candidate-set for 11 is given by $C_1 = \{24, 32, 39, 40, 52, 68, 73\}$, thus in the next level, we will try to extend 11 with $24, 32, \cdots, 73$, and so on, recursively. For our running example, when $S_{p+1} = 11$, $S_y = 24$, then $S'_y = \{11, 24\}$. Also $t(S_{p+1}) = \{2, 3, 4, 9\}$, and $t(S_y) = \{2, 3, 4, 5\}$, which gives $t(S'_y) = \{2, 3, 4\}$ (see Figure 3). As $p = 1$, we use the interestingness measure for pruning the search (line 21), i.e., the second case in Equation 4. With $thresh_{SCHISM}(1) = 0.21$, $n_1/n = 3/9 = 0.33 > 0.22$; thus S'_y is interesting, and we add 24 to the candidate set. Proceeding in this manner, we get the lattice shown in Fig.3. The rectangles shaded in gray are the elements of MIS.

Assigning Points to Clusters Let A correspond to the d-subspace surrounding a point p_i, and let B correspond to a mined p-subspace. Let Y and y be the random variable denoting the number and the true number, respectively, of

Figure 4. Assigning points to clusters

dimensions in which subspaces A and B are identically constrained. Under the default uniform distribution, each dimension is independent of the other and Y is a binomial random variable with mean $E[Y] = b/\xi$, where $b = E[\|B\|]$ is the expected number of dimensions in which B is constrained. Using Chernoff-Hoeffding bounds again, under a uniform distribution, if $Pr[Y \geq y] \leq exp(-2bt^2) \leq \tau$ for reasonably small user-specified threshold τ, it implies that the similarity between A and B is unusually high and the point in A is with high probability generated from the subspace B. Now, $exp(-2bt^2) \leq \tau$ implies that $t \geq \sqrt{\frac{1}{2b} ln\left(\frac{1}{\tau}\right)}$. Substituting t in $y = E[Y] + bt = \frac{b}{\xi} + bt$, we get $ThresholdSim = \frac{b}{\xi} + \sqrt{\frac{b}{2} ln\left(\frac{1}{\tau}\right)}$. We set $b = d/2$.

Fig. 1, line 4 of SCHISM assigns each point to the most similar maximal interesting subspace (lines 2-3), or else labels it as an outlier (line 4). Figure 4 shows these steps. Additionally, we have to examine if the similarity is statistically significant by using $ThresholdSim$ computed above.

5. Experiments

We perform tests on a range of synthetic high-dimensional datasets using our data generator and a couple of real datasets. We evaluate SCHISM based on two metrics: i) speed: the time taken to find the interesting subspaces in the dataset, and ii) accuracy: measured in terms of entropy and coverage. For a clustering C, *entropy* is defined as $E(C) = -\sum_{C_j}\left(\frac{n_j}{n}\sum_i p_{ij} \log(p_{ij})\right)$, where $p_{ij} = \frac{n_{ij}}{n}$, C_j is the jth cluster in C, n_j is the number of points in C_j, and n_{ij} is the number of points of C_j that actually belong to subspace i. The lower the $E(C)$, the better the clustering. *Coverage* is the fraction of points in DB which are accurately labeled as not being outliers. Ideally this is 1.

5.1. Synthetic datasets

We generate synthetic datasets using our own data generator which employs techniques similar to those mentioned in [2, 3, 20]. We embed k multivariate Gaussian clusters in a dataset of n points and d dimensions. Each dimension of a seed center is constrained to a single interval, with probability c; integer values are chosen in $[0, 1000]$. By not setting all dimensions of a seed center, we produce subspaces. If a center is set in any dimension, then the next center to be generated has the same dimension constrained with probability o. This ensures that the subspaces have different volumes and they can overlap in some dimensions. If the points are normally distributed about their cluster centers, the standard deviation for each dimension, for each cluster, is distributed uniformly in the range [10,30]. Let x be the fraction of the points generated as outliers and let the fraction of points generated for the i-th subspace be α_i, such that $x + \sum_{i=1}^{k} \alpha_i = 1$. In order that the number of points in the subspaces differ, we use a parameter

$\kappa = \frac{\max_i \alpha_i}{\min_i \alpha_i}$ i.e., the ratio of the α_is of the subspace with the most points to the subspace with the least points. An outlier has each dimension chosen uniformly in [0,1000]. The points for each subspace are independently and normally distributed about its center and the coordinates for dimensions in which the center is unbounded are chosen uniformly in [0,1000]. Thus, the subspaces generated in the dataset are oriented parallel to the axes. For all experiments, unless otherwise mentioned, we set as parameters to our data generator, $k = 5$, $n = 1000$, $d = 50$, $c = 0.5$, $o = 0.5$, $\kappa = 4.0$, $x = 0.05$. Also, we set support threshold $u = 0.05$, $\tau = 1/n$, $\xi = 10$ as the parameters to SCHISM. Also, we use $f(p) = \frac{p}{d}$.

Experiments were carried out on a Sun Sparc 650 MHz machine running on a Solaris O/S with 256 MB RAM. Since we have the seed subspaces we can easily evaluate the accuracy of SCHISM. We first mine the subspaces and partition the points in the space, so that they either belong to some interesting subspace or they are classified as outliers. Each of the following graphs, unless otherwise mentioned, shows the variation in performance, as a measure of two evaluation metrics: execution time and coverage (shown on y-axis), as a parameter of either SCHISM or the synthetic dataset is varied (shown on x-axis). *The entropy for all these experiments is below 0.004 and hence not shown.* This implies that SCHISM mines very pure clusters from our synthetic datasets. Ideally, the running time curve should be flat or linear and the coverage curve should be flat at 1.0.

5.1.1 Effect of varying dataset parameters

Effect of dataset size and dimensionality In Fig. 5, it is evident that as the dataset size increases, the coverage remains constant, while the running time grows linearly.

Note that in Fig. 6, as the dimensionality of the dataset increases, the coverage remains more or less constant, but the running time seems to grow exponentially initially, and then grows linearly from dimensions 200-300. In the worst case, this algorithm has exponential complexity in the number of dimensions, but in practice as shown here, the DFS algorithm coupled with the varying threshold function, significantly prunes the search space.

Effect of subspace size and dimensionality In Fig. 7, we observe the variation in coverage and running time, as the ratio $\kappa = \frac{\max_i \alpha_i}{\min_i \alpha_i}$ increases from 2 to 12. We observe that as the ratio κ increases, the coverage dips marginally and the running time remains constant. The coverage decreases because the subspaces which contain a smaller number of points have, on average, as large a volume as those containing a larger number of points, leading to a lower density. A smaller fraction of their enclosing subspaces are likely to be identified as 'interesting' and hence only a small fraction of their points are detected as non-outliers, as compared to when the ratio is not so large.

In Fig. 8, we observe the variation in coverage and running time, as the probability of constraining a dimension in a subspace c, increases from 0.3 to 0.9. We observe that as c increases, the running time remains constant but larger fractions of the dataset are constrained to smaller volumes, making them more 'interesting' and hence coverage improves somewhat.

Effect of subspace overlap Subspaces may overlap in terms of the dimensions in which they are constrained or in terms of the specific intervals they are constrained to. Accordingly, we have two experiments. In the first, we test the effect on performance due to increased overlap between constrained dimensions of subspaces generated consecutively. By increasing o from 0.1 to 0.9, we increase the likelihood of different subspaces being constrained to the same intervals of the same dimensions. In Fig. 9, we observe that running time stays constant but coverage decreases as o increases. This occurs because it becomes more likely that points belong to multiple 'interesting' subspaces simultaneously and hence only one is discovered, which may not completely cover the other.

In the second experiment, if $C_{i,j}$ is the jth co-ordinate of the center of the ith subspace, then if we constrain the jth co-ordinate of the $(i+1)$th center as well, we set it so $C_{i+1,j} \in \{C_{i,j} - 2\sigma_{i,j}, C_{i,j} + 2\sigma_{i,j}\}$, where $\sigma_{i,j}$ is the standard deviation in the jth dimension of the points corresponding to the ith subspace. From Fig. 10, we observe that SCHISM does not perform too well in this test and fails to find some of the clusters as the dimensionality rises, again because a point may now belong to multiple subspaces.

Performance on datasets with less dense subspaces In this experiment we run SCHISM on Gaussian and hyper-rectangular datasets. We decrease the density of the Gaussian datasets by increasing the standard deviation of each constrained dimension in each subspace. For hyper-rectangular subspaces, each constrained dimension is constrained to an interval of width, chosen uniformly in [0.5w,1.5w]. Thus, the density is decreased by increasing w; the volume of the subspace and keeping the number of points assigned to it is the same.

From Fig. 11 and Fig. 12, it is clear that as density decreases, SCHISM's performance deteriorates. This is because a smaller percentage of the subspace's points tend to fall into the same interval as that of the subspace center, as the volume increases. In such a case, decreasing the number of intervals in the dimension (ξ) might help or we must search for less 'interesting' subspaces, i.e., decrease τ.

Effect of number of clusters k Note from Fig. 13, that the running time remains constant as the number of embedded subspaces (k) increases, while coverage worsens after $k = 8$ as some clusters become very small and hence not 'interesting'.

5.1.2 Effects of varying algorithm parameters

Effect of τ In Fig. 14, we decrease the user specified interestingness threshold τ from 10^{-12} to $10^{-.25}$, and observe its effect on the coverage and running time. Note that the coverage increases rapidly, implying that τ *is the main parameter* which determines how much of the search space is mined and hence running time drops rapidly too. Our experiments on the effect of u on SCHISM performance (which are not shown due to lack of space), indicate that τ has a more precise control on pruning than u.

Effect of ξ From Fig. 15, we observe that, varying the number of intervals into which each dimension is discretized (ξ), has a small effect on SCHISM's performance for a considerable range of values for ξ. This is because the term ξ is incorporated into $thresh_{SCHISM}$. Outside this range however ($\xi > 15$), performance is severely degraded as the interval size becomes so small that very few contain enough points to be considered 'interesting'.

Effect of $thresh()$ function on performance Here we compare the performance of the $thresh()$ function given

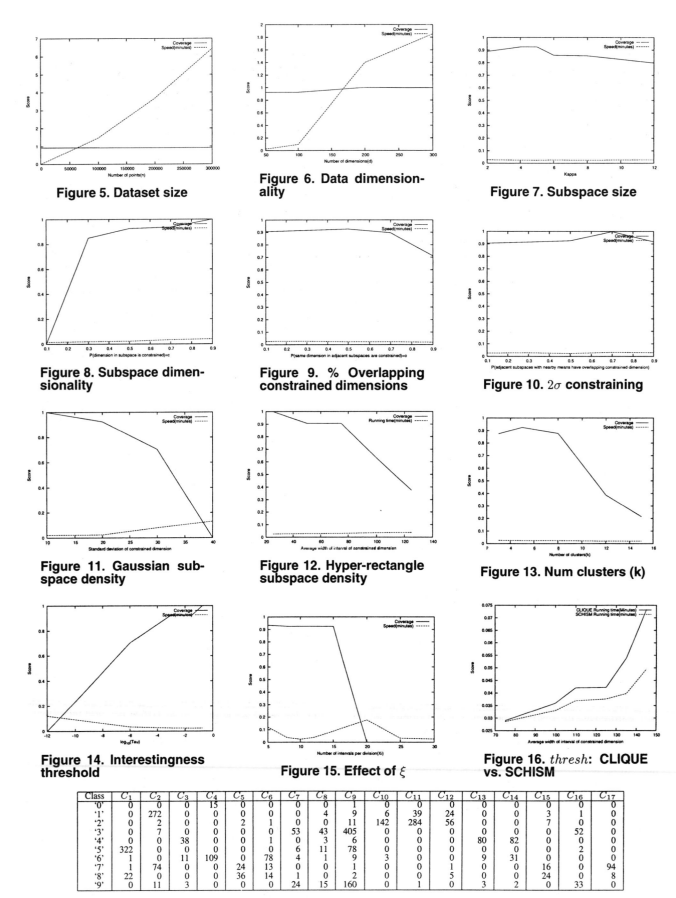

Figure 5. Dataset size

Figure 6. Data dimensionality

Figure 7. Subspace size

Figure 8. Subspace dimensionality

Figure 9. % Overlapping constrained dimensions

Figure 10. 2σ constraining

Figure 11. Gaussian subspace density

Figure 12. Hyper-rectangle subspace density

Figure 13. Num clusters (k)

Figure 14. Interestingness threshold

Figure 15. Effect of ξ

Figure 16. *thresh*: CLIQUE vs. SCHISM

Class	C_1	C_2	C_3	C_4	C_5	C_6	C_7	C_8	C_9	C_{10}	C_{11}	C_{12}	C_{13}	C_{14}	C_{15}	C_{16}	C_{17}
'0'	0	0	0	15	0	0	0	0	1	0	0	0	0	0	0	0	0
'1'	0	272	0	0	0	0	0	4	9	6	39	24	0	0	3	1	0
'2'	0	2	0	0	2	1	0	0	11	142	284	56	0	0	7	0	0
'3'	0	7	0	0	0	0	53	43	405	0	0	0	0	0	0	52	0
'4'	0	0	38	0	0	1	0	3	6	0	0	0	80	82	0	0	0
'5'	322	0	0	0	0	0	0	6	11	78	0	0	0	0	0	2	0
'6'	1	0	11	109	0	78	4	1	9	3	0	0	9	31	0	0	0
'7'	1	74	0	0	24	13	0	0	1	0	0	1	0	0	16	0	94
'8'	22	0	0	0	36	14	1	0	2	0	0	5	0	0	24	0	8
'9'	0	11	3	0	0	0	24	15	160	0	1	0	3	2	0	33	0

Figure 17. Confusion matrix for PenDigits dataset

in Eq. 4, with that of CLIQUE on the synthetic datasets. From Fig. 16, we observe that as the density of the hyper-rectangular clusters dips due to increase in the width of its constrained dimensions, the running time of CLIQUE [4] increases rapidly over that of SCHISM. Also, CLIQUE tends to split clusters into smaller ones. Its performance closely mirrors that of SCHISM for datasets having well-defined distinct clusters. However, when clusters overlap in a number of dimensions, the coverage and entropy suffers.

5.2. Real datasets

We apply SCHISM to two well researched datasets from different domains. The PenDigits dataset [5] [6] contains 7,494 16-dimensional vectors. 30 different writers wrote approximately 250 digits, sampled randomly from the digit set [0,9] on a pressure-sensitive tablet. Each vector corresponds to the (x, y) coordinates of 8 points, spatially sampled from each of these handwritten digits. Note that the embedded subspaces, i.e., the digits 0-9, overlap considerably in the 16-dimensional space. SCHISM outputs 128 subspaces in 4 seconds, of which the 17 clusters with the highest entropies are shown in the confusion matrix in Figure 17. It achieves a coverage of 69% and an entropy of 0.365 ($u = .01, \tau = 0.018$). CLIQUE achieves a coverage of 60.7% and an entropy of 0.49 in approximately 4 seconds too. As in DOC, ORCLUS, we provide a confusion matrix (Figure 17), which is interpreted as follows: cell (i, j) of the matrix denotes the number of points having true class i, which were clustered by SCHISM into subspace j. Ideally, each row and each column have only a single non-zero entry implying E(C)=0. Note that samples of the digits $\{3, 9\}$ are both assigned by SCHISM to clusters C_7, C_8, C_9 due to their similarity in structure. The clusters not shown typically have all their samples from the same digit class.

The other dataset is the gene expression data for the yeast cell cycle [6], obtained for 2884 genes (rows) at 17 (columns) points in time. We obtained a number of clusters of which a few were highly populated and the others relatively empty. Ideally, clustering gene expression data should produce clusters of genes which are similar in function. However, almost all the genes have multiple functions and hence genes cannot be labeled by a single class. The highly populated clusters we mined using SCHISM, contained groups of genes which are known to have strong similarity in terms of function, e.g., out of 5 genes in our dataset known (see www.yeastgenome.org) to be involved in ribonuclease MRP activity, 4 (POP4,POP5,POP8,SNM1) are assigned to the same cluster, 4 genes (SEC7,AGE1,SFT1,COG6) out of 6 involved in intra-Golgi transport, are assigned to the same cluster, etc. ($\xi = 5, \tau = 0.018$). While SCHISM finds 59 such groups of genes which are clustered together in larger clusters, CLIQUE finds only 33, both doing so in approximately 8.5 seconds.

While, we attempted to compare our algorithm performance with that of SUBCLU [17], we found default parameter setting for SUBCLU to be unsatisfactory and manual setting to be extremely hard, as it took an unreasonably long time (on the order of a number of hours) to produce output for our synthetic and real datasets. The clusters produced generally split the embedded clusters into distinct clusters.

---

[4]Our implementation of CLIQUE involves simply replacing $thresh_{SCHISM}$ with $thresh_{CLIQUE}$ in our implementation to test the significance of our threshold function.

[5]See ftp://ftp.ics.uci.edu/pub/machine-learning-databases/pendigits

[6]See http://arep.med.harvard.edu/biclustering/yeast.matrix

6. Conclusions

We define a new interestingness measure which provides absolute guarantees to the user about the interestingness of the subspaces reported, as per our definition of interesting. We use the interestingness measure itself to prune our search, as opposed to traditional methods[21], which determine interestingness of patterns after the search is completed, making the process faster. We use an algorithm which requires parameters which are relatively easy to set intuitively. These contributions can also be applied to the problem of finding interesting itemsets. The code for SCHISM is available at www.cs.rpi.edu/ sequek/schism

References

[1] C. Aggarwal. Towards systematic design of distance functions for data mining applications. In *SIGKDD Conf*, 2003.

[2] C. Aggarwal, C. Procopiuc, J. Wolf, P. Yu, and J. Park. A framework for finding projected clusters in high dimensional spaces. In *SIGMOD Conf*, 1999.

[3] C. Aggarwal and P. Yu. Finding generalized projected clusters in high-dimensional spaces. In *SIGMOD Conf*, 2000.

[4] R. Agrawal, J. Gehrke, D. Gunopulos, and P. Raghavan. Automatic subspace clustering of high dimensional data for data mining applications. In *SIGMOD Conf*, 1998.

[5] R. Agrawal, T. Imielinski, and A. Swami. Mining association rules between sets ofitems in large databases. In *SIGMOD Conf*, 1993.

[6] F. Alimoglu and E. Alpaydin. Methods of combining multiple classifiers based on different representations for pen-based handwriting recognition. In *Turkish AI and Neural Networks Symp*, 1996.

[7] K. Beyer, J. Goldstein, R. Ramakrishnan, U. Shaft. When is nearest neighbors meaningful? *ICDT Conf*, 1999.

[8] M. Brusco and J. Cradit. A variable selection heuristic for k-means clustering. *Psychometrika*, 66:249–270, 2001.

[9] K. Chakrabarti and S. Mehrotra. Local dimensionality reduction: A new approach to indexing high dimensional spaces. In *VLDB Conf*, 2000.

[10] C. Cheng, A. Fu, Y. Zhang. Entropy-based subspace clustering for mining numerical data. In *SIGKDD Conf*, 1999.

[11] H. Chernoff. A measure of asymptotic efficiency for tests of a hypothesis based on the sum of observations. *Annals of Math. Statistics*, 23:493–509, 1952.

[12] C. Ding, X. He, H. Zha, and H. Simon. Adaptive dimension reduction for clustering high-dimensional data. In *ICDM Conf*, 2002.

[13] K. Gouda and M. Zaki. Efficiently mining maximal frequent itemsets. In *ICDM Conf*, 2001.

[14] J. Han and M. Kamber. *Data Mining: Concepts and Techniques*. Morgan Kaufmann, San Francisco, CA, 2001.

[15] A. Hinneburg and D. Keim. Optimal grid-clustering: Towards breaking the curse of dimensionality in high-dimensional clustering. In *VLDB Conf*, 1999.

[16] W. Hoeffding. Probability inequalities for sums of bounded random variables. *J. American Statistical Association*, 58:13–30, 1963.

[17] K. Kailing, H. Kriegel, and P. Kroger. Density-connected subspace clustering for high-dimensional data. In *SIAM Data Mining Conf*, 2004.

[18] K. Kailing, H. Kriegel, P. Kroger, and S. Wanka. Ranking interesting subspaces for clustering high-dimensional data. In *European PKDD Conf*, 2003.

[19] H. Nagesh, S. Goil, and A. Choudhary. Adaptive grids for clustering massive data sets. In *SIAM Data Mining Conf*, 2001.

[20] C. Procopiuc, M. Jones, P. Agarwal, and T. Murali. A monte-carlo algorithm for fast projective clustering. In *SIGMOD Conf*, 2002.

[21] P. Tan, V. Kumar, and J. Srivastava. Selecting the right interestingness measure for association patterns. In *SIGKDD Conf*, 2002.

A Transaction-based Neighbourhood-driven Approach to Quantifying Interestingness of Association Rules

B. Shekar
Quantitative Methods and Information Systems Area
Indian Institute of Management Bangalore
Bannerghatta Road, Bangalore – 560 076
Karnataka, INDIA.
shek@iimb.ernet.in

Rajesh Natarajan
Information Technology and Systems Group
Indian Institute of Management Lucknow
Prabandh Nagar, Lucknow-226 013
Uttar Pradesh, INDIA.
rajeshn@iiml.ac.in

Abstract

In this paper, we present a data-driven approach for ranking association rules (ARs) based on interestingness. The occurrence of unrelated or weakly related item-pairs in an AR is interesting. In the retail market-basket context, items may be related through various relationships arising due to mutual interaction, 'substitutability' and 'complementarity.' Item-relatedness is a composite of these relationships. We introduce three relatedness measures for capturing relatedness between item-pairs. These measures use the concept of function embedding to appropriately weigh the relatedness contributions due to complementarity and substitutability between items. We propose an interestingness coefficient by combining the three relatedness measures. We compare this with two objective measures of interestingness and show the intuitiveness of the proposed interestingness coefficient.

1. Introduction

An important problem in association rule (AR) mining is the generation of a large number of mined rules. Usage of interestingness measures to rank ARs is a solution. Objective measures [1, 12, 13] quantify the interestingness of a rule in terms of rule structure and the underlying data used in rule generation. Subjective measures [2, 3, 4, 5, 6, 8, 10, 18], in addition incorporate views of the user while evaluating interestingness of patterns.

Here, we consider the retail market-basket context. ARs reveal items that are likely to be purchased together. ARs that contain weakly related or unrelated items are interesting. This is because frequent co-occurrence of such items is unexpected. We present a data-driven approach to evaluating interestingness.

The paper is organized as follows. In the following section, we adopt a functional point of view to classify

item interactions and the relationships arising from them. It should be noted that we consider only the transactions containing customer purchases. We introduce and intuitively evolve three measures for capturing various aspects of item-relatedness namely, MI (a modification of confidence), CI and SI. We present an illustrative example. The three item-relatedness measures are then combined to evolve a total relatedness coefficient (TR). We then develop an interestingness coefficient (I_C) using the basic relationship - relatedness and interestingness are mutually inverse concepts. We compare I_C with two commonly used objective measures of interestingness and bring out its intuitiveness.

2. Item Relatedness

Any item possesses many attributes or properties. A subset of these properties implies a function – the purpose for which the item is manufactured. We consider only this *primary function*. In addition, an item may also possess many secondary functions. We define a *simple function*, as a function that cannot be sub-divided i.e. it is atomic. A *compound function* is one that is realized by combining one or more simple or compound functions. A scenario or situation may consist of many such functions. A set of items possessing these functions to varying extents satisfies the scenario either partially or completely. A combination of many related scenarios constitutes a context, for example, a household context, an industrial context, etc.

Interacting functions give rise to relationships between the items. Any two items can be related through many such relationships. *Item-relatedness* is a composite of these relationships. Relatedness is influenced by two attributes, strength of a relationship and cardinality of the set of relationships. Relatedness is directly proportional to the strength and also to the cardinality. Consider two items x and y. When they are brought together in a context, their primary functions may interact in one of the following ways.

2.1. Complementarity

Two items may be termed complementary if they together find application. The primary function of item x may need the primary function of item y when they are used together. This interaction between the two primary functions gives rise to a new compound function f. For example, a knife and a fork can be considered complementary to each other. The attribute of sharpness enables a knife to cut objects. A fork is needed to hold the object. Absence of any one of the items usually inhibits the effective execution of the compound function.

We identify two shades of complementarity; *intrinsic* and *flexible*. The primary functions of two items, say x and y, may be inextricably bound together. Also, x and y may not serve any meaningful function independently. The compound function f, implied by the primary functions of items x and y can be realized if and only if the two items function together. We refer to this type of complementarity as *intrinsic complementarity*. For example, consider the case of a 0.5 mm clutch pencil and 0.5 mm leads. Though these items are sold separately in a retail store they are intrinsically complementary to each other. Neither of them can be used separately for writing on a piece of paper. Consider another situation in which the primary functions of two items not only interact with each other but also combine with primary functions of other items to imply different functions. For example, items x and y may interact with item z in one situation to imply function f_1. In another scenario, the same two items may interact with item w to imply function f_2. *Flexible complementarity* is the ability of the primary functions of two items to serve multiple functions. In general, complementary items tend to be purchased together in purchase transactions.

2.2. Substitutability

An item functionally *substitutes* another item if it serves the other's function to a significant extent. Thus, a pen can substitute a pencil as far as the function of writing on paper is concerned. Substitutes have similar or closely related primary functions. In general, substitutes belong to the same generic category. Generally, substitution is with respect to one single function in a particular context. Although substitutes are not used together, they are strongly related. Two items that substitute each other are likely to possess many similar or closely related attributes. If two items are substitutes to each other, then they are not likely to be purchased in the same transaction. However, two substitutable items are likely to be bought with identical or similar items that go with them, in separate transactions.

2.3. Non-dependence

In case of *non-dependence*, the primary functions of x and y do not interact with each other to serve any other compound function. Primary functions of x and y, however, may separately find application in different domains and different contexts. Since their functions do not interact, the likelihood of being used together in the same or similar contexts is quite low. Non-dependent items are likely to be from different domains, for example, kitchen knife and 0.5 mm lead. A combination of non-dependent items is unlikely to be purchased with a frequency higher than the product of the expected frequencies of the individual items.

Relatedness between two items increases if complementarity and substitutability increases. A pair of items can take shades of complementarity and substitutability depending on the context. Therefore, on some occasions, we do find substitutes being purchased together in the same transaction. Two items can exhibit different relationships depending on the function demanded and the context. In this paper, we are concerned only with the primary functions of items.

3. Measures for Item Relatedness

We clarify some of the assumptions regarding customer purchasing behaviour that we make in our approach to item relatedness. First, we assume that items are purchased mainly for their primary function. Hence, we are concerned mainly with primary functions of items. Next, we assume that customers purchase items mainly for self or family consumption over a short period. Consequently, item usage patterns get reflected in customer purchasing behaviour. Hence, we draw conclusions about relatedness of items by examining customer transactions.

Consider a database of retail market-basket transactions. Let I be the set of items available for sale in the retail market. I= {a, b, c, ...}. Database D consists of a set of transactions, T. Each transaction t consists of a set of items purchased by a customer on a single buying instance at a retail store. Thus, $x \in t \Rightarrow x \in I$; $t \subseteq I$.

Let x and y be two items occurring in an association rule whose relatedness is of interest to us. This means that $\frac{|t_{xy}|}{|t|} \geq minsup$ where |t| is the total number of transactions in the database. Let t_x represent the set of transactions that contains item x but not y; t_y represent the set consisting of transactions containing item y but not x, and t_{xy} represent the set consisting of transactions containing both x and y. Each transaction in t_x, t_y and t_{xy} might contain items other than x and y accordingly. The remaining transactions contain neither of the two items. In order to compute relatedness between items x and y, we need to examine t_{xy} and neighbourhood items in t_x, t_y and t_{xy}. Other items purchased with items x and y, can also contribute substantially to their relatedness if they are similar. This is because x and y might find applicability with other items in many more contexts than all by themselves. This increases their usefulness and relatedness.

Let Z be the set of items/item-sets purchased together with x and y. In particular, an item-set $z \in$ Z if

$$\frac{|t_{xyz}|}{|t_{xy}|} \geq minsup$$ where *minsup* is user-specified threshold.

The item-set z and the set Z are called *co-occurring neighbour* of {x,y} and *co-occurring neighbourhood* respectively. Co-occurring neighbours are likely to be used together with items {x,y}. Therefore, a relationship exists between co-occurring neighbours and item-pair {x,y}. Similarly, let M and N be item-sets that are purchased with items x and y in transaction sets t_x and t_y respectively. Then, M∩N is the set of item-sets that are purchased with each of x and y separately. We call set M∩N the *non co-occurring neighbourhood* of {x,y} and each item w∈ M∩N the *non co-occurring neighbour*. It should be noted that "neighbourhood", as defined above, represents the item-set frequently purchased along with a specific item-pair. A context, on the other hand, is a combination of many related scenarios each of which may refer to a set of items. A context is not specific to any particular item-pair. All neighbours of {x,y} need not occur in a context containing {x,y}. Here again we assume that items comprising sets M and N occur in respective transactions in significant numbers. In addition, transaction sets t_x and t_y are also assumed to be significant.

3.1. M_I (Mutual Interaction)

A customer is likely to purchase items that are used together in the same transaction. Thus, two items x and y, are related if they are purchased together in large numbers. The more the co-occurrence, greater is the relatedness. Co-occurrence of the two items implies that the function of item x and the function of items y interact with each other in a useful way. This gives rise to a compound function. However, the frequency of item x in transactions containing y need not equal the frequency of item y in transactions containing x. The presence of item x in transactions containing y can be stronger than the presence of item y in transactions containing x. This aspect is not captured if we consider only t_{xy}. We try to capture this aspect through mutual interaction measure, M_I, given by:

$$M_I = 0.5 \times \left[\frac{f(xy)}{f(x)} + \frac{f(xy)}{f(y)} \right] \quad (1)$$

where, f(xy) is the total number of transactions containing items x and y together i.e. $|t_{xy}|$; f(x) is the total number of transactions in which item x occurs, either alone or along with other items which is $|t_x|+|t_{xy}|$; f(y) is the total number of transactions in which item *y* occurs which is $|t_y|+|t_{xy}|$.

From (1), it can be seen that M_I equals the average confidence of ARs x→y and y→x. In other words, M_I gives the predictive ability of the presence of one item given the other. Thus, M_I gives us a numerical estimate of the mutual interaction of items x and y in the database. It does not consider the presence of other items that may occur with x, y, or both. M_I can take a value in the range [0,1]. When items x and y are never purchased with each other, then M_I takes a value of 0. If the two items are intrinsically complementary to each other (x always occurring with y and vice versa) then the values of f(xy), f(x) and f(y) become equal and M_I takes a value of 1. Suppose x and y are perfectly substitutable with respect to their primary functions. This is reflected in their never being purchased together in transactions. Then, the value of f(xy) approaches 0 and M_I also approaches 0. It should be noted that M_I is computed by considering the value of f(xy) only. On the other hand, the statistical measure correlation [11] considers both the presence and absence of items while computing linear dependency between items. A large positive correlation coefficient does not distinguish between presence (of both the items) and absence. Either of f(xy), f(¬x¬y) might be large.

3.2. Function Embedding

The concept of *function embedding* helps us in deciding the relevant relationships to be included while calculating relatedness between items. Consider P={x, a, b, c}. We do not consider transactions containing P while evaluating its subsets as frequent/infrequent. While calculating its relatedness we need to assign a larger weight to it as compared to its frequently purchased subsets {x, a}, {x, b} and {x, a, b}. Transaction data decides the relevance of a particular function. Consider subset {x, a, c} of P. This subset does not imply a relevant function since it does not feature in the frequently purchased market baskets. Therefore, while assigning a weight to P we do not consider subset {x, a, c}.

The implied function of a set assigns a weight of 1 to it. In addition, each of its subsets purchased in separate transactions and in significant numbers assigns a weight of 1. Thus, set P is assigned a weight of 4. Sets {x, a}, {x, b} and {x, a, b} each contribute a weight of 1 to it. Similarly, {x, a, b} is assigned a weight of 3. It should be noted that while calculating the weight of P, {x, a, b}'s contribution is 1 (and not 3). This is because {x, a, b} implies one function different from its subsets. The functions of its subsets {x, a} and {x, b} have already been taken into account by their contributions to the weight of P. By assigning a weight of 1 to {x, a, b} we avoid double counting the weights of {x, a} and {x, b}. Note that the number of non-empty subsets of P is 15.

3.3. C_I (Intensity of Complementarity)

Two items {x, y} are complementary if they are used together in significant numbers. Other items purchased with {x, y} give an indication of the different relationships that may exist between x and y. Complementarity of {x,y} increases if this pair can be used together with other items in different situations. Note that an item-set {a, b} and its subset {a} can both be considered as co-occurring neighbours of {x, y} if and only if both are individually purchased with {x, y} in significant numbers. While considering the significance of the occurrence of set {a} along with {x, y} we do not consider its occurrence in set {a, b}. This is because we consider sets {a} and {a, b} as separate sets that serve different functions.

Let Z be the set of all co-occurring neighbours of {x, y}. Note that each element of Z can be either a single item or a set of items. The intensity of complementarity is given by:

$$C_I = 0 \qquad \text{if } |Z|=0 \text{ i.e. } Z=\phi$$
$$= \frac{1}{f(xy)} \times \sum_{z \in Z} [Wt(z) \times f(xyz)] \quad \text{(Otherwise)} \qquad (2)$$

where, $Wt(z)$ is the weight of the itemset z. The weight of item set z is assigned as follows. $Wt(z)=1+p$, where p is the number of subsets of z that occur in Z. Thus, C_I measures the intensity of flexible complementarity only and not intrinsic complementarity.

3.4. S_I (Intensity of Substitutability)

Item-sets in the non co-occurrence neighbourhood of {x,y} contribute to this relatedness between them. Consider an item w present in the non co-occurrence neighbourhood of {x,y}. Thus, items x and y can substitute each other in the presence of item set $w \in (M \cap N)$. If there are many such cases of x and y substituting each other with respect to different item sets from their non co-occurring neighbourhood the relatedness of {x, y} increases. This is because items x and y can substitute each other with respect to many functions. Common attributes between x and y in turn imply greater relatedness. We try to capture this aspect through measure S_I. S_I is given by:

$$S_I = 0 \qquad \text{if } (M \cap N)=\phi$$
$$= \sum_{w \in M \cap N} Wt(w) \times [1 - |\alpha_w - \beta_w|] \quad \text{(Otherwise)} \qquad (3)$$

where, $\alpha_w = \dfrac{f(xw) - f(xyw)}{f(x) - f(xy)}$ and $\beta_w = \dfrac{f(yw) - f(xyw)}{f(y) - f(xy)}$.

$\alpha_w, \beta_w \geq Sig$, where Sig is a user-defined threshold. $Wt(w)$ is the weightage of the item set w. $Wt(w)=1+v$; where v is the number of subsets of $w \in M \cap N$.

The weight of an item-set gives an indication of the number of useful functions implied by w. α_w gives the proportion of transactions containing x (and not y) with item set w in it. Similarly, β_w gives the proportion of transactions containing y (and not x) with w. $\alpha_w, \beta_w \geq Sig$ ensures that item-set w occurs in a significant portion of t_x and t_y. $|\alpha_w - \beta_w|$ gives the deviation of this proportionate occurrence of item-set w with items x and y in t_x and t_y respectively. Intuitively, we can expect substitutes to interact in a similar manner with respect to items they substitute. Therefore, if x and y substitute each other perfectly with respect to w, α_w and β_w can be expected to be nearly equal and $|\alpha_w-\beta_w|$ will take a value close to 0. At this point the deviation is the lowest and we should get highest value for substitutability contribution i.e. weight of the item-set w. Greater the deviation $|\alpha_w- \beta_w|$, lower the relatedness. Therefore, we subtract $|\alpha_w- \beta_w|$ from 1 to give the contribution of w to relatedness due to substitutability.

We have used two filters to ensure that substitutability contributions from non co-occurring neighbours are significant. The first filter ensures that the size of t_x is significant. This is done by checking if $\dfrac{|t_x|}{|t_x| + |t_{xy}|}$ is greater than a threshold, say, *minsup*. If it is less, then we can say that none of the non co-occurring neighbours of the set {x,y} will contribute significantly to substitutability. Then, S_I can be directly assigned a value of 0. The second filter considers the frequency of non co-occurring neighbours of x in t_x. $\alpha_w, \beta_w \geq Sig$ ensures that item-set w occurs in a significant portion of t_x and t_y of the database.

3.5. Total Relatedness (TR) Coefficient

Total relatedness coefficient TR is the sum of the values of the three relatedness measures. Thus,

$$TR= M_I + C_I + S_I \qquad (4)$$

The rationale for the summation is as follows. Relatedness between x and y is a composite of relationships existing between them. Stronger and larger number of relationships implies greater relatedness. Therefore, TR includes both the strength of relationships and the number of relationships between x and y. As can be observed from Equation 1, M_I reveals the strength of only one relationship i.e. mutual interaction between x and y. Its value varies in the range [0, 1]. C_I and S_I bring out the intensity of complementarity and substitutability between the two items. Complementarity is due to the interaction between item sets present in {x,y}'s co-occurring neighbourhood and {x,y}. On the other hand, substitutability is a consequence of the

Table 1. A sample data set

Tran-saction	Nos.	Tran-saction	Nos.	Tran-saction	Nos.	Tran-saction	Nos.	Tran-saction	Nos.	Tran-saction	Nos.
{a,d,f}	3	{a,b}	2	{a,e}	2	{b,c,e,f}	4	{b,e,f}	3	{c,d,e}	4
{d,f}	1	{a,b,c}	4	{a,e,f}	3	{b,c,e}	4	{a,b,c,d}	3	{c.d}	5
{b,e}	2	{a,b,d}	4	{a,f}	2	{b,d}	3	{b,f}	1		

Table 2. Relatedness values for item-pairs occurring in association rules

Sr. No.	Pair	Z *	M∩N *	M_I	C_I	S_I	TR
1	{a, b}	{{c}, {d}, {c, d}}	{{e}, {e, f}}	0.4993	1.3077	2.6705	**4.4775**
2	{e, f}	{{a}, {b}, {b, c}}	{{a}, {b}}	0.5214	1.4	1.8571	**3.7785**
3	{b, e}	{{c}, {f}, {c, f}}	{a}	0.5121	1.4615	0.8954	**2.869**
4	{b, c}	{{a}, {a, d}, {e}, {e, f}}	{d}	0.5625	1.4667	0.575	**2.6042**
5	{c, e}	{{b}, {d}, {b, f}}	{φ}	0.5227	1.3333	0	**1.856**

Z and M∩N are the respective co-occurring and non co-occurring neighbourhoods.

interaction between {x,y}'s non co-occurring neighbourhood and {x,y}. Each item set that interacts with {x, y} contributes to one instance of a relationship. The strength of the relationship is revealed by the frequency of occurrence of the item set. Therefore, C_I and S_I are assigned values depending on the cardinality and strength of relationships between x and y. Consequently, values of C_I and S_I may exceed 1.

Table 1 shows every transaction and the number of occurrences in the database. Each transaction, a subset of the set of six items {a, b, c, d, e, f}, represents purchases by a customer during a single buying instance at a mall. Though the data set given in Table 1 is small, with respect to both transactions and items, it is sufficient to demonstrate the efficacy of the relatedness measures. Item b that occurs in 30 transactions is the most frequently occurring item. {b, c} is the most frequent 2-itemset with 15 occurrences. The most frequent 3-itemset {b, c, e} occurs in 8 transactions. ARs were mined using a minimum support threshold of 15% and a minimum confidence threshold of 50%. This gave rise to ten ARs satisfying the minimum support and minimum confidence constraints. Relatedness measures M_I, C_I and S_I were computed for those item pairs that occurred in at least one AR. The first filter (checking for the significance of t_x and t_y) was not applied while calculating S_I. However, the second filter (α_w, $\beta_w \geq 0.10$) was applied during the computation of S_I. The results of the computations are given in Table 2.

4. From Relatedness to Interestingness

TR reveals the total relatedness of an item-pair based on information contained in transactions. Relatedness contributions due to substitutability and complementarity components for two unrelated items such as {beer, diaper} may not be high. Hence, TR will be assigned a low value. On the other hand, two related items may be expected to have similar or closely related properties. Many complementarity and substitutability relationships may arise due to these closely related properties. Hence two related items, such as {bread, butter}, can be expected to have a high TR value. From the relatedness perspective, a rule containing {beer, diaper} would be deemed more interesting than a rule containing {bread, butter}. However, in general, an AR contains more than one item-pair. Therefore, we need one consolidated value that represents the AR rather than any one of its item-pairs. It can be intuitively argued that the relatedness of a set of items is driven by the least related item-pair in it [6]. Let $\{a_1, a_2, ..., a_n\} \rightarrow \{b_1, b_2, ..., b_m\}$ represent an AR. $^{(m+n)}C_2$ item pairs can be formed from this AR. Let the least related item-pair among these $^{(m+n)}C_2$ item-pairs be {x,y} and its total relatedness coefficient be TR(x,y).

Since relatedness and interestingness are opposing notions, the interestingness of an AR can be given by:

$$I_C = \frac{^{(m+n)}C_2 \times k}{TR(x,y)} \quad (5)$$

In Equation 5, we have weighted the interestingness coefficient by the number of item-pairs in the rule.

Table 3. Comparison of I_C with Conviction (V) and Interest (Int)

Sr. No.	Association Rule	Support	Confidence	TR*	I_C	Conviction (V)	Interest (Int)
1	{c, e}→{b}	0.16	0.6667	1.8560	1.6164	1.2000	1.1100
2	{b, e}→{c}	0.16	0.6154	1.8560	1.6164	1.3520	1.2821
3	{b, c}→{e}	0.16	0.5333	1.8560	1.6164	1.2000	1.2121
4	{c}→{e}	0.24	0.50	1.8560	0.5388	1.12	1.1364
5	{e}→{c}	0.24	0.5454	1.8560	0.5388	1.144	1.1364
6	{b}→{c}	0.30	0.50	2.6042	0.3840	1.04	1.0417
7	{c}→{b}	0.30	0.625	2.6042	0.3840	1.0667	1.04167
8	{e}→{b}	0.26	0.5909	2.869	0.3486	0.9778	0.9848
9	{f}→{e}	0.20	0.588	3.7785	0.2647	1.3600	1.3368
10	{a}→{b}	0.26	0.5652	4.4775	0.2233	0.92	0.9420

TR value of the least related item-pair in a rule is displayed when the rule has more than two items.

Consider two ARs: AR_1 and AR_2. Let the least-related item pair in both rules be the same. If AR_1 has more items than AR_2, then AR_1 can be more interesting than AR_2. This is because AR_1 brings out more relationships with the most interesting pair. This intuition leads us to weighing the interestingness of an AR by the cardinality of item-pairs in it. In Equation 5, k is the constant of proportionality. The importance given to the cardinality of item-pairs in a rule can be altered by assigning an appropriate value to 'k'. A value of k<1 decreases the contribution of the cardinality of item pairs to I_C. Here, I_C has been calculated using k=1. Finally, we note that TR(x,y) can never be zero. This is because each item-pair of an AR has a relatedness component due to co-occurrence, namely M_I. Since {x, y} is selected from an AR, M_I will have a value not less than the minimum support. Note that in any AR, $\dfrac{f(x,y)}{f(x)} \geq \dfrac{f(x,y)}{|D|}$, since $|D| \geq f(x)$, $|D|$ being the total number of transactions in the database.

Table 3 contains information about the 10 ARs mined from the transaction set given in Table 1. The ARs have been ordered in the descending order of their interestingness using I_C. I_C assigns identical values (0.5388) to rules {c}→{e} and {e}→{c}. This is because the TR coefficient from which I_C is derived, considers antecedent and consequent of a rule in a symmetric fashion. M_I component of TR considers the average predictive ability of an item in the presence of the other.

Rule {c,e}→{b} gets the highest I_C value of 1.6164. This is due to two factors: the presence of the least related item-pair {c,e}, and the weight accorded to the number of item-pairs in the rule. Item-pair {c,e} has a low TR value of 1.856. In addition, the rule has three item-pairs. We can

contrast this to a single item-pair AR, {c}→{e}. It is assigned an I_C value of 0.5388. This is despite {c}→{e} having the same least related item-pair as in rule {c,e}→{b}. Thus, we observe that I_C is larger if: (1) The least related item-pair of the rule has a low relatedness value. (2) The rule has many item-pairs.

Rule {a}→{b} is assigned the lowest I_C value of 0.2233. It has the highest TR value. This is because items a and b are effective substitutes of each other. They are not strongly related due to co-occurrence or complementarity. This component of relatedness due to substitutability is ignored by support and confidence.

From Table 3, it can be seen that the most interesting rule does not have the highest support. In addition, some of the least interesting rules, namely {a}→{b} and {f}→{e} have high confidence values of 0.5652 and 0.588 respectively. This is because support and confidence do not consider the other relationships considered by I_C, namely substitutability and complementarity. This observation corroborates our viewpoint that all relationships between item-pairs need to be examined to bring out the item-pair's interestingness. Support and confidence may be used as preliminary filters to select significant rules. The selected rules can then be ordered by I_C.

5. Comparative Analysis

We compare I_C with two commonly used objective measures of interestingness present in the data mining literature. The chosen measures are *Conviction* (V) [12, 15] and *Interest* (Int) [12, 15, 16, 19]. *Conviction* is considered to have an edge over *confidence* with respect to measuring implication [15]. Int is essentially a measure of departure from independence. Int=1 if the two items are completely independent. However, by being symmetric it measures only co-occurrence and not implication.

Consider the 2-item rules. V measures the strength of implication. Therefore, in general we can say that higher V values mean antecedent items and consequent items are strongly related. Rules having higher V-values should be less interesting from relatedness viewpoint. Thus, higher values of conviction should be related to lower I_C values. Consider rule $\{f\} \rightarrow \{e\}$. This rule is assigned a high V-value of 1.3600. Its I_C value is also low (0.2647). In this example, V and I_C seem to be related as expected. We note that item-pair $\{f,e\}$ has a high TR- value of 3.7785 due to the large contribution from S_I.

However, from Table 3 we see that in general, rules having higher I_C values have higher V values. For example, rule $\{e\} \rightarrow \{c\}$ has an I_C and V value of 0.5388 and 1.144 respectively. On the other hand, rule $\{b\} \rightarrow \{c\}$ which has a lower I_C value of 0.3840 also has a lower V-value (1.04) as compared to $\{e\} \rightarrow \{c\}$. According to V, relatedness of $\{e,c\}$ is more than that of $\{b,c\}$. The V-values imply that $\{b,c\}$ is more interesting than $\{e,c\}$, while I_C values seem to suggest the reverse. This apparent counter intuitive result can be explained if we examine the TR components for pairs $\{e,c\}$ and $\{b,c\}$. The pair $\{e, c\}$ has a lower TR value as compared to the pair $\{b, c\}$ mainly due to $\{e, c\}$'s S_I value being assigned a value of 0. This results in $\{e,c\}$ being assigned a higher I_C value than $\{b,c\}$. Since V ignores components of relatedness due to substitutability and complementarity, interesting rules brought out by V may not give the complete picture.

Consider the Int values. Brijs, et al. [19] give an 'economical' interpretation of *Interest*. For an AR $\{a\} \rightarrow \{b\}$, *Interest* > 1 indicates complementarity effects between a and b while *Interest* < 1 indicates substitutability effects. Items a and b are conditionally independent when *Interest* = 1. Consider rule $\{e\} \rightarrow \{b\}$. It has an Int value of 0.9848 and an I_C value of 0.3486. From the economic interpretation of Int, items e and b should be substitutes. However, from Table 2 we see that C_I value of $\{e, b\}$ (1.4615) is greater than its S_I value (0.8954). Thus, items e and b are also complementary. This aspect is not brought out by Int.

Consider rule $\{a\} \rightarrow \{b\}$. It has an Int-value of 0.9420 while I_C assigns a value of 0.2233 to it. The Int value indicates that a and b are substitutes for each other. This is confirmed by the S_I component (2.6705) of the TR coefficient for $\{a, b\}$. There also exists some degree of complementarity between items a and b. This again is not brought out by Int. Another observation pertaining to rule $\{c,e\} \rightarrow \{b\}$ is as follows. I_C assigns the highest value of 1.6164 to it, whereas the values assigned by V and Int are 1.200 and 1.11 respectively. We cannot infer from the V and Int values that the rule $\{c, e\} \rightarrow \{b\}$ is the most interesting one of the ten rules.

V and Int do not explicitly account for the number of item pairs in a rule or give additional weightage to the most interesting pair in a rule. This might result in counter-intuitive results as shown in the following example. Consider the rule $\{c,e\} \rightarrow \{b\}$ and its sub-rule $\{c\} \rightarrow \{b\}$. We note that the item pair $\{c,e\}$ in $\{c,e\} \rightarrow \{b\}$ is less related than $\{c,b\}$. Also, $\{c,e\} \rightarrow \{b\}$ has three item pairs while $\{c\} \rightarrow \{b\}$ has only one. Therefore, according to I_C rule $\{c,e\} \rightarrow \{b\}$ (1.6164) is more interesting than $\{c\} \rightarrow \{b\}$ (0.3840). V values for $\{c,e\} \rightarrow \{b\}$ and $\{c\} \rightarrow \{b\}$ are 1.20 and 1.0667 respectively. This means that the items in the first rule are more dependent on each other and hence less interesting. Similarly, Int values for $\{c,e\} \rightarrow \{b\}$ and $\{c\} \rightarrow \{b\}$ are 1.110 and 1.04167 respectively. This seems to suggest that item c and item b are more independent and hence rule $\{c\} \rightarrow \{b\}$ is more interesting. This seems to be counter-intuitive as $\{c\} \rightarrow \{b\}$ is contained in $\{c,e\} \rightarrow \{b\}$. In addition, it conveys less knowledge about the domain than $\{c,e\} \rightarrow \{b\}$.

All items in the antecedent and consequent are considered while computing V and Int. This can lead to the masking of the contribution of the least related item-pair. V and Int do not consider substitutability and complementarity relationships explicitly. Therefore, interestingness rankings based on I_C values are more intuitive than those due to V and Int.

6. Discussions

Objective measures like *support* [1, 12], *confidence* [1, 12], *conviction* [12, 15] and *interest* [12, 15, 16] have been extensively used in data mining studies. Hilderman and Hamilton [13] survey seventeen interestingness measures from the data mining literature. Tan, Kumar and Srivatsava [12] have described several key properties that can be used to select the right objective measure for a given application. Our approach is different from the traditional approaches [12, 13]. Jaroszewicz and Simovici [17] have proposed a measure that is a generalization of many conditional and unconditional classical measures. Omiecinski [7] has proposed three alternative interestingness measures for associations: any-confidence, all-confidence and bond. Our work is quite different from these two studies on two counts. We consider classical association rules in a retail-market basket context. Secondly, in the studies mentioned, relationships have not explicitly been taken into account.

Meo [14] has proposed a new model to evaluate dependencies in data mining problems. Our study also focuses on dependencies between items. However, we try to discern interestingness of ARs by using relatedness based on relationships between item-pairs. Brijs, et al. [19] have introduced a micro-economic integer-programming model for product selection (PROFSET).

Our approach considers the simultaneous existence of complementarity and substitutability unlike Brijs, et al. [19]. Substitution rules were introduced by Teng and others [20]. According to them, an item-set X is a substitute for Y if X and Y are negatively correlated along with the existence of a negative AR ($X \rightarrow \neg Y$) in mined rule set. On the other hand, in our approach, the degree of substitutability (a component of relatedness) of an item pair {x, y} is computed by identifying item-sets that occur in {x, y}'s non co-occurring neighbourhood. Other relationships like flexible complementarity and mutual interaction have also been considered in our approach. Dong and Li [9] have presented a method of evaluating interestingness of ARs in terms of neighbourhood-based unexpectedness. The neighbourhood of a rule is defined in terms of a distance function on rules. In our work, we consider both co-occurring and non co-occurring neighbours of items. We also compare our interestingness coefficient (I_C) with two objective measures of interestingness *Conviction* (V) and *Interest* (Int). It is seen that I_C compares favourably with V and Int in ranking ARs. I_C also takes into account aspects of relatedness not accounted for by V and Int, thus making it more intuitively appealing. I_C treats the antecedent and consequent of an AR in a symmetric fashion. As a part of our future work, we propose to examine the feasibility of generalizing I_C to account for directionality of ARs. In addition, we also propose to apply the suggested framework on real-life datasets.

7. References

[1] A. A. Freitas. On Rule Interestingness Measures. *Knowledge-Based Systems*, 12, 1999, pp. 309-315.

[2] A. Silberschatz, and A. Tuzhilin. What makes Patterns Interesting in Knowledge Discovery Systems. *IEEE Transactions on Knowledge and Data Engineering*, 8(6), 1996, pp. 970-974.

[3] B. Liu, W. Hsu, L. Mun, and H. Lee. Finding Interesting Patterns Using User Expectations. *IEEE Transactions on Knowledge and Data Engineering*, 11(6), 1999, pp. 817-832.

[4] B. Liu, W. Hsu, S. Chen, and Y. Ma. Analyzing the Subjective Interestingness of Association Rules. *IEEE Intelligent Systems*, 15(5), 2000, pp. 47-55.

[5] B. Padmanabhan, and A. Tuzhilin. Unexpectedness as a Measure of Interestingness in Knowledge Discovery. *Decision Support Systems*, 27(3), 1999, pp. 303-318.

[6] B. Shekar, and R. Natarajan. A Framework for Evaluating Knowledge-based Interestingness of Association Rules. *Fuzzy Optimization and Decision Making*, 3(2), June 2004, pp. 157-185.

[7] E. R. Omiecinski. Alternative Interest Measures for Mining Associations in Databases. *IEEE Transactions on*

[8] G. Adomavicius, and A. Tuzhilin. Discovery of Actionable Patterns in Databases: The Action Hierarchy Approach. *Proceedings of the Third International Conference on Knowledge Discovery and Data Mining(KDD –1997)*, AAAI, 1997, pp. 111-114.

[9] G. Dong, and J. Li. Interestingness of Discovered Association Rules in Terms of Neighborhood-Based Unexpectedness. *Proceedings of the Second Pacific-Asia Conference on Knowledge Discovery and Data Mining*, 1998, pp.72-86.

[10] J. F. Roddick, and S. Rice. What's Interesting About Cricket? – On Thresholds and Anticipation in Discovered Rules. *SIGKDD Explorations*, 3(1), 2001, pp. 1-5.

[11] P. Tan, and V. Kumar. Interestingness Measures for Association Patterns: A Perspective. *KDD'2000 Workshop on Postprocessing in Machine Learning and Data Mining*, Boston, MA, August 2000.

[12] P. Tan, V. Kumar, V. and J. Srivastava. Selecting the Right Interestingness Measure for Association Patterns. *Information Systems*, 29(4), June 2004, pp. 293-331.

[13] R. J. Hilderman, and H. J. Hamilton. Knowledge Discovery and Interestingness Measures: A Survey, *Technical Report*, Department of Computer Science, University of Regina, Canada, 1999.

[14] R. Meo. Theory of Dependence Values. *ACM Transactions on Database Systems*, 25(3), September 2000, pp. 380-406.

[15] S. Brin, R. Motwani, and C. Silverstein. Beyond Market Baskets: Generalizing Association Rules to Correlations. *Proceedings of the 1997 ACM SIGMOD International Conference on Management of Data*, May 1997, pp.265-276.

[16] S. Brin, R. Motwani, J. D. Ullman, and S. Tsur. Dynamic Itemset Counting and Implication Rules for Market Basket Data. *Proceedings of the ACM SIGMOD International Conference on Management of Data*, May 1997, pp. 255-264.

[17] S. Jaroszewicz, and D. A. Simovici. A General Measure of Rule Interestingness. *Proceedings of the 5th European Conference on Principles of Data Mining and Knowledge Discovery (PKDD 2001)*, Springer-Verlag, LNAI 2168, Freiburg, September 2001, pp. 253-266.

[18] S. Sahar. Interestingness Via What is Not Interesting. Proceedings of the 5th ACM, SIGKDD International Conference on Knowledge Discovery and Data Mining, 1999, pp. 332-336.

[19] T. Brijs, G. Swinnen, K. Vanhoof, and G. Wets. Building and Association Rules Framework to Improve Product Assortment Decisions. *Data Mining and knowledge Discovery*, 8, 2004, pp. 7-23.

[20] W. Teng, M. Hsieh, and M. Chen. On the Mining of Substitution Rules for Statistically Dependent Items. *Proceedings of IEEE International Conference on Data Mining (ICDM'02)*, 2002, pp. 442-449.

Probabilistic Principal Surfaces for Yeast Gene Microarray Data Mining

Antonino Staiano, Lara De Vinco, Angelo Ciaramella, Giancarlo Raiconi, Roberto Tagliaferri
Dipartimento di Matematica ed Informatica
Università di Salerno
Via Ponte don Melillo, 84084 Fisciano (Sa), Italy
{astaiano, ciaram, gianni, robtag}@unisa.it

Roberto Amato, Giuseppe Longo, Ciro Donalek, Gennaro Miele
Dipartimento di Scienze Fisiche
Università Federico II di Napoli and INFN Napoli Unit
Polo delle Scienze e della Tecnologia
via Cintia 6, 80136 Napoli, Italy
{longo, donalek, miele}@na.infn.it

Diego Di Bernardo
Telethon Institute for Genetics and Medicine
Via Pietro Castellino 111 I-80131 Napoli, Italy
dibernard@tigem.it

Abstract

The recent technological advances are producing huge data sets in almost all fields of scientific research, from astronomy to genetics. Although each research field often requires ad-hoc, fine tuned, procedures to properly exploit all the available information inherently present in the data, there is an urgent need for a new generation of general computational theories and tools capable to boost most human activities of data analysis. Here we propose Probabilistic Principal Surfaces (PPS) as an effective high-D data visualization and clustering tool for data mining applications, emphasizing its flexibility and generality of use in data-rich field. In order to better illustrate the potentialities of the method, we also provide a real world case-study by discussing the use of PPS for the analysis of yeast gene expression levels from microarray chips.

1 Introduction

Across a wide variety of fields, data is being collected and accumulated at a dramatic pace. There is an urgent need for a new generation of computational theories and tools to assist humans in extracting useful information (knowledge) from rapidly growing volumes of data. These theo-ries and tools are usually labeled as Knowledge Discovery in Databases (KDD). At an abstract level, the *KDD* field is concerned with the development of methods and techniques aimed at extracting *meaning* out of data. The full and effective scientific exploitation of these massive data sets calls for the implementation of automatic tools capable to perform a large fraction of data mining and data analysis work, and is posing considerable technical problems and even more challenging methodological ones. Traditional data analysis methods, in fact, are inadequate to cope with such exponential growth in the data volume and especially in the data complexity (ten or hundreds of dimensions of the parameter space) [10]. For example, in genetics, gene-expression microarrays, commonly called "gene-chips", make it possible to simultaneously measure the expression of each of the thousands of genes that are present (transcribed) in a cell or tissue. One can use these comprehensive snapshots of biological activity to infer regulatory pathways in cells, identify novel targets for drug design, and improve diagnosis, prognosis, and treatment planning for those suffering from disease. However, the amount of data this new technology produces is well beyond what can be manually analyzed. Hence, the need for automated analysis of microarray data offers an opportunity for machine learning to have a significant impact on biology and medicine (see [12] [13]). Among the data mining methodologies, visualization plays a key role in developing good models for data especially when the quantity of data is large. In this context PPS represent a very powerful tool for characterizing and visualizing high-D data. PPS [3, 4] are a nonlinear extension of principal components, in that each node on the PPS is the average of all data points that projects near/onto it. From a theoretical point of view, the PPS is a generalization of the Generative Topographic Mapping (GTM) [2], which on the other hand, can be seen as a parametric alternative to the well known Self Organizing Maps (SOM) [7]. Some advantages of PPS over less sophisticated methods includes the parametric and flexible formulation for any geometry/topology in any dimension, and the guaranteed convergence (indeed the PPS training is accomplished through the Expectation-Maximization algorithm). A PPS is governed by its latent topology and owing to the flexibility of the PPS, a variety of PPS topologies can be created, among which also that of a $3D$ sphere. The sphere is finite and unbounded, with all nodes distributed at the edge, making it ideal for emulating the sparseness and peripheral property of high-D data. Furthermore, the sphere topology can be easily comprehended by humans and thereby used for visualizing high-D data. We shall go in details over all these issues in the next sections, which are organized as follows: in section 2 latent variable models are presented focusing on GTM and PPS, while section 3 shows the visualization possibilities offered by PPS illustrating a number of visualization methods proposed and implemented by us. Finally, in section 4 a real case-study concerning with the analysis of yeast gene expression levels from microarray data is presented, and in section 5 some preliminary conclusions are drawn.

2 Latent Variable Models

A latent variable model builds the distribution $p(\mathbf{t})$ of a variable $\mathbf{t} = (t_1, \ldots, t_D)$ lying in an input data space, in terms of a smaller number of latent variables $\mathbf{x} = (x_1, \ldots, x_Q)$, lying in the so called "latent space", where $Q < D$. The mapping between the input and the latent spaces is given by

$$\mathbf{t} = \mathbf{y}(\mathbf{x}; \mathbf{w}) + \mathbf{u} \qquad (1)$$

where $\mathbf{y}(\mathbf{x}; \mathbf{w})$ is a function of the latent variable $\mathbf{x}$ with parameters $\mathbf{w}$, and $\mathbf{u}$ is an $\mathbf{x}$-independent noise process. Geometrically, the function $\mathbf{y}(\mathbf{x}; \mathbf{w})$ defines a manifold in data space given by the image of the latent space. By assuming that the components of $\mathbf{u}$ are uncorrelated and by defining a distribution $p(\mathbf{x})$ in the latent space, we can define the joint distribution as:

$$p(\mathbf{t}, \mathbf{x}) = p(\mathbf{x})p(\mathbf{t}|\mathbf{x}) = p(\mathbf{x}) \prod_{d=1}^{D} p(t_d|\mathbf{x}), \qquad (2)$$

where $p(\mathbf{t}|\mathbf{x})$ is the conditional distribution of the data variables given the latent variables. The type of the mapping $\mathbf{y}(\mathbf{x}; \mathbf{w})$ determines the specific latent variable model.

The desired model for the distribution $p(\mathbf{t})$ of the data is obtained by marginalizing over the latent variables

$$p(\mathbf{t}) = \int p(\mathbf{t}|\mathbf{x})p(\mathbf{x})d\mathbf{x}. \qquad (3)$$

This integration will, in general, be analytically intractable except for specific forms of the distributions $p(\mathbf{t}|\mathbf{x})$ and $p(\mathbf{x})$.

2.1. Generative Topographic Mapping

The *GTM* defines a non-linear, parametric mapping $\mathbf{y}(\mathbf{x}; \mathbf{W})$ from a Q-dimensional latent space ($\mathbf{x} \in \mathbb{R}^Q$) to a D-dimensional data space ($\mathbf{t} \in \mathbb{R}^D$), where normally $Q < D$. The mapping $\mathbf{y}(\mathbf{x}; \mathbf{W})$ (defined continuous and differentiable) maps every point in the latent space to a point into the data space. Since the latent space is Q-dimensional, these points will be confined to a Q-dimensional manifold non-linearly embedded into the D-dimensional data space. If we define a probability distribution over the latent space, $p(\mathbf{x})$, this will induce a corresponding probability distribution into the data space which will be zero outside of the embedded manifold. However, this constraint is unrealistic since the points do not lie exactly on a Q-dimensional manifold and, therefore, a noise model for the variable $\mathbf{t}$ is added as

$$p(\mathbf{t}|\mathbf{x}, \mathbf{W}, \beta) = \left(\frac{\beta}{2\pi}\right)^{\frac{D}{2}} exp\left\{-\frac{\beta}{2}\sum_{d=1}^{D}(t_d - y_d(\mathbf{x}, \mathbf{W}))^2\right\}$$
$$(4)$$

where $\mathbf{t}$ is a point in the data space and β^{-1} denotes the noise variance.

By marginalizing over the latent variables, the probability distribution in the data space, expressed as a function of the parameters β and $\mathbf{W}$, is obtained

$$p(\mathbf{t}|\mathbf{W}, \beta) = \int p(\mathbf{t}|\mathbf{x}, \mathbf{W}, \beta)p(\mathbf{x})d\mathbf{x}. \qquad (5)$$

By choosing $p(\mathbf{x})$ as a set of M equally weighted delta functions on a regular grid,

$$p(\mathbf{x}) = \frac{1}{M}\sum_{m=1}^{M}\delta(\mathbf{x} - \mathbf{x}_m), \qquad (6)$$

we render the (5) analytically tractable since it turns in into a sum,

$$p(\mathbf{t}|\mathbf{W}, \beta) = \frac{1}{M}\sum_{m=1}^{M}p(\mathbf{t}|\mathbf{x}_m, \mathbf{W}, \beta). \qquad (7)$$

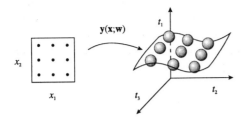

Figure 1. The prior distribution $p(\mathbf{x})$ consists of a superposition of delta functions located at the nodes of a regular grid in latent space. Each node $\mathbf{x}_m$ is mapped into a corresponding point $\mathbf{y}(\mathbf{x}_m; \mathbf{w})$ in the data space and forms the center of a corresponding Gaussian distribution.

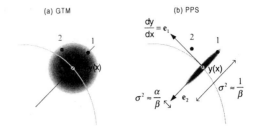

Figure 2. Under a spherical Gaussian model of the *GTM*, points 1 and 2 have equal influences on the center node $y(\mathrm{x})$ (a) *PPS* have an oriented covariance matrix so point 1 is probabilistically closer to the center node $y(\mathrm{x})$ than point 2 (b).

Each delta function center maps into the center of a Gaussian which lies in the manifold embedded in the data space, as illustrated in Figure 1. Equation 7 defines a constrained mixture of Gaussians (all of which share the same variance with the priors all fixed to $\frac{1}{M}$), since the centers of the mixture components cannot move independently of each other, but all depend on the mapping $\mathbf{y}(\mathbf{x}; \mathbf{W})$. The parameters $\mathbf{W}$ and β of the mixture are computed by means of the Expectation-Maximization algorithm used for optimizing the model log-likelihood function with respect to $\mathbf{W}$ and β themselves. The form of the mapping $\mathbf{y}(\mathbf{x}; \mathbf{w})$ is defined as a generalized linear regression model

$$\mathbf{y}(\mathbf{x}; \mathbf{w}) = \mathbf{W}\phi(\mathbf{x}) \tag{8}$$

where the elements of $\phi(\mathbf{x})$ consist of L fixed basis functions $\{\phi_l(\mathbf{x})\}_{l=1}^{L}$, and $\mathbf{W}$ is a $D \times L$ matrix.

2.2. Probabilistic Principal Surfaces

The *PPS* generalizes the GTM model by building a unified model and share the same formulation as the GTM, except for an oriented covariance structure for the Gaussian mixture in $\mathbb{R}^D$. This means that data points projecting near a principal surface node (i.e., a Gaussian center of the mixture) have higher influences on that node than points projecting far away from it. This is illustrated in Figure 2.

Therefore, each node $\mathbf{y}(\mathbf{x}; \mathbf{w})$, $\mathbf{x} \in \{\mathbf{x}_m\}_{m=1}^{M}$, has covariance

$$\mathbf{\Sigma}(\mathbf{x}) = \frac{\alpha}{\beta} \sum_{q=1}^{Q} \mathbf{e}_q(\mathbf{x})\mathbf{e}_q^T(\mathbf{x}) + \frac{(D - \alpha Q)}{\beta(D - Q)} \sum_{d=Q+1}^{D} \mathbf{e}_d(\mathbf{x})\mathbf{e}_d^T(\mathbf{x}),$$
$$\tag{9}$$
$$0 < \alpha < \frac{D}{Q}$$

where

- $\{\mathbf{e}_q(\mathbf{x})\}_{q=1}^{Q}$ is the set of orthonormal vectors tangential to the manifold at $\mathbf{y}(\mathbf{x}; \mathbf{w})$,

- $\{\mathbf{e}_d(\mathbf{x})\}_{d=Q+1}^{D}$ is the set of orthonormal vectors orthogonal to the manifold in $\mathbf{y}(\mathbf{x}; \mathbf{w})$.

The complete set of orthonormal vectors $\{\mathbf{e}_d(\mathbf{x})\}_{d=1}^{D}$ spans $\mathbb{R}^D$. The parameter α is a clamping factor and determines the orientation of the covariance matrix. The unified *PPS* model reduces to GTM for $\alpha = 1$ and to the manifold-aligned GTM for $\alpha > 1$

$$\mathbf{\Sigma}(\mathbf{x}) = \begin{cases} 0 < \alpha < 1 & \perp \text{ to the manifold} \\ \alpha = 1 & I_D \text{ or spherical} \\ 1 < \alpha < D/Q & \parallel \text{ to the manifold.} \end{cases}$$

The EM algorithm can be used to estimate the PPS parameters W and β, while the clamping factor is fixed by the user and is assumed to be constant during the EM iterations. If we choose a $3D$ latent space, a spherical manifold can be constructed using a PPS with nodes $\{\mathbf{x}_m\}_{m=1}^{M}$ arranged regularly on the surface of a sphere in $\mathbb{R}^3$ latent space, with the latent basis functions evenly distributed on the sphere at a lower density. After a PPS model is fitted to the data, the data themselves are projected into the latent space as points onto a sphere (Figure 3). The latent manifold coordinates $\hat{\mathbf{x}}_n$ of each data point $\mathbf{t}_n$ are computed as

$$\hat{\mathbf{x}}_n \equiv \langle \mathbf{x}|\mathbf{t}_n \rangle = \int \mathbf{x}p(\mathbf{x}|\mathbf{t})d\mathbf{x} = \sum_{m=1}^{M} r_{mn}\mathbf{x}_m$$

where r_{mn} are the latent variable responsibilities defined as

$$r_{mn} = p(\mathbf{x}_m|\mathbf{t}_n) = \frac{p(\mathbf{t}_n|\mathbf{x}_m)P(\mathbf{x}_m)}{\sum_{m'=1}^{M} p(\mathbf{t}_n|\mathbf{x}_{m'})P(\mathbf{x}_{m'})} = \frac{p(\mathbf{t}_n|\mathbf{x}_m)}{\sum_{m'=1}^{M} p(\mathbf{t}_n|\mathbf{x}_{m'})}.$$

These coordinates lie within a unit sphere.

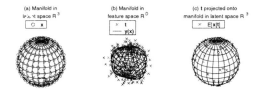

Figure 3. (a) The spherical manifold in $\mathbb{R}^3$ latent space. (b) The spherical manifold in $\mathbb{R}^3$ data space. (c) Projection of data points t onto the latent spherical manifold.

3 Spherical PPS Visualizations

In order to make as much interactive as possible the user-data relation, we have integrated a number of functionalities in a user-friendly graphical user interface which provides a unified tool for the training of the PPS model, and then, after the completion of the training phase, it allows to accomplish all the functions for the visualization and the investigation of a given data set [10]. The implemented prototype was developed under the Matlab computing environment exploiting and adapting the LANS Matlab Toolbox [1] and Netlab Toolbox [8]. Basically, the user is allowed to

- easily interact with the data into the latent space, hence with the data onto the sphere in several ways,

- to visualize the data probability density in the latent space in order to obtain a first understanding of the clusters in the data,

- to fix a number of clusters and visualize the points therein. Eventually, at the end of this phase one could still interact with the data by selecting data points in a given cluster and then make several types of comparisons.

All the graphics representation above described can be properly investigated by rotating the sphere.

3.1. Selecting points on the sphere

Having projected the data into the latent sphere, it is advisable for a data analyzer to localize the most interesting data points (obviously, this depends on the specific application). For instance, the ones lying far away from more dense areas, or the ones lying in the overlapping regions between clusters, and to gain some information about them, by linking the data points on the sphere with their position in the data set which contains all the information about the typology of the data. These possibilities are fundamental

[1] http://www.lans.ece.utexas.edu/ lans/lans/

for the user who may be able to extract important meanings from the data and for all the data mining activities. Furthermore, the user is also allowed to select a latent variable and coloring all the points for which that specific latent variable is responsible (Figure 4).

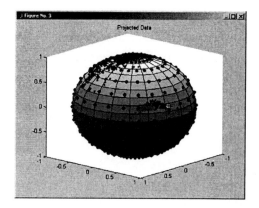

Figure 4. Data points selection phase. The bold black circles represent the latent variables; the blue points represent the projected input data points. While selecting a latent variable, each projected point for which the variable is responsible is colored. By selecting a data point the user is provided with information about it: coordinates and index corresponding to the position in the original catalog.

3.2. Visualizing the latent variable responsibilities on the sphere

The projections of the data points onto the sphere provide only partial information about the clusters inherently present in the data: if the points are strongly overlapped the data analyzer cannot derive any information at all. A first insight on the number of agglomerates localized in the spherical latent manifold is provided by the mean of the responsibility for each latent variable. Furthermore, if we build a spherical manifold which is composed by a set of faces each one delimited by four vertices, then we can color each face with colors varying in intensity on the base of the values of the responsibility associate to each vertex (and hence, to each latent variable). The overall result is that the sphere will contain regions denser than other and this information is easily visible and understandable (see, for example, Figure 6). Obviously, what may happen is that a denser area of the spherical manifold could contain more than one cluster, and this can be validated by further investigations.

3.3. Cluster computation and visualization

Once the user or a data analyzer has gained an overall idea of the number of clusters on the sphere, he can exploit this information through the use of classical objective function-based clustering techniques (such as hard or fuzzy k-means [1]) or agglomerative hierarchical clustering techniques [6] to find out the prototypes of the clusters (only in the case of objective function clustering techniques) and the data therein contained. Whatever clustering procedure the user will choose, the clustering is accomplished on the latent variables images in the data space. Afterwards, the clusters are visualized in the latent space and eventually, one may proceed by coloring each cluster with a given color (Figure 8).

4. Spherical PPS and yeast gene expression data

4.1. Preliminaries: gene-expression microarrays

Gene-expression microarrays measure the expression of a gene in a cell by measuring the amount of mRNA (messenger ribonucleic acid) present for that gene. In the following we take a look on how a DNA microarray works. The nucleotide sequences for a few thousands genes are printed on a glass slide. A target sample and a reference sample are labeled with red and green dyes, and each are hybridized with the DNA on the slide. Through fluoroscopy, the log (red/green) intensities of RNA hybridizing at each site is measured. The result is a few thousand numbers, typically ranging from -6 to 6, measuring expression level of each gene in the target relative to the reference sample. Positive values, indicate higher expression in the target versus the reference, and vice versa for the negative values. A gene expression data set collects together the expression values from a series of DNA microarray experiments, with each column representing an experiment. There are therefore several thousand rows representing individual genes, and tens of columns representing experiments.

4.2. The problem and the data

[9] provides a comprehensive catalog of yeast genes whose transcript levels vary periodically within the cell cycle. In order to produce the catalog, samples from yeast cultures synchronized with different experiments were used. In [9] a type of agglomerative hierarchical clustering [5] was used in order to identify clusters of genes behaving similarly in each experiment and which represent groups of apparently co-regulated genes. These clusters provide a solid basis for understanding the transcriptional mechanism of cell cycle regulation. The data set used by us, consist of a set of 6125 genes subject to four different experiments. Each experiment consists of a series of measurements at different time points. The overall data set consist, therefore, of 6125 genes and 73 parameters. In order to make this data set more tractable by the PPS, we applied a preprocessing phase in which through the use of a nonlinear PCA [11] we reduced each experiment to 8 measurements and eliminated the genes whose experiments had too much missing data. Hence, the used data set consists of 5425 genes and 32 features.

4.3. PPS experiments

We used a PPS with 266 latent variables and 40 latent basis functions and a clamping factor α set to 0.5. This parameter setting is the result of empirical trials aimed at finding a good compromise between the data representation and the model complexity. Obviously, different values for the parameters also lead to satisfactorily results provided the number of latent variables and basis functions is not too low with respect to the data complexity (in fact, the mapping $y(\mathbf{x}; \mathbf{W})$ between the latent and the data spaces would not be sufficiently smooth to build a probability density function in the data space able to fit the true distribution of the points therein). After the completion of the training phase we projected the data onto the latent space and computed the responsibility for each latent variable as shown in Figures 5 and 6, respectively. A $3D$ PCA of the data is shown in Figure 7 to show the difficulty of visualizing this kind of data. On the basis of the probability density function visualized in Figure 6 we decided to identify 30 clusters through the k-means algorithm. The results are depicted in Figure 8. For each cluster we plotted the prototype trend with respect to the 32 features, as it can be seen in Figure 9, which highlights the periodic behavior of each gene belonging to the cluster. In figure 10 we show the comparison between

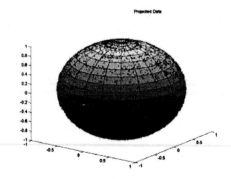

Figure 5. Data point projections on the spherical latent space.

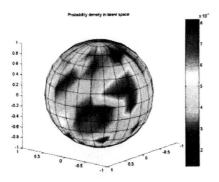

Figure 6. The latent variable responsibilities for the entire data set. Note how the red areas corresponds to higher density locations.

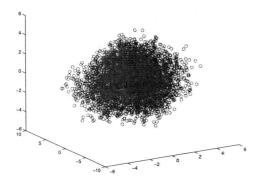

Figure 7. $3D$ PCA of the yeast gene data.

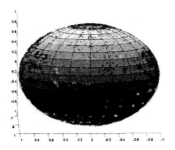

Figure 8. PPS clusters computed by k-means.

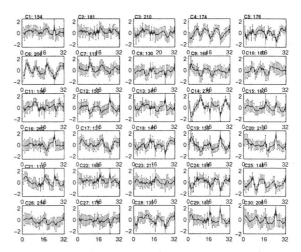

Figure 9. Cluster prototype periodic behaviors and error bars showing the standard deviation of genes from the prototypes for a fixed cluster. On top of each subplot the cluster number and the number of genes within each cluster is reported.

the Spellman clustering and ours. The table was obtained by projecting the 250 genes used by Spellman into our 30 clusters. Each element (i, j) of the table gives the fraction of genes belonging to the $j - th$ Spellman's cluster which are classified by our algorithm in our $i - th$ cluster (bold face marks the maximum values). It must be noticed that we were obliged to use only 8 out of the 9 Spellman's clusters since no information were available on the composition of Spellman's $9 - th$ cluster.

5. Conclusions

Even at first sight, Figure 10 shows interesting trends. Before discussing the table, we wish to stress that the two clustering procedures were completely different: Spellman in fact, clustered the gene properties using a priori knowledge on their characteristics, while our algorithm made use of the statistical properties of the data with no a priori knowledge. In spite of this, some remarkable patterns may be detected: Spellman's cluster number 1 is broken by us in two clusters, 80.6% of the objects being in cluster 25 and

19.4% in cluster 4; Spellman's clusters number 2 and 8 are statistically speaking undistinguishable (our cluster number 6); Spellman's cluster number 5 appears to be a sort of "statistical" waste basket which groups together rather different clusters identified by us (number 8, 27 and 30, plus several others with lower significance) which, however are topological neighbors in the PPS latent space and can therefore be considered as "sub-structures" of a larger cluster. It has, however, to be noticed that cluster 30 is dominated by genes belonging to Spellman's cluster number 7. The most relevant result, however seems to be the fact that many (11 out of 30) of our clusters are not mapped by any of the 250 genes in the Spellman's sample. Whether this clusters have or have not biological significance will be the subject of future studies.

	1	2	3	4	5	6	7	8
1	0	0	0	0	0	0	0	0
2	0	0	0	10	0	0	0	0
3	0	0	0	0	0	0	0	0
4	19.355	0	0	0	0	13.333	0	0
5	0	0	12.5	0	0	0	0	0
6	0	87.5	0	0	0	0	0	96.296
7	0	0	0	0	0	0	0	0
8	0	0	0	0	9.0909	0	0	0
9	0	0	0	0	0	0	0	0
10	0	0	0	0	0	60	0	0
11	0	0	0	0	0	0	0	0
12	0	0	0	0	3.0303	6.6667	4.5455	0
13	0	0	0	0	3.0303	0	4.5455	0
14	0	0	0	0	0	0	0	0
15	0	0	0	10	0	0	0	0
16	0	0	0	0	0	0	0	0
17	0	10	0	30	3.0303	0	0	0
18	0	0	0	0	0	0	0	0
19	0	0	0	0	6.0606	0	0	0
20	0	0	0	0	6.0606	0	0	0
21	0	0	0	0	0	0	0	0
22	0	0	0	0	0	0	0	0
23	0	0	0	10	6.0606	0	0	0
24	0	0	0	0	0	20	0	0
25	80.645	0	0	0	12.121	0	0	0
26	0	0	0	40	3.0303	0	4.5455	0
27	0	0	0	0	30.303	0	4.5455	3.7037
28	0	2.5	87.5	0	3.0303	0	0	0
29	0	0	0	0	0	0	0	0
30	0	0	0	0	15.152	0	81.818	0

Figure 10. PPS and Spellman cluster comparisons. On each row are reported the 30 PPS clusters, while on the columns are the clusters computed by Spellman. The A_{ij}-th entry of the table correspond to the fraction of Spellman's cluster j falling in the PPS cluster i.

References

[1] J. C. Bezdek, J. Keller, R. Krisnapuram, and N. Pal. *Fuzzy Models and Algorithms for Pattern Recognition and Image Processing*. Kluwer Academic Publisher, 1999.

[2] C. M. Bishop, M. Svensen, and C. K. I. Williams. Gtm: The generative topographic mapping. *Neural Computation*, 1998.

[3] K. Chang. *Nonlinear Dimensionality Reduction Using Probabilistic Principal Surfaces*. PhD thesis, The University of Texas at Austin, USA, 2000.

[4] K. Chang and J. Ghosh. A unified model for probabilistic principal surfaces. *IEEE Transactions on Pattern Analysis and Machine Intelligence, vol.23, no.1*, 2001.

[5] M. B. Eisen, P. T. Spellman, P. O. Brown, and D. Botstein. Cluster analysis and display of genome-wide expression patterns. *PNAS*, 95:14863–14868, 1998.

[6] T. Hastie, R. Tibshirani, and J. Friedman. *The Elements of Statistical Learning - Data Mining, Inference, and Prediction*. Springer-Verlag, 2001.

[7] T. Kohonen. *Self-Organizing Maps*. Springer-Verlag, Berlin, 1995.

[8] I. T. Nabney. *NETLAB - Algorithms for Pattern Recognition*. Springer-Verlag, 2002.

[9] P. T. Spellman, G. Sherlock, M. Q. Zhang, V. R. Iyer, K. Anders, M. B. Eisen, P. O. Brown, D. Botstein, and B. Futcher. Comprehensive identification of cell cycle-regulated genes of the yeast saccharomyces cerevisiae by microarray hybridization. *Molecular Biology of the Cell*, 9:3273–3297, December 2001.

[10] A. Staiano. *Unsupervised Neural Networks for the Extraction of Scientific Information from Astronomical Data*. PhD thesis, Universià di Salerno, Italy, 2003.

[11] R. Tagliaferri, A. Ciaramella, L. Milano, F. Barone, and G. Longo. Spectral analysis of stellar light curves by means of neural networks. *Astronomy and Astrophysics Supplement Series*, 137:391–405, 1999.

[12] P. Tamayo, D. Slonim, J. Mesirov, Q. Zhu, S. Kitareewan, E. Dmitrovsky, E. S. Lander, and T. R. Golub. Interpreting patterns of gene expression with self-organizing maps: Methods and application to hematopoietic differentiation. *PNAS*, 96:2907–2912, March 1999.

[13] P. Toronen, M. Kolehmainen, G. Wong, and E. Castren. Analysis of gene expression data using self-organizing maps. *FEBS Letters*, 451:142–146, 1999.

On Local Spatial Outliers

Pei Sun
University of Sydney
School of Information Technologies
Sydney, NSW, Australia
psun2712@it.usyd.edu.au

Sanjay Chawla
University of Sydney
School of Information Technologies
Sydney, NSW, Australia
chawla@it.usyd.edu.au

Abstract

We propose a measure, Spatial Local Outlier Measure (SLOM) which captures the local behaviour of datum in their spatial neighborhood. With the help of SLOM we are able to discern local spatial outliers which are usually missed by global techniques like "three standard deviations away from the mean". Furthermore the measure takes into account the local stability around a data point and supresses the reporting of outliers in highly unstable areas, where data is too heterogeneous and the notion of outliers is not meaningful. We prove several properties of SLOM and report experiments on synthetic and real data sets which show that our approach is novel and scalable to large data sets.

1 Introduction and Related Work

Of all the data mining techniques, outlier detection seems closest to the definition of "discovering nuggets of information" in large databases. When an outlier is detected, and determined to be genuine, it can provide insights which can radically change our understanding of the underlying process. We give a historical example of how the discovery of outliers led to a better understanding and prediction of global weather patterns known as El Niño and La Niña.

In the early 1900s, Sir Gilbert Walker, a British meterologist discovered that extreme variations in surface pressure over the equator close to Australia are correlated with monsoon rainfall and drought in India and other parts of the world. This variation is captured in a measure , which is now called the Southern Osscillation Index (SOI). The SOI is defined as the normalized surface air pressure difference between the islands of Tahiti and Darwin, Australia. As shown in the upper graph in Figure 1(Reprinted from [6]), when the SOI index attains outlier values, i.e., when it is two or more standard deviations away from the mean, the sea surface temperature over the Pacific Ocean also rises

and falls sharply (lower graph). Thus a SOI of two standard deviations below the mean corresponds to a rise in surface temperature and is known as El Niño. The opposite phenomenon, i.e., when SOI is two or more standard deviations above the mean which corresponds to a fall in surface temperature is known as La Niña. Notice how in 1998 the sea surface temperature reached more than 3 degrees above normal and that was one of most dramatic El Niño years in recorded history. Also notice that the relationship between SOI and El Niño is sharper than that between SOI and La Niña.

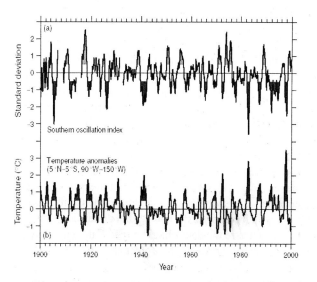

Figure 1. The relationship between the Southern Oscillation Index(SOI) and sea surface temperature. High tempeature anomolies correspond to El Niño and low to La Niña. The relationship was discovered by Sir Gilbert Walker and clearly shows how outlier detection can provide penetrating insights about the underlying phenomenon, global weather patterns in this case [6]

Thus an automated or partially-automated system of outlier detection can serve as a trigger for unlocking secrets about the underlying process which has generated the data.

The classic definition of an outlier is due to Hawkins [2] who defines *"an outlier is an observation which deviates so much from other observations as to arouse suspicions that it was generated by a diferrent mechanism."* Several different approaches has been taken in order to operationalize this definition. For example, it is standard to use variations of the Chebyshev's inequality,

$$P(|X - \mu| \geq k\sigma) \leq \frac{1}{k^2}$$

where μ and σ are the mean and variance of a random variable X which models the underlying mechanism. When additional information is available, like the distributional assumption of X, this inequality can be sharpened. For example, when X follows a normal distribution, it can be shown that 99.7% of the data lies between three standard deviations, as opposed to 88.8% given by the general Chebyshev's inequality.

Knorr and Ng [3] were the first to propose the definition of distance-based outlier, which was free of any distributional assumptions and was readily generalizable to multidimensional dataset. They gave the following definition of $DB(p, D)$ outlier: *"An object o in a dataset T is a DB(p,D)-outlier if at least fraction p of the objects in T lie at a greater distance than D from o."*

The authors proved that this definition generalized the folk definition of outliers "three standard deviations away from the mean". For example, if the dataset T is generated from a normal distribution, with mean μ and standard deviation δ, and $t \in$ T is such that $\frac{t-\mu}{\delta} > 3$, then t is a $DB(p, D)$ outlier with $p = 0.9988$ and $D = 0.13\delta$. Similar extensions were shown for other well-known distribution including the Possion.

For spatial data, both statistical and data mining approaches have to be modified because of the qualitative difference between spatial and non-spatial dimensions. The attributes which comprise the non-spatial dimensions intrinsically characterize the data while the spatial dimensions provide a locational index to the object and are not instrinsic to the object. However, the physical neighborhood plays a very important role in analysis of spatial data. For example, in Figure 2 the data value 8 indexed at location $(8, 1)$ is an outlier however the same value 8 indexed at $(3, 8)$ is not an outlier.

Shekhar et al. [7] proposed the following definition of spatial outlier: *"A spatial outlier is a spatially referenced object whose non-spatial attribute values are significantly different from those of other spatially referenced objects in its spatial neighborhood."*

A spatial neighborhood may be defined based on spatial attributes, e.g., location, using spatial relationships such as distance or adjacency. Comparisons between spatially referenced objects are based on non-spatial attributes.

There are two types of spatial outlier: multi-dimensional space-based outliers and graph-based outliers. The only difference between them is that they use different spatial neighborhood definitions. Multi-dimensional space-based outliers use Euclidean distances to define spatial neighborhoods, while graph-based outliers use graph connectivity.

Thus given a function f defined on a spatial grid S, a natural approach is to transform f into g such that $g(o) = f(o) - \frac{1}{|N(o)|} \sum_{p \in N(o)} f(p)$, where $N(o)$ is the spatial neighborhood of o. Now, a Chebyshev inequality like approach, can be undertaken in order to identify those points o which are candidate outliers. Indeed this is the state of the art [9, 8, 4, 5].

However the approach of using a statistical test is useful for discovering global outliers but may not be able to discover local outliers which are likely to be of more interest. For example, again consider the data value 8 indexed at location $(8, 1)$ in Figure 2. Clearly this point is a local outlier as it is forms a local maxima in its neigborhood however the value 8 is not a global outlier in the sense that even after transformation it still is within three standard deviations from the mean.

Thus clearly an approach is needed which can efficiently capture spatial local outliers. In fact our method will go further and associate a SLOM score with each data point. The SLOM defines the "degree of outlierness" of each point very much along the lines proposed by Breunig et. al. [1]. However besides the qualitative difference between spatial and non-spatial attributes, spatial data exhibits spatial autocorrelation (non-independence) and heteroscedasticity(non-constant variance) both of which must be factored into SLOM.

1.1 Problem Definition

Given: A large spatial database with multi-dimensional non-spatial attributes.
Design: A measure which assigns a "degree of outlierness" to each element in the database.

Constraints:
Spatial autocorrelation : The value of each element in the database is affected by its spatial neighbors.
Spatial Heteroscedasticity: The variance of the data is not uniform and is a function of the spatial location.

Together these two constraints imply that the IID (Identical and Independent Distribution) assumption cannot be assumed to hold in the context of spatial data.

	0	1	2	3	4	5	6	7	8	9
0	−16	−9	−16	4	8	25	−2	20	−11	9
1	−3	−1	9	−12	1	1	−1	−2	−4	−2
2	14	1	11	2	−13	15	4	3	11	19
3	−10	16	−11	−2	−10	−11	−17	4	8	−15
4	−5	20	−11	4	−5	8	6	6	−2	−1
5	15	10	−9	7	12	−9	−18	16	8	−6
6	0	0	0	0	−21	−5	12	−15	−5	11
7	0	0	0	0	5	6	1	1	−9	3
8	0	8	0	0	−9	−8	−1	−2	9	5
9	0	0	0	0	19	−1	−2	−7	−3	−12

Figure 2. Original data matrix

1.2 Key Insights and Contributions

- The first insight which guides our approach can be described with the help of an example. Consider the cell with value 8 indexed at location $(8, 1)$ in Figure 2. Clearly in the local neighborhood, 8 is an outlier. An obvious way to capture the relationship between a point and its neighbors is to define a measure $d(o)$ for each point o as

$$d(o) = \frac{1}{|N(o)|} \sum_{p \in N(o)} dist(o, p)$$

where $dist(o, p)$ is a definition of (euclidean) distance between the non-spatial components of o and p and $N(o)$ are the neighboring points of o.

In Figure 2, the value of $d(o)$ is 8 for object o located at $(8, 1)$. However, for a point p in the neighborhood of o, which is not an outlier, the influence of o can overwhelm p's relationship with its other neighbors. In order to factor out the effect of o on p, a modified measure, $\tilde{d}(o)$ is defined as follows.

First, define $maxd(o) = max\{dist(o, p) | p \in N(o)\}$ as the maximum non-spatial distance between o and its neighbors. Then define

$$\tilde{d}(o) = \frac{\sum_{p \in N(o)} dist(o, p) - maxd(o)}{|N(o)| - 1}$$

Now notice that for the point 8 (location (8,1)) in Figure 2, $\tilde{d}(o) = d(o)$ but for points in the

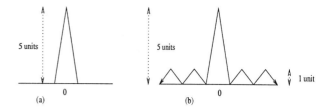

Figure 3. Both (a) and (b) have the same $\tilde{d}$ value however the the β values in (a) is higher than (b) because of the instability around (b)

neighborhood of this point: $0 = \tilde{d}(p) < d(p) = 1$.

Thus the advantage of using $\tilde{d}(o)$ instead of $d(o)$ is that if o is an outlier, then $\tilde{d}$ suppresses the effect of o in its neighborhood or in other words stretches the difference between an outlier and its neighbors.

Thus $\tilde{d}$ stretches the difference between an outlier and its neighbors compared to d.

The definition of $\tilde{d}$ is similar to that of *trimmed mean*, where a certain percentage of the largest and smallest values around the mean are removed [10]. The trimmed mean is less sensitive to outliers like the median but retains some of the averaging behavior of the mean.

- The second insight that underpins our approach is that outliers which are in unstable areas should have lower precedence than outliers in stable areas. Stability around a point o can be captured using the variance, however we have used a statistic which can be deterministically bounded. In particular we have defined a statistic β which captures the net oscillation with respect to the average value around o (details in Section 2). For example, Figure 3 shows the plot of $\tilde{d}$ around the point o. For both the figures $\tilde{d}(o)$ is the same but $\beta(o)$ in Figure 3(a) is higher than Figure 3(b).

- Another novel contribution of our work is related to system integration. All the spatial data remain database *in-situ*. We manage this by exploiting the growing list of spatial features that are now standard features in commercial database systems such as Oracle9i. In particular, we use R-trees to access the database and spatial sql to retrieve data based on spatial relationships.

The rest of the paper is as follows. In Section 2, we introduce a series of definitions which will culminate in the definition of the Spatial Local Outlier Measure (SLOM). Along the way we will explain how each component of SLOM address spatial autocorrelation and heteroscedasticity. In Section 3, we analyze the complexity of our method and describe two database strategies to efficiently interact with the database in order to reduce the I/O overhead. In Section 4, we report the results of our experiments on synthethic and real data sets. In Section 5, we conclude with a summary and directions for future work.

2 Definitions

We now formally define SLOM and prove several properties. Recall that our objective is to design a measure which can capture both spatial autocorrelation and heteroscedasticity (non-constant variance). We have already defined $\tilde{d}$ in Section 1 which factors out the effect of spatial autocorrelation and now define β which penalizes for oscillating behavior around a potential outlier.

For an object o, we can define its SLOM value as $\frac{\sum_{p \in N(o)} \frac{\tilde{d}(o)}{\tilde{d}(p)}}{|N(o)|}$, just like the method used in [1]. However, this definition has two drawbacks.

1. First, one extreme (small) value of $\tilde{d}(p)$ will result in a very large $SLOM$ value of an object o.

2. Second, it is possible that the value of $\tilde{d}(p)$ is zero, which will make the value of $SLOM = \infty$.

We begin by quantifying the average of a $\tilde{d}$ in its neighborhood.

- Let $N_+(o)$ denote the set of all the objects in o's neighborhood and o itself and $avg(N_+(o)) = \frac{\sum_{p \in N_+(o)} \tilde{d}(p)}{|N_+(o)|}$.

- Oscillating parameter $\beta(o)$:
  For an object o, if it has large value for $\tilde{d}(o)$ and small $\tilde{d}$ value in o's neighborhood then this means it is a good candidate for an outlier. On the other hand even though it may have the largest value in its neighborhood, if all neighbors also have large values, this means that o inhabits an unstable (oscillating) area, so it is a poor candidate for an outlier. We define a parameter $\beta(o)$, which can capture the oscillation of an area, which intuitively is the net number of times the values around o are bigger or smaller than $avg(N_+(o))$. We calculate $\beta(o)$ using the following pseudo-code.

  1. $\beta(o) \leftarrow 0$
  2. For each $p \in N_+(o)$
       if $\tilde{d}(p) > avg(N_+(o))$
          $\beta(o) + +$
       else if $\tilde{d}(p) < avg(N_+(o))$

$\beta(o) - -$
3. End for
4. $\beta(o) = |\beta(o)|$
5. $\beta(o) = \frac{max(\beta(o),1)}{(|N_+(o)|-2)}$
6. $\beta(o) = \frac{\beta(o)}{1+avg\{\tilde{d}(p)|p \in N(o)\}}$

While step one to four are self-explanatory, we explain step 5 and 6. There are two reasons why we divide $\beta(o)$ by $|N_+(o)| - 2$ in step 5. First, we need to correct for boundary terms where the number of neighbors is fewer than that in the interior. The second motivation is that for a local region like that in Figure 2 where the data value 8 at location $o = (8,1)$ is surrounded by constant values, $\beta(o) = 1$, the highest value β can assume.

However, if we have stopped at step 5 then β cannot distinguish between the two cases shown in Figure 3. In order to do that we divide $\beta(o)$ by $1 + avg\{\tilde{d}(p)|p \in N(o)\}$. This allows us to penalize the situation where large values of $\tilde{d}$ exist around the point o. However in order to bound this term we have to normalize the original data so that the maximum value that denominator can assume is $1 + \sqrt{d}$, where d is the dimensionality of the non-spatial attributes. Thus in Figure 3(a) and (b) the β values are 1 and 0.5 respectively.

- We are ready to define SLOM. For a point o,

$$SLOM(o) = \tilde{d}(o) * \beta(o)$$

A high value of SLOM indicates that the point is good candidate for an outlier. The $\tilde{d}$ term is analogous to the expectation of the first derivative of a smooth random variable, while the β term is analogous to the standard deviation of the first derivative of a smooth random variable.

Lemma 1 *For all $o \in S$, $\frac{1}{(|N_+(o)|-2)(1+\sqrt{d})} < \beta(o) \leq 1$, where d is the dimensionality of the non-spatial attributes.*

Proof: After step 4 of computing $\beta(o)$, the maximum value of $\beta(o)$ is $|N_+(o)| - 2$. This happens when $\tilde{d}(p)$ is the only value that is greater than (or smaller than) $avg(N_+(o))$. The minimum value of $\beta(o)$ is 0. After step 5, the maximum value of $\beta(o)$ becomes 1, and the minimum value becomes $\frac{1}{|N_+(o)|-2}$. In step 6, the maximum value of $avg\{\tilde{d}(p)|p \in N(o)\}$ is $\sqrt{d}$ and the minimum value is 0. So, after step 6, the maximum value of $\beta(o)$ becomes 1, and minimum value becomes $\frac{1}{(|N_+(o)|-2)(1+\sqrt{d})}$.

Lemma 2 *For all $o \in S$, $0 \leq SLOM(o) \leq \sqrt{d}$.*

Proof: The value of $\tilde{d}(o)$ is between 0 and $\sqrt{d}$, and the value of $\beta(o)$ is between $\frac{1}{(|N_+(o)|-2)(1+\sqrt{d})}$ and 1. $SLOM(o)$ is the product of $\tilde{d}(o)$ and $\beta(o)$, so its value must be between 0 and $\sqrt{d}$

3 Complexity Analysis

For distance-based outlier detection [3] the key step is a method to search for nearest neighbors. This search must be performed on the complete dataset and is the computational bottleneck, especially in high-dimensional space.

However, for spatial outlier detection the neighborhood is defined by it spatial information, which is usually bounded by three dimensions. Here we can use a spatial R-tree index in order to perform this step efficiently.

Given that we have N objects and each object has a maximum of k spatial neighbors($k \leq 8$ for a 2D grid), the calculation of SLOM for the full data set involves the following steps.

1. The first step is to normalize the nonspatial attributes to between $[0, 1]$. Here we can take advantage of the summary statistics (min, max, avg) that are stored in the database catalog. Thus this step can be done in one database pass and the computational cost is $O(Nd)$, where d is the number of non-spatial dimensions.

2. To compute $\tilde{d}(o)$ we need to find the spatial neighbors of each object and calculate the distance between them. The cost of a single k-NN query using an R-tree is $O(k log N)$ and the cost of computing the nonspatial distance is $O(kd)$. Thus the cost of this step is $O(Nk log N + kdN)$.

3. After the computation of $\tilde{d}(o)$, we need to compute $\beta(o)$. This involves another round of nearest neighbor queries followed by a summation to compute the neighborhood average of $\tilde{d}(o)$. The cost of this step is thus $O(Nk log N + dN)$.

4. To compute the SLOM we multiply the $\tilde{d}$ and β for each object. The cost is $O(N)$.

5. Finally we sort the objects by SLOM and report the top-n outliers for which the cost is $O(N log N)$.

6. Thus the final cost of the whole operation is $O(Nk log N + kdN)$.

While the spatial dimensionality is bounded by three, the spatial part of the data set can be quite large and complicated, especially if the spatial objects are complex polygons (like the boundaries of countries). Even though the R-tree index can speed up the processing of the nearest neighbor search, finding the k nearest neighbors is still a very time

	0	1	2	3	4	5	6	7	8	9
0	0.21	0.15	0.25	0.15	0.19	0.49	0.14	0.48	0.24	0.26
1	0.13	0.19	0.22	0.27	0.16	0.13	0.15	0.11	0.21	0.19
2	0.25	0.18	0.22	0.18	0.18	0.41	0.12	0.09	0.20	0.34
3	0.35	0.31	0.30	0.15	0.18	0.20	0.43	0.06	0.13	0.41
4	0.33	0.41	0.28	0.21	0.16	0.30	0.21	0.14	0.16	0.13
5	0.21	0.24	0.23	0.21	0.26	0.25	0.40	0.31	0.18	0.13
6	0.05	0.05	0.04	0.10	0.46	0.23	0.30	0.31	0.18	0.23
7	0.0	0.0	0.0	0.04	0.16	0.18	0.11	0.12	0.22	0.13
8	0.0	0.17	0.0	0.04	0.20	0.17	0.05	0.06	0.23	0.15
9	0.0	0.0	0.0	0.04	0.46	0.08	0.03	0.10	0.11	0.28

Figure 4. The matrix of the values of $\tilde{d}$

consuming task. We have two options in order to avoid accessing the original spatial data twice (steps 2 and 3 above).

The first option is that we store the neighborhood information in main memory when we compute $\tilde{d}$. Then, when computing $\beta(O)$ we can access this information from memory rather than the database. The prerequisite for this is that the main memory should be large enough to hold all relevant information.

The second option is that we use an R-tree index to generate the neighborhood information and store it into a table beforehand. When computing $\tilde{d}$ and β, we visit this table instead of the original table that stores the spatial information. Since spatial data enjoys slow updates this is a very attractive option and can result in huge savings in the running time as we can amortize the cost of creating the neighborhood table over subsequent k-NN queries.

4 Experiments, Results and Analysis

We have carried out detailed experiments on synthetic and real datasets in order to

1. Test whether SLOM can pick up *local outliers* and supress the reporting of *global outliers* in unstable areas. Intuitively a point is a global outlier, if its determination, that it is an outlier, depends upon a comparison with all other points in the data set. A point is classified as a local outlier if its determination is based on a comparsion with points in its neighborhood.

2. Compare the SLOM approach with the the family of

213

Position (SLZ method)	g(x) value (SLZ method)	Position (our method)	SLOM value
(0,7)	24.0	(0,5)	0.4277
(0,5)	23.6	(2,5)	0.2479
(6,4)	-23.0	(0,7)	0.2061
(9,4)	22.6	(8,1)	0.1739
(3,9)	-22.0	(3,9)	0.1727

Table 1. Outliers found by different method on the same dataset

	0	1	2	3	4	5	6	7	8	9
0	0.09	0.06	0.05	0.03	0.08	0.43	0.06	0.21	0.10	0.11
1	0.03	0.02	0.03	0.03	0.06	0.08	0.05	0.01	0.02	0.04
2	0.05	0.02	0.08	0.02	0.11	0.25	0.05	0.03	0.02	0.14
3	0.14	0.03	0.03	0.05	0.11	0.07	0.15	0.02	0.05	0.17
4	0.06	0.05	0.03	0.02	0.06	0.10	0.02	0.05	0.10	0.11
5	0.04	0.09	0.09	0.02	0.03	0.03	0.05	0.04	0.07	0.03
6	0.02	0.02	0.02	0.01	0.06	0.08	0.03	0.04	0.02	0.05
7	0.0	0.0	0.0	0.02	0.02	0.06	0.01	0.01	0.03	0.03
8	0.0	0.17	0.0	0.02	0.03	0.02	0.01	0.02	0.09	0.03
9	0.0	0.0	0.0	0.02	0.10	0.02	0.02	0.02	0.05	0.12

Figure 5. The SLOM matrix

	0	1	2	3	4	5	6	7	8	9
0	-11.6	-3.6	-14.2	6.0	4.2	23.6	-10.6	24.0	-15.2	14.7
1	-0.8	0.13	11.5	-12.7	-2.8	-3.6	-9.0	-4.5	-9.9	-6.8
2	13.4	-2.1	10.8	5.4	-11.0	20.8	5.0	2.6	9.6	19.4
3	-19.2	14.9	-16.1	2.1	-9.8	-9.5	-21.3	1.6	4.9	-22.0
4	-15.2	20.6	-15.3	7.6	-4.9	14.5	8.6	5.4	-4.5	0.4
5	10.0	8.8	-12.7	10.8	14.6	-7.6	-20.3	17.0	7.5	-8.2
6	-5.0	-2.0	-1.0	0.8	-23.0	-3.5	14.9	-15.7	-6.1	12.8
7	-1.6	-1.0	-1.0	3.1	9.6	9.3	2.5	2.3	-9.9	0.8
8	-1.6	8.0	-1.0	-1.9	-11.6	-10.2	0.5	-0.6	12.0	7.4
9	-2.7	-1.6	-1.6	-2.0	22.6	-0.8	1.8	-7.2	-1.6	-15.6

Figure 6. Result from the SLZ method

methods to discover spatial outliers proposed in [9, 8, 4].

3. Test how the running time changes as we vary the number of nearest neighbors used in the experiments.

One of the strengths of our approach is that the data always remains database *in-situ*, i.e., we never have to extract the data from the database into a flat file in order to carry out the data mining exercise. In particular all the spatial k-NN queries are carried out inside the database.

We accomplish this using the set of spatial features that are increasingly becoming a standard component in commercial and open source DBMS like Oracle and Postgres respectively. In particular these systems provide an R-tree structure to index spatial data and also support extensions of SQL to formulate queries which involve spatial relationships. We used Oracle9i to store all spatial and non-spatial data.

In our experiments, all the spatial objects are polygons. For an object *o*, all the spatial objects that directly touch its boundaries are defined to be its neighbors. We use the following SQL statement to generate the neighborhood in formation:

select a.id, b.id
from spatial a, spatial b
where sdo_relate(a.geom,b.geom,
'mask=touch querytype=window')='true'

In the table `spatial`, $GEOM$ is a special column that stores the boundary information of each object, and a R-tree index is created on it to speed up the processing of this query.

If the spatial objects are points, and the neighborhood is defined to be the k nearest neighbors, then the following SQL statement can be use to generate the neighborhood information.

select a.id, b.id
from spatial a, spatial b
where sdo_nn(a.geom,b.geom,'sdo_num_res=k')='true'

4.1 Result on a Synthetic Dataset

We have created a synthetic data set consisting of one non-spatial attribute in order to explain and compare our method with the prototype method proposed in [8, 9, 5]. We

County Name	SLOM value	Area	Pop. den.	Neighbor	area	Pop. den.
Yukon-Koyukuk,AK	0.2896	157094.25	0.05	Bethel Census Area,AK	41080.34	0.33
				Wade Hampton,AK	17121.14	0.34
				Southeast Fairbanks,AK	25989.64	0.23
				Fairbanks North S. B.,AK	7361.16	10.56
				Matanuska-Susitna B.,AK	24689.41	1.61
				Nome Census Area,AK	23008.59	0.36
				North Slope B.,AK	87845.38	0.07
				Northwest Arctic B.,AK	35856.31	0.17
Philadelphia,PA	0.1884	135.11	11735.78	Burlington,NJ	804.63	490.99
				Delaware,PA	184.19	2973.23
				Montgomery,PA	483.06	1403.78
				Bucks,PA	607.54	890.76
				Camden,NJ	222.29	2261.98
				Gloucester,NJ	324.81	708.36
Suffolk,MA	0.1831	58.51	11347.16	Essex,MA	497.98	1345.59
				Norfolk,MA	399.54	1542.01
				Middlesex,MA	823.40	1698.40
Bronx,NY	0.1633	42.02	28645.75	Bergen,NJ	234.16	3524.80
				Nassau,NY	286.72	4489.89
				New York,NY	28.37	52428.34
				Westchester,NY	432.81	2021.36
				Queens,NY	109.38	17842.16
Northwest A. B.,AK	0.1489	35856.31	.17	Nome Census Area,AK	23008.59	0.36
				Yukon-Koyukuk,AK	157094.25	0.05
				North Slope B.,AK	87845.38	0.07

Table 2. Top five outliers and their neighbors

will refer to this method as SLZ (Shekhar, Lu and Zhang). The core idea of SLZ is that given a function f defined on the spatial set S, the neighborhood effect can be captured by the transformation $g(x) = f(x) - \sum_{y \in N(x)} f(y)$. This is followed by an application of a statistical test on g inspired from Chebyshev's inequality to determine the outliers of f.

Our synthetic data set consists of one hundred spatial objects organized as a 10×10 matrix. We used a Gaussian generator to produce the values of non-spatial attribute, and they are listed in Figure 2. The location of some values were deliberately changed so that all the zeros appeared at the lower-left corner and an 8 showed up at the location (8,1).

The top five outliers detected by SLZ (at a confidence interval of 95 percent) and SLOM are listed in Table 1. The $\bar{d}$, SLOM and the SLZ matrices are shown in Figures 4, 5 and 6 respectively. The objects located at position (0,7),(0,5) and (3,9) are marked as outliers by both methods. This means that they are both global and local outliers. The objects located at position (6,4) and (9,4) are captured as one of the top five outliers by SLZ but not by SLOM . This means that they are global outliers but not local outliers as they are located in unstable areas. This can be seen from

their SLOM values which are 0.06 and 0.10. The objects located at position (8,1) and (2,5) are captured as outliers by SLOM, but not SLZ. This means they are local but not global outliers. Again their SLOM values are 0.17 and 0.25 respectively.

4.2 Result on a Real Dataset

The real data set that we have used is from the U.S Census Bureau and consists of spatial and non-spatial information about all the counties in the United States. In order to make the results easily comprehensible we have selected two non-spatial attributes: area and population density. The informaton about the top five outliers counties and their neighbors is listed in Table 2. Not surprisingly the top 5 outliers consist of counties which have large areas or large population densities. However they are truly local outliers. For example, the area of the Yukon-Koyukuk county in Alaska is almost twice as big as the area of any of its neighboring counties, and its population density (except for the North Slope county) is three times smaller. For urban areas notice that Philadelphia is more "outlierish" compared to the Bronx even though it has a bigger area and smaller popula-

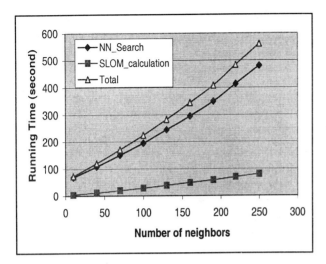

Figure 7. The break-up of the total running time into NN search and SLOM value calculation as a function of the number of nearest neighbors

tion density again because its neighborhood is relative more stable.

4.3 Break-up of the total running time

The total running time of our algorithm mainly consists of two part: the time to search the nearest neighbors (NN_Search) and the time to calculate the SLOM values ($SLOM\_Calculation$). The break up is shown in Figure 7 from which it is clear that most of the running time is consumed by the nearest neighbor search.

5 Summary and Future Work

We have proposed a new measure "Spatial Local Outlier Measure"(SLOM) which captures both spatial autocorrelation and spatial heteroscedasticity (non-constant variance). The effects of spatial autocorrelation are factored out by a new measure $\tilde{d}$ which reduces the effects of outliers on its neighbors. The variance of a neighborhood is captured by $\beta(o)$ which quantifies the oscillation and instability of an area around o. The use of β, instead of standard-deviation, was motivated by a desire to deterministically bound a variance-like measure. We have compared our approach with the current state-of-the-art methods and have shown that SLOM is sharper in detecting local outliers. Local outliers may be more interesting than global outliers because they are likely to be less known and therefore more surprising. Another novel feature of our approach is related to system integration. The spatial data never leaves

the database and we use an R-tree index to carry out nearest neighbor queries directly in the database.

For future work we would like to apply our method to large climate databases and discover potentially useful patterns like the Southern Oscillation Index (SOI).

References

[1] M. M. Breunig, H.-P. Kriegel, R. T. Ng, and J. Sander. Lof: Identifying density-based local outliers. In W. Chen, J. F. Naughton, and P. A. Bernstein, editors, *Proceedings of the 2000 ACM SIGMOD International Conference on Management of Data, May 16-18, 2000, Dallas, Texas, USA*, pages 93–104. ACM, 2000.

[2] D. Hawkins. *Identification of Outliers*. Chapman and Hall, London, 1980.

[3] E. M. Knorr and R. T. Ng. Algorithms for mining distance-based outliers in large datasets. In *Proceedings of 24rd International Conference on Very Large Data Bases, August 24-27, 1998, New York City, New York, USA*, pages 392–403. Morgan Kaufmann, 1998.

[4] C.-T. Lu, D. Chen, and Y. Kou. Algorithms for spatial outlier detection. In *Proceedings of the 3rd IEEE International Conference on Data Mining (ICDM 2003), 19-22 December 2003, Melbourne, Florida, USA*, pages 597–600. IEEE Computer Society, 2003.

[5] C.-T. Lu, D. Chen, and Y. Kou. Detecting spatial outliers with multiple attributes. In *Proceedings of 15th IEEE International Conference on Tools with Artificial Intelligence (ICTAI 2003), 3-5 November 2003, Sacramento, California, USA*, pages 122–128. IEEE Computer Society, 2003.

[6] M. McPhadden. El nino and la nina: Causes and global consequences. In *Encyclopedia of Global Environmental Change*, pages 353–370, 2002.

[7] S. C. Shashi Shekhar. *Spatial Databases: A Tour*. Prentice Hall, 2003.

[8] S. Shekhar, C.-T. Lu, and P. Zhang. Detecting graph-based spatial outliers: algorithms and applications (a summary of results). In *Proceedings of the seventh ACM SIGKDD international conference on Knowledge discovery and data mining, August 26-29, 2001, San Francisco, CA, USA. ACM, 2001*, pages 371–376, 2001.

[9] S. Shekhar, C.-T. Lu, and P. Zhang. A unified approach to detecting spatial outliers. *GeoInformatica*, 7(2):139–166, 2003.

[10] R. Wilcox. *Applying Contemporary Statistical Techniques*. Elseiver Science, 2003.

MMAC: A New Multi-class, Multi-label Associative Classification Approach

Fadi A. Thabtah
*Modelling Optimisation
Scheduling And Intelligent
Computing Research Centre
Fabdelja@bradford.ac.uk*

Peter Cowling
*Modelling Optimisation
Scheduling And Intelligent
Computing Research Centre
P.i.Cowling@bradford.ac.uk*

Yonghong Peng
*Department of Computing,
University of Bradford, BD7
1DP, UK
Y.h.Peng@bradford.ac.uk*

Abstract

Building fast and accurate classifiers for large-scale databases is an important task in data mining. There is growing evidence that integrating classification and association rule mining together can produce more efficient and accurate classifiers than traditional classification techniques. In this paper, the problem of producing rules with multiple labels is investigated. We propose a new associative classification approach called multi-class, multi-label associative classification (MMAC). This paper also presents three measures for evaluating the accuracy of data mining classification approaches to a wide range of traditional and multi-label classification problems. Results for 28 different datasets show that the MMAC approach is an accurate and effective classification technique, highly competitive and scalable in comparison with other classification approaches.

1. Introduction

Classification is a well-known task in data mining that aims to predict the class of an unseen instance as accurately as possible. While single label classification, which assigns each rule in the classifier the most obvious label, has been widely studied [9, 11, 13, 18], little work has been done on multi-label classification. Most of the work to date on multi-label classification is related to text categorisation [10, 15]. There are many approaches for building single class classifiers from data, such as divide-and-conquer [14] and separate-and-conquer [8]. Most traditional learning techniques derived from these approaches, such as decision trees [7, 13], and statistical and covering algorithms [11], are unable to treat problems with multiple labels.

The most common multi-label classification approach is one-versus-the rest (OvR) [17], which constructs a set of binary classifiers obtained by training on each possible class versus all the rest. OvR approach performs the winner-take-all strategy that assigns a real value for each class to indicate the class membership.

Another known approach in multi-label classification is one-versus-one (OvO) [15], which constructs a classifier that has been trained on each possible pair of classes. For K classes, this results in $(K-1)$ $K/2$ binary classifiers, which may be problematic if K is large. On the other hand, the OvR approach has been criticised for training on several separate classification problems, since each class can easily be separated from the rest, and therefore problems a rise, like contradictory decisions, i.e. whenever two or more rules predict the test instance, and no decision, i.e. whenever none of the resulting rules can predict the test instance [6].

Another important task in data mining is the discovery of all association rules in data. Classification and association rule discovery are similar, except that there is only one target to predict in classification, i.e., the class, while association rule can predict any attribute in the data. In recent years, a new approach that integrates association rule with classification, named associative classification, has been proposed [9, 12]. A few accurate classifiers that use associative classification have been presented in the past few years, such as CBA [12], CMAR [9], and CPAR [18].

In existing associative classification techniques, only one class label is associated with each rule derived, and thus rules are not suitable for the prediction of multiple labels. However, multi-label classification may often be useful in practise. Consider for example, a document which has two class labels "Health" and "Government", and assume that the document is associated 50 times with the "Health" label and 48 times with the "Government" label, and the number of times the document appears in the training data is 98. A traditional associative technique like CBA generates the rule associated with the "Health" label simply because it has a larger representation, and discards the other rule. However, it is very useful to generate the other rule, since it brings up useful knowledge having a large representation in the training data, and thus could take a role in classification. In this paper, a novel approach for multi-class and multi-label classification, named multi-class, multi-label associative classification (MMAC), is introduced. It assumes that for each instance that passes certain thresholds, there is a rule associated with not only the most obvious class, but with the second, third,…, k_{th} possible class label. Three evaluation methods are presented in this research paper in order to evaluate classifiers derived by MMAC on different application themes, and compare them to other approaches.

The multi-label classification problem is introduced in Section 2. Basic concepts of association rule and associative classification are discussed in Section 3. The MMAC approach and our methods for evaluation of traditional and multi-label classifiers are presented in Section 4, and the experimental results are given in Section 5. Finally the conclusions are presented in Section 6.

2. Multi-label Classification

Most of the research conducted on classification in data mining has been devoted to single label problems. A traditional classification problem can be defined as follows: let D denote the domain of possible training instances and Y be a list of class labels, let H denote the set of classifiers for $D \rightarrow Y$, each instance $d \in D$ is assigned a single class y that belongs to Y. The goal is to find a classifier $h \in H$ that maximises the probability that $h(d) = y$ for each test case (d, y). In multi-label problems, however, each instance $d \in D$ can be assigned multiple labels $y1, y2, …, y_k$ for $y_i \in y$, and is represented as a pair $(d, (y1, y2, …, y_k))$ where $(y1, y2, …, y_k)$ is a list of ranked class labels from y associated with the instance d in the training data.

3. Classification Based on Association Rule

3.1 Frequent Items, Support and Confidence

Let T be the training data with n attributes $A_1, A_2, …, A_n$ and C is a list of class labels. A particular value for attribute A_i will be denoted a_i, and the class labels of C are denoted c_j.

Definition 1: An item is defined by the association of an attribute and its value (A_i, a_i), or a combination of between 1 and n different attributes values, e.g. $< (A_1, a_1)>$, $< (A_1, a_1), (A_2, a_2)>$, $(A_1, a_1), (A_2, a_2), (A_3, a3)>$, … etc.

Definition 2: A rule r for multi-label classification is represented in the form:

$$(A_{i1}, a_{i1}) \wedge (A_{i2}, a_{i2}) \wedge … \wedge (A_{1m}, a_{i_m}) \rightarrow c_{i1} \vee c_{i2} \vee … \vee c_{im}$$

where the condition of the rule is an item and the consequent is a list of ranked class labels.

Definition 3: The actual occurrence (*ActOccr*) of a rule r in T is the number of cases in T that match r's condition.

Definition 4: The support count (*SuppCount*) of r is the number of cases in T that matches r's condition, and belong to a class c_i. When the item is associated with multiple labels, there should be a different *SuppCount* for each label.

Definition 5: A rule r passes the minimum support threshold (*MinSupp*) if for r, the *SuppCount*(r)/ $|T| \geq$ *MinSupp*, where $|T|$ is the number of instances in T.

Definition 6: A rule r passes the minimum confidence threshold (*MinConf*) if *SuppCount*(r)/*ActOccr*$(r) \geq$ *MinConf*.

Definition 7: Any item in T that passes the *MinSupp* is said to be a frequent item.

3.2 Associative Classification

Generally, in association rule mining, any item that passes *MinSupp* is known as a frequent item. If the frequent item consists of only a single value, i.e. items $< (A1, x1)>$, $< (A1, x2)>$ and $< (A2, y1)>$ in Table 1, it is said to be a frequent single item. The frequent single items are inputs to the process of finding possible frequent pairs of items, the frequent pairs of items are input to discover frequent triples of items, and so on. Associative classification techniques generate frequent items by making multiple passes over the training data. In the first pass, they count the support of single items and determine whether it is frequent, and then in each subsequent pass, they start with items found to be frequent in the previous pass in order to produce new possible frequent items.

After frequent items have been discovered, associative classification methods derive a complete set of class-association-rules (CAR) for those frequent items that pass *MinConf*. These kinds of techniques are often called confidence-based methods, since they generate only the most obvious class per association rule. One of the first algorithms to bring up the idea of using an association rule for classification was proposed in [12]. It has been named CBA. It consists of two main phases; phase one implements the famous Apriori algorithm [2] in order to discover frequent items. Phase two involves building the classifier. Experimental results indicated that CBA produced classifiers which are competitive to popular learning methods like decision trees [13].

Table 1. Training data 1

RowIds	A1	A2	Single Class
1	x1	y1	c1
2	x1	y2	c2
3	x1	y1	c2
4	x1	y2	c1
5	x2	y1	c2
6	x2	y1	c1
7	x2	y3	c2
8	x1	y3	c1
9	x2	y4	c1
10	x3	y1	c1

4. MMAC

Our proposed algorithm consists of three phases: rules generation, recursive learning and classification. In the first phase, it scans the training data to discover and generate a complete CAR. In the second phase, MMAC proceeds to discover more rules that pass the *MinSupp* and *MinConf* thresholds from the remaining unclassified instances, until no further frequent items can be found. In the third phase, the rules sets derived at each iteration will be merged to form a global multi-class label classifier that will then tested against test data. Figure 1 represents a general description of our proposed method, which we will explain in more detail below. Training attributes can be categorical, i.e. attributes with limited distinct values, or continuous, i.e., real and integer attributes. For categorical attributes, we assume that all possible values are mapped to a set of positive integers. At the present time, our method does not treat continuous attributes.

Input: Training data, confidence and support (σ) thresholds
Output: A set of multi-label rules and the classification accuracy
Phase 1:
❖ Scan the training data T with n columns to discover frequent items
❖ Produce rules set$_i$ by converting any frequent item that passes *MinConf* into a rule.
❖ Rank the rules set according to (confidence, support, …, etc).
❖ Evaluate the rules set$_i$ in order to remove redundant rules.
Phase 2:
❖ Discard instances P_i associated with rules set$_i$
❖ Generate new training data $T^{'} \leftarrow T - P_i$
❖ Repeat phase 1 on $T^{'}$ until no further frequent item is found
Phase 3:
❖ Merge rules sets generated at each iteration to produce a multi-label classifier
❖ Classify test objects

Figure 1. MMAC algorithm

4.1 Building the Classifier

4.1.1 Frequent Items Discovery and Rules Generation.
To increase the efficiency of frequent items discovery and rules generation, MMAC employs a new technique based on an intersection method that has been presented in [21]. We have extended their method to accomplish classification. Our method scans the training data once to count the occurrences of single items, from which it determines those that pass *MinSupp* and *MinConf* thresholds, and stores them along with their occurrences (rowIds) inside fast access data structures. Then, by intersecting the rowIds of the frequent single items discovered so far, we can easily obtain the possible remaining frequent items that involve more than one attribute. The rowIds for frequent single items are useful information, and can be used to locate items easily in the training data in order to obtain support and confidence values for rules involving more than one item.

To clarify the picture, consider for instance frequent single items A and B, if we intersect the rowIds sets of A and B, then the resulting set should represent the tuples where A and B happen to be together in the training data, and therefore the classes associated with A^B can be easily located, in which the support and confidence can be accessed and calculated, which they will be used to decide whether or not A^B is a frequent item and a candidate rule in the classifier. Since the training data have been scanned once to discover and generate the rules, this approach is highly effective in runtime and storage because it does not rely on the traditional approach of discovering frequent items [1], which requires multiple scans.

Once an item has been identified as a frequent item, MMAC checks whether or not it passes the *MinConf* threshold. If the item confidence is larger than *MinConf*, then it will be generated as a candidate rule in the classifier. Otherwise, the item will be discarded. Thus, all items that survive *MinConf* are generated as candidate rules in the classifier.

4.1.2 Ranking of Rules and Pruning.
In order to ensure a subset of effective rules form the classifier, a detailed ranking technique, which is shown in Figure 2, is presented. It reduces the need for random selection and aims to ensure that high confidence general and detailed

---

Definition 8: Given two rules, r_a and r_b, r_a precedes r_b if :
1. The confidence of r_a is greater than that of r_b
2. The confidence values of r_a and r_b are the same, but the support of r_a is greater than that of r_b
3. The confidence and support values of r_a and r_b are the same, but r_a has larger *ActOccr* than r_b in the training data
4. Both confidence and support and *ActOccr* values of r_a and r_b are the same, but r_a has fewer conditions in its left hand side (LHS) than that of r_b
5. All above criteria are identical for r_a and r_b, but r_a was generated before r_b

Figure 2. Rules ranking technique of MMAC

---

rules are kept for classification. Pruning takes place by discarding any item that has a support value less than the *MinSupp,* and a confidence value less than the *MinConf* threshold. Another pruning of the rules occurs in the rule evaluation which we will discuss in the next subsection.

4.1.3 Rules Evaluation. A rule *r* is said to be significant if and only if it covers at least one training instance. After a set of rules is generated and ranked, an evaluation step takes place to test each rule in order to remove redundant rules. If a rule correctly classifies at least a single instance, then it will be marked as a survivor, and a good candidate rule. In addition, all instances correctly classified by it will be deleted from the training data. In the case that a rule has not classified any training instance, it will then be removed from the rules set.

4.1.4 Recursive Learning. For given training instances *D*, other associative classification algorithms like CBA and CPAR derive a single label rules set, and form a default class for the remaining unclassified instances in *D*. On the other hand, the MMAC derives more than one rules set, and merges them to form a multi-label classifier. For *D*, the proposed method produces the first rules set in which each rule is associated with the most obvious class label. Once this rules set is generated, all training instances associated with it will be discarded. The remaining unclassified instances will then become new training data, say D', and the MMAC checks whether there are still any more frequent items remaining undiscovered in D' (rules derived from *D* which may be associated with more than one class label). If so, a new set of rules will be generated from D', and the remaining unclassified instances in D' will form new training data, and so forth. The algorithm proceeds with learning until no more frequent items could be discovered. At that stage, any remaining unclassified instance will form a default class.

This process results in learning from several subsets of the original training data and generating few rules sets. Consider for example the training data shown in Table 2. Assume that the *MinSupp* and *MinConf* have been set to 20% and 40%, respectively. At the first iteration, MMAC derives a set of rules that covers the instances that are not underlined in Table 2, which eventually will be discarded at the end of the iteration. The remaining unclassified instances which are underlined will represent the new training data for

Table 2. Training data

RowId	A1	A2	Class
1	x1	y1	c1
2	x1	y2	c2
3	x1	y1	c2
4	x1	y2	c1
5	x2	y1	c2
6	x2	y1	c1
7	x2	y3	c2
8	x1	y3	c1
9	x2	y4	c1

iteration two, in which two more rules will be learned and produced to form the second rules set. When the learning process is finished, a merging of the rules sets which have been produced at iterations 1 and 2 will be performed to obtain a global multi-label classifier. In many cases, a rule will be presented in more than one rules set and is associated with different class labels like item <(A1, x1)> which has two representations in Table 2, one with class label "c1" in rules set 1, and one with class label "c2" in rules set 2. A good question will be how one can rank the class labels in a rule to represent this item.

4.1.5 Ranking of Class Labels. Definition 9: A class label $l_1 < l_2$, also known as l_1, precedes l_2 in a rule *r* if it has a larger representation in the training data. Consider, for example, an item $< (A, a)(B, b)>$ which is associated with three labels ("c1", "c2", "c3"). Assume that it has 100 representation in the training data in which it is associated with labels "c1", "c2" and "c3", 50, 30, and 20 times. Moreover, assume that this item has passed *MinSupp* and *MinConf* thresholds when associated with "c1", "c2" and "c3". MMAC ranks these labels based on their number of occurrences ("c1"<"c2"<"c3"), and a rule will be presented for this instance in the following form: $(A,a) \wedge (B,b) \rightarrow c1 \vee c2 \vee c3$.

4.2 Classification

In classification, let *R* be the set of generated rules and *T* the training data. The basic idea of the proposed method is to choose a set of high confidence rules in *R* to cover *T*. In classifying a test object, the first rule in the set of rules that matches the test object condition classifies it. This process ensures that only the highest ranked rules classify test objects.

4.3 Comparison of MMAC and CBA

CBA and MMAC were applied on the training data shown in Table 1 by using a *MinSupp* of 20% and *MinConf* of 40% to illustrate the effectiveness of the rules sets derived by both algorithms. Table 3a represents the classifier generated by CBA, which consists of two rules and covers 8 training instances, which are (1, 2, 3, 4, 5, 6, 8, 10). The remaining two instances form a default class rule that covers 20% of the entire data.

Table 3b represents the classifier produced by MMAC on the same training data, in which more rules have been discovered, i.e. two more rules than the CBA classifier. The rules extracted will be then ranked and merged to form a multi-class label classifier in which some of its rules are associated with a list of ranked class labels. In this particular example, there is only one rule derived by our proposed algorithm from Table 1 that has

RuleId	Frequent Item	Support	Confidence	Class Label
1	x1	3/10	3/5	C1
3	y1	3/10	3/5	C1
default				C2

Table 3b. MMAC classifier

RuleId	Frequent Item	Support	Confidence	Class Label
1a	x1	3/10	3/5	C1
1b	x1	2/10	2/5	C2
2	x2	2/10	2/4	C2
3	y1	3/10	3/5	C1
default				C1

multiple labels which is $(A1, x1) \rightarrow c1 \lor c2$. The MMAC classifier covers nine training instances, and the remaining one forms the default class. Unlike the CBA algorithm that was unable to produce rules with multiple labels, our proposed method generates rules that can predict multiple labels. Moreover, the default rule of MMAC classifier covers only 10% of the training data, and therefore it has less impact on the classification of unseen data that may significantly affect the accuracy in the classification, and could lead to deterioration in the overall error rate.

Generally, the main differences between MMAC and other associative algorithms are the following:

- MMAC presents not only a single class classifier but also a multi-label one, in which each instance is associated with its ranked list of classes.
- Other associative classification techniques often use multiple passes to discover frequent items. Alternatively, MMAC uses a new technique for discovering the rules, which requires only one scan.
- MMAC introduces a detailed rule ranking technique that minimises randomisation when a choice point among two or more rules occurs in the rules ranking process.
- The proposed method presents a recursive learning phase that discovers more rules, and minimises the role of the default class in classifying test objects.
- Other associative techniques discover frequent items in one phase, and generate the rules in a separate phase. The proposed method discovers and generates rules in one phase.

4.4 Evaluation Measures

Since multi-label classification has been investigated mostly in text categorisation, there is very little work conducted on developing evaluation measures for its classifiers. There are no standard evaluation techniques applicable to the multi-label classification problems. Moreover, the right measure is often problematic and depends heavily on the features of the conducted problem, such as those used in [3]. In this section, we introduce three evaluation measures suitable for the majority of binary, multi-class and multi-label classification problems.

4.4.1 Top-label. This evaluation measure takes into consideration only the top-ranked class label and ignores any other labels associated with an instance. For traditional classification task where there is only one class label to assign to the test object, and given an instance and its associated class label $<d, y>$, a classifier H predicts a list of ranked class labels $Y_j = \left\langle Y_j^1, Y_j^2, ..., Y_j^k \right\rangle$, if the predicted first class label matches the true class label y of the instance, i.e. $Y_j^1 = y$, then the classification is correct. The top-label method estimates how many times the top-ranked class label is the correct class label. So, for a set of single-class instances $I = <(x_1, y_1), (x_2, y_2),...,(x_m, y_m)>$, the top-label is $\frac{1}{m} \sum_{j=1}^{m} (Y_j^1 = y_j)$, where m represents the number of instances.

4.4.2 Any-label. This evaluation technique measures how many times any of the predicted labels of an instance matches the actual class label in all cases of that instance in the test data. If any of the predicted class labels of an instance d matches the true class label y, i.e. $Y_j^i = y$, then the classification is correct. For a set of single-class instances $I = <(x_1, y_1), (x_2, y_2),...,(x_m, y_m)>$, the any-label is $\frac{1}{m} \sum_{j=1}^{m} (Y_j^i = y_j)$, where m represents the number of instances.

4.4.3 Label-weight. This technique enables each predicted label for an instance to play a role in classifying a test case based on its ranking, and therefore it could be considered as a multi-label evaluation measure. An instance may belong to several class labels, each one associated with it by a number of occurrences in the training data. Each class label can be assigned a weight according to how many times that label has been associated with the instance. Let rule r_j be associated with a list of ranked labels $Y_j = \left\langle Y_j^1, Y_j^2, ..., Y_j^k \right\rangle$, and denote w_j^k as the set of weights for Y_j where $\sum_{j=1}^{k} w_j^k = 1$. A classifier H is defined as $D \rightarrow Y$ such that it assigns a weight of the correct class label to an instance as $H(d) = W^i$, where $d \in D$, and $W^i \in W_j^k$. For a set of single-class instances $I = <(x_1, y_1), (x_2, y_2),...,(x_n, y_n)>$, the label-weight

$$is \frac{1}{m} \sum_{k=1}^{m} \left(w^i * \left\langle \delta(H(d_i), y_i) \right\rangle \right) \qquad , \qquad \text{where}$$

$$\delta(x, y) = \begin{cases} 1 & if & x = y \\ 0 & if & x \neq y \end{cases}.$$

For example, if an item (A ,a) is associated with class labels "c1", "c2" and "c3", 7, 5 and 3 times, respectively, in the training data. Each class label will be assigned a weight, i.e. 7/15, 5/15, and 3/15, respectively, for labels "c1", "c2" and "c3". This technique assigns the predicted class label weight to the case if the predicted class label matches the case class label. For instance if label "c2" of item (A, a) matches a case in the test data that has "c2" as its class, then the case will be considered a hit, and 5/15 will be assigned to the case.

5. Experimental Results

We investigated our approach against 19 different datasets from [20] as well as a different datasets for forecasting the behaviour of an optimisation heuristic within a hyperheuristic framework [5, 16]. Stratified ten-fold cross-validation was used to derive the classifiers and error rates in the experiments. Cross-validation is a standard evaluation measure for calculating error rate on data in machine learning. Three popular classification techniques a decision tree rule (PART), RIPPER and CBA have been compared to MMAC in terms of classification accuracy, in order to evaluate the predictive power of the proposed method.

The choice of such learning methods is based on the different strategies they use to generate the rules. Since the chosen techniques are only suitable for traditional classification problems where there is only one class assigned to each training instance, we therefore used classification accuracy derived by only the top-label evaluation measure for fair comparison.

All experiments were conducted on a Pentium IV 1.6 GH PC. The experiments of PART and RIPPER were conducted using the *Weka* software system [20]. *Weka* stands for Waikato Environment for Knowledge Analysis. It is an open java source code for the machine teaching community that includes implementations of different methods for several different data mining tasks such as classification, clustering, association rule and regression. CBA experiments were conducted using a VC++ implementation version provided by [19]. Finally, MMAC was implemented using Java.

We have evaluated 19 selected datasets from *Weka* data collection [20], in which, a few of them (6) were reduced by ignoring their integer and/or real attributes. Several tests using ten-fold cross-validation have been performed to ensure that the removal of any real/integer attributes from some of the datasets does not significantly affect the classification accuracy. To do so, we only considered datasets where the error rate was not more than 6% worse than the error rate obtained on the same dataset before the removal of any real/integer attributes. Thus, the ignored attributes do not impact on the error rate too significantly.

Many studies have shown that the support threshold plays a major role in the overall classification accuracy of the set of rules produced by existing associative classification techniques [9, 12]. Moreover, the support value has a larger impact on the number of rules produced in the classifier and the processing time and storage needed during the algorithm rules discovery and generation. From our experiments, we noticed that the support rates that ranged between 2% to 5% usually achieve the best balance between accuracy rates and the size of the resulted classifiers. Moreover, the classifiers derived when the support was set to 2% and 3% achieved high accuracy, and most often better than that of decision trees rule (PART), RIPPER and CBA. Thus, the *MinSupp* was set to 3% in the experiments. The confidence threshold, on the other hand, is less complex and does not have a large effect on the behaviour of any associative classification method as support value, and thus it has been set to 30%.

Table 4 represents the classification rate of the classifiers generated by PART, RIPPER, CBA and MMAC against 19 benchmark problems from *Weka* data

Table 4. Classification accuracy of PART, RIPPER, CBA and MMAC

Dataset	PART	RIPPER	CBA	MMAC
Tic-Tac	92.58	97.54	98.60	99.29
Contact-lenses	83.33	75.00	66.67	79.69
Led7	73.56	69.34	72.39	73.20
Breast-cancer	71.32	70.97	68.18	72.10
Weather	57.14	64.28	85.00	71.66
Heart-c	81.18	79.53	78.54	81.51
Heart-s	78.57	78.23	71.20	82.45
Lymph	76.35	77.70	74.43	82.20
Mushroom	99.81	99.90	98.92	99.78
primary-tumor	39.52	36.28	36.49	43.92
Vote	87.81	87.35	87.39	89.21
CRX	84.92	84.92	86.75	86.47
Sick	93.90	93.84	93.88	93.78
Balance-scale	77.28	71.68	74.58	86.10
Autos	61.64	56.09	35.79	67.47
Breast-w	93.84	95.42	94.68	97.26
Hypothyroid	92.28	92.28	92.29	92.23
zoo	91.08	85.14	83.18	96.15
kr-vs-kp	71.93	70.24	42.95	68.75

collection. The accuracy of MMAC has been derived using the top-label evaluation measure. Our algorithm outperforms the rule learning methods in terms of accuracy rate, and the won-loss-tied records of MMAC against PART, RIPPER and CBA 13-6-0, 15-4-0 and 15-4-0, respectively.

The evaluation measures of MMAC have been compared on 9 solution runs produced by the Peckish hyperheuristic [5] with regard to accuracy, and number of rules produced. Figures 3a and 3b represent the relative prediction accuracy that indicates the difference of the classification accuracy of MMAC evaluation measures with respect to those derived by CBA and PART, respectively. In other words, how much better or worse MMAC measures perform with respect to CBA and PART learning methods. The relative prediction accuracy numbers shown in Figures 3a and 3b are conducted using the formula

$$\frac{(Accuracy_{MMAC} - Accuracy_{PART})}{Accuracy_{PART}}$$ and

$$\frac{(Accuracy_{MMAC} - Accuracy_{CBA})}{Accuracy_{CBA}}$$ respectively. After

analysing the charts, we found out that there is consistency between the top-label and label-weight measures, since both of them consider only one class in the prediction. The top-label takes into account the top-ranked class, and the label-weight considers only the weight for the predicted class that matches the test case. Thus, both of these evaluation measures are applicable to traditional single-class classification problems. On the other hand, the any-label measure considers any class in the set of the predicted classes as a hit whenever it matches the predicted class regardless of its weight or rank. Is should be noted that, the relative accuracy of MMAC evaluation methods against dataset number 8 in Figure 3a and 3b, is negative since CBA and PART achieved a higher classification rate against this particular dataset.

A comparison of the knowledge representation produced by our method, PART and CBA has been conducted to evaluate the effectiveness of the set of rules derived. Figure 4 represents the classifiers generated form the hyperheuristic datasets. Analysis of the rules sets indicated that MMAC derives a few more rules than PART and CBA for the majority of the datasets. In particular, the proposed method produced more rules than PART and CBA on 8 and 7 datasets, respectively. A possible reason for extracting more rules is based on the recursive learning phase that MMAC employs to discover more hidden information that most of the associative classification techniques discard, since they only extract the highest confidence rule for each frequent item that survives *MinConf*.

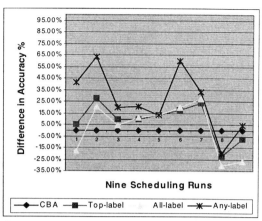

Figure 3a. Difference of accuracy between MMAC evaluation measures and CBA algorithm.

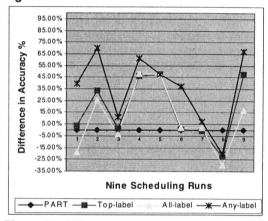

Figure 3b. Difference of accuracy between MMAC evaluation measures and PART algorithm.

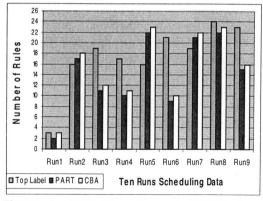

Figure 4. Classifier sizes of MMAC (top-label), PART and CBA algorithms against the scheduling data.

6. Conclusions

A new approach for multi-class, and multi-label classification has been proposed that has many distinguishing features over traditional and associative classification methods in that it (1) produces classifiers that contain rules with multiple labels, (2) presents three evaluation measures for evaluating accuracy rate, (3) employs a new method of discovering the rules that require only one scan over the training data, (4) introduces a ranking technique which prunes redundant rules, and ensures only high effective ones are used for classification, and (5) integrates frequent items set discovery and rules generation in one phase to conserve less storage and runtime. Performance studies on 19 datasets from *Weka* data collection and 9 hyperheuristic scheduling runs indicated that our proposed approach is effective, consistent and has a higher classification rate than the-state-of-the-art decision tree rule (PART), CBA and RIPPER algorithms. In further work, we anticipate extending the method to treat continuous data and creating a hyperheuristic approach to learn "on the fly" which low-level heuristic method is the most effective.

References

[1] R. Agrawal, T. Amielinski and A. Swami. Mining association rule between sets of items in large databases. *In Proceeding of the 1993 ACM SIGMOD International Conference on Management of Data*, Washington, DC, May 26-28 1993, pp. 207-216.

[2] R. Agrawal and R. Srikant. Fast algorithms for mining association rule. *In Proceeding of the 20th International Conference on Very Large Data Bases,* 1994, pp. 487 – 499.

[3] M. Boutell, X. Shen, J. Luo and C. Brown. Multi-label semantic scene classification. Technical report 813, Department of Computer Science, University of Rochester, Rochester , NY 14627 & Electronic Imaging Products R & D, Eastern Kodak Company, September 2003.

[4] A. Clare and R.D. King. Knowledge discovery in multi-label phenotype data. In L. De Raedt and A. Siebes, editors, *PKDD01*, volume 2168 of Lecture Notes in Artificial Intelligence, Springer - Verlag, 2001, pp. 42-53.

[5] P. Cowling and K. Chakhlevitch. Hyperheuristics for Managing a Large Collection of Low Level Heuristics to Schedule Personnel. *In Proceeding of 2003 IEEE conference on Evolutionary Computation*, Canberra, Australia, 8-12 Dec 2003.

[6] R. Duda, P. Hart, and D. Strok. *Pattern classification.* Wiley, 2001.

[7] E. Frank and I. Witten. Generating accurate rule sets without global optimisation. In Shavlik, J., ed., *Machine Learning: In Proceedings of the Fifteenth International Conference*, Madison, Wisconsin. Morgan Kaufmann Publishers, San Francisco, CA, pp. 144-151.

[8] J. Furnkranz. Separate-and-conquer rule learning. *Technical Report* TR-96-25, Austrian Research Institute for Artificial Intelligence, Vienna, 1996.

[9] W. Li, J. Han and J. Pei. CMAR: Accurate and efficient classification based on multiple class association rule. In *ICDM'01*, San Jose, CA, Nov. 2001, pp. 369-376.

[10] T. Joachims. Text categorisation with Support Vector Machines: Learning with many relevant features. *In Proceeding Tenth European Conference on Machine Learning*, 1998, pp. 137-142.

[11] T. S. Lim, W. Y. Loh and Y. S. Shih. A comparison of prediction accuracy, complexity and training time of thirty-three old and new classification algorithms. *Machine Learning*, 39, 2000.

[12] B. Liu, W. Hsu and Y. Ma. Integrating Classification and association rule mining. *In KDD '98*, New York, NY, Aug. 1998.

[13] J.R. Quinlan. C4.5: *Programs for Machine Learning*. San Mateo, CA: Morgan Kaufmann, San Francisco, 1993.

[14] J.R. Quinlan. Generating production rules from decision trees. *In Proceeding of the 10th International Joint Conferences on Artificial Intelligence*, Morgan Kaufmann, San Francisco, 1987, pp. 304-307.

[15] R. Schapire and Y. Singer, "BoosTexter: A boosting-based system for text categorization," *Machine Learning*, vol. 39, no. 2/3, 2000, pp. 135-168.

[16] F. Thabtah, P. Cowling and Y. Peng. Comparison of Classification techniques for a personnel scheduling problem. *In Proceeding of the 2004 International Business Information Management Conference, Amman, July 2004.*

[17] Y. Yang. An evaluation of statistical approaches to text categorisation. Technical Report CMU-CS-97-127, Carnegie Mellon University, April 1997.

[18] X. Yin and J. Han. CPAR: Classification based on predictive association rule. In *SDM 2003*, San Francisco, CA, May 2003.

[19] CBA:http://www.comp.nus.edu.sg/~dm2/ p_download.html

[20] Weka: Data Mining Software in Java: http://www.cs.waikato.ac.nz/ml/weka.

[21] M. J. Zaki, S. Parthasarathy, M. Ogihara, and W. Li. New algorithms for fast discovery of association rules. *In Proceedings of the 3rd KDD Conference*, Aug. 1997, pp.283-286.

Analysis of Consensus Partition in Cluster Ensemble

Alexander P. Topchy   Martin H. C. Law   Anil K. Jain
Dept. of Computer Science and Engineering
Michigan State University
East Lansing, MI 48824, USA
{topchyal, lawhiu, jain}@cse.msu.edu

Ana L. Fred
Dept. of Electr. and Comp. Engineering
Instituto Superior Tecnico
1049-001, Lisbon, Portugal
afred@lx.it.pt

Abstract

In combination of multiple partitions, one is usually interested in deriving a consensus solution with a quality better than that of given partitions. Several recent studies have empirically demonstrated improved accuracy of clustering ensembles on a number of artificial and real-world data sets. Unlike certain multiple supervised classifier systems, convergence properties of unsupervised clustering ensembles remain unknown for conventional combination schemes. In this paper we present formal arguments on the effectiveness of cluster ensemble from two perspectives. The first is based on a stochastic partition generation model related to re-labeling and consensus function with plurality voting. The second is to study the property of the "mean" partition of an ensemble with respect to a metric on the space of all possible partitions. In both the cases, the consensus solution can be shown to converge to a true underlying clustering solution as the number of partitions in the ensemble increases. This paper provides a rigorous justification for the use of cluster ensemble.

1 Introduction

Recent research on data clustering is increasingly focusing on combining multiple data partitions as a way to improve the robustness of clustering solutions. It has been shown that a meaningful consensus of multiple clusterings is possible by using a consensus function that maps a given ensemble (a collection of different partitions of a data set) to a combined clustering result. Several efficient consensus functions have been derived from statistical, graph-based and information-theoretic principles. A variety of known consensus functions are based on co-association matrix [5, 6, 7], hypergraph cuts [13, 9], mutual information [15], mixture models [14] and voting [3, 4]. Extensive experiments with these functions indicate that a combination of clusterings is capable of detecting novel cluster structures. Empirical evidence also supports the idea that requirements for individual clustering algorithms can be significantly relaxed in favor of weaker and inexpensive partition generation.

With all this progress, we are still lacking a rigorous understanding of why clustering ensembles can converge to a better consensus solution as compared with individual components of an ensemble. Basic properties of the consensus solutions have not been rigorously analyzed for existing consensus functions. The challenge of explaining the cluster ensembles is two-fold. First, a consensus of unsupervised classifications does not conform to the rules established for multiple classifier systems due to the invariance of clustering to class label permutations. All the partitions which differ only in cluster labeling are identical. Second, analysis of consensus solutions must include both consensus functions as well as assumptions about the ensemble generation mechanism. Indeed, clustering ensembles merely represent a more sophisticated class of clustering algorithms utilizing a two-step process – ensemble generation and search for consensus.

Several difficulties must be resolved in providing the "proof of consensus". Primarily, we need a good probabilistic model of individual unsupervised classifications as the components of ensemble. Many studies use the k-means algorithm and its randomness in choosing the initial cluster centers to generate diverse components. Unfortunately, at present we are unable to formally characterize the distribution of the k-means partitions of a data set produced from random initializations. In general, it is very difficult to make any analytic statement about a partition generated by a clustering algorithm. Moreover, some consensus functions, which act on the samples from such distributions of partitions, are either heuristic in nature or have no explicit objective function. For instance, the consensus results of hypergraph partitioning or agglomerative clustering algorithms for co-association matrices are difficult to predict.

Research supported by ONR grant no. N00014-04-1-0183.

To circumvent these difficulties, we have made several simplifying assumptions. As in the case of analyzing classifier combinations in supervised learning, we model the output of a clustering algorithm without referring to any property of the algorithm. Rather, the partition generated by an algorithm is interpreted as a noisy version of the ground-truth partition of the data set. Two approaches of analysis are considered. The first is based on the assumption that the unsupervised classifications of data are produced in two steps: each partition is a noisy version of the true partition, where all the cluster labels undergo a random permutation. The goal of consensus function is to discover the true underlying partition. As we explain below, voting with re-labeling can detect the true partition with probability approaching to 1 as the size of ensemble increases. Our second approach is based on the fact that a consensus function can be regarded as finding a "mean" partition of different partitions in a cluster ensemble, with respect to a metric defined on a space of partitions. By using results of large deviation theory, we can show that the chance of failing to discover the true partition drops exponentially with increasing number of partitions in the ensemble.

The notation used in this paper is as follows. A data set which we want to cluster into k clusters is represented by $\mathcal{X} = \{x_1, \ldots, x_n\}$, with $|\mathcal{X}| = n$. The set of all possible partitions of $\mathcal{X}$ into k clusters is denoted by $\mathbb{P}$, with $\mathbb{P} = \{P_1, P_2, \ldots, P_m\}$, where each P_i represents a partition of $\mathcal{X}$ into k clusters. The cardinality of $\mathbb{P}$, also known as the Stirling number of the second kind, is denoted by m. The (unknown) "ground-truth" partition of $\mathcal{X}$ is denoted by C. The cluster ensemble of N partitions is denoted by $D_N = (C_1, \ldots, C_N)$, where C_i represents a random partition of $\mathcal{X}$ that follows the probability measure μ, i.e., $P(C_i = P_j) = \mu(P_j)$, and $\sum_j \mu(P_j) = 1$.

2   Consensus based on voting

In this section, we analyze consensus solution obtained by plurality voting. We first define the probabilistic model for generating partitions that is based on mis-labeling and label permutation in section 2.1. Section 2.2 discusses the process of re-labeling, and section 2.3 shows that plurality voting used in the consensus function can indeed recover the ground truth partition, even with an imperfect collection of partitions.

2.1   Stochastic partition generation model

The true partition C of the data set $\mathcal{X}$ can be written as $C = \{C(x_1), C(x_2), \ldots, C(x_n)\}$, where $C(x_j) = l$, if the object x_j belongs to the l-th cluster, $l \in \{1, \ldots, k\}$. The cluster labels by themselves are irrelevant and simply used to specify the partition. Let the first n_1 objects belong to the

cluster 1, next n_2 objects belong to the cluster 2, etc., such that $n_1 + n_2 + \cdots + n_k = n$. Each observed partition C_i in the ensemble D_s is generated by two transformations of the true partition C: noise $C' = F(C)$ and label permutation $C^* = T(C')$.

First, a random noise with probability $(1 - p)$ is applied to a cluster label $C(x_j)$ of each object x_j, $j = 1, 2, \ldots, n$. The value $C(x_j)$ is replaced by a new random label l from $\{1, \ldots, k\}$ with equal probability q, for all values $l \neq C(x_j)$. Hence, an object keeps a correct label $C(x_j)$ with probability p, and acquires an incorrect label with probability $(1 - p)$. We assume that all the incorrect labels are equally probable:

$$q = \frac{1 - p}{k - 1}.$$

We say that the first step generates a noisy version $C'(X)$ of the true partition C:

$$C' = \{C'(x_1), C'(x_2), \ldots, C'(x_n)\}.$$

The second step performs a random permutation of the labels in a noisy partition C'. The label permutation $T = \{\sigma(1), \sigma(2), \ldots, \sigma(k)\}$ is drawn from a set of all possible permutations of k labels with uniform probability. The partition $C^*(X) = T(C(X))$ becomes a member of an ensemble:

$$C^* = \{C^*(x_1), C^*(x_2), \ldots, C^*(x_n)\},$$

and C_1, the first partition in the cluster ensemble, takes this value of C^*. The above process is repeated with different realizations of $F(.)$ and $T(.)$ to generate other partitions C_i in the ensemble. The observed ensemble D_N is just the collection of N random partitions:

$$D_N = \{C_1, C_2, \ldots, C_N\}.$$

The label permutation, which is absent in supervised classifier combination, is a major difficulty in deriving a consensus solution from multiple clusterings. One can note that this ensemble generation procedure can be also described as a sampling of object's labels from a finite mixture of multivariate multinomial components. A mixture model admits maximum likelihood solution for consensus clustering, but is difficult to analyze in terms of convergence. That is why we proceed with the voting-type consensus function, where explicit parallels with the supervised case of multiple experts are possible. Figure 1 illustrates ensemble generation with 4 partitions of 7 objects.

2.2   Voting consensus function

A consensus function maps a given set of partitions in the ensemble to a single consensus partition. Voting procedure can be used to find a target partition if (i) all the

true	Noisy partitions					relabeled partitions				
1	X1	1	1	1	2	X1	2	3	1	3
1	X2	1	1	2	1	X2	2	3	3	2
2	X3	3	2	2	2	X3	1	2	3	3
2	X4	2	3	1	2	X4	3	1	1	3
2	X5	2	2	2	1	X5	3	2	3	2
3	X6	3	3	3	3	X6	1	1	2	1
3	X7	3	2	2	1	X7	1	2	3	2

Figure 1. An example of ensemble generation.

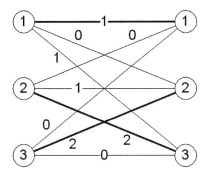

Figure 2. The bipartite graph for two partitions C_r and C_t.

ensemble's partitions use exactly the same set of cluster labels and (ii) clusters in different partitions are *consistently* labeled. A notion of consistent labeling can be made precise using our assumption about partition generation process: the best possible labeling of clusters in the ensemble should minimize the number of incorrectly labeled objects in comparison with the true partition. In order to achieve the most consistent labeling of clusters in a partition, we must solve an assignment problem equivalent to maximum weight bipartite matching problem. Equivalent matching problem is constructed from a contingency table between two partitions. A contingency table contains a number of cluster label co-occurrences counted for two partitions of the same set of objects. For example, for two partitions $C_r = \{1, 1, 2, 2, 2, 3, 3\}$ and $C_t = \{3, 1, 3, 3, 2, 2, 2\}$, we find the following contingency table

$$
\begin{array}{c|ccc}
 & \multicolumn{3}{c}{C_t} \\
 & 1 & 2 & 3 \\
\hline
C_r \quad 1 & 1 & 0 & 1 \\
2 & 0 & 1 & 2 \\
3 & 0 & 2 & 0 \\
\end{array}
$$

and the equivalent weighted bipartite graph (figure 2). The minimum number of misassigned objects in partition C_t

with respect to C_r is achieved by the re-labeling: $1 \leftrightarrow 1$, $2 \leftrightarrow 3$, $3 \leftrightarrow 2$ (shown by bold edges in the graph). Hence, the most consistent re-labeling would return $C_t = \{2, 1, 2, 2, 3, 3, 3\}$. In general, minimization of clustering error with respect to the true partition is equivalent to maximization of the weight of complete bipartite matching:

$$
\max_{\{y_{ij}\}} \sum_{i=1}^{k} \sum_{j=1}^{k} w_{ij} y_{ij} \tag{1}
$$
$$
\text{Subject to } \sum_{j=1}^{k} y_{ij} = \sum_{i=1}^{k} y_{ij} = 1, y_{ij} \in \{0,1\},
$$

where $\{w_{ij}\}$ are the values in the contingency table, and $\{y_{ij}\}$ are indicator variables which determine the correspondence between the clusters in the two partitions. An optimal solution of the problem (1) can be found by Hungarian algorithm [12] with the complexity $O(k^3)$.

A consistent re-labeling of all the partitions in the ensemble can be obtained by using a single common reference partition C_r. Ideally, the true partition is the best choice for a reference partition C_r, which, of course, is unavailable to us. In practice, any partition from the ensemble can be chosen as a reference partition. Then, all the remaining components of the ensemble can be relabeled by solving the problem in Equation (1) for every pair of partitions $(C_r, C_i), i = 1, ..., N, i \neq r$. Once all the partitions are re-labeled, plurality voting can be used to determine a consensus label for each object. *Plurality* voting decides in favor of a label, which is most frequently selected by individual experts in the ensemble for the given object. Unlike majority voting, more than half of the votes are not required for plurality consensus. Clearly, the accuracy of the consensus solution depends on the accuracy of: (i) decisions made by individual experts (clusterings), and (ii) their correct re-labeling through a solution of the matching problem. Both these procedures are analyzed in detail now.

2.3 Supervised plurality consensus

Suppose that a re-labeling of an ensemble has been done. We make this assumption before considering the accuracy of such a re-labeling in the next section. Given this, one has to deal with the ensemble of experts (partitions in the ensemble) where each expert is accurate with probability p^*. Note that the probability p^* that an object has a correct true label is generally different than the probability p, that the object label was not changed by noise $F(.)$, because of additional label permutation $T(.)$. Our first goal is to demonstrate that the accuracy of consensus solution, p_c, improves with the increasing ensemble size if each expert performs better than random. Specifically, we expect that ensemble accuracy p_c for k-class problem using the plurality voting combination rule satisfies:

$$\lim_{q \to \infty} p_c(p^*, q) = 1, \text{ for } p^* > \frac{1}{k} . \tag{2}$$

Note that p_c is a function of p^* and q because the performance of the ensemble, in general, depends on the noise level. The correctness of Equation (2) is commonly assumed in the literature for multiple classifier systems, yet its proof was given only recently for $k = 3$ and for general k with "best" non-independent classifiers [2]. Here, we would like to provide a simple proof of this convergence property for independent classifiers. Further, it will be utilized for unsupervised case as well.

We will assume that all the individual experts are independent. We shall focus on the label of a particular object x_l. Each decision on the object's class (label) is correct with probability h. All the incorrect decisions are equally probable for any given object. Let Z_1 be the number of votes in favor of the correct class and Z_i be the number of votes for an incorrect class i, $2 \le i \le k$. Given N independent decisions, the joint probability of random variables $Z_1, Z_2, \ldots, Z_k$ is a multinomial:

$$P(Z_1 = N_1, Z_2 = N_2, \ldots, Z_K = N_k)$$
$$= \frac{N!}{N_1! N_2! \ldots N_k!} h^{N_1} g^{N_2} \ldots g^{N_k} \tag{3}$$

Here, $g = (1 - h)/(k - 1)$ is probability of each possible incorrect class, and $N = N_1 + N_2 + \ldots + N_k$. The probability, p_c, of correct classification by N experts using plurality voting is:

$$
\begin{aligned}
p_C &= P(Z_1 > Z_2, Z_1 > Z_3, \ldots, Z_1 > Z_k) \\
&= 1 - P(Z_1 \le Z_2 \text{ or } Z_1 \le Z_3 \text{ or } \ldots \text{ or } Z_1 \le Z_k) \\
&\ge 1 - \sum_{i=2}^{k} P(Z_1 \le Z_i)
\end{aligned}
\tag{4}
$$

Consider any term $P(Z_1 \le Z_i)$ in the sum in Equation (4). We intend to show that for all $i > 1$, as $P(Z_1 \le Z_i) \to 0$ as $N \to \infty$, that would also imply $p_c \to 1$ as stated in Equation (2). Probability $P(Z_1 \le Z_i)$ can be rewritten as $P(Y_i \le 0)$, with $Y_i = (Z_1 - Z_i)/N$. Expected value and variance of Y_i can be obtained from multinomial distribution in Equation (3):

$$E[Y_i] = \frac{Nh - Ng}{N} = h - g,$$

$$Var[Y_i] = \frac{1}{N^2} \begin{bmatrix} 1 & -1 \end{bmatrix} Cov\left(\begin{bmatrix} X_1 \\ X_i \end{bmatrix}\right) \begin{bmatrix} 1 \\ -1 \end{bmatrix},$$

$$\text{where } Cov\left(\begin{bmatrix} X_1 \\ X_i \end{bmatrix}\right) = N \begin{bmatrix} h(1-h) & -hg \\ -hg & g(1-g) \end{bmatrix}$$
$$\tag{5}$$

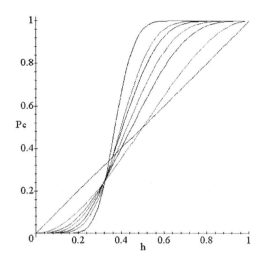

Figure 3. Accuracy of plurality voting

Since each expert is better than random, $h \ge 1/k$, we find that $E[Y_i] = h - g > 0$. Furthermore, Equation (5) implies $\lim_{N \to \infty} Var[Y_i] = 0$, which leads to $\lim_{N \to \infty} P(Y_i \le 0) = 0$. As a result, perfect accuracy is asymptotically achieved:

$$\lim_{N \to \infty} p_c = \lim_{N \to \infty} P(Z_1 > Z_2, Z_1 > Z_3, \ldots, Z_1 > Z_K) = 1 \tag{6}$$

Figure 3 illustrates the dependence of plurality voting accuracy p_c for $N = 1, 4, 7, 10, 15, 20, 50$ when $k = 3$. The value of ensemble accuracy in this case is given as:

$$
\begin{aligned}
p_c &= \sum_{i=\lceil \frac{N+1}{2} \rceil}^{N} \frac{N!}{i!(N-i)!} h^N (1-h)^{N-i} \\
&+ \sum_{i=\lceil \frac{N+1}{3} \rceil}^{\lceil \frac{N+1}{2} \rceil - 1} \sum_{j=N-2i+1}^{N-1} \frac{N!}{i!j!(N-i-j)!} h^i \left(\frac{1-h}{2}\right)^{N-i}
\end{aligned}
\tag{7}
$$

For $k > 3$, the complexity of similar expressions quickly becomes prohibitive for closed form analysis. Certain Monte-Carlo estimations of the values of p_c were obtained in [10]. Note that for small values of N, combination accuracy p_c can be smaller than the accuracy h of each member of an ensemble if $1/k < h < 1/2$.

2.4 Probability of label permutation

The stochastic partition generation process in section 2.1 includes a label permutation step $T(.)$ because the Hungarian algorithm that matches the cluster labels of C_r with those of C_i can make an error. Consequently, the probability that an expert (an aligned partition in the ensemble) assigns the correct label to an object, p^* (defined in section

2.3), can be less than p. Strictly speaking, an expert can give the correct label to an object even when the Hungarian algorithm has made a mistake, because the expert may as well have assigned a wrong label to the object, and these two types mistakes can to cancel each other. This does not affect our analysis below, however, because we are only interested in an upper bound on the probability of error. Also, these "double mistakes" are rare and ignoring it does not have any practical consequences.

It is, however, difficult to conduct a probabilistic analysis of the result of the cluster label matching process, because Hungarian algorithm is defined only algorithmically. It is hard to obtain the distribution of its output based on a distribution of the input. Instead, we try to find bounds on the probabilities of the output. Without loss of generality, suppose the correct matching between the partitions C_i and C_r is to match the j-th cluster in C_i to the j-th cluster in C_r. Hungarian algorithm is guaranteed to find this matching if the (j, j)-th entry in the j-th row of the contingency table is the largest for all j. Since the conversion of the cluster label $C(x_l)$ to $C'(x_l)$ due to noise is assumed to be independent for different l, each row of the contingency table can be considered separately. It is easy to see that the entries in each row of the contingency table follow a multinomial distribution. Let γ_j be the probability that the (j, j)-th entry is not the largest in the j-th row in the contingency table. We have

$$\gamma_j \leq P(\ (j,j)\text{-th entry } \leq n_j/2)$$
$$= \sum_{i=0}^{\lceil \frac{n_j}{2} \rceil} \frac{n_j!}{(n_j - i)!i!} p^i (1-p)^{n-i},$$

where n_j is the size of the j-th cluster. If n_j is large, by large deviation principle [1], the summand above can be approximated using $I(x)$, the rate function of Bernoulli trial, defined as

$$I(x) = x \log \frac{x}{p} + (1-x) \log \frac{1-x}{1-p}. \quad (8)$$

Assuming $p > 0.5$, we obtain $\gamma_j \leq e^{-n_j I(0.5)} = (4p(1-p))^{n_j/2}$. The probability that the Hungarian algorithm makes a mistake can be upper bounded by $ke^{-n_j I(0.5)} = k(4p(1-p))^{n_j/2}$. So, a lower bound for p^* in section 2.3 is

$$p^* \geq p(1 - k(4p(1-p))^{n_j/2}), \quad (9)$$

under the approximation that the dependence between the error of the Hungarian algorithm and the error of labeling an individual object by the expert is negligible. Since the argument in section 2.3 requires only $p^* > 1/k$, a lower bound of p^* is sufficient to derive the convergence of the consensus of a cluster ensemble to the true partition.

3 Consensus as the mean partition

In this section, we present an alternative proof of the effectiveness of cluster ensemble by considering the properties of the mean partition with respect to a metric on a space of partitions.

3.1 Definitions

Let $d(P_i, P_j)$ denote a metric for two elements in $\mathbb{P}$. Many metrics have been proposed in the literature to compare two partitions of a data set, such as Rand index, Jaccard coefficient, Fowlkes and Mallows index, and Hubert's Γ, all of which are discussed in [8]. Although these are similarity measures, they can be easily converted to metrics because their values are upper bounded by one and the upper bound is attained if and only if two partitions are identical. Recently, normalized mutual information [7] and variation of information [11] have been used to compare two partitions. Here, we only require $d(.,.)$ to be symmetric, non-negative and $d(P_i, P_j) = 0$ only when P_i and P_j are the same. In particular, we do not require $d(.,.)$ to satisfy the triangle equality. One interpretation of consensus function is that it attempts to find the "mean" of the partitions in the ensemble. Formally, a consensus function applied to ensemble D_s of size s should return partition $\hat{C}$ such that

$$\hat{C} = \arg\min_{P_j \in \mathbb{P}} \sum_{i=1}^{s} d(P_j, C_i). \quad (10)$$

One such example is the consensus function based on voting, which uses the Hamming distance between P_j and C_i, after the matching of cluster labels by the Hungarian algorithm, as the metric. The consensus function based on mutual information in [15] can be regarded as another example, though, in this case, the partition that maximizes the sum of a similarity measure is returned instead.

The second tool for our analysis is a probability measure μ on $\mathbb{P}$, which characterizes the noise process that distorts the ground-truth partition. Each partition C_i in the ensemble D_s is a random variable sampled according to this measure, i.e., $P(C_i = P_j) = \mu(P_j)$. In order for C to be interpreted as the ground-truth, we require C to be the "mean" according to μ, i.e.,

$$C = \arg\min_{P \in \mathbb{P}} \sum_{i=1}^{m} \mu(P_i) d(P, P_i). \quad (11)$$

Intuitively, the distance of C from all the partitions in the ensemble should be the smallest. This is consistent with the definition of mean in the usual sense. There are two ways to specify probability measure μ. Usually, a stochastic partition generation process can be specified (as in section 2.1) that automatically induces a probability measure on $\mathbb{P}$, given C. Alternatively, μ can be defined using distance $d(.,)$:

$$\mu(P_i) \propto \exp(-\lambda d(P_i, C)) \quad (12)$$

where C is a location-type parameter and λ is a scale-type parameter. The proportionality constant ommited in Equation (12), in general, depends on C.

3.2 Analysis of a simple case

The final goal of our analysis is to answer the question: what is the probability that the consensus partition $\hat{C}$ in Equation (10) is equal to the true partition C? Will this probability approach to 1 when the size of the ensemble increases indefinitely? The answer is affirmative. For simplicity, we shall assume Equation (11) has only one solution, i.e., P is unique.

We begin by studying a simpler version of the problem. Consider two arbitrary partitions, α and β, such that α is more "appropriate" mean partition than β, in the sense that

$$u \equiv \sum_{i=1}^{m} \mu(P_i)d(\alpha, P_i) - \sum_{i=1}^{m} \mu(P_i)d(\beta, P_i) < 0. \quad (13)$$

Intuitively, the average distance (with respect to the distribution μ) from α to all the partitions is smaller than that from β. Consider a random ensemble $D_s = (Y_1, \ldots, Y_s)$ of s partitions, such that $Y_i \in \mathbb{P}$ are i.i.d. random variables drawn from the distribution μ. If, for a particular realization of D_k, $\sum_{i=1}^{s} d(\alpha, Y_i) \geq \sum_{i=1}^{s} d(\beta, Y_i)$ is satisfied, then β is more appropriate than α as the mean partition. Hence ensemble D_s leads to a wrong consensus solution. We want to estimate the probability for this error to occur. Let $Z_i = d(\alpha, Y_i) - d(\beta, Y_i)$ be a real-valued random variable. Assuming that μ gives positive probabilities to both partitions α and β, we can see that $v \equiv \text{Var}[Z_i]$, the variance of Z_i, is positive. Error (incorrect consensus) occurs if $\sum_{i=1}^{s} Z_i \geq 0$. Define

$$\Gamma(\lambda) \equiv \log E[e^{\lambda Z_i}] = \log \sum_{i=1}^{m} \mu(P_i)e^{\lambda Z_i}, \quad (14)$$

$$\Gamma^*(x) \equiv \sup_{\lambda \in \mathbb{R}} (\lambda x - \Gamma(\lambda)), \quad (15)$$

where $\Gamma(\lambda)$ ($\lambda \in \mathbb{R}$) is the logarithm of the moment generating function of Z_i, also known as the cumulant generating function. $\Gamma^*(x)$ ($x \in \mathbb{R}$) is the Fenchel-Legendre transform of $\Gamma(\lambda)$ [1]. Since for all λ, $\Gamma(\lambda)$ is now finite, continuous, and the variance of Z_i is non-zero (implying the second derivative of $\Gamma(\lambda)$ evaluated at $\lambda = 0$ is positive), $\Gamma^*(x)$ is a continuous convex function with minimum value 0. This minimum value is attained only at $x = E[z_i] = u$. By

Cramer's theorem [1] and the continuity of $\Gamma^*(x)$, we have

$$\lim_{s \to \infty} \frac{1}{s} \log P((\frac{1}{s} \sum_{i=1}^{s} Z_i) \in [0, \infty]) = - \inf_{x \in [0, \infty]} \Gamma^*(x) \quad (16)$$

Since $\Gamma^*(x)$ is the smallest when $x = u < 0$, $\inf_{x \in [0, \infty]} \Gamma^*(x)$ is simply $\Gamma^*(0)$ and we write $e \equiv \inf_{\lambda \in \mathbb{R}} \Gamma(\lambda) = \Gamma^*(0) > 0$. Since e is a positive constant, substituting α by the true mean partition C leads to the following theorem.

Theorem 3.1. *If $s \to \infty$, the probability of obtaining any partition β other than C as the mean partition of an ensemble D_s decreases exponentially with respect to s: $O(\exp(-se))$, where e is a positive constant.*

The exact value of constant e depends on the minimum value of the moment generation function. If $d(.,.)$ and μ were given, we could, in principle, find the minimum of $\Gamma(\lambda)$ by setting its derivative to zero. However, such optimization can be very complicated and requires complete knowledge of μ. A reasonable approximation of e only from the values of $u = E[Z_i]$ and $v = VAR[Z_i]$ is possible. By the Central Limit Theorem, $\frac{1}{s} \sum_{i=1}^{s} Z_i$ is approximately normal with mean u and variance v/s. Using the rate function of the normal distribution, e can then be approximated as $u^2/(2v)$.

Consider one intuitive interpretation of this result. Suppose α and β are far apart and lie in regions of $\mathbb{P}$ with high and low probabilities, respectively. In this case β should be a much better estimate of the mean partition than α. The values of $d(\alpha, P_i) - d(\beta, P_i)$ are negative for most partitions $\{P_i\}$ with high probability, meaning that u takes a large negative value. So, e is large too, and the probability of error decreases very rapidly with s. This agrees with our expectation.

In practice, both u and v are hard to compute unless the support of μ contains only few elements. We can approximate u and v by either summation over P_i such that $\mu(P_i)$ are significant, or by adopting Monte Carlo simulation. The later is particularly appropriate when μ is defined only implicitly in an algorithmic form as a process to corrupt the true partition, such as the generation model described in section 2.1. The sampling according to distribution μ can be accomplished by following the noise model.

3.3 Analysis of the general problem

We now consider the general problem: what is the probability that the estimated consensus $\hat{C}$ (defined in Equation 10) based on D_s is different from C? $\hat{C}$ is different if there exists a partition $\beta \in \mathbb{P}$ such that β is more "central" than

C. In other words,

$$\text{Prob}(\hat{C} \neq C) =$$

$$\text{Prob}(\bigcup_{\beta \in \mathbb{P}, \beta \neq C} \{\sum_{i=1}^{s} (d(C, C_i) - d(\beta, C_i)) \geq 0\})$$

$$\leq \sum_{j=1, P_j \neq c}^{m} \text{Prob}(\sum_{i=1}^{s} (d(C, Y_i) - d(P_j, C_i)) \geq 0)$$

$$\approx \sum_{j=1, P_j \neq C}^{m} e^{-se(j)} \quad \text{when } s \rightarrow \infty$$

Here, we denote the dependence of e on β by writing $e(j)$, with $\beta = P_j$, and m is the total number of possible partitions. In the limiting case as s goes to infinity, the above summand will be dominated by the term with the smallest $e(j)$, i.e.,

$$\lim_{s \to \infty} \text{Prob}(\hat{C} \neq C) \leq e^{-s \min_j e(j)},$$

assuming there is a unique minimum of $e(j)$. The probability of a incorrect consensus decreases exponentially with increasing s, with the rate determined by the smallest $e(j)$.

Another possibility to obtain the decreasing rate of the error is to invoke the multi-dimensional version of the Cramer's theorem. Let $C = P_j$. Let Z_j be a random vector in $\mathbb{R}^{m-1}$ with $Z_i \equiv (d(C_i, C) - d(C_i, P_1), \ldots, d(C_i, C) - d(C_i, P_{j-1}), d(C_i, C) - d(C_i, P_{j+1}), \ldots, d(C_i, C) - d(C_i, P_m))$. The event that the consensus partition is correct corresponds to the event that all the components of $\sum_{i=1}^{s} Z_i$ are non-negative. Let A denote the subset of $\mathbb{R}^{m-1}$ such that all the coordinates are non-negative. Let λ and x denote a $(m-1)$-dimensional vector of real numbers, and let $< x, y >$ denote the inner product between x and y. Define

$$\Gamma(\lambda) \equiv \log E[e^{<\lambda, Z_i>}] = \log \sum_{i=1}^{m} \mu(P_i) e^{<\lambda, Z_i>}, \quad (17)$$

$$\Gamma^*(x) \equiv \sup_{\lambda \in \mathbb{R}^{m-1}} (< \lambda, x > -\Gamma(\lambda)), \quad (18)$$

The Cramer's theorem states that

$$\lim_{s \to \infty} P(\frac{1}{s} \sum_{i=1}^{s} Z_i \in A) = - \inf_{x \in A} \Gamma^*(x), \quad (19)$$

and $\inf_{x \in A} \Gamma^*(x)$ is positive, assuming the variance of Z_i is non-zero. Once again we have the exponentially decreasing probability of error when s goes to infinity. This result is more of theoretical interest, however, because typical values of the number of partitions is exponential large with respect to the number of objects and estimating $\inf_{x \in A} \Gamma^*(x)$ is very difficult.

4 Conclusion

In this paper we have presented two approaches to prove the utility of the consensus partition of a cluster ensemble. The first approach is based on a plurality voting argument, while the second is based on a metric and a probability measure on the space of partitions. In both cases, we have shown that the consensus partition indeed converges to the true partition when the ensemble consists of a large number of partitions. Convergence of voting consensus solutions is guaranteed as long as each expert (partition) gives a better than random clustering result. In the second approach, we give an estimate of the rate of convergence. The current paper complements the existing empirical literature on cluster ensembles and provides rigorous proof of the utility of consensus partition.

References

[1] A. Dembo and O. Zeitouni. *Large Deviations Techniques and Applications*. Jones and Bartlett Publishers, 1993.

[2] M. Demirekler and H. Altincay. Plurality voting based multiple classifier systems: Statistically independent with respect to dependent classifier sets. *Pattern Recognition*, 35:2365–2379, 2002.

[3] S. Dudoit and J. Fridlyand. Bagging to improve the accuracy of a clustering procedure. *Bioinformatics*, 19(9):1090–1099, 2003.

[4] B. Fischer and J. M. Buhmann. Bagging for path-based clustering. *IEEE Transactions on Pattern Analysis and Machine Intelligence*, 25(11):1411–1415, 2003.

[5] A. Fred. Finding consistent clusters in data partitions. In *Multiple Classifier Systems, volume LNCS 2096*, pages 309–318. Springer, 2001.

[6] A. Fred and A. K. Jain. Data clustering using evidence accumulation. In *Proc. of Sixteenth International Conference on Pattern Recognition*, pages IV:276–280, 2002.

[7] A. Fred and A. K. Jain. Robust data clustering. In *Proc. of IEEE Computer Society Conference on Computer Vision and Pattern Recognition*, pages II–128–133, 2003.

[8] A. K. Jain and R. C. Dubes. *Algorithms for Clustering Data*. Prentice Hall, 1988.

[9] G. Karypis and V. Kumar. A fast and high quality multilevel scheme for partitioning irregular graphs. *SIAM Journal of Scientific Computing*, 20(1):359–392, 1998.

[10] X. Lin, S. Yacoub, J. Burns, and S. Simske. Performance analysis of pattern classifier combination by plurality voting. *Pattern Recognition Letters*, 24(12):1959–1969, Aug. 2003.

[11] M. Meila. Comparing clusterings by the variation of information. In *Proc. of Computational Learning Theory*, pages 173–187, 2003.

[12] J. Munkres. Algorithms for the assignment and transportation problems. *J. SIAM*, 5:32–38, Mar. 1957.

[13] A. Strehl and J. Ghosh. Cluster ensembles – a knowledge reuse framework for combining multiple partitions. *Journal of Machine Learning Research*, 3:583–617, December 2002.

[14] A. Topchy, A. Jain, and W. Punch. A mixture model for clustering ensembles. In *Proc. SIAM Data Mining*, pages 379–390, 2004.

[15] A. Topchy, A. K. Jain, and W. Punch. Combining multiple weak clusterings. In *Proc. IEEE International Conference on Data Mining*, pages 331–338, 2003.

Privacy-Preserving Outlier Detection

Jaideep Vaidya
Rutgers University
180 University Avenue
Newark, NJ 07102-1803
jsvaidya@rbs.rutgers.edu

Chris Clifton
Purdue University
250 N. University St.
W. Lafayette, IN 47907-2066
clifton@cs.purdue.edu

Abstract

Outlier detection can lead to the discovery of truly unexpected knowledge in many areas such as electronic commerce, credit card fraud and especially national security. We look at the problem of finding outliers in large distributed databases where privacy/security concerns restrict the sharing of data. Both homogeneous and heterogeneous distribution of data is considered. We propose techniques to detect outliers in such scenarios while giving formal guarantees on the amount of information disclosed.

1. Introduction

Advances in information technology and the ubiquity of networked computers have made personal information much more available. This has lead to a privacy backlash. Unfortunately, "data mining" has been the whipping-boy for much of this backlash, witness a United States Senate proposal to forbid all "data-mining activity" by the U.S. Department of Defense[7]. Much of this is based on a mistaken view of data mining; the above-cited act specifically discusses search for individuals. Most data mining is not about individuals, but generalizing information.

Data mining does raise legitimate privacy concerns; the process of data mining often results in greater integration of data, increasing potential for misuse. If the data mining results do not pose an inherent privacy threat, privacy-preserving data mining techniques enable knowledge discovery without requiring disclosure of private data. Privacy-preserving methods have been developed for numerous data mining tasks; many are described in [13].

To our knowledge, privacy-preserving outlier detection has not yet been addressed. Outlier detection has wide application; one that has received considerable attention is the search for terrorism. Detecting previously unknown suspicious behavior is a clear outlier detection problem. The search for terrorism has also been the flash point for at-tacks on data mining by privacy advocates; the U.S. Terrorism Information Awareness program was killed for this reason[18].

Outlier detection has numerous other applications that also raise privacy concerns. Mining for anomalies has been used for network intrusion detection[1, 17]; privacy advocates have responded with research to enhance anonymity[20, 10]. Fraud discovery in the mobile phone industry has also made use of outlier detection[6]; organizations must be careful to avoid overstepping the bounds of privacy legislation[5]. Privacy-preserving outlier detection will ensure these concerns are balanced, allowing us to get the benefits of outlier detection without being thwarted by legal or technical counter-measures.

This paper assumes data is distributed; the stewards of the data are allowed to use it, but disclosing it to others is a privacy violation. The problem is to find distance-based outliers without any party gaining knowledge beyond learning which items are outliers. Ensuring that data is not disclosed maintains privacy, i.e., no privacy is lost beyond that inherently revealed in knowing the outliers. Even knowing which items are outliers need not be revealed to all parties, further preventing privacy breaches.

The approach duplicates the results of the outlier detection algorithm of [14]. The idea is that an object O is an outlier if more than a percentage p of the objects in the data set are farther than distance dt from O. The basic idea is that parties compute the portion of the answer they know, then engage in a secure sum to compute the total distance. The key is that this total is (randomly) split between sites, so nobody knows the actual distance. A secure protocol is used to determine if the actual distance between any two points exceeds the threshold; again the comparison results are randomly split such that summing the splits (over a closed field) results in a 1 if the distance exceeds the threshold, or a 0 otherwise.

For a given object O, each site can now sum all of its shares of comparison results (again over the closed field). When added to the sum of shares from other sites, the result is the correct count; all that remains is to compare it with the percentage threshold p. This addition/comparison is also done with a secure protocol, revealing only the result: if O is an outlier.

We first discuss the problem we are facing: the different problems posed by vertically and horizontally partitioned datasets, and the formal definition of outlier detection. Section 3 gives privacy-preserving algorithms for both horizontally and vertically partitioned data. We prove the security of the algorithms in Section 4, and discuss the computational and communication complexity of the algorithms in Section 5. We conclude with a discussion of areas for further work on this problem.

2. Data Partitioning Models

The problem as we define it is that the data is inherently distributed; it is sharing (or disclosure to other parties) that violates privacy. The way the data is distributed / partitioned results in very different solutions. We consider two different data partitions: horizontal and vertical. In either case, assume k different parties, $P_0, \ldots, P_{k-1}$; m attributes; and n total objects. We now describe the specifics of the different data models considered.

2.1. Horizontally Partitioned Data

With horizontally partitioned (viz. distributed homogeneous) data, different parties collect the same information (features) for different objects. Each party collects information about m attributes, $A_1, \ldots, A_m$. Party P_i collects information about n_i objects, such that $\sum_{i=0}^{k-1} n_i = n$ (different parties collect information about different entities). Consider the case of several banks that collect similar data about credit card transactions but for different clients. Clearly, the data is horizontally partitioned. Outlier detection is particularly useful in this case to determine potentially fraudulent transactions.

2.2. Vertically Partitioned Data

With vertically partitioned (viz. distributed heterogeneous) data, different parties collect different features for the same set of objects. Party P_i collects information about m_i attributes, $A_{i,1}, \ldots, A_{i,m_i}$. The total number of attributes, $\sum_{p=0}^{k-1} m_p = m$. All of the parties also hold information about the same n objects. Thus, there are a total of n transactions (with data for each transaction really being split between the parties). Consider the case of an airline, banking institution and federal databases. By cross correlating information and locating outliers we may hope to spot potential terrorist activities.

2.3. Outlier Detection

Our goal is to find Distance Based Outliers. Knorr and Ng [14] define the notion of a Distance Based outlier as follows: *An object O in a dataset T is a DB(p,dt)-outlier if at least fraction p of the objects in T lie at distance greater than dt from O.* Other distance based outlier techniques also exist[15, 19]. The advantages of distance based outliers are that no explicit distribution needs to be defined to determine unusualness, and that it can be applied to any feature space for which we can define a distance measure. We assume Euclidean distances, although the algorithms are easily extended to general Minkowski distances. There are other non distance based techniques for finding outliers as well as significant work in statistics [2], but we do not consider those in this paper and leave that for future work.

3. Privacy Preserving Outlier Detection

We now present two algorithms for Distance Based Outliers meeting the definition given in Section 2.3. The first is for horizontally partitioned data, the second for vertically partitioned data. The algorithm is based on the obvious one: Compare points pairwise and count the number exceeding the distance threshold. The key is that all intermediate computations (such as distance comparisons) leave the results randomly split between the parties involved; only the final result (if the count exceeds $p\%$) is disclosed.

The pairwise comparison of all points may seem excessive, but early termination could disclose information about relative positions of points (this will be discussed further in Section 5.) The asymptotic complexity still equals that of [14].

Note that to obtain a secure solution, all operations are carried out modulo some field. We will use the field D for distances, and F for counts of the number of entities. The field F must be over twice the number of objects. Limits on D are based on maximum distances; details on the size are given with each algorithm.

3.1. Horizontally Partitioned Data

The key idea behind the algorithm for horizontally partitioned data is as follows. For each object i, the protocol iterates over every other object j. If the party holding i also holds j, it can easily find the distance and compare against the threshold. If two different parties hold the two objects, the parties engage in a distance calculation protocol (Section 3.1.1) to get *random shares* of the distance. A second protocol allows comparing the shares with the threshold, returning 1 if the distance exceeds the threshold, or 0 if it does not. The key to this second protocol is that the 1 or 0 is actually two shares r'_q and r'_s, such that $r'_q + r'_s = 1$ (or 0) (mod F). From one share, the party learns nothing.

Once all points have been compared, the parties sum their shares. Since the shares add to 1 for distances exceeding the distance threshold, and 0 otherwise, the total sum (mod F) is the number of points for which the distance exceeds the threshold. The parties do not actually compute this sum; instead all parties pass their (random) shares to a designate to add, and the designated party and the party holding the point engage in a secure protocol that reveals only if the sum of the shares exceeds $p\%$. This ensures that no party learns anything except whether the point is an outlier.

Algorithm 1 gives the complete details. Steps 5-23 are the pairwise comparison of two points, giving each party random shares of a 1 (if the points are far apart) or 0 (if the points are within the distance threshold dt). The random split of shares ensures that nothing is learned by either party. In steps 25-28, the parties (except the party P_q holding the object being evaluated) sum their shares. Again, since each share is a random split (and P_q holds the other part of the split), no party learns anything. Finally, P_{q-1} and P_q add and compare their shares, revealing only if the object o_i is an outlier. Note that the shares of this comparison are split, and could be sent to any party (P_q in Algorithm 1, but it need not even be one of the P_r). Only that party (e.g., a fraud prevention unit) learns if o_i is an outlier, the others learn nothing.

3.1.1 Computing distance between two points

Step 13 of Algorithm 1 requires computing a distance, but leaving random shares of that distance with two parties rather than revealing the result. For convenience, we actually compute shares of the *square* of the distance, and compare with the square of the threshold. (This does not change the result, since squaring is a monotonically increasing function.) We now give an algorithm based on secure scalar product for computing shares of the square of the Euclidean distance.

Formally, let there be two parties, P_1 and P_2. All computations are over a field D larger than the square of the maximum distance. P_1's input is the point X, P_2's input is the point Y. The outputs are r_1 and r_2 respectively (independently uniformly distributed over D), such that $r_1 + r_2 = Distance^2(X, Y)$ (mod D), where $Distance(X, Y)$ is the Euclidean distance between the points X and Y.

Let there be m attributes, and a point X be represented by its m-dimensional tuple $(x_1, \ldots, x_m)$. Each co-ordinate represents the value of the point for that attribute.

The square of the Euclidean distance between X and Y

Algorithm 1 Finding DB(p,D)-outliers

Require: k parties, $P_0, \ldots, P_{k-1}$; each holding a subset of the objects O.

Require: Fields D larger than the maximum distance squared, F larger than $|O|$

1: **for all** objects $o_i \in O$ {Let P_q be the party holding o_i} **do**
2:     **for all** parties P_r **do**
3:         $num_r \leftarrow 0$ (mod F) {Initialize counters}
4:     **end for**
5:     **for all** objects $o_j \in O, o_j \neq o_i$ **do**
6:         **if** P_q holds o_j **then**
7:             **if** $Distance(o_i, o_j) > dt$ {Computed locally at P_q} **then**
8:                 At P_q: $num_q \leftarrow num_q + 1$ (mod F)
9:             **end if**
10:        **else**
11:           {Let P_s hold o_j}
12:           {Using the distance computation protocol (Section 3.1.1)}
13:           $P_q \leftarrow r_q$ and $P_s \leftarrow r_s$ such that $r_q + r_s$ (mod D) $= Distance^2(o_i, o_j)$
14:           {Using the secure comparison protocol (Section 3.3)}
15:           $P_q \leftarrow r'_q$ and $P_s \leftarrow r'_s$ such that:
16:           **if** $r_q + r_s$ (mod D) $> dt^2$ **then**
17:              $r'_q + r'_s = 1$ (mod F)
18:           **else**
19:              $r'_q + r'_s = 0$ (mod F)
20:           **end if**
21:        **end if**
22:        At P_q: $num_q \leftarrow num_q + r'_q$
23:        At P_s: $num_s \leftarrow num_s + r'_s$
24:     **end for**
25:     **for all** P_r except P_q and P_{q-1} (mod k) **do**
26:        P_r sends num_r to P_{q-1}
27:     **end for**
28:     At P_{q-1}: $num_{q-1} \leftarrow \sum_{i \neq q} num_i$
29:     {Using the secure comparison of Section 3.3}
30:     $P_q \leftarrow temp_q$ and $P_{q-1} \leftarrow temp_{q-1}$ such that:
31:     **if** $num_q + num_{q-1}$ (mod F) $> |O| * p\%$ **then**
32:        $temp_q + temp_{q-1} \leftarrow 1$ {o_i is an outlier}
33:     **else**
34:        $temp_q + temp_{q-1} \leftarrow 0$
35:     **end if**
36:     P_{q-1} sends $temp_{q-1}$ to P_q, revealing to P_q if o_i is an outlier.
37: **end for**

---

is given by

$$
\begin{aligned}
Distance^2(X,Y) &= \sum_{r=1}^{m}(x_r - y_r)^2 \\
&= x_1^2 - 2x_1y_1 + y_1^2 + \ldots \\
&\quad \ldots + x_m^2 - 2x_my_m + y_m^2 \\
&= \sum_{r=1}^{m} x_r^2 + \sum_{r=1}^{m} y_r^2 - \sum_{r=1}^{m} 2x_ry_r
\end{aligned}
$$

P_1 can independently calculate $\sum_r x_r^2$. Similarly, P_2 can calculate $\sum_r y_r^2$. As long as there is more than one attribute (i.e., $m > 1$), the remaining sum $\sum_r (2x_r)(-y_r)$ is simply the scalar product of two m-dimensional vectors. P_1 and P_2 engage in a secure scalar product protocol to get random shares of the dot product. This, added to their prior calculated values, gives each party a random share of the square of the distance. There are many scalar product protocols proposed in the literature [4, 21, 11]; any of these can be used.

Assuming that the scalar product protocol is secure, applying the composition theorem of [8] shows that the entire protocol is secure.

3.2. Vertically Partitioned Data

Vertically partitioned data introduces a different challenge. Each party can compute a *share* of the pairwise distance locally; the sum of these shares is the total distance. However, the distance must not be revealed, so a secure protocol is used to get shares of the pairwise comparison of distance and threshold. From this point, it is similar to horizontal partitioning: Add the shares and determine if they exceed $p\%$.

An interesting side effect of this algorithm is that the parties need not reveal any information about the attributes they hold, or even the number of attributes. Each party locally determines the distance threshold for its attributes (or more precisely, the share of the overall threshold for its attributes). Instead of computing the local pairwise distance, each party computes the difference between the local pairwise distance and the local threshold. If the sum of these differences is greater than 0, the pairwise distance exceeds the threshold.

Algorithm 2 gives the full details. In steps 5-9, the sites sum their local distances. The random x added by P_0 masks the distances from each party. In steps 11-18, Parties P_0 and P_{k-1} get shares of the pairwise comparison result, as in Algorithm 1. The comparison is a test if the sum is greater than 0 (since the threshold has already been subtracted.) These two parties keep a running sum of their shares. At the end, these shares are added and compared with the percentage threshold, again as in Algorithm 1.

Algorithm 2 Finding DB(p,D)-outliers

Require: k parties, $P_0, \ldots, P_{k-1}$; each holding a subset of the attributes for all objects O.

Require: dt_r : local distance threshold for P_r (e.g., $dt^2 + m_r/m$).

Require: Fields D larger than twice the maximum distance value (e.g., for Euclidean this is actually $Distance^2$), F larger than $|O|$

1: **for all** objects $o_i \in O$ **do**
2:    $m_0' \leftarrow m_{k-1}' \leftarrow 0 \pmod{F}$
3:    **for all** objects $o_j \in O, o_j \neq o_i$ **do**
4:       P_0: Randomly choose a number x from a uniform distribution over the field D; $x' \leftarrow x$
5:       **for** $r \leftarrow 0, \ldots, k-2$ **do**
6:          At P_r: $x' \leftarrow x' + Distance_r(o_i, o_j) - dt_r \pmod{D}$ {$Distance_r$ is local distance at P_r}
7:          P_r sends x' to P_{r+1}
8:       **end for**
9:       At P_{k-1}: $x' \leftarrow x' + Distance_{k-1}(o_i, o_j) - dt_{k-1} \pmod{D}$
10:      {Using the secure comparison protocol (Section 3.3)}
11:      $P_0 \leftarrow m_0$ and $P_{k-1} \leftarrow m_{k-1}$ such that:
12:      **if** $0 < x' + (-x) \pmod{D} < |D|/2$ **then**
13:         $m_0 + m_{k-1} = 1 \pmod{F}$
14:      **else**
15:         $m_0 + m_{k-1} = 0 \pmod{F}$
16:      **end if**
17:      At P_0: $m_0' \leftarrow m_0' + m_0 \pmod{F}$
18:      At P_{k-1}: $m_{k-1}' \leftarrow m_{k-1}' + m_{k-1} \pmod{F}$
19:    **end for**
20:    {Using the secure comparison of Section 3.3}
21:    $P_0 \leftarrow temp_0$ and $P_{k-1} \leftarrow temp_{k-1}$ such that:
22:    **if** $m_0' + m_{k-1}' \pmod{F} > |O| * p\%$ **then**
23:       $temp_0 + temp_{k-1} \leftarrow 1$ {o_i is an outlier}
24:    **else**
25:       $temp_0 + temp_{k-1} \leftarrow 0$
26:    **end if**
27:    P_0 and P_{k-1} send $temp_0$ and $temp_{k-1}$ to the party authorized to learn the result; if $temp_0 + temp_1 = 1$ then o_i is an outlier.
28: **end for**

Theorem 1 *Proof of Correctness: Algorithm 2 correctly returns as output the complete set of points that are global outliers.*

PROOF. In order to prove the correctness of Algorithm 2, it is sufficient to prove that a point is reported as an outlier if and only if it is truly an outlier. Consider point q. If q is an outlier, in steps 12-16 for at least $p\% * |O| + 1$ of the other points, $m_0 + m_{k-1} = 1 \pmod{F}$. Since $|F| > |O|$, it follows that $m'_0 + m'_{k-1} > |O| * p\%$. Therefore, point q will be correctly reported as an outlier. If q is not an outlier, the same argument applies in reverse. Thus, in steps 12-16 at most $p\% * |O| - 1$ points, $m_0 + m_{k-1} = 1 \pmod{F}$. Again, since $|F| > |O|$, it follows that $m'_0 + m'_{k-1} \leq |O| * p\%$. Therefore, point q will not be reported as an outlier. $\square$

3.3. Modified Secure Comparison Protocol

At several stages in the protocol, we need to securely compare the sum of two numbers, with the output split between the parties holding those numbers. This can be accomplished using the generic circuit evaluation technique first proposed by Yao[23]. Formally, we need a modified secure comparison protocol for two parties, A and B. The local inputs are x_a and x_b and the local outputs are y_a and y_b. All operations on input are in a field F_1 and output are in a field F_2. $y_a + y_b = 1 \pmod{F_2}$ if $x_a + x_b \pmod{F_1} > 0$, otherwise $y_a + y_b = 0 \pmod{F_2}$. A final requirement is that y_a and y_b should be independently uniformly distributed over F (clearly the joint distribution is not uniform).

This builds on the standard secure multiparty computation circuit-based approach for solving this problem[8]. Effectively, A chooses y_a with a uniform distribution over F, and provides it as an additional input to the circuit that appropriately computes y_b. The circuit is then securely evaluated, with B receiving the output y_b. The complexity of this is equivalent to the complexity of Yao's Millionaire's problem (simple secure comparison).

4. Security Analysis

The security argument for this algorithm uses proof techniques from Secure Multiparty Computation. The idea is that since what a party sees during the protocol (its shares) are randomly chosen from a uniform distribution over a field, it learns nothing in isolation. (Of course, collusion with other parties could reveal information, since the *joint* distribution of the shares is not random.) The idea of the proof is based on a simulation argument: If we can define a simulator that uses the algorithm output and a party's own data to simulate the messages seen by a party during a real execution of the protocol, then the real execution isn't giving away any new information.

To formalize this, we will first give some definitions from [8]. We then give the proofs of security for Algorithms 1 and 2.

4.1 Secure Multi-Party Computation

Yao first postulated the two-party comparison problem (Yao's Millionaire Protocol) and developed a provably secure solution[23]. This was extended to multiparty computations by Goldreich et al.[9]. They developed a framework for secure multiparty computation, and in [8] proved that computing a function privately is equivalent to computing it securely.

We start with the definitions for security in the semi-honest model. A semi-honest party follows the rules of the protocol using its correct input, but is free to later use what it sees during execution of the protocol to compromise security. A formal definition of private two-party computation in the semi-honest model is given below.

Definition 1 *(privacy w.r.t. semi-honest behavior):[8]*

Let $f : \{0,1\}^* \times \{0,1\}^* \longmapsto \{0,1\}^* \times \{0,1\}^*$ be probabilistic, polynomial-time functionality, where $f_1(x,y)$ (respectively, $f_2(x,y)$) denotes the first (resp., second) element of $f(x,y)$; and let Π be two-party protocol for computing f.

Let the view of the first (resp., second) party during an execution of protocol Π on (x,y), denoted $view_1^\Pi(x,y)$ (resp., $view_2^\Pi(x,y)$), be $(x, r_1, m_1, \ldots, m_t)$ (resp., $(y, r_2, m_1, \ldots, m_t)$). r_1 represent the outcome of the first (resp., r_2 the second) party's internal coin tosses, and m_i represent the ith message it has received.

The output of the first (resp., second) party during an execution of Π on (x,y) is denoted $output_1^\Pi(x,y)$ (resp., $output_2^\Pi(x,y)$) and is implicit in the party's view of the execution.

Π privately computes f if there exist probabilistic polynomial time algorithms, denoted S_1, S_2 such that

$$\{(S_1(x, f_1(x,y)), f_2(x,y))\}_{x,y \in \{0,1\}^*} \equiv^C$$
$$\{(view_1^\Pi(x,y), output_2^\Pi(x,y))\}_{x,y \in \{0,1\}^*}$$
$$\{(f_1(x,y), S_2(x, f_1(x,y)))\}_{x,y \in \{0,1\}^*} \equiv^C$$
$$\{(output_1^\Pi(x,y), view_2^\Pi(x,y))\}_{x,y \in \{0,1\}^*}$$

where $\equiv^C$ denotes computational indistinguishability.

As we shall see, our protocol is actually somewhat stronger than the semi-honest model, although it does not meet the full malicious model definition of [8].

Privacy by Simulation The above definition says that a computation is secure if the view of each party during the execution of the protocol can be effectively simulated given the input and the output of that party. Thus, in all of our proofs of security, we only need to show the existence of a simulator for each party that satisfies the above equations.

This does not quite guarantee that private information is protected. Whatever information can be deduced from the final result obviously cannot be kept private. For example, if a party learns that point A is an outlier, but point B which is close to A is not an outlier, it learns an estimate on the number of points that lie between the space covered by the hypersphere for A and hypersphere for B. Here, the result reveals information to the site having A and B. The key to the definition of privacy is that nothing is learned *beyond* what is inherent in the result.

A key result we use is the composition theorem. We state it for the semi-honest model. A detailed discussion of this theorem, as well as the proof, can be found in [8].

Theorem 2 (*Composition Theorem for the semi-honest model*): *Suppose that g is privately reducible to f and that there exists a protocol for privately computing f. Then there exists a protocol for privately computing g.*

PROOF. Refer to [8]. □

4.2. Horizontally Partitioned Data

Theorem 3 *Algorithm 1 returns as output the set of points that are global outliers, and reveals no other information to any party provided parties do not collude.*

PROOF. Presuming that the number of objects $|O|$ is known globally, each party can locally set up and run its own components of Algorithm 1 (e.g., a party only needs to worry about its local objects in the "For all objects" statements at lines 1 and 5.) In the absence of some type of secure anonymous send[20, 10] (e.g., anonymous transmission with public key cryptography to ensure reception only by the correct party), the number of objects at each site is revealed. Since at least an upper bound on the number of items is inherently revealed by the running time of the algorithm, we assume these values are known.

The next problem is to simulate the messages seen by each party during the algorithm. Communication occurs only at steps 13, 15, 26, 30, and 36. We now describe the simulation independently.

Step 13: P_q and P_s each receive a share of the square of the distance. As can be seen in Section 3.1.1, all parts of the shares are computed locally except for shares of the scalar product. Assume that the scalar product protocol chooses shares by selecting the share for P_q (call it

s_q) randomly from a uniform distribution over D. Then $\forall x \in D, Pr(s_q = x) = \frac{1}{|D|}$. Thus, s_q is easily simulated by simply choosing a random value from D. Let the result $r = \sum_r (2x_r)(-y_r)$ be fixed. Then $\forall x \in F, Pr(s_s = x) = Pr(r - s_q = y) = Pr(s_q = r - y) = \frac{1}{|D|}$. Therefore, the simulator for P_s can simulate this message by simply choosing a random number from an uniform distribution over D. Assuming that the scalar product protocol is secure, applying the composition theorem shows that step 13 is secure.

Steps 15 and 30: The simulator for party P_q (respectively P_s) again chooses a number randomly from a uniform distribution, this time over the field F. By the same argument as above, the actual values are uniformly distributed, so the probability of the simulator and the real protocol choosing any particular value are the same. Since a circuit for secure comparison is used, using the composition theorem, no additional information is leaked and step 15 is secure.

Step 26: P_{q-1} receives several shares num_r. However, note that num_r is a sum, where all components of the sum are random shares from Step 15. Since P_{q-1} receives only shares from the P_s in step 15, and receives none from P_q, all of the shares in the sum are independent. The sum num_r can thus be simulated by choosing a random value from a uniform distribution over F.

Step 36: Since P_q knows the results (1 if o_i is an outlier, 0 otherwise), and $temp_q$ was simulated in step 30, it can simulate $temp_{q-1}$ with the results (1 or 0) $-temp_q \mod F$.

The simulator clearly runs in polynomial time (the same as the algorithm). Since each party is able to simulate the view of its execution (i.e., the probability of any particular value is the same as in a real execution with the same inputs/results) in polynomial time, the algorithm is secure with respect to Definition 1. □

While the proof is formally only for the semi-honest model, it can be seen that a malicious party in isolation cannot learn private values (regardless of what it does, it is still possible to simulate what it sees without knowing the input of the other parties.) This assumes that the underlying scalar product and secure comparison protocols are secure against malicious behavior. A malicious party can cause incorrect results, but it cannot learn private data values.

4.3. Vertically Partitioned Data

Theorem 4 *Algorithm 2 returns as output the set of points that are global outliers while revealing no other information to any party, provided parties do not collude.*

PROOF. All parties know the number (and identity) of objects in O. Thus they can set up the loops; the simulator just runs the algorithm to generate most of the simulation. The only communication is at lines 7, 11, 21, and 27.

Step 7: Each party P_s sees $x' = x + \sum_{r=0}^{s-1} Distance_r(o_i, o_j)$, where x is the random value chosen by P_0. $Pr(x' = y) = Pr(x + \sum_{r=0}^{s-1} Distance_r(o_i, o_j) = y) = Pr(x = y - \sum_{r=0}^{s-1} Distance_r(o_i, o_j)) = \frac{1}{|D|}$. Thus we can simulate the value received by choosing a random value from a uniform distribution over D.

Steps 11 and 21: Each step is again a secure comparison, so messages are simulated as in Steps 15 and 30 of Theorem 3.

Step 27: This is again the final result, simulated as in Step 36 of Theorem 3. $temp_0$ is simulated by choosing a random value, $temp_1 = result - temp_0$. By the same argument on random shares used above, the distribution of simulated values is indistinguishable from the distribution of the shares.

Again, the simulator clearly runs in polynomial time (the same as the algorithm). Since each party is able to simulate the view of its execution (i.e., the probability of any particular value is the same as in a real execution with the same inputs/results) in polynomial time, the algorithm is secure with respect to Definition 1. □

Absent collusion and assuming a malicious-model secure comparison, a malicious party is unable to learn anything it could not learn from altering its input. Step 7 is particularly sensitive to collusion, but can be improved (at cost) by splitting the sum into shares and performing several such sums (see [12] for more discussion of collusion-resistant secure sum).

5. Computation and Communication Analysis

Both Algorithms 1 and 2 suffer the drawback of having quadratic computation complexity due to the nested iteration over all objects.

Due to the nested iteration, Algorithm 1 requires $O(n^2)$ distance computations and secure comparisons (steps 12-20), where n is the total number of objects. Similarly, Algorithm 2 also requires $O(n^2)$ secure comparisons (steps 10-16). While operation parallelism can be used to reduce the round complexity of communication, the key practical issue is the computational complexity of the encryption required for the secure comparison and scalar product protocols.

Achieving lower than quadratic complexity is challenging. Failing to compare all pairs of points is likely to reveal

information about the relative distances of the points that *are* compared. Developing protocols where such revelation can be proven not to disclose information beyond that revealed by simply knowing the outliers is a challenge. When there are three or more parties, assuming no collusion, we can develop much more efficient solutions that reveal some information. While not completely secure, the privacy versus cost tradeoff may be acceptable in some situations. An alternative (and another approach to future work) is demonstrating lower bounds on the complexity of fully secure outlier detection.

5.1. Horizontally Partitioned Data

With horizontally partitioned data, we can use a semi-trusted third party to perform comparisons and return random shares. The two comparing parties just give the values to be compared to the third party to add and compare. As long as the third party does not collude with either of the comparing parties, the comparing parties learn nothing.

The real question is, what is disclosed to the third party? Basically, since the data is horizontally partitioned, the third party has no idea about the respective locations of the two objects. All it can find out is the distance between the two objects. While this is information that is not a part of the result, by itself it is not very significant and allows a tremendous increase in efficiency. Now, the cost of secure comparison reduces to a total of 4 messages (which can be combined for all comparisons performed by the pair, for a constant number of rounds of communication) and insignificant computation cost.

5.2. Vertically Partitioned Data

The simple approach used in horizontal partitioning is not suitable for vertically partitioned data. Since all of the parties share all of the points, partial knowledge about a point does reveal useful information to a party. Instead, one of the remaining parties is chosen to play the part of completely untrusted non-colluding party. With this assumption, a much more efficient secure comparison algorithm has been postulated by Cachin [3] that reveals nothing to the third party. The algorithm is otherwise equivalent, but the cost of the comparisons is reduced substantially.

6. Conclusion

In this paper, we have presented privacy-preserving solutions for finding distance based outliers in distributed data sets, and proven their security. One contribution of the paper is to point out that quadratic complexity is a necessity for secure solutions to the problem – at most constant-time improvements are possible over the algorithms given.

We are currently implementing these schemes and integrating them into software packages (e.g., Weka [22]) to enable a practical evaluation of the computational cost. Another important problem is to figure out privacy-preserving methods of space transformation[16], allowing additional distance-based operations to be done in a secure manner.

References

[1] D. Barbará, N. Wu, and S. Jajodia. Detecting novel network intrusions using bayes estimators. In *First SIAM International Conference on Data Mining*, Chicago, Illinois, Apr. 5-7 2001.

[2] V. Barnett and T. Lewis. *Outliers in Statistical Data*. John Wiley and Sons, 3rd edition, 1994.

[3] C. Cachin. Efficient private bidding and auctions with an oblivious third party. In *Proceedings of the 6th ACM conference on Computer and communications security*, pages 120–127. ACM Press, 1999.

[4] W. Du and M. J. Atallah. Privacy-preserving statistical analysis. In *Proceeding of the 17th Annual Computer Security Applications Conference*, New Orleans, Louisiana, USA, December 10-14 2001.

[5] Directive 95/46/EC of the european parliament and of the council of 24 october 1995 on the protection of individuals with regard to the processing of personal data and on the free movement of such data. *Official Journal of the European Communities*, No I.(281):31–50, Oct. 24 1995.

[6] K. J. Ezawa and S. W. Norton. Constructing bayesian networks to predict uncollectible telecommunications accounts. *IEEE Expert*, 11(5):45–51, Oct. 1996.

[7] M. Feingold, M. Corzine, M. Wyden, and M. Nelson. Datamining moratorium act of 2003. U.S. Senate Bill (proposed), Jan. 16 2003.

[8] O. Goldreich. *The Foundations of Cryptography*, volume 2, chapter General Cryptographic Protocols. Cambridge University Press, 2004.

[9] O. Goldreich, S. Micali, and A. Wigderson. How to play any mental game - a completeness theorem for protocols with honest majority. In *19th ACM Symposium on the Theory of Computing*, pages 218–229, 1987.

[10] D. Goldschlag, M. Reed, and P. Syverson. Onion routing. *Commun. ACM*, 42(2):39–41, Feb. 1999.

[11] I. Ioannidis, A. Grama, and M. Atallah. A secure protocol for computing dot-products in clustered and distributed environments. In *The 2002 International Conference on Parallel Processing*, Vancouver, British Columbia, Aug. 18-21 2002.

[12] M. Kantarcıoğlu and C. Clifton. Privacy-preserving distributed mining of association rules on horizontally partitioned data. *IEEE Transactions on Knowledge and Data Engineering*, 16(9):1026–1037, Sept. 2004.

[13] Special section on privacy and security. *SIGKDD Explorations*, 4(2):i–48, Jan. 2003.

[14] E. M. Knorr and R. T. Ng. Algorithms for mining distance-based outliers in large datasets. In *Proceedings of 24th International Conference on Very Large Data Bases (VLDB 1998)*, pages 392–403, New York City, NY, USA, Aug.24-27 1998.

[15] E. M. Knorr, R. T. Ng, and V. Tucakov. Distance-based outliers: algorithms and applications. *The VLDB Journal*, 8(3-4):237–253, 2000.

[16] E. M. Knorr, R. T. Ng, and R. H. Zamar. Robust space transformations for distance-based operations. In *Proceedings of the seventh ACM SIGKDD international conference on Knowledge discovery and data mining*, pages 126–135, San Francisco, California, 2001. ACM Press.

[17] A. Lazarevic, A. Ozgur, L. Ertoz, J. Srivastava, and V. Kumar. A comparative study of anomaly detection schemes in network intrusion detection. In *SIAM International Conference on Data Mining (2003)*, San Francisco, California, May 1-3 2003.

[18] M. Lewis. Department of defense appropriations act, 2004, July 17 2003. Title VIII section 8120. Enacted as Public Law 108-87.

[19] S. Ramaswamy, R. Rastogi, and K. Shim. Efficient algorithms for mining outliers from large data sets. In *Proceedings of the 2000 ACM SIGMOD international conference on Management of data*, pages 427–438. ACM Press, 2000.

[20] M. K. Reiter and A. D. Rubin. Crowds: Anonymity for Web transactions. *ACM Transactions on Information and System Security*, 1(1):66–92, Nov. 1998.

[21] J. Vaidya and C. Clifton. Privacy preserving association rule mining in vertically partitioned data. In *The Eighth ACM SIGKDD International Conference on Knowledge Discovery and Data Mining*, pages 639–644, Edmonton, Alberta, Canada, July 23-26 2002.

[22] I. H. Witten and E. Frank. *Data Mining: Practical Machine Learning Tools and Techniques with Java Implementations*. Morgan Kaufmann, San Fransisco, Oct. 1999.

[23] A. C. Yao. How to generate and exchange secrets. In *Proceedings of the 27th IEEE Symposium on Foundations of Computer Science*, pages 162–167. IEEE, 1986.

SUMMARY: Efficiently Summarizing Transactions for Clustering *

Jianyong Wang and George Karypis
Department of Computer Science, Digital Technology Center, & Army HPC Research Center
University of Minnesota, Minneapolis, MN 55455
{jianyong, karypis}@cs.umn.edu

Abstract

Frequent itemset mining was initially proposed and has been studied extensively in the context of association rule mining. In recent years, several studies have also extended its application to the transaction (or document) classification and clustering. However, most of the frequent-itemset based clustering algorithms need to first mine a large intermediate set of frequent itemsets in order to identify a subset of the most promising ones that can be used for clustering. In this paper, we study how to directly find a subset of high quality frequent itemsets that can be used as a concise summary of the transaction database and to cluster the categorical data. By exploring some properties of the subset of itemsets that we are interested in, we proposed several search space pruning methods and designed an efficient algorithm called SUMMARY. Our empirical results have shown that SUMMARY runs very fast even when the minimum support is extremely low and scales very well with respect to the database size, and surprisingly, as a pure frequent itemset mining algorithm it is very effective in clustering the categorical data and summarizing the dense transaction databases.

1 Introduction

Frequent itemset mining was initially proposed and has been studied extensively in the context of associa-tion rule mining [2, 3, 24, 29, 15, 9, 18, 35]. In recent years, some studies have also demonstrated the use-fulness of frequent itemset mining in serving as a con-densed representation of the input data in order for an-swering various types of queries [22, 8], and the trans-actional data (or document) classification [5, 20, 19, 4] and clustering [32, 7, 11, 34, 33].

Most frequent-itemset based clustering algorithms need to first mine a large intermediate set of frequent itemsets (in many cases, it is the complete set of fre-quent itemsets), on which some further post-processing can be performed in order to generate the final result set which can be used for clustering purposes. In this paper we consider directly mining a final subset of fre-quent itemsets which can be used as a concise summary of the original database and to cluster the categorical data. To serve these purposes, we require the final set of frequent itemsets have the following properties: (1) it maximally covers the original database given a minimum support; (2) each final frequent itemset can be used as a description for a group of transactions, and the transactions with the same description can be grouped into a cluster with approximately maxi-mal intra-cluster similarity. To achieve this goal, our solution to this problem formulation is that for each transaction we find one of the longest frequent itemsets that it contains and use this longest frequent itemset as the corresponding transaction's description. The set of so mined frequent itemsets is called a *summary set*.

One significant advantage of directly mining the fi-nal subset of frequent itemsets is that it provides the possibility of designing a more efficient algorithm. We proved that each itemset in the *summary set* must be closed, thus some search space pruning methods proposed for frequent closed itemset mining can be borrowed to accelerate the *summary set* mining. In addition, based on some properties of the *summary set*, we proposed several novel pruning methods which greatly improve the algorithm efficiency. By incorpo-rating these pruning methods with a traditional fre-

*This work was supported in part by NSF CCR-9972519, EIA-9986042, ACI-9982274, ACI-0133464, and ACI-0312828; the Digital Technology Center at the University of Minnesota; and by the Army High Performance Computing Research Center (AH-PCRC) under the auspices of the Department of the Army, Army Research Laboratory (ARL) under Cooperative Agreement num-ber DAAD19-01-2-0014. The content of which does not neces-sarily reflect the position or the policy of the government, and no official endorsement should be inferred. Access to research and computing facilities was provided by the Digital Technology Center and the Minnesota Super-computing Institute.

quent itemset mining framework, we designed an efficient *summary set* mining algorithm, SUMMARY. Our thorough empirical tests show that SUMMARY runs very fast even when the minimum support is extremely low and scales very well w.r.t. the database size, and its result set is very effective in clustering the categorical data and summarizing the dense transaction databases.

The rest of this paper is organized as follows. Section 2 and Section 3 introduce the problem definition and some related work, respectively. Section 4 describes the algorithm in detail. Section 5 presents the empirical results. Section 6 shows an application of the algorithm in clustering categorical data, and the paper ends with some discussions and conclusion in Section 7.

2 Problem Definition

A *transaction database TDB* is a set of transactions, where each transaction, denoted as a tuple $\langle tid, X \rangle$, contains a set of items (i.e., X) and is associated with a unique transaction identifier *tid*. Let $I = \{i_1, i_2, \ldots, i_n\}$ be the complete set of distinct items appearing in TDB. An *itemset* Y is a non-empty subset of I and is called an *l-itemset* if it contains l items. An itemset $\{x_1, \ldots, x_l\}$ is also denoted by $x_1 \cdots x_l$. A transaction $\langle tid, X \rangle$ is said to *contain* itemset Y if $Y \subseteq X$. The number of transactions in TDB containing itemset Y is called the (absolute) *support* of itemset Y, denoted by $sup(Y)$. In addition, we use $|TDB|$ and $|Y|$ to denote the number of transactions in database TDB, and the number of items in itemset Y, respectively.

Given a minimum support threshold, *min_sup*, an itemset Y is *frequent* if $sup(Y) \geq min\_sup$. Among the longest frequent itemsets supported by transaction T_i, we choose any one of them and denote it by SI_{T_i}. SI_{T_i} is called the *summary itemset* of T_i[1]. The set of the *summary itemsets* w.r.t. the transactions in TDB (i.e., $\cup_{i=1}^{|TDB|}\{SI_{T_i}\}$) is called a *summary set* w.r.t. database TDB. Note that the *summary set* of a database may not be unique, this is because a transaction may support more than one *summary itemset*.

Given a transaction database TDB and a minimum support threshold *min_sup*, the problem of this study is to find any one of the *summary sets* w.r.t. TDB.

Example 2.1 The first two columns in Table 1 show the transaction database TDB in our running example. Let *min_sup*=2, we sort the list of frequent items in support ascending order and get the sorted item list which is called *f_list*. In this example *f_list* = <a:3, b:4,

---

[1]Transaction T_i may support no frequent itemset, in this case SI_{T_i} is empty and T_i can be treated as an outlier.

Tid	Set of items	Ordered frequent item list
01	a, c, e, g	a, c, e
02	b, d, e	b, d, e
03	d, f, i	d, f
04	e, f, h	e, f
05	a, b, c, d, e, f	a, b, c, d, e, f
06	b, c, d	b, c, d
07	a, c, f	a, c, f
08	e, f	e, f
09	b, d	b, d

Table 1. A transaction database TDB

c:4, d:5, e:5, f:5>. The list of frequent items in each transaction are sorted according to *f_list* and shown in the third column of Table 1. It is easy to figure out that $\{ace$:2, acf:2, bcd:2, bd:4, bde:2, df:2, ef:3$\}$ is one *summary set* w.r.t. TDB. □

3 Related Research

Since the introduction of the association rule mining [2, 3], numerous frequent itemset mining algorithms have been proposed. In essence, SUMMARY is a projection-based frequent itemset mining algorithm [18, 1] and adopts the natural matrix structure instead of the FP-tree to represent the (conditional) database [26, 12]. It grows a current prefix itemset by physically building and scanning its projected matrix. In [15] an algorithm was proposed to mine all most specific sentences, however, both the problem and the algorithm in this study are different from those in [15].

In Section 4 we prove that each *summary itemset* must be closed, thus some pruning methods previously proposed in the closed (or maximal) itemset mining algorithms [6, 25, 27, 10, 35, 30, 23, 21] can be used to enhance the efficiency of SUMMARY. Like several itemset mining algorithms with length-decreasing support constraint [28, 31], SUMMARY adopts some pruning methods to prune the unpromising transactions and prefixes. However, because the problem formulations are different, the pruning methods in SUMMARY are different from the previous studies.

One important application of the SUMMARY algorithm is to concisely summarize the transactions and cluster the categorical data. There are many algorithms designed for clustering categorical data, typical examples include ROCK [14] and CACTUS [13]. Recently several frequent-itemset based clustering algorithms have also been proposed to cluster categorical or numerical data [7, 11, 34]. These methods first mine an intermediate set of frequent itemsets, and some postprocessing are needed in order to get the clustering solution. SUMMARY mines the final subset of frequent itemsets which can be directly used to group the transactions to form clusters and enables us to design more effective pruning methods to enhance the performance. **Contributions.** The contributions of this paper can be summarized as follows.

1. We proposed a new problem formulation of mining the *summary set* of frequent itemsets with the application of summarizing transactions and clustering categorical data.

2. By exploring the properties of the *summary set*, we have proposed several pruning methods to effectively reduce the search space and enhance the efficiency of the SUMMARY algorithm.

3. Thorough performance study has been performed and shown that SUMMARY has high efficiency and good scalability, and can be used to cluster categorical data with high accuracy.

4 SUMMARY: An Efficient Algorithm to Summarize the Transactions

In this section we first briefly introduce a traditional framework for enumerating the set of frequent itemsets, which forms the basis of the SUMMARY algorithm. Then we discuss how to design some pruning methods to speed up the mining of the *summary set*. Finally we present the integrated SUMMARY algorithm, and discuss how to revise SUMMARY to mine all the *summary itemsets* for each transaction.

4.1 Frequent Itemset Enumeration

Like some other projection-based frequent itemset mining algorithms, SUMMARY employs the *divide-and-conquer* and *depth-first search* strategies [18, 30], which are applied according to the *f_list* order. In Example 2.1, SUMMARY first mines all the frequent itemsets containing item a, then mines all frequent itemsets containing b but no a, ..., and finally mines frequent itemsets containing only f. In mining itemsets containing a, SUMMARY treats a as the current prefix, and builds its conditional database, denoted by $TDB|_a = \{\langle 01, ec \rangle, \langle 05, efc \rangle, \langle 07, fc \rangle\}$ (where the local infrequent items b, d, and g have been pruned and the frequent items in each projected transaction are sorted in support ascending order). By recursively applying the *divide-and-conquer* and *depth-first search* methods to $TDB|_a$, SUMMARY can find the set of frequent itemsets containing a. Note instead of using the FP-tree structure, SUMMARY adopts the natural matrix structure to store the physically projected

database [12]. This is because the matrix structure allows us to easily maintain the *tid*s in order to determine which set of transactions the prefix itemset covers. In addition, in the above enumeration process, SUMMARY always maintains the current longest frequent itemset for each transaction T_i that was discovered first so far. In the following we call it the *current Longest Covering Frequent itemset* w.r.t. T_i (denoted by LCF_{T_i}).

4.2 Search Space Pruning

The above frequent itemset enumeration method can be simply revised to mine the *summary set*: Upon getting a frequent itemset, we check if it is longer than the current longest covering frequent itemset w.r.t. any transaction that this itemset covers. If so, this newly mined itemset becomes the current longest covering frequent itemset for the corresponding transactions. Notice that this naïve method is no more efficient than the traditional all frequent itemset mining algorithm. However, the above algorithm for finding the *summary set* can be improved in two ways. First, as we will prove later in this section, any *summary itemset* must be closed and thus, the pruning methods proposed for closed itemset mining can be used. Second, since during the mining process we maintain the length of the current longest covering itemset for each transaction, we can employ additional *branch-and-bound* techniques to further prune the overall search space.

Definition 4.1 *(Closed itemset)* An itemset X is a **closed itemset** if there exists no proper superset $X' \supset X$ such that $sup(X') = sup(X)$. □

Lemma 4.1 *(Closure of a summary itemset) Any summary itemset w.r.t. a transaction T_i, SI_{T_i}, must be a closed itemset.*

Proof. We will prove it by contradiction. Assume SI_{T_i} is not closed, which means there must exist an itemset Y, such that $SI_{T_i} \subset Y$ and $sup(SI_{T_i}) = sup(Y)$. Thus, Y is also supported by transaction T_i and is frequent. However, $|Y| > |SI_{T_i}|$ contradicts with the fact that SI_{T_i} is the summary itemset of transaction T_i. □

Lemma 4.1 suggests that any pruning method proposed for closed itemset mining can be used to enhance the performance of the *summary set* mining. In SUMMARY, only one such technique, *item merging* [30], is adopted that works as follows. For a prefix itemset P, the complete set of its local frequent items that have the same support as P are merged with P to form a new prefix, and these items are removed from the list of the local frequent items of the new prefix. It is easy to see that such a scheme does not affect the correctness of the algorithm [30].

Example 4.1 Assume the current prefix is $a:3$, whose local frequent item list is $<e:2, f:2, c:3>$, among which $c:3$ can be merged with $a:3$ to form a new prefix $ac:3$ with local frequent item list $<e:2, f:2>$. □

Besides the above pruning method, we developed two new pruning methods called *conditional transaction* and *conditional database* pruning that given the set of the currently maintained longest covering frequent itemsets w.r.t. TDB, they remove some conditional transactions and databases that are guaranteed not to contribute to and generate any *summary itemsets*.

Specifically, let P be the prefix itemset that is currently under consideration, $sup(P)$ its support, and $TDB|_P = \{\langle T_{P_1}, X_{P_1}\rangle, \langle T_{P_2}, X_{P_2}\rangle, \cdots, \langle T_{P_{sup(P)}}, X_{P_{sup(P)}}\rangle\}$ its conditional database. Note that some (or all) of the transactions X_{P_i} ($1 \le i \le sup(P)$) can be empty.

Definition 4.2 *(Invalid conditional transaction)* A conditional transaction T_{P_i} in $TDB|_P$ (where $1 \le i \le sup(P)$), is an **invalid** conditional transaction if it falls into one of the following two cases:

1. $|X_{P_i}| \le (|LCF_{T_{P_i}}| - |P|)$;

2. $|X_{P_i}| > (|LCF_{T_{P_i}}| - |P|)$, but $|\{ \forall j \in [1..sup(P)], T_{P_j} \mid |X_{P_j}| > (|LCF_{T_{P_i}}| - |P|) \}| < min\_sup$.

*Otherwise, T_{P_i} is called a **valid** conditional transaction.* □

The first condition states that a conditional transaction is invalid if its size is no greater than the difference between its current longest covering frequent itemset and the length of the prefix itemset, whereas the second condition states that the number of conditional transactions which can be used to derive itemsets longer than $LCF_{T_{P_i}}$ by extending prefix P is smaller than the minimum support.

Lemma 4.2 *(Unpromising summary itemset generation) If T_{P_i} is an invalid conditional transaction, there will be no frequent itemset derived by extending prefix P that T_{P_i} supports and is longer than $LCF_{T_{P_i}}$.*

Proof. Follows directly from Definition 4.2. (i) If a transaction T_{P_i} is invalid because of the first condition, it will not contain sufficient items in its conditional transaction to identify a longer covering itemset. (ii) If a transaction T_{P_i} is invalid because of the second condition, the conditional database will not contain a

sufficiently large number of long conditional transactions to obtain an itemset that is longer than $LCF_{T_{P_i}}$ and frequent. □

Note it is possible for an invalid conditional transaction to be used to mine summary itemsets for other valid conditional transactions w.r.t. prefix P; thus, we cannot simply prune any invalid conditional transaction. Instead, we can safely prune some invalid conditional transactions according to the following Lemma.

Lemma 4.3 *(Conditional transaction pruning) An invalid conditional transaction, T_{P_i}, can be safely pruned, if it satisfies:*

$$|X_{P_i}| \le \min_{\forall j,\ T_{P_j}\ is\ valid} (|LCF_{T_{P_j}}| - |P|) \qquad (1)$$

Proof. Consider an invalid conditional transaction T_{P_i} that satisfies Equation 1. Then in order for a frequent itemset supported by the conditional transaction T_{P_i} and prefix P to replace the current longest covering frequent itemset of a valid conditional transaction T_{P_j}, T_{P_i} needs to contain more than $|X_{P_i}|$ items in its conditional transaction. As a result, T_{P_i} can never contribute to the support of such an itemset and can be safely pruned from the conditional database. □

Lemma 4.3 can be used to prune from the conditional database some unpromising transactions satisfying Equation 1 even when there exist some valid conditional transactions. However, in many cases, there may exist no valid conditional transactions, in this case the whole conditional database can be safely pruned.

Lemma 4.4 *(Conditional database pruning) Given the current prefix itemset P and its projected conditional database $TDB|_P$, if each of its conditional transactions, T_{P_i}, is invalid, $TDB|_P$ can be safely pruned.*

Proof. According to Lemma 4.2, for any invalid conditional transaction, T_{P_i}, we cannot generate any frequent itemsets longer than $LCF_{T_{P_i}}$ by growing prefix P. This means that if each conditional transaction is invalid, we can no longer change the current status of the set of the currently maintained longest covering frequent itemsets w.r.t. prefix P, $\cup_{i=1}^{sup(P)} \{LCF_{T_{P_i}}\}$, by extending P; thus, $TDB|_P$ can be safely pruned. □

Example 4.2 Assume the prefix is $c:4$ (i.e., $P=c$). From Table 1 we get that $TDB|_c=\{\langle 01, e\rangle, \langle 05, def\rangle, \langle 06, d\rangle, \langle 07, f\rangle\}$, and $LCF_{01}=ace:2$, $LCF_{05}=ace:2$, $LCF_{06}=bcd:2$, and $LCF_{07}=acf:2$. Conditional transactions $\langle 01, e\rangle$, $\langle 06, d\rangle$, and $\langle 07, f\rangle$ fall into case 1 of Definition 4.2, while $\langle 05, def\rangle$ falls into case 2 of Definition 4.2, thus all the conditional transactions in $TDB|_c$ are invalid. According to Lemma 4.4, conditional database $TDB|_c$ can be pruned. □

INPUT: (1) *TDB: a transaction database*, and (2) *min_sup: a minimum support threshold.*
OUTPUT: (1) *SI: the summary set.*
```
01. for all t_i ∈ TDB
02.    SI_{t_i} ← ∅;
03. call summary(∅, TDB);
```

SUBROUTINE 1 : **summary**(*pi, cdb*)

INPUT: (1) *pi: a prefix itemset*, and (2) *cdb: the conditional database w.r.t. prefix pi.*
```
04. I ← find_frequent_items(cdb,min_sup);
05. S ← item_merging(I);  pi ← pi ∪ S;  I ← I - S;
06. if(pi ≠ ∅)
07.    for all t_i ∈ cdb
08.       if(|SI_{t_i}| < |pi|)
09.          SI_{t_i} ← pi;
10. if(I ≠ ∅)
11.    if(conditional_database_pruning(I,pi,cdb))
12.       return;
13.    cdb ← conditional_transaction_pruning(I,pi,cdb);
14.    for all i∈I do
15.       pi' ← pi ∪ {i};
16.       cdb' ← build_cond_database(pi', cdb);
17.       call summary(pi', cdb');
```

4.3 The Algorithm

By pushing deeply the search space pruning methods of Section 4.2 into the frequent itemset mining framework described in Section 4.1, we can mine the *summary set* as described in the SUMMARY algorithm shown in ALGORITHM 1. It first initializes the summary itemset to empty for each transaction (lines 01-02) and calls the SUBROUTINE 1 (i.e., *summary(∅, TDB)*) to mine the *summary set* (line 03). SUBROUTINE *summary(pi, cdb)* finds the set of local frequent items by scanning conditional database *cdb* once (line 04) and applies the search space pruning methods such as the *item_merging* (line 05), *conditional_database_pruning* (lines 11-12), and *conditional_transaction_pruning* (line 13), updates the *summary set* information for conditional database *cdb* w.r.t. prefix itemset *pi* (lines 06-09), and grows the current prefix, builds the new conditional database, and recursively calls itself under the projection-based frequent itemset mining framework (lines 14-17).

Discussion. A transaction may be covered by multiple summary itemsets. In this paper we mainly focus on the SUMMARY algorithm, which for each transaction, only inserts into the *summary set* the summary itemset that was discovered first. However, it is rather straightforward to revise SUMMARY to find all the summary itemsets supported by each transaction. Specifically, if we change the '≤' to '<' in case 1 of Definition 4.2, all the '>' to '≥' in case 2 of Definition 4.2, the '≤' to

'<' in Equation 1 of Lemma 4.3, and the '<' to '≤' in line 08 of ALGORITHM 1, the revised SUMMARY algorithm will find all the summary itemsets. We denote the so-derived algorithm by SUMMARY-all.

5 Experimental Results

We have implemented both the SUMMARY and SUMMARY-all algorithms, and performed a thorough experimental study to evaluate the effectiveness of the pruning methods, their algorithmic efficiency, and their overall scalability. All the experiments except the efficiency test were performed on a 2.4GHz Intel PC with 1GB memory and Windows XP installed. In our experiments, we used some databases which were popularly used in evaluating various frequent itemset mining algorithms [35, 30, 16], such as *connect, chess, pumsb*, mushroom*, and *gazelle*, and some categorical databases obtained from the UCI Machine Learning repository, such as *SPECT, Letter Recognition*, and so on.

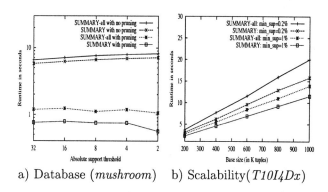

a) Database (*mushroom*)   b) Scalability(*T10I4Dx*)

Figure 1. Effectiveness of the pruning methods and the scalability test

Effectiveness of the Pruning Methods. We first evaluated the effectiveness of the pruning methods by comparing SUMMARY and SUMMARY-all themselves with or without the *conditional database* and *transaction* pruning methods. Figure 1a shows that the algorithms with pruning can be over an order of magnitude faster than the corresponding algorithms without pruning for database *mushroom*. This illustrates that the pruning methods newly proposed in this paper are very effective in reducing search space.

Scalability. We also tested the algorithm scalability using the IBM synthetic database series *T10I4Dx* by setting the average transaction length at 10 and changing the number of transactions from 200K to 1000K. We ran both SUMMARY and SUMMARY-all at two different minimum relative supports of 0.2% and 1%.

Figure 1b shows that these two algorithms scale very well against the database size.

Efficiency. To mine the *summary set*, a naïve method is to first mine the complete set of frequent closed itemsets, from which the *summary set* can be further identified. Our comparison with FPclose [17], one of the most recently developed efficient closed itemset mining algorithms [16], shows that such a solution is not practical when the minimum support is low. As we will discuss in Section 6, such low minimum support values are beneficial for clustering applications. The efficiency comparison was performed on a 1.8GHz Linux machine with 1GB memory by varying the absolute support threshold and turning off the output of FPclose. The experiments for all the databases we used show consistent results. Due to limited space, we only report the results for databases *connect* and *gazelle*.

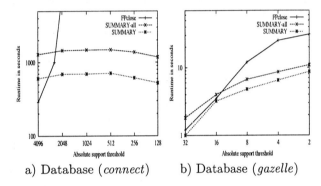

a) Database (*connect*)   b) Database (*gazelle*)

Figure 2. Efficiency test for *connect* **and** *gazelle*

Figure 2 shows the runtime for databases *connect* and *gazelle*. It shows that both SUMMARY and SUMMARY-all scale very well w.r.t. the support threshold, and for *connect* database, they even run faster at low support value of 128 than at high support value of 512. This is because these two algorithms usually mine longer itemsets at lower support, which makes the pruning methods more effective in removing some short transactions and conditional databases. Because the FP-tree structure adopted by FPclose is very effective in condensing dense databases, at high support FPclose is faster than SUMMARY and SUMMARY-all for dense databases like *connect*, but once we continue to lower the support, it can be orders of magnitude slower. While for sparse databases like *gazelle*, FPclose can be several times slower. In addition, the above results also show that SUMMARY always runs a little faster than SUMMARY-all, this is because SUMMARY-all mines more *summary itemsets* than SUMMARY. For example, at absolute minimum support threshold of 32, on average SUMMARY-

all finds 11.1 *summary itemsets* for each transaction of database *mushroom*, and finds 1.3 *summary itemsets* for each transaction of database *gazelle*.

6 Application - *Summary Set* based Clustering

One important application of the SUMMARY algorithm is to cluster the categorical data by treating each summary itemset as a cluster description and grouping the transactions with the same cluster description into a cluster. In SUMMARY, we adopt a prefix tree structure to facilitate this task, which has been used extensively in performing different data mining tasks [18, 30]. For each transaction, T_i, if its summary itemset SI_{T_i} is not empty, we sort the items in SI_{T_i} in lexicographic order and insert it into the prefix tree. The tree node corresponding to the last item of the sorted summary itemset represents a cluster, to which the transaction T_i belongs.

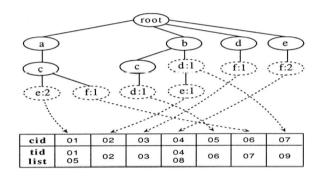

Figure 3. Clustering based on *summary set*

Example 6.1 The summary itemsets for the transactions in our running example are $SI_{01}=ace$, $SI_{02}=bde$, $SI_{03}=df$, $SI_{04}=ef$, $SI_{05}=ace$, $SI_{06}=bcd$, $SI_{07}=acf$, $SI_{08}=ef$, and $SI_{09}=bd$. If we insert these summary itemsets into the prefix tree in sequence, we can get seven clusters with cluster descriptions *ace*, *bde*, *df*, *ef*, *bcd*, *acf*, and *bd*, as shown in Figure 3. From Figure 3 we see that transactions 01 and 05 are grouped into cluster 01, transactions 04 and 08 are grouped into cluster 04, while each of the other transactions forms a separate cluster of their own. Note that a non-leaf node *summary itemset* in the prefix tree represents a non-maximal frequent itemset in the sense that one of its proper supersets must be frequent. For example, *summary itemset bd* is non-maximal, because *summary itemset bde* is a proper superset of *bd*. In this case, we have an alternative clustering option: merge the non-leaf node clusters with their corresponding leaf node

246

clusters to form larger clusters. In Figure 3, we can merge cluster 07 with cluster 02 to form a cluster. □

Clustering Evaluation. We have used several categorical databases to evaluate the clustering quality of the SUMMARY algorithm, including *mushroom*, *SPECT*, *Letter Recognition*, and *Congressional Voting*, which all contain class labels and are available at *http://www.ics.uci.edu/~mlearn/*. We did not use the class labels in mining the *summary set* and clustering, instead, we only used them to evaluate the clustering accuracy, which is defined by the number of correctly clustered instances (i.e., the instances with dominant class labels in the computed clusters) as a percentage of the database size. SUMMARY runs very fast and can achieve very good clustering accuracy for these databases, especially when the minimum support is low. Due to limited space, we only show results for *mushroom* and *Congressional Voting* databases, which have been widely used in the previous studies [14, 32, 34].

The *mushroom* database contains some physical characteristics of various mushrooms. It has 8124 instances and two classes: poisonous and edible. Table 2 shows the clustering results for this database, including the *minimum support* used in the tests, the *number of clusters* found by SUMMARY, the *number of misclustered instances*, *clustering accuracy*, *compression ratio* and *runtime* (in seconds) for both the *summary set* discovery and clustering. The compression ratio is defined as the total number of items in the database divided by the total number of items in the *summary set*. We can see that SUMMARY has a clustering accuracy higher than 97% and a runtime less than 0.85 seconds for a wide range of support thresholds. At support of 25, it can even achieve a 100% accuracy. The MineClus algorithm is one of the most recently developed clustering algorithm for this type of databases [34]. Its reported clustering solution for this database finds 20 clusters with an accuracy 96.41% and in the meantime declares 0.59% of the instances as outliers, which means it misclusters about 290 instances and treats about another 48 instances as outliers. Compared to this algorithm, SUMMARY is very competitive in considering both of its high efficiency and clustering accuracy. In addition, the high compression ratios demonstrate that the *summary set* can be used as a concise summary of the original database (Note in each case of Table 2, the *summary set* covers each instance of the original database, which means there is no outlier in our solution).

The *Congressional Voting* database contains the 1984 United States Congressional Voting Records and has two class labels: Republican and Democrat. In our

sup.	# clu.	# miscl.	accur.	com. rat.	time
1400	30	32	99.6	660	0.38s
1200	35	32	99.6	549	0.42s
1000	37	32	99.6	509	0.44s
800	63	208	97.4	268	0.48s
400	128	8	99.9	120	0.66s
200	140	6	99.93	97	0.77s
100	197	32	99.6	62	0.81s
50	298	1	99.99	37	0.79s
25	438	0	100	23	0.75s

Table 2. Clustering *mushroom* database

cid	# Rep.	# Demo.	cid	# Rep.	# Demo.
1	2	244	4	1	3
2	155	16	5	2	1
3	5	0	6	1	1

Table 3. Clustering *Congressional Voting* database

experiments, we removed four outlier instances whose most attribute values are missing and used the left 431 instances. Table 3 shows the clustering solution of SUMMARY at a minimum support of 245, at which point the clusters produced by SUMMARY covers the entire database (while a minimum support higher than 245 will make SUMMARY miss some instances), and SUMMARY only uses 0.001 seconds to find the six clusters with an accuracy higher than 95% and a compression ratio higher than 1164. Even we simply merge the four small clusters with the two large clusters in order to get exact two clusters, the accuracy is still higher than 93% in the worst case (e.g., clusters 3 and 5 are merged into cluster 1, and clusters 4 and 6 are merged into cluster 2), and is much better than the reported accuracy, 86.67%, of the MineClus algorithm [34].

7 Discussions and Conclusion

In this paper we proposed to mine the *summary set* that can maximally cover the input database. Each *summary itemset* can be treated as a distinct cluster description and the transactions with the same description can be grouped together to form a cluster. Because the *summary itemset* of a cluster is one of the longest frequent itemsets that is common among the corresponding transactions of the same cluster, it can approximately maximize the intra-cluster similarity, while different clusters are dissimilar with each other because they support distinct *summary itemsets*. In addition, we require each *summary itemset* be frequent in order to make sure it is statistically significant.

Directly mining the *summary set* also enabled us to design an efficient algorithm, SUMMARY. By exploring some properties of the *summary set*, we developed two novel pruning methods, which significantly reduce the search space. Our performance study showed that SUMMARY runs very fast even when the minimum support is extremely low and the *summary set* is very effective in clustering categorical data. In addition, we also evaluated SUMMARY-all, a variant of SUMMARY, which mines all the summary itemsets for each transaction. In future, we plan to explore how to choose the one among the summary itemsets supported by a transaction which can reduce the number of clusters while achieving a high clustering accuracy.

References

[1] R. Agarwal, C. Aggarwal, V. Prasad. A Tree Projection Algorithm for Generation of Frequent Item Sets, Journal of Parallel and Distributed Computing. 61(3), 2001.

[2] R. Agrawal, T. Imielinski, A. Swami. *Mining Association Rules between Sets of Items in Large Databases*, SIGMOD'93.

[3] R. Agrawal, R. Srikant. *Fast Algorithms for Mining Association Rules*, VLDB'94.

[4] M. Antonie, O. Zaiane. *Text Document Categorization by Term Association*, ICDM'02.

[5] R.J. Bayardo. *Brute-force Mining of High-confidence Classification rules*, KDD'97.

[6] R.J. Bayardo. *Efficiently Mining Long Patterns from Databases*, SIGMOD'98.

[7] F. Beil, M. Ester, X. Xu. *Frequent Term-Based Text Clustering*, KDD'02.

[8] J. Boulicaut, A. Bykowski, C. Rigotti. *Free-Sets: A Condensed Representation of Boolean Data for the Approximation of Frequency Queries*, Journal of Data Mining and Knowledge Discovery. 7(1), 2003.

[9] S. Brin, R. Motwani, J.D. Ullman, S. Tsur. *Dynamic Itemset Counting and Implication Rules for Market Basket Data*, SIGMOD'97.

[10] D. Burdick, M. Calimlim, J. Gehrke. *MAFIA: A Maximal Frequent Itemset Algorithm for Transactional Databases*, ICDE'01.

[11] B. Fung, K. Wang, M. Ester. *Hierachical Document Clustering Using Frequent Itemsets*, SDM'03.

[12] K. Gade, J. Wang, G. Karypis. *Efficient Closed Pattern Mining in the Presence of Tough Block Constraints*, KDD'04.

[13] V. Ganti, J. Gehrke, R. Ramakrishnan. *CACTUS: Clustering Categorical Data Using Summaries*, KDD'99.

[14] S. Guha, R. Rastogi, K. Shim. *ROCK: A Robut Clustering Algorithm for Categorical Attributes*, ICDE'99.

[15] D. Gunopulos, H. Mannila, S.Saluja. *Discovering All Most Specific Sentences by Randomized Algorithms*, ICDT'97.

[16] B. Goethals, M. Zaki. *An Introduction to FIMI'03 Workshop on Frequent Itemset Mining Implementations*, ICDM-FIMI'03.

[17] G. Grahne, J. Zhu. *Efficiently Using Prefix-trees in Mining Frequent Itemsets*, ICDM-FIMI'03.

[18] J. Han, J. Pei, Y. Yin. *Mining Frequent Patterns without Candidate Generation*, SIGMOD'00.

[19] W. Li, J. Han, J. Pei. *CMAR: Accurate and Efficient Classification based on multiple class-association rules*, ICDM'01.

[20] B. Liu, W. Hsu, Y. Ma. *Integrating Classification and Association Rule Mining*, KDD'98.

[21] G. Liu, H. Lu, W. Lou, J. X. Yu. *On Computing, Storing and Querying Frequent Patterns*, KDD'03.

[22] H. Mannila, H. Toivonen. *Multiple Uses of Frequent Sets and Condensed Representations*, KDD'96.

[23] F. Pan, G. Cong, A.K.H. Tung, J. Yang, M. Zaki. *CARPENTER: Finding Closed Patterns in Long Biological Datasets*, KDD'03.

[24] J. Park, M. Chen, P. S. Yu. *An Effective Hash Based Algorithm for Mining Association Rules*, SIGMOD'95.

[25] N. Pasquier, Y. Bastide, R. Taouil, L. Lakhal. *Discovering Frequent Closed Itemsets for Association Rules*, ICDT'99.

[26] J. Pei, J. Han, H. Lu, S. Nishio, S. Tang, D. Yang. *H-Mine: Hyper-structure Mining of Frequent Patterns in Large Databases*, ICDM'01.

[27] J. Pei, J. Han, R. Mao. *CLOSET: An Efficient Algorithm for Mining Frequent Closed Itemsets*, DMKD'00.

[28] M. Seno, G. Karypis. *LPMiner: An Algorithm for Finding Frequent Itemsets Using Length-Decreasing Support Constraint*, ICDM'01.

[29] H. Toivonen. *Sampling Large Databases for Association Rules*, VLDB'96.

[30] J. Wang, J. Han, J. Pei. *CLOSET+: Searching for the Best Strategies for Mining Frequent Closed Itemsets*, KDD'03.

[31] J. Wang, G. Karypis. *BAMBOO: Accelerating Closed Itemset Mining by Deeply Pushing the Length-Decreasing Support Constraint*, SDM'04.

[32] K. Wang, C. Xu, B. Liu. *Clustering Transactions using Large Items*, CIKM'99.

[33] H. Xiong, M. Steinbach, P. Tan, V. Kumar. *HICAP: Hierarchial Clustering with Pattern Preservation*, SDM'04.

[34] M. Yiu, N. Mamoulis. *Frequent-Pattern based Iterative Projected Clustering*, ICDM'03.

[35] M. Zaki, C. Hsiao. *CHARM: An Efficient Algorithm for Closed Itemset Mining*, SDM'02.

Bottom-Up Generalization: A Data Mining Solution to Privacy Protection *

Ke Wang
Simon Fraser University
wangk@cs.sfu.ca

Philip S. Yu
IBM T. J. Watson Research Center
psyu@us.ibm.com

Sourav Chakraborty
Simon Fraser University
chakrabo@cs.sfu.ca

Abstract

The well-known privacy-preserved data mining *modifies existing data mining techniques to randomized data. In this paper, we investigate data mining as a technique for masking data, therefore, termed* data mining based privacy protection. *This approach incorporates partially the requirement of a targeted data mining task into the process of masking data so that essential structure is preserved in the masked data. The idea is simple but novel: we explore the data generalization concept from data mining as a way to hide detailed information, rather than discover trends and patterns. Once the data is masked, standard data mining techniques can be applied without modification. Our work demonstrated another positive use of data mining technology: not only can it discover useful patterns, but also mask private information.*

We consider the following privacy problem: a data holder wants to release a version of data for building classification models, but wants to protect against linking the released data to an external source for inferring sensitive information. We adapt an iterative bottom-up generalization from data mining to generalize the data. The generalized data remains useful to classification but becomes difficult to link to other sources. The generalization space is specified by a hierarchical structure of generalizations. A key is identifying the best generalization to climb up the hierarchy at each iteration. Enumerating all candidate generalizations is impractical. We present a scalable solution that examines at most one generalization in each iteration for each attribute involved in the linking.

1 Introduction

The increasing ability to accumulate, store, retrieve, cross-reference, mine and link vast number of electronic records brings substantial benefits to millions of people. For example, cross-mining personal records on chemical exposure and death records could help identify cancer-causing substances. These advances also raise responsibility and privacy concerns because of the potential of creating new information. An example given in [11] is that a *sensitive* medical record was uniquely linked to a *named* voter record in a publicly available voter list through the shared attributes of Zip, Birth date, Sex. Indeed, since "the whole is greater than the sum of the parts", protection of individual sources does not guarantee protection when sources are cross-examined. A relevant research topic is finding ways to safeguard against inferring private information through record linkage while continuing to allow benefits of information sharing and data mining.

1.1 Our contribution

Information becomes sensitive when they are specific to a small number of individuals. Data mining, on the other hand, typically makes use of information shared by some minimum number of individuals to ensure a required statistical significance of patterns. As such, sensitive information are to be discarded for reliable data mining. This observation motivates us to apply the requirement of an intended data mining task to identify useful information to be released, therefore, sensitive information to be masked. This approach, called *data mining based privacy protection*, turns data mining from a threat into a solution to privacy protection.

We consider the following *anonymity problem* [10]. A data holder wants to release a person-specific data R, but wants to prevent from linking the released data to an external source E through shared attributes $R \cap E$, called the *virtual identifier*. One approach is to generalize specific values into less specific but semantically consistent values to create K-*anonymity*: if one record r in R is linked to some external information, at least $K - 1$ other records are similarly linked by having the same virtual identifier value as r. The idea is to make the inference ambiguous by creating extraneous linkages. An example is generalizing "birth date" to "birth year" so that every body born in the same year are

*Research was supported in part by a research grant from Emerging Opportunity Fund of IRIS, and a research grant from the Natural Science and Engineering Research Council of Canada

linked to a medical record with that birth year, but most of these linkages are non-existing in the real life.

We focus on the use of data for building a classifier. We propose a data mining approach, an iterative bottom-up generalization, to achieve the required K anonymity while preserving the usefulness of the generalized data to classification. The generalization space is specified by a taxonomical hierarchy per attribute in the virtual identifier. The key is identifying the "best" generalization to climb up the hierarchy at each iteration. Evaluating all possible candidates at each iteration is not scalable because each evaluation involves examining data records. We present a scalable solution that examines *at most one generalization per attribute in the virtual identifier in each iteration*, where the work for examining one generalization is proportional to the number of (distinct) virtual identifier values that are actually generalized. We evaluate both quality and scalability of this approach.

1.2 Related work

A well-studied technique for masking sensitive information, primarily studied in statistics, is *randomizing* sensitive attributes by adding random error to values [2, 3, 4, 8]. Recently, this technique was studied in data mining [1]. In these works, privacy was quantified by how closely the original values of a randomized attribute can be estimated. This is very different from the K-anonymity that quantifies how likely an individual can be linked to an external source. The *privacy-preserving data mining* in [1] extends traditional data mining techniques to handle randomized data. We investigate data mining itself as a technique for masking data. The masked data does not require modification of data mining techniques in subsequent data analysis.

Instead of randomizing data, *generalizing* data makes information less precise. Grouping continuous values and suppressing values are examples of this approach. Compared to randomization, generalization has several advantages. First, it preserves the "truthfulness" of information, making the released data meaningful at the record level. This feature is desirable in exploratory and visual data mining where decisions often are made based on examining records. In contrast, randomized data are useful only at the aggregated level such as average and frequency. Second, preferences can be incorporated through the taxonomical hierarchies and the data recipient can be told what was done to the data so that the result can be properly interpreted.

Generalization was used to achieve anonymity in Datafly system [10] and μ-Argus system [6]. Their works did not consider classification or a specific use of released data. In fact, data distortion was simply measured by the number of hierarchy levels climbed up [6]. Each iteration selected the attribute having most number of distinct values in the

Datafly system or values not having K occurrences in the μ-Argus system to generalize or suppress. Such selection did not address the quality for classification where there is a different impact between generalization within a class and that across classes.

To our knowledge, [7] is the only work that has considered the anonymity problem for classification, and presented a genetic algorithm to search for the optimal generalization of the data. As noted in [7], their solution took 18 hours to generalize 30K records. We uses an entirely different approach, the iterative bottom-up generalization, and we focused on the scalability issue. We used an information/privacy trade-off to *select* a generalization, whereas [7] used the privacy requirement to filter a *selected* generalization. Furthermore, the sequence of generalizations produced by our approach can be used to determine a desired trade-off point between privacy and quality. The genetic evolution of random nature does not serve this purpose, neither does the final generalized data because the same final state can be reached by many generalization sequences.

Bottom-up generalization was previously used for extracting patterns, see [5] for example. The new lights in our work are the consideration on privacy protection, quality preservation, and the related scalability issue.

2 The Problem

Consider that a data holder wants to release a person-specific data $R(D_1, \cdots, D_n, C)$ to the public. A record has the form $< v_1, \cdots, v_n, cls >$, where v_i is a domain value from the attribute D_i and cls is a class in C. Suppose that R shares some attributes with an external source E, denoted $R \cap E$. If a value on $R \cap E$ is so specific that the probability of having this value by chance is negligible, each linking from a record in R to some information in E through this value has a good chance of identifying a real life fact. The data holder protects against such linkages by requiring a minimum number of records linkable through each value on $R \cap E$.

Definition 1 (Anonymity) The *virtual identifier*, denoted VID, is the set of attributes shared by R and E. $a(vid)$ denotes the number of records in R with the value vid on VID. The *anonymity* of VID, denoted $A(VID)$, is the minimum $a(vid)$ for any value vid on VID. If $a(vid) = A(VID)$, vid is called an *anonymity vid*. R satisfies the anonymity requirement $< VID, K >$ if $A(VID) \geq K$, where K is specified by the data holder. ■

We transform R to satisfy the anonymity requirement by generalizing specific values on VID into less specific but semantically consistent values. The generalization increases the probability of having a given value on VID by chance, therefore, decreases the probability that a linking through this value represents a real life fact. The generalization space is specified through a taxonomical hierarchy per attribute in VID, provided by either the data holder or the data recipient. A hierarchy is a tree with leaf nodes representing domain values and parent nodes representing less specific values. R is generalized by a sequence of generalizations, where each generalization replaces all child values c with their parent value p in a hierarchy. Before a value c is generalized, all values below c should be generalized to c first.

Definition 2 (Generalization) A *generalization*, written $\{c\} \to p$, replaces all child values $\{c\}$ with the parent value p. A generalization is *valid* if all values below c have been generalized to c. A vid is *generalized* by $\{c\} \to p$ if the vid contains some value in $\{c\}$. ∎

Relationship	Race	Workclass	$a(vid)$	C
c_1	b_2	a_3	4	0Y4N
c_1	b_2	c_3	4	0Y4N
c_1	b_2	d_3	3	0Y3N
c_1	c_2	a_3	3	2Y1N
c_1	c_2	b_3	4	2Y2N
d_1	c_2	b_3	4	4Y0N
d_1	c_2	e_3	2	2Y0N
d_1	d_2	b_3	3	2Y1N
d_1	d_2	e_3	2	2Y0N

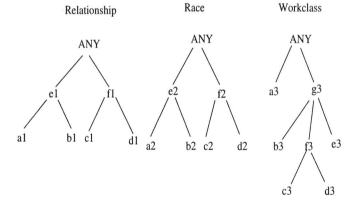

Figure 1. Data and hierarchies for VID

Example 1 Consider

$$VID = \{Relationship, Race, Workclass\},$$

and the hierarchies and vids in Figure 1. We have compressed all records having the same value on VID into a single row with the distribution of the Y/N class label and the count $a(vid)$. Initially, the generalizations at

e_1, f_1, e_2, f_2, f_3 are valid, $A(VID) = 2$, and $d_1 c_2 e_3$ and $d_1 d_2 e_3$ are anonymity vids. The requirement of $K = 3$ can be satisfied by applying $\{c_2, d_2\} \to f_2$, which generalizes the vids $d_1 c_2 e_3$ and $d_1 d_2 e_3$ into a single vid $d_1 f_2 e_3$ with $a(d_1 f_2 e_3) = 4$. ∎

Definition 3 (Anonymity for Classification) Given a relation R, an anonymity requirement $< VID, K >$, and a hierarchy for each attribute in VID, generalize R, by a sequence of generalizations, to satisfy the requirement and contain as much information as possible for classification. ∎

The anonymity requirement can be satisfied in more than one way of generalizing R, and some lose more information than others with regard to classification. One question is how to select a sequence of generalizations so that information loss is minimized. Another question is how to find this sequence of generalizations efficiently for a large data set. We like to answer these questions in the rest of the paper.

3 Metrics for generalization

We consider a metric for a single generalization, which is used to guide the search of a sequence of generalizations in the next section. A "good" generalization should preserve information for classification *and* focus on the goal of achieving the K-anonymity. Let us formalize this criterion.

Consider a generalization $G : \{c\} \to p$. Let R_c denote the set of records containing c, and let R_p denote the set of records containing p after applying G. $|R_p| = \Sigma_c |R_c|$, where $|x|$ is the number of elements in a bag x. The effect of G is summarized by the "information loss" and "anonymity gain" after replacing R_c's with R_p.

We adapt the entropy based information loss, which can be substituted by other information measures:

$$I(G) = Info(R_p) - \Sigma_c \frac{|R_c|}{|R_p|} Info(R_c),$$

where $Info(R_x)$ is the *impurity* or *entropy* of R_x [9]:

$$Info(R_x) = -\Sigma_{cls} \frac{freq(R_x, cls)}{|R_x|} \times log_2 \frac{freq(R_x, cls)}{|R_x|}.$$

$freq(R_x, cls)$ is the number of records in R_x with the class label cls.

The anonymity gain is $A_G(VID) - A(VID)$, where $A(VID)$ and $A_G(VID)$ denote the anonymity before and after applying G, respectively. $A_G(VID) \geq A(VID)$. In the case of $A_G(VID) > K$, $A_G(VID) - K$ is the "surplus" of anonymity. While more anonymity is always preferred for privacy protection, it comes at the expense of losing more information. If such a "surplus" really outweighs the information concern, the data holder should specify a larger K in the first place. This consideration leads to the modified anonymity gain:

$$P(G) = x - A(VID)$$

where $x = A_G(VID)$ if $A_G(VID) \leq K$, and $x = K$ otherwis.

Information-Privacy Metric. To minimize the information loss for achieving a given K-anonymity, our criterion is to favor the generalization having the minimum information loss for each unit of anonymity gain:

$$Minimize : IP(G) = I(G)/P(G).$$

$IP(G)$ is ∞ if $P(G) = 0$. If $P(G) = 0$ for all (valid) generalizations G, we compare them based on $I(G)$. This metric also maximizes the anonymity gain for each unit of information loss. We use $I(G)/P(G)$ instead of $I(G) - P(G)$ because differentiating semantically different quantities makes little sense.

Unlike the "penalty" metric in [7] that focuses on information distortion alone, $IP(G)$ takes into account both information and anonymity. The anonymity consideration helps focus the search on the privacy goal, therefore, has a look-ahead effect. However, this presents a new challenge to scalability because the effect on anonymity is only available after applying a generalization. We will examine this issue in subsequent sections.

4 Bottom-Up Generalization

Algorithm 1 describes our bottom-up generalization process. In the ith iteration, we generalize R by the "best" generalization G_{best} according to the IP metric. This algorithm makes no claim on efficiency because Line 2 and 3 requires computing $IP(G)$ for all candidate generalizations G. Let us look at this computation in more details.

Consider a candidate generalization $G : \{c\} \rightarrow p$ in an iteration. $|R_c|$ and $freq(R_c, cls)$ can be maintained after each iteration. $|R_p|$ and $freq(R_p, cls)$ can be obtained by aggregating $|R_c|$ and $freq(R_c, cls)$. Therefore, $I(G)$ can be easily computed, i.e., without accessing vids. In fact, any metric on a single attribute (plus the class label) can be computed this way. $A(VID)$ is available as a result of applying the previous generalization. Computing $A_G(VID)$, however, depends on the "effect" of G, which is only available after applying G, and requires accessing vids. This is a new challenge to scalability.

Our insight is that most generalizations G do not affect $A(VID)$, therefore, $A_G(VID) = A(VID)$. In fact, if a generalization G fails to generalize *all* anonymity vids, G will not affect $A(VID)$. For such G, $P(G) = 0$ and $IP(G) = \infty$, and our metric does not need $A_G(VID)$. Therefore, we can focus on "critical generalizations" as defined below.

Algorithm 1 The bottom-up generalization

1: **while** R does not satisfy the anonymity requirement **do**
2:   **for all** generalization G **do**
3:     compute $IP(G)$;
4:   **end for**;
5:   find the best generalization G_{best};
6:   generalize R by G_{best};
7: **end while**;
8: output R;

Definition 4 (Critical generalization) G is *critical* if $A_G(VID) > A(VID)$. ∎

A critical generalization G has a non-zero $P(G)$ and a finite $IP(G)$, whereas a non-critical generalization G has a zero $P(G)$ and infinite $IP(G)$. Therefore, so long as one generalization is critical, all non-critical generalizations will be ignored by the IP metric. If all generalizations are non-critical, the IP metric will select the one with minimum $I(G)$. In both cases, $A_G(VID)$ is not needed for a non-critical generalization G. Based on this observation, we optimize Algorithm 1 by replacing Line 2 and 3 with

2:   **for all** critical generalization G **do**
3:     compute $A_G(VID)$;

Three questions remain: how to identify all critical generalizations without actually computing $A_G(VID)$ for all generalizations; how many generalizations are critical, therefore, need to compute $A_G(VID)$; and how to apply a generalization without scanning all vids. We answer these questions in the next section.

5 Pruning Strategies

A key issue in our approach is how to identify critical generalizations without computing $A_G(VID)$ for all candidate G. First, we present an efficient structure for applying a given generalization.

5.1 The data structure

We store all distinct vids in a tree structure, called *Taxonomy Encoded Anonymity* (TEA) index. Each level of the tree represents the current generalization of a particular attribute, and each path represents a particular vid with $a(vid)$ stored in the leaf node. In addition, the TEA index links up the vids according to the generalizations that generalize them. Each time a generalization is applied, the TEA index is updated by adjusting the vids linked to this generalization. The purpose of this index is to prune the number of candidate generalizations to no more than $|VID|$ at each iteration, where $|VID|$ is the number of attributes in VID.

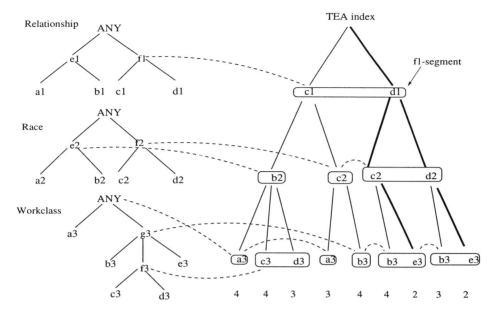

Figure 2. The TEA index for VID

Definition 5 (TEA index) The *Taxonomy Encoded Anonymity* (TEA) index for $VID = \{D_1, \cdots, D_k\}$ is a tree of k levels. The level $i > 0$ represents the current values for D_i. Each root-to-leaf path represents an existing vid in the data, with $a(vid)$ stored at the leaf node. For a generalization $G : \{c\} \rightarrow p$, a *segment* of G is a maximal set of sibling nodes, $\{s_1, \cdots, s_t\}$, such that $\{s_1, \cdots, s_t\} \subseteq \{c\}$, where t is the size of the segment. All segments of G are linked up. A vid is *generalized* by a segment if the vid contains a value in the segment. ∎

Intuitively, a segment of G represents a set of sibling nodes in the TEA index that will be merged by applying G. To apply G, we follow the link of the segments of G and merge the nodes in each segment of G. The merging of sibling nodes implies inserting the new node into a proper segment and recursively merging the child nodes having the same value if their parents are merged. The merging of leaf nodes implies summing up $a(vid)$ stored at such leaf nodes. The cost is proportional to the number of vids generalized by G.

Example 2 Figure 2 shows the TEA index for the vids in Example 1. A rectangle represents a segment, and a a dashed line links up the segments of the same generalization. For example, the left-most path represents the vid $c_1 b_2 a_3$, and $a(c_1 b_2 a_3) = 4$. $\{c_1, d_1\}$ at level 1 is a segment of f_1 because it forms a maximal set of siblings that will be merged by f_1. $\{c_1 c_2\}$ and $\{d_1 c_2, d_1 d_2\}$ at level 2 are two segments of f_2. $\{c_1 b_2 c_3, c_1 b_2 d_3\}$ at level 3 is a segment of f_3. $d_1 d_2 e_3$ and $d_1 c_2 e_3$, in bold face, are the anonymity vids.

Consider applying $\{c_2, d_2\} \rightarrow f_2$. The first segment of

f_2 contains only one sibling node $\{c_1 c_2\}$, we simply re-label the sibling by f_2. This creates new vids $c_1 f_2 a_3$ and $c_1 f_2 b_3$. The second segment of f_2 contains two sibling nodes $\{d_1 c_2, d_1 d_2\}$. We merge them into a new node labeled by f_2, and merge their child nodes having the same label. This creates new vids $d_1 f_2 b_3$ and $d_1 f_2 e_3$, with $a(d_1 f_2 b_3) = 7$ and $a(d_1 f_2 e_3) = 4$. ∎

Observation 1. G is critical *only if* every anonymity vid is generalized by some size-k segment of G, $k > 1$. In Figure 2, no anonymity vid is generalized by the (only) size-2 segment of f_3, so f_3 is not critical. The two anonymity vids are generalized by the (only) segment size-2 of f_1, but f_1 is still not critical.

Observation 2. At each level of the TEA index, each vid is generalized by *at most* one segment. This observation implies that the "only if" condition in Observation 1 holds for at most one generalization at each level of the TEA index.

Theorem 1 G is critical only if every anonymity vid is generalized by some size-k segment of G, where $k > 1$. At most $|VID|$ generalizations satisfy this "only if" condition, where $|VID|$ denotes the number of attributes in VID. ∎

By checking the "only if" condition in Theorem 1, we can prune the computation of $A_G(VID)$ for all but at most $|VID|$ generalizations, and are still guaranteed to find all critical generalizations. Note that $|VID|$ is a very small constant, for example, 3 in Example 1. We implement this pruning strategy in three steps.

5.2 Step 1: pruning generalizations

This step finds all generalizations satisfying the "only if" condition in Theorem 1, denoted $Cand$. We start at the leaf nodes for the anonymity vids in the TEA index, walk up their paths synchronously one level at a time. At each level, we check if every anonymity vid is generalized by some size-k segment of the *same* generalization G, $k > 1$. If not, no critical generalization exists at the current level. If yes, we add G to $Cand$. We then move up to the next level in the TEA index.

5.3 Step 2: finding the best generalization

This step finds the best generalization by computing $IP(G)$ for *every* (valid) generalization G. $A(VID)$ and $I(G)$ are available or easily computed from the result of the previous iteration. For every G not in $Cand$, G is non-critical (Theorem 1), so $IP(G) = I(G)$. So, we focus on computing $A_G(VID)$ for $G \in Cand$. We present a method that examines only the vids actually generalized by G, not all vids.

Let A_G^n be the minimum $a(vid)$ for the new vids produced by applying G. Let A_G^o be the minimum $a(vid)$ for all old vids not generalized by G. $A_G(VID) = min\{A_G^n, A_G^o\}$. To compute A_G^n, we apply G to the TEA index as described in Section 5.1, except that the effect is made permanent only if G is actually the best generalization.

To compute A_G^o, we keep track of the number of vids not generalized by G such that $a(vid) = i$, stored in $O[i]$, for $1 \leq i \leq K$. K is typically a few hundreds, so this is a small cost. Before applying G, $O[i]$ is available from the previous iteration. Each time a vid having $a(vid) = i$ is generalized by G, we decrement $O[i]$. At the end of applying G, $O[i]$ stores the correct value. Now, if $O[i] > 0$ for some $1 \leq i \leq K$, let A_G^o be the smallest such i. If $O[i] = 0$ for $1 \leq i \leq K$, we consider two cases: if $A_G^n \leq K$, then $A_G(VID) = A_G^n$; if $A_G^n > K$, then $A_G(VID) > K$, but such $A_G(VID)$ is never used in our metric.

The cost in this step is proportional to the number of vids generalized by G, not all vids.

5.4 Step 3: applying the best generalization

This step applies the best generalization G_{best} found in Step 2. If G_{best} is in $Cand$, we just make the effect of G in Step 2 permanent. If G_{best} is not in $Cand$, we apply G_{best} to the TEA index. In this case, $Cand$ must be empty, otherwise G_{best} must come from $Cand$ following the remark below Definition 4.

5.5 Analysis

The TEA index is typically smaller than the database because a vid may occur in multiple records, but is stored only once in the TEA index. Once the TEA index is created, the bottom-up generalization depends only on the TEA index, not the database. The number of iterations is bounded by the number of possible generalizations, which is equal to the number of non-leaf nodes in all hierarchies. The analysis below focuses on a single iteration.

Step 1 involves walking up the anonymity vids in the TEA index. This cost is bounded by the number of anonymity vids, which is typically small because of the constraint $a(vid) = A(VID)$. Step 2 and 3 together apply at most $|VID|$ generalizations (Theorem 1). The cost of applying a generalization is bounded by the number of vids actually generalized, not the number of all vids.

6 Experimental Validation

Our first objective is to evaluate the quality of generalized data for classification, compared to that of the unmodified data. Our second objective is to evaluate the scalability of the proposed algorithm. All experiments were performed on a 2.4GHz Pentium IV processor with 512MB memory. The implementation language is C++.

6.1 Data quality

We adapted the publicly available "Adult" data [1], used previously in [7]. "Adult" has 6 continuous attributes and 8 categorical attributes. The class label represents two income levels, $\leq$50K or >50K. There are 45,222 records without missing values, pre-split into 30,162 and 15,060 records for training and testing. We used the same 7 categorical attributes used in [7], shown in Table 1, and obtained their hierarchies from the authors of [7]. [7] also used the numeric attribute Age. We did not include Age because our current algorithm handles only categorical attributes. In effect, this data is equivalent to their data with Age generalized into ANY in advance. This puts us in a non-favorable position because we do not have other choices of generalizing Age. VID contains all 7 attributes.

We generalized the training set on VID and built a C4.5 decision tree on the generalized data. The found generalization was then applied to the testing set and the error E was collected on the generalized testing set. We compared this error with two errors. B denotes the "baseline error" where the data was not generalized at all, which is 17.4%. W denotes the "worst error" where all the attributes in VID were generalized to ANY, which is 24.6%. $W - B$ measures the

---
[1] http://www.ics.uci.edu/ñlearn

254

Hierarchy	# Leaf nodes	# Levels
Occupation	14	3
Education	16	5
Country	41	4
Martial_status	7	3
Sex	2	2
Race	5	2
Work_class	8	3

Table 1. The hierarchies for "Adult" data

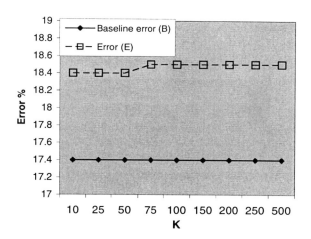

Figure 3. Error versus K

contribution of the attributes in VID, and $E - B$ measures the quality lost by our generalization. Figure 3 shows E for various thresholds K. Below are the main findings.

First, $E - B$ is no more than 1.1% for all K in the range from 10 to 500, which is significantly lower than $W - B = 7.2\%$. On one hand, the large $W - B$ implies that the attributes generalized are important. On the other hand, the small $E - B$ implies that the generalizations required for the K-anonymity does not harm the quality much. We observed that most generalizations tended to focus on over-fitting values for the K tested, and if a generalized attribute became less discriminating, some previously unused alternatives emerged and were picked by C4.5 classifiers. Our approach takes advantage of such "health generalizations" and "multiple structures" typically present in the data for masking sensitive information while preserving quality.

Second, our results are comparable to the best results in [7] but take much less time. [7] reported the errors from 17.3% to 18.5% for K up to 500, with the baseline error of 17.1%. Our errors ranged from 18.4% to 18.5%, but our data has the baseline error of 17.4%. The error increase relative to the baseline is similar in both cases. On the other hand, our algorithm took no more than 7 seconds to create the index and no more than 22 seconds to generalize the data for all K tested, whereas the genetic algorithm took 18 hours as reported in [7].

6.2 Scalability

This experiment evaluated the scalability of the proposed algorithm by enlarging the "Adult" data. First, we merged the training set and testing set into one set, which gave 45,222 records. For each original record t in the merged set, we added $\sigma - 1$ "variations" of t, where $\sigma > 1$ is the *scale factor*. A variation of t took random values on ρ attributes randomly selected from VID, and agreed with t on the remaining attributes in VID. ρ is called the *novelty factor*. Random values came from the leaves in the corresponding hierarchy. The enlarged data has the 45,222 original records plus all variations, giving a total of $\sigma * 45,222$ records. We used σ and ρ to control the number of distinct vids.

Figure 4 (from top to bottom) plots the time versus the threshold K, scale factor σ, and novelty factor ρ. Another 50 seconds or less were spent on creating the index. As one parameter varied, the other two were fixed. "Pruning-based" refers to the implementation that uses the pruning discussed in Section 5. "Index-based" refers to the implementation that uses the TEA index for performing a generalization, but not pruning.

In all experiments, both methods finished in less than 730 seconds. The longest time was took at $\sigma = 30$, $K = 150$ and $\rho = 3$ (the middle figure) where the data has $45,222 * 30 = 1,356,660$ records and 127,831 distinct vids. These experiments showed a much better scalability than the genetic algorithm in [7].

The first figure shows that K has some but not major effect on the time. The second figure shows that "pruning-based" scales up much better than "index-based" for a large scale factor. In this experiment, we observed that the scale factor has more impact on scalability than the novelty factor in that it increased the number of distinct vids faster. When the number of distinct vids is large, the effectiveness of the pruning in "pruning-based" became more significant.

7 Conclusion

We have investigated data mining as a technique for masking data, called *data mining based privacy protection*. The idea is to explore the data generalization concept from data mining as a way to hide detailed information, rather than discover trends and patterns. Once the data is masked, standard data mining techniques can be applied without modification. Our work demonstrated another positive use of the data mining technology: not only can it discover useful patterns, but also mask private information.

In particular, we presented a bottom-up generalization for transforming specific data to less specific but seman-

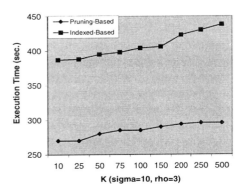

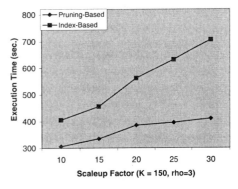

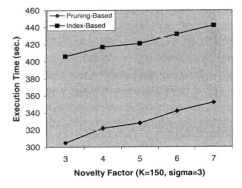

Figure 4. Scalability

tically consistent data for privacy protection. We focused on two key issues, quality and scalability. The quality issue was addressed by a trade-off of information and privacy and an iterative bottom-up generalization process. The scalability issue was addressed by a novel data structure for focusing on good generalizations. The proposed approach achieved a similar quality but much better scalability compared to existing solutions. Our current algorithm greedily hill-climbs a k-anonymity state, therefore, has the possibility of getting stuck at a local optimum. As suggested by one reviewer, local optimum can be escaped by introducing stochastic elements to this greedy heuristic or by using Simulated annealing. We plan to study this possibility in future work.

We believe that the framework of bottom-up general-

ization is amenable to several extensions that will make it more practical: incorporating different metrics, handling data suppression where a value is taken out entirely, and partial generalization where not necessarily all child values are generalized altogether, and generalizing numeric attributes without a pre-determined hierarchy. We plan to investigate these issues further.

Acknowledgement. Finally, we wish to thank the reviewers for constructive and helpful comments.

References

[1] R. Agrawal and R. Srikant. Privacy preserving data mining. In *SIGMOD*, 2000.

[2] C. F. Clark. The introduction of statistical noise to utility company data on a microdata tape with that data matched to annual housing survey data. In *Draft Project Report, Bureau of The Census, Washington, D.C.*, 1978.

[3] W. A. Fuller. Masking procedures for microdata disclosure limitation. *Journal of Official Statistics*, 9(2):383–406, 1993.

[4] B. Greenberg. Disclosure avoidance research at the census bureau. In *Proceedings of the 1990 Annual Research Conference of the Bureau of the Census, Washington, D.C.*, 1990.

[5] J. Han, Y. Cai, and N. Cercone. Knowledge discovery in databases: an attribute-oriented approach. In *VLDB*, 1992.

[6] A. Hundepool and L. Willenborg. μ- and τ-argus: software for statistical disclosure control. In *Third International Seminar on Statistical Confidentiality, Bled*, 1996.

[7] V. S. Iyengar. Transforming data to satisfy privacy constraints. In *SIGKDD*, 2002.

[8] J. Kim and W. Winkler. Masking microdata files. In *ASA Proceedings of the Section on Survey Research Methods*, 1995.

[9] R. J. Quinlan. *C4.5: Programs for Machine Learning*. Morgan Kaufmann, 1993.

[10] L. Sweeney. Achieving k-anonymity privacy protection using generalization and suppression. *International Journal on Uncertainty, Fuzziness and Knowledge-based Systems*, 10(5):571–588, 2002.

[11] L. Sweeney. k-anonymity: a model for projecting privacy. *International Journal on Uncertainty, Fuzziness and Knownledge-based Systems*, 10(5):557–570, 2002.

A Probabilistic Approach for Adapting Information Extraction Wrappers and Discovering New Attributes*

Tak-Lam Wong   and   Wai Lam
Department of Systems Engineering and Engineering Management
The Chinese University of Hong Kong, Shatin
Hong Kong
{wongtl,wlam}@se.cuhk.edu.hk

Abstract

We develop a probabilistic framework for adapting information extraction wrappers with new attribute discovery. Wrapper adaptation aims at automatically adapting a previously learned wrapper from the source Web site to a new unseen site for information extraction. One unique characteristic of our framework is that it can discover new or previously unseen attributes as well as headers from the new site. It is based on a generative model for the generation of text fragments related to attribute items and formatting data in a Web page. To solve the wrapper adaptation problem, we consider two kinds of information from the source Web site. The first kind of information is the extraction knowledge contained in the previously learned wrapper from the source Web site. The second kind of information is the previously extracted or collected items. We employ a Bayesian learning approach to automatically select a set of training examples for adapting a wrapper for the new unseen site. To solve the new attribute discovery problem, we develop a model which analyzes the surrounding text fragments of the attributes in the new unseen site. A Bayesian learning method is developed to discover the new attributes and their headers. EM technique is employed in both Bayesian learning models. We conducted extensive experiments from a number of real-world Web sites to demonstrate the effectiveness of our framework.

1. Introduction

Tremendous amount of Web documents available from the World Wide Web provide a good source for users to access various useful information electronically. Normally, users search for information with the assistance of Web search engines. By entering the key phrases to a search

*The work described in this paper was substantially supported by grants from the Research Grant Council of the Hong Kong Special Administrative Region, China (Project Nos: CUHK 4187/01E and CUHK 4179/03E) and CUHK Strategic Grant (No: 4410001).

Figure 1. An example of Web page about book catalog.

engine, numerous related Web sites or Web pages will be returned. To locate the exact and precise information, human effort is required to examine each of the Web sites or Web pages. This brings the need for information extraction systems which aim at automatically extracting precise text fragments from the pages. Another application of information extraction from Web documents is to support automated agent systems which collect precise information or data as input for conducting certain intelligent tasks such as price comparison shopping agent [6] and automated travel assistance agent [1]. A common information extraction technique known as wrappers can solve the automatic extraction problem. A wrapper normally consists of a set of extraction rules which can precisely identify the text fragments to be extracted from Web pages. In the past, these extraction rules are manually constructed by human. This manual effort is tedious, boring, error-prone and requires a high level of expertise. Recently, several wrapper learning approaches are proposed for automatically learning wrappers from training examples [2, 4, 11]. Wrapper learning systems significantly reduce the amount of human effort in constructing wrappers.

Consider a Web page shown in Figure 1 collected from a Web site under the book domain[1]. To learn the wrapper for automatically extracting information from this Web

[1]The URL of the Web site is *http://www.halfpricecomputerbooks.com.*

site, one can manually provide some training examples via a simple GUI by just highlighting the appropriate text fragments. The training example contains the basic composition of a book record. For example, a user may highlight the text fragment "Game Programming Gems 2" as the title and the text fragment "Mark Deloura" as the corresponding author. The wrapper learning system automatically learns the wrapper based on the information embedded in the training examples.

Typically, although the learned wrapper can effectively extract information from the same Web site and achieve very good performance, the learned wrapper cannot be applied to other Web sites for information extraction even the Web sites are in the same domain. Wrapper adaptation aims at automatically adapting a previously learned wrapper from the source Web site to new unseen sites. It can significantly reduce the human effort in preparing training examples for learning the wrappers for the new unseen sites. Figure 2 depicts a Web page collected from a Web site different from the one shown in Figure 1[2]. Wrapper adaptation can automatically adapt the wrapper previously learned from the source Web site shown in Figure 1 to the new unseen site shown in Figure 2. The adapted wrapper can then be applied to the Web pages in the new unseen site for automatically extracting the data records.

The attributes extracted by the learned wrapper are dependent on the training examples provided. For example, refer to the Web site shown in Figure 1, the learned wrapper can only extract the two attributes, namely, title and author. Some other attributes such as price and publication date of the book record cannot be extracted by the learned wrapper because these attributes are not indicated in the training examples. To make the learned wrapper able to extract the publication date of the book records, the related attribute must be provided in the training examples.

In wrapper adaptation, similar problem is encountered. For instance, if the previously learned wrapper only contains extraction rules for the title and author from the source Web site shown in Figure 1, the adapted wrapper can at best extract the title and author from the new unseen site shown in Figure 2. However, the new unseen site may contain some new attributes which are not present in the previously learned wrapper. For example, the book records in Figure 2 contain the attribute ISBN that does not exist in the previously learned wrapper as shown in Table **??**. The ISBN of the book records in the unseen sites cannot be extracted.

Both wrapper induction and wrapper adaptation pose a limitation on the attributes to be extracted. The wrapper learned or adapted can only extract the pre-specified attributes. The goal of new attribute discovery is to extract new attributes that are not specified in the current learned wrapper and also discover the header text fragments (if any)

Figure 2. An example of Web page about book catalog collected from a different Web site shown in Figure 1.

associated with these new attributes. "Our Price" and "Your Price" are examples of header text fragments for the attribute price in the Web sites shown in Figure 1 and Figure 2 respectively. Different Web sites may use different headers for the same attribute, but the headers normally contain some semantic meaning. By discovering the header text fragments for the new attributes, we are not only able to discover the new attribute items, but also understand some semantic meanings of the items newly discovered and extracted. New attribute discovery is particularly useful when combining with wrapper adaptation as illustrated in the above example. Some attributes in the new unseen site may not be present in the source Web site. In this case, the adapted wrapper can only extract incomplete information in the new unseen site. New attribute discovery can be applied to extract more useful information embodied in the new site.

Several techniques such as bootstrapping [16] and active learning [9, 15] have been developed for reducing the human effort in preparing training examples. ROADRUNNER [5], DeLa [17] and MDR [13] are approaches developed for completely eliminating human effort in extracting items in Web sites. The idea of ROADRUNNER is to compare the similarities and differences of the Web pages. If two different strings occur in the same corresponding positions of two Web pages, they are believed to be the items to be extracted. DeLa discovers repeated patterns of the HTML tags within a Web page and expresses these repeated patterns with regular expression. The items are then extracted in a table format by parsing the Web page to the discovered regular patterns. MDR first discovers the data regions in the Web page by building the HTML tag tree and making use of string comparison techniques. The data records from each data region are extracted by applying some heuristic knowledge of how people commonly present data objects in Web pages. The above three approaches do not require any human involvement in training and extraction. However, they suffer from one common shortcoming; they cannot differentiate the type of information extracted

---

[2]The URL of the Web site is *http://www.discount-pcbooks.com.*

and hence the items extracted by these approaches require human effort to interpret the meaning.

Wrapper adaptation aims at adapting the previously learned extraction knowledge to a new unseen site in the same domain automatically. This can significantly reduce the human work in labeling training examples for learning wrappers for different sites. Golgher et al. [8] proposed to solve the problem by applying bootstrapping technique and a query-like approach. This approach searches the exact matching of items in an unseen Web page. However their approach assumes that the seed words, which refer to the elements in the source repository in their framework, must appear in the unseen Web page. Cohen and Fan designed a method for learning page-independent heuristics for extracting item from Web pages [3]. Their approach is able to extract items in different domains. However, one major disadvantage of this method is that training examples from several Web sites must be collected to learn such heuristic rules. KNOWITALL [7] is a domain independent information extraction system. Its idea is to make use of online search engines and bootstrap from a set of domain independent and generic patterns from the Web. However, one limitation of KNOWITALL is that the proposed generic patterns can only be applied to the free text portions of the Web pages. It is not able to extract information from the semi-structured text documents which contain a mix of HTML tags and data text fragments in the Web pages.

We have developed a preliminary wrapper adaptation method called WrapMA in our previous work [18]. One of the limitation of WrapMA is that it requires human effort to scrutinize the intermediate discovered data in the adaptation process. An improvement from our previous work called IEKA which attempts to tackle the wrapper adaptation problem in a fully automatic manner [20] have been developed. One common shortcoming of WrapMA and IEKA is that the attributes to be extracted by the adapted wrapper are fixed as specified from the source Web site. The adapted wrapper cannot extract new attributes which appear in the unseen target site. In this paper, we describe a novel probabilistic framework for solving the wrapper adaptation with new attribute discovery. This new approach is able to automatically adapt a previously learned wrapper from a source Web site to a new unseen site. The adapted wrapper can also extract new attribute items together with the associated header text fragments. We have conducted extensive experiments which offer a very encouraging results for our wrapper adaptation with new attribute discovery approach.

2. Overview

We develop a probabilistic framework for wrapper adaptation with new attribute discovery. This framework is based on a generative model for the generation of text fragments related to attribute items and formatting data in a Web page as depicted in Figure 3. In each domain, there is an

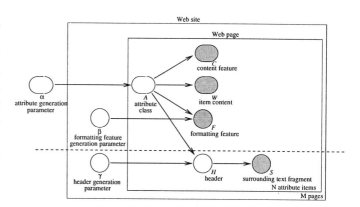

Figure 3. The generative model for attribute generation. Shaded nodes represent Observable variables and unshaded nodes represent unobservable variables. Circle nodes represent site dependent variables and oval nodes represent site invariant variables.

attribute generation parameter α which is domain dependent and site invariant. This parameter controls the attribute classes of the items contained in the Web pages. For each of the N attribute items contained in one of the M pages under the same Web site, the attribute class, A, is assumed to be generated from the distribution $P(A|\alpha)$. Refer to the Web site shown in Figure 1, this Web site consists of several Web pages and each of them contains a number of attribute items. The attribute classes of the items generated are *title*, *author*, *price*, *published year*, etc. Based on the attribute classes generated, the item content, W, and the content feature, C, are then generated from the distribution $P(W|A)$ and $P(C|A)$ respectively. W is to represent the orthographic information of the attribute. For example, the item content W for the title of the first record in Figure 1 is the character sequence "Game Programming Gems 2". The content feature C is to represent the characteristics of the attributes such as the number of words starting with capital letter. W and C are conditionally independent to each other and both of them are dependent on A which in turn is dependent on α. Therefore, W and C are site invariant. Given the same domain and same attribute class, W and C remain largely unchanged in the Web pages collected from different Web sites. Within a particular Web site, there is a formatting feature generation parameter denoted by β. The formatting feature F of the attributes is to represent the formatting information and the context information and it is generated from the distribution $P(F|A, \beta)$. As F is dependent of β which is site dependent, F is also site dependent and the format of the same attribute in different Web sites are different. For example, the title of the book record in Figure 1 is bolded and underlined while the title of the book record in Figure 2 is only bolded. Within a Web site, there is a random variable called header (denoted by H) generated from $P(H|A; \gamma)$ where γ is a binomial distribution parameter. Similar to β, γ is site dependent and hence H is also site dependent. The surrounding text fragment of the attribute denoted by S is then generated with $P(S|H)$ and S is also site dependent. For example, the text fragment "Mark Deloura" in Figure 1 is surrounded by the text fragment "Author" which is the header for the attribute author whereas the other text fragment "List Price" is not the header. The joint probability distribution can be expressed as :

$$P(W, C, F, S, H, A|\alpha, \beta, \gamma) = P(W|A)P(C|A)P(F|A;\beta)P(S|H)P(H|A;\gamma)P(A|\alpha) \quad (1)$$

Our wrapper adaptation with new attribute discovery is a two-stage probabilistic framework based on this generative model. At the first stage, the objective is to tackle the wrapper adaptation problem which aims at automatically adapting a previously learned wrapper from the source Web site to a new unseen site. This stage first identifies the set of useful text fragments from the new unseen Web site by considering the document object model[3] (DOM) representation of Web pages and designing an information-theoretic method. The related information of a useful text fragment can be represented by (W, C, F) and is observable. Next, these useful text fragments are categorized into one of the attribute classes by employing an automatic text fragment classification model. We consider the probability $P(A|W, C, F; \alpha, \beta)$ which represents the probability that the useful text fragment represented by (W, C, F) belongs the attribute class A. Two kinds of information from the source Web site providing useful clues are considered. The first kind of information is the knowledge contained in the previously learned wrapper which contains rich knowledge about the semantic content of the attribute. The second kind of information is the items previously extracted or collected from the source Web site which embodies the characteristics of the attributes. These items can be used for inferring training examples for the new unseen site because they contain information about C and W, which are site invariant, of the attributes. However, they are different from ordinary training examples because they do not contain any information about F of the unseen site. We call this property *partially specified*. Our approach uses the partially specified training examples to estimate the probability $P(A|W, C, F; \alpha, \beta)$ for each of the useful text fragments. We then apply Bayesian learning technique and expectation-maximization (EM) algorithm to construct the model for finding the attribute class for each of the useful text fragments. It corresponds to the generative model depicted in the upper part of Figure 3. As a result, the corresponding attributes for the useful text fragments can be discussed.

Certain useful text fragments belong to previously unseen, or new attribute classes. One example for such attribute classes is the ISBN attribute shown in Figure 2.

---

[3]The details of the Document Object Model can be found in *http://www.w3.org/DOM/*.

At the second stage of our framework, we attempt to discover new or previously unseen attributes for those useful text fragments which do not associate with any known attributes after the inference process in the first stage. It is achieved by another level of Bayesian learning by analyzing the relationship between the useful text fragments and their surrounding text fragments. It corresponds to the generative model depicted in the lower part of Figure 3. Recall that S consists of the surrounding text fragments of the attributes. For example, the text fragment "Scott Urman" is surrounded by "Author :" and "ISBN :" and the text fragment "0072121467" is surrounded by "ISBN :" and "MSRP" in the first record in Figure 2. From the inference of our wrapper adaptation approach in the first stage, we know that the text fragment "Scott Urman" belongs to the attribute author. Suppose we also know that "Author :" is the header for the attribute author. We can then infer the relationship between the headers and the attributes in the Web site from their relative position and other characteristics of the headers. We can discover that it is highly probable that "ISBN :" is the header for the text fragment "0072121467". To model this idea, we consider the joint probability as depicted in Equation 1 and obtain the following conditional probability:

$$P(H|W, C, F, S; \alpha, \beta, \gamma) = \frac{\sum_A P(W, C, F|A; \beta)P(S|H)P(H|A; \gamma)P(A|\alpha)}{\sum_H \sum_A P(W, C, F|A; \beta)P(S|H)P(H|A; \gamma)P(A|\alpha)} \quad (2)$$

Equation 2 essentially means how likely that the surrounding text fragment S is the header of the useful text fragment which is represented by the tuple (W, C, F). we can apply maximum likelihood technique and EM algorithm to estimate the parameters in Equation 2.

3. Probabilistic Model for Wrapper Adaptation

As mentioned above, the first stage of our framework is to conduct wrapper adaptation. It mainly consists of two major steps. The first step is to identify a set of useful text fragments. The second step is to categorize the useful text fragment into one of the attribute classes.

For the first step, its aim is to identify a set of useful training text fragments from the Web pages in the new unseen Web site. We observe that in different pages within the same Web site, the text fragments regarding the attribute are different, while the text fragments regarding the formatting or context are similar. This observation provides some clues in identifying the useful text fragments. A Web page can be represented by a DOM structure. A DOM structure is an ordered tree consisting of two types of nodes. The first type of node is called the element node which is used to represent HTML tag information. These nodes are labeled with the element name such as "<table>", "<a>", etc. The other type of node is called the text node which includes the text displayed in the browser and labeled simply with the corresponding text. We develop an information-theoretic algorithm that can effectively locate the informative text nodes in the DOM structure. These text fragments become the useful text fragments for the new unseen site. The details of this useful text fragment identification step can be found in [19].

The second step of wrapper adaptation is to categorize these useful text fragments by employing an automatic text fragment classification algorithm. We first select the useful text fragments containing the same semantic classes as the ones contained in the target pattern components of the previously learned wrapper from the source Web site. The selected useful text fragments will then be categorized into different attribute classes by using a classification model. The generative model is depicted in the upper part of Figure 3. The probability for generating a particular (W, C, F, A) given the parameters α and β is expressed as:

$$P(W, C, F, A | \alpha, \beta) = P(W|A)P(C|A)P(F|A; \beta)P(A|\alpha) \quad (3)$$

The probability for generating the set of all the attributes, Λ, in a Web page is as follows:

$$P(\Lambda | \alpha, \beta) = \prod_{i=1}^{N} P(W_i, C_i, F_i, A_i | \alpha, \beta) \quad (4)$$

Combining Equations 3 and 4, we can obtain the following log likelihood function $L(\alpha, \beta; \Lambda)$:

$$L(\alpha, \beta; \Lambda) = \sum_{i=1}^{N} \log \sum_{A_{ij} \in A} P(W_i | A_{ij}) P(C_i | A_{ij}) P(F_i | A_{ij}, \beta) P(A_{ij} | \alpha) \quad (5)$$

where A_{ij} means the i-th useful text fragment belongs to the j-th attribute class. As A_{ij} in the above equation is an unobservable variable, we can derive the following expected log likelihood function $L'(\alpha, \beta; \Lambda)$:

$$L'(\alpha, \beta; \Lambda) = \sum_{i=1}^{N} \sum_{A_{ij} \in A} P(A_{ij} | \alpha) \log P(W_i | A_{ij}) P(C_i | A_{ij}) P(F_i | A_{ij}, \beta) \quad (6)$$

By Jensen's inequality and the concavity of the logarithmic function, it can be proved that $L(\alpha, \beta; \Lambda)$ is bounded below by $L'(\alpha, \beta; \Lambda)$ [14, 19]. The EM algorithm is employed to increase $L'(\alpha, \beta; \Lambda)$ iteratively until convergence. The E-Step and M-Step are as described as follows:
E-Step:

$$P(A|W, C, F; \alpha_t, \beta_t) \propto P(W|A)P(C|A)P(F|A; \beta_t)P(A|\alpha_t)$$

M-Step:

$$(\alpha_{t+1}, \beta_{t+1}) = \arg \max_{\alpha, \beta} L'(\alpha, \beta; \Lambda, \alpha_t, \beta_t)$$

To initialize the EM algorithm, we have to first estimate $P(A|W, C, F; \alpha_0, \beta_0)$. Recall that W is largely unchanged

for the attributes in the Web pages collected from the same domain. Therefore, we utilize the partially specified training examples collected from the source Web site and employ a two-level edit distance approach to compute on initial approximation of this probability. The details of the two-level edit distance algorithm can be found in our previous work [20]. We define $D(W, l_i^j)$ as the distance between the the useful text fragment with item content W and the i-th partially specified training example for the j-th attribute. Then we approximate $P(A|W, C, F; \alpha_0, \beta_0)$ by:

$$P(A_j | W, C, F; \alpha_0, \beta_0) \sim \frac{1}{K} (\max_i \{D'(W, l_i^j)\}) \quad (7)$$

where $D'(W, l_i^j) = 1 - D(W, l_i^j)$ and K is a normalization factor.

After obtaining the parameters, we can calculate the probability $P(A|W, C, F; \alpha, \beta)$ for each useful text fragment and determine their attribute classes by the following formulae:

$$P(A|W, C, F; \alpha, \beta) = \frac{P(W, C, F|A; \beta)P(A|\alpha)}{\sum_A P(W, C, F|A; \beta)P(A|\alpha)} \quad (8)$$

$$\hat{A} = \arg \max_{A_i \in A} P(W, C, F|A_i; \beta)P(A_i|\alpha) \quad (9)$$

For each attribute class, those useful text fragments with the probability of belonging to this attribute higher than a certain threshold will be selected as training examples for learning the new wrapper for the new unseen Web site. Users could optionally scrutinize the discovered training examples to improve the quality of the training examples. However, in our experiments, we did not conduct manual intervention and the adaptation was conducted in a fully automatic way. We employ the same wrapper learning method used in the source site [12].

4. New Attribute Discovery

As described before, the goal of the second stage in our framework is to discover previously unseen attributes for those useful text fragments which do not associate with any known attributes after the inference process in the first stage. We develop a Bayesian learning model to achieve this task. The model is learned from the previously categorized useful text fragments in the first stage. After the model is learned, it can be applied to discover previously unseen attributes.

By Bayes theorem, $P(W, C, F|A; \beta)P(A|\alpha) = P(A|W, C, F; \alpha, \beta)P(W, C, F)$. From Equation 2, we have:

$$P(H|W, C, F, S; \alpha, \beta, \gamma)$$
$$= \frac{\sum_A P(A|W, C, F|\alpha, \beta)P(S|H)P(H|A; \gamma)P(W, C, F)}{\sum_H \sum_A P(A|W, C, F; \alpha, \beta)P(S|H)P(H|A; \gamma)P(W, C, F)} \quad (10)$$

Since H and A are both unobservable, we can then derive the following expected log likelihood as follows:

$$L''(\gamma; \Lambda, \alpha, \beta,) = \sum_{i=1}^{N} \sum_H \sum_{A_{ij} \in A}$$
$$\{P(A_{ij}|W, C, F; \alpha, \beta)P(H|A_{ij}; \gamma) \log P(W, C, F)P(S|H)\} \quad (11)$$

In Equation 11, the term $P(A_{ij}|W, C, F; \alpha, \beta)$ can be determined in the first stage of our framework. Therefore, the EM algorithm proceeds as follows:

E-Step:

$$P(H|W, C, F, S; \alpha, \beta, \gamma_t)$$
$$\propto \sum_{A_{ij} \in A} P(A_{ij}|W, C, F; \alpha, \beta) P(S|H) P(H|A_{ij}; \gamma_t)$$

M-Step:

$$\gamma_{t+1} = \arg\max_{\gamma} L''(\gamma; \gamma_t, \alpha, \beta; \Lambda)$$

After estimating the parameters, the attribute headers can be predicted by the following reasoning. Since the candidate useful text fragments belong to some new or unseen attribute classes, we assume the terms $P(A|W, C, F; \alpha, \beta)$ are equal for all A. We replace the term $P(H|A; \gamma)$ by $E_A[H|A; \gamma]$ as H is binomially distributed with H being either zero or one. Next we observe that $P(H|W, C, F, S; \alpha, \beta, \gamma) \propto E_A[H|A; \gamma] P(S|H)$. By representing S with a set of features $f_k(S)$ such as the relative position of S to the candidate useful text fragments, the number of characters of S, etc., we can obtain $P(S|H) = \prod_k P(f_k(S)|H)$ by the independence assumption. We can derive the following formula:

$$P(H|W, C, F, S; \alpha, \beta, \gamma) \propto E_A[H|A; \gamma] \prod_k P(f_k(S)|H) \quad (12)$$

Equation 12 can be used for estimating the probability that the surrounding text fragment S is the header of the useful text fragment (W, C, F).

5. Experimental Results

We conducted extensive experiments on several real-world Web sites in the book domain to demonstrate the performance of our framework for wrapper adaptation with new attribute discovery. Table 1 depicts the Web sites used in our experiment. The first column shows the Web site labels. The second column shows the names of the Web site and the corresponding Web site addresses. The third and forth columns depict the number of pages and the number of records collected from the Web site for evaluation purpose respectively.

5.1. Evaluation on Wrapper Adaptation

To evaluate the performance of our wrapper adaptation approach, we first provide five training examples in each Web site for learning a wrapper. The attribute classes of interest are title and author. After obtaining the learned wrapper for each of the Web sites, we conducted two sets of experiments. The first set of experiments is to simply apply the learned wrapper from one particular Web site *without* wrapper adaptation to all the remaining sites for information extraction. For example, the wrapper learned from S1 is directly applied to S2 - S10 to extract items. This experiment can be treated as a baseline for our adaptation approach. The second set of experiments is to adapt the learned wrapper from one particular Web site *with* wrapper adaptation to

	Web site (URL)	# pp.	# rec.
S1	Half Price Computer Books (http://www.halfpricecomputerbooks.com)	5	100
S2	Discount-PCBooks.com (http://www.discount-pcbooks.com)	14	110
S3	mmistore.com (http://www.mmistore.com)	11	110
S4	Amazon.com (http://www.amazon.com)	5	125
S5	Jim's Computer Books (http://www.vstore.com/cgi-bin/pagegen /vstorecomputers/jimsbooks/)	7	139
S6	1Bookstreet.com (http://www.1bookstreet.com)	5	125
S7	Barnes & Noble.com (http://www.barnesandnoble.com)	5	120
S8	bookpool.com (http://www.bookpool.com)	5	124
S9	half.com (http://half.ebay.com)	6	120
S10	DigitalGuru Technical Bookshops (http://www.digitalguru.com)	17	102

Table 1. Web sites collected for experiments. # pp. and # rec. refer to the number of pages and number of records respectively.

all the remaining sites. The extraction performance is evaluated by two commonly used metrics called *precision* and *recall*. Precision is defined as the number of items for which the system correctly identified divided by the total number of items it extracts. Recall is defined as the number of items for which the system correctly identified divided by the total number of actual items. The attribute items for evaluation in the first set of experiments are title and author.

The experimental results of the first set of experiments reveal that all learned wrappers are not able to adapt to extract records from other Web sites. The is due to the fact that the format of the Web pages from different sites are different. The extraction rules learned from a particular Web site cannot be applied to other sites to extract information. In addition, we also evaluated an existing system called WIEN [10] to perform the same adaptation task[4]. The wrapper learned by WIEN for a particular Web site cannot extract items in other Web sites.

Table 2 shows the results of the second set of experiments. The first column shows the Web sites (source sites) from which the wrappers are learned from given training examples. The first row shows the Web sites (new unseen sites) to which the learned wrapper of a particular Web site is adapted. Each cell in Table 2 is divided into two sub-columns and two sub-rows. The two sub-rows represent the extraction performance on the attributes title and author respectively. The two sub-columns represent the precision (P) and recall (R) for extracting the items respectively. These results are obtained by adapting a learned wrapper from one Web site to the remaining sites using our wrapper adaptation approach. The results indicate that the extraction performance is very satisfactory. Table 3 summarizes the average

---

[4]WIEN is available in the Web site: *http://www.cs.ucd.ie/staff/nick/research/research/wrappers/wien/.*

	S1		S2		S3		S4		S5		S6		S7		S8		S9		S10	
	P	R	P	R	P	R	P	R	P	R	P	R	P	R	P	R	P	R	P	R
S1	-	-	85.4	87.2	100.0	90.0	99.2	97.6	100.0	95.7	100.0	100.0	98.9	73.3	100.0	96.0	100.0	95.0	97.1	66.7
	-	-	42.7	87.2	100.0	90.0	100.0	97.6	100.0	54.7	100.0	100.0	100.0	65.0	100.0	100.0	94.8	48.7	93.3	68.6
S2	100.0	33.0	-	-	100.0	90.0	99.2	97.6	100.0	95.7	100.0	33.6	98.9	73.3	100.0	96.0	100.0	95.0	97.1	66.7
	100.0	90.0	-	-	100.0	90.0	100.0	97.6	100.0	54.7	100.0	100.0	100.0	65.0	100.0	100.0	94.8	48.7	93.3	68.6
S3	100.0	33.0	42.7	87.2	-	-	99.2	97.6	100.0	95.7	100.0	100.0	98.9	73.3	100.0	96.0	100.0	95.0	97.1	65.7
	100.0	90.0	42.7	87.2	-	-	100.0	97.6	100.0	54.7	100.0	100.0	100.0	65.0	100.0	100.0	94.8	48.7	93.3	67.6
S4	100.0	33.0	42.7	87.2	100.0	90.0	-	-	100.0	95.7	100.0	100.0	98.9	73.3	100.0	96.0	100.0	95.0	97.1	66.7
	100.0	90.0	42.7	87.2	100.0	90.0	-	-	100.0	54.7	100.0	100.0	100.0	65.0	100.0	100.0	94.8	48.7	93.3	68.6
S5	100.0	33.0	42.7	87.2	100.0	90.0	99.2	97.6	-	-	100.0	100.0	0.0	0.0	100.0	96.0	100.0	90.0	97.1	66.7
	100.0	90.0	0.0	0.0	100.0	90.0	100.0	97.6	-	-	100.0	100.0	100.0	65.0	100.0	100.0	94.5	46.0	93.3	68.6
S6	100.0	33.0	42.7	87.2	100.0	90.0	99.2	97.6	100.0	95.7	-	-	0.0	0.0	100.0	96.0	100.0	90.0	97.1	66.7
	100.0	90.0	42.7	87.2	100.0	90.0	100.0	97.6	100.0	54.7	-	-	98.9	74.2	100.0	100.0	94.5	46.0	52.9	8.8
S7	100.0	33.0	42.7	87.2	100.0	90.0	99.2	97.6	100.0	95.7	100.0	100.0	-	-	100.0	96.0	100.0	95.0	97.1	66.7
	100.0	90.0	42.7	87.2	100.0	90.0	100.0	97.6	100.0	54.7	100.0	100.0	-	-	100.0	100.0	94.8	48.7	93.3	68.6
S8	100.0	33.0	42.7	87.2	100.0	90.0	99.2	97.6	100.0	95.7	100.0	100.0	98.9	73.3	-	-	100.0	90.0	97.1	66.7
	100.0	90.0	42.7	87.2	100.0	90.0	100.0	97.6	100.0	54.7	100.0	100.0	100.0	65.0	-	-	94.5	46.0	93.3	68.6
S9	100.0	33.0	42.7	87.2	100.0	90.0	99.2	97.6	100.0	95.7	100.0	100.0	98.9	73.3	100.0	96.0	-	-	97.1	66.7
	100.0	90.0	42.7	87.2	100.0	90.0	100.0	97.6	100.0	54.7	100.0	100.0	100.0	65.0	100.0	100.0	-	-	93.3	68.6
S10	100.0	33.0	42.7	87.2	100.0	90.0	99.2	97.6	100.0	95.7	100.0	100.0	98.9	73.3	100.0	96.0	100.0	95.0	-	-
	100.0	90.0	42.7	87.2	100.0	90.0	100.0	97.6	100.0	54.7	100.0	100.0	100.0	65.0	100.0	100.0	94.8	48.7	-	-

Table 2. Experimental results of adapting a learned wrapper from one Web site to the remaining Web sites. P and R refer to precision and recall (in percentages) respectively.

	Title				Author			
	Without Adaptation		With Adaptation		Without Adaptation		With Adaptation	
	P	R	P	R	P	R	P	R
S1	0.0	0.0	97.8	89.1	0.0	0.0	92.3	79.1
S2	0.0	0.0	99.5	75.7	0.0	0.0	98.7	79.4
S3	0.0	0.0	93.1	82.6	0.0	0.0	92.4	79.0
S4	0.0	0.0	93.2	81.9	0.0	0.0	92.3	78.2
S5	0.0	0.0	82.1	73.4	0.0	0.0	87.5	73.0
S6	0.0	0.0	82.1	72.9	0.0	0.0	87.7	72.1
S7	0.0	0.0	93.2	84.6	0.0	0.0	92.3	81.9
S8	0.0	0.0	93.1	81.5	0.0	0.0	92.3	77.7
S9	0.0	0.0	93.1	82.2	0.0	0.0	92.9	83.7
S10	0.0	0.0	93.4	85.3	0.0	0.0	93.1	81.5
Average	0.0	0.0	92.1	80.9	0.0	0.0	92.2	78.6

Table 3. Average extraction performance on title and author for the book domain for the cases of without adaptation and with adaptation when training examples of one particular Web site are provided. P and R refer to precision and recall (in percentages) respectively.

extraction performance for the cases of without adaptation and with adaptation. The first column shows the Web sites where training examples are given. Each row summarizes the results obtained by using the learned wrapper of the Web site in the first column and applying to all other sites for extraction. The results indicate that the wrapper learned from a particular Web site cannot be directly applied to others without adaptation for information extraction. After applying our wrapper adaptation approach, the wrapper learned from a particular Web site can be adapted to other sites. A very promising performance is achieved especially compared with the performance obtained without adaptation.

5.2. Evaluation on New Attribute Discovery

In each of the Web sites shown in Table 1, there exists some other attributes apart from title and author. For example, S1 contains attributes such as book type, list price, our price, etc. We conducted some experiments to evaluate our new attribute discovery approach for discovering those previously unseen attributes. Recall (NewR) and pre-

cision (NewP) are used for evaluating the performance with the ground truth consisting of all new attributes in the Web sites. Table 4 shows the results of the experiments. The first column depicts the Web sites where we attempt to discover the new attributes. The second column depicts the new or previously unseen attributes that are discovered. The third column depicts the new attributes that are not able to be discovered. The last two columns show the precision (NewP) and recall (NewR) of all new attributes in the Web sites respectively. For example, in S1, the new attributes "publication date", "list price", "you save", and "our price" can be discovered by our approach. Among the new attributes, the precision and recall for identifying items belonging to new attributes are 100.0% and 95.0% respectively. The results show that our new attribute discovery approach achieves a very good performance with average precision and recall reaching 99.8% and 74.3% respectively. We can also correctly identify the headers for the discovered attributes from Web pages in S1 to S4. In S5, since all attributes are not associated with any headers in the Web pages, no header information is available. For S6-S10, since no headers are associated with title or author, no evidence can be used for inferring the headers of new attributes.

6. Conclusions

We have developed a probabilistic framework for adapting information extraction wrappers with new attribute discovery. Our framework is based on a generative model for generating text fragments related to attribute items and formatting data. For wrapper adaptation, one feature of our framework is that we utilize the extraction knowledge contained in the previously learned wrapper from the source Web site. We also consider previously extracted or collected items. A set of training examples for learning the new wrapper for the unseen site can be identified by using a Bayesian learning approach. For new attribute discovery, we analyze the relationship between the attributes and their surrounding

	New attributes correctly discovered	New attribute not discovered	NewP	NewR
S1	publication date, list price, you save, our price	-	100.0	95.0
S2	ISBN. MSRP, your price, you save	-	100.0	87.5
S3	publisher, publication date, ISBN, list price, our price, edition	shipping status	100.0	69.6
S4	list price, our price, buy used, buy collectible, shipping status	book type	100.0	39.3
S5	book type, number of pages, publication date, price	-	100.0	73.4
S6	book type, regular price, you save, our price, shipping status	-	98.3	100.0
S7	shipping status, publication date our price, you save	publisher, book type	100.0	63.9
S8	publisher, publication date, ISBN, edition, book type, our price, your save, inventory	-	100.0	96.3
S9	price, save	book type, publication date	100.0	45.0
S10	publisher, publication date, reading level, online price	you save	100.0	73.1
Ave.	-	-	99.8	74.3

Table 4. Experimental results for new attribute discovery. NewP and NewR refer to precision and recall of all new attributes in the Web sites (in percentages) respectively. Ave. refers to the average performance.

text fragments. A Bayesian learning model is developed to extract the new attributes and their headers from the unseen site. We employ EM technique in the learning algorithm of both Bayesian models. Experiments from some real-worlds Web sites show that our framework achieves a very promising performance in wrapper adaptation with new attribute discovery.

References

[1] J. Ambite, G. Barish, C. Knoblock, M. Muslea, J. Oh, and S. Minton. Getting from here to there: Interactive planning and agent execution for optimizing travel. In *Proceedings of the Forteenth Innovative Applications of Artificial Intelligence Conference*, pages 862–869, 2002.

[2] D. Blei, J. Bagnell, and A. McCallum. Learning with scope, with application to information extraction and classification. In *Proceedings of the Eighteenth Conference on Uncertainty in Artificial Intelligence (UAI-2002)*, pages 53–60, 2002.

[3] W. Cohen and W. Fan. Learning page-independent heuristics for extracting data from Web pages. *Computer Networks*, 31(11-16):1641–1652, 1999.

[4] W. Cohen, M. Hurst, and L. Jensen. A flexible learning system for wrapping tables and lists in HTML documents. In *Proceedings of the Eleventh International World Wide Web Conference (WWW-2002)*, pages 232–241, 2002.

[5] V. Crescenzi, G. Mecca, and P. Merialdo. ROADRUNNER: Towards automatic data extraction from large web sites. In *Proceedings of the 27th Very Large Databases Conference (VLDB-2001)*, pages 109–118, 2001.

[6] R. B. Doorenbos, O. Etzioni, and D. S. Weld. A scalable comparison-shopping agent for the World-Wide Web. In *Proceedings of the First International Conference on Autonomous Agents*, pages 39–48, February 1997.

[7] O. Etzioni, M. Cafarella, D. Downey, A. Popescu, T. Shaked, S. Soderland, D. S. Weld, and A. Yates. Methods for domain-independent information extraction from the web: An experimental comparison. In *Proceedings of the Nineteenth National Conference on Artificial Intelligence (AAAI-2004)*, 2004.

[8] P. Golgher and A. da Silva. Bootstrapping for example-based data extraction. In *Proceedings of the Tenth ACM International Conference on Information and Knowledge Management (CIKM-2001)*, pages 371–378, 2001.

[9] T. Kristjansson, A. Culotta, P. Viola, and A. McCallum. Interactive information extraction with constrained conditional random fields. In *Proceedings of the Nineteenth National Conference on Artificial Intelligence (AAAI-2004)*, 2004.

[10] N. Kushmerick and B. Grace. The wrapper induction environment. In *Proceedings of the Workshop on Software Tools for Developing Agents (AAAI-1998)*, pages 131–132, 1998.

[11] N. Kushmerick and B. Thomas. Adaptive information extraction: Core technologies for information agents. In *Intelligents Information Agents R&D In Europe: An AgentLink Perspective*, pages 79–103, 2002.

[12] W. Y. Lin and W. Lam. Learning to extract hierarchical information from semi-structured documents. In *Proceedings of the Ninth International Conference on Information and Knowledge Management (CIKM-2000)*, pages 250–257, 2000.

[13] B. Liu, R. Grossman, and Y. Zhai. Mining data records in web pages. In *Proceedings of the Ninth ACM SIGKDD International Conference on Knowledge Discovery and Data Mining (SIGKDD-2003)*, pages 601–606, 2003.

[14] G. J. McLachlan and T. Krishnan. *The EM Algorithm and Extensions*. John Wiley & Sons, Inc., 1997.

[15] I. Muslea, S. Minton, and C. Knoblock. Selective sampling with redundant views. In *Proceedings of the Seventeenth National Conference on Artificial Intelligence (AAAI-2000)*, pages 621–626, 2000.

[16] E. Riloff and R. Jones. Learning dictionaries for information extraction by multi-level bootstrapping. In *Proceedings of the Sixteenth National Conference on Artificial Intelligence (AAAI-1999)*, pages 1044–1049, 1999.

[17] J. Wang and F. H. Lochovsky. Data extraction and label assignment for Web databases. In *Proceedings of the Twelfth International World Wide Web Conference (WWW-2003)*, pages 187–196, 2003.

[18] T. L. Wong and W. Lam. Adapting information extraction knowledge for unseen web sites. In *Proceedings of the 2002 IEEE International Conference on Data Mining (ICDM-2002)*, pages 506–513, 2002.

[19] T. L. Wong and W. Lam. A probabilistic approach for adapting wrappers and discovering new attributes. In *The Chinese University of Hong Kong, Department of Systems Engineering and Engineering Management Technical Report*, 2004.

[20] T. L. Wong and W. Lam. Text mining from site invariant and dependent features for information extraction knowledge adaptation. In *Proceedings of the 2004 SIAM International Conference on Data Mining (SDM-2004)*, pages 45–56, 2004.

Aligning Boundary in Kernel Space for Learning Imbalanced Dataset

Gang Wu & Edward Y. Chang
Department of Electrical & Computer Engineering
University of California, Santa Barbara 93106
{gwu@engineering, echang@ece}.ucsb.edu

Abstract

An imbalanced training dataset poses serious problem for many real-world supervised learning tasks. In this paper, we propose a kernel-boundary-alignment algorithm, which considers training-data imbalance as prior information to augment SVMs to improve class-prediction accuracy. Using a simple example, we first show that SVMs can suffer from high incidences of false negatives when the training instances of the target class are heavily outnumbered by the training instances of a non-target class. The remedy we propose is to adjust the class boundary by modifying the kernel matrix, according to the imbalanced data distribution. Through theoretical analysis backed by empirical study, we show that our kernel-boundary-alignment algorithm works effectively on several datasets.

1. Introduction

Support Vector Machines (SVMs) are a core machine learning technology. They have strong theoretical foundations and excellent empirical successes in many pattern-recognition applications such as handwriting recognition, image retrieval [6], and text classification [13]. However, for applications such as video-event recognition [25], fraud detection [10], and medical-image analysis, where the training instances of the target class are significantly outnumbered by the other training instances, the class-boundary learned by SVMs can be severely skewed toward the target class. As a result, the false-negative rate can be excessively high in identifying important target objects (e.g., a surveillance event or a disease-causing agent), and can result in catastrophic consequences.

Skewed class boundary is a subtle but severe problem that arises from using an SVM classifier—in fact from using *any* classifier—for real-world problems with imbalanced training data. To understand the nature of the problem, let us consider it in a binary classification setting (positive vs. negative). We know that the Bayesian framework estimates the posterior probability using the class conditional and the prior [11]. When the training data are highly imbalanced, it can be inferred that the state of the nature favors the majority class. Hence, when ambiguity arises in classifying a particular sample because of similar class conditional densities for the two classes, the Bayesian framework will rely on the large class prior in favor of the majority class to break the tie. Consequently, the decision boundary will skew toward the minority class.

While the Bayesian framework gives the optimal results (in terms of the smallest average error rate) in a theoretical sense, one has to be careful in applying it to real-world applications. In a real-world application such as security surveillance and disease diagnosis, the risk (or consequence) of mispredicting a positive event (a false negative) far outweighs that of mispredicting a negative event (a false positive). It is well known that in a binary classification problem, Bayesian risks are defined as:

$$R(\alpha_p|\mathbf{x}) = \lambda_{pp}P(\omega_p|\mathbf{x}) + \lambda_{pn}P(\omega_n|\mathbf{x})$$
$$R(\alpha_n|\mathbf{x}) = \lambda_{np}P(\omega_p|\mathbf{x}) + \lambda_{nn}P(\omega_n|\mathbf{x})$$

where p and n refer to the positive and negative events, respectively, λ_{np} refers to the risk (or cost) of a false negative, and λ_{pn} the risk of a false positive. Which action (α_p or α_n) to take—or which action has a smaller risk—is affected not just by the event likelihood (which directly influences the misclassification error), but also by the risk of mispredictions (λ_{np} and λ_{pn}).

How can we factor risk into SVMs to compensate for the effect caused by $P(\omega_n|\mathbf{x}) >> P(\omega_p|\mathbf{x})$? Examining the class prediction function of SVMs [20],

$$sgn\left(f(\mathbf{x}) = \sum_{i=1}^{n} y_i\alpha_i K(\mathbf{x}, \mathbf{x}_i) + b \right), \qquad (1)$$

we see that three parameters can affect the decision outcome: b, α_i, and K. Our theoretical analysis backed up by empirical study will show that the the only effective method for improving SVMs is through adaptively modifying K based on the training data distribution. To modify K, we propose in this paper the kernel-boundary-alignment

(KBA) algorithm, which addresses the imbalanced training-data problem in three complementary ways.

1. *Improving class separation.* KBA increases intra-class similarity and decreases inter-class similarity through changing the similarity scores in the kernel matrix. As a consequence, instances in the same class are better clustered in the feature space $\mathcal{F}$ away from those in the other classes.

2. *Safeguarding overfitting.* To avoid overfitting, KBA uses the existing support vectors to guide its boundary-alignment procedure.

3. *Improving imbalanced ratio.* By adjusting the similarity scores between majority instances properly, KBA can reduce the number of support vectors at the majority side and hence improve the imbalanced support-vector ratio.

Our experimental results on both UCI and real-world image/video datasets show the kernel-boundary-alignment algorithm to be effective in correcting the skewed boundary caused by imbalanced training data.

The rest of this paper is organized as follows. Section 2 discusses related work. In Section 3, we describe the kernel-boundary-alignment algorithm for addressing the imbalanced training-data problem. Section 4 presents the setup and the results of our empirical studies. We offer our concluding remarks in Section 5.

2. Related Work

Approaches for addressing the imbalanced training-data problem can be divided into two main categories: the data processing approach and the algorithmic approach. The data processing approach can be further divided into two methods: under-sample the majority class, and over-sample the minority class. The one-sided selection proposed by Kubat [16] is a representative under-sampling approach which removes noisy, borderline, and redundant majority training instances. However, these steps typically can remove only a small fraction of the majority instances, so they might not be very helpful in a scenario with a majority-to-minority ratio of more than 100:1 (which is becoming common in many emerging pattern-recognition applications). Multi-classifier training [5] and Bagging [3] are two other under-sampling methods. These methods do not deal with noisy and border-line data directly, but use a large ensemble of sub-classifiers to reduce prediction variance.

Over-sampling [22] is the opposite of the under-sampling approach. It duplicates or interpolates minority instances in the hope of reducing the imbalance. The over-sampling approach can be considered as a "phantom-transduction" method. It assumes the neighborhood of a positive instance to be still positive, and the instances between two positive instances positive. The validity of assumptions like these, however, can be data-dependent.

The algorithmic approach, which is traditionally[1] orthogonal to the data-processing approach, is the focus of this paper. Nugroho [19] suggests combining a competitive learning network and a multilayer perceptron as a solution for the class imbalance problem. Kubat et al. [16] modify the decision-tree generator to improve its learning performance on imbalanced datasets. For SVMs, few attempts [15, 18, 21] have dealt with the imbalanced training-data problem. These methods modify parameters b and α_i in Eqn. 1. Karakoulas et al. [15] proposed an approach to modify the bias (or parameter b) in the class prediction function (Eqn. 1). Veropoulos et al. [18, 21] use different pre-defined penalty constants (based on some prior knowledge) for different classes of data. The effectiveness of this method is limited since the Karush Kuhn Tucker (KKT) conditions [17] use the penalty constants as the upper bounds, rather than the lower bounds, of misclassification costs. Moreover, the KKT condition $\sum_{i=1}^{n} \alpha_i y_i = 0$ imposes an equal total influence from the positive and negative support vectors. The increases in some α_i's at the positive side will inadvertently increase some α_i's at the negative side to satisfy the constraint. These constraints can make the increase of C^+ on minority instances ineffective. (Validation is presented in Section 4.)

Another algorithmic approach to improve the SVMs for imbalanced training is to modify the employed kernel function K. In kernel-based methods, such as SVMs, the kernel K represents a pairwise similarity measurement among the data. Because of the central role of the kernel, a poor K will lead to a poor performance of the employed classifier [8, 20]. Our prior work ACT [23] falls into this category by modifying the K using (quasi-) conformal transformation so as to change the spatial resolution around the class boundary. However, ACT works only when data have a fixed-dimensional vector-space representation, since the algorithm relies on information in the input space. The kernel-boundary alignment algorithm (KBA) that we propose in this paper is a more general approach, which modifies kernel matrix[2] $\mathbf{K}$ instead of kernel function K, and hence does not require the data to have a vector-space representation. This relaxation is important so that we can deal with a large class of sequence data (motion trajectories, DNA sequences, sensor-network data, etc.), which may have differ-

---

1   Although our algorithmic approach focuses on aligning class boundary, it can effectively remove redundant majority instances as a by-product. Details will be discussed in Section 3.

2   Given a kernel function K and a set of instances $\mathcal{X}_{train} = \{\mathbf{x}_i, y_i\}_{i=1}^{n}$, the kernel matrix (Gram matrix) is the matrix of all possible inner-products of pairs from X_{train}, $\mathbf{K} = (k_{ij} = K(\mathbf{x}_i, \mathbf{x}_j))$.

ent length. Furthermore, KBA provides greater flexibility in adjusting the class boundary. (We present details in Section 3).

Recently, several kernel alignment algorithms [8, 14] have been proposed in the Machine Learning community to learn a kernel function or a kernel matrix from the training data. The motivation behind these methods is that a good kernel should be data dependent, and a systematic method for learning a good kernel from the data is useful. All these methods are based on the notion of the kernel target alignment proposed by Cristianini et al. [8]. The alignment score is used for measuring the quality of a given kernel matrix. To address the imbalanced training-data problem, Kandola et al. [14] propose an extension to kernel-target alignment by giving the alignment targets of $\frac{1}{n^+}$ to the positive instances and $-\frac{1}{n^-}$ to the negative instances. (We use n^+ and n^- to denote the number of minority and majority instances, respectively.) Unfortunately, when $\frac{n^+}{n^-}$ is small (when n^+ does not remain $O(n^+ + n^-)$), the concentration property upon which that kernel-target alignment relies may no longer hold. In other words, the proposed method can deal only with imbalanced data that are not very imbalanced. Our proposed KBA algorithm is based on maximizing the separation margin of the SVMs, and is more effective in its solution.

3. Kernel Boundary Alignment

Let us consider a two-class classification problem with training dataset $\mathcal{X}_{train} = \{\mathbf{x}_i, y_i\}_{i=1}^n$, where $\mathbf{x}_i \in \Re^m$ and $y \in \{-1, +1\}$. Kernel-based methods, such as SVMs, introduce a mapping function Φ which embeds the $\mathcal{I}$ into a high-dimensional $\mathcal{F}$ as a curved Riemannian manifold $\mathcal{S}$ where the mapped data reside [4]. A Riemannian metric $g_{ij}(\mathbf{x})$ is then defined for $\mathcal{S}$, which is associated with the kernel function $K(\mathbf{x}, \mathbf{x}')$ by

$$g_{ij}(\mathbf{x}) = \left(\frac{\partial^2 K(\mathbf{x}, \mathbf{x}')}{\partial x_i \partial x_j'} \right)_{\mathbf{x}'=\mathbf{x}}. \quad (2)$$

The metric g_{ij} shows how a local area around $\mathbf{x}$ in $\mathcal{I}$ is magnified in $\mathcal{F}$ under the mapping of Φ. The idea of conformal transformation in SVMs is to enlarge the margin by increasing the magnification factor $g_{ij}(\mathbf{x})$ along the classification boundary and to decrease it around other areas. This could be implemented by a conformal transformation[3] of the related kernel $K(\mathbf{x}, \mathbf{x}')$ according to Eqn. 2, so that the spatial relationship between the data would not be affected too much [1]. Such a (quasi-) conformal transformation can be

---

[3] Usually, it is difficult to find a totally-conformal mapping function to transform the kernel. As suggested in [1], we can choose a quasi-conformal mapping function for kernel transformation.

Symbol	Meaning
$D(\mathbf{x})$	Conformal transformation function
τ_b^2	Parameters of $D(\mathbf{x})$
M	Nearest neighborhood range
$|\mathbf{SI}|$	Number of support instances
$|\mathbf{SI}^+|$	Number of minority support instances
$|\mathbf{SI}^-|$	Number of majority support instances
$\mathbf{x}^+, \Phi(\mathbf{x}^+)$	A minority support instance
$\mathbf{x}^-, \Phi(\mathbf{x}^-)$	A majority support instance
$\mathbf{x}_b, \Phi(\mathbf{x}_b)$	An interpolated boundary instance
β	Weight parameter of interpolation
$\mathcal{X}_{train}$	Set of the training instances
$\mathcal{X}_b^*$	Sets of the interpolated boundary instances
$\mathcal{X}_{mis}^+$	Set of the misclassified minority test instances
$\mathcal{X}_{mis}^-$	Set of the misclassified majority test instances

Table 1: Notations Used in ACT and KBA

depicted as

$$\tilde{K}(\mathbf{x}, \mathbf{x}') = D(\mathbf{x})D(\mathbf{x}')K(\mathbf{x}, \mathbf{x}'), \quad (3)$$

where $D(\mathbf{x})$ is a properly defined positive (quasi-) conformal function. $D(\mathbf{x})$ should be chosen in such a way that the new Riemannian metric $\tilde{g}_{ij}(\mathbf{x})$, associated with the new kernel function $\tilde{K}(\mathbf{x}, \mathbf{x}')$, has larger values near the decision boundary. (More details are presented in [23].)

To deal with the skew of the class boundary caused by imbalanced classes, we propose to modify the kernel, according to Eqn. 3, by considering the imbalanced data distribution as the prior information. In our prior work [23], we proposed an adaptive conformal transformation (ACT) in SVMs to modify the kernel function K directly in input space $\mathcal{I}$, so as to deal with the imbalanced training-dataset problem. (Please refer to [23] for the details.) ACT relies on the data information in $\mathcal{I}$, and hence the fixed-dimensional input space must exist.

However, for data that do not have a vector-space representation (e.g., sequence data), it may not be feasible to transform kernel function K conformally by relying on the information in the input space $\mathcal{I}$. Our kernel-boundary-alignment (KBA) algorithm bypasses this limitation by modifying the kernel matrix $\mathbf{K}$ by only relying on the mapped data information in the feature space $\mathcal{F}$. Indeed, as long as the resulting kernel matrix $\mathbf{K}$ maintains the positive (semi-) definite property, the modification is mathematically valid. We will at the end of this section point out the differences between KBA and ACT, and in particular, the additional flexibility hat KBA enjoys in adjusting similarity measures. To assist the reader, Table 1 lists key notations used in this section.

KBA modifies kernel matrix $\mathbf{K}$ based on the training-data distribution in $\mathcal{F}$. Kernel matrix $\mathbf{K}$ encodes all pairwise-similarity information between the instances in the training dataset. Hence, modifying the kernel matrix transforms the kernel function indirectly. (Notice that

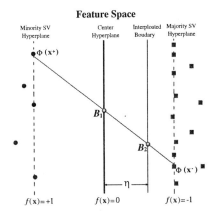

Feature Space

Minority SV Hyperplane   Center Hyperplane   Interploated Boundary   Majority SV Hyperplane

$\Phi(\mathbf{x}^+)$

B_1

B_2

$\Phi(\mathbf{x}^-)$

η

$f(\mathbf{x})=+1$ $f(\mathbf{x})=0$ $f(\mathbf{x})=-1$

Figure 1: Estimate Boundary Instances in $\mathcal{F}$.

KBA is certainly applicable to data that *do* have a vector-space representation, since $\mathbf{K} = (k_{ij} = K(\mathbf{x}_i, \mathbf{x}_j)).$) Now, because a training instance $\mathbf{x}$ might not be a vector, we introduce a more general term, *support instance*[4], to denote $\mathbf{x}$ if its embedded point via $\mathbf{K}$ is a support vector in $\mathcal{F}$.

In the following subsections, we will first propose a data-dependent way to estimate the "ideal" class boundary in $\mathcal{F}$ (Section 3.1). We then choose a feasible alignment function $D(\mathbf{x})$, which can assign a larger spatial resolution along the estimated "ideal" boundary in $\mathcal{F}$ (Section 3.2). Finally, we present KBA's iterative training procedure (Section 3.3).

3.1. Estimation of Boundary

Performing transformation on K or $\mathbf{K}$ aims to magnify the spatial resolution along the decision boundary, thereby improving the class separation. According to the work of [1, 23], maximal magnification should be performed along the class boundary. Unfortunately, locating the class boundary in input space $\mathcal{I}$ is difficult [1]. Instead, KBA locates the class boundary in feature space $\mathcal{F}$ through interpolation. In $\mathcal{F}$, the class boundary learned from the training data is the center hyperplane in the margin. When the training dataset is balanced, the center hyperplane approximates the "ideal" boundary well. However, when the training dataset is imbalanced, the decision boundary is skewed toward the minority class. To compensate for this skew, KBA gives the maximal magnification to an interpolated boundary between the center hyperplane and the hyperplane formed by the majority support instances in $\mathcal{F}$.

Figure 1 illustrates how the interpolation procedure works. $\Phi(\mathbf{x}^+)$ and $\Phi(\mathbf{x}^-)$ in the figure denote a

minority support instance and a majority support instance, respectively. A boundary instance $\Phi(\mathbf{x}_b)$ on the "ideal" boundary should reside between the center hyperplane (the thick line in the middle of Figure 1) and the majority support-instance hyperplane (the dash line on the right-hand side of the figure). We can thus estimate the location of $\Phi(\mathbf{x}_b)$ by interpolating the positions of $\Phi(\mathbf{x}^+)$ and $\Phi(\mathbf{x}^-)$ as follows:

$$\Phi(\mathbf{x}_b) = (1-\beta)\Phi(\mathbf{x}^+) + \beta\Phi(\mathbf{x}^-), \quad \frac{1}{2} \leq \beta \leq 1. \quad (4)$$

When the training dataset is balanced, β is $\frac{1}{2}$, and $\Phi(\mathbf{x}_b)$ lies on the center hyperplane (e.g., point B_1 in the figure). In this balanced case, the estimated "ideal" boundary coincides with the learned boundary. When the training dataset is imbalanced, however, we need to adjust β to estimate the "ideal" boundary. The key research question to answer is: "How to determine β in a data-dependent way?"

We propose a cost function for measuring the loss caused by false negatives and false positives when different values of β are introduced. We choose the β which can achieve the minimal cost. Let $\mathcal{X}_{mis}^+$ denote the set of the misclassified minority test-instances and $\mathcal{X}_{mis}^-$ the set of the misclassified majority test-instances. We define the cost functional $C(\cdot)$ for any scalar decreasing loss functions $c_p(\cdot)$ and $c_n(\cdot)$ as follows:

$$C(\eta) = \sum_{i=1}^{|\mathcal{X}_{mis}^+|} c_p\left(y_i f'(\mathbf{x}_i)\right) + \sum_{i=1}^{|\mathcal{X}_{mis}^-|} c_n\left(y_i f'(\mathbf{x}_i)\right),$$
$$where \; f'(\mathbf{x}_i) = f(\mathbf{x}_i) + \eta, \quad 0 \leq \eta \leq 1$$

In the equation above, $f(\mathbf{x}_i)$ is the SVM predication score for test instance $\mathbf{x}_i$, η is the offset of the interpolated boundary from the center hyperplane, as shown in Figure 1, and $y_i f'(\mathbf{x}_i)$ is the associated margin in $\mathcal{F}$ of the instance $\mathbf{x}_i$ with respect to the interpolated class boundary. The loss functions $c_p(\cdot)$ and $c_n(\cdot)$ are used to penalize the misclassified[5] minorities (false negative) and majorities (false positive), respectively. Each loss function, $c_p(\cdot)$ or $c_n(\cdot)$, can be chosen as any scalar decreasing function of the margin $y_i f'(\mathbf{x}_i)$ according to the prior knowledge. When no prior knowledge is available, usually, we can choose the exponential loss function as $c_p(\cdot)$ and the log-likelihood loss function as $c_n(\cdot)$, i.e,

$$c_p(y_i f'(\mathbf{x}_i)) = \exp(-y_i f'(\mathbf{x}_i)),$$
$$c_n(y_i f'(\mathbf{x}_i)) = \ln(1 + \exp(-y_i f'(\mathbf{x}_i))).$$

The justification of choosing them as the loss functions comes from boosting [12], where the exponential loss criterion concentrates much more influence (exponentially) on

---

4   In the KBA algorithm, if $\mathbf{x}$ is a support instance, we call both $\mathbf{x}$ and its embedded support vector via $\mathbf{K}$ in $\mathcal{F}$ *support instance*.

5   In KBA, we only consider the misclassified test instances in the margin so as to reduce the influence from the outliers. Their SVM scores $f(\mathbf{x})$ range from -1 to $+1$.

observations with large negative margins ($y_i f'(\mathbf{x}_i) < 0$), and the log-likelihood loss concentrates relatively less influence (linearly) on such observations. Since KBA aims to concentrate on false negatives, we use the exponential loss as $c_p(\cdot)$ and the log-likelihood loss as $c_n(\cdot)$.

The optimal η^* is then chosen by minimizing the total loss induced by all test instances falling into the margin of SVMs,

$$\eta^* = \arg\min_{\eta} C(\eta), \quad 0 \le \eta \le 1.$$

The optimal η^* can be calculated from $\frac{\partial C(\eta)}{\partial \eta} = 0$ and truncated between 0 and 1. After the optimal position η^* of the interpolated boundary is calculated, we can obtain β in Eqn. 4 as follows:

$$\beta = \frac{1 + \eta^*}{2}.$$

3.2. Selection of $D(\mathbf{x})$

After interpolating a boundary in the margin, we then magnify the spatial resolution along the boundary by modifying the Riemannian metric $g_{ij}(\mathbf{x})$ according to Eqn. 2 and Eqn. 3. When given a prior kernel, $g_{ij}(\mathbf{x})$ is determined by the conformal function $D(\mathbf{x})$. As what we discussed in the beginning of Section 3, a good $D(\mathbf{x})$ function should be larger when $\mathbf{x}$ is closer to the boundary in $\mathcal{F}$ so as to achieve a larger spatial resolution around the boundary. According to this criteria, we choose $D(\mathbf{x})$ as a set of Gaussian functions:

$$D(\mathbf{x}) = \frac{1}{|\mathcal{X}_b^*|} \sum_{\mathbf{x}_b \in \mathcal{X}_b^*} \exp\left(-\frac{\|\Phi(\mathbf{x}) - \Phi(\mathbf{x}_b)\|^2}{\tau_b^2}\right), \quad (5)$$

where τ_b^2 is a parameter controlling the magnitude of each exponential function in $D(\mathbf{x})$. For a given instance $\mathbf{x}$, $D(\mathbf{x})$ is calculated as the average of all exponential functions, each of which is related with one interpolated boundary instance $\Phi(\mathbf{x}_b)$ in $\mathcal{X}_b^*$ set. In addition, $\|\Phi(\mathbf{x}) - \Phi(\mathbf{x}_b)\|^2$ is calculated via the kernel trick as follows

$$\|\Phi(\mathbf{x}) - \Phi(\mathbf{x}_b)\|^2 \qquad (6)$$
$$= \|\Phi(\mathbf{x}) - (1 - \beta)\Phi(\mathbf{x}^+) - \beta\Phi(\mathbf{x}^-)\|^2$$
$$= k_{\mathbf{xx}} + (1 - \beta)^2 k_{\mathbf{x}^+\mathbf{x}^+} + \beta^2 k_{\mathbf{x}^-\mathbf{x}^-}$$
$$- 2(1 - \beta)k_{\mathbf{xx}^+} - 2\beta k_{\mathbf{xx}^-} + 2\beta(1 - \beta)k_{\mathbf{x}^+\mathbf{x}^-},$$

where $k_{\mathbf{xx}'}$ is from the kernel matrix $\mathbf{K}$. When the instance $\mathbf{x}$ is an unseen test instance, $k_{\mathbf{xx}'}$ is computed using the pre-defined similarity measurement which generates the kernel matrix $\mathbf{K}$.

According to [1, 20], we have the following corollary to guarantee the kernel transformation induced by $D(\mathbf{x})$, as defined in Eqn. 5, performs a mathematically valid conformal transformation.

Corollary 1 *The function $D(\mathbf{x})$ defined in Eqn. 5 gives a valid conformal transformation on feature space $\mathcal{F}$ induced by the pre-defined kernel matrix $\mathbf{K}$.*

Proof. Please refer to [24].

In KBA, we adaptively choose τ_b^2 in a data-dependent way as

$$\tau_b^2 = \mathrm{AVG}_{i \in \{Dist^2(\mathbf{x}_i, \mathbf{x}_b) < M\}} \left(Dist^2(\mathbf{x}_i, \mathbf{x}_b)\right), \quad (7)$$

where the neighborhood range M is the margin value. The distance $Dist^2(\mathbf{x}_i, \mathbf{x}_b)$ between two interpolated boundary instances $\mathbf{x}_i$ and $\mathbf{x}_b$ is $\|\Phi(\mathbf{x}_i) - \Phi(\mathbf{x}_b)\|^2$ and can be computed using Eqn. 4 and Eqn. 6. Notice that we do not need to scale τ_b^2 as in ACT [23] for dealing with the imbalanced training-data problem, since we have considered this factor when interpolating the class boundary and selecting $D(\mathbf{x})$.

We believe that our adjusted interpolation procedure and selection of $D(\mathbf{x})$ enjoy two benefits.

1. *Improved class-prediction accuracy.* In the imbalanced situation, most of misclassified minority instances fall into the margin area between the center hyperplane and the majority support-vector hyperplane. By maximizing the spatial resolution in this area, we expect to move those ambiguous instances as far away from the decision boundary as possible, so as to improve class-prediction accuracy.

2. *Improved imbalance ratio.* Since the majority support instances are located nearer the interpolated boundary than the minority support instances ($\frac{1}{2} \le \beta \le 1$ in Eqn. 4), by choosing a proper form of $D(\mathbf{x})$ as in Eqn.5, we can increase the degree of similarity between majority support instances and make them close each other in feature space after kernel transformation. This increase can lead to a reduction of the number of majority support instances, and hence improve the imbalanced support-instance ratio.

3.3. Retraining

After choosing $D(\mathbf{x})$, KBA modifies the given kernel matrix $\mathbf{K} = (k_{ij})$ in the following way.

$$\tilde{k}_{ij} = D(\mathbf{x}_i) \times D(\mathbf{x}_j) \times k_{ij}. \quad (8)$$

The new kernel matrix $\tilde{\mathbf{K}}$ after modification is then put back into the regular SVM algorithm for retraining. We have the following corollary, supported by the work of [20], to guarantee that the new kernel matrix after transformation in Eqn. 8 is a valid kernel matrix.

Corollary 2 *When given a positive (semi-)definite kernel matrix $\mathbf{K}$, the kernel transformation defined in Eqn. 8 results in a new kernel matrix $\tilde{\mathbf{K}}$ which is also positive (semi-)definite.*

Proof. Please refer to [24].

DATASET	# ATTRIB	# POS	# NEG	$\frac{|SI^-|}{|SI^+|}$	SVMs	SMOTE	ACT	KBA
SEGMENTATION	19	30	180	1.8:1	98.1 ± 5.1	98.1 ± 5.1	98.1 ± 5.1	$\mathbf{98.1 \pm 5.1}$
GLASS	10	29	185	2.0:1	89.9 ± 6.3	91.8 ± 6.5	93.7 ± 6.7	$\mathbf{93.7 \pm 6.6}$
EUTHYROID	24	238	1762	1.5:1	92.8 ± 3.6	92.4 ± 4.3	94.5 ± 3.0	$\mathbf{94.6 \pm 2.9}$
CAR	6	69	1659	1.8:1	99.0 ± 2.2	99.0 ± 2.3	99.9 ± 0.2	$\mathbf{99.9 \pm 0.2}$
YEAST	8	51	1433	3.0:1	59.0 ± 12.1	69.9 ± 10.0	78.5 ± 4.5	$\mathbf{82.2 \pm 7.1}$
ABALONE	8	32	4145	9.0:1	0.0 ± 0.0	0.0 ± 0.0	51.9 ± 7.6	$\mathbf{57.8 \pm 5.4}$

Table 2: Mean and standard deviation of g-Means prediction accuracy on UCI datasets.

4. Experimental Results

Our empirical study examined the effectiveness of the kernel-boundary-alignment algorithm in two aspects.

1. *Vector-space evaluation.* We compared KBA with other algorithms for imbalanced-data learning. We used six UCI datasets and an image dataset to conduct this evaluation. (We present the datasets shortly.)

2. *Non-vector-space evaluation.* We evaluated the effectiveness of KBA on a set of video surveillance data, which are represented as spatio-temporal sequences that do not have a vector-space representation.

In our experiments, we used C-SVMs as our yardstick to measure how other methods perform. We employed Laplacian kernels of the form $\exp(-\gamma|\mathbf{x} - \mathbf{x}'|)$ as $K(\mathbf{x}, \mathbf{x}')$ of C-SVMs. Then we used the following procedure: The dataset was first randomly split into training and test subsets generated in a certain ratio which was empirically chosen to be optimal on each dataset for the regular C-SVMs. Hyperparameters (C and γ) of $K(\mathbf{x}, \mathbf{x}')$ were obtained for each run using 7-fold cross-validation. All training, validation, and test subsets were sampled in a stratified manner ensuring each of them had the same negative/positive ratio [16]. We repeated this procedure seven times, computed average class-prediction accuracy, and compared the results. The detailed choices of parameters are presented in Sections 4.1.1 and 4.1.2.

4.1. Vector-space Evaluation

For this evaluation, we used six UCI datasets and a 116-category image dataset. The six UCI datasets we experimented with are *abalone* (19), *car* (3), *segmentation* (1), *yeast* (5), *glass* (7), and *euthyroid* (1). The class-label in the parentheses indicates the target class we chose. Table 2 shows the characteristics of these six datasets organized according to their negative-to-positive training-instance ratios. The top three datasets (segmentation, glass, and euthyroid) are not-too-imbalanced. The middle two (car and yeast) are mildly imbalanced. The bottom dataset (abalone) is the most imbalanced (the ratio is about 130:1).

The image dataset contains 20K images in 116 categories collected from the Corel Image CDs[6]. Each image is represented by a vector of 144 dimensions including color, texture, and shape features [6]. To perform class prediction, we employed the one-per-class (OPC) ensemble [9], which trains 116 classifiers, each of which predicts the class membership for one class. The class prediction on a testing instance is decided by voting among the 116 classifiers.

4.1.1. Results on UCI Benchmark Datasets. Tables 2 and 3 report the experimental results with the six UCI datasets. In addition to conducting experiments with SVMs, ACT, and KBA, we also implemented and tested one popular minority-oversampling strategy SMOTE [7]. We used the L_2-norm RBF function for $D(\mathbf{x})$ in ACT. In each run, the training and test subsets were generated in the ratio 6:1. For SMOTE[7], the minority class was over-sampled at 200%, 400% and 1000% for each of three groups of UCI datasets in Table 2, respectively.

We report in Table 2 using the Kubat's g-means metric defined as $\sqrt{a^+ \cdot a^-}$, where a^+ and a^- are positive (the target class) and negative testing accuracy, respectively [16]. Means and standard deviations of the experimental results are both reported in the table. In all the six datasets, KBA achieves the highest or ties for the highest accuracy. (The best results are marked in bold.) When the data is very imbalanced (the last row abalone of Table 2), both SVMs and SMOTE cannot make accurate predictions. KBA achieves 57.8% mean class-prediction accuracy (in g-means), and shows 5.9 percentile points improvement over ACT.

We also report in Table 3 using AUC [2] defined as the area under an ROC curve to compare the four strategies on the six UCI datasets. An ROC curve demonstrates the trade-off between true-positive rate and false-positive rate in binary classification problems as a function of varying a classification threshold. In our experiments, since all four strategies use Eqn. 1 as the decision function for classification, we varied the classification threshold θ by $sgn(f(\mathbf{x}) - \theta)$ to determine the label of $\mathbf{x}$, so as to draw the ROC curves. Means and standard deviations of the AUC scores are reported in the table. For readability, we report AUCs as percentages between 0% and 100%, instead of between 0 and

---

the Boston category contains various subjects, e.g., architectures, landscapes, and people, of Boston.)

7   For the datasets in Table 2 from top to bottom, for SMOTE, the optimal γ was 0.002, 0.003, 0.085, 0.3, 0.5, and 0.084, respectively. For SVMs, ACT, and KBA, the optimal γ was 0.004, 0.003, 0.08, 0.3, 0.5, and 0.086, respectively. All optimal C's were $1,000$.

---

6   We exclude from our testbed those categories that cannot be classified automatically, such as "industry", "Rome", and "Boston". (E.g.,

DATASET	SVMs	SMOTE	ACT	KBA
SEGMENTATION	100.0 ± 0.0	100.0 ± 0.0	100.0 ± 0.0	100.0 ± 0.0
GLASS	96.9 ± 3.0	97.1 ± 3.1	98.5 ± 2.5	$\mathbf{98.9 \pm 2.6}$
EUTHYROID	96.6 ± 2.2	96.0 ± 2.8	98.2 ± 1.8	$\mathbf{98.8 \pm 1.5}$
CAR	99.8 ± 0.2	99.8 ± 0.2	$\mathbf{99.9 \pm 0.1}$	$\mathbf{99.9 \pm 0.1}$
YEAST	89.2 ± 5.4	91.1 ± 5.0	93.8 ± 2.2	$\mathbf{95.2 \pm 2.5}$
ABALONE	62.5 ± 12.1	62.5 ± 12.1	80.2 ± 7.1	$\mathbf{87.4 \pm 6.8}$

Table 3: Mean and standard deviation of AUCs (in %) on UCI datasets.

1. Again, KBA achieves the highest mean AUCs in all six UCI datasets. Compared to ACT, KBA generated better results especially for the last datasets (yeast and abalone), with 1.4 and 7.2 percentile points improvement, respectively. Such gains bear out the flexibility and superiority of KBA working in feature space $\mathcal{F}$. Statistically, the higher AUCs from KBA means that our KBA algorithm will favor in classifying a positive (target) instance with a higher probability than other algorithms and hence could well tackle the imbalanced training-dataset problem.

4.1.2. Results on 20K Image Dataset. The image dataset is more imbalanced than the UCI datasets. We first set aside $4K$ images to be used as the test subset; the remaining $16K$ images were used for training and validation. We compared four schemes: SVMs, BP (the biased penalty method of [18, 21]), ACT, and KBA. Notice that in this experiment, we used the L_1-norm RBF function for $D(\mathbf{x})$ in ACT, since the L_1-norm RBF works best for the image dataset [6].

Table 4 presents the prediction accuracy for twelve representative categories out of 116, sorted by their imbalance ratios. KBA improves the accuracy over SVMs by 5.3, 5.9, and 15.5 percentile points on the three subgroup datasets, respectively. KBA achieves the best prediction accuracy for nine out of twelve categories among all schemes (marked by bold font). BP outperforms SVMs, but only slightly. (We have predicted BP's ineffectiveness, due to the KKT conditions, in Section 2.)

Remark. From Table 4, we can see that on this challenging dataset of several diversified classes, the results of all algorithms, including KBA, are not stellar (class-predication accuracy is less than 50% for almost all classes). This low accuracy is caused partly by a large number of classes (116), and partly by not-so-perfect image-feature extraction (due to the state of the available image processing technologies).

4.2. Non-vector-space Evaluation

For our multi-camera video-surveillance project, we recorded video data at a campus parking lot. We collected trajectories depicting five motion patterns: *circling* (30 instances), *zigzag-pattern* or *M-pattern* (22 instances), *back-forth* (40 instances), *go-straight* (200 instances), and *parking* (3, 161 instances). We divided these events into benign and suspicious categories and aimed to detect suspicious events with high accuracy. The benign-event category consists of patterns *go-straight* and *parking*, and the

CATEGORY	RATIO	SVMs	BP	ACT	KBA
MOUNTAIN	34:1	24.8	24.8	33.3	**34.5**
SNOW	37:1	46.4	47.8	**54.6**	52.3
DESERT	39:1	33.7	34.3	**39.1**	36.8
DOG	44:1	32.9	35.2	41.5	**42.7**
WOMAN	54:1	27.9	26.2	35.3	**39.1**
CHURCH	66:1	**21.8**	**21.8**	20.0	20.6
LEAF	80:1	26.1	24.8	32.6	**37.2**
LIZARD	101:1	13.9	15.1	22.2	**25.4**
PARROT	263:1	7.1	7.1	14.3	**18.4**
HORSE	264:1	14.3	14.3	28.6	**32.9**
LEOPARD	283:1	7.7	7.7	23.1	**23.1**
SHARK	1232:1	0.0	0.0	**16.6**	**16.6**

Table 4: Image-dataset prediction accuracy.

suspicious-event category consists of the other three patterns.

For each experiment, we chose 60% of the data as the training set, keeping the remaining 40% to use as our testing data. We employed a sequence-alignment kernel to compute similarity between two trajectories [25]. Figure 2(a) reports the means and standard deviations of sensitivities of using SVMs and two methods of improving the SVMs. Both methods, BP and KBA, can improve sensitivity. However, our KBA achieves significantly larger magnitude of improvement over SVMs, around 30 percentile points. Figure 2(b) shows that all methods maintain high specificity. Overall, BP does not work effectively, which bears out our prediction in Section 2.

5. Conclusion

We have proposed the kernel-boundary-alignment algorithm for tackling the imbalanced training-data challenge. Through theoretical justifications and empirical studies, we show this method to be effective. We believe that kernel-boundary alignment is attractive, not only because of its accuracy, but also because it can be applied to learning both vector-data and sequence-data (e.g., DNA sequences and spatio-temporal patterns) through modifying the kernel matrix directly.

6. Acknowledgement

We would like to thank the support of two NSF grants NSF Career IIS-0133802 and NSF ITR IIS-0219885.

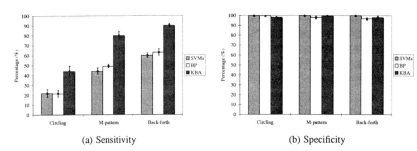

(a) Sensitivity   (b) Specificity

Figure 2: Sensitivity vs. Specificity on trajectory dataset.

References

[1] S. Amari and S. Wu. Improving support vector machine classifiers by modifying kernel functions. *Neural Networks*, 12(6):783–789, 1999.

[2] A. P. Bradley. The use of the area under the roc curve in the evaluation of machine learning algorithms. *Pattern Recognition*, 30:1145–1159, 1997.

[3] L. Breiman. Bagging predictors. *Machine Learning*, 24:123–140, 1996.

[4] C. Burges. Geometry and invariance in kernel based methods. in adv. in kernel methods: Support vector learning. pages 89–116, 1999.

[5] P. Chan and S. Stolfo. Learning with non-uniform class and cost distributions: Effects and a distributed multi-classifier approach. *Workshop Notes KDD-98 Workshop on Distributed Data Mining*, pages 1–9, 1998.

[6] E. Y. Chang, K. Goh, G. Sychay, and G. Wu. Content-based soft annotation for multimodal image retrieval using bayes point machine. *IEEE Transactions on Circuits and Systems for Video Technology Special Issue on Conceptual and Dynamical Aspects of Multimedia Content Description*, 13(1):26–38, January 2003.

[7] N. Chawla, K. Bowyer, L. Hall, and W. P. Kegelmeyer. Smote:synthetic minority over-sampling technique. *International Conference on Knowledge Based Computer Systems*, 2000.

[8] N. Cristianini, J. Kandola, A. Elisseeff, and J. Shawe-Taylor. On kernel target alignment. *Journal Machine Learning Research*, 1, 2002.

[9] T. Dietterich and G. Bakiri. Solving multiclass learning problems via error-correcting output codes. *Journal of Artifical Intelligence Research*, 2:263–286, 1995.

[10] T. Fawcett and F. Provost. Adaptive fraud detection. *In Data Mining and Knowledge Discovery*, 1(3):291–316, 1997.

[11] K. Fukunaga. *Introduction to Statistical Pattern Recognition*. Academic Press, Boston, MA, 2 edition, 1990.

[12] T. Hastie, R. Tibshirani, and J. Friedman. *The Elements of Statistical Learning: Data Mining, Inference, and Prediction*. Springer, New York, 2001.

[13] T. Joachims. Text categorization with support vector machines: learning with many relevant features. In *Proceedings of ECML-98, the tenth European Conference on Machine Learning*, pages 137–142, 1998.

[14] J. Kandola and J. Shawe-Taylor. Refining kernels for regression and uneven classification problems. In *Proceedings of the ninth International Workshop on Artificial Intelligence and Statistics*, 2003.

[15] G. Karakoulas and J. S. Taylor. Optimizing classifiers for imbalanced training sets. In *Advances in Neural Information Processing Systems*, 1999.

[16] M. Kubat and S. Matwin. Addressing the curse of imbalanced training sets: One-sided selection. In *Proceedings of the fourteenth International Conference on Machine Learning*, pages 179–186, 1997.

[17] H. W. Kuhn and A. W. Tucker. *Non-linear programming*. Proc. 2nd Berkeley Syrup. on Mathematical Statistics and Probability, Univ. Calif. Press, 1961.

[18] Y. Lin, Y. Lee, and G. Wahba. Support vector machines for classification in nonstandard situations. *Machine Learning*, 46:191–202, 2002.

[19] A. Nugroho, S. Kuroyanagi, and A. Iwata. A solution for imbalanced training sets problem by combnet-ii and its application on fog forecasting. *IEICE Transaction on Information and Systems*, E85-D(7):1165–1174, July 2002.

[20] B. Scholkopf and A. Smola. *Learning with Kernels: Support Vector Machines, Regularization, Optimization, and Beyond*. MIT Press, Cambridge, MA, 2002.

[21] K. Veropoulos, C. Campbell, and N. Cristianini. Controlling the sensitivity of support vector machines. *Proceedings of the International Joint Conference on Artificial Intelligence*, pages 55–60, 1999.

[22] G. M. Weiss and F. Provost. The effect of class distribution on classifier learning: An empirical study. *Technical Report ML-TR-44, Department of Computer Science, Rutgers University*, August 2001.

[23] G. Wu and E. Y. Chang. Adaptive feature-space conformal transformation for imbalanced data learning. In *Proceedings of the twentieth International Conference on Machine Learning*, pages 816–823, August 2003.

[24] G. Wu and E. Y. Chang. Kernel boundary alignment for imbalanced-data training. Technical report, http://mmdb.ece.ucsb.edu/~gangwu/Papers/kba.pdf, May 2004.

[25] G. Wu, Y. Wu, L. Jiao, Y.-F.Wang, and E. Y. Chang. Multi-camera spatio-temporal fusion and biased sequence-data learning for security surveillance. *ACM International Conference on Multimedia*, November 2003.

IRC: An Iterative Reinforcement Categorization Algorithm for Interrelated Web Objects

Gui-Rong Xue[1]   Dou Shen[2]   Qiang Yang[4]   Hua-Jun Zeng[3]   Zheng Chen[3]

Yong Yu[1]   WenSi Xi[5]   Wei-Ying Ma[3]

[1]Computer Science and Engineering
Shanghai Jiao-Tong University
Shanghai 200030, P.R.China

grxue@sjtu.edu.cn, yyu@cs.sjtu.edu.cn

[2]Computer Science and Technology
TsingHua University
Beijing 100084, P.R.China

shendou@mails.tsinghua.edu.cn

[3]Microsoft Research Asia
5F, Sigma Center, 49 Zhichun Road
Beijing 100080, P.R.China

{hjzeng, zhengc, wyma}@microsoft.com

[4]Hong Kong University of
Science and Technology
Clearwater Bay, Kowloon, Hong Kong

qyang@cs.ust.hk

[5]Computer Science
Virginia Polytechnic Institute and State University
Virginia, U.S.A

xwensi@vt.edu

Abstract

Most existing categorization algorithms deal with homogeneous Web data objects, and consider interrelated objects as additional features when taking the interrelationships with other types of objects into account. However, focusing on any single aspects of these interrelationships and objects will not fully reveal their true categories. In this paper, we propose a novel categorization algorithm, the Iterative Reinforcement Categorization algorithm (IRC), to exploit the full interrelationships between the heterogeneous objects on the Web. IRC attempts to classify the interrelated Web objects by iterative reinforcement between individual classification results of different types via the interrelationships. Experiments on a clickthrough log dataset from MSN search engine show that, with the F1 measures, IRC achieves a 26.4% improvement over a pure content-based classification method, a 21% improvement over a query metadata-based method, and a 16.4% improvement over a virtual document-based method. Furthermore, our experiments show that IRC converges rapidly.

1. Introduction

We are concerned with categorizing Web pages into meaningful semantic categories. Traditional *content-based* categorization approaches use simple representation schemes that are based on word occurrence statistics. However, several problems are concluded that may affect the performance of such algorithms. First, most Web pages contain noisy information. Sometimes non-text objects, such as images and scripts that are

unusable by text classifiers, are part of the page content. Second, the Web pages are created by different authors who may have no coherent page-construction style, languages or even structures.

Our key observation here is that the Web consists of many types of objects such as queries, Web pages and users, while these types of objects are highly interrelated with each other. The intuitive approach is to augment the features of Web objects by using their interrelated Web objects as additional features since related objects are likely to have similar properties. For example, in Web pages categorization, the feature vector of a Web page can be constructed by combining its content and the queries that are associated with the page through the clickthrough log [1][19]. We denote these methods as *virtual-document* categorization. In our experiment, this kind of categorization has a little improvement over the content-based categorization approach. Thus there is still head room for harnessing such interrelationships between the heterogeneous objects.

Since the interrelated heterogeneous objects are likely to have similar topic, they are also likely to share similar category information. Therefore, after classifying the objects based on their content, is it possible to impose category information of the interrelated objects in improving the categorization performance? In fact, the heterogeneous objects form a graph within which the mapping is really many-to-many rather than one-to-many. In this paper, we propose a novel classification algorithm, the Iterative Reinforcement Categorization (IRC), to fully exploit the many-to-many relationships on such graph. In this approach, the category information of one object is reinforced by the category information of all its interrelated objects; and the updated category information of the object will consequently reinforce the category information of its interrelated objects. That is to say, it is an iterative reinforcement process until it converges to a conclusive result. The difference of our method to *virtual-document* method is that we use the category information instead of the content feature of queries. Furthermore, one Web page is usually interrelated to a few queries while the dimension of the query vector space is very high (up to 46,000), the *virtual-document* categorization algorithm will suffer from severe data sparseness. The problem is also solved in IRC.

The novelty of our work can be seen from several aspects. First, we extend the traditional classification methods to multi-type interrelated data objects. We aim to classify interrelated data objects of different types simultaneously using both their content features and their relationship with other types of objects. Second, we present a reinforcement algorithm to classify interrelated Web data objects on a bipartite graph. In this algorithm, the category of one type is propagated to reinforce the categorization of other interrelated data objects, vice versa, as an iterative process.

We perform comprehensive experiments on the clickthrough log dataset from MSN search engine to evaluate the proposed approach. Our experiments show that, with the F1 measurements, IRC achieves a 26.4% improvement over a pure content-based classification method, a 21% improvement over a query metadata-based method, and a 16.4% improvement over a virtual document-based method.

The rest of the paper is organized as follows. In Section 2, we review some related work on Web classification and log analysis. In Section 3, we explain the IRC algorithm and analyze the properties of the algorithm. Experimental results are reported in Section 4. We give conclusions and discuss future works in Section 5.

2. Related work

The first collection of related works is about classification which can be divided into content-based or link-analysis-based classification techniques. The former relies on the text representation of data objects being classified. Joachims [13] proposed a method of using Support Vector Machines (SVMs) to classify documents. Dumais and Chen [7] use text representation to organize search results into an existing hierarchical structure. They could not achieve high performance on Web pages in some cases due to the noise contained in the Web pages, especially for pages with non-text information such as images and scripts that are unusable for text classifiers.

In the link-analysis-based classification techniques, learning algorithms are applied to handle both text components of the Web pages and the hyperlink relationship among them. Slattery et al. [16] explored the

hyperlink topology using an extended HITS algorithm. Similarly, Cohn et al. [6] and Glover et al. [9] showed that classification performance can be improved by combining link-based and content-based techniques. Chakrabarti et al. [2] proposed a probabilistic model to utilize both text and linkage information to classify a database of patents and a small Web collection. They showed that directly incorporating words from neighboring pages might reduce classification performance. However, incorporating category information, such as hierarchical category prefixes, improves performance. Oh. et al. [14] reported similar results on a collection of encyclopedia articles. Getoor et al. [8] proposed the PRMs to combine the content feature and its relationship with other objects. Our work is different from the hyperlink-based classification methods in that we could classify the heterogeneous data objects across different data types, such as Web pages, search queries and users by fully exploited interrelated relationship through an iterative process.

A second group of related work is query log analysis Beeferman et al. [1] proposed an innovative query clustering method based on clickthrough data. In their work, they treat clickthrough data sets as a bipartite graph and identify the mapping between queries and the associated URLs. Queries with similarly clicked URLs can be clustered together. In this work, they deal with the query clustering problem while our algorithm deals with categorization problem (for both query and Web pages). Another difference is that we use the interrelationship to infer probability that a query/webpage belong to a class, while [1] only used the interrelationship as additional feature for clustering. The analogous method [12] is also used in finding similar objects, which iteratively calculate the similarities between the objects through the link relationship. Wen et al. [19] described a query clustering method that makes use of user logs. Chuang et al. [4] proposed a technique for categorizing Web query terms from the clickthrough logs into a pre-defined subject taxonomy based on their popular search interests. Wang et al. [17] proposed a method of using query clickthrough log to iteratively reinforce query and Web page clusters.

To the best of our knowledge, our work on multi-type data objects classification on the Web is one of the first to integrate content information with relationships across different data types to improve the performance of classification.

3. Categorization of interrelated objects

In this section, we first define the problem of interrelated objects categorization, followed by our IRC algorithm to iteratively exploit the relationship between the heterogeneous data objects. In this paper, two types of Web objects--the query and Web page--are considered, and we are concerned with the problem of categorizing Web pages into categories.

3.1. Problem definition

The Web could be modeled as a *weighted directed bipartite graph* $G=(V, E)$, where the nodes in V represent queries and Web pages, and the edges E represent the clickthrough information from a query to a browsed Web page. We can divide V into two subsets $Q=\{q_1, q_2, ..., q_m\}$ and $D=\{d_1, d_2, ..., d_n\}$ where Q represents the queries and D represents the Web pages. A matrix M is used to represent the adjacency matrix, whose (i, j)-element is the weight from Web page i to query j. In this paper, we simply deem the weight as the frequency of the page being clicked to the query.

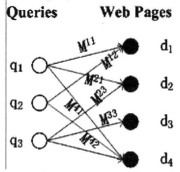

Figure 1. Interrelation between queries and Web pages

Based on such a relationship graph, our problem is how to exploit the graph, which is constructed using two types of objects, to enhance the performance of categorization. Formally, given a bipartite graph $G=(V, E)$, we want to classify the Web pages D and queries Q into a set of predefined categories $C=\{c_1, c_2, ..., c_k\}$, where k is the number of categories.

We can use vectors $P_i=\{p_{i1}, p_{i2}, ..., p_{ik}\}$ and $R_i=\{r_{i1}, r_{i2}, ..., r_{ik}\}$ to represent the probabilities of the testing Web page d_i and the testing query q_i belongs to each category, respectively, where $0 \leq p_{ij}, r_{ij} \leq 1$. Thus, a probability matrix $P_{n \times k}$ ($R_{m \times k}$) for all n Web pages (m queries) can be constructed, where each entry p_{ij} (r_{ij}) is the probability that Web page d_i (query q_i) belongs to category j.

3.2. Iterative reinforcement algorithm

First, we classify the Web pages according to their content feature, such as the plain text, the title and the metadata of the page, etc.

To fully utilize the relationship in the bipartite graph, we propose a novel iterative reinforcement classification method. The basic idea is to propagate the categories computed for one type of object to all related objects by updating their probability of belonging to a certain category. This process is iteratively performed until the classification results for all object types converge.

We divide the Web pages D into training set D_t and testing set D_s. We consider all queries as being part of the test set Q_s, because we have no training set for the queries. Our iterative reinforcement algorithm is described as follows:

Iterative Reinforcement Categorization Algorithm (IRC)
Input: D_s, D_t, Q_s
Output: The categories of D_s, Q_s
1. Calculate the probability distribution of the Web pages in D_s on the k categories based on the content feature;
2. Calculate the probability distribution of queries on the k categories according to the probability distribution of the interrelated Web pages in D_t and D_s;
3. Label the query q with the category c where $c = \arg\max_{c_i}[P(c_i | q)]$;
4. Update the probability distribution of Web pages on the k categories according to the probability distribution of the interrelated queries in Q_s of the moment from the probability distribution calculated in Step 1 (see Equations 1 to 8 below);
5. Label the Web page p as the category c where $c = \arg\max_{c_i}[P(c_i | p)]$;
6. Update the probability distribution of queries on the k categories according to the probability distribution of the interrelated Web pages in D_t and D_s of the moment;
7. Repeat Steps 3 to 6 until the probability distributions reach a fixed point.

In the following, we illustrate the process in detail.

3.2.1. Classifying queries based on a bipartite graph.

After initially classifying Web pages according to their contents, we could infer the probability of *queries* belonging to categories according to their interrelated Web pages through the M matrix. This propagation of probability is based on the assumption that the queries of a certain category are usually followed by clicks on Web pages of the same category.

In general, for any query, its interrelated Web pages in our experiment may be from two different sets: the training set D_t and the testing set D_s. Since the categories of Web pages in the training data set are known and the categories of Web pages in the testing data set are predicted, the role played by the training data and the testing data on the queries should be differentiated. We denote M_T (M_S) as the adjacency matrix between training Web pages (testing Web pages) and queries. In particular, the entry r_{ij} of the query probability matrix R, denoting the probability that query i belongs to category j, is computed through the following equation:

$$r_{ij} = \alpha \frac{\sum\limits_{m:d_m \in D_T \cap O_i} M_T^{mi} p_{mj}}{\sum\limits_{m:d_m \in D_T \cap O_i} M_T^{mi}} + \beta \frac{\sum\limits_{n:d_n \in D_S \cap O_i} M_S^{ni} p_{nj}}{\sum\limits_{n:d_n \in D_S \cap O_i} M_S^{ni}} \quad (1)$$

where O_i is the set of Web pages associated with the query q_i; α and β are the parameters to be tuned to reflect the relative importance between the training data and the testing data.

We denote the matrix T and S as the row normalized matrix M_T' and M_S' (M_T' and M_S' are the transpose of M_T and M_S). Formula (1) could be re-written with a matrix form:

$$R_S = \alpha T P_T + \beta S P_S \quad (2)$$

where P_t and P_s are the probability matrices of D_t and D_s on k categories, respectively.

3.2.2. Classifying Web pages based on a bipartite graph.
Just as the Web pages can affect the queries, the classification result on queries could also affect the Web pages. After acquiring the categorization of queries, we could re-classify Web pages through the relationship between queries and pages. In this step, we both take the content and the categories of the associated queries into consideration. The element p_{ij} of the matrix P, denoting the probability that page i belongs to category j, is computed through the following equation:

$$p_{ij} = \alpha' p_{ij} + \beta' \frac{\sum\limits_{n:q_n \in I_i} M_S^{in} r_{nj}}{\sum\limits_{n:q_n \in I_i} M_S^{in}} \quad (3)$$

where I_i is the set of queries interrelated with the Web page p_i; α' and β' are the parameters we tune to show the relative importance of the content of the Web pages and their associated queries. We denote the matrix U as the row normalized matrix M_S. This equation could also be re-written in matrix form as follows:

$$P_S = \alpha' P_S + \beta' U R_S \quad (4)$$

3.2.3. Iterative reinforcement categorization (IRC).
Only using the above two steps, we still have not fully utilized the interrelationships between Web pages and queries. Therefore we continue to perform an iterative reinforcement on the categorization by exploiting the bipartite graph. Such calculation is an iterative process in which the categories are propagated from one side to the other side. Let R_S^i denote the probability matrix of interrelated queries and P_S^i denote the probability matrix of Web pages after ith iteration. The algorithm could be re-written in the following matrix:

$$R_S^{i+1} = \alpha T P_T^0 + \beta S P_S^i \quad (5)$$

$$P_S^{i+1} = \alpha' P_S^0 + \beta' U R_S^{i+1} \quad (6)$$

Based on the Equations (5) and (6), we could derive the following:

$$P_S^{i+1} = \alpha' P_S^0 + \alpha \beta' U T P_T^0 + \beta \beta' U S P_S^i \quad (7)$$

Taken $\alpha' P_S^0 + \alpha \beta' U T P_T^0$ as P, the formula could be written in the following form:

$$P_S^{i+1} = P + \omega U S P_S^i \quad (8)$$

Where ω is equal to $\beta \beta'$. The equation implies that the probability matrix of Web pages is affected by the probability calculated on the content of Web pages and the relationship of the adjacent matrix.

Similar to Equation (6), the computation of the probability matrix for *queries* is derived as follows:

$$R_S^{i+1} = \alpha T P_T^0 + \alpha' \beta S P_S^0 + \beta \beta' S U R_S^i \quad (9)$$

Taken $\alpha T P_T^0 + \alpha' \beta S P_S^0$ as R, the formula could be written in the following form:

$$R_S^{i+1} = R + \omega S U R_S^i \quad (10)$$

After several iterations, the P_S and R_S would reach a fixed point. Then, the category of p is taken to be $\arg\max\limits_{c_i}[P(c_i \mid p)]$, while the category of q is $\arg\max\limits_{c_i}[P(c_i \mid q)]$.

The above computation is performed iteratively until the Euclidean length of the residual vector $\| P_S^{i+1} - P_S^i \|$ becomes less than a predefined δ for some $i > 0$.

3.2.4. Convergence of IRC.
We now give a claim that the iterative procedure converges to a fixed point eventually.

Lemma 1. S and U are nonnegative matrices and sum of each row is equal to 1.

Proof. It is a direct induction from definition of S and U.

Lemma 2. US is a Markov matrix and therefore $(US)^i$ is also a Markov matrix for any integer i.

Proof. US is a nonnegative square matrix and it is easy to verify that the entries in each row of US sum to 1. So it is a Markov matrix. Also from the Markov Chain theory [10], $(US)^i$ is also a Markov matrix for any integer i.

Theorem 1. The IRC algorithm can converge to a fixed point.

Proof. Without loss of generality, we only prove that the matrix P_S^i can converge to a fixed point.

S, U are Markov matrices (Lemma 1), and ω ($0 < \omega < 1$)
From equation (8),

$$P_S^{i+1} = P + \omega U S P_S^i$$
$$= P + \omega U S P + (\omega U S)^2 P + \ldots + (\omega U S)^i P + (\omega U S)^{i+1}$$

Now we see the convergence as following:

$$\lim_{i \to \infty} \| P_S^{i+1} - P_S^i \|$$

$$= \lim_{i \to \infty} \| (\omega US)^i (P + \omega US - E) \|$$

$$= \lim_{i \to \infty} \| \omega^i (US)^i (P + \omega US - E) \|$$

Since,

$$\lim_{i \to \infty} \omega^i = 0 \quad (0 < \omega < 1)$$

$(US)^i$ is a Markov matrix too (Lemma 2).

So $(US)^i$ is nonnegative and sum of each row is equal to 1.

Thus, $\quad \lim_{i \to \infty} \| (\omega US)^i \| = \lim_{i \to \infty} \| \omega^i (US)^i \| = 0$

Finally, $\quad \lim_{i \to \infty} \| P_S^{i+1} - P_S^i \| = 0$

It is obvious that P_S^i will converge to its respective fixed point eventually. Analogously, R_S^i can also converge to its respective fixed point eventually.

4. Experiments

4.1. Data set

To evaluate the performance of our algorithm, experiments were performed using a set of classified Web pages extracted from the Open Directory Project (ODP) (http://dmoz.org/). ODP contains about 1.2 million Web pages, in which each Web page is classified by human experts into 17 top level categories (*Arts, Business and Economy, Computers and Internet, Games, Health, Home, Kids and Teens, News, Recreation, Reference, Regional, Science, Shopping, Society, Sports, Adult and World*). Because the Web pages in the regional category are also included in other categories and the Web pages in the category of the world are not written in English, these two categories are removed in our experiments. Accordingly, 15 categories in all are used in the experiments.

A real MSN query clickthrough log is collected as our experiment data set. The collect log contains about 1.2 million query requests recorded over 12 hours in August 2003. The log we obtained has been already processed into a predefined format; i.e. each query request is associated with one or more clicked Web pages, forming a "query session", which can be defined as follows:

*Query Session: = query text [clicked Web page *]*

Some preprocessing steps are applied to queries and Web pages in the raw log. All queries are converted into lower-case, and are stemmed using the Porter algorithm. The stop words are removed too. The query sessions sharing the same query and the same URL are merged into one query session, with the frequencies summed up.

Since we only have 12 hours of query log on hand, some of Web pages in the ODP data set are not in our query clickthrough log. Hence, in our experiment, we only

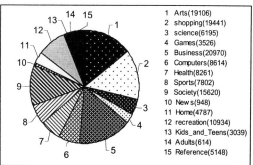

Figure 2. Distribution of Web pages in the 15 categories

deal with the common pages which appeared in both the ODP data set and the query clickthrough log. Finally, we got 131,788 Web pages in 15 top-level categories, 199,564 associated queries and 468,696 query sessions. Figure 2 shows the distribution of the number of Web pages in 15 categories.

We test the relevancy of queries to the contents of Web pages from the users' perspective. We randomly select three subsets which contain 600 query sessions in total. Ten volunteer graduate students are chosen as our evaluation subjects. They are asked to evaluate whether the queries are relevant to the Web pages according to the content of the pages. The result is shown in Table 1, that about 81.7% of queries on average are relevant to the contents of the Web pages.

Table 1. Relevance between the queries and Web page

Subset	Session	Relevant	Ratio
1	300	247	0.82
2	300	262	0.87
3	300	228	0.76
Average			**0.817**

Table 2. A sample of raw MSN clickthrough data

Query	URL	Category
software bugs	http://www.cpsr.org/program/y2k	Computer
	http://www.bugnet.com/	Computer
softball hitting	http://www.hitranger.com	Shopping
	http://www.decatursports.com/softball_drills_page.htm	Sports
playing mantis	http://www.playingmantis.com	Games
	http://www.johnnylightning.com/	Recreation
sniper rifles	http://www.sniperworld.com	Sports
	http://www.snipercentral.com	Sports
	http://www.norcalprecision.com/	Sports

Before the experiment, we also conducted another statistics test to see whether query terms can introduce extra information for Web categorization. Several examples of Query session in the raw data are shown in Table 2. From the examples we may come to a conclusion intuitively that the pages linked by the same query belong to the same category. Statistically 68.4% Web pages fall into the same ODP category when they are clicked by the same query.

4.2. Other setting

4.2.1. Feature selection and Classifier.
To speed up the classification, a simple feature selection method, known as "Information Gain (*IG*)"[20], is applied in our experiments. SVM is a promising classification algorithm developed by Vapnik [3][13]. In this paper, we use linear SVM because of its high accuracy when used for text categorization. The SVM[light] software package is used [15]. In all experiments, the trade-off parameter C is set to 1. The widely used one-against-all approach is used for the multi-class case. In the rest of this paper, we only consider the probability of the data objects that belong to the categories, so we utilize the method in [18] to assign each category with a probability.

4.2.2. Evaluation Criteria.
The performance of the proposed methods was evaluated using the conventional precision, recall and F_1 measures. Precision p is defined as the proportion of correctly classified examples in the set of all examples assigned to the target class. Recall r is defined as the proportion of the correctly classified examples out of all the examples having the target class. F_1 is a combination of precision and recall defined as follows:

$$F_1 = \frac{2pr}{p+r} \qquad (11)$$

Furthermore, micro-averaging and macro-averaging [20] were applied to get single performance values over all classification tasks.

4.3. Performance

The *content-based classification method* is taken to be the baseline. Since most queries are relevant to the semantics of the corresponding Web pages, we can intuitively take the interrelated queries could be taken as an additional feature for their corresponding pages. Consider the example in Figure 1. Web page d_i is clicked by users for queries $q_1, q_2, ..., q_m$ with different frequencies. Thus $M^{i1} \cdot q_1 + M^{i2} \cdot q_2 + ... + M^{im} \cdot q_m$ can be taken as additional metadata for Web page d_i where M^{ik} means the frequency that users click on d_i following query q_k. We consider how to utilize the query metadata. First, we can use the query metadata as additional features of Web page directly. We denote this method as *query-metadata*

based classification. Second, we can integrate the query metadata and the content of the Web page together and take them a *virtual document* of the Web page; for the importance of the query metadata, we try different weights of the metadata and integrate them with the content of the Web pages. For example, if we set "content: metadata" as 1:2, the query metadata is twice as important as the content of the Web page. After removing stop words and feature selection, the dimension of the Vector Space for the content of collection, the query metadata of collection and the virtual document collection are 258,669, 46,002, and 281,259 respectively.

We fixed several parameters for the rest of the experiments: the ratio between the content of Web pages and the query metadata is set as 1: 2 when constructing the virtual documents; α and β in equation 1 are set as 6 and 4; α' and β' in equation 3 are set as 7 and 3; and iteration times equals five. These parameters are determined based on an experiment conducted on a subset of training data.

Table 3. Performance of the four algorithms

MICRO			
	Precision	Recall	F1
Content	0.561	0.561	0.561
Query metadata	0.586	0.586	0.586
Virtual document	0.609	0.609	0.609
IRC	**0.709**	**0.709**	**0.709**
MACRO			
	Precision	Recall	F1
Content	0.642	0.470	0.496
Query metadata	0.523	0.554	0.523
Virtual document	0.575	0.583	0.568
IRC	0.671	0.664	0.68

We start by analyzing how each source of information such as content, query metadata and virtual document performs without using the iterative algorithm. Table 3 shows the micro-averaged *F1* values for the different classifiers. The highest values for each classifier are shown in bold face. The content-based classifiers, as expected, showed poor results, indicating that the text of the Web pages does not provide sufficient information to reliably classify the Web pages. Since queries are relevant to the Web page topics, which could be used to improve the performance.

IRC achieves the higher performance than the other three methods in comparison. Relatively speaking, the IRC under the F_1-micro-averageing measure improved over the content method by 26.4%, over the query metadata method by 21%, and over the virtual document method by 16.4%. The reason for the improvement lies in the fact that our algorithm could fully exploit the relationship between the Web pages and the queries.

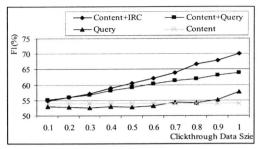

Figure 3. Performance on the different clickthrough data size

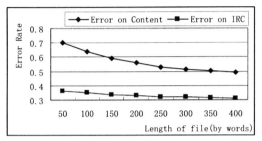

Figure 4. Error rate on different file length

We conducted a further experiment to show the effect of the clickthrough data by increasing the clickthrough data size as displayed in Figure 3. We randomly selected 10% data from the clickthrough data at the first time and 20% at the second time and so on. We found that the performance of the content-based categorization is quite poor. When clickthrough data is introduced, the performance of the Web page categorization is improved.

The page length has also an important effect on the performance of classification based on content feature. In order to verify such an intuition, two experiments are conducted and results are shown in Table 4 and Figure 4.

Table 4. Effect of the length of file on classification

	Wrongly Classified	Correctly Classified	Total
Number of files	6060	7113	13173
Ave.Length of files	180.85	375.28	285.84

When processing the data, we find many pages that contain too few words to indicate their main topics though they are meaningful with plentiful non-text resources such as picture and video. Thus it is hard to identify their labels only based on such words. However, these pages may still be retrieved and clicked by users when they are relevant to the query given by the users. In these cases, the query logs may be especially effective to predict the labels of these pages. In Figure 4, we can see the error rate of the content-based categorization gradually increasing in a large scale with the shorter length of pages while our IRC show a very small change in error rate.

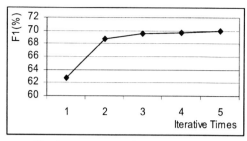

Figure 5. Performance on different iteration counts

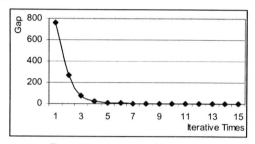

Figure 6. Convergence of the iterative algorithm

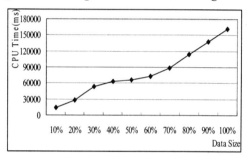

Figure 7. Execution time on different data size

Figure 5 shows the performance of the IRC algorithm with the iteration times. The implicit relationships are exploited more and more thoroughly with the increase of the iterations and these relationships contribute to the improvement of the classification performance.

The convergence curve of our iterative algorithm is shown in Figure 6. The gap $\| P_S^{i+1} - P_S^i \|$ denotes the difference between the current iteration and the previous iteration. Figure 6 shows the IRC algorithm will converge after five iterations.

We run the IRC algorithm on the Pentium 1.9G PC with 512M of memory. Figure 7 shows the execution time of the algorithm on different data size, where the CPU time is linear with the size of the clickthrough data, which shows that the algorithm scales up well with large data.

5. Conclusions and future work

In this paper, we proposed an iterative reinforcement classification algorithm to categorize interrelated data objects from different data types simultaneously. The proposed algorithm considers both the content feature of data objects and the relationship across the different data types in the iterative classification process. The intermediate results of each type will be used to reinforce the classification of their related data types. Experiments on real MSN query clickthrough log datasets show that IRC can significantly improve the Web page classification under the F_1 measure after introducing the relationships between the Web pages and queries. In the future, it would be interesting to see whether it is possible to effectively integrate multiple types of relationships such as hyperlinks and user access patterns to improve the classification effectiveness.

6. References

[1] D. Beeferman and A. Berger. Agglomerative clustering of a search engine query log. In Proceedings of the sixth ACM SIGKDD International Conference on Knowledge Discovery and Data Mining, pages 407-415, 2000.

[2] S. Chakrabarti, B. Dom, and P. Indyk. Enhanced hypertext categorization using hyperlinks. In Proceedings of the ACM SIGMOD International Conference on Management of Data, pages 307-318, Seattle, Washington, June 1998.

[3] C.Cortes and V. Vapnik. Support Vector Networks. Machine Learning, 20:1-25, 1995.

[4] S. L. Chuang and L. F. Chien. Enriching Web taxonomies through subject categorization of query terms from search engine logs. Decision Support System, Volume 35, Issue 1, April 2003.

[5] H. Cui, J. R. Wen, J. Y. Nie, and W. Y. Ma. Query Expansion by Mining User Logs, IEEE Transaction on Knowledge and Data Engineering, Vol. 15, No. 4, July/August 2003.

[6] D. Cohn and T. Hofmann. The missing link - a probabilistic model of document content and hypertext connectivity. In Advances in Neural Information Processing Systems 13, pages 430-436.MIT Press, 2001.

[7] S. Dumain and H. Chen. Hierarchical Classification of Web Content. In Proceedings of the 23rd annual international ACM SIGIR Conference on Research and Development in Information Retrieval, 2000.

[8] L. Getoor, N. Friedman, D. Koller, and B. Taskar. "Learning Probabilistic Models of Relational Structure," In Proceeding of the 18th International Conference on Machine Learning, 2001.

[9] E. J. Glover, K. Tsioutsiouliklis, S. Lawrence, D. M. Pennock, and G. W. Flake. Using Web structure for classifying and describing Web pages. In Proceedings of WWW-02, International Conference on the World Wide Web, 2002.

[10] G. Grimmett and D. Stirzaker. Probability and Random Processes, 2nd ed. Oxford, England: Oxford University Press, 1992.

[11] C. K. Huang, L. F. Chien, and Y. J. Oyang. Relevant term suggestion in interactive Web search based on contextual information in query session logs. JASIST 54(7): 638-649, 2003.

[12] G. Jeh and J. Widom. SimRank: A Measure of Structural-Context Similarity. Proceedings of the Eighth ACM SIGKDD International Conference on Knowledge Discovery and Data Mining, pages 538-543, Edmonton, Canada, July 2002.

[13] T. Joachims. Text categorization with support vector machines: learning with many relevant features. In Proceedings of ECML-98, 10th European Conference on Machine Learning, pages 137-142, Chemnitz, Germany, April 1998.

[14] H. J. Oh, S. H. Myaeng, and M. H. Lee. A practical hypertext categorization method using links and incrementally available class information. In Proceedings of the 23rd annual international ACM SIGIR conference on Research and development in information retrieval, pages 264-271. ACM Press, 2000.

[15] Sequential Minimal Optimization, http://research. micro-soft.com/~jplatt/smo.html.

[16] S. Slattery and M. Craven. Discovering test set regularities in relational domains. In Proceedings of ICML-00, 17th International Conference on Machine Learning, pages 895-902, Stanford, US, 2000.

[17] J. D. Wang, H. J. Zeng, Z. Chen, H. J. Lu, L. Tao, and W.-Y Ma. ReCoM: reinforcement clustering of multi-type interrelated data objects. In Proceedings of the ACM SIGIR Conference on Research and Development in Information Retrieval, pages 274-281, Toronto, CA, July 2003.

[18] J. Platt. Probabilistic outputs for support vector machines and comparisons to regularized likelihood methods. In A. Smola, P. Bartlett, B. Sch olkopf, and D. Schuurmans, editors, Advances in Large Margin Classi ers. MIT Press, 1999.

[19] J. R. Wen, J. Y. Nie, and H. J. Zhang. Clustering user queries of a search engine. In Proceedings of the Tenth International World Wide Web Conference, Hong Kong, May 2001.

[20] Y. Yang and J.O. Pedersen. A comparative study on feature selection in text categorization, in Proceeding of the Fourteenth International Conference of Machine Learning, 1997.

A Polygonal Line Algorithm based Nonlinear Feature Extraction Method

Feng Zhang

Texas A&M University
College Station, Texas 77843
zhangfeng@neo.tamu.edu

Abstract

We propose a polygonal line based principal curve algorithm for nonlinear feature extraction, in which the nonlinearities among the multivariable data can be described by a set of local linear models. The proposed algorithm integrates the linear PCA approach with the polygonal line algorithm to represent complicated nonlinear data structure. Statistical redundancy elimination for high dimensional data is also discussed for describing the underlying principal curves without much loss of information among the original data sets. The polygonal line algorithm can produce robust and accurate nonlinear curve estimation for different multivariate data types, and it is helpful in reducing the computation complexity for existing principal curve approaches when the sample size is large.

1. Introduction

The goal of dimension reduction is to obtain a compact, accurate representation of the multivariate data or eliminate statistically redundant component without loss useful information. One classic way for linear dimension reduction is PCA. Suppose that $x = [x_1, x_2, \ldots, x_d]^T$ with mean vector μ_x and covariance matrix Σ_x. PCA involves the analysis of the eigenvectors $\{z_i : i = 1, 2, \ldots, d\}$ of Σ_x and their associated eigenvalues λ_i arranged in descending order. Though PCA is a global linear technique to represent x in the reduced $\Re^r$ space, it fails to detect nonlinearities in the data structure due to its limitation on the linear assumptions. Some nonlinear approaches are expected to provide better representation with lower distortion, which has naturally motivated various developments of nonlinear feature extraction methods to retain the properties of linear PCA, such as principal curves [4, 8]. A principal curve $f \in \Re^d$ is a one-dimensional smooth curve explicitly ordered by projection index $t \in \Re$, that passes through the middle of data x, i.e. $f(t) = E[x|t_f(x)=t]$ where t_f is the projection index. In short, each point on the principal curve is the average of all points projecting onto it. It is shown that f is the collection of points that minimizes the squared Euclidean distance function $\Delta(f) = E\|x - f(t_f(x))\|^2$ given some smooth constraints.

In [4], the Principal Curve algorithm (HS throughout this paper) starts with $f(t) = \mu_x + tz_1$, then iterates between the projection step and conditional expectation step, until convergence. Applications of the principal curves can be envisaged in fitting and recognizing complex nonlinear patterns in signal and image processing [1, 2, 4, 7]. Another definition of principal curve as a continuous curve of specified length was proposed [7] to develop a piecewise principal curve that minimizes the average squared distance between the curve and the multivariate observations. Finite Gaussian mixture models were also used in nonlinear feature extraction and dimension reduction [3, 5, 9]. The standard method to fit finite mixture models is EM algorithm, which converges to a maximum likelihood estimate of the mixture parameters. However, the EM algorithm is a local method and sensitive to initialization because the likelihood function of a mixture model is not necessarily unimodal.

Several problems exist with the aforementioned methods. When the sample data are concentrated around a highly bended curve or the model assumptions are not satisfied, these methods exhibit poor performance. This is due to their fixed topology on the latent data space or to bad initialization [8]. We will develop a polygonal line method to avoid the poor solutions by fitting the line segments without any mapping or length constraints. The complexity of principal curve estimation is another implementation factor when the size of sample is large. For N data points, the HS algorithm actually produces polygonal lines with N segments and the computational complexity is mostly determined by the sample size. In the present study, we take a new approach by estimating principal curves as continuous curves which minimize the mean square distance between the curve and data points. The new learning scheme chooses a curve from a class of polygonal lines with K segments to minimize the distance measure. The segment number, K, when optimally chosen, is usually much less than N. Therefore, the polygonal line algorithm can achieve reduced computational expense.

In the present paper we propose the polygonal line based principal curve method for nonlinear feature extraction in order to capture the interdependencies and nonlinearities among different variables by a combination of local linear PCA models. Each local partition of the data space may be represented by some line segments, with the vertices points connecting neighbor partitions searched by a global optimization criterion. This criterion lies upon the utilization of a common Euclidean distance function.

2. Polygonal Lines for Nonlinear Patterns

2.1 Piecewise Linear Curve

A straight line $s(t)$ is the first principal component, if and only if,

$$E[\min_t \|x - s(t)\|^2] \leq E[\min_t \|x - \tilde{s}(t)\|^2] \qquad (1)$$

for any other straight line. We would like to generalize this property of the first principal component and define principal curves so that they minimize the expected squared distance over a class of curves, rather than only being critical points of the distance function. To do this, it is necessary to constrain the length of the curve since, otherwise, for any x with a density and any $\varepsilon > 0$, there exists a smooth curve f such that $\Delta(f) \leq \varepsilon$ and, thus, a minimizing f has infinite length. On the other hand, if the distribution of x is concentrated on a polygonal line and is uniform there, the infimum of the square distances $\Delta(f)$ is 0 over the class of smooth curves, but no smooth curve can achieve this infimum. For this reason, we relax the requirement that f should be differentiable and, instead, we constrain the length of f by defining it to be a polygonal line with fine line segments. Note that, by the polygonal line definition of principal curves, f is still continuous.

In what follows, we consider the problem of polygonal line estimation based on a set of sample data. Suppose that N independent copies $x_1, x_2, \ldots, x_N$ of x are given. The goal is to use the sample data to construct a curve with line segments at most K whose expected square loss is close to that of the unknown principal curve for x.

Let $\Delta(x, f) = \min_t \|x - f(t)\|^2$ be the square distance between a point $x \in \Re^d$ and the curve f. For any f, the empirical square error is the sample average

$$J = (1/N) \Sigma_{n=1}^{N} \Delta(x_n, f). \qquad (2)$$

For a K-segment polygonal line, f consists of $K+1$ vertices $\{v_1, v_2, \ldots, v_{K+1}\}$. Denote $f_k(t) = v_k + (t - t_k) \dfrac{v_{k+1} - v_k}{\|v_{k+1} - v_k\|} \equiv c_k + t u_k$ as the kth line segment defined over $[t_k, t_{k+1}] \subset \Re$ ($k = 1, 2, \ldots K$), the way the distance of point x and the line segment is measured depends on the value of the projection index, $t_{f_k}(x)$. Formally,

$$\Delta(x, f_k) = \begin{cases} \|x - v_k\|^2 & t_{f_k}(x) = t_k, \\ \|x - v_{k+1}\|^2 & t_{f_k}(x) = t_{k+1}, \\ \|x - c_k\|^2 - ((x - c_k)^T u_k)^2 & o.w. \end{cases}$$
(3)

And the distance in (2) is $\Delta(x_n, f) = \min_k\{\Delta(x_n, f_k)\}$.

2.2 Piecewise Linear Basis Function

The K-segment polygonal line $f(t)$ can be readily written as a piecewise linear basis function :

$$f(t) = \mathbf{W} b_w(t), \ t \in [t_1, t_{K+1}] \qquad (4)$$

where $\mathbf{W} = [v_1 \ v_2 \ldots v_{K+1}]$, and the basis function $b_w(t)$ is

$$b_{w,i}(t) = \begin{cases} (t - t_{i-1})/(t_i - t_{i-1}), & t_{i-1} < t \leq t_i \\ (t_{i+1} - t)/(t_i - t_{i-1}), & t_i < t \leq t_{i+1} \\ 1, & t = t_i \\ 0, & otherwise \end{cases} \qquad (5)$$

where t_i are the projection index of the vertices onto the polygonal line. Without loss of generality, it is convenient requiring the basis functions to be non-negative and to form a partition of unity for all t.

The piecewise linear curves have an important computational advantage over all completely nonlinear types, since the latter ones require to solve a non-convex optimization problem for the estimation of principal curves, which may be computationally expensive. In addition, the curve can be always easily be parameterized in terms of arc length, which only requires that the interval between neighboring projection indices corresponds to the actual distance between the associated vertices.

3. The Polygonal Line Algorithm

In this section, we will introduce a local PCA based algorithm for approximate principal curves using polygonal lines. The accuracy of approximation depends on some factors such as the number of line segments and sample size. Each line segment defines an associated local partition of the data space, as discussed in Section 3.2. Thus the sample data generated from the underlying principal curve are partitioned into different local regions. Each local partition may be best represented by the first eigenvector if the number of dominating eigenvalues is equal to one; otherwise, this local partition lies in a linear subspace with dimension greater than one and needs multiple line segments to represent, so we have to add one line segment by determining the location of new vertices.

3.1 Initialization of the Polygonal Line Approximation

The polygonal line algorithm can start with a straight line (i.e. $K = 1$) to find a more accurate piecewise linear cure by increasing the number of line segments K. Usually to speed up the polygonal line searching procedure, we can initialize an r piecewise linear curve ($r > 1$) with some prior knowledge of the data structure, followed by the optimization for the coordinates of the $r + 1$ vertices.

An intuitive and effective way to achieve this task is to project all the N data points onto the first dominant eigenvector $\hat{z}_1$ of sample covariance matrix, then start from either one end point of the projection along the eigenvector direction and set the location of $r + 1$ points such that the number of projected data within every two neighboring of these points almost equal to N/r. Now these $r + 1$ projection points on $\hat{z}_1$ are set as the initial guess of vertices for the polygonal line. The experimental results showed that this initialization of polygonal line is always efficient on computation time and accuracy.

3.2 Vertices Optimization

Given the initialization of the vertices, in this step, the new coordinate positions of all the vertices v_i will be updated. The sum of square distance is minimized subject to the constraint that the piecewise curve is one with K segments.

The global vertices optimization step needs to calculate the gradients of the performance objective function in (2) with respect to unknown $K+1$ vertex points $\mathbf{W} = [v_1 \, v_2 \, ... \, v_{K+1}]$ in d-dimensional space.

Let x_n be any arbitrary sample data, and v_i and v_{i+1} be the two neighboring vertices such that the line segment (v_i, v_{i+1}) is the closest one among these K segments to data x_n. For simplicity, denote J_n as the minimal square Euclidean distance from x_n to the line segment (v_i, v_{i+1}), and the overall performance function can be represented as $J = \sum_n J_n$. To implement the optimization procedure, we also calculate the gradient and Hessian for J_n with respect to the $K+1$ vertices. For notation simplicity, let $Vec(\mathbf{W})$ be a $d(K+1)$ vector containing the stacked columns of $\mathbf{W}$.

Then, for each J_n, the gradient with respect to the unknown $K+1$ vertices, $dJ_n / dVec(\mathbf{W})$, will be derived given the following two distinct geometrical cases.

Case I: The closest point on f_i to x_n is one end point of this segment. Assume v_i to be such a vertex, then

$$J_n = (v_i - x_n)^{\mathrm{T}}(v_i - x_n), \text{ and}$$

$$\frac{dJ_n}{dVec(\mathbf{W})} = \begin{bmatrix} 0 \\ \vdots \\ 2(v_i - x_n) \\ 0 \\ \vdots \\ 0 \end{bmatrix}.$$

Case II: The closest point on f_i to x_n is some point other than the vertex points. Then, the distance J_n is

$$J_n = (v_i - x_n)^{\mathrm{T}}(v_i - x_n) - \frac{(v_i - x_n)^{\mathrm{T}}(v_{i+1} - v_i)(v_{i+1} - v_i)^{\mathrm{T}}(v_i - x_n)}{(v_{i+1} - v_i)^{\mathrm{T}}(v_{i+1} - v_i)}.$$

And the corresponding gradient vector is

$$\frac{dJ_n}{dVec(\mathbf{W})} = \begin{bmatrix} 0 \\ \vdots \\ \partial J_n / \partial v_i \\ \partial J_n / \partial v_{i+1} \\ \vdots \\ 0 \end{bmatrix},$$

where

$$\frac{\partial J_n}{\partial v_i} = 2(v_i - x_n) - \frac{2(v_i - x_n)^{\mathrm{T}}(v_{i+1} - v_i)}{(v_{i+1} - v_i)^{\mathrm{T}}(v_{i+1} - v_i)}(v_{i+1} + x_n - 2v_i)$$

$$- \frac{2[(v_i - x_n)^{\mathrm{T}}(v_{i+1} - v_i)]^2}{[(v_i - v_i)^{\mathrm{T}}(v_{i+1} - v_i)]^2}(v_{i+1} - v_i), \text{ and}$$

$$\frac{\partial J_n}{\partial v_{i+1}} = \frac{2[(v_i - x_n)^{\mathrm{T}}(v_{i+1} - v_i)]^2}{[(v_i - v_i)^{\mathrm{T}}(v_{i+1} - v_i)]^2}(v_{i+1} - v_i) - \frac{2(v_i - x_n)^{\mathrm{T}}(v_{i+1} - v_i)}{(v_{i+1} - v_i)^{\mathrm{T}}(v_{i+1} - v_i)}(v_i - x_n).$$

Given the gradients for all N sample data, the gradient vector of J with respect to the vertices vector $Vec(\mathbf{W})$ is obtained, and the conjugate methods could be applied to the optimal search for $K + 1$ vertices.

Recall that the method of steepest descent method uses only the first derivatives (gradients) in selecting a suitable search direction. This strategy is not always the most effective in the sense of convergence. If higher derivatives are incorporated, the resulting iterative optimization algorithm may perform better than the gradient methods. Before the derivation of the second derivatives, i.e. Hessian matrix for J, we first define:

$$g_{n,i} = \frac{(v_i - x_n)^{\mathrm{T}}(v_{i+1} - v_i)}{(v_{i+1} - v_i)^{\mathrm{T}}(v_{i+1} - v_i)}.$$

Then, the Hessian matrix $\mathbf{H}_n$ for J_n is

$$\mathbf{H}_n = \frac{d^2 J_n}{dVec(\mathbf{W})dVec(\mathbf{W})^{\mathrm{T}}} = \begin{bmatrix} \frac{\partial(\frac{\partial J_n}{\partial v_1})}{\partial v_1^{\mathrm{T}}} & \cdots & \frac{\partial(\frac{\partial J_n}{\partial v_1})}{\partial v_{K+1}^{\mathrm{T}}} \\ \vdots & & \vdots \\ \frac{\partial(\frac{\partial J_n}{\partial v_{K+1}})}{\partial v_1^{\mathrm{T}}} & \cdots & \frac{\partial(\frac{\partial J_n}{\partial v_{K+1}})}{\partial v_{K+1}^{\mathrm{T}}} \end{bmatrix}$$

As the above gradients calculation, the second derivatives of J_n with respect to the vertices ($v_1, v_2, ..., v_{k+1}$) depend on the two geometrical cases.

For case I, $\mathbf{H}_n = Diag\{0, ..., 2\mathbf{I}_{d \times d}, 0, ..., 0\}$ where $2\mathbf{I}_{d \times d}$ is the ith diagonal block of the Hessian matrix $\mathbf{H}_n$.

For case II,

$$\mathbf{H}_n = \begin{bmatrix} \mathbf{0}_{d\times d} & \mathbf{0}_{d\times d} & \cdots & & \cdots & \mathbf{0}_{d\times d} & \mathbf{0}_{d\times d} \\ \vdots & \ddots & & & & & \vdots \\ & & \dfrac{\partial(\frac{\partial J_n}{\partial v_i})}{\partial v_i^{\mathsf{T}}} & \dfrac{\partial(\frac{\partial J_n}{\partial v_i})}{\partial v_{i+1}^{\mathsf{T}}} & & & \\ \mathbf{0}_{d\times d} & & & & & \mathbf{0}_{d\times d} & \\ & & \dfrac{\partial(\frac{\partial J_n}{\partial v_{i+1}})}{\partial v_i^{\mathsf{T}}} & \dfrac{\partial(\frac{\partial J_n}{\partial v_{i+1}})}{\partial v_{i+1}^{\mathsf{T}}} & & & \\ \vdots & & & & & & \vdots \\ \vdots & & & & & & \vdots \\ \mathbf{0}_{d\times d} & \mathbf{0}_{d\times d} & \cdots & & \cdots & \mathbf{0}_{d\times d} & \mathbf{0}_{d\times d} \end{bmatrix},$$

where the four non-zero $d\times d$ matrices are calculated by

$$\frac{\partial(\frac{\partial J_n}{\partial v_i})}{\partial v_i^{\mathsf{T}}} = (2 + 4g_{n,i} + 2g_{n,i}^2)\mathbf{I} - \frac{2(v_{i+1} + x_n - 2v_i)(v_{i+1} + x_n - 2v_i)^{\mathsf{T}}}{(v_{i+1} - v_i)^{\mathsf{T}}(v_{i+1} - v_i)}$$
$$- \frac{4[(v_{i+1} + x_n - 2v_i)(v_{i+1} - v_i)^{\mathsf{T}} + (v_{i+1} - v_i)(v_{i+1} + x_n - 2v_i)^{\mathsf{T}}]g_{n,i}}{(v_{i+1} - v_i)^{\mathsf{T}}(v_{i+1} - v_i)}$$
$$+ \frac{8g_{n,i}^2(v_{i+1} - v_i)(v_{i+1} - v_i)^{\mathsf{T}}}{(v_{i+1} - v_i)^{\mathsf{T}}(v_{i+1} - v_i)};$$

$$\frac{\partial(\frac{\partial J_n}{\partial v_i})}{\partial v_{i+1}^{\mathsf{T}}} = (-2g_{n,i} - 2g_{n,i}^2)\mathbf{I} - \frac{2(v_{i+1} + x_n - 2v_i)(v_i - x_n)^{\mathsf{T}}}{(v_{i+1} - v_i)^{\mathsf{T}}(v_{i+1} - v_i)}$$
$$- \frac{4[(v_{i+1} + x_n - 2v_i)(v_{i+1} - v_i)^{\mathsf{T}} - (v_{i+1} - v_i)(v_i - x_n)^{\mathsf{T}}]g_{n,i}}{(v_{i+1} - v_i)^{\mathsf{T}}(v_{i+1} - v_i)}$$
$$+ \frac{8(v_{i+1} - v_i)(v_{i+1} - v_i)^{\mathsf{T}} g_{n,i}^2}{(v_{i+1} - v_i)^{\mathsf{T}}(v_{i+1} - v_i)};$$

$$\frac{\partial(\frac{\partial J_n}{\partial v_{i+1}})}{\partial v_i^{\mathsf{T}}} = \left[\frac{\partial(\frac{\partial J_n}{\partial v_i})}{\partial v_{i+1}^{\mathsf{T}}} \right]^{\mathsf{T}};$$

$$\frac{\partial(\frac{\partial J_n}{\partial v_{i+1}})}{\partial v_{i+1}^{\mathsf{T}}} = 2g_{n,i}^2\mathbf{I} - \frac{2(v_i - x_n)(v_i - x_n)^{\mathsf{T}}}{(v_{i+1} - v_i)^{\mathsf{T}}(v_{i+1} - v_i)}$$
$$+ \frac{4[(v_{i+1} - v_i)(v_i - x_n)^{\mathsf{T}} + (v_i - x_n)(v_{i+1} - v_i)^{\mathsf{T}}]g_{n,i}}{(v_{i+1} - v_i)^{\mathsf{T}}(v_{i+1} - v_i)}$$
$$+ \frac{8(v_{i+1} - v_i)(v_{i+1} - v_i)^{\mathsf{T}} g_{n,i}^2}{(v_{i+1} - v_i)^{\mathsf{T}}(v_{i+1} - v_i)}.$$

One advantage of this polygonal line algorithm is that the optimization step can simultaneously determine the optimal coordinates of all vertices, and reduces the computation time on polygonal line estimation, compared to the algorithm in [7]. Their approach searches the optimal location of only one vertex by fixing the other vertices in each inner loop. Therefore, updating the vertices when a new vertex was added will need $K+1$ inner loops and the final coordinate locations were suboptimal.

3.3 Partition Data Space into Local Regions

In the proposed polygonal line learning algorithm, we need to partition the sample data into some local regions for linear principal component analysis. Let X be a set of N samples from $\mathfrak{R}^d$. Given the current K line segments, Define the local regions $V_1, V_2, \ldots, V_K$ as
$$V_i = \{x \in X \mid i = \arg\min_k \Delta(x, f_k)\}. \tag{6}$$

Hence, V_i contains all data points for which the ith line segment f_i is the closest. The way to construct the local partition by projecting the overall sample data into specific number of regions is built on Euclidean distance. The mean vector $\hat{\mu}_i$ of local partition V_i is defined as sample mean. For the data partitions, we apply PCA to the sample covariance matrix $\hat{\Sigma}_i$ for each V_i to estimate the dominant eigenvalues. The dimension number r_i of the local linear variety is estimated accordingly. If there is some partition with r_i greater than 1, it implies that partition V_i should be represented by multiple line segments. When there are multiple local regions V_i with more than one dominant eigenvalues, we choose the local region in which its second dominant eigenvalues contributes more percentage of variance to the total variance within V_i ($i = 1, 2, \ldots, K$). The midpoint of the corresponding line segment then serves as the initialization of the new vertex point. This incremental scheme that increases the number of line segments by one will help avoid the over-fitting problem in polygonal line estimation.

Newton's method in the vertices optimization step uses the first and second derivatives and indeed performs better than the steepest descent method on the convergence property when the starting point is near the optimal solution. To provide a good initialization for the vertices when a new vertex point is added, we propose the following projection-regression scheme for obtaining the initial values of vertices. The basic scheme arises from the piecewise linear basis function form (4) for the polygonal line, which iterates between two estimation steps:

Projection Step: Given some values for the weights of $\mathbf{W}$ in (4), the projection step requires the estimation of the projection index t along the line segments represented by $\mathbf{W}$. The basis function $b_w(t)$ is then calculated according to (5).

Regression Step: Given the values of basis function $b_w(t)$, the regression-step requires the estimation of the optimal function parameters (weights)
$$\hat{\mathbf{W}} = \arg\min_{\mathbf{W}} \sum_{n=1}^{N} \left\| x_n - \mathbf{W} b_w(t_n) \right\|^2.$$

It is straightforward to obtain:
$$\hat{\mathbf{W}} = [x_1 \ x_2 \ \cdots \ x_N]\mathbf{B}_t^{\mathsf{T}}(\mathbf{B}_t\mathbf{B}_t^{\mathsf{T}})^{-1},$$
where $\mathbf{B}_t = [b_w(t_1) \ b_w(t_2) \ldots b_w(t_N)]$.

Since the projection-step and regression-step minimize the same distance error function with respect to t and $\mathbf{W}$, respectively, it is easy to see that the non-negative error is monotonously decreasing and therefore, the proposed initialization scheme should converge to a suboptimal estimation for vertices.

3.4 Computational Complexity

The complexity of the data partition is dominated by the complexity of the projection step, which is $O(NK)$. In the vertices optimization step as described in Section 3.2, the complexity of the algorithm to obtain f is $O(NK+K^3)$. As the experimental studies showed, the optimal number of line segments K is much smaller compared to the sample size of data, N (usually $K << N^{2/3}$), the computational complexity of the polygonal line algorithm is reduced, which is slightly better than the $O(N^2)$ complexity of the HS algorithm. The complexity can be dramatically decreased in certain situations. One can also set K to be a constant if the data size is large, since increasing K beyond a certain threshold brings only diminishing returns. These simplifications work well in certain situations, but the original algorithm is more robust.

4. Polygonal line algorithm for high dimensional data

In the spirit of [8], we assume that a multivariate observation x can be modeled by
$$x = f(t) + w,$$
where $f(t)$ is the underlying principal curve, t is a random scalar and w is a zero-mean random noise vector with covariance matrix Σ_w. Unless otherwise noted, it will be assumed that $\Sigma_w = \sigma^2 \mathbf{I}$, a scalar multiple of the identity matrix.

Let $\mathbf{M}$ denote an r-dimensional subspace of $\mathfrak{R}^d$. We denote by $a_0 + \mathbf{M}$ the r-dimensional linear variety that results from translating $\mathbf{M}$ by the constant vector a_0. Actually in many high dimensional situations we would find a principal curve in which a lower dimensional linear variety lies. The random vector x which is assumed to generate the data set $\mathbf{X} = \{x_1, ..., x_N\} \subset \mathfrak{R}^d$ can be interpreted to be composed of a signal part which varies in an r dimensional subspace and an isotropic Gaussian noise part. And any nonlinear principal curve can be approximated arbitrarily closely by a piecewise continuous linear curve.

Suppose that for all t, $f(t)$ lies in an r-dimensional linear variety $a_0 + \mathbf{M}$. Assume also that no other linear variety in which $f(t)$ lies has dimension smaller than r. It was shown [10] that standard PCA can be used to identify this linear subspace. The dimension r of the linear variety is exactly the number of dominant eigenvalues from PCA. The linear subspace $\mathbf{M}$ itself is given by the span of the first r principal eigenvectors.

Therefore, the results of PCA help us to estimate $f(t)$ by first estimating the principal curve $h(t)$ based on the PCA scores in $\mathfrak{R}^r$ and then transform back $h(t)$ to the d-dimensional principal curve by $f(t) = \mathbf{Z}h(t)$, where the $d \times r$ matrix $\mathbf{Z} = [z_1 \ z_2 \ ... \ z_r]$ is constructed from the first r eigenvectors.

If r is much less than d, however, considerable savings in computational expense can also be achieved as follows. Note that since each transformed sample data $x_{z,n} = \mathbf{Z}\mathbf{Z}^T(x - \mu_x) + \mu_x$ lies in the linear variety $\mu_x + \mathbf{M}$, minimizing $\sum_{n=1}^{N} \left\| x_{z,n} - f(t) \right\|^2$ must always result in an $f(t)$ that also lies in $\mu_x + \mathbf{M}$. Consequently, there is no loss in generality in restricting our search for $f(t) \in \mathfrak{R}^d$. This can be accomplished by working with the r-dimensional vectors of PCA scores $y_n = \mathbf{Z}^T(x_n - \mu_x)$, where y_n consists of the coefficients of $x_{z,n} - \mu_x$ using $\{z_i, i = 1, ..., r\}$ as a basis for the r-dimensional subspace $\mathbf{M}$. Similarly define $h(t) = \mathbf{Z}^T(f(t) - \mu_x)$ to be the coefficients of $f(t) - \mu_x$ in $\mathbf{M}$, and it follows that $f(t) = \mathbf{Z}h(t) + \mu_x$. For any t we have
$$x_{z,n} - f(t) = \mathbf{Z}\mathbf{Z}^T[x_n - \mu_x] + \mu_x - [\mathbf{Z}h(t) + \mu_x] = \mathbf{Z}[y_n - h(t)]$$

so that
$$\left\| x_{z,n} - f(t) \right\|^2 = \left\| \mathbf{Z}[y_n - h(t)] \right\|^2 = [y_n - h(t)]^T \mathbf{Z}^T \mathbf{Z}[y_n - h(t)] = \left\| y_n - h(t) \right\|^2.$$

In other words, choosing $f(t)$ to minimize $\sum_{n=1}^{N} \left\| x_{z,n} - f(t) \right\|^2$ is equivalent to choosing $h(t)$ to minimize $\sum_{n=1}^{N} \left\| y_n - h(t) \right\|^2$ and then recovering $f(t)$ from $h(t)$. For the polygonal line algorithm proposed in the present paper, we thus first estimate the piecewise linear curve $h(t) = \mathbf{W}_h b_{wh}(t)$ for the sample PCA scores y_n and then transform $h(t)$ to get the higher dimensional polygonal line $f(t) = \mathbf{Z}\mathbf{W}_h b_{wh}(t) + \mu_x$. The advantage of working with the r-dimensional vectors y_n, as opposed to the original data $x_n \in \mathfrak{R}^d$, is that computational complexity is reduced roughly by a factor of r/d [10, 2].

5. Experimental Study

In this section, we evaluate the performance of the proposed algorithm, and start with a generative model
$$x_n = f(t_n) + w, n = 1, ..., N.$$

If not stated otherwise, the noise w would be assumed to be spherical Gaussian, that is, $w \sim N_d(\mathbf{0}, \sigma^2 \mathbf{I})$. In the simulation examples, the performance of our algorithm is compared with other principal curve algorithm on the basis of how closely the estimated curve follows the generating curve.

Given a true principal curve $f(t)$, the estimate from HS standard algorithm is denoted as $\hat{f}_{HS}(t)$, $\hat{f}_{LPCA}(t)$ and $\hat{f}_{KP}(t)$ are used to represent the estimate resulting from our algorithm and Kegl's principal curve algorithm. The average squared distance between the estimates and the true principal curve $f(t)$ is chosen as the comparison performance measure, i.e.

$$d = \frac{1}{N}\sum_{n=1}^{N}\min_{v}\left\|\hat{f}(t_f(x_n)) - f(v)\right\|^2.$$

In the simulations, 10,000 Monte Carlo replications were averaged to obtain the comparison data in Table 1 ~ 3.

5.1 Smooth Curves in Low Dimensional Space

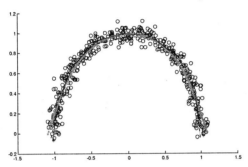

Figure 1. The polygonal line (solid line) compared with HS curve (dotted line) and Kegl's curve (dashed line).

In this case, we tested our algorithm on a smooth half circle, as shown in Figure 2. For various N and σ, the figure and corresponding simulation results in Table 1 showed that the curve produced by our algorithm was closer to the true curve than that from the HS principal curve algorithm, especially when N larger and noise size smaller. It is natural to expect the algorithm to approximate the true curve well when sample size N grows up.

Table 1. Performance comparison

N	σ	$d_{HS(\times 10^{-3})}$	$d_{KP(\times 10^{-3})}$	$d_{LPCA(\times 10^{-3})}$
100	0.05	0.48	0.49	0.46
100	0.1	0.82	0.88	0.91
200	0.05	0.46	0.45	0.39
200	0.1	0.78	0.79	0.76
400	0.05	0.44	0.39	0.30
400	0.1	0.75	0.71	0.72

5.2 Zigzag Curves in Low Dimensional Space

Another generating shape of the principal curve is considered in this case study, in which a sharp curve or zigzag curve was generated by the previous introduced generative model. Figure 2 demonstrated the robustness

and accuracy of the polygonal approximation algorithm with local PCA interpretation. In this scenario, the generating curve $f(t)$ is consist of 6 segments of equal line length such that the two consecutive segments join at a right angle. In the simulation cases, the sample data were evenly distributed along each line segment.

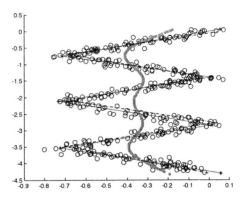

Figure 2. The polygonal line (solid line) compared with HS curve (dotted line) and Kegl's curve (dashed line).

Like the first case, we also introduced noise with different stand variance ($\sigma = 0.05$ and 0.1) to the generating curve to compare the performance measures between these algorithms. In both noise cases, our algorithm produced curves that fit the true curve more closely. Table 2 also illustrated that the polygonal line algorithm by local PCA exhibits better when sample data dimensional number d or sample size N increases.

Table 2. Performance comparison

d	N	σ	$d_{HS(\times 10^{-3})}$	$d_{KP(\times 10^{-3})}$	$d_{LPCA(\times 10^{-3})}$
2	100	0.05	15.0	0.6	0.4
2	100	0.1	17.4	3.3	2.9
2	200	0.05	14.9	0.3	0.2
2	200	0.1	17.2	2.6	1.8
2	400	0.05	14.4	0.2	0.1
2	400	0.1	16.9	1.8	1.1
3	100	0.05	16.3	0.9	0.5
3	100	0.1	18.5	3.7	3.2
3	200	0.05	16.2	0.7	0.3
3	200	0.1	17.9	2.5	1.7
3	400	0.05	16.1	0.4	0.2
3	400	0.1	17.5	1.6	1.0

In this simulation, both our algorithm and Kegl's algorithm achieved high estimation accuracy due to the characteristic of polygonal line approximation. The estimated curve from our algorithm is hard to distinguish from the true generating curve, while the HS algorithm over smoothed the estimated curve and fail to recover the zigzag shape of $f(t)$.

5.3 Piecewise Linear Curves in High Dimensional Space

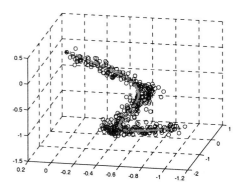

Figure 3. For illustration only, the high dimensional curve (solid line, $n = 3$, $r = 3$) estimated by the local PCA polygonal line algorithm, compared with HS curve.

In previous 2 cases, we focus on the applications of low dimensional data. Now some multivariate data ($d \gg 2$) are analyzed here, as shown in Figure 3 (used for illustration only). For this high dimensional case, the $p = r = 3$ line segments were chosen to be orthogonal and of unit length so that the noise variance size σ_w could be meaningful with respect to $f(t)$ as in the low dimensional experiment situations.

Table 3. Performance comparison

d	N	σ	$d_{HS\,(\times 10^{-3})}$	$d_{LPCA\,(\times 10^{-3})}$
8	100	0.05	5.6	1.2
8	100	0.1	8.5	3.7
8	200	0.05	5.4	0.7
8	200	0.1	7.7	3.0
8	400	0.05	5.3	0.4
8	400	0.1	6.6	2.1
16	100	0.05	7.4	1.5
16	100	0.1	11.9	5.1
16	200	0.05	6.5	0.8
16	200	0.1	10	3.9
16	400	0.05	6.0	0.5
16	400	0.1	7.5	2.3
32	100	0.05	9.9	2.0
32	100	0.1	19.3	7.9
32	200	0.05	9.6	1.1
32	200	0.1	13.1	5.0
32	400	0.05	7.6	0.6
32	400	0.1	10.1	3.1

Experiments gave us results what we expected and demonstrated in the previous case of Table 1~2. Over varying d, N and σ, the local PCA based polygonal line method improved the estimation accuracy than HS algorithm to a great extent. Even in the worst case of $d = 8$, $N = 100$ and $\sigma = 0.1$, our method also provided the estimation error less than the half of the error from the HS estimation, which is a positive improvement on the accuracy or made the calculated curve more close to the generating principal curve.

In a practical sense, the number p of segments plays a more important role in determining the computation complexity than in controlling the curve approximation accuracy, which was shown by the above experiments also. So in real applications where computation time or complexity has high priority than other considerations, it is appropriate to use a smaller number of line segments to estimate the principal curve.

5.4 Nonlinear Pattern Recognition Application

Factor analysis (FA) model assumes that the d-dimensional observation data x is generated as a linear transformation of lower r-dimensional latent variable v plus additive Gaussian noise, that is,

$x = Cv + \mu + w$,

where C is the factor loading matrix and μ is the mean vector. FA as a dimensionality reduction model extracts a linear subspace underlying the observed data. A mixture of FA is an extension of FA [5] by extracting finite r-dimensional locally linear manifolds $x_k = C_k v_k + \mu_k + w$, for $k = 1, 2, \ldots, K$, where K is the total number of local linear subspaces. Mixture of FA thus performs clustering and dimensionality reduction by providing a global nonlinear data model.

The piecewise linear basis model (4) is also applicable to pattern recognition situations as the mixture model, since once the former model is fitted to the data, we can cluster the data by assigning each data point to some finite linear manifold, followed by the general factor analysis in each cluster.

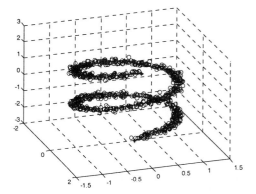

Figure 4. Result by the piecewise principal curves based algorithm for a one-dimensional manifold extraction problem.

Figure 4 shows results of extracting a one-dimensional manifold from three-dimensional noisy spiral data using the piecewise principal curves algorithm by setting $r = 1$ for each subspace. In this case, each factor loading matrix C_k becomes a three-dimensional vector corresponding to each line between two "*" in the plot. As the experimental results in the previous case studies, our nonlinear reduction algorithm successfully extracted the data manifolds and gave the number of mixture subspace $K = 11$ shown in Figure 4, and it also avoid the initialization and parameter boundary problems arising in EM based finite mixture model methods..

6. Conclusion

In this paper, we propose a polygonal line approximation algorithm for nonlinear feature extraction and dimension reduction, in which the local PCA interpretation has been utilized extensively. The extended experimental results with multivariate data indicate that this nonlinear dimensional reduction method outperforms linear techniques. Also the proposed method helps decrease the noise effect in estimation accuracy and computation complexity by approximating the underlying nonlinear curve in a reduced data space. The polygonal line algorithm is believed to be practical and effective to extract nonlinear features from multivariate data sets.

References

[1] J. D. Banfield and A.E. Raftery, "Ice Floe Identification in Satellite Images Using Mathematical Morphology and Clustering about Principal Curves," *JASA* **87**(1992), 7-16.

[2] K. Chang and J. Ghosh, "Principal Curves for Nonlinear Feature Extraction and classification," *SPIE Applications of Artificial Neural Networks in Image Processing* **3307**(1998), 120-129.

[3] Z. Ghahramani and G.E. Hinton, "The EM Algorithm for Mixtures of Factor Analyzers," *Technical Report CRG-TR-96-1*, University of Toronto, 1996.

[4] T. Hastie and W. Stuetzle, "Principal Curves," *Journal of the American Statistical Association* **84**(1989), 502-516.

[5] G. E. Hinton, M. Revow and P. Dayan, "Recognizing Handwritten Digits using Mixtures of Linear Models," *NIPS* **7** (1995), The MIT Press.

[6] N. Kambhatla and T. K. Leen, "Dimension Reduction by Local PCA," *Neural Computation* **9**(1997), 1493-1510.

[7] B. Kégl, A. Krzyzak, T. Linder and K. Zeger, "Learning and Design of Principal Curves," *IEEE TPAMI* **22**(2000), 281-297.

[8] R. Tibshirani, "Principal Curves Revisited," *Statistics and Computing* **2**(1992), 183-190.

[9] M.E. Tipping and C. M. Bishop, "Mixtures of Probabilistic Principal Component Analysers," *Neural Computation* **11**(1999), 443-482.

[10] D. Apley and F. Zhang, "Nonlinear Variation Pattern Identification using Principal Curves Methods," submitted to *IIE Transactions*, 2004.

AVT-NBL: An Algorithm for Learning Compact and Accurate Naïve Bayes Classifiers from Attribute Value Taxonomies and Data

Jun Zhang   and   Vasant Honavar
Artificial Intelligence Research Laboratory
Department of Computer Science
Iowa State University
Ames, Iowa 50011-1040, USA
{jzhang, honavar}@cs.iastate.edu

Abstract

In many application domains, there is a need for learning algorithms that can effectively exploit attribute value taxonomies (AVT) - hierarchical groupings of attribute values - to learn compact, comprehensible, and accurate classifiers from data - including data that are partially specified. This paper describes AVT-NBL, a natural generalization of the Naïve Bayes learner (NBL), for learning classifiers from AVT and data. Our experimental results show that AVT-NBL is able to generate classifiers that are substantially more compact and more accurate than those produced by NBL on a broad range of data sets with different percentages of partially specified values. We also show that AVT-NBL is more efficient in its use of training data: AVT-NBL produces classifiers that outperform those produced by NBL using substantially fewer training examples.

1. Introduction

Synthesis of accurate and compact pattern classifiers from data is one of the major applications of data mining. In a typical inductive learning scenario, instances to be classified are represented as ordered tuples of attribute values. However, attribute values can be grouped together to reflect assumed or actual similarities among the values in a domain of interest or in the context of a specific application. Such a hierarchical grouping of attribute values yields an attribute value taxonomy (AVT). Such AVT are quite common in biological sciences. For example, the Gene Ontology Consortium is developing hierarchical taxonomies for describing many aspects of macromolecular sequence, structure, and function [1]. Undercoffer et al. have developed a hierarchical taxonomy which captures the features that are observable or measurable by the target of an attack or by a

system of sensors acting on behalf of the target [22]. Several ontologies being developed as part of the Semantic Web related efforts [2] also capture hierarchical groupings of attribute values. Kohavi and Provost have noted the need to be able to incorporate background knowledge in the form of hierarchies over data attributes in e-commerce applications of data mining [11]. Against this background, algorithms for learning from AVT and data are of significant practical interest for several reasons:

a. An important goal of machine learning is to discover comprehensible, yet accurate and robust classifiers [18]. The availability of AVT presents the opportunity to learn classification rules that are expressed in terms of *abstract* attribute values leading to simpler, accurate and easier-to-comprehend rules that are expressed using familiar hierarchically related concepts [24] [11].

b. Exploiting AVT in learning classifier can potentially perform regularization to minimize overfitting when learning from relatively small data sets. A common approach used by statisticians when estimating from small samples involves *shrinkage* [15] to estimate the relevant statistics with adequate confidence. Learning algorithms that exploit AVT can potentially perform *shrinkage* automatically thereby yielding robust classifiers and minimizing over-fitting.

c. Presence of explicitly defined AVT allows specification of data at different levels of precision, giving rise to *partially specified instances* [25]. The attribute value of a particular attribute can be specified at different levels of precision in different instances. For example, the medical diagnostic test results given by different institutions are presented at different levels of precision. Partially specified data are unavoidable in knowledge acquisition scenarios which call for integration of information from semantically heterogeneous information sources [4]. Semantic differences between information sources arise as a direct consequence of differences in ontological commitments [2]. Hence, algorithms for learning classifiers from AVT and partially specified data are of great interest.

Against this background, this paper introduces AVT-NBL, an AVT-based generalization of the standard algorithm for learning Naïve Bayes classifiers from partially specified data. The rest of the paper is organized as follows: Section 2 formalizes the notions on learning classifiers with AVT taxonomies; Section 3 presents the AVT-NBL algorithm; Section 4 discusses briefly on alternative approaches; Section 5 describes our experimental results and Section 6 concludes with summary and discussion.

2 Preliminaries

In what follows, we formally define AVT, and its induced instance space. We introduce the notion of partially specified instances, and formalize the problem of learning from AVT and data.

2.1 Attribute Value Taxonomies

Let $\mathbf{A} = \{A_1, A_2, ..., A_N\}$, be an ordered set of attributes and $\mathbf{C} = \{c_1, c_2, ..., c_M\}$ a finite set of mutually disjoint classes. Let $Values(A_i)$ denote the set of values (the domain) of attribute A_i. Instances are represented using ordered tuples of attribute values. Each instance belongs to a class in $\mathbf{C}$.

Let T_i be an Attribute Value Taxonomy $AVT(A_i)$ defined over the possible values of attribute A_i. We use T_i and $AVT(A_i)$ interchangeably to represent AVT for attribute A_i. Let $Nodes(T_i)$ represent the set of all values in T_i, and $Root(T_i)$ stand for the root of T_i. The set of leaves of the tree, $Leaves(T_i) = Values(A_i)$, corresponds to the set of *primitive values* of attribute A_i. The internal nodes of the tree correspond to *abstract values* of attribute A_i. For example, Figure 1 shows two attributes with corresponding AVTs for describing students in terms of their *student status* and *work status*.

We define two operations on AVT T_i associated with an attribute A_i.

- $depth(T_i, v(A_i))$ returns the length of the path from root to an attribute value $v(A_i)$ in the taxonomy;

- $leaf(T_i, v(A_i))$ returns a Boolean value indicating if $v(A_i)$ is a leaf node in T_i, that is if $v(A_i) \in Leaves(T_i)$.

After Haussler [9], we define a cut γ_i for $AVT(A_i)$ as follows.

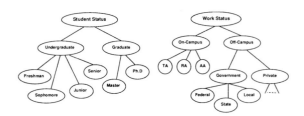

Figure 1. Illustrative taxonomies on student status and work status

Definition 1 (Cut) *A cut γ_i is a subset of elements in $AVT(A_i)$ satisfying the following two properties: (1) For any leaf $l \in Leaves(T_i)$, either $l \in \gamma_i$ or l is a descendant of an element $n \in \gamma_i$; and (2) For any two nodes $f, g \in \gamma_i$, f is neither a descendant nor an ancestor of g.*

A cut γ_i induces a partition of elements of $Values(A_i)$. For example in Figure 1, {*On-Campus, Government, Private*} defines a partition over the primitive values of the *work status* attribute.

Let $\mathbf{T} = \{T_1, T_2, ..., T_N\}$ denote the ordered set of AVTs associated with $A_1, A_2, \cdots A_N$. For each T_i, define Δ_i to be the set of all valid cuts in T_i. Let $\boldsymbol{\Delta} = \times_i \Delta_i$ denote the cartesian product of the cuts through the individual AVTs. Let $\Gamma = \{\gamma_1, \gamma_2, ..., \gamma_N\}$ be an ordered set that defines a global cut through $T_1, T_2, \cdots T_N$ accordingly, where $\gamma_i \in \Delta_i$ and $\Gamma \in \boldsymbol{\Delta}$.

Let $\psi(v, T_i)$ be the set of descendants of a node corresponding to value v in the AVT T_i; $\pi(v, T_i)$, the set of all children (direct descendants) of a node with value v in T_i; $\Lambda(v, T_i)$ the list of ancestors, including the root, for v in T_i.

Definition 2 (Refinements) *We say that a cut $\hat{\gamma}_i$ is a refinement of a cut γ_i if $\hat{\gamma}_i$ is obtained by replacing at least one attribute value $v \in \gamma_i$ by its descendants $\psi(v, T_i)$. Conversely, γ_i is an abstraction of $\hat{\gamma}_i$. We say that a set of cuts $\hat{\Gamma}$ is a refinement of a set of cuts Γ if at least one cut in $\hat{\Gamma}$ is a refinement of a cut in Γ. Conversely, the set of cuts Γ is an abstraction of the set of cuts $\hat{\Gamma}$.*

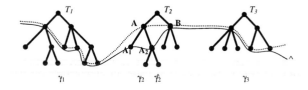

Figure 2. A demonstrative refinement process

Figure 2 illustrates a refinement process. $\gamma_2 = \{A, B\}$ in T_2 has been refined to $\hat{\gamma}_2 = \{A_1, A_2, B\}$ by replacing A with its two children A_1, A_2. Therefore, $\hat{\Gamma} = \{\gamma_1, \hat{\gamma}_2, \gamma_3\}$ is a refinement of $\Gamma = \{\gamma_1, \gamma_2, \gamma_3\}$.

2.2 AVT-Induced Instance Space

Definition 3 (Abstract Instance Space) *Any choice* Γ *of* $\Delta = \times_i \Delta_i$ *defines an abstract instance space* $\mathbf{I}_\Gamma$. *When* $\exists i \, \gamma_i \in \Gamma$ *such that* $\gamma_i \neq Leaves(T_i)$, *the resulting instance space is an abstraction of the original instance space* **I**. *The original instance space is given by* $\mathbf{I} = \mathbf{I}_{\Gamma_0}$, *where* $\forall i \, \gamma_i \in \Gamma_0$, $\gamma_i = Values(A_i) = Leaves(T_i)$, *that is, the primitive values of the attributes* $A_1 \cdots A_N$.

Definition 4 (AVT-Induced Abstract Instance Space) *A set of AVTs* $\mathbf{T} = \{T_1 \cdots T_N\}$ *associated with a set of attributes* $\mathbf{A} = \{A_1 \cdots A_N\}$ *induces an instance space* $\mathbf{I_A} = \cup_{\Gamma \in \Delta} \mathbf{I}_\Gamma$ *(the union of instance spaces induced by all of the the cuts through the set of AVTs* $\mathbf{T}$*).*

2.3 Partially Specified Data

Definition 5 (Partially Specified Data) *An instance* X_j *is represented by a tuple* $= (v_{1j}, v_{2j}, ..., v_{Nj})$. X_j *is:*

- *a completely specified instance if* $\forall i \, v_{ij} \in Leaves(T_i)$
- *a partially specified instance if one or more of its attribute values are not primitive:* $\exists v_{ij} \in X_j$, $depth(T_i, v_{ij}) \geq 0 \wedge \neg leaf(T_i, v_{ij})$

Thus, a partially specified instance is an instance in which at least one of the attributes is partially specified. Relative to the AVT shown in Figure 1, the instance (*Senior, TA*) is a fully specified instance. Some examples of partially specified instances are: (*Undergraduate, RA*), (*Freshman, Government*), (*Graduate, Off-Campus*).

Definition 6 (A Partially Specified Data Set) *A partially specified data set* $\mathbf{D_T}$ *(relative to a set* $\mathbf{T}$ *of attribute value taxonomies) is a collection of instances drawn from* $\mathbf{I_A}$ *where each instance is labelled with the appropriate class label from* **C***. Thus,* $\mathbf{D_T} \subseteq \mathbf{I_A} \times \mathbf{C}$.

2.4 Learning Classifiers from Data

The problem of learning classifiers from AVT and data is a natural generalization of the problem of learning classifiers from data without AVT. The original data set D is simply a collection of labelled instances of the form (X_j, c_j) where $X_j \in \mathbf{I} = \times_i Values(A_i) = \times_i Leaves(T_i)$, and $c_j \in \mathbf{C}$ is a class label. A classifier is a hypothesis in the form of a function $h : \mathbf{I} \to \mathbf{C}$, whose domain is the instance space **I** and whose range is the set of classes **C**. A hypothesis space **H** is a set of hypotheses that can be represented in some hypothesis language or by a parameterized family of functions (e.g., decision trees, Naive Bayes classifiers, SVM, etc.). The task of learning classifiers from the original data set D entails identifying a hypothesis $h \in \mathbf{H}$ that

satisfies some criteria (e.g., a hypothesis that is most likely given the training data D).

The problem of learning classifiers from AVT and data can be stated as follows: Given a user-supplied set of AVTs **T** and a data set $\mathbf{D_T}$ of (possibly) partially specified labelled instances, construct a classifier $h_T : \mathbf{I_A} \to \mathbf{C}$ for assigning appropriate class labels to each instance in the instance space $\mathbf{I_A}$. Of special interest are the cases in which the resulting hypothesis space $\mathbf{H_T}$ has structure that makes it possible to search it efficiently for a hypothesis that is both concise as well as accurate.

3 AVT-Based Naïve Bayes Learner

3.1 Naïve Bayes Learner (NBL)

Suppose each attribute A_i takes a value from a finite set of values $Values(A_i)$. An instance X_p to be classified is represented as a tuple of attribute values $(v_{1p}, v_{2p}, \cdots, v_{Np})$ where each $v_{ip} \in Values(A_i)$. The Bayesian approach to classifying X_p is to assign it the most probable class $c_{MAP}(X_p)$. Naïve Bayes classifier operates under the assumption that each attribute is independent of others given the class. Hence, we have:

$$
\begin{aligned}
c_{MAP}(X_p) &= \underset{c_j \in C}{\mathrm{argmax}} \, P(v_{1p}, v_{2p}, \cdots, v_{Np} | c_j) p(c_j) \\
&= \underset{c_j \in C}{\mathrm{argmax}} \, p(c_j) \prod_i P(v_{ip} | c_j)
\end{aligned}
$$

Hence, the task of the Naive Bayes Learner (NBL) is to estimate $\forall c_j \in \mathbf{C}$ and $\forall v_{i_k} \in Values(A_i)$, relevant class probabilities $p(c_j)$ and the class conditional probabilities $P(v_{i_k} | c_j)$ from training data D. These probabilities, which completely specify a Naive Bayes classifier, can be estimated from D using standard probability estimation methods [17] based on relative frequencies of the corresponding classes and attribute value and class label cooccurrences observed in D. These relative frequencies summarize *all* the information relevant for constructing a Naive Bayes classifier from a training set D, and hence constitute *sufficient statistics* for NBL [3, 4].

3.2 AVT-NBL

Given a user-supplied ordered set of AVTs $\mathbf{T} = \{T_1, \cdots, T_N\}$ corresponding to the attributes $A_1 \cdots A_N$ and a data set $D = \{(X_p, c_p)\}$ of labelled examples of the form (X_p, c_p) where $X_p \in \mathbf{I_A}$ is a partially or fully specified instance and $c_p \in \mathbf{C}$ is the corresponding class label, the task of AVT-NBL is to construct a Naïve Bayes classifier for assigning X_p to its most probable class $c_{MAP}(X_p)$. As in the case of NBL, we assume that each attribute is independent of the other attributes given the class.

Let $\Gamma = \{\gamma_1, \gamma_2, \cdots, \gamma_N\}$ be a set of cuts where, γ_i stands for a cut through T_i. A Naive Bayes classifier defined on the instance space $\mathbf{I}_\Gamma$ is completely specified by a set of class conditional probabilities for each value of each attribute. Suppose we denote the table of class conditional probabilities associated with values in γ_i by $CPT(\gamma_i)$. Then the Naive Bayes classifier defined over the instance space $\mathbf{I}_\Gamma$ is specified by $h(\Gamma) = \{CPT(\gamma_1), CPT(\gamma_2), \cdots, CPT(\gamma_N)\}$.

If each cut $\gamma_i \in \Gamma$ is chosen to correspond to the primitive values of the respective attribute i.e., $\forall i\, \gamma_i = Leaves(T_i)$, $h(\Gamma)$ is simply the standard Naïve Bayes Classifier based on the attributes $A_1, A_2, \cdots, A_N$. If each cut $\gamma_i \in \Gamma$ is chosen to pass through the root of each AVT, i.e., $\forall i\, \gamma_i = \{Root(T_i)\}$, $h(\Gamma)$ simply assigns each instance to the class that is a priori most probable.

AVT-NBL starts with the Naïve Bayes Classifier that is based on the most abstract value of each attribute (the most general hypothesis in $\mathbf{H_T}$) and successively refines the classifier (hypothesis) using a criterion that is designed to tradeoff between the accuracy of classification and the complexity of the resulting Naïve Bayes classifier. Successive refinements of Γ correspond to a partial ordering of Naive Bayes classifiers based on the structure of the AVTs in $\mathbf{T}$. For example, in Figure 2, $\hat{\Gamma}$ is a refinement of Γ, and hence corresponding hypothesis $h(\hat{\Gamma})$ is a refinement of $h(\Gamma)$

3.2.1 Class Conditional Frequency Counts

Let $\sigma_i(v|c_j)$ be the frequency count of value v of attribute A_i given class label c_j in a training set D and $p_i(v|c_j)$, the estimated class conditional probability of value v of attribute A_i given class label c_j in a training set D.

Given an attribute value taxonomy T_i for attribute A_i, we can define a tree of class conditional frequency counts $CCFC(A_i)$ such that there is a one-to-one correspondence between the nodes of the AVT T_i and the nodes of the corresponding $CCFC(A_i)$. It follows that the class conditional frequency counts associated with a non leaf node of $CCFC(A_i)$ should correspond the aggregation of the corresponding class conditional frequency counts associated with its children. Because each cut through an AVT T_i corresponds to a partition of the set of possible values $Nodes(A_i)$ of the attribute A_i, the corresponding cut through $CCFC(A_i)$ specifies a valid class conditional probability table for the attribute A_i.

When all of the instances in the data set D are fully specified, estimation of $CCFC(A_i)$ for each attribute is straightforward: we simply estimate the class conditional frequency counts associated with each of the primitive values of A_i from the data set D and use them recursively to compute the class conditional frequency counts associated with the non-leaf nodes of $CCFC(A_i)$. When some of the

data are partially specified, we can use a 2-step process for computing $CCFC(A_i)$: First we make an upward pass aggregating the class conditional frequency counts based on the specified attribute values in the data set. Then we propagate the counts associated with partially specified attribute values down through the tree, augmenting the counts at lower levels according to the distribution of values along the branches based on the subset of the data for which the corresponding values are fully specified. This procedure is a simplified case of EM (Expectation Maximization) algorithm to estimate expected sufficient statistics for $CCFC(A_i)$. The procedure is shown below.

1. Calculate frequency counts $\sigma_i(v|c_j)$ for each node v in T_i using the class conditional frequency counts associated with the specified values of attribute A_i in training set D.

2. For each attribute value v in T_i which received non-zero counts as a result of step 1, aggregate the counts upward from each such node v to its ancestors $\Lambda(v, T_i)$:
$\sigma_i(w|c_j)_{w \in \Lambda(v,T_i)} \leftarrow \sigma_i(w|c_j) + \sigma_i(v|c_j)$

3. Starting from the root, recursively propagate the counts corresponding to partially specified instances at each node v downward according to the observed distribution among its children to obtain updated counts for each child $u_l \in \pi(v, T_i)$:

$$\sigma_i(u_l|c_j) \leftarrow \sigma_i(u_l|c_j)\left(1 + \frac{\sigma_i(v|c_j) - \sum_{k=1}^{|\pi(v,T_i)|}\sigma_i(u_k|c_j)}{\sum_{k=1}^{|\pi(v,T_i)|}\sigma_i(u_k|c_j)}\right)$$

$$If \sum_{k=1}^{|\pi(v,T_i)|}\sigma_i(u_k|c_j) \neq 0;$$

$$\sigma_i(u_l|c_j) \leftarrow \left(\frac{v_i(v|c_j)}{|\pi(v,T_i)|}\right) Otherwise.$$

Let $\Gamma = \{\gamma_1, \cdots, \gamma_N\}$ be a set of cuts where γ_i stands for a cut through $CCFC(A_i)$. The estimated conditional probability table $CPT(\gamma_i)$ associated with the cut γ_i can be calculated from $CCFC(A_i)$ using Laplace estimates [17, 12].

$$p_i(v|c_j)_{v \in \gamma_i} \leftarrow \frac{1/|D| + \sigma_i(v|c_j)}{|\gamma_i|/|D| + \sum_{u \in \gamma_i}\sigma_i(u|c_j)}$$

Recall that the Naïve Bayes Classifier $h(\Gamma)$ based on a chosen set of cuts Γ is completely specified by the conditional probability tables associated with the cuts in Γ: $h(\Gamma) = \{CPT(\gamma_1), \cdots, CPT(\gamma_N)\}$.

3.2.2 Searching for a Compact Naïve Bayes Classifier

We use a variant of the minimum description length (MDL) principle [20] to capture the tradeoff between the complexity and accuracy of Naive Bayes classifiers that correspond to different choices of cuts through the AVTs. Friedman et al [8] suggested the use of a conditional MDL (CMDL) score in the case of hypotheses that are used for classification (as opposed to modelling the joint probability distribution of a set of random variables) to capture this tradeoff. In general, computation of CMDL score is not feasible for Bayesian networks with arbitrary structure. However, in the case of Naive Bayes classifiers induced by a set of AVT, as shown below, it is possible to efficiently calculate the CMDL score.

$$CMDL(h|D) = \left(\frac{\log|D|}{2}\right) size(h) - CLL(h|D)$$

$$where, CLL(h|D) = |D| \sum_{p=1}^{|D|} \log P_h(c_p|v_{1p}, \cdots, v_{Np})$$

Here, $P_h(c_p|v_{1p}, \cdots, v_{Np})$ denotes the conditional probability assigned to the class $c_p \in C$ associated with the training sample $X_p = (v_{1p}, v_{2p}, \cdots, v_{Np})$ by the classifier h, $size(h)$ is the number of parameters used by h, $|D|$ the size of the data set, and $CLL(h|D)$ is the conditional log likelihood of the data D given a hypothesis h. In the case of a Naïve Bayes classifier h, $size(h)$ corresponds to the total number of class conditional probabilities needed to describe h. Because each attribute is assumed to be independent of the others given the class in a Naïve Bayes classifier, we have:

$$CLL(h|D) = |D| \sum_{p=1}^{|D|} \log\left(\frac{P(c_p) \prod_i P_h(v_{ip}|c_p)}{\sum_{j=1}^{|C|} P(c_j) \prod_i P_h(v_{ip}|c_j)}\right)$$

where $P(c_p)$ is the prior probability of the class c_p which can be estimated from the observed class distribution in the data D.

There are two cases in the calculation of the conditional likelihood $CLL(h|D)$ when D contains partially specified instances. The first case is when a partially specified value of attribute A_i for an instance lies on the cut γ through $CCFC(A_i)$ or corresponds to one of the descendants of the nodes in the cut. In this case, we can treat that instance as though it were fully specified relative to the Naïve Bayes classifier based on the cut γ of $CCFC(A_i)$ and use the class conditional probabilities associated with the cut γ to calculate its contribution to $CLL(h|D)$. The second case is when a partially specified value (say v) of A_i is an ancestor of a subset (say λ) of the nodes in γ. In this case, $p(v|c_j) = \sum_{u_i \in \lambda} p(u_i|c_j)$, such that we can aggregate the class conditional probabilities of the nodes in λ to calculate the contribution of the corresponding instance to $CLL(h|D)$.

Because each attribute is assumed to be independent of others given the class, the search for the AVT-based Naïve Bayes classifier (AVT-NBC) can be performed efficiently by optimizing the criterion independently for each attribute. This results in a hypothesis h that intuitively trades off the complexity of Naïve Bayes classifier (in terms of the number of parameters used to describe the relevant class conditional probabilities) against accuracy of classification. The algorithm terminates when none of the candidate refinements of the classifier yield statistically significant improvement in the CMDL score. The procedure is outlined below.

1. Initialize each γ_i in $\Gamma = \{\gamma_1, \gamma_2, \cdots, \gamma_N\}$ to $\{Root(T_i)\}$.

2. Estimate probabilities that specify the hypothesis $h(\Gamma)$.

3. For each cut γ_i in $\Gamma = \{\gamma_1, \gamma_2, \cdots, \gamma_N\}$:

   A. Set $\delta_i \leftarrow \gamma_i$

   B. Until there are no updates to γ_i

      i. For each $v \in \delta_i$

         a. Generate a refinement γ_i^v of γ_i by replacing v with $\pi(v, T_i)$, and refine Γ accordingly to obtain $\hat{\Gamma}$. Construct corresponding hypothesis $h(\hat{\Gamma})$

         b. If $CMDL(h(\hat{\Gamma})|D) < CMDL(h(\Gamma)|D)$, replace Γ with $\hat{\Gamma}$ and γ_i with γ_i^v

      ii. $\delta_i \leftarrow \gamma_i$

4. Output $h(\Gamma)$

4 Alternative Approaches to Learning Classifiers from AVT and Data

Besides AVT-NBL, we can envision two alternative approaches to learning classifiers from AVT and data:

The first approach is to treat each partially specified (and hence partially missing) attribute value as if it were (totally) missing, and handle the resulting data set with missing attribute values using standard approaches for dealing with missing attribute values in learning classifiers. A main advantage of this approach is that it requires no modification to NBL.

A second approach to learn classifiers from AVT and data uses AVT to construct a set of Boolean attributes from each (original) attribute A_i, a set of boolean attributes corresponds to nodes in T_i. Thus, each instance in the original data set defined using N attributes is turned into a Boolean instance specified using $\tilde{N}$ Boolean attributes where $\tilde{N} = \sum_{i=1}^{N} |Nodes(A_i)|$. The Boolean attributes that correspond to descendants of the partially specified attribute value are treated as unknown.

Note that the Boolean features created by the propositionalization technique described above are not independent given the class. A Boolean attribute that corresponds to any node in an AVT is necessarily correlated with Boolean attributes that correspond to its descendants as well as its ancestors in the tree. For example, the boolean attribute (Student Status = *Undergraduate*) is correlated with (Student Status = *Junior*). (Indeed, it is this correlation that enables us to exploit the information provided by AVT in learning classifiers from AVT and data). Thus, a Naïve Bayes classifier that would be optimal in the Maximal a Posteriori sense [14] when the original attributes are independent given class, would no longer be optimal when applied to *propositionalized* data sets because of the strong dependencies among the Boolean attributes derived from an AVT.

5 Experiments and Results

Our experiments were designed to explore the performance of AVT-NBL relative to that of the standard Naïve Bayes algorithm (NBL) and a Naïve Bayes Learner applied to a propositionalized version of the data set (PROP-NBL).

Although partially specified data and hierarchical AVT are common in many application domains, at present, there are few standard benchmark data sets of partially specified data and the associated AVT. We select 8 data sets (with only nominal attributes) from the UC Irvine Machine Learning Repository. For three of them (i.e., *Mushroom*, *Soybean*, and *Nursery*), AVTs were supplied by domain experts. For the rest data sets, the AVTs were generated using AVT-Learner, a Hierarchical Agglomerative Clustering (HAC) algorithm to construct AVTs [10].

The first set of experiments compares the performance of AVT-NBL, NBL, and PROP-NBL on the original (fully specified) data. The second set of experiments explores the performance of the algorithms on data sets with different percentages of totally missing and partially missing attribute values. Three data sets with a pre-specified percentage (10%, 30%, or 50%) of totally or partially missing attribute values were generated by assuming that the missing values are uniformly distributed on the nominal attributes [25]. In each case, the error rate and the size (as measured by the number of class conditional probabilities used to specify the learned classifier) were estimated using 10-fold cross-validation, and we calculate 90% confidence interval on the error rate.

A third set of experiments were designed to investigate the performance of classifiers generated by AVT-NBL, Prop-NBL, and NBL as a function of the training set size. We divided each data set into two disjoint parts: a training pool and a test pool. Training sets of different sizes, corresponding to 10%, 20%, ..., 100% of the training pool, were sampled and used to train Naïve Bayes classifier using AVT-NBL, Prop-NBL, and NBL. The resulting classifiers were evaluated on the entire test pool. The experiment was repeated 9 times for each training set size. The entire process was repeated using 3 different random partitions of data into training and test pools. The accuracy of the learned classifiers on the examples in the test pool were averaged across the 9×3=27 runs.

5.1 Results

AVT-NBL yields lower error rates than NBL and PROP-NBL on the original fully specified data. Table 1 shows the estimated error rates of the classifiers generated by the AVT-NBL, NBL, and PROP-NBL on 8 original benchmark data sets. The error rate of AVT-NBL is substantially smaller than that of NBL and PROP-NBL, with the differ-

ence in error rates being most pronounced in the case of *Mushroom, Soybean, Audiology* and *Zoo* data. It is worth noting that PROP-NBL (NBL applied to a transformed data set using Boolean features that correspond to nodes of the AVTs) generally produces classifiers that have higher error rates than NBL. This can be explained by the fact that the Boolean features generated from an AVT are generally not independent given the class.

Table 1. Comparison of error rate and size of classifiers generated by NBL, PROP-NBL and AVT-NBL on benchmark data

% Error rates using 10-fold cross validation with 90% confidence interval; The size of the classifiers for each data set is constant for NBL and Prop-NBL, and for AVT-NBL, the size shown represents the average across the 10-cross validation experiments.

DATA SET	NBL		PROP-NBL		AVT-NBL	
	ERROR	SIZE	ERROR	SIZE	ERROR	SIZE
Audiology	26.55 (±5.31)	3696	27.87 (±5.39)	8184	23.01 (±5.06)	3600
Breast-Cancer	28.32 (±4.82)	84	27.27 (±4.76)	338	27.62 (±4.78)	62
Car	14.47 (±1.53)	88	15.45 (±1.57)	244	13.83 (±1.50)	80
Dermatology	2.18 (±1.38)	876	1.91 (±1.29)	2790	2.18 (±1.38)	576
Mushroom	4.43 (±1.30)	252	4.45 (±1.30)	682	0.14 (±0.14)	202
Nursery	9.67 (±1.48)	135	10.59 (±1.54)	355	9.67 (±1.48)	125
Soybean	7.03 (±1.60)	1900	8.19 (±1.72)	4959	5.71 (±1.45)	1729
Zoo	6.93 (±4.57)	259	5.94 (±4.25)	567	3.96 (±3.51)	245

Table 2. Comparison of error rates on data with partially or totally missing values

% Error rates using 10-fold cross validation with 90% confidence interval

DATA METHODS		PARTIALLY MISSING			TOTALLY MISSING		
		NBL	PROP-NBL	AVT-NBL	NBL	PROP-NBL	AVT-NBL
MUSHROOM	10%	4.65(±1.33)	4.69(±1.34)	0.30(±0.30)	4.65(±1.33)	4.76(±1.35)	1.29(±071)
	30%	5.28 (±1.41)	4.84(±1.36)	0.64(±0.50)	5.28 (±1.41)	5.37(±1.43)	2.78(±1.04)
	50%	6.63(±1.57)	5.82(±1.48)	1.24(±0.70)	6.63(±1.57)	6.98(±1.61)	4.61(±1.33)
NURSERY	10%	15.27(±1.81)	15.50(±1.82)	12.85(±1.67)	15.27(±1.81)	16.53(±1.86)	13.24(±1.70)
	30%	26.84(±2.23)	26.25(±2.21)	21.19(±2.05)	26.84(±2.23)	27.65(±2.24)	22.48(±2.09)
	50%	36.96(±2.43)	35.88(±2.41)	29.34(±2.29)	36.96(±2.43)	38.66(±2.45)	32.51(±2.35)
SOYBEAN	10%	8.76(±1.76)	9.08(±1.79)	6.75(±1.57)	8.76(±1.76)	9.09(±1.79)	6.88(±1.58)
	30%	12.45(±2.07)	11.54(±2.00)	10.32(±1.90)	12.45(±2.07)	12.31(±2.05)	10.41(±1.91)
	50%	19.39(±2.47)	16.91(±2.34)	16.93(±2.34)	19.39 (±2.47)	19.59(±2.48)	17.97(±2.40)

AVT-NBL yields classifiers that are substantially more compact than those generated by PROP-NBL and NBL. The shaded columns in Table 1 compare the total number of class conditional probabilities needed to specify the classifiers produced by AVT-NBL, NBL, and PROP-NBL on original data. The results show that AVT-NBL is effective in exploiting the information supplied by the AVT to generate accurate yet compact classifiers. Thus, AVT-guided learning algorithms offer an approach to compressing class conditional probability distributions that is different from the statistical independence-based factorization used in Bayesian Networks.

AVT-NBL yields significantly lower error rates than NBL and PROP-NBL on partially specified data and data with totally missing values. Table 2 compares the estimated error rates of AVT-NBL with that of NBL and PROP-NBL in the presence of varying percentages (10%,

30% and 50%) of partially missing attribute values and totally missing attribute values. Naïve Bayes classifiers generated by AVT-NBL have substantially lower error rates than those generated by NBL and PROP-NBL, with the differences being more pronounced at higher percentages of partially (or totally) missing attribute values.

AVT-NBL produces more accurate classifiers than NBL and Prop-NBL for a given training set size. Figure 3 shows the plot of the accuracy of the classifiers learned as a function of training set size for *Audiology* data. We obtained similar results on other benchmark data sets used in this study. Thus, AVT-NBL is *more efficient* than NBL and Prop-NBL in its use of training data.

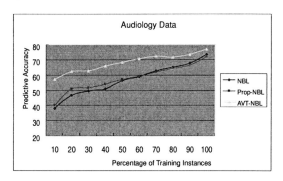

Figure 3. Classifier accuracy as a function of training set size

6 Summary and Discussion

6.1 Summary

In this paper, we have described AVT-NBL [1], an algorithm for learning classifiers from attribute value taxonomies (AVT) and data. Our experimental results show that AVT-NBL is able to generate classifiers that are substantially more compact and accurate than those produced by NBL on a broad range of data sets with different percentages of partially specified values. We also show that AVT-NBL is more efficient in its use of training data: AVT-NBL produces classifiers that outperform those produced by NBL using substantially fewer training examples. Thus, AVT-NBL offers an effective approach to learning compact (hence more comprehensible) accurate classifiers from data - including data that are *partially specified*. AVT-guided learning algorithms offer a promising approach to knowledge acquisition from autonomous, semantically heterogeneous information sources, where domain specific AVTs are often available and data are often partially specified.

6.2 Related Work

There is some work in the machine learning community on the problem of learning classifiers from attribute value taxonomies (sometimes called tree-structured attributes) and fully specified data in the case of decision trees and rules (see [25] for a review) desJardins et al [7] suggested the use of Abstraction-Based Search (ABS) to learn Bayesian networks with compact structure. Zhang and Honavar [25] describe AVT-DTL, an efficient algorithm for learning decision tree classifiers from AVT and partially specified data. With the exception of AVT-DTL, to the best of our knowledge, there are no algorithms for learning classifiers from AVT and partially specified data.

There has been some work on the use of class taxonomy (CT) in the learning of classifiers in scenarios where class labels correspond to nodes in a predefined class hierarchy [6][13].

There is a large body of work on the use of domain theories to guide learning. AVT can be viewed as a restricted class of domain theories. However, the work on exploiting domain theories in learning has not focused on the effective use of AVT to learn classifiers from partially specified data.

Chen et al. [5] proposed database models to handle imprecision using partial values and associated probabilities where a partial value refers to a set of possible values for an attribute. McClean et al [16] proposed aggregation operators defined over partial values. While this work suggests ways to aggregate statistics so as to minimize information loss, it does not address the problem of learning from AVT and partially specified data.

Automated construction of hierarchical taxonomies over attribute values and class labels is beginning to receive attention in the machine learning community. Examples include distributional clustering [19], extended FOCL and statistical clustering [23], information bottleneck [21]. Such algorithms provide a source of AVT in domains where none are available. The focus of work described in this paper is on algorithms that use AVT in learning classifiers from data.

6.3 Future Work

Some directions for future work include:

(1) Development AVT-based variants of other machine learning algorithms for construction of classifiers from partially specified data from distributed, semantically heterogeneous data sources [3][4].

(2) Extension of the algorithms like AVT-DTL and AVT-NBL to handle taxonomies defined over ordered and numeric attribute values.

---

[1]A Java implementation of AVT-NBL and the data sets and AVTs used in this study are available at:
http://www.cs.iastate.edu/~jzhang/ICDM04/index.html

(3) Further experimental evaluation of AVT-NBL, AVT-DTL, and related learning algorithms on a broad range of data sets in scientific knowledge discovery applications e.g., computational biology.

Acknowledgments

This research was supported in part by grants from the National Science Foundation (NSF IIS 0219699) and the National Institutes of Health (GM 066387).

References

[1] M. Ashburner, et al. Gene ontology: tool for the unification of biology. The Gene Ontology Consortium. Nat Genet. 25(1), 2000.

[2] T. Berners-Lee, J. Hendler and O. Lassila. The semantic web. Scientific American, May 2001.

[3] D. Caragea, A. Silvescu, and V. Honavar. A Framework for Learning from Distributed Data Using Sufficient Statistics and its Application to Learning Decision Trees. International Journal of Hybrid Intelligent Systems. Vol. 1 2004.

[4] D. Caragea, J. Pathak, and V. Honavar. Learning Classifiers from Semantically Heterogeneous Data. In: Proceedings of the 3rd International Conference on Ontologies, Databases, and Applications of Semantics for Large Scale Information Systems, ODBASE-2004.

[5] A. Chen, J. Chiu, and F. Tseng. Evaluating aggregate operations over imprecise data. IEEE Trans. On Knowledge and Data Engineering, 8, 1996.

[6] A. Clare, R. King. Knowledge Discovery in Multi-label Phenotype Data. In: Lecture Notes in Computer Science. Vol. 2168, 2001.

[7] M. desJardins, L. Getoor, D. Koller. Using Feature Hierarchies in Bayesian Network Learning. Lecture Notes in Artificial Intelligence 1864, 2000.

[8] N. Friedman, D. Geiger. Goldszmidt, M.: Bayesian Network Classifiers. Machine Learning, Vol: 29, 1997.

[9] D. Haussler. Quantifying Inductive Bias: AI Learning Algorithms and Valiant's Learning Framework. Artificial Intelligence, 36, 1988.

[10] D. Kang, A. Silvescu, J. Zhang, and V. Honavar. Generation of Attribute Value Taxonomies from Data for Data-Driven Construction of Accurate and Compact Classifiers. To appear: Proceedings of The Fourth IEEE International Conference on Data Mining, 2004.

[11] R. Kohavi, P. Provost. Applications of Data Mining to Electronic Commerce. Data Mining and Knowledge Discovery, Vol. 5, 2001.

[12] R. Kohavi, B. Becker, D. Sommerfield. Improving simple Bayes. Tech. Report, Data Mining and Visualization Group, Silicon Graphics Inc., 1997.

[13] D. Koller, M. Sahami. Hierarchically classifying documents using very few words. In: Proceedings of the 14th Int'l Conference on Machine Learning, 1997.

[14] P. Langley, W. Iba, K. Thompson. An analysis of Bayesian classifiers Proceedings of the Tenth National Conference on Artificial Intelligence, 1992.

[15] A. McCallum, R. Rosenfeld, T. Mitchell, A. Ng. Improving Text Classification by Shrinkage in a Hierarchy of Classes. Proceedings of the 15th Int'l Conference on Machine Learning, 1998.

[16] S. McClean, B. Scotney, M. Shapcott. Aggregation of Imprecise and Uncertain Information in Databases. IEEE Transactions on Knowledge and Data Engineering (6), 2001.

[17] T. Mitchell. Machine Learning. Addison-Wesley, 1997.

[18] M. Pazzani, S. Mani, W. Shankle. Beyond concise and colorful: Learning Intelligible Rules. In Proceedings of the 4th International Conference on Knowledge Discovery and Data Mining, 1997.

[19] F. Pereira, N. Tishby, L. Lee. Distributional clustering of English words. In: Proceedings of the Thirty-first Annual Meeting of the Association for Computational Linguistics, 1993.

[20] J. Rissanen. Modeling by shortest data description. Automatica, vol. 14, 1978.

[21] N. Slonim, N. Tishby. Document Clustering using Word Clusters via the Information Bottleneck Method. ACM SIGIR, 2000.

[22] J. Undercoffer, et al. A Target Centric Ontology for Intrusion Detection: Using DAML+OIL to Classify Intrusive Behaviors. To appear, Knowledge Engineering Review - Special Issue on Ontologies for Distributed Systems, Cambridge University Press, 2004.

[23] T. Yamazaki, M. Pazzani, C. Merz. Learning Hierarchies from Ambiguous Natural Language Data. In: Proceedings of the 12th Int'l Conference on Machine Learning, 1995.

[24] J. Zhang, A. Silvescu, and V. Honavar. Ontology-Driven Induction of Decision Trees at Multiple Levels of Abstraction. Proceedings of Symposium on Abstraction, Reformulation, and Approximation 2002. Lecture Notes in Artificial Intelligence 2371, 2002.

[25] J. Zhang, V. Honavar. Learning From Attribute Value Taxonomies and Partially Specified Instances. In: Proceedings of the 20th Int'l Conference on Machine Learning, 2003.

Cost-Guided Class Noise Handling for Effective Cost-Sensitive Learning

Xingquan Zhu   and   Xindong Wu

Department of Computer Science, University of Vermont, Burlington VT 05405, USA
{xqzhu, xwu}@cs.uvm.edu

Abstract

Recent research in machine learning, data mining and related areas has produced a wide variety of algorithms for cost-sensitive (CS) classification, where instead of maximizing the classification accuracy, minimizing the misclassification cost becomes the objective. However, these methods assume that training sets do not contain significant noise, which is rarely the case in real-world environments. In this paper, we systematically study the impacts of class noise on CS learning, and propose a cost-guided class noise handling algorithm to identify noise for effective CS learning. We call it Cost-guided Iterative Classification Filter (CICF), because it seamlessly integrates costs and an existing Classification Filter [1] for noise identification. Instead of putting equal weights to handle noise in all classes in existing efforts, CICF puts more emphasis on expensive classes, which makes it especially successful in dealing with datasets with a large cost-ratio. Experimental results and comparative studies from real-world datasets indicate that the existence of noise may seriously corrupt the performance of CS classifiers, and by adopting the proposed CICF algorithm, we can significantly reduce the misclassification cost of a CS classifier in noisy environments.

1. Introduction

Inductive learning such as rule and decision tree induction, linear and neural classifiers, and Bayesian learning usually aims at forming a generalized description of a given set of data, so that further unseen instances can be classified with a minimal error rate. A common assumption behind these algorithms is that all errors have the same cost, which is seldom the case in real-world problems. For example, in medical diagnosis, the errors committed in diagnosing a patient as healthy when he/she actually has a life-threatening disease is usually considered to be far more serious (thus, a higher cost) than the opposite type of error – diagnosing a patient as ill when he/she is in fact healthy.

Recently a body of work has attempted to address this issue, with techniques known as cost-sensitive learning [2-6], where the "cost" could be interpreted as misclassification cost, training cost, test cost, or others [7]. Among all different types of costs, the misclassification cost is the most popular one. In general, misclassification cost is described by a cost matrix C, with $C(i,j)$ indicting the cost of predicting that an example belongs to class i when in fact it belongs to class j. With this type of cost, the objective of a CS learner is to form a generalization from training instances such that the average cost on previously unobserved instances is minimized. Obviously, this minimal cost is determined by two most important factors: (1) the inductive bias of the CS learner; and (2) the quality of the training data.

Many efforts have been conducted to explore efficient CS learning algorithms. Roughly, these efforts fall into two categories: (1) developing specific learners or effective pruning mechanisms for cost-sensitive classification [2][6][8][12], which includes the methods specific for decision trees [2][6][8], neural networks [12] etc.; and (2) making a normal classifier cost-sensitive [4][10-11], including using Bayes theory to wrap the training instances with the lowest expected cost class [4] or using sampling mechanisms to modify the distribution of training examples before applying the learning algorithm [9-11]. These existing efforts assume that datasets are noise-free or noise in the datasets is less significant. However, real-world data is never perfect and can often suffer from noise that may impact models created from the data. In [13], noise is classified into two categories: class noise and attribute noise, and *in this paper, we only deal with class noise, which means the errors introduced in the class labels*. When the users are unsure whether their dataset is noise-free or not, they may raise two possible concerns: (1) if the dataset is not noise-free, how does noise impact the CS learner? and (2) if noise does bring serious troubles, how can we handle noise for effective CS learning?

For normal learning algorithms (non-CS), the existence of noise actually brings trained classifiers various negative impacts such as decreasing the classification accuracy, and increasing the training time and the tree size [1][14][23]. Accordingly, the problem of learning in noisy environments for non-CS algorithms has been the focus of much attention in machine learning and most inductive learning algorithms have a mechanism for handling noise. For example, pruning in decision trees is designed to reduce the chance that the trees are overfitting to noise [15]. As suggested by Gamberger et al. [17], handling noise from the data before hypothesis formation has the advantage that noise does not influence hypothesis construction. Accordingly, when learning from noisy datasets, a logical solution to enhance the learners is to cleanse noise in some way. Nevertheless all these conclusions are made for normal inductive learning, where maximizing classification accuracy is the goal. The objective of CS learning, however, is to minimize the misclassification cost, where the accuracy becomes less important, especially when the misclassification of some classes becomes much more expensive than misclassifying others, *i.e.*, $C(i,j) >> C(j,i)$, $i{\neq}j$, or vice versa. A simple analysis may imply that the existence of noise could have less impact on CS learning, because decreasing the accuracy does not necessarily increase the misclassification cost of a CS classifier (given that a CS learner usually sacrifices accuracy for minimal costs). Unfortunately, rare research has systematically addressed the behavior of CS learners in noisy environments, which leaves noise handing for effective CS learning still an open problem.

In this paper, we report our recent research efforts in resolving the above concerns. We systematically study the noise impacts on CS learning (Section 2) and propose a unique cost-guided noise handing approach for effective CS learning (Section 3). The experimental results from 20 real-world datasets collected from the UCI data repository [18] and KDD Archive [19] indicate that in noisy environments, the CS classification could be seriously corrupted, and by adopting the proposed algorithm, we can significantly reduce the average cost of the learned CS classifier.

2. Noise Impacts on Cost-sensitive Learning

To study the impact of noise on cost-sensitive learning, we systematically design the following experiments for quantitative evaluations. Given a dataset D, we use 10-fold cross-validation to construct a training set (E) and a test set (T). We then use the techniques introduced in Section 4.1 to manually introduce a certain level of noise in E and construct a noisy dataset E'. Meanwhile, assuming a noise cleansing technique is adopted to remove all noisy instances from E', we can therefore get a cleansed dataset E''. We observe the performances of a CS learner on E, E', and E'' to evaluate the impact of noise. In addition, because costs between classes may also affect the performance of a CS learner, we will assign the cost-ratio (defined by Eq. (5)) to three values: 2, 5, and 10 to evaluate their impacts. We use the WDBC dataset [23] (a two-class problem) to demonstrate results, because a two-class problem can help us explore the impacts of noise and cost-ratio on cost-sensitive learning. To train CS classifiers in our experiments, we use the C5.0 cost-sensitive classification tree [16].

To systematically study the impacts of noise, we first adopt the *Total Random Corruption* (*TRC*) model (see Section 4.1) to introduce noise and evaluate the system performance. Nevertheless, a possible concern with *TRC* is that it equally introduces noise to all classes and will change the class distribution after the noise corruption, which may possibly become the main reason of the cost increase (*i.e.*, increasing the misclassification cost by changing the class distribution). Accordingly, in addition to *TRC*, we also adopt a *Proportional Random Corruption* (*PRC*) model, where the class distribution remains constant during noise corruption. Because *TRC* equally introduces noise to all classes, the intended noise level and the actual noise level are the same. For *PRC*, however, these two noise levels are different. For detailed comparisons, we will report both of them in the results, as denoted by the first and second rows of the x-axis in Figs. 1 and 2.

2.1 Noise Impacts on Misclassification Costs

In Fig. 1, we report the impact of noise on the cost of a CS learner where Fig. 1(a) and Fig. 1(b) represent the results from different noise corruption models. The first and second rows of the x-axis represent the intended and the actual noise levels in the dataset. The y-axis indicates the cost of CS classifiers. CS_E' and CS_E'' represent the average cost of a CS classifier trained from E' and E'' (before and after noise cleaning) in classifying test instances in T, and r is the cost-ratio defined by Eq. (5).

As we can see from Fig. 1, with both noise corruption models, the average cost of a CS classifier proportionally increases with the value of r, even if the dataset is noise-free.

This does not surprise us, because in our experiments we fix the cost of $C(i, j)$ to 100 and set the cost of $C(j, i)$ to 100·r. So raising the value of r will increase the average cost of a CS classifier. Meanwhile, we find that *when noise is introduced in the dataset, the average cost will inevitably increase, regardless of the noise corruption model and the value of r*. The higher the noise level, the larger is the average cost of a CS classifier (given a fixed cost-ratio r). On the other hand, removing noisy instances can actually keep the average cost almost the same as that of the noise-free dataset (E). This observation indicates that *removing noisy instances is an effective way to reduce the impacts of noise on CS learning*.

Although noise increases the cost of trained CS classifiers no matter what the cost-ratio (r) is, when comparing costs from three r values, we can find that their patterns of increase are different. As shown in Fig. 1(a), when r is small, increasing noise levels will gradually increase the average cost, but at lower noise levels, the impacts of noise are less significant. On the other hand, when r becomes large, introducing a small portion of noise will quickly increase the average cost, but increasing the noise level further does not show significant extra impacts. Taking the results from r=2 and r=10 in Fig. 1(a) as examples, when the dataset actually contains 10% noise, the cost increase for r=2 is 4.89 (from 9.77 to 14.66), but for r=10 the increase is about 26 (from 27.08.13 to 52.95). Although the above observations likely conclude that noise does more harm to a dataset with a high cost-ratio, one possible concern with Fig. 1(a) is that *TRC* has already changed the class distribution of the dataset, therefore, it is not clear that given the same amount of noise in the dataset who is responsible for the significant increase of the cost, the change of the class distribution or the large cost-ratio r? We then turn to Fig. 1(b) for answers, where the class distribution is constant during noise corruption.

As we can see from Fig. 1(b), due to the unequal class distribution of the dataset, the actual noise level in the dataset is always lower than the intended corruption level. When the actual noise level is 0.1, the intended level is about 0.13 (please refer to Section 4 and Tab. 1 for the reason). At this noise level, the cost increase for r=2 is 4.35 (from 9.77 to 14.12), and for r=10 the increase is about 18 (from 27.08 to 44.89). It is obvious that given the same amount of noise in the dataset, even if the noise does not change the class distribution, a dataset with a large cost-ratio appears to be more error prone and therefore receives a large misclassification cost. These observations indicate that *when the dataset has a large cost-ratio value, the existence of noise becomes especially fatal, and a small portion of noise can corrupt the results significantly*.

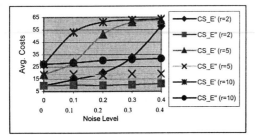

(a) WDBC Dataset, total random noise (*TRC*)

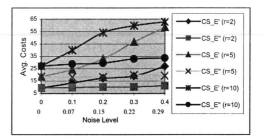

(b) WDBC Dataset, proportional random noise (*PRC*)

Fig. 1. Impacts of class noise on the average cost of a *CS* classification algorithm

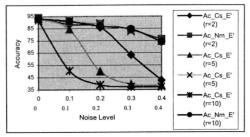

(a) WDBC Dataset, total random noise (*TRC*)

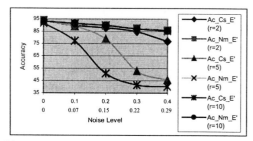

(b) WDBC Dataset, proportional random noise (*PRC*)

Fig. 2. Impacts of class noise on the classification accuracy of normal and *CS* classification algorithms

When applying a *CS* learner on a noisy dataset, it seems that the trained *CS* classifier has a "saturation" point in reacting to noise impacts. When the noise level is less than this point, noise will continuously bring impacts to the *CS* classifier. However, once the noise level is beyond the "saturation" point, the classifier becomes less sensitive to noise. A simple analysis will indicate that this "saturation" point is determined by two most important factors: the value of r and the class distribution. Given a two-class problem, assume that the class distribution is α_1: α_2, where α_1 indicates the distribution of the major class, and that the cost of predicting a minor class instance to the major class is $cs_{min} \cdot r$, where cs_{min} is the counter cost (from the major class to the minor class). For a test set with ε classification error rate, the average misclassification cost, CS_{Avg} (the left side of Eq. (1)), should satisfy Eq. (1), because the right side of Eq. (1) is the average cost of predicting that all instances belong to the minor class (which is the optimal solution for a *CS* classifier with low confidence, denoted by CS_{Sat}). For this purpose the error rate ε should be less than a critical value ε^* defined by Eq. (2). *I.e.*, the higher the cost-ratio r, the lower the ε^*, and the more likely the classifier tends to approach the "saturation" point.

$$\underbrace{\frac{\varepsilon \cdot \alpha_1}{\alpha_1 + \alpha_2} cs_{min} + \frac{\varepsilon \cdot \alpha_2}{\alpha_1 + \alpha_2} r \cdot cs_{min}}_{CS_{Avg}} \leq \underbrace{\frac{\alpha_1}{\alpha_1 + \alpha_2} cs_{min}}_{CS_{Sat}} \quad (1)$$

$$\varepsilon^* = \frac{\alpha_1}{\alpha_1 + r \cdot \alpha_2} \quad (2)$$

With Section 4 and Tab. 1, we know that α_1: α_2=0.627:0.373 and cs_{min}=100 for the WDBC dataset, so CS_{Sat} is 62.7, which is consistent with the results in Fig. 1. This concludes that *class noise does not continuously bring impacts to the CS classifier all the time, and after noise reaches a certain level, the CS classifier may simply stick to the "expensive" class, and then the impact of noise likely becomes constant. The higher the cost-ratio, the more likely the classifier tends to do so.*

2.2 Noise Impacts on Classification Accuracy

The above observations suggest that eliminating noise from a dataset with a relatively small cost-ratio likely brings contributions to a *CS* classifier. Two questions should be answered before we take any further action to handle noisy instances: (1) why is a dataset with a large cost-ratio especially sensitive to noise? and (2) to develop a noise handling algorithm for effective *CS* learning, shall we trust a normal classifier or a *CS* classifier? We refer to experimental comparisons between the classification accuracy of a normal (non-*CS*) classifier and a *CS* classifier for answers, as shown in Fig. 2, where *Ac_Cs_E′* and *Ac_Nm_E′* indicate the accuracies of a normal and a *CS*

classifier trained from *E′* respectively. As shown in Fig. 2, when the cost-ratio is small (r=2), the differences between the accuracies of normal and *CS* classifiers are small, and the accuracy of the *CS* classifier is relatively worse. This is understandable, because a *CS* classifier likely sacrifices the accuracy for minimal costs. However, when the cost-ratio gets larger (r=5 or higher), the accuracy of the *CS* classifier becomes significantly worse than the normal classifier. If we compare Fig. 2(a) with Fig. 1(a), we can find that this is actually the reason a dataset with a large cost-ratio is more willing to approach to the "saturation" point. In this situation, a small portion of noise will make the CS classifier ignore the classification accuracy and stick to the "expensive" classes. On average we can find that the accuracy of a normal classifier is always better (or much better). This indicates that *in noisy environments, if we want to adopt a noise identification mechanism, we shall trust a normal classifier rather than a CS classifier*, because the former always has a higher accuracy in determining the right class of an instance.

2.3 Further Investigations

Now, let's have a little more discussion on the theoretical background of cost-sensitive learning, which shall also answer why a dataset with a large cost-ratio is especially sensitive to noise. If, for a given example I_k, we know the probability of each class j $P(j|I_k)$, the Bayes optimal prediction for I_k is the class i that minimizes the conditional risk [4][20], as defined by Eq. (3). The conditional risk $P(i|I_k)$ is the expected cost of predicting instance I_k belongs to class i. The Bayes optimal prediction is guaranteed to achieve the lowest possible overall cost (*i.e.*, the lowest expected cost over all possible examples I_k, weighted by their probabilities $P(I_k)$). $C(i, j)$ and $P(j|I_k)$ together with the rule above imply a partition of the example space X into j regions, such that class j is the optimal (least-cost) prediction in region j. The goal of cost-sensitive classification is to find the frontiers between these regions, explicitly or implicitly. However, this is complicated by their dependence on the cost matrix C: in general, as misclassifying examples of class j becomes more expensive relative to misclassifying others, the region where j should be predicted will expand at the expense of the regions of other classes, even if the class probabilities $P(j|I_k)$ remain unchanged. In noisy environments, the probability of each class j $P(j|I_k)$ becomes less reliable, and the error rate introduced in $P(j|I_k)$ is going to be magnified by the adopted cost matrix $C(i, j)$ (the CS classifier tends to prefer those "expensive" classes). Therefore, the higher the cost-ratio in the dataset, the more sensitive the *CS* classifier behaves to noise.

$$R(i \mid I_k) = \sum_j P(j \mid I_k) C(i, j) \quad (3)$$

3. Cost-guided Iterative Classification Filter

To identify noisy instances, various approaches have been proposed [1][14][17]. However, none of them was originally designed for *CS* classification, where the cost variance implies that some classes are inherently important than others, so the noise handling should take the cost into consideration for better performances. In this section we propose a cost-guided noise identification algorithm which seamlessly integrates cost and the general noise handling algorithm for effective *CS* learning.

Among all existing noise handling efforts, the Classification Filter (*CF*) [1] appears to be a successful algorithm. Generally *CF* simplifies noise elimination as a filtering operation where noise is characterized as instances that are incorrectly classified by the noise classifiers. The main procedure of *CF* is shown in Fig. 3. An inherent disadvantage of *CF* is that the noise classifiers (H_y) are organized in a parallel way so they cannot benefit each other in noise identification. As we can see, the noise levels for all formed subsets E_y are theoretically equal. Therefore none of the learned noise classifiers is better than others. However, if we can organize the noise classifiers in such a way that the current classifier could benefit from the results of former classifiers, and in addition, when conducting noise handling, each noise classifier also takes the costs into consideration, we may expect better results in identifying noise for effective *CS* learning. Motivated by these observations, we propose a Cost-guided Iterative Classification Filter (*CICF*) for noise identification. The main procedure is given in Fig. 4.

Procedure: Classification_Filter()
Input: E'(noisy dataset); **Output:** E''(cleansed dataset).
Parameter: n (# of subsets, typically 10)
(1) Form n disjoint equal size subset E_i, where $\cup_i E_i = E'$.
(2) $A \leftarrow \varnothing$
(3) For $i=1, \dots, n$
(4)   Form $E_y \leftarrow E' \setminus E_i$
(5)   Induce H_y based on examples in E_y.
(6)   For every $I_k \in E_i$
(7)   If H_y incorrectly classify I_k
(8) $A \leftarrow A \cup \{I_k\}$
(9) Return ($E'' \leftarrow E' \setminus A$)

Fig. 3. Classification Filter

As shown in Fig. 4, *CICF* needs the users to specify the number of iterations (n) in advance. This number is also used to determine the number of subsets to partition the original dataset. *CICF* first partitions the original noisy dataset E' into n subsets (as *CF* does). Given the first iteration $It=1$, *CICF* first aggregates $n-1$ subsets (excluding subset E_1), and trains the first noise classifier H_1. The examples in E_1, which are incorrectly classified by H_1, are forwarded to a noise subset (A), and all other instances are forwarded to a good instance subset (G). The above steps are the same as in *CF*. But the difference is that after H_1 has identified noisy instances from E_1, *CICF* will introduce a cost-guided rejection sampling [21] (Section 3.1) to remain all good instances in E_1 and randomly removes identified noise in E_1, by putting a heavier penalty (removing more) to the noise in cheaper classes. So the removed noisy instances will not take part in the following noise identification steps, and meanwhile, the noise classifier can still put an emphasis on the expensive classes. It is obvious that such a procedure will change the data distribution in E_1. After the first round, *CICF* conducts the

second iteration by aggregating another 9 subsets (excluding subset E_2), identifies noise from E_2 and conducts a cost-guided rejection sampling on E_2. *CICF* iteratively executes the above procedure until n iterations are accomplished, and provides the user with a cleansed dataset E''.

Procedure: Cost_guided_Iterative_Classification_Filter()
Input: E'(noisy dataset); C (cost matrix).
Output: E''(cleansed dataset).
Parameter: n (# of iterations, typically 10)
(1) Form n disjoint equal size subset E_i, where $\cup_i E_i = E'$.
(2) $A \leftarrow \varnothing; B \leftarrow \varnothing; G \leftarrow \varnothing$;
(3) **For** ($It=1$; $It \leq n$; It ++)
(4) | $B \leftarrow \cup_i E_i$, $i \neq It$
(5) | Induce H_{It} based on examples in B.
(6) | **For** each instance I_k in E_{It}
(7) | | **If** H_{It} correctly classifies I_k
(8) | | $G \leftarrow G \cup \{I_k\}$ // Good instance subset
(9) | | **Else**
(10) | | $A \leftarrow A \cup \{I_k\}$ // Noise subset
(11) | **End for**
(12) | **For** each instance I_k in E_{It}
(13) | **If** H_{It} correctly classifies I_k // Keep good instances
(14) | Remain I_k in E_{It}
(15) | **Else** // invoke a rejection sampling for noisy instances
(16) | $OgCls = Class(I_k)$
(17) | $PrdCls = H_{It}(I_k)$
(18) | $SaplChance = \dfrac{C(PrdCls, OgCls)}{\sum_{i,j \in \{prdCls, OgCls\}} C(i,j)}$
(19) | **If** $Random() < SaplChance$
(20) | Remain I_k in E_{It} // Keep noisy instances
(21) | **Else**
(22) | Remove I_k from E_{It} // Reject noisy instances
(23) | **End for**
(24) **End for**
(25) Return ($E'' \leftarrow G$)

(Steps (13) to (23) are bracketed and labelled "Cost-guided rejection sampling")

Fig. 4. Cost-guided Iterative Classification Filter

3.1. Cost-guided Rejection Sampling

The above observations have indicated that all noise classifiers in *CF* are organized in parallel, so they cannot benefit each other in noise identification. Accordingly, instead of conducting parallel noise filtering, we construct a sequential mechanism, where given the current iteration It, the noise identification results from the former iterations i, $i=1, 2, .., It-1$, can possibly contribute to noise handling in E_{It}. Such a procedure is demonstrated in steps (12) to (23) in Fig. 4, where $Class(I_k)$ returns the class label of I_k, and $Random()$ produces a random value within the constraint [0, 1]. To this end, the most intuitive solution is to remove all identified noisy instances from E_{It}, $It=1, 2, .., n$, so in the following iterations, the identified noise are discarded from training the noise classifier. We call this intuitive solution an *Iterative Classification Filter* (*ICF*). In Fig. 4, if we set *SaplChance* to 0, the algorithm works exactly as *ICF*, and if we set *SaplChance* to 1, the algorithm becomes *CF*.

Although *ICF* progressively lowers the noise level in each round to train the classifier, our experimental results in Section 4 will indicate that the disadvantage of *ICF* is that any falsely identified noisy instance are removed and will not be used to train noise classifiers in the following iterations. The negative impacts from *ICF* become especially severe when the accuracy of the noise classifier is low and the cost-ratio in the dataset in relatively large, because the expensive classes obviously cannot bear the same level of information loss as cheap classes. *CF*, on the other hand, keeps all identified noisy instances in training the noise classifiers, which obviously suffers from a low noise identification accuracy. Accordingly, instead of either removing or keeping all identified noisy instances, we adopt a sampling mechanism by taking costs into consideration.

When conducting cost-sensitive learning, some algorithms [9-11] have used sampling mechanisms to modify the distribution of training examples. The intuitive idea behind these approaches is to put more emphasis (a higher density) on expensive classes, so the classifier learned from the modified dataset becomes cost-sensitive. This motivates us to adopt similar ideas in noise handing, where at each iteration *It*, the identified noisy instances are randomly sampled and removed from the dataset, therefore two objectives could be achieved through this procedure: (1) putting more focus on the expensive classes, so the classifier could have more investigation on them; and (2) lowering the noise level in the succeeding iterations, so a higher noise identification accuracy could be achieved. For these purposes, rejection sampling [21] was adopted.

Given the current iteration *It*, *It*=1, 2, .., *n*, assuming A_{It} denotes the subset consisting of all identified noisy examples from E_{It}, the original distribution in E_{It} is D_{It}, and the transformed distribution (after the sampling) is $D_{It}{}'$, we conduct rejection sampling by drawing examples from A_{It}, and then keeping (or accepting) the sample with a probability proportional to $D_{It}{}'/D_{It}$. Here, we have $D_{It}{}'/D_{It} \propto C$, so we keep an example (I_k) with probability *SaplChance*, which is defined by Eq. (4).

$$SapleChance=C(PrdCls, OgCls) / \sum_{i, j \in \{PrdCls, OgCls\}} C(i, j) \quad (4)$$

where *OrgCls* and *PrdCls* indicate the original and predicted class of I_k. The higher the misclassification cost of I_k, the more likely I_k is going to be kept, as shown in steps (16) to (22) in Fig. 4. With such a procedure, the identified noise in E_{It} is independently sampled (*w.r.t* the misclassification cost of the instance) to form a modified dataset E_{It} (where some identified noisy instances are removed). Accordingly, the original distribution D_{It} was transformed to $D_{It}{}'$, with less focus on cheap classes. Hopefully, classifiers learned from $D_{It}{}'$ will have better a performance to handle noise from expensive classes.

The merits of such a rejection sampling based noise handling mechanism is twofold: (1) rejection sampling independently draws instances to form a new distribution, and it is inherently superior to other sampling mechanisms like sampling with/without replacement, because instances are not independently drawn from the latter approaches [10]; and (2) instead of either keeping (like in *CS*) or removing (like in *ICF*) all identified noisy instances, *CICF* randomly keeps identified noise (*w.r.t* the cost of the instance), so the noise classifier could be learned from the environments with a relatively low noise level but still emphasize on the expensive instances.

4. Experimental Evaluations
4.1 Experiment Settings

The majority of our experiments use C5.0 (Quinlan, 1997). We evaluate different algorithms on 20 benchmark datasets [18-19], as shown in Tab. 1, where *class ratio* indicates the ratio between the most common and the least common classes. Due to size restrictions, we will mainly report the results of several representative datasets. The summarized results from all benchmark datasets are reported in Figs. 5 and 6.

For most datasets we used, they don't actually contain much noise (at least we do not know which instance is noisy), so we implement two manual corruption mechanisms, *Total Random Corruption* (*TRC*) and *Proportional Random Corruption* (*PRC*), to introduce noise and evaluate the algorithms. With *TRC*, when the users specify an intended corruption level *x·100%*, we will randomly introduce noise to all classes. That is, an instance with its label *i* has a *x·100%* chance to be mislabeled as another random class (excluding class *i*). As we can see, if there are only two classes in the dataset, *TRC* is actually the pairwise corruption model that has been popularly used by many existing efforts [1][14]. *TRC*, however, changes the class distribution in the dataset when corrupting noise, which becomes a big concern in *CS* Learning, because modifying the class distribution may change the average cost considerably. We then propose *PRC*, which keeps the class distribution constant during noise corruption. Given a dataset with *M* classes, assume the original class distribution is π_1, π_2,..,π_M, with $\sum_i^M \pi_i$ =1, where π_1 and π_M are the percentage of the most and least common classes respectively. With *PRC*, when the users specify an intended corruption levels *x·100%*, we proportionally introduce random noise to different classes, where an instance with its label *i* has a (π_I /π_i)· *x·100%* chance to be corrupted as another random class. That is, we use the least common class as the baseline, and proportionally introduce noise to different classes. It is obvious that with *PRC*, the actual noise level is less (or even much less) than the intended corruption level.

For each experiment, we perform 10 times 3-fold cross-validation and use the average accuracy as the final result. In each run, the dataset is randomly (with proportional partitioning) divided into a training set *E* and a test set *T*. We form a noisy dataset *E′* by introducing noise in *E* with the above methods, and use *T* to evaluate the system performance.

To assign the values for the misclassification cost matrix, we adopt a proportional cost (*PC*) model that integrates the class distribution of the dataset. Given two classes *i* and *j*, *i≠j*, we first check their class distribution π_i and π_j. Without losing the generality, let's assume $\pi_i > \pi_j$, which means that class *j* is relatively rarer than *i*. Then we assign a fixed cost value to *C(j, i)*, e.g. 100, and assign the value of *C(i, j)* as 100·*r*, where *r* is the cost-ratio, as defined by Eq. (5). In our experiments, we set *r∈* [1, 10], which indicates that we prefer to assign higher costs to rarer classes. This is consistent with the reality, because assigning a large cost to the common class simply does not make sense, and if we really do so, the *CS* learner will tend to ignore all rare classes (because they are less in quantity and cheap in cost). In our experiments, the cost matrix is generated at the beginning of each trail of 10 time cross-validation.

$$r = C(i, j) / C(j, i) \quad (5)$$

We use average costs to evaluate the improvement of the proposed algorithm in enhancing *CS* learning. To evaluate the performance of noise identification mechanisms, we adopt three measures: *False Positive* (*FP*), *False Negative* (*FN*) and *Noise identification Precision* (*NP*), which are defined by Eq. (6), where |*X*| denotes the number of examples in *X*, *A* is the set of examples that are identified as noise, $\widetilde{A}$ is *A*'s complement, *G* is the set of non-noisy examples, and *N* is the set of noise.

$$FP = \frac{|A \cap G|}{|G|} \qquad FN = \frac{|\widetilde{A} \cap N|}{|N|} \qquad NP = \frac{|A \cap N|}{|A|} \quad (6)$$

Tab. 1. Benchmark dataset characteristics

Dataset	# of Classes	Class Ratio	Dataset	# of Classes	Class Ratio
Adult	2	0.76:0.24	Auto-mpg	3	0.63:0.18
Credit	2	0.56:0.44	Car	4	0.70:0.04
Krvskp	2	0.52:0.48	Glass	6	0.36:0.04
Monks-3	2	0.53:0.47	KDD99	5	$0.79:10^{-4}$
Mushroom	2	0.52:0.48	LED24	10	0.12:0.09
Sick	2	0.94:0.06	Lympho	4	0.55:0.01
Tictactoe	2	0.65:0.35	Nursery	5	$0.33:10^{-4}$
Vote	2	0.61:0.39	Soybean	19	0.13:0.01
WDBC	2	0.63:0.37	Splice	3	0.52:0.24
Wisc. Ca.	2	0.66:0.34	Wine	3	0.40:0.27

Tab. 2. Noise identification results (*TRC* corruption)

Dataset	Noise (%)	FP (×10) CF	FP (×10) ICF	FP (×10) CICF	FN (×10) CF	FN (×10) ICF	FN (×10) CICF	NP (×10) CF	NP (×10) ICF	NP (×10) CICF
Car	10	**1.24**	1.09	1.13	0.45	**0.64**	0.56	4.64	**4.92**	4.86
	20	**1.38**	1.19	1.25	0.53	**0.70**	0.62	6.27	**6.56**	6.47
	30	**1.60**	1.39	1.45	0.55	**0.81**	0.71	7.16	**7.37**	7.33
	40	**1.87**	1.60	1.71	0.68	**0.92**	0.78	7.68	**7.89**	7.81
KDD99	10	0.12	**0.13**	0.12	0.03	0.03	0.03	**9.02**	8.98	9.01
	20	0.15	0.15	0.15	0.03	0.04	0.04	9.43	**9.44**	9.44
	30	**0.17**	0.16	0.15	0.04	**0.05**	0.04	9.62	**9.66**	9.63
	40	**0.31**	0.21	0.22	**0.08**	0.05	0.06	9.56	**9.69**	9.67
Sick	10	0.21	0.21	0.20	0.19	**0.23**	0.22	8.38	**8.43**	8.39
	20	0.24	0.24	0.23	0.23	**0.26**	0.25	9.12	**9.14**	9.12
	30	**0.35**	0.32	0.32	0.35	**0.38**	0.36	9.22	**9.29**	9.28
	40	**0.57**	0.55	0.55	0.56	**0.65**	0.59	9.16	9.18	**9.19**
Splice	10	**0.82**	0.72	0.77	0.38	**0.49**	0.42	5.67	**5.95**	5.80
	20	**1.11**	0.86	0.96	0.57	**0.65**	0.61	6.79	**7.31**	7.16
	30	**2.15**	1.35	1.70	1.09	**1.24**	1.14	6.43	**7.37**	6.92
	40	**3.78**	2.47	3.01	1.89	**2.21**	1.97	5.91	**6.80**	6.36
WDBC (Ca.)	10	**0.89**	0.73	0.81	0.97	**1.24**	1.11	5.33	**5.74**	5.56
	20	**1.15**	0.93	1.00	1.25	**1.46**	1.32	6.50	**6.88**	6.78
	30	**1.41**	1.32	1.37	1.26	**1.82**	1.52	**7.28**	7.27	7.27
	40	**2.78**	2.21	2.44	2.85	**3.09**	2.90	6.38	**6.82**	6.65

4.2 Noise Identification Results

We test each dataset at four noise levels and report the results (*CF*, *ICF* and *CICF*) in Tab. 2, where the text in bold indicates the largest value of the measure.

The results in Tab. 2 show three conclusions. (1) Among all three approaches, *ICF* usually has the highest noise identification precision, and in comparison with *CF* and *CICF*, the improvement from *ICF* could be as much as 9% and 4.4% (e.g. the Splice dataset) respectively. This is consistent with our original design. *ICF* iteratively involves identified good instances from former iterations to train a noise classifier in the current round (H_{it}). With the decrease of noise level in the training set, the accuracy of H_{it}, AC_{it}, likely increases, *i.e.* $AC_1 \leq AC_2 \ldots \leq AC_n$. For *CF*, the accuracy of all noise classifiers is theoretically equal, which is the accuracy of the first iteration in *ICF*. Therefore, *ICF* tends to have a better accuracy than *CF*. (2) Tab. 2 also indicates that *ICF* tends to have the highest *FN* value, which means *ICF* is more conservative than *CF* and *CICF* (keeps more noise unidentified). The reason is that with *ICF*, the identified noise was discarded from training the noise classifier in the succeeding rounds. The knowledge from falsely removed instances will never be recovered in the following noise classifiers. So *ICF* appears to be the most conservative. (3) Among the three approaches, *CF* usually suffers from the highest *FP* value, where *FP* from *CF* could be as much as 13% and 6.7% worse than *ICF* and *CICF* respectively (e.g. the Splice dataset), which indicates that *CF* is much more aggressive than

ICF and *CICF*. Given that normal datasets usually come with a certain level of domain redundancy [22], being aggressive likely does not show much negative impact to normal learners. This is the reason that *CF* receives good performance in improving the classification accuracy [1], even if its *NP* is relatively low. However, **when applying noise handling for *CS* learning, being aggressive with expensive classes may actually do more harm, because the expensive class obviously should not bear the same level of information loss as cheap classes.** This leaves space for *CICF* to improve the system performance by adjusting the emphasis on classes with different costs.

4.3 Cost Improvement through Noise Cleansing

To evaluate the effectiveness of the different mechanisms in improving the performance of a *CS* learner, we perform experiments on two types of datasets (two-class and multi-class) with different noise levels and provide the results in Tabs. 3 and 4, where CS_{wt} represents the average cost of a *CS* classifier trained from a noisy dataset (E') without any noise cleansing, and CS_{CF}, CS_{ICF}, and CS_{CICF} denote the average cost of the *CS* classifier learned from the cleansed dataset (E'') which adopts *CF*, *ICF* and *CICF* respectively. In Tabs. 3 and 4, the text in bold indicates the lowest cost value. We also summarize results from all 20 datasets in Figs. 5 and 6.

For each two-class dataset, we assign three cost-ratio values ($r=2$, 5 and 10) and evaluate the results. For multi-class datasets, we randomly select the value of r for each class pair $C(i, j)$.

When evaluating the results from two-class datasets (Tab. 3), it is not hard for us to conclude that a dataset, which adopts noise cleansing (either *CF*, *ICF* or *CICF*), likely makes the *CS* classifier improve its performance significantly, where the improvement can be as significant as 10 times better (e.g., *ICIF* on the Sick dataset with 40% noise). This shows the effectiveness and importance of noise handling for *CS* learning.

Meanwhile, we also notice that when the cost-ratio is relatively small, e.g., $r=2$, the improvements could be found from almost all datasets in Tab. 3, regardless of noise levels, where involving noise handing almost always shows better performances. However, when the cost-ratio becomes larger, *e.g.*, $r=5$ or more, the improvement turns to be less significant. In this situation, applying noise handing on some datasets (at some noise levels) may increase the average costs of trained *CS* classifiers. As we have analyzed in Section 2, when the cost-ratio in the dataset is large, it's actually hard to achieve significant improvement through noise cleansing (due to the bias of *CS* learners). In such a situation, if a noise cleansing mechanism is less accurate, it may actually decrease the system performance rather than enhance it.

When taking a further investigation on the performances of the three noise handling mechanisms, we can find that *ICF* appears to be very unstable. Some times *ICF* shows good performance (e.g., the Vote dataset with $r=2$ and 30% noise), but some times, it appears to be the worst. As we have analyzed in the above sections, *ICF* prohibits noise identified in each round from taking part in training the noise classifiers at later stages, which may possibly result in a bias and make the noise classifier be too conservative. This disadvantage becomes especially severe when the datasets have a large cost-ratio, because removing valuable information from expensive classes can significantly impact the *CS* learner. In conclusion, removing all noisy instances identified in each round appears to be an inferior solution to training noise classifiers for *CS* learning.

By integrating cost-guided rejection sampling and iterative noise handling, *CICF* receives very attractive results. When the cost ratio is low, e.g., *r*=2, *CICF* is comparable to *CF*, and in Tab.3, they almost equally win the lowest cost. However, when the cost ratio becomes higher, e.g., *r*=5 or more, we can easily find that *CICF* is dominant and outperforms *CF*. This demonstrates that a noise handling mechanism which takes the cost into consideration is promising for *CS* learning, especially when some classes are much expensive than others. Instead of equally handling noise in different classes, we shall pay more attention to noise in expensive classes, and it will finally benefit the *CS* classifier learned from the noise cleansed dataset.

Tab. 4 provides the results from multi-class datasets (to save space we omit the results of *ICF*), which also demonstrate that involving noise handling usually results in a better *CS* learner.

4.4 Experimental Result Summarization

In Figs. 5 and 6, we summarize the results from all benchmark datasets and provide two types of comparisons: (1) the cost between *CICF* and the original noisy dataset (Fig. 5); and (2) the cost between *CF* and *CICF* (Fig. 6). In Fig. 5, the *x*-axis and *y*-axis represent the cost of the *CS* classifier trained from the noisy dataset with and without adopting *CICF* respectively. Each point corresponds to a dataset evaluated at one noise level and one type of cost matrix (so each figure has 40 points). Points above the *y*=*x* line are those which receive a better performance by adopting *CICF*. In Fig. 6, *x*-axis and *y*-axis represent the cost of the *CS* classifier trained from the dataset cleansed by *CICF* and *CF* respectively. Therefore, points above the *y*=*x* line are those which receive a better performance from *CICF* than from *CF*.

As we can see from Fig. 5(a), when the cost-ratio is small, adopting *CICF* can improve the performance of the *CS* classifier from almost all datasets (there are three points below *y*=*x*, which are from Krvskp at noise level 20%, Adult at noise level 10%, and Tictactoe at noise level 10%). However, when *r* increases from 2 to 5, ten points are actually below *y*=*x*. When *r* becomes 10, there are 14 points below *y*=*x*, which means about 35% (14/40) points receive negative impacts.

When evaluating the results from Fig. 5(d), we can find that on average the performance from multi-class datasets are less attractive than two-class datasets. Among all 40 points, there are 13 points actually below the *y*=*x* line, which is 32.5%. Our further analysis indicates that on average, the noise identification precision for multi-class datasets is less accurate, in comparison with two-class datasets. As a result, noise cleansing likely removes valuable information and corrupts the performance of the *CS* learner. In addition, we randomly assign cost-ratio values *r* to multi-class datasets, which likely results in relatively large cost-ratio values.

When comparing *CICF* with *CF* (Fig. 6), a clear trend could be drawn, which is that the higher the cost-ratio, the more obvious *CICF* is dominant and outperforms *CF*. As we can see, when *r* is small, e.g., *r*=2, *CICF* and *CF* are comparable. However, when the cost-ratio becomes higher, *CICF* appears to be "always" better than *CF*. In these situations, the improvement from *CICF* (in comparison with *CF*) becomes significant. It clearly supports our motivation in designing *CICF*. When handling noise for *CS* learning, we should pay more attention to expensive classes, and prevent a noise classifier from misidentifying noise from expensive classes. The higher the cost-ratio, the more necessary we need to do so. With cost-guided rejection sampling, *CICF* inherently attains this goal by two facts: (1) iteratively lowering the overall noise level by removing more suspicious instances in cheap classes, and (2) putting more efforts on investigating noise in expensive classes.

Tab. 3. Cost improvements from two-class datasets (*TRC*)

Dataset	Noise (%)	r=2				r=5				r=10			
		CS_{wt}	CS_{CF}	CS_{ICF}	CS_{CICF}	CS_{wt}	CS_{CF}	CS_{ICF}	CS_{CICF}	CS_{wt}	CS_{CF}	CS_{ICF}	CS_{CICF}
Credit	10	21.88	20.66	20.79	**19.42**	34.73	32.47	36.26	**32.16**	52.67	**51.15**	52.65	51.49
	20	29.16	21.84	23.27	**20.86**	46.54	**32.15**	41.97	32.22	55.48	51.44	55.01	**48.42**
	30	34.74	29.33	30.79	**28.07**	54.70	**35.95**	42.56	36.89	55.51	51.62	56.37	**51.33**
	40	46.05	44.58	46.42	**43.21**	55.52	55.26	58.16	**51.87**	55.48	64.08	67.38	**53.65**
Monks-3	10	4.25	2.38	**2.28**	2.30	14.66	4.15	4.11	**2.96**	37.39	6.49	4.92	**3.89**
	20	10.89	**3.54**	4.17	**3.54**	43.88	6.08	4.61	**4.33**	51.90	13.68	13.06	**12.02**
	30	26.88	**19.68**	20.93	22.42	52.77	25.09	28.11	**23.58**	52.75	41.76	50.20	**36.28**
	40	49.01	**41.02**	48.03	43.45	**52.72**	74.68	80.16	56.70	**52.82**	97.99	98.92	80.57
Sick	10	3.57	**3.21**	3.34	3.26	14.71	6.57	6.55	**6.14**	68.14	10.93	11.31	**10.34**
	20	4.26	**3.41**	3.54	3.53	87.75	6.25	6.42	**6.12**	92.43	11.64	13.72	**11.03**
	30	10.84	**4.52**	5.1	4.53	93.68	8.02	7.69	**7.64**	93.77	14.24	18.32	**13.02**
	40	92.44	9.91	10.55	**9.37**	93.83	21.64	22.66	**20.03**	93.87	36.91	39.52	**32.17**
Vote	10	8.93	**6.49**	7.41	6.82	17.81	7.49	10.42	**7.07**	34.67	**12.02**	14.84	**12.02**
	20	12.73	7.16	6.75	**6.47**	41.04	10.18	10.96	**8.16**	58.31	11.70	13.14	**10.08**
	30	27.24	9.41	**8.76**	10.13	59.37	15.69	16.63	**14.25**	61.36	24.74	20.38	**18.95**
	40	46.67	27.78	**26.36**	28.08	61.51	44.73	44.71	**37.71**	61.41	46.87	58.11	**37.79**
WDBC	10	15.34	**11.39**	11.64	11.45	28.11	19.24	20.60	**18.06**	53.16	34.55	34.45	**32.37**
	20	20.66	13.44	**12.99**	13.49	50.08	24.01	24.92	**22.45**	59.48	38.45	38.35	**34.27**
	30	34.60	18.65	19.64	**17.45**	59.68	32.33	34.51	**31.70**	62.15	52.78	58.37	**47.19**
	40	60.87	37.29	**36.14**	36.14	**62.30**	80.43	74.68	65.44	**62.79**	116.35	124.89	101.41

Tab. 4. Cost improvements from multi-class datasets (*TRC*)

Noise (%)	Car			KDD-99			Soybean			Splice			Wine		
	CS_{wt}	CS_{CF}	CS_{CICF}	CS_{wt}	CS_{CF}	CS_{CICF}	CS_{wt}	CS_{CF}	CS_{CICF}	CS_{wt}	CS_{CF}	CS_{CICF}	CS_{wt}	CS_{CF}	CS_{CICF}
10	**31.81**	42.94	40.69	6.37	4.32	**4.09**	**37.50**	47.97	46.61	21.57	13.94	**13.90**	30.98	**30.26**	32.51
20	50.82	51.35	**47.92**	46.39	6.28	**6.00**	57.03	**46.11**	46.35	34.52	17.46	**17.26**	48.58	45.47	**44.21**
30	67.26	49.28	**44.75**	69.14	6.52	**6.21**	75.71	53.01	**50.93**	62.33	28.12	**25.98**	62.21	61.30	69.70
40	85.13	63.23	**57.08**	81.20	4.98	**4.82**	87.84	60.91	**60.17**	66.52	43.97	**40.38**	81.19	66.78	**64.06**

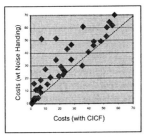 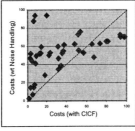 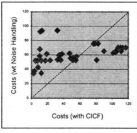 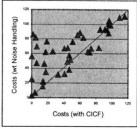

| (a) Two Class (r=2) | (b) Two Class (r=5) | (c) Two Class (r=10) | (d) Multi-class (Random r) |

Fig. 5. Experimental summaries of cost improvements between *CICF* and no noise handling mechanism (20 datasets)

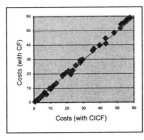 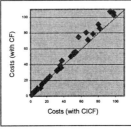 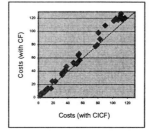 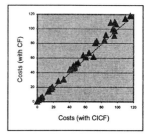

| (a) Two Class (r=2) | (b) Two Class (r=5) | (c) Two Class (r=10) | (d) Multi-class (Random r) |

Fig. 6. Experimental comparisons of cost improvement between *CF* and *CICF* from all 20 benchmark datasets

All observations above conclude that when the cost-ratio in datasets is relatively small, adopting noise cleaning is an effective way to enhance *CS* learning; however, when the cost-ratio becomes large, we need to be careful in adopting noise cleaning, especially for multi-class datasets. When handling noise for *CS* learning, instead of putting equal weighs to all classes, we need to take costs into consideration and put more emphasis on expensive classes, and such a mechanism becomes especially successful for datasets with a large cost-ratio.

5. Conclusions

In this paper, we have empirically studied the impacts of class noise on cost-sensitive learning, and conclude that the existence of noise can bring serious troubles for cost-sensitive classification, especially when misclassifying some classes becomes extremely expensive. Meanwhile, removing noisy instances will significantly improve the performance of a cost-sensitive classifier learned from noisy environments. Motivated by these observations, we have proposed a Cost-guided Iterative Classification Filter (*CICF*) algorithm to identify and remove noise for effective *CS* learning. Two novel features make *CICF* distinct from existing approaches. (1) It provides a general framework which seamlessly integrates the cost of the instance for noise handling, where more emphasis is put on expensive classes. It can be easily demonstrated that this framework is general enough to allow any existing noise handling efforts to be incorporated to make themselves cost-sensitive in handling noise. (2) *CICF* iteratively involves noise identification results in former iterations to train the noise classifier in the current round. As a result, the system can progressively improve the accuracy of noise identification and finally benefits from noise handling for *CS* learning. Experimental results and comparative studies have indicated that by applying *CICF* on noisy datasets, we can significantly reduce the average cost of a *CS* classifier.

References

[1] C. Brodley & M. Friedl, Identifying mislabeled training data, *J. of AI Research*, 11:131-167, 1999.

[2] J. Bradford, C. Kunz, R. Kohavi, C. Brunk, & C. Brodley, Pruning decision trees with misclassification costs. *Proc. of ECML*, 1998.

[3] L. Breiman, J. Friedman, R. Olshen, & C. Stone, *Classification and Regression Trees*. Wadsworth & Brooks, CA, 1984.

[4] P. Domingos, MetaCost: a general method for making classifiers costsensitive. *Proc. of KDD*, 1999.

[5] M. Pazzani, C. Merz, P. Murphy, K. Ali, T. Hume & C. Brunk, Reducing misclassification costs, *Proc. of ICML*, 1994.

[6] V. Zubek & T. Dietterich, Pruning improves heuristic search for cost-sensitive learning, *Proc. of ICML*, 2002.

[7] P. Turney, Cost-sensitive learning bibliography, http://purl.org/peter.turney/bibliographies/cost-sensitive.html,

[8] M. Tan, Cost-sensitive learning of classification knowledge and its applications in robotics, *Machine Learning*, 13:7-33, 1993.

[9] P. Chan & S. Stolfo, Toward scalable learning with non-uniform class and cost distributions, *Proc. of KDD*, 1998.

[10] B. Zadrozny, J. Langford & N. Abe, Cost-sensitive learning by cost-proportionate example weighting, *Proc. of ICDM*, 2003.

[11] N. Abe & B. Zadrozny, An iterative method for multi-class cost-sensitive learning, *Proc. of KDD*, 2004.

[12] P. Geibel & F. Wysotzki, Perceptron based learning with example dependent and noisy costs, *Proc. of ICML* 2003.

[13] X. Wu, *Knowledge acquisition from databases*, Ablex Pulishing Corp., USA, 1995.

[14] X. Zhu, X. Wu, & Q. Chen, Eliminating class noise in large datasets, *Proc. of 20th ICML*, 2003.

[15] J. Quinlan, *C4.5: programs for machine learning*, Morgan Kaufmann, San Mateo, CA, 1993.

[16] J. Quinlan, http://rulequest.com/see5-info.html, 1997.

[17] D. Gamberger, N. Lavrac, & C. Groselj, Experiments with noise filtering in a medical domain, *Proc. of 16th ICML*, 1999.

[18] C. Blake & C. Merz, *UCI Data Repository*, 1998.

[19] S. Hettich & S. Bay, *The UCI KDD Archive*, 1999.

[20] R. Duda & P. Hart, *Pattern classification and scene analysis*, Wiley, New York, 1973

[21] J. Von Neumann, Various techniques used in connection with random digits, *National bureau of standards applied mathematics series*, 12, 36-38, 1951.

[22] M.Moller, Supervised learning on large redundant training sets, *Int. J. of Neural Systems*, 4(1), 1993.

[23] X. Zhu & X. Wu, Class noise vs attribute noise: A quantitative study of their impacts, *Artificial Intelligence Review, in press*, 2004.

Dynamic Classifier Selection for Effective Mining from Noisy Data Streams

Xingquan Zhu, Xindong Wu, and Ying Yang

Department of Computer Science, University of Vermont, Burlington VT 05405, USA

{xqzhu, xwu, yyang}@cs.uvm.edu

Abstract

Recently, mining from data streams has become an important and challenging task for many real-world applications such as credit card fraud protection and sensor networking. One popular solution is to separate stream data into chunks, learn a base classifier from each chunk, and then integrate all base classifiers for effective classification. In this paper, we propose a new dynamic classifier selection (DCS) mechanism to integrate base classifiers for effective mining from data streams. The proposed algorithm dynamically selects a single "best" classifier to classify each test instance at run time. Our scheme uses statistical information from attribute values, and uses each attribute to partition the evaluation set into disjoint subsets, followed by a procedure that evaluates the classification accuracy of each base classifier on these subsets. Given a test instance, its attribute values determine the subsets that the similar instances in the evaluation set have constructed, and the classifier with the highest classification accuracy on those subsets is selected to classify the test instance. Experimental results and comparative studies demonstrate the efficiency and efficacy of our method. Such a DCS scheme appears to be promising in mining data streams with dramatic concept drifting or with a significant amount of noise, where the base classifiers are likely conflictive or have low confidence.

1. Introduction

The ultimate goal of effective mining from data streams (from the classification point of view) is to achieve the best possible classification performance for the task at hand. This objective has traditionally led to an intuitive solution: separate stream data into chunks, and then integrate the classifiers learned from each chunk for a final decision [11, 22, 24]. Given a huge volume of data, such an intuitive solution can easily result in a large number of base classifiers, where the techniques from Multiple Classifier Systems (*MCS*) [1-2] are involved to integrate base classifiers. The fact behind the merit of *MCS* is from the following underlying assumption: Each participating classifier in the *MCS* has a merit that deserves exploitation [3], i.e., each base classifier has a particular subdomain from which it is most reliable, especially when different classifiers are built using different subsets of features, different subsets of the data, and/or different mining algorithms.

Roughly, existing integration techniques can be distinguished into two categories:

1. Combine base classifiers for the final decision. When classifying a test instance, the results from all base classifiers are combined to work out the final decision. We refer it to *Classifier Combination* (*CC*) techniques.
2. Select a single "best" classifier from base classifiers for the final decision, where each base classifier is evaluated with an evaluation set to explore its domain of expertise. When classifying an instance, only the "best" classifier is used to determine the classification of the test instance. We name it *Classifier Selection* (*CS*) techniques.

In [4], the *CC* techniques were categorized into three types, depending on the level of information being exploited. Type 1 makes use of class labels. Type 2 uses class labels plus a priority ranking assigned to each class. Finally, Type 3 exploits the measurements of each classifier and provides each classifier with some measure of support for the classifier's decision. The *CS* takes the opposite direction. Instead of adopting the combining techniques, it selects the "best" classifier to classify a test instance. Two types of techniques are usually adopted:

1. *Static Classifier Selection* (*SCS*). The selection of the best classifier is specified during a training phase, prior to classifying a test instance [5-6].
2. *Dynamic Classifier Selection* (*DCS*). The choice of a classifier is made during the classification phase. We call it "dynamic" because the classifier used critically depends on the test instance itself [7-10].

Many existing data stream mining efforts are based on the *Classifier Combination* techniques [11, 22-24], and as they have demonstrated, a significant amount of improvement could be achieved through the ensemble classifiers. However, given a data stream, it usually results in a large number of base classifiers, where the classifiers from the historical data may not support (or even conflict with) the learner from the current data. This situation is compounded when the underlying concept of the data stream experiences dramatic changes or evolving, or when the data suffers from a significant amount of noise, because the classifiers learned from the data may vary dramatically in accuracy or in their domain of expertise (i.e., they appear to be conflictive). In these situations, choosing the most reliable one becomes more reasonable than relying on a whole bunch of likely contradictive base classifiers.

In this paper, we propose a new *DCS* mechanism for effective mining from noisy data streams. Our intuitive assumption is that the data stream at hand suffers from dramatic concept drifting, or a significant amount of noise, so the existing *CC* techniques become less effective. We will first review related work in Section 2; and then propose our new method in Section 3. In Section 4, we discuss about applying the proposed *DCS* scheme in noisy datasets. Our experimental results and comparative studies in Section 5 indicate that the proposed *DCS* scheme outperforms most *CC* or *CS* methods in many situations and appears to be a good solution for mining real-world data.

2. Related Work

The two main reasons of employing multiple classifiers for data stream mining are efficiency and accuracy. Although the efficiency could be the most attractive reason for adopting multiple classifiers, because a data stream can always involve a huge volume of data which turns to be a nightmare for any single learner. The accuracy of *MCS* in handling stream data is also remarkable: especially when the concept in the data stream is subject to evolving, changing or drifting [11, 24]. Like many partitioning-based or scale-up learning algorithms (e.g., Bagging [12], Boosting [13] and Meta learning [14]) have demonstrated, by partitioning the whole dataset into subsets, the system efficiency can be dramatically improved, with a limited sacrifice of the accuracy.

When adopting *MCS* in stream data, the most intuitive (and probably also the simplest) scheme is simple voting which is also called Select All Majority (*SAM*) [7], where the prediction from each base classifier is equally weighted to vote for the final prediction. Although simple, *SAM* has been proved to be effective to integrate multiple classifiers, and many revised versions [11, 22, 24] have been successfully developed to handle data streams. In comparison with *CC* based schemes, the *CS* schemes select one classifier for the final decision, where two kinds of techniques, *SCS* and *DCS*, are usually adopted. Among all *SCS* schemes, the most intuitive one is Cross-Validation Majority (*CVM*)[5]. In *CVM*, cross-validation is adopted and the base classifier with the highest classification accuracy from the cross-validation is selected to classify all test instances.

In comparison with *SCS* where the "best" classifier has been selected before the testing phase, *DCS* dynamically selects the "best" classifier for each test instance. Among different *DCS* schemes, the most representative one is *Dynamic Classifier Selection by Local Accuracy* (*DCS_LA*) [10] which explores a local community for each test instance to evaluate the base classifiers, where the local community is characterized as the k *Nearest Neighbors* (*kNN*) of the test instance in the evaluation set Z. Although *DCS_LA* has been widely integrated in many systems, it suffers from the following three disadvantages:

(1) The selection of k and the adopted distance function critically affect the system performance.

(2) The speed factor. Given a test instance, *DCS_LA* has to go through the whole evaluation set to find its neighborhood. Its time complexity is unbearable for stream data.

(3) Sensitive to noise. Usually, the number of instances in a local community is relatively small, the existence of noise will critically affect the performance of *DCS_LA*.

Intuitively, for real-world datasets, not all attributes have the same importance in classification. Instead of using all attributes to evaluate the base classifiers, a more reasonable way may consider the important attributes of each base classifier. Accordingly, a referee based dynamic classifier selection scheme was proposed in [9] where referees, in the form of decision trees, partition the whole evaluation set into subsets, and each base classifier is evaluated with these subsets to explore its domain of expertise. The advantage of the Referee is that it partitions the evaluation set into subsets by joining the features of the base classifiers. The less important attributes won't be used in partitioning the evaluation set, and the partitioned subsets tend to be more reasonable in exploring the domain expertise. However, the drawbacks are threefold: (1) to learn each referee, one has to explore the features of each base classifier; (2) it uses the learned decision trees to partition the original training set into subsets, and the system performance will critically depend on the quality of learned decision trees; and (3) because each classifier has its own referee, and the reliabilities from different referees are evaluated from different subsets. Without the same measurements, the selected classifier might not work well.

The above review shows that in order to explore the domain expertise of each base classifier, the *DCS* schemes have to evaluate the classifiers from either an entire or partial evaluation set to determine which classifier is the best for the test instance at the current stage. Such a mechanism inherently provides an adaptive scheme that is most suitable for mining data streams with dramatic changes, where most existing mining efforts appear to be less effective. However, all existing *DCS* approaches use either distance-based schemes or classification trees (or classification rules) to partition the evaluation set into subsets, where the quality of the partitioned subsets critically depends on the performance of adopted distance functions or classification trees. In this paper, we present a new *DCS* scheme that evaluates base classifiers with subsets of the evaluation set, where the subsets are constructed with statistical information of attribute values. We believe such a partitioning scheme is more natural and intuitive in exploring the domain expertise of each base classifier for effective data stream mining.

3. AO-DCS: Attribute-Oriented Dynamic Classifier Selection

In this section, we present a new dynamic classifier selection scheme, called AO-DCS (*Attribute-Oriented Dynamic Classifier Selection*). We use attribute values of instances to partition the evaluation set into subsets for evaluation purpose. If the instances in a dataset have only one attribute, and we use this attribute to partition the evaluation set into disjoint subsets with each subset corresponding to one value of this attribute, the classification accuracy of each base classifier with these subsets is the performance of the classifier with the instances characterized by each attribute value. Then each base classifier's performance will reflect its domain of expertise. Our AO-DCS takes the following three steps.

1. Statically partition the evaluation set into subsets by using the attribute values of the instances. We denote the aggregation of all constructed subsets by Π.

2. Evaluate the classification accuracy of each base classifier on all subsets in Π. We call this accuracy "attribute-oriented" classification accuracy.

3. For a test instance, use its attribute values to select the corresponding subsets from Π, and select the base classifier C_j that has the highest classification accuracy from the selected subsets as the "best" classifier to classify the test instance.

3.1 Constructing Subsets

Given a dataset D, let X, Y and Z be the training, test and evaluation set, with the numbers of instances in X, Y and Z denoted by N_X, N_Y and N_Z respectively, and C_1, C_2..., C_L be the L base classifiers from X. The objective of AO-DCS is to select the "best" classifier C^* to classify each instance $\hat{I}_x$ in Y. Our algorithm first acquires statistical attribute information of all instances in D. Assuming the instances in D have M attributes A_1, A_2,..,A_M, and each attribute A_i contains n_i values $V_1^{A_i}$,..,$V_{n_i}^{A_i}$ (we will discretize numerical attributes into discrete values). For an attribute A_i, we use its values to partition the evaluation set Z into n_i subsets $S_1^{A_i}$,..,$S_{n_i}^{A_i}$, where $S_1^A \cup..\cup S_{n_i}^A = Z$. To partition Z, we design a procedure in Fig. 1.

Procedure	PartitionEvaluationSet (A_i)
Input:	Attribute A_i of the evaluation set Z.
Output:	n_i subsets $S_1^{A_i},.., S_{n_i}^{A_i}$ determined by A_i.

(1) $S_1^{A_i} \leftarrow \varnothing, S_2^{A_i} \leftarrow \varnothing, .., S_{n_i}^{A_i} \leftarrow \varnothing$

(2)   **For** $k = 1; k \le N_Z; k{+}{+}$

(3)   For $r = 1; r \le n_i; r{+}{+}$

(4) $S_r^{A_i} = S_r^{A_i} \cup \{I_k \mid I_k \in Z, I_k^{A_i} = V_r^{A_i}\}$

     End for

Fig. 1. Evaluation set partitioning by attribute values

In Fig. 1, $I_k^{A_i}$ denotes instance I_k's value on attribute A_i in the evaluation set Z. Given A_i, we can use its values to partition the evaluation set Z into n_i disjoint subsets, and instances with the same values on A_i are put in the same subset. We partition the evaluation set Z by each attribute, and we can hereby construct $\sum_i^M n_i$ subsets from all attribute values. An example of evaluation set partitioning from a dataset containing only two attributes A_1 and A_2 is pictorially depicted in Fig. 2, where the x-axis denotes the values of attribute A_1, and the y-axis represents the values of attribute A_2 (assuming A_1 and A_2 contain 3 and 4 values respectively). The x-axis and y-axis span the space ($\Re$) of all instances in this dataset. Using three attribute values $V_1^{A_1}$, $V_2^{A_1}$ and $V_3^{A_1}$ of A_1, we construct three subsets, $S_1^{A_1}$, $S_2^{A_1}$ and $S_3^{A_1}$, with $S_1^{A_1} \cap S_2^{A_1} \cap S_3^{A_1} = \varnothing$ and $S_1^{A_1} \cup S_2^{A_1} \cup S_3^{A_1} = \Re$. Four subsets constructed by A_2 are also depicted in Fig. 2. Any two subsets from A_1 and A_2, e.g., $S_1^{A_1}$ and $S_3^{A_2}$, have a small portion of overlapping, and the overlapping region indicates the instances that have the same attribute values on A_1 and A_2.

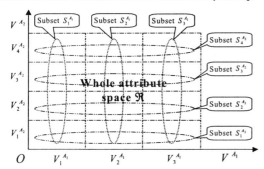

Fig. 2. An example of subset partitioning with two attributes (V^{A_1} and V^{A_2})

After we have constructed $\sum_i^M n_i$ subsets by all attributes, we calculate the classification accuracy of each base classifier $C_1, .. C_j, .., C_L$ on each of these $\sum_i^M n_i$ subsets, and we evaluate the classification accuracy of each base classifier on each subset with the procedure in Fig. 3. We denote the acquired accuracy matrix by $Acy_{C_j}^{S_l^{A_i}}$, $i = 1, .., M$; $l = 1, .., n_i$; $j = 1, .., L$.

Finally, the classification accuracy of each base classifier from all constructed subsets ($\sum_i^M n_i$) can be worked out. An example accuracy matrix is given in Fig. 4, where the first column denotes the base classifiers, and the first row represents the subsets constructed from all attribute values. Each $(i, j)^{\text{th}}$ cell indicates the classification accuracy of classifier C_i on subset S_j.

Procedure	GenerateAccuracyMatrix()
Input:	An evaluation set Z
Output:	The accuracy matrix $Acy_{C_j}^{S_l^{A_i}}$

(1) **For** $i = 1; i \le M; i{+}{+}$

(2)   For each attribute A_i

(3)   PartitionEvaluationSet(A_i);

(4)   For $l = 1; l \le n_i; l{+}{+}$

(5)   **For** $j = 1; j \le L; j{+}{+}$

(6)   Calculate $Acy_{C_j}^{S_l^{A_i}}$, i.e., the classification accuracy of classifier C_j on dataset $S_l^{A_i}$;

     End

End for

Fig. 3. Evaluating each base classifier on constructed subsets

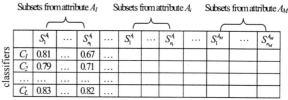

		Subsets from attribute A_1			Subsets from attribute A_i				Subsets from attribute A_M		
		$S_1^{A_1}$	…	$S_{n_1}^{A_1}$	…	$S_1^{A_i}$	…	$S_{n_i}^{A_i}$	…	$S_1^{A_M}$	…	$S_{n_M}^{A_M}$
classifiers	C_1	0.81	…	0.67	…							
	C_2	0.79	…	0.71	…							
	…	…	…	…	…							
	C_L	0.83	…	0.82	…							

Fig. 4. The classification accuracy from the base classifiers on all constructed subsets

3.2 Dynamic Classifier Selection

With the acquired classification matrix, $Acy_{C_j}^{S_l^{A_i}}$, $i = 1, .., M$, $l = 1, .., n_i$; $j = 1, .., L$. given a test instance $\hat{I}_x$, AO-DCS performs classifier selection with the procedure below:

Procedure	DynamicClassifierSelection($\hat{I}_x$)
Input:	A test instance $\hat{I}_x$ and a classification matrix $Acy_{C_j}^{S_l^{A_i}}$, $i = 1, .., M$; $l = 1, .., n_i$; $j = 1, .., L$
Output:	The best classifier for instance $\hat{I}_x$, $C^*(\hat{I}_x)$.

(1) AverageAcy[] $\leftarrow 0$;

(2) **For** $j = 1; j \le L; j{+}{+}$

(3)   **For** $i = 1; i \le M; i{+}{+}$

(4)   AverageAcy[j]= AverageAcy[j]+ $Acy_{C_j}^{S_l^{A_i}} \mid l = \arg_b\{V_b^{A_i} = \hat{I}_x^{A_i}; b = 1, .. n_i\}$;

     End for

(5)   AverageAcy[j]= AverageAcy[j] / M;

    End for

(6) $C^*(\hat{I}_x) = C_k(\hat{I}_x) \mid k = \arg_j\{\max\{\underset{j=1,2,...,L}{AverageAcy [j]}\}\}$;

Fig. 5. Dynamic classifier selection of AO-DCS

In Fig. 5, $\hat{I}_x^{A_i}$ denotes $\hat{I}_x$'s value on A_i. Given $\hat{I}_x$, AO-DCS first acquires $\hat{I}_x$'s values on all attributes $\hat{I}_x^{A_i}$, $i = 1, .., M$. These attribute values can be used to find specific subsets that were constructed by similar instances in the evaluation set. The classifier that receives the highest average accuracy with all selected subsets is identified as the "best" classifier for $\hat{I}_x$.

3.3 Remarks on Relevant Research Efforts

Our method can accommodate both missing values and numerical attributes. A missing value is treated as a specific additional value. Numerical attributes can be converted into nominal ones using discretization techniques. In our system, we adopt the k-means clustering algorithm [15] to convert numerical attributes into nominal ones.

By using attribute values to partition the evaluation set into subsets in advance, AO-DCS works similar to the static dynamic classifier selection in [16] where it also partitions the evaluation set into subsets to evaluate the performance of base classifiers. However, there are two key distinctions:

> - The method in [16] directly assigns the best classifier for each predefined region. AO-DCS, however, creates some small regions by using the attribute values from the evaluation set, and uses each test instance to determine the final subsets for evaluating the base classifiers.
> - Instead of adopting a clustering technique that has to use distance functions to find small regions, we use attribute values to partition an evaluation subset, which is more natural and intuitive from the data viewpoint.

By using attribute values to partition the evaluation dataset into subsets, our method is also somewhat similar to the rudimentary rule induction algorithm — 1R [17]. This method generates a one-level decision tree, which is expressed in the form of a set of rules that all test on one particular attribute. 1R is a simple, cheap method that often comes up with quite good rules for characterizing the structure in data. Perhaps this is because the structure underlying many real-world datasets is rudimentary, and just one attribute is sufficient to determine the class of an instance accurately. With the surprising results from the 1R algorithm, we can find that using a single attribute to explore the domain of expertise might be more reasonable to some degree, especially in noisy environments.

4. Applying AO-DCS in Data Stream Mining

In many applications, data is not static but arrives in data streams, and the stream data is also characterized by drifting concepts. In other words, the underlying data generation models, or the concepts that we try to learn from the data, are constantly evolving, even dramatically. Meanwhile, real-world stream data is never perfect and can often suffer from corruptions (noise) that may impact interpretations of the data, models created from the data and decisions made based on the data [25]. Due to the inherent huge volume of the size, it is actually hard to apply general data cleansing mechanisms [18] to stream data for better data quality. Therefore, the above two facts (concept drifting and noise) imply that the classifiers learned from a small portion of the stream may vary significantly in performance, which makes DCS a promising solution for effective mining from a real-world data stream. In this section, we propose a framework to apply AO-DCS to mine noisy data streams. This framework is general enough to allow any exiting learning algorithms to be incorporated to handle any real-world data streams.

As shown in Fig. 6, we first partition streaming data into a series of chunks, $S_1, S_2, .. S_i,..$, each of which is small enough to be processed by an induction algorithm at one time. Then we learn a base classifier C_i from each chunk S_i. To evaluate all base classifiers (in the case that the number of base classifiers is too large, we can keep only the most recent K classifiers) and

determine the "best" one for each test instance, we will dynamically construct an evaluation set Z (using the most recent instances, because they are likely consistent with the current test instances). When classifying a test instance, I_k, we will employ AO-DCS (and the evaluation set Z) to integrate existing base classifiers and select the "best" classifier to classify I_k.

In real-world situations, many data streams contain a certain level of noise. There are two common types of noise: attribute noise and class noise [18]. In this paper, we assume the data stream suffers from a certain level of class noise (which means the errors are introduced in the class labels), and will extensively evaluate the performance of different DCS schemes in handling noisy data, where various levels of class noise are manually introduced (before the data partitioning) to simulate real-world scenarios. This should provide interested readers with valuable knowledge about mining from real-world data streams.

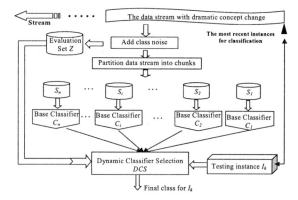

Fig. 6. Applying DCS in noisy data streams

5. Experimental Results and Comparisons

In this section, we design two sets of experiments, (1) DCS from classifiers that vary significantly in performance; and (2) DCS in classifying noisy datasets, to evaluate the performance of our proposed scheme. We take 8 datasets (including synthetic [19] and real-world data from the UCI database repository [20]) as benchmark data streams (by assuming the data comes in a time series manner) to evaluate the system performance.

Our purpose of the first set of experiments is to evaluate DCS in mining data streams with dramatic concept drifting. Unfortunately, although mining data streams with concept drifting has been addressed by many research efforts, we cannot find any benchmark dataset with dramatic concept changes (most existing efforts evaluate their algorithms with synthetic data). So we use the following design to simulate the scenarios in this regard. Given a dataset X, we first execute c4.5rules [21] on X to learn a classifier C_0, and then split X into 2^η chunks (using proportional partitioning [14]), and randomly select one chunk to induce a base classifier C_η, until we get η base classifiers $C_1, C_2,.. C_\eta$. Normally, given a dataset X, the less the instances are used for training, the worse is the learned classifier in addressing the genuine concept of X. Therefore, from C_1 to C_η, the classifier becomes weaker and weaker in performance (we assume it is the result of the dramatic change of the underlying concept). We use $C_1, C_2,.., C_\eta$ to evaluate the proposed DCS algorithms. In the second set of experiments, DCS schemes are used to integrate classifiers learned from noisy datasets.

We compare the proposed *AO-DCS* with four multiple classifier mechanisms: *SAM* [7], *CVM* [5], *DCS_LA* [10] and *Referee* [9]. For *DCS_LA*, we use the overall accuracy from the *k* nearest neighbors to evaluate the local accuracy. Meanwhile, we set *k*=10 for all experiments (as recommended by the original authors). For *Referee*, we use decision rules [21] as the referee, because decision rules are easier to manage. To compare the results of *DCS* schemes in classifying noisy data streams, we implement the *Arbiter* scheme proposed by Chang [14].

For each experiment, we execute 10-fold cross-validation and use the average accuracy as the final result. The classification accuracy in all tables and figures below denotes the accuracy evaluated from the test sets.

To add class noise, we adopt a pairwise scheme [18]: given a pair of classes (ε_x, ε_y) and a noise level γ, an instance with its label ε_x has a $\gamma \cdot 100\%$ chance to be corrupted and mislabeled as ε_y, so does an instance of class $\varepsilon_{|y}$. We use this method because in realistic situations, only certain types of classes are likely to be mislabeled. With this scheme, the percentage of the entire training set that is corrupted will be less than $\gamma \cdot 100\%$ because only some pairs of classes are considered problematic. In experiments below, we corrupt only one pair of classes (usually the pair of classes with the highest proportion of instances) in each dataset and only report the value γ in all tables and figures.

5.1 DCS from Classifiers Vary Significantly in Performance

5.1.1 Classification accuracy of base classifiers

To evaluate whether base classifiers actually vary significantly in performance, we add different levels of noise into the data and generate 5 (η=5) base classifiers. We then compare the accuracy of each base classifier with *SAM*, *CVM* and *AO-DCS*, and demonstrate the results in Table 1, where the first column indicates the noise level, columns 2 to 6 represent the accuracy of each base classifier, and column 7 is the average accuracy of all base classifiers.

Table 1 illustrates that in most situations, the accuracy from C_1 to C_5 is getting worse. However, in a single run, there may have exceptions, Fig. 7 shows the accuracy of the base classifiers from 10 runs (with 15% noise). One can find that from C_1 to C_5, the overall accuracy is getting worse, but in a single run, the accuracy of the base classifiers can be different from this trend. E.g., in the third run of Fig. 7, the accuracy of C_3 is better than C_1 and C_2. Actually, the same phenomenon has been found from some of the other datasets. From Fig. 7, one can find that by dynamic selecting the "best" classifier, the *AO-DCS* outperforms all base classifiers in any single run.

Table 1 also indicates that at most noise levels, the classification accuracy from the classifier selection schemes (*CVM* and *AO-DCS*) is better than the combination scheme (*SAM*). However, when the noise becomes extremely serious, the results from *SAM* become closer to (or even better than) *CVM* and *AO-DCS*, as demonstrated on the eighth to tenth columns of Table 1. One possible reason is that when the noise level increases, each base classifier becomes weaker. In the case that all base classifiers have a low confidence, combing results from base classifiers becomes more reasonable. Comparing the results from *CVM* and *AO-DCS*, one can find that the latter outperforms the former at almost every noise level. As we analyzed before, *CVM* statistically selects the single best classifier by evaluating

the overall performance of the base classifiers. And by integrating the proposed *DCS* scheme, we can explore the merit of each base classifier and improve the system performance.

Table 1. Classification accuracy of base classifiers with various MCS schemes (Car dataset, 5 base classifiers)

Noise Level %	C_1 (%)	C_2 (%)	C_3 (%)	C_4 (%)	C_5 (%)	AVG (%)	SAM (%)	CVM (%)	AO-DCS (%)
0	88.5	85.1	81.6	77.9	76.1	81.8	85.4	88.5	88.8
10	87.0	84.0	78.5	73.8	71.9	79.1	83.7	87.9	88.2
20	80.4	77.6	73.0	73.7	71.6	75.2	80.4	80.4	81.2
30	74.0	74.5	68.3	64.2	63.9	69.0	76.8	74.6	76.4
40	61.4	62.9	61.0	62.8	57.4	61.1	67.1	60.7	63.4

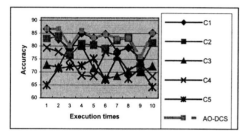

Fig. 7. Classification accuracy of base classifiers and AO-DCS from 10 runs (Car dataset, 15% noise)

5.1.2 Comparative studies on accuracy

In this subsection, we compare *AO-DCS* with three *CS* algorithms (*DCS_LA*, *Referee*, and *CVM*) and one *CC* scheme (*SAM*). We add various levels of noise into original data (and the evaluation set) to evaluate the performance of various algorithms in noisy environments. Table 2 shows the results from the Car dataset, where the first column indicates the noise level and the other columns denote the accuracy from different methods.

From Table 2, one can find that with five base classifiers varying in degrees of accuracy, the *CS* schemes achieve better performances than the *CC* scheme (*SAM*) at most noise levels. When the noise level is low, all *CS* methods outperform *SAM* with *DCS_LA* attaining the highest performance. However, with the increase of the noise level, *DCS_LA* receives the most dramatic decline in comparison with *Referee* and *AO-DCS*. Meanwhile, although the accuracy of *Referee* is usually lower than *AO-DCS* and *DCS_LA*, it was found to be the most noise tolerant, i.e., it receives the lowest decline caused by the increase of the noise level. In Table 2, when noise increases from 0% to 40%, the performance of *DCS_LA* and *AO-DCS* drops 30.57% (from 90.65% to 62.94%) and 29.58% respectively. But, Referee receives only 21.14% decrease. Actually, our analysis in Section 5.2 will indicate that Referee is more sensitive to the increase of the chunk number, and *DCS_LA* is more sensitive to noise.

Table 2. DCS accuracies from Car dataset (5 base classifiers)

Noise Level (%)	SAM (%)	CVM (%)	Referee (%)	DCS_LA (%)	AO-DCS (%)
0	85.72	89.23	89.56	90.65	89.73
10	82.33	82.75	85.03	87.33	85.46
20	78.45	77.83	80.31	80.26	78.15
30	71.86	73.03	77.43	73.84	74.65
40	61.62	61.49	70.63	62.94	63.19

5.1.3 Comparative studies on efficiency

The time complexity of *DCS* schemes comes from two phases: 1) evaluate the classification accuracy of base classifiers with predefined subsets, TS_1; and 2) select the "best" classifier for test instances, TS_2. Given a dataset D with M attributes, assume the numbers of instances in the evaluation and test sets are N_Z and N_Y respectively, and the number of induced base classifier is L. Assume further that *DCS_LA* selects k nearest neighbors for each test instance, and no indexing structure is adopted to facilitate the *kNN* search. For each test instance, TS_1 of *DCS_LA* is zero, and TS_2 is the time to go through all N_Z evaluation instances to find the k nearest neighbors and rank L base classifiers accordingly, which is $O(N_Z \log k + L \log L)$. For N_Y test instances, the total complexity is denoted by Eq. (1)

$$Complexity_{DCS\_LA} = O(\underbrace{0}_{TS_1} + \underbrace{N_Y N_z \log k + N_Y L \log L}_{TS_2}) \quad (1)$$

For the *Referee* method, TS_1 is the time to construct the referee for each base classifier by using instances in the evaluation set, and we assume a quadratic complexity for such a procedure (Although other better (less that quadratic) learning algorithms are available, we assume the quadratic complexity for the worst case), where the complexity to construct L referees is $O(L \cdot (N_Z)^2)$. TS_2 is the time to pass all referees and select the "best" classifier, which is $O(L \log L)$. Therefore for N_Y test instances, the total complexity denoted by Eq. (2).

$$Complexity_{Referee} = O(\underbrace{L \cdot (N_Z)^2}_{TS_1} + \underbrace{N_Y L \log L}_{TS_2}) \quad (2)$$

For *AO-DCS*, TS_1 is the time to evaluate the accuracy of each base classifier with the subsets constructed by attributes, where each classifier needs to go through the evaluation set for M times (where M is the number of attributes). So TS_1 of *AO-DCS* is $O(LMN_Z)$. TS_2 for *AO-DCS* is the time to select the "best" classifier that has the highest accuracy with the subsets determined by the test instance, which is $O(M \log L)$. For N_Y test instances the total complexity of *AO-DCS* is denoted by Eq. (3).

$$Complexity_{AO-DCS} = O(\underbrace{LMN_Z}_{TS_1} + \underbrace{N_Y M \log L}_{TS_2}) \quad (3)$$

For normal datasets, it is obvious that $(M, L, k) \ll (N_Y, N_Z)$, therefore complexity of *AO-DCS* appears to be the lowest one.

In addition to the above theoretical analysis, we also perform an empirical analysis. Table 3 shows the execution times of these three schemes from the Mushroom dataset, where we present the actual execution time (in seconds) of each method and their ratio values (We used a PC with Intel Pentium 4 with 2 GHz speed and 512 MB memory). In Table 3, the first column indicates the percentage of the size of the evaluation set in

comparison with the size of the whole dataset, and *TS* is the sum of TS_1 and TS_2. RatioA and RatioB are given in Eqs. (4) and (5).

$$RatioA = TS \text{ of } Referee \text{ / } TS \text{ of } AO\text{-}DCS \quad (4)$$

$$RatioB = TS \text{ of } DCS\_LA \text{ / } TS \text{ of } AO\text{-}DCS \quad (5)$$

From the results in Table 3, one can find that *AO-DCS* comprehensively improves the system performance in terms of time efficiency. When the size of the evaluation set increases, both *DCS_LA* and *Referee* suffer from spending a lot of time on finding the nearest neighborhood or inducing referee rules from the evaluation set, which is obviously a nonlinear increase with the size of the evaluation set. But increase the size of the evaluation set has less influence on *AO-DCS*.

5.2 DCS in Classifying Noisy Data Datasets

5.2.1 Experiments with noise levels

To evaluate the performances of *DCS* schemes in classifying partition-based noisy data datasets, we equally split the dataset into 9 non-overlapping chunks (using proportional sampling). We use c4.5rules to construct a base classifier from each chunk, and apply *DCS* schemes to integrate these base classifiers. In addition, we also add certain levels of class noise into the original data. The experimental results are shown in Tables 4 and 5, where the first column indicates the noise level, the second to seventh columns represent the classification accuracy of each scheme, and the eighth and ninth columns give the average and variance of the 9 base classifiers' accuracy.

From Tables 4 and 5, when we compare the performances of the three *DCS* schemes with *SAM*, *CVM* and *Arbitrator*, we can find that *DCS* schemes receive relatively better performances at various noise levels. If we compare the second and eighth columns, we can find that *SAM*'s accuracy is higher than the average accuracy of all base classifiers, where the improvement from *SAM* can be 2% to 10% compared to the average accuracy of all base classifiers. This confirms that *SAM* works surprisingly (or embarrassingly) well in many circumstances. From the ninth column, one can find that when the noise level increases, the variance of the base classifiers' accuracy becomes large, which indicates that the performance of the base classifier varies significantly. Usually, if the variance of the base classifiers' accuracy becomes significant, *DCS* can receive relatively large improvement.

When we compare the fourth to sixth columns, we can find *DCS_LA* is more sensitive to noise. When the noise level increases, the performance of *DCS_LA* decreases dramatically. The reason is that this method uses the nearest neighbors to evaluate base classifiers, and in high noise-level environments, the selected neighbors may be seriously corrupted by noise. Both *Referee* and *AO-DCS* use statistical information of the evaluation set, so noise has less negative impact on them.

Table 3. Execution time (in seconds) of different DCS schemes from Mushroom dataset (20% noise, 5 base classifiers)

Evaluation Set (%)	Referee (s)			DCS_LA (s)			AO-DCS (s)			RatioA	RatioB
	TS₁	TS₂	TS	TS₁	TS₂	TS	TS₁	TS₂	TS		
10	1.040	0.034	1.074	0	0.788	0.788	0.186	0.039	0.225	4.77	3.50
30	7.450	0.030	7.480	0	2.178	2.178	0.346	0.039	0.385	19.43	5.66
50	29.990	0.034	30.024	0	3.63	3.630	0.582	0.037	0.619	48.50	5.86
70	74.280	0.038	74.318	0	5.210	5.210	0.701	0.037	0.738	100.70	7.06
90	127.609	0.034	127.643	0	6.842	6.842	0.808	0.036	0.844	151.25	8.11
100	173.689	0.032	173.721	0	7.824	7.824	0.861	0.041	0.902	192.60	8.67

When we compare *SAM* (the second column) and *Arbiter* (the seventh column), one can find that *Arbiter* generally outperforms *SAM* in most situations. However, when the noise level reaches a relatively high level (30% ~ 40%), the improvement from *Arbiter* disappears. The reason is that when the noise level goes higher, more noisy instances are used to train the Arbiter. Consequently, the ability of the learned Arbiter becomes weaker.

Table 4. Experimental comparisons at different noise levels from Car dataset (9 chunks)

Noise level (%)	SAM (%)	CVM (%)	Referee (%)	DCA_LA (%)	AO-DCS (%)	Arbiter (%)	Avg. (%)	Var. (%)
0	84.4	84.6	85.5	91.3	86.6	86.0	81.5	2.4
10	83.1	82.2	81.8	89.2	83.8	83.9	79.1	3.8
20	80.1	80.5	78.8	83.9	82.0	81.0	76.2	6.2
30	76.0	76.9	78.1	80.2	80.4	79.0	70.7	8.7
40	71.6	67.1	74.3	64.6	73.7	69.5	65.6	11.3

Table 5. Experimental comparisons at different noise levels from Krvskp dataset (9 chunks)

Noise level (%)	SAM (%)	CVM (%)	Referee (%)	DCA_LA (%)	AO-DCS (%)	Arbiter (%)	Avg. (%)	Var. (%)
0	97.1	97.2	97.4	98.2	97.5	96.8	95.7	0.3
10	95.1	95.8	96.0	97.0	95.9	95.7	93.5	0.9
20	93.9	93.8	94.2	93.5	94.3	93.7	90.9	1.2
30	92.2	92.4	92.7	84.5	93.1	91.1	82.9	10.1
40	72.9	73.0	76.9	66.9	75.2	71.6	62.6	13.2

5.2.2 Experiments with variable number of chunks

In this subsection, we address the impact of the number of chunks on the performance of the proposed algorithms. We partition the dataset into a different number of chunks (from 3 to up to 63). Meanwhile, we run the experiments at two noise levels (0% and 25%), and show the results in Figs. 9 to 14. From Figs. 9 to 14, we can find that when the number of chunks increases, the overall accuracy from all schemes decreases. However, in a certain range, the chunk number may have less impact on the classification accuracy (and the increase of the number of chunks can even increase the classification accuracy). This phenomenon might come from the intrinsic characteristics of each dataset, e.g., the level of redundancy.

For noise-free datasets, *DCS_LA* can usually acquire the best performance. However, in noisy environments, *DCS_LA* receives less improvement, especially when the number of chunks is relatively large. As shown in Fig. 9(b), where the noise level is 25%, while the number of chunks increases, the performance of *DCS_LA* receives less improvement than *AO-DCS*. The same phenomenon has been found from most other datasets (except from Krvskp, in Fig. 11 (b), where the Referee scheme receives the highest classification accuracy).

When comparing the three *DCS* schemes, we find *Referee* is most sensitive to the number of chunks. Take Fig. 9 as an example. When the chunk number increases from 3 to 63, the performance of *Referee* drops 19.79% (from 90.24% to 72.38%) which is the largest among all three *DCS* schemes (the drop of *DCS_LA* and *AO-DCS* in the same range is 3.93% and 10.17% respectively). The reason behind this phenomenon is that with the increase of the chunk number, the number of instances in each

chunk is decreased. Each learned base classifier then tends to bias to only one or two attributes. Consequently, the learned referee of each classifier cannot comprehensively partition the evaluation set into small subsets to explore the domain expertise of each base classifier. Moreover, as we have mentioned in Section 2, Referee uses different subsets to evaluate different base classifiers (each classifier has its own referee), and without the same measurements, the selected "best" classifier might not work well.

The experimental results in Figs. 9 to 14 indicate that with a large number of chunks, the *Arbiter* scheme likely receives the same classification accuracy as *SAM*. The reason is that with the increase of the number of chunks (the number of base classifiers), the learned Arbiter will have less influence on the classification accuracy, because the arbitration rules take effect only if the base classifiers cannot have a majority classification. Meanwhile, the existence of noise could also be fatal to the Arbiter, because the arbiter is learned from uncertain data collected from different chunks. In noisy datasets, there is no doubt that the uncertain data collected from different chunks usually contain significant noise. Then, the learned arbiter has a very limited ability to improve the system performance.

We have performed comparisons with different datasets at two noise levels (0% and 25%). One can go through all figures below to get detailed comparisons. Clearly, these results indicate that *DCS* acquires much better performance than simple classifier combining, especially when a large number of base classifiers is adopted. This conclusion supports our initial motivation that each base classifier has its own merit that deserves exploitation, and finding the domain of expertise of each classifier supplies a new way to improve the system performance.

Notes: Figs. 9 to 14 report the number of chunks and the system performance on 6 datasets, where (a) is tested on noise-free data; and (b) is tested with 25% class noise. In Figs. 9 to 14, the *x*-axis denotes the number of chunks and the y-axis represents the classification accuracy, and each curve denotes one method that is specified in Fig. 8.

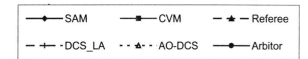

Fig. 8. The meaning of each curve in Figs 9 to 14

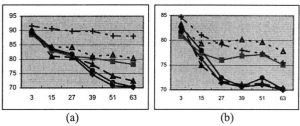

(a)   (b)

Fig. 9. Results from Car dataset

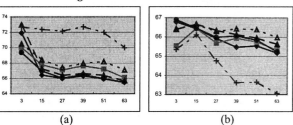

(a)   (b)

Fig. 10. Results from Connect-4 dataset

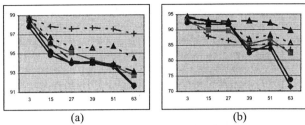

(a)   (b)

Fig. 11. Results from Krvskp dataset

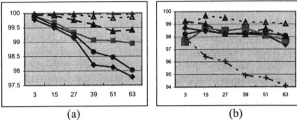

(a)   (b)

Fig. 12. Results from Mushroom dataset

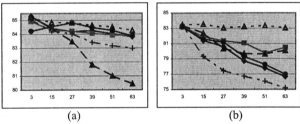

(a)   (b)

Fig. 13. Results from Adult dataset

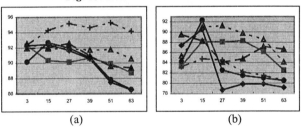

(a)   (b)

Fig. 14. Results from WDBC dataset

6. Conclusions

Traditional data mining algorithms are challenged by two most important features of data streams: huge volumes of data and the underlying concept drifting. These two challenges raise the need for incorporating ensemble classifiers in existing stream mining efforts. This intuitive solution, however, ignores the fact that the base classifier learned from a portion of a data stream carries two important features: (1) weak (even conflictive with others) in overall performance; but (2) still reliable in a specific domain. This fact becomes especially clear if the data stream suffers from dramatic concept drifting or a significant amount of noise. Consequently, instead of adopting any *combination* scheme, we have presented a new *DCS* algorithm that selects the "best" classifier once a time for each test instance in the data stream. We use each attribute to partition the evaluation set into disjoint subsets. We evaluate the classification accuracy of each base classifier on each subset. This accuracy indicates the ability of the base classifiers in classifying the instances characterized by each attribute, and hopefully, helps us explore the merit of each base classifier. Given a test instance, its attribute values will determine the subsets that have been constructed by similar instances in the evaluation set. The base classifier that has the highest accuracy with all these determined subsets is selected to classify the test instance.

Our experimental results have demonstrated that in comparison with classifier combination schemes, the *DCS* algorithms can possibly acquire more accuracy improvement, especially when the performances of the base classifiers vary significantly. When the real-world data suffers from dramatic concept drifting or a certain level of noise, *AO-DCS* turns to be a better choice in integrating multiple classifiers to enhance the system performance.

References

[1] Ali K. & Pazzani M., Error reduction through learning multiple description, *Machine Learning, vo.24, no.3, 1996*.

[2] Huang Y. S. & Suen C. Y., A method of combining multiple experts for the recognition of unconstrained handwritten numerals, *IEEE Trans. on PAMI, 17(1), pp.90-94, 1995*.

[3] Ueda N., Optimal linear combination of neural networks for improving classification perform., *IEEE Trans. on PAMI, 22, 2000*.

[4] Xu L., Krzyak A. & Suen C., Methods of combining multiple classifiers and their application to handwriting recognition, *IEEE Trans. on Sys., Man and Cyber., 22, 1992*.

[5] Schaffer C., Selecting a classification method by cross-validation, *Machine Learning, vol.13, pp.135-143, 1993*.

[6] Breiman L., Friedman J. H., Olshen R.A. & Stone C. J., Classification and regression trees, *Belmont, CA, 1984*.

[7] Merz C. J., Dynamical selection of learning algorithms, *In: D.Fisher, H.-J.Lenz (eds.), Learning from Data, Artificial Intelligence and Statistics, Springer-Verlag, NY (1996)*.

[8] Merz C. J., Using correspondence analysis to combine classifiers, *Machine Learning, vo.36 (1-2), pp.33-58, 1999*.

[9] Ortega J., Koppel M. & Argamon S., Arbitrating among competing classifiers using learned referees, *Knowledge and Information Systems, vol.3, no.4, 2001*.

[10] Woods K., Kegelmeyer W. P. & Bowyer K., Combination of multiple classifiers using local accuracy estimation, *IEEE Transactions on PAMI, vol.19, no.4, Apr., 1997*.

[11] Wang H., Fan W., Yu P. & Han J., Mining concept-drifting data streams using ensemble classifiers, Proc. of KDD 2003.

[12] Breiman L., Stacked regressions, *Machine Learning*, 24, 1996.

[13] Schapire R., The strength of weak learnability, *Machine Learning*, vol.5, no.2, pp.197-227, 1990.

[14] Chan P., An extensible meta-learning approach for scalable and accurate inductive learning, *Ph.D thesis, Columbia Univ., 1996*.

[15] Jain Anil K. & Dubes R. C., Algorithms for clustering data. *Prentice Hall, 1998*.

[16] Kucheva L.I., Switching between selection and fusion in combining classifiers: An experiment, *IEEE Trans. SMC, 32(2), 2002*.

[17] Holte R.C., Very simple classification rules perform well on most commonly used datasets, *Machine Learning, 11, 1993*.

[18] Zhu X., Wu X. & Chen Q., Eliminating class noise in large datasets, *Prof. of 20th ICML Conf., Washington DC, 2003*.

[19] IBM Almaden Research, Synthetic data generator, http://www.almaden.ibm.com/software/quest/Resources/datasets/syndata.html#classSynData

[20] Blake C. L. & Merz, UCI Data Repository, 1998.

[21] Quinlan R., C4.5 programs for machine learning, San Mateo, CA, Morgan Kaufmann publisher, 1993.

[22] Domingos P. & Hulten G., Mining high-speed data streams, *Proc. of SIGKDD*, 2000.

[23] Nasraoui O., Cardona C., Rojas C. & González F., TECNO-STREAMS: Tracking Evolving Clusters in Noisy Data Streams with a Scalable Immune System Learning Model, *Proc. of ICDM*, 2003.

[24] Kolter J. & Maloof M., Dynamic weighted majority: a new ensemble method for tracking concept drift, *Proc. of ICDM*, 2003

[25] Zhu X. & Wu X., Class noise vs attribute noise: A quantitative study of their impacts, *Artificial Intelligence Review, in press*, 2004.

Short Papers

Using Emerging Patterns and Decision Trees in Rare-class Classification

Hamad Alhammady and Kotagiri Ramamohanarao
Department of Computer Science and Software Engineering
The University of Melbourne, Australia
Email: {hhammady, rao}@cs.mu.oz.au

Abstract

The problem of classifying rarely occurring cases is faced in many real life applications. The scarcity of the rare cases makes it difficult to classify them correctly using traditional classifiers. In this paper, we propose a new approach to use emerging patterns (EPs) [3] and decision trees (DTs) in rare-class classification (EPDT). EPs are those itemsets whose supports in one class are significantly higher than their supports in the other classes. EPDT employs the power of EPs to improve the quality of rare-case classification. To achieve this aim, we first introduce the idea of generating new non-existing rare-class instances, and then we over-sample the most important rare-class instances. Our experiments show that EPDT outperforms many classification methods.

1. Introduction

The problem of classifying rare cases is an important issue in data mining. It implies processing an imbalanced dataset to distinguish rarely-occurring cases from other overwhelming cases. An example of this problem is the identification of intruders accessing a networking system by guessing passwords. In this case, the number of intrusion sessions can be very low (5% to 10%) compared to the overall number of legal sessions. The most important challenge in classifying such datasets is the scarcity of the rare class. This scarcity limits the information gained from the rare cases. Hence, traditional classifiers fail to classify these rare cases. For example, C4.5 decision tree [7] is one of the powerful classifiers, however, it fails to perform well in rare-class classification. The reason of this failure is that the scarcity of the rare class biases most of the decisions in the tree toward the major class.

In this paper we propose a new approach to use the advantage of emerging patterns (EPs) and decision trees (DTs) to classify rare cases in imbalanced datasets. Our approach (called EPDT) aims at improving the

performance of decision trees by biasing the decisions toward the rare class. This is achieved through two stages. The first stage involves using the rare-class EPs to create new non-existing rare-class instances. The second stage involves using the rare-class EPs to over-sample the most important rare-class instances.

Traditional classification accuracy (percentage of correctly classified instances in all classes) is not a suitable metric to measure the performance in rare-case classification. For example, suppose we have an imbalanced dataset consisting of two classes, and the major class contributes 95% of the instances. Then, the traditional accuracy can be increased to at least 95% by classifying all instances as major class. In this paper we adopt the *weighted accuracy* [11], and the *f-measure* [8] as they are suitable metrics for measuring the performance of rare-case classification.

2. Definitions

Let $obj = \{a_1, a_2, a_3, ... a_n\}$ is a data object following the schema $\{A_1, A_2, A_3, ... A_n\}$. $A_1, A_2, A_3.... A_n$ are called *attributes*, and $a_1, a_2, a_3, ... a_n$ are *values* related to these attributes. We call each pair (attribute, value) an *item*.

Let I denote the set of all items in an encoding dataset D. *Itemsets* are subsets of I. We say an instance Y contains an itemset X, if $X \subseteq Y$.

Definition 1. Given a dataset D, and an itemset X, the support of X in D is defined as the number of instances in D containing X over the total number of instances in D.

Definition 2. Given two different classes of datasets D_1 and D_2. Let $s_i(X)$ donates the support of the itemset X in the dataset D_i. The growth rate of an itemset X from D_1 to D_2 is defined as the ratio of $s_2(X)$ over $s_1(X)$.

Definition 3. Given a growth rate threshold $p > 1$, an itemset X is said to be a *p-emerging pattern* (p-EP or simply EP) from D_1 to D_2 if its growth rate >= p.

For example, the Mushroom dataset, from the UCI Machine Learning Repository [4], contains a large number of EPs between the poisonous and the edible mushroom classes. Figure 1 shows two examples of these EPs. e1 is an EP from the poisonous mushroom class to the edible mushroom class. It never exists in the former class, and exists in 63.9% of the instances in the later class; hence, its growth rate is ∞ (63.9 / 0). On the other hand, e2 is an EP from the edible mushroom class to the poisonous mushroom class. It exists in 3.8% of the instances in the former class, and in 81.4% of the instances in the later class; hence, its growth rate is 21.4 (81.4 / 3.8).

EP	Support in poisonous mushrooms	Support in edible mushrooms	Growth rate
e1	0%	63.9%	∞
e2	81.4%	3.8%	21.4

Figure 1. Examples of EPs

The problem of rare classes is also referred to as the problem of imbalanced datasets. It is defined as follows.

Definition 4. Given a training dataset T with an assigned set of class labels $C = \{c_R, c_M\}$, and an attribute set $A=\{A_1, A_2, A_3, \dots A_n\}$, where n is small (10s or a few 100s). The proportion of the class $C= c_M$ in the training set T is relatively much larger (90% or more) than the proportion of the class $C= c_R$ (10% or less) in the same training set. Under these constraints, the problem is to have a classifier $F : A \rightarrow C$, such that the evaluation metric $E(F)$ is optimized over any unknown test set S, where S follows the same attribute set A, and is a part of the population to which T is related.

3. EPs and DTs in rare-class classification

3.1. Overall system

Our proposed approach, EPDT, consists of four stages; 1) mining EPs from the training dataset, 2) creating new non-existing rare-class instances, 3) over-sampling important rare-class instances, and 4) classification. In the first stage we use an existing algorithm [2] to mine EPs. For the fourth stage we use C4.5 decision tree for classification.

3.2. Creating new rare-class instances

As mentioned earlier, our approach aims at employing the power of EPs in the problem of rare-class classification. Our first step toward this aim is to use the rare-class EPs to create new rare-class instances. Given a training dataset and a set of rare-class EPs, the attribute values that have the highest growth rate from the major class to the rare class in the training dataset are found. The set of rare-class EPs is divided into a number of groups such that EPs of each group have attribute values for most of the elements in the attribute set. The new rare-class instances are created by combining the EPs in each group.

If a value for an attribute is missing from a group, it is substituted by the value that has the highest growth rate for the same attribute. Figure 2 shows an example of this process. Suppose we have a dataset consisting of 7 attributes $\{A_1, A_2, A_3, A_4, A_5, A_6, A_7\}$. The values that have the highest growth rate for these attributes are $\{V_1, V_2, V_3, V_4, V_5, V_6, V_7\}$. Table a in figure 2 represents a group of three rare-class EPs. These EPs are $E_1\{(A_1=1), (A_2=X_1)\}$, $E_2\{(A_5=Y_1), (A_6=2), (A_7=3)\}$, and $E_3\{(A_2=X_2), (A_3=4), (A_5=Y_2)\}$. Notice that none of these EPs has a value for attribute A_4. As a result, the value that has the highest growth rate for attribute A_4, V_4, will be used as described earlier. The three EPs and the value chosen for attribute A_4 are combined to create four new rare-class instances. The intersected values (X_1 and X_2 for attribute A_2, and Y_1 and Y_2 for attribute A_5) are used one after the other to create the new instances. The four created instances are shown in table b in figure 2. After creating all the new rare-class instances using all the EP groups, the duplicated instances or those instances that already exist in the original training dataset are filtered out.

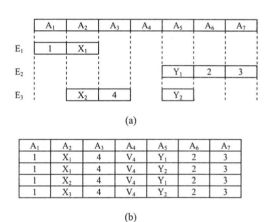

(a)

A_1	A_2	A_3	A_4	A_5	A_6	A_7
1	X_1	4	V_4	Y_1	2	3
1	X_1	4	V_4	Y_2	2	3
1	X_2	4	V_4	Y_1	2	3
1	X_3	4	V_4	Y_2	2	3

(b)

Figure 2. Creating new rare-class instances

3.3. Over-sampling rare-class instances

We adopt over-sampling some rare-class instances to balance the rare-class dataset. The over-sampling process helps C4.5 decision tree, which we use, improve its performance. However, over-sampling the rare-class instances randomly [9] may affect the performance negatively because of the possibility of noise amplification. Our over-sampling stage overcomes this problem by dealing with the most important instances only. This is achieved by duplicating those instances that contain rare-class EPs. We believe that these instances have the most important information that can aid the classification process and do not contribute the noise in the space of rare-class instances. The reason for this belief is that they contain the rare-class EPs which themselves can be considered as the most important information (as described in section 3) that represent the rare-class space. The over-sampling process we adopt has a great impact on C4.5 decision tree. Firstly, it helps increase the rare-class population. As a result, the degree of imbalance in the training dataset will be decreased. Secondly, the increase in the training dataset helps C4.5 decision tree carve the instance space to finer partitions. Thirdly, the increase in the probability of some attribute values will bias the decisions of the tree toward the rare-class.

4. System validation

We carry out a number of controlled experiments to prove the validity of our system. Due to the limited space for this paper, we present a simplified description of these experiments. We use balanced datasets (no rare class exists). We reserve 10% of each dataset for the testing purpose (*test*). We use the remaining 90% for training (*train1*). We convert *train1* to a rare-class dataset by eliminating most of the instances related to a certain class (*train-mid*). We apply our approach to *train-mid* to generate more instances for the rare class (*train2*). We run C4.5 tree using (*train1, test*) and (*train2, test*). The results of these two runs are very close. This proves that our approach successfully creates instances with the necessary information to support classification.

5. Experimental evaluation

In order to investigate the performance of our approach, we carry out a number of experiments. We use five challenging rare-class databases with different numbers of attributes and distributions of data between the major and rare classes. These datasets are the home insurance dataset [5], the network intrusion dataset [4], the disease dataset [4], the hypothyroid dataset [4], and the sick-euthyroid dataset [4]. We compare our approach to other methods such as our previous approach, EPRC [1], PNrule [10], C4.5 [7], Metacost [6], and over-sampling [9]. C4.5 is used as a basic classifier for our approach, Metacost, and over-sampling. The main difference between EPRC [1] and EPDT is that the former generates more rare-class EPs to enable EP-based classifiers to cope with the problem of rare-class classification. On the other hand, EPDT generates more rare-class instances which can be used by any standard classifier in the same problem. The comparison we present is based on the recall, precision, and F-measure. We perform two sets of experiments. In the first set, we compare our approach to the other methods using the test sets supplied by the owners of the datasets we use. In the second set of experiments, we compare our approach to the other

methods using 10-fold cross-validation. The later set of experiments helps explore the reliability of our approach. That is, 10-fold (or other numbers of folds) cross-validation commonly helps getting an overall reliable evaluation metric for a learning algorithm on a dataset.

5.1. 10-fold cross-validation

In this section we apply 10-fold cross-validation on the five datasets using our proposed approach and the other methods. The aim of this experiment is to test the reliability of our approach. The results are shown in table 1. Our proposed approach outperforms all other methods in all datasets. These results show that our proposed approach is reliable.

5.2. Test set evaluation

In this section we compare our approach, EPDT, to EPRC [1], PNrule [10], C4.5 [7], Metacost [6], and over-sampling [9] using the test sets supplied with the datasets. For the PNrule method, we present the results for the home insurance and network intrusion datasets only. Unfortunately, we did not have access to results of this method on the other datasets. The results are shown in table 2. Our proposed approach outperforms all other methods in all datasets in terms of f-measure. In terms of weighted accuracy, it outperforms all other methods in three datasets. Moreover, it scores the second highest weighted accuracy in the other two datasets. This performance is achieved by balancing both the recall and the precision. Achieving a very high result in either recall or precision does not guarantee achieving the highest weighted accuracy and f-measure. For example, in the home insurance test, Metacost trades off precision (5.92%) to obtain the highest recall (99.57%). As a result, the weighted accuracy (49.80%) and the f-measure (11.18%) are very low.

6. Conclusions

In this paper, we propose a new EP-based approach to enhance the performance of decision trees in classifying rare cases. Our approach, called EPDT, introduces the idea of generating new rare-class instances. Moreover, it adopts the idea of over-sampling existing rare-class instances. The two previous techniques are based on EPs. We experimentally demonstrate how our approach outperforms other classifiers (EPRC, PNrule, C4.5, Metacost, and over-sampling) on a number of challenging rare-class datasets. Furthermore, our approach can be thought of as an avenue to extend the applications of EPs to cover a wide range of problems in data mining.

References

[1] H. Alhammady, and K. Ramamohanarao. The Application of Emerging Patterns for Improving the Quality of Rare-class Classification. In Proceedings of 2004 Pacific-Asia Conference on Knowledge Discovery and Data Mining (PAKDD '04), Sydney, Australia.

[2] H. Fan, and K. Ramamohanarao. An Efficient Single-Scan Algorithm For Mining Essential Jumping Emerging Patterns for Classification. In Proceedings of 2002 Pacific-Asia Conference on Knowledge Discovery and Data Mining (PAKDD '02), Taipei, Taiwan.

[3] G. Dong, and J. Li. Efficient Mining of Emerging Patterns: Discovering Trends and Differences. In Proceedings of 1999 International Conference on Knowledge Discovery and Data Mining (KDD '99), San Diego, CA, USA.

[4] C. Blake, E. Keogh, and C. J. Merz. UCI repository of machine learning databases. Department of Information and Computer Science, University of California at Irvine, CA, 1999. http://www.ics.uci.edu/~mlearn/MLRepository.html.

[5] P. van der Putten, M. de Ruiter, and M. van Someren. The CoIL Challenge 2000 report. June 2000. http://www.liacs.nl/~putten/library/cc2000

[6] P. Domingos. MetaCost: A General Method for Making Classifiers Cost-Sensitive. In Proceedings of 1999 International Conference on Knowledge Discovery and Data Mining (KDD'99), San Diego, CA, USA.

[7] I. H. Witten, E. Frank. Data Mining: Practical Machine Learning Tools and Techniques with Java Implementations. Morgan Kaufmann, San Mateo, CA., 1999.

[8] C. J. van Rijsbergan. Information Retrieval. Butterworths, London, 1979.

[9] C. X. Ling, and C. Li. Data Mining for Direct Marketing: Problems and Solutions. In Proceedings of 1998 International Conference on Knowledge Discovery and Data Mining (KDD'98), New York, NY, USA.

[10] M. V. Joshi. Learning Classifier Models for Predicting Rare Phenomena. PhD thesis, University of Minnesota, November, 2002.

[11] J. Cheng, C. Hatzis, H. Hayashi, M. Krogel, S. Morishita, D. Page, and J. Sese. KDD Cup 2001 report. ACM SIGKDD Explorations, January, 2002.

Table 1. The results of the 10-fold cross validation experiments

Classifier	Weighted accuracy	Recall	Precision	F-measure
Home insurance				
EPDT	59.41	22.70	27.14	24.72
EPRC	58.42	21.83	21.71	21.77
C4.5	53.42	10.91	14.55	12.47
Metacost	52.93	10.05	13.25	11.43
Over-sampling	53.06	10.34	13.48	11.70
Network intrusion				
EPDT	57.93	15.91	50.69	24.22
EPRC	56.73	13.47	77.50	22.96
C4.5	52.56	5.13	95.16	9.73
Metacost	53.80	7.65	29.53	12.15
Over-sampling	52.56	5.13	77.63	9.62
Disease				
EPDT	87.52	75.55	70.83	73.11
EPRC	85.33	71.11	72.72	71.91
C4.5	79.80	60.00	71.05	65.06
Metacost	81.87	64.44	60.41	62.36
Over-sampling	81.26	63.04	67.44	65.16
Hypothyroid				
EPDT	96.21	92.66	95.20	93.91
EPRC	94.25	88.66	96.37	92.36
C4.5	94.81	90.00	92.46	91.21
Metacost	95.35	91.33	87.82	89.54
Over-sampling	95.60	92.00	85.18	88.46
Sick-euthyroid				
EPDT	93.72	88.35	88.05	88.20
EPRC	92.66	86.30	90.00	88.11
C4.5	92.48	86.30	86.89	86.59
Metacost	92.96	87.32	86.44	86.88
Over-sampling	92.79	86.98	86.39	86.68

Table 2. The results of the test set experiments

Classifier	Weighted accuracy	Recall	Precision	F-measure
Home insurance				
EPDT	62.74	39.07	15.39	22.09
EPRC	63.89	44.95	14.20	21.59
PNrule	58.91	26.89	15.80	19.90
C4.5	52.87	9.66	13.52	11.27
Metacost	49.80	99.57	5.92	11.18
Over-sampling	57.39	32.25	10.43	15.77
Network intrusion				
EPDT	56.57	13.31	82.70	22.93
EPRC	56.53	13.23	81.76	22.78
PNrule	56.44	13.05	82.09	22.52
C4.5	52.61	5.23	96.35	9.92
Metacost	52.98	7.44	21.76	11.09
Over-sampling	52.60	5.25	88.64	9.92
Disease				
EPDT	68.76	38.46	35.71	37.03
EPRC	65.07	30.76	40.00	34.78
C4.5	61.17	23.07	30.00	26.08
Metacost	53.68	7.69	25.00	11.76
Over-sampling	64.91	30.76	30.76	30.76
Hypothyroid				
EPDT	96.44	93.54	85.29	89.23
EPRC	97.92	96.77	81.08	88.23
C4.5	93.28	87.09	87.09	87.09
Metacost	93.31	87.09	88.52	87.80
Over-sampling	94.25	91.93	52.29	66.66
Sick-euthyroid				
EPDT	95.53	93.15	81.92	87.17
EPRC	95.46	93.15	80.95	86.62
C4.5	91.83	84.93	87.32	86.11
Metacost	90.91	82.87	88.97	85.81
Over-sampling	90.90	84.24	77.84	80.92

Discovery of Functional Relationships in Multi-relational Data using Inductive Logic Programming

Alexessander Alves, Rui Camacho and Eugenio Oliveira
LIACC, Rua do Campo Alegre, 823, 4150 Porto, Portugal
FEUP, Rua Dr Roberto Frias, 4200-465 Porto, Portugal
alves@ieee.org {rcamacho,eco}@fe.up.pt
tel: +351 22 508 1849   fax: +351 22 508 1443

Abstract

ILP systems have been largely applied to datamining classification tasks with a considerable success. The use of ILP systems in regression tasks has been far less successful. Current systems have very limited numerical reasoning capabilities, which limits the application of ILP to discovery of functional relationships of numeric nature.

This paper proposes improvements in numerical reasoning capabilities of ILP systems for dealing with regression tasks. It proposes the use of statistical-based techniques like Model Validation and Model Selection to improve noise handling and it introduces a new search stopping criterium based on the PAC method to evaluate learning performance.

We have found these extensions essential to improve on results over machine learning and statistical-based algorithms used in the empirical evaluation study.

1 Introduction

Inductive logic programming (ILP) offers several advantages for data mining, such as the expressiveness and intelligibility of first-order logic as hypothesis representation language; the ability to use structured, complex and multi-relational data; the compact and natural description of relations; the ability to use various forms of background knowledge; and the possibility to use language bias provided by the user to define the search space of the relational patterns considered. These advantages enabled ILP to achieve a considerable success in domains like biochemistry, and language processing since in these domains, the background knowledge is mainly of a relational nature and the data attributes are of categorical nature.

Theoretically there is no impediment of using whatever knowledge is useful for the induction of a theory. For some applications it would be quite useful to include as back-

ground knowledge methods and algorithms of a numerical nature. Such an ILP system would be able to harmoniously combine relations with "numerical methods" in the same *model*. A proper approach to deal with numerical domains would therefore extend the applicability of ILP systems to regression data mining tasks.

Current ILP approaches [9] to numerical domains usually carry out a search through the model (hypothesis) space looking for a minimal value of a cost function like the Root Mean Square Error (RMSE). Systems like TILDE [2] are of that kind. One problem with the minimisation of RMSE in noisy domains is that the models tend to be brittle. The error is small when covering a small number of examples. The end result is a large set of clauses to cover the complete set of examples. This is a drawback on the intelligibility of ILP induced models. This aspect is also an obstacle to the induction of a *numerical theory*, since we end up with small locally fitted *sub-models*, that may not correspond to the overall structure of the underlying process that generated data.

In this paper we introduce improvements on the numerical reasoning capabilities of ILP systems by adopting statistical-based noise handling techniques such as model validation and model selection, as well as a new stopping criterium based on the PAC [10] method to evaluate learning performance. The experimental results show that an ILP system extended with such procedures compares very well with statistical methods and other data mining techniques found on the published literature.

The rest of the paper is organised as follows. Section 2 identifies the steps of a basic ILP algorithm that are subject to improvements proposed in this paper. The proposals for Model Validation are discussed in Section 3. In Section 4 we propose the stopping criterium. The proposals for Model Selection are discussed in Section 5. Section 6 presents the experimental findings. Finally, in Section 7 we draw the conclusions.

2 Search Improvements

In ILP, the search procedure is usually an iterative greedy set-covering algorithm that finds the best clause on each iteration and removes the covered examples. Each hypothesis generated during the search is evaluated to determine their quality. In numerical domains it is common to use the RMSE or Mean Absolute Error (MAE) as a score measure [9]. Algorithm 1 presents an overview of the procedure and identifies the steps modified by our proposals.

Algorithm 1 A basic greedy set-covering ILP algorithm

1: **repeat**
2:    **repeat**
3:       synthesise an hypothesis
4:       accept an hypothesis (Model Validation)
5:       Update best hypothesis (Model Selection)
6:    **until** Stopping Criterium satisfied
7:    Remove explained examples
8: **until** "All" examples explained

We propose an improvement to step 4 where an hypothesis is checked if it is a satisfactory approximation of the underlying process that generated data. Step 5 is improved using a model selection criterium to mitigate the over-fitting problem. Our proposal for step 6 is inspired on the PAC [10] method to evaluate learning performance.

2.1 Dealing with multi-relational data

Multi relational data is naturally handled by ILP systems. The relation that holds the target concept is declared separately of the remaining relations, which are handled by the ILP system in a similar fashion to the background knowledge relations. While this setting is a straightforward technique to include multi-relational data, it is more demanding in what regards heap memory requirements, however, the effects were negligible in the empirical evaluation.

3 Model Validation

In most applications, the true nature of the model is unknown, therefore, it is of fundamental importance to assess the goodness-of-fit of each conjectured hypothesis. This is performed in a step of the induction process called *Model Validation*. Model Validation allows the system to check if the hypothesis captures the structure of the underlying process that generated the data.

There are various ways of checking if a model is satisfactory. The most common approach is to examine the residuals. If the model fits correctly data, the residuals are the random process formed from the differences between the observed and predicted values of a variable, and by definition independently drawn. Hypotheses whose residuals are not random may be rejected using specific statistical tests that check randomness, like run tests and the Ljung-Box test [4]. Other statistical tests may be also incorporated to check the user assumptions regarding error structure, like for example tests for normality.

The Model Validation step accepts a hypothesis if the scored p-value on the statistical tests is greater than a predefined level of significance α established by the user. The residuals of hypotheses accepted by this method will be incompressible according to the definition of statistical independence. In this context, Muggleton and Srinivasan [8] also proposed to check for noise imcompressibility to evaluate hypothesis significance on classification problems.

The usage of Model Validation tests to restrict the set of acceptable hypothesis is supported by the White theorem [7], which states that for a fixed set of models and a battery of validation tests, as the sample size tends to infinity and increasingly smaller test sizes are employed, the test battery will with probability 1 select the best model. The results of White theorem are asymptotic, which is not enough to assure good results in the sample sizes typically used in datamining, nevertheless we have found good results in the empirical evaluation.

4 Stopping Criterium

The stopping criterium proposed is based on the PAC [10] method to evaluate learning performance: $P(|z| > \epsilon) < \delta$. The search is stopped whenever the probability of the error be greater than the accuracy (ϵ) is less than the confidence interval (δ). Different degrees of "goodness" will correspond to different values of ϵ and δ. In this section we propose a method to calculate the bound, δ, for any unknown distribution. For that, we assume the usage of the Ljung-Box test in the model validation step. The null hypothesis of the Ljung-Box test is a strict white noise process, which means that residuals are independent and identically distributed (i.i.d.). Theorem 1, proves the existence of that bound for a single clause (hypothesis) and provides a procedure to calculate the error probability for a given accuracy level. Corollary 1, generalises the bound on the error probability to multi-clausal theories.

Theorem 1 (Bounding Error Probability of an Hypothesis)
Let z be the residuals from the hypothesis h_i. Assume z is independent and identically distributed (i.i.d.) with distribution variance σ^2. Then the probability of the error being greater then ϵ is bounded by:

$$P(|z| > \epsilon \mid h_i) < \delta, \quad \delta = \frac{\sigma^2}{\epsilon^2} \qquad (1)$$

Proof: Let the residuals $z_1, z_2, \ldots, z_n$ be a sequence of i.i.d. random variables each with finite mean μ and σ. if $\bar{z} = (z_1 + \ldots + z_n)/n$ is the average of $z_1, z_2, \ldots, z_n$, then, it follows from the week law of large numbers [4] that:

$$\bar{z} \xrightarrow{P} \mu \qquad (2)$$

Let the sample variance be $S_n = \frac{1}{n}\sum_{j=1}^{n}(z_j - \bar{z})^2 = \frac{1}{n}\sum_{j=1}^{n} z_j^2 - \bar{z}^2$, where $\bar{z}$ is the sample average. It follows from the Slutski's lemma [4] that:

$$S_n \xrightarrow{P} \sigma \qquad (3)$$

Assuming the residuals z of the hypothesis h_i pass the null hypothesis of the Ljung-Box test, then they will comply with a strict white noise process with zero mean and finite variance, yielding thereby:

$$\mu = 0, \qquad \sigma < \infty \qquad (4)$$

Following Conditions (2) and (3), each observation may be considered drawn from the same ensemble distribution. Thus, the sample mean and variance of the joint distribution converge to the ensemble mean and variance. Moreover, condition (4) states that both values are finite and, therefore, for all $\epsilon > 0$, the Chebishev's inequality bounds the probability of the residuals value, z, being greater then ϵ to:

$$P(|z| > \epsilon \mid h_i) < \frac{\sigma^2}{\epsilon^2} \qquad (5)$$

■

Corollary 1 (Bounding Error Probability of a Theory)
Let H be a set of hypothesis (clauses) that describes a given theory T. Assume:

$$P(|z| > \epsilon \mid h_i) < \delta, \quad \forall_{h_i \in H} \qquad (6)$$

then, for theory T, the probability of the error, z, being greater than ϵ, is also bounded by $P(|z| > \epsilon) < \delta$.

We recall that just one clause is activated at each time thus all clauses of a non-recursive theory are mutually exclusive regarding example coverage, i.e.

$$h_i \cap h_j = \emptyset \quad \forall_{i \neq j} \qquad (7)$$

We also recall that the prior probability of h_i, $P(h_i)$ may be estimated calculating the frequency of h_i on the training set and dividing it by the coverage of the theory. Because the sum of the frequencies of all hypotheses is equal to the theory coverage, then

$$\sum_{\forall_{h_i \in H}} P(h_i) = 1 \qquad (8)$$

Proof: Let conditions (7) and (8) hold, then it follows from the *total probability theorem* that:

$$P(|z| > \epsilon) = \sum_{\forall_{h_i \in H}} P(|z| > \epsilon \mid h_i)P(h_i). \qquad (9)$$

Let condition (6) hold, then we may substitute $P(|z| > \epsilon \mid h_i)$ by δ in equation (9), yielding thereby: $P(|z| > \epsilon) < \delta \sum_{\forall_{h_i \in H}} P(h_i)$. Since $\sum_{\forall_{h_i \in H}} P(h_i) = 1$ and $P(|z| > \epsilon \mid h_i) < \delta, \quad \forall_{h_i \in H}$, then:

$$P(|z| > \epsilon) < \delta \qquad (10)$$

■

5 Model Selection

The evaluation of conjectured hypotheses is central to the search process in ILP. Given a set of hypotheses of the underlying process that generated data, we wish to select the one that best approximates the "true" process. The process of evaluating candidate hypothesis is termed *model selection* in statistical inference.

Hypotheses with larger number of adjustable parameters have more flexibility to capture complex structures in data but also to fit noise, leading to the problem of overfitting. Hence, any criterium for model selection should establish a trade-off between descriptive accuracy and hypothesis complexity. In numerical domains, a common measure of complexity is the number of adjusted parameters to data of an hypothesis [5]. A hypothesis with fewer degrees of freedom generically will be less able to fit statistical artifacts in small data sets and will therefore be less prone to the so-called "generalisation error". There are several model selection criteria using this complexity measure, an example is the Maximum Description Length [5] (MDL).

Dimension consistent criteria like MDL tend to choose oversimplified models when the true model is not on the set of candidate hypotheses. A criterium that mitigates this problem is the Akaike Information Criterium Corrected for small sample bias (AICC) [5], however, AICC is not optimal, which means that model complexity may increase as more data is supplied. Since this is a prediction task, one may drop optimality for the sake of prediction performance, adopting AICC instead. Formally, AICC $= -2\ln(L) + 2k\frac{n}{n-k+1}$, where the hypothesis likelihood function, L, with k adjusted parameters shall be estimated from data assuming a prior distribution. In this context, the Gaussian distribution plays an important role in the characterisation of the noise, fundamentally due to the central limit theorem. Assuming error is i.i.d. drawn from a Gaussian distribution then, the likelihood of an hypothesis given the data [5] is: $\ln(L) = -\frac{n}{2}(1 + \ln(2\pi) + \ln(\hat{\sigma}_r^2))$, where $\hat{\sigma}_r^2 = \frac{1}{n}\sum_{i=1}^{n} z_i^2$, and z are the residuals of the induced hypothesis. Usually the compared hypotheses have different coverages, Box and Jenkins [3](pg. 201) suggest the normalisation of those criteria by the sample size. This approach has the advantage of indirectly biasing the search to favour hypothesis with higher coverage, and consequentially, theories with less clauses.

Other authors presented similar work in this area. Zelezni [11] derives a model selection criterium under similar assumptions that uses a different complexity measure and requires the calculation of the "generality" function for each induced hypothesis.

6 Experiments

This section presents a diversified set of experiments consisting of regression tasks to illustrate the general character, and to provide empirical evidence for the proposals made on this paper. Due to space constraints we present here a summary of the results and provide a technical report [1] separately with the experiments details.

The datasets used were collected from data mining, statistics and time series literature. The *MPG* dataset concerns to the city-cycle fuel consumption in miles per gallon, to be predicted in terms of 3 multivalued discrete and 5 continuous attributes. The remaining datasets will be predicted in terms of its historical values, formally $\tilde{x}_t \leftarrow h(X_s) + \epsilon, s < t$, where $\tilde{x}$ is the predicted argument and X is the vector of arguments of an example. The *G7* dataset concerns to the G7 Industrial Production Index of each country. the *USA* dataset concerns to the USA Unemployment rate; the *ECG* dataset concerns the heart beat rate of a patient with sleep apnea; and the *VBR* dataset concerns to the VBR Traffic of an MPEG video. Theories induced by the raw IndLog system are compared with the IndLog system with Model Validation and Model Selection activated (IndLog*) as well as other data mining, and statistical time series models described in the papers referring the datasets. The recall number of the theories induced with IndLog* for the USA, G7, VBR, and ECG datasets are respectively: 100%, 96%, 94%, and 78%. The recall number for the MPG dataset is 100%. The results obtained with these methodologies are presented on table 1.

7 Conclusions

In this paper we have proposed improvements in the numerical reasoning capabilities of ILP systems. The improvements proposed are: model validation; model selection criteria and; a stopping criterium.

Our proposals were incorporated in the IndLog [6] system and evaluated on regression tasks. The ILP results compared well with statistics-based time series prediction models, as well as other classical machine learning methods

Table 1. Relative RMSE

Algorithm	MPG	USA	G7	VBR	ECG
IndLog*	0.98	0.91	0.85	0.93	0.82
IndLog	1.03	1.11	1.04	0.96	0.93
CART	1.04	–	–	–	–
AR	–	1.04	0.98	0.94	0.97
SARIMA	–	1.00	1.00	–	–
MSA	–	1.19	–	–	–
MSC	–	–	1.00	–	–
MSMH	–	–	0.98	–	–
MSIAH	–	–	1.20	–	–
SETAR	–	–	1.19	–	–
TAR	–	1.00	–	1.00	–
RBFN	–	–	–	–	1.00
BAR	–	1.20	–	–	–
Benchmark	2.18	1.59E-1	4.44E-3	12.9E3	4.53

like neural networks, support vector machines and regression trees. The ILP system also discovered a new switching model based on the possibility of varying the delay on the activation rule of each sub-model of a TAR model.

References

[1] A. Alves, R. Camacho, and E. Oliveira. Multi-relational data mining in numerical domains with ILP. Technical report, University of Porto, 2004.

[2] H. Blockeel, L. D. Raedt, and J. Ramon. Top-down induction of clustering trees. In J. Shavlik, editor, *15th ICML*, pages 55–63. Morgan Kaufmann, 1998.

[3] J. Box and Reinsel. *Time Series Analysis, Forecasting and Control*. Prentice Hall, Englewood Cliffs, N.J., USA, 3rd edition edition, 1994.

[4] P. Brockwell and R. Davis. *Time series: theory and methods*. Springer, N.Y., 1991.

[5] K. Burnham and D. Anderson. *Model Selection and Multimodel Inference*. Springer, New York, 2002.

[6] R. Camacho. *Inducing Models of Human Control Skills using Machine Learning Algorithms*. PhD thesis, Universidade do Porto, July 2000.

[7] K. Hoover and S. Perez. Data mining reconsidered: encompassing and the general-to-specific approach to specification search. *Econometrics Journal*, 93(2):167–191, 1999.

[8] S. Muggleton, A. Srinivasan, and M. Bain. Compression, significance and accuracy. In D. e. a. Sleeman, editor, *ML92*, pages 338–347. Morgan Kauffman, 1992.

[9] A. Srinivasan and R. Camacho. Numerical reasoning with an ILP system capable of lazy evaluation and customised search. *J. Logic Prog.*, 40(2-3):185–213, 1999.

[10] L. Valiant. A theory of the learnable. *Commun. ACM*, 27(11):1134–1142, 1984.

[11] F. Zelezny. Learning functions from imperfect positive data. In *International Workshop on Inductive Logic Programming*, pages 248–260, 2001.

Attribute Measurement Policies for Time and Cost Sensitive Classification

Andrew Arnt and Shlomo Zilberstein
Department of Computer Science
University of Massachusetts at Amherst
Amherst, MA 01003
[arnt,shlomo]@cs.umass.edu

Abstract

Attribute measurement is an important component of classification algorithms, which could limit their applicability in realtime settings. The time taken to assign a value to an unknown attribute may reduce the overall utility of the final result. We identify three different costs that must be considered, including a time sensitive utility function. We model this attribute measurement problem as a Markov decision process (MDP), and build a policy to control this process using AO* heuristic search. The results offer a cost-effective approach to attribute measurement and classification for a variety of realtime applications.

1. Introduction

Machine learning classifiers predict labels for instances using many attributes measured or computed from the instance. Computing some of these attributes may be computationally intensive or rely on slow external sources of information. It may be impractical to measure all possible attributes for each instance in a realtime setting. To address these issues, we develop a model that allows the system to quickly decide which attributes to measure, what order to measure them in, and when to stop measurement and classify the current instance. We take a decision theoretic approach, where we try to minimize the expected value of a cost function reflecting the quality of service of the system.

Managing the tradeoff between classifier accuracy and costs incurred is a challenging problem. Myopic methods such as those used in [3] will not perform well due to interactions between attributes: when not all attributes can be measured, the ordering of measurements becomes very important. By framing the attribute measurement problem as an MDP where the state contains both the current attribute vector and the current time, we can find an optimal attribute measurement policy. Due to the potentially large size of the MDP, AO* heuristic search will be used to compute the policy. We examine the use of statistical pruning and inadmissible heuristics to cope with exceptionally difficult searches.

2. Types of cost in realtime classification

In standard classification systems, the goal of the classifier is to correctly predict the actual label of a problem instance (represented as a vector of attributes). The goal of this work is to develop a system for realtime classification that provides a high quality of service by allowing a tradeoff between the time required to process an instance, the cost of observing attributes in that instance, and the risk of misclassifying an instance. A cost function C, composed of three types of cost, is designed so that minimizing C will cause the system to provide the highest quality of service.

Misclassification costs In many applications, not all misclassifications have the same value. There may be a significant difference between the problems caused by a false negative versus those caused by a false positive. We denote this portion of the cost function which handles misclassification penalties as $C_L(l_p|l_a)$, which is the cost incurred by classifying an instance with actual label l_a with the predicated label l_p.

The misclassification (MC) cost component depends on the actual label l_a of an instance, which is unknown, except in training data. Thus, in practice we need to use the *expected* MC cost, given that the classifier predicts label l_p: $EC_L(\text{cl}(l_p)|\mathbf{f}) = \sum_{l_a \in L} C_L(l_p|l_a)p(l_a|\mathbf{f})$, where L is the complete set of labels that an instance may have. The probability that an instance with the current measured attribute vector $\mathbf{f}$ has the actual label of l_a is estimated from training data: $p(l_a|\mathbf{f}) = \frac{|train(l_a,\mathbf{f})|}{|train(\mathbf{f})|}$, where $train(\mathbf{f})$ is the set of all training examples such that for every measured attribute in $\mathbf{f}$, the training example has the same value, and $train(l_a, \mathbf{f})$ is the subset of examples in $train(\mathbf{f})$ that have label l_a.

For classification actions, algorithm will choose the label that incurs the minimum expected MC cost on a set of training data: $l_p = \arg \min_{l \in L} EC_L(\text{cl}(l)|\mathbf{f})$.

Attribute measurement costs An individual attribute f_i may have a deterministic cost to measure: $C_M(\text{m}(f_i))$.

Response time costs The cost function should also reflect the timeliness with which we wish the classifier to act. In many systems (especially those that interact with humans), a labeling decision made quickly will be worth more than one that takes a very long time.

Therefore the cost function has a final component $C_T(t)$, which will typically have an exponential form, which provides a good approximation of a user's perceived utility of a system when they are forced to wait for a result. In general, however, the time cost component can take on any form, so long as the time cost is nondecreasing over time.

Combining cost function components To combine the three components of the cost function, it suffices to perform a simple weighted addition. The cost of assigning predicted label l_p to an instance $\mathbf{f}$ with measured attributes $\text{meas}(\mathbf{f})$ and actual label l_a in t time units is:

$$C(\mathbf{f}, t) = w_L E C_L(\text{cl}(l_p)|\mathbf{f}) + w_T C_T(t) + w_M \sum_{f_i \in \text{meas}(\mathbf{f})} C_M(\text{m}(f_i))$$

3. Cost effective policies

Given a set of training data, we want to find the attribute measurement and classification policy that minimizes the expected cost of classification of future instances.

Our strategy for time and cost sensitive policy learning builds on the work of [4]. We frame the attribute measurement and classification problem as an MDP. The "optimal" policy (quoted because it is optimal only with respect to a set of labeled training data) can then be found using AO* search, a classical heuristic search technique. We extend their model to handle time-sensitive utility costs.

Cost effective classification as an MDP MDPs are a popular framework for sequential decision making problems. An agent in an MDP takes *actions* which cause stochastic transitions between *states*. A typical formulation (and the one used here) has an agent with the goal of minimizing the costs incurred while transitioning to some terminal state. The mapping from states to actions that minimizes cost is called the *optimal policy*.

The states $s \in S$ in the model presented in [4] are simply the set of all possible attribute vectors $\mathbf{f}$, including those with unmeasured attributes, augmented to include the current waiting time of the task: $s = \langle \mathbf{f}, t \rangle$ for all values of $\mathbf{f}$ and t (time is discretized and bounded empirically), in addition to an additional absorbing termination state E that is transitioned to when an instance is classified. The starting state of the MDP is the state with no measured attributes and no elapsed waiting time.

The actions in this model are to either measure an unmeasured attribute f_i, denoted 'm(f_i)', or to classify the current instance using the label l_p, denoted 'cl(l_p)'.

There are three types of cost related to taking an action. $C_M(\text{m}(f_i))$ is the deterministic cost to measure attribute f_i. There are also incremental time costs $C_\Delta(\delta|t)$ which

indicate the portion of the end cost $C_T(t)$ incurred by waiting δ additional time units to classify an instance that has already been waiting t time units. Given a time cost function $C_T(t)$, it is straightforward to compute the incremental time cost function: $C_\Delta(\delta|t) = C_T(t + \delta) - C_T(t)$. The expected immediate cost of taking the action $\text{m}(f_i)$ is then $C_M(\text{m}(f_i)) + \sum_{\delta \in T_i} p(T_i = \delta)C_\Delta(\delta|t)$.

The probability of transitioning from state $s = \langle \mathbf{f}, t \rangle$ to state $s' = \langle \mathbf{f} \cup f_i = x, t + \delta \rangle$ (where $\mathbf{f} \cup f_i = x$ refers to $\mathbf{f}$ with attribute f_i set to x) is $p(s'|s, \text{m}(f_i)) = p(f_i = x|\mathbf{f})p(T_i = \delta)$. The probability that attribute f_i will take on value x given the incomplete attribute vector $\mathbf{f}$ is estimated from training data: $p(f_i = x|\mathbf{f}) = \frac{|train(\mathbf{f} \cup f_i = x)|}{|train(\mathbf{f})|}$. The probability that attribute f_i takes δ time units to measure is denoted as $p(T_i = \delta)$, and is estimated from training data or from some other source of prior experience.

The probability of arriving in terminal state E when the classification action is taken is: $p(E|s, \text{cl}(l_p)) = 1$

AO* search AO* search is an heuristic search algorithm for searching AND/OR graphs. MDP policies can be represented as an AND/OR graph: at an OR node, the agent must choose a single action to take so as to minimize future cost. However, since the environment is stochastic, taking an action causes the agent to transition probabilistically to one of a number of states. Therefore all these states are successors of the original state and their costs must be AND ed together to compute the best action.

AO* works by iteratively improving upon the current best partial solution policy until an optimal policy is found. Each iteration of AO* search is composed of two parts. First, the current best partial solution is expanded (its successors are added to the search graph) by picking an unexpanded search state within the current policy. Next, state values and best action choices are updated in a bottom-up manner, starting from the newly expanded state. The estimated value of a state s during the search is $f(s)$: an optimistic estimate of the cost to get from s to a terminal state.

Heuristic A heuristic is necessary to guide AO*. The heuristic value of a state is the optimistic estimate of how much cost will be incurred before reaching a terminal state. For an optimal policy to be found, the heuristic must be *admissible*: it must never overestimate the cost from a state to the terminal state. We use the optimistic one-step lookahead heuristic of [4] with the inclusion of incremental time costs. Given an unexpanded state s, the heuristic value $h(s)$ is the cost of the action (classifying or measuring an attribute) giving the smallest immediate cost:

$$h(s) = \min_{f_i \notin \text{meas}(\mathbf{f})} \begin{cases} EC_L(\text{cl}(l_p)|\mathbf{f}) \\ C_M(\text{m}(f_i)) + \sum_{\delta \in T_i} p(T_i = \delta)C_\Delta(\delta|t) \end{cases}$$

Pruning strategies For classification problems where instances have a large number of measurable attributes, each of which can take on many values, pruning of the search space is essential for efficient search. A pruning strategy that preserves the optimality of the policy hinges on the fact that the terminal state E can be reached by from any state of this MDP by taking a single classification action [4]. This property, which is not applicable for general MDP models, allows for some significant pruning of the search space. An upper bound $\hat{h}(s)$ value is computed at each node; this value represents the expected cost of following the current *best known* policy from search state s.

Therefore, any unexpanded search node s' with parent node s where $\hat{h}(s) < h(s')$ can be pruned, as the expansion of s' cannot lead to an improved policy since we will always choose the action at s that provides the minimal $\hat{h}(s)$.

[4] also examine statistical pruning of the search space due to sparsities of training data. This is an important consideration, since the amount of training data that is being used to direct the search gets smaller and smaller as measurement actions are taken. Eventually, the search reaches a depth where there is insufficient training data to justify choosing any one action over any other. A statistical test can be performed prior to node expansion to determine if the expansion of the node is justified by the training data matching that node. This pruning has two benefits: the search space is reduced, and overfitting of the training data is avoided.

Evaluation function decomposition   [2] show that the evaluation function in AO* search can be decomposed into $f(s) = g(s) + h(s)$. $g(s)$ represents the portion of the solution cost of the policy rooted at s that is *known*; That is, the $g(s)$ cost has been explicitly computed using just costs incurred on transitions to generated states, with no $h()$ values being considered. The $h(s)$ value represents the costs in the policy rooted at s that are just estimated using the h estimates at unexpanded nodes. Generated but not yet expanded states s have $g(s) = 0$, and $h(s)$ as defined earlier.

This decomposition of the value function allows a weighted version of AO* that gives more emphasis to the heuristic estimate. Instead of using $f(s) = g(s) + h(s)$, the estimated cost can be given more weight: $f'(s) = (1 - \omega)g(s) + \omega h(s)$. As ω increases from 0.5 to 1.0, the heuristic becomes inadmissible and the search becomes increasingly greedy, producing policies of decreasing quality. The search space explored also shrinks, allowing a trade-off between quality of results and computability for large search spaces. This results in a bounded loss of optimality, but also can significantly reduce the number of search states that must be evaluated.

4. Experimental results

We created a 3000 instance data set with binary labels using a naive Bayes network. For each of the 10 binary attributes in an instance, $p(f_i = l_a) = 0.6$ and $p(f_i \neq l_a) =$ 0.4, except for a single attribute independent of the label with probability 0.5 of being 1. $C_M(m(f_i))$ is zero for all attributes. For all attributes, the distribution of measurement time is $p(T_i = 1) = 0.3$, $p(T_i = 2) = 0.4$, $p(T_i = 3) = 0.2$, $p(T_i = 10) = 0.1$, except for the last two attributes which are measured instantaneously. The time utility function used is $C_T(t) = e^{0.3t} - 1$. The MC cost is a simple 0-1 function where $C_L(l_p|l_a) = 1$ if $l_p = l_a$ and 0 otherwise.

We hold w_T fixed at 1 and vary w_L to simulate a variety of domains. When w_L is small, the time costs tend to dominate the search, resulting in shallow searches that quickly terminate with a policy that chooses to observe very few of the time consuming attributes. When w_L is very large, MC costs dominate, and the resulting search space is very large, and results in policies that generally measure all attributes of an instance. AO* search is terminated after 250000 nodes generated, returning a policy that takes the current best known action at each state. 2000 instances of the data set were used for training.

We also examine the performance of a myopic algorithm that greedily chooses to observe the attribute that will provide the largest expected immediate reduction in cost, given that the next action will be to classify. Classification is performed when none of the attributes are expected to reduce cost. This algorithm is akin to an offline version of the expected value of computation work of Horvitz [3].

Comparison of search strategies   Figure 1 (top) shows the number of nodes expanded for AO* with and without statistical pruning of search nodes at a confidence level of 95%. Note from the inset that the number of nodes generated grows quickly as w_L increases, until the memory limit of 250000 nodes is hit when $w_L \geq 256$. Note that the pruning searches tend to generate less nodes, as expected.

Figure 1 (bottom) shows the average total cost achieved on testing data for policies learned by each of the methods. Since the total costs for different values of w_L are not directly comparable, results are given as a fraction of the worst total cost received by any of the three methods. We see that the greedy policy is by far the worse method for all tasks except the shallow $w_L = 16$ and difficult case where $w_L = 512$. Statistical pruning results in significantly better policies when the memory limit is a factor.

Non-admissible heuristics   When faced with large search spaces that cause AO* search to prematurely terminate because memory is exhausted, it is advantageous to use a non-admissible heuristic.

Figure 2 shows the behavior in both number of nodes generated and the total cost of the learned policies on test data for $w_L = 512$ and ω varying from 0.5 (the standard admissible heuristic) to 1.0 (a greedy search that focuses only on minimizing future costs from a state). For total cost of the greedy policy is also given. The 250000 node memory limit is encountered when $\omega \leq 0.7$. In this case using a very

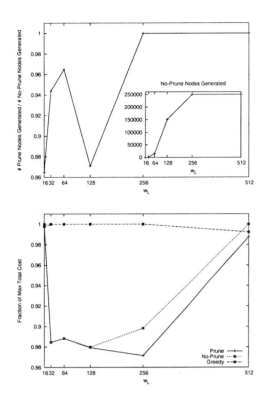

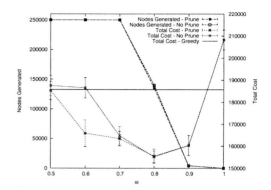

Figure 2. Varying ω **for** $w_L = 512$

model by augmenting the incremental time cost component: $C_{\Delta}'(\delta|t,\mathbf{q}) = C_{\Delta}(\delta|t) + C_{OC}(\delta|\mathbf{q})$, and expanding the state space to $s = \langle \mathbf{f}, t, \mathbf{q} \rangle$. The MDP transition model must also be augmented: the probability of transitioning from state $s = \langle \mathbf{f}, t, \mathbf{q} \rangle$ to state $s' = \langle \mathbf{f} \cup f_i = x, t + \delta, \mathbf{q}' \rangle$ is

$$p(s'|s, \mathrm{m}(f_i)) = p(f_i = x|\mathbf{f})p(T_i = \delta)p(\mathbf{q}'|\mathbf{q}, \delta)$$

where $p(\mathbf{q}'|\mathbf{q}, \delta)$ is the probability of the queue going from state $\mathbf{q}$ to $\mathbf{q}'$ during a time interval of δ time units. This quantity can be estimated from past experience.

6. Conclusions

Existing cost-sensitive classification algorithms have focused solely on misclassification and attribute measurement costs. Yet for many applications, good responsiveness is a desirable and often necessary property. We have shown how AO* search combined with statistical pruning and inadmissible heuristics can be used to learn policies for attribute measurement and classification in these settings.

The problem of time sensitive classification is further compounded when dealing with a stream of instances. If future instances are not considered while choosing which attributes to measure for the current task, there is the risk of large penalties for the delay in classifying those future tasks. Future work will explore this problem in more detail.

References

[1] A. Arnt, S. Zilberstein, J. Allan, and A. I. Mouaddib. Dynamic composition of information retrieval techniques. *Journal of Intelligent Information Systems*, 2004.

[2] P. P. Chakrabarti, S. Ghose, and S. DeSarkar. Admissibility of AO* when heuristics overestimate. *Artificial Intelligence*, 34:97–113, 1988.

[3] E. Horvitz and G. Rutledge. Time-dependent utility and action under uncertainty. In *Proc. 7th Conf. on Uncertainty in Artificial Intelligence*, pages 151–158, 1991.

[4] V. B. Zubek and T. Dietterich. Pruning improves heuristic search for cost-sensitive learning. In *Proc. 19th Intl. Conf. on Machine Learning*, pages 27–34, 2002.

Figure 1. Training: Avg nodes generated (top), Testing: Avg cost incurred (bottom)

inadmissible heuristic allows the search to terminate normally with all of the search space explored, resulting in better policies than those searches that terminate prematurely with a significant amount of search space unexplored.

Note that using statistical pruning also allows for improved policies for cases where search terminates abnormally. The pruning of unnecessary nodes allows the search to make for effective use of the available memory.

5. Sequences of classification tasks

The above procedures do not account for other tasks that need to be classified. Indeed, suppose that instead of a single classification task to process, the system has to handle a *stream* of classification tasks arriving over time. Therefore, when deciding which attributes to measure in the current task, we must also consider the potential for utility loss due to delay in processing of all other tasks waiting to be classified. [1] refer to this as the *opportunity cost* (OC), the loss of expected value due to delay in the starting of work on the remaining tasks. They show that for a similar problem, the OC function can be quickly and effectively approximated by examining simple attributes of the queue of waiting tasks, such as number of tasks waiting and average waiting time of each task. Call this vector $\mathbf{q}$.

The OC component can be introduced to the MDP

Detecting Patterns of Appliances from Total Load Data Using a Dynamic Programming Approach

Michael Baranski

Member IEEE, VDE,

baranski@nek.upb.de

Jürgen Voss

Member IEEE, VDE

voss@nek.upb.de

Abstract

Nonintrusive Appliance Load Monitoring (NIALM) systems require sufficient accurate total load data to separate the load into its major appliances. The most available solutions separate the whole electric energy consumption based on the measurement of all three voltages and currents. Aside from the cost for special measuring devices, the intrusion into the local installation is the main problem for reaching a high market distribution. The use of standard digital electricity meters could avoid this problem but the loss of information of the measured data has to be compensated by more intelligent algorithms and implemented rules to disaggregate the total load trace of only the active power measurements. The paper presents a new NIALM approach to analyse data, collected form a standard digital electricity meter. To disaggregate the consumption of the entire active power into its major electrical end uses, an algorithm consisting of clustering methods, a genetic algorithm and a dynamic programming approach is presented. The genetic algorithm is used to combine frequently occuring events to create hypothetical finite state machines to model detectable appliances. The time series of each finite state machine is optimized using a dynamic programming method similar to the viterbi algorithm.

1. Introduction and Overview NIALM

Non-intrusive appliance load monitoring (NIALM) is, since the midnineties, a mature technique for disaggregating the entire electrical load into the major end uses of domestic homes cf. [2],[4] and [6]. The evaluation is often based on measuring of both, the active and reactive power fluctuations on all three phases of the household connection, so that the information with regard to the energy and power consumption can be analysed with a resolution of about one second. However, the costs for the measuring instrumentation and the essential intrusion into the electrical installation of a household play against an area wide distribution. To minimise the essential intrusions, the consump-

tion data could be collected by a low cost optical sensor clamped on the existing electricity meter cf. [10]. Typical NIALM systems with automatic setup use pattern recognition methods based on a priori knowledge from connected expert systems to detect appliances. Some other (cf. [4] and [6]) need initial training periods with manual entering of data. This NIALM approach tries to find recurring appliance patterns without manually entering of initial data.

The developed methods could also be used to analyse any other time series data to detect patterns of finite state machines (FSM) automaticly. Further applications could be found in data mining or pattern detection and recognition systems like financial or speech analysis.

2. Pattern Detection approach consisting of genetic algorithm and dynamic programming methods

The discrete time series of the total active power of a private home is measured with the above mentioned optical sensor with time resolution of one second. State changes in total load trace are detected and handled as events. The algorithm only focusses on recognisable electric appliances which could be handled as finite state machines (FSM). The detected events from a time period of one day are clustered to group frequently occuring power steps which probably represent state transitions of finite state machines. Different combinations of these transition values are combined to find frequently occuring patterns of unknown electric appliances. This could be done by searching the complete tree of possible combinations but, with respect to the great number of detected events ($\approx 10^4$ per day) and number of clusters (> 25), the use of more time efficient methods like gentic algorithms is necessary.

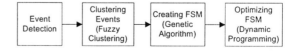

Fig. 1: Structure of the main algorithm

After creating hypothetic model of FSM according to the results of the genetic algorithm, the corresponding switch events are distributed to the created list of FSM. For each FSM, a shortest path problem is solved simultanously, stressing a dynamic programming approach. To avoid multiple assignments of single switch events to different FSMs, the optimisation has to be repeated until all of them are solved.

So let $\{S_t\}$ be the series of detected switch events from the total load data $\{P_t\}$. The difference series is computed to eliminate the offset of the load.

$$\Delta P_t = P_t - P_{t-1} \qquad (1)$$

Neighbouring values ΔP_t are assigned to a switch event due to the following rule

$$\Delta P_t \in \begin{cases} S_j & \text{if } |\Delta P_t| > \delta \wedge sgn(\Delta P_t) = sgn(\Delta P_{t-1}) \\ S_{j+1} & \text{if } |\Delta P_t| > \delta \wedge sgn(\Delta P_t) \neq sgn(\Delta P_{t-1}) \end{cases} \qquad (2)$$

where δ describes a threshold value in dependency of the accuracy of the used power sensor. Each event is treated as an abstract object, containing a subseries of ΔP_t values. Summing up all difference values results the active power step $P(S_j)$ of each event S_j. Further properties like the point of time or the duration are also available.

After clustering these events, using fuzzy clustering (cf. [11]) techniques or self organised maps (cf. [12]), each one is finally distributed to its best matching cluster. The power step values $P(C_i)$ of the cluster centres are assumed to represent state transitions of typical different appliances V_i, handled as FSM for further explanations. By altering the binary values c_{ij} in (3), 2^{N_C} possible combinations of transition values could be generated representing different appliances.

$$\mathcal{A}_i = \left\{ c_{i,1}P(C_1), .., c_{i,N_C}P(C_{N_C}) \right\} = \left\{ A_{i,1}, ..., A_{jk} \right\} \qquad (3)$$

The set of state transition $\mathcal{A}_i$ related to V_i could be evaluated by a combined quality function like

$$Q_{V_i} = \gamma_1 Q_{V_i}^{(1)} + \gamma_2 Q_{V_i}^{(2)} + \gamma_3 Q_{V_i}^{(3)} \qquad (4)$$

$$Q_{V_i}^{(1)} = \frac{\left| \sum_{j=1}^{N_C} c_{i,j} P(C_j) \right|}{\max_{c_{ji}=1} \left(\left\{ |c_{ji}P(C_j)| \right\} \right)} \qquad (5)$$

$$Q_{V_i}^{(2)} = \frac{\left| \sum_{j=1}^{N_C} h(C_j) c_{ji} P(C_j) \right|}{\max_{c_{ji}=1} \left(\left\{ |c_{ji} P(C_j)| \right\} \right)} \qquad (6)$$

$$Q_{V_i}^{(3)} = \frac{1}{N_C} \left| \sum_{i=1}^{N_C} c_{ji} \right| \qquad (7)$$

where $h(C_i)$ denotes the standardised number of events assigned to cluster C_j. Equation (5) computes the sum of all positive and negative state transition, resulting in zero for

an optimal appliance, (6) is related to the frequency and (7) addresses the total number of different states.

The use of a genetic algorithm reduces execution time when the number of different clusters exceeds about 25. The implemented GA is similar to the pseudo code GA presented in [8].

For each V_i, different variations of state transitions

$$\underline{A}_i^{(v)} = \left[A_{i,1}, ..., A_{i,k} \right] \qquad (8)$$

have to be investigated creating different sets of states by

$$Z_{i,k} = Z_{j,k-1} + A_{j,k}; \quad k = 1, ..., N_{Z_i} - 1 \qquad (9)$$

where N_{Z_i} denotes the number of different state transitions. Variations of (8), which violate the non negativity constraint of electric appliances in households specified by

$$Z_{i,k} \geq 0 \quad \forall k \in \left\{ 1, ..., N_{Z_i} \right\} \qquad (10)$$

have to be discarded. Each state computed by (9) represents a possible power state of appliance V_i. The corresponding switch events referenced by the clusters, linked to apliiance V_i according to (3), are then stressed to model the time series $\{P_{i,t}\}$ of appliance V_i by

$$P_{i,t} = \sum_{\tau=1}^{t} u_{i,t_j} P(S_j) \sigma(\tau - t_j) \qquad (11)$$

using the well known step-function $\sigma(t)$ and keeping in mind the following constraints:

$$0 \leq P_{i,t} \leq \max(Z_1, ..., Z_k) \quad \forall t \qquad (12)$$

$$P_{i,t} \leq P_t \quad \forall t \qquad (13)$$

Each V_i holds its own vector $\underline{u}_i^T$ containing N_s binary $u_{i,t}$, referencing every detected switch event. The binary values $u_{i,t}$ in (11) could be altered to model the behavior of all V_i optimising a suitable quality criterion. This job could be transformed to solve a shortest path problem. If we include the following additional assumptions for our appliances:

i)   The time series $\{P_{i,t}\}$ of any detectable appliances should be considered as a recurring pattern with parameters range in a limited area around their expectation value

ii) Every state from the set of states defining a FSM is activated exactly one time in each sequence

iii) Every sequence has the same fixed order of states to pass through (not necessary)

Each series $\{P_{i,t}\}$ could be subdivided into a finite number of sequences Γ_l stressing i) to iii),

$$P_{i,t} = \sum_{l=1}^{N_\Gamma} \Gamma_{i,l} \quad \text{with} \quad \Gamma_{i,l} = \left\{ A_{i,1}, A_{i,2}, ..., A_{i,k} \right\} \qquad (14)$$

where the power value of $A_{i,k}$ is replaced by the power step of the corresponding switch event linked to $A_{i,k}$.

A quality criterion similar to Shannons entropy cf. [5] leads to suitable results evaluating the quality of each sequence by

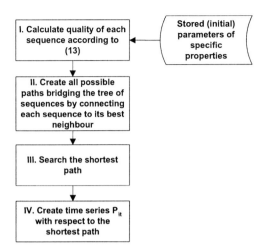

Fig. 3: Finding the shortest path according to fixed model paramters

$$Q_{r_{i,l}} = -\sum_{r}^{N_{E_i}} \Delta e_{i,r} \log |\Delta e_{i,r}| \qquad (15)$$

with

$$\Delta e_{i,r} = \left| \frac{\mathcal{E}_{i,r}(\Gamma_{i,l}) - \mathcal{E}_{i,r}(\Gamma_{i,c})}{\mathcal{E}_{i,r}(\Gamma_{i,c})} \right| + e_0 \qquad (16)$$

where $\mathcal{E}_{i,r}$ denotes the N_{E_i} different properties like time duration between state transitions or deviations of $u_{i,t}P(S_j)$ to $A_{i,k}$ calculated with respect to the cluster centres (avaraged values) containing the special event S_j. In (16) $\mathcal{E}_{i,r}(\Gamma_{i,c})$ describes the properties of a sequence assumed to be the optimal pattern of appliance V_i.

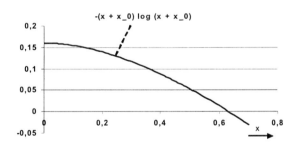

Fig. 2: Quality function of (14)

In Figure 2, $f(x) = -x \log |x|$ is shifted by $x_0 = 0{,}3678$, the x value to maximize f(x) if a parameter of the corresponding sequence deviates minimum (x= 0) to it's optimum cf. (15).

The best path crossing the tree of all valid sequences for each appliance could be found by searching the maximum quality value summing the quality of connected sequences

$$Q_p = \sum_{l=1}^{N_{T_p}} Q_l \qquad (17)$$

for each path. Using the quality function from (15), sequences with properties deviating more than 60% (cf. Fig. 2) relative according to their optimum decrease the quality value and will be omitted. After choosing the best path (series of sequeces), the time series $\{P_{i,t}\}$ is generated by setting all $u_{j,t}$ in (11) according to the corresponding best path. Figure 3 gives a short overview of this algorithm. The whole procedure could be repeated varying the optimal paramters (optimal properties of the sequences) referring to block number IV in Fig. 4. to improve the quality.

The procedures IV to VI in Fig. 4 are repeated until the requested quality of computed sequences is reached. The altering of parameters could be done by an evolutionary strategy with respect to the deviation of those parameters (cf. the algorithm from Rechenberg and Schwefel in [8]).

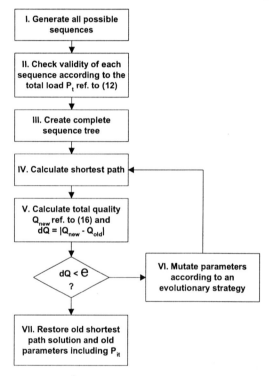

Fig. 4: Global algorithm to optimize the parameters, detecting structures

After optimising each finite state machine simultaneously, several switch events might be connected to different appliances. These overlappings could be solved step by step, linking the affected switch events to the appliance with the best quality value and repeating the complete optimisation without altering the $u_{i,t}$ of the next best finite state machine. Not later than N_V iterations all overlappings, due to multiple assigned events are solved, the algorithm quits.

Figure 5 shows an example of a series of state transitions of an appliance with three different transition values $A_{j,1}, A_{j,2}$ and $A_{j,3}$. To create the sequence tree, first, subsequences of combinations containing two state transitions are built. These subsequences are then connected to create sequences with respect to avoid overlappings in time. The arrows in Fig. (5) describe possible combinations to create subsequences. The vertical lines describe transition states, where subsequences could be connected to sequences.

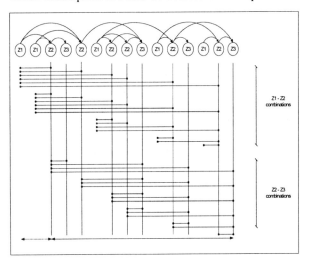

Fig. 5: Creating sequences of three different state transitions A_1, A_2 and A_3

3. Summary

The presented algorithm is designed to analyse rough data from ordinary electricity meters and has been tested with simulated and real data from different domestic homes. The analysed real data was collected with an optical sensor clamped on the already installed electricity meter in domestic homes.

If the clustering method results in 30 different state transitions to create FSMs, the genetic algorithm reduces the number evaluated combinations to find finite state machines from about $2^{30} \approx 10^9$ to $1,5 \cdot 10^4$ with sufficient quality. Every iteration, the lower 50% of individuals ordered by quality are displaced by new individuals generated by the upper 50%. Number of individuals takes 150 when 30 clusters are generated.

The gentic algorithm offers a variety of parameters to be tuned to improve the detection of appliances or to assimilate data sources of different applications.

To find typical appliance patterns, data from about five to ten days has to be analysed simultaneously. A daily set of data is used to update temporary stored parameters of detected appliances of each household.

The results show, that patterns of chief consumer load devices like refrigerators, electric flow heaters, stoves or a cookers could be detected. Additional tests are affordable to elaborate a suitable and robust parameter set to detect appliances for a wide spectrum of electric appliances of do-

mestic homes. The technical specification of the developed system is designed to be integrated in smart home applications based on the use of standard communication techniques and a standard pc. The total execution time ranges about ten minutes computed by a 2,4 GHz-personal computer.

An online NIALM system could be a suitable application for consumers to remote control special appliances of their home in absence. The results could be compared to existing references by connecting the system to an extended expert system via internet.

4. References

[1] Forney, G.D.: "The Viterbi Algorithm", Proceedings of the IEEE, Vol. 61, No.3, 1973, pp 268-278

[2] Hart, George W.:"Nonintrusive Appliance Load Monitoring", Proceedings of the IEEE, Vol. 80, No. 12, December 1992

[3] Bezdek, James C.:"Fuzzy Models For Pattern Recognition, Methods That Search For Structre In Data",IEEE Press, 1991

[4] Zmeureanu, Radu; Farinaccio, Linda:"Using a pattern recognition approach to disaggregate the total electricity consumption in a house into the major end-uses", Energy and Buildings 30 (1999), pp 245-259

[5] Shannon, C.E.: "A Mathematical Theory of Communication", The Bell System Technical Journal, Vol 27, pp379-423, 623-656, July, October, 1948

[6] Zmeureanu, Radu; Farinaccio, Linda: "Use of soft computing techniques for the evaluation of energy performance of equipments in buildings", Department of Building, Civil and Enviromental Engineering Concordia University, Montreal, Quebec, CANADA

[7] VDN Lastenheft "Elektronischer Haushaltszähler", Draft Version 0.9 from 14.11.2003, VDN (network operator association) at The German Electricity Association VDEW, www.vdn-berlin.de

[8] Schöneburg E., Heinzmann F., Feddersen S., "Genetische Algorithmen und Evolutionsstrategien", Addison Wesley, 1994

[9] Rabiner, Lawrence R.: "A Tutorial on Hidden Markov Models and Selected Applications in Speech Recognition", Proceedings of the IEEE, Vol. 77, No. 2, Feb. 1989

[10] Baranski M., Voss J.:"Non-Intrusive Appliance Load Monitoring based on an Optical Sensor", IEEE 2003 Bologna PowerTech, Bologna, Italy, June 23- June 262003, Paper BPT03-256

[11] Bandemer H.:"Ratschläge zum Mathematischen Umgang mit Ungewissheit", Teubner Verlag, Stuttgart, 1997, ISBN: 3-8154-2118-7,

[12] Kohonen T.:"Self-Organizing Maps", Springer Series in Information Siences, Springer Verlag, Heidelberg, Germany, 1995, ISBN: 3-540-58600-8

Text Classification by Boosting Weak Learners based on Terms and Concepts

Stephan Bloehdorn
University of Karlsruhe
Institute AIFB, Knowledge Management Group
D-76128 Karlsruhe, Germany
bloehdorn@aifb.uni-karlsruhe.de

Andreas Hotho
University of Kassel
Knowledge and Data Engineering Group
D-34121 Kassel, Germany
hotho@cs.uni-kassel.de

Abstract

Document representations for text classification are typically based on the classical Bag-Of-Words paradigm. This approach comes with deficiencies that motivate the integration of features on a higher semantic level than single words. In this paper we propose an enhancement of the classical document representation through concepts extracted from background knowledge. Boosting is used for actual classification. Experimental evaluations on two well known text corpora support our approach through consistent improvement of the results.

1 Introduction

Most of the explicit knowledge assets of today's organizations consist of unstructured textual information in electronic form. Systems that contextualize information by automatically classifying text documents into predefined thematic classes help users to organize and exploit the ever growing amounts of textual information.

During the last decades, a large number of machine learning methods have been proposed for text classification tasks [8]. They are, however, typically built around the *Bag-of-Words model* known from information retrieval. In this representation, documents are considered to be bags of words, each term or term stem being an independent feature of it's own – typically represented through binary indicator variables, absolute frequencies or more elaborated measures like TFIDF [7]. Learning algorithms are thus restricted to detecting patterns in the used *terminology* only, while *conceptual* patterns remain ignored. Specifically, systems using only words as features exhibit a number of inherent deficiencies:

1. *Multi-Word Expressions* with an own meaning like *"European Union"* are chunked into pieces with possibly very different meanings like *"union"*.

2. *Synonymous Words* like *"tungsten"* and *"wolfram"* are mapped into different features.
3. *Polysemous Words* are treated as one single feature while they may actually have multiple distinct meanings.
4. *Lack of Generalization*: there is no way to generalize similar terms like "beef" and "pork" to their common hypernym "meat".

In this paper, we show how background knowledge in form of simple ontologies can improve text classification results by directly addressing these problems. We propose a hybrid approach for document representation based on the common term stem representation enhanced with concepts extracted from the used ontologies. For actual classification we suggest to use the AdaBoost algorithm which has proven to produce accurate classification results in many experimental evaluations and seems to be well suited to integrate different types of features. Evaluations on two well known text corpora show that our approach leads to consistent improvements.

2 Conceptual Document Representation

Ontologies The background knowledge we will exploit further on is encoded in a *core ontology*. For the purpose of this paper, we present only important parts of our more extensive ontology definition described in [2].

Definition 2.1 (Core Ontology) *A core ontology is a structure $\mathcal{O} := (C, <_C)$ consisting of a set C, whose elements are called concept identifiers, and a partial order $<_C$ on C, called generalization hierarchy or taxonomy. The partial order $<_C$ relates the concepts in an ontology in form of specialization/generalization relationships.*

Definition 2.2 (Lexicon for an Ontology) *A lexicon for an ontology $\mathcal{O}$ is a tuple $Lex := (S_C, Ref_C)$ consisting of a set S_C, whose elements are called signs for concepts (symbols), and a relation $Ref_C \subseteq S_C \times C$ called lexical reference for concepts, where $(c, c) \in Ref_C$ holds for all $c \in C \cap S_C$. Based on Ref_C, for $s \in S_C$ we define $Ref_C(s) := \{c \in C | (s, c) \in Ref_C\}$.*

For the purpose of actual evaluation in the experiments, we have used two different resources, namely *WordNet* and the *MeSH Tree Structures Ontology*. Although not explicitly designed as an ontology, *WordNet*[1] largely fits into the ontology definitions given above. The WordNet database organizes 152,059 lexical index terms into a total of 115,424 so called *synonym sets (synsets)*, each of which represents an underlying concept and links these through semantic relations.

The *MeSH Tree Structures Ontology* is an ontology that has been compiled out of the Medical Subject Headings (MeSH) controlled vocabulary thesaurus of the United States National Library of Medicine (NLM)[2]. The ontology itself was ported into and accessed through the Karlsruhe Ontology and Semantic Web Infrastructure (KAON) infrastructure[3]. The ontology contains more than 22,000 concepts, each enriched with synonymous and quasi-synonymous language expressions.

Concept Extraction from Texts We have developed a process for extracting concepts from texts given a specific ontology. We shortly describe these steps in the following. The interested reader is referred to [1] for a more detailed description.

Due to the existence of multi-word expressions, the mapping of terms to concepts can not be accomplished by querying the lexicon directly for single words. We have addressed this issue by defining a *candidate term detection strategy* that builds on the basic assumption that finding the longest multi-word expressions that appear in the text and the lexicon will lead to a mapping to the most specific concepts. Our algorithm moves a window of a given length over the input text, analyzes the window content and either decreases the window size if the content can not be found in the lexicon or moves the window further to the next candidate expression. Querying the lexicon directly for any candidate expression in the window is likely to result in a large number of unnecessary queries. To increase efficiency and at the same time improve the concept retrieval quality we have incorporated a *syntactical analysis* step. By defining appropriate POS patterns (e.g. patterns for noun phrases) and matching the window content against these, expressions that will surely not symbolize concepts can be excluded in the first hand and different syntactic categories can be disambiguated.

Typically, the lexicon will not contain all inflected forms of its entries. If the lexicon interface is capable of performing the morphological transformations for base form reduction (e.g. in WordNet), queries can be processed directly. If the lexicon interface does not provide such functionalities, a separate index of stemmed forms is maintained. If a first query for the inflected forms on the original lexicon turned

out unsuccessful, a second query for the stemmed expression is performed.

Having detected a lexical entry for an expression, this does not necessarily imply a one-to-one mapping to a concept in the ontology. Although multi-word-expression support and POS pattern matching reduce ambiguity, there may arise the need to disambiguate an expression versus multiple possible concepts. In our experiments, we have used three simple *Word Sense Disambiguation* strategies [5]:

1. The 'all' strategy uses all possible concepts (no disambiguation).
2. The 'first' strategy exploits WordNet's capability to return synsets ordered with respect to usage frequency by choosing the most frequent among several concepts.
3. The 'context' strategy performs disambiguation based on a simple approach that also considers the overall document context for disambiguation as proposed in [5].

The last step in the process is about going from the specific concepts found in the text to more general concept representations. This is realized by compiling, for every concept, all superconcept up to a maximal distance h into the concept representation. Note that the parameter h needs to be chosen carefully as climbing up the taxonomy too far is likely to obfuscating the concept representation.

3 Boosting

Boosting is a relatively young, yet extremely powerful machine learning technique. The main idea behind boosting algorithms is to combine multiple *weak learners* – classification algorithms that perform only slightly better than random guessing – into a powerful composite classifier. In this paper, we will concentrate on the well known AdaBoost algorithm [4] given on the next page and on simple indicator function decision stumps as base learners. These latter have the form:

$$h(x) = \begin{cases} c & \text{if } x^j = 1 \\ -c & \text{else.} \end{cases}$$

where $c \in \{-1, 1\}$. These decision stumps take binary features (e.g. word or concept occurrences) as inputs. The index j identifies a specific binary feature whose presence either supports a positive classification decision, i.e. $c = 1$ or a negative decision, i.e. $c = -1$.

4 Experiments

Evaluation Metrics We have used a standard set of evaluation metrics commonly used in IR to assess the performance of our approach, namely the *classification error*, *precision*, *recall*, the F_1 *measure* and break-even point (BEP). To average evaluation results of binary classifications on the per-class level, two conventional methods exist. The *macro-averaged* figures are meant to be averages over the individual results of the different classes while *micro-averaged* fig-

---

[1] see http://www.cogsci.princeton.edu/~wn/
[2] see http://www.nlm.nih.gov/mesh/
[3] see http://kaon.semanticweb.org/

Algorithm 1 The AdaBoost algorithm.

Input: training sample $S_{train} = \{(x_1, y_1), \ldots, (x_n, y_n)\}$
with $(x_i, y_i) \in \mathbb{X} \times \{-1, 1\}$ and $y_i = f(x_i)$, number of iterations T.
Initialize: $D_1(i) = \frac{1}{n}$ for all $i = 1, \ldots, n$.
  for $t = 1$ to T **do**
    train base classifier h_t on weighted training set
    calculate the weighted training error:

$$\epsilon_t \leftarrow \sum_{i=1}^{n} D_t(i) \, I_{y_i \neq h_t(x_i)} \qquad (1)$$

compute the optimal update step as:

$$\alpha_t \leftarrow \frac{1}{2} \ln \frac{1 - \epsilon_t}{\epsilon_t} \qquad (2)$$

update the distribution as:

$$D_{t+1}(i) \leftarrow \frac{D_t(i) \, e^{-\alpha_t y_i h_t(x_i)}}{Z_t} \qquad (3)$$

where Z_t is a normalization factor ensuring that $\sum_{i=1}^{n} D_{t+1}(i) = 1$
    if $\epsilon_t = 0$ or $\epsilon_t = \frac{1}{2}$ **then**
      break
    end if
  end for
Result: composite classifier given by:

$$\hat{f}(x) = \text{sign}\left(\hat{f}_{soft}(x)\right) = \text{sign}\left(\sum_{t=1}^{T} \alpha_t h_t(x)\right) \qquad (4)$$

ures are calculated over all individual documents. Refer to [8] for a detailed description of these measures.

Evaluation on the Reuters-21578 Corpus

A first set of evaluation experiments was conducted on the well-known Reuters-21578 collection. We used the "ModApte" split which divides the collection into 9,603 training documents, 3,299 test documents and 8,676 unused documents.

In the first stage of the experiment, term stems[4] and WordNet concepts were extracted as features from the documents in the training and test corpus. As a result, 17,525 distinct term stems and – depending on the chosen disambiguation strategy and maximal generalization (hypernym) distance – 10,259 to 27,236 distinct concept features. Using AdaBoost, we performed binary classification on the top 50 categories containing the highest number of positive training documents. The number of boosting iterations for training was fixed at 200 rounds for all feature combinations.

As a general finding, the results obtained in the experiments suggest that AdaBoost typically achieves better classification for both macro- and micro-averaged results when used with a combination of term-based and concept-based features. Table 1 summarizes the results of the experiments for different feature types with the best values being highlighted. The relative gains on the F_1 value, which is influ-

enced both by precision and recall, compared to the baseline show that in all but one cases the performance can be improved by including conceptual features, peaking at an relative improvement of 3.29 % for macro-averaged values and 2.00 % for micro-averaged values. Moderate improvements are achieved through simple concept integration, while larger improvements are achieved in most cases through additional integration of more general concepts.

Feature Type	Error	macro-averaged (in percentages)			
		Prec	Rec	F_1	BEP
term	00.65	80.59	66.30	72.75	74.29
term & synset.first	00.64	80.66	67.39	73.43	75.08
term & synset.first.hyp5	00.60	80.67	**69.57**	74.71	74.84
term & synset.first.hyp10	00.62	80.43	68.40	73.93	**75.58**
term & synset.context	00.63	79.96	68.51	73.79	74.46
term & synset.context.hyp5	00.62	79.48	68.34	73.49	74.71
term & synset.all	00.64	80.02	66.44	72.60	73.62
term & synset.all.hyp5	**00.59**	**83.76**	68.12	**75.14**	75.55

Feature Type	Error	micro-averaged (in percentages)			
		Prec	Rec	F_1	BEP
term	00.65	89.12	79.82	84.21	85.77
term & synset.first	00.64	88.75	80.79	84.58	85.97
term & synset.first.hyp5	00.60	89.16	**82.46**	85.68	85.91
term & synset.first.hyp10	00.62	88.78	81.74	85.11	86.14
term & synset.context	00.63	88.86	81.46	85.00	85.91
term & synset.context.hyp5	00.62	89.09	81.40	85.07	85.97
term & synset.all	00.64	88.82	80.99	84.72	85.69
term & synset.all.hyp5	**00.59**	**89.92**	82.21	**85.89**	86.44

Table 1. Evaluation Results for Reuters-21578.

Evaluation on the OHSUMED Corpus

A second series of experiments was conducted using the 1987 portion of the OHSUMED collection[5] consisting of 54,708 titles and abstracts from medical journals indexed with MeSH descriptors. About two thirds, 36,369 documents, were randomly selected as training documents, the remaining 18,341 documents were used for testing. For term stems, a total number of 38,047 distinct features could be identified. WordNet and the MeSH Tree Structures Ontology were used to extract conceptual features. With WordNet, all different disambiguation strategies were used resulting in 16,442 to 34,529 synset features. For the MeSH Tree Structures Ontology, only the "all" strategy was used, resulting in 11,572 to 13,663 MeSH concept features. Again, binary classification was performed with AdaBoost on the top 50 categories where the number of boosting iterations was set to 1000 rounds. Different runs of the classification stage were performed based on the different features, leading to often substantially different results.

Table 2 summarizes the macro- and micro-averaged results. Again, the general finding is that complementing the term stem representation with conceptual features significantly improves classification performance. The relative improvements for the F_1 scores compared to the term stem baseline range from 2.40 % to 6.98 % on the macro

---

[4]In this and in the next experiment term stem extraction comprises the removal of the standard stopwords for English defined in the SMART stopword list and stemming using the porter stemming algorithm.

[5]see http://trec.nist.gov/data/t9_filtering.html

level and from 1.96 % to 6.53 % on the micro level. The relative improvements achieved on OHSUMED are generally higher than those achieved on the Reuters-21578 corpus. This makes intuitively sense as the documents in the OHSUMED corpus are taken from the medical domain and are therefore typically suffering from the problems described in section 1, especially synonymous terms and multi-word expressions. The even better results achieved through hypernym integration with WordNet indicate that also the highly specialized language is a problem that can be remedied through integration of more general concepts.

Feature Type	Error	macro-averaged (in percentages)			
		Prec	Rec	F_1	BEP
term	00.53	52.60	35.74	42.56	45.68
term & synset.first	00.52	53.08	36.98	43.59	46.46
term & synset.first.hyp5	00.52	53.82	38.66	45.00	48.01
term & synset.context	00.52	52.83	37.09	43.58	46.88
term & synset.context.hyp5	**00.51**	**54.55**	**39.06**	**45.53**	**48.10**
term & synset.all	00.52	52.89	37.09	43.60	46.82
term & synset.all.hyp5	00.52	53.33	38.24	44.42	46.73
term & mesh	00.52	53.65	37.56	44.19	47.31
term & mesh.sc1	00.52	52.91	37.59	43.95	46.93
term & mesh.sc3	00.52	52.77	38.06	44.22	46.90
term & mesh.sc5	00.52	52.72	37.57	43.87	47.16

Feature Type	Error	micro-averaged (in percentages)			
		Prec	Rec	F_1	BEP
term	00.53	55.77	36.25	43.94	46.17
term & synset.first	00.52	56.07	37.30	44.80	47.01
term & synset.first.hyp5	00.52	56.84	38.76	46.09	48.31
term & synset.context	00.52	56.30	37.46	44.99	47.34
term & synset.context.hyp5	**00.51**	**58.10**	**39.18**	**46.81**	**48.45**
term & synset.all	00.52	56.19	37.44	44.94	47.32
term & synset.all.hyp5	00.52	56.29	38.24	45.54	46.73
term & mesh	00.52	56.81	37.84	45.43	47.78
term & mesh.sc1	00.52	56.00	37.90	45.20	47.49
term & mesh.sc3	00.52	55.87	38.26	45.42	47.45
term & mesh.sc5	00.52	55.94	37.94	45.21	47.63

Table 2. Evaluation Results for OHSUMED.

5 Related Work

To date, the work on integrating semantic background knowledge into text classification or other related tasks is quite scattered and has often lead to disappointing results. For example, a comparison of a number of approaches based on word-sense document representations reported in [6] ends with the conclusion of the authors that *"the use of word senses does not result in any significant categorization improvement"*.

Improvements resulting from feature representations based on ontological concepts were reported in text clustering settings [5]. Very good results with a feature representation mixed of terms and "concepts" computed statistically by means of Probabilistic Latent Semantic Analysis (pLSA) were recently reported in [3]. The experiments reported therein are of particular interest as the classification was also based on boosting combined term-concept representation, the latter being however automatically extracted from the document corpus using pLSA.

6 Conclusions

In this paper, we have proposed an approach to incorporate concepts from background knowledge into document representations for text document classification. AdaBoost, was used for actual classifications. Experiments on the Reuters and OHSUMED datasets clearly show that the integration of concepts into the feature representation improves classification results. The scores achieved are highly competitive with other published results. A series of statistical significance tests we have ommitted in full detail due to space restrictions indicates that the reported relative improvements can be assessed significant in most cases.

A comparative analysis of the improvements for different concept integration strategies revealed that these are due to two separate effects. Firstly, some improvements can be attributed to the detection of multi-word expressions and conflation of synonyms achieved through basic concept integration. Building on this initial improvement, further improvements can be achieved by generalization through superconcept retrieval and integration.

Acknowledgements This research was partially supported by the European Commission under contract FP6-001765 aceMedia. The expressed content is the view of the authors but not necessarily the view of the aceMedia project as a whole.

References

[1] S. Bloehdorn and A. Hotho. Boosting for Text Classification with Semantic Features. In *Proceedings of the MSW 2004 Workshop at the 10th ACM SIGKDD Conference on Knowledge Discovery and Data Mining* , Seattle, WA, USA, 2004.

[2] E. Bozsak et al. KAON – Towards a Large Scale Semantic Web. In *Proc. of the 3rd International Conference on E-Commerce and Web Technologies (EC-Web 2002)*, Aix-en-Provence, France, 2002.

[3] L. Cai and T. Hofmann. Text Categorization by Boosting Automatically Extracted Concepts. In *Proc. of the 26th Annual Int. ACM SIGIR Conference on Research and Development in Informaion Retrieval*, Toronto, Canada, 2003.

[4] Y. Freund and R. E. Schapire. A Decision Theoretic Generalization of On-Line Learning and an Application to Boosting. In *Second European Conference on Computational Learning Theory (EuroCOLT-95)*, Barcelona, Spain, 1995.

[5] A. Hotho, S. Staab, and G. Stumme. Wordnet improves Text Document Clustering. In *Proceedings of the Semantic Web Workshop at the 26th Annual International ACM SIGIR Conference*, Toronto, Canada, 2003.

[6] A. Kehagias, V. Petridis, V. G. Kaburlasos, and P. Fragkou. A Comparison of Word- and Sense-Based Text Categorization Using Several Classification Algorithms. *Journal of Intelligent Information Systems*, 21(3):227–247, 2000.

[7] G. Salton. *Automatic Text Processing*. Addison-Wesley Publishing Inc, Boston, MA, USA, 1989.

[8] F. Sebastiani. Machine Learning in Automated Text Categorization. *ACM Computing Surveys*, 34(1):1–47, 2002.

Matching in Frequent Tree Discovery

Björn Bringmann
Machine Learning Lab, University of Freiburg
Georges-Köhler-Alle, Geb. 079, 79098 Freiburg, Germany
bbringma@informatik.uni-freiburg.de

Abstract

Various definitions and frameworks for discovering frequent trees in forests have been developed recently. At the heart of these frameworks lies the notion of matching, which determines when a pattern tree matches a tree in a data set. We introduce a novel notion of tree matching for use in frequent tree mining and we show that it generalizes the framework of Zaki while still being more specific than that of Termier et al. Furthermore, we show how Zaki's TreeMinerV algorithm can be adapted towards our notion of tree matching. Experiments show the promise of the approach.

1. Introduction

In the past few years, interest has grown in extending the frequent item set paradigm to more expressive pattern types such as graphs, trees and sequences. Special attention has been devoted to semi-structured and tree-structured data [3, 5, 7, 2, 6, 1, 8]. Most of these approaches aim at finding all frequent trees in a forest of trees. They differ in the algorithms and implementation details, and more importantly also in the underlying notion of tree matching. When does one tree match another one? Asai *et al.*, Zaki and Termier *et al.* [1, 8, 6] provide different answers to this question. Asai's notion is more restrictive than Zaki's, which is in turn more restrictive than Termier's. Termier *et al.* have also shown that it can be beneficial to work with more permissive notions of matching. However, this typically comes at a computational price. Indeed, due to the expressiveness of their framework, Termier *et al.* cannot guarantee completeness, whereas Zaki and Asai *et al.* do.

The key contribution of this paper is a novel notion of tree matching. It fills the gap between the approaches of Zaki and Termier *et al.*. We also argue that – in the context of web mining – it is a natural way to look at tree matching. Furthermore, we extend Zaki's algorithm, introduce a new pruning technique, and experimentally evaluate our approach.

2. Frequent Tree Mining

A rooted k-tree t is a set of k nodes V_t where each $v \in V_t$, except one called root, has a parent denoted $\pi(v) \in V_t$. We use $\lambda(v)$ to denote the label of a node and an operator $\prec$ to denote the order from left to right among the children of a node. The transitive closure of π will be denoted π^*. Let $\mathcal{L}$ be a formal language composed of all labeled, ordered, rooted trees and $\mathcal{D} \subset \mathcal{L}$ a database. To count trees $t \in \mathcal{D}$ containing a pattern p we define a function $d_t : \mathcal{L} \to \{0,1\}$ to be 1 iff p matches the tree t and 0 otherwise. The frequency of p in $\mathcal{D}$ can then be defined as $\sigma_{\mathcal{D}}(p) =_{\text{def}} \Sigma_{t \in \mathcal{D}} d_t(p)$. Given a set of trees $\mathcal{D}$ and a minimum frequency α, the task of tree-mining is to find all patterns p such that $\sigma_{\mathcal{D}}(p) \geq \alpha$.

Tree Matching. Termier *et al.* [6] present three notions of tree matching. Formally speaking:

Definition 1 *A tree t matches a tree t' iff a mapping $\varphi : V_t \to V_{t'}$ exists such that*
$$\forall u, v \in V_t : \lambda(u) = \lambda(\varphi(u)) \wedge u \prec v \Leftrightarrow \varphi(u) \prec \varphi(v).$$

Now, each of the notions of matching imposes further constraints for two trees to match. More specifically, *tree inclusion* requires $\forall u, v \in V_t : \pi(u) = v \Leftrightarrow \pi(\varphi(u)) = \varphi(v)$. The more relaxed notion of *tree embedding* requires $\forall u, v \in V_t : \pi^*(u) = v \Leftrightarrow \pi^*(\varphi(u)) = \varphi(v)$. Finally, in *tree subsumption* there has to be a mapping $\varphi : V_t \to 2^{V_{t'}}$ from V_t to the powerset of $V_{t'}$ preserving the labels and $\forall u, v \in V_t : \pi^*(u) = v \Rightarrow \pi^*(\varphi(u)) = \varphi(v)$. This notion does *not* preserve the order of the child nodes.

The novel notion of tree matching, to which we will refer as *tree incorporation*, is more relaxed than *tree embedding* since a π^* relationship in the data does not have to hold in the pattern. It is more restrictive than *tree subsumption* as φ is a mapping to $V_{t'}$ rather than to $2^{V_{t'}}$, and it attempts to preserve the order of the children. More formally speaking:

Definition 2 *A tree t is incorporated in a tree t' iff there exists a mapping $\varphi : V_t \to V_{t'}$ such that*
$$\begin{aligned} \forall u, v \in V_t : \quad & \lambda(u) = \lambda(\varphi(u)) \\ \wedge \quad & u \prec v \Leftarrow \varphi(u) \prec \varphi(v) \\ \wedge \quad & \pi^*(u) = v \Rightarrow \pi^*(\varphi(u)) = \varphi(v). \end{aligned}$$

The relation among the different notions of matchings is captured by the following theorem (proof omitted).

Theorem 1 *For all trees t, t',*
t is included in $t' \Rightarrow t$ is embedded in $t' \Rightarrow$
t is incorporated in $t' \Rightarrow t$ is subsumed by t'.

As a consequence, the set of frequent trees w.r.t. a data set $\mathcal{D}$ for tree inclusion is smaller than for tree embedding, which is in turn smaller than for tree incorporation and this one is again smaller w.r.t. tree subsumption. This motivates the use of the notion of matching as a parameter of frequent tree discovery tasks. Basically our novel definition fills the gap between *tree embedding* and *tree subsumption*. The toy-example of an online shop (figure 1) compares tree

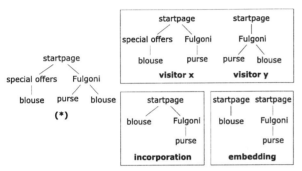

Figure 1. Two subtrees from a master-tree (*) and respective *most-specific* **patterns**

incorporation and embedding. While the novel definition yields only one *most specific* pattern, the notion of tree embedding yields two. According to tree embedding some visitors looked at the blouse and some at the Fulgoni purse. The single most specific pattern according to the novel notion offers more information: The visitors looking at the blouse and the visitors looking at the purse are the **same persons**. This knowledge might be helpful when restructuring the online-shop to improve accessibility or placement of advertisements. Technically, incorporated trees can be discovered by an algorithm similar to the fast and complete TreeMinerV algorithm [8]. In our implementation the user can select between the notions of tree inclusion, embedding, and incorporation as a constraint similar to minimum frequency. A further optimization of the algorithm is described in section 3.

3. Frequent Tree Mining Algorithms

In this section, we discuss frequent tree mining w.r.t. *tree incorporation*. We explain candidate tree generation, candidate counting, and a novel pruning technique.

Candidate Tree Generation. To generate candidate patterns we use a method called *rightmost expansion* to canonically enumerate all labeled, ordered, rooted trees. This technique was independently proposed by Zaki and Asai *et al.*

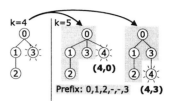

Figure 2. Rightmost expansion and equivalence classes (EQ).

[8, 1]. It works in a levelwise manner adding a single node to a known frequent pattern in such a way that every possible candidate pattern will be generated exactly once. Basically a k-tree is expanded to several $k + 1$-trees by adding new nodes only to its rightmost path as shown in figure 2. The new node n_{k+1} is called *rightmost leaf* (RML) and the subtree without its RML is called *prefix* of the tree. For efficient candidate generation the anti-monotonicity of frequent patterns is used (i.e. a specialization s of a pattern p is not more frequent than p). Thus, we consider only frequent patterns for extension. With focus on the *rightmost extension*, patterns are organized in so called *equivalence classes* (EQ). An EQ contains all patterns that have the same prefix, i.e. differ only in their RMLs. It contains the pattern prefix only once and for each pattern P_i a tuple $(\lambda(\text{RML}_i), \pi(\text{RML}_i))$. At this point it is important to note that in the same EQ every pattern (λ, j) with $j > p$ is a *specialization* of a pattern (λ, p) with respect to the novel definition. Hence, a φ exists that maps the nodes of (λ, p) to the nodes of (λ, j) with respect to definition 2. For example the left 5-tree in figure 2 is a pattern for the right 5-tree, but not vice versa. Due to this relationship there is a large number of generalizations for every pattern. By using the notion of extended instance lists which we will define below, the algorithm generates only the necessary ones to find all patterns of the most specific border (*s-set*). The resulting pattern set is a superset of the s-set w.r.t. the notion of tree incorporation.

To efficiently count the support of a pattern the algorithm needs information about the instances of the pattern in the data. Let pattern X be a k-subtree occurring in a tree T, φ the mapping from the pattern-nodes to the nodes of T, and x_k refers to the RML of X. Following Zaki, we use $\mathcal{I}(X)$ to refer to the *instance-list* (i.e. *scope-list*) of X. Each element of $\mathcal{I}$ is a triple (t, s, m) identifying an instance of X. t is the id of a tree T in which X occurs, $m =_{def} \{\varphi(n) \mid n \in (X \setminus x_k)\}$ is called *match label* of the prefix of X, and s is the scope of the rightmost leaf $\varphi(x_k)$. These instance lists contain all instances of a pattern w.r.t. *tree embedding*. For the novel definition, we introduce the notation of *extended instance lists* $\mathcal{I}^*(X) = \mathcal{I}^*(\lambda, p) =_{def} \cup_{j \geq p} \mathcal{I}(\lambda, j)$ containing all instances that support a pattern X. When two patterns A and B of the same EQ are joined, the information in the instance lists $\mathcal{I}^*(A), \mathcal{I}^*(B)$ is used to track the patterns in the same way as described in [8]. Only in the case of an *outscope-*

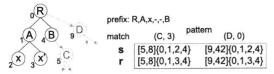

prefix: R,A,x,-,-,B

match	pattern (C, 3)	(D, 0)
s	[5,8]{0,1,2,4}	[9,42]{0,1,2,4}
r	[5,8]{0,1,3,4}	[9,42]{0,1,3,4}

Figure 3. Instances s or r would be removed by instance pruning.

join the condition has to be changed, such that a join is also possible if a new node D is a descendant or left-sibling of A, not only if D is a left-sibling of A. The interested reader is referred to [8] for more information.

Instance Pruning. Besides simpler pruning techniques like *node pruning* and *edge pruning* that are also used by Zaki [8] and Termier *et al.* [6] we introduce a new technique called *instance pruning* (*IP*) that reduces the average computation time to 50%. It is not only applicable to the algorithm working on the novel pattern definition, but also to the algorithm provided by Zaki. As stated before, $d_t(X)$ returns a 1 if there is at least one occurrence of pattern X in tree t, otherwise it returns 0. Hence, the frequency of a pattern depends only in part on the number of instances. If there are different instances of a pattern (x, i) in tree t, they are represented in the instance list $\mathcal{I}(x, i)$ as $I_{1,0} = (t, a_0, s)$ and $I_{2,0} = (t, b_0, r)$. If the pattern (x, i) is joined with another pattern (y, j) all instances in I_1 and I_2 will be joined with the respective instances of (y, j). Consider two groups of instances of the tree t with match labels r, s and triples $(t, a_{0\cdots m}, s), (t, b_{0\cdots n}, r)$, as shown in figure 3. If for every triple (t, b_k, r) there exists a triple (t, a_l, s) with $a_l = b_k$, all triples with the match label r can be removed from the EQ. This is possible, as for instances in the same tree with the same match label, only the nodes a_l (or b_k) are of relevance for the extension of the instances. If a match label s includes all nodes b_k of a match label r, no instance can be created out of instances with match label r that cannot be created out of instances with match label s. This reduction of instances can efficiently reduce the memory footprint of the process. Even more important than the substantially lowered memory usage is the reduction in computation time. Not only the removed instances themselves are not joined anymore, but also the ones that would have been created by joining them. When the number of labels is low in relation to the number of nodes in the trees, *IP* can reduce the computation time even to 20%.

Algorithm. Figure 4 shows the algorithm used to compute frequent patterns w.r.t. tree incorporation. As stated before, the algorithm is an extended version of Zaki's TreeMinerV algorithm. The main differences are the usage of the extended instance lists and a new condition for the *out-scope* test. The sets containing all frequent 1-trees (i.e. nodes) and 2-trees are computed before the main loop. The function *Enumerate-Frequent-Subtrees* generates all possible refinements of patterns in an EQ $[P]$. This is done by joining

MINEFREQUENTTREES($\mathcal{D}$, *minsup*):
  F_1 = { frequent 1-subtrees };
  F_2 = { classes $[P]_1$ of frequent 2-subtrees };
  for all $[P]_1 \in F_2$ do *Enumerate-Frequent-Subtrees*($[P]_1$);
ENUMERATE-FREQUENT-SUBTREES($[P]$):
  for each element $(x, i) \in [P]$ do $[P_x] = \emptyset$
    for each element $(y, j) \in [P]$ with $i \geq j$ do
      $R = \{(x, i) \otimes (y, j)\}$;
      $\mathcal{I}(R) = \{\mathcal{I}^*(x, i) \cap_\otimes \mathcal{I}^*(y, j)\}$;
      if for any $p \in R$, p is frequent then $[P_x] = [P_x] \cup \{p\}$;
    Enumerate-Frequent-Subtrees($[P_x]$);

Figure 4. TreeMining Algorithm

every pair $(x, i) \otimes (y, j)$ of patterns in $[P]$ including self-joins. Due to the rightmost expansion it is not allowed to join $(x, i) \otimes (y, j)$ with $i < j$ which would result in non-canonical expansions. A join results in one or two new patterns (R). Afterwards the according instance lists are created by joining the instance lists of the patterns (x, i) and (y, j). Any new pattern that turns out to be frequent is then added to the new EQ $[P_x]$. If all frequent patterns of the new EQ $[P_x]$ are computed further refinements of these patterns are generated. Thus, the algorithm proceeds depth-first.

4. Experimental Results

A number of experiments were conducted on real-world and synthetic datasets. The real-world dataset (legcare [4]) consists of an online shop's weblog, containing 234942 visits. Each visit is regarded as a subtree of the hierarchically structured website. There where 694 unique labels for the database. For the synthetic dataset we implemented a data generator as described by Zaki [8]. All the experiments were performed on a 3.2GHz Intel Pentium 4 with 2GB main memory, running SUSE 9.0. The algorithms were implemented in C++. For the tree embedding and tree incorporation, *instance pruning* is available. We compared the number of frequent patterns found by the algorithms and the size of the s-set on both datasets with different minimum support. To calculate the s-set an additional post-processing step was performed. Figure 5 shows the number of patterns generated during the search and the number of patterns contributing to the s-set for tree embedding and tree incorporation on the legcare dataset. As mentioned earlier, our novel definition is more relaxed than tree embedding such that more patterns are generated and discovered during the search. In contrast to the figures shown here (figure 5), there is no order between the notions w.r.t. the size of the according s-set. All three notions have in common that they grow exponentially in the number of most specific patterns as well as in patterns considered during the search when reducing the minium support. For the legcare-dataset there was no effect on computation time with and without *IP*. However, using *IP*, the memory consumption dropped

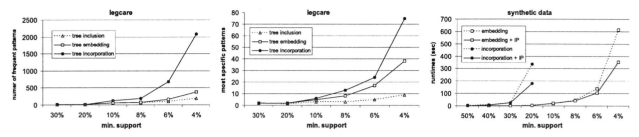

Figure 5. Comparing embedding and incorporation w.r.t. patterns found, s-set size, and *IP*.

dramatically for computing frequent pattern sets with minimum support below 10%. For the experiments with the synthetic data, a master-tree with 100 unique labels and 10000 nodes was generated with a maximum depth and fanout of 10. From this hypothetical website we generated 10000 visits, each a smaller subtree of the master-tree, as database. The right graph in figure 5 shows the results of experiments on this dataset regarding computation time and the effect of instance pruning. The plot clearly indicates an exponential growth in computation time when lowering the minimum support. The solid lines depict the required time with *IP*. Both, tree embedding and tree incorporation, show a significant speedup for low minimum support levels with *IP*.

5. Conclusions and Related Work

The algorithm presented in this paper improves and expands the TreeMinerV algorithm with our novel pattern definition. The introduced *instance pruning* reduces the computation time as well as the memory usage of the algorithm in many cases. Unfortunately we are not yet able to deal with low minimum support levels. Since the amount of frequent patterns in large databases grows fast when lowering the minimum support, it appears to be useful to calculate only the set of all most specific patterns. Until now an additional post processing step is necessary to do this which requires additional computation time. We hope to be able to incorporate this step directly into the mining process to reduce the post processing time. Furthermore, it would be nice to have more constraints, such as a most-general or most-specific pattern, to enable the user to focus the search as in [2] or to extend the tree-mining process to first order logic. On the other hand the frequent patterns discovered could also be used as features for some classifier as in [9]. Considering our novel notion we still have to evaluate if the additional cost in time and memory is justified by 'better' patterns. Finally, it depends on the data and on the requirements of the user which tree matching notion is the best.

Related Work. The most directly related work to this paper is Zaki's TreeMinerV as well as Termier's TreeFinder and FreqT by Asai [8, 6, 1]. Zaki uses a smart, so called *vertical representation* to facilitate the candidate count enabling a fast mining process that scales well, even with large

datasets. We adopted this idea for our pattern definition, which is more specific than tree subsumption used by Termier. Since our definition is more general than Zaki's we find much more patterns than with tree embedding. Therefore, it is not surprising that the algorithm is slower than TreeMinerV. Using our algorithm to mine embedded trees there is a significant speedup compared to TreeMinerV due to our pruning technique. Compared to TreeFinder, it uses a less general pattern definition, but is complete.

Other algorithms like AGM [3], FSM [5] and gSpan [7] work on graphs rather than trees. They are restricted to subgraphs consisting of edges and if applied to trees would only discover frequent trees in the sense of subtree inclusion.

Acknowledgments. The real world dataset was kindly provided by Blue Martini Software. The author thanks Luc De Raedt for encouragement for writing this paper and Mohammed Zaki for providing the TreeMiner source code. Also many thanks to Andreas Karwath, Albrecht Zimmermann, and the anonymous reviewers whose comments helped to improve the paper. This research was supported by the European Project: IST-2000-26469, cInQ.

References

[1] T. Asai, K. Abe, S. Kawasoe, H. Arimura, H. Sakamoto, and S. Arikawa. Efficient substructure discovery from large semi-structured data. In *Proc. of SIAM SDM*, pages 158–174, 2002.
[2] L. De Raedt and S. Kramer. The levelwise version space algorithm and its application to molecular fragement finding. In *Proc. of IJCAI-01*, pages 853–862, 2001.
[3] A. Inokuchi, T. Washio, and H. Motoda. An apriori-based algorithm for mining frequent substructures from graph data. In *Proc. of PKDD*, pages 13–23, 2000.
[4] R. Kohavi, C. Brodley, B. Frasca, L. Mason, and Z. Zheng. KDD-Cup 2000 organizers' report: Peeling the onion. *SIGKDD Explorations*, 2(2):85–98, 2000.
[5] M. Kuramochi and G. Karypis. Frequent subgraph discovery. In *Proc. of ICDM*, 2001.
[6] A. Termier, M.-C. Rousset, and M. Sebag. Treefinder: a first step towards xml data mining. In *Proc. of ICDM*, 2002.
[7] X. Yan and J. Han. gspan: Graph-based substructure pattern mining. In *Proc. of ICDM*, 2002.
[8] M. Zaki. Efficiently mining frequent trees in a forest. In *Proc. of KDD*, 2002.
[9] M. J. Zaki and C. C. Aggarwal. Xrules: An effective structural classifier for xml data. In *Proc. of SIGKDD 03*, 2003.

A biobjective model to select features with good classification quality and low cost*

Emilio Carrizosa

Facultad de Matemáticas. Universidad de Sevilla (Spain)

ecarrizosa@us.es

Belen Martin-Barragan

Facultad de Matemáticas. Universidad de Sevilla (Spain)

belmart@us.es

Dolores Romero Morales

Saïd Business School. University of Oxford (United Kingdom)

dolores.romero-morales@sbs.ox.ac.uk

Abstract

In this paper we address a multi-group classification problem in which we want to take into account, together with the generalization ability, cots associated with the features. This cost is not limited to an economical payment, but can also refer to risk, computational effort, space requirements, etc. In order to get a good generalization ability, we use Support Vector Machines (SVM) as the basic mechanism by considering the maximization of the margin. We formulate the problem as a biobjective mixed integer problem, for which Pareto optimal solutions can be obtained.

1. Introduction

Support Vector Machine (SVM) has shown to have good performance, and is widely used for classification problems, see e.g. [1, 5, 6, 12]. In the case of two groups, SVM builds the *maximum margin hyperplane*, which is the hyperplane that maximizes the minimum distance from itself to the closest point. Generalizations to the multi-group case are not straightforward. Some methods have been proposed in the literature, such as the so-called 'one-against-the-rest' [17] and 'one-against-one' [11] classifiers, see [12], which are based on combining some two-group classifiers.

In real-world classification problems, an usual concern is costs. The most studied type of cost associated with classification is the misclassification cost. Turney [16] proposed

*This research was partially supported by projects BFM2002-11282-E and BFM2002-04525-C02-02 of Ministerio de Ciencia y Tecnología (Spain) and FQM-329 of Plan Andaluz de Investigación (Andalucía, Spain).

other types of cost, for instance the test cost, where each test (attribute, measurement, feature) has an associated cost, such as economical payment, computational effort or some kind of complexity. The typical example is medical diagnosis, where some tests are much more expensive than others. If the classification rule does not use variables based on the most expensive tests, classifying new patients will be much cheaper, perhaps without deteriorating significantly the quality of classification.

In this paper, we address classification problems in which both misclassification and testing costs are relevant. To do this, we formulate a biobjective program of simultaneous minimization of misclassification and testing costs. Efficient solutions, i.e. classifiers that cannot be improved at the same time in both objectives, are sought.

We have structured the paper as follows. In Section 2 the problem is formally introduced and an extension of the definition of margin to more than two classes is stated. In Section 3 we model the first goal: the testing cost. Maximizing the margin, as a surrogate of minimizing the misclassification cost, will be our second goal. A Biobjective Mixed Integer Program formulation is given in Section 4.

2. The problem

We have a finite set of classes $\mathcal{C} = \{1, 2, \ldots, C\}$, and a set of objects Ω, each object u having two components $u = (x^u, c^u)$. The first component x^u is called the *predictor vector* and takes values in a set X. The set X is usually assumed to be a subset of $\mathbb{R}^p$, and then, the components x_l, $l = 1, 2, \ldots, p$, of the predictor vector x are called *predictor variables*. The other component c^u, with values in the set of classes $\mathcal{C}$, is called the *class-membership* of object u. Object u is said to belong to class c^u.

In general, class-membership of objects in Ω is known only for a subset I, called the *training sample*: both predictor vector and class-membership are known for $u \in I$, whereas only x^u is known for $u \in \Omega \setminus I$.

Denote by $I_c = \{u \in I : c^u = c\}$, the set of objects of class c, for every $c \in \mathcal{C}$. We assume that each class is represented in the training sample, i.e., $I_c \neq \emptyset \, \forall c \in \mathcal{C}$.

We use a classification model in which a *score function*, $f = (f_c)_{c \in \mathcal{C}}$ with $f_c : X \longrightarrow \mathbb{R}$, enables us to classify (allocate) any $z \in X$ to the class c^* whose score function is highest:

$$c^* = \arg\max_{c \in \mathcal{C}} f_c(z). \qquad (1)$$

Notice that in case of ties, the object will be unclassified by this rule, and can be later allocated randomly or by a prefixed order to some class in $\arg\max_{c \in \mathcal{C}} f_c(z)$. Following a worst-case approach, we will consider those objects as misclassified throughout the paper. Score functions f_c are assumed to have the form

$$f_c(x) = \sum_{k=1}^{N} \alpha_k^c \phi_k(x) + \beta^c, \qquad (2)$$

where $\mathcal{G} = \{\phi_1, \phi_2, \ldots, \phi_N\}$ is a finite set of real valued functions on X. Hence, each f_c belongs to a vector space $\mathcal{F}$, generated by $\mathcal{G}$. Linear classifiers correspond to scores generated by

$$\mathcal{G} = \{x_1, x_2, \ldots, x_p\}, \qquad (3)$$

whereas quadratic classifiers, [8, 9], are obtained by setting

$$\mathcal{G} = \{x_1, x_2, \ldots, x_p\} \bigcup \{x_i x_j : 1 \leq i \leq j \leq p\} \qquad (4)$$

i.e., the set of monomials of degree up to 2.

The framework also includes voting classifiers, such as boosting, e.g. [7, 10] in which $\mathcal{C} = \{1, 2\}$, a set of primitive classifiers $\phi_k : X \to \{0, 1\}$

$$\phi_k(x) = 1 \text{ iff } x \text{ is allocated to class 1 via the } k\text{-th classifier,} \qquad (5)$$

are combined linearly into a single score function of the form (2). For a very promising strategy for generating such primitive classifiers see e.g. [3].

Denote the coefficients of the score function by $A = (\alpha^1, \ldots, \alpha^C)$ with $\alpha^c \in \mathbb{R}^N$, and $b = (\beta^1, \ldots, \beta^C) \in \mathbb{R}^C$. The problem of choosing f is reduced to the choice of its coefficients (A, b).

Hereafter, unless explicitly stated, we assume that $\mathcal{F}$ is rich enough to enable separability, i.e., there exists $f = (f_c)_{c \in \mathcal{C}}$, with $f_c \in \mathcal{F}$, such that

$$f_{c^u}(x^u) > f_j(x^u) \; \forall j \neq c^u, \quad \forall u \in I. \qquad (6)$$

In other words, we assume there exists a score function in $\mathcal{F}$ that correctly classifies all the objects in the training sample I. This definition of separability depends on the generator $\mathcal{G}$. Under weak assumptions, there exists a generator, $\mathcal{G}$, rich enough to enable separability of $\{I_c : c \in \mathcal{C}\}$. For more details, see [4].

This assumption ensures the existence of score functions f that correctly classifies all the objects in I. It is easy to see ([4]) that uniqueness never holds. We thus need a criterion for choosing one of such score function. In the two group case, SVM is based on the idea of choosing the hyperplane with maximal margin. In Cristianini and Shawe-Taylor ([6]), a formal definition of the so-called (geometrical) margin are introduced. The extension of such definition to the multi-group case is given below.

Definition 1 *The geometrical margin of a score function (A, b) with respect to a training sample I is the quantity*

$$\xi^I(A, b) = \min_{u \in I} \min_{j \neq c^u} \left\{ \frac{f_{c^u}(x^u) - f_j(x^u)}{\|A\|} \right\}. \qquad (7)$$

The term $\|A\|$ is introduced in order to normalize the quantities $\hat{\xi}^u(A, b) = f_{c^u}(x^u) - f_j(x^u)$, to be able to compare score functions.

Now, we consider the problem of maximizing the margin

$$\max_{A \neq 0, \, b \in \mathbb{R}^C} \xi^I(A, b). \qquad (8)$$

Such problem can be reformulated as follows:

$$\begin{array}{ll} \max & \min_{u \in I} \hat{\xi}^u(A, b) \\ s.t.: & \|A\| \leq 1 \\ & (A, b) \in \mathbb{R}^{NC} \times \mathbb{R}_+^C \end{array} \qquad (9)$$

Property 2 *Problems (8) and (9) are equivalent in the sense that every optimal solution of (9) is also optimal for (8) and for any optimal solution of (8), (A^*, b^*), there exists an optimal solution (A, b) of (9), that is also optimal in (8).*

The proof and other details can be found in [4].

3. Inspection costs

Finding classifiers separating conveniently the groups is a plausible criterion when obtaining the predictor vector x^u is costless. When this is not the case, we should also take into account the cost associated with performing classification.

In many practical applications, as medical diagnosis, the predictor variables of the data may be some diagnosis test (blood test, ...) that have associated a cost, either money, or risk/damage incurred to the patient. If the classifier built does not depend on some of these variables, we could avoid their measurement (and the corresponding cost) in the diagnosis of new patients. In this situation, we should seek a classifier that enjoys good generalization properties, and at the same time, has low cost.

Several authors have addressed inspection cost issues related with classification. For instance, [13, 14, 15] consider classification trees whose branching rule takes such costs into account. See [16] for a comparison of such methods and [2, 16] and the references therein for other proposals. However, as far as the authors are aware of, inspection costs have not been formally introduced in SVM models.

In this paper, costs are modelled as follows: Denote by Π_k the cost associated with evaluating the feature $\phi_k \in \mathcal{G}$ at a given x. For instance, if we are following a linear approach, as given by (3), Π_l represents the cost of measuring the predictor variable l in a new object.

Given the parameter $A = (\alpha^1, \dots, \alpha^C)$, define

$$S(A) = \{k = 1, 2, \dots, N : \alpha_k^c \neq 0 \text{ for some } c \in \mathcal{C}\}.$$

In other words, $S(A)$ represents the set of features we have to use in order to classify new objects. In principle, these are the features we have to pay for, so a score function with coefficients (A, b) will have associated a testing cost equal to

$$\pi(A, b) = \sum_{k \in S(A)} \Pi_k. \qquad (10)$$

Pure linearity, as assumed in (10), may be unrealistic in some practical situations. For instance, it may be the case that, once we have incurred a cost for obtaining some feature ϕ_k, some other features may be given for free or at reduced cost. This may happen, for example, in a medical context when the measurement of a variable requires a blood extraction, and some other variables can be measured using the same blood test. Another context where one encounters this, is the case in which some features are functions of other features: In model (4), feature $\phi(x) = x_i x_j$ is obtained for free if both features $\phi(x) = x_i$ and $\phi(x) = x_j$ have been previously inspected.

In Table 1 one can see the costs of a simple example with two classes $C = 2$, and $\mathcal{G} = \{\phi_1, \dots, \phi_5\}$ with different costs.

features	ϕ_1	ϕ_2	ϕ_3	ϕ_4	ϕ_5
costs	2	5	3	0	2

Table 1. Example of feature cost.

The score function $f = (f_1, f_2)$ given by $f_1 = \phi_1 + 4\phi_5$ and $f_2 = 3\phi_1 + 2$ supposes a cost of $2 + 2 = 4$.

Suppose that precedence constraints, in the form of a partial order $\prec$ between the features, is given. This means that

if $h \preceq k$, the use of the feature ϕ_k requires the payment for feature ϕ_h. Moreover, in computing the total cost, the cost for every feature has to be summed at most once. In order to formalize this, define an auxiliary variable $z_k \in \{0, 1\}$ for each $k = 1, \dots, N$, representing

$$z_k = \begin{cases} 1 & \text{if payment of } \Pi_k \text{ is needed} \\ 0 & \text{otherwise} \end{cases} \qquad (11)$$

in other words:

$$z_k = \begin{cases} 1 & \text{if } h \in S(A) \text{ for some } h \text{ with } k \preceq h \\ 0 & \text{otherwise} \end{cases} \qquad (12)$$

Thus, cost associated with a score function with coefficients (A, b) will be

$$\pi(A, b) = \sum_{k=1}^{N} z_k \Pi_k. \qquad (13)$$

Minimizing (13) will be one of our goals. However, our main goal is finding classifiers with good generalization properties. We use the margin maximization, described in Section 2, as a surrogate of the good generalization. In the following section we describe how to manage both objectives simultaneously.

4. A biobjective approach

In the last sections we have described the two objectives of our problem, namely, maximizing the margin and minimizing the cost. Hence we have the following biobjective problem:

$$\begin{aligned} &\max && \hat{\xi}(A, b) \\ &\min && \pi(A, b) \\ &s.t.: && \|A\| \leq 1 \\ & && (A, b) \in \mathbb{R}^{NC} \times \mathbb{R}_+^C \end{aligned} \qquad (14)$$

where $\hat{\xi}(A, b)$ denotes $\min_{u \in I} \hat{\xi i}^u(A, b)$.

In [4] it is proved that the set of Pareto efficient outcomes of the biobjective problem (14) is finite. Moreover, for particular choices of $\|\cdot\|$, this can be rewritten as a biobjective mixed integer linear problem, as stated below.

Property 3 *Let* $\|\cdot\|_1$ *be the* L_1-norm, $\|A\|_1 = \sum_{k=1}^{N} \sum_{c=1}^{C} |\alpha_k^c|$. *Then, Problem (14) can be formu-*

lated as the following Biobjective Mixed Integer Problem,

$$
\begin{aligned}
\max \quad & y \\
\min \quad & \sum_{k=1}^{N} \Pi_k z_k \\
s.t.: \quad & \sum_{k=1}^{N} \phi_k(x^u) \left(\alpha_{+k}^i - \alpha_{-k}^i - \alpha_{+k}^j + \alpha_{-k}^j \right) \\
& \quad + \beta^i - \beta^j - y \geq 0, \\
& \qquad\qquad \forall i \neq j;\ i,j \in \mathcal{C},\ u \in I_i \\
& \sum_{c=1}^{C} \sum_{k=1}^{N} \left(\alpha_{+k}^c + \alpha_{-k}^c \right) \leq 1, \\
& \sum_{h:k \preceq h} \sum_{c=1}^{C} \left(\alpha_{+k}^c + \alpha_{-k}^c \right) \leq z_k, \\
& \qquad\qquad \forall k = 1, 2, \dots, N \\
& y \text{ unrestricted}, \\
& \alpha_{+k}^c \geq 0, \qquad \forall k = 1, 2, \dots, N;\ c \in \mathcal{C} \\
& \alpha_{-k}^c \geq 0, \qquad \forall k = 1, 2, \dots, N;\ c \in \mathcal{C} \\
& \beta^c \geq 0, \qquad\qquad \forall c \in \mathcal{C} \\
& z_k \in \{0, 1\}, \qquad \forall k = 1, 2, \dots, N \\
& \qquad\qquad\qquad\qquad\qquad\qquad (15)
\end{aligned}
$$

Property 4 *Let $\|\cdot\|_\infty$ be the L_∞-norm, $\|A\|_\infty = \max_{1 \leq k \leq N;\ c \in \mathcal{C}} |\alpha_k^c|$. Then, Problem (14) can be reformulated as the following Biobjective Mixed Integer Problem,*

$$
\begin{aligned}
\max \quad & y \\
\min \quad & \sum_{k=1}^{N} \Pi_k z_k \\
s.t.: \quad & \sum_{k=1}^{N} \phi_k(x^u) \left(\alpha_k^i - \alpha_k^j \right) + \beta^i - \beta^j - y \geq 0, \\
& \qquad\qquad \forall i \neq j;\ i,j \in \mathcal{C},\ u \in I_i \\
& -z_k \leq \sum_{h:k \preceq h} \sum_{c=1}^{C} \alpha_k^c \leq z_k, \\
& \qquad\qquad \forall k = 1, 2, \dots, N \\
& \alpha_k^c \text{ unrestricted}, \qquad \forall k = 1, 2, \dots, N;\ c \in \mathcal{C} \\
& y \text{ unrestricted}, \\
& \beta^c \geq 0, \qquad\qquad \forall c \in \mathcal{C} \\
& z_k \in \{0, 1\}, \qquad \forall k = 1, 2, \dots, N \\
& \qquad\qquad\qquad\qquad\qquad\qquad (16)
\end{aligned}
$$

Our objective is to generate Pareto efficient solutions of Problem (14) for the L_1-norm or the L_∞-norm, by using formulations (15) or (16) respectively. Both (15) and (16) are biobjective mixed integer linear problems, which can be tackled for instance, by adapting the two-phase method of [18] designed for solving biobjective knapsack problems. In [4] the reader can find a detailed description of the two-phase method specifically adapted to Problem (14) and computational results for the L_1 norm case.

References

[1] E. Allwein, R. Schapire, and Y. Singer. Reducing multiclass to binary: A unifying approach for margin classifiers. *Journal of Machine Learning Research*, 1:369–409, 2000.

[2] V. Bayer Zubek. *Learning Cost-Sensitive Diagnostic Policies from Data*. PhD thesis, Oregon State University, July 2003. http://eecs.oregonstate.edu/library/?call=2003-13.

[3] E. Boros, P. L. Hammer, T. Ibaraki, and A. Kogan. A logical analysis of numerical data. *Mathematical Programming*, 79:163–190, 1997.

[4] E. Carrizosa, B. Martín-Barragán, and D. R. Morales. Minimum-cost feature selection for classification: A biobjective model. Working Paper, 2004.

[5] C. Cortes and V. Vapnik. Support-vector network. *Machine Learning*, 1:113–141, 1995.

[6] N. Cristianini and J. Shawe-Taylor. *An introduction to support vector machines*. Cambridge University Press, 2000.

[7] A. Demiriz, K. P. Bennett, and J. Shawe-Taylor. Linear programming boosting via column generation. *Machine Learning*, 46(1):225–254, 2002.

[8] A. Duarte Silva and A. Stam. Second order mathematical programming formulations for discriminant analysis. *European Journal of Operational Research*, 72:4–22, 1994.

[9] J. Falk and V. Karlov. Robust separation of finite sets via quadratics. *Computers and Operations Research*, 28:537–561, 2001.

[10] Y. Freund and R. Schapire. A decision-theoretic generalization of on-line learning and an application to boosting. *Journal of Computer and System Sciences*, 55(1):119–139, 1997.

[11] T. Hastie and R. Tibshirani. Classification by pairwise coupling. *The Annals of Statistics*, 26(2):451–471, 1998.

[12] R. Herbrich. *Learning Theory Classifiers. Theory and Algorithms*. MIT Press, 2002.

[13] S. Norton. Generating better decision trees. In *Proceedings of the Eleventh International Joint Conference on Artificial Intelligence, IJCAI-89*, pages 800–805, Detroit, Michigan, 1989.

[14] M. Núñez. The use of background knowledge in decision tree induction. *Machine Learning*, 6:231–250, 1991.

[15] M. Tan. Cost-sensitive learning of classification knowledge and its applications in robotics. *Machine Learning*, 13:7–33, 1993.

[16] P. Turney. Cost-sensitive classification: Empirical evaluation of a hybrid genetic decision tree induction algorithm. *Journal of Artificial Intelligence Research*, 2:369–409, 1995.

[17] V. Vapnik. *Statistical learning theory*. Wiley, 1998.

[18] M. Visée, J. Teghem, M. Pirlot, and E. Ulungu. Two-phases method and branch and bound procedures to solve the biobjective knapsack problem. *Journal of Global Optimization*, 12:139–155, 1998.

Incremental Mining of Frequent XML Query Patterns

Yi Chen[1]   Liang Huai Yang[2]   Yu Guo Wang[1]
[1]*Institute of Software, Chinese Academy of Sciences*
[2]*Department of Computer Science, Peking Univerity*

Abstract

Recently, the discovering of frequent XML query patterns gains its focus due to its many applications in XML data management, and several algorithms have been proposed to discover frequent query patterns using the frequent structure mining techniques. In this paper we consider the problem of incremental mining of frequent XML query patterns. We propose a novel method to minimize the I/O and computation requirements for handling incremental updates.

1. Introduction

With XML being the standard for data encoding and exchange over Internet, how to manage XML data efficiently becomes a critical issue. The knowledge of frequently occurred query patterns can play an important role in XML data management. Recently, [4, 5] proposed to discover frequent XML query patterns using frequent subtree mining techniques. Given the user logs composed of a set of XML queries, [4, 5] model them as unordered trees with descendant edges or wildcards, and frequent structure mining techniques are extended to extract frequent subtrees based on the semantics of XML queries.

In [4, 5], the user logs are assumed to be static, the frequencies of candidate query patterns are created from scratch periodically and their creation is based on checking the entire log database. Their methods are not suitable in the settings where the log database is updated frequently since re-running the discovering program on the set of all transactions might produce significant expense.

In this paper we propose a novel algorithm, *increQPMiner*, for the incremental mining of frequent query patterns. We adapt the schema-guided rightmost expansion method [4] to enumerate candidate patterns in the incremental settings. To update the mining result, candidate patterns of the incremental database are checked against candidate patterns of the original database to decide whether existing frequent patterns should be removed or new ones should be introduced.

2. Problem statement

In this paper, we consider query patterns in the syntax of XPath [1], which are generally modeled as query pattern trees [2]. A query pattern tree is a labeled tree QPT $= (V, E)$, where V is the vertex set, E is the edge set. Each vertex v has a label, denoted by v.label, whose value is in tagSet$\cup$"*"}, where tagSet is the set of all element names in the context. An edge can be a child edge representing the parent-child relationship or a descendant edge representing the ancestor-descendant relationship. Figure 1 shows five QPTs, where descendant edges are shown with dotted lines, and tree nodes are shown with circles, the symbols in the circles are their labels.

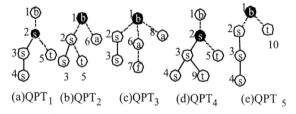

(a)QPT$_1$ (b)QPT$_2$ (c)QPT$_3$ (d)QPT$_4$ (e)QPT$_5$

Figure 1. Query pattern trees

Given a QPT $qpt = (V, E)$, we also refer to V and E with qpt if it's clear from the context. Given an edge $e = (v_1, v_2) \in qpt$ where v_2 is a child of v_1, v_2 will also be denoted as a d-child of v_1 if e is a descendant edge, and as a c-child otherwise. Let qpt be a pattern tree, the size of qpt is defined by the number of its nodes | qpt |.

Given a QPT qpt, a *rooted subtree* RST of qpt is a subtree of QPT such that root(RST) = root(qpt) holds. An RST of size $k+1$ will also be denoted as a k-edge RST. An RST will also be denoted as a single branch RST if it has only one leaf node, and as a multi-branch RST otherwise.

The occurrence of a tree pattern in the transaction database is tested using the concept of tree subsumption [2]. Given two QPTs qpt and qpt', qpt is *subsumed* in qpt', denoted as $qpt \subseteq qpt'$, iff we can construct a simulation relation $sim \subseteq \{(p, q)| p \in qpt, q \in qpt'\}$, such that:
1. (root(qpt), root(qpt'))$\in sim$;
2. v.label = v'.label or v'.label = "*", if $(v, v')\in sim$;

3. For each (u, v) ∈ *qpt*, if *v* is a c-child (or d-child respectively) of *u* and (u, u')∈ *sim*, then there must exist v' ∈ *qpt'*, such that (v, v')∈ *sim*, and v' is a c-child (or proper descendant) of u'.

Given a transaction database $D = \{ qpt_i \mid i = 1,..., n \}$, we say RST *rst* occurs in *D* if *rst* is subsumed in a QPT qpt_i ∈ *D*. The *frequency* of *rst*, denoted as Freq(*rst*), is the number of QPTs of *D* in which *rst* occurs, and supp(*rst*) = Freq(*rst*)/|*D*| is its *support rate*. Given a transaction database *D* and a positive number 0<σ≤1 called the minimum support, the frequent set of *D* is the set $F_D = \{rst_1, ..., rst_m\}$, such that for each *rst* ∈ F_D, supp(*rst*) ≥ σ.

Suppose that a set *d* of new query pattern trees is about to be added to the transaction database *D*. Our purpose is to discover the set of all frequent RSTs of the updated database with minimal possible re-computation.

3. Candidate generation

Next, we will adapt schema-guided rightmost expansion method [4] to enumerate candidate RSTs for incremental mining. Given a transaction database $D=\{qpt_i \mid i = 1,..., n\}$, its *global query pattern tree* G-QPT is a special query pattern tree constructed by merging all QPTs in *D*. Each node *v* of the G-QPT is associated with an identifier, denoted as *v*.id, whose value is set as follows: Initially, the G-QPT is a QPT with only a root node, and we set its identifier to one. Whenever a new tree node is inserted into the G-QPT, its identifier will be set to |G-QPT|+1.

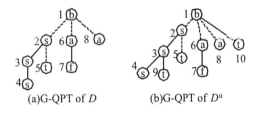

(a)G-QPT of *D*   (b)G-QPT of D^u

Figure 2. Global query pattern tree

Let *D* be the *original database* composed of the three QPTs QPT_1, QPT_2 and QPT_3 as shown in Figure 1, *d* the *incremental database* composed of QPT_4 and QPT_5, and $D^u = D+d$ the *updated database*. Figure 2(a) and (b) show G-QPTs of *D* and D^u respectively. In the diagram, identifiers of G-QPT nodes are shown with numbers outside of the circles. Because each node *u* of *qpt*∈*D* is merged with a unique node *v* of the G-QPT, *u* has the same identifier with *v*. For example, in Figure 1, numbers outside of the circles are identifiers of corresponding tree nodes. Given the G-QPT under consideration, we also use g_i to refer to the G-QPT node with identifier *i*. Since each QPT can be taken as a subtree of the G-QPT, g_i can also be used to refer to the QPT node with identifier *i*.

After labeling each node with an identifier, the representation of QPTs can be simplified to strings as in [4], which will be called as *string encodings* of QPTs.

Given a *k*-edge RST *rst* and its string encoding *s*, an *i-length prefix* of *s* is defined as the list of nodes up to *i*-th node in *s*, and is denoted as prefix(*rst, i*). Given a *k*-edge RST *rst*, we define the equivalence class [*rst*] ={*rst'*| *rst'* is a *k*+1-edge RST such that prefix(*rst, k*+1)= prefix(*rst'*, *k*+1)}.

Given two different (*k*+1)-edge RSTs rst_1 and rst_2 in the same equivalence class [rst^k], we define the order between rst_1 and rst_2 as follows: Let u_1 and u_2 are the rightmost leaves of rst_1 and rst_2 respectively, and v_1 and v_2 parents of u_1 and u_2 respectively. Then rst_1 precedes rst_2, or $rst_1 \geq rst_2$, iff 1) v_1.id < v_2.id; or 2) v_1.id = v_2.id and u_1.id > u_2.id.

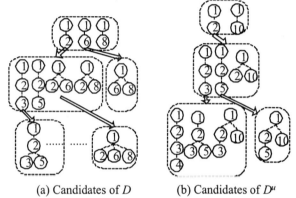

(a) Candidates of *D*   (b) Candidates of D^u

Figure 3. Enumeration of candidate RSTs

After the construction of G-QPT, the enumeration of candidates is reduced to the enumeration of all RSTs of the G-QPT. It's not difficult to prove that all RSTs of the G-QPT can be generated with the rightmost leaf node expansion and the join operation defined in [4], and all RSTs in each equivalence class will be sorted in ascending order automatically. Given a RST *rst*, if it's generated through join of two RSTs rst_1 and rst_2, then rst_1 and rst_2 are called its generating RSTs; if it's generated through RMLNE of rst_1, then rst_1 is called its generating RST. Figure 3(a) and (b) illustrate the enumeration of candidates of *D* and D^u respectively.

In this section, we propose a new numbering scheme to assign identifiers to G-QPT nodes and give a new definition of the order between candidates. Our numbering scheme and definition of the order have the following property: no matter how many new nodes are inserted into the G-QPT and how they are inserted, the string encodings of existing candidates and the order between them will remain unchanged. In [4], identifiers of G-QPT nodes are assigned according to their position in a pre-order traversal, and RSTs in the same equivalence class are sorted according to the identifiers of their rightmost leaf nodes. The numbering scheme and the definition of the order used in [4] are unsuitable for incremental mining because with them, whenever a new node is inserted into the G-QPT, we need to re-number the nodes of G-QPT and existing RSTs and re-sort candidates in each equivalence class. Clearly it might increase the complexity of the mining task.

4. Incremental mining

4.1. Algorithm *increQPMiner*

In this section, we present our algorithm *increQPMiner* for the incremental mining of frequent RSTs. The main framework of *increQPMiner* is shown in Figure 4. In the algorithm, $F^k(D)$, $F^k(d)$, and $F^k(D+d)$ are the sets of k-edge RSTs that are frequent in D, d, and $D+d$, N^k is the set of all k-edge RSTs that have new G-QPT nodes, $C^k(d)$ is the set of k-edge candidates of d. Our algorithm organizes RSTs in the frequent set in the compact tree structure, the ECTree, proposed in [4], and for each frequent RST, we maintain its support.

```
Algorithm: increQPMiner(D, d, ectree)
Input: D—the original database
       d—the incremental database
       ectree—ECTree of the original database
Output: ECTree of the updated database
(1) k = 1;
(2) while C^k(d) is not null and F^k(D) is not null
(3)   for each rst ∈ C^k(d)
(4)     if rst ∈ N^k
(5)       rst.getOcc(D+d); rst.countSupp(D+d);
(6)       if rst is frequent in D+d
(7)         insert rst into ectree;
(8)     if rst ∉ N^k
(9)       rst.getOcc(d); rst.countSupp(d);
(10)      if rst ∈ F^k(D) and rst ∈ F^k(d)
(11)        update support of rst;
(12)      if rst ∉ F^k(D) and rst ∈ F^k(d)
(13)        rst.getOcc(D); rst.countSupp(D);
(14)        if rst is frequent in D+d
(15)          insert rst into ectree;
(16)      if rst ∈ F^k(D) and rst ∉ F^k(d)
(17)        if rst is not frequent in D+d
(18)          remove rst and its supertrees from ectree;
(19)  for each rst ∈ F^k(D) − C^k(d)
(20)    rst.getOcc(d); rst.countSupp(d);
(21)    if rst is not frequent in D+d
(22)      remove rst and its super-trees from ectree;
(23)  C^{k+1}(d) = candidate-gen(F^k(D+d)∩(F^k(d)∪N^k));
(24)  k = k +1;
```

Figure 4. Update of the frequent set

IncreQPMiner processes candidates level-wise. At level k, it enumerates k-edge candidates, gets their supports in the updated database to update the frequent set.

Let's consider RSTs in $C^k(d)$. At the first level, $C^1(d)$ is composed of all 1-edge RSTs of QPTs in the incremental database, and at the succeeding levels, $C^k(d)$ is generated by the function candidate-gen() (see line 23 of Figure 4). Given any $k \geq 1$, let $S = F^k(D+d) \cap (F^k(d) \cup N^k)$. Then candidate-gen() produces the set $C^{k+1}(d)$ of candidates in two setps: 1) for each RST $rst \in S$, candidate-gen() produces candidates through RMLNE of rst; 2) given any two RSTs rst_1, $rst_2 \in S$, if there exists a RST rst^{k-1} such that rst_1, $rst_2 \in [rst^{k-1}]$ holds, then candidate-gen() produces candidates through join of rst_1 and rst_2.

For those RSTs in $C^k(d)$ that have new G-QPT nodes, the algorithm gets their supports in D^u (line 5), and those frequent in D^u are inserted into the ECTree (lines 6-7). The supports of candidates are computed using the functions getOcc() and countSupp(), which will be discussed in next subsection.

Given any RST rst that is in $C^k(d)$ but not in N^k, the algorithm gets its support in d (line 9), and then:

1. If rst is frequent in both D and d, then it must also be frequent in D^u, and the algorithm has to update its support (line 11).
2. If rst is frequent in d but not in D, the algorithm has to get its support in D (line 13) to check whether rst is frequent in D^u. Those frequent in D^u are inserted into the ECTree as new frequent RSTs (lines 14-15).
3. If rst is frequent in D but not in d, the algorithm has to check whether it remains frequent in D^u (line 17). Those that become infrequent in D^u are removed, and their super-trees are also removed based on the anti-monotone property of tree subsumption (line 18).

Since candidate-gen() only produces candidates from RSTs that are frequent in both d and D^u, some RSTs in $F^k(D)$ are possibly not included in $C^k(d)$. To check whether these RSTs remain frequent in D^u, the algorithm has to get their supports in d (line 20), and remove them and their super-trees from the ECTree if they are infrequent in D^u (line 22).

4.2. Computation of supports

In this subsection, we propose a new method to count the support values of candidates based on the notion of distinguished occurrence.

Given a QPT, if it's a single branch QPT, then we define the parent node of its leaf node as its *distinguished node*; if it's a multi-branch QPT, then we define as its *distinguished node* the node that has more than one child, but none of whose ancestors has more than one child.

Given two QPTs QPT and QPT' such that QPT $\subseteq$ QPT', and $v \in$ QPT, we use $sim(v$, QPT, QPT'$)$ to denote the set of nodes of QPT' that can be matched with v according the definition of tree subsumption, or formally, $sim(v$, QPT, QPT'$) = \{v' | \forall v'$ such that $(v, v') \in$ *simulation*, where *simulation* is any simulation relation between nodes of QPT and QPT'}.

Given a RST *rst* and a QPT *qpt*, if $rst \subseteq qpt$ and v is the distinguished node of *rst*, then we define the set dist(*rst*, *qpt*) = *sim*(v, *rst*, *qpt*) as *the set of distinguished occurrences of rst in qpt*.

After associating each QPT with a transaction identifier, denoted as QPT.tid, the distinguished occurrences of a candidate in all QPTs can also be recorded vertically. Given a RST *rst* and a transaction database D, let G-QPT be the global query pattern tree of D, v a node of *rst*, and g_i the node of G-QPT whose identifier is i. We define tidList(*rst*, v, g_i) as the set { qpt.tid| $\forall qpt \in D$ such that its node $g_i \in sim(v, rst, qpt)$}.

With the above definition, given a RST *rst* and its distinguished node v, the sets of its distinguished occurrences in QPTs in D can be vertically represented as the set dist(*rst*, D) = {tidList(*rst*, v, g_i)| $\forall g_i \in$ G-QPT}.

The notion of distinguished occurrence is useful because supports of candidates can be directly derived from the sets of their distinguished occurrences. Given a RST *rst* with distinguished node v, $rst \subseteq$ QPT holds iff the transaction identifier of QPT is in the set S ={tid | $\exists$ tidList(*rst*, v, g_i)$\in$ dist(*rst*, D) such that tid$\in$ tidList(*rst*, v, g_i)}. Thus, Freq(*rst*) = $|S|$.

Next, let's investigate how to obtain the distinguished occurrences of candidates efficiently. While constructing the G-QPT, we maintain the transaction information in the G-QPT as in [3]. We associate each G-QPT node u with a list of transaction IDs, denoted as u.tidList. While merging node v of QPT with node u of G-QPT, if v is a leaf node of QPT, then QPT.tid is inserted into u.tidList.

After associating the G-QPT with transaction IDs, the distinguished occurrences of single branch RSTs can be obtained from the information provided by the G-QPT.

Lemma 1: Given a single branch RST *rst*, let v be its leaf node and u its distinguished node. We have: for each $g_i \in$ G-QPT, if $g_i \in sim(u, rst, $ G-QPT$)$, then tidList(*rst*, u, g_i) = {tid| tid $\in g_j$.tidList, or $\exists g_k \in$ descendant(g_j) such that tid $\in g_k$.tidList, where g_j is any G-QPT node such that $(u, v) \subseteq (g_i, g_j)$}; otherwise, tidList(*rst*, u, g_i) = ϕ. Hence, dist(*rst*, D) = {tidList(*rst*, u, g_i)| $g_i \in sim(u, rst, $ G-QPT$)$}. □

Next, Let's investigate how to obtain distinguished occurrences of multi-branch RSTs. Given a RST *rst* and its node v, we call v a computation node if it's a leaf node or it has more than one child. Given two computation nodes v and u such that u is a descendant of v, we call u a supporting node of v if there doesn't exist any other computation node in the path from v to u.

Lemma 2: Given a multi-branch RST *rst*, let c be one of its computation nodes, for each G-QPT node g_i, we define list(*rst*, c, g_i) as follows:

1. If c is a leaf node, then list(*rst*, c, g_i) = {tid| tid $\in g_i$.tidList, or $\exists g_j \in$ descendant(g_i) such that tid $\in g_j$.tidList}.
2. Otherwise, assume that $S = \{s_1, s_2, ..., s_n\}$ is the set of supporting nodes of c. For each $s_j \in S$, let $G_j = \{g_k | \forall g_k \in$ G-QPT such that $(c, s_j) \subseteq (g_i, g_k)$ holds}. Then we set
$$\text{list}(rst, c, g_i) = \bigcap_{s_j \in S}(\bigcup_{g_k \in G_j} list(rst, s_j, g_k)).$$

Given the distinguished node v of RST, for each G-QPT node $g_i \in sim(v, rst, $ G-QPT$)$, we have tidList(*rst*, v, g_i) = list(*rst*, v, g_i). □

We also designed a method to obtain distinguished occurrences of a multi-branch RST *rst* through set operations on the sets of distinguished occurrences of its two supporting subtrees, which are formed by cutting off the rightmost leaf node or leftmost leaf node of *rst* respectively. However, the details will not be given here due to the space limitation.

In our algorithm, we implement the function getOcc() to obtain the distinguished occurrences of candidates based on the above discussion, and implement the function countSupp() to derive supports of candidates from their distinguished occurrences.

5. Conclusion

In this paper, we consider the incremental mining of frequent XML query patterns. We propose an efficient algorithm, *increQPMiner*, to update the mining results incrementally.

We performed a sets of experiments to evaluate the performance of the *increQPMiner* algorithm. Experiments show that our method results in substantial performance gains, and the running time of *increQPMiner* scales almost linearly with the number of transactions in the database.

References

[1] J. Clark and S. DeRose. XML Path Language (XPath) version 1.0 w3c recommendation. Technical Report REC-xpath- 19991116, World Wide Web Consortium, 1999.
[2] Gerome Miklau, Dan Suciu: Containment and Equivalence for an XPath Fragment. PODS 2002: 65-76.
[3] Y. Xiao, J-F Yao, Z. Li, and M. Dunham. Efficient data mining for maximal frequent subtrees. In *Proc. of the 2003 IEEE Int. Conf. on Data Mining (ICDM'03)*, 2003.
[4] L.H. Yang, M.L. Lee, W. Hsu, S. Acharya. Mining Frequent Query Patterns from XML Queries. DASFAA, 2003, pp:355-362, 2003.
[5] L.H. Yang, M.L. Lee, W. Hsu. Efficient Mining of Frequent Query Patterns for Caching. In Proc. Of 29th VLDB Conference, 2003.

Spam Filtering using a Markov Random Field Model with Variable Weighting Schemas

Shalendra Chhabra
UC Riverside
Riverside, California, USA
schhabra@cs.ucr.edu

William S. Yerazunis
MERL
Cambridge, Massachusetts, USA
wsy@merl.com

Christian Siefkes
GKVI*/ FU Berlin
Berlin, Germany
christian@siefkes.net

Abstract

In this paper we present a Markov Random Field model based approach to filter spam. Our approach examines the importance of the neighborhood relationship (MRF cliques) among words in an email message for the purpose of spam classification. We propose and test several different theoretical bases for weighting schemes among corresponding neighborhood windows. Our results demonstrate that unexpected side effects depending on the neighborhood window size may have larger accuracy impact than the neighborhood relationship effects of the Markov Random Field.

1 Introduction and Related Work

Spam filtering problem can be seen as a particular instance of the Text Categorization problem, in which only two classes are possible: *spam* and *legitimate email or ham*. In this paper, we present spam filtering based on the MRF Model with different weighting schemes of feature vectors for variable neighborhood of words. We present theoretical justification for our approach and conclude with results.

Recently Sparse Binary Polynomial Hash (SBPH), a generalization of the Bayesian method [9] and Markovian discrimination [10] have been reported for spam filtering. The classifier model in [10] uses empirically derived ad-hoc superincreasing weights. We develop more on [10], correlate it with MRFs, choose variable neighborhood windows for features using Hammersley-Clifford theorem [4] and present different weighting schemes for the corresponding neighborhood window. We tested these weighting schemes in CRM114 Discriminator Framework [3]. Our results reflect the effect of neighborhood relationship among features and provide evidence that this model is superior to existing Bayesian models used for spam filtering.

*The work of this author is supported by the German Research Society (DFG grant no. GRK 316).

2 Markov Random Fields

Let $\mathbf{F} = \{F_1, F_2 \ldots, F_m\}$ be a family of random variables defined on the discrete set of sites $\mathbf{S}$, in which each random variable F_i takes a value f_i in the discrete label set $\mathbf{L}$. The family $\mathbf{F}$ is called a random field. The notation $F_i = f_i$ denotes the event that F_i takes the value f_i and the notation $(F_1 = f_1, \ldots, F_m = f_m)$ denotes the joint event. A joint event (abbreviated as $\mathbf{F} = f$ where $f = \{f_1, \ldots f_m\}$) is a *configuration* of $\mathbf{F}$, corresponding to a realization of the field. For the label set $\mathbf{L}$, the probability that random variable F_i takes the value f_i is denoted by $P(F_i = f_i)$, and abbreviated as $P(f_i)$. The joint probability is denoted by $P(F = f) = P(F_1 = f_1, \ldots F_m = f_m)$ but abbreviated as $P(f)$. A site in the context of spam classification refers to the relative position of the word in a sequence and a label maps to word values. $\mathbf{F}$ is said to be a MRF on $\mathbf{S}$ with respect to a neighborhood N iff the following conditions hold:

1. $P(f) > 0, \forall f \in F$ (*positivity*)

2. $P(f_i|f_{S-\{i\}}) = P(f_i|f_{N_i})$ (*Markovianity*)

where $\mathbf{S} - \{i\}$ is the set difference, $f_{S-\{i\}}$ denotes the set of labels at the sites in $\mathbf{S} - \{i\}$ and $f_{N_i} = \{f_{i'}|i' \in N_i\}$ stands for the set of labels at the sites neighboring i. When the positivity condition is satisfied, the joint probability of any random field is uniquely determined by its local conditional probabilities [2]. The Markovianity depicts the local characteristics of $\mathbf{F}$. Only neighboring labels have direct interactions with each other. It is always possible to select sufficiently large N_i so that the Markovianity holds. Any $\mathbf{F}$ is a MRF with respect to such a neighborhood system.

3 Markov Random Fields and CRM114

We have implemented our scheme in CRM114 Discriminator Framework[1][3]. Like other binary document classi-

[1]The current version of CRM114 [3] is similar in spirit to MRF with lot of tweaks and hacks.

fiers, the CRM114 Discriminator associates a binary class value $S \in \{spam, nonspam\}$ with any given document $\omega = (\omega_1, \ldots, \omega_n)$. As a word context sensitive classifier CRM114 does not treat the input document ω as a bag of independent words, but rather considers all relations between neighboring words to matter, for neighborhoods with variable window size (for example: up to 3, 4, 5, 6 words etc.).

We now derive a *possible* MRF model based on this neighborhood structure, thereby casting the classification problem as a partial Bayesian inference problem. Our MRF model consists of a probability measure P defined on a set of configurations Ω. The elements $\omega \in \Omega$ represent all possible documents of interest, with the i-th component ω_i representing the i-th word or token. A random class function C is defined over Ω, $C : \Omega \to \{spam, nonspam\}$, such that C indicates the class of the document, and whose law is given by P.

In this framework the document classification problem can be treated as the problem of computing the probability $P(C(w) = s|\omega)$, or more precisely for MAP estimation (i.e. maximum a posteriori). The optimal class s^* is chosen as $s^* = \arg\max_{s \in S} P(C(w) = s|\omega)$.

Let us define a k-neighborhood consisting of k consecutive token positions in a document. The cliques are defined to be all possible subsets of a neighborhood. Thus if $\omega = (\omega_1, \ldots, \omega_n)$ is a document, then the first 3-neighborhood is $\{1, 2, 3\}$, and the associated cliques are $\{1\}, \{2\}, \{3\}, \{1, 2\}, \{1, 3\}, \{2, 3\}$. We assume that the measure P is an exponential form Markov Random Field conditioned on $C(w)$. This postulate is natural in view of the characterization by Hammersley and Clifford [4], in terms of conditional distributions on cliques. The functional form of P is therefore fixed as
$$P(\omega|C(\omega) = s) = Z_s^{-1} \exp\left(\sum_i V_i^s(\omega_i) + \sum_{ij} V_{ij}^s(\omega_i, \omega_j) + \cdots + \sum_{i_1, \ldots, i_k} V_{i_1, \ldots, i_k}^s(\omega_{i_1}, \ldots, \omega_{i_k})\right),$$
where Z_s is the appropriate normalizing constant which guarantees that $\sum_\omega P(\omega|C(\omega)) = 1$ when summed over all possible documents ω (*emails*). By the Hammersley and Clifford [4] characterization of MRFs, the functions V are nonzero if and only if the indices form a clique.

We can identify the conditional MRF with a specific CRM114 instance by assigning the required V functions from the local probability formulas. For example,
$$V_{ij}^s(\omega_i, \omega_j) = \log \Pi_{ij}(\omega, s),$$
where $\Pi_{ij}(\omega, s) = (local\ probability\ for\ (\omega_i, \omega_j), given$ $C(\omega) = s)$. $\Pi_{ij}(\omega, s)$ cannot be interpreted directly as conditional probabilities, however an easy product form solution is obtained i.e.
$$P(\omega|C(\omega) = spam) = Z_{spam}^{-1} \prod_{cliques\ c} \Pi_c(\omega, spam)$$

which is quite different from a naive Bayesian model. In the special case of neighborhoods with $k = 1$, this reduces to a naive Bayesian model. With this solution, Bayes' rule can be applied to obtain the class probability, given a document:
$$P(C(\omega) = spam|\omega) = \frac{P(\omega|C(\omega) = spam)P(spam)}{P(\omega)}.$$

In the Bayesian framework, the two unknowns on the right are $P(spam)$ (the prior) and $P(\omega)$. Normally, $P(\omega)$ is ignored, since it doesn't influence the MAP estimate, but it can also be expanded in the form
$$P(\omega) = Z_{spam}^{-1} \prod_{cliques\ c} \Pi_c(\omega, spam)P(spam) + Z_{nonspam}^{-1} \prod_{cliques\ c} \Pi_c(\omega, nonspam)(1 - P(spam))$$
While these Z^{-1} terms are unknown a possible value can be approximated by setting bounds based on the neighborhood structure of the clique.

4 Features Vectors in the Neighborhood

An incoming document *(email)* has to be broken into features to generate feature vectors. These feature vectors can be assigned weights so that the learning algorithms can compensate for the inter-word dependence. This is done by re-defining the learnable features to be both single tokens and groupings of sequential tokens, and by varying the length of the grouping window. By forcing the shorter groupings of sequential tokens to have smaller weightings, the inter-word dependence of natural language can be compensated that a Naive Bayesian Model normally ignores. The larger groupings have greater clique potentials and the smaller groupings have smaller clique potentials. In our scheme(s) feature vectors are assigned weights in a superincreasing fashion. The basic idea of superincreasing weights is to have a non linear classifier that is not bound by the limits of the Perceptron theorem [5]. This superincreasing classifier can cut the feature hyperspace along a curved (and possibly disconnected) surface, in contrast to a linear Bayesian classifier that is limited to a flat hyperplane. We now propose some weighting schemes with superincreasing weights.

Let n-*sequence* denote a feature containing n sequential nonzero tokens, not separated by placeholders; n-*term* denotes a feature containing n nonzero tokens, ignoring placeholders; e.g. "A B C" would be a 3-sequence and a 3-term, "A B ? D" would be a 3-term, but not a sequence. For each n-sequence, there are $Num(n) = 2^n - 2$ subterms (-2 because the empty feature (containing only placeholders) and the full n-sequence feature are both ignored). The number of subterms with k tokens is given by the binomial coefficient: $Num(n, k) = \binom{n}{k}$, for $0 < k < n$.

The weight $W(n)$ of a n-sequence should be larger than the weight of all subterms considered for this sequence i.e.

$$W(n) > \sum_{k=1}^{n-1} \left(\binom{n}{k} \times W(k) \right) \qquad (1)$$

Minimum Weighting Sequences: The minimum weighting scheme for a superincreasing set of weights, can be evaluated as $W(n) = \sum_{k=1}^{n-1} \left(\binom{n}{k} \times W(k) \right) + 1$.

Exponential Weighting Sequences: For any given window length, the exponential weighting $W(k) = base^{k-1}$ can be evaluated as:

$$base^{n-1} > \sum_{k=1}^{n-1} \left(\binom{n}{k} \times base^{k-1} \right) \qquad (2)$$

Applying the Binomial Theorem and setting $a=1$, $b=base$, we get: $2 \times base^n + 1 > (base + 1)^n$.

The resulting weighting schemas are shown in table 1.

n	MWS	ES
1	1	1
2	1, 3	1, 3
3	1, 3, 13	1, 5, 25
4	1, 3, 13, 75	1, 6, 36, 216
5	1, 3, 13, 75, 541	1, 7, 49, 343, 2401
6	1, 3, 13, 75, 541, 4683	1, 8, 64, 512, 4096, 32768

Table 1. Minimum & Exponential Weightings

5 Training and Prediction using CRM114

For evaluation, we used the same corpus and testing procedure as described in [10]. The 4147 messages (1397 spam, 2750 nonspam), were shuffled into ten different standard sequences. The last 500 messages of each standard sequence formed the *testing set* used for accuracy evaluation.

5.1 Models Tested

Four different weighting methodologies for differential evaluation of increasingly long matches were tested. These models correspond to increasingly accurate descriptions of known situations in the Markov Field Model.

The first model tested was Sparse Binary Polynomial Hashing (SBPH), which uses a constant weighting of 1.0 for all matches, irrespective of the length. With a window length of 1, SBPH is identical to the common Naive Bayesian model without discarding any features as "too uncommon" or "too ambivalent". Testing showed that best results occurred when the maximum window length was five tokens.

The second model tested was the exponential superincreasing model (ESM), which uses an empirically-derived formula that yields weights of 1, 4, 16, 64, 256, and 1024 for matches of one, two, three, four, five, and six words, respectively.

The third model tested was the Minimum Weighting System (MWS) model. This model uses the minimum weight increase necessary to assure that a single occurrence of a feature of length N words can override a single occurrence of all of its internal features (that is, all features of lengths $1, 2, \ldots, N-1$). This is a different notion than the superincreasing ESM model, and produces weights of 1, 3, 13, 75, 541 and 4683 as deduced above.

The fourth model tested uses a variable base to form an exponential series (ES), with a base chosen to assure that the values are always above the MWS threshold for any value of window length used. For our tests, we used a base of 8, yielding weights of 1, 8, 64, 512, 4096, and 32768. A summary of the term weighting length is shown in table 2.

Note that the ESM weight sequence is not larger than the MWS weight sequence for features of length 4 or longer. Thus, a long ESM-weighted feature may not be capable of overriding the weighting of it's internal subfeatures.

An example of the weighting model used for these tests is presented in the table 3. Here, the phrase "Do you feel lucky?" is broken into a series of subfeatures, and the respective weightings given to those subfeatures in each of SBPH, ESM, MWS, and ES are shown.

For each of these weighting schemes, these weights are used as multiplicative factors when calculating the local probability of each subfeature as it is evaluated in an otherwise-conventional Bayesian Chain Rule evaluation. The local probability of each class in CRM114 is given by

$$P = 0.5 + (((f_c * w) - (f'_c * w))/(m * ((f_{totalhits} * w) + n))) \qquad (3)$$

where f_c is the number of feature hits in this class, f'_c is the number of feature hits in the other class, $f_{totalhits}$ is the number of the total hits and w is the weight. In our implementation, $m = 16$ and $n = 1$. These experimentally determined constants generate probabilities close enough to 0.5 so as to avoid numerical underflow errors even over thousands of repeated applications of the Bayesian Chain Rule.

Model	Weighing Sequence
SBPH	1, 1, 1, 1, 1, 1
ESM	1, 4, 16, 64, 256, 1024
MWS	1, 3, 13, 75, 541, 4683
ES	1, 8, 64, 512, 4096, 32768

Table 2. A Summary of Tested Models with their Weighting Sequences

Text	SBPH	ESM	MWS	ES
Do	1	1	1	1
Do you	1	4	3	8
Do *<skip>*feel	1	4	3	8
Do you feel	1	16	13	64
Do *<skip><skip>*lucky?	1	4	3	8
Do you *<skip>*lucky?	1	16	13	64
Do *<skip>*feel lucky?	1	16	13	64
Do you feel lucky?	1	64	75	512

Table 3. Example Subphrases and Relative Weights with the Models Tested

5.2 Test Results and Discussion

In our tests we varied the window length parameter and the term weighting length table. All four models with a window length of 1 are exactly equivalent to each other and to a pure Bayesian model as postulated by Graham [1]. Each of these advanced models is also more accurate than a pure Bayesian model in every window length > 1.

The results are shown in the table 4. Figure 1 shows that even though ESM has a theoretical weakness due to coefficients less than the MWS for window lengths of four or greater, it has the best accuracy for all tested setups.

Size	1	2	3	4	5	6
SBPH	97.98	98.56	98.6	98.62	98.68	98.48
ESM	97.98	98.46	98.66	98.76	98.88	98.28
MWS	97.98	98.44	98.72	98.76	98.80	98.26
ES	97.98	98.48	98.58	98.32	98.80	98.16

Table 4. Accuracy (%) per 5000 test messages With Varying Window Sizes

6 Conclusion and Future Work

We have derived a generalized form of weighting schemas for classifiers with superincreasing weights. The weighting sequences define a set of clique potentials, where the neighborhood of a single word is given by the words surrounding it. For a window of size 2, "pairwise only dependence" is reflected [2].

Determining a generalized optimal window size may be the subject of future work. An interesting direction of future research is the combination of Sparse Binary Polynomial Hashing (SBPH) and feature weighting with other learning algorithms. Recently we have obtained significant improvements by combining SBPH with a variant of the *Winnow* algorithm [6] using TIES [8] [7].

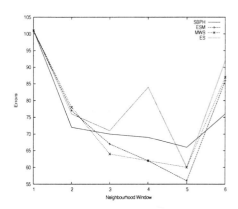

Figure 1. Errors in the Tested Models with Variable Neighborhood Windows

Acknowledgments

The authors are grateful to Laird Arnault Breyer, University of Lancaster, U.K. for fruitful discussions.

References

[1] A Plan for Spam. http://www.paulgraham.com/spam.html.

[2] J. Besag. Spatial Interaction and the Statistical Analysis of Lattice Systems. In *Journal of the Royal Statistical Society, Series B*, volume 36, pages 192–236, 1974.

[3] CRM114 Discriminator - The Controllable Regex Mutilator. http://crm114.sourceforge.net/.

[4] J. M. Hammersley and P. Clifford. Markov Field on Finite Graphs and Lattices. In *Unpublished*, 1971.

[5] Minsky and Papert. Perceptrons. 1969.

[6] Nick Littlestone. Learning Quickly When Irrelevant Attributes Abound: A New Linear-threshold Algorithm. *Machine Learning*, 2:285–318, 1988.

[7] C. Siefkes, F. Assis, S. Chhabra, and W. S. Yerazunis. Combining Winnow and Orthogonal Sparse Bigrams for Incremental Spam Filtering. In *Proceedings of ECML/PKDD 2004*, LNCS. Springer Verlag, 2004.

[8] TIES - Trainable Incremental Extraction System. http://www.inf.fu-berlin.de/inst/ag-db/software/ties/.

[9] W. S. Yerazunis. Sparse Binary Polynomial Hashing and the CRM114 Discriminator. In *MIT Spam Conference*, 2003.

[10] W. S. Yerazunis. The Spam Filtering Accuracy Plateau at 99.9 Percent Accuracy and How to Get Past It. In *MIT Spam Conference*, 2004.

An Adaptive Learning Approach for Noisy Data Streams

Fang Chu   Yizhou Wang   Carlo Zaniolo

Computer Science Department, University of California, Los Angeles, CA 90095

{fchu, wangyz, zaniolo}@cs.ucla.edu

Abstract

Two critical challenges typically associated with mining data streams are concept drift and data contamination. To address these challenges, we seek learning techniques and models that are robust to noise and can adapt to changes in timely fashion. We approach the stream-mining problem using a statistical estimation framework, and propose a fast and robust discriminative model for learning noisy data streams. We build an ensemble of classifiers to achieve timely adaptation by weighting classifiers in a way that maximizes the likelihood of the data. We further employ robust statistical techniques to alleviate the problem of noise sensitivity. Experimental results on both synthetic and real-life data sets demonstrate the effectiveness of this new model learning approach.

1. Introduction

There is much current research interest in continuous mining of data streams. Applications involving stream data abound and include network traffic monitoring, credit card fraud detection and stock market trend analysis. Practical situations pose three fundamental issues to be addressed.

Adaptation Issue. Unlike traditional learning tasks where data is stationary, the concept generating a data stream drifts with time due to changes in the environment. These changes cause the model learned from old data obsolete, and model updating is necessary.

Robustness Issue. The noise problem is more severe for stream data mining, because it is difficult to distinguish noise from changes caused by concept drift. If an algorithm is too eager to adapt to concept changes, it may overfit noise by falsefully interpreting it as data from a new concept. If it is too conservative and slow to adapt, it may overlook important changes.

Performance Issue. To assure on-line responses with limited resources, continuous mining should be "fast and light", that is: (1) learning should be done very fast, preferably in one pass of the data; and (2) algorithms should make light demands on memory resources.

To address these issues, we propose a novel discriminative model for adaptive learning for noisy data streams, with modest resource consumption. The model takes a form of a weighted ensemble, whose member classifiers and their weights are adaptively updated. For a learnable concept, the class of a sample conditionally follows a Bernoulli distribution. Our method assigns classifier weights in a way that maximizes the training data likelihood with the learned distribution. This weighting scheme has theoretical guarantee of adaptability, and can also boost a collection of weak classifiers into a strong ensemble. Weak classifiers are desirable because they learn faster and consume less resources.

The adaptive weighting scheme distinguishes our approach from previous work using ensemble methods for data stream learning, such as the work in [4] and [5]. In [4], uniform votes are taken among members, while in [5], classifier votes are weighted proportionally to their estimated accuracy. As shown in the experiment section, our approach outperforms both methods, For ease of references in our comparative study, we name them 'Bagging' and 'Weighted Bagging', respectively. (The name " bagging" derives from their analogy to traditional bagging ensembles.)

Our outlier detection differs from previous off-line approaches which assume an unchanging data model. The truth is that outliers are directly defined by the current concept, so the outlier identifying strategy needs to be modified whenever the concept drifts away. In our approach, the outlier detection is integrated into the model learning, so that they mutually reinforce each other.

The "fast and light" learning is achieved by boosting weak classifiers into strong ensembles. This is illustrate by learning strong ensembles of small decision trees, each with very few nodes.

2. Adaptation to Concept Drift

Ensemble weighting is the key to fast adaptation. Here we show that this problem can be formulated as a statistical optimization problem solvable by logistic regression.

We first look at how an ensemble is constructed and maintained. The data stream is simply partitioned into small blocks of fixed size, then classifiers are learned from blocks. The most recent K classifiers comprise the ensemble, and old classifiers retire sequentially by age. A separate set of training examples are prepared for classifier weighting by sampling the training data streams. When sufficient training data is collected for classifier learning and ensemble weighting, the following steps are conducted: (1) learn a new classifier from the training block; (2) replace the oldest classifier in the ensemble with this newly learned; and then (3) weigh the ensemble.

For simplicity, we consider a two-class classification setting. The training data for ensemble weighting is represented as

$$(\mathcal{X}, \mathcal{Y}) = \{(\mathbf{x}_i, y_i); i = 1, \cdots, N\}$$

$\mathbf{x}_i$ is a vector-valued sample attribute, and $y_i \in \{0, 1\}$ is the sample class label. An ensemble of classifiers is denoted in a vector form as

$$\mathbf{f} = (f_1(\mathbf{x}), \cdots, f_K(\mathbf{x}))^T$$

where each $f_k(\mathbf{x})$ is a classifier function producing a value for the belief on a class. The individual classifiers in the ensemble may be weak or out-of-date. It is the goal of our discriminative model $\mathcal{M}$ to make the ensemble strong by weighted voting. Classifier weights are model parameters, denoted as

$$\mathbf{w} = (w_1, \cdots, w_K)^T$$

where w_k is the weight associated with classifier f_k. The model $\mathcal{M}$ also specifies a weighted voting scheme:

$$\mathbf{w}^T \cdot \mathbf{f}$$

Because the ensemble prediction $\mathbf{w}^T \cdot \mathbf{f}$ is a continuous value, yet the class label y_i to be decided is discrete, a standard approach is to assume that y_i conditionally follows a Bernoulli distribution parameterized by a latent score η_i:

$$\begin{aligned} y_i | \mathbf{x}_i; \mathbf{f}, \mathbf{w} &\sim \text{Ber}(q(\eta_i)) \\ \eta_i &= \mathbf{w^T} \cdot \mathbf{f} \end{aligned} \quad (1)$$

where $q(\eta_i)$ is the logit transformation of η_i:

$$q(\eta_i) \triangleq \text{logit}(\eta_i) = \frac{e^{\eta_i}}{1 + e^{\eta_i}}$$

Eq.1 states that y_i follows a Bernoulli distribution with parameter q, thus the posterior likelihood is

$$p(y_i | \mathbf{x}_i; \mathbf{f}, \mathbf{w}) = q^{y_i}(1 - q)^{1-y_i} \quad (2)$$

The above description leads to optimizing classifier weights using logistic regression. Logistic regression is a well-established regression method, widely used in traditional areas when the regressors are continuous and the responses are discrete [3]. In our problem, given a data set $(\mathcal{X}, \mathcal{Y})$ and an ensemble $\mathbf{f}$, the logistic regression technique optimizes the classifier weights by maximizing the likelihood of the data. The optimization problem has a closed-form solution which can be computed quickly.

3. Robustness to Outliers

Regression is adaptive because it always tries to fit the data from the current concept, but can potentially overfit outliers. We integrate the following outlier detection technique into the model learning.

We define outliers as samples with a small likelihood under a given data model. The goal of learning is to compute a model that best fits the bulk of the data, that is, the inliers. Since we do not know the outliers, we use the EM approach discussed in the next section.

Previously we have described a training data set as $\{(\mathbf{x}_i, y_i), i = 1, \cdots, N\}$, or $(\mathcal{X}, \mathcal{Y})$. This is an *incomplete* data set, as the outlier information is missing. A *complete* data set is a triplet

$$(\mathcal{X}, \mathcal{Y}, \mathcal{Z})$$

where

$$\mathcal{Z} = \{z_1, \cdots, z_N\}$$

is a hidden variable that distinguishes the outliers from the inliers. $z_i = 1$ if $(\mathbf{x}_i, y_i)$ is an outlier, $z_i = 0$ otherwise. This $\mathcal{Z}$ is not observable and needs to be inferred. After $\mathcal{Z}$ is inferred, $(\mathcal{X}, \mathcal{Y})$ can be partitioned into an inlier set

$$(\mathcal{X}_0, \mathcal{Y}_0) = \{(\mathbf{x}_i, y_i, z_i), \mathbf{x}_i \in \mathcal{X}, y_i \in \mathcal{Y}, z_i = 0\}$$

and an outlier set

$$(\mathcal{X}_\phi, \mathcal{Y}_\phi) = \{(\mathbf{x}_i, y_i, z_i), \mathbf{x}_i \in \mathcal{X}, y_i \in \mathcal{Y}, z_i = 1\}$$

The samples in $(\mathcal{X}_0, \mathcal{Y}_0)$, which all come from one underlying distribution, and are used to fit the model parameters.

To infer the outlier indicator $\mathcal{Z}$, we introduce a new model parameter λ. It is a threshold value of sample likelihood. That is,

$$z_i = \text{neg}\big(\log p(y_i | \mathbf{x}_i; \mathbf{f}, \mathbf{w}) - \lambda\big) \quad (3)$$

where neg() returns 1 for a negative value, 0 otherwise.

This λ, together with $\mathbf{f}$ (classifier functions) and $\mathbf{w}$ (classifier weights) discussed earlier, constitutes the complete set of parameters of our discriminative model $\mathcal{M}$, which has a four tuple representation $\mathcal{M}(\mathbf{x}; \mathbf{f}, \mathbf{w}, \lambda)$.

4. Model Learning

The goal of model learning is to compute the optimal values of parameters $\mathbf{w}$ and λ, so that the discriminative model $\mathcal{M}$ gives the best fit on the data $(\mathcal{X}, \mathcal{Y})$. The problem is thus an optimization problem. The score function to be maximized involves two parts: (i) the log-likelihood term for the inliers $(\mathcal{X}_0, \mathcal{Y}_0)$, and (ii) a penalty term for the outliers $(\mathcal{X}_\phi, \mathcal{Y}_\phi)$.

Each inlier sample $(\mathbf{x}_i, y_i) \in (\mathcal{X}_0, \mathcal{Y}_0)$ is assumed to be drawn from an independent identical distribution belonging to a probability family characterized by parameters $\mathbf{w}$, denoted by a density function $p((\mathbf{x}, y); \mathbf{f}, \mathbf{w})$. The problem is to find the values of $\mathbf{w}$ that maximizes the log-likelihood of $(\mathcal{X}_0, \mathcal{Y}_0)$ in the probability family:

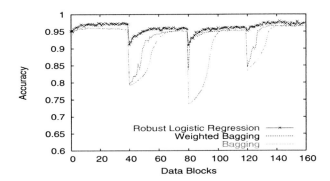

Figure 1. Adaptability comparison of the ensemble methods on data with three abrupt shifts.

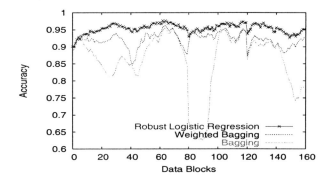

Figure 2. Adaptability comparison of the ensemble methods on data with three abrupt shifts mixed with small shifts.

$$\log\ p((\mathcal{X}_0, \mathcal{Y}_0)|\mathbf{f}, \mathbf{w})$$

A parametric model for outlier distribution is not available. We use instead a non-parametric statistics:

$$e \cdot \|(\mathcal{X}_\phi, \mathcal{Y}_\phi)\|$$

This term penalizes having too many outliers. The optimization problem is then formalized as:

$$
\begin{aligned}
(\mathbf{w}, \lambda)^* \ = \ &\arg\max_{(\mathbf{w}, \lambda)} \big(\log\ p((\mathcal{X}_0, \mathcal{Y}_0)|\mathbf{f}, \mathbf{w}) \\
&- e \cdot \|(\mathcal{X}_\phi, \mathcal{Y}_\phi)\| \big)
\end{aligned}
\tag{4}
$$

The score function to be maximized is not differentiable because of the non-parametric penalty term. We have to resort to a more elaborate technique based on the Expectation-Maximization (EM) [1] algorithm to solve the problem.

The EM is a general method for maximizing data likelihood in problems where data is incomplete. The algorithm iteratively performs an Expectation-Step (*E-Step*) followed by an Maximization-Step (*M-Step*). In our case,

1. E-Step: to impute / infer the outlier indicator $\mathcal{Z}$ based on the current model parameters $(\mathbf{w}, \lambda)$, as in Eq.3.
2. M-Step: to compute new values for $(\mathbf{w}, \lambda)$ that maximize the score function in Eq.4 with current $\mathcal{Z}$. This step is actually a Maximum Likelihood Estimation (MLE) problem.

Due to space limitation, we refer the readers to a full version of this work ([2]) for detailed model computation.

5. Experiments and Discussions

On both synthetic and real-life data, our robust regression method is shown to be superior to the previously mentioned approaches: *Bagging* [4] and *Weighted Bagging* [5]. The base learner we have used is the C4.5 decision tree.

The synthetic data consists of points in a 3-dimension unit cube: $\mathbf{x} = \langle x_1, x_2, x_3 \rangle$, $x_i \in [0, 1], i = 0, 1, 2$. Two classes are separated by a sphere inside the cube. Concept drift is simulated by moving the center of the sphere between adjacent blocks with a step of $\pm\delta$. The value of

δ controls the level of shifts. In our setting, we consider a concept shift small if δ is around 0.02, and relatively large if δ around 0.1. To study robustness, we insert noise by randomly flipping the class labels with a certain probability.

The real-life application is to build a weighted ensemble to detect fraudulent credit card transactions. Concept drift is simulated by sorting transactions by transaction amount.

Detailed data descriptions are given in [2].

Evaluation of Adaptation We have two sets of experiments, both have large changes, with $\delta = 0.1$, occurring at block 40, 80 and 120. In one setting, data remains stationary between these changing points, while in the other, small shifts are mixed between the abrupt ones, with $\delta \in (0.005, 0.03)$. Noise level is 10%.

As shown in Fig.1 and Fig.2, the robust regression model always gives the best performance. The two bagging ensembles are seriously impaired at the concept changing points, but the robust regression is able to catch up with the new concept quickly.

Robustness in the Presence of Outliers Fig. 3 shows the ensemble performance for different noise levels. We see that the robust regression is always the most accurate, and it also gives the least performance drops when noise increases.

To better understand why the robust regression method is less impacted by outliers, we record the outliers in blocks 0-59 in the experiments shown in Fig.2. Outliers consist mostly of noisy samples and samples from a newly emerged concept. As shown in Fig.4, true noise dominates the identified outliers. Even at block 40 where a large concept drift occurs and a bit more samples reflecting the new concept are falsefully reported as outliers, still more true noisy samples are detected.

Discussions on Performance Issue Robust regression ensembles can build strong ensembles from boost weak classifiers, i.e., decision trees with a few terminal nodes (8, 16, or 32). Actually, as shown in Fig.5, robust regression

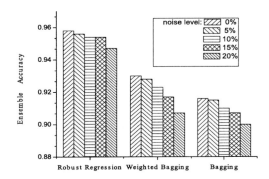

Figure 3. Robustness comparison of the ensembles.

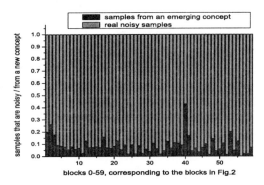

Figure 4. In the outliers detected, the normalized ratio of (1) true noisy samples (the upper bar), vs. (2) samples from an emerging concept (the lower bar). The bars correspond to blocks 0-59 in the experiments shown in Fig.2

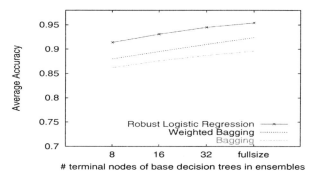

Figure 5. Comparison of the ensemble methods with classifiers of different size.

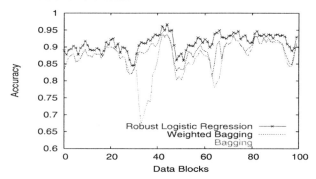

Figure 6. Performance of the ensembles on credit card data. Base trees have no more than 16 terminal nodes.

ensembles of smaller trees are comparable or even better than the two bagging ensembles of larger trees, even full-sized trees.

In terms of computation time, we verify that robust regression is compatible to the other two methods. Running over 40 blocks with full-grown trees, learning and evaluation time totals a 138 seconds for unweighted bagging, 163 seconds for weighted bagging, and 199 seconds for robust regression. If small decision trees are used instead, logistic regression learning can further be sped up, and yet perform better than the other two methods with full grown trees.

Experiments on Real Life Data We study the ensemble performance using different block size (1k–4k), and base classifiers of different size. Fig.6 shows the results obtained for block size 1k and base models having at most 16 terminal nodes. Results of other experiments are similar. The curve shows fewer and smaller drops in accuracy for the robust regression. These drops occur when the transaction amount jumps.

6. Summary and Future Work

We propose an adaptive and robust model learning method that is highly adaptive to concept changes and is robust to noise. The model produces a weighted ensem-

ble. Classifier weighting is computed by logistic regression, which ensures good adaptability. This weighting scheme is also capable to boost weak classifiers, thus achieving the goal of fast and light learning. Outlier detection is further integrated into the model learning, which leads to the robustness of the resulting ensemble.

Acknowledgement This work was supported in part by NCR TeraData, and by the National Science Foundation grant NSF-IIS 0339259.

References

[1] J. Bilmes. A gentle tutorial on the em algorithm and its application to parameter estimation for gaussian mixture and hidden markov models. In *Technical Report ICSI-TR-97-021*, 1998.

[2] F. Chu, Y. Wang, and C. Zaniolo. An adaptive learning approach for noisy data streams. In *Technical report 040029, UCLA Computer Science*, 2004.

[3] T. Hastie, R. Tibshirani, and J. Friedman. *The Elements of Statistical Learning, Data Mining,Inference and Prediction*. Springer, 2000.

[4] W. Street and Y. Kim. A streaming ensemble algorithm (sea) for large-scale classification. In *Int'l Conf. on Knowledge Discovery and Data Mining (SIGKDD)*, 2001.

[5] H. Wang, W. Fan, P. Yu, and J. Han. Mining concept-drifting data streams using ensemble classifiers. In *Int'l Conf. on Knowledge Discovery and Data Mining (SIGKDD)*, 2003.

Scalable Multi-Relational Association Mining

Amanda Clare*
Department of Computer Science,
University of Wales Aberystwyth,
Aberystwyth, SY23 3DB, UK
afc@aber.ac.uk

Hugh E. Williams   Nicholas Lester
School of Computer Science and Information Technology,
RMIT University, GPO Box 2476V,
Melbourne, Australia 3001.
{hugh,nml}@cs.rmit.edu.au

Abstract

We propose the new RADAR *technique for multi-relational data mining. This permits the mining of very large collections and provides a new technique for discovering multi-relational associations. Results show that* RADAR *is reliable and scalable for mining a large yeast homology collection, and that it does not have the main-memory scalability constraints of the Farmer and Warmr tools.*

1. Introduction

Large collections of multi-relational data present significant new challenges to data mining. These challenges are reflected in the annual KDD Cup competition, which involved relational datasets in 2001 and 2002, and network mining in 2003. The July 2003 edition of the ACM SIGKDD Explorations is devoted to position papers outlining the current frontiers in multi-relational data mining. Similar problems exist in bioinformatics databases — such as those at MIPS[1] — that provide integrated data on a genome-wide scale for whole organisms, with multiple cross references to other databases.

The vast majority of association mining algorithms are designed for single table, propositional datasets. We propose a novel technique for multi-relational association mining that permits efficient and scalable discovery of relationships. To our knowledge, the only existing multi-relational association mining algorithms are upgrades of Apriori [1] and, with the field in its infancy, there is much scope for improving the scalability of these solutions. Our technique uses an *inverted index*, a largely disk-based search structure that is used to support querying in all practical Information Retrieval systems and web search engines.

*This work carried out at and supported by the School of Computer Science and Information Technology at RMIT University.

[1]See: http://mips.gsf.de/

2. Inverted Indexes

An inverted index is a well-known structure used in all practical text retrieval systems [8]. It consists of an in-memory (or partially in-memory) search structure that stores the *vocabulary* of searchable terms, and on-disk *postings* that store, for each term, the location of that term in the collection. In practice, the vocabulary is typically the words that occur in the collection [8].

Using the notation of Zobel and Moffat [10], each term t has postings $< f_{d,t}, d >$, where $f_{d,t}$ is the frequency f of term t in document d. Consider an example for the term "mining" that occurs in four documents:

$$< 2, 11 > \quad < 1, 19 > \quad < 1, 72 > \quad < 2, 107 >$$

This *postings list* shows that the word "mining" occurs twice in document 11, once in document 19, once in document 72, and twice in document 107. The documents themselves are ordinally numbered, and a *mapping table* associates each document number to its location on disk. Despite its simplicity, this inverted index structure is sufficient to support the popular ranked query mode that is used by most search engine users.

The organisation, compression, and processing of postings lists is crucial to retrieval system performance. Compression is important for three reasons: first, a compressed representation requires less storage space than an uncompressed one; second, a retrieval system is faster when compression is used, since the cost of transferring compressed lists and decompressing them is typically much less than the cost of transferring uncompressed data; and, last, caching is improved because more lists fit into main-memory than when uncompressed lists are used. Scholer et al. [7] recently showed that compression of postings lists more than halves query evaluation times than when no compression is used.

3. Multi-Relational Association Mining

The first mining technique to find associations in multi-table relational data was Warmr [4]. Warmr is a first-order upgrade of Apriori, with the additional introduction of a user-defined language bias to restrict the search space. Blockeel et al. [2] have been investigating enhancements — such as query packs — to the underlying Prolog compiler to address efficiency issues. They have also implemented techniques to allow the user to limit the amount of data required to be loaded into main-memory. With Warmr, the user has the full power of the Prolog programming language for specifying the data and background knowledge.

PolyFARM [3] was based on the ideas of Warmr and written for distribution on a Beowulf cluster by partitioning the data to be counted. Unfortunately, although the size of the database is reduced by partitioning, the size of the candidate associations held in main-memory can grow impractically large.

Nijssen and Kok's Farmer [6] is a new multi-relational mining technique, with a running time that is an order of magnitude improvement over Warmr; indeed, on small data sets, Farmer can be astonishingly fast. However, they still require that all data is available in main-memory — a still significant problem for large datasets — and the main-memory use increases steadily throughout each search.

4. RADAR

We propose RADAR, the Relational Association Datamining AlgoRithm[2]. RADAR is the first multi-relational association mining algorithm that uses compressed inverted indexing techniques to provide a scalable solution for mining large databases.

Our aim is to count all *frequent associations* in a database. We use the language of first order logic to represent the associations. A frequent association is a conjunction or set of atoms that occurs with at least the minimum support frequency in the database [4]. For example, "a chardonnay wine that is made by an Australian grower" is represented by the association:

$$\text{wine}(W) \wedge \text{chardonnay}(W) \wedge \text{grower}(W, G) \wedge \text{australian}(G)$$

Inspired by the Eclat algorithm [9], we propose to mine these frequent associations by flattening the database, building an inverted index of the flattened database, and repeatedly joining postings lists.

In a multi-table relational database, we must decide which field in which table is our main key or notion of *transaction*, that is, what we are counting. For example, in a database representing wines, retailers, and growers, we

[2]The RADAR software and sample databases are available from http://www.aber.ac.uk/compsci/Research/bio/dss/radar/

Figure 1 Five tables representing molecules by atoms and bonds.

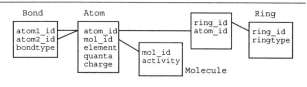

Figure 2 Example of the two-column flattened database with keys. For example, line 2 describes a double bond in mol 12 between atoms 10 and 11.

Keys (Arguments)	Attributes (Predicate Symbols)
m12	inactive
m12, a10, a11	bond_double
m12, a10	elem_carbon, quanta_27, charge_medium
m12, a11, a12	bond_double
m12, a11, a13	bond_single
m12, a11	elem_carbon, quanta_22, charge_medium
m12, r47, a10	ring_benzene
m12, r47, a11	ring_benzene
m12, r47, a12	ring_benzene

must decide if we are interested in counting the number of Australian growers that make chardonnay wines, or the number of chardonnay wines that are made by Australian growers. We refer to this field as the COUNTKEY, so as to distinguish it from the common notion of a database key field.

To prepare for indexing, the database is flattened into a single table with a two-column format. The first column stores the database keys (which represent the arguments to the predicates), and the second column stores the database items, that is, descriptive attributes (which represent the predicate names). We refer to these as *keys* and *predicate symbols* respectively. Each row of the flattened database can hold multiple keys and multiple predicate symbols.

The attributes in a simple multi-table relational database describing molecules represented by bonds and atoms are shown in Figure 1. Selected flattened rows from this database are shown in Figure 2. Flattening can be made more or less explicit depending on the application requirements.

Keys are used to form the arguments to the predicates. For example, if grower($Wine, Grower$) is to be a possible atom in associations, then any row in the flattened database that contains an instance of the grower term in the second column must always have both Wine and Grower keys listed in the first column of that row.

To create an inverted index for the flattened database, we number each row sequentially and use these numbers as the document numbers. All terms within a row are indexed, that

356

Figure 3 A section of the inverted index of the flattened database from Figure 2. For compactness, the postings list show only document numbers; we have omitted $f_{d,t}$.

Term (t)	Postings list ($d_1 \ldots d_{f,t}$)
inactive	1
bond_double	2,4
bond_single	5
elem_carbon	3,6
ring_benzene	7,8,9
quanta_22	6
m12	1,2,3,4,5,6,7,8,9
a10	2,3,7
a11	2,4,5,6,8

is, both keys and attributes. A section of the inverted index for Figure 2 is shown in Figure 3.

To mine the data, the user provides the flattened database and a *language bias* (the set of factors that influence and direct the search). In our case, this is a list of the COUNTKEYS, a list of all the predicates for use in associations, the types and modes of their arguments, and other constraints. Associations are then generated depth-first.

All arguments to the predicates in an association are variables that can be satisfied by particular database keys. To count how frequently an association appears in the database — with respect to the COUNTKEY — we need to test whether, for each possible COUNTKEY, there is a set of keys that satisfy this relationship. This means that when we have multi-relational data we cannot simply intersect postings lists for predicates that appear within the same association because we are seeking to identify predicates that share the correct set of keys that hold the relationships between the predicates. The algorithm for counting associations using our compressed inverted index is shown in Figure 4.

5. Results

We present results of using RADAR, Warmr, and Farmer. All measurements were carried on a 1.66 GHz AMD Athlon-based workstation running Linux with 2 GB of main-memory. We used two small collections — for which RADAR is not optimised, but that are well-known and well-suited to the other schemes — and a large collection that illustrates the scalability of RADAR. MUTA is a well-known mutagenesis dataset [5], consisting of descriptions of molecules, including their atoms, bonds, and ring structures. KDD2002 is the collection used in Task 2 of the KDD 2002 Cup competition[3], that describes yeast proteins and their interactions. YEASTHOM is a large collection[4] that de-

---

[3]See: http://www.biostat.wisc.edu/~craven/kddcup/
[4]http://www.aber.ac.uk/compsci/Research/bio/dss/yeastdata/

Figure 4: Algorithm for counting an association

```
function countassoc (association)
    v₁..vₙ ← fetch postings lists for each predicate p₁..pₙ in
            association
    foreach countkey in countkeys do
        ck_postings ← fetch postings list for countkey
        join ck_postings with each appropriate vᵢ
        if all vᵢ are non-empty then
            if other args exist then
                if doargs(1, v₁..vₙ, association) then
                    total++
            else
                total++
    return total

function doargs (argnum, v₁..vₙ, association)
    docs ← find shortest docs list amongst appropriate predicates
    foreach doc in docs do
        key ← key of appropriate type for argnum from doc
        k_postings ← fetch postings list for key
        join k_postings with each appropriate vᵢ
        if all vᵢ are non-empty then
            if other args exist then
                if doargs(argnum + 1, v₁..vₙ, association) then
                    return true
            else
                return true
    return false
```

scribes homologous relationships between yeast genes and proteins in the SwissProt database.

We compared RADAR to Warmr (version ACE 1.2.6) and Farmer (2003). A fair, direct comparison is not straightforward as each algorithm has its own distinct properties. In particular, Farmer does not allow a limit on the length of the association, but only on the maximum use of each individual predicate. This means that we cannot stop Farmer from finding more, longer associations than the other algorithms.

Table 1 shows the results of our experiments. The results for MUTA and KDD2002 illustrate the general properties of the schemes: RADAR uses 34 Mb of main-memory for both collections, while the memory use of the other schemes varies significantly with the number of discovered associations (from 25 to 119 Mb for Warmr, and from 387 to 11 Mb for Farmer). Constant memory use comes at a price for small collections: RADAR is two to three times slower than the other schemes on the MUTA task, and unacceptably slow on the KDD2002 task compared to the fast Farmer.

The results for YEASTHOM illustrate the advantages of RADAR, and the disadvantages of the other approaches. RADAR is highly scalable: despite the almost thousand-fold increase in data size from KDD2002 to YEASTHOM, main-memory use only increases from 34 Mb to 56 Mb. Farmer — which is impressive on small datasets — is unsuitable for this task: main-memory use increases steadily throughout the lifetime of the task, since it holds the database and as-

Data	Algorithm	Data size		Maximum Memory	Time	Associations
		Original	Compiled	Use (Mb)		Found
MUTA	Warmr	823 kb	1,292 kb	25	7.8 mins	2,756
	Farmer	823 kb	—	387	10.9 mins	95,715
	RADAR	596 kb	526 kb	34	25.0 mins	12,530
KDD2002	Warmr	1,407 kb	1,556 kb	119	31.1 mins	7,523
	Farmer	1,407 kb	—	11	0.1 mins	20,359
	RADAR	1,023 kb	418 kb	34	361.0 mins	9,130
YEASTHOM	Warmr	841 Mb	880 Mb	800	*25 days*	7,712*
	Farmer	1,465 Mb	—	1,254	18 days	698,974
	RADAR	1,565 Mb	163 Mb	56	*25 days*	34,782*

Table 1. Experiments on the MUTA, KDD2002 **and** YEASTHOM **collections. For** MUTA, **support = 20 molecules (10.6%), max. assoc. length = 3 predicates (excluding** $\mathrm{mol}(X)$**). Farmer continued to find associations to length 11. For** KDD2002, **support = 20 ORFs (0.84%), max. assoc. length = 3 predicates (excluding** $\mathrm{orf}(X)$**). Farmer continued to find associations to length 8. For** YEASTHOM, **support = 20 ORFs (0.31%), max. assoc. length = 3 predicates (excluding** $\mathrm{orf}(X)$**). Italicised figures indicate that the algorithm was still running. Farmer continued to find associations to length 7 but stopped before completion due to main memory exhaustion. Warmr's maximum memory use was set to 800 Mb.**

sociations in memory. Indeed, after 18 days, main-memory was exhausted. Warmr processes associations in *packs* that group together common subparts for faster counting. This means that no results are given until a whole level is complete. For the YEASTHOM collection, associations of length two were produced after about six hours, and then the system gave no further output for several weeks.

RADAR is structured — similarly to Farmer — as an *anytime* algorithm that produces continuous output. Further, RADAR can be seeded with an association, so that the application can be restarted at any time. This aspect is useful for large-scale mining problems that run for weeks.

6. Conclusion

Large multi-relational collections are the next frontier for data mining. In this paper we have shown how compressed inverted indexes used in text retrieval systems can be adapted for multi-relational data mining. Our technique, RADAR, is both scalable and reliable on large amounts of data. It produces output continuously, with the option of stopping and resuming the mining process later. For small datasets — for which RADAR is not designed — the Warmr and Farmer techniques should be used in preference.

Acknowledgements

This work was supported by the Australian Research Council.

References

[1] R. Agrawal and R. Srikant. Fast algorithms for mining association rules in large databases. In *20th International Conference on Very Large Databases (VLDB 94)*, 1994.

[2] H. Blockeel et al. Improving the efficiency of Inductive Logic Programming through the use of query packs. *Journal of Artificial Intelligence Research*, 16:135–166, 2002.

[3] A. Clare and R. D. King. Data mining the yeast genome in a lazy functional language. In *Practical Aspects of Declarative Languages (PADL'03)*, 2003.

[4] L. Dehaspe. *Frequent Pattern Discovery in First Order Logic*. PhD thesis, Department of Computer Science, Katholieke Universiteit Leuven, 1998.

[5] R. King, S. Muggleton, A. Srinivasan, and M. Sternberg. Structure-activity relationships derived by machine learning. *Proc. Nat. Acad. Sci. USA*, 93:438–442, 1996.

[6] S. Nijssen and J. N. Kok. Efficient frequent query discovery in FARMER. In *13th International Conference on Inductive Logic Programming (ILP 2003)*, 2003.

[7] F. Scholer, H. E. Williams, J. Yiannis, and J. Zobel. Compression of inverted indexes for fast query evaluation. In K. Järvelin, M. Beaulieu, R. Baeza-Yates, and S. H. Myaeng, editors, *Proc. ACM-SIGIR International Conference on Research and Development in Information Retrieval*, pages 222–229, Tampere, Finland, 2002.

[8] I. Witten, A. Moffat, and T. Bell. *Managing Gigabytes: Compressing and Indexing Documents and Images*. Morgan Kaufmann Publishers, Los Altos, CA 94022, USA, second edition, 1999.

[9] M. J. Zaki. Scalable algorithms for association mining. *IEEE Transactions on Knowledge and Data Engineering*, 12(3):372–390, 2000.

[10] J. Zobel and A. Moffat. Exploring the similarity space. *ACM SIGIR Forum*, 32(1):18–34, 1998.

An Evaluation of Approaches to Classification Rule Selection

Frans Coenen and Paul Leng

Department of Computer Science, The University of Liverpool, Liverpool, L69 3BX

{frans,phl}@csc.liv.ac.uk

Abstract

In this paper a number of Classification Rule evaluation measures are considered. In particular the authors review the use of a variety of selection techniques used to order classification rules contained in a classifier, and a number of mechanisms used to classify unseen data. The authors demonstrate that rule ordering founded on the size of antecedent works well given certain conditions. **Keywords:** *Classification rule evaluation measures.*

1. Introduction

Classification Association Rule Mining (CARM) is based on the observation that a subset of the Association Rules (ARs) generated by Association Rule Mining (ARM) algorithms can effectively be used for the purpose of classification [2]. ARs [1] are rules of the form $A \Rightarrow C$ where A and C (Antecedent and Consequent) are disjoint subsets of a set of binary valued attributes defined by the input data set. In the case of Classification Rules (CRs) the variable C is a unary subset of a set of classes defined with respect to the input data. The notation $r.A$ and $r.C$ will be used to indicate respectively the antecedent and consequent (class) of a rule r.

Once a classifier has been established (usually presented in the form of a list of rules), regardless of the methodology used to generate it, there are a number of proposed mechanisms for using the resulting classifier to classify unseen data. These can be itemised as follows (given a particular case):

1. **Best Rule:** Select the first "best" rule that satisfies the given case according to some ordering imposed on the rule listing. The ordering can be defined according to many different ordering schemes, including:

   (a) **CSA:** Combinations of confidence, support and size of antecedent, with confidence being the most significant factor. Example CARM systems that use CSA ordering include CBA [7],

   and (only during the early stages of processing) CMAR [6]).

   (b) **WRA:** The weighted relative accuracy which reflects a number of rule "interestingness" measures as proposed in [5].

   (c) **Laplace Accuracy** Laplace accuracy measures as used in PRM and CPAR [8].

   (d) χ^2 **Testing:** χ^2 values as used, in part, in CMAR [6].

   An alternative to CSA, that has not been considered in the literature to date is to make use of the size of the antecedent as the most significant factor followed by confidence and support, i.e. **ACS** ordering.

2. **Best K rules:** Select the first best K rules that satisfy the given case and then select a rule according to some averaging process as used for example, in CPAR [8]. "Best" in this case is defined according to an imposed ordering of the form described in 1.

3. **All rules:** Collect all rules in the classifier that satisfy the given case and then evaluate this collection to identify a class. One well known evaluation method in this category is *Weighted χ^2* (WCS) testing as used in CMAR [6].

In this paper we compare the above satisfaction/ordering techniques which are described in some further detail in the following two Sections. The evaluation of the techniques is carried out using a number of sets of CRs, generated using the Apriori-TFPC CARM algorithm which is briefly reviewed in Section 4. The evaluation is discussed in detail in Section 5 and some conclusions offered in Section 6.

2. Rule Ordering

As noted in the introduction to this paper five different rule ordering strategies are considered here, four established strategies and one new strategy. Each is described in more detail in the following five sub-sections.

2.1. CSA ordering

The confidence-Support framework remains very common amongst current ARM algorithms. Given a CR, r, the support for r ($sup(r)$) is the proportion of occurrences of the set $r.A \cup r.C$ in the input data compared to the number of records in the input. The confidence of r ($conf(r)$) is then given as $sup(r)/sup(r.A)$. CSA (Confidence, Support, size of Antecedent) ordering is defined as follows:

1. **Confidence**: A rule r_1 has priority over a rule r_2 if $conf(r_1) > conf(r_2)$.

2. **Support**: A rule r_1 has priority over a rule r_2 if $conf(r_1) = conf(r_2)$ and $sup(r_1) > sup(r_2)$.

3. **Size of antecedent**: A rule r_1 has priority over a rule r_2 if $conf(r_1) = conf(r_2)$, $sup(r_1) = sup(r_2)$ and $|r_1.A| < |r_2.A|$.

Given that confidence values are normally calculated as real numbers it is unusual to have CRs with identical confidence values other than in the case of "100% confidence rules". Where 100% rules are found the associated supported value "comes into play". The size of the antecedent is seldom used in CSA ordering.

It should be noted that CARM algorithms that use the support/confidence framework, usually also make use of user defined minimum support/confidence threshold values during the CR generation process. Consequently rules contained in the final classifier will be such that $sup(r) > min\ support\ threshold$ and $conf(r) > min\ conf\ threshold$.

2.2. Weighted Relative Accuracy (WRA)

The use of WRA (Weighted Relative Accuracy) was proposed in [5] as a unifying mechanism for determining CR expected accuracy. The idea is that the WRA measure is a synthesis of a number of rule "interestingness" measures. The WRA for a rule r is calculated using the identity $wra(r) = weighting \times relative\ accuracy$ Where relative accuracy is equal to $confidence(r) - sup(r.C)$.

The term "relative" is used in the sense that the support for a rule is compared with its expected support — a concept not dissimilar to the idea under-pinning χ^2 testing. A negative relative accuracy indicates that the accuracy associated with r is less than the fixed rule $true \Rightarrow C$. So that rules with a low "generality" (i.e. a low $sup(r.A)$ value) are not given a high accuracy measure the support value for the rule antecedent is used to weight the relative accuracy: $wra(r) = sup(r.A) \times (confidence(r) - sup(r.C))$.

2.3. Laplace Accuracy

The *Laplace expected accuracy estimate*, given a rule r, is defined in [8] as follows:

$$Laplace\ accuracy(r) = \frac{sup(r.A \cup r.C) + 1}{sup(r.A) + k}$$

where k is the number of classes. Note that in this case support is defined as the actual number of records (in the training or test set) that contain $r.A \cup r.C$ or $r.A$.

2.4. χ^2 Testing

χ^2 testing is a well known statistical technique used to determine whether two variables are independent of one another by comparing a set of *observed values* (O) against a set of *expected values* (E) — values that would be expected if there were no association between the variables. A χ^2 value is calculate using the identity:

$$\chi^2 = \sum_{1 \leq i \leq n} (0_i - E_i)^2 / E_i$$

where n is the number of observed/expected values (this is always 4 in the case of CARM). If the result is above a given *critical threshold value* then it can be said that a relationship between the variables exists, otherwise there is no relationship. For CMAR a critical threshold value of 3.8415 was used (this value has also been used in this paper).

2.5. ACS or Specificity ordering

In this paper it is proposed that a good alternative ordering to CSA (as described above) is ACS ordering (size of Antecedent, Confidence and Support) which is defined in a similar manner to CSA (see above) but with size of antecedent placed first. The intuition behind this ordering is that more specific rules should be "triggered" before more general rules are attempted. For example we may have a classifier, ordered using CSA, comprising two rules as follows:

#	Rule	Conf.
1	$\{ab\} \Rightarrow \{y\}$	80%
2	$\{abcd\} \Rightarrow \{x\}$	75%

Given a case $\{abc\}$ this would be classified, using "best first" case satisfaction, as belonging to class y when intuitively class x would be more likely to be the correct class. ACS ordering thus ensures that specific rules have a higher precedence than more general rules so that in the above example the class x would be returned. It should be noted, however, that for ACS to work well a high confidence threshold value should be used. An appropriate mechanism to prevent *overfitting* must also be incorporated.

3 Classification

In the introduction to this paper three alternative case/record classification mechanisms were identified. Two of these, "best k" and "χ^2 testing" are briefly discussed below so as to provide some necessary further detail ("best first" has the obvious interpretation).

3.1. Best K Testing

The intuition behind "best k testing" is that 'one cannot expect that any single rule can perfectly predict the class label for every example satisfying its body' [8]. Given a case n to be classified the best K approach is as follows: (1) obtain all rules that satisfy n; (2) keep only best K rules for each class, or all rules if there are less than K rules for a particular class; (3) for each group determine some average expected value to be maximised (e.g. confidence, size of antecedent, Laplace accuracy, χ^2 value); (4) Select the class associated with the best average. In [8] a value of 5 was suggested as an appropriate value for K.

3.2. Weighted χ^2 Testing

Weighted χ^2 Testing is used in a number of CARM algorithms, such as CMAR [6], to classify data by considering entire groups of rules that satisfy a given case. With respect to CMAR, given a case n to be classified, the procedure commences by first collecting all rules that satisfy n. Then if the consequents of all rules are identical, or only one rule is found, classify case according to the consequents; otherwise group rules according to class and determine the combined effect of the rules in each group (the class associated with the "strongest group" is then selected). The strength of a group is calculate using the WCS (Weighted χ Squared) value. The class associated with the group of rules with the highest WCS value is then selected as the class to be allocated to the case.

4. Apriori-TFPC

The Apriori-TFPC classification rule generation algorithm is founded on the Apriori-TFP (Total From Partial) ARM algorithm [4][1]. This algorithm generates frequent sets that are placed as nodes in a set enumeration tree. To evaluate the above approaches a number of variations of the algorithm were created, each reflecting one of the identified approaches.

Uniquely, in Apriori-TFPC CRs are generated as part of the "frequent set identification process". As the tree is

developed nodes in branches whose root represents a classifier are tested for their appropriateness as classification rules using a confidence threshold (to evaluate the different techniques considered in this paper this can equally well be achieved using a χ^2 threshold, Laplace accuracy or a WRA measure). If a node represents a suitable CR, the rule is placed in a list and the node not processed any further. Nodes are also pruned during the generation process according to a user supplied support threshold. This tree pruning is intended to prevent *overfitting*.

The different ordering and case satisfaction techniques considered in this paper can be combined into eleven different variations of Apriori-TFPC (see Table 1). With respect to ACS ordering, note that tree pruning is still carried out according to confidence. In the case of experiments using "best K" techniques K was set to 5.

5. Evaluation

Experiments were conducted using a range of data sets taken from the UCI Machine Learning Repository [3]. The chosen datasets were discretized using the LUCS-KDD DN software[2], where appropriate continuous attributes were ranged using five sub-ranges. The experiments were run on a 1.2 GHz Intel Celeron CPU with 512 Mbyte of RAM running under Red Hat Linux 7.3.

The first set of evaluations undertaken used a confidence threshold value of 50% and a support threshold value of 1% (as used in the published evaluations of CMAR [6] and CBA [7]). The results are presented in Table 1 where the best accuracy obtained for each of the data sets is highlighted in bold print. The row labels describe the key characteristics of each data set: for example, the label *adult.D*131.*N*48842.*C*2 denotes the "adult" data set, which includes 48842 records in 2 classes, with attributes that for the experiments described here have been discretised into 131 binary categories.

It should be noted that the datasets were rearranged so that occurences of classes were distributed evenly throughout the datasets. This then allowed the datasets to be divided in half with the first half used as the training set and the second half as the test set. Although a "better" accuracy figure might have been obtained using Ten-Cross Validation, it is the relative accuracy that is of interest here and not the absolute accuracy.

From Table 1 it can be seen that with a 50% confidence threshold the proposed ACS ordering worked reasonably well but not as well as was hoped. It is surmised that this is probably because many specific rules with relatively low confidence were given a high precedence over higher confidence but more general rules. The last four columns of

---

[1] Apriori-TFP and Apriori-TFPC my be obtained from http://www.csc.liv.ac.uk/ frans/KDD/Software.

[2] The LUCS-KDD DN is available at http://www.csc.liv.ac.uk/ frans/KDD/Software/LUCS-KDD-DN/.

Table 1 show the results of a further set of experiments conducted using a confidence threshold of 75%. In this case best results were obtained using "best first" and ACS. ACS with "best first" also produces the greatest number of best accuracies (10 out of 22). The experiment also illustrated that by reducing the overall number of rules (by increasing the confidence requirement) the "best K" approach deteriorated.

Kaufman, pp487-499.

[2] Bayardo, R.J. (1997). *Brute-Force Mining of High-Confidence Classification Rules*. Proc. of 3rd Int. Conf. on Knowledge Discovery and Data Mining, AAAI, pp123-126.

| Data Set | confidence = 50% | | | | | | | | | | | confidence = 75% | | | |
| | Best first | | | | | Best K first | | | | | All | Best first | | Best K first | |
	CSA	ACS	WRA	Lap.	χ^2	CSA	ACS	WRA	Lap.	χ^2	WCS	CSA	ACS	CSA	ACS
adult.D131.N48842.C2	76.1	76.1	65.2	76.1	32.8	76.0	**76.3**	57.8	76.1	33.7	76.1	80.7	76.1	**80.9**	76.4
anneal.D106.N798.C6	**85.5**	**85.5**	68.4	83.7	59.1	79.4	79.5	69.2	82.2	42.3	80.7	88.0	85.5	**89.5**	**89.5**
auto.D142.N205.C7	12.7	19.6	**54.9**	48.0	19.6	13.7	13.7	32.4	43.1	12.7	20.6	13.7	12.7	12.7	**19.6**
breast.D47.N699.C2	**98.0**	**98.0**	81.1	96.6	83.1	93.4	93.4	72.2	91.7	88.5	**98.0**	98.0	98.0	98.0	97.1
con4.D129.N67557.C3	65.8	65.8	37.3	65.8	61.1	65.8	65.8	62.4	65.8	**65.9**	65.8	65.8	65.8	**65.9**	**65.9**
glass.D52.N214.C7	**49.5**	38.3	34.6	46.7	13.1	42.1	42.1	26.2	43.0	13.1	13.1	32.7	36.4	**46.7**	45.8
heart.D53.N303.C5	49.7	54.3	**57.6**	55.0	55.0	53.0	53.0	56.3	55.0	55.0	55.0	43.0	**54.3**	29.8	29.8
hepatitis.D58.N155.C2	71.4	79.2	67.5	79.2	20.8	**80.5**	**80.5**	70.1	79.2	28.6	61.0	64.9	**79.2**	53.2	53.2
horseCol.D94.D368.C2	67.9	78.2	**83.7**	77.8	62.5	70.7	70.1	78.3	66.8	51.1	62.5	60.9	**77.1**	47.8	58.7
iono.D172.N351.C2	81.7	**91.4**	76.0	87.4	84.6	77.1	88.0	62.9	82.9	69.7	62.9	91.4	91.4	66.3	**94.3**
iris.D23.N150.C3	**94.7**	**94.7**	93.3	93.3	93.3	92.0	92.0	93.3	92.0	89.3	**94.7**	89.3	**94.7**	88.0	88.0
led7.D24.N3200.C10	67.1	57.2	32.9	66.6	26.0	66.2	66.3	31.9	66.8	19.1	**73.8**	63.4	**64.6**	64.1	64.1
letRec.D106.N20000.C26	**44.2**	34.9	16.9	42.4	28.1	41.0	41.2	8.1	41.3	25.6	38.1	28.6	**29.1**	28.5	28.4
mushr'm.D127.N8124.C2	96.0	89.1	47.5	46.7	88.4	71.1	69.7	66.9	69.8	85.6	53.1	**96.2**	89.1	82.0	81.9
nursery.D32.N12960.C5	80.0	74.4	70.6	80.0	70.6	69.8	69.9	70.3	70.6	68.6	85.3	**89.6**	87.2	87.6	88.3
pageBl'ks.D55.N5473.C5	**89.8**	**89.8**	79.6	**89.8**	3.4	**89.8**	**89.8**	68.5	**89.8**	5.4	2.0	89.8	89.8	89.8	89.8
penDig.D90.N10992.C10	79.5	40.6	33.1	78.1	49.9	54.4	54.8	35.2	55.0	46.8	70.8	**83.0**	79.3	71.0	71.2
pimaInd.D42.N768.C2	74.2	74.2	**76.0**	74.5	65.1	71.3	73.7	66.9	70.6	62.0	70.6	76.0	**76.8**	73.7	73.7
ticTacToe.D29.N958.C2	66.6	66.0	65.8	66.0	65.8	64.3	51.4	54.9	64.9	65.8	**78.9**	**69.1**	66.2	55.9	55.7
wave.D108.N5000.C3	66.2	61.1	62.5	66.4	62.5	57.8	58.3	60.0	58.7	60.0	**77.6**	**76.4**	67.8	66.0	66.8
wine.D68.N178.C3	70.8	82.0	86.5	**92.1**	**92.1**	67.4	67.4	71.9	80.9	84.3	91.0	70.8	**83.1**	27.0	28.1
zoo.D43.N101.C7	88.0	80.0	54.0	62.0	74.0	70.0	74.0	58.0	62.0	62.0	**92.0**	**86.0**	78.0	66.0	66.0
Average	71.6	69.6	61.1	71.6	55.0	66.7	66.9	57.9	68.6	51.6	64.7	70.8	71.9	63.2	65.1

Table 1 *Classification accuracy (minsup = 1%)*

6. Conclusion

In this paper a number of alternative rule ordering and case satisfaction strategies have been considered. Four established ordering strategies were examined. In addition the authors proposed a fifth strategy, ACS, where more specific rules are given a higher precedence than less specific rules (but using confidence as the most significant factor for tree pruning during the generation process).

The principal findings of the evaluation are as follows: (1) there is no overall best ordering suited to all the data sets used in the experiments, (2) the "best first" case satisfaction mechanism works better than "best k" in all the data sets tested, (3) ACS ordering produces the best result provided that a relatively high confidence threshold is used (a threshold of 75% is suggested), (4) for lower confidence thresholds (50% to 75%) CSA and Laplace ordering coupled with a "best first" case satisfaction produced good results.

References

[1] Agrawal, R. and Srikant, R. (1994). *Fast algorithms for mining association rules*. Proc. VLDB'94, Morgan

[3] Blake, C.L. and Merz, C.J. (1998). *UCI Repository of machine learning databases.* http://www.ics.uci.edu/ mlearn/MLRepository.html, Irvine, CA: University of California.

[4] Coenen, F., Leng, P., Goulbourne, G. (2004). *Tree Structures for Mining Association Rules.* Jo. of Data Mining and Knowledge Discovery, 8(1), pp25-51.

[5] Lavrač, N., Flach, P. and Zupan, B. (1999) *Rule Evaluation Measures: A Unifying View* Proc. 9th Int. Workshop on Inductive Logic Programming (ILP'99), Springer-Verlag, pp174–185.

[6] Li W., Han, J. and Pei, J. (2001). *CMAR: Accurate and Efficient Classification Based on Multiple Class-Association Rules.* Proc ICDM 2001, pp369-376.

[7] Liu, B. Hsu, W. and Ma, Y (1998). *Integrating Classification and Association Rule Mining.* Proceedings KDD-98, AAAI, pp80-86.

[8] Yin, X. and Han, J. (2003). *CPAR: Classification based on Predictive Association Rules.* Proc. SIAM Int. Conf. on Data Mining (SDM'03), pp331-335.

Mining Frequent Closed Patterns in Microarray Data

Gao Cong, Kian-Lee Tan, Anthony K.H. Tung, Feng Pan
School of Computing
National University of Singapore
3 Science Drive 2, Singapore
{conggao, atung, tankl, panfeng}@comp.nus.edu.sg

Abstract

Microarray data typically contains a large number of columns and a small number of rows, which poses a great challenge for existing frequent (closed) pattern mining algorithms that discover patterns in item enumeration space. In this paper, we propose two new algorithms that explore the row enumeration space to mine frequent closed patterns. Several experiments on real-life gene expression data show that the new algorithms are faster than existing algorithms, including CLOSET, CHARM, CLOSET+ and CARPENTER.

1. Introduction

Microarray datasets may contain up to thousands or tens of thousands of columns (genes) but only tens or hundreds of rows (samples). Discovering frequent patterns from microarray datasets is very important and useful, especially in the following: 1) To discover association rules, which can not only reveal biological relevant associations between genes and environments/categories to identify gene regulation pathways but also help to uncover gene networks [1]. 2) To discover bi-clustering of gene expression as shown in [8].

However, these high-dimensional microarray datasets pose a great challenge for existing frequent pattern discovery algorithms. While there are a large number of algorithms that have been developed for frequent pattern discovery and closed pattern mining [3, 4, 7], their basic approaches are based on *item enumeration* in which combinations of items are tested systematically to search for frequent (closed) patterns. As a result, their running time increases exponentially with increasing average length of the records. The high dimensional microarray datasets render most of these algorithms impractical.

It was first shown in [2] that the complete frequent closed patterns can also be obtained by searching in the *row enu-*

meration space, which was also observed in [5] [1]. Moreover, [2] proposed an algorithm, CARPENTER, to explore the row enumeration search space by constructing projected transposed database recursively.

Considering that many algorithms have been proposed to mine frequent (closed) patterns by item enumeration, it would be interesting to investigate whether some ideas can be borrowed from these algorithms to search row enumeration space more efficiently. In this paper, we developed two new efficient algorithms, RERII and REPT, to explore the row enumeration space to discover frequent closed patterns. Algorithm RERII is inspired by algorithms that mine patterns from vertical layout data [7], while algorithm REPT is inspired by algorithms that are based on FP-tree [4]. But RERII and REPT are very different from them in that both of them adopt row enumeration. Compared with CARPENTER, RERII and REPT use different implementation methods and employ more powerful pruning methods. Several experiments are performed on real-life microarray data to show that the new algorithms are much faster than the existing algorithms, including CLOSET [4], CHARM[7], CLOSET+[6] and CARPENTER[2].

2. Problem definition and preliminary

Let $I=\{i_1, i_2, .., i_m\}$ be a set of items. Let D be the dataset (or table) which consists of a set of rows $R=\{r_1, .., r_n\}$ with each row r_i consisting of a set of items in I, i.e $r_i \subseteq I$. Figure 1 shows an example dataset. To simplify notation, in the sequel, we will denote a set of row numbers like $\{r_2, r_3, r_4\}$ as "234". Likewise, a set of items like $\{a, c, f\}$ will also be represented as acf. Given a set of items I', the number of rows in the dataset that contain I' is called the **support** of I'. A set of items $I' \subseteq I$ is called a **closed pattern** if there exists no I'' such that $I' \subset I''$ and the set of rows containing I'' is not the same as the set of rows containing I'. A set of items $I' \subseteq I$ is called a **fre-**

---

[1]The submission date of the paper [5] is 1 month after that of [2].

i	r_i
1	b,d,e,f
2	a,c,e,f
3	a,c,d,e
4	a,b,c,d,e,g
5	a,b,c,d,e,f

Figure 1. Example Table

i_j	rows containing i_j
a	2,3,4,5
b	1,4,5
c	2,3,4,5
d	1,3,4,5
e	1,2,3,4,5
f	1,2,5
g	4

Figure 2. Transposed Table

quent closed pattern if (1) the support of I' is higher than a minimum support threshold, $minsup$; (2) I' is a closed pattern.

Problem Definition: Given a dataset D which contains records that are subset of a set of items I, the problem is to discover all frequent closed patterns with respect to a user given support threshold $minsup$. In addition, we assume that the database satisfies the condition $|R| << |I|$.

Preliminary: CARPENTER is designed based on two basic concepts. One is (projected) transposed table and the other is row enumeration. Table in Figure 2 is a transposed version of table in Figure 1. Let X be a subset of rows. Given the transposed table TT, a X-**projected transposed table**, denoted as $TT|_X$, is a subset of tuples from TT such that: 1) For each tuple x in TT, there exists a corresponding tuple x' in $TT|_X$. 2) x' contains all rows in x with row ids larger than any row in X. A complete row enumeration tree on table in Figure 2 is shown in Figure 3.

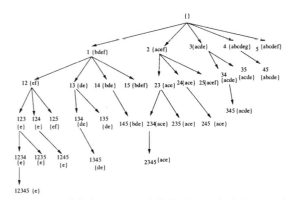

Figure 3. The row enumeration tree.

3. Algorithm RERII

In RERII, each node X in Figure 3 will be represented with a three-element group $X = \{itemlist, sup, childlist\}$, where $itemlist$ is the closed pattern corresponding to node X, sup is the number of rows at the node and $childlist$ is the list of child nodes of X. For example, the root of the tree can be represented with $\{\{\}, 0, \{1, 2, 3, 4, 5\}\}$ and the node "12" can be represented with $\{\{1, 2\}, 2, \{3, 4, 5\}\}$.

Given a node X in the row enumeration tree, we will perform an intersection of the $itemlist$ of node X with the $itemlists$ of all its sibling nodes after X. Each intersection will result in a new node (Note that the intersection may be pruned as discussed later) whose $itemlist$ is the intersection, whose sup is $X.sup + 1$ and whose $childlist$ will be available at next level intersection. And each new node will be intersected with its afterward siblings. In this way, the row enumeration tree will be recursively expanded in a depth-first way.

Lemma 3.1 *Let Xr_i and Xr_j be two sibling nodes, where $Xr_i < Xr_j$. The following five properties will hold:*

1) If $Xr_i.itemlist \cap Xr_j.itemlist = \emptyset$, nothing needs to be done.

2) If $Xr_i.itemlist = Xr_j.itemlist$, Xr_j will be integrated into Xr_i, i.e. $Xr_i.sup = Xr_i.sup + 1$ and any further expansion below Xr_j will be pruned.

3) If $Xr_i.itemlist \subset Xr_j.itemlist$, $Xr_i.sup = Xr_i.sup + 1$ and Xr_j will not expand Xr_i.

4) If $Xr_i.itemlist \supset Xr_j.itemlist$, any further expansion below Xr_j will be pruned and Xr_j will become a candidate extension of Xr_i. (Note that whether Xr_j will be a true extension of Xr_i is pending other checking introduced later.)

5) If $Xr_i.itemlist \neq Xr_j.itemlist$, Xr_j will become a candidate extension of Xr_i.

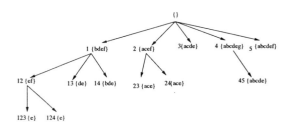

Figure 4. The pruned row enumeration tree.

Example 1 *We now illustrate the Lemma 3.1 with the example table in Figure 1. Suppose minimum support = 1, let us look at how to apply Lemma 3.1 to prune the complete row enumeration tree shown in Figure 3. Consider node 1, its itemlist is a subset of that of node 5 (case 2) while the intersection of its itemlist with the others satisfies the case 5. As a result, we increase the support of node 1 by 1 and extend node 1 with nodes 2, 3 and 4 to get three child nodes. Next we process the node 12, the intersection of the itemlist* *of 12 with the itemlist of 13 and 14 satisfies the case 5 and we extend 12 with 13 and 14. At the node 123, the intersection of its itemlist with that of 124, i.e. e satisfies with case 2. In this way, we get a close pattern {e} with support=4. Next we proceed to node 13 and the intersection of its itemlist with that of node 14, i.e. {de}, satisfies case 3. Thus we get a closed pattern de with support =3. The extension is done in a depth-first way. The nodes that are actually checked are shown in the Figure 4.*

Algorithm RERII(D, minsup)

---

1. Scan database D to find the set of frequent items F
2. Remove the infrequent items in each row r_i of D
3. Each r_i forms a node in the first level of row enumeration tree and let N be the set of nodes
4. RERIIdepthfirst(N, FCP)
5. Let CF be the set of closed items in F, $FCP = FCP \cup CF$ and return FCP

Procedure: RERIIdepthfirst(N, FCP)

6.   **for** each node n_i in N
7. N_i = null
8.   **if** the left row enumeration cannot be frequent **return**
9.   **for** each n_j in N, where $n_j > n_i$
10.   compute the frequency of items to do support pruning
11.   d = $n_i.itemlist \cap n_j.itemlist$
12.   **if** $|d| > 1$
13.   **if** $n_i.itemlist = n_j.itemlist$
14.   remove n_j from N
15.   increase $n_i.sup$ and $n'.sup$ $(n' \in N_i)$ by 1
16.   **if** $n_i.itemlist \subset n_j.itemlist$
17.   increase $n_i.sup$ and $n'.sup$ $(n' \in N_i)$ by 1
18.   **if** $n_i.itemlist \supset n_j.itemlist$
19.   remove n_j from N
20.   **if** $n_i.itemlist \cup d$ is not discovered before
21.   add n' $(n'.sup = n_i.sup + 1, n'.itemlist = d)$ to N_i
22.   **if** $(n_i.itemlist \neq n_j.itemlist)$
23.   **if** $n_i.itemlist \cup d$ is not discovered before
24.   add n' $(n'.sup = n_i.sup + 1, n'.itemlist = d)$ to N_i
25.   **end for**
26.   **if** $n_i.sup \geq minsup$, add $n_i.itemset$ to FCP
27.   **if** $N_i \neq \emptyset$ and N_i satisfies support pruning
28.   call RERIIdepthfirst(N_i, FCP)
29. **end for**

Figure 5. Algorithm RERII

We give the pseudo code of algorithm RERII in Figure 5. We further optimize the algorithm RERII using three techniques that will be explained as follows.

Single Item Pruning. RERII has already discovered the set of frequent single items by scanning the database once, we only need to discover those frequent closed patterns longer than 1. Therefore, if RERII finds that an enumeration node cannot result in pattern longer than 1, that node will be pruned. Algorithm RERII applies such an optimization at line 3 and line 12.

Support Pruning. RERII tries to utilize support pruning at three levels.

Level 1. This pruning is done at line 8 of RERI-Idepthfirst(). Given a node X with k child nodes $Xr_1, Xr_2, ..., Xr_k$, for any child node Xr_i, if $Xr_i.sup + k - i < minsup$, there is no need to do any further enumeration below node Xr_i.

Level 2. This pruning is done at line 10 of RERI-Idepthfirst(). Given a node X with k child nodes $Xr_1, Xr_2, ..., Xr_k$, for any child node Xr_i, we compute the supports for items in $X.itemlist$ $(= i_1, i_2, ...i_m)$ in all nodes Xr_j such that $i \leq j \leq k$. The counter $support(i_l)$ for each item i_l in $X.itemlist$ is initialized with $X.sup$ and will be increased by 1 if the item is in $Xr_j.itemlist$. On the basis of *single item pruning*, we only need to discover patterns longer than 1. We can derive the following two pruning methods. First, if there are fewer than two items such that $i_l \in Xr_i$ and $support(i_l) \geq minsup$, there is no need to do any further enumeration below node Xr_i. Second, if there are fewer than two items such that $i_l \in X.itemset$ and $support(i_l) \geq minsup$, there is no need to do any further enumeration below nodes Xr_j $(i \leq j \leq k)$.

Level 3. This pruning is done at line 27 of RERIIdepth-first() after N_i is filled, i.e. the child nodes of n_i are obtained. The detailed approach is similar to that in Level 2.

Redundant Pruning. On the basis of the lemma 3.1, at a node X, if pattern $X.itemlist$ has already been discovered in an earlier enumeration, we can prune node X and any further enumerations below X.

4. Algorithm REPT

Like CARPENTER, algorithm REPT traverses the row enumeration tree with the help of projected transposed table. Its first main difference from CARPENTER is that REPT represents (projected) transposed table with prefix trees, which can help in saving memory and saving computation in counting frequency. The second main difference of REPT from CARPENTER lies in pruning method. The prefix tree used to represent transposed table is similar to the FP-tree used in [4] to represent original table. In FP-tree, each node represents an item while the node of prefix tree used in REPT represents a row. The algorithm details are ignored here because of space limitation.

5. Performance Studies

In this section, we will evaluate RERII and REPT in terms of both the efficiency and memory usage. All our experiments were performed on a PC with a Pentium IV 2.4 Ghz CPU, 1GB RAM running Linux and a PC with Pentium IV 2.6, 1 G RAM running Windows XP. Algorithms were coded in Standard C. We compare RERII and REPT against three other closed pattern discovery algorithms [2], CARPENTER [2], CHARM [7] and CLOSET [4] on Linux and against CLOSET+ [6] on Windows.

Our experiments are performed on 2 real-life datasets, which are the clinical data on breast cancer (BC) [3] and ALL-AML leukemia (ALL) [4]. In the BC dataset, there are 97 tissue samples and each sample is described by the activity level of 24481 genes. In the ALL dataset, there are 72 tissue samples each described by the activity level of 7129 genes. The datasets are discretized by doing a equal-width partition for each column with 50 buckets.

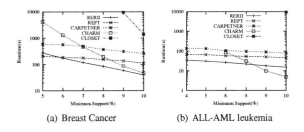

(a) Breast Cancer   (b) ALL-AML leukemia

Figure 6. Runtime Performance

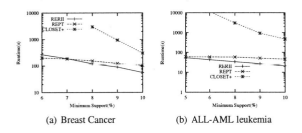

(a) Breast Cancer   (b) ALL-AML leukemia

Figure 7. Comparison with CLOSET+

Figure 6 shows the experimental results on our three datasets. Note that the y-axes of these graphs are in logarithmic scale. At some points in Figure 6(b), the runtime of CHARM is not shown because CHARM cannot finish by reporting error after using up all available memory. We do not give the runtime of CLOSET on all points because it is too slow and showing them will make the differences in runtime of other algorithms unclear in these graphs. Among the five algorithms, we find that RERII is usually the fastest while CLOSET is the slowest and has the steepest increases in run time as $minsup$ is decreased. CHARM is generally 1 order of magnitude slower than RERII and REPT at low support. Compared to CARPENTER, RERII is usually 2-4 times faster and REPT is usually 1-2 times faster. These re-

sults clearly show that the two proposed algorithms in this paper are efficient.

Figure 7 shows the comparison results with CLOSET+. CLOSET+ cannot finish by reporting error after using up all available memory at $minsup = 7\%$ on BC. Figure 7 shows that both RERII and REPT are usually 1 order of magnitude faster than CLOSET+.

In our experiments, we also observe the memory usage, which usually follows the following relation: CHARM > RERII > CLOSET, CARPENTER, CLOSET+ > REPT. REPT needs the least memory while CHARM is the most memory consuming. It is also interesting to note that tree-based schemes (e.g., CLOSET, REPT using FP-tree or prefix tree) generally consume less memory, while non-tree-based algorithms(e.g., CHARM, RERII) are typically more efficient on the data that we use.

6. Conclusions

In this paper, we have proposed two new algorithms, RERII and REPT, to discover frequent closed patterns. Several experiments showed that the proposed algorithms are faster than existing algorithms, including CLOSET, CHARM, CLOSET+ and CARPENTER.

References

[1] C. Creighton and S. Hanash. Mining gene expression databases for association rules. *Bioinformatics*, 19, 2003.

[2] F. Pan, G. Cong, A. K. H. Tung, J. Yang, and M. J. Zaki. CARPENTER: Finding closed patterns in long biological datasets. In *Proc. ACM SIGKDD Int'l Conf. on Knowledge Discovery and Data Mining(KDD)*, 2003.

[3] N. Pasquier, Y. Bastide, R. Taouil, and L. Lakhal. Discovering frequent closed itemsets for association rules. In *Proc. 7th Int'l Conf. Database Theory (ICDT)*, 1999.

[4] J. Pei, J. Han, and R. Mao. CLOSET: An efficient algorithm for mining frequent closed itemsets. In *Proc. ACM-SIGMOD Int'l Workshop Data Mining and Knowledge Discovery (DMKD)*, 2000.

[5] F. Rioult, J.-F. Boulicaut, B. Cremileux, and J. Besson. Using transposition for pattern discovery from microarray data. In *Proc. ACM-SIGMOD Int'l Workshop Data Mining and Knowledge Discovery (DMKD)*, 2003.

[6] J. Wang, J. Han, and J. Pei. CLOSET+: Searching for the best strategies for mining frequent closed itemsets. In *Proc. ACM SIGKDD Int'l Conf. on Knowledge Discovery and Data Mining (KDD)*, 2003.

[7] M. J. Zaki and C. Hsiao. CHARM: An efficient algorithm for closed association rule mining. In *Proc. SIAM Int'l Conf. on Data Mining (SDM)*, 2002.

[8] Z. Zhang, A. Teo, B. Ooi, and K.-L. Tan. Mining deterministic biclusters in gene expression data. In *4th Symposium on Bioinformatics and Bioengineering*, 2004.

---

[2] We are grateful to Dr. Mohammed Zaki for the Linux version source code of CHARM and Dr. Jiawei Han and Dr. Jianyong Wang for the executable code of CLOSET+ running on Windows

[3] http://www.rii.com/publications/default.htm

[4] http://www-genome.wi.mit.edu/cgi-bin/cancer

Clustering on Demand for Multiple Data Streams

Bi-Ru Dai, Jen-Wei Huang, Mi-Yen Yeh, and Ming-Syan Chen
Department of Electrical Engineering
National Taiwan University
Taipei, Taiwan, ROC
E-mail:mschen@cc.ee.ntu.edu.tw, {brdai, jwhuang, miyen}@arbor.ee.ntu.edu.tw

Abstract

In the data stream environment, the patterns generated by the mining techniques are usually distinct at different time because of the evolution of data. In order to deal with various types of multiple data streams and to support flexible mining requirements, we devise in this paper a Clustering on Demand framework, abbreviated as COD framework, to dynamically cluster multiple data streams. While providing a general framework of clustering on multiple data streams, the COD framework has two major features, namely one data scan for online statistics collection and compact multi-resolution approximations, which are designed to address, respectively, the time and the space constraints in a data stream environment. Furthermore, with the multi-resolution approximations of data streams, flexible clustering demands can be supported.

1 Introduction

In recent years, several query problems and mining capabilities have been explored for the data stream environment [2], including those on the statistics [3], the aggregate query [4], association rules [8], frequent patterns [10], data clustering [1][5][9], and data classification [6], to name a few. For data stream applications, the volume of data is usually too huge to be stored on permanent devices or to be scanned thoroughly more than once. It is hence recognized that both approximation and adaptivity are key ingredients for executing queries and performing mining tasks over rapid data streams.

In this paper, the problem of clustering multiple data streams is addressed. It is assumed that at each time stamp, data points from individual streams arrive simultaneously, and the data points are highly correlative to previous ones in the same stream. Unlike that of prior studies, the objective in this work is to partition these data streams, rather than their data points, into clusters. Note that the data streams

are not of a fixed length. Instead, they are still evolving when the clustering results are observed at users' requests. The problem studied in this paper is different from the one discussed in [7], which focuses on clustering the windows of a single streaming time series. On the other hand, clustering of evolving streams is discussed in [11]. However, the objective in [11] is to continuously report clusters satisfying the specified distance threshold. To further enhance these techniques, clustering requests of flexible time ranges are supported in our framework.

In the data stream environment, the patterns generated by the mining techniques are usually distinct at different time because of the evolution of data. Depending on different applications, the frequency for patterns in data streams to change varies. For example, the streams gathered from adjacent sensors may always be in the same cluster. However, for stock prices, some companies are probably within the same cluster during several months but in different clusters afterward. The clusters obtained hence change frequently. Therefore, an important question arises: "*Can we design a scheme for modeling both fast and slow evolving patterns adaptively?*" Furthermore, the clustering request is unknown when the data is collected and processed. After the time range of clustering request reveals, recommendations for short-term or long-term investments are desired to be offered precisely. This leads to another important issue: "*Can we provide a system to support various clustering requirements at the same time?*" Consequently, we devise in this paper a framework of *Clustering on Demand*, abbreviated as *COD framework*, to dynamically cluster multiple data streams. While providing a general framework of clustering on multiple data streams, the proposed COD framework has two advantageous features: (1) one data scan for online statistics collection, and (2) compact multi-resolution approximations, that are designed to address, respectively, the time and the space constraints in a data stream environment. Furthermore, with the multi-resolution approximations of data streams, flexible clustering demands can be supported. Note that since the clustering algorithms are only applied to the statistics maintained rather than to the original data streams, the COD proposed is very efficient in practice.

The COD framework proposed consists of two phases, namely the *online maintaining phase* and the *offline clustering phase*. The online maintaining phase provides an efficient algorithm to maintain the summary hierarchies of the data streams with multiple resolutions in the time complexity linear to both the number of streams and the number of data points in each stream. On the other hand, an *adaptive clustering algorithm* is devised for the offline phase to retrieve the approximations of the desired sub-streams from the summary hierarchies as precisely as possible according to the clustering queries specified by the users. In general, we keep finer approximations for more recent data and coarser approximations for more obsolete data. The COD framework performs very efficiently in the data stream environment while producing clustering results of very high quality.

The rest of this paper is organized as follows. Preliminaries and advantages of the COD framework are described in Section 2. The online maintaining phase and the offline clustering phase of the COD framework are presented in Section 3. This paper concludes with Section 4.

2 Clustering on Demand Framework

2.1 Framework Definitions

The COD framework has two phases, i.e., the *online maintaining phase* and the *offline clustering phase*. In the online maintaining phase, the arriving data streams are processed and only very brief summaries are maintained. The offline clustering phase deals with the clustering queries. The COD framework supports clustering queries with a flexible window size and a desired number of windows to observe. For example, a clustering query could be 12 windows with the window size of 30 days to observe the clusters of each month during a year. Based on the limited space property in the data stream environment, the raw data streams are parsed only once and then discarded. Therefore, the clustering algorithm in our framework is applied to the statistics maintained by the online phase rather than to the original streams, as illustrated in Figure 1.

At any time stamp, each stream receives a new value simultaneously, and there are totally n data streams. More specifically, we have the n streams $\{S_1, S_2, ..., S_n\}$ at time stamp m where $S_i = \{f_i^1, f_i^2, ..., f_i^m\}$, for $1 \leq i \leq n$, and f_i^j is the value of stream S_i that arrives at time j. First, we introduce the *offline clustering phase*. Let k denote the number of clusters, and let w be the window size of the clustering query submitted at time stamp t_{now}. The algorithm proposed will generate at most p windows of k-clustering results where

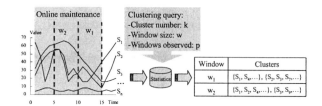

Figure 1. Clustering of multiple data streams by COD at $t_{now} = 15$, for a query of $k = 2$, $w = 5$ and $p = 2$.

$Cl(w_i) = \{C_1(w_i), C_2(w_i), ..., C_k(w_i)\}$, for $1 \leq i \leq p$, which minimizes each clustering cost $Cost(Cl(w_i))$ of the sub-streams in the interval $(t_{now} - w \times i, t_{now} - w \times (i-1)]$. Note that $C_j(w_i)$ is the jth cluster of window w_i with the properties of $\bigcap_{j=1}^{k} C_j(w_i) = \phi$ and $\bigcup_{j=1}^{k} C_j(w_i) = \{S_1(w_i), S_2(w_i), ..., S_n(w_i)\}$, where $S_q(w_i) = \{f_q^{(t_{now} - w \times i)+1}, f_q^{(t_{now} - w \times i)+2}, ..., f_q^{(t_{now} - w \times i)+w}\}$, for $1 \leq q \leq n$.

Example 1: Consider the first three data streams $\{S_1, S_2, S_3\}$ in Figure 1 at time stamp t_{now}=15, where
S_1={64,48,16,32,56,56,48,24,32,24,16,16,24,32,40},
S_2={24,38,46,52,54,56,40,16,24,26,34,28,20,14,8}, and
S_3={32,46,54,60,62,64,66,64,58,50,42,36,28,22,16}.
Assume that the clustering query is $k = 2$, $w = 5$, and $p = 2$. The algorithm will generate at most 2 windows of 2-clustering results, $Cl(w_1) = \{C_1(w_1), C_2(w_1)\}$ and $Cl(w_2) = \{C_1(w_2), C_2(w_2)\}$. Note that the resulting clusters of window w_1 are $C_1(w_1) = \{S_1\}$ and $C_2(w_1) = \{S_2, S_3\}$ since S_2 is more similar to S_3 in the interval $(15 - 5 \times 1, 15 - 5 \times (1-1)] = (10, 15]$. In window w_2, the clusters are $C_1(w_2) = \{S_1, S_2\}$ and $C_2(w_2) = \{S_3\}$ since S_2 is more similar to S_1 in the interval $(15 - 5 \times 2, 15 - 5 \times (2-1)] = (5, 10]$. ∎

We next describe the *online maintaining phase*. To support various clustering queries in the offline clustering phase, adequate information has to be preserved during the online maintaining phase for discovering fast and slowly evolving patterns. Note that the resolution of statistics maintained could affect the patterns obtained. With a small interval used for summarization, short-term patterns can be observed, but long-term patterns are likely to be neglected. Also, the summaries are possibly affected by noises and oscillations, and the summaries should be updated or reconstructed frequently. On the other hand, if a large interval is used, long-term patterns can be observed while neglecting short-term patterns. Also, the patterns may not catch up with the changes of the data streams. Moreover, the patterns could be very rough because of the generalization/summarization of streams. Therefore, we devise a hierarchical structure to store data summaries at different resolutions in the online maintaining phase. Whenever a clustering query is submitted, the algorithm of the offline clustering phase will select the approximations from appropriate levels of the summary hierarchies to support the requirements of the clustering query. Details of the online and offline phases will be described in following sections.

2.2 Advantages of the COD Framework

Since the summaries maintained in the summary hierarchies are at multiple resolutions, the COD framework is able to support the *clusters for variable window sizes*. Applying the conventional time series clustering algorithms to the raw streams with the desired window sizes is not practical in the streaming environment because there is not enough space for the storage of continuous streams. On the other hand, the summarization techniques which maintain the streams with a fixed resolution do not perform well for various window sizes. Although the prior work [11] for clustering of evolving streams continuously reports clusters within the given distance threshold, it does not allow the user to specify a desired window size to be observed. In our COD framework, even though the data streams are collected and summarized into the summary hierarchies before the clustering queries are submitted, the clusters with various window sizes can be obtained directly from the existing summary hierarchies without parsing the data streams again to construct the summaries for the desired resolutions. For example, suppose that the summary hierarchies of the stock prices have been kept for the prices in ten years. Then, clusters in one day, one month, or even one year can be observed very efficiently without resorting to the old prices again.

From the definition of clustering query, at most p windows of clustering results can be obtained for a query. It is very efficient to *observe the trends and changes of clusters* at one time. The behaviors of the clusters, such as the moving paths of clusters, the merges and splits of clusters, and the streams jumping between clusters, can be investigated from the results of a clustering query. Consider the example of stock prices again. Assume that the window size is one month and 12 windows are inspected. We might find out that stock A and stock B are in the same cluster for one month and then stock A jumps to another cluster for the following several months. Such trends and changes within one year can be extended from the results of this clustering query.

3 The Framework of COD

3.1 Online Maintaining Phase

The main objective of this online maintaining phase is to provide a one scan algorithm of the incoming multiple data streams for statistics collection. A summary hierarchy

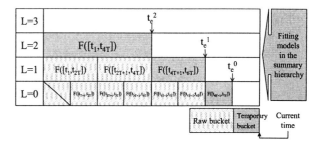

Figure 2. The illustration of summary hierarchy, where $F(h)$ represents the fitting model in the time interval $h = [t_s, t_e]$, and $\alpha = 6$.

is maintained incrementally to provide multi-resolution approximations for a stream. Multiple levels in the hierarchy correspond to various resolutions.

A **fitting model** $F(h)$ is defined as an approximation of a raw sub-stream in the interval $h = [t_s, t_e]$ by some summarization techniques. The fitting model on level L is generated by the aggregation of B_h models on level $(L-1)$, and each level keeps the time stamp of the latest data point, which has been summarized to that level, as the end time t_e of the level. The procedure of generating and updating the summary hierarchy of a stream is described as follows.

Procedure of the online maintaining phase

1 For each incoming value, put it in the temporary bucket.

2 If the number of items in the temporary bucket is less than the bucket size B_t, go to Step 1. Else:

  2.1 A new fitting model of level 0 is generated according to the values in the temporary bucket.

  2.2 Update the end time t_e^0 of level 0.

  2.3 Move all the items from the temporary bucket to the raw bucket.

  2.4 If the number of items in the raw bucket is more than α, remove the oldest items to keep the number no larger than α.

3 For each level L, if B_h new models are accumulated:

  3.1 A new model of level $(L+1)$ will be generated by aggregating the latest B_h models in level L.

  3.2 Update the end time t_e^{L+1} of level $(L+1)$.

  3.3 If the number of models in level $(L+1)$ is larger than α, remove the oldest model from that level.

As shown in the procedure, to achieve the space limitation in the streaming environment, the number of fitting models maintained at each level is limited to be the maximum number of α. Note the α should be set to a number no smaller than B_h in order to have enough fitting models for the model generation in a higher level. Figure 2 gives an example of the summary hierarchy.

3.2 Offline Clustering Phase

As the clustering query shown in Section 2.1, the users want to inspect clusters with window size w, and at most p windows will be observed. Note that the window size desired could be different from those maintained in the summary hierarchy. In this situation, we have to select the fitting models from appropriate levels of the hierarchy to approximate the desired windows. We have the following theorems for adaptive level selection.

Theorem 1: The highest level to approximate a sub-stream with window size w is $L_{max} = \left\lfloor log_{B_h}(\frac{w}{B_t}) \right\rfloor$.

Theorem 2: The lowest level to approximate a sub-stream with window size w is $L_{min} = \min_{L} \left\{ w \leq (t_{now} - t_e^L) + \alpha_L \times h_L \right\}$, where α_L is the exact number of fitting models in level L, and $h_L = B_t \times (B_h)^L$ is the window size of the fitting models in level L.

From the above theorems, fitting models in the levels between L_{min} and L_{max} are able to approximate the sub-streams in the windows of clustering queries. The fitting models in higher levels span longer intervals and thus provide more generalized fittings to the original streams. In contrast, the fitting models in lower levels possess shorter spans and can thus provide more specific and accurate fittings to the original streams. However, only α models are maintained in each level. Therefore, we devise an *adaptive clustering algorithm* for the offline clustering phase to approximate each window of data streams with the fitting models as accurately as possible. Note that the offline clustering phase is not designed for a specific clustering algorithm. Therefore, users can adopt any traditional clustering algorithm with minor modification if so necessary.

Procedure of adaptive clustering algorithm

1. Calculate L_{min} and L_{max}. For each data stream, do Step 2 and 3.

2. If the end time $t_e^{L_{min}}$ of level L_{min} is not equal to the current time, aggregate the models of lower levels (from $L_{min} - 1$ to 0) and the temporary bucket to generate a temporary model characterizing the interval between $t_e^{L_{min}}$ and the current time. Then, aggregate this temporary model to the latest model in level L_{min}.

3. Encapsulate the fitting models between level L_{min} and L_{max} to generate at most p entries, where each entry represents a window with size w. Set $L = L_{min}$ initially. For the windows from w_1 to w_p, if the range of a desired window is covered by the interval of the fitting models in level L, encapsulate an appropriate number of fitting models into that entry. Else, increase L by one to look for the fitting models with enough coverage. This step stops when p entries have been retrieved or when L exceeds the maximum level L_{max} with p_r entries obtained, where $p_r \leq p$.

4. Run the clustering algorithm to cluster these sub-streams by the retrieved entries for each window.

4 Conclusions

In order to deal with various types of multiple data streams and to support flexible mining requirements, we devised a COD Framework to dynamically cluster multiple data streams. While providing a general framework of clustering on multiple data streams, COD framework had two major advantages, namely one data scan for online statistics collection and compact multi-resolution approximations. The online maintaining phase of COD provided an efficient algorithm to maintain the summaries of the data streams with multiple resolutions. On the other hand, an adaptive clustering algorithm was devised for the offline phase of COD to retrieve the approximations of the desired sub-streams from the summary hierarchies as precisely as possible according to the clustering queries. The COD framework performed very efficiently in the data stream environment while producing clustering results of very high quality.

Acknowledgement

The work was supported in part by the National Science Council of Taiwan, R.O.C., under Contract NSC93-2752-E-002-006-PAE.

References

[1] C. C. Aggarwal, J. Han, J. Wang, and P. S. Yu. A framework for clustering evolving data streams. In *Proc. of VLDB*, 2003.

[2] B. Babcock, S. Babu, M. Datar, R. Motwani, and J. Widom. Models and issues in data stream systems. In *Proc. of PODS*, June 2002.

[3] A. Bulut and A. K. Singh. Swat: Hierarchical stream summarization in large networks. In *Proc. of ICDE*, pages 303–314, Mar. 2003.

[4] A. Dobra, M. N. Garofalakis, J. Gehrke, and R. Rastogi. Processing complex aggregate queries over data streams. In *Proc. of ACM SIGMOD*, pages 61–72, June 2002.

[5] S. Guha, N. Mishra, R. Motwani, and L. O'Callaghan. Clustering data streams. In *Proc. of FOCS*, pages 359–366, 2000.

[6] G. Hulten, L. Spencer, and P. Domingos. Mining time-changing data streams. In *Proc. of ACM SIGKDD*, pages 97–106, Aug. 2001.

[7] E. Keogh, J. Lin, and W. Truppel. Clustering of time series subsequences is meaningless: Implications for past and future research. In *Proc. of ICDM*, Nov. 2003.

[8] G. S. Manku and R. Motwani. Approximate frequency counts over streaming data. In *Proc. of VLDB*, pages 346–357, Aug. 2002.

[9] L. O'Callaghan, N. Mishra, A. Meyerson, S. Guha, and R. Motwani. Streaming-data algorithms for high-quality clustering. In *Proc. of ICDE*, 2002.

[10] W.-G. Teng, M.-S. Chen, and P. S. Yu. A regression-based temporal pattern mining scheme for data streams. In *Proc. of VLDB*, Sep. 2003.

[11] J. Yang. Dynamic clustering of evolving streams with a single pass. In *Proc. of ICDE03*, Mar. 2003.

Extensible Markov Model[1]

Margaret H. Dunham and Yu Meng
*Department of Computer Science and
Engineering
Southern Methodist University
Dallas, Texas 75275-0122
mhd(ymeng)@engr.smu.edu*

Jie Huang
*The University of Texas Southwestern
Medical Center at Dallas,
5323 Harry Hines Blvd.
Dallas, Texas 75390-9041
jie.huang@utsouthwestern.edu*

Abstract

A Markov Chain is a popular data modeling tool. This paper presents a variation of Markov Chain, namely Extensible Markov Model (EMM). By providing a dynamically adjustable structure, EMM overcomes the problems caused by the static nature of the traditional Markov Chain. Therefore, EMMs are particularly well suited to model spatiotemporal data such as network traffic, environmental data, weather data, and automobile traffic. Performance studies using EMMs for spatiotemporal prediction problems show the advantages of this approach.

1. Introduction

In this paper we investigate a new modeling tool targeting spatiotemporal problems. An interesting, yet crucial, aspect of this type of data is that any modeling approach must be able to handle the fact that the data changes over time. For example, traffic data changes as a city grows. *Markov Chain (MC)* and its variations are some of the most powerful tools available to engineers and scientists for analyzing complex systems. In many real applications, such as spatiotemporal event prediction, problems with the use of MCs include:

1. The required structure of the MC may not be certain at the model construction time.
2. As the real world being modeled by the MC changes, so should the structure of the MC.

This paper presents a new data modeling technique, named *Extensible Markov Model (EMM)*. EMM is essentially a time varying Markov Chain. It has the advantage of learning and adjusting its structure (number of states) as well as state transition probabilities based on the input data seen. Applications initially examined using the EMM approach include prediction of river flow rate/water level, prediction of traffic volumes for both networks and roadways, identification of rare events in roadways, and identification of rare events for network traffic.

In the next section we provide an overview of previous related work. Section 3 introduces EMM,

Section 4 provides preliminary results of performance experiments, and we conclude the paper in Section 5.

2. Related Work

A first order Markov Chain is a finite or countably infinite sequence of events $\{E_1, E_2, \ldots \}$ over discrete time points, where $P_{ij} = P(E_j \mid E_i)$, and at any time the future behavior of the process is based solely on the current state [1]. Throughout this paper, we use a view of Markov Chain as depicted by a directed graph. The graph has a fixed structure although the labels of the arcs may change. (Note that in this paper we use arc, link and transition interchangeably; and use node, to specifically refer to a vertex in the MC (EMM).) The Markov Property states that the next transition depends only on the current state regardless of the past history, which implies that $P_{12\ldots j} = P(E_1)P(E_2 \mid E_1) \ldots P(E_j \mid E_{j-1})$. Although higher order Markov Chains can be studied, in this paper we only look at first order Markov Chains.

An MC is used to model the transition of real world events (states). Each node in the MC corresponds to a real world state. An MC is typically created by two steps: determine the states in the model and determine the suitable state transition probabilities. Usually the structure is defined by a domain expert to reflect the classification of real world observations and events. Transition probabilities may be determined by learning or assignment from a domain expert. Learning occurs by observing and counting how many times each transition in the model has been taken versus how many times the state actually occurred in the training data.

There have been several proposals to extend the static MC which we briefly examine in the following paragraphs.

One approach is to start with a single state model and create new states by splitting an existing state until a good model is found for the training data. This model construction measure is employed in several applications when using a *Hidden Markov model (HMM)* [2]. The determination of appropriate state to split is complicated and requires an exhaustive search of the model space.

Another approach of dynamically constructing an MC was proposed in [4], where certain states and their

---

1   This material is based upon work supported by the National Science Foundation under Grant No. IIS-0208741.

transitions were cloned (duplicated) due to satisfaction of certain criteria. The number of states could grow with the input data, whereas the number of state representatives is still the same, no new state representatives are identified with the input data coming in.

Dani Goldberg and Maja Mataric came up with a so called *Augmented Markov Model (AMM)* [6], which created new states if the input data has never been seen in the model, and transition probabilities are adjusted according to the traverse times kept with the link versus the number of times in the transit from state. After the model is constructed in a dynamic manner, it will not be updated in prediction phase.

3. Extensible Markov Model Overview

Our proposed EMM model is similar to AMM, but is more flexible:

1) EMM continues to learn during the application (prediction, etc.) phase.

2) The EMM is a generic incremental model whose nodes can have any kind of representatives.

3) State matching is determined using a clustering technique.

4) EMM not only allows the creation of new nodes, but deletion (or merging) of existing nodes. This allows the EMM model to "forget" old information which may not be relevant in the future. It also allows the EMM to adapt to any main memory constraints for large scale datasets.

5) EMM performs one scan of data and therefore is suitable for online data processing.

Definition 1: Extensible Markov Model (EMM): at any time t, EMM consists of an MC with designated current node, N_n, and algorithms to modify it, where algorithms include:

1) *EMMCluster*, which defines a technique for matching between input data at time $t + 1$ and existing states in the MC at time t.

2) *EMMIncrement* algorithm, which updates MC at time $t + 1$ given the MC at time t and clustering measure result at time $t + 1$.

3) *EMMDecrement* algorithm, which removes nodes from the EMM when needed.

It is crucial to keep in mind that each node in the EMM represents a cluster of a set of real world events/states which belong to that cluster. The labeling of a node actually depends on the clustering approach used as well as the representative identified for that cluster. We propose the use of a centroid or medoid for this labeling. Future work will examine the use of Birch [9] and in that case the labeling of a node would be the CF-feature for that cluster.

At any point in time, t, one node in the graph is designated as the current node, N_c. This node is the one in the graph which represents the cluster to which

the the previous input state was determined to belong. *EMMCluster* is used to place a given event at time t, E_t, into one of the clusters represented by the nodes in the EMM, G. If the current event is not sufficiently "close enough" to any current cluster, a new node (and thus a new cluster) is created. For simplicity, we assume a nearest neighbor algorithm [5]. However any incremental algorithm can be used *EMMIncrement* is called by *EMMCluster* to update and add nodes incrementally to an EMM.

EMMIncrement calculates transition probabilities by keeping counts that indicate the number of times a node has been found to be the current node. Note that we use CN_i to represent the size of the cluster represented by node N_i and CL_{ij} to be the number of times the transition from N_i to N_j has occurred. We initially define the state transition probability to be $P_{ij} = (CL_{ij} / CN_i)$. Example 1 illustrates the use of *EMMCluster* and *EMMIncrement*.

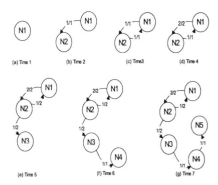

Figure 1. EMMIncrement example

Example 1. This example uses hypothetical automobile traffic data shown below:

Time 1: < 20 50 100 30 25 4 10 >
Time 2: < 20 80 50 20 10 10 10 >
Time 3: < 40 30 75 20 30 20 25 >
Time 4: < 15 60 30 30 10 10 15 >
Time 5: < 40 15 25 10 35 40 9 >.
Time 6: < 5 5 40 35 10 5 4 >
Time 7: < 0 35 55 2 1 3 5 >

Each real world state can be viewed as a vector of seven values obtained from sensors located at specific points on roads. Each sensor collects a count of the number of vehicles which have crossed this sensor in the preceding time interval. In the following we show the steps involved in the construction of the EMM for the above data. Figure 1, shows the creation of the EMM. We assume the use of Jaccard similarity with a threshold of 0.8 and a nearest neighbor clustering technique

Time 1: Initialize $N_1 = V_1 = < 20 50 100 30 25 4 10 >$, $CN_1 = 0$.

Time2: $Sim_{Jaccard} (V_2, N_1) = 0.7342$. A new state N_2 is created and represented by vector. $N_2 = V_2 = < 20 80 50 20 10 10 10 >$. A state transition from N_1 to N_2 has been made. Update $CL_{12} = 1$ and $CN_1 = 1$.

<u>Time 3</u>: Sim(V_3, N_1) = 0.8497, Sim(V_3, N_2) = 0.6559. Therefore V_3 is mapped to state N_1. The state transition is from N_2 to N_1. Update the parameters CN_2 = 1 and CL_{21} = 1.

Processing continues in this manner.

If the EMM is determined to be too large, *EMMDecrement* can be executed to decrease the size of the EMM. Our initial version of this algorithm is assumed to be executed manually, although it could be merged with *EMMIncrement* to develop a complete EMM construction algorithm. We also assume that with each execution of *EMMDecrement*, one node in the graph is removed. The node to be decremented, N_d, is input. When the node is removed, each incoming arc is replaced with the same number of arcs as N_d initially had as outgoing. The associated transition probabilities are the products of the probabilities found in the incoming-outgoing arc pairs.

If multiple nodes are to be removed, this can be performed in an incremental manner. Each connected subgraph to be removed can be compressed into one node and *EMMDecrement* applied to each. *EMMDecrement* can be executed at any time, but will probably be used only when memory space is an issue or if it is known that certain portions of the graph are no longer applicable

Example 2. To illustrate the EMMDecrement process, we describe the removal of node N_2 from Figure 2(a). Initially this node has two incoming arcs and three outgoing arcs. When it is removed, each of the incoming arcs will be replaced with three outgoing arcs. Figure 2(b) illustrates this.

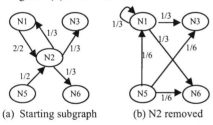

(a) Starting subgraph   (b) N2 removed

Figure 2. EMMDecrement example

As indicated earlier, EMM is a modeling tool. It can be used by many different types of applications. We have initially investigated its use with prediction (forecasting) and rare event detection. The prediction application predicts a future node (or cluster) value at some time point in the future. Prediction is made using the outgoing link with the highest transition probability from the current node. Prediction for multiple time points into the future is made by taking the subsequent links with highest probability. The likelihood of this future event is determined to be the product of the probabilities along the associated path. Example 3 describes the use of EMM for prediction.

Example 3 – Prediction. At time 3 in Figure 1, the current state is N_1. Based on the EMM at this state, Figure 2 (c), we predict the state at the next time to be state N_2. If we were to predict two time points into the future, we would predict N_1.

Rare event detection is somewhat more complicated and space limitations prevent us from discussing this application in detail. The basic idea is that a rare event is detected if an input event, E_t, is determined not to belong to any existing cluster (node in EMM), if the cardinality of the associated cluster (CN_n) is small, or it the transition from the current node to the new node small.

4. Performance

Experiments were performed with actual implementations using Matlab. Three different datasets were used for testing. MnDot is traffic data collected from freeways of the Minnesota Twin City metropolis [7]. In our experiments, the traffic volume data collected every 5 minutes in March of 2004 at Monitor Stations 119 and 120 located near I-494/I-35W are used. Ouse and Serwent are river sensor readings at two different catchments in the United Kingdom [8] [3]. Ouse sensors are located at three river level gauges. The sensors read every 15 minutes. There are three groups of data: 480 data are readings from August 25, 1986 to August 29, 1986; 672 data are readings from December 25, 1994 to December 31, 1994 and 768 data are from January 26, 1995 to February 2, 1995. Serwent data is obtained from seven sensors in the upper Serwent catchment where water flow rate (m^3/s) is read from every location once per day. The date range that all seven locations have data available is from December 1971 to January 1977.

4.1. Clustering Impact

Table 1. Clustering impact on number of EMM nodes

Data	Sim	Threshold				
		0.99	0.992	0.994	0.996	0.998
Ser went	Jaccrd	156	190	268	389	667
	Dice	72	92	123	191	389
	Cosine	11	14	19	31	61
	Ovrlap	2	2	3	3	4
Ouse	Jaccrd	56	66	81	105	162
	Dice	40	43	52	66	105
	Cosine	6	8	10	13	24
	Ovrlap	1	1	1	1	1

Initial experiments examined the use of different similarity measures [5] using the nearest neighbor clustering algorithm. Table1 shows the number of states created in EMM using the Ouse and Serwant datasets, four different similarity measures, and five thresholds for clustering. As can be seen, there is a dramatic difference in the size of the respective EMM graphs. Ongoing work is examining the use of more sophisticated clustering techniques such as Birch.

4.2. Size

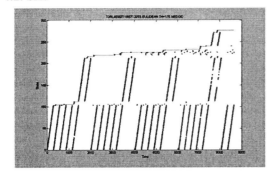

Figure 3. State growth of EMM for MnDot dataset

We now examine the growth rate of EMM using MnDot traffic data In Figure 3, each entry on the y-axis represents a unique node in the EMM. Over time, as events occur, these nodes may be reused (as the event is placed into an already existing cluster). Thus the real benefit of the EMM model is illustrated when multiple real world events are placed into the same cluster (node). This is shown by repeated y values for multiple x values. Figure 3 shows that of the MnDot. If a horizontal line is drawn on the graph, the number of intersections which occur indicate the actual size of the cluster at that point. Of course, this depends on the data. In fact in this figure not only the unique clustering of weekday vs. weekend traffic is captured, but also the occurrence of some anomalous behavior is identified on the upper right hand corner of this graph. During this last weekend, there was an extremely low amount of traffic at these locations.

4.3. Prediction Accuracy

Performances of predictions are evaluated by two metrics, Normalized Absolute Ratio Error (NARE) and Root Means Square (RMS), as defined below:

$$\text{NARE} = \frac{\sum_{t=1}^{N} |O(t) - P(t)|}{\sum_{t=1}^{N} O(t)} \quad \text{RMS} = \sqrt{\frac{\sum_{t=1}^{N} (O(t) - P(t))^2}{N}}$$

Where $O(t)$ is the observed profile and $P(t)$ is the predicted profile, N is the length of the dataset and t is the time variable or the tth tuple in the input dataset.

Table 2. Water level prediction of EMM and RLF

		NARE	*RMS*	*No of States*
RLF		0.321423	1.5389	
EMM	Th=0.95	0.068443	0.43774	20
	Th=0.99	0.046379	0.4496	56
	Th=0.995	0.055184	0.57785	92

Using Ouse data, Table 2 compares the water level prediction accuracy of EMM to that of a neural network solution provided with the RLF system that is available on-line [8]. The data clearly shows that for this experiment the prediction accuracy of EMM is higher than that of the neural network approach, a typical non-linear regression method.

5. Summary and Future Work

We have introduced a new spatiotemporal modeling tool, Extensible Markov Model (EMM). We have very briefly reported our ongoing EMM performance experiments. To summarize, we have found that the size of EMM grows at a sublinear rate being able to take advantage of the clustering aspect of nodes. The degree of clustering (and thus the EMM size) depends on the clustering technique, as well as the dataset. Prediction accuracy is good, and at least as good as one available neural network approach specifically designed for the dataset studied. Future work will look at EMMs and rare event detection in more detail. Birch and other more sophisticated clustering algorithms will be examined.

6. Acknowledgements

The authors gratefully acknowledge the Transportation Data Research Laboratory of the Minnesota Department of Transportation, the Ridings Area Office of the Environment Agency North-East and the British National River Flow Archive for providing the training and testing data, and Nathaniel Ayewah and Zhigang Li for their helpful information.

7. References

[1] U. Narayan Bhat and Gregory K. Miller, *Elements of Applied Stochastic Processes Third Edition,* John Wiley & Sons, 2002.
[2] M.J. Black and Y. Yacoob, "Recognizing facial expressions in image sequences using local parameterized models of image motion", *Int. Journal of Computer Vision*, 25(1), 1997, 23-48.
[3] British National River Flow Archive, http://www.nercwallingford.ac.uk/ih/nrfa/index.html.
[4] G. V. Cormack, R. N. S. Horspool. "Data compression using dynamic Markov Modeling," *The Computer Journal,* Vol. 30, No. 6, 1987.
[5] Margaret H. Dunham. *Data Mining Introductory and Advanced Topics.* Prentice Hall, 2002.
[6] Dani Goldberg, Maja J Mataric. "Coordinating mobile robot group behavior using a model of interaction dynamics," *Proceedings, the Third International Conference on Autonomous Agents* (agents '99), Seattle, Washington, May.
[7] Minnesota Department of Transportation (MnDot), http://tdrl1.d.umn.edu/services.htm.
[8] River Level Forecaster (RLF/1), http://www.ccg.leeds.ac.uk/simon/intro.html.
[9] Tian Zhang, Raghu Ramakrishnan, and Miron Livny, "BIRCH: An Efficient Data Clustering Method for Very Large Databases," *Proceedings of the ACM SIGMOD Conference,* 1996, pages 103-114.

Using Representative-Based Clustering for Nearest Neighbor Dataset Editing

Christoph F. Eick , Nidal Zeidat, and Ricardo Vilalta
Dept. of Computer Science, University of Houston
{ceick, nzeidat, vilalta}@cs.uh.edu

Abstract

The goal of dataset editing in instance-based learning is to remove objects from a training set in order to increase the accuracy of a classifier. For example, Wilson editing removes training examples that are misclassified by a nearest neighbor classifier so as to smooth the shape of the resulting decision boundaries. This paper revolves around the use of representative-based clustering algorithms for nearest neighbor dataset editing. We term this approach supervised clustering editing. The main idea is to replace a dataset by a set of cluster prototypes. A novel clustering approach called supervised clustering is introduced for this purpose. Our empirical evaluation using eight UCI datasets shows that both Wilson and supervised clustering editing improve accuracy on more than 50% of the datasets tested. However, supervised clustering editing achieves four times higher compression rates than Wilson editing.

1. Introduction

Nearest neighbor classifiers have received considerable attention by the research community (for a survey see Toussaint [3]). Most of the research aims at producing time-efficient versions of the algorithm. For example, several condensing techniques have been proposed that replace the set of training examples O by a smaller set $O_C \subset O$ such that all examples in O are still classified correctly by a NN-classifier that uses O_C.

Data set editing techniques, on the other hand, aim at replacing a dataset O with a, usually smaller, dataset O_E with the goal of improving the accuracy of a NN-classifier. A popular technique in this category is *Wilson editing* [5]; it removes all examples that have been misclassified by the 1-NN rule from a dataset. Wilson editing cleans interclass overlap regions, thereby leading to smoother boundaries between classes. It has been shown by Penrod and Wagner [2] that the accuracy of a Wilson edited nearest neighbor classifier converges to Bayes' error as the number of examples approaches infinity. Figure 1a shows a hypothetical dataset where examples that are misclassified using the 1-NN-rule are

marked with circles around them. Figure 1.b shows the reduced dataset after applying Wilson editing.

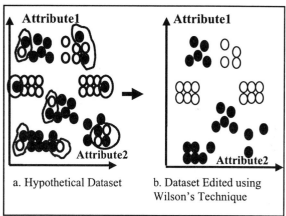

a. Hypothetical Dataset   b. Dataset Edited using Wilson's Technique

Figure 1: Wilson editing for a 1-NN classifier.

In addition to analyzing the benefits of Wilson editing, this paper proposes a new approach to nearest neighbor editing that replaces a dataset by a set of cluster prototypes using a *supervised clustering* algorithm [6]. We will refer to this editing technique as *supervised clustering editing* (SCE) and to the corresponding nearest neighbor classifier as *nearest representative (NR) classifier*. Section 2 introduces supervised clustering editing. Section 3 discusses experimental results that compare Wilson editing, supervised clustering editing, and traditional, "unedited" nearest-neighbor classifiers. Section 4 summarizes the results of this paper.

2. Using Supervised Clustering for Dataset Editing

Due to its novelty, the goals and objectives of supervised clustering will be discussed in the first subsection. The subsequent subsections will explain how supervised clustering can be used for dataset editing.

2.1. Supervised Clustering

Supervised clustering deviates from traditional clustering in that it is applied on classified examples with the objective of identifying clusters having not only strong cohesion but also class purity. Moreover, in supervised clustering, we try to keep the number of clusters small, and objects are assigned to clusters using a notion of closeness with respect to a given distance function. Consequently, supervised clustering evaluates a clustering based on the following two criteria:

- *Class impurity, Impurity(X).* Measured by the percentage of minority examples in the different clusters of a clustering X. A minority example is an example that belongs to a class different from the most frequent class in its cluster.
- *Number of clusters, k.* In general, we favor a low number of clusters.

In particular, we use the following fitness function in our experimental work (lower values for q(X) indicate 'better' quality of clustering X).

$$q(X) = \text{Impurity}(X) + \beta * \text{Penalty}(k) \quad (1)$$

Where

$$\text{Impurity}(X) = \frac{\text{\# of Minority Examples}}{n},$$

$$\text{Penalty}(k) = \begin{cases} \sqrt{\dfrac{k-c}{n}} & k \geq c \\ 0 & k < c \end{cases}$$

With n being the total number of examples and c being the number of classes in a dataset. Parameter β ($0 < \beta \leq 3.0$) determines the penalty that is associated with the number of clusters, k; i.e., higher values for β imply larger penalties as the number of clusters increases.

2.2 Representative-Based Supervised Clustering Algorithms

Representative-based clustering aims at finding a set of k representatives that best characterizes a dataset. Clusters are created by assigning each object to the closest representative. Representative-based supervised clustering algorithms seek to accomplish the following goal: *Find a subset O_R of O such that the clustering X, obtained by using the objects in O_R as representatives, minimizes q(X).*

As part of our research, we have designed and evaluated several supervised clustering algorithms [1,6,7]. Among the algorithms investigated, one named <u>S</u>ingle <u>R</u>epresentative <u>I</u>nsertion/<u>D</u>eletion Steepest Decent <u>H</u>ill <u>C</u>limbing with Randomized <u>R</u>estart (SRIDHCR for short) performed quite well. This greedy algorithm starts by randomly selecting a number of examples from the dataset as the initial set of representatives. Clusters are then created by assigning examples to their closest

representative. The algorithm tries to improve the quality of the clustering by adding a single non-representative example to the set of representatives as well as by removing a single representative from the set of representatives. The algorithm terminates if the solution quality (measured by q(X)) of the current solution does not improve. Moreover, SRIDHCR is run r times, reporting the best solution found as its result.

2.3 Using Cluster Prototypes for Dataset Editing

Figure 2 gives an example illustrating how supervised clustering is used for dataset editing. Figure 2.a shows a dataset that was partitioned into 6 clusters using a supervised clustering algorithm. Cluster representatives are marked with small circles around them. Figure 2.b shows the result of supervised clustering editing.

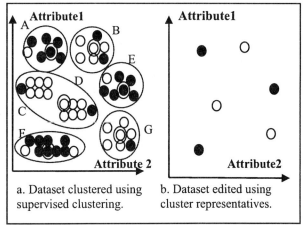

a. Dataset clustered using supervised clustering.   b. Dataset edited using cluster representatives.

Figure 2: Editing a dataset using supervised clustering.

3. Experimental Results

To evaluate the benefits of Wilson editing and supervised clustering editing, we applied these techniques to a benchmark consisting of eight UCI datasets [4] (see. Table 1).

Table1: Datasets used in the experiments.

Dataset name	# of objects	# of attributes	# of classes
Glass	214	9	6
Heart-Statlog	270	13	2
Heart-H	294	13	2
Iris Plants	150	4	3
Pima Indians Diabetes	768	8	2
Image Segmentation	2100	19	7
Vehicle Silhouettes	846	18	4
Waveform	5000	21	3

All datasets were normalized using a linear interpolation function that assigns 1 to the maximum value and 0 to the minimum value. Manhattan distance was used to compute the distance between two objects.

Table 2: Prediction accuracy for the four classifiers.

β	NR	Wilson	1-NN	C4.5
Glass **(214***)*				
0.1	0.636	0.607	0.692	0.677
0.4	0.589	0.607	0.692	0.677
1.0	0.575	0.607	0.692	0.677
Heart-Stat Log **(270)**				
0.1	0.796	0.804	0.767	0.782
0.4	0.833	0.804	0.767	0.782
1.0	0.838	0.804	0.767	0.782
Diabetes **(768)**				
0.1	0.736	0.734	0.690	0.745
0.4	0.736	0.734	0.690	0.745
1.0	0.745	0.734	0.690	0.745
Vehicle **(846)**				
0.1	0.667	0.716	0.700	0.723
0.4	0.667	0.716	0.700	0.723
1.0	0.665	0.716	0.700	0.723
Heart-H **(294)**				
0.1	0.755	0.809	0.783	0.802
0.4	0.793	0.809	0.783	0.802
1.0	0.809	0.809	0.783	0.802
Waveform **(5000)**				
0.1	0.834	0.796	0.768	0.781
0.4	0.841	0.796	0.768	0.781
1.0	0.837	0.796	0.768	0.781
Iris-Plants **(150)**				
0.1	0.947	0.936	0.947	0.947
0.4	0.973	0.936	0.947	0.947
1.0	0.953	0.936	0.947	0.947
Segmentation (2100)				
0.1	0.938	0.966	0.956	0.968
0.4	0.919	0.966	0.956	0.968
1.0	0.890	0.966	0.956	0.968

The parameter β of q(X) has a strong influence on the number k of representatives chosen by the supervised clustering algorithm. In general, an editing technique reduces the size n of a dataset to a smaller size k. We define the dataset compression rate of an editing technique as:

$$\text{Compression Rate} = 1 - \frac{k}{n} \qquad (2)$$

In order to explore different compression rates for supervised clustering editing, three different values for parameter β were used in the experiments: 1.0, 0.4, and

0.1. Prediction accuracies were measured using 10-fold cross-validation throughout the experiments. Representatives for the nearest representative (NR) classifier were computed using the SRIDHCR supervised clustering algorithm that was restarted 50 times. Accuracies and compression rates were obtained for a 1-NN-classifier that operates on subsets of the 8 datasets obtained using Wilson editing. We also computed prediction accuracy for a traditional 1-NN classifier that uses all training examples when classifying a new example. Finally, we report prediction accuracy for the decision-tree learning algorithm C4.5 that was run using its default parameter settings. Table 2 reports the accuracies obtained by the four classifiers evaluated in our experiments. Table 3 reports the average dataset compression rates for supervised clustering editing and Wilson editing. It also reports the average, minimum, and maximum number of representatives found on the 10 runs for SCE.

If we inspect the results displayed in Table 2, we can see that Wilson editing is a quite useful technique for improving traditional 1-NN-classfiers. Using Wilson editing leads to higher accuracies for 6 of the 8 datasets tested and only shows a significant loss in accuracy for the Glass dataset. The SCE approach, on the other hand, accomplished significant improvement in accuracy for the Heart-Stat Log, Waveform, and Iris-Plants datasets, outperforming Wilson editing by at least 2% in accuracy for those datasets. It should also be mentioned that the achieved accuracies are significantly higher than those obtained by C4.5 for those datasets. However, our results also indicate a significant loss in accuracy for the Glass and Segmentation datasets.

More importantly, looking at Table 3, we notice that SCE accomplishes compression rates of more than 95% without a significant loss in prediction accuracy for 6 of the 8 datasets. For example, for the Waveform dataset, a 1-NN classifier that only uses at an average 28 representatives outperforms the traditional 1-NN classifier that uses all 4500 training examples[1] by 7.3% (76.8% to 84.1%).

As mentioned earlier, Wilson editing reduces the size of a dataset by removing examples that have been misclassified by a k-NN classifier, which explains the low compression rates for the Iris and Segmentation datasets. Condensing approaches, on the other hand, reduce the size of a dataset by removing examples that have been classified correctly by a nearest neighbor classifier. Finally, supervised clustering editing reduces the size of a

---

[1] Due to the fact that we use 10-fold cross-validation, training sets contain 0.9*5000=4500 examples.

dataset by removing examples that have been classified correctly as well as examples that have not been classified correctly. A representative-based supervised clustering algorithm is used that aims at finding clusters that are dominated by instances of a single class, and tends to pick as cluster representatives[2] objects that are in the center of the region associated with the cluster.

Table 3: Dataset compression rates for SCE and Wilson editing.

B	Avg. k [Min-Max] for SCE	SCE Compression Rate (%)	Wilson Compression Rate (%)
Glass (214)			
0.1	34 [28-39]	84.3	27
0.4	25 [19-29]	88.4	27
1.0	6 [6 – 6]	97.2	27
Heart-Stat Log (270)			
0.1	15 [12-18]	94.4	22.4
0.4	2 [2 – 2]	99.3	22.4
1.0	2 [2 – 2]	99.3	22.4
Diabetes (768)			
0.1	27 [22-33]	96.5	30.0
0.4	9 [2-18]	98.8	30.0
1.0	2 [2 – 2]	99.7	30.0
Vehicle (846)			
0.1	57 [51-65]	97.3	30.5
0.4	38 [26-61]	95.5	30.5
1.0	14 [9-22]	98.3	30.5
Heart-H (294)			
0.1	14 [11-18]	95.2	21.9
0.4	2	99.3	21.9
1.0	2	99.3	21.9
Waveform (5000)			
0.1	104 [79-117]	97.9	23.4
0.4	28 [20-39]	99.4	23.4
1.0	4 [3-6]	99.9	23.4
Iris-Plants (150)			
0.1	4 [3-8]	97.3	6.0
0.4	3 [3 – 3]	98.0	6.0
1.0	3 [3 – 3]	98.0	6.0
Segmentation (2100)			
0.1	57 [48-65]	97.3	2.8
0.4	30 [24-37]	98.6	2.8
1.0	14	99.3	2.8

4. Conclusion

The goal of dataset editing in instance-based learning is to remove objects from a training set in order to increase the accuracy of the learnt classifier. This paper evaluates the benefits of Wilson editing using a benchmark consisting of eight UCI datasets. Our results show that Wilson editing enhanced the accuracy of a traditional nearest neighbor classifier on six of the eight datasets tested, achieving an average compression rate of about 20%. It is also important to note that Wilson editing, although initially proposed for nearest neighbor classification, can easily be used for other classification tasks. For example, a dataset can easily be *"Wilson edited"* by removing all training examples that have been misclassified by a decision tree classification algorithm.

In this paper, we introduced a new technique for dataset editing called supervised clustering editing (SCE). The idea of this approach is to replace a dataset by a subset of cluster prototypes. Experiments were conducted that compare the accuracy and compression rates of SCE, with Wilson editing, and with a traditional, unedited, 1-NN classifier. Results show SCE accomplished significant improvements in prediction accuracy for 3 out of the 8 datasets used in the experiments, outperforming the Wilson editing based 1-NN classifier by more than 2%. Moreover, experimental results show that for 6 out the 8 datasets tested, SCE achieves compression rates of more than 95% without significant loss in accuracy. In summary, surprisingly, high accuracy gains were achieved using only a very small number of representatives for several datasets. In general, our empirical results stress the importance of centering more research on dataset editing techniques.

5. References

[1] Eick, C., Zeidat, N., and Zhao, Z., *"Supervised Clustering – Algorithms and Applications.* submitted for publication.
[2] Penrod, C. and Wagner, T., *"Another look at the edited nearest neighbor rule"*, IEEE Trans. Syst., Man, Cyber., SMC-7:92–94, 1977.
[3] Toussaint, G., *"Proximity Graphs for Nearest Neighbor Decision Rules: Recent Progress"*, Proceedings of the 34th Symposium on the INTERFACE, Montreal, Canada, April 17-20, 2002.
[4] University of California at Irving, Machine Learning Repository. http://www.ics.uci.edu/~mlearn/MLRepository.html
[5] Wilson, D.L., *"Asymptotic Properties of Nearest Neighbor Rules Using Edited Data"*, IEEE Transactions on Systems, Man, and Cybernetics, 2:408-420, 1972.
[6] Zeidat, N., Eick, C., *"Using k-medoid Style Algorithms for Supervised Summary Generation"*, Proceedings of MLMTA, Las Vegas, June 2004.
[7] Zhao, Z., *"Evolutionary Computing and Splitting Algorithms for Supervised Clustering"*, Master's Thesis, Dept. of Computer Science, University of Houston, May 2004.

---

[2] Representatives are rarely picked at the boundaries of a region dominated by a single class, because boundary points have the tendency to attract points of neighboring regions that are dominated by other classes, therefore increasing cluster impurity.

Decision Tree Evolution Using Limited Number of Labeled Data Items from Drifting Data Streams

Wei Fan[1]   Yi-an Huang[2]   Philip S. Yu[1]

[1]IBM T. J. Watson Research, Hawthorne, NY 10532

{weifan,psyu}@us.ibm.com

[2]College of Computing, Georgia Institute of Technology, Atlanta, GA 30332

yian@cc.gatech.edu

Abstract

Most previously proposed mining methods on data streams make an unrealistic assumption that "labelled" data stream is readily available and can be mined at anytime. However, in most real-world problems, labelled data streams are rarely immediately available. Due to this reason, models are reconstructed only when labelled data become available periodically. This passive stream mining model has several drawbacks. We propose a new concept of demand-driven active data mining. In active mining, the loss of the model is either continuously guessed without using any true class labels or estimated, whenever necessary, from a small number of instances whose actual class labels are verified by paying an affordable cost. When the estimated loss is more than a tolerable threshold, the model evolves by using a small number of instances with verified true class labels. Previous work on active mining concentrates on error guess and estimation. In this paper, we discuss several approaches on decision tree evolution.

1 Introduction

Most previous work on mining data streams concentrates on capturing time-evolving trends and patterns with "labeled" data. However, one important aspect that is often ignored or unrealistically assumed is the availability of "class labels" of data streams. Most algorithms make an implicit and impractical assumption that labeled data is readily available. Most works focus on how to detect the change in patterns and how to update the model to reflect such changes when there are labelled instances to be mined. However, for many applications, the class labels are not "immediately" available unless dedicated efforts and substantial costs are spent to investigate these labels right away. If the true class labels were readily available, data mining models would not

be very useful - we might just wait. In credit card fraud detection, we usually do not know if a particular transaction is a fraud until at least one month later after the account holder receives and reviews the monthly statement. As another example, in large organizations, data mining engine normally runs on a data warehouse, while the real-time data streams are stored, processed and maintained on a separate production server. In most cases, the data on the production server is summarized, de-normalized, cleaned up and transferred to the data warehouse periodically such as over night or over the weekend. The true class labels for each transaction are usually kept and maintained in several database tables. It is very hard to provide the true labels to the learner at real time due to volume and quality issues. Most current applications obtain class labels and update existing models in preset frequency, usually synchronized with data refresh. As a summary, the passive life cycle of today's stream data mining is: "given labeled data → train initial model → classify data stream → passively wait for labeled data → re-train model ...". The effectiveness of the passive mode is dictated by some application-oriented constraints, yet not by the demand for a better model with a lower loss. Such a passive mode to mine data streams results in a number of potential undesirable consequences that contradict the notions of "streaming and continuous". If either the concept or data distribution drifts rapidly at an un-forecasted rate that application-dependent constraints do not catch up, the models is likely to be out-of-date on the data stream and important business opportunities might be missed. If there is neither conceptual nor distributional change, periodic passive model refresh and re-validation is a waste of resources.

Demand-driven Active Mining of Data Streams The demand-driven active stream data mining process is originally proposed in [Fan et al., 2004]. There are three simple steps:

1. Detect potential changes of data streams on the fly

when the existing model classifies continuous data streams. The detection process does not use or know any true labels of the stream. One of the change detection methods is a guess of the actual loss or error rate of the model on the new data stream.

2. If the guessed loss or error rate of the model in Step 1 is much higher than an application-specific tolerable maximum, we choose a small number of data records in the new data stream to investigate their true class labels. With these true class labels, we statistically estimate the true loss of the model.

3. If the statistically estimated loss in Step 2 is verified to be higher than the tolerable maximum, we reconstruct or evolve the old model using the same true class labels sampled in the previous step.

We extend the classification tree algorithm to implement active mining. Previous work in [Fan et al., 2004] concentrates on the first two steps of the active mining or error estimation. In this paper, we describe a solution to the third step or an extension to evolve existing decision trees using limited number of labelled instances.

2 The Approaches

If the loss of a decision tree on the data stream is suspected to be higher than an empirically tolerable threshold, it is necessary to reconstruct the tree in order to reduce its loss. Since the data stream doesn't have true class labels at the moment and verifying every single true class label is impossible, we choose to verify the true class labels of a small number of instances selected from the data stream. We then use these sampled true class labels to reconstruct the decision tree at the leaf node level by either replacing the class probability distribution or expanding a leaf node.

Class Distribution Replacement The basic idea is to use those examples with verified true class labels, that are classified by the leaf node, to estimate the current class probability distribution at this leaf node. When the estimated class distribution based on examples with verified true class labels is significantly different from the original class distribution at this leaf node, the class distribution will be replaced with the new distribution.

At a particular leaf, the probability distribution of class labels is a "proportion statistics". For many practical loss-function, such as 0-1 loss and cost-sensitive loss, we are only interested in the probability of one class, usually the positive or rare class. Assume that p (shorthand for $p(c|\mathbf{x})$) is the probability estimated from the sample that examples classified at this leaf node is of class c, the confidence limits

for examples classified by this leaf to be of class c is

$$p \pm \left[t\sqrt{1-f}\sqrt{pq/(n'-1)} + \frac{1}{2n'} \right] \quad (1)$$

where $q = 1 - p$, N' is the total number of examples from the data stream that is classified by the leaf, n' is the number of examples among N' that are verified with their true class labels, and $f = \frac{n'}{N'}$. Exact methods exist, however this normal approximation is good enough in practice. It is obvious that the standard error is a function of both the estimated probability p and sample size n'. When the difference in distribution is significant with high confidence and the difference results in less loss, the distribution of the sample will replace that in the leaf.

To give an example under 0-1 loss, assume that we have two labels $\{-, +\}$. The original distribution of a leaf node is $P(+|\mathbf{x}) = 0.7$ and the prediction will be $+$ since it is the majority label. If the distribution of those examples with verified true class labels is $p(+|\mathbf{x}) = 0.45$ with confidence limit of 0.1 at 99.7% confidence interval, we will change the distribution and the majority label will be - instead of +. However, if the confidence limit is 0.3, we can not make a decision, but keep the original class distribution until we can afford to verify the true class labels of more instances.

Leaf Node Expansion Leaf node expansion is necessary if the replaced class label distribution cannot improve the loss at this node. For example, under 0-1 loss, if the new distribution is 51% positive, it means that 49% of examples classified by this node as positive are actually negative. However, this leaf node can be expanded or further grown by invoking the tree growing function. Decision tree algorithms, such as C4.5, expands a node as much as possible until the number of examples reaches the minimum threshold (2 by default in C4.5). However, if the cumulative loss by growing a node into a branch is the same as the original node, the original node is kept.

3 Experiments

We conducted extensive experiments on both synthetic and real life data streams. Our goals are to evaluate the impact of the frequency and magnitude of both the distribution and concept drifts on prediction accuracy of the extended classification tree, and to analyze the advantage of our approach over complete re-training on the new data streams. The decision tree algorithm was modified from C4.5.

Streaming Data We use both synthetic dataset and real life datasets in our experiments. Detailed description about the synthetic and credit card fraud datasets can be found in [Fan et al., 2004]. The adult dataset from UCI repository. We use the natural split of training and test sets. In order to simulate pattern-drifting streams, we sample different portions of positive and negatives to generate the new data stream, i.e, {10/90,20/80,...,90/10}.

Experiment Setup Each of the three datasets have one training set and a series of data stream chucks with increasing percentage of either distribution or concept drifts from the original training set. An original classification tree, or sometimes called old decision tree in the rest of paper, is constructed from the original training set. Then the series of data stream chunks are applied on this original classification tree to compute its error. When the data stream chunks arrive, a small percentage of them are sampled to verify their true class labels to evolve the original decision tree. The resultant tree is called either evolved decision tree or reconstructed decision tree. For comparative studies, we also compute a new decision tree "from scratch" using every data item of the new data chunk.

3.1 Experimental Results

Class Distribution Replacement The results by replacing the class distribution at the leaf nodes are plotted in Figure 1. The total number of examples with verified true class labels is 10% of data item from the data stream. There are three curves in each plot. For the synthetic and adult datasets, the curve on the top is the loss of the original decision tree on the new data stream. The curve in the middle is the loss of the evolved decision tree, and the curve at the bottom is the loss of the new decision tree. Since we use benefits (average amount of recovered money per transaction) in the credit card datasets, the order of the curves reverses, i.e., the original decision tree is the one with the least benefits and it is at the bottom. To simulate concept-changing data streams, the transactions are sorted with decreasing transaction amount and the overhead to investigate a fraud is $90. The old decision tree actually starts to produce negative benefits after the x-axis is more than 5. This is because the extra overhead of false positives exceeds the amount recovered from true positives.

The general observation among all three datasets is that the evolved decision tree is lower in loss than the original decision tree. In addition, for the credit card fraud and adult datasets, the evolved decision tree has accuracy very close to that of the completely re-trained decision tree. Comparing the synthetic dataset result with that of credit card fraud and adult datasets, the evolved decision tree improved the accuracy of the old tree by a relatively small amount. We suspect this is probably due to the relative small size of the data chunk, and the algorithm cannot pass the significance test to replace the class probability distribution at most of the leaf nodes.

Leaf Node Expansion We first experimented to use the same 10% of true labels, as used in class probability distribution, to expand leaf nodes. However, most of the nodes do not have enough examples to justify the need for an expansion. We then increased the percentage to 20%. But there were still a lot of nodes that could not be expanded due to statistical insignificance. In the end, we increased the number of sampled true class labels to 30%. The plots on tree evolution via leaf node expansion are shown in Figure 2. There are 4 curves in each plot, including the loss of the original decision tree on the data streams, the loss of the reconstructed decision by leaf node expansion (either unpruned or pruned after expansion), and the loss of the newly trained decision tree on the complete data stream. The credit card dataset uses benefits (average amount of recovered money per transaction) rather than cost, and the order of the curves reverses. A pruned reconstructed decision tree removes statistically insignificant expansions of a reconstructed unpruned decision tree.

There are a few observations from the plots. Reconstructed decision tree is more accurate than the original decision tree. Pruned reconstructed decision tree is more accurate than unpruned reconstructed decision tree in general. Comparing with the results of class probability distribution replacement, as in Figure 1, evolving decision trees via leaf node expansion is more accurate than class distribution replacement only for the synthetic dataset. Leaf node expansion and class probability replacement results on credit card fraud detection and adult datasets are very similar.

4 Related Work

Data stream processing has recently become a very important research domain. Much work has been done on modeling [Babcock et al., 2002], querying [Gao and Wang, 2002], mining [Hulten et al., 2001], regression analysis [Chen et al., 2002], clustering [Guha et al., 2000] as well as visualization [Aggarwal, 2003]. A most recent updated list of stream processing related work appeared in a tutorial given in [Pei et al., 2004]. The most closely related work to this paper appears in [Fan et al., 2004]. The substantial difference of this paper from [Fan et al., 2004] is on the reconstruction of streaming models with limited number of labelled data, while the focus of [Fan et al., 2004] is on change detection and loss estimation either without labelled data or with very limited number of targeted data items. The work in this paper compliments the work of [Fan et al., 2004].

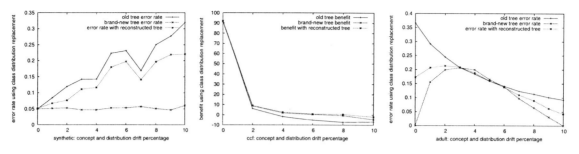

Figure 1. Loss on reconstructed tree via replacing class distribution

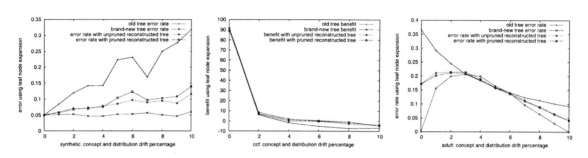

Figure 2. Loss on reconstructed tree via leaf node expansion

5 Conclusion

We extended a new framework to mine data streams that solves one important problem, that the true labels of the data stream are not immediately available. However, model evolution is necessary whenever loss of the current model is suspected to be higher than a tolerable maximum. We proposed two approaches to evolve the old decision tree by either i) replacing existing class probability distribution or, ii) expanding the leaf nodes. Experimental studies were conducted on both synthetic and real-life data streams. We have found that the evolved decision tree using from 10% to 30% of true class labels is significantly more accurate than the original decision tree on concept-drifted data streams, and is comparable to a brand new decision tree constructed using all available data items of the new data chunk. Between the two decision tree evolution methods, we also find that leaf node expansion requires more examples with true class labels than class probability distribution replacement, in order to pass the statistical significance test.

References

[Aggarwal, 2003] Aggarwal, C. C. (2003). A framework for diagnosing changes in evolving data streams. In *Proceedings of ACM SIGMO 2003*, pages 575–586.

[Babcock et al., 2002] Babcock, B., Babu, S., Datar, M., Motawani, R., and Widom, J. (2002). Models and issues in data stream systems. In *ACM Symposium on Principles of Database Systems (PODS)*.

[Chen et al., 2002] Chen, Y., Dong, G., Han, J., Wah, B. W., and Wang, J. (2002). Multi-dimensional regression analysis of time-series data streams. In *Proc. of Very Large Database (VLDB)*, Hongkong, China.

[Fan et al., 2004] Fan, W., an Huang, Y., Wang, H., and Yu, P. S. (April 2004). Active mining of data streams. In *Proceedings of 2004 SIAM International Conference on Data Mining*, pages 457–461.

[Gao and Wang, 2002] Gao, L. and Wang, X. (2002). Continually evaluating similarity-based pattern queries on a streaming time series. In *Int'l Conf. Management of Data (SIGMOD)*, Madison, Wisconsin.

[Guha et al., 2000] Guha, S., Milshra, N., Motwani, R., and O'Callaghan, L. (2000). Clustering data streams. In *IEEE Symposium on Foundations of Computer Science (FOCS)*, pages 359–366.

[Hulten et al., 2001] Hulten, G., Spencer, L., and Domingos, P. (2001). Mining time-changing data streams. In *Int'l Conf. on Knowledge Discovery and Data Mining (SIGKDD)*, pages 97–106, San Francisco, CA. ACM Press.

[Pei et al., 2004] Pei, J., Wang, H., and Yu, P. S. (August 2004). Tutorial: Online mining data streams: Problems, applications and progress. In *A tutorial for 2004 ACM SIGKDD International Conference on Knolwedge Discovery and Data Mining(KDD'2004)*, Seattle, Washington, USA.

A Machine Learning Approach to Improve Congestion Control over Wireless Computer Networks

Pierre Geurts, Ibtissam El Khayat, Guy Leduc
University of Liège, Sart Tilman, B28
Liège 4000 - Belgium
{geurts, elkhayat, leduc}@montefiore.ulg.ac.be

Abstract

In this paper, we present the application of machine learning techniques to the improvement of the congestion control of TCP in wired/wireless networks. TCP is suboptimal in hybrid wired/wireless networks because it reacts in the same way to losses due to congestion and losses due to link errors. We thus propose to use machine learning techniques to build automatically a loss classifier from a database obtained by simulations of random network topologies. Several machine learning algorithms are compared for this task and the best method for this application turns out to be decision tree boosting. It outperforms ad hoc classifiers proposed in the networking literature.

1 Introduction

Nowadays computer networks combine a large diversity of different technologies (hybrid networks that combine wired, wireless, and satellite links) and must respond to a large variety of tasks with very different requirements in terms of quality of service (e.g. e-mail, videoconference, streaming). Furthermore, the behavior of these networks depends on a large number of external factors (user behaviours, load of the networks, link capacities...) that are difficult to appraise. Hence, data mining and machine learning are certainly tools of choice to improve our understanding of networks and to help in the design of control solutions.

In this paper, we propose a specific application of machine learning techniques to the improvement of TCP over hybrid wired/wireless networks. We first discuss the drawback of TCP congestion control algorithm and how we propose to solve this problem with machine learning techniques. Section 4 then describes the database that has been generated for this study and Section 5 the different machine learning methods that have been compared. Experiments with the new protocol are described in Section 6. Further

details about this study may be found in [9] and [5].

2 TCP over wired/wireless networks

TCP, for "Transmission Control Protocol", is the most widely used protocol in the Internet. Its success lies in its reliable file transfer and its capacity in avoiding congestion. A congestion arises in the network when routers are not able to process the data that arrive to them and this causes buffer overflows at these routers that result in the loss of some packets of data. The only solution to relax a congestion is to reduce the load of the network. TCP congestion protocol is based on the definition of a congestion window that controls the rate at which packets are sent by a sender to a receiver and a mechanism to adapt the value of this window size according to the state of the network. The idea is to increase the rate steadily (i.e. additively) when everything works fine and to reduce it more abruptly (i.e. multiplicatively) as soon as a loss occurs. Further details about congestion control mechanisms in TCP may be found in RFC-2581.

This congestion control mechanism thus makes the hypothesis that packet losses are due to buffer overflows and it works fairly well in the case of wired networks where this is indeed the case. However, in wireless links, losses caused by error in the link (for example by signal fading) are not so unlikely. TCP has no mechanism to distinguish loss caused by a link error from losses caused by a congestion and it reduces systematically its rate. This reduction is not justified when there is no congestion and the consequence is that the throughput of TCP over wireless link is lower than what it could be. Several studies have highlighted the bad behaviour of TCP over wireless link (e.g. [14]).

3 Proposed machine learning solution

A straightforward solution to increase the throughput of TCP over wireless links is to prevent it from reducing its rate when it faces a loss due to a link error. The approach adopted in this paper is to endow one of the end systems (i.e the sender or the receiver) with an algorithm able to determine the cause of a packet loss only from information available at this end system. With such a classifier, the modified protocol will divide its congestion window only if the loss is classified as a congestion loss. Otherwise, it will maintain its congestion window constant.

Several rough classification rules for losses have been proposed in the literature based on heuristics or analytical derivations (e.g. in Veno [8] or Westwood [13]). In this paper, we propose to use supervised machine learning techniques to automatically derive a classification model for loss causes. This model will use as inputs statistics computed on packets received by the sender or by the receiver and it will be induced from a database obtained by simulations of random network topologies.

For this application to be practically feasible and useful, two specific constraints should be taken into account when choosing a classifier. First, because classifications are done in real-time, the computing times to make a prediction and the computer resource needed to store the model are not to be neglected. Second, since TCP is so popular in nowadays networks, any new protocol should be TCP-Friendly ([11]). A TCP-Friendly protocol is a protocol that, when sharing the network with TCP, allows this latter to have a throughput similar to the one it would get if it were in competition with another TCP in similar conditions.

In [5], we show that it is possible to derive analytically an upper bound on the misclassification error on congestion losses that ensures TCP-friendliness. This bound is of the form:

$$Err_C \leq f(RTT, p), \qquad (1)$$

where Err_C is the probability of misclassifying a congestion loss as a link error loss, RTT is the round-trip-time[1], and p is the actual loss rate, i.e. the percentage of lost packets whatever the cause. Since this bound may change with time, our solution to ensure TCP-friendliness will be to dynamically adapt the classifier such that it always satisfies the constraint given the current RTT and p values.

4 Database generation

To solve our problem of loss classification, each observation $< x_i, y_i >$ of our learning sample will be an input/output pair where the inputs x_i are some variables that describe the state of the network at the occurrence of a loss and the (discrete) output y_i is either C to denote a loss due to a congestion or LE to denote a loss due to a link error.

The database[2] was generated by simulations with a net-

---

[1] the time between the sending of a packet and the reception of its acknowledgment by the sender

[2] The database is available electronically at http://www.montefiore.ulg.ac.be/~geurts/publications/BD-Fifo.dat.gz.

work simulator called ns-2[12]. To generate our observations of losses, we have used the following procedure: a network topology is generated randomly and then the network is simulated during a fixed amount of time, again by generating the traffic randomly. At the end of the simulation, all losses that have occurred within this time interval are collected in the database. In our study, we have collected 35,441 losses (among which 22,426 are due to congestion) that correspond to more than one thousand different random network topologies.

At the end system (sender or receiver), the only information we can measure to predict a congestion is some statistics on the packet departure and arrival times. So, to define our inputs, we have computed different statistics relating the one-way delay and the inter-packet time of several packets surrounding the loss. All in all, this results in a set of 40 numerical input variables.

5 Machine learning techniques

In this study, we propose to compare several machine learning algorithms which are:

Decision trees. The main advantage of this method for our application is that pruned trees are usually quite small and the computation of a prediction is very fast. To build a decision tree, we have adopted the standard CART algorithm described in [4].

Decision tree ensembles. Ensemble methods are generic techniques that improve a learning algorithm by learning several models and then by aggregating their predictions. In our experiment, we have compared four ensemble methods that have been proposed for decision trees, namely Bagging [2], Random forests [3], Boosting [7], and Extra-trees [10]. All these methods have been used with their default parameter setting.

Artificial Neural Networks. This method usually gives more accurate models than decision trees but it is also much more demanding in terms of computing times and computer resources. In our experiments, we have used multilayer perceptrons with Levenberg-Marquardt optimization [1].

k-Nearest Neighbors. An important drawback of this method for this application is that the computation of a prediction is quite demanding and furthermore it requires to store the entire learning sample.

As discussed above, one important characteric of the chosen classifier is that it should be possible to adjust its error on congestion losses dynamically to ensure TCP-friendliness. Actually, all these methods not only provide a class prediction for each value of the inputs x but also provide an estimate of the conditional probability of each class, C or LE, given the inputs x. In the two class case, the default use of the model is to classify a loss as a congestion loss if the probability estimate $\hat{P}(C|x)$ is greater than 0.5.

However, by using a user defined threshold P_{th} different from 0.5, we can change the misclassification probability of each class and hence adjust our classifier to satisfy (1).

A natural way to evaluate our models independently of the value of P_{th} is to use receiver operating characterisic (ROC) curves (see [6] for an introduction). A ROC curve plots for every possible value of the threshold P_{th} the true positive rate versus the false positive rate of a given class (among two classes). In our case, the true positive rate is taken as $1 - Err_C$ and the false positive rate is the probability of misclassifying a link error loss, that will be denoted Err_{LE}. While ROC curves are two-dimensional, a common one-dimensional summary of a ROC curve to compare classifiers is the area under the ROC curve (AUC) which we will also use to rank our packet loss classifiers. ROC curves and AUC are computed according to the algorithms presented in [6].

6 Experiments

First, we evaluate classifiers and then we evaluate the new protocol with the best classifier only.

6.1 Comparison of loss classifiers

To make a reliable estimate of the error of each model, we have randomly divided the whole database into two parts: a learning set of 25,000 cases and a validation set containing the remaining 10,441 cases. A classification model is built with every method on the learning sample and its ROC curve, AUC, and error rate are evaluated on the validation sample. The methods are compared from these criteria in Table 1 and in Figure 1. We also give in Table 1 the time needed to classify the validation set with each method. For ensemble methods, we build $T = 25$ trees. As the ROC curves of all ensemble methods are very close, we only give the results obtained by boosting in Figure 1. The value of k for the k nearest neighbors was determined by leave-one-out cross-validation (the optimum is $k = 7$). For the MLP, we tried several structures of one and two layers with a number of neurons going from 10 to 50 neurons in each layer. Table 1 only shows the best result that was obtained with two layers of 30 neurons.

The results are quite good considering the diversity of the network topologies represented in the database. The decision tree has the lowest AUC but it is by far the fastest method to make a prediction. The k-NN has a better AUC than decision tree but its ROC curve is worst for small values of Err_C, which is the region of interest of our application. It is also the slowest method in terms of computing times. MLP improves upon both methods in terms of accuracy but it remains below ensemble methods in terms of

Table 1. Comparison of different ML methods

Method	AUC	Error (%)	Time (msec)
DT	0.9424	8.92	150
Bagging	0.9796	6.65	650
Random forests	0.9823	6.48	600
Extra-trees	0.9813	6.91	940
Boosting	0.9840	6.34	570
MLP	0.9761	7.67	1680
k-NN	0.9541	10.16	316,870
Veno	0.7260	34.52	-
Westwood	0.6627	41.54	-

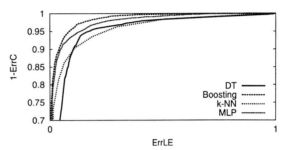

Figure 1. Comparison of the ROC curves of different ML methods

accuracy and computing times. All ensemble methods are very close but boosting is superior along the two criteria.

For comparison, we put also in Table 1 the result obtained on the validation set by two ad-hoc classification rules that have been proposed in the networking literature in the context of two extensions of TCP for wireless networks called Veno [8] and Westwood [13]. The results obtained by these rules are far below the results obtained by machine learning algorithms. This clearly shows the interest of a machine learning approach in the context of this application, both to improve existing classifiers but also to assess their validity.

6.2 Simulations of the modified protocol

We propose to use the boosting classifier in the following way to improve TCP. Each time a loss occurs, the minimal value of P_{th} such that (1) is satisfied is determined from the current (estimated) values of RTT and p. Then, the ensemble of trees together with this value of P_{th} are used to classify the loss. If the loss is predicted as caused by a congestion, TCP works as usual. Otherwise, it maintains its congestion window constant.

The main criteria to evaluate this protocol are bandwidth usage in the case of wireless links and TCP-friendliness in the case of wired networks. In this paper, we only describe two simple experiments showing the interest of the machine

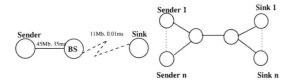

Figure 2. Two topologies used in simulations

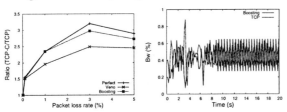

Figure 3. Top, the gain in wireless link, bottom, TCP-Friendliness

learning solution along these criteria. A more detailed validation of the protocol may be found in [5].

Improvement on wireless links. To illustrate the gain of our protocol over wireless link, we simulated the simple hybrid network illustrated in the left part of Figure 2 with ns-2. The first link is wired and the second one that constitutes the bottleneck is wireless. We compare the ratio between the throughput obtained by the classifier and the one obtained by a standard TCP when we vary the packet loss rate from 0 to 5% over the wireless link. To have some points of comparison, we run also simulations with the classification rule proposed in Veno and, as our system is simulated, with a hypothetic perfect classification rule. The left graph of Figure 3 illustrates the ratio obtained by TCP enhanced with the three classifiers. The superiority of boosting over Veno and standard TCP is clear. It is also very close to the perfect model. Its gain with respect to TCP reaches about 300% when the loss rate is equal to 3%.

TCP-friendliness. To test the behaviour of our protocol when it competes with another TCP, we use the classical topology in the right part of Figure 2 with $n = 2$. The experiment consists in running a standard TCP in competition with our TCP plus the boosting classifier. The right part of Figure 3 shows the evolution of the throughput obtained by each traffic. This figure shows that the link is fairly shared between the two protocols. The same experiment was run with Veno's classification rules and in this case, the bandwidth used by Veno was five times higher than that of TCP.

7 Conclusions

In this paper, we have presented the application of machine learning techniques to the improvement of conges-

tion control protocol in wireless networks. The application of the boosting classifier shows a significant improvement of bandwidth usage in wireless networks and no deterioration in traditional wired networks. The resulting classifier also compares very favorably to existing ad-hoc classification rules that have been proposed in the networking literature. This study thus shows the interest of the application of machine learning techniques to help designing new protocol in computer networks.

Acknowledgment

This work has been partially supported by the Belgian Science Policy in the framework of the IAP program (Motion P5/11 project). P. Geurts is a post-doctoral researcher at the FNRS, Belgium.

References

[1] C. Bishop. *Neural Networks for Pattern Recognition*. Oxford: Oxford University Press, 1995.

[2] L. Breiman. Bagging predictors. *Machine Learning*, 24(2):123–140, 1996.

[3] L. Breiman. Random forests. *Machine learning*, 45:5–32, 2001.

[4] L. Breiman, J. Friedman, R. Olsen, and C. Stone. *Classification and Regression Trees*. Wadsworth International (California), 1984.

[5] I. El Khayat, P. Geurts, and G. Leduc. Classification of packet loss causes in wired/wireless networks by decision tree boosting. Technical report, University of Liège, 2004.

[6] T. Fawcett. Roc graphs: Notes and practical considerations for researchers. Technical report, HP Labs, 2004.

[7] Y. Freund and R. E. Schapire. A decision-theoretic generalization of on-line learning and an application to boosting. In *Proceedings of the second European Conference on Computational Learning Theory*, pages 23–27, 1995.

[8] C. P. Fu and S. C. Liew. TCP veno: TCP enhancement for transmission over wireless access networks. *IEEE (JSAC) Journal of Selected Areas in Communications*, Feb. 2003.

[9] P. Geurts, I. El Khayat, and G. Leduc. A machine learning approach to improve congestion control over wireless computer networks. Technical report, University of Liège, 2004.

[10] P. Geurts, D. Ernst, and L. Wehenkel. Extremely randomized trees. Submitted, 2004.

[11] M. Mathis, J. Semke, Mahdavi, and T. Ott. The macroscopic behavior of the TCP congestion avoidance algorithm. *ACM Computer Communication Review*, 3:67–82, July 1997.

[12] S. McCanne and S. Floyd. *The LBNL Network Simulator*. Lawrence Berkeley Laboratory, 1997.

[13] R. Wang, M. Valla, M. Sanadidi, B. Ng, and M. Gerla. Efficiency/friendliness tradeoffs in TCP westwood. In *In Proceedings of the 7th IEEE Symposium on Computers and Communications*, 2002.

[14] G. Xylomenos, G. Polyzos, P. Mahonen, and M. Saaranen. TCP performance issues over wireless links. *Communications Magazine, IEEE*, 39(4):52–58, 2001.

LOADED: Link-based Outlier and Anomaly Detection in Evolving Data Sets

Amol Ghoting, Matthew Eric Otey and Srinivasan Parthasarathy *
Department of Computer Science and Engineering, The Ohio State University
{ghoting, otey, srini}@cse.ohio-state.edu

Abstract

In this paper, we present LOADED, an algorithm for outlier detection in evolving data sets containing both continuous and categorical attributes. LOADED is a tunable algorithm, wherein one can trade off computation for accuracy so that domain-specific response times are achieved. Experimental results show that LOADED provides very good detection and false positive rates, which are several times better than those of existing distance-based schemes.

1 Introduction

Webster's Dictionary defines an outlier as "one which lies, or is, away from the main body." In the context of this work, an outlier is a sample point that is distinct from most, if not all, other points in the data set. The problem of efficient outlier detection has recently drawn increased attention due to its wide applicability in areas such as fraud and intrusion detection [4, 14], data cleaning, and scientific and biomedical analysis [13].

There are several approaches to outlier detection. One approach is that of model-based outlier detection, where the data is assumed to follow a parametric (typically univariate) distribution [2]. Such approaches do not work well in even moderately high-dimensional spaces and finding the right model is often a difficult task in its own right. To overcome these limitations, researchers have turned to various non-parametric approaches including clustering-based approaches [8, 14], distance-based approaches [3, 9] and density-based approaches [5, 12] that characterize outliers based on their distance from "normal" points in the data set. There are several challenges that still need to be addressed.

First, almost all non-parametric approaches rely on some well-defined notion of distance to measure the proximity between two data points. However, many real-world data sets contain not only continuous attributes, but *categorical* attributes as well, which have serious implications for a well-defined notion of distance. Simply disregarding categorical attributes may result in the loss of information important for effective outlier detection. Moreover, distance in this categorical space being ill-defined, finding an overall distance in the combined space of categorical and continuous attributes is no longer an additive operation. We address this challenge by defining a metric that allows for outlier detection using efficient determination of dependencies (a) within a categorical attribute space, (b) within a continuous attribute space and (c) between categorical and continuous attributes.

Second, an outlier detection scheme needs to be sensitive to *response time constraints* imposed by the domain. For instance, an application such as network intrusion detection requires on-the-fly outlier detection. Most existing distance-based approaches require multiple passes over the data set which, if not impossible, are prohibitive in such a scenario. To address this challenge we present an efficient *flexible-pass* algorithm (including a single pass version suitable for streaming data), LOADED, that can be tuned to application needs.

2 Algorithms

Capturing dependencies using Links: Informally, two data points p_i and p_j are considered linked if they are considerably similar to each other. Moreover, associated with each link is a link strength, which captures the degree of linkage, and is determined using a similarity metric defined on the two points. We consider a data set M in which, each data point (record) p_i has N categorical attributes. We represent p_i as an ordered set $\{(attribute_1, value_1), \ldots, (attribute_N, value_N)\}$ consisting of N attribute-value pairs. Two data points p_i and p_j are *linked* in a categorical attribute space if they have at least one attribute-value pair in common. The associated link strength is equal to the number of attribute-value pairs shared in common between the two points.

Using these definitions, we define an outlier in a categorical attribute space as a data point that has either (a) very few links to other points or (b) very weak links to other points. A score function that would generate high scores for outliers would assign scores to a point that are inversely proportional to the sum of the strengths of all its links. To estimate this score efficiently, we rely on ideas from frequent itemset mining. Let I be the set of all possible attribute-value pairs in the data set M. Let $D = \{d : d \in PowerSet(I) \land \forall_{i,j:i\neq j} d_i.attribute \neq d_j.attribute\}$, the set of all itemsets, where an attribute only occurs once per itemset. We define $sup(d)$ as the number of points p_i in the data set where $d \subseteq p_i$, otherwise known as the *support* of d. We also define $|d|$ as the number of attribute-value pairs in d.

We can then define our score function as:

$$Score_1(p_i) = \sum_{d \subseteq p_i} \left(\frac{1}{|d|} : sup(d) \leq s \right)$$

where the user-defined threshold s is the minimum support. The score is proportional to the number of *infrequent* itemsets, and inversely proportional to the size of those infrequent itemsets (i.e. the link strength). We note that the function $sup(d)$ has the downward-closure (*apriori*) property.

* This work is supported by an NSF CAREER grant (IIS-0347662), an NSF NGS grant (CNS-0406386) and a grant from Pfizer Inc.

Lemma 1 *If* $sup(d) > s$ *then* $sup(d') > s$ $\forall d' \subseteq d$.

Approximation scheme: We also note that the number of itemsets is, in the worst case, exponential in the number of categorical attributes. To alleviate this problem, we use the above property to precisely estimate the score for a point by only maintaining frequency counts for itemsets that are in the positive border of the itemset lattice. We can also get an approximate solution by only maintaining and using itemsets between the positive border and some maximal set size $MAXLEVEL$, where $MAXLEVEL < N$. The key benefit here is improved execution time, as a smaller subset of the itemset lattice will be maintained, with only a small cost to accuracy.

Handling Mixed Attribute Data: As motivated previously, we would like to capture the dependencies between the continuous and categorical attributes in a domain-independent manner. We choose a unified approach to capture these dependencies. We incrementally maintain a correlation matrix that stores Pearson's Correlation Coefficient between every pair of continuous attributes. This matrix is maintained for each itemset in D. Since we are maintaining this matrix for each itemset, we are inherently capturing the dependence between the values in the categorical and continuous data spaces. We note that this can lead to large memory requirements in high dimensional data sets and we address this by storing a discretized representation of the true correlation coefficients such that each value is stored in a byte. We maintain 256 equi-width bins to represent the range (-1,1). Furthermore, the approximation scheme presented above allows us to relax the memory requirements even further.

A point is defined to be linked to another point in the mixed data space if they are linked together in the categorical data space and if their continuous attributes adhere to the joint distribution as indicated by the correlation matrix. Points that violate these conditions are defined to be outliers. We modify our score function for mixed attribute data as follows.

$$Score_2(p_i) = \sum_{d \subseteq p_i} \left(\frac{1}{|d|} : (C1 \vee C2) \wedge C3 \text{ is true} \right)$$

where *C1*: $sup(d) \leq s$, *C2*: at least $\delta\%$ of the correlation coefficients disagree with the distribution followed by the continuous attributes for point p_i, and *C3*: *C1* or *C2* hold true for every superset of d in p_i. Condition *C1* is the same condition used to find outliers in a categorical data space using $Score_1$. Condition *C2* adds continuous attribute checks to $Score_1$. Condition *C3* is a heuristic and allows for more efficient processing because if an itemset does not satisfy conditions *C1* and *C2*, then none of its subsets will be considered. The rationale for *C3* is as follows. First, as stated by the Apriori property in Lemma 1, subsets of frequent itemsets will also be frequent and thus, will not satisfy *C1*. Second, correlation coefficients intuitively tend to be less discriminatory as the size of the itemset is reduced and thus, are less likely to satisfy *C2*.

The LOADED Algorithm: LOADED finds outliers based on the score estimation function $Score_2$. It also provides extensions to operate over dynamic data and supports intelligent itemset lattice management.

Score estimation using LOADED: The LOADED algorithm for outlier detection is presented in Figure 1. The score function $Score_2$ requires that we iterate over all possi-

```
Procedure: Find Outliers
Input: FrequencyThreshold, CorrelationThreshold, ΔScore,
        ScoreWindowSize, MAXLEVEL
Output: Outliers discovered in one pass
  For each incoming point p:
    G = Enumeration of all itemsets of size MAXLEVEL for point p
    For each g ∈ G
      Get frequency count freq for g from the hash table
      Update frequency and correlation coefficients for g in the hash table
      If freq < FrequencyThreshold
        score = score + 1/|g|
        Add all subsets of g of size |g| − 1 into G
        If these subsets of g do not have an entry in the hash table
          Get precise a frequency count from MAXLEVEL itemsets
          Insert frequency count into hash table
      Else
        If number of continuous attribute pairs that disagree with
          the correlation coefficients > CorrelationThreshold
          score = score + 1/|g|
          Add all subsets of g of size |g| − 1 into G
          If these subsets of g do not have an entry in the hash table
            Get precise a frequency count from MAXLEVEL itemsets
            Insert frequency count into hash table
    End For
    If score > (Avg. score in ScoreWindow × ΔScore)
      Flag as Outlier
    Else
      Normal
      Update the Score window of size ScoreWindowSize if the point is normal
  End For
end
```

Figure 1. The LOADED Algorithm for outlier detection

ble itemsets in $PowerSet(p_i)$. There are several approaches to maintaining frequency counts for these subsets, such as Lossy Counting [11], or using a disk-based approach [6] that retrieves counts from disk when needed. However, these approaches are expensive and so are not suitable for our algorithm. One of the ways to make the algorithm efficient is to minimize the number of itemsets in the itemset lattice that we must examine when a new point arrives. Lemma 1 states the Apriori property that if an itemset is frequent then all of its subsets must also be frequent. An anomaly score for a point is calculated based on the number of infrequent itemsets that it contains (as per function $Score_1$). Furthermore, due to condition *C3*, we need only access all itemsets at or above the positive border of the itemset lattice. Since the positive border can shift during execution, we may later need frequency counts for itemsets below the current positive border. By Lemma 2 we can obtain frequency for these itemsets when necessary.

Lemma 2 *The frequency of itemset* $g \in G$ *(Figure 1) can be precisely estimated using frequency counts from all* $MAXLEVEL$ *itemsets in* G.

Extensions for Dynamic Data: As motivated previously, several applications (e.g. network intrusion detection) demand outlier detection over dynamic data. In order to capture concept drift and other dynamics of the data, we need to update our model to capture the most recent trends in the data. We achieve this by introducing a bias towards recent data. We maintain the itemsets together with their frequency counts in a hash table and the bias is introduced in the following two ways. First, we maintain an itemset together with its frequency count in the hash table only if it appears at least once every W points. Second, the frequency for every itemset in the hash table will be decremented by a value Δf every W points. We apply these biases using smart hash-table management coupled with a down-counting approach described in Figure 2.

```
┌─────────────────────────────────────────────────────┐
│ Hash Table Management:                                │
│ Let i be the index of the point that just arrived     │
│ If i mod W = 0,                                       │
│    Then create a new hash table with index i div W    │
│    delete the hash table with index i div W − 2       │
│                                                       │
│                                                       │
│ Frequency Estimation:                                 │
│ When estimating the frequency for an itemset          │
│ from a point with index i:                            │
│ If an itemset for the iᵗʰ point is found in hash table │
│    with index i div W                                 │
│    Increment and use the freq. from this hash table   │
│ Else                                                  │
│    If itemset is found in hash table with index i div W − 1 │
│       insert it into the hash table with index i div W, │
│       set freq = freq in table (i div W − 1) + 1 − Δf  │
│       and then use this freq.                         │
│    Else                                               │
│       insert it into the hash table with index i div W │
│       with freq. = 1                                  │
└─────────────────────────────────────────────────────┘
```

Figure 2. Algorithm for hash table management and frequency estimation

For every W points, we create a new hash table and delete the oldest hash table. Thus, at every instant in time, we maintain at most two hash tables. We estimate the frequency for an itemset based on the its frequency in the two hash tables. Moreover, for every W points, relevant itemsets will have their frequencies biased with a value of $-\Delta f$. The oldest hash table is deleted every W points and the two most recent hash tables will contain all the relevant itemsets with their biased frequencies.

Single-Pass vs Multi-Pass LOADED: For an application such as network intrusion detection, providing an interactive response time is crucial. This enforces a one-pass processing requirement over the data set and the score is estimated using itemset frequency counts maintained over a recent window of time. On the other hand, an application may need a higher detection accuracy, arguing for a two-pass approach. In the first pass, we find itemset frequency counts over the entire data set and in the second pass, we find outliers based on what we have learned. The two-pass approach is beneficial as points that were mistaken as outliers during the first pass (due to a lack of information about the entire data set) will not be flagged as outliers in the second pass.

Complexity: LOADED's time complexity grows linearly in the size of the data set and quadratically in the number of continuous attributes. We partially alleviate the complexity associated with the expensive operation of lattice management by operating between $MAXLEVEL$ and the positive border. Moreover, a decade of research [1] has shown that under practical considerations, an itemset lattice can be managed in an efficient and scalable fashion, which is also evident in our experimental results.

3 Experimental Results

All experiments were performed on a 1GHz Pentium III processor with 1GB RAM running Linux kernel 2.4. We evaluate LOADED[1] using the following real data sets[2]: (a) The KDDCup 1999 network intrusion detection data set with labels indicating attack type (32 continuous and 9 categorical

---

[1] For all experiments unless otherwise noted, we run LOADED with the following parameter settings: *FrequencyThreshold=10, CorrelationThreshold=0.3, ΔScore=10, ScoreWindowSize=40.*

[2] We have also evaluated LOADED over other real data sets with good results, but due to space limitations those results are not included in this paper.

Attack Type	Detection Rate (10% Training) LOADED/ORCA	Detection Rate (Testing) LOADED/ORCA	Detection Rate (Training) LOADED
Apache 2	n/a	100%/0%	n/a
Buffer Overflow	94%/63%	90%/100%	91%
Back	100%/5%	n/a	97%
FTP Write	28%/88%	n/a	33%
Guess Password	100%/21%	100%/0%	100%
Imap	100%/13%	n/a	100%
IP Sweep	42%/3%	28%/0%	37%
Land	100%/66%	n/a	100%
Load Module	100%/100%	n/a	100%
Multihop	94%/57%	100%/75%	94%
Named	n/a	100%/40%	n/a
Neptune	92%/1%	n/a	98%
Nmap	94%/8%	n/a	91%
Perl	100%/100%	n/a	100%
Phf	0%/25%	20%/100%	0%
Pod	45%/12%	100%/18%	53%
Port Sweep	100%/13%	100%/3%	100%
Root Kit	33%/70%	n/a	33%
Satan	75%/9%	n/a	72%
Saint	n/a	100%/1%	n/a
Sendmail	n/a	50%/50%	n/a
Smurf	24%/1%	21%/0%	22%
Snmpgetattack	n/a	52%/0%	n/a
Spy	100%/100%	n/a	100%
Teardrop	50%/1%	n/a	49%
Udpstorm	n/a	0%/0%	n/a
Warez Client	48%/3%	n/a	43%
Warez Master	0%/15%	n/a	0%
Xlock	n/a	50%/66%	n/a
Xsnoop	n/a	100%/100%	n/a

Table 1. Detection rates - LOADED (single pass) and ORCA on 10% KDDCup1999 training data set and entire testing data set, LOADED (single pass) on entire training data set

attributes); (b) the Adult data set extracted from US Census Bureau's Income data set with labels indicating the individual's yearly income level (6 continuous and 8 categorical attributes); (c) the Congressional Votes data set consisting of a representatives votes on 16 issues together with a label indicating if the representative was a Republican or Democrat (16 categorical attributes).

Qualitative Evaluation: *KDDCup 1999:* We modified the KDDCup data set to ensure that attacks (outliers) comprise 2% of the data set as the original data set has an unrealistic percentage of attacks[3]. We compare our approach against ORCA [3] [4] which uses the Euclidean and Hamming distances as similarity measures for continuous and categorical attributes respectively. ORCA finds the top-k outliers in a data set, with k being a user supplied parameter. We set k equal to the number of outliers in the data set. For the comparison between ORCA and LOADED, we used the 10% subset of the KDDCup 1999 training data as well as the testing data set, as ORCA did not complete in a reasonable amount of time on the full training data set. We do present results of LOADED on the full training and testing data set. Detection rates for the two approaches are reported in Table 1 (Note that "n/a" indicates that the attack was not present in the particular data set). Overall, our detection rates are very good and much higher than those detected by ORCA. *Our approach gives us a false positive rate of 0.35%, which is extremely good for anomaly detection schemes, especially considering our high detection rates.* ORCA has a false positive rate of 0.43%, but this is not as significant considering its lower detection rates.

---

[3] This reflects typical intrusion scenario and details are provided in a related report [7]

[4] We would like to thank Stephen Bay for providing us with his implementation of ORCA.

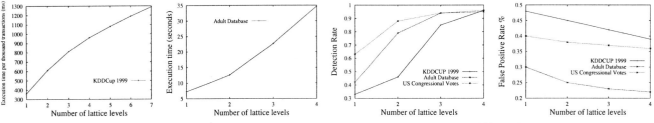

Figure 3. (a) and (b) - Execution time variation with increase in lattice levels, (c) and (d) - Detection and false positive rates

LOADED's low false positive rate can be attributed to a better representation for anomalous behavior obtained by capturing the dependence between categorical attributes and their associated continuous attributes. The attacks in the training data set for which we do poorly are *Phf, Warez Master, FTP Write, IP Sweep, Smurf* and *Rootkit*. For *Phf, Warez Master* and *FTP Write*, ORCA is able to provide better detection rates but for the others it does worse, sometimes significantly so. The intrusions for which LOADED does poorly are detected in a second pass of the algorithm. The rationale for this behavior can be explained by the distribution of their arrivals. For instance, *smurf* attacks, which tend to be grouped attacks (DOS), arrive in the first part of the data set. In our one-pass algorithm the first few *smurf* attacks are flagged but the later ones are not since at that point in time only a small part of the data set has been read and the percentage contribution of smurfs is quite high. A similar rationale extends to the other intrusions with low detection rates. On the testing data set our approach is able to detect most of the unknown attacks (a problem for almost all of the KDDCup 1999 participants). Note that our approach is a general anomaly detection scheme and has not been trained to catch specific intrusions – one can use this approach in conjunction with a signature detector to handle this problem [10]. In terms of execution time, LOADED processed the 10% sample of the KDDCup 1999 training data set in approximately 8 *minutes*. ORCA, on the other hand, took 212 *minutes* to process the same data set.

Adult Database: This being a static data set is processed in two passes. Here we are unable to make a comparison with ORCA, since this data set does not provide us with labeled outliers. The following data records are marked as the top outliers: *(a) A 39 year old self-employed male with a doctorate, working in a Clerical position making less than 50,000 dollars per year (b) A 42 year old self-employed male from Iran, with a bachelors degree, working in an Executive position making less than 50,000 dollars per year (c) A 38 year old Canadian female with an Asian Pacific Islander origin working for the US Federal Government for 57 hrs per week and making more than 50,000 dollars per year.* Apart from these, the other outliers we find tend to come from persons from foreign countries that are not well represented in this data set.

Congressional Votes: As in the previous case, this data set was processed in two passes. We are unable to compare with ORCA because, as in the previous case, this data set does not contain labeled outliers. Many of the top outliers contain large numbers of missing values, though there are examples in which this is not the case. One such example is a Republican congressman, who has four missing values, but also voted significantly differently from his party on four other bills. According to the conditional probability tables supplied with the data set, the likelihood of a Republican voting in a such a

manner is very low.

Benefits of the Approximation Scheme: In our experiments, we measure the execution time, detection rate and the false positive rate as a function of the number of itemset lattice levels maintained. The primary benefit of our approximation scheme is that far better execution times can be achieved if we maintain fewer lattice levels, as can be seen in Figure 3. However, our false positive rates increase and detection rates decrease as the number of lattice levels decrease. From Figure 3, one can see that number of lattice levels has a greater affect on the detection rate in the case of the KDDCup data set than in the other data sets. This can be attributed to larger categorical attribute dependencies being used in the detection process for the KDDCup data set. The number of lattice levels maintained does not affect the false positive rate as much as they affect the detection rate. We also note that the processing rate per 1000 network transactions is within reasonable response time rates even for a lattice level equal to four. Ideally, one would like to tune the application based on the learning curves in an application specific manner, as each application will exhibit a specific dependence behavior. Empirically, it appears from Figure 3 that execution time grows near-linearly with the number of lattice levels.

4 Conclusion

Applying existing distance-based outlier detection algorithms to mixed attribute data has a major limitation in that distance is ill-defined in the categorical data space. In this paper, we presented LOADED, an algorithm that uses a robust unifying similarity metric that combines a link-based approach (for categorical attributes) with correlation statistics (for continuous attributes). It is a flexible-pass algorithm that can operate on evolving data sets, with an approximation mechanism to reduce its memory requirements and execution time, with a small cost to accuracy. We evaluated LOADED on several real mixed attribute data sets with good results.

References

[1] R. Agrawal and R. Srikant. Fast algorithms for mining association rules. In *VLDB*, 1994.

[2] V. Barnett and T. Lewis. *Outliers in Statistical Data*, 1994.

[3] S. Bay and M. Schwabacher. Mining distance-based outliers in near linear time with randomization and a simple pruning rule. In *SIGKDD*, 2003.

[4] R. Bolton and D. Hand. Statistical fraud detection: A review. In *Statistical Science*, 2002.

[5] M. Breunig *et al.* LOF: Identifying density-based local outliers. In *SIGMOD*, 2000.

[6] A. Ghoting and S. Parthasarathy. DASPA: A disk-aware stream processing architecture. In *SIAM High Performance Data Mining Workshop*, 2003.

[7] A. Ghoting *et al.* LOADED: Link-based outlier and anomaly detection in evolving data sets. Technical report, CSE,The Ohio State University, 2004.

[8] S. Guha *et al.* ROCK: A robust clustering algorithm for categorical attributes. In *Information Systems*, 2000.

[9] E. Knorr *et al.* Distance-based outliers: Algorithms and applications. In *VLDB Journal*, 2000.

[10] M. Mahoney and P. Chan. Learning non-stationary models of normal network traffic for detecting novel attacks. In *SIGKDD*, 2002.

[11] G. Manku and R. Motwani. Approximate frequency counts over data streams. In *VLDB*, 2002.

[12] S. Papadimitriou *et al.* LOCI: Fast outlier detection using the local correlation integral. In *ICDE*, 2003.

[13] K. Penny *et al.* A comparison of multivariate outlier detection methods for clinical laboratory safety data. *The Statistician, Journal of the Royal Statistical Society*, 2001.

[14] K. Sequeira and M. Zaki. ADMIT: Anomaly-based data mining for intrusions. In *SIGKDD*, 2002.

SVD based Term Suggestion and Ranking System

David Gleich
Harvey Mudd College
Claremont, CA
dgleich@cs.hmc.edu

Leonid Zhukov
Yahoo! Research Labs
Pasadena, CA
leonid.zhukov@overture.com

Abstract

In this paper, we consider the application of the singular value decomposition (SVD) to a search term suggestion system in a pay-for-performance search market. We propose a novel positive and negative refinement method based on orthogonal subspace projections. We demonstrate that SVD subspace-based methods: 1) expand coverage by reordering the results, and 2) enhance the clustered structure of the data. The numerical experiments reported in this paper were performed on Overture's pay-per-performance search market data.

1. Introduction

In a pay-for-performance search market, advertisers compete in online auctions by bidding on search terms for sponsored listings in affiliated search engines. Because of the competitive nature of the market, each search term may have bids from many advertisers, and almost every advertiser bids on more than one search term. The practical motivation for our work was creating a "term suggestion" tool, which, for any given search term, provides a sorted list of relevant search term suggestions from the existing database. One of the desired features of this term suggestion tool is a smoothly controlled level of "generality" of suggested terms. To that end, we decided to use both a vector space model and a singular value decomposition (SVD) [5] based approach to term ranking and suggestion.

It is well known that Latent Semantic Indexing (LSI) [3, 4], an SVD based-method, can help to expose semantic information within a dataset. Most papers cite the use of LSI to enhance text information retrieval systems [1]. In this context, LSI is used to compute a document-query similarity score for each document in the collection. However, as noticed in [3], we can also compute the similarity between documents and other documents, between documents and terms, and between terms and other terms. In this paper, we focus on using SVD for term-term similarity.

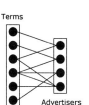
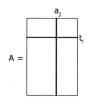

(a) Bipartite Graph Representation.

(b) Vector Space Representation.

Figure 1. Data representation.

The vector space approach allows retrieval of all terms directly correlated with the search term – we call this an exact match. Using SVD, we can also perform a conceptual match [1, 3], which might expand the number of suggested terms and also change their ranking. In other words, SVD enables us to match terms globally, or conceptually, without the need for explicit connections.

The main goal of this paper is to investigate the use of SVD as a suggestion tool for relational data, establish a better understanding of its behavior, and provide a new method for interactive refinement of search results.

2. Data

In this study, we use a small, densely connected subset of Overture's US market data with 10,000 bidded search terms, 8,850 advertisers, and more than 250,000 bids.

The "advertiser–search term" relationship can be represented by a bipartite graph with edges connecting advertisers to keywords. The advertisers are on one side of the graph and the keywords are on the other side as depicted in Fig. 1(a). The edges of the graph might also contain bid values. In this representation all correlated terms are connected through the same advertiser, i.e. are next nearest neighbors.

An alternative representation for the data can be given by an "advertiser–search term" matrix, A, Fig. 1(b) whose columns correspond to advertisers and rows to bidded search terms. The number of rows in this matrix, m, is equal to the number of unique bidded search terms, and the number of columns, n, is the number of unique advertisers active on the market. Thus, every column of this matrix represents an advertiser vector described in the bidded terms space and every row is a bidded term vector in the advertiser space.

The matrix A is strictly non-negative and sparse. It is normalized using the binary frequency variant of term-frequency, inverse document frequency normalization [1].

3. Method

Similarity Measure For any two terms, t_i and t_j, we define the similarity metric as a cosine of the angle between corresponding vectors,

$$sim(t_i, t_j) = \cos(t_i, t_j) = \frac{t_i^T \cdot t_j}{||t_i|| \, ||t_j||}. \quad (1)$$

In a subspace defined by its orthogonal projection $\hat{P}_k$, the similarity (cosine of the angle) between vector projections is

$$sim(\hat{P}_k t_i, \hat{P}_k t_j) = \frac{(\hat{P}_k t_i)^T \cdot (\hat{P}_k t_i)}{||\hat{P}_k t_i|| \, ||\hat{P}_k t_j||}. \quad (2)$$

Below we consider an orthogonal subspace constructed by SVD

$$A = USV^T. \quad (3)$$

The first k columns of the matrix V form the truncated orthogonal subspace, V_k. The number of columns in V_k is equal to the rank of the subspace we use, and every column of V_k is a basis vector. The Eckart and Young theorem [5] guarantees that the matrix formed by the top k singular vectors provides the best (closest in the L_2 norm sense) approximation of the data matrix A in any basis of order k.

An orthogonal projection on a subspace spanned by V_k is given by a projection operator $\hat{P}_k = V_k V_k^T$.

Search Terms Ranking A query q is a search term represented in the advertiser space, or in other words, a query is a column a_i of the matrix A^T. Mathematically, it is convenient to express $q_i = a_i = A^T e_i$, where e_i is a column vector of all zeros except for a position corresponding to the column of interest in the matrix A^T, or row in the matrix A. The angle between a query vector and any other term vector in the matrix is

$$sim(t_i, q_j) = \cos(t_i, q_j) = \frac{(AA^T)_{ij}}{||a_i|| \, ||a_j||}, \quad (4)$$

which is a normalized inner product of A^T columns, or A matrix rows.

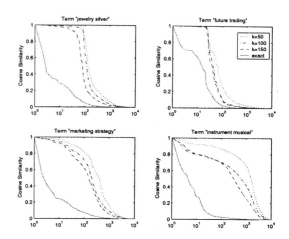

Figure 2. The exact and SVD subspace cosine similarity scores between four search terms and the data.

The similarity for the same vectors in the SVD orthogonal subspace is given by

$$sim(\hat{P}_k^T t_i, \hat{P}_k^T q_j) = \frac{(SU_k^T)_i^T (SU_k^T)_j}{||(SU_k^T)_i^T|| \, ||(SU_k^T)_j||}. \quad (5)$$

Iterative Refinement We can iteratively refine the suggested results when the user chooses terms from the returned set to reinforce or reject the ranking, thus performing *positive* or *negative* refinements or relevance feedback.

By positive refinement, we mean the user selects positive, reinforcing examples to add to the query from the provided term list. Then, instead of using q_0 as a query we can construct a new, extended query that spans the space $\{q_0, a_{j1}, a_{j2}, ..a_{jp}\}$, where a_j is the j-th column of A^T corresponding to the term that the user chooses to reinforce the query. Notice, that we are not computing the centroid for a new query as in [1], but rather are measuring the angle between the terms and an extended query subspace. If the space is formed by non-orthogonal vectors, the projection operator on that subspace is given by [5].

$$\hat{P}_Q = Q(Q^T Q)^{-1} Q^T. \quad (6)$$

The angle between a term and the positive term subspace is defined as the angle between a term and its orthogonal projection on that subspace. Formally,

$$sim(t_i, Q) = \frac{t_i^T (\hat{P}_Q t_i)}{||t_i|| \, ||\hat{P}_Q t_i||}. \quad (7)$$

This feedback mechanism works in both the entire space and the SVD subspace. For the SVD subspace, instead of t_i we use $t_{ik} = V_k V_k^T t_i$ and Q is formed using $a_{ik} = V_k V_k^T a_i$.

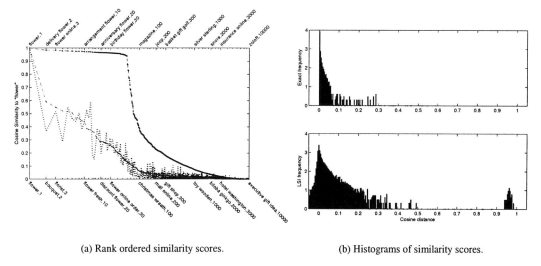

(a) Rank ordered similarity scores.

(b) Histograms of similarity scores.

Figure 3. The suggested results for the term "flower" from the exact cosine method and the SVD method with $k = 100$.

Negative refinement allows users to choose irrelevant documents and force the search results to be orthogonal to them. Thus, we are looking for a vector term in the collection with the smallest angle with the query and, at the same time, orthogonal to the negative term vectors specified by the user. Again, we want to emphasize that our method will produce results orthogonal to the entire subspace spanned by negative examples and not to only those terms. In this case, we need to build a complementary projector to the negative examples space, $\hat{P}_{Qn} = I - \hat{P}_Q$.

Then the new similarity score becomes

$$sim(t_i, Q) = \frac{t_i^T (I - \hat{P}_{Qn}^T) t_i}{||t_i|| \, ||(I - \hat{P}_{Qn}^T) t_i||}. \qquad (8)$$

and search results are ranked according to this similarity.

4. Implementation

We developed two programs for this work. The first is a program to compute the truncated SVD of a sparse matrix using the Implicitly Restarted Lanczos Method implemented in ARPACK and ARPACK++ libraries [6]. The second is a Java program to query a dataset and retrieve results between general and specific associations.

While the formulas presented in the previous section provide a compact description of the operations, they are extremely inefficient as written. For example, while the original matrix A is around 3 MB in a sparse matrix representation, the matrix AA^T is more than 300 MB. Thus, the implementation is solely based on sparse and dense matrix vector multiplications.

5. Results

Figure 2 demonstrates the cosine similarity scores for all terms in the dataset to four different search terms using four methods: exact match and SVD projections into rank $k = 50, 100, 150$ subspaces.

A more detailed example is given in Fig. 3, where we present the suggested results for the term "flower" from the exact cosine method and the SVD method with $k = 100$. In this example, we directly compare the two similarity curves based on their values and the ordering each method generates. The corresponding term suggestions for the query "flower" are shown in Table 1. There is little difference between the top set of results (1-5). The second set of results (74-78) demonstrates the benefits of LSI.

The system is designed for suggestion of search terms to an advertiser which sells flowers. Hence, the suggestion of "cooking" and "cosmetic" are not relevant. However, the suggestion of "stuffed bear" and "gourmet basket" are relevant in that many companies which sell flowers also sell these items. Many other terms suggested for LSI are holidays or events where flowers are frequently given as gifts, i.e. "valentine's day" and "birthday" – good terms for an advertiser selling flowers.

Precision and Recall With relevance judgments, we evaluated precision and recall for the top 10 to 10000 results from the various methods. Fig. 4(a) presents the precision and recall curves from the exact and the SVD method with $k = 100$ for the term "flower." The results show when precision is high, the methods are all roughly equivalent. As precision decreases, the results from SVD are better. Fi-

"flower" (full)			"flower" (SVD $k = 100$)		
1	flower	1	1	flower	1
2	deliver flower	0.591	2	bouquet	0.983
3	flower online	0.548	3	florist	0.983
4	flower send	0.520	4	floral	0.977
5	florist	0.516	5	flower online	0.977
74	sunflower	0.106	74	gourmet basket	0.579
75	birthday	0.106	75	valentine day	0.565
76	cooking	0.106	76	wreath	0.552
77	baby	0.100	77	fruit basket gift	0.519
78	cosmetic	0.098	78	birthday	0.501

Table 1. Comparison of exact and SVD $k = 100$ similarity scores

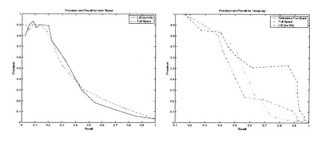

(a) Precision and Recall for "flower".

(b) Precision and Recall for "cheap isp."

Figure 4. Precision and recall curves

nally, when the precision is low ($\approx< 0.3$), the methods all show bad results, although SVD appears moderately worse.

Next, Fig. 4(b) demonstrates the results for the query "internet provider" with positive relevance feedback on "cheap isp" obtained by the subspace projection method. The results after refinement are more relevant to the concept behind the query, i.e. inexpensive internet access

Expanded Coverage By expanded coverage, we refer to the increase in recall at moderate precision (0.3-0.7). The change in coverage happens due to the change in ranking caused by SVD. When projected onto SVD subspace, the angles between term vectors change non-uniformly. This change results in differences in ranking (ordering) of search results for a given search term from the exact match method to the SVD approximate match method. This, in turn, leads to the increase in coverage through SVD subspace projections.

The reordering (change in ranking) caused by SVD is only local. The dotted line in the middle of Fig. 3(a) shows the similarity values from the exact cosine sorting results using the ordering from the SVD results. Of note in this figure is that there is very little reordering of the results beyond the plateau, thus SVD only performs a *local reordering* of the results.

Clustering Behavior Figure 3 also demonstrates the *clustering behavior* that occurs with SVD. The plateau at the top of the SVD curve represents a set of results whose similarity scores are high. If we take the histogram of the distances, as in Fig. 3(b) this behavior becomes even more apparent. The cluster at the right of the SVD histogram represents the "flower" cluster in the data; the steep decline of the SVD curve corresponds to the end of related terms.

The clustering behavior is also due to a non-uniform change in angles in subspace projection. Vectors that are close in the original data get closer when projected into the SVD subspace. Likewise, vectors that were distant in the original data become more distant in the SVD subspace [2].

This behavior, however, does not occur for all terms in the dataset. In Fig. 2, the terms "marketing strategy" and "instrument musical" do not display any clear clustering behavior.

Since the steep decline in the SVD curve corresponds to the end of the related terms for the query "flower", identifying this cutoff suggests a natural way to cluster a dataset using SVD. For the terms, "marketing strategy" and "instrument musical," then, there is no good cluster in the data for these terms.

6. Conclusions

We investigated the effect of SVD subspace projections on data from Overture's advertising market. We developed a tool to suggest related terms at varying levels of generality and a novel relevance feedback system for positive and negative examples using subspaces.

References

[1] M. Berry, Z. Drmac, and E. Jessup. Matrices, vector spaces, and information retrieval. *SIAM Review*, 41(2):335–362, 1999.

[2] M. Brand and K. Huang. A unifying theorem for spectral embedding and clustering. In C. M. Bishop and B. J. Frey, editors, *Proceedings of the Ninth International Workshop on Artificial Intelligence and Statistics*, January 2003.

[3] S. C. Deerwester, S. T. Dumais, T. K. Landauer, G. W. Furnas, and R. A. Harshman. Indexing by latent semantic analysis. *Journal of the American Society of Information Science*, 41(6):391–407, 1990.

[4] S. Dumais. Improving the retrieval of information from external sources. *Behavior Research Methods, Instruments, and Computers*, 23(2), 1991.

[5] G. H. Golub and C. F. V. Loan. *Matrix Computations*. John Hopkins Univ. Press, 1989.

[6] R. Lehoucq, D. Sorensen, and C. Yang. *ARPACK Users' Guide: Solutions of Large-Scale Eigenvalue Problems with Implicitly Restarted Arnoldi Methods*, 1997.

The Anatomy of a Hierarchical Clustering Engine
for Web-page, News and Book Snippets *

Paolo Ferragina   Antonio Gullì

Dipartimento di Informatica, Università di Pisa, Italy

Current search engines return a ranked list of web pages that contain the keywords of the user query together with some *contextual information*, in the form of a page excerpt, the so called *(page or web) snippet*. The key difficulty in the searching process relies in what is *"relevant"* to the user. The same set of keywords may abstract different user needs that may also vary over the time according to the context in which the user is formulating his/her own query. Recently, there has been a surge of commercial interest in novel IR-tools that help the users in their difficult search task by means of novel ways for reporting the query results. Two success stories are represented by Vivisimo and Dogpile that were elected as the best meta-search engines of the last three years 2000-03 by a jury composed by more than 500 web users, as reported by SearchEngineWatch.com. Other commercial tools are Mooter, Copernic, iBoogie, Kartoo, and Groxis. These IR-tools add to the flat list of query results a *hierarchy of clusters* built on-the-fly over the snippets. Each node of this hierarchy is properly *labeled* via a meaningful sentence that captures the "theme" of the snippets (and, thus, of the corresponding web pages) contained into its cluster. As a result, users are provided with a small, but intelligible, picture of the query results at various levels of details. So that the user has no longer to browse through tedious pages of results, but may navigate through labeled folders.

In this paper, we investigate the *web snippet hierarchical clustering* problem in its full extent by devising an algorithmic solution, and a software prototype called SnakeT (accessible at http://roquefort.di.unipi.it/), that: **(1)** draws the snippets from 16 Web search engines, the Amazon collection of books a9.com, the news of Google News and the blogs of Blogline; **(2)** builds the clusters on-the-fly (ephemeral clustering [10]) in response to a user query without adopting any pre-defined organization in categories; **(3)** labels the clusters with sentences of variable length, drawn from the snippets and possibly missing some terms, pro-

vided they are not too many;

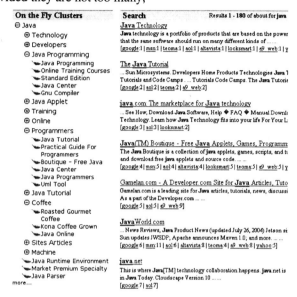

Figure 1. SnakeT's Clusters for *"Java"*.

(4) uses some ranking functions which exploit *two knowledge bases* properly built by our engine at preprocessing time for the *sentences selection and cluster-assignment process*; **(5)** organizes the clusters into a hierarchy, and assigns to the nodes intelligible sentences in order to allow post-navigation for query refinement. Our clustering algorithm possibly let the clusters overlap at different levels of the hierarchy.

We remark that the problem we have in our hands is different from the canonical clustering which is persistent since "in normal circumstances, the cluster structure is generated only once, and cluster maintenance can be carried out at relatively infrequent intervals" [11]. Moreover this problem is made difficult by the fact that, for efficiency issues, the labeling must exploit just the snippets and they are less informative than their documents because consist of about 100 words. In summary, our result is innovative in two respects: it introduces novel algorithmic ideas, and it is the first in the literature to address the ephemeral clustering of three kinds of heterogeneous collections such as the Web,

---
*Partially supported by the Italian MIUR projects ALINWEB, ECD, the "Italian Grid Project", "Distributed high-performance platform", and by the Italian Registry of ccTLD.it. Contact: {ferragina,gulli}@di.unipi.it

catalogues of books and rapid evolving collections of news and blogs.

1 The software architecture

Figure 2 illustrates the software architecture of SnakeT. There are two types of computations: an off-line computation that builds two knowledge bases at preprocessing time; and an on-line computation that is executed at query time and groups the snippets into clusters, extracts meaningful sentences to label them and produces a hierarchy. An extended description is in [3].

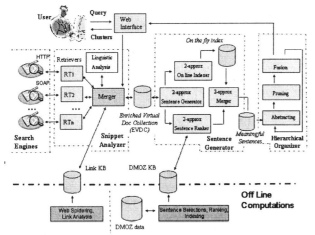

Figure 2. The architecture of SnakeT.

1.1 The two knowledge bases

The Anchor Text and the Link Database. Several search engines exploit the hyperlinks among Web pages as a source of information for ranking and retrieval. We use this information to cluster the snippets by modelling each Web page p as a *virtual document* consisting of two sets of terms: The set $A(p)$ formed by the terms contained in p, and the set $B(p)$ formed by the terms contained in the (anchor) text surrounding each hyperlink that points to p. Our experiments showed that $B(p)$ often provides a precise, yet concise, description of p. Unfortunately, common search engines do not return $B(p)$. Hence, we deployed the *Nutch's open source spider* to collect more than 200 millions Web pages selected among the top-cited ones. Hereafter, this index is denoted by $\mathcal{A}_{\text{link}}$.

The Semantic Knowledge Base. We introduce this KB to *rank* a set of candidate sentences, and select the most meaningful ones for our labeling purposes. There are many proposals in the literature to rank individual terms, either based on precomputed archives (e.g. ontologies, dictionaries and lexical databases, as WordNet and AppliedSemantics) or on frequency information, e.g. TFxIDF. To exploit the positive features of both approaches, we designed our clustering engine based on a *mixed* strategy. We indexed DMOZ, a high-quality directory freely available on

the Web, and developed a *ranking engine* upon it, hereafter denoted by $\mathcal{R}_{\text{dmoz}}$. This engine exploits more than three millions single terms and implements an ad-hoc *DMOZ-category*-centered TFxIDF measure, taking into account single terms, pairs of terms, longer sentences and their positions in the DMOZ tree. As a result, we are implicity exploiting a whole Web directory, but unlike [2], we are using it only for *ranking* the candidate sentences which, we remark, are created on-the-fly from the snippets at query time.

1.2 First module: The Snippet Analyzer

The task of this module is to forward the user query to a set of selected, remote search engines and to retrieve and merge the returned snippets. Currently we request an average of 40 Web snippets to each search engine using async I/O. The merged snippets are enriched with information retrieved from $\mathcal{A}_{\text{link}}$ and processed by a *Linguistic Analyzer* which filters a *stop list* in 12 different languages; stems the result by using a variant of the Snowball stemmer; and finally extracts Part of Speeches and Named Entities. The result is the Enriched Virtual Document Collection (EVDC).

1.3 Second module: The Sentences Generator

The task of this module is to create a set of meaningful labels as "approximate" sentences extracted from the EVDC. These labels will be then used to form and name the *clusters* and all nodes in the *hierarchy*. We are interested in long and intelligible sentences which are much more useful than a single term, but their extraction and management introduces some difficulties. For example, the sentences "John Fitzegerald Kennedy", and "Kennedy John" are syntactically different, but it would be desirable to consider them as the "same sentence". Grouper and the other academic tools [15, 17, 12, 4] did not deal with this problem because they treated sentences *formed by contiguous terms*. Nevertheless it is clear from the "future directions of research" of [15, 10] that the extraction of sentences involving not contiguous terms might boost the precision of the cluster labels and, in turn, the usefulness of the cluster hierarchy to humans. Vivisimo makes indeed use of approximate sentences as it is clear from its working. To the best of our knowledge, we are the first to design a clustering engine that tries to cluster together Web snippets containing *almost the same sentences*.

First phase: Construction. We generate "2-*approximate sentences*" by drawing all the pairs of (non contiguous) terms that occur within a proximity d in each sentence identified by the Snippet Analyzer. Stop words are skipped. Of course, some of the term pairs could introduce artificial meanings. Hence, we apply a simple rule: We say that (t_h, t_k) is a *valid* term-pair if either the two terms t_h and t_k appear contiguously in some other document of the

EVDC or they appear contiguously in $\mathcal{R}_{\text{dmoz}}$. Sentences not valid are discarded.

Second phase: Ranking. The 2-approximate sentences are ranked using both $\mathcal{R}_{\text{dmoz}}$ and the frequency information derived from the snippets themselves. Our ranking has two peculiarities: it exploits *"local"* information, via a set of statistics collected from the Web snippets, and *"background"* information, via a judgement on the importance of a 2-approximate sentence assigned according to $\mathcal{R}_{\text{dmoz}}$. 2-approximate sentences below a threshold are removed.

Third phase: Merging. The filtered 2-approximate sentences participate to a merging process whose aim is to form longer *k-approximate sentences*. Here, we exploit an index based upon a combination of bitmaps and inverted lists, and built *on-the-fly* on the filtered sentences.

1.4 Third module: The Hierarchical Organizer

Given the k-approximate sentences, we postulate that *"virtual documents sharing the same k-approximate sentences belong to the same cluster"*. According to this policy, a single document may occur in many clusters, being this consistent with the observation that a Web page can cover *multiple themes*. The result of this initial clustering step is a flat pool of clusters (leaves of our hierarchy), each one having assigned a k-approximate sentence as meaningful label. This label is hereafter called the *primary label* of that cluster. Primary labels indeed occur within all the (virtual) documents forming a cluster and they are the sentences reporting the largest rank. They are therefore of *high quality* but are often *too much specific* to generate the labels of the nodes in the higher levels of the hierarchy. Our next key choice has been then to associate to each (leaf) cluster also a *set of secondary labels* defined as follows: they are k-approximate sentences which have a *good rank* and occur in *at least* the $c\%$ of the documents contained in the cluster. If c is sufficiently large the secondary labels provide a description for the cluster at a coarser level of detail (than the primary label), and are thus more useful for hierarchical formation and labeling. In order to manage primary and secondary labels efficiently, we concatenate them into a single string, separated by a special symbol $, called the *signature* of the cluster.

The hierarchy formation process consists actually of three phases executed repeatedly until a few number of superclusters remain: *abstraction*, *pruning* and *fusion*. The abstraction phase aims at building another level of the hierarchy starting from a set of (super)clusters $SC_1, \ldots SC_z$, each having its own signature. We compare the signatures of all SC_is and extract the common substrings which do not include the special symbol $. If the signatures of $SC_{i_1}, \ldots, SC_{i_z}$ contain the substring s, then we form a new supercluster SC' whose primary label is s and whose documents are given by the union of the documents of $SC_{i_1}, \ldots, SC_{i_z}$.

We can look at SC' as the *father* of $SC_{i_1}, \ldots, SC_{i_z}$ in the hierarchy. The rank of s is computed as a function of the rank of the (primary or secondary) labels having s as a substring. We exploit the properties of the signatures to execute an all-against-all comparison among these signatures in almost linear time. Moreover we point out that, s is not necessarily a contiguous substring of the original Web snippets since it is a substring of a k-approximate sentence. The final pruning phase aims at simplifying the hierarchy obtained so far, by removing the *redundant* superclusters. We formalize this as a *covering* problem and solve it via a greedy approach. Finally, we compute the secondary label of each remaining supercluster, by uniting the secondary labels of its children and by discarding those labels which occur in less than $c\%$ of its included documents. At this point we have re-established the inductive conditions on the superclusters at the current level, and we can repeat the above three phases.

2 Related Works and Experimental Results

Various papers have been recently published onto this challenging problem [7, 15, 17, 12, 4, 10, 5, 9, 16, 8, 13]. Grouper [15] uses *contiguous phrases* of variable length drawn from the Web snippets by means of a Suffix Tree data structure. SHOC [17] uses instead a Suffix Array and organizes the clusters in a hierarchy via an SVD approach. In Lexical Affinities Clustering [10], the indexing unit consists of a *pair of words* (not necessarily contiguous) that are linked by a lexical affinity (LA). All the above softwares are **no longer available** as the authors communicated to us. FIHC [4] uses Frequent Itemsets , WebCat [5] uses Transactional K-Means, Retriever [7] uses robust relational fuzzy clustering. These three approaches do not form any hierarchy and the labels are *single keywords*. [14] proposes to combine links and content in a k-means framework. The problem is that search engines don't provide an easy access to the links graph, as we discuss in section 1.1. [1, 2] use *static classification* and exploit statistical techniques to learn a model based on a labeled set of training documents. The model is then applied to new documents to determine their categories. We believe that using a predefined set of categories is not flexible enough to capture the different, fine themes of the pages answering to a given user query. Hearst [6] in fact suggested that ".. clusters [should be] created as a function of which documents were retrieved in response to a query, and therefore have the potential to be more closely tailored to characteristics of a query than independent, static, clustering.". The most recent results come from Microsoft and IBM. [16] extracts sentences of variable length but contiguous, via five different measures through regression. The approach is not hierarchical, and in fact the authors highlight the need of (1) a hierarchical clustering, and (2) external taxonomies for improving labels precision.

This is actually what we do with SnakeT. [8] proposes a greedy algorithm to build the hierarchy based on a minimization of an objective function similar to ours. However, their labels are contiguous sentences and usually consist of single words. We point out that [16, 8] **didn't provide us with an access** to their software, so that a fair comparison with them has been not yet possible to be performed.

A Web interface is instead provided by three software: CIIRarchies [9] extracts sentences using a pre-computed language model and builds the hierarchy via a recursive algorithm; Highlight [13] adopts lexical analysis and a probabilistic framework for hierarchy construction, and Carrot2 [12] being an open source implementation of Grouper. These softwares have been checked against SnakeT. We performed several user studies running our system on a Linux PC with a CPU P4 and RAM 1.5Gb. The first study was aimed at understanding whether a Web clustering engine is an useful complement to the flat, ranked list of results. We asked to 45 people, of intermediate web ability, to use VIVISIMO during their day by day search activities. After a test period of 20 days, 85% of them reported that using the tool "[..] get a good sense of range alternatives with their meaningful labels", and 72% said that the most useful feature is "[..] the ability to produce on-the-fly clusters in response to a query, with labels extracted from the text". Then, we selected 18 queries belonging to many different topics (*iraq, bush, data mining, bill gates, last minute, car rental, mp3, divx, sony, final fantasy, ipo, equity, google ipo, warterlo, second war, aids, allergy, nasa*, and asked three users to compare our results against those provided by Mooter, CIIRarchies, Highlight, Carrot2. For a large part of the queries users did not like Mooter, since it provides single terms clusters. Carrot2 often tends to create a number of clusters which exceed the number of snippets itself (!!), thus reducing the need of such IR-tool. Carrot2 also fails to cluster together similar labels such as "knowledge, knowledge discovery", "mining and knowledge", and furthermore labels the hierarchy paths with sentences which are one the substring of the other. Highlight obtains its first-level's labels by using classification, so that they are few and of little use. In many cases (e.g. "data mining"), the clustering process produces identical subtrees under different top level categories and a number of clusters which exceeds the number of snippets themselves (e.g 160 clusters for the "iraq" query). CIIRarchies provides good hierarchies but, as the authors themselves admit, they are often not compact, have large depth and contain some non content-bearing words which tend to repeat (e.g ""DivX download" occurs under 5 different fathers and at different depths). CIIRarchies and Highlight are significantly slower than SnakeT. Our third study was aimed at drawing a preliminary evaluation of our software against Vivisimo. We selected 20 students of the University of Pisa and asked them

to execute the above queries on VIVISIMO and SnakeT. 75% of them were satisfied of the quality of our hierarchy and its labels.

In summary, no academic result has achieved a performance comparable to the one provided by Vivisimo, and no one proposed a unifying clustering system with a Web interface for both Web Search, Books, News and Blog domains. This is one of our main achievements with SnakeT. Moreover we claim that the architecture of SnakeT (Fig. 2) is simple and its blocks can be used easily by other researchers. In the light of the experimental results, some issues remain to be further investigated. We are: (1) extending and refining our users' studies on free queries and on a larger and more variegate set of users; (2) investigating the benefits carried out by each module of SnakeT; and (3) studying some forms of mathematical evaluation for the "quality of the labeled hierarchy of clusters". This is an interesting research problem as stated in [8].

References

[1] G. Attardi, A. Gulli, and F. Sebastiani. Theseus: categorization by context. In *WWW99*.

[2] H. Chen and S. T. Dumais. Bringing order to the web: automatically categorizing search results. In *SIGCHI00*.

[3] P. Ferragina and A. Gulli. The anatomy of a clustering engine. Technical report, TR04-04 Informatica, Pisa, 2004.

[4] B. Fung, K. Wang, and M. Ester. Large hierarchical document clustering using frequent itemsets. In *SDM03*.

[5] F. Giannotti, M. Nanni, and D. Pedreschi. Webcat: Automatic categorization of web search results. In *SEBD03*.

[6] M. A. Hearst and J. O. Pedersen. Reexamining the cluster hypothesis: Scatter/gather on retrieval results. In *SIGIR-96*.

[7] Z. Jiang, A. Joshi, R. Krishnapuram, and L. Yi. Retriever: Improving web search engine results using clustering. In *Managing Business with Electronic Commerce 02*.

[8] K. Kummamuru. A hierarchical monothetic document clustering algorithm for summarization and browsing search results. In *WWW04*.

[9] D. J. Lawrie and W. B. Croft. Generating hiearchical summaries for web searches. In *SIGIR03*.

[10] Y. S. Maarek, R. Fagin, I. Z. Ben-Shaul, and D. Pelleg. Ephemeral document clustering for web applications. Technical Report RJ 10186, IBM Research, 2000.

[11] G. Salton and M. McGill. *Introduction to Modern Information Retrieval*. McGraw Hill, 1983.

[12] D. Weiss and J. Stefanowski. Web search results clustering in polish: Experimental evaluation of carrot. In *IIS03*.

[13] Y. Wu and X. Chen. Extracting features from web search returned hits for hierarchical classification. In *IKE03*.

[14] M. K. Yitong Wang. On combining link and contents information for web page clustering. In *DEXA02*.

[15] O. Zamir and O. Etzioni. Grouper: a dynamic clustering interface to Web search results. In *Computer Networks 98*.

[16] H. Zeng, Q. He, Z. Chen, and W. Ma. Learning to cluster web search results. In *SIGIR04*.

[17] D. Zhang and Y. Dong. Semantic, hierarchical, online clustering of web search results. In *WIDM01*.

Query-Driven Support Pattern Discovery for Classification Learning *

Yiqiu Han   and   Wai Lam

Department of Systems Engineering and Engineering Management
The Chinese University of Hong Kong
Shatin, Hong Kong

Abstract

We propose a novel query-driven lazy learning algorithm which attempts to discover useful local patterns, called support patterns, for classifying a given query. The learning is customized to the query to avoid the horizon effect. We show that this query-driven learning algorithm can guarantee to discover all support patterns with perfect expected accuracy in polynomial time. The experimental results on benchmark data sets also demonstrate that our learning algorithm really has prominent learning performance.

1. Introduction

Many eager classification learning algorithms, such as Decision Tree [5] or rule-based classification learning [4, 3], attempt to search for useful classification rules or a decision tree in a greedy manner. The learning is conducted by partitioning the training data iteratively or recursively. However, as the heuristic used for partitioning looks no further than the next attribute to select, it may not be guaranteed that the learned trees or rules will be optimal. This problem is usually called horizon effect [1]. Several extensions have been proposed to cope with this problem by providing look ahead capabilities, multi-attribute splitting tests, or supporting constructive induction.

We propose a query-driven or lazy learning algorithm called QUery-driven Support Pattern Learning (QUSUP). The learning is conducted in a customized way for the unseen instance to be classified, which is called the *query*. QUSUP attempts to discover local classification rules, i.e., *support patterns*, for the current query. The discovery process starts with the query. By gradually removing some attribute values, QUSUP obtains more general support patterns for consideration. At each step QUSUP will investi-

gate the associated class distribution of the current support pattern to decide whether it should be selected or discarded.

If common eager classification rule learning algorithms can be viewed as conducting "drill down" operations to produce more concrete rules from the current set of rules, QUSUP can be viewed as conducting "scroll up" operations from the current query to produce more general support patterns. Since the learning is customized to the query, QUSUP can search the hypothesis space more thoroughly and efficiently. Therefore, QUSUP can avoid the horizon effect as QUSUP can guarantee to discover any support patterns with perfect (100%) expected accuracy in polynomial time. QUSUP can also guarantee a low probability to reject any useful support pattern with an expected accuracy higher than a specified value.

In order to evaluate the effectiveness of QUSUP, we conducted extensive experiments on benchmark data sets. QUSUP shows prominent classification performance on benchmark data sets. Also, We examined the decision tree discovered by common eager learning, and the support patterns discovered by QUSUP on a data set. This investigation explains why QUSUP outperforms common eager learning algorithms on some data sets.

2. Discovering Support Patterns for a Query

2.1. Background

Given a query $\mathbf{t}$ denoted by a full set of attribute values $\{t_1, t_2, \ldots, t_n\}$, its support patterns can be viewed as subsets of the set $\{t_1, t_2, \ldots, t_n\}$. We denote the cardinality of a support pattern $\mathbf{A}$ as $|\mathbf{A}|$ where $\mathbf{A} \subseteq \mathbf{t}$. Although there are 2^n subsets of the set $\{t_1, t_2, \ldots, t_n\}$, the number of valid support patterns is usually much smaller with polynomial growth, because a valid support pattern must have some associated training instances sharing the same subset of attribute values with the query $\mathbf{t}$.

Since support patterns must be supported by training instances, the operations on support patterns can be transformed into operations on training instances. In QUSUP,

---

*The work described in this paper was substantially supported by grants from the Research Grant Council of the Hong Kong Special Administrative Region, China (Project Nos: CUHK 4187/01E and CUHK 4179/03E) and CUHK Strategic Grant (No: 4410001).

support patterns are explored from the largest cardinality. Suppose the largest cardinality is k. QUSUP starts with support patterns whose cardinalities equal to k. They must be associated with some training instances which share exactly the same k attribute values with the query. Hence support patterns with the largest cardinality can be enumerated and explored by investigating all qualified training instances.

For a valid support pattern $\mathbf{S}$ with cardinality l where $l < k$, its associated training instances must share l or more attribute values with the query. Hence $\mathbf{S}$ must satisfy one of the following conditions.

Cond1: $\mathbf{S}$ has associated training instances which share exactly l identical attribute values with the query.

Cond2: $\mathbf{S}$ is a common subset of two or more explored support patterns whose cardinalities are all larger than l.

Cond3: $\mathbf{S}$ is a pure subset of an explored support pattern whose cardinality is larger than l. All $\mathbf{S}$'s associated training instances are also inherited from the explored support pattern. This condition need not to be considered in the exploration of support patterns, as discussed in Rule 4 below.

Therefore, all valid support patterns with cardinality l can be exhaustively enumerated by two ways. The first way is to explore all training instances which share exactly l identical attribute values with the query. The second way is to check all common subsets of explored valid support patterns with cardinalities larger than l. Consequently, QUSUP can explore all valid support patterns systematically, from the largest cardinality to the smallest cardinality. The whole process is implemented by examining all available training instances. Then the number of valid support patterns is constrained by both 2^n and the number of training instances that have at least one identical attribute value with the query $\mathbf{t}$. They can be ranked according to their number of identical attribute values with the query $\mathbf{t}$. Thus at each step only a small fraction of training data need to be read into memory. As we discuss below, QUSUP usually completes the learning process after only examining a small fraction of training data which bears some relationships with the query $\mathbf{t}$. For problems with large attribute dimensions but relatively sparse training data, QUSUP has obvious advantage in the capability of exploring all valid support patterns. Even for problems with both large attribute dimensions and large number of data instances, QUSUP can still efficiently reduce the search space and discover useful support patterns with the aid of a set of rules, as discussed below.

2.2. Rules of Exploring Support Patterns

Given two valid support patterns $\mathbf{S_1}$ and $\mathbf{S_2}$ with sufficient training instances, if $\mathbf{S_1} \subseteq \mathbf{S_2}$, $\mathbf{S_2}$ is obviously more useful in classification because it is closer to the query. QUSUP then considers $\mathbf{S_2}$ and ignores $\mathbf{S_1}$. In QUSUP, two support patterns can only be compared with each other when they have the subset relationship. This can significantly improve the learning efficiency. This approach also avoids introducing any apriori assumptions such as dependence or independence of attributes, a global Euclidean distance metric, or a weighting scheme for different attributes. This makes the learning from support patterns more flexible and more robust.

To facilitate the utilization of the subset relationship to explore support patterns, we develop the following rules. Suppose a support pattern has x associated training instances among which y instances share the same majority class label. y/x is called the *majority rate* of that support pattern. It can also be viewed as the empirical accuracy of applying that particular support pattern for classification. Consider two support patterns $\mathbf{S_1}$ and $\mathbf{S_2}$, where $\mathbf{S_1} \subseteq \mathbf{S_2} \subseteq \mathbf{t}$. Obviously, $\mathbf{S_1}$ is more general while $\mathbf{S_2}$ is more close to the query $\mathbf{t}$. Then we have:

Rule 1: If $\mathbf{S_1}$ has sufficiently high majority rate, then $\mathbf{S_2}$ has a greater chance to have a high majority rate. As an extreme case, if $\mathbf{S_1}$ has a 100% majority rate, so does $\mathbf{S_2}$. If $\mathbf{S_2}$ is observed to has low majority rate, it implies that $\mathbf{S_1}$ also cannot have 100% majority rate.

Rule 2: If $\mathbf{S_2}$ has been selected by QUSUP, which means that it has sufficiently high majority rate and sufficient associated training instances, then $\mathbf{S_1}$ should not be considered any more because $\mathbf{S_1}$ is a generalization of $\mathbf{S_2}$ and contains less information.

Rule 3: If $\mathbf{S_2}$ is discarded, then $\mathbf{S_1}$ should not be considered any more due to the same reason as the Rule 2. This rule can also be regarded as an extension of the Rule 1. A formal discussion is presented in Section 2.3.

Rule 4: If $\mathbf{S_2}$ has the same associated training instance set as $\mathbf{S_1}$, $\mathbf{S_2}$ need not to be considered as a valid support pattern since $\mathbf{S_1}$ can replace it without any cost.

The rules above show that support patterns can be exploited by analyzing their relationship and observing their class distributions. Whether to select or discard a particular support pattern will trigger a family of support patterns to be pruned.

2.3. Posterior Property

In classical association rule learning, it uses an useful concept called *Apriori Property* to reduce the search space. It can be expressed as "nonempty subsets of a frequent itemset must also be frequent." In our query-driven learning, we introduce another concept called *Posterior Property*, which can be viewed as the inverse of Apriori Property.

Posterior Property can be expressed as "A superset of a good support pattern is also a good support pattern". It is based on the following observation: if a support pattern $\mathbf{S_1}$ of a given query $\mathbf{t}$ has perfect (100%) accuracy in classification, its superset $\mathbf{S_2}$ satisfying $\mathbf{S_1} \subset \mathbf{S_2} \subseteq \mathbf{t}$ can be used alternatively in classifying $\mathbf{t}$ if available.

This property can be extended to process support patterns with high but less than 100% accuracy. Suppose a user requires an useful support pattern to be with p or higher accuracy. If a support pattern $\mathbf{S_1}$ can meet this requirement, then the probability of observing y training instances of the majority class among its x associated training instances is expressed as follows:

$$P(y/x) = \frac{x!}{y!(x-y)!} p^y (1-p)^{x-y} \qquad (1)$$

If $P(y/x)$ is less than γ for an accuracy higher than p, we will discard it. In other words, QUSUP uses a minimum probability threshold γ (e.g., 10%) and a minimum expected accuracy p (e.g., 85%) to select useful support patterns and discard those unlikely support patterns. Thus the search space can be effectively reduced. Therefore, QUSUP only has less than γ chance to reject an useful support pattern with expected accuracy higher than p. We can further prune any support pattern S_2 where $S_2 \subset S_1 \subseteq t$, because the observed class distribution of S_1 can also be regarded as coming from S_2. Even if the majority class label of S_1 is different from that of S_2, the observed class distribution of S_1 can still be used to evaluate S_2. Suppose the majority class of support pattern S_2 has a frequency z in S_1, we also observe y positive training instances of the majority class among S_1's x associated training instances. Then if the following equation holds, QUSUP will reject S_2 as with p or higher accuracy.

$$\left(\frac{z}{x} \leq \frac{y}{x} \leq p\right) \wedge \left(\frac{x!}{y!(x-y)!} p^y (1-p)^{x-y} \leq \gamma\right) \qquad (2)$$

Equation 2 explains why all subsets of a discarded support pattern will also be discarded as Rule 3 stated. It should be noted that a support pattern S_1 with few training instances generally cannot make Equation 2 hold, avoiding the pruning of potentially useful support patterns incorrectly.

If we are only interested in support patterns with perfect (100%) accuracy, then we just need to consider the support patterns whose associated training instances have the same class label. In other words, QUSUP can guarantee to discover all support patterns with 100% accuracy in polynomial time.

A support pattern is considered to be qualified by QUSUP only when "the probability that this support pattern has an expected classification accuracy less than q is no more than γ", which implies:

$$\left(\frac{y}{x} \geq q\right) \wedge \left(\frac{x!}{y!(x-y)!} q^y (1-q)^{x-y} \leq \gamma\right) \qquad (3)$$

Similar to Equation 2, if QUSUP decides that support pattern is qualified for classification, then all of its children support patterns are pruned (Rule 2). Therefore, QUSUP only has less than γ (e.g., 10%) chance to select an unreliable support pattern with expected accuracy less than q (e.g., the majority rate of the whole training data set).

If a support pattern is neither selected nor discarded, QUSUP then stores this support pattern. The common subsets of stored patterns are used to generate new support patterns as stated by Cond2 mentioned in Section 2.2.

2.4. Support Pattern Based Classifier

The details of how QUSUP explores support patterns is depicted in Figure 1. A dynamic memory pool Δ is constructed for exploring support patterns. It is initialized by the set of training instances that have at least one identical attribute value with the query t. QUSUP searches support patterns from the largest cardinality to the lowest. The rules and Posterior Property we discussed are utilized to select or prune support patterns as shown in Steps 7, 11, 17, and 21 in Figure 1. The search completes when the dynamic memory pool Δ is empty. A set of qualified support patterns are discovered for the query. If the training data is sparse for the query and no qualified support patterns are selected by QUSUP, the support patterns with the largest cardinality will be automatically selected for classification.

Then QUSUP combines their associated training instances to classify the query t. The final prediction is made by summarizing the frequency of each class on all selected support patterns, the class with the maximal frequency serves as the predictor for the class label of the given query. In this combining process, since a particular single training instance may appear in different support patterns, we can observe that it may be sampled multiple times proportional to its contribution to the learning. This usually happens when a training instance exhibits relatively high similarities to the query.

3. Empirical Experiments

We have also extensive experiments on 20 benchmark data sets from the UCI repository of machine learning database [2] to evaluate our QUSUP framework. These data sets are collected from different real-world problems in various domains. We partitioned each data set into 10 even portions and then conducted 10-fold cross-validation. The performance is measured by the classification accuracy. In these experiments, we have also investigated the performance of Naive Bayesian, SVM, kNN, and Decision Tree (J48) provided by Weka-3-2-6 machine learning software package [6]. All the runs were conducted on the same computer platform. All these models except for kNN use default settings during the entire evaluation process. For kNN, we set $k = 10$ for all data sets.

The results of experiments are depicted in Table 1, which show the average of classification accuracy (in percentage) on different data sets. Compared with existing approaches, in most data sets, QUSUP achieves good performance. For some data sets such as Labor, Sonar, and Contact, QUSUP outperforms all other classical classifiers. The results also show that QUSUP excels at handling data sets with unsatisfactory data quality or incomplete attribute information. The reason is due to the flexible framework of QUSUP. On average, the classification accuracy of QUSUP on these 20 benchmark data sets is 89.1%, which shows improvement over other classical eager or lazy learning models.

```
1   Sort training instances according to |S(d⁽ⁱ⁾, t)|.
      //S(d⁽ⁱ⁾, t) denotes the support pattern shared by d⁽ⁱ⁾ and t.
2   Put all training instances satisfying |S(d⁽ⁱ⁾, t)| > 0 into Δ.
3   Initialize the active set u and the final set r to be empty.
4   FOR j = n to 1
5     FOR every d⁽ⁱ⁾ in Δ satisfying |S(d⁽ⁱ⁾, t)| = j
6       IF S(d⁽ⁱ⁾, t) cannot satisfy Equation 1
7         Remove all d⁽ᵏ⁾ satisfying S(d⁽ᵏ⁾, t) ⊆ S(d⁽ⁱ⁾, t).
8       ELSE
9         IF S(d⁽ⁱ⁾, t) is selected as qualified
10          Insert d⁽ⁱ⁾ into r.
11          Remove all d⁽ᵏ⁾ satisfying S(d⁽ᵏ⁾, t) ⊆ S(d⁽ⁱ⁾, t).
12        ELSE
13          Insert S(d⁽ⁱ⁾, t) into u.
14          Produce intersections using S(d⁽ⁱ⁾, t) and u.
15    FOR every x in u satisfying |x| = j
16      IF x does not satisfy Equation 1
17        Remove all d⁽ᵏ⁾ satisfying S(d⁽ᵏ⁾, t) ⊆ x.
18      ELSE
19        IF x is selected as qualified
20          Insert x into r.
21          Remove all d⁽ᵏ⁾ satisfying S(d⁽ᵏ⁾, t) ⊆ x.
22        ELSE
23          Insert x into u.
24          Produce intersections using x and u.
25    IF |Δ| == 0
26      BREAK
27    IF |r| = 0
28      Move all S(d⁽ⁱ⁾, t) with the largest cardinality into r.
29    Return the discovered support pattern set r.
```

Figure 1. The outline of QUSUP algorithm

We examined the behavior of learning algorithms for the Labor data set, to investigate why QUSUP outperforms the common eager learning algorithms such as Decision Tree (J48). For this data set, the Decision Tree algorithm returns a simple tree learned from the full training data set. This decision tree only contains 3 leaves and utilizes 2 attributes out of the 16 attributes. One possible reason is that eager learning algorithm inherently constructs a decision tree satisfying certain global constraints. It may be affected by missing attribute values or the horizon effect. On the contrary, QUSUP achieves a satisfying performance (96.5%) on this data set. Although this data set is small and has considerable amount of missing attribute values, QUSUP can discover more than 12 useful support patterns. These discovered support patterns provide more knowledge about the data set by utilizing more attributes and capturing more useful patterns of class distribution on the attribute space.

Data Set	QUSUP	kNN	NaiveBayes	J48	SVM
Annealing	97.1	96.1	86.5	**98.4**	97.9
Breast(W)	96.7	96.4	96.0	95.3	**97.0**
Colic	80.4	82.4	79.1	**85.9**	82.6
Contact(L)	**87.5**	68.2	75.0	83.3	81.7
Credit(A)	84.9	85.8	77.7	**86.0**	84.9
Diabetes	72	72.5	75.8	74.1	**77.5**
Glass	**75.0**	63.5	48.5	67.2	71.0
Heart(C)	82.6	82.2	**84.5**	79.2	84.5
Hepatitis	**90.0**	82.6	83.8	79.4	85.8
Ionosphere	90.3	84.6	82.4	**90.9**	88.0
Iris	**96.0**	96.0	96.0	95.3	85.3
Kr-vs-Kp	96.5	94.9	87.6	**99.5**	95.7
Labor	**96.5**	89.3	94.7	78.7	92.7
Letter	86.8	**94.8**	64.2	87.8	81.7
Lymph	83.1	81.8	83.8	77.0	**86.5**
Mushroom	99.8	99.9	95.8	**100**	100
Sonar	**87.04**	73.0	65.9	74.1	77.8
Soybean	92.1	87.1	92.8	92.2	**94.0**
Vowel	**91.5**	57.2	61.4	78.3	47.6
Zoo	**96.2**	88.2	95.2	92.1	92.1
Average	**89.1**	83.8	81.3	85.7	85.2

Table 1. Classification performance of QUSUP and other classifiers.

References

[1] D. W. Aha. Relating relational learning algorithms. In S. Muggleton, editor, *Inductive Logic Programming*, pages 233–260. Academic Press, 1992.

[2] C. Blake, E. Keogh, and C. Merz. UCI repository of machine learning databases. http://www.ics.uci.edu/~mlearn/MLRepository.html.

[3] W. Li, J. Han, and J. Pei. CMAR: Accurate and efficient classification based on multiple class-association rules. In *Proceedings of the IEEE International Conference on Data Mining (ICDM)*, pages 369–376, 2001.

[4] B. Liu, W. Hsu, and Y. Ma. Integrating classification and association rule mining. In *Proceedings of the Fourth International Conference on Knowledge Discovery and Data Mining (KDD'98)*, pages 80–86, 1998.

[5] L. R. Quinlan. Induction of decision trees. *Machine learning*, 1:81–106, 1986.

[6] I. Witten and E. Frank. *Practical Machine Learning Tools and Techniques with Java Implementations*. Morgan Kaufmann, 2000.

Evolutionary Algorithms for Clustering Gene-Expression Data[*]

Eduardo R. Hruschka, Leandro N. de Castro, Ricardo J. G. B. Campello
Universidade Católica de Santos (UniSantos)
{erh,lnunes,campello}@unisantos.br

Abstract

This work deals with the problem of automatically finding optimal partitions in bioinformatics datasets. We propose incremental improvements for a Clustering Genetic Algorithm (CGA), culminating in the Evolutionary Algorithm for Clustering (EAC). The CGA and its modified versions are evaluated in five gene-expression datasets, showing that the proposed EAC is a promising tool for clustering gene-expression data.

1. Introduction

Microarray technology has produced massive amounts of genetic data, and has highlighted the need for new pattern recognition techniques that can mine and discover biological meaningful knowledge in large datasets [1]. Clustering is a useful exploratory technique for gene-expression data that provides groups of similar genes or experiments (or both), allowing the identification of potentially meaningful relationships between them. Several clustering algorithms have been applied to gene expression data, but there is no method of choice in the bioinformatics community. Moreover, there are a few works that deal with the problem of finding the *right* number of clusters (e.g. see [2] and references therein).

The present work describes evolutionary algorithms that automatically find clusters of genes. We consider that clustering involves the partitioning of a set **X** of objects into a collection of mutually disjoint subsets C_i of **X**. Many methods proposed in the literature assume that the number of clusters (k) is given by the user [3]. This approach assumes domain knowledge and usually has the disadvantage of searching for the solution in a small subset of the search space. Another alternative involves optimizing k according to numeric criteria. However, the problem of finding an optimal solution to the partition of N objects into k clusters is NP-complete and, provided that the number of distinct partitions of N data into k clusters increases approximately as $k^N/k!$, attempting to find a globally optimal solution is usually not feasible. This difficulty has stimulated the development of efficient approximated algorithms. Genetic algorithms are widely believed to be effective on NP-complete global optimization problems and they can provide good sub-optimal solutions in reasonable time. Under this perspective, the Clustering Genetic Algorithm (CGA), designed to optimize both the number of clusters and the corresponding clusterings, was introduced in [4] and is adopted here as a *starting point algorithm*, from which more efficient algorithms are designed.

2. Main Features of the CGA

The CGA [4] is based on a simple encoding scheme. Let us consider a data set formed by N objects. Then, a genotype is an integer vector of (N+1) positions. The i-th position (gene) represents the i-th object, whereas the last gene represents the number of clusters (k). For instance, in a dataset composed of 20 objects, a possible genotype is: 22345123453321454552 5. In this case, five objects {1,2,7,13,20} form the cluster whose label is 2.

The CGA crossover operator combines clustering solutions coming from different genotypes. It works in the following way. First, 2 genotypes (**G1,G2**) are selected. Then, assuming that **G1** represents k_1 clusters, the CGA randomly chooses $c \in \{1,2,...,k_1\}$ clusters to copy into **G2**. The unchanged clusters of **G2** are maintained and the changed ones have their objects allocated to the corresponding nearest clusters (according to their centroids). This way, offspring **G3** is obtained. The same procedure is employed to get offspring **G4**, but now considering that the changed clusters of **G2** are copied into **G1**. Two operators for mutation are used. The first operator works only on genotypes that encode more than 2 clusters. It eliminates a randomly chosen cluster, placing its objects into the nearest remaining clusters. The second operator splits a randomly selected cluster into 2 new ones. The first cluster is formed by the objects closer to the original centroid, whereas the other cluster is formed by those objects closer to the farthest object from the centroid.

The objective function is based on the silhouette [3]. Let us consider an object i belonging to cluster **A**. So, the average dissimilarity of i to all other objects of **A** is denoted by $a(i)$. Now let us take into account cluster **B**. The average dissimilarity of i to all objects of **B** will be called $d(i,\mathbf{B})$. After computing $d(i,\mathbf{B})$ for all clusters **B**≠**A**, the smallest one is selected, i.e. $b(i) = \min d(i,\mathbf{B})$, **B**≠**A**. This value represents the dissimilarity of i to its neighbor cluster. The silhouette $s(i)$ is given by Equation (1). It is easy to verify that $-1 \leq s(i) \leq 1$. If cluster **A** is a singleton,

[*] This work was supported by both FAPESP and CNPq.

403

then $s(i)$ is not defined and the most neutral choice is to set $s(i) = 0$ [3]. The objective function is the average of $s(i)$ over $i = 1,2,...,N$ and the best clustering is achieved when its value is maximized.

$$s(i) = \frac{b(i) - a(i)}{\max\{a(i), b(i)\}} \quad (1)$$

The genotypes corresponding to each generation are selected according to a normalized roulette wheel strategy [4]. In addition, the best genotype is always copied and maintained into the succeeding generation. The CGA does not employ crossover and mutation probabilities, i.e., it is assumed that 50% of the selected genotypes are crossed-over, 25% are mutated by operator 1 and 25% are mutated by operator 2. The initial populations are randomly generated in such a way that each gene takes a random value from the set $\{1,2, \cdots, k\}$.

3. From CGA to EAC

Considering the CGA [4], we evaluate 3 incremental modifications: (i) including the k-means algorithm [3] as a local search procedure; (ii) applying an objective function based on centroids; and (iii) eliminating the crossover operator, obtaining the proposed Evolutionary Algorithm for Clustering (EAC). The CGA [4] will be named CGA-I and the modified algorithms will be called CGA-II, CGA-III and EAC, respectively. The CGAs (I, II and III) were previously compared in a toy problem [5].

3.1. CGA-II

The k-means algorithm partitions a dataset of N objects into k clusters, minimizing the sum of distances between objects of a cluster and its centroid. It has two main drawbacks: (i) it may get stuck at suboptimal centroids; and (ii) the user has to provide the number of clusters (k). On the one hand, these problems are lessened by CGA-I, which can find the *best* clustering in a dataset in terms of both the number of clusters and centroids. The genetic operators of CGA-I are suitable for clustering problems because they merge, split, and eliminate clusters, thus trying to find better partitions. These partitions, in turn, may represent better *initial* centroids for the k-means, thus reducing the probability of getting stuck at suboptimal solutions. On the other hand, the k-means also improves CGA-I by fine-tuning rough solutions. In summary, the only difference between CGA-II (Fig.1) and CGA-I is that, in the latter, Step 2 is not performed. The computational cost of CGA-I is estimated as $O(N^2)$, whereas the cost of the k-means algorithm is $O(N)$. Hence, in principle, CGA-II is as costly as CGA-I. However, the use of k-means together with the standard CGA can speed up the CGA-I convergence, as shown in Section 4. From a different perspective, one can consider

that the CGA provides an approach to automatically optimize the k-means algorithm, both in relation to the initial centroids and in relation to the number of clusters. This interpretation of CGA-II seems to be particularly useful for the bioinformatics community, in which the k-means algorithm is quite popular [1,2].

1. Initialize a population of random genotypes;
2. Apply the k-means algorithm to each genotype;
3. Evaluate each genotype according to its silhouette;
4. Apply a linear normalization (ranking);
5. Select genotypes by proportional selection;
6. Apply crossover and mutation;
7. Replace the old genotypes by the ones formed in Step 6;
8. If convergence is attained, stop; else, go to Step 2.

Figure 1. Main steps of CGA-II (CGA-I + k-means).

3.2. CGA-III

The second modification proposed concerns improving the efficiency of the CGA-II objective function. In this sense, the traditional silhouette function [3], which depends on the computation of all distances among all objects, is replaced with one based on the distances among objects and centroids of the clusters currently available. The parameter $a(i)$ of Eqn. (1) now corresponds to the dissimilarity of object i to its corresponding cluster (**A**) centroid. Similarly, instead of computing $d(i,\mathbf{C})$ as the average dissimilarity of i to all objects of $\mathbf{C}$, $\mathbf{C} \neq \mathbf{A}$, we propose to compute the distances between i and the centroid of $\mathbf{C}$. These modifications significantly reduce the computational cost of the algorithm and cause a synergy between the objective function and the k-means algorithm to take place, for they are now both based on centroids. Thus, CGA-III is only different from CGA-II in Step 3, which makes the CGA-III complexity to be $O(N)$.

3.3. Evolutionary Algorithm for Clustering-EAC

In a nutshell, the EAC is derived by equipping CGA-III with more powerful mutation operators designed to make up for the removal of the crossover operator. Our motivation to propose the EAC comes from the fact that the mutation operators are much less computationally expensive than the crossover operator. Besides, we also intend to evaluate the influence of the crossover operator (which basically combines clustering solutions) when compared with more powerful mutation operators. To do so, the modified mutation operators are allowed to act in more than one cluster. Thus, the mutation operator 1 eliminates one or more clusters $(1,...,k-2)$. The second mutation operator splits one or more clusters $(1,..,k)$, which must be formed by at least two objects to be eligible for this operator, each of which into two new clusters. The basic mechanisms of the CGA operators are still valid in the EAC, considering that 50% of the genotypes are mutated by operator 1 and the others are mutated by operator 2.

4. Simulations Using Bioinformatics Datasets

The assessment of clustering accuracy requires datasets for which the clusters are *a priori* known. However, one rarely has *a priori* knowledge of which objects should be clustered together, especially in the case of clustering genes [2]. To overcome this limitation, Yeung et al. [2] created synthetic array datasets with error distributions taken from real data. These datasets, in which the clusters are known, are crucial for the development and testing of clustering algorithms [2]. Thus, we employed the datasets (without repeated measurements and with low noise levels) proposed in [2] to test CGA-I, CGA-II, CGA-III and EAC. These datasets are formed by 400 genes and 20 attributes. There are 6 clusters in each dataset. These *known clusters* will, from now on, be called *classes*, whereas the term *cluster* will refer to each group of similar objects found by the clustering algorithms. In this sense, our simulations were designed to verify the accuracy (according to the classes) and efficiency (computational effort) of our evolutionary clustering algorithms. Although the classes of each gene are known *a priori*, this information is not used in the clustering process. The algorithms CGA-I, CGA-II, CGA-III and EAC were implemented in *C Language*, *incrementally* from CGA-I to EAC, and using only the strictly necessary additional commands. This way, more uniform efficiency comparisons can be performed.

In our simulations, populations formed by 4 genotypes were used. This is the smallest possible population in the context of the CGAs. By doing this, we can show how effective the proposed methods are in the most adverse situation. In order to perform fair comparisons, the EAC was also evaluated employing 4 genotypes. The Euclidean norm was used to compute dissimilarities between objects. The data were normalized within the interval [0,1]. The *k*-means algorithm was programmed to stop when one of the following criteria is satisfied: (i) 5 iterations; or (ii) the maximum absolute difference between centroids in 2 consecutive iterations is less than or equal to 0.001.

Initially, we performed simulations considering initial populations randomly generated, in which each genotype represents 100 clusters. This is a reasonable value to this parameter, because it can be assumed that the maximum number of clusters is equal to 200 (clusters formed by at least two objects) and that the minimum number of clusters is 2. Thus, considering that the number of clusters

is unknown, it is reasonable to use an approximate mean value of the aforementioned extreme values.

For each algorithm/dataset, 15 simulations were run in a Pentium IV, 1.8 GHz CPU, 512 MB RAM, until one of the following criteria is met: (i) the objective function value (OFV) corresponding to the *right* or a better solution is found; or (ii) 10,000 generations are performed. The OFV for the right and found solutions are shown in Table 1. It is important to emphasize that the algorithms have different objective functions (see Section 3 for further details). The employed clustering algorithms have provided similar results in terms of accuracy, and Table 2 summarizes these results.

Table 1. *Right* (classes) and found (clusters) Objective Function Values (OFVs) in dataset D.

D	Right CGA-{I,II}	Found CGA-{I,II}	Right CGA-III/EAC	Found CGA-III/EAC
1	0.671	0.671	0.774	0.774
2	0.502	0.705	0.597	0.799
3	0.395	0.722	0.530	0.807
4	0.728	0.728	0.816	0.816
5	0.661	0.659/0.661	0.765	0.765

Table 2. Number of clusters in each dataset. Numbers between parentheses indicate labels of *mixed* classes.

D	CGA-I	CGA-II	CGA-III	EAC
1	6	6	6	6
2	5 (1∪2)	5 (1∪2)	5 (1∪2)	5 (1∪2)
3	4 (1∪2;3∪4)	4 (1∪2;3∪4)	4 (1∪2;3∪4)	4 (1∪2;3∪4)
4	6	6	6	6
5	5 (1∪4)	6	6	6

In datasets 1, 4 and 5, all algorithms have found the right classes (OFVs given in Table 1), except for simulations with CGA-I and CGA-II in the fifth dataset. In this dataset, CGA-I found 5 clusters, which provided an OFV equal to 0.659, by joining classes 1 and 4 in the same cluster. This *error* represents a difference of 0.3%, which could be cancelled out in a higher number of generations. CGA-II, in turn, found 7 clusters (the correct classes and a singleton, formed by the second gene) in 7 simulations. Doing so, the OFV is equal to 0.662, slightly better than 0.661 (6 classes). This fact points out that this gene is somewhat different from the other ones of its class. In a real application, one could better investigate the characteristics of this gene, which could also be considered an outlier. Indeed, this is an interesting characteristic for tools aimed at exploratory data analysis.

In datasets 2 and 3, all algorithms have systematically joined classes. In fact, the OFVs actually found in these datasets are higher than those given by the classes (Table 1). This situation happens when the classes are so similar that it is better (under the perspective of the employed objective function) to join them. However, good estimations of the correct number of clusters were obtained. In real-world datasets, one could focus on a number of clusters around the obtained values.

We have also used the OFVs (Table 1) as a basis to evaluate the computational cost of each clustering solution. Specifically, when the algorithms reach those values, their computing times are stored. A summary of the simulation results is described in Table 3, where μ_i and σ_i represent the average and the standard deviation for each dataset (D) i over 15 simulations, respectively.

Table 3. Computing times in seconds: μ_i-σ_i ($k_{initial}$ =100).

D	CGA-I	CGA-II	CGA-III	EAC
1	154.10-66.33	12.80-5.09	12.38-5.11	8.33-1.73
2	87.85-42.66	18.44-7.79	26.37-10.60	9.59-4.29
3	129.89-51.41	15.51-8.95	19.35-12.89	7.29-1.40
4	103.33-62.64	10.87-2.32	14.96-4.34	9.21-3.77
5	39.26-27.24	22.36-27.07	15.63-3.48	9.42-2.60

Table 3 indicates that, in general, increasingly better results in terms of reduction in CPU time were obtained from CGA-I to EAC. In fact, this hypothesis was statistically tested by means of the Wilcoxon/Mann-Whitney test. In summary, we concluded that, at α=5%, our simulations support that the average CPU times of CGA-II are less than those of CGA-I, i.e. the incorporation of k-means into the CGA has speeded up its convergence. The CGA-III, by its turn, has not shown such a superior performance when compared to CGA-II. In fact, even in datasets 1 and 5, where apparent performance gains were achieved, there is no sample evidence to support that CGA-III is more efficient than CGA-II at the α=5% level. We believe that this result is due to the information loss caused by their centroid-based objective functions. This loss may make up for the computational savings resulting from using centroid-based objective functions, depending on the dataset and on the initial population. Therefore, this subject deserves further investigations.

An interesting aspect to be observed in these simulations is the superior efficiency of EAC in relation to the CGAs (α=5%). Also, the simulation results obtained for initial populations randomly generated with k=100 are very encouraging, because they have a practical appeal. From a different perspective, these simulations have also represented scenarios in which the values of k were overestimated. However, it is also important to evaluate the performance of our algorithms in another *extreme* scenario in terms of the number of clusters, namely, choosing initial populations in which all genotypes represent two clusters (minimum amount). These simulations are intended to show that our evolutionary algorithms are also able to increase underestimated values for the number of clusters. Table 4 shows the simulation results in terms of CPU time for 15

simulations in this scenario. In what concerns accuracy, the results are equal to those described in Table 2.

Table 4 shows that the average CPU times of CGA-II were less than those of CGA-I. This result is supported by the Wilcoxon/Mann-Whitney test with α = 5%. However, unlike the previous scenario ($k_{initial}$=100), the efficiency of CGA-III was better than that of CGA-II in four out of five datasets (at the α=5% level). Indeed, CGA-III has even shown similar performances to the EAC ones in two out of five datasets and has provided better results in other two, whereas the EAC has shown to be more efficient in the fifth dataset. We also believe that more significant differences (in favor of EAC) were not observed because the initial number of clusters was set very close to the right number of clusters.

Table 4. Computing times in seconds: μ_i-σ_i ($k_{initial}$ =2).

D	CGA-I	CGA-II	CGA-III	EAC
1	169.53-114.08	69.75-39.19	1.08-0.51	2.31-1.47
2	12.29-13.15	1.77-2.05	0.83-0.20	0.84-0.50
3	10.05-18.35	0.93-0.22	0.62-0.45	0.61-0.38
4	33.15-45.02	1.68-0.67	1.21-0.52	2.24-1.58
5	991.48-1172.80	45.05-45.01	52.26-46.63	4.17-3.16

5. Conclusions and Future Work

This work tackled the problem of clustering genes by means of evolutionary algorithms that estimate the *right* number of clusters. Several simulations in bioinformatics datasets were performed. All algorithms have shown good results in terms of accuracy, and the proposed Evolutionary Algorithm for Clustering (EAC) has shown better or similar performances, in terms of efficiency, in 80% of the simulations. Considering future works, we are going to evaluate our algorithms (mainly the EAC) in real-world datasets as well as to investigate structural improvements to the genetic operators.

6. References

[1] Valafar, F., Pattern Recognition Techniques in Microarray Data Analysis: A Survey, Annals of NY Acad Sci, 980, 41-64, Techniques in Bioinformatics and Medical Informatics, 2002.
[2] Yeung, K.Y., Medvedovic, M., Bumgarner, R.E., Clustering gene-expression data with repeated measurements, Genome Biology, v.4, issue 5, article R34, 2003.
[3] Kaufman, L., Rousseeuw, P. J., Finding Groups in Data – An Introduction to Cluster Analysis, Wiley Series in Probability and Mathematical Statistics, 1990.
[4] Hruschka, E.R., Ebecken, N.F.F., A genetic algorithm for cluster analysis, Intelligent Data Analysis (7), pp. 15-25, IOS Press, 2003.
[5] Hruschka, E.R., Campello, R.J.G.B., de Castro, L.N., Improving the Efficiency of a Clustering Genetic Algorithm, Proc. of the Iberamia 2004 (LNAI), to appear.

Mining Ratio Rules Via Principal Sparse Non-Negative Matrix Factorization

Chenyong Hu[1],Benyu Zhang[2],Shuicheng Yan[3],Qiang Yang[4],Jun Yan[3],Zheng Chen[2],Wei-Ying Ma[2]

[1] *Institute of Software, CAS,Beijing, P.R. China*
huchenyong@itechs.iscas.ac.cn

[2]*Microsoft Research Asia, Beijing*
{byzhang,zhengc,wyma}@microsoft.com}

[3]*LMAM, Peking University, Beijing, P.R. China*
yanjun@math.pku.edu.cn
v-scyan @msrchina.research.microsoft.com
[4]*Hong Kong University of Science and Technology*
qyang@cs.ust.hk

Abstract

Association rules are traditionally designed to capture statistical relationship among itemsets in a given database. To additionally capture the quantitative association knowledge, F.Korn et al recently proposed a paradigm named Ratio Rules [4] for quantifiable data mining. However, their approach is mainly based on Principle Component Analysis (PCA) and as a result, it cannot guarantee that the ratio coefficient is non-negative. This may lead to serious problems in the rules' application. In this paper, we propose a new method, called Principal Sparse Non-Negative Matrix Factorization (PSNMF), for learning the associations between itemsets in the form of Ratio Rules. In addition, we provide a support measurement to weigh the importance of each rule for the entire dataset.

1. Introduction

Association rules are one of the major representations in representing the knowledge discovered from large databases. The problem of association rule mining (ARM) in large transactional databases was introduced in [1, 3], Its basic idea is to discover important and interesting associations among the data items. The form of such association is as following:

$$\{bread,milk\} => butter \ (80\%)$$

To find association rules, most prevalent approaches assume the transactions only carry Boolean information and ignore the valuable knowledge inherent in the quantities of the items. In fact, considering that the quantities of the items normally contain valuable information for us, it is necessary to provide a definition of quantitative association rules when the datasets contain quantitative attributes. Several efficient algorithms for mining quantitative association rules have been proposed in the past [2, 7]. A notable algorithm is the work [4], where they provided a stronger set of rules as *Ratio Rules*. A rule under this framework is expressed in the following form:

$$bread : milk : butter = a : b : c$$

$$(a,b,c \ is \ arbitrary \ numerical \ values)$$

This rule states that for each *a* amount spent on bread, a customer normally spends *b* amount on milk and *c* amount on butter.

Principal Component Analysis (PCA) is often used to discover the *eigen-vectors* of a dataset. Ratio Rules [4] can represent the quantitative associations between items as the principal *eigen-vectors*, where the values *a*, *b* and *c* in the example above correspond to the projections of the eigenvector. Because the element of *eigen-vector* can be either positive or negative, sometime the ratio coefficient of Ratio Rules may contain negative value, such as

$$Shoe: Coat: Hat = 1: -2: -5$$

Obviously, such rule loses the intuitive appeal of associations between items, because a customer's spending should always be positive.

Our method amounts to a novel application of non-negative matrix factorization (NMF) [5]. However, we cannot directly apply NMF for our purpose, because it is still difficult to explain that these latent components represent the latent association between items in a quantifiable dataset. We need to provide a bridge to bring NMF closer to association rules.

In this work, we propose a novel method called *Principal Sparse Non-Negative Matrix Factorization* (PSNMF), which adds the sparsity constraint as well as the non-negativity constraint in the standard NMF[5].

The rest of the paper is organized as follows: Section 2 describes the problem and the intuition behind the Ratio Rules. Section 3 introduces our new algorithm (PSNMF). Section 4 presents the experimental results. Section 5 concludes the paper. The convergence of PSNMF learning procedure is provided in Appendix.

2. Problem Definition

The problem that we tackle is as follows. Given a $N \times M$ matrix V (e.g., market basket databases), the entity v_{ij} gives the amount spent by customers on the product. The goal is to find all Ratio Rules of the form:

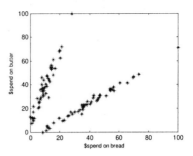 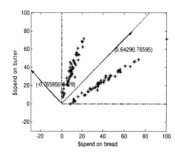 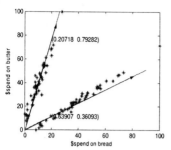

(a) A data matrix with 2-dimension   (b) Ratio Rules identified by PCA   c)Ratio Rules identified by PSNMF

Fig 1. A data matrix and latent associations discovered by PCA and PSNMF

$$v_1 : v_2 : v_3 : ... : v_M \quad (v_i \geq 0)$$

The above form means that customers who buys the items will spend v_1, v_2 ... respectively on each itemset.

Fig1.(a) lists distribution of the matrix V which is organized with N customers and M ($M = 2$) products Here we assume that the dataset is consisted with two clusters. Our goal is to capture the associations between items. We list two Ratio Rules discovered by PCA[4] in Fig.1 (b), where one contains negative values:

$$bread : butter = -0.77 : 0.64$$

Obviously, the negative association between items ("bread" and "butter") does not make sense. Furthermore, it is obvious that the Ratio Rules deviate with the latent associations behind the distribution of these points.

In fact, from Fig 1.(a), we find that the latent associations are not mutually orthogonal, while the method by PCA imposes the orthogonality constraint on these ratio rules. Therefore, Ratio Rules based on PCA cannot truly reflect the latent associations among the items correctly. Compared to Fig.1 (b), Fig 1(c) illustrates the Ratio Rules captured by our proposed PSNMF. Surprisingly, each rule could be treated as an association in the two clusters respectively.

3. Principal Sparse Non-Negative Matrix Factorization (PSNMF)

Given a $M \times N$ non-negative matrix V, denote a set of $P \ll M$ basis components by a $M \times P$ matrix W, where each transaction (column vector) can be represented as a linear combination of the basis components using the approximate factorization:

$$V \approx WH \qquad (1)$$

where H is a $P \times N$ coefficients matrix.

3.1 Non-negative Matrix Factorization(NMF)

Because the entries of W and H calculated by PCA

may contain negative values, NMF [5] is proposed as a procedure for matrix factorization which imposes non-negative instead of orthogonal constraint, and NMF uses the I-divergence of V from Y, which is defined as

$$D(V \| Y) = \sum_{i,j}(v_{ij}\log\frac{v_{ij}}{y_{ij}} - v_{ij} + y_{ij}) \qquad (2)$$

As the measurement of fitness for factorizing V into $WH \triangleq Y = [Y_{ij}]$, a NMF factorization is defined as

$$\min_{W,H} D(V \| WH) \quad s.t \ W, \ H \geq 0, \ \sum_i w_{ij} = 1 \ \forall j \qquad (3)$$

The above optimization can be done by using multiplicative update rules [5].

3.2 Sparse Non-negative Matrix Factorization (SNMF)

Although NMF is successful in Matrix Factorization, the NMF model does not impose the sparse constraints. Therefore, it can hardly yield a factorization, which reveals local sparse features in the data V. Related sparse coding is proposed in the work of [6] for matrix factorization.

Inspired by the original NMF and sparse coding, the aim of our work is to propose Sparse Non-negative Matrix Factorization (SNMF), which imposes the sparse and non-negative constraint. Therefore, we put forward the following constrained divergence as objective function:

$$D(V \| Y) = \sum_{i,j}(v_{ij}\log\frac{v_{ij}}{y_{ij}} - v_{ij} + y_{ij}) + \lambda\sum_j\|l_j\|_1 \qquad (4)$$

$$l_j = (h_{1j}, h_{2j}, h_{3j}, ..., h_{pj})^T \ denotes \ the \ column \ of \ H.$$

where $WH \triangleq Y = [Y_{ij}]$, and λ obtained by experience was assumed a positive constant. As the measurement of fitness for factorizing V into $WH \triangleq Y = [Y_{ij}]$, a SNMF factorization is defined as:

$$\min_{W,H} D(V \| WH) \qquad (5)$$

$$s.t \ \forall i,j: \ W_{ij} \geq 0, \ H_{ij} \geq 0, \ and \ \forall i \ \|w_i\|_1 = 1$$

Notice that we have chosen to measure sparseness by a linear activation penalty (i.e. minimum the 1-norm of the column of H). A Sparse solution to the above constrained minimization can be found by the following update rules:

$$h_{kl} = h_{kl} \sum_i v_{il} \frac{w_{ik}}{\sum_k (w_{ik} h_{kl})} \bigg/ \left(\sum_i w_{ik} + \lambda \right) \qquad (6)$$

$$w_{kl} = w_{kl} \sum_j v_{kj} \frac{h_{lj}}{\sum_l w_{kl} h_{lj}} \bigg/ \sum_j h_{lj} \qquad (7)$$

To make the solution unique, we further require that the 1-normal of the column vector in matrix W is one. In addition, matrix H needs to be adjusted accordingly.

$$w_{kl} = w_{kl} \bigg/ \sum_k w_{kl} \qquad (8)$$

$$h_{kl} = h_{kl} \sum_k w_{kl} \qquad (9)$$

It is proved that the objective function is non-increasing under the above iterative updating rules, and the convergence of the iteration is guaranteed (in Appendix).

3.3 Principal SNMF

When the dataset V is decomposed with W and H, each column value of H represents the corresponding projection on the basis space W. As a whole, the sum of every row vector of H represents the importance of corresponding base. Therefore, we define a *support* measurement after normalizing every column of H:

$$h_{kl} = h_{kl} \bigg/ \sum_k h_{kl} \qquad (10)$$

Definition. For every rule (column vector) of W, we define a support measurement:

$$support(w_i) = \sum_j h_{ij} \bigg/ \sum_{ij} h_{ij} \qquad (11)$$

Consequently, we can measure the importance of each rule for the entire dataset by their *support* values. The more value of *support* implies the more importance of such rule for the whole dataset.

In order to select the principal k rules as Ratio Rules, firstly, we rank the whole rules in descending by the *support* value. And then, retain the first k principal rules as Ratio Rules because they are more important than others. About the selection of k value, a simple method is taken such as:

$$\min_k \left(\frac{\sum_{i=1}^{k} support(w_i)}{\sum_{i=1}^{M} support(w_i)} > threshold \right) \qquad (12)$$

From above (12), Ratio Rules are obtained effectively according that the sum of k *support* values of rules cover *threshold (i.e.90%)* of the grand total *support* values.

4. Experiments

Synthetic dataset:

We have applied both the PSNMF and the PCA to a dataset that consists of two clusters, which contains 25

Gaussian distribution points on x-y plain (generated with mu=[3;5], sigma=[1,1.2;1.2,2]) and 50 points on y-z plain. (Fig2.)(Generated with mu=[3;5], sigma=[2,1.6;1.6,2]).

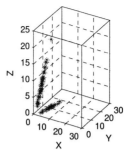

Fig 2.Dataset with two clusters

Table 1. Ratio Rules based on PSNMF and PCA

PSNMF	RR_1	RR_2	RR_3
(X)	0.000	0.696	0.020
(Y)	0.493	0.304	0.980
(Z)	0.507	0.000	0.000
$Sum(w_i)$	49.88	21.64	3.488
$Support(w_i)$	0.665	0.289	0.046

PCA	RR_1	RR_2
(X)	-0.52	0.72
(Y)	-0.77	-0.15
(Z)	-0.38	-0.68

(a)Based on PSNMF   (b) Based on PCA

Table 1.(a) lists all the rules and corresponding *support* values. After ranking such rules, Ratio Rules are obtained since $support(w_1) + support(w_2) = 0.9535 > 90\%$.

$$rule_1 :: \quad X:Y:Z => 0:0.493:0.507 \qquad (0.6650)$$
$$rule_2 :: \quad X:Y:Z => 0.696:0.304:0 \qquad (0.2885)$$

For example, 2/3 transactions (the cluster with distribution on y-z plain) are mostly depended on $rule_1$ and others on $rule_2$. Therefore, the corresponding *support* value (0.665) of $rule_1$ does not contradict with intuition. Otherwise, Table 1.(b) lists the Ratio Rules by PCA which is difficult to explain the negative association obviously.

Real Dataset: NBA (459×11)

This dataset comes from basketball statistics obtained from the 97-98 season, including minutes played, Point per Game, Assist per Game, etc. The reason why we select this dataset is that it can give a intuitive meaning of such latent associations. Table 2 presents the first three Ratio Rules (RR_1, RR_2, RR_3) by the PSNMF. Based on a general knowledge of basketball, we conjecture the RR_1 represent the agility of a player, which gives the ratio of Assists per Game and Steals, is $0.206:0.220 \approx 1:1$. It means that the average player who possess one time of assist per game will be also steal the ball one time, and so does $RR_2 (0.117:0.263 \approx 1:2.25)$. In this case, traditional method cannot give such information behind the dataset.

Table 2. Ratio Rules by PSNMF from NBA

field	RR_1	RR_2	RR_3
Games			0.450
Minute			0.013
Points Per Game			0.010
Rebound Per Game		0.117	
Assists per Game	0.206		
Steals	0.220		
Fouls		0.263	
3Points			

5. Conclusion

In this work, we proposed Principal Sparse Non-Negative Matrix Factorization (PSNMF) for learning sparse non-negative components in matrix factorization. It aims to learn latent components which are called Ratio Rules. Experimental results illustrate that our Ratio Rules are more suited for representing associations between items than that by PCA.

References

[1] Agrawal, R., Imielinski, T. and Swami, A.N., Mining association rules between sets of items in large databases. In *the Proc. of the ACM SIGMOD*, (1993), 207-216.

[2] Aumann, Y. and Lindell, Y., A statistical theory for quantitative association rules. In *the Proc. KDD*, (1999).

[3] Han, J. and Fu, Y., Discovery of Multiple-Level Association Rules from Large Databases. In *Proc. of the VLDB*, (1995), 420--431.

[4] Korn, F., Labrinidis, A., Kotidis, Y. and Faloutsos, C., Ratio rules: A new paradigm for fast, quantifiable data mining. In *the Proc. of the VLDB*, (1998), 582-593.

[5] Lee, D.D. and Seung, H.S., Algorithms for nonnegative matrix factorization. In *Proc. of the Advances in Neural Information Processing Systems 13*, (2001), 556-- 562.

[6] Olshausen, B.A. and Field, D.J. Emergence of simple-cell receptive field properties by learning a sparse code for natural images. *Nature 381(1996)*. 607--609.

[7] Srikant, r. and Agrawal, R., Mining quantitative association rules in large relational tables. In *Proc. of the ACM SIGMOD* (1996).

Appendix

To prove the convergence of the leaning algorithm (6)-(7), an auxiliary function $G(H, Z')$ is given for objective function $L(Z)$ with the properties that $G(Z, Z') \geq L(Z))$ and $G(Z, Z) = L(Z)$, we will show that the multiplicative update rule corresponds to setting ,at each iteration ,the new state vector to the values that minimize the auxiliary function:

$$Z^{(t+1)} = \arg\min_z G(Z, Z') \qquad (13)$$

Then the objective function $L(Z)$ is non-increasing when Z is updated using (13), because of

$$L(Z^{(t+1)}) \leq G(Z^{(t+1)}, Z') \leq G(Z', Z') = L(Z') .$$

Updating H : with W fixed, H is updated by minimizing $L(H) = D(V \| WH)$. An auxiliary function is constructed for $L(H)$ as:

$$G(H, H') = \sum_{i,j} v_{ij} \log v_{ij} - \sum_{i,j,k} v_{ij} \frac{w_{ik} h_{kj}'}{\sum_k w_{ik} h_{kj}'} \left(\log \left(w_{ik} h_{kj} \right) - \log \frac{w_{ik} h_{kj}'}{\sum_k w_{ik} h_{kj}'} \right)$$
$$+ \sum_{i,j} y_{ij} - \sum_{i,j} v_{ij} + \lambda \sum_{i,j} h_{ij}$$

Since it is easy to verify $\sum_j \|l_j\|_1 = \sum_{i,j} h_{ij}$, therefore it is not difficult to testify $G(H, H) = L(H)$. The following proves $G(H, H') \geq L(H)$. Because $\log(\sum_k w_{ik} h_{kj})$ is a convex function, the following holds for all i,j and $\sum_k \mu_{ijk} = 1$:

$$-\log(\sum_k w_{ik} h_{kj}) \leq -(\sum_k \mu_{ijk} \log \frac{w_{ik} h_{kj}}{\mu_{ijk}}) \quad (where \ \mu_{ijk} = \frac{w_{ik} h_{kj}'}{\sum_k w_{ik} h_{kj}'})$$

thus

$$-\log(\sum_k w_{ik} h_{kj}) \leq -(\sum_k \frac{w_{ik} h_{kj}'}{\sum_k w_{ik} h_{kj}'} \left(\log w_{ik} h_{kj} - \log \frac{w_{ik} h_{kj}'}{\sum_k w_{ik} h_{kj}'} \right)$$

Thus, $G(H, H') \geq L(H)$.

To minimize $L(H)$, we update H by:

$$H^{(t+1)} = \arg\min_H G(H, H') \qquad (14)$$

for all kl

$$\frac{\partial G(H, H')}{\partial h_{kl}} = -\sum_i v_{il} \frac{w_{ik} h_{kj}'}{\sum_k w_{ik} h_{kj}'} \frac{1}{h_{kl}} + \sum_i b_{i.k} + \lambda = 0$$

Solving for H, this gives:

$$h_{kl} = h_{kl}' \sum_i v_{il} \frac{w_{ik}}{\sum_k \left(w_{ik} h_{kl}' \right)} \Big/ \left(\sum_i w_{ik} + \lambda \right)$$

which is the desired updated H.

Updating W : with H fixed, W is updated by minimizing $L(W) = D(V \| WH)$. The auxiliary function is

$$G(W, W') = \sum_{i,j} v_{ij} \log v_{ij} - \sum_{i,j,k} v_{ij} \frac{w_{ik}' h_{kj}}{\sum_k w_{ik}' h_{kj}} \left(\log \left(w_{ik} h_{kj} \right) - \log \frac{w_{ik}' h_{kj}}{\sum_k w_{ik}' h_{kj}} \right)$$
$$+ \sum_{i,j} y_{ij} - \sum_{i,j} v_{ij} + \lambda \sum_{i,j} h_{ij}$$

It is easily to prove $G(W, W) = L(W)$ and $G(W, W') \geq L(W)$ likewise. we can get:

$$w_{kl} = w_{kl}' \sum_j v_{kj} \frac{h_{lj}}{\sum_k w_{kl}' h_{lj}} \Big/ \sum_j h_{lj}$$

This completes the proof.

Feature Selection via Supervised Model Construction

Y Huang, PJ. McCullagh, ND. Black

*School of Computing and Mathematics, Faculty of Engineering, University of Ulster, Jordanstown,
BT37 0QB, Northern Ireland, UK
E-mail: yhuang@infj.ulst.ac.uk, {pj.mccullagh, nd.black}@ulst.ac.uk*

Abstract

ReliefF is a feature mining technique, which has been successfully used in data mining applications. However, ReliefF is sensitive to the definition of relevance that is used in its implementation and when handling a large data set, it is computationally expensive. This paper presents an optimisation (Feature Selection via Supervised Model Construction) for data transformation and starter selection, and evaluates its effectiveness with C4.5. Experiments indicate that the proposed method gave improvement of computation efficiency whilst maintaining classification accuracy of trial data sets.

Keywords: *Feature Selection, ReliefF*

1. Introduction

Feature selection is the process of identifying and removing as much of the irrelevant and redundant information as possible. It may be used to satisfy the general goal of maximizing the accuracy of the classifier while minimizing the associated measurement costs; improve accuracy by reducing irrelevant and possibly redundant features; reduce the complexity and the associated computational cost; and improve the chances that a solution will both understandable and practical [1].

This paper presents an optimized approach, called FSSMC (Feature Selection via Supervised Model Construction), by augmenting a typical feature subset selection algorithm ReliefF. The resulting algorithm is simpler and faster to execute on different data sets as a result of a reduction of the training data.

2. Relief and ReliefF

The Relief method was initially introduced in by Kira Rendell in 1992 [2]. It is a feature weight-based algorithm inspired by instance-based learning algorithms. The Relief family of algorithms (Relief, ReliefF and RReliefF) have commonly been viewed as feature subset selection methods that are applied in a pre-processing step before the model is learned, and are amongst the most successful algorithms [3]. The majority of the heuristic measures for estimating the quality of the attributes assume the conditional (upon the target variable) independence of the attributes and are therefore less appropriate in problems which possibly involve *much* feature interaction. Relief algorithms do not make this assumption. They are efficient, aware of the contextual information, and can correctly estimate the quality of attributes in problems with strong dependencies between attributes.

The key idea of original Relief is to estimate the quality of attributes according to how well their values distinguish among instances that are near to each other. The rationale is that a good attribute should differentiate between instances from different classes and should have the same value for instances of the same class.

ReliefF, the extension of Relief, solves the multi-class data sets problem, and can deal with noisy and incomplete data. ReliefF smoothes the influence of noise in the data by averaging the contribution of k nearest neighbours from the same and opposite class of each sampled instance, instead of the single nearest neighbour. Selection of the number of nearest neighbours is the basic difference to Relief and ensures greater robustness of the algorithm with regards to noise. User-defined parameter k controls the locality of the estimates. Multi-class data sets are handled by finding the nearest neighbours from each class that are different from the current sampled instance, and weighting their contributions by the prior probability of each class estimated form the training data [2].

3. The optimization of ReliefF

Although ReliefF has been successfully applied in many aspects [4,5], two issues are worth investigating.
1) The way to deal with different attributes. ReliefF did not address the problem of multi valued attributes [2]. At present, the similarity measurement is a numerical-oriented method. So when coping with the categorical attributes, if the two selected instances have the same value, the result of difference function is 0, otherwise is 1. This definition cannot measure the contribution of multi-class (>=3) discrete value to class label respectively [6,7].
2) The setting of parameter m, which is the number of instances sampled from the data set. Usually it is set

empirically or the entire data are analysed. In this research, an instance selecting method has been used to find typical instances that can represent the whole data, generate *m* automatically and improve the efficiency of the algorithm.

3.1. Data transformation

In order to improve the performance of data mining techniques, data transformation techniques are applied. Data transformation is one of the most important steps of the knowledge discovery process, which affects the accuracy of the results greatly [6].

In the research, we applied the frequency based encoding scheme [7] to transform categorical data to numerical data. We represent the categorical code of a particular variable with a numerical value derived from its relation frequency among the outcomes (Class label) as defined below:

$$y_{jk} = P(C_k)_{ij} / \sum_{k=1}^{K} P(C_k)_{ij}$$

Where
y_{jk} is the new numerical value of categorical variable y_j;
$P(C_k)$ is the probability of being Class C_k coming from category *i* of attribute *j*;
K is the class number of class label.

3.2. Supervised Model Construction for Starter Selection

In ReliefF, users choose an appropriate value for *m*, and the performance of feature selection is significantly dependent on *m* and the initially selected instances.

The conventional method is to use the entire data for analysis or run the algorithms many times with different values and then decide which has the best performance. When *m* is not the whole data, the instance used for finding the nearest neighbours is randomly selected from the database.

Obviously, if *m* is equal to the number of all the training instances, the best results can be achieved. When the data set is not large, the result will be very successful. But in contrast, it will be a significant computational burden if there are a large number of records in the database.

In order to overcome this problem, the novel algorithm by Supervised Model Construction [8] is applied for starter selection. This approach eliminates the dependency on the selection of a "good value" for *m*. The motivation is to improve the efficiency of ReliefF whilst preserving the accuracy.

The basic idea of FSSMC is to find the representatives of the total training data for feature selection, i.e. building an inductive learning model from the training dataset and using this model (set of representatives) for feature selection.

For example, there is a training data set with two classes {cross, point} distributed in two-dimensional data space. In this example, Euclidean distance has been used as the similarity measurement.

It is clear that many data points with the same class label are close to each other in many local areas. So these points can be grouped, averaging their values, using the centre point as a good representation of the local region (Figure 1). Thus the size of the training data can be significantly reduced and improve the efficiency of next stage of analysis.

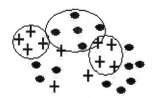

Figure 1. Grouped data points

The key issue is how to determine the scope of the local region. In the model construction process, we first randomly select an instance *I* from the training data, calculating the distance (similarity function) between instance *I* and all the other instances in the training data. And then the nearest instance R_x with same class label is grouped to the group G_i. The procedure will be repeated until meeting the first instance with a different class label. Next, another ungrouped instance will be selected until all the training data has been grouped.

The algorithm is described in Figure 2.

Obviously, it is unnecessary to choose a specific *m* for further analysis. The parameter *m* can be generated automatically in the model construction procedure, and will be different when applying to different data sets.

4. Classification based on FSSMC

There are many possible measures for evaluating feature selection algorithms [9]. Classification accuracy and computing time of feature selection have been used to compare the performance of FSSMC algorithm to InfoGain and ReliefF.

The UCI Repository is a widely-used repository of databases, domain theories and data generators collected by the machine learning community for the empirical analysis of machine learning algorithms [10]. Nine benchmark datasets are applied to study the performance of these feature selection techniques.

Information about the data sets and the dimensionality reduction of Feature Selection summarized in Table 1.

```
Algorithm FSSCM
Input: for each training instance a vector of attribute values and
the class value
Output: the vector W of estimations of the qualities of attributes


1.   for A:=1 to a do
2.       if (A is Categorical) then TransferToNum(A1, A);
3.   set all weights W[A]:=0;
4.   m:=StarterSet();
5.   for i:=1 to m do begin
6.       Select instance R_i from StarterSet();
7.       Find k nearest hits H_j of R_i;
8.       for each class C ≠ class(R_i) do
9.           from class C find k nearest misses M_j(C);
10.  for A:=1 to a do
```

$$W[A] := W[A] - \sum_{j=1}^{k} diff(A, R_i, H_j)/(m \bullet k) +$$

$$\sum_{C \neq class(R_i)} [\frac{P(C)}{1 - P(class(R_i))} \sum_{j=1}^{k} diff(A, R_i, M_j(C))]/(m \bullet k);$$

```
11.  end.
```

TransferToNum(A1,A): the function to transfer categorical attributes, *A1* is newly generated attribute of *A*

StarterSet(): the function to identify the instance for further analysis, return the value of selected instance number

m: the number of randomly selected instances, the value is generated by *StarterSet()*

diff(A, I_x, I_v): calculating the difference between the values of the attribute *A* for two instances I_x and I_y.

****

Function StarterSet()
Input: the entire training data
Output: the *m* selected instances from the training data

```
1.   Sign 'UnGroup' to all the training data
2.   Randomly select an instance I from 'UnGroup' instances,
     mark it as 'Grouped', and create a new empty instance set
     Group G_i;
3.   Add I to Group G_i;
4.   for j:=1 to n do
5.       if (R_j is 'UnGroup') then Sim(I, R_j)
6.   Select the nearest neighbour R_x of I with the same class
     label
7.   Sign R_x 'Grouped', add it to Group G_i;
8.   Search another instance with high similarity and same
     class from 'UnGroup' data, repeat 6;
9.   Until meeting a new instance with different class label;
10.  Repeat 2. Until all instances have been 'Grouped'.
11.  Calculate the centre of each group, add them in newly
     instance set GG;
12.  Return m.
```

n: the number of instances in training data
Sim(R_i, R_j): Similarity calculation function
G_i: the *i*th group of the training data

Figure 2. Pseudo code of FSSMC algorithm

Table 1. Number of the Selected Attributes

Data Set	Cases No	Attri- No	IG	RF	FSSMC
Breast	699	9	8	7	7
Credit	690	16	11	11	11
Diabetes	768	8	4	4	4
Glass	214	9	7	7	7
Heart	294	13	5	3	9
Iris	150	4	2	2	2
Labour	57	17	9	7	9
Mushroom	8124	22	13	11	13
Soybean	683	35	26	26	27

IG: InforGain; RF: ReliefF

To evaluate the effect of each method on the performance of a standard decision tree classifier C4.5, ten-fold cross-validation is used as the sampling strategy. For each data set, C4.5 has been tested on the following four subsets of features:

1) Before feature selection (the set of all available attributes)
2) After InfoGain (the feature subset selected by Information Gain)
3) After Relief (the feature subset selected by Relief)
4) After FSSMC (the feature subset selected by FSSMC)

5. Experimental Results and Discussion

From Table 1, the best dimensionality reducer is ReliefF, which considers as relevant only 59.4% of features (on average). FSSMC removes the least number of features. This result suggests that the relevance of some features to the target may be revealed only by a feature selection procedure, which is able to evaluate subsets of features rather than individual features only. We need to emphasize that the attribute subsets generated by each feature selection approach is different. The quality of the features selected by all these strategies is examined below.

The running time of different feature selection methods are demonstrated in Table 2. The analysis is running on the computer with Intel Pentium 4 processor. The InfoGain is the fastest method of feature selection. FSSMC significantly decreases the computational burden resulting from ReliefF for a large data set.

Table 2 also presents the classification accuracy generated by decision tree C4.5 before and after different feature selection methods.

As one can see from Table 2, the algorithm FSSMC appears to be the best method among the three feature selection techniques, and ReliefF has better performance than InfoGain, with respect to the accuracy of the C4.5 classifier. However, compared with the results generated by ReliefF, there is no significant classification accuracy improvement of FSSMC except the data set *Soybean*. The reason is that the data set is not large and complicated enough to show the advantages of FSSMC. In addition, decision tree schemes have inherent feature selection mechanism. During the procedure to construct a tree, they select the key predictor gradually.

Table 2. Feature Selection running time (sec.) / Classification Accuracy (%)

Data Set	C4.5			
	Before FS	InfoGain	ReliefF	FSSMC
Breast	0/94.6	0.16/94.8	2.05/95.3	0.15/95.3
Credit	0/86.4	1.15/86.7	3.58/86.4	1.20/86.8
Diabetes	0/74.5	1.26/74.1	2.63/75.8	1.34/75.8
Glass	0/65.4	0.44/69.2	0.56/69.6	0.67/69.6
Heart	0/76.2	0.22/79.9	0.32/80.6	0.41/81.2
Iris	0/95.3	0.05/95.3	0.10/95.3	0.23/95.3
Labour	0/73.7	0.22/75.4	0.41/75.4	0.51/75.4
Mushroom	0/100	0.65/100	446/100	5.86/100
Soybean	0/79.1	0.34/71.2	5.92/79.2	1.73/89.2
Average	0/80.8	0.50/83.0	51.2/84.2	1.34/85.4

In Table 2, the accuracy was reduced after applying InfoGain on the data sets *Diabetes* and *Soybean*. Because InfoGain assumes that attributes are independent, it is not applicable in domains with strong dependencies between attributes.

Although FSSMC retained the most attributes on average, combined computing time (running time of feature selection and classification model construction) is still comparable with the other two. Evaluating the classification accuracy and computational efficiency of the three feature selection strategies, FSSMC can achieve the best combined result. Therefore, FSSMC overcomes the computational problem of ReliefF and has the best performance for feature selection when comparing to ReliefF and InfoGain.

6. Conclusion

In this paper, we presented an optimisation called FSSMC for ReliefF, which can be applied to data sets containing a mixture of nominal and continuous attributes. FSSMC significantly improves the efficiency of ReliefF by reducing the training data set for further analysis. The algorithm performance vs. ReliefF and InfoGain has been evaluated by applying C4.5 on nine benchmark data sets to selected features. Experimental results are encouraging and show promise for FSSMC as a practical feature estimator for common machine learning algorithms. FSSMC has been proved in this study to preserve the accuracy of the full set classifier in most data sets, while using the selected available variables.

References

[1] Steppe. J., K.W. Bauer, "Feature Saliency Measures", *Computers & Mathematics with Applications*, Vol 33, No. 8, 1997, pp. 109-126.

[2] Kononenko I., "Estimating attributes: Analysis and Extension of Relief", *Proceeding of the Seventh European Conference in Machine Learning*, Springer-Verlag, 1994, pp. 171-182.

[3] Robnik M., Kononenko I., *Machine Learning*, Kluwer Academic Publishers, 53, 2003, pp. 23-69.

[4] Kononenko I., Simec E., "Induction of Decision Trees using RELIEFF", *Proceeding of ISSEK Workshop on Mathematical and Statistical Methods in Artificial Intelligence*, Springer, 53, 1995, pp. 199-220.

[5] Robnik M., Kononenko I., "Discretization of continuous attributes using ReliefF", *Proceeding of Electr. and Comp. Sci. Cof.*, ERK-95, 1995, pp. 149-152

[6] Fayyad, U.M, Piatesky-Shapiro, and G., Smytth P., "From Data Mining to Knowledge Discovery: An Overview", *Advances in Knowledge Discovery and Data Mining*, AAAI Press/The MIT Press, 1996, pp. 1-34.

[7] Kauderer H., Mucha H., "Supervised Learning with Qualitative and Mixed Attributes", *Classification, Data Analysis, and Data Highways*, Springer-Verlag, 1997, pp. 374-382.

[8] Guo G., Wang H., Bell D., Bi Y., Greer K., "KNN Model-Based Approach in Classification", *CoopIS/DOA/ODBASE 2003*, Springer-Verlag, 2003, pp. 986-996.

[9] Molina L., Belanche L., Nebot A., "Feature Selection Algorithms: A Survey and Experimental Evaluation", *Proceeding of IEEE International Conference on Data Mining*, IEEE, 2002, pp. 306-313

[10] Blake, C.L. & Merz, C.J., UCI Repository of machine learning databases, *www.ics.uci.edu/~mlearn/*. Irvine, CA: University of California, Department of Information and Computer Science. 1998

Mining Generalized Substructures from a Set of Labeled Graphs

Akihiro Inokuchi

Tokyo Research Laboratory, IBM Japan

1623-14, Shimo-tsuruma, Yamato, Kanagawa, 242-8502, Japan

inokuchi@jp.ibm.com

Abstract

The problem of mining frequent itemsets in transactional data has been studied frequently and has yielded several algorithms that can find the itemsets within a limited amount of time. Some of them can derive "generalized" frequent itemsets consisting of items at any level of a taxonomy [7]. Recently, several approaches have been proposed to mine frequent substructures (patterns) from a set of labeled graphs. The graph mining approaches are easily extended to mine generalized patterns where some vertices and/or edges have labels at any level of a taxonomy of the labels by extending the definition of "subgraph". However, the extended method outputs a massive set of the patterns most of which are over-generalized, which causes computation explosion. In this paper, an efficient and novel method is proposed to discover all frequent patterns which are not over-generalized from labeled graphs, when taxonomies on vertex and edge labels are available.

1 Introduction

Data mining has been thoroughly studied and led to several algorithms that can find characteristic patterns and useful knowledge. They are applied to various kinds of data, such as transactional data, sequences, vectors, time-series, geographical data, multi-relational data, graphs, trees, semi-structured data, and unstructured data (text). Mining graphs is one of problems attracting a lot of attention recently. Modeling objects using such complex structures allows us to represent arbitrary relationships among entities [6]. In this paper, a novel method is proposed to discover useful patterns from a set of labeled graphs and a taxonomy on their vertex labels and edge labels.

The existing methods for mining frequent subgraphs discover patterns (substructures) contained as subgraphs in the graphs in a dataset [3]. Given graphs G and G_s, G_s is a subgraph of G if a function $\phi : V(G_s) \to V(G)$ holds

1. $\forall v \in V(G_s)$, $lb(v) = lb(\phi(v))$, and

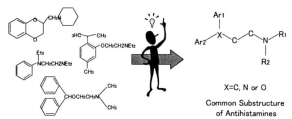

Figure 1. Common Substructure of Antihistamines

2. $\forall(v_i, v_j) \in E(G_s)$, $lb(v_i, v_j) = lb(\phi(v_i), \phi(v_j))$,

where $V(G)$ and $E(G)$ are sets of vertices and edges in the graph G, respectively, and lb is a function to assign a label to a vertex or an edge. The methods for frequent subgraph mining may miss important patterns, because they cannot use vertex and edge labels at various levels in a taxonomy on the labels. For example, the four chemical compounds in Figure 1 are antihistamines and the right-hand pattern in the figure is known to be their common substructure, where X is either C (carbon), N (nitrogen), or O (oxygen). Assume that the existing methods are applied to the compounds where each atom, chemical bond, atom type, and bond type in a compound correspond to a vertex, edge, vertex label, and edge label in its graph, respectively. The methods for frequent subgraph mining cannot discover the patterns that contain vertex labels at any level of the taxonomy, because the methods use exact matching to check whether a candidate pattern is contained in a labeled graph in the dataset. Therefore, a method to mine the generalized subgraph patterns in Figure 1 is needed.

The second reason is that many of the discovered subgraph patterns are not meaningful. For example, we consider two labeled graphs, a taxonomy on vertex labels, and a minimum support are given as input as shown in Figure 2. Each of the graphs in the input consists of six vertices (atoms) and each vertex connects to two other vertices with aromatic bonds. The taxonomy shows that A is a generalization of C and N. When the straightforward approach is applied to them, the number of frequent subgraph patterns

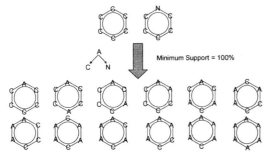

Figure 2. Over-generalized Patterns

consisting of six vertices is 12 as shown in Figure 2. We would like to discover only the upper-left one, because the others are over-generalized.

2 Problem Statement

A labeled graph G is represented as $G = (V, E, L_V, L_E, lb)$, where $V = \{v_1, \ldots, v_k\}$ is a set of vertices, $E = \{(v_i, v_j) | v_i, v_j \in V\}$ is a set of edges, $L_V = \{lb(v_i) | \forall v_i \in V\}$ is a set of vertex labels, $L_E = \{lb(v_i, v_j) | \forall (v_i, v_j) \in E\}$ is a set of edge labels, and lb is a function defined as $lb : (V \rightarrow L_V) \cup (E \rightarrow L_E)$. The sets of vertices, edges, vertex labels, and edge labels of the graph G are represented as $V(G)$, $E(G)$, $L_V(G)$, and $L_E(G)$, respectively. The *topology* of the graph G is defined as a graph $G_T(G) = (V, E)$ that does not contains any labels.

Let T be a directed acyclic graph (DAG) whose nodes have labels in $L_V \cup L_E$. An edge in T represents an *is-a* relationship and T represents a set of taxonomies on the vertex labels and edge labels. If there is an edge from a to d in the transitive-closure of T, a is called an *ancestor* of d and d is called a *descendant* of a. (a is a generalization of d.) A node in T is not an ancestor of itself, since T is acyclic. The taxonomy is modeled as a DAG rather than a forest to allow for multiple taxonomies. Given a label x, $\tau(x)$ is defined as a set of labels which consists of x and its ancestors. For example, Figure 3 shows a taxonomy on vertex labels. The value of $\tau(A)$ is equal to $\{A, C\}$.

Given graphs G and G_s, if a function $\phi : V(G_s) \rightarrow V(G)$ satisfies

1. $\forall v \in V(G_s)$, $lb(v) \in \tau(lb(\phi(v)))$, and

2. $\forall (v_i, v_j) \in E(G_s)$, $lb(v_i, v_j) \in \tau(lb(\phi(v_i), \phi(v_j)))$,

G_s is a subgraph of G, which is represented as $G_s \sqsubseteq G$. The function ϕ is injective and is not surjection. For the graphs G and G_s, total occurrence of G_s in G with respect to the function ϕ is represented as $total(\phi)$, where $total(\phi)$ does not contain any duplications of occurrences. For example, given a taxonomy on vertex labels and two labeled

graphs G_i and P_1 in Figure 3, although vertices $(1, 2)$ of P_1 correspond to vertices $(3, 1), (3, 2), (3, 4)$, and $(4, 3)$ of G_i, respectively, $total(\phi)$ is equal to $\{(3, 1), (3, 2), (3, 4)\}$, because $(3, 4)$ and $(4, 3)$ are duplicates.

Given a set of labeled graph $GD = \{G_1, G_2, \cdots, G_N\}$, the support $sup(P)$ of a graph pattern P is defined as $sup(P) = \frac{|\{G_i | G_i \in GD, P \sqsubseteq G_i\}|}{|GD|}$. We call a substructure whose support is greater than 0% a *pattern*. We call a graph pattern whose support is greater than or equal to a given minimum support level a *frequent subgraph*. The extracted patterns are the graph patterns contained as subgraph in the graphs in the database. Let the total occurrences of a pattern P in the graph data G_i be $total(\phi_i)$. The *weighted support* of the pattern P is defined as $sup_w(P) = \sum_{G_i \in GD} |total(\phi_i)|$.

If the topologies of P_1 and P_2 are isomorphic and $P_1 \sqsubseteq P_2$, P_1 is called a *generalized pattern* of P_2. (P_2 is called a *specialized pattern* of P_1.) In addition, if P_1 is a generalized pattern of P_2 and $sup(P_1) = sup(P_2)$, P_1 is called an *over-generalized pattern*. As examples, given P_1 and P_2 in Figure 3, P_1 is a generalized pattern of P_2, and this relationship is denoted as $P_1 \sqsubseteq P_2$.

The *expansion* of a pattern P is to add some vertices or some edges in order to generate a larger pattern P'. P is a subgraph of P'. For example, AGM [?], FSG [6], gSpan [8], FREQT [1], and TreeMiner [9] generate patterns of size k from frequent patterns of size $k - 1$ if and only if certain conditions are fulfilled.

When a dataset which consists of a set of labeled graphs, a minimum support, and a taxonomy on vertex labels and edge labels are given as inputs, the problem is to discover all frequent subgraph patterns which are contained as subgraphs from the dataset, where the over-generalized patterns are not output.

3 Properties of weighted Supports

For the sake of simplicity, it is assumed that vertices in graphs have labels and edges do not have labels in this section. Therefore, we consider only a taxonomy on vertex labels. In addition, we consider the vertex expansion.

A straightforward approach to derive a complete set of frequent subgraphs that does not contain over-generalized patterns is to first enumerate all frequent subgraphs with the conventional methods that are integrated with the ex-

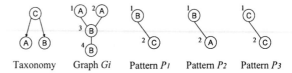

Figure 3. Generalized Patterns

416

tended definition of a subgraph, and then to remove the over-generalized patterns in post-processing. However, the set of frequent subgraphs obtained in the first step becomes too large. If we can remove the over-generalized patterns during the computation, it would be efficient. Let P_1 be a generalized pattern of P_2 which satisfies $sup(P_1) = sup(P_2)$. Let P_1' and P_2' be patterns into which P_1 and P_2 are expanded, respectively. For the patterns P_1' and P_2', $sup(P_1') = sup(P_2')$ does not always hold, so P_1 can not be removed just because $sup(P_1) = sup(P_2)$. In this section, it is shown that over-generalized patterns P_1 that fulfill certain conditions can be removed.

Property 1. If P_1 is a generalized pattern of P_2 and $sup_w(P_1) = sup_w(P_2)$ holds, then $sup(P_1) = sup(P_2)$ also holds. □

Let P_1 be a generalized pattern of P_2, and the pattern P_2' be a pattern into which P_2 is expanded by adding a vertex with the label l and some edges. When P_1 is expanded into P_1' to make its topology isomorphic to the topology of P_2 by adding a vertex with the label l and some edges, this expansion is called an *isomorphic expansion* of P_1 and P_2 as shown in Figure 4. P_1' is a generalized pattern of P_2'.

Property 2. If a pattern P_1 is a generalized pattern of P_2 and $sup_w(P_1) = sup_w(P_2)$ holds, then the support values of the patterns P_1' and P_2' generated by the isomorphic expansion of P_1 and P_2 are equal. □

Property 3. If P_1 is an generalized pattern of P_2 and $sup_w(P_1)$ is equal to $sup_w(P_2)$, the supports of patterns generated by applying isomorphic expansions to P_1 and P_2 one or more times are always equal. □

If P_1 is a generalized pattern of P_2 and their weighted support values are equal, we can remove P_1, which does not affect the set of discovered patterns. In other words, patterns which should be output are never pruned from the search space.

4 Experiments

The proposed method to prune over-generalized patterns was integrated into AcGM (Apriori-based connected Graph

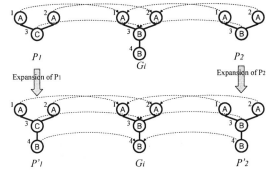

Figure 4. Isomorphic Expansion of P_1 and P_2

Mining) algorithm which is an optimized version of AGM to mine only frequent *connected* subgraphs [4]. The integrated method was implemented using C++, and an IBM IntelliStation (R) with Windows (R) XP was used for the evaluation experiments, with a Xeon-2.4 GHz CPU and 2 GB of main memory installed. For testing, a real world chemistry dataset was used. In this experiment, each atom, chemical bond, atom type, or bond type in a compound corresponds to a vertex, edge, vertex label, or edge label in a graph, respectively. The molecular structure data of carcinogenic compounds was analyzed. This data was provided by Predictive Toxicology Evaluation[1], and contains information on 340 compounds. Each data entry is categorized into either active or inactive. A total of 182 compounds are categorized into active and 155 compounds are categorized as inactive. There were 24 types of atoms in the compounds. The atomic bonds, which correspond to edges in a graph, have 4 types. The average size of the graph data is approximately 27 atoms, and the maximum size is 214.

Three methods are compared. One of them, called $Method_1$, is a conventional AcGM algorithm that does not use taxonomy. The second methods, called $Method_2$, is an AcGM algorithm that uses a taxonomy and prunes over-generalized patterns during the computations. The other, called $Method_3$, is an AcGM algorithm that uses the same taxonomy and does not prune the over-generalized patterns. $Method_2$ counts both support values and weighted support values for each pattern, although $Method_1$ and $Method_3$ count only the support values. A taxonomy on vertex labels as shown in Figure 2 was used in this experiment. Figure 5 shows the results for computation times and the numbers of discovered frequent subgraphs for various minimum support values for 340 compounds. The bar chart and the line chart in the figure show the number of discovered frequent subgraphs, and the computation time, respectively. When $Method_1$ is compared with $Method_2$ and $Method_3$, the results show that $Method_2$ and $Method_3$ need more computation time, because they use the taxonomy and the number of potential patterns becomes too large. When $Method_2$ is compared with $Method_3$, $Method_2$ can find all of the frequent subgraphs that have supports greater than 2%, although $Method_3$ could find the subgraphs with supports greater than 6% within 2 hours. The more complex the taxonomy on labels becomes, the greater the difference between the computation times of $Method_2$ and $Method_3$. This experiment shows that the pruning method proposed in this paper is very effective to mine generalized patterns.

The usefulness of discovered generalized patterns is examined for 337 compounds whose classes are known. Atoms with aromatic bonds were distinguished from atoms without them in this experiment. The taxonomy on vertex labels as shown in Figure 6 was used. $Method_1$

[1] http://oldwww.comlab.ox.ac.uk/oucl/groups/machlearn/PTE

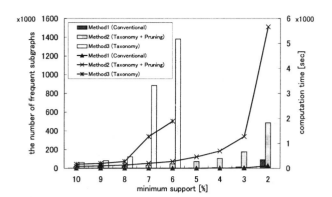

Figure 5. Comp. Time and the Number of Frequent Subgraph v.s. Minimum Supports

and $Method_2$ were applied to discover the rules as $P \Rightarrow$ *positive (negative)*, where P is a pattern. Each rule was evaluated by using a chi-square measure according to [2]. Figure 7 shows the results of the distributions of the chi-square values for the discovered rules, when the 100 most significant rules with respect to the measure were mined by both methods. The maximum chi-square value among the discovered rules by the proposed method was 28.8, while the maximum value for the conventional method was 15.8. Figure 8 shows the discovered patterns, each of which have its maximum chi-square values. Figure 8 that the left pattern is contained in 7 chemical compounds with carcinogenic activity and 26 compounds without such activity. Figures 7 and 8 show that the proposed method can discover rules that are more significant than the existing mining algorithms.

5   Conclusion

In this paper, an efficient method was proposed to prune over-generalized patterns and discover generalized frequent subgraphs, when a set of labeled graphs and a taxonomy on vertex and edge labels are available. It abandons over-generalized patterns whose weighted supports are equal to those of their specialized patterns earlier in the computations, and thereby accelerates the overall performance. The performance has been evaluated using a real world dataset and the efficiency and effectiveness of the approach have been confirmed with respect to the computation time and usefulness of the discovered patterns.

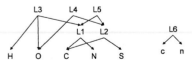

* Lower cases show the atom types which have aromatic bonds.

Figure 6. Taxonomy Used in Experiment 2

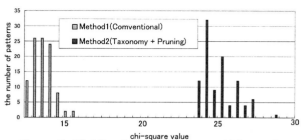

Figure 7. Distribution of Chi-square Values of Discovered Patterns

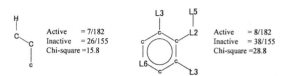

Figure 8. Discovered Patterns

References

[1] T. Asai, K. Abe, S. Kawasoe, H. Arimura, H. Sakamoto, & S. Arikawa. Efficient Substructure Discovery from Large Semi-structured Data. *Proc. of SIAM Int'l Conf. on Data Mining*, pp. 158-174, 2002.

[2] S. Brin, R. Motwani, & C. Silverstein. Beyond Market Baskets: Generalizing Association Rules to Correlations. *Proc. of SIGMOD Conf. on Management of Data*, pp. 265-276, 1997.

[3] A. Inokuchi, T. Washio, & H. Motoda. An Apriori-based Algorithm for Mining Frequent Substructures from Graph Data. *Proc. of European Conf. on Principles of Data Mining and Knowledge Discovery*, pp. 13–23, 2000.

[4] A. Inokuchi, T. Washio, Y. Nishimura, & H. Motoda. A Fast Algorithm for Mining Frequent Connected Subgraphs. *IBM Research Report*, RT0448 Feb., 2002.

[5] A. Inokuchi. Mining Generalized Substructures from a Set of Labeled Graphs. *IBM Research Report*, RT0577 Aug., 2004.

[6] M. Kuramochi & G. Karypis. Frequent Subgraph Discovery. *Proc. of Int'l Conf. on Data Mining*, pp.313–320, 2001.

[7] R. Srikant & R. Agrawal. Mining Generalized Association Rules. *Proc. of Very Large Data Bases Conference*, pp. 407–419, 1995.

[8] X. Yan & J. Han. gSpan: Graph-Based Substructure Pattern Mining. *Proc. of Int'l Conf. on Data Mining*, pp. 721–724, 2002.

[9] M. Zaki. Efficiently Mining Frequent Trees in a Forest. *Proc. of Int'l Conf. on Knowledge Discovery and Data Mining*, pp. 71–80, 2002.

Divide and Prosper: Comparing Models of Customer Behavior From Populations to Individuals

Tianyi Jiang
Stern School of Business
New York University
tjiang@stern.nyu.edu

Alexander Tuzhilin
Stern School of Business
New York University
atuzhili@stern.nyu.edu

Abstract

This paper compares customer segmentation, 1-to-1, and aggregate marketing approaches across a broad range of experimental settings, including multiple segmentation levels, marketing datasets, dependent variables, and different types of classifiers, segmentation techniques, and predictive measures. Our experimental results show that, overall, 1-to-1 modeling significantly outperforms the aggregate approach among high-volume customers and is never worse than aggregate approach among low-volume customers. Moreover, the best segmentation techniques tend to outperform 1-to-1 modeling among low-volume customers.

1. Introduction

Customer segmentation, such as customer grouping by the level of family income or education, is considered as one of the standard techniques used by marketers for a long time [11]. Its popularity comes from the fact that segmented models usually outperform aggregated models of customer behavior [3]. More recently, there has been much interest in the marketing and data mining communities in building individual models of customer behavior within the context of 1-to-1 marketing [15] and personalization [1]. Although there have been many claims made about the benefits of 1-to-1 marketing [15], there has been little scientific evidence provided to this regard and no systematic studies comparing individual, aggregate and segmented models of customer behavior have been reported in the literature.

In this paper, we address this issue and provide a systematic study in which we compare performance of individual, aggregate and segmented models of customer behavior across a broad spectrum of experimental settings. We found that in general, there exists a tradeoff between the sparsity of data for individual customer models and customer heterogeneity in aggregate models: individual models may suffer from sparse data, while aggregate models suffer from high levels of customer heterogeneity. We study this tradeoff across different experimental settings and show that the individual level models significantly outperform aggregate and segment level models for high-volume customers and are never worse than aggregate models for low-volume customers across these experimental settings. Moreover, the best segmentation techniques perform significantly better than the aggregate and individual level models for low-volume customers. We also present other comparison results for aggregate, segmentation and individual approaches.

2. Problem Formulation

To build predictive models on customer behaviors, we used panelist datasets that track a set of customers' transaction histories over time. Let C be the customer base consisting of N customers, each customer C_i is defined by the set of m demographic attributes $A = \{A_1, A_2, ..., A_m\}$, k_i transactions $Trans(C_i) = \{TR_{i1}, TR_{i2}, ..., TR_{ik}\}$ performed by customer C_i (such as purchasing transactions), and h summary statistics $S_i = \{S_{i1}, S_{i2}, ..., S_{ih}\}$ (such as average dollar amount of purchase), computed from the transactional data $Trans(C_i)$.

Given this data, we learn predictive models of customer behavior of the form

$$Y = \hat{f}(X_1, X_2, ..., X_p) \qquad (1)$$

where X_1, X_2, ..., X_p are some of the demographic attributes from A and some of the transactional attributes from T, and Y is one of the class labels which we try to predict. Function $\hat{f}$ is a predicative model learned via different types of machine learning classifiers.

Various models of customer behavior can be built at different levels of analysis as customers are grouped into various *segments* of different levels of granularity based on some of their demographic and behavioral characteristics. We consider the following levels of customer analysis:

- *Aggregate level* – the unit of analysis is the *whole* customer base, and only *one* predictive model of type (1) is built for the whole customer base.
- *Segmentation level* – "similar" customers are grouped into progressively finer *segments,* and the model(s) of customer behavior are built at each segment level based on the transactions and the demographic data of *that* particular grouping of customers. In this case, we still use the model of type (1) but learn it from the data pertaining *only* to the selected segment of customers. Moreover, we do this for *each* customer segment. In our study, the degree of customer similarity is determined by clustering summary statistics S_i, across customers.

- *Individual (or 1-to-1) level* – the unit of analysis is an individual customer, the model of customer behavior is built based *only* on the purchase transactions of *that* customer and his or her demographic data.

As we progress from the aggregate to the segmented and then to the individual models of customer behavior, we would create increasingly more "homogenous" customer groups for which predictive models are theorized to be more accurate. However, while we consider more refined customer segments, less data is contained in each such segment, and thus function $\hat{f}$ in (1) is estimated using fewer data points, potentially resulting in less accurate estimates.

Thus the general research question is to *determine which level of analysis would provide better prediction of customer behavior*, as defined by some measure of predictive performance of models of type (1). The answer to this question depends on the tradeoff between the sparsity of data for individual customer models and customer heterogeneity in aggregate models. In this paper, we study this tradeoff experimentally by comparing predictive models of type (1) across the three levels of analysis (i.e. individual vs. aggregate, individual vs. segmentation, and segmentation vs. aggregate) and six dimensions of different types of data sets; types of customers (high vs. low-volume); types of predictive models; dependent variables; performance measures; and segmentations techniques:

Types of datasets. We used two real world marketing datasets, ComScore panelist dataset from Media Merix on Internet buying behavior and Beverage panelist dataset from a major market research firm on household beverage purchase behavior. These datasets differed greatly in terms of the type of purchase transactions (Internet vs. physical purchases), variety of products, number of individual families covered, and demographics.

Types of customers. We partitioned our datasets into high and low volume customers to study the effect of data sparsity (details of data partitioning is described in [9])

Types of predictive models. We build predictive models using three different types of classifiers via Weka 3.4 system [18]: C4.5 decision tree [16], Naïve Bayes [10], and rule based classifier RIPPER [5] for building predictive models. These are chosen because they represent popular and fast classifiers.

Dependent variables. We built various models to make predictions on transactional variables, TR_{ij}, to compare discussed approaches across different experimental settings. The data we used to train any one model are customer C_i's independent variables $X_1, X_2, ..., X_p$, except TR_{ij}.

Performance measures. We use the following performance measures: percentage of correctly classified instances (CCI), root mean squared error (RME), and relative absolute error (RAE)[18].

Given models α and β, α is considered "better" than β when $\left(CCI_\alpha > CCI_\beta\right) \wedge \left(RME_\alpha < RME_\beta\right) \wedge \left(RAE_\alpha < RAE_\beta\right)$

Segmentation techniques. We use clustering algorithms to generate customer groupings across five levels of segment/sub-segment hierarchy. For Random clustering, customers are grouped together arbitrarily. The clustering techniques used are: *Random, SimpleKMeans[18], FarthestFirst[8]*, and *Expectation Maximization*. Detailed description is presented in [9].

3. Related Work

The problem of building individual and segmented models of customer behavior is related to the work on (a) user modeling and customer profiling in data mining, (b) customer segmentation in marketing, and (c) building local vs. global models in statistics. We examine the relationship of our work to these areas in this section.

There has been much work done in data mining on modeling customer behavior and building customer profiles. Customer profiles can be built in terms of simple factual information represented as a vector or as a set of attributes. Customer profiles can also be defined by sets of rules defining behavior of the customer [2], sets of sequences such as sequences of Web browsing activities [7, 14, 17], and signatures, used to capture the evolving behavior learned from data streams of transactions [6].

There has also been some work done on modeling personalized customer behavior by building appropriate probabilistic models of customers [4, 12]. However, all these approaches focus on the task of building good profiles and models of customers and do not study the performance of individual vs. segmented and vs. aggregate models of customer behavior.

Comparison of segmentation vs. aggregate models of customer behavior has also been done by marketing researchers who demonstrated that segmented models of customer behavior exhibit better performance characteristics than aggregate models [3]. However, this work has not been extended to the 1-to-1 case and no comparison has been made between aggregate and individual, and between individual and segmented models.

Our work is also related to the work on clustering that partitions the customer base and their transactional histories into homogeneous clusters for the purpose of building better models of customer behavior using these clusters [19]. However, we go beyond simple partitioning to compare performance of aggregated vs. segmented and vs. individual models of customer behavior.

Finally, our work is related to the problem of building local vs. global models in data mining and statistics [7]. Rather than building one global aggregated model of customer behavior, it is often better to build several local models that would produce better performance results. Furthermore, this method can be carried to the extreme when a local model is built for *each* customer, resulting in 1-to-1 customer modeling. We pursue this approach and compare the performance of aggregate, segmented and individual models of customer transactions.

4. Comparing Individual vs. Aggregate Levels of Customer Modeling

In this section, we compare individual vs. aggregate levels of customer modeling. More specifically, we compare predictive accuracy of function (1) estimated from data $Trans(C_i)$ for all the *individual* customer models and compare its performance with the performance of function (1) estimated from the transactional data for the *whole* customer base. In particular, we explore the aforementioned tradeoff between the heterogeneity of customer base and the sparsity of data.

To determine whether individual modeling performs statistically better than aggregate level modeling, we use a variant of the non-parametric Mann-Whitney rank test [13] to test whether the accuracy score of the one aggregate model is statistically different from a random variable with a distribution generated from individual accuracy results of the individual level models.

We conducted significance test for all customer type datasets across different dependent variables and classifiers. While performances of classifiers vary, our results clearly show that *for high-volume customers, modeling customer behavior at the individual level will yield significantly better results than the aggregate case.* In fact, modeling low-volume customers at the individual level will not be worse off than the aggregate level approach. The details of our experimental results are reported in [9].

5. Comparing Individual vs. Segmentation vs. Aggregate Levels of Customer Modeling

In this section, we compare individual vs. segmentation and aggregate vs. segmentation levels of customer modeling. More specifically, we compare predictive accuracy of function (1) estimated from the transactional data $Trans(C_i)$ for the segmentation level models, and compare its performance with the performance results obtained in Section 4. To do this, we generate progressively finer customer sub-segment levels as explained in Section 2.

5.1 Performance Curves

To compare the clustering algorithms against aggregate and individual level models, we first compute the *best performing segmentation level* for a clustering algorithm as follows:

$$\text{Best Segment Level} = \arg\max\left(\overline{CCI}_l - \overline{RME}_l - \overline{RAE}_l\right),$$

where $l = 1 \ldots 5$ levels, and $\overline{CCI}_l, \overline{RME}_l, \overline{RAE}_l$ are the average CCI, RME, and RAE for all the groups at level l as defined in Section 2. We took the difference between these performance measures in order to compare the performance of various models as explained in Section 2.

As we compare various segmentation models against that of aggregate and individual models, we found that different clustering algorithms can produce significantly different patterns. To gain a better understanding of the various factors that influence the performance of our models across the three levels of analysis, we plot the *performance curves*, which plot a performance measure across different segmentation levels. For example, in Fig. 1, the performance curves plot the $\overline{CCI}$ measure across all levels of segmentation ranging from aggregate to the individual level. Out of the overall 260 performance curves of $\overline{CCI}$ generated in our experiments, three dominating patterns are presented in Fig. 1: (A) for *high-volume* customers and "well-behaved" clustering (clustering that performed significantly better than Random clustering), algorithms, we see a monotonically increasing curve; (B) for *low-volume* customer datasets and "well-behaved" clustering algorithms, we see a convex curve; (C) for low-volume customer datasets and "badly-behaved" clustering algorithms, we see a "concave" pattern. These dominant performance patterns help guide the interpretation of our subsequent findings.

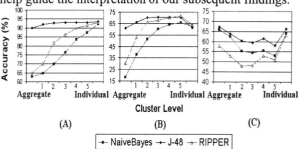

Figure 1. General Performance Curve Shapes

5.2 Segmenting Customers Using Clustering

We compare aggregate model to the best segment level using the same Mann-Whitney rank test we employed in Section 4. Our results show that best Segment Level significantly dominates aggregate level models across all customer types (Fig. 1-A,B). However, there is a significant number of instances where the aggregate level models performed better than best segment level models (Fig. 1-C). Further clustering performance analysis showed that this occurred because of some of the clustering algorithms produced poor performance results (see detailed results in [9]).

Comparisons of individual models to the best segment level models show that individual level models significantly dominate best segment level models for

421

high-volume customers (Fig. 1-A). However, for low-volume customers, the best segment level models performed better in more instances than individual level models (Fig. 1-B). In particular, clustering analysis showed that the best segment level models in the best performing clustering algorithms significantly dominate individual level models.

We found significant differences in performances among the 3 non-random clustering techniques when compared against that of Random clustering method described in Section 2. When we focused our analysis on "well-behaved" clustering algorithms, such as FarthestFirst, we found that, as expected, the best segment level model performs significantly better than aggregate model across all customer types (Fig. 1-A,B). However, while individual level outperforms best segment level for the *high-volume* customers (Fig. 1-A), best segment level clearly dominates for the *low-volume* customers (Fig. 1-B). As mentioned in Section 4, there is general tradeoff between customer heterogeneity and data sparsity when building customer segmentation models. Our results strongly suggest that *aggregation of idiosyncratic customers with insufficient data outperforms individual level models*.

6. Conclusions

We conducted a comparative study of aggregate, segmentation, and individual level modeling across multiple dimensions of analysis such as different types of datasets, customers, predictive models, dependent variables, performance measures, and segmentation techniques. We identified four factors that significantly influence the prediction outcomes of customer behavior models: customer heterogeneity, data sparsity, quality of segmentation techniques, and levels of segmentation.

Our results show that, given sufficient transactional data, 1-to-1 modeling significantly outperforms other types of models of customer behavior. However, when modeling customers with very little transaction data, segmentation dominates individual modeling for the best segmentation techniques and the best level (granularity) of segmentation. What is surprising is that 1-to-1 modeling is never worse than aggregate level modeling in our experiments, even in the case of sparse data. However, we do not want to over-generalize this claim to arbitrary datasets since this phenomenon needs further study. We also showed that poor segmentation techniques could lead to poor performance results that are comparable to random segmentation.

We performed further analysis of the four influencing factors by plotting *performance curves* across all levels of customer segmentation and observed three dominating patterns presented in Fig. 1. The first monotone pattern occurs for high-volume customers and "well-behaved" clustering algorithms, and shows that we can build models of idiosyncratic customer behavior all the way to the individual level without running into the data sparsity problem. The second convex pattern occurs for low-volume customers and "well-behaved" clustering algorithms, and shows that we will eventually run into the problem of data sparsity while trying to build progressively finer models of customer behavior. The last concave pattern occurs primarily for low-volume customers and "poorly-behaved" clustering algorithms (i.e. clustering algorithms yielding statistically equivalent performance results as that of Random clustering). It occurs because heterogeneous customers are grouped into same segments by poorly-behaved clustering algorithms.

In the future, we would like to study the problem of predicting customer behaviors via different levels of segmentation under a more general class of experimental settings. We also need to gain a better understanding on the nature of the tradeoff between customer heterogeneity and data sparsity at a more theoretical level.

7. References
[1]. *Comm of ACM*, in *Special Issue on Personalization*. 2000.
[2]. Adomavicius, G. and A. Tuzhilin, *Expert-driven validation of rule-based user models in personalization applications*. Data Mining and Knowledge Discovery, 2001. **5**((1/2)): p. 33-58.
[3]. Allenby, G.M. and P.E. Rossi, *Marketing Models of Consumer Heterogeneity*. J. of Econometrics, 1999. **89**.
[4]. Cadez, I.V., P. Smyth, and H. Mannila, *Predictive profiles for transaction data using finite mixture models* 2001 UC Irvine
[5]. Cohen, W.W. *Fast Effective Rule Induction. ICML* 1995
[6]. Cortes, C., et al. *Hancock: a language for extracting signatures from data streams. ACM SIGKDD* 2000
[7]. Hand, D., H. Mannila, and P. Smyth, *Principles of Data Mining*. 2001: MIT Press. Sections 6.3.2-6.3.3
[8]. Hochbaum, S.D. and B.D. Shmoys, *A Best Possible Heuristic for the K-Center Problem*. Mathematics of Operational Research, 1985. **10**(2): p. 180-184.
[9]. Jiang, T. and A. Tuzhilin, *Divide and Prosper: Comparing Models of Customer Behavior From Populations to Individuals*, Stern *Working Paper, CeDER-0405*. NYU. 2004
[10]. John, G.H. and P. Langley. *Estimating Continuous Distributions in Bayesian Classifiers. UAI* 1995
[11]. Kotler, P., *Marketing Management*. 11 ed. 2003: Pren Hall
[12]. Manavoglu, E., D. Pavlov, and C.L. Giles. *Probabilistic User Behavior Models. ICDM* 2003
[13]. Mendenhall, W. and R.J. Beaver, *Introduction to probability and statistics*. 9th ed. 1994: Thomson Publishing
[14]. Mobasher, B., et al. *Using Sequential and Non-Sequential Patterns for Predictive Web Usage Mining Tasks. ICDM* 2002
[15]. Peppers, D. and M. Rogers, *The One-to-One Future*. 1993, New York, NY: Doubleday
[16]. Quinlan, R., *C4.5: Programs for Machine Learning*. 1993
[17]. Spiliopoulou, M., et al., *A Framework for the Evaluation of Session Reconstruction Heuristics in Web Usage Analysis*. INFORMS Journal of Computing, 2003: p. 15(2).
[18]. Witten, I.H. and E. Frank, *Data Mining: practical machine learning tools and techniques with Java implementations*. 2000
[19]. Yang, Y., B. Padmanabhan. *Segmenting Customer Trans. Using a Pattern-Based Clustering Approach. ICDM* 2003

Filling-in Missing Objects in Orders

Toshihiro Kamishima   Shotaro Akaho

National Institute of Advanced Industrial Science and Technology (AIST)

AIST Tsukuba Central 2, Umezono 1-1-1, Tsukuba, Ibaraki, 305-8568 Japan

mail@kamishima.net (http://www.kamishima.net/)   s.akaho@aist.go.jp

Abstract

Filling-in techniques are important, since missing values frequently appear in real data. Such techniques have been established for categorical or numerical values. Though lists of ordered objects are widely used as representational forms (e.g., Web search results, best-seller lists), filling-in techniques for orders have received little attention. We therefore propose a simple but effective technique to fill-in missing objects in orders. We built this technique into our collaborative filtering system.

1 Introduction

We developed a technique to fill-in missing objects in orders, and built this technique into our collaborative filtering system based on order responses.

An *order* is a sorted sequence of objects, in which the only meaningful determination is which object precedes or succeeds the others. Such orders are widely used as representational forms. For example, Web search engines return page lists sorted according to their relevance to queries. Further, best-seller lists, which are item-sequences sorted according to the volume of sales, are used on many E-commerce sites. In spite of their importance, the methods of processing orders have received little attention. Filling-in missing objects in orders is one such processing task. This task is important, since missing values are frequently observed in real data. Specifically, given a set of sample orders, we developed a method of determining the rank of an object that doesn't appear in one order among the samples, based on the summaries of samples. This is an analogy for filling-in missing numerical values by means of samples.

We were motivated to develop our filling-in technique to perform better recommendation in collaborative filtering (*CF* for short). CF is a framework for recommending items based on the other users' preference patterns [2, 8]. Almost all CF methods adopt the Semantic Differential (SD) method [7] to measure users' preferences. In this method,

the users expose their preference by using, for example, a five-point-scale on which *1* and *5* indicate *don't prefer* and *prefer*, respectively. One alternative is a ranking method. Users' preference patterns are obtained in the form of response orders, which are lists of objects sorted according to the degrees of the users' preferences. We previously called a CF framework incorporating this ranking method, *Nantonac Collaborative Filtering*[1] [4]; using it, more appropriate recommendations could be performed. However, it was not as advantageous if the length of response orders was short, because it becomes difficult to evaluate similarities between users' preferences. Such short responses can be easily collected using Joachims' procedure [3]. We therefore wanted to improve recommendations in such a condition by introducing a filling-in technique.

We describe filling-in methods for orders in Section 2 and a nantonac CF task in Section 3. Section 4 and 5 show our experimental results and our conclusions, respectively.

2 Filling-in Missing Objects in Orders

We first describe our basic notations. x_j denotes an object, entity, or substance to be sorted. The universal object set, X^*, consists of all possible objects. The order is denoted by $O = x_1 \succ x_2 \succ \cdots \succ x_3$. The meaning of the order, $x_1 \succ x_2$, is "x_1 precedes x_2." The object set X_i is composed of all the objects in the order O_i; thus $|X_i|$ is equal to the length of the order O_i. An order of all objects, i.e., O_i s.t. $X_i = X^*$, is called a complete order; otherwise, it is an incomplete order. The rank, $r(O_i, x_j)$, is the cardinal number that indicates the position of the object x_j in the order O_i. For example, $r(O_i, x_2), O_i = x_1 \succ x_3 \succ x_2$ is 3. For two orders, O_1 and O_2, consider an object pair x_a and x_b, such that $x_a, x_b \in X_1 \cap X_2, x_a \neq x_b$. We say that the orders O_1 and O_2 are concordant w.r.t. x_a and x_b, if two objects are placed in the same order, i.e.,

$$(r(O_1, x_a) - r(O_1, x_b))(r(O_2, x_a) - r(O_2, x_b)) \geq 0;$$

---

[1]The word *nantonac* originates from Japanese, *nantonaku*, which means "unable to explain specifically, but I think such and such is the case."

otherwise, they are discordant. O_1 and O_2 are concordant if O_1 and O_2 are concordant w.r.t. all object pairs such that $x_a, x_b \in X_1 \cap X_2, x_a \neq x_b$. The distance, $d(O_a, O_b)$, is defined between two orders consisting of the same objects, that is, $X_a = X_b (\equiv X)$. *Spearman's distance* $d_S(O_a, O_b)$ [5] is a typical dissimilarity; that is defined as the sum of the squared differences between ranks. We adopted Spearman's distance, because its statistical properties have been well studied and its computational complexity is relatively small. By normalizing the distance range to be $[-1, 1]$, the *Spearman's rank correlation* ρ is defined as

$$\rho = 1 - 6 \times d_S / (|X|^3 - |X|). \tag{1}$$

We then describe the task of filling-in missing objects. To calculate the distance between two orders, we use

$$O_a = x_1 \succ x_3 \succ x_6 \text{ and } O_b = x_5 \succ x_3 \succ x_2 \succ x_6. \tag{2}$$

Distance is defined between two orders consisting of the same objects, but X_a and X_b differ; that is to say, both orders include missing objects. The missing objects for O_a are $\tilde{X}_a = \{x \,|\, x \notin O_a \wedge x \in X_b\} = \{x_2, x_5\}$, and those for O_b are $\{x_1\}$. Hence, it is not possible to directly calculate the distance. One way to overcome this difficulty is to ignore the missing objects and to calculate the distance over common objects, i.e., $X_a \cap X_b$. For example, by ignoring missing objects, both O_a and O_b are converted into $x_3 \succ x_6$; accordingly, the Spearman's distance $d_S = 0$. But since useful information might be contained in these ignored objects, ignoring them would lessen the precision or the confidence in the calculation of distances. Moreover, if $X_a \cap X_b = \emptyset$, the distance cannot be obtained. If samples of orders are available, the ranks of such missing objects can be filled-in based on the summary statistics of the samples. Such techniques would be highly beneficial to the derivation of more appropriate distances. Note that, in this paper, we assume that objects are uniformly missing. For example, top-3-orders do not satisfy this assumption, because only the top three objects are observed and objects at the bottom portions of the order are always missing.

2.1 Traditional Filling-in Methods for Orders

In literature on psychological statistics, these missing values are commonly processed by considering a set of orders instead of a single order. We describe the notion of an *Incomplete Order Set* (IOS)[2] [5], which is defined as a set of orders that are concordant with the given incomplete order. Formally, let O be the order consisting of the object set X, and $\tilde{X}$ be the set of missing objects. An IOS is defined as

$$\text{ios}(O, \tilde{X}) = \{O_i' | O_i' \text{ is concordant with } O, X_i' = X \cup \tilde{X}\}.$$

[2]In the cited book, this notion is referred to by the term *incomplete ranking*, but we have adopted IOS to insist that this is a set of orders.

This idea is not fit for large-scale data sets because the size of the set is $|X'|!/|X|!$, which grows exponentially in accordance with $|X'|$. Furthermore, there are some difficulties in defining the distances between the two sets of orders. One possible definition is to adopt the arithmetic mean of the distances between orders in each of the two sets. However, this is not distance because $d(\text{ios}_a, \text{ios}_a)$ may not be 0.

To avoid the above difficulties in IOS, we proposed the idea of *default rank* [4]. The idea is to rank missing objects into the middle of the filled-in orders, since such ranks can be considered as being neutral. However, default ranks were not found to be effective. We had thought that the middle ranks in orders would represent neutral values, but this was not the case. For example, suppose that there is an object ranked at the lowest in almost all the sample orders. If this object was ranked at the middle, the filled-in order would indicate that the object is ranked relatively high.

2.2 A Default Order

We propose a new idea, *default orders*. In the case of numerical or nominal variables, missing values can be replaced with the summary statistics of samples, for example, the means or the modes. By analogy, we try to fill the ranks of missing objects by using the centers of orders in sample orders, S. The central order $\bar{O}_S$ [5] is defined as

$$\bar{O}_S = \arg\min_O \sum_{O_i \in S} d(O_i, O).$$

Note that $\bar{O}_S$ is composed of objects $\bar{X}_S = \cup_{O_i \in S} X_i$. Except for a few special cases, deriving the strict central orders is not tractable. Hence, we employ the Thurstone's paired comparison method, which is based on the model of the Thurstone's law of comparative judgment [9]. This model sorts objects, x_j, according to their utilities, which follow the normal distribution $N(\mu_j, \sigma)$. By applying the least square method to this model [6], the μ_j' (a linear transformation of the μ_j) is derived as

$$\mu_j' = \frac{1}{|X|} \sum_{x \in \bar{X}_S} \Phi^{-1}\big(\Pr[x_j \succ x]\big), \tag{3}$$

where $\Phi(\cdot)$ is the normal distribution function. The probability that the object x_j precedes x, $\Pr[x_j \succ x]$, can be estimated by simply counting the ordered pairs appearing in the sample set. We approximate the central order by sorting objects according to the corresponding μ_j'.

A default order is an order that is concordant with a central order and is composed of missing objects. For example, supposing the orders in Equation (2) are given, and let the central order of samples be $x_1 \succ x_5 \succ x_2 \succ x_3 \succ x_4 \succ x_6$. The missing objects for O_a and for O_b are $\{x_2, x_5\}$ and $\{x_1\}$, respectively. Accordingly, the default order for O_a is $\tilde{O}_a = x_5 \succ x_2$. Similarly, that for O_b is $\tilde{O}_b = x_1$. We propose to fill-in the ranks of missing objects by using these default

424

orders. For this purpose, the observed order and its default order have to be merged. By definition, no objects are commonly included in both orders; thus, the traditional merging methods for orders cannot be applied. We hence propose a new merging method based on order statistics.

Consider the case that the observed order O and its default order $\tilde{O}$ are merged into the filled order O'. These three orders respectively consist of object sets, X, $\tilde{X}$, and X'. By definition, $X' = \tilde{X} \cup X$ and $X \cap \tilde{X} = \emptyset$. Instead of directly modeling this merging process, we consider the division process. Because we assumed that objects are uniformly missing, suppose that $|O|$ of objects are uniformly sampled from objects in the X' without replacement. These are then sorted so as to be concordant with the O', so that O is obtained. In this case, for the i-th object $x_{i:O}$ in O, the expectation of ranks in O' becomes

$$\mathrm{E}[r(O', x_{i:O})] = i \times \frac{|O'| + 1}{|O| + 1},$$

according to [1]. Similarly, for the j-th object in $\tilde{O}$, the expectation is $j(|O'| + 1)/(|\tilde{O}| + 1)$. We assigned these expectations of rank to the objects in X and $\tilde{X}$; then O' is formed by sorting according these expectations. In the example of Equation (2), $O_a = x_1 \succ x_3 \succ x_6$ and its default order $\tilde{O}_a = x_5 \succ x_2$ are merged. To the second object x_3 in O_a, the expected rank $2 \times (5+1)/(3+1) = 3$ is assigned. These expectations are assigned to all the remaining objects in a similar way. Consequently, by sorting objects according to these expectations, we obtain the order $O'_a = x_1 \succ x_5 \succ x_3 \succ x_2 \succ x_6$. Similarly, $O'_b = x_5 \succ x_3 \succ x_1 \succ x_2 \succ x_6$. This filling-in technique is very simple; thus, its computational complexity is small, $O(\max(|X'|, |\tilde{X}| \log |\tilde{X}|))$, if the central order is calculated in advance. Hence this filling-in method can be applied to large-scale data.

3 Nantonac CF with Filling-in Objects

We built the above filling-in technique based on default orders into our nantonac CF method.

We first describe a *nantonac collaborative filtering* task [4]. The aim of a CF task is to predict the preferences of a particular user (an active user) based on the preference data collected on other users (a user DB). The system shows a set of objects, X_i, to the user i, and the user sorts these objects according to his/her preferences. The sorted sequences are denoted by $O_i = x_1 \succ x_2 \succ \cdots \succ x_{|X_i|}$. The user DB, $D_S = \{O_1, \ldots, O_{|D_S|}\}$, is a set of all O_i. Sample users are people who provided orders in the DB. Let O_a be the order sorted by the active user, and the order is composed of objects in X_a. Given O_a and D_S, the goal of a nantonac CF task is to estimate which of the objects are preferred by the active user.

A simple correlation method (SCR) [4] is a basic method for performing a nantonac CF task. In this method, objects are recommended to active users through almost the same process as that used in the GroupLens [8]. Rating scores are simply substituted by ranks $r(O_i, x_j)$, which is the rank of object j in the sample order of the user i. The system estimates the active user's preferences for the object j by the function:

$$\hat{r}_{aj} = \frac{\sum_{i \in I_j} R_{ai}\left(r(O_i, x_j) - \bar{r}_i\right)}{\sum_{i \in I_j} |R_{ai}|}, \qquad (4)$$

where $\bar{r}_i$ denotes the mean ranks over $X_{ai} = X_a \cap X_i$. I_j is a set of indices of sample users who evaluated the object j; i.e., $\{i \mid O_i \in D_S \text{ s.t. } x_j \in X_i\}$. R_{ai} is a Pearson correlation between the ranks of the active user and the user i concerning objects in X_{ai}. The objects are sorted in ascending order of estimated preferences, and highly ranked objects are recommended. Note that the objects missing in the other order are ignored, but the ranks are not renumbered. For example, for $O_a = x_1 \succ x_2 \succ x_3$ and $O_i = x_3 \succ x_1$, the object x_2 in O_a is missing in O_i, so x_2 is ignored. However, the rank of x_3 remains $r(O_a, x_3) = 3$, not 2. Hence, this correlation is different from Spearman's ρ.

In accordance with the decrease of $|X_i|$ relative to $|X^*|$, the frequency of the event $X_a \cap X_i = \emptyset$ increases. Because R_{ai} is always 0 in such cases, the similarities between users can no longer be precisely measured, and an inappropriate recommendation will be made. Improving recommendations for short response orders, especially those with a length of two, is an important objective. One of the obstacles to performing CF is that users often take the trouble of representing their preferences. To overcome this obstacle, Joachims proposed a method for collecting preference orders of length two [3].

In the case of CF adopting the SD method, Breese et al. [2] proposed to fill-in missing scores and to calculate the correlation between users' responses over $X_a \cup X_i$, not $X_a \cap X_i$. We introduce this idea into the nantonac CF method. The procedures are the same as the original SCR except for filling-in missing objects of O_a and O_i. The central order $\tilde{O}_S$ over the user DB is derived in advance. Before calculating the correlation R_{ai}, missing objects in the response orders are filled-in by using $\tilde{O}_S$ as the default order. The Spearman's rank correlations between filled orders are used as R_{ai}. Note that filled orders are used only for calculating R_{ai}. The $\hat{r}_{aj}$ of Equation (4) is derived from the R_{ai} between filled orders and the original rank $r(O_i, x_j)$.

4 Experiments

To test the efficiency of using default orders, the above CF methods were applied to preference data in sushi. Data collection and experimental procedures were the same as

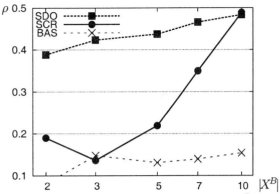

Figure 1. Changes of ρ according to $|X^B|$

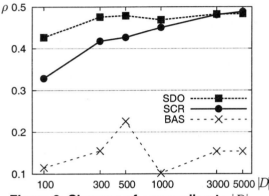

Figure 2. Changes of ρ according to $|D|$

those of [4], except that the data size was expanded to 5000. The quality of the recommendation was measured by means of the Spearman's ρ (Equation (1)) between the estimated and the true preference order. Note that a larger ρ indicates a better estimation.

We compared the nantonac CF methods using default orders (SDO) with two baselines. One was the original simple correlation method (SCR) in [4]. The other was a non-personalized recommendation (BAS); for all active users, the objects were sorted so as to be concordant with the central orders of the user DB. That is to say, the central orders were treated as a best-seller list, and popular objects were recommended.

Figure 1 shows the changes according to the lengths of the response orders $|X^B|$ when fixing $|D|$=5000 (the size of data sets). The SDO method was clearly superior to the SCR, and the differences were statistically significant, if $|X^B| \leq 7$. The shorter the response orders were, the more inappropriately the similarities between users were evaluated in the case of the SCR. Therefore, the SDO was remarkably effective for the shorter orders relative to the SCR. Figure 2 shows the changes according to the sizes of the data sets $|D|$ when fixing $|X^B|$=10. The SDO was superior to the SCR if $|D| \leq 500$, and the differences were

significant if $|D|$=300, 500. If sample sizes decrease, the number of sample users that rank the objects commonly ranked by the active user ranked decrease. The SCR therefore becomes ineffective. However, since such sample users disappear, the SDO could make better recommendation.

We then observed results for the other baseline, the BAS method. If all users had a shared preference, the central order itself would have provided better recommendations. However, this non-personalized method was apparently worse than the SDO method. This indicates that the advantage of the SDO was not due to the specific characteristics of the users' sharing common preferences, but arose from the ability of the SDO method to provide well-personalized recommendations.

5 Conclusions

In this paper, we have proposed the notion of default orders to fill-in missing objects in orders. The performance of nantonac CF was improved by using default orders.

Acknowledgments: A part of this work is supported by the grant-in-aid 14658106 and 16700157 of the Japan society for the promotion of science.

References

[1] B. C. Arnold, N. Balakrishnan, and H. N. Nagaraja. *A First Course in Order Statistics*. John Wiley & Sons, Inc., 1992.

[2] J. S. Breese, D. Heckerman, and C. Kadie. Empirical analysis of predictive algorithms for collaborative filtering. In *Uncertainty in Artificial Intelligence 14*, pages 43–52, 1998.

[3] T. Joachims. Optimizing search engines using clickthrough data. In *Proc. of The 8th Int'l Conf. on Knowledge Discovery and Data Mining*, pages 133–142, 2002.

[4] T. Kamishima. Nantonac collaborative filtering: Recommendation based on order responses. In *Proc. of The 9th Int'l Conf. on Knowledge Discovery and Data Mining*, pages 583–588, 2003.

[5] J. I. Marden. *Analyzing and Modeling Rank Data*, volume 64 of *Monographs on Statistics and Applied Probability*. Chapman & Hall, 1995.

[6] F. Mosteller. Remarks on the method of paired comparisons: I — the least squares solution assuming equal standard deviations and equal correlations. *Psychometrika*, 16(1):3–9, 1951.

[7] C. E. Osgood, G. J. Suci, and P. H. Tannenbaum. *The Measurement of Meaning*. University of Illinois Press, 1957.

[8] P. Resnick, N. Iacovou, M. Suchak, P. Bergstrom, and J. Riedl. GroupLens: An open architecture for collaborative filtering of Netnews. In *Proc. of The Conf. on Computer Supported Cooperative Work*, pages 175–186, 1994.

[9] L. L. Thurstone. A law of comparative judgment. *Psychological Review*, 34:273–286, 1927.

Orthogonal Decision Trees

Hillol Kargupta*and Haimonti Dutta
Department of Computer Science and Electrical Engineering
University of Maryland Baltimore County, 1000 Hilltop Circle Baltimore, MD 21250
{hillol, hdutta1}@cs.umbc.edu

Abstract

This paper introduces orthogonal decision trees that offer an effective way to construct a redundancy-free, accurate, and meaningful representation of large decision-tree-ensembles often created by popular techniques such as Bagging, Boosting, Random Forests and many distributed and data stream mining algorithms. Orthogonal decision trees are functionally orthogonal to each other and they correspond to the principal components of the underlying function space. This paper offers a technique to construct such trees based on eigen-analysis of the ensemble and offers experimental results to document the performance of orthogonal trees on grounds of accuracy and model complexity.

1. Introduction

Decision tree [7] ensembles are frequently used in data mining and machine learning applications. Boosting [3], Bagging[1], Stacking [9], and random forests [2] are some of the well-known ensemble-learning techniques. Many of these techniques often produce large ensembles that combine the outputs of many trees for producing the overall output. Large ensembles pose several problems to a data miner. They are difficult to understand and the overall functional structure of the ensemble is not very "actionable" since it is difficult to manually combine the physical meaning of different trees in order to produce a simplified set of rules that can be used in practice. Moreover, in many time-critical applications such as monitoring data streams [8], particularly for resource constrained environments [4], maintaining a large ensemble is computationally challenging. So it will be useful if we can develop a technique to construct a redundancy free meaningful compact representation of large ensembles. This paper offers a technique to do that.

This paper presents a technique to construct redundancy-free decision trees-ensembles by constructing orthogonal decision trees. The technique first constructs an algebraic representation of trees using multi-variate discrete Fourier bases. The new representation is then used for eigen-analysis of the covariance matrix generated by the decision trees in Fourier representation. The proposed approach con-

verts the corresponding principal components to decision trees using a technique reported elsewhere [4]. These trees are functionally orthogonal to each other and they span the underlying function space. These orthogonal trees are in turn used for accurate (in many cases with improved accuracy) and redundancy-free (in the sense of orthogonal basis set) compact representation of large ensembles.

Section 2 presents a brief overview of the Fourier spectrum of decision trees. Section 3 describes the construction of orthogonal decision trees. Section 4 presents experimental results. Finally, Section 5 concludes this paper.

2. Fourier Transform of Decision Trees

This section briefly discusses the background material [4] necessary for the development of the proposed technique to construct orthogonal decision trees. The proposed approach makes use of linear algebraic representation of the trees. In order to do that that we first need to convert the trees into a numeric tree just in case the attributes are symbolic. This can be done by simply using a codebook[4] that replaces the symbols with numeric values in a consistent manner. Since the proposed approach of constructing orthogonal trees uses this representation as an intermediate stage and eventually the physical tree is converted back, the exact scheme for replacing the symbols (if any) does not matter as long as it is consistent.

Once the tree is converted to a discrete numeric function, we can also apply any appropriate analytical transformation if necessary. Fourier transformation is one interesting possibility for reasons to be discussed later. Fourier bases are orthogonal functions that can be used to represent any discrete function. Consider the set of all ℓ-dimensional feature vectors where the i-th feature can take λ_i different categorical values. The Fourier basis set that spans this space is comprised of $\Pi_{i=0}^{\ell} \lambda_i$ basis functions. Each Fourier basis function is defined as,

$$\psi_{\mathbf{j}}^{\overline{\lambda}}(\mathbf{x}) = \frac{1}{\sqrt{\Pi_{i=1}^{l} \lambda_i}} \Pi_{m=1}^{l} \exp^{\frac{2\pi i}{\lambda_m} x_m j_m}$$

where $\mathbf{j}$ and $\mathbf{x}$ are strings of length ℓ; x_m and j_m are m-th attribute-value in $\mathbf{x}$ and $\mathbf{j}$, respectively; $x_m, j_m \in \{0, 1, \cdots \lambda_i\}$ and $\overline{\lambda}$ represents the feature-cardinality vector, $\lambda_0, \cdots \lambda_\ell$; $\psi_{\mathbf{j}}^{\overline{\lambda}}(\mathbf{x})$ is called the $\mathbf{j}$-th basis function. The

---

*Also affiliated with AGNIK, LLC, USA.

vector **j** is called a *partition*, and the *order* of a partition **j** is the number of non-zero feature values it contains. A Fourier basis function depends on some x_i only when the corresponding $j_i \neq 0$. If a partition **j** has exactly α number of non-zeros values, then we say the partition is of order α since the corresponding Fourier basis function depends only on those α number of variables that take non-zero values in the partition **j**.

A function $f : \mathbf{X}^\ell \to \Re$, that maps an ℓ-dimensional discrete domain to a real-valued range, can be represented using the Fourier basis functions: $f(\mathbf{x}) = \sum_{\mathbf{j}} w_{\mathbf{j}} \overline{\psi}_{\mathbf{j}}^{\lambda}(\mathbf{x})$. where $w_{\mathbf{j}}$ is the Fourier Coefficient (FC) corresponding to the partition **j** and $\overline{\psi}_{\mathbf{j}}^{\lambda}(\mathbf{x})$ is the complex conjugate of $\psi_{\mathbf{j}}^{\lambda}(\mathbf{x})$; $w_{\mathbf{j}} = \sum_{\mathbf{x}} \psi_{\mathbf{j}}^{\lambda}(\mathbf{x}) f(\mathbf{x})$. The *order* of a Fourier coefficient is nothing but the order of the corresponding partition. We shall often use terms like *high order* or *low order* coefficients to refer to a set of Fourier coefficients whose orders are relatively large or small respectively. Energy of a spectrum is defined by the summation $\sum_{\mathbf{j}} w_{\mathbf{j}}^2$. Let us also define the inner product between two spectra $\mathbf{w}_{(1)}$ and $\mathbf{w}_{(2)}$ where $\mathbf{w}_{(i)} = [w_{(i),1} w_{(i),2}, \cdots w_{(i),|J|}]^T$ is the column matrix of all Fourier coefficients in an arbitrary but fixed order. Superscript T denotes the transpose operation and $|J|$ denotes the total number of coefficients in the spectrum. The inner product, $< \mathbf{w}_{(1)}, \mathbf{w}_{(2)} > = \sum_{\mathbf{j}} w_{(1),\mathbf{j}} w_{(2),\mathbf{j}}$. We will also use the definition of the inner product between a pair of real-valued functions defined over some domain Ω. This is defined as $< f_1(\mathbf{x}), f_2(\mathbf{x}) > = \sum_{\mathbf{x} \in \Omega} f_1(\mathbf{x}) f_2(\mathbf{x})$.

Fourier transformation of a bounded-depth decision tree has several properties that make it an efficient one. More details can be found elsewhere [4, 5, 6]. Let us also note that,

1. the Fourier spectrum of a decision tree can be efficiently computed [4] and

2. the Fourier spectrum can be directly used for constructing the tree [6].

In other words, we can go back and forth between the tree and its spectrum. This is philosophically similar to the switching between the time and frequency domains in the traditional application of Fourier analysis for signal processing.

Fourier transformation of decision trees also preserves inner product. The functional behavior of a decision tree is defined by the class labels it assigns. Therefore, if $\{\mathbf{x}_1, \mathbf{x}_2, \cdots \mathbf{x}_{|\Omega|}\}$ are the members of the domain Ω then the functional behavior of a decision tree $f(\mathbf{x})$ can be captured by the vector $[f]_{x \in \Omega} = [f(\mathbf{x}_1) f(\mathbf{x}_2) \cdots f(\mathbf{x}_{|\Omega|})]^T$, where the superscript T denotes the transpose operation. The following section describes a Fourier analysis-based technique for constructing redundancy-free orthogonal representation of ensembles.

3 Removing Redundancies from Ensembles

Existing ensemble-learning techniques work by combining (usually a linear combination) the output of the base classifiers. They do not structurally combine the classifiers themselves. As a result they often share a lot of redundancies. The Fourier representation offers a unique way to fundamentally aggregate the trees and perform further analysis to construct an efficient redundancy-free representation.

Let $f_e(\mathbf{x})$ be the underlying function representing the ensemble of m different decision trees where the output is a weighted linear combination of the outputs of the base classifiers. Then we can write,

$$
\begin{aligned}
f_e(\mathbf{x}) &= \alpha_1 \tau_{(1)}(\mathbf{x}) + \alpha_2 \tau_{(2)}(\mathbf{x}) + \cdots + \alpha_m \tau_{(m)}(\mathbf{x}) \\
&= \alpha_1 \sum_{\mathbf{j} \in \mathcal{J}_1} w_{(1),\mathbf{j}} \overline{\psi}_{\mathbf{j}}^{\lambda}(\mathbf{x}) \cdots + \alpha_m \sum_{\mathbf{j} \in \mathcal{J}_m} w_{(m),\mathbf{j}} \overline{\psi}_{\mathbf{j}}^{\lambda}(\mathbf{x}).
\end{aligned}
$$

Where α_i is the weight of the ith decision tree and Z_i is the set of all partitions with non-zero Fourier coefficients in its spectrum. Therefore, $f_e(\mathbf{x}) = \sum_{\mathbf{j} \in \mathcal{J}} w_{(e),\mathbf{j}} \overline{\psi}_{\mathbf{j}}^{\lambda}(\mathbf{x})$, where $w_{(e),\mathbf{j}} = \sum_{i=1}^{m} \alpha_i w_{(i),\mathbf{j}}$ and $\mathcal{J} = \cup_{i=1}^{m} \mathcal{J}_i$. Therefore, the Fourier spectrum of $f_e(\mathbf{x})$ (a linear ensemble classifier) is simply the weighted sum of the spectra of the member trees.

Consider the matrix D where $D_{i,j} = \tau_{(j)}(\mathbf{x_i})$, where $\tau_{(j)}(\mathbf{x_i})$ is the output of the tree $\tau_{(j)}$ for input $\mathbf{x_i} \in \Omega$. D is an $|\Omega| \times m$ matrix where $|\Omega|$ is the size of the input domain and m is the total number of trees in the ensemble.

An ensemble classifier that combines the outputs of the base classifiers can be viewed as a function defined over the set of all rows in D. If $D_{*,j}$ denotes the j-th column matrix of D then the ensemble classifier can be viewed as a function of $D_{*,1}, D_{*,2}, \cdots D_{*,m}$. When the ensemble classifier is a linear combination of the outputs of the base classifiers we have $F = \alpha_1 D_{*,1} + \alpha_2 D_{*,2} + \cdots \alpha_m D_{*,m}$, where F is the column matrix of the overall ensemble-output. Since the base classifiers may have redundancy, we would like to construct a compact low-dimensional representation of the matrix D. However, explicit construction and manipulation of the matrix D is difficult, since most practical applications deal with a very large domain.

In the following we demonstrate a novel way to perform a PCA of the matrix D, defined over the entire domain. The approach uses the Fourier spectra of the trees and works without explicitly generating the matrix D.

The following analysis will assume that the columns of the matrix D are mean-zero. This restriction can be easily removed with a simple extension of the analysis. Note that the covariance of the matrix D is $D^T D$. Let us denote this covariance matrix by C. The (i, j)-th entry of the matrix,

$$C_{i,j} = <D(*,i), D(*,j)> = <\tau_{(i)}(\mathbf{x}), \tau_{(j)}(\mathbf{x})>$$
$$= \sum_{\mathbf{p}} w_{(i),\mathbf{p}} w_{(j),\mathbf{p}} = <\mathbf{w}_{(i)}, \mathbf{w}_{(j)}> \qquad (1)$$

Now let us the consider the matrix W where $W_{i,j} = w_{(j),(i)}$, i.e. the coefficient corresponding to the i-th member of the partition set $\mathcal{J}$ from the spectrum of the tree $\tau_{(j)}$. Equation 1 implies that the covariance matrices of D and W are identical. Note that W is an $|\mathcal{J}| \times m$ dimensional matrix. For most practical applications $|\mathcal{J}| << |\Omega|$. Therefore analyzing W using techniques like PCA is significantly easier. The following discourse outlines a PCA-based approach.

PCA of the matrix W produces a set of eigenvectors which in turn defines a set of Principal Components, $V_1, V_2, \cdots V_k$. Let $\gamma_{(j),q}$ be the j-th component of the q-th eigenvector of the matrix $W^T W$.

$$V_q = \sum_{j=1}^{n} \gamma_{(j),q} D(*,j) = \left[\sum_{\mathbf{i}} a_{\mathbf{i},q} \overline{\psi}_{\mathbf{i}}^{\overline{\lambda}}(\mathbf{x}) \right]_{\mathbf{x} \in \Omega}.$$

Where $a_{\mathbf{i},q} = \sum_{j=1}^{n} \gamma_{(j),q} w_{(j),\mathbf{i}}$. The eigenvalue decomposition constructs a new representation of the underlying domain where the feature corresponding to column vector V_q is $v_q = \sum_{\mathbf{i}} a_{\mathbf{i},q} \overline{\psi}_{\mathbf{j}}^{\overline{\lambda}}(\mathbf{x})$ i.e., $V_q = [v_q]_{\mathbf{x} \in \Omega}$. Note that v_q is a linear combination of a set of Fourier spectra and therefore it is also a Fourier spectrum. Also note that V_q-s are orthogonal which is proved in the following.

The inner product between V_q and V_r for $q \neq r$ is, $<V_q, V_r> = <[v_q]_{\mathbf{x}}, [v_r]_{\mathbf{x}}> = 0$. Therefore, we conclude that the spectra corresponding to the orthonormal basis vectors V_q and V_r are themselves orthonormal. Let f_q and f_r be the functions corresponding to the spectra $\mathbf{a}_q$ and $\mathbf{a}_r$. In other words, $f_q(\mathbf{x}) = \sum_{\mathbf{i}} a_{\mathbf{i},q} \psi_{\mathbf{i}}(\mathbf{x})$ and $f_r(\mathbf{x}) = \sum_{\mathbf{i}} a_{\mathbf{i},r} \psi_{\mathbf{i}}(\mathbf{x})$. Therefore, we can also conclude that, $<V_q, V_r> = <\mathbf{a}_q, \mathbf{a}_r> = <f_q(\mathbf{x}), f_r(\mathbf{x})>$. This implies that the inner product between the output vectors of the corresponding functions are also orthonormal to each other.

The principal components $V_1, V_2, \cdots V_k$ computed using the eigenvectors of the covariance matrix C are orthogonal to each other themselves. Since each of these principal components is a Fourier spectrum in itself we can always construct a decision tree from this spectrum using technique noted in Section 2 and detailed elsewhere [4]. Although the tree looks physically different from the Fourier spectrum, they are functionally identical. Therefore, the trees constructed from the principal components $V_1, V_2, \cdots V_k$ also maintain the orthogonality condition. These orthogonal trees now can be used to represent the entire ensemble in a very compact and efficient manner. The following section reports some experimental results.

Method of classification	Error Percentage
C4.5	24.5989 (%)
Bagging (40 trees)	20.85 (%)
Aggregated Fourier Trees (40 trees)	19.78(%)
Orthogonal Decision Trees	8.02(%)

Table 1. Classification error for SPECT data.

4. Experimental Results

This section reports the experimental performance of orthogonal decision trees on the Single Proton Emission Computed Tomography (SPECT) data set. [1] The following four different experiments were performed to test classification accuracies: (1) **C4.5 classifier**, (2) **Bagging**, (3) **Aggregated Fourier Tree:** The training set was uniformly sampled, with replacement and C4.5 decision trees were built on each sample. A Fourier representation of each tree was obtained(preserving approximately 99(%) of the total energy), and these were aggregated with uniform weighting, to obtain a Fourier tree. The classification accuracy of this aggregated Fourier tree was reported. (4) **Orthogonal Decision Tree:** The matrix containing the Fourier coefficients of the decision trees (obtained from step 3 above) was subjected to principle component analysis. Orthogonal trees were built, corresponding to the significant components and they were combined using an uniform aggregation scheme. The accuracy of the orthogonal trees was reported.

We report classification accuracies using 10-fold cross-validation and tree complexity, in terms of the number of nodes in the tree. In case of the orthogonal trees, tree complexity refers to the average number of nodes in each tree projected along significant components.

The dataset of 267 SPECT image sets (corresponding to different patients) was processed to extract 22 binary feature patterns that summarize the original SPECT images. The training data set consisted of 80 instances while the test data consists of 187 instances. The class label is binary.

Figure 1 illustrates four decision trees built on the uniformly sampled training data set(each of size 20). The first tree has a complexity 7 and considers attribute 7, 15 and 10 as ideal for splits. Before pruning, only one instance is misclassified giving an error of 5(%). After pruning, there is no change in structure of the tree. The estimated error percentage is 28.5(%). The second, third and fourth decision trees have complexities 7, 5, and 3 respectively. An orthogonal decision tree obtained from the first principle component, is shown in Figure 2. Table 1 illustrates the error percentage obtained in each of the four different classification schemes. For Bagging, only 40 trees are used in the ensemble, since

---

[1] Available from the University of California Irvine, Machine Learning Repository.

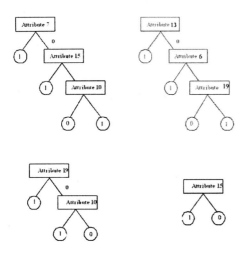

Figure 1. Decision trees built from the four different samples of the SPECT data set.

Figure 2. An orthogonal Decision Tree.

Method of classification	Tree Complexity
C4.5	13
Bagging (average of 40 trees)	5.06
Aggregated Fourier Trees (40 trees)	3
Orthogonal Decision Tree	3

Table 2. Tree complexity for SPECT data.

and random forests [2].

The proposed approach exploits the earlier work done by the first author and his colleagues [4, 6] on the Fourier analysis of decision trees. Although, the paper considers the Fourier representation, this is clearly not the only available linear representation around and other representations should be explored. This work also opens up several other possibilities. Linear systems theory offers many tools for analyzing properties like stability and convergence. For example, eigenvalues of a linear system are directly associated with the stability of the system. We plan to explore these issues for tree-ensembles in the future.

Acknowledgments

The authors acknowledge supports from NSF CAREER award IIS-0093353, NSF grant IIS-0203958, and NASA grant NAS2-37143.

References

[1] L. Breiman. Bagging predictors. *Machine Learning*, 24(2):123–140, 1996.

[2] L. Breiman. Random forests. *Machine Learning*, 45(1):5–32, 2001.

[3] H. Drucker and C. Cortes. Boosting decision trees. *Advances in Neural Information Processing Systems*, 8:479–485, 1996.

[4] H. Kargupta and B. Park. A fourier spectrum-based approach to represent decision trees for mining data streams in mobile environments. *IEEE Transactions on Knowledge and Data Engineering*, 16(2):216–229, 2002.

[5] N. Linial, Y. Mansour, and N. Nisan. Constant depth circuits, fourier transform, and learnability. *Journal of the ACM*, 40:607–620, 1993.

[6] B. H. Park and H. Kargupta. Constructing simpler decision trees from ensemble models using fourier analysis. In *Proceedings of the 7th Workshop on Research Issues in Data Mining and Knowledge Discovery, ACM SIGMOD*, pages 18–23, 2002.

[7] J. R. Quinlan. Induction of decision trees. *Machine Learning*, 1(1):81–106, 1986.

[8] W. N. Street and Y. Kim. A streaming ensemble algorithm (sea) for large-scale classificaiton. In *Seventh ACM SIGKDD International Conference on Knowledge Discovery and Data Mining*, San Francisco, CA, 2001.

[9] D. Wolpert. Stacked generalization. *Neural Networks*, 5:241–259, 1992.

this gives the best classification accuracy for the data set.

For orthogonal trees, the coefficient matrix was projected onto the first five most significant principal components. The equivalent eigenvectors captured, 99.4416(%), 0.3748(%), 0.0925(%), 0.0240(%), 0.0156(%) of the variance respectively. Orthogonal trees performed significantly better. Table 2 illustrates the tree complexity for this data set. The aggregated Fourier tree and the orthogonal trees were found to be smaller in complexity, thus reducing the complexity of the ensemble. The following section concludes this paper.

5 Conclusions

This paper introduced the notion of orthogonal decision trees and offered a methodology to construct them. Orthogonal decision trees are functionally orthogonal to each other and they provide an efficient redundancy-free representation of large ensembles that are frequently produced by techniques like Boosting [3], Bagging[1], Stacking [9],

Integrating Multi-Objective Genetic Algorithms into Clustering for Fuzzy Association Rules Mining

Mehmet KAYA
Department of Computer Engineering
Fırat University
23119, Elazığ, Turkey
kaya@firat.edu.tr

Reda ALHAJJ
ADSA Lab, Department of Computer Science
University of Calgary
Calgary, Alberta, Canada
alhajj@cpsc.ucalgary.ca

Abstract

In this paper, we propose an automated method to decide on the number of fuzzy sets and for the autonomous mining of both fuzzy sets and fuzzy association rules. We compare the proposed multi-objective GA based approach with: 1) CURE based approach; 2) Chien et al clustering approach. Experimental results on 100K transactions extracted from the adult data of United States census in year 2000 show that the proposed method exhibits good performance over the other two approaches in terms of runtime, number of large itemsets and number of association rules.

1. Introduction

In general, quantitative mining algorithms either ignore or over-emphasize elements near the boundary of an interval. The use of sharp boundary intervals is also not intuitive with respect to human perception. Some work has recently been done on the use of fuzzy sets in discovering association rules for quantitative attributes, e.g., [1, 4, 8, 9, 11]. However, in existing approaches fuzzy sets are either supplied by expert or determined by applying clustering algorithm. The former is not realistic because it is extremely hard for an expert to specify fuzzy sets. The latter approaches have not produced satisfactory results. They do not considered the optimization of membership functions; a user specifies the number of fuzzy sets and membership functions are tuned accordingly.

In this paper, we propose a clustering method that employs multi-objective GA for the automatic discovery of membership functions used in determining fuzzy quantitative association rules. Our approach optimizes the number of fuzzy sets and their ranges according to multi-objective criteria in a way to maximize the number of large itemsets with respect to a given minimum support value. So, we defined two objective parameters in terms of large itemsets and the time required to determine fuzzy sets. These two are in conflict with each other. So, we use a GA with multiple objective optimization capabilities known as *Pareto GA* [10].

Experimental results demonstrate the effectiveness of the proposed approach. Also, we compared the proposed approach, in terms of the number of produced large itemsets and interesting association rules, with CURE based approach [2] and Chien *et al* approach [3], which is an efficient hierarchical clustering algorithm based on variation of density to solve the problem of internal partitioning.

The rest of this paper is organized as follows. Fuzzy association rule is defined in Section 2. Utilizing GA to determine membership functions is described in Section 3. A brief overview of CURE based approach and Chien *et al* work is given in Section 4. Experimental results are given in Section 5. Section 6 is summary and conclusions.

2. Fuzzy Association Rules

Consider a database of transactions $T=\{t_1, t_2,...,t_n\}$, where each t_j represents the j-th tuple in T. We use $I=\{i_1, i_2,...,i_m\}$ to represent all attributes that appear in T; each quantitative attribute i_k is associated with at least two fuzzy sets. The degree of membership of each value of i_k in any of its fuzzy sets is directly based on the evaluation of the membership function of the particular fuzzy set with the value of i_k as input. The value falls in the interval [0, 1], with the lower bound 0 strictly indicates "not a member", the upper bound 1 indicates "total membership"; and all other values between 0 and 1, exclusive, specify "partial membership". Finally, we use the following form for fuzzy association rule:

If $Q=\{u_1, u_2, ..., u_p\}$ is $F_1=\{ f_{1_1}, f_{1_2}, ..., f_{1_p} \}$ then

$R=\{v_1, v_2, ..., v_q\}$ is $F_2=\{ f_{2_1}, f_{2_2}, ..., f_{2_q} \}$,

where $Q \subset I$ and $R \subset I$ are itemsets with $Q \cap R = \phi$, F_1 and F_2, respectively, contain the fuzzy sets associated with corresponding attributes in Q and R, i.e., f_{1i} is a fuzzy set related to attribute u_i and f_{2j} is related to attribute v_j.

3. Multi-Objective GA for Automated Clustering

We consider as objective functions the number of large itemsets and the gain in time, inverse of the time required to find all large itemsets in a given database. It is assumed that each of the n components of the objective vector is to be maximized. An optimal solution can be defined as: *a solution not dominated by any other solution in the search space*. Such a solution is called *Pareto optimal*, and the entire set of optimal trade-offs is called *Pareto-optimal set* [10].

Each individual represents the base values of membership functions for a quantitative attribute from the given database. We used membership functions in triangular shape.

To illustrate the utilized encoding scheme, consider a quantitative attribute, say i_k, having 3 fuzzy sets, the corresponding membership functions and their base variables are shown in Figure 1. Each base variable takes finite values. For instance, the search space of the base value $b_{i_k}^1$ lies between the minimum and maximum values of attribute i_k, denoted $\min(D_{i_k})$ and $\max(D_{i_k})$, respectively. Enumerated next to Figure 1 are the search intervals of all the base values and the intersection point R_{i_k} of attribute i_k.

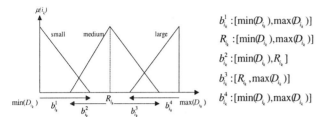

$b_{i_k}^1 : [\min(D_{i_k}), \max(D_{i_k})]$

$R_{i_k} : [\min(D_{i_k}), \max(D_{i_k})]$

$b_{i_k}^2 : [\min(D_{i_k}), R_{i_k}]$

$b_{i_k}^3 : [R_{i_k}, \max(D_{i_k})]$

$b_{i_k}^4 : [\min(D_{i_k}), \max(D_{i_k})]$

Figure 1 Membership functions and base variables of attribute i_k

We used 8 quantitative attributes in the experiments of this study and assumed that each attribute can have at most 7 fuzzy sets. So, a chromosome consisting of the base lengths and the intersecting points is represented in the form:

$$w_{i_1} b_{i_1}^1 b_{i_1}^{12} R_{i_1}^1 b_{i_1}^2 b_{i_1}^3 R_{i_1}^2 b_{i_1}^4 b_{i_1}^5 R_{i_1}^3 b_{i_1}^6 b_{i_1}^7 R_{i_1}^4 b_{i_1}^8 b_{i_1}^9 R_{i_1}^5 b_{i_1}^{10} b_{i_1}^{11} \ldots w_{i_8} b_{i_8}^1 b_{i_8}^{12} \ldots R_{i_8}^5 b_{i_8}^{10} b_{i_8}^{11}$$

where gene w_{i_j} denotes the number of fuzzy sets for attributes i_j. If the number of fuzzy sets is 2, then while decoding the individual, the first two base variables are considered and the others are omitted. However, if w_{i_j} is 3, then the next three variables are also taken into account. So, as long as the number of fuzzy sets increases, the number of variables to be taken into account is enhanced too.

We used real-valued coding, where chromosomes are represented as floating point numbers and their genes are the real parameters. While the value of a gene is reflected under its own search interval, the following formula is employed:

$$b_{i_j}^k = \min(b_{i_j}^k) + \frac{g}{g_{\max}}(\max(b_{i_j}^k) - \min(b_{i_j}^k)),$$ where g is the value of the gene in search, $g_{\max}$ is the maximum value that gene g may take, $\min(b_{i_j}^k)$ and $\max(b_{i_j}^k)$ are the minimum and the maximum values of the reflected area, respectively. Also, we used Pareto-based ranking procedure, where the rank of an individual is the number of solutions encoded in the population by which its corresponding decision vector is dominated. Individuals who are strong according to parent selection policy are candidates to form a new population. We adapted the *elitism* selection policy in our experiments. Finally, after selecting chromosomes with respect to the evaluation function, genetic operators such as, crossover and mutation, are applied to these individuals.

To generate fuzzy association rules, the following formula is used to calculate the fuzzy support of itemset Z and its corresponding set of fuzzy sets F, denoted $S_{<Z,F>}$:

$$S_{<Z,F>} = \frac{\sum_{t_i \in T} \prod_{z_j \in Z} \mu_{z_j}(f_j \in F, t_i[z_j])}{|T|},$$ where $|T|$ denotes the number of transactions in database T.

Each large itemset, say L, is used in deriving all association rules $(L-S) \Rightarrow S$, for each $S \subset L$. The strong association rules discovered are chosen by considering only

rules with confidence over a pre-specified minimum confidence. However, not all of these rules are interesting enough to be presented to the user. Whether a rule is interesting or not can be judged either subjectively or objectively. Ultimately, only the user can judge if a given rule is interesting or not, and this judgment, being subjective, may differ from one user to another. However, objective interestingness criterion based on the statistics behind the data can be used as one step towards the goal of weeding out presenting uninteresting rules to the user.

4. Overview of CURE and Chein et al Work

The process of CURE can be summarized as follows. Starting with individual values as individual clusters, at each step the closest pair of clusters are merged to form a new cluster. This is repeated until only k clusters are left. As a result, the values of each attribute in the database are distributed into k clusters. The centroids of the k clusters are the set of midpoints of the fuzzy sets for the corresponding attribute. Here, note that in the process to obtain the membership functions by CURE clustering algorithm, the number of clusters, i.e., number of fuzzy sets should be given by the user beforehand. To overcome this restriction, we integrated a GA with CURE clustering approach.

A GA finds the most appropriate number of clusters according to a predefined fitness function. In the GA process used in this study, each variable holds the number of fuzzy sets only. This is because CURE clustering algorithm itself adjusts the base values of the membership functions.

As Chien *et al* clustering approach is concerned, it is an efficient hierarchical clustering algorithm based on variation of density to solve the problem of interval partitioning. For this purpose, two main characteristics for clustering numerical data are defined first. Then, a reasonable interval can be generated automatically by giving a proper parameter α to determine the importance of relative closeness and relative inter-connectivity. The reader is referred to [3] for more details about this clustering technique.

5. Experimental Results

Effectiveness of the proposed approach has been demonstrated by comparison with two existing clustering approaches: CURE based approach and Chien *et al* work. We concentrate on testing the time requirements as well as changes in the main factors that affect the proposed clustering process: finding nondominated sets, number of large itemsets, and number of association rules. The experiments have been conducted on Pentium III 1.4 GHz CPU with 512 MB memory and running Windows 2000. As experiment data, we used 100K transactions from the adult data of US census in 2000; we concentrated our analysis on 8 quantitative attributes. Further, in all the experiments conducted in this study, the GA process started with a population of 80 individuals for the GA-based approach and 30 individuals for the other approach. As the termination criteria for the developed GA programs, the maximum number of generations has been fixed at 500. Finally, in all the experiments in which GA have been used, the minimum support was set to 10%, unless otherwise specified, and the maximum number of fuzzy sets has been specified as 7 for each of the three methods.

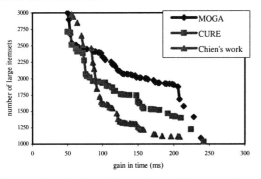

Figure 2 Nondominated set using 20K transactions

The first experiment is dedicated to find the nondominated set for each of the three different methods using 20K transactions. We decided to use 20K transactions because according to the next two experiments, the three approaches perform almost the same up to 20K transactions. The results are reported in Figure 2, where the three approaches are labeled as MOGA, CURE and Chein's work, to represent the proposed approach, CURE based approach and Chien *et al* work based approach, respectively. MOGA mostly outperforms the others for both objectives.

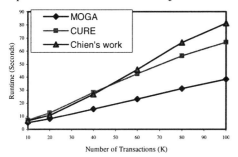

Figure 3 Runtime to find large itemsets for optimum case

The second experiment compares the runtime of the three approaches to find large itemsets for different numbers of transactions, varying from 10K to 100K. The results are reported in Figure 3. The runtime here represents the time required to find all large itemsets after the number of fuzzy sets and their ranges have been determined by employing the corresponding method. MOGA outperforms the other two approaches for all numbers of transactions. Finally, the curves plotted in Figure 3 demonstrate that the three methods are scalable with respect to the number of transactions.

The third experiment compares the runtime of the three approaches to find large itemsets when the number of fuzzy sets is fixed at 5. The results are reported by the curves plotted in Figure 4. We have decided on considering 5 fuzzy sets in this experiment because it is approximately the average number of fuzzy sets found by each of the three approaches. From Figure 4, the other two approaches

outperform MOGA; the extra time in MOGA is spent on optimizing membership functions.

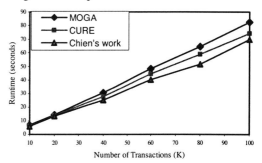

Figure 4 Runtime to find large itemsets for 5 fuzzy sets

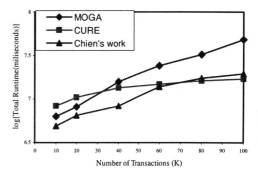

Figure 5 Total runtime required to find optimum fuzzy sets

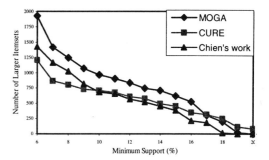

Figure 6 Number of large itemsets for optimum fuzzy sets

The fourth experiment compares the total runtime required for each of the three methods to find optimum fuzzy sets for different numbers of transactions. The results are reported in Figure 5; the total runtime of MOGA is smaller than the other two approaches up to around 40K transactions; after that, MOGA requires higher execution time than the other two approaches. The extra runtime is spent on optimizing membership functions. Figure 5 shows that all the three approaches scale well on the number of transactions.

The fifth experiment compares the change in the number of large itemsets for different values of minimum support. All the 100K transactions have been utilized and the optimum solution case has been considered. The results are reported by the curves plotted in Figure 6; MOGA finds larger number of large itemsets than the other two approaches. This is quite consistent with our intuition, simply because MOGA puts more effort on the optimization process and this has been reflected into finding better results than classical clustering approaches.

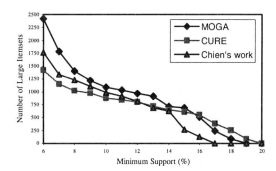

Figure 7 Number of large itemsets for 5 fuzzy sets

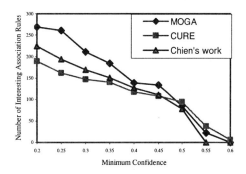

Figure 8 Number of association rules for optimum case

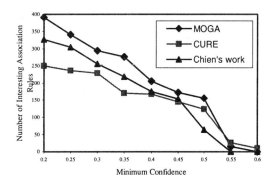

Figure 9 Number of association rules for 5 fuzzy sets

The sixth experiment is similar to the fifth but here 5 fuzzy sets are considered instead of the optimum case. The three curves plotted in Figure 7 show the number of large itemsets for different values of minimum support. For small values of minimum support, the difference between the three curves is larger than the difference for the optimum solution case shown in Figure 6. Finally, for the two cases plotted in Figures 6 and 7, the curves become smoother and the difference between them decreases as the minimum support increases. This is true because as the minimum support increase, the number of large itemsets decreases and approaches zero.

The last two experiments report the correlation between minimum confidence and number of interesting association rules discovered for each of the three approaches. Figure 8 reports the values for the optimum solution case. Figure 9 gives the results in case the number of clusters is set to 5 for each of the three methods. MOGA optimizes the ranges of the membership functions and the number of fuzzy sets in a way that outperforms the other two approaches.

6. Summary and Conclusions

In this paper, we proposed a multi-objective GA based clustering method, which automatically adjusts the fuzzy sets to provide large number of large itemsets in low duration. This is achieved by tuning together, for each quantitative attribute, the number of fuzzy sets and the base values of the membership functions. In addition, we demonstrated through experiments that using multi-objective GA has 3 important advantages over CURE and Chien *et al* work. First, the number of clusters for each quantitative attribute is determined automatically. Second, the GA-based approach optimizes membership functions of quantitative attributes for a given minimum support. So, it is possible to obtain more appropriate solutions by changing the minimum support in the desired direction. Finally, the number of large itemsets and interesting association rules obtained using the GA-based approach are larger. As a result, all these advantages show that the proposed approach is more appropriate and can be used more effectively to achieve optimal solutions than the classical clustering algorithms described in the literature.

References

[1] K.C.C. Chan and W.H. Au, "Mining Fuzzy Association Rules," *Proc. of ACM CIKM*, pp.209-215, 1997.

[2] S. Guha, R. Rastogi and K. Shim, "CURE: An Efficient Clustering Algorithm for Large Databases," *Information Systems*, Vol.26, No.1, pp.35-58, 2001.

[3] B.C. Chien, Z.L. Lin and T.P. Hong, "An Efficient Clustering Algorithm for Mining Fuzzy Quantitative Association Rules," *Proc. of IFSA World Congress and NAFIPS Conference*, Vol.3, pp.1306-1311, 2001.

[4] T.P. Hong, C.S. Kuo and S.C. Chi, "Mining Association Rules from Quantitative Data," *Intelligent Data Analysis*, Vol.3, pp.363-376, 1999.

[5] B. Lent, A. Swami and J. Widom, "Clustering Association Rules," *Proc. of IEEE ICDE*, pp.220-231, 1997.

[6] R.J. Miller and Y. Yang, "Association Rules over Interval Data," *Proc. of the ACM SIGMOD*, pp.452-461, 1997.

[8] R. Srikant and R. Agrawal. "Mining Quantitative Association Rules in Large Relational Tables," *Proc. of ACM SIGMOD*, pp.1-12, 1996.

[8] R.R. Yager, "Fuzzy Summaries in Database Mining," *Proc. of Artificial Intelligence for Application*, pp.265-269, 1995.

[9] W. Zhang, "Mining Fuzzy Quantitative Association Rules," *Proc. of IEEE ICTAI*, pp.99-102, 1999.

[10] E. Zitzler and L. Thiele, "Multi-objective Evolutionary Algorithms: A Comparative Case Study and the Strength Pareto Approach," *IEEE TEC*, Vol.3, pp.257-271, 1999.

[11] M. Kaya and R. Alhajj, "Multi-Objective Genetic Algorithm Based Method for Mining Optimized Fuzzy Association Rules," *Proc. of IDEAL*, Springer, Aug. 2004.

Feature-Based Prediction of Unknown Preferences for Nearest-Neighbor Collaborative Filtering

Hyungil Kim[*], Juntae Kim[*], and Jonathan Herlocker[**]

[*]Department of Computer Engineering, Dongguk University, Seoul, Korea
{hikim, jkim}@dongguk.edu
[**] School of Electrical Engineering and Computer Science, Oregon State University, Corvallis, Oregon, USA
herlock@cs.orst.edu

Abstract

Recommendation systems analyze user preferences and recommend items to a user by predicting the user's preference for those items. Among various kinds of recommendation methods, collaborative filtering (CF) has been widely used and successfully applied to practical applications. However, collaborative filtering has two inherent problems: data sparseness and the cold-start problems. In this paper, we propose a method of integrating additional feature information of users and items into CF to overcome the difficulties caused by sparseness and improve the accuracy of recommendation. Several experimental results that show the effectiveness of the proposed method are also presented.

1. Introduction

Recommender systems analyze a user's preference and suggest items such as books, movies, music, web pages, etc., by computing the prediction value of preference for items for the user. Among various approaches, collaborative filtering (CF) has been successfully applied to recommender systems [2,6,7].

Collaborative filtering recommendation systems use each user's rating information on various items. The most common approach compares the rating information between users, discovers similar users, and then predicts a user's preference for a certain item based on the similar users' preference for that item. Because the collaborative method does not require any information on the contents of items, it can recommend items like music or movies, for which the contents are difficult to analyze.

Collaborative filtering has many advantages and has been applied successfully for various applications. However, it has limitations due to the sparseness of data. If there are very few known preferences, it is difficult to find many similar users, and therefore the accuracy of recommendation is degraded. This weakness is more serious in the initial stage of the system, and when a recommendation is to be made to a new user. This is called a cold-start problem.

One possibility to overcome the data sparseness and the cold-start problem is to use the additional feature information on users and items. In this paper, we propose a method of integrating feature information into CF to overcome the difficulties caused by the sparseness and improve the accuracy of recommendation. In our method, we first predict the unknown preference values by using the probability distribution of feature values, and then apply collaborative filtering with the modified data to produce recommendations. We call this method of filling unknown preference values as *data blurring*.

2. Backgrounds

Collaborative filtering is a method of utilizing ratings on items from many users to recommend items to a given user. Nearest neighbor-based CF compares the rating information between users, finds out similar users, and then predicts a user's preference for certain items based on the similar user's preferences. A user similarity can be computed by statistical methods such as Pearson correlation [7] or vector similarity [3]. Once similarity is computed, user preference for a certain item is predicted by computing the weighted average of similar user's ratings on that item. The correlation-based method was used to quantify user similarities and predictions in many CF systems like GroupLens [7]. Also, various modifications have been proposed to improve the accuracy of recommendations [2,3,6].

As mentioned previously, collaborative filtering has problems of data sparseness and cold-start. For example, if the user's preference is recorded by the purchase history and each user purchases only several items among thousands of items, the vector similarity between users will be zero in most cases. However, usually we have some feature information on users and items, with which the sparseness problem can be alleviated.

There have been various attempts to combine content information into the collaborative filtering. Basu et al. presented a hybrid collaborative and content-based recommender [1]. Pazzani combined collaborative, content-based, and demographic information by representing them into user profiles [9]. Good et al. used a content-based software agent to generate ratings to reduce data sparseness [5]. Condliff et al. tried to incorporate user and item features with user ratings in the Bayesian mixed-effect model [4]. Melville et al. used textual information describing each movie to enhance the user preference data, and performed CF [8]. Popescul et al. suggested a unified probabilistic model that combines the user-item co-occurrence data with the content data (words describing items) in a three-way aspect model [10]. Our method differs from these in integrating both user and item features while maintaining the basic CF framework.

3. Integrating feature information

3.1 The concept

In many practical applications, we have some information on user and item features, such as user's age or item's category, in addition to the preference data itself. By using such information, we can improve the performance of collaborative filtering by alleviating the problems of data sparseness and cold-start.

For example, let's assume that the original user preference data is as shown in Table 1. U represents users, I represents items, and the '1' in the table means the user has preference for the item.

Table 1. A basic user preferences (with features)

	Genre	A	A	C	C	D	D
Gender		I1	I2	I3	I4	I5	I6
M	U1	1	0	1	0	0	0
M	U2	0	1	0	1	0	0
F	U3	0	0	0	0	1	1
F	U4	0	0	0	0	1	1
F	U5	0	0	0	0	0	0

Table 2. The predicted unknown preferences

	Genre	A	A	C	C	D	D
Gender		I1	I2	I3	I4	I5	I6
M	U1	1	0.5	1	0.5	0	0
M	U2	0.5	1	0.5	1	0	0
F	U3	0	0	0	0	1	1
F	U4	0	0	0	0	1	1
F	U5	0	0	0	0	0.67	0.67

With this data only, U1 and U2 are not similar users because there are no common preferences found, and U5 cannot have any similar users at all since U5 has preference vector 0. Therefore, it is impossible to make CF-based recommendation for U1 or U5. The U1 case is

an example of data sparseness problem, and the U5 case is an example of cold-start problem.

Now, let's consider the feature values. With these values, we may conclude that U1 and U2 are somewhat similar with each other, since both of them prefer an item with genre A and C. Likewise, U3, U4, and U5 may be similar users because they all have gender feature value of F. In our proposed method, we use such additional information to fill up the "unknown" preferences (the 0's in the user preference data). We call this a *data blurring*. The basic concept is that if a user prefers an item with feature value x, then we assume that the user also have some preference for other items with feature value x.

In our example, from the fact that U1 prefers I1 and I1's genre feature value is A, we predict the U1's preference for I2 as 0.5 because it also has genre feature value A. 0.5 is an average preference of U1 to items with genre feature value A. This method can apply to user features too. From the fact that item I6 is preferred by U3, U4 with gender feature value F, we predict the preference for I6 from U5 as 0.67 because U5 also has gender feature value F. Table 2 shows the example blurring result.

3.2 Computing blurring values

In this section, we present our proposed data blurring method in more formal way. We assume that only implicit ratings such as purchasing items are obtained. Therefore, an item is either 'preferred' or 'unknown'. Let's assume the following.

- P is a Boolean user-item preference matrix. $P_{ij} = 1$ if user U_i prefers item I_j, and $P_{ij} = 0$ if we have no information regarding U_i's preference for item I_j.
- The users have n features named $f_1, f_2, \ldots, f_n$
- The items have m features named $g_1, g_2, \ldots, g_m$
- Associated with each user U_i is a vector $X_i = <x_1, x_2, \ldots, x_n>$, x_k is the value of f_k for user U_i
- Associated with each item I_j is a vector $Y_j = <y_1, y_2, \ldots, y_m>$, y_k is the value of g_k for item I_j
- For $P_{ij} = 0$, we want to make it to non-zero value by using blurring.

We can predict the value of P_{ij} either by using item feature information or by using user feature information. We call the former as a *row-wise blurring* and the later as a *column-wise blurring*.

The row-wise blurring is filling the unknown value P_{ij} by using the item feature information. Let $SI(Y_j)$ be the set of items with feature vector Y_j (same as I_j's). The probability that the user U_i has preference for item I_j is the probability that user U_i has preference for $SI(Y_j)$, multiplied by the probability that item I_j is preferred among $SI(Y_j)$. Therefore, it can be computed by using the probability distribution of item features as follows:

$$P(I_j | U_i) = P(I_j | y_1,..., y_m) \cdot P(y_1,..., y_m | U_i) \quad (1)$$

$$\approx P(I_j | y_1,..., y_m) \cdot \prod_{k=1}^{m} P(y_k | U_i) \quad (2)$$

$$\approx \frac{N(I_j)}{N(y_1,...,y_m)} \cdot \frac{N(U_i, y_1)+1}{N(U_i)+k_1} \cdot ... \cdot \frac{N(U_i, y_m)+1}{N(U_i)+k_m} \quad (3)$$

In equation (2), we approximate the probability value by assuming the independence between item features. The probabilities are computed by counting 1's in matrix P. In equation (3), $N(I_j)$ is the number of preferences for item I_j (total number of 1's in column j in matrix P), and $N(y_1, y_2, ... , y_m)$ is the total number of known preferences for items with feature value $y_1, y_2, ... , y_m$. $N(U_i)$ is user U_i's total number of preferences (total number of 1's in row i in matrix P), and $N(U_i, y_1)$ denotes user U_i's number of preferences for the items with y_1 feature value. The Laplace's approximation is used to eliminate the problem of zero probability.

The column-wise blurring is filling the unknown value P_{ij} by using the user feature information. Let $SU(X_i)$ be the set of users with feature vector X_i (same as U_i's). Then the probability of item I_j being preferred by user U_i is the probability of item I_j being preferred by $SU(X_i)$, multiplied by the probability of U_i among $SU(X_i)$.

$$P(U_i | I_j) = P(U_i | x_1,..., x_n) \cdot P(x_1,..., x_n | I_j) \quad (4)$$

$$\approx P(U_i | x_1,..., x_n) \cdot \prod_{k=1}^{n} P(x_k | I_j) \quad (5)$$

$$\approx \frac{N(U_i)}{N(x_1,...,x_n)} \cdot \frac{N(I_j, x_1)+1}{N(I_j)+l_1} \cdot ... \cdot \frac{N(I_j, x_n)+1}{N(I_j)+l_n} \quad (6)$$

In equation (6), $N(x_1, x_2, ... , x_n)$ is the total number of known preferences of users with feature value $x_1, x_2, ... , x_n$. $N(I_j, x_1)$ denotes the number of preferences for the item I_j from users with x_1 feature value.

From the result of row-wise and column-wise blurring, the final value is determined as a weighted average of those blurring values. After all the unknown preference values are predicted, the modified preference matrix is used to generate CF recommendations.

4. Experiments

The dataset used for the experiment is selected from the EachMovie dataset. The EachMovie dataset has rating information from a web-based movie recommender on 1,628 movies by 72,916 users. The EachMovie data contains ratings for movies on a discrete six-level scale ranging from 0.0 to 1.0. The data also contains user information such as user id, age, gender, and item information such as movie title and movie genre.

In this experiment, we randomly selected 1,000 users and 1,000 movies, and converted the rating values to Boolean values according to the following procedure: each user's rating average is computed, and then rating values larger than the average is converted to 1 and the remaining values are converted to 0. All the missing preferences are also 0. In this new dataset, we only have positive preference information. The '1' in the preference matrix means 'preferred', and the '0' means 'unknown'.

We divide our 1000 users into 10 equal-size groups. We select one group as a test set and use the other nine groups as a training set, and repeat this process for each of the groups (10-fold cross validation).

First, we blur the training set by using the feature information (all the 0's in the preference matrix are filled with the blurring value). We use 'genre' as the item feature, and 'age' and 'gender' as the user features. Then, for each '1' in the test set in turn, we change it to '0' (this is the "target item") and blur the test set. Finally, with the blurred sets, we perform CF to predict the previously unknown preferences and select the top-N items with the highest prediction values. If the "target item" is found in the top-N list, we call it a "hit". The final accuracy is measured in terms of the hit ratio, which is the total number of hits divided by total number of targets. The hit ratio is compared for different values of k and N. The accuracy of the recommendation with the blurred data is compared to the accuracy of the recommendation with the original data.

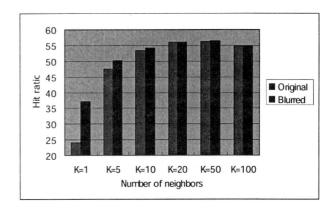

Figure 1. The accuracy of top-20 recommendations – original vs. blurred data.

In the dataset, the number of known preferences (1's in the preference matrix P) is 15,226, which is 1.5% of total possible preferences. These preferences are not evenly distributed. Several items are more popular than others. The top-10 most preferred items occupy 16% of known preferences, and the top-20 most preferred items occupy 28% of known preferences. It means that we can achieve about 28% top-20 hit ratio if we always recommend most popular top-20 items.

Figure 1 compares the accuracy of recommendation with the original data and the blurred data for top-20 recommendation case. For most of cases, the blurred data produced a higher hit ratio. The highest accuracy achieved is 56.3% when K=50 with the blurred data. The improvement in accuracy is greater for smaller values of K. This is because the sparseness has greater effect for smaller values of K. Since the blurred data reflects the probability obtained from the feature information, it is possible to make recommendations even if the data is very sparse or there are no known preferences available.

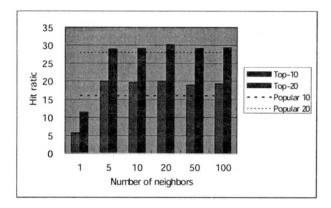

Figure 2. The accuracy of cold-start recommendations (when no preferences are known for the target user).

As we mentioned in previous sections, the cold-start problem represents one major weakness of CF recommendation. When there are no known preferences, CF can not recommend items because it can not find similar users. However, if we predict (blur) the target user's preference values based on known attributes of the user, then CF recommendation is possible.

Figure 2 shows the accuracy of recommendation with blurred data when we assume no known preferences. For this experiment, we eliminate all 1s in target user's preference vector, blur the vector, and check whether each target item known to be good is hit in top-10 and top-20 recommendations. The result shows that for the number of neighbors more than 5, the accuracy of CF recommendations with blurred data is higher than the accuracy of recommending most popular N items. This result suggests that the blurring can help to make recommendations for new users.

5. Conclusion

Although Collaborative Filtering (CF) has been successfully used for recommendation, it suffers from the data sparseness. CF is also challenged to produce good recommendations in early startup stages, when little training data is available, either for a user or for an item. In this paper, we proposed a data blurring method, in which the feature information of users and items are integrated into CF to overcome those difficulties.

The original preference data is blurred by using the distributions of feature values, such as age and gender of users, and genre or supplier of items. Since the blurred data is not sparse – unknown preferences are filled with the predicted values, blurring can alleviate the problems caused by the data sparseness. Experimental results with a movie rating dataset show that the accuracy of recommendation is improved by using the proposed data blurring method.

References

1. C. Basu, H. Hirsh, and W. Cohen, "Recommendation as classification: Using social and content-based information in recommendation," *Proceedings of the 15th National Conference on Artificial Intelligence*, 1998.
2. D. Billsus and M. Pazzani, "Learning Collaborative Information Filters," *Proceedings of the 15th International Conference on Machine Learning*, 1998.
3. J. Breese, D. Heckerman, and C. Kadie, "Empirical Analysis of Predictive Algorithms for Collaborative Filtering," *Proceedings of the 14th Conference of Uncertainty in Artificial Intelligence*, 1998.
4. M. Condliff, D. Lewis, D. Madigan, and C. Posse, "Baysian mixed-effect models for recommender systems," *Proceedings of Recommender Systems Workshop at SIGIR-99*, 1999.
5. N. Good, J. B. Schafer, J. A. Konstan, A. Borchers, B. Sarwar, J. Herlocker, and J. Riedl, "Combining Collaborative Filtering with Personal Agents for Better Recommendations," *Proceedings of the 6th Conference of American Association of Artificial Intelligence*, 1999.
6. J. Herlocker, J. Konstan, A. Borchers, and J. Riedl, "An Algorithmic Framework for Performing Collaborative Filtering," *Proceedings of the 22nd Conference on Research and Development in Information Retrieval*, 1999.
7. J. Konstan, B. Miller, D. Maltz, J. Herlocker, L. Gordon and J. Riedl, "GroupLens: Applying collaborative filtering to usenet news," *Communications of the ACM*, March 1997.
8. P. Melville, R. Mooney, and R. Nagarajan, "Content-boosted collaborative filtering," *Proceedings of the SIGIR-2001 Workshop on Recommender Systems*, 2001.
9. M. Pazzani, "A framework for collaborative, content-based and demographic filtering," *Artificial Intelligence Review*, 13 (5-6), 1999.
10. A. Poposcul, L. Ungar, D. Pennock, and S. Lawrence, "Probabilistic models for unified collaborative and content-based recommendation in sparse-data environment," *Proceedings of the 17th Conference on Uncertainty in Artificial Intelligence*, 2001.

GREW—A Scalable Frequent Subgraph Discovery Algorithm*

Michihiro Kuramochi and George Karypis
Department of Computer Science and Engineering
University of Minnesota
{kuram, karypis}@cs.umn.edu

Abstract

Existing algorithms that mine graph datasets to discover patterns corresponding to frequently occurring subgraphs can operate efficiently on graphs that are sparse, contain a large number of relatively small connected components, have vertices with low and bounded degrees, and contain well-labeled vertices and edges. However, for graphs that do not share these characteristics, these algorithms become highly unscalable. In this paper we present a heuristic algorithm called GREW to overcome the limitations of existing complete or heuristic frequent subgraph discovery algorithms. GREW is designed to operate on a large graph and to find patterns corresponding to connected subgraphs that have a large number of vertex-disjoint embeddings. Our experimental evaluation shows that GREW is efficient, can scale to very large graphs, and find non-trivial patterns.

Keywords frequent pattern discovery, frequent subgraph, graph mining.

1 Introduction

In the last five years, an ever increasing body of research has focused on developing efficient algorithms to mine frequent patterns in large graph datasets that employ different mining strategies, are designed for different input graph representations, and find patterns that have different characteristics and satisfy different constraints (e.g., [1, 9, 4, 3, 6, 5]).

A key characteristic of all of these algorithms is that they are complete in the sense that they are guaranteed to find all subgraphs that satisfy the specific constraints. Even though completeness is intrinsically a very important and desirable property, one can not ignore the fact that it also imposes very strong limitations on the types of graph datasets that can be mined in a reasonable amount of time. In general, the algorithms can only operate efficiently on input datasets that are sparse, contain a large number of relatively small connected components, have vertices with low and bounded degrees, and contain well-labeled vertices and edges. On the other hand, existing heuristic algorithms, which are not guaranteed to find the complete set of subgraphs, as SUBDUE [2] and GBI [10], tend to find an extremely small number of patterns and are not significantly more scalable. For example, the results reported in a recently published study showed that SUBDUE was able to find 3 subgraphs in 5,043 seconds, while VSIGRAM (a recently developed complete algorithm) was able to find 3,183 patterns in just 63 seconds from a graph containing 33,443 vertices and 11,244 edges [6].

To overcome the limitations of existing algorithms (either complete or heuristic) we developed an algorithm called GREW. GREW is a heuristic algorithm, designed to operate on a large graph and to find patterns corresponding to connected subgraphs that have a large number of vertex-disjoint embeddings. Because of its heuristic nature, the number of patterns discovered by GREW is significantly smaller than those discovered by complete algorithms. However, as our experiments will show, GREW can operate effectively on very large graphs (containing over a quarter of a million vertices) and still find long and meaningful/interesting patterns. At the same time, compared to existing heuristic algorithms GREW is able to find significantly more and larger patterns at a fraction of their runtime.

We experimentally evaluate the performance of GREW on four different datasets containing 29,014–255,798 vertices that are derived from different domains including cocitation analysis, VLSI, and web link analysis. Our experiments show that GREW is able to quickly find a large number of non-trivial size patterns.

The rest of this paper is organized as follows. Section 2 provides a detailed description of GREW and its various

*This work was supported in part by NSF ACI-0133464 and ACI-0312828; the Digital Technology Center at the University of Minnesota; and by the Army High Performance Computing Research Center (AHPCRC) under the auspices of the Department of the Army, Army Research Laboratory (ARL) under Cooperative Agreement number DAAD19-01-2-0014. The content of which does not necessarily reflect the position or the policy of the government, and no official endorsement should be inferred. Access to research and computing facilities was provided by the Digital Technology Center and the Minnesota Supercomputing Institute.

computational steps. Section 3 shows a detailed experimental evaluation of GREW on datasets from different domains and compares it against existing algorithms. Finally, Section 4 provides concluding remarks.

2 GREW—Scalable Frequent Subgraph Discovery Algorithm

GREW is a heuristic algorithm, designed to operate on a large graph and to find patterns corresponding to connected subgraphs that have a large number of vertex-disjoint embeddings. Specifically, the patterns that GREW finds satisfy the following two properties:

Property 1 The number of vertex-disjoint embeddings of each pattern is guaranteed to be at least as high as the user-supplied minimum frequency threshold.

Property 2 If a vertex contributes to the support of multiple patterns $\{G_1, G_2, \ldots, G_k\}$ of increasing size, then G_i is a subgraph of G_{i+1} for $i = 1, \ldots, k-1$.

GREW discovers frequent subgraphs in an iterative fashion. During each iteration, GREW identifies vertex-disjoint embeddings of subgraphs that were determined to be frequent in previous iterations and merges certain subgraphs that are connected to each other via one or multiple edges. This iterative frequent subgraph merging process continues until there are no such candidate subgraphs whose combination will lead to a larger frequent subgraph. Note that unlike existing subgraph growing methods used by complete algorithms (e.g., [1, 9, 4, 3, 6, 5]), which increase the size of each successive subgraph by one edge or vertex at a time, GREW, in each successive iteration, can potentially double the size of the subgraphs that it identifies. At the same time, compared to some of the most efficient heuristic subgraph discovery algorithms (e.g., B-GBI [8]), GREW can discover larger subgraphs faster by using a greedy MIS algorithm to identify and contract concurrently multiple edge-types and by collapsing subgraphs that are connected by multiple edges.

The key feature that contributes to GREW's efficiency is that it maintains the location of the embeddings of the previously identified frequent subgraphs by rewriting the input graph. As a result of this graph rewriting, the vertices involved in each particular embedding are *collapsed* together to form a new vertex (referred to as **multi-vertex**), whose label uniquely identifies the particular frequent subgraph that is supported by them. Within each multi-vertex, the edges that are not part of the frequent subgraph are added as loop edges. To ensure that the rewritten graph contains all the information present in the original graph, these newly created loop-edges, as well as the edges of the

---

Algorithm 1 GREW-SE(G, f)

1: ▷ G is the input graph.
2: ▷ f is the minimum frequency threshold.
3: $\mathcal{F} \leftarrow \emptyset$
4: $\hat{G} \leftarrow$ augmented graph representation of G
5: **while true do**
6:     $\mathcal{E} \leftarrow$ all edge-types in $\hat{G}$ that occur at least f times
7:     order $\mathcal{E}$ in decreasing frequency
8:     **for each** edge-type e **in** $\mathcal{E}$ **do**
9:        $G_o \leftarrow$ overlap graph of e
10:        ▷ each vertex in G_o corresponds to an embedding of e in $\hat{G}$
11:        $\mathcal{M}_{\text{MIS}} \leftarrow$ obtain MIS for G_o
12:        $e.f \leftarrow |\mathcal{M}_{\text{MIS}}|$
13:        **if** $e.f \geq f$ **then**
14:           $\mathcal{F} \leftarrow \mathcal{F} \cup \{e\}$
15:           **for each** embedding m **in** $\mathcal{M}_{\text{MIS}}$ **do**
16:              mark m
17:     **if** no marked edge in $\hat{G}$ **then**
18:        **break**
19:     update $\hat{G}$ by rewriting all of its marked edges
20: **return** $\mathcal{F}$

---

original graph that are incident to a multi-vertex, are augmented to contain information about (i) the label of the incident vertices, and (ii) their actual end-point vertices within each multi-vertex (with respect to the original graph), which is referred to as the *augmented graph*. Using the augmented graph representation, GREW identifies the sets of embedding-pairs to be merged by simply finding the frequent edges that have the same augmented edge-label. In addition, GREW obtains the next level rewritten graph by simply contracting together the vertices that are incident to the selected edges.

2.1 GREW-SE—Single-Edge Collapsing

The simplest version of GREW, which is referred to as GREW-SE, operates on the augmented graph and repeatedly identifies frequently occurring edges and contracts them in a heuristic fashion. The overall structure of GREW-SE is shown in Algorithm 1. It takes as input the original graph G and the minimum frequency threshold f, and on completion, it returns the set of frequent subgraphs $\mathcal{F}$ that it identified. During each iteration (loop starting at line 5), it scans the current augmented graph $\hat{G}$ and determines the set of edge-types $\mathcal{E}$ that occur at least f times in $\hat{G}$.

Each of these edge-types represent identical subgraphs, and as a result each edge-type in $\mathcal{E}$ can lead to a frequent subgraph. However, because some vertices can be incident to multiple embeddings of the same (or different) frequent edge-types, the frequencies obtained at this step represent upper-bounds, and the actual number of the vertex-disjoint embeddings can be smaller. For this reason, GREW-SE further analyzes the embeddings of each edge-type to select a maximal set of embeddings that do not share any vertices with each other or with embeddings selected previously for other edge-types (lines 8–16). This step (the loop starting at line 8) is achieved by constructing the overlap graph G_o for the set of embeddings of each edge-type e and using a greedy maximal independent set algorithm to quickly identify a large number of vertex-disjoint embeddings. If the size of this maximal set is greater than the minimum frequency threshold, this edge-type survives the current iteration and the embeddings in the independent set are marked. Otherwise the edge-type is discarded as it does not lead to a frequent subgraph in the current iteration. After processing all the edge-types, the contraction operations are performed, graph $\hat{G}$ is updated, and the next iteration begins.

2.2 GREW-ME—Multi-Edge Collapsing

A result of successive graph rewriting operations is the creation of multiple loops and multiple edges in $\hat{G}$. In many cases, there may be the same set of multiple edges connecting similar pairs of vertices in $\hat{G}$, all of which can be collapsed together to form a larger frequent subgraph. To take advantage of this and quickly identify large frequent subgraphs, we developed the GREW-ME algorithm that in addition to collapsing vertices connected via a single edge, it also analyzes the sets of multiple edges connecting pairs of vertices to identify any frequent subsets of edges. This is achieved by using a traditional frequent closed itemset mining algorithm as follows. For each pair of vertices that are connected via multiple edges (or a single vertex with multiple loops), GREW-ME creates a list that contains the multiple edge-types that are involved, and treats each list as a transaction whose items corresponds to the multiple edges. Then, by running a closed frequent itemset mining algorithm, GREW-ME finds all the frequent sets of edges whose raw frequency is above the minimum threshold. Each of these multiple sets of edges is treated as a different edge-type, and GREW-ME proceeds in a fashion identical to GREW-SE.

3 Experimental Evaluation

In this section, we study the performance of the proposed algorithms with various parameters and real datasets. All experiments were done on Intel Pentium 4 processor (2.6 GHz) machines with 1 Gbytes main memory, running the Linux operating system. All the reported runtimes are in seconds.

Datasets We evaluated the performance of GREW on four different datasets, each obtained from a different domain. The basic characteristics of these datasets are shown in Table 1. Note that even though some of these graphs consist of multiple connected components, GREW treats them as one large graph. Those datasets are originally from the Aviation Safety Reporting System Database, the International Symposium on Physical Design '98 (ISPD98) benchmark ibm05, KDD Cup 2003 and the 2002 Google Programming Contest (see [7] for the details).

Table 1. Datasets used in the experiments

Dataset	Vertices	Edges	Labels		Connected Components
			Vertex	Edge	
Aviation	101,185	133,113	6,173	52	1,049
Citation	29,014	294,171	742	1	3,018
VLSI	29,347	81,353	11	1	1
Web	255,798	317,247	3,438	1	25,685

Results Table 2 shows the runtime, the number of frequent patterns found, and the size of the largest frequent patterns obtained by GREW-SE and GREW-ME for the four datasets. A dash ("—") indicates the computation was aborted because of memory exhaustion.

Both GREW-SE and GREW-ME can find large frequent patterns in a reasonable amount of time. For example, GREW-SE can mine the Web dataset, which contains over 250,000 vertices, with the minimum frequency of five in around four minutes. Looking at the characteristics of the algorithms, as the minimum frequency threshold decreases, we can see that, as expected, they are able to find both a larger number of frequent patterns and patterns that are in general longer.

Comparing the relative performance of GREW-SE and GREW-ME, we can see that overall, they perform quite similarly, as they both find similar number of patterns, and their longest patterns are of similar sizes. However, there are some dataset dependencies. For example, GREW-SE performs better for the Citation dataset, whereas GREW-ME performs better for the VLSI dataset. In terms of runtime, GREW-ME is somewhat slower than GREW-SE. This is because (i) GREW-ME incurs the additional overhead of finding closed frequent itemsets, and (ii) it processes a larger number of distinct edge-types (as each closed itemset is represented by a different edge-type). In addition, the memory overhead associated with storing these larger number of edge-types is the reason why GREW-ME run out of memory for some parameter combinations with the Aviation and Web datasets.

Example Subgraphs To illustrate the types of subgraphs that GREW can discover, we analyzed the subgraphs that were identified in the Web dataset. Each vertex in this graph corresponds to an actual web-page, each edge to a hyperlink between two web-pages, and each vertex-label to the subdomain of the server that hosts the web-page. Moreover, this graph was constructed by removing any hyperlinks between web-pages that have the same subdomain. As a result, a frequently occurring subgraph will represent a particular cross-linking structure among a specific set of institutions that occurs often, and it can identify common cross-university collaborations, interdisciplinary teams, or topic-specific communities.

Figure 1 shows two representative examples of the subgraphs discovered by GREW. The first subgraph (Fig-

Table 2. GREW-SE and GREW-ME

Aviation					Citation				
Method	f	t	#	Size	Method	f	t	#	Size
GREW-SE	1000	336	38	13	GREW-SE	100	9	87	3
	500	213	72	16		50	20	150	7
	200	129	117	32		20	48	306	16
	100	2151	175	53		10	105	533	31
GREW-ME	1000	370	38	13		5	683	1061	63
	500	396	72	16	GREW-ME	100	18	86	3
	200	—	—	—		50	34	150	7
	100	—	—	—		20	74	305	8
						10	130	546	25
						5	555	1077	47

VLSI					Web				
Method	f	t	#	Size	Method	f	t	#	Size
GREW-SE	100	20	54	17	GREW-SE	100	6	296	1
	50	20	84	18		50	15	554	3
	20	23	145	43		20	45	1254	7
	10	23	239	27		10	89	2430	9
	5	29	445	33		5	259	4822	13
GREW-ME	100	23	55	15	GREW-ME	100	8	296	1
	50	23	90	18		50	20	553	3
	20	24	146	20		20	66	1256	5
	10	26	238	36		10	220	2461	14
	5	38	417	44		5	—	—	—

f: the minimum frequency threshold
t: runtime in seconds
#: the number of frequent patterns discovered
Size: the size of the largest frequent patterns found

ure 1(a)) has a star topology and connects together various web-servers that are part of California's University System. The star-node corresponds to web-servers that are part of the University of California's Office of the President with various web-servers that are located at Berkeley, UCI, UCLA, UCSD, and UCSF. The second subgraph (Figure 1(b)) has a more complex topology with a higher degree of connectivity and connects together various web-servers at Harvard, National Radio Astronomy Observatory (nrao.edu), and Space Telescope Science Institute (stsci.edu). An analysis of the complete uniform resource locators (URLs) of the embeddings of this subgraph showed that all the web-pages had to do with astronomy and astrophysics. These examples suggest that the patterns that GREW finds are interesting and can be used to gain insights on the underlying graph datasets.

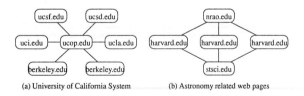

(a) University of California System   (b) Astronomy related web pages

Figure 1. Patterns discovered by GREW

3.1 Comparison with SUBDUE

We ran SUBDUE [2] version 5.1.0 (with the default set of parameters) on our four benchmark datasets and measured the runtime, the number of patterns discovered, their size, and their frequency. Although we gave SUBDUE eight hours to mine each of the datasets, SUBDUE could finish within the eight hour window only for the Aviation dataset. It took SUBDUE more than 6 hours and discovered three most interesting patterns according to the Minimum Description Length (MDL) principle. Their sizes are either 9 or 10 and their frequencies are all 13. On the other hand, as shown in Table 2, GREW-SE and GREW-ME can find 72 patterns of up to size 16 whose frequency is at least 500, which is about 38 times more than the frequency of the best three patterns reported by SUBDUE. The runtime of GREW-SE and GREW-ME is also significantly shorter than that of SUBDUE. GREW-SE spends 213 seconds and GREW-ME spends 396 seconds.

4 Conclusions

In this paper we presented a heuristic algorithm called GREW to find frequent connected subgraphs from a single undirected input graph, and evaluated its efficiency and scalability by various experiments using graphs directly created from the four real datasets. Our results showed that GREW is highly scalable, can operate on very large graphs, and find a large and diverse set of patterns.

Acknowledgment We thank Drs. Hiroshi Motoda, Takashi Washio, Tetsuya Yoshida and Takashi Matsuda of Osaka University for their useful comments and kindly providing the implementation of B-GBI.

References

[1] C. Borgelt and M. R. Berthold. Mining molecular fragments: Finding relevant substructures of molecules. In *Proc. ICDM'02*, 2002.

[2] D. J. Cook and L. B. Holder. Substructure discovery using minimum description length and background knowledge. *J. Artificial Intelligence Research*, 1, 1994.

[3] J. Huan, W. Wang, and J. Prins. Efficient mining of frequent subgraph in the presence of isomorphism. In *Proc. ICDM'03*, 2003.

[4] A. Inokuchi, T. Washio, and H. Motoda. Complete mining of frequent patterns from graphs: Mining graph data. *Machine Learning*, 50(3), 2003.

[5] M. Kuramochi and G. Karypis. An efficient algorithm for discovering frequent subgraphs. *IEEE TKDE*, 16(9), 2004.

[6] M. Kuramochi and G. Karypis. Finding frequent patterns in a large sparse graph. In *Proc. SDM04*, 2004.

[7] M. Kuramochi and G. Karypis. Grew—a scalable frequent subgraph discovery algorithm. Technical Report 04-024, University of Minnesota, Dept. of Computer Science, 2004.

[8] T. Matsuda, H. Motoda, T. Yoshida, and T. Washio. Mining patterns from structured data by beam-wise graph-based induction. In *Proc. DS2002*, 2002.

[9] X. Yan and J. Han. gSpan: Graph-based substructure pattern mining. In *Proc. ICDM'02*, 2002.

[10] K. Yoshida and H. Motoda. CLIP: Concept learning from inference patterns. *Artificial Intelligence*, 75(1), 1995.

Predicting Density-Based Spatial Clusters Over Time

Chih Lai   Nga T. Nguyen
Graduate Programs in Software Engineering
University of St. Thomas
St. Paul, MN 55125
clai@stthomas.edu   ntnguyen1@stthomas.edu

Abstract

Most of existing clustering algorithms are designed to discover snapshot clusters that reflect only the current status of a database. Snapshot clusters do not reveal the fact that clusters may either persist over a period of time, or slowly fade away as other clusters may gradually develop. Predicting dynamic cluster evolutions and their occurring periods are important because this information can guide users to prepare appropriate actions toward the right areas during the right time for the most effective results. In this paper we developed a simple but effective approach in predicting the future distance among object pairs. Objects that will be close in distance over different periods of time are then processed to discover density-based clusters that may occur or change over time.

1. Introduction

Clustering is the process of grouping data into clusters so that objects within a cluster have high similarity or close distance [1][2][3][6]. However, most of existing clustering algorithms are designed to discover snapshot clusters that reflect only the current status of a database. Such snapshot clusters conceal the fact that some clusters may persist over periods of time, and some clusters may slowly fade away as other clusters may gradually develop. If we can compute the change rates of individual objects from past data and consider these change rates in the clustering process, clusters that may expand, shrink, disappear, emerge, or remain unchanged over time can be predicted. Predicting these cluster changes over time have many important applications.

For example, if we can predict the periods and areas of future concentration of incoming missiles or enemies, preemptive actions, such as firing intercepted weapons to the predicted areas in a specific time window, can be prepared and executed in advance for the most effective results. Other usages include predicting periods and areas of congestions for air traffic control, or city growing plan.

One solution in discovering future dense clusters is to repeatedly execute the clustering algorithms discussed in [1][2] on extrapolated data at regular intervals. Unfortunately, if the selected intervals are not small enough, many cluster changes over time may not be detected. Although, at the expense of high computation cost, executing more frequent clustering at shorter intervals can alleviate this problem, there is no short enough interval that can cover infinite time points on a timeline. If no future cluster is detected by this interval-checking approach, keep shortening the interval may simply waste more system resources because there may not have any future cluster in some databases.

It is our goal in this paper to develop a simple but effective approach in predicting density-based clusters over time. We first modify our previous work [4] on air traffic control and develop a simple formula that can check which paired objects will be in the ε–neighborhood [1] of each other. From these pair-wise ε–neighborhood relationships, we can then calculate which objects will become *Core Objects Over Time* (*COOTs*) during what periods in which areas. *COOTs* tell users where, when, and how long the concentrations may happen so that effective actions can be taken toward the right places at the right time. If detailed cluster contents and their periods are needed, our algorithm can also produce *Clusters Over Time* (*COTs*) from these pair-wise ε–neighborhood relationships. Each *COT* contains two major items: a set of clusters with their containing objects, and a time period in which the *COT* remains unchanged.

On the temporal domain, our approach is general enough to predict *COOTs* and *COTs* that may happen any where in a timeline (i.e. in the future and/or in the past). That is the reason we use the general term "over time", instead of specific terms such as "future". In fact, our approach also offers an option that allows users to provide a *Specified Prediction Windows* (*SPW*) for predicting *COOTs* and *COTs* (i.e. within next two to four hours). *SPW* not only reduces unnecessary computations and space by filtering out uninteresting ε–neighborhood relationships from unwanted periods, it also allows users to guide the prediction process to produce more focused results in the periods where users are able to react to the cluster changes. On the functional domain, our algorithms can be applied to 2D/3D spatial applications, or it can be generalized to high dimensional feature space.

In Section 2, we give the formal definitions for *Core Objects Over Time* (*COOTs*) and *Clusters Over Time*

443

(*COTs*). In Section 3.1, we first develop a simple formula for predicting the ε–neighborhood relationships of each object pair over time. Section 3.2 discuss algorithms for discovering *COOTs* and *COTs*. Section 4 concludes our study.

2. Problem Definition

In order to predict cluster changes over time, we first need to predict the periods of ε–neighborhood relationships among objects. Core objects and their present periods can then be identified from these ε–neighborhood relationships among objects. After the core objects and their present periods are identified, objects that are density-connected to the core objects during these periods can then be grouped into clusters that exist over certain periods of time. In this section, we extend the definitions for ordinary core objects and density-based clusters to incorporate timing information.

Let $D = \{O_1, O_2, \ldots O_n\}$ be a database that contains n objects at current time. Let each object O_i ($1 \leq i \leq n$) have $m \geq 1$ attributes, then the status of O_i can be denoted as an m-tuple $O_i = <o_{i,1}, o_{i,2}, \ldots, o_{i,m}>$. We use another m-tuple $V_i = <v_{i,1}, v_{i,2}, \ldots, v_{i,m}>$ to denote the rates of changes (velocity) for the object O_i, where $v_{i,j}$ is the rate of change for the jth attribute of O_i. Hence, the status (position) of O_i at any time T will be referred to as O_i^T, and it can be expressed as a function of time as: $O_i^T = <o_{i,1} + v_{i,1} \times T, o_{i,2} + v_{i,2} \times T, \ldots, o_{i,m} + v_{i,m} \times T>$.

Definition 1. An object O_i will become a **C**ore **O**bject **O**ver **T**ime (*COOT*) in the period of [j, k] if $|N_\varepsilon(O_i)| \geq MinPts$ is true in [j, k]. We denote such core object over time as $COOT_{i,j,k}$.

If O_i is identified as a *COOT* during the period of [j, k], that means $COOT_{i,j,k}$ (or O_i) will move from O_i^j to O_i^k in the period of [j, k]. Note that the period of a $COOT_{i,j,k}$ is always a closed period: the period of $COOT_{i,j,k}$ includes the begin and the end time points j and k. This may not be the case for *COTs*, as we will define *COTs* shortly.

Since different objects may move in or out the ε–neighborhood of O_i over time and O_i itself is moving, O_i may become a *COOT* in different time periods. To avoid reporting the same object as *COOTs* for multiple times in overlapped periods, we required that any $COOT_{i,j,k}$ must satisfy the following condition: $\forall COOT_{i,j',k'}$, if [j, k] $\cap$ [j', k'] $\neq \varnothing$, then $j = j'$ and $k = k'$.

At any time T when new *COOTs* emerge, or when the objects that are within the ε–neighborhood of present *COOTs* change, we need to report a set of **C**lusters **O**ver **T**ime (*COT*) that stay unchanged (wrt. constituting objects) until sometime right before T so that all the different clusters over time can be captured. In other words, we need to first report an existing *COT* before we

can update its contents to reflect the changes occurred at time T. Detailed examples can be found in [5].

We denote *COTs* that are reported in the period between q and r as $COT_{p,q,r}$. That is, q and r specify the time segment in which the constituting objects of $COT_{p,q,r}$ remain unchanged, and $p \in \{1, 2, 3, 4\}$ is used to indicate the openness of the time segment at time q and r. The openness of this time segment can be in one of the four situations: [q, r], [q, r), (q, r], or (q, r), denoted by 1, 2, 3, or 4, respectively. Note that a bracket indicates a closed time point and a parenthesis indicates an open time point.

The openness of a *COT* period can be determined by the previous and the current ε–neighborhood relationship events as given in Table 1. If multiple ε–neighborhood relationships begin and end at the same time point, the begin events will be processed before the end events so that a surge of concentration can also be captured. We refer readers to [5] for detailed examples.

Table 1. Openness rules for a *COT*'s period.

		Previous ε–Relationship Event	
Current		Begin	End
ε–Relationship	Begin	$p=2$, [q,r)	$p=4$, (q,r)
Event	End	$p=1$, [q,r]	$p=3$, (q,r]

Since *COTs* can develop or change only when *COOTs* emerge or change, every cluster that is included in $COT_{p,q,r}$ must satisfy the following condition: it contains only the objects that are density-reachable from some $COOT_{a,b,c}$ such that $b \leq q \leq r \leq c$. In other words, the period of a *COT* must be covered by the period of at least one *COOT*. Let $\lfloor n / MinPts \rfloor$ be the maximum number of clusters that can develop in D at any time, we have the following formal definition:

Definition 2. $COT_{p,q,r} = \{C_x \mid x \geq 1\}$, where $C_x \subseteq D$ is a cluster and $|COT_{p,q,r}| \leq \lfloor n / MinPts \rfloor$. $\forall O_i, O_j \in C_x$, $\exists COOT_{a,b,c}$ such that at any time T with $b \leq q \leq T \leq r \leq c$, O_i^T and O_j^T are density-reachable from O_a^T.

3. Algorithms

In Section 3.1 we develop efficient formulas for predicting which objects will be in the ε–neighborhood of each other over time. From these ε–neighborhood relationships, algorithms discussed in Section 3.2 can calculate which objects will become *COOTs* in which *COTs* during what periods. Section 3.3 discusses a simple approach to further reduce time/space complexity, and produce more focused *COOT* and *COT* predictions.

3.1. Predicting ε–Neighborhood Over Time

In order to construct clusters that may happen over time, we first need to identify objects that may become core objects over time. To obtain this information, we first need to know the distance between each distinct pair of objects over time. These distance measurements can then be compared against ε to determine which objects are within the ε-neighborhood of each other. More specifically, we need to answer following two questions:

1. Will any two different objects O_i and O_j be within the ε-neighborhood of each other over time?
2. What will be the period the ε-neighborhood relationship exists between O_i and O_j?

We first define all the distinct pairs of objects in a database D as a set $D_P = \{<O_i, O_j> \mid \forall 1 \leq i, j \leq n, O_i, O_j \in D, i \neq j$ and $i < j\}$. As we also defined in the previous section that, at any time T, the status (position) of an object O_i with m attributes can be expressed as a function of time as: $<o_{i,1} + v_{i,1} \times T, o_{i,2} + v_{i,2} \times T, \ldots, o_{i,m} + v_{i,m} \times T>$. The Euclidean distance E between any paired objects $<O_i, O_j> \in D_P$ at any time T can then be computed as:

$$E^2 = \sum_{k=1}^{m} ((o_{i,k} + v_{i,k} \times T) - (o_{j,k} + v_{j,k} \times T))^2$$

Let $\Delta o_k = o_{i,k} - o_{j,k}$ and $\Delta v_k = v_{i,k} - v_{j,k}$, we now have:

$$E^2 = \sum_{k=1}^{m} (\Delta o_k + \Delta v_k \times T)^2 \text{, or}$$

$$E^2 = T^2 \times (\Delta v_1^2 + \ldots + \Delta v_m^2) + 2 \times T \times (\Delta o_1 \times \Delta v_1 + \ldots + \Delta o_m \times \Delta v_m)$$

$$+ (\Delta o_1^2 + \ldots + \Delta o_m^2) \qquad (1)$$

If $E \leq \varepsilon$ or $E^2 \leq \varepsilon^2$, O_i and O_j are within the ε-neighborhood of each other. The difference between E^2 and ε^2 at any time T can be expressed as a function $f_{ij}(T) = E^2 - \varepsilon^2$. More precisely, this difference function $f_{ij}(T)$ describes the ε-neighborhood relationship between O_i and O_j over time. Substituting E^2 of $f_{ij}(T)$ with the right hand side of equation (1), we have equation (2):

$$T^2 \times (\Delta v_1^2 + \ldots + \Delta v_m^2) + 2 \times T \times (\Delta o_1 \times \Delta v_1 + \ldots + \Delta o_m \times \Delta v_m)$$

$$+ (\Delta o_1^2 + \ldots + \Delta o_m^2) - \varepsilon^2 = f_{ij}(T) \qquad (2)$$

That is, if O_i and O_j are evolving based on their change rates, their ε-neighborhood relationship will begin and end at the time when $f_{ij}(T) = E^2 - \varepsilon^2 = 0$, or simply $E = \varepsilon$.

Let $A = (\Delta v_1^2 + \ldots + \Delta v_m^2)$, $B = 2 \times (\Delta o_1 \times \Delta v_1 + \ldots + \Delta o_m \times \Delta v_m)$, and $C = e^2 - \varepsilon^2$, respectively. Note that $e = (\Delta o_1^2 + \ldots + \Delta o_m^2)^{1/2}$ represents the distance between O_i and O_j at current time. Equation (2) can then be rewritten as equation (3):

$$AT^2 + BT + C = f_{ij}(T) \qquad (3)$$

It follows that this ε-neighborhood relationship function can be analyzed as a parabola function. More precisely, the existence of ε-neighborhood relationship between O_i and O_j can be easily tested by equation (4):

$$B^2 - 4 \times A \times C \geq 0 \qquad (4)$$

If $B^2 - 4 \times A \times C \geq 0$, the parabola intersects with the $f_{ij}(T) = 0$ axis. That is, if $B^2 - 4 \times A \times C \geq 0$, then $E \leq \varepsilon$ (or $E^2 \leq \varepsilon^2$) will be true somewhere in a timeline, indicating the existence of an ε-neighborhood relationship between O_i

and O_j over time. If this relationship exists, it will occur in the period defined by one of the following equations:

$$(-B \pm \sqrt{B^2 - 4 \times A \times C}) / (2 \times A) \quad \text{if } (A \neq 0) \qquad (5)$$

$$-\infty \text{ to } \infty \qquad \text{if } (A = 0) \text{ AND } (C = e^2 - \varepsilon^2 \leq 0) \qquad (6)$$

When O_i and O_j have the same change rates on all m attributes, A (and B) will be zero and there is no solution for equation (3). Under this case, if the current distance between O_i and O_j is not greater than ε (i.e. $C = e^2 - \varepsilon^2 \leq 0$ or $e^2 \leq \varepsilon^2$), the ε-neighborhood relationship between O_i and O_j persists forever from $-\infty$ to ∞ (equation 6). However, if $A = 0$ and the current distance between O_i and O_j is greater than ε (i.e. $C = e^2 - \varepsilon^2 > 0$), no ε-neighborhood relationship between O_i and O_j will occur over time.

Example 1. Let ε be set to 1 and a database D contain three objects $\{O_1, O_2, O_3\}$. Assume each object has two attributes, and their current statuses are given as $O_1 = <5, 0>$, $O_2 = <0, 1>$, $O_3 = <0, 5>$, respectively. Let the change rates for O_1, O_2, and O_3 be $V_1 = <0, 1>$, $V_2 = <1, 0>$, $V_3 = <1, 0>$, respectively. The ε-neighborhood relationships among these objects over time can be studied by $f_{ij}(T)$.

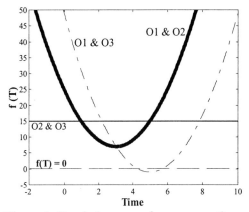

Figure 1. Parabola curves for representing ε-neighborhood relationships over time.

Based on equation (3), the ε-neighborhood relationship between O_1 and O_2 over time can be described as $f_{1,2}(T) = 2T^2 - 12T + 25$. Similarly, the ε-neighborhood relationship between O_1 and O_3, O_2 and O_3 can be expressed as $f_{1,3}(T) = 2T^2 - 20T + 49$ and $f_{2,3}(T) = 15$, respectively. The curves for $f_{1,2}(T)$, $f_{1,3}(T)$, and $f_{2,3}(T)$ are shown in Figure 1. Since only $f_{1,3}(T)$ has $B^2 - 4 \times A \times C \geq 0$, we know only O_1 and O_3 will be in the ε-neighborhood of each other. This can also be observed in Figure 1 where only $f_{1,3}(T)$ has $E \leq \varepsilon$ or $E^2 - \varepsilon^2 \leq 0$. Moreover, the period of this ε-neighborhood relationship between O_1 and O_3 can be computed by equation (5) as [4.29289, 5.70711].

Weighted distance [3] can also be used with our approach to measure the distance between O_i and O_j:

$$W^2 = \sum_{k=1}^{m} w_k \times ((o_{i,k} + v_{i,k} \times T) - (o_{j,k} + v_{j,k} \times T))^2$$

w_k is the weight assigned to each of the m variables according to its perceived importance. If weighted distance is used, then coefficients A, B, and C in equation (3) can be replaced by the followings: $A = (w_1 \times \Delta v_1^2 + \ldots + w_m \times \Delta v_m^2)$, $B = 2 \times (w_1 \times \Delta o_1 \times \Delta v_1 + \ldots + w_m \times \Delta o_m \times \Delta v_m)$, and $C = (w_1 \times \Delta o_1^2 + \ldots + w_m \times \Delta o_m^2) - \varepsilon^2$.

3.2. Finding COOTs and COTs

In the previous section we discussed a simple but effective approach for checking the ε-neighborhood relationships between paired objects O_i and O_j over time. If an ε-neighborhood relationship between O_i and O_j never occurs, no further action is needed. But, if such relationship exists between O_i and O_j, the period of this relationship, denoted as $[x, y]$, can be computed by equations (5) or (6).

The start time (x) and the end time (y) of this period along with the $<O_i, O_j>$ pair will be inserted into a modified $B+$ tree β for sorting and mining. β has a similar structure as an ordinary $B+$ tree except for its leaf nodes. In β, each entry on a leaf node has three tuples: $<T, BList, EList>$. T is used as an indexed key as in an ordinary $B+$ tree, and it represents a time point at which some ε-neighborhood relationships start and end. $BList$ and $EList$ are lists of paired objects $<O_i, O_j>$ that have their ε-relationships start and end at time T, respectively.

When inserting x into β, the search and insertion methods of an ordinary $B+$ tree are used to locate a right leaf node for storing x. If x is a new key value, one entry will be created on the allocated leaf node of β with the following settings: T is set to x, and $<O_i, O_j>$ pair is appended to $BList$. If an entry with $T = x$ is found on a leaf node of β, then no new entry will be created. Instead, $<O_i, O_j>$ pair will be appended to $BList$ of the found entry. When inserting y value into β, the same procedure will take place, except $EList$ is used, not $BList$.

After creating β, each entry on a leaf node of β represents begin and end of ε-neighborhood relationships between paired objects held in $BList$ and $EList$ of the entry. Moreover, these entries, from left to right, are sorted in an ascending order wrt. T. Hence, if we scan these leaf node entries from left to right (referred to as a *scanning process*), we can count which objects will have at least *MinPts* objects within their ε-neighborhood over what periods of time. These objects are declared as *COOTs*. If, for each *COOTs*, we keep track exactly which objects are within its ε-neighborhood during the scanning process, cluster contents over time can also be constructed. We refer readers to [5] for more detailed algorithms and complexity analysis.

3.3. Specified Prediction Window (*SPW*)

If users want to focus the *COOTs* and *COTs* predictions in a particular time period (i.e. from current time to next hour), users can provide a time segment $[s_1, s_2]$, referred to as a *Specified Prediction Window* (*SPW*), to filter out ε-neighborhood relationships that do not have their periods intersect with *SPW*. That is, an ε-neighborhood relationship occurs in a time segment $[x, y]$ will be discarded if $y < s_1$ or $s_2 < x$. If $s_1 \leq x \leq s_2$ or $s_1 \leq y \leq s_2$, this relationship with its period set to $[x', y'] = [s_1, s_2] \cap [x, y]$ will be inserted into β for prediction. More precisely, $x' = \max(x, s_1)$, and $y' = \min(y, s_2)$. A set of disconnected *SPWs* can also be used if needed.

4. Conclusion

Most of existing clustering algorithms focus on discovering snapshot clusters that do not reveal important information such as how long the present clusters will persist, or where and when the future clusters may occur. This information is important because it can guide users to prepare appropriate actions toward the right places at right time for the most effective results.

In this study, we propose a simple but effective approach in predicting density-based clusters over time. We first utilizes efficient formulas in determining the future ε-neighborhood relationships among object pairs. Object pairs that will never be in the ε-neighborhood of each other are filtered out. The *COOT* and *COT* algorithms then process the remaining pairs to discover concentrated areas *COOTs* and detailed cluster contents *COTs*, respectively. *SPW* can further reduce unnecessary computations and space by filtering out uninteresting object pairs from unwanted periods. Our experiments in [5] confirm that our approach not only has much higher precision in predicting clusters over time than the interval-checking method, it is also much more efficient.

5. References

[1] M. Ester, H. Kriegel, J. Sander and X. Xu, "A Density-Based Algorithm for Discovery Clusters in Large Spatial Databases with Noise", *In Proc. of 2nd Int'l Conf. On Knowledge Discovery and Data Mining*, 1996, pp. 226-231.

[2] M. Ester, H. Kriegel, J. Sander, M. Wimmer and X. Xu, "Incremental Cluster for Mining in a Data Warehousing Environment", *In Proc. of 24th Int'l Conf. Of VLDB*, 1998, pp. 323-333.

[3] J. Han, M. Kamber, *Data Mining: Concepts and Techniques*, Morgan Kaufmann, 2001

[4] C. Lai, "Method for Determining Conflicting Paths Between Mobile Airborne Vehicles and Associated System", U.S. Patent 6-564-149, European Patent EP1299742, 2003.

[5] C. Lai, N. Nguyen, "Predicting Density-Based Spatial Clusters Over Time", **http://personal1.stthomas.edu/clai/**.

[6] T. Zhang, R. Ramakrishnan, M. Livny, "BIRCH: An Efficient Data Clustering Method for Very Large Database", *In Proc. ACM SIGMOD Int'l Conf. On Management of Data*, 1996, pp. 103-114.

Dynamic Daily-living Patterns and Association Analyses in Tele-care Systems

B.-S. Lee[1], T. P. Martin[1], N. P. Clarke[1], B. Majeed[2], and D. Nauck[2]

[1]*Dept. of Engineering Mathematics, University of Bristol, Bristol, UK.*
[2]*Intelligent Systems Lab, Research & Venturing, British Telecom PLC, Ipswich, UK.*
rom.lee@bris.ac.uk, travor.martin@bris.ac.uk, nick.clarke@bris.ac.uk,
basim.majeed@bt.com, detlef.nauck@bt.com

Abstract

Tele-care systems aim to carry out intelligent analyses of a person's wellbeing using data about their daily activities. This is a very challenging task because the massive dataset is likely to be erroneous, possibly with misleading sections due to noise or missing values. Furthermore, the interpretation of the data is highly sensitive to the lifestyle of the monitored person and the environment in which they interact. In our tele-care project, sensor-network domain knowledge is used to overcome the difficulties of monitoring long-term wellbeing with an imperfect data source. In addition, a fuzzy association analysis is leveraged to implement a dynamic and flexible analysis over individual- and environment-dependent data.

1. Introduction

The UK is currently home to an ageing population that places increasingly greater demands on the care sector in order to maintain quality of life for all. The vast majority of these people, some 80%, wish to remain in familiar surroundings rather than gradually move through increasingly supervised and less personal environments traditionally offered by the social services [1]. The demand therefore for a low cost, client-centric home based health solution is immediate.

The direction now taken by various research groups is to create what are called "tele-care" systems able to monitor the behaviour of all vulnerable types of people over time. The majority of the current tele-care systems [2] [3] have placed more emphasis on identifying emergency situations rather than evaluating general wellbeing. Our tele-care system, sponsored by BT, the Department of Trade and Industry (DTI), and Liverpool city council, focuses on analysing long-term trends to identify signs of deteriorating health as early as possible. This information can then be used to ensure the health and social wellbeing of an individual. The overview of the data analysis of our system is shown in Figure 1.

To carry out intelligent analyses, the sensors are grouped together according to the domain knowledge and specific activities of interest. Each sensor may belong to more than one sensor group. By maintaining these groups, analyses using individual or environment specific information focus only on the relevant sensors. In the analysis phase, three things are monitored: long-term trends, significant patterns, and associations among patterns. Then, the substantial or gradual changes in daily activities are reported to the client's care-giver with the detailed analysis conveyed in a fashion allowing a non-expert in data analysis to easily understand the results.

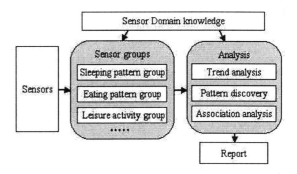

Figure 1. Data analysis overview

The main focus of this paper is on the details of how fuzzy association analysis is used to handle individual- and environment-dependent time series data. Section 2 discusses how the data with missing values and noise is pre-processed before any analysis. Section 3 illustrates the procedure of fuzzy association analysis step by step with sample data. Other issues not covered by these sections will be briefly examined in the discussion and future work section, followed by concluding remarks.

2. Data pre-processing

The sensors installed at the client's house can be classified into two types: location sensor type and activity sensor type. The location sensor type is usually a passive infrared (PIR) sensor that is used to detect movements. The second type of sensor provides information on the activities happening at a specific location. The current location of the client provides crucial information in wellbeing analysis. However, in some cases detailed activities may need to be monitored to carry out an in-depth activity analysis.

Besides ensuring the proper installation and maintenance of the sensors and the network, the information of the layout of the client's house and the location of each sensor are used to correct the erroneous data. The same information is also used to overcome environment dependencies in analysis caused by clients having unique house layouts. In addition, the sensors are abstracted into different sensor groups depending on the daily activities that are important in measuring the type of wellbeing. For example, activities during the sleeping time and the relevant sensors are grouped together to monitor the sleeping pattern. Instead of depending on just a particular sensor, by observing the overall events of the relevant sensors, robustness can be achieved despite erroneous data.

3. Fuzzy association analysis

This section explains how the fuzzy membership functions for each sensor are dynamically obtained and updated. In addition, we will discuss how these membership functions are used to fuzzify the original data into a reduced data set to obtain the significant patterns and associations among them.

3.1. Data reduction

An activity can occur at any arbitrary time of day (StartTime) and usually with a variety of duration (Duration). These are important sensor event properties that are significant with regard to the person's wellbeing. The time of day when the event occurs, the duration of the event, the frequency of the event, and the day of week when the event occurs are just some examples of these factors. For illustrative purposes, only the first two factors and the sensor name are considered in this paper.

First, these quantitative values are discretized using fuzzy membership functions. This procedure is required so as to satisfy some mining criteria, such as maximizing the confidence or compactness of the rules mined.

The fuzzy membership functions for StartTime segment the whole day into 12 overlapping groups. Its partial fuzzy membership graph is shown in Figure 2.

Unlike the fuzzy membership functions for StartTime, constructing the fuzzy memberships for Duration is rather complex and each sensor has to have its own Duration membership functions because each sensor has a unique duration range. To construct these fuzzy membership functions we used statistical distributions detailed in section 3.2. A fuzzy membership

graph for the duration of bedroom occupancy is shown in Figure 3.

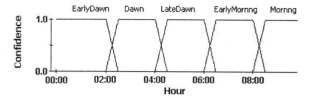

Figure 2. StartTime membership functions

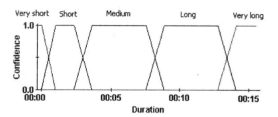

Figure 3. Duration membership functions

In addition to the data reduction by fuzzification of quantitative time values, the two types of fuzzy variables (StartTime and Duration) are combined with the sensor name and represented as a categorical attribute for association analysis. For example, assume a bedroom occupancy event occurred at 04:05:00 lasting about 3 hours. This produces *Dawn* StartTime with membership 0.1 and *LateDawn* StartTime with membership 0.3 and *Short* Duration with membership 0.9. This will result into two categorical attributes, *BedOccupancy Dawn Short* with membership 0.09 (0.1 multiplied by 0.9) and *BedOccupancy LateDawn Short* with membership 0.27 (0.3 multiplied by 0.9).

3.2. Obtaining the baseline period

Before fuzzifying time series values into categorical attributes, a representative period of daily activities has to be obtained. This is a period of days during which the person has maintained normal or typical activities. This is carried out by looking at the trend of a significant sensor activity that doesn't have much variation. We keep track of the weighted moving average of this sensor activity. If there are no major changes in the trend for a long period time, the data during this stable period is considered to be representative. An example trend of the bed occupancy duration is shown in Figure 4. The stable period is shaded in gray.

In addition, the data during this period is used to calculate the statistical values for each sensor. For example, the average and the semi-quartile range of the duration of bed occupancy are obtained as 05:41:47 and 01:51:24 respectively, allowing a normal duration to be interpreted as lying within the range of 03:50:23 and 07:33:11.

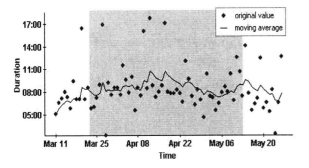

Figure 4. Baseline period

These statistical values are obtained to construct fuzzy membership functions according to the data distributions. The duration fuzzy membership functions for each sensor are *VeryLong, Long, Medium, Short,* and *VeryShort.* Given the average (AVG) value and the semi-quartile range (SQR) value and an overlapping gap value (G) between adjacent fuzzy member functions, each membership function is calculated as follows:

VeryShort = [RightLinear, AVG-SQR-G, AVG-SQR+G]
Short = [Trapezoid, AVG-SQR-G, AVG-SQR+G,
        AVG-SQR/3-G, AVG-SQR/3+G]
Medium = [Trapezoid, AVG-SQR/3-G, AVG-SQR/3+G,
        AVG+SQR/3-G, AVG+SQR/3+G]
Long = [Trapezoid, AVG+SQR/3-G, AVG+SQR/3+G,
        AVG+SQR-G, AVG+SQR+G]
VeryLong = [LeftLinear, AVG+SQR-G, AVG+SQR+G]

The values in the brackets indicate the shape of each fuzzy membership function followed by the parameters for the shape. Note that the construction of fuzzy membership functions described here is slightly different in its goal from other methods [4]. The resulting fuzzy membership function in our project is used not for classification or clustering for rule mining but rather for data partitioning purpose. Also, note that this approach is different from fuzzy partition methods used in [5], which use intervals of quantitative attributes to obtain categorical attributes instead of fuzzy membership functions.

3.3. Fuzzy association rules

Once the fuzzy membership functions are obtained by finding a baseline period and the data set is reduced, an extended version of Apriori algorithm is applied to this data set to find associations among activity patterns. This

algorithm is the same Apriori algorithm proposed in [7], except that the weights for each item in a transaction may vary. These weights are calculated by multiplying `StartTime` and `Duration` memberships as described in Section 3.1.

As an example, let's say that a data set is collected in the morning of a certain day as listed in Table 1.

Table 1. Original data set

Sensor	StartTime	Duration
HALL	10:43:57	00:01:18
FRONTDOOR	10:44:00	00:01:14
UTILITY	10:46:38	00:00:19
BACKDOOR	10:47:00	00:00:00
UTILITY	10:47:00	00:00:17

Using the following fuzzy membership functions calculated during a baseline period, each data item is fuzzified into a categorical attribute with its membership. The fuzzy variable `StartTime` for every data item in this case belongs only to *LateMorning* with membership 1, which can be seen in the following `StartTime` membership functions of a trapezoid shape:

Morning = [08:00:00, 08:30:00, 10:00:00, 10:30:00]
LateMorning = [10:00:00, 10:30:00, 12:00:00, 12:30:00]
EarlyAfternoon = [12:00:00, 12:30:00, 14:00:00, 14:30:00]

The fuzzy `Duration` variables for each sensor have membership functions constructed using statistical values as follows (only one of the four membership functions is shown here due to the space limit):

FRONTDOOR
VeryShort=[RightLinear, 00:00:14, 00:00:21]
Short=[Trapazoid, 00:00:14, 00:00:21, 00:00:42, 00:00:49]
Medium=[Trapazoid, 00:00:42, 00:00:49, 00:01:10, 00:01:17]
Long=[Trapazoid, 00:01:10, 00:01:17, 00:01:38, 00:01:45]
VeryLong=[LeftLinear, 00:01:38, 00:01:45]

Note that the FRONTDOOR event at 10:44:00 with duration 00:01:14 belongs to two fuzzy members, *Long* and *Medium*. The event is thus converted using both of these categorical attributes as shown in Table 2.

Table 2. Fuzzified data set

Sensor	StartTime	Duration	Membership
HALL	*LateMorning*	*VeryLong*	1
FRONTDOOR	*LateMorning*	*Long*	0.5
FRONTDOOR	*LateMorning*	*Medium*	0.5
UTILITY	*LateMorning*	*VeryShort*	1
BACKDOOR	*LateMorning*	*VeryShort*	1
UTILITY	*LateMorning*	*VeryShort*	1

Once all the sensor events and their `StartTime` and `Duration` are fuzzified in a categorical representation, a set of these fuzzified categorical attributes for each day will be treated as one transaction (or a basket in the familiar association term). Afterwards, the Apriori algorithm is applied to find associations among daily activities. Table 3 shows one example of the resulting association rules.

From these results, the association rules produced are interesting and convey much information about the daily activity patterns. By looking at the changes in these patterns and associations over time, we can observe the significant changes in the person's wellbeing. For example, the client used to spend significant amount of time cooking in the afternoon and ate before going to bed. However, the person now begins to spend less time cooking and skips meals before going to bed.

Table 3. Association rules

Antecedent	Consequent	Support	Conf.
KITCHEN *LateMorning Medium*	FRIDGEDOOR *LateMorning Short*	0.587	0.942
FRIDGEDOOR *Morning Short*	FRONTDOOR *LateMorning VeryShort*	0.815	0.847
LIVROOM *LateMorning VeryShort* AND LIVCHAIR *EarlyMorning VeryShort*	KITCHEN *LateMorning Short*	0.624	0.821

Some of the association rules merely reflect the layout of the house or the location of the sensor, and do not carry particularly useful information. For example, the first entry in the table tells us that the fridge is located in the kitchen. However, the second association in the table, namely FRIDGEDOOR *Morning Short* and FRONTDOOR *LateMorning VeryShort*, can be interpreted as the person usually uses the fridge before going out in the late morning.

5. Conclusion

The aim of this tele-care project is to deliver a solution whereby a care-giver can constantly observe the behavior of a person remotely, changing the provision of assistance to a more efficient and less intrusive on-demand basis. Intelligent data analyses are used to monitor the long-term wellbeing of vulnerable persons living at home, with primarily trend analysis, pattern discovery, and association analyses applied to capture comprehensive information about a person's daily activities.

The analysis of wellbeing is very challenging, as normal patterns of behaviour are difficult to obtain. In addition to this fact, what is considered to be normal for one person can be abnormal for another. More over, people have a tendency to change the way they do things without necessarily being affected by deterioration in their physical or mental abilities. Therefore interactive and adaptive algorithms are necessary to handle such analysis with the particularities of each individual in mind.

The focus of this paper was placed on explaining how the erroneous data is preprocessed to provide a cleaner data set for the further analysis using sensor network domain knowledge. An illustration is given to explain how the fuzzy association rules are obtained with dynamically updated fuzzy membership functions for the fuzzification of quantitative values. In summary, our tele-care system is developed to carry out an objective data analysis over the data set which is highly individual- and environment-dependent.

6. References

[1] P. Garner, Telecare: Freedom for the Frail, Internal report, BT Exact Centre for Care in the Community, Mar. 2004.

[2] S. P. Nelwan, T. B. van Dam, P. Klootwijk and S. H. Meij, Ubiquitous Mobile Access to Real-time Patient Monitoring Data. Computers in Cardiology, 2000, vol. 29, pp. 557-560.

[3] N. Barnes et al, Lifestyle Monitoring - Technology for Supported Independence, Computing & Control Engineering Journal, Aug. 1998, vol.9, no.4, pp. 169-174.

[4] M. Skubic and R. A. Volz, Identifying Contact Formations from Sensory Patterns and Its Applicability to Robot Programming by Demonstration, in Proceedings of the 1996 IEEE/RSJ Intl. Conf. On Intelligent Robots and Systems, Osaka, Japan, Nov. 1996, vol. 2, pp. 458-464.

[5] Y.-C. Hu, G.-H. Tzeng, R.-S. Chen, Discovering Fuzzy Concepts for Competence Set Expansion, Proceedings of 2nd International Symposium on Advanced Intelligent Systems, Daejon, Korea, Aug. 2001, pp. 396-401.

[6] R. Agrawal, T. Imielinski, and A. Swami, Mining Association Rules between Sets of Items in Large Databases, In Proceedings of the ACM SIGMOD Conference on Management of Data, Washington DC, USA, 1993, pp. 207-216.

Mining Temporal Patterns Without Predefined Time Windows

Tao Li

School of Computer Science

Florida International University

Miami, FL 33199

taoli@cs.fiu.edu

Sheng Ma

IBM T.J. Watson Research Center

Hawthorne, NY 10532

shengma@us.ibm.com

Abstract

This paper proposes algorithms for discovering temporal patterns without predefined time windows. The problem of discovering temporal patterns is divided into two sub-tasks: (1) using "cheap statistics" for dependence testing and candidates removal (2) identifying the temporal relationships between dependent event types. The dependence problem is formulated as the problem of comparing two probability distributions and is solved using a technique reminiscent of the distance methods used in spatial point process, while the latter problem is solved using an approach based on Chi-Squared tests. Experiments are conducted to evaluate the effectiveness and scalability of the proposed methods.

1. Introduction

In many real-world applications, an overwhelming amount of data are generated and collected in the form of temporal events. We consider the problem of discovering temporally dependent patterns with some time relationships (e.g., event a followed by b in about 5 seconds) and propose algorithms that discover the temporal patterns without predefined time windows. Specifically, the algorithms enable to discover the following two types of temporal patterns:

Loose temporal patterns. These patterns assert dependency between events. The patterns of this type assert that an event a "usually" precedes another event b or a usually follows by b before time t. Intuitively, this pattern characterizes the situation that a leads to b, but the time is not precise.

Stringent temporal patterns. Patterns of this type specify time distance between two events in loose temporal patterns. Usually, it can be described as "event a happens after event b, say, about 5 minutes".

In the rest of the paper, we refer this two types of patterns as **t-patterns**. In both patterns, the dependence and the temporal relationships are essential factors to be discovered. Such temporal patterns of our interest appear naturally in all the real-world applications. In specific, a computer system problem may trigger a series of symptom events/activities. Such a sequence of symptom events provides a natural signature for identifying the root cause [4].

Previous work of temporal mining focuses on frequent itemsets with a predefined time window. It fails to address two important aspects often required by applications. First, the fixed time-window scheme can not explore precise temporal information within a window, and misses the opportunity to mine temporal relationship longer than the window size. To apply association mining techniques a predefined time window has to be used [8, 7] thereby reducing temporal data to basket data. As we shall see later in our experimental results on system management applications, the temporal relationships discovered have time distance ranging from one second to one day. The fixed time-window scheme can not discover all such patterns and a new mechanism is needed to discover temporal relationship specific to an individual pattern. Second, as well-known for transaction data, frequent pattern framework misses significant, but infrequent patterns. In most network management applications, frequent patterns are normal operations and service disruptions are usually infrequent but significant.

In this paper, ideas from spatial statistics are used to characterize the inter-arrival time of events. The dependence problem is formulated as the comparison of two probability distributions and our technique for testing the dependence is reminiscent of the distance methods in spatial point process. Distance methods make use of precise information on the arrival time of events and have the advantage of independent of choices of window size [3, 2]. Also, the statistical properties imposed on the patterns provide meaningful characterizations and they are usually robust against noise. As a first step, we focus on pairwise patterns. Pairwise patterns can be easily interpreted by domain experts, and be easily visually presented. In addition, pairwise patterns can be extended to longer temporal patterns using a level-wise strategy.

2. Notations and Problem Formulation

2.1. Notations

An event has two basic components: the event type and the time stamp (occurrence time or arrival time). Throughout the paper, we assume a finite set E of event types. Examples of event types include "router up" or "switch down" etc. We use the symbol e, possibly with subscripts to denote event types. An event is then a pair $< e, t >$ where $e \in E$ is an event type and t is the timestamp of e. Our data, called an event sequence, is then a collection of all events occurred within some time range (say, between 0 and T)

$$D = \{< e_1, t_1 >, < e_2, t_2 >, \ldots, < e_n, t_n >\},$$

where $e_i \in E, t_i \in [0, T]$, and $t_i \leq t_{i+1}$. Define the shortest distance from a point z to the point process a by $d(z, T_a) = \inf_{x \in T_a, x \geq z} ||x - z||$. Intuitively, the distance is defined to be the distance from the point z to its closest neighbor in T_a. Since each event can be viewed as a point process, to test the dependence between events is to test the dependence of the two point processes. Denote $t_i = b_i - b_{i-1}$ as the inter-arrival time for T_b, where $i = 1, \ldots, n_b$ and $b_0 = 0$. Let $n'_a = N_a([0, T'])$ denote the number of points in T_a within the time range $[0, T']$. For each point $a_i, 1 \leq i \leq n'_a$, denote d_i as the distance from a_i to the nearest b occurring after b_i, i.e., $d_i = d(a_i, T_b)$.

2.2. Two Interarrival Distributions

Let T_a and T_b be two point processes for event a and b respectively. We would like to check whether T_b is dependent on T_a. Our approach is motivated from the methods of measuring spatial associations between spatial point patterns developed in statistical community [2, 3]. The idea of the approach is based on the observation: *if the occurrence of event type b could be predictable by event type a, then the conditional distribution which modeling the waiting time of event type b from event type a's presence would be different from the unconditional one.*

We now formally introduce the concept of two interarrival distributions. These concepts are described in detail in [3, 1] and our description here is adapted to suit our purpose for event data.

Definition 1 *The unconditional distribution of the waiting time of event b is defined as $F_b(r) = \mathcal{P}\{d(x, T_b) \leq r\}$.*

The distribution can be interpreted as the probability of having event type b within $[0, r]$.

Definition 2 *The conditional distribution for the waiting time of event b with respect to event a is defined as: $F_b^a(r) = \mathcal{P}(d(x, T_b) \leq r | x \in T_a) = \mathcal{P}^x(d(x, T_b) \leq r)$ where $\mathcal{P}^x$ denotes the Palm distribution [3] at an arbitrary point x with respect to the process a.*

The conditional distribution can can be regarded as the conditional probability distribution given there is an event of a at time x. So, the dependent relationships between event types are then defined based on the two distributions.

Definition 3 *Given two event types a and b, Denote their arrival times as T_a and T_b. We say that b is directly dependent on a if the two distributions $F_b(r)$ and $F_b^a(r)$, defined respectively in Definition 1 and Definition 2, are different.*

3. Two-Stage Approach

Statistical testing for spatial data has been developed in statistical community and has been used for geostatistical data and lattice data etc [3]. Our main contributions are two-fold. First, we extend the existing results to temporal events and propose estimation methods to compute the statistics. Second, we develop a two-stage algorithm that scales up the hypothesis testing. In the first stage, we do a simple statistical test based on low order statistics. As we shall see, such a simple test may generate false positives, but not false negatives. It helps to eliminate candidate space dramatically. Then, the second stage performs more detailed analysis in determining temporal relationships. Due to space limit, we only present the sketch of our idea in the paper. For detailed description, please refer to [5].

3.1. Stage One: Testing the Dependences

Estimating the Two Distributions. Since the true distributions are not available, we have to first estimate them. Under the stationarity assumption, the distribution of $d(x, T_b)$ does not depend on the location of x. The assumption of stationary is a pragmatic simplification which justifies the use of relatively simple estimation methods [3]. The two distributions can be estimated as follows: let T' be the last arrival time of event type b, i.e., $T' = b_{n_b}$. We use the information in $[0, T']$ for estimation. $F_b(r)$ can be estimated by measuring the distance $d(x, b)$ from each of several arbitrary test points to the nearest event occurrence in b and forming an empirical distribution. Similarly, $F_b^a(r)$ can be estimated by measuring the distance from each occurrence a_i of the point process a to the nearest arrival of event type b, and forming an empirical distribution function.

Dependency Tests On First Moments. Under the null hypothesis that there is no dependency between event type a and b, it is expected that $F_b = F_b^a$. For efficient comparison, we have developed efficient computation approaches to first test the differences between the estimated distributions and remove candidates of dependent pairs. Our computation is based on the first moment difference between the distributions. It is easy to see that if $F_b = F_b^a$, so are their first moments. Counterexamples can be constructed in which a and b are dependent but the first moments of two distribution functions are the same. However, stage one only serves as a preprocessing step for reducing the candidate space, the conservative property of the test ensures that we don't get rid of any true dependent pairs. It can be shown that, under certain assumptions, the first moments can be directly computed from the inter-arrival times.

3.2. Stage Two: Identifying the Relationships

After preprocessing via "cheap statistics" in stage one, the next task is identifying the dependence between the candidate pairs and finding the waiting period (or lag) between two dependent events. Let δ be the time tolerance accounting for factors such as phase shifts and lack of clock synchronization.

Definition 4 *Given b is dependent on a, we say that the waiting period of b after a is p if the distance sequence $D_{ab} = (d_1, \cdots, d_{n'_a})$, has a period p with time tolerance δ.*

The discovery of the waiting periods is carried out using the Chi-Squared test based approach first introduced in [7]. Consider an arbitrary element τ in D_{ab} and a fixed δ. Let C_τ be the total number of elements of D_{ab} that fall into the interval $[\tau - \delta, \tau + \delta]$. Intuitively, if τ is not a period p, C_τ should be small; otherwise it should be large. The idea here is to compare C_τ with the number of elements in $[\tau - \delta, \tau + \delta]$ that would expected from a random sequence. The procedure for identifying the relationship, as described in *Algorithm 1*, is essentially a one dimensional clustering process. $|D_{ab}|$, the possible candidate, is a sequence for a direct dependence between two event types and it is a much shorter sequence than raw data that contains a mixture of event types. Note that $|C - d_i|$ is the distance between C and d_i. It is not hard to see that Step 1 to Step 3 in *Algorithm 1* perform a one-pass clustering. In particular, Step 3.2.1 computes the cluster center (i.e., the mean of the samples in the cluster) in an incremental fashion. P' stores the cluster center and the size of each cluster. The cluster centers obtained from the *Algorithm 1* are candidates for the lags. It can be shown that: the distance from any cluster center to the sample belonging to the cluster is kept within the time tolerance δ.

4. Experiments

4.1. Synthetic Data

All the experiments are performed on a P3 1GHz machine with 256M memory running Linux 2.4.20-19.9. We first test our algorithm on synthetic data. The synthetic datasets are characterized by the duration of time, number of t-patterns, number of event types, total number of events and NSR ratio. Noise events are randomly and uniformly generated. Our first experiment is to test the effectiveness of the algorithm in the presence of noise. We set the number duration of time to $[0, 500]$, the number of t-pattern to 10, the number of event type to 40 and

---

Algorithm 1 Procedure for Lag Detection

Input: D_{ab}; δ: Time tolerance
Output: P: set of lags, (initialized to be $\emptyset$)
1.   Randomly pick a point d in D_{ab}
2.   Set $N(d) = 1$, $P' = \{(d, N(d))\}$;
3.   For $d_i \in D_{ab}$ Begin
3.1 C = the point in P "closest" to d_i
3.2   If $|C - d_i| \leq \delta$ Begin
3.2.1 $C = \frac{N(C)}{N(C)+1}C + \frac{1}{N(C)+1}d_i$
3.2.2 $N(c) = N(c) + 1$; End
3.3   Else Begin
3.3.1   Set $N(d_i)=1$;
3.3.2   Add $(d_i, N(d_i))$ to P'; End
     End
4.   For each C in P' Begin
4.1   Compute the threshold C'_C as in [7]
4.2   If $N(C) > C'_C$, then insert C into the output P
     End

---

the total number of events to 40000. Figure 1 shows the effectiveness of the algorithm with different NSR ratio in both tabular and graph formats. A run is effective if there is no false negative, i.e., all t-patterns are correctly discovered. The effectiveness is defined as the percentage of the correctly discovered patterns. We observe that the effectiveness is 100% if NSR less than 1 and gradually decreases as NSR increases above 1. Especially when NSR is greater than 4, the effectiveness falls beyond 50%. The

NSR	Effectiveness
0.1 to 1	100%
1.5	80%
2	70%
2.5	70%
3	60%
3.5	50%
4	50%
4.5	40%
5	30%
10	30%

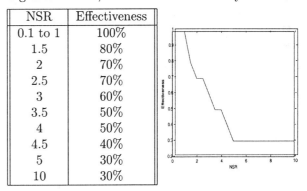

Figure 1. Effectiveness Results with Different NSR.

second experiment is to assessing the scalability results of the algorithm. NSR ratio is controlled between $0.5 - 1$ and the number of events per type is controlled between $2000 - 5000$. Figure 2 plots the average CPU time in the run against the number of events.

4.2. Product Data

Now, we apply our algorithms to mine t-patterns in real data. Here our evaluation criteria are more subjective in that we must rely on the domain knowledge to

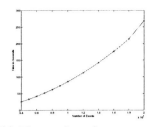

(a) The number of events per type is 2000.

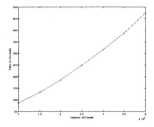

(b) The number of events per type is 5000.

Figure 2. CPU time vs. the number of events

decide whether the results is correct or not. We review the discovered patterns with operation staff. In addition, whenever possible, we also use the Event Browser [6] to visualize and verify the results. Four datasets are considered. These datasets were collected from either an Intranet containing hundreds of network elements (e.g.,routers, hubs and servers) or from outsourcing centers that support multiple application servers across a large geographical regions. Events in these datasets are either application-oriented (e.g., the CPU utilization of a server is above threshold) or network-oriented (e.g, the link is down for a router). An event in these datasets consists of three key attributes: *Host ID*, which is the source of event; *Event ID*, which specify what happened (e.g., port up); and the time stamp of when the event occurred. In our preprocessing, we map each distinct pair of host ID and event ID into a unique event type. The datasets and their characteristics are list in Table 1.

Dataset	Number of Events	Number of Event Types	Min:Max Count
Dataset 1	1000	6	6: 480
Dataset 2	10549	312	2:1738
Dataset 3	11204	1496	1:1849
Dataset 4	46069	1784	1:2422

Table 1. Datasets characteristics. Column 4 is the range of the occurrence counts for each event type.

The experimental results are summarized in Table 2. Several factors account for the dependence behaviors in these datasets. The first factor is a result of periodic monitoring that is initiated when a high severity event occurs. The second factor is a sequence of installation policies, such as rebooting some severs every morning. The third factor is the instable network connection or server which often leads a sequence of events. We reviewed the discovered patterns with the operation staff and it turned out that many of the t-patterns related to underlying problems. We found several patterns of interest. For example, the "port up" and "port down" are loose temporal patterns that signify a mobile user's login and logout; "router link down" followed by "Router

down" in 10 second signifies a typical router down sequence: a router "down" results in its link down. Further, a sequence of four SNMP_requests (5, 10, 15, seconds apart in sequences) raises up a security concern of port_scans in a regular way. Another stringent pattern about a performance measurement crossing critical threshold and resetting, leads to further investigation and final discovery of a wrong threshold setting problem.

Dataset	Possible Pairs	dependent pairs	Min: Max Lags
Dataset 1	36	9	0:100
Dataset 2	97344	257	0:1-day
Dataset 3	2238016	1039	0:1-day
Dataset 4	3182656	1496	0:1-day

Table 2. Experimental Results On The Datasets. Column 2 show the number of possible dependent event type pairs, Column 3 indicates the number of discovered dependent pairs and Column 4 shows the range of the lags.

5. Discussions and Conclusions

Existing temporal mining approaches faces two fundamental problems: the temporal correlation of events and the characteristics of interesting patterns. This paper proposes algorithms to find temporal patterns without predefined time windows. The problem is divided into two stages: testing the dependence and finding the lags. By formulating the dependence problem as the comparison of two probability distributions, our technique for testing the dependence resembles the distance methods in spatial point process and hence overcome the difficulties associated with traditional window techniques. The lag detection is solved with an approach based on Chi-Squared test.

References

[1] P. Andersen, O. Borgan, R. Gill, and N. Keiding. *Statistical Models based on Counting Processes*. Springer, 1993.

[2] M. Berman. Testing for spatial association between a point process and another stochastic process. *Applied Statistics*, 35(1):54–62, 1986.

[3] N. A. Cressie. *Statistics for spatial data*. John Wiley & Sons, 1991.

[4] J. L. Hellerstein, S. Ma, and C.-S. Perng. Discovering actionable patterns in event data. *IBM System Journal*, 41(3):475–493, 2002.

[5] T. Li. *Knowledge Discovery from Labeled and Unlabeled Data*. PhD thesis, University of Rochester, 2004.

[6] S. Ma and J. L. Hellerstein. Eventbowser: A flexible tool for scalable analysis of event data. In *DSOM'99*.

[7] S. Ma and J. L. Hellerstein. Mining partially periodic event patterns with unknown periods. In *ICDE'01*.

[8] H. Mannila, H. Toivonen, and I. Verkamo. Discovering frequent episodes in sequences. In *KDD'95*.

Classifying Biomedical Citations without Labeled Training Examples

Xiaoli Li*, Rohit Joshi, Sreeram Ramachandaran, Tze-Yun Leong*

School of Computing, National University of Singapore
*Computer Science Program, Singapore MIT Alliance**

Abstract

In this paper we introduce a novel technique for classifying text citations without labeled training examples. We first utilize the search results of a general search engine as original training data. We then proposed a mutually reinforcing learning algorithm (MRL) to mine the classification knowledge and to "clean" the training data. With the help of a set of established domain-specific ontological terms or keywords, the MRL mining step derives the relevant classification knowledge. The MRL cleaning step then builds a Naive Bayes classifier based on the mined classification knowledge and tries to clean the training set. The MRL algorithm is iteratively applied until a clean training set is obtained. We show the effectiveness of the proposed technique in the classification of biomedical citations from a large medical literature database.

1. Introduction

Traditional text classification needs a large number of labeled training examples in order to build an accurate classifier. Manual labelling, however, is very labour intensive and time consuming. To deal with the problem of labeling a large training set in classification, recently several techniques are designed. Blum and Mitchell [5] and Nigam et. al. [10] proposed a technique using a small set of labeled data of every class and a large unlabeled set for classifier building. It was shown that the unlabeled data does help classification. Li and Liu [7], Liu et. al. [8], and Yu et. al. [11] also proposed techniques to learn from only positive and unlabeled data.

In this paper, we explore a novel technique to build classifiers without labeled training examples. The ability to build classifiers without labeled training data is particularly useful if one needs to do classification for different topics. For example, a doctor needs to track the new development of a few diseases simultaneously, e.g., colorectal cancer, SARS, bird flu, etc. Furthermore, given a particular disease, he/she would like to classify documents into predefined categories: diagnostic procedures, risk factors, screening methods, and treatment therapies. Following traditional classification, for each disease (topic), labeling of training examples for every category is needed. Obviously, techniques that can provide accurate classification without manual labelling any document will be preferred.

This paper proposes a novel technique to build a robust classifier without labeled training examples. The main idea of the proposed technique is as follows: given a particular user's query (e.g., colorectal cancer), our approach first constructs an original training set for each category by utilizing the results from a search engine (such as Google). This set of returned pages by the search engine acts as the initial set of labeled training documents. With the help of a set of established domain-specific ontological concepts, our proposed Mutually Reinforcing Learning (*MRL*) algorithm then tries to derive classification knowledge from original training set. *MRL* then builds a Naive Bayes classifier based on the mined classification knowledge and tries to clean the training set. The *MRL* algorithm is iteratively applied until a clean training set is obtained. Finally, an accurate classifier will be built to classify any future documents.

The reason that this technique works is because our mining step in *MRL* can obtain the discriminative semantic concepts (we call them *knowledge phrases*) for each category from the original training set. Our cleaning step in *MRL* thus builds a classifier based on the discriminative concepts and revises the label of training set. When the *MRL* algorithm is applied again in the next iteration, we can get better discriminative concepts and consequently a more accurate *NB* classifier will be built. We believe that the quality of features used in classification has profound effects on the performance of classifier. Correspondingly, the classification techniques based on the semantic concepts of a domain can produce better classifiers than those based only on the words or the keywords. Our results show that the proposed technique is highly effective. We believe this is a promising method for text classification.

2. The proposed technique

Our proposed technique first constructs the original training set using a search engine. Then a Mutually Reinforcing Learning (*MRL*) algorithm, which contains the mining step and the cleaning step, is applied.

In order to build an original classifier, we query a search engine (i.e., Google) to construct the original training set. For a set of predefined classes, $C = \{C_1, C_2, \ldots, C_{|C|}\}$, we generate search query $Q_1, Q_2, \ldots, Q_{|C|}$ by combining the user's query and category descriptive words. For example "colorectal cancer" +"screening" are combined for the class "colorectal cancer and screening methods". The set of returned pages by the search engine acts as the initial set of labeled training documents: $\{T_1, T_2, \ldots, T_{|C|}\}$.

2.1. Mining step: Mining classification knowledge

The target of this step is to derive the semantic concepts that have discriminative power to support the classification. We want to automatically extract some characteristic phrases for each class, which we call *knowledge phrases* of the class. Different kinds of features can be extracted as the *knowledge phrases* from the original training set, for example, keywords, concepts, and semantic types etc. Those *knowledge phrases* that have definite meanings and higher discriminating power will be extracted out as important keywords for each class. In order to get the *knowledge phrases*, a pre-processing step is needed to label the semantic information of original training examples. For a particular domain, there exist some established domain-specific ontological terms or concepts available. For example, for a phrase "virtual colonoscopy", Unified Medical Language System (UMLS) ontology provides its semantic information such as the mapping concept word, synonyms (meta-candidates: "Colonoscopy", "Colonoscope", …) and semantic types("Diagnostic Procedure"). Semantic types are more generic concepts (hypernyms). For a phrase "irinotecan", its semantic type is "Organic Chemical, Pharmacologic Substance". Obviously, the semantic information, providing the phrase with the definite meanings and higher discriminating power, can play important roles in classifier building.

The association rule mining algorithm was proposed by Agrawal [4]. Given a dataset D which is set of transaction T, an association rule is of the form: $\mathbf{X} \rightarrow \mathbf{Y}$ ($\mathbf{X}$ implies $\mathbf{Y}$), where $\mathbf{X}$ and $\mathbf{Y}$ are mutually exclusive sets of items. An association rule $\mathbf{X} \rightarrow \mathbf{Y}$ presents the pattern when $\mathbf{X}$ occurs, $\mathbf{Y}$ also occurs with certain probability. The rule's statistical significance is measured by its *support*, and the rule's strength by its *confidence*. The mining algorithm tries to find all the rules that satisfy the user-specified *minimum support* (*minsup*) and *minimum confidence* (*minconf*).

In our case, we want to find those *knowledge phrases* that have discriminating power to indicate which class a text citation may belong to. So, $\mathbf{X}$ is a phrase from the Mining object set M = {keywords, concepts, semantic types} and $\mathbf{Y} \in C = \{C_1, C_2, \dots, C_{|C|}\}$. The problem is how to set the *minsup* and *minconf* in noisy environment.

Since mining is done in noisy training data, we set the lower *confident degree* value (*minconf*=60%) in order not to miss some true *knowledge phrases*. In this setting, we can get the rules with high *recall*. We set *minsup* as $\sum_w freq(w)/|V|$, which is the average word frequency of all the words in training set (w is a word and V is the vocabulary of training set).

We define the basic *candidate rules set* CR= {$\mathbf{X} \rightarrow \mathbf{Y}$ |

$\mathbf{X} \rightarrow \mathbf{Y}$ .conf> minconf & $\mathbf{X} \rightarrow \mathbf{Y}$.sup> $\sum_Z freq(Z)/|V|$ }.

Obviously, it is possible that there are still some undesirable rules in CR. Our heuristic filtering strategy will filter some rules with less *semantic support*.

For any candidate rule $(\mathbf{X} \rightarrow C_i) \in$ CR, a phrase $\mathbf{X}$ in CR should have some *semantic support* concepts within a class C_i. The *semantic support* of X are synonyms with the same semantic types.

1 Loop for all the term t in the CR
2   CS = CS $\cup$ { t.semantic types or t.synonyms};
3 Loop for all the term t in the CR
4   **If** t is the phrase,
5   Search its *synonyms* and *semantic types* in CS;
6   Loop for each *synonym* and *semantic type* of t
7   **If** (t.semantic types or t. synonyms) $\in$ CS
8   t.sup++;
9   **Else** // t is a semantic type
10   Loop all the concept c in CS;
11   **If** c.semantic types = t
12   t.sup++;
13   **If** t.sup < δ
14   CR= CR –{t}
15 Loop for all the rules in CR
16 K_{Ci} ={ X | X $\rightarrow$ C_i $\in$ CR }

Figure 1 filter the undesired rules from CR

If any concept in CR has very few *semantic support* concepts within the corresponding class, then it is considered as an occasional case and is filtered out. Specifically, for all the phrases in CR, we first search the synonyms and semantic types and store them into a set CS. If X is a phrase, then we compute the *semantic support* by checking how many times its synonyms and semantic types occurred in CS. Similarly, if $\mathbf{X}$ is a semantic type, we compute its *semantic support* by counting the number of times the concepts in CS has $\mathbf{X}$ as their semantic type. A concept $\mathbf{X}$ is filtered if its *semantic support* is less than a predefined threshold (δ =2). After filtering, we can get high precision rules. In the end, we construct the *knowledge phrases* set K_{Ci} for each class C_i: K_{Ci} ={ X | X $\rightarrow$ C_i $\in$ CR }.

2.2. Cleaning step: Building NB classifiers

To clean the original training set, we build a classifier using the noisy training set with the classification knowledge mined. Then we classify the training examples and revise the labels of the training set according to the classification results.

The Naïve Bayes classifier [9, 10] builds a classifier using a set of labeled training examples D. Each example document is considered an ordered list of words. We use $w_{d_i, k}$ to denote the word in position k of document d_i, where each word is from the vocabulary $V = \{w_1, w_2, \dots, w_{|v|}\}$. A set of pre-defined classes is $C = \{c_1, c_2, \dots, c_n\}$. In order to perform classification, we need to compute the posterior probability $P(c_j|d_i)$, where c_j is a class and d_i is a document. Based on the Bayesian probability and the multinomial model, we have

$$P(c_j) = \frac{\sum_{i=1}^{|D|} P(c_j \mid d_i)}{|D|} \qquad (1)$$

and with Laplacian smoothing,

$$P(w_t \mid c_j) = \frac{1 + \sum_{i=1}^{|D|} N(w_t, d_i) P(c_j \mid d_i)}{|V| + \sum_{s=1}^{|V|} \sum_{i=1}^{|D|} N(w_s, d_i) P(c_j \mid d_i)} \qquad (2)$$

where $N(w_t, d_i)$ is the count of the number of times the word w_t occurs in document d_i and $P(c_j|d_i) \in \{0,1\}$ depending on the class label of the document.

Finally, assuming that the probabilities of words are independent given the class, we obtain the NB classifier:

$$P(c_j \mid d_i) = \frac{P(c_j) \prod_{k=1}^{|d_i|} P(w_{d,k} \mid c_j)}{\sum_{r=1}^{|C|} P(c_r) \prod_{k=1}^{|d_i|} P(w_{d,k} \mid c_r)} \qquad (3)$$

Next, we will introduce how to use *knowledge phrases* mined to boost the classifier building. We modify the standard NB classifier in two ways.

1. Add *knowledge phrases* { K_{Ci} }, i = 1, 2, …, |C| into vocabulary set V and computed the condition probability $P(w_t \mid c_j)$ for all $w_t \in K_{Ci}$.

$V = V \bigcup$ { K_{Ci} }, i = 1, 2, …, |C|, for $w_t \in K_{Ci}$, we modify the computation of the conditional probability $P(w_t \mid c_j)$ in equation (2) in the following way:

$$\begin{cases} \textbf{If } j = i, \\ \quad \text{replace } \sum_{i=1}^{|D|} N(w_t, d_i) P(c_j \mid d_i) \text{ with } \sum_{i=1}^{|D|} N(w_t, d_i); \\ \textbf{Else } \text{set } \sum_{i=1}^{|D|} N(w_t, d_i) P(c_j \mid d_i) = 0; \end{cases}$$

w_t is one of *knowledge phrases* of class C_i and it has discriminating power to distinguish C_i from other categories, so we no longer use its word distribution information among the classes to estimate the conditional probability $P(w_t \mid c_i)$. Instead, in equation (2), if $j = i$, we use the total word frequency of w_t in all classes, replace word frequency only in C_i. Correspondingly if $j \neq i$, we set $\sum_{i=1}^{|D|} N(w_t, d_i) P(c_j \mid d_i) = 0$ since w_t should only occur in class C_i in purer training set.

2. Emphasize the *knowledge phrases* when we classify a document. In other words, we give high weights to *knowledge phrases*. We use the equation (4) to replace the equation (3) to classify any document.

$$P(c_j \mid d_i) = \frac{P(c_j) \prod_{k=1}^{|d_i|} P(w_{d,k} \mid c_j) * \mu(w_{d,k})}{\sum_{r=1}^{|C|} P(c_r) \prod_{k=1}^{|d_i|} P(w_{d,k} \mid c_r) * \mu(w_{d,k})} \qquad (4)$$

Here $\mu(w_{d,k})$ is the weight we assign to word $w_{d,k}$. If

$w_{d,k}$ is one of *knowledge phrases*, then we give it a high weight. In effect, we build two NB classifiers. Classifier NB1 is a normal classifier, which used the original training set. Classifier NB2 is a classifier based on *knowledge phrases*. The final classifier NB is more depend on the classifier NB2 since a high weight of NB2:

$$P(c_j, d_i)_{NB} = \mu_1 * P(c_j, d_i)_{NB1} + (1 - \mu_1) * P(c_j, d_i)_{NB2}$$

Where we set $\mu_1 = 0.1$ in our experiment, which makes use of the discriminating power of *knowledge phrases*.

2.3. Mutually Reinforcing Learning Algorithm

Below, we present the MRL algorithm through combining the two main components: the mining step and the cleaning step. The NB classifier built with knowledge words aids in assigning the correct label to each citation in the training set. This will result in a purer training set. Furthermore, if the mining step of MRL is done with the purer training set, we will get better *knowledge phrases*, which will in-turn build an accurate classifier in the cleaning step. Figure 2 gives the Mutually Reinforcing Learning (MRL) algorithm.

1. Loop for each document $d \in T$
2. Assigned semantic information to d using domain specific ontological terms;
3. Loop if the labels in training set T change
4. Perform mining step to get rule set CR for each C_i;
5. Filtering rules use Figure 1 algorithm;
6. Extending the *knowledge phrases* for each C_i;
7. Build final classifier NB using the mined *knowledge phrases*;
8. Classify the training set using NB;
9. Revised the label of training set of T according to NB's classification results;

Figure 2 Mutually Reinforcing Learning algorithm

3. Experimental Results

Now we evaluate the proposed technique on the biomedical citations in a large medical literature database, i.e., **MEDLINE**. We classify two disease types "colorectal cancer" and "SARS" into 4 classes: diagnosis", "risk factor", "screening", and "treatment". In order to construct the training set, we query a search engine Google and restrict Google only to search from **MEDLINE.** The set of returned pages by Google acts as the initial set of labeled training documents (each class 100 documents). We manually label 500 citations from **MEDLINE** as test set.

We compare our proposed technique with the Expected Maximization (EM) [6, 10] algorithm. In order to evaluate the separate contributions of *knowledge phrases* and filtering step, we include the results of several techniques: EM without *knowledge phrases* (EM_wo_know), EM with *knowledge phrases* but without filtering (EM_wo_filt) and EM with both *knowledge phrases* and filtering (EM_w_know_filt). Note all the three EM based techniques, compared with MRL, do not have the cleaning step to revise the label of the training set.

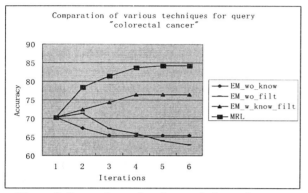

Figure 3 Comparison of various techniques for query "colorectal caner"

Figure 3 gives us the accuracy results for "colorectal cancer" of each iteration using three EM-based techniques and *MRL*. Here the baseline NB classifier gets 70.3%. The accuracy of EM_wo_know decreases with the iterations of EM. In other words, without the help of *knowledge phrases*, EM can not improve the NB's results. The accuracy of EM_wo_filt increases first but then decreases. So filtering is a very important step and directly using concepts mined will hurt the performance of a classifier. With the help of *knowledge phrases* (with filtering), EM_w_know_filt gets the 76.4%, 6.1% higher than NB's results. Our proposed MRL technique achieves the accuracy of 84.2%, which improves the NB and EM_w_know_filt by 13.9% and 7.8% respectively.

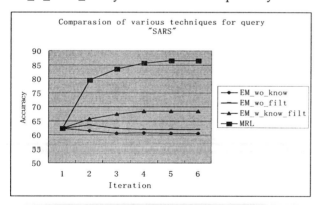

Figure 4 Comparison of various techniques for query "SARS"

The second experiment is to classify "SARS" documents. Figure 4 shows the accuracy results of various techniques. Both EM_wo_know and EM_wo_filt cannot improve the NB's results. The accuracy of EM_w_know_filt is 6.1% higher than the NB's result. MRL obtains the best results 86.5%, 18.1% higher than EM_w_know_filt.

From figures 3 and 4, we conclude that qualified *knowledge phrases* does help learning algorithm EM and MRL to build an accurate classifier. Moreover, the cleaning step of *MRL* makes it perform significantly better than the EM algorithm.

4. Conclusion

In this paper, we propose a new approach to build a classifier to classify citations in the **MEDLINE** database without a labeled training dataset. In this approach, we utilize the search results from a general search engine as the original training data. With the help of a set of established domain-specific ontological terms or keywords, a mutually reinforcing learning algorithm *MRL* is applied iteratively to extract the classification knowledge and cleaning the training data. Experimental results show this is very promising approach for text classification.

Acknowledgments: This research is partially supported by the Singapore-MIT Alliance and the Research Grant No. BM00/007 from the Agency for Science, Technology, and Research (A*Star) and the Ministry of Education in Singapore.

5. References

[1] **MEDLINE**, http://www.ncbi.nlm.nih.gov/PubMed/

[2] **UMLS**, http://umlsks.nlm.nih.gov/

[3] **Google**, http://www.google.com

[4] Agrawal R., Srikant R., "Fast Algorithms for Mining Association Rules", *Proc. of 20th Intl.Conf. on Very Large Data Bases*, pages 487-499, 1994.

[5] Blum, A., Mitchell, T. "Combining labeled and unlabeled data with co-training," *Proc. of the 11th Intl. Conf. on Computational Learning Theory*, pp. 92-100, 1998.

[6] Dempster, A., Laird, N. M. & Rubin. D. "Maximum likelihood from incomplete data via the EM algorithm." *Journal of the Royal Statistical Society*, B:39, pp. 1-38, 1977.

[7] Li X., Liu B. Learning to classify text using positive and unlabeled data. *Proc. of 11th Intl. Conf. on Artificial Intelligence*, pp. 587-594, 2003.

[8] Liu, B., Lee, W. S., Yu, P., and Li, X. "Partially supervised classification of text documents." *Proc. of 19th Intl. Conf. on Machine Learning*, pp. 387-394.

[9] McCallum, A., Nigam, K. "A comparison of event models for naïve Bayes text classification." *AAAI-98 Workshop on Learning for Text Categorization*, pp. 41-48, 1998.

[10] Nigam, K., McCallum, A., Thrun, S. and & Mitchell, T. "Text classification from labeled and unlabeled documents using EM." *Journal of Machine Learning*, Vol 39, pp. 103-134, 2000.

[11] Yu, H., Han, J. & Chang, K. "PEBL: Positive example based learning for Web page classification using SVM." *Proc. 8th Intl. Conf. Knowledge Discovery in Databases*, pp. 239-248, 2002.

Improving the Reliability of Decision Tree and Naive Bayes Learners

David Lindsay,
Computer Learning Research Centre,
Royal Holloway, University of London,
Egham, Surrey, TW20 OEX, UK,
davidl@cs.rhul.ac.uk

Siân Cox
School of Biological Sciences,
Royal Holloway, University of London,
Egham, Surrey, TW20 OEX, UK
s.s.e.cox@rhul.ac.uk

Abstract

The C4.5 Decision Tree and Naive Bayes learners are known to produce unreliable *probability forecasts. We have used simple Binning [11] and Laplace Transform [2] techniques to improve the reliability of these learners and compare their effectiveness with that of the newly developed Venn Probability Machine (VPM) meta-learner [9]. We assess improvements in reliability using loss functions, Receiver Operator Characteristic (ROC) curves and Empirical Reliability Curves (ERC). The VPM outperforms the simple techniques to improve reliability, although at the cost of increased computational intensity and slight increase in error rate. These trade-offs are discussed.*

1. Introduction

Probability forecasting is a generalisation of the standard pattern recognition problem. Rather than attempting to find the "best" label, the aim is to estimate the conditional probability (otherwise known as a probability forecast) of a possible label given an observed object.

The problem of making *effective* probability forecasts is a well studied problem [3][4][7]. Dawid (1985) gives two simple criteria for describing how effective probability forecasts are:

1) **Reliability** - The probability forecasts "should not lie". When a probability $\hat{p}$ is assigned to an event, there should be roughly $1 - \hat{p}$ relative frequency of the event not occurring. This is also referred to as being *well-calibrated*.

2) **Resolution** - The probability forecasts should be practically useful and enable the observer to easily rank the events in order of their likelihood of occurring. This criterion is more related to classification accuracy.

Investigations to improve the reliability of probability forecasts output by popular machine learners such as Naive Bayes and Decision Tree have been considered [11][6]. In this study, we investigate the effectiveness of two simple

approaches to improve reliability, namely the Laplace transform [2] for the C4.5 learner and re-calibration using 'binning' [11] for the Naive Bayes and C4.5 learners. We compare the effectiveness of these simple techniques to that of the recently developed Venn Probability Machine (VPM) meta-learner [9]. Unlike the simpler approaches the VPM has proven ability to produce reliable probability forecasts [9]. This study describes the first-ever implementation of the VPM on top of the Naive Bayes and Decision Tree learners and we show that the VPM outperforms simpler techniques to improve reliability. However this comes at a cost of increased computational intensity and a slight increase in error rate. We discuss the implications of these trade-offs and the practical advantages of reliable probability forecasts.

2. Reliability: a Machine Learning Perspective

Our notation will extend upon the commonly used supervised learning approach to pattern recognition. Nature outputs information pairs called *examples*. Each example $(\mathbf{x}_i, y_i)$ consists of an *object* $\mathbf{x}_i$ and its *label* $y_i \in \mathbf{Y} = \{1, 2, \ldots, |\mathbf{Y}|\}$. Adapting formulation as in [4], let us consider a sequence of n probability forecasts for the $|\mathbf{Y}|$ possible labels output by a learner Γ. Let $\hat{P}(y_i = j \mid \mathbf{x}_i) = \hat{p}_{i,j}$ represent the estimated conditional probability of the jth label matching the true label for the ith object tested. To calculate reliability for a finite number of forecasts a method of discretising probability forecasts must be used. For predicted probabilities $\hat{p}_{i,j}$ of each class $j \in \mathbf{Y}$ we define a set of 'bins' (disjoint sub-intervals) B_j, for example one possible bin choice would be to choose k equal bins $B_j = \left\{ [0, \frac{1}{k}), [\frac{1}{k}, \frac{2}{k}), \ldots, [\frac{k-1}{k}, 1] \right\}$. Of course a learner's probability forecasts are rarely uniformly distributed and so equal width intervals may not be sufficient [1]. Let

---

[1]For our ERC [6], VPM [9] and binning [11] meta-learner implementations, we used the Discretize filter provided by WEKA [10] which uses an MDL criterion to optimally define bin interval sizes [5].

$n_b^j = \sum_{i=1}^n \mathbb{I}_{\{\hat{p}_{i,j} \in b\}}$ count the number of forecasts $\hat{p}_{i,j}$ for class $j \in \mathbf{Y}$ that fall within bin interval $b \in B_j$. There are many possible choices of bin sizes, however we aim to specify bin sizes which encompass enough forecasts (make n_b^j as large as possible for each bin) to obtain practically useful estimates.

Once the sets of bins $B_j, j \in \mathbf{Y}$ have been defined, we can define reliability by calculating various statistics from the individual bins $b \in B_j$. Reliability ensures that for each bin of forecasts with predicted values $\approx \hat{p}$, the frequency of this label not occurring in that bin is $\approx 1 - \hat{p}$. To obtain a practically useful estimate of the predicted value represented by each bin we use the average predicted probability $\phi_n^j(b) = \frac{\sum_{i=1}^n \mathbb{I}_{\{\hat{p}_{i,j} \in b\}} \hat{p}_{i,j}}{n_b^j}$ for each bin interval b. The empirical frequency $\rho_n^j(b) = \frac{\sum_{i=1}^n \mathbb{I}_{\{y_i = j\}} \mathbb{I}_{\{\hat{p}_{i,j} \in b\}}}{n_b^j}$ of each bin b calculates the proportion of predictions in that bin that had true class $y_i = j$. To determine whether a bin b contains enough forecasts to be practically useful to gather the $\rho_n^j(b)$ and $\phi_n^j(b)$ statistics an extra weighting term $\nu_n^j(b) = \frac{n_b^j}{n}$ is used. Every learner's performance in calibration criteria can be categorised using the above functions. Using them intuitively defines reliability. A learner is *well calibrated* (reliable) if its forecasts $\{\hat{p}_{1,1}, \ldots, \hat{p}_{1,|\mathbf{Y}|}, \ldots, \hat{p}_{n,1}, \ldots, \hat{p}_{n,|\mathbf{Y}|}\}$ and a fixed specification of bins $B_j, j \in \mathbf{Y}$ satisfy $R(\Gamma, n) = \sum_{j=1}^{|\mathbf{Y}|} \sum_{b \in B_j} \nu_n^j(b) |\rho_n^j(b) - \phi_n^j(b)| \approx 0$.

3. Methods for Assessing Reliability

At present the most popular techniques for assessing the quality of probability forecasts are *square loss* [10], *log loss* [10] and *ROC curves* [8]. The problem of defining effective scoring rules or loss functions for evaluating probability forecasts has been considered in depth [4]. Each loss function assesses a combination of reliability and resolution, with different biases on the individual components [7]. The area under the ROC curve is commonly used as a measure of the usefulness of the probability forecasts; the larger the area, the better the forecasts.

The *Empirical Reliability Curve* (ERC) is a visual interpretation of the theoretical definition of reliability [6]. Unlike the previous methods, the ERC allows visualisation of over- and under-estimation of probability forecasts. For more detail about ERC implementation please refer to [6]. In brief, each coordinate (marked as a cross) on the ERC represents the statistics computed for each bin b, and the cross is coloured according the weighting of that bin $\nu(b)$ (black = 1, 1 > shades of grey > 0, white = 0). A reliable classifier will have ERC coordinates $(\phi(b), \rho(b))$ close to the diagonal line of calibration $(0,0) \rightarrow (1,1)$ (where predicted probability equals empirical frequency). A trend

line is predicted from these coordinates using a weighted regression algorithm [1] (each training example weighted according to the value $\nu(b)$). This allows the coordinates which relate to a bin containing a large sample of forecasts to have a greater influence on the shape of the curve.

4. The Venn Probability Machine (VPM)

The Venn Probability Machine (VPM) framework was designed to complement predictions made by traditional learning algorithms with provably reliable probability forecast bounds in the online setting (where data is continually updated) [9]. However, there is much empirical evidence (as given in this study) to support the fact that these bounds are also reliable for the offline learning setting. The VPM "*sits on top*" of existing learners and can be easily modified from generating bounds to useful point estimates. Essential to the working of the VPM is the $|\mathbf{Y}| \times |\mathbf{Y}|$ dimensional *Venn probability matrix* $\mathbf{M}$.

The VPM is self calibrated by the definition of a fixed method for grouping examples $z_i = (\mathbf{x}_i, y_i)$ into 'types'. The intuition behind this is that a reasonable statistical forecast would take into account *only* objects $\mathbf{x}_i$ which are *similar* to the object of interest to obtain reliable estimates. We choose a finite set of types $\{\lambda_1, \ldots, \lambda_{|\Lambda|}\} = \Lambda$ to cluster examples into apriori. We assign types to each example using a *type defining function* $T_n : \mathbf{Z}^n \rightarrow \Lambda^n$, with the requirement that the function is *invariant* (i.e. the order in which the training examples are presented to the learning machine does not affect the resulting types assigned for each example). In practical implementations the underlying learning algorithm is used to define the types. For the implementations of VPM Naive Bayes and VPM Decision Tree we take the underlying learners' probability forecasts and discretise them using the same MDL criterion [5] used in the construction of the ERC plots. These discretised forecasts act as the types for our VPM learner; with this method the number of types is defined dynamically as the algorithm classifies data.

Of course, there are many different choices of types Λ to cluster examples into, and many different ways of defining these functions T_n. As soon as we specify the type information, the corresponding VPM is defined automatically in a simple way as detailed below. In particular, the learning component of the VPM always lies in the type definitions [9]. For each new test object $\mathbf{x}_{n+1}$ we compute the $n + 1$ types of the n training examples and the new test object with a tentatively assigned label $T(z_1, \ldots, z_n, (\mathbf{x}_{n+1}, j)) = (t_1, \ldots, t_n, t_{n+1})$. Once we have computed the types for each tentatively assigned class label $y_{n+1} = j$ of the new test object $\mathbf{x}_{n+1}$, we compute a row of the $|\mathbf{Y}| \times |\mathbf{Y}|$ dimensional Venn probability matrix $\mathbf{M}$. The rows of the matrix $\mathbf{M}$ represent the frequency count of each class label in the set of training examples which have the *same type* as the new test example $M_{ij} = \frac{\sum_{k=1}^{n+1} \mathbb{I}_{\{t_k=t_{n+1}\}} \mathbb{I}_{\{y_k=i\}}}{\sum_{k=1}^{n+1} \mathbb{I}_{\{t_k=t_{n+1}\}}}$. The rows of each matrix have the property $\Sigma_{i=1}^{|\mathbf{Y}|} M_{ij} = 1$, which guarantees that the predicted probabilities (averages of each column) will sum to one. To extract conditional probabilities for each possible label $l \in \mathbf{Y}$ from the VPM learner the average of each column of $\mathbf{M}$ is calculated $\hat{P}(y_{n+1} = l \mid \mathbf{x}_{n+1}) = \frac{\sum_{k=1}^{|\mathbf{Y}|} M_{kl}}{|\mathbf{Y}|}$.

5. Experimental Results

Further details regarding the experimental conditions, datasets and programs used can be found at: http://www.clrc.rhul.ac.uk/people/davidl/ICDMResults.html In brief, we used 6 real life datasets, five from the UCI data repository and one (Abdominal Pain) from Edinburgh Hospital, UK. All datasets were tested using 10-fold cross validation on an AMD Athlone 2Ghz PC. All programs used are extensions of the WEKA data mining system [10]. Figure 1 shows several Empirical Reliability Curves (ERC) to solely assess the reliability of probability forecasts output by the C4.5 Decision Tree and Naive Bayes learners when tested on the Satellite Image and Abdominal Pain datasets respectively. The solid diagonal line represents the *line of calibration*, where predicted probability (*horizontal*) equals observed empirical frequency of occurrence (*vertical*). Under and over estimation of probability forecasts are represented by the reliability curve (dashed black line) deviating above and below the line of calibration respectively. On their own, both learners display over and under estimation (unreliability) in their probability forecasts. For example, when the Naive Bayes learner makes a prediction with estimated probability 0.9, the empirical frequency of the label occurring is only 0.7 (over estimation). In contrast when a prediction is made with estimated probability 0.2, the empirical frequency of label occurrence is actually $\approx$ 0.3 (under estimation). This phenomenon reiterates the fact that both learners' probability forecasts are too 'extreme'.

Application of the Laplace transform to the C4.5 learner and the Binning technique to both learners improves the reliability of the probability forecasts, as shown by the ERC plots realigning with the ideal line of calibration (Fig. 1). Despite improvement in reliability by the Laplace transform to the C4.5 learner there is still a dramatic over estimation of forecast values $\hat{p} \approx 0.8$; this effect is also observed with the Binning approach, but to a lesser extent. VPM implementations of the Naive Bayes and C4.5 Decision Tree learners produce probability forecasts which are very reliable - as shown by their well-aligned ERC plots (Fig. 1).

We used several assessment scores (Error Rate, ERC deviation area, ROC area, Square & Log loss) to determine the effectiveness of probability forecasts output by the C4.5

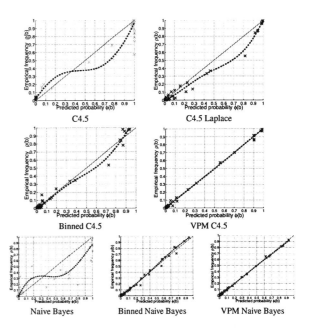

Figure 1. ERC plots visualising reliability of probability forecasts output by various Naive Bayes and C4.5 Decision Tree learners.

Decision Tree and Naive Bayes learners (and their variants) across six datasets. When scores were ranked, they all ranked differently from the traditionally studied error rate (results not shown), indicating that reliability and classification accuracy do not always go 'hand in hand' [6]. The ERC deviation, ROC area and loss scores supported the improvement in reliability shown by the ERC plots in Fig. 1.

Table 1 gives a summary of the average percentage change (across all six datasets) for each assessment score with respect to the underlying Naive Bayes or C4.5 Decision Tree learner. The VPM C4.5 Decision Tree results indicate a dramatic improvement in terms of the quality of the probability forecasts as compared with the Laplace transform and Binning technique (i.e. ERC deviation decreased by 79% for VPM C4.5 as compared with 12% for C4.5 Laplace and 61% for Binned C4.5). This pattern of improvement is also observed for the Naive Bayes learner, however the difference between the binning approach and VPM is less striking. It is interesting that the ROC area is increased by all techniques applied to the Decision Tree learner yet not for the Naive Bayes learners. This could be because the ROC area may be biased toward measuring the resolution criterion and not reliability [6]. In this instance, the VPM and Binning techniques for the Naive Bayes learner may be forfeiting resolution for reliability. Indeed with VPM implementations of both learners there is on average a slight decrease in classification accuracy. Across all data the VPM is observed to be the slowest in terms of computation

Table 1. Summary of Results on UCI Datasets

Average Percentage Change For C4.5 Across Data (%)						
Learner	Error	ERC Dev	ROC Area	Sqr Loss	Log Loss	Time
C4.5 Laplace	0	-12.1	+27.1	-8.4	-61.5	+39.5
Binned C4.5	-0.4	-61.6	+23.1	-10.6	-58.9	+90.6
VPM C4.5	+2.9	-79.2	+32.2	-16.4	-65.6	+1386.5

Average Percentage Change For Naive Bayes Across Data (%)						
Learner	Error	ERC Dev	ROC area	Sqr Loss	Log Loss	Time
Binned Naive Bayes	-6.1	-76.4	-3.2	-15.6	-60.6	+452.6
VPM Naive Bayes	+0.7	-78.6	-4.1	-18.4	-64.1	+672.2

time compared to other techniques tested. This increase in time is most apparent with the VPM Decision Tree with an increase of +1386.5% as opposed to +672.2% with VPM Naive Bayes. This is because the C4.5 Decision Tree is not incremental by design and, unlike the Naive Bayes, when a new example is added to the training data the C4.5 algorithm must be re-run. As indicated earlier, the VPM learner classifies each test example by adding it into the training data with all possible labels tentatively assigned. If the learner's hypothesis can be cached in memory for the training data and simply updated (as with Naive Bayes) then huge computational shortcuts may be made.

6. Discussion

We have tested three methods to improve the reliability of the Naive Bayes and C4.5 Decision Tree learners: Laplace transform, Binning and VPM. The VPM meta-learner outperforms the other techniques in terms of improving reliability, however this is at the cost of slightly increased error rate and increased computation time. Unlike the simpler techniques tested the VPM has the ability to output provably reliable probability forecasts. The C4.5 Decision Tree learner is often limited by small sample sizes settling at leaves of the tree, a problem that is not experienced with VPM as it gains its statistics from the larger sets of the training data (i.e. examples with the same type). The Naive Bayes learner makes simplifying assumptions about the underlying probability distribution (independence of attributes) that rarely hold for real data. In contrast, the VPM learner makes no assumption *further* than the data being *i.i.d.*, which is far more realistic; the only necessary condition for reliability is that the VPM's type defining function is invariant with respect to the order of the training examples. Indeed another advantage of the VPM approach is that there are many possible type defining functions that could be investigated to yield better results.

One major limitation of the VPM is its computational complexity; if the learner is not naturally incremental, as is the case with the C4.5 Decision Tree, then the computation time can be much larger than for simpler learners, and with large datasets with many possible labels this could be-

come infeasible. It would be interesting therefore to investigate whether incremental versions of Decision Tree learners could be implemented successfully. Another limitation of the VPM is that it can decrease classification accuracy. However we argue that the practical benefit of significantly improving reliability outweighs possible slight increases in error rate. Knowing the reliability of probability forecasts will provide the user with an alternative perspective of a learner's performance, enabling the user to know whether to 'trust' a learner's predictions [6]. Suppose a user is presented with *differing predictions* from two distinct learners with similar classification accuracy. If reliability is overlooked, the user will probably trust the prediction output by the most accurate learner. However an ERC plot of the probability forecasts made by this learner may reveal gross over estimation. In our view, as practitioners in machine learning we should aim to create learners which are both accurate *and* reliable.

Acknowledgements

We thank A. Gammerman, Z. Luo, and V. Vovk for their comments. DL was funded by an EPSRC Studentship Grant.

References

[1] C. G. Atkeson, A. W. Moore, and S. Schaal. Locally weighted learning. *Artificial Intelligence Review*, 11:11 73, 1997.

[2] B. Cestnik. Estimating probabilities: A crucial task in machine learning. In *Proc. of the 9th Euro. Conf. on Artificial Intelligence*, 1990.

[3] A. P. Dawid. Calibration-based empirical probability (with discussion). *Annals of Statistics*, 13:1251–1285, 1985.

[4] M. H. DeGroot and S. E. Feinberg. The comparison and evaluation of forecasters. *The Statistician*, 32:12–22, 1982.

[5] U. Fayyad and K. Irani. The attribute selection problem in decision tree generation. In *Proc. of 10th Nat. Conf. on Artificial Intelligence*, 1992.

[6] D. Lindsay. Visualising and improving reliability - a machine learning perspective. CLRC-TR-04-01, Royal Holloway University of London, England, 2004.

[7] A. H. Murphy. A new vector partition of the probability score. *Journal of Applied Meteorology*, 12:595–600, 1973.

[8] F. Provost and T. Fawcett. Analysis and visualisation of classifier performance: Comparision under imprecise class and cost distributions. In *Proc. of the 3rd Int. Conf. on Knowledge Discovery and Data Mining*, 1997.

[9] V. Vovk, G. Shafer, and I. Nouretdinov. Self-calibrating probability forecasting. In *Advances in Neural Information Processing Systems 16*, 2003.

[10] I. Witten and E. Frank. *Data Mining - Practical Machine Learning Tools and Techniques with Java Implementations*. Morgan Kaufmann, San Francisco, 2000.

[11] B. Zadrozny and C. Elkan. Obtaining calibrated probability estimates from decision trees and naive bayesian classifiers. In *Proc. of the 18th Int. Conf. on Machine Learning*, 2001.

Revealing True Subspace Clusters in High Dimensions

Jinze Liu, Karl Strohmaier, and Wei Wang
Department of Computer Science, University of North Carolina, Chapel Hill, NC 27599
{liuj, strohma, weiwang}@cs.unc.edu

Abstract

Subspace clustering is one of the best approaches for discovering meaningful clusters in high dimensional space. One cluster in high dimensional space may be transcribed into multiple distinct maximal clusters by projecting onto different subspaces. A direct consequence of clustering independently in each subspace is an overwhelmingly large set of overlapping clusters which may be significantly similar. To reveal the true underlying clusters, we propose a similarity measurement of the overlapping clusters. We adopt the model of Gaussian tailed hyper-rectangles to capture the distribution of any subspace cluster. A set of experiments on a synthetic dataset demonstrates the effectiveness of our approach. Application to real gene expression data also reveals impressive meta-clusters expected by biologists.

Keywords: Subspace Clustering, Overlapping Cluster, Adhesion, Gaussian Tails, Cluster Intersection, Local Grid, Gene Expression

1 Introduction

Clustering has become one of the most popular and effective data mining techniques to reveal characteristics of large amounts of data. Because of the curse of the dimensionality, there have been many studies [2, 1, 3, 4] on designing new models and efficient algorithms for capturing subspace clusters.

Recent methods result in subspace clusters that are either *disjoint subspace clusters* or *overlapping subspace clusters*. In the model of disjoint clusters, each object may belong to at most a single cluster, regardless of the subspace in which the cluster is present. These disjoint clusters are succinct. In contrast, the model of overlapping clusters allows an object to naturally be included in multiple clusters, which offer indisputable advantages in real-world applications. For example, a gene may have multiple functions, each of which may be manifested in a specific metabolic pathway. It is biologically relevant to discover that one gene may appear in multiple gene clusters. However, the flexibility offered by this model poses substantial challenges

in the design of the cluster model and mining algorithm. Due to efficiency concerns, existing models often discretize the data space and assume that all clusters are hyper-rectangles consisting of adjacent grids in their subspaces. Density and entropy measures based on data distribution within a subspace are applied to determine the existence of a subspace cluster. Since this decision is made independently for each subspace, clusters in different subspaces may overlap. In fact, the degree of cluster overlap may be very high, even if we only keep the set of maximal subspace clusters[1]. The number of subspace clusters can be large, which may degrade the significance of each cluster and hinder the posterior analysis. In this paper, we propose a new similarity measure for subspace clusters to accommodate the difference in subspaces, based on solid statistical theory. The application of our model to gene expression data revealed biologically relevant clusters with significantly reduced number of clusters.

Section 2 addresses related work in subspace clustering and cluster merging. Section 3 defines the model proposed in the paper. A greedy algorithm is presented in Section 4. The experiment is reported in Section 5. Section 6 concludes the paper and discusses some future work.

2 Related Work

Our work is related to grid and density-based subspace clustering, as well as cluster similarity analysis and cluster merging. Density- and grid-based approaches view clusters as regions of the data space in which objects are dense and are separated by regions of low object density. CLIQUE[2], MAFIA[4] and ENCLUS[3] are three such algorithms. The resolution of the grid ultimately determines the computation efficiency. These algorithms detect independent clusters in the highest dimensional subspaces, which may lead to a large number of clusters.

Previous work on cluster similarity assessment solely handles clusters in the full space. Classical hierarchical

---

[1]The formal definition of *maximal subspace cluster* is in Section 3. Intuitively, a maximum subspace cluster is a subspace cluster that cannot include more objects or dimensions without violating the clustering criteria.

clustering algorithms use the distance between clusters to measure similarity among clusters. In fuzzy clustering[5], the similarity of a pair of clusters is defined as the maximum percentage of data points of each cluster falling in the intersection of the two clusters. However, extra caution has to be used when merging clusters from different subspaces.

3 Model

Let $\mathcal{A} = \{A_1, A_2, ..., A_d\}$ be a set of ordered, numerical dimensions (attributes) with bounded domains $\mathcal{V} = A_1 \times A_2 \times ... \times A_d$ a d-dimensional vector space. We refer to each individual A_i $(i = 1, ..., d)$ as a dimension (or attribute) of $\mathcal{V}$. The inner product of any subset of $\mathcal{A}$ forms a subspace of $\mathcal{V}$, which is denoted as $\mathcal{S}$. We assume that each dimension A_i has been normalized to range $[0, 1]$. Let the database $\mathcal{O}$ be a set of data points (or objects) in $\mathcal{S}$. Each data point x is a d-dimensional unit vector.

We adopt the space discretization of CLIQUE[2] by superimposing a grid of non-overlapping rectangular units (cells) onto $\mathcal{S}$, given the size of the interval, λ, and the density threshold ξ. A *cluster* in a subspace is a maximum set of connected dense units. To discriminate from the cluster model we will propose later in the paper, we call it a *base cluster*. A base cluster is denoted as a tuple $C = < \mathcal{O}, \mathcal{S}, \mathcal{R} >$, where $\mathcal{O}(C)$ denotes the set of data points, $\mathcal{S}(C)$ denotes its subspace, and $\mathcal{R}(C)$ denotes the minimum bounding rectangle containing the cluster. A cluster within a k-dimensional subspace is called a k-dimensional subspace cluster. A cluster C is *maximum* if there does not exist another cluster C' such that $O(C) \subseteq O(C')$, and $S(C) \subseteq S(C')$. Given a subspace $\mathcal{S}$, let $\mathcal{CL}(\mathcal{S})$ be the set of base clusters generated by function $\mathcal{CL}$ in subspace $\mathcal{S}$.

3.1 Scenarios of Overlapping among Base Clusters

In our study, we classify the cluster overlap as *inclusive* overlap or *non-inclusive* overlap.

Lemma 3.1 *Given a maximal base cluster C in k-dimensional space $\mathcal{S}$, $\forall$ $(k-1)$ dimensional subspace $\mathcal{S}'$, $\mathcal{S}' \subset \mathcal{S}$, there exists $C' \in \mathcal{CL}(\mathcal{S}')$ such that $\mathcal{O}(C) \subseteq \mathcal{O}(C')$.*

Lemma 3.1 can be proven by the Apriori property of dense units in [2]. Given cluster C, the set of dense and connected units composing C are also dense and connected when they are projected onto any its $(k-1)$-dimensional subspace. Therefore, those dense and connected $(k-1)$-dimensional dense units may be equal to or part of a cluster C'. Lemma 3.1 describes the nested *inclusion* relationship occurring between clusters illustrated in Figure 1(a).

Corollary 3.1 *Given a k-dimensional space $\mathcal{S}$, let $\{\mathcal{S}'_1, \mathcal{S}'_2, ..., \mathcal{S}'_k\}$, $\mathcal{S}'_i \subset \mathcal{S}$, all be $k-1$-dimensional subspaces of $\mathcal{S}$. Given a cluster C, $C \in \mathcal{CL}(\mathcal{S})$, there exists $C'_i \in \mathcal{CL}(\mathcal{S}'_i)$ such that $\mathcal{O}(C) \subseteq \cap_{0 < i \leq k} \mathcal{O}(C'_i)$.*

Beside inclusive overlap, base clusters residing in non-inclusive subspaces, where $\mathcal{S}' \subseteq \mathcal{S}$ and $\mathcal{S} \subseteq \mathcal{S}'$, may have non-inclusive overlap, where neither cluster is a subset of the other, as illustrated in Figure 1(b). Those overlapping clusters might be different views of one underlying cluster when they are projected onto corresponding subspaces.

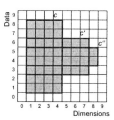 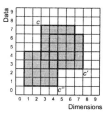

(a)Inclusive overlap   (b) Non-inclusive overlap

Figure 1. Two typical cases of cluster relationships.

In this study, all the base clusters are represented by minimum hyper-rectangular *kernels* defined by a pair of vectors $\vec{R^l}$ and $\vec{R^h}$, which are the lower and upper boundaries. The union of a set of base clusters is referred to as a *meta-cluster*. They are described by the hyper-rectangular kernels with softened Gaussian boundaries.

3.2 Adhesion Strength between Overlapping Clusters

Given two clusters, the *adhesion strength* is a measure of how tightly one cluster attaches to the other. Intuitively, two clusters have strong adhesion strength if both clusters have a large percentage of data points closely located. In addition, exclusive data points in the exclusive subspaces should not form statistically significant outliers.

Definition 3.1 *Given two clusters $C = \mathcal{O}(C) \times \mathcal{S}(C)$ and $C' = \mathcal{O}(C') \times \mathcal{S}(C')$, defined by two hyper-rectangular kernels R and R', the **adhesion score** of C to C' is defined as*

$$\mathcal{H}(C, C') = \sqrt[|S(C)|]{\prod_{i \in \mathcal{S}(C)} h(C, C', i)} \qquad (1)$$

where the adhesion score along each dimension i is defined as

$$h(C, C', i) = \frac{|\vec{R_i} \wedge \vec{R_i'}|}{|\vec{R_i}|} \frac{\mathcal{Q}(\vec{R_i} \wedge \vec{R_i'}, C)}{\mathcal{Q}(\vec{R_i}, C)} \qquad (2)$$

where function $\mathcal{Q}(\overrightarrow{R}, C)$ returns the number of points in C that falls in region $\overrightarrow{R}$, and $\overrightarrow{R_i} \wedge \overrightarrow{R'_i}$ is

(i). 0,
$$\text{if } (i \in \mathcal{S}(C) \cap \mathcal{S}(C'))$$
$$\textbf{and } (max(\overrightarrow{R_i^l}, \overrightarrow{R'_i^l}) > min(\overrightarrow{R_i^h}, \overrightarrow{R'_i^h})),$$
$$(Figure\ 2(b)(1));$$

(ii). $[min(\overrightarrow{R_i^h}, \overrightarrow{R'_i^h}), max(\overrightarrow{R_i^l}, \overrightarrow{R'_i^l})]$,
$$\text{if } (i \in \mathcal{S}(C) \cap \mathcal{S}(C'))$$
$$\textbf{and } (min(\overrightarrow{R_i^h}, \overrightarrow{R'_i^h}) > max(\overrightarrow{R_i^l}, \overrightarrow{R'_i^l})),$$
$$(Figure\ 2(b)(2.1\&2.2));$$

(iii). $[min_{x \in \mathcal{O}(C')} x_i, max_{x \in \mathcal{O}(C')} x_i] \wedge \overrightarrow{R_i}$
$$\textbf{if } (i \in \mathcal{S}(C)) \textbf{ and } (i \notin \mathcal{S}(C')).$$

$$(3)$$

The adhesion strength is asymmetric and can be used to construct a similarity measure between two clusters.

$$Similarity(C, C') = \min\{\mathcal{H}(C, C'), \mathcal{H}(C', C)\}.$$

In Equation 2, the adhesion strength from one cluster to the other in each dimension depends on the ratio between the intersection area and the cluster boundary, as well as the percentage of data points falling in the intersection region. In each dimension, the adhesion strength h of two clusters is captured in terms of both data points and physical space. Two clusters can adhere to each other only if they have a common kernel(Figure 2(b) 2.1&2.2), which is the intersection of their hyper-rectangular kernels. Furthermore, both of the clusters should have a large percentage of data points falling within the kernel. This is determined by function $\mathcal{Q}$. If two clusters do not have a boundary intersection in any dimension of their subspaces, the adhesion strength is 0 (Figure 2 (b) 1). In the exclusive dimensions, when only the cluster who owns the dimension has a kernel boundary, we approximate the other kernel boundary using the maximum and minimum of the common points in that dimension (Case (iii) in Definition 3.1). The overall adhesion strength across all unified dimensions is the geometric average of the adhesion strength in each dimension. The asymmetric property of adhesion strength enables its use in describing the scenario when one cluster is much smaller than the other but is strongly coupled to it. If the similarity between a pair of clusters is high, we may merge them into a new meta-cluster. If C and C' are the two meta-clusters of high similarity, the new meta-cluster C'' will be in the subspace $\mathcal{S}(C) \cup \mathcal{S}(C')$ and include objects $\mathcal{O}(C) \cup \mathcal{O}(C')$. To determine the hyper-rectangular kernel of the new meta-cluster, a Gaussian tailed rectangular kernel is fit onto the cluster based on the model proposed in [8].

3.2.1 Rectangular Kernel Determination

Let C_1 and C_2 be the two clusters with kernels $[\overrightarrow{R^{l_1}}, \overrightarrow{R^{h_1}}]$ and $[\overrightarrow{R^{l_2}}, \overrightarrow{R^{h_2}}]$. They are to be merged to

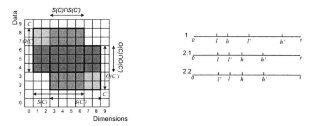

(a)Two overlapping clusters.   (b) Two intervals relationships.

Figure 2. Illustration of Definition 3.1.

generate a meta-cluster C.

$$LL(x) = (-|O_1 \cup O_2| \ln(\sqrt{2\pi}\sigma_i + \overrightarrow{R_i^{h3}} - \overrightarrow{R_i^{l3}}))$$
$$+ \sum_{x \in O_1 \cup O_2} -\frac{1}{2}(\frac{x_i - closest(x_i, \overrightarrow{R_i^{l3}}, \overrightarrow{R_i^{h3}})}{\sigma_i})$$

$$(4)$$

The optimal values of $\overrightarrow{R_i^{l3}}$ and $\overrightarrow{R_i^{h3}}$ should be the ones that maximize $LL(x)$ in Equation 4. The golden ratio optimizer [7] can be used to locate the optimal values of $\overrightarrow{R_i^{l3}}$ and $\overrightarrow{R_i^{h3}}$, starting with the initial values $[\overrightarrow{R_i^{l3}}, \overrightarrow{R_i^{h3}}] = [\overrightarrow{R_i^{l1}}, \overrightarrow{R_i^{h1}}] \wedge [\overrightarrow{R_i^{l2}}, \overrightarrow{R_i^{l2}}]$, as defined in Definition 3.1. The intersection area for measuring adhesion strength is set as the initial kernel to meet its density requirement. Once we determine the initial kernel of the meta-cluster, we may apply the MLE of the Gaussian tailed hyper-rectangular distribution to compute its optimal kernel.

4 A Greedy Algorithm

This algorithm evaluates every pair of clusters at each iteration, and picks the pair having the best adhesion score and merges it. After that, the adhesion score of those pairs having one of the clusters being merged is updated with the new meta-cluster and reordered. If there still exists a pair of clusters having an adhesion score above the threshold, the merging continues. This algorithm is simple and straightforward. The time complexity is $O(N^3 logN)$, where N is the total number of clusters.

Algorithm *MergeGreedy*(C, δ)
Input: C: A set of unique dense subspace clusters; δ: similarity threshold
Output: C': A set of unique subspace clusters
1.   Compute the similarity score of $\frac{|C| * (|C| - 1)}{2}$ cluster pairs
2.   Sort the list of cluster pairs in decreasing order of the score
3.   **while** Head of the list having a similarity score$> \delta$
4.   **do** Merge C_i, C_j with highest score.
5.   Remove cluster pairs containing C_i or C_j
6.   Recompute the similarity score.
7.   Insert them into the list of cluster pairs in decreasing order of the score.
8.   **return**.

5   Performance Evaluation

We compare the meta-clusters with the base clusters generated by CLIQUE in terms of the cluster quality using both synthetic data sets and real gene expression data. All implementations are in C++ and tested on a machine with an 800MHz Pentium III processor and 2GB of main memory.

5.1   Effect of Meta-Clustering

The synthetic high dimensional data set is generated by embedding clusters in the subspaces. The clusters are points following a Gaussian tailed hyper-rectangular distribution. For each cluster, the number of data points and the hyper-rectangular kernel are first determined by selecting the dimensionality of the subspace, and the upper and lower bounds of the hyper-rectangular kernel. Let p be the percentage of data points we want to put in the kernel. We have $\sigma = \frac{(1-p)(\mathcal{R}^h - \mathcal{R}^l)}{\sqrt{2\pi}}$. A random generator is used to distribute data points into the kernel, $\pm\sigma$ outside the kernel and $\pm2\sigma$ outside the kernel for each dimension, accordingly.

In this group of experiments, we embedded 5 6-dimensional meta-clusters in the data set with 1500 20-dimensional data points. The experiment varies the adhesion score from 0.4 to 1 in steps of 0.1. The number of clusters in each dimension is presented in Figure 3. The clusters generated when the adhesion score is 1 are actually the base clusters, which corresponds to the top curve in the figure. The general trend is that fewer meta-clusters are generated with a lower adhesion score because more clusters may be valid for merging. The big gap between the curves of adhesion scores 0.6 and 0.7 suggests that 0.6 to 0.7 may be a good point to have a reasonable number of meta-clusters matching well with the underlying real clusters.

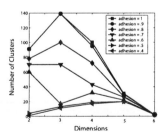

Figure 3. Number of clusters in different subspaces with varying adhesion score.

5.2   Meta-Clustering on real data

Two types of cell lines derived from basal epithelium and luminal epithelium respectively were treated under the chemotherapeutics. The expression levels of genes of both cell lines are recorded during the treatment at 12, 24, and 36 hours. Multiple samples are generated at each time point. After certain filtering of noise, we selected 1034 genes and 26 columns for analysis. Each type of cell line has 13 columns in the gene expression matrix. On the advice of biologists, we normalized the expression levels using logarithms and then transformed them into [-1, 1]. We divided each dimension into 5 intervals with length 0.4. The density threshold is 0.01. The whole clustering process took less than two minutes, and given an adhesion threshold of 0.6, it generated 28086 base clusters, from which 4130 meta clusters were generated. That is only 14% of the number of base clusters. This number is reasonable considering the very low density threshold and the number of subspaces.

6   Conclusion

In this paper, we provide a framework to organize the overlapping subspace clusters generated in grid and density-based algorithms. We show that significant overlap among clusters is very common in subspace clustering and can result in redundancy in identifying real clusters embedded in a data space. Adhesion strength is defined to measure the similarity between two clusters with a Gaussian tailed hyper-rectangular shape. Experiments on both synthetic and real datasets highlight the effectiveness of the adhesion strength in measuring the similarity of subspace clusters. Our ongoing work includes developing simple and efficient algorithms for meta-clustering.

Acknowledgement

We thank Dr. Chuck Perou and his lab at UNC for their valuable help with gene expression experiments.

References

[1] C. Aggarwal, C. Procopiuc, J.L.Wolf, P.S.Yu and J.S.Park. A Framework for Finding Projected Clusters in high dimensional spaces. In SIGMOD, 1999.

[2] R.Agrawal, J.Gehrke, D.Gunopulos, and P.Raghavan. Automatic subspace clustering of high dimensional data for data mining applications. In SIGMOD, 1998.

[3] C.H. Cheng, A.W. Fu, Y. Zhang, Entropy-based Subspace Clustering for Mining Numerical Data. In SIGKDD, Aug 1999.

[4] S. Goil, Harsha and Alok Choudhary. MAFIA: Efficient and scalable subspace clustering for very large data sets. In ICDE, 2000.

[5] U.Kaymak, and M.Setnes. Extended Fuzzy Clustering Algorithms. Discussion paper of Erasmus Research Institute of Management (ERIM), Erasmus University Rotterdam, 2000.

[6] J. Liu, K. Strohmaier and W. Wang. Revealing Subspace Clusters in High Dimensional Space. UNC-CH CS technical report.

[7] W.H.Press, S.A. Teukolsky, W.T.Vetterling, B.P.Flannery. Numerical recipes in C, 2_{nd} edition.

[8] Dan Pelleg, Andrew Moore, Mixtures of Rectangles:Interpretable Soft Clustering, ICML, 2001

An Adaptive Density-Based Clustering Algorithm for Spatial Database with Noise

Daoying Ma and Aidong Zhang
Department of Computer Science and Engineering
State University of New York at Buffalo
Email: {daoma,azhang}@cse.buffalo.edu

Abstract

Clustering spatial data has various applications. Several clustering algorithms have been proposed to cluster objects in spatial databases. Spatial object distribution has significant effect on the results of clustering. Few of current algorithms consider the distribution of objects while processing clusters. In this paper, we propose an adaptive density-based clustering algorithm, ADBC, which uses a novel adaptive strategy for neighbor selection based on spatial object distribution to improve clustering accuracy. We perform a series of experiments on simulated data sets and real data sets. A comparison with DBSCAN and OPTICS shows the superiority of our new approach.

1 Introduction

Huge amounts of spatial data have been collected by satellites, radars, and other equipments in recent years. Designing efficient and effective algorithms to analyze tremendous amounts of spatial data is critical to numerous potential applications in military battlefields analysis[5, 2], geographic information systems, and Global Positioning Systems (GPS)[4].

One primary data analysis of spatial data is cluster detection. Existing clustering algorithms can be broadly classified into partitioning[11, 10, 12], hierarchical[10, 7, 9, 13], and density-based [6, 1, 8] clustering algorithms. When process clustering, most of the clustering algorithms do not take the variety of the data distribution into account. However, the distribution of objects has significant influence on the result of clustering. In this paper, we propose an adaptive density-based clustering (ADBC) algorithm for the purpose of clustering spatial databases with respect to the data distribution.

In Section 2, we first present the motivation of our design, and then our new adaptive density-based clustering algorithm is introduced. In Section 3, we provide an experimental evaluation comparing our approach to previous approaches, such as DBSCAN and OPTICS. Concluding remarks are offered in Section 4.

2 Clustering database with respect to the data distribution

The density-based clustering algorithms can discover arbitrary shape clusters with noise. They have received significant attention in spatial clustering. The key idea of density-based clustering is to continue growing a given cluster as long as the density (ρ) is larger than some threshold. The density is calculated by the area of neighboring region (ξ) and the number of objects in the region ($|N_\xi(q)|$). In the classic density-based clustering algorithm DBSCAN, there are two types of objects in a cluster: core objects and border objects. For each core object q, the density of neighboring region with center q must be larger than the threshold:

$$\rho = \frac{|N_\xi(q)|}{\xi} \geq \frac{MinPts}{\pi Eps^2},\tag{1}$$

where Eps is the radius of the neighboring region and $MinPts$ is the minimum number of objects in the region.

The parameters, Eps and $MinPts$, are critical inputs for DBSCAN. Since a cluster in DBSCAN contains at least one core object, $MinPts$ also defines the minimum number of objects in a cluster. So $MinPts$ must be large enough to distinguish noise and clusters. Eps defines the radius of the neighboring region. If Eps is set too small, a cluster might be divided into several sub-clusters or noise. If the Eps is set too large, noise can not be isolated from clusters, and/or multiple clusters might become one large cluster (chain affection). Therefore, if the neighboring region is not chosen properly, the clustering results won't be accurate.

We propose the following two definitions to measure the quality of density in DBSCAN.

Definition 1 *(Density pad) A density pad is a convex region inside a circle with radius Eps that includes all the useful objects.*

Definition 2 *(void pad) An void pad is the region inside the circle with radius Eps that is not density pad.*

Obviously, the larger void pad is, the more chance to include noise data into a cluster, which can cause chain affection, and hence lower quality of density. The void pad in Figure 1(b) is larger than in Figure 1(a), therefore the quality of density in Figure 1(b) is lower than that in Figure 1(a).

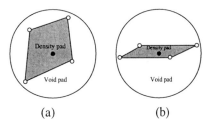

Figure 1. Density pad and void pad

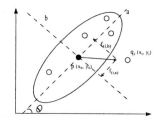

Figure 2. Neighbor selection

There are two ways to minimize the void pad to achieve better quality of density. First method is setting Eps as small as possible. However, Eps must be large enough to avoid clusters to be divided into sub-clusters or noise. The second method is using different measures to select an object's neighbors. In DBSCAN, a circle is used to define the neighboring region. Only when the distribution of data objects inside the circle are spherical shapes, the large void pad will not occur. If the objects in the circle don't follow that distribution, using different measurement might help to improve the quality of density.

2.1 Neighbor Selection

The method used to define the neighboring region is very important to avoid void pad in density-based clustering algorithms. It can dramatically improve the clustering accuracy. The ideal method should be able to cover as many neighbors as possible, at the same time, have as small void pad as possible. Therefore, the neighboring region should be defined properly to reflect the data distribution of an object's neighbors. Since the shape of the neighboring region is arbitrary, the circle used in DBSCAN actually limits the effectiveness of the clustering algorithm to large extent.

We propose to use a dynamic ellipse which can not only adjust with different radiuses but also rotate according to the distribution of the neighbors of an object. Newton's Universal Law of Gravitation states that any two objects exert gravitational force of attraction on each other. The direction of the force is along the line joining the objects. For example, there are two objects p and q. In the initial step, we consider the force in each direction is the same. So the neighboring region of object p is initialized as a circle with area = ξ. The circle is considered as an extensible string. If there is force between objects p and q, the string will be extended in the direction of the force. At the same time, we keep p as the center and the area covered by the string same all the time. Thus, the circle becomes an ellipse with long radius following the direction of the force.

For each given object p, we first find out the gravitational force between p and it's neighbors. Then, the directions and lengths of the long radius and the short radius of the ellipse can be adjusted according to the force. The direction of the long radius can be decided by θ, which is the angle between

the long radius and the x-axis. θ can be calculated by:

$$\theta = \frac{\sum_1^n(\theta_1 + ... + \theta_n)}{n}, \qquad (2)$$

where n is the number of neighbors, and $\theta_1,...,\theta_n$ is the direction of force between object p and its neighbors.

After we decide the long radius direction of the ellipse, we then transform all the force between p and other objects into the directions of the long and short radiuses. The lengths of the long and short radiuses of the ellipse can be decided according to the force on the directions of the long and short radiuses. For example, in Figure 2, the position of an object p is (x_0, y_0). It has n neighbors, q_1, ..., q_n. The force between p and neighbor q_i is f_i. After rotating the ellipse by θ, we split the force into the direction of the long and short radiuses, $f_{(i,a)} = f_i \times cos(\phi)$ and $f_{(i,b)} = f_i \times sin(\phi)$, where ϕ is the angle between f_i and the long radius. The total force on the direction of the long and short radiuses are f_a and f_b, respectively.

$$f_a = |f_{(1,a)}| + ... + |f_{(i,a)}| + ... + |f_{(n,a)}|. \qquad (3)$$

$$f_b = |f_{(1,b)}| + ... + |f_{(i,b)}| + ... + |f_{(n,b)}|. \qquad (4)$$

The relation of the length of the long radius, a, and the short radius, b, of the ellipse is:

$$a/b = \frac{f_a}{f_b} = \frac{|f_{(1,a)}| + ... + |f_{(i,a)}| + ... + |f_{(n,a)}|}{|f_{(1,b)}| + ... + |f_{(i,b)}| + ... + |f_{(n,b)}|}. \qquad (5)$$

The area of the ellipse is equal to the initial circle's area which is ξ. So,

$$\pi ab = \xi; a = \sqrt{\frac{\xi f_a}{\pi f_b}}; b = \sqrt{\frac{\xi f_b}{\pi f_a}}. \qquad (6)$$

Therefore, the ellipse region is:

$$1 = \frac{[(x-x_0)^2 + (y-y_0)^2]cos^2[atan(\frac{y-y_0}{x-x_0}) - \theta]}{a^2}$$
$$+ \frac{[(x-x_0)^2 + (y-y_0)^2]sin^2[atan(\frac{y-y_0}{x-x_0}) - \theta]}{b^2}. \qquad (7)$$

We use $MaxRds$ and $MinRds$, which are the longest and shortest radiuses allowed, to help us decide the neighboring region for each object. The area for the neighbor region is as follows: $\xi = \pi \times MaxRds \times MinRds$. When consider the data distribution, the longer the distance between two objects, the less the impact they can have on each other. Therefore, we only focus on the objects that have significant effect on each other, which are the ones may fall into the neighboring region. For each object p, if the distance between an object and p is larger than $MaxRds$, we ignore the force between them. Otherwise, we set the force between the two objects to one unit force. Then we use the scheme described above to find the ellipse neighboring region for the object p.

2.2 Algorithm

We define two types of relationship among objects of a density-based cluster. The first, directly border-reachable, is the relationship between the core objects and the border objects.

Definition 3 *(Directly border-reachable) An object p is directly border-reachable from an object q with respect to $MinPts$ and ξ, if*

(1) p is a border object ($|N_\xi(p)| < MinPts$),
(2) q is a core object ($|N_\xi(q)| \geq MinPts$),
(3) $p \in N_\xi(q)$, where $N_\xi(q)$ denotes the neighboring region defined by Equation 7, $|N_\xi(q)|$ denotes the number of objects in the region.

Next, we define the relationship between two core objects. In a cluster, any two core objects can reach each other directly or indirectly. If the two core objects are not directly connected, there must exist a chain, which connects these two core objects. We use the following definitions, directly core-connected and core-connected, to reflect the relationship:

Definition 4 *(Directly core-connected) A core object p is directly core-connected to a core object q with respect to $MinPts$ and ξ, if $p \in N_\xi(q)$ and $q \in N_\xi(p)$.*

Definition 5 *(Core-connected) An object p is core-connected to an object q with respect to $MinPts$ and ξ, if there is a chain of objects $p_1, ..., p_n, p_1 = q, p_n = p$ such that p_{i+1} is directly core-connected from p_i.*

Based on the three definitions, we then define the density-based notion of a cluster. For any pair of core objects in a cluster, they are core-connected to each other. For any border objects, it can be directly reached by at least one core object in the cluster.

Definition 6 *(Cluster) Let D be a database of objects. A cluster C with respect to $MinPts$ and ξ is a non-empty subset of D satisfying the following conditions:*
(1) Maximality: $\forall p$, if there is an core object $q \in C$ and p is directly border-reachable from q or p is core-connected with q with respect to ξ and $MinPts$, then $p \in C$.
(2) Connectivity: $\forall p, q \in C$, if p and q are core objects, then p core-connected to q with respect to ξ and $MinPts$.
(3) Reachability: $\forall p$ in C, if p is border object, there must have a core object q in C and p is directly border-reachable from q with respect to ξ and $MinPts$.

ExpandCluster($object$, $ClusterID$)

1. $object.ClusterID := ClusterID$;
2. put $object$ into $Seeds$;
3. **while** $Seeds$ not empty **do**
       $p := Seeds.first()$
       if p is a core object **do**
           for each object q of p's neighbor **do**
               if q has not been processed **do**
                   if p and q are directly core-connect **do**
                       put q into $Seeds$
                       $q.clusterID := ClusterID$;
                   else
                     if p and q are directly border-reachable
                       $q.clusterID := ClusterID$;
               endif
           endif
           endfor
       endif
   endwhile

Since all the core objects in a cluster are core-connected, we first find one core object and then form a cluster based on the core object and its core-connected objects. In the main steps of our ADBC algorithm, we check each object in the *Database*. If it has not been processed, we first check whether it is a core object or not. If the number of objects covered by the ellipse neighboring region of the object is less than the $MinPts$, the object is either a border object or noise. Otherwise, the object is a core object and we pass it to ExpandCluster to start forming a cluster based on the core object.

Since the *object* is a core object, all the objects, which are directly core-connected to *object*, also belong to the same cluster. We put all the newly discovered core objects into a queue, named *Seeds*, for future expansion. The checking procedure stops when all objects in *Seeds* have been processed. By doing so, all the core objects of the cluster are collected. One border object may be directly border-reachable for more than one core object which belongs to different clusters. In our algorithm, we assign a border object to the cluster which first discovers the border object.

The run-time of our algorithm is similar to DBSCAN. The total run-time for both algorithm is $O(n \times \text{run-time of a}$ neighbor query). When use a tree-based spatial index, such as R*-tree [3], the run-time of our algorithm is $O(nlogn)$.

3 Experimental Results

To evaluate the effectiveness of the ADBC algorithm, we performed comprehensive experiments on different data sets. One important measurement of the quality of density-

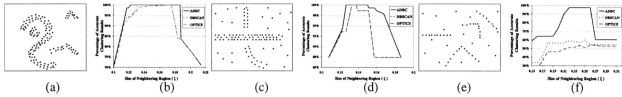

Figure 3. Valid ranges of different clustering algorithms for different data sets

based clustering algorithms is the valid range of the algorithms. In the example shown in Figure 3(b), x-axis is the size of neighboring region and y-axis is the percentage of the accurate clustering results of a density-based algorithm. If we want at least 95% of the objects are correctly classified, the valid rang of the DBSCAN for this data set is [0.125, 0.17]. Obviously, the wider the valid range of a density-based algorithm is, the more flexibility it can provide users to choose different neighboring region parameters and at the same time obtain accurate clustering results.

It has been proved that DBSCAN has better performance than partitioning and hierarchical algorithms for spatial data mining, so we only compare our algorithm with DBSCAN and OPTICS. We examine our algorithm on different data sets. The first data set (Figure 3(a)) is used in DBSCAN study, the second data set (Figure 3(c)) is simulated GPS data, and the last one (Figure 3(e)) is a military data set. We observe that the valid range using our algorithm is much wider than DBSCAN and OPTICS. OPTICS considers the global data distribution when detecting clusters, but it still uses the similar measurement used in DBSCAN to select density neighboring region. Most of the clusters in GPS and military data sets are organized into certain lineal formation in order to travel efficiently as well as gain tactical advantage. Thus make it even tougher for DBSCAN to detect density region. DBSCAN must set *Eps* large enough to detect some clusters. However, because objects are organized into lineal formations, the larger *Eps* is, the larger void pad is. Since there are a lot of noise data, DBSCAN with larger *Eps* is likely to include those noise data and cause chain affection, forming serval larger clusters instead of small individual clusters. As shown in Figure 3(f), DB-SCAN and OPTICS all fail to detect all the clusters. In our algorithm, the neighboring region of an object can be automatically adjusted to reflect its neighbors' distribution. So it can cover as much objects as possible, at the same time, have a smaller void pad to avoid noise. Therefore, it can dramatically reduce the affect caused by noise data and improve the quality of the clustering results.

4 Conclusions

In this paper, we proposed a novel adaptive strategy for neighbor selection based on spatial object distribution to improve density-based clustering accuracy. The neighboring region formed in our algorithm reflects the neighbors'

distribution. Experimental results demonstrated that our clustering algorithm can provide significant improvement of accuracy of the cluster detecting, especially for objects with arbitrary and linear distribution.

References

[1] M. Ankerst, M. Breuning, H.-P. Kriegel, and J. Sander. Optics: Ordering points to identify the clustering structure. *Proc. 1999 ACM-SIGMOD Int. Conf. Management of Data (SIGMOD'99)*, pages 49–60, 1999.

[2] Y. Bar-Shalom and W. D. Blair. *Multitarget-Multisensor Tracking: Applications and Advances Volume III*. Artech House, Norwood, MA, 2000.

[3] N. Beckmann, H.-P. Kriegel, R. Schneider, and B. Seeger. The r*-tree: An efficient and robust access method for points and rectangles. *Proc. 1990 ACM-SIGMOD Int. Conf. Management of Data (SIGMOD'90)*, pages 322–331, 1990.

[4] B.Hofmann-Wellenhof, H.Lichtenegger, and J.Collins. *Global Positioning System: Theory and Practice*. Springer-Verlag Wien, New York, 1994.

[5] S. Blackman and R. Popoli. *Design and Analysis of Modern Tracking Sysytem*. Artech House, Norwood, MA, 1999.

[6] M. Ester, H.-P. Kriegel, J. Sander, , and X. Xu. A density-based algorithm for discovering clusters in large spatial databases. *Proc. 1996 Int. Conf. Knowledge Discovery and Data Mining(KDD'96)*, pages 226–231, 1996.

[7] S. Guha, R. Rastogi, and K. Shim. Cure: An efficient clustering algorithm for large databases. *Proc. 1998 ACM-SIGMOD Int. Conf. Management of Data (SIGMOD'98)*, pages 73–84, 1998.

[8] A. Hinneburg and D. A. Keim. An efficient approach to clustering in large multimedia database with noise. *Proc. 1998 Int. Conf. Knowledge Discovery and Data Mining(KDD'98)*, pages 58–65, 1998.

[9] G. Karypis, E.-H. Han, and V. Kumar. Chameleon: A hierarchical clustering algorithm using dynamic modeling. *Computer*, 32:68–75, 1999.

[10] L. Kaufman and P. J. Rousseeuw. *Finding Groups in Data: An introduction to Cluster Analysis*. John Wiley and Son, New York, 1990.

[11] J. McQueen. Some methods for classification and analysis of multivariat observations. *Proc. of the Fifth Berkeley Symposium on Mathematical Statistics and Probability*, 1:281–297, 1967.

[12] R. Ng and J. Han. Clarans: A method for clustering objects for spatial data mining. *IEEE Trans. on Knowledge and Data Engineering*, vol. 14, no. 5, 2002.

[13] T. Zhang, R. Ramakrishnan, and M. Livny. Birch: An efficient data clustering method for very large databases. *Proc. 1996 ACM-SIGMOD Int. Conf. Management of Data (SIGMOD'96)*, pages 103–114, 1996.

Finding Constrained Frequent Episodes Using Minimal Occurrences *

Xi MA[1]   HweeHwa PANG[2]   Kian-Lee TAN[1]

[1]Department of Computer Science   [2]Institute for Infocomm Research
National University of Singapore   21 Heng Mui Keng Terrace
3 Science Dr 2, Singapore 117543   Singapore 119613

Abstract

Recurrent combinations of events within an event sequence, known as episodes, often reveal useful information. Most of the proposed episode mining algorithms adopt an apriori-like approach that generates candidates and then calculates their support levels. Obviously, such an approach is computationally expensive. Moreover, those algorithms are capable of handling only a limited range of constraints. In this paper, we introduce two mining algorithms — Episode Prefix Tree (EPT) and Position Pairs Set (PPS) — based on a prefix-growth approach to overcome the above limitations. Both algorithms push constraints systematically into the mining process. Performance study shows that the proposed algorithms run considerably faster than MINEPI [4].

1. Introduction

Recurrent combinations of events within an event sequence, known as episodes, often reveal valuable information regarding the applications. With the explosive growth of data in the form of event sequences, episode mining algorithms, as a tool for discovering episodes, become a practical necessity.

The frequent episode mining problem was first introduced by Mannila [5]: Given a sequence of events, episode mining aims to find all of the episodes with occurrence frequencies satisfying the user-specified minimum support. Several episode mining algorithms have been proposed, where the representative algorithms are WINEPI [5] and MINEPI [4]. However, almost all of them are based on the apriori property which states that *any super-pattern of a non-frequent pattern cannot be frequent.* Those apriori-like algorithms involve the generation of potentially huge sets of candidate episodes, and require as many full sequence scans as the longest episode. In [2], two methods, slice scan and selective hash, are introduced to address the drawbacks. However, it is still a candidate generation approach. Furthermore, most of the existing algorithms, like WINEPI, employ the sliding window technique, e.g. a win-

dow slides across the event sequence one unit a time, where the size of the discovered episodes becomes limited by the window width. A related research area is sequential pattern mining on transaction data. GSP [7] and SPADE [8] use an apriori-like approach while Prefixspan [1] adopt pattern growth strategy. However, those algorithms are not applicable for episode mining, as they have different input formats and definitions of occurrence.

In order to improve the quality of the results and to reduce the processing time, a mining algorithm should allow the user to specify constraints on the desired patterns. The algorithms in [5] allow users to express arbitrary unary constraints on individual events. In [4], Mannila et al expand those constraints to include binary conditions on pairs of events. However, many constraints are not covered. That restricts the usefulness of algorithms, especially in realtime-response mining tasks. In sequential pattern mining area, Srikant and Agrawal [7] introduce time constraints, sliding window, and user-defined taxonomy. Garofalakis et al [3] propose regular expressions as constraints and develop a family of SPIRIT algorithms. In [6], a general property of constraints, prefix-monotone, is identified and applied in PrefixSpan [1], which covers several constraints. However, those proposed techniques for supporting constraints cannot apply directly to episode mining, as there is as yet no prefix-growth algorithm for episode mining.

The above requirements motivate us to find new episode mining solutions that overcome the limitations of existing techniques. In particular, they should satisfy these design objectives: 1) better efficiency and scalability, 2) avoid sliding windows, 3) support general constraints. In this paper, we present two such algorithms – Episode Prefix Tree (EPT) and Position Pairs Set (PPS). EPT is designed to mine frequent episodes by growing their prefixes in the form of a prefix tree. PPS provides a divide-and-conquer strategy to avoid the iterative full sequence scans in EPT. Both algorithms are based on *minimal occurrences* of episodes, which was first introduced in [4]: *an occurrence of an episode P at $[t, t^{'}]$ is minimal if P does not occur at any proper subinterval $[u, u^{'}] \subset [t, t^{'}]$.* In addition to being simple and efficient, this heuristic definition implies that events in episodes are more likely to occur close to each other in time, which is often true in real-life applications.

---

*A full version of this paper can be retrieved from http://www.comp.nus.edu.sg/ tankl/publication/2004/episodes04full.pdf

The remaining of the paper is organized as follows. Section 2 introduces the EPT and PPS algorithms, while Section 3 presents a performance evaluation. Section 4 concludes the paper and discusses future research issues.

2. Episode mining algorithms

This section introduces two algorithms – Episode Prefix Tree (EPT) and Position Pairs Set (PPS). As both algorithms are based on the prefix-growth technique, we will discuss the common components together after introducing the two algorithms. Following that, a comparison of the two proposed algorithms with established algorithms is given.

2.1. Problem description

In the episode model, an event sequence S is a history of events. Given the set $R = \{A_1, ..., A_m\}$ of event attributes with domains $D_{A_1}, ..., D_{A_m}$ respectively, an event e over R is a $(m + 1)$ tuple $(a_1, ... a_m, t)$, where $a_i \in D_{A_i}$ and t is a real number, the time of e. There are three kinds of episodes: 1) serial, defined as an ordered list of events; 2) parallel, defined as a set of events; and 3) composite, defined as an ordered list of sets of events. Constrained frequent episodes are a particular type of episodes that satisfy certain constraints, noted by C, and their occurrences in S satisfy a specified minimum support, noted by min_sup. The mining task is to find the complete set of constrained frequent episodes.

For simplicity, the episodes as mentioned in the rest of this paper refer to serial episodes comprising consecutive events; support for gaps in adjacent events and parallel and composite episodes will be discussed in sections 2.4 and 2.5.

Example 1 *An example of event sequence is shown in Figure 1. With a minimum support of 2, the event sequence contains two possible episodes, $\langle ED \rangle$ and $\langle BC \rangle$.*

Fig. 1: A sequence of event.

2.2. Episode prefix tree (EPT) algorithm

Definition 1 (EPT-tree). An EPT-tree stores the episode prefixes that are at most k in length, where k is a constant called *Depth Threshold*.

- It consists of one root labelled as "null".
- Each internal node registers two pieces of information: the label of an event, and an occurrence count.
- For any node N in the tree, the nodes in the path from root to N (inclusive) form a prefix of episode ending with the event associated with N. The count of N registers the number of occurrences of the corresponding episode.

Property 1 *Non-growth path: A non-growth path ends at a leave node with a counter below the min_sup. Frequent episodes cannot have a prefix that constitutes a non-growth path.*

Property 2 *Depth threshold: The process of building an EPT-tree with depth threshold k and removing non-growth paths can be accomplished in two steps: 1) build an EPT-tree with depth threshold k_1 ($0 < k_1 < k$) then remove non-*

growth paths; and 2) *extend remaining branches by k_2 such that $k_1 + k_2 = k$, then remove non-growth paths. This property can be generalized so that the EPT-tree is constructed in more than two steps.*

Based on the above properties, we have Algorithm 1, which takes as input a series of depth thresholds, $\{k_1, k_2, ..., k_n\}$. The basic idea of the algorithm is to grow the EPT-tree in multiple phases. In each phase, we grow the EPT-tree to the next depth threshold, k_i, and prune all non-growth paths, which entails a scan through S. The algorithm stops there is not more path to grow.

Algorithm 1 EPT
---
i=1
repeat
    scan the event sequence S.
    for all events e_j in S **do**
        find the node nd_j at level $\sum_{l=1}^{i-1} k_l$ in the tree associated with e_j by re-recognizing the prefixes.
        call extend_node (nd_j, S, C, k_i)
    cache the frequent parts of those non-growth paths.
    prune all non-frequent and non-growth paths.
    i=i+1
until there is no path left in the EPT-tree.
output episodes from the cache.

Algorithm 2 extend_node(et, nd, S, C, k_i)

Input: et:the exploring event. nd:the node to be expanded.
if depth $(et) \geq \sum_{l=1}^{i} k_l$ **then**
    return.
next-events set $= \{e_j | e_j$ follows et and satisfies $C\}$
for all events $e_j \in$ *next-events set* **do**
    create a child node $node_j$ of nd associated with e_j if it not present.
    call extend_node($e_j, node_j, S, C, k$)

Correctness Analysis: Let α be a length-l path, and $\{\beta_1, \beta_2, \cdots, \beta_m\}$ be the set of all frequent length-$(l + 1)$ paths having prefix α. Considering the enumeration of event patterns in the above algorithm, the complete set of paths having prefix α can only be composed of elements in the β set and those non-frequent pruned paths, which means the prefix space is searched completely. Hence, EPT returns the complete set of episodes.

Depth Threshold: A finely-tuned threshold series should balance between speed and space consumption, which at present can only be preset by users through trial and error.

2.3. Position pair set (PPS) algorithm

Although the EPT does not generate candidates by growing the episode prefixes, it still leaves ample room for improvement. First, it is tedious to repeatedly scan the sequence and re-recognize the episode prefixes. Moreover, during the next scan a lot of effort is wasted in growing non-frequent branches to k_{i+1} in depth. The PPS algorithm is designed to overcome those costly operations by caching the position of the beginning and ending events of an occurrence of an episode prefix, called *position-pair*.

Prefix	Position-pair sets	Prefix	Position-pair sets
$\langle A \rangle$	(20),(31),(32),(38)	$\langle E \rangle$	(26), (29)
$\langle B \rangle$	(22),(23),(34),(41)	$\langle BC \rangle$	(23,24),(34,35)
$\langle C \rangle$	(24),(35),(39)	$\langle ED \rangle$	(26,28),(29,30)
$\langle D \rangle$	(28), (30)		

Table 1: The prefixes and their position-pairs after adding window-size.

Property 3 *Position-pair: If occurrences of all prefixes of an episode follow the definition of minimal occurrence, then, for each prefix, a position-pair uniquely locates its items in the event sequence. For example, given an event sequence, $\langle CABEBDE \rangle$, the position-pair of episode $\langle ABD \rangle$, is $(2, 6)$, where A is at 2, B at 2 and D at 6.*

Like EPT, PPS works by growing frequent prefixes. However, the strategy that PPS employs is quite different. Whenever an episode prefix is found, all position-pairs of that prefix are cached. During subsequent growth of this episode prefix, only the slices immediately following those position-pairs need to be examined instead of the whole sequence. In other words, position-pairs are used to effectively split S into smaller slices, so that when growing the prefixes, only those slices need to be examined.

Example 2 *Consider the sequence shown in Figure 1 and suppose $min\_sup = 2$. The set of events is $\{A, B, C, D, E, F, G\}$. The frequent episodes in S can be mined in following steps.*

*Step 1. **Find length-1 episodes and their associated position-pairs.** Scan S once to find all frequent episodes. They are A, B, C, D and E.*

*Step 2. **Divide the search space.** The complete set of episodes can be partitioned into the following five subsets according to the five prefixes: (1) those having prefix A; ... ; and (5) those having prefix E.*

*Step 3. **Grow each prefix separately and recursively.** We look for episodes beginning with event E. By checking the event following each position-pair of E, we obtain a frequent episode $\langle ED \rangle$. We then continue to grow the prefix $\langle ED \rangle$ by examining the events following its position-pairs, until no further growth. Table 1 lists the result.*

The PPS algorithm is shown in Algorithm 3; it explores the search space in a depth-first search (DFS) manner.

The correctness of PPS mining algorithm can be proved the same way as for EPT. Due to the introduction of *position-pair*, PPS requires the entire sequence to be hold in main memory. Since all algorithms for finding frequent episodes are CPU-bound, this assumption is not very limiting in practice.

2.4. Constraint support

To support constraints in EPT and PPS, only those events that satisfy the constraints are appended when growing the episodes prefixes, leading to an easy implementation of the numeric prefix constraints such as *time constraints*, *regular expression*, *length constraint*, *duration constraints* and so on. Here, we take the *time constraints* for example, which mainly include: 1)*max-gap*: the maximum allowed time difference between two successive occurrences of events; 2)*min-gap*: the minimum required time difference between

---

Algorithm 3 PPS

> scan S once for 1-length episodes; add them to *active-set*.
> scan S again; find their associated *position-pairs*.
> **while** *active-set* is not empty **do**
>> get next prefix pf_i from the head of *active-set* and its associated *position-pairs*.
>> **for all** $pp_j \in position\text{-}pairs$ **do**
>>> *next-events set =* $\{e_k | e_k$ is in the following slice of pp_j and satisfies $C\}$.
>>> **for all** events $e_k \in next\text{-}events$ set **do**
>>>> append e_k to pf_i and record the *position-pairs* of the new formed prefixes.
>>> **if** $frequency$(new formed prefixes) $> min\_sup$ **then**
>>>> add the new formed prefixes to *active-set*.
>>> **else**
>>>> cache pf_i.
> output episodes from the cache.

---

two successive occurrences of events; 3)*max-during*: the maximum allowed time difference between the latest and earliest occurrences of events. Below is an example involving PPS; EPT operates in a similar way.

Example 3 *Consider the sequence shown in Figure 1, and suppose max-gap=3, min-gap=1. The next-events after the first B is $\{B:[(23)], C:[(24)]\}$, thus two prefixes $\langle BB \rangle$ and $\langle BC \rangle$ are found instead of one prefix in the no-constraint case. The 2-length and 3-length prefixes are listed in Table 2. Note that the max-gap and min-gap constraints introduce gaps between adjacent events.*

Prefix	Position-pair sets	Prefix	Position-pair sets
$\langle AB \rangle$	(20,22),(32,34),(38,41)	$\langle ED \rangle$	(26,28),(29,30)
$\langle AC \rangle$	(32,35),(38,39)	$\langle ABC \rangle$	(20,24),(32,35)
$\langle BC \rangle$	(23,24),(34,35)		

Table 2: The prefixes and their position-pairs after applying time-constraints.

2.5. Parallel episode and composite episode

Up till this point, we have discussed only serial episodes. The two proposed algorithms can also mine parallel and composite episodes; the former are specialized forms of the latter. To mine composite episodes, we extend the definition of episode prefixes to include parallel components. That is, we allow this forms of prefix, $\langle A(BC)D \rangle$ where the relative order between B and C is immaterial. The mining process is the same as that for serial episodes, except that appending an event from *next-events* to a prefix leads to two extended prefixes — one is appended as a separate component of the prefix, while the other is merged into the last component of the prefix. For example, after appending E to $\langle A(BC)D \rangle$, we get $\langle A(BC)DE \rangle$ and $\langle A(BC)(DE) \rangle$.

2.6. Discussion

Both proposed algorithms utilize an episode-growth strategy, thus no candidate episode is generated. Therefore, EPT and PPS search a much smaller space compared to Apriori-like algorithms. Our algorithms do not have sliding windows, so there is no restriction on the length of discovered episodes. While MINEPI does not apply sliding windows either, it cannot identify some occurrences of episodes due to algorithm limitation. For example, in slice $\langle ABBC \rangle$, the minimal occurrence of $\langle AB \rangle$ and $\langle BC \rangle$ do not overlap, so MINEPI cannot recognize the candidate ABC. In contrast, our proposed algorithms can correctly identify those episodes.

3. Performance study

In this section, we present a performance comparison of EPT and PPS with MINEPI that also uses the minimal occurrences. Nevertheless, in most cases, the mining result of MINEPI is slightly different from our proposed algorithms due to its own limitation (see Section 2.6). All the experiments are performed on an Intel PC with a 2 GHz Pentium 4 CPU, 512 MB memory.

Parameter	Description	Range
$S_{sequence}$	Size of the event sequence	20,000~2,000,000
T_{event}	Number of event type	300~10,000
N_{fe}	Number of frequent episodes	100~5,000
L_{avg_fe}	Average length of episodes	5~100

Table 3: Synthetic Database Parameter.

The experiments are conducted on both synthetic and real sequences. The synthetic single sequences are generated by a modified version of the data generator from IBM AssocGen [7] and labelled with the parameters in Table 3, e.g. *T500N100L5S200k* indicates a sequence generated with $T = 500, N = 100, L = 5, S = 200,000$. The real sequences are derived from a collection of text documents. Due to the consistent results we report here only results for *L2* which has 153799 events with 8345 event types.

The parameters required by the mining algorithms are min_sup and C such as *max-gap, max-span*. The default depth threshold series for EPT is $\{1, 1, 1, \ldots\}$. The primary performance metric is the runtime inclusive of CPU time and I/O time.

Figures 2 and 3 show the execution times of algorithms with different min_sup. On synthetic sequences, PPS is much more efficient than EPT and MINEPI, while EPT is faster than MINEPI at low support thresholds. On real-data sequences *L2*, unlike MINEPI, EPT and PPS degrade much slower as the minimum support decreases. MINEPI performs the worst because it generates too many candidates. Similar results can be observed in experiments varying $S_{sequence}$, as the effect of increasing $S_{sequence}$ is similar to that of decreasing the min_sup.

As shown in Figure 4, EPT and PPS cope better with longer episodes, whereas MINEPI cannot handle long episodes well. This is because, unlike MINEPI, EPT and PPS do not generate many short episodes.

To evaluate the effect of a constraint, we define the selectivity of a constraint as the ratio of the number of episodes satisfying the constraint over the total number of episodes. The results of *max-during* constraints are shown in Figure 5. When the selectivity is low, i.e., many episodes do not satisfy the constraints, significant gains can be observed for both PPS and EPT.

To summarize, we can safely conclude that PPS outper-

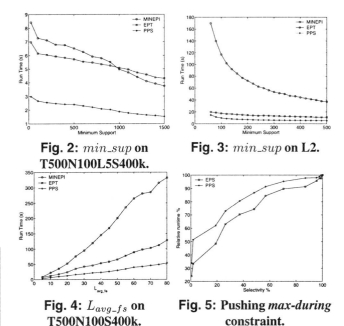

Fig. 2: min_sup on **T500N100L5S400k.**

Fig. 3: min_sup on L2.

Fig. 4: L_{avg_fs} on **T500N100S400k.**

Fig. 5: Pushing *max-during* constraint.

forms EPT and MINEPI by a large margin. PPS achieves good execution times with varying min_sup, $S_{sequence}$ and L_{avg_fs}. PPS also occupies the least memory due to the DFS search strategy despite the entire sequence in memory. The related experiments is not included due to space limit.

4. Conclusion

Existing episode mining algorithms have two limitations: 1) restricting the length of result episodes, caused by the use of sliding window; 2) lack of flexible constraints-support ability, and inefficiency especially at low support thresholds, caused by the apriori-like mining methodology. In this paper, we introduce two algorithms, Episode Prefix Tree (EPT) and Position Pairs Set (PPS), to overcome those limitations. Based on *minimal occurrences* of episodes, both algorithms mine for frequent episodes by growing their prefixes and allow a systematic way to push various constraints into the mining process. Performance study shows that the proposed algorithms run considerably faster than MINEPI [4], especially on real datasets. Between the two algorithms, PPS is more efficient and requires less memory than EPT. For future work, we will extend the proposed algorithms toward mining data streams.

References

[1] J. Pei, J.-W. Han et al. Prefixspan: Mining sequential patterns efficiently by prefix-projected pattern growth. In *ICDE'01*.
[2] C.-R. Lin, C.-H. Yun, and M.-S. Chen. Utilizing slice scan and selective hash for episode mining. In *KDD'01*.
[3] M. Garofalakis, R. Rastogi et al. Spirit: Sequential pattern mining with regular expression constraints. In *VLDB'99*.
[4] H. Mannila and H. Toivonen. Discovering generalized episodes using minimal occurrences. In *KDD'96*.
[5] H. Mannila, H. Toivonen, and A. Verkamo. Discovering frequent episodes in sequences. In *KDD'95*.
[6] J. Pei, J. Han, and W. Wang. Mining sequential patterns with constraints in large databases. In *CIKM'02*.
[7] R. Srikant and R. Agrawal. Mining sequential patterns: Generalizations and performance improvements. In *EDBT'96*.
[8] M. J. Zaki. SPADE: An efficient algorithm for mining frequent sequences. *Machine Learning*, 2001.

Estimation of False Negatives in Classification [*][†]

Sandeep Mane, Jaideep Srivastava
Department of Computer Science
University of Minnesota
Minneapolis, USA
{smane, srivasta}@cs.umn.edu

San-Yih Hwang
Department of Information Management
National Sun-Yat-Sen University
Kaohsiung, Taiwan
shwang@cs.umn.edu

Jamshid Vayghan
IBM Corporation
Minneapolis, USA
vayghan@us.ibm.com

Abstract

In many classification problems such as spam detection and network intrusion, a large number of unlabeled test instances are predicted negative by the classifier. However, the high costs as well as time constraints on an expert's time prevent further analysis of the "predicted false" class instances in order to segregate the false negatives from the true negatives. A systematic method is thus required to obtain an estimate of the number of false negatives. A capture-recapture based method can be used to obtain an ML-estimate of false negatives when two or more independent classifiers are available. In the case for which independence does not hold, we can apply log-linear models to obtain an estimate of false negatives. However, as shown in this paper, lesser the dependencies among the classifiers, better is the estimate obtained for false negatives. Thus, ideally independent classifiers should be used to estimate the false negatives in an unlabeled dataset. Experimental results on the spam dataset from the UCI Machine Learning Repository are presented.

1 Introduction

Detecting intrusions in a computer network can be considered as a 2-class classification problem. The task is to analyze each network flow and label it as 'suspicious' or 'normal'. [1] There are some unique characteristics of this problem. First, the rate of data generation is very high, e.g. 200,000-300,000 connections per minute. Second, the oc-

currence of 'intrusions' is much rarer than the occurrence of 'normal' traffic. For such a dataset, a classifier will label relatively very few instances as positive as compared to those labeled negative. The predicted positive instances can be given to an expert who can further analyze them in order to separate the true positives from the false positives. However, the negatively classified instances, being much larger in number, would require an unacceptable amount of time to separate the false negatives from the true negatives. Thus, getting a complete picture of classifier accuracy, e.g. ROC curves, is infeasible. However, since the cost of a false negative may be much higher than of a false positive, e.g. an actual attack being missed, obtaining at least an estimate of false negatives predicted by the classifier is required. This, for example, can be used to estimate false negatives detected by two intrusion detection systems (say SNORT – *http://www.snort.org/* and MINDS – *http://www.cs.umn.edu/research/minds/MINDS.htm*) for an unlabeled dataset, and then comparing their performance.

In the commercial domain, an example of this problem is the estimation of missed opportunities during the sales opportunity analysis process (Vayghan et al. [11]). Here, once a sales opportunity has been classified as negative (not promising) by a human expert (e.g. a business manager), there is no further analysis of that opportunity in order to verify whether it was actually unprofitable or there was a judgment error. A method for estimating the number of false negatives predicted by the decision maker would be useful to estimate the accuracy of the human expert w.r.t. the ground truth (actual outcome). Furthermore, for an individual decision maker, it will help identify strengths and weakness in different domains of opportunities, e.g. the ability to identify 'hardware-selling opportunities' vs. the ability to identify 'software-services opportunities'.

The examples above motivate the need for estimating false negatives for a classifier on an unlabeled dataset. In this paper we present a methodology for obtaining such an estimate for false negatives based on the classical capture-recapture method for parameter estimation in statistics. In addition, we also illustrate a number of important issues

---

[*] Sandeep Mane's and Jaideep Srivastava's work was supported in part by NSF Grant ISS-0308264, ARDA Grant F30602-03-C-0243, and a grant from IBM. San-Yih Hwang's work was supported by a Fulbright scholarship. Jamshid Vayghan's work was supported by the IBM Corporation.

[†] The authors would like to acknowledge comments from Prof. Vipin Kumar and Dr. Philip Yu which led to the formulation of this problem.

[1] Data mining is suitable for detecting novel, i.e. previously unseen, attacks. In such a case, automated techniques can only identify unusual or suspicious behavior. An expert analyst must then examine it to determine if it is truly an intrusion.

that need to be explored in making the application of this method practicable. The remainder of this paper is organized as follows: section 2 provides a brief overview of the approach and related work, section 3 presents experimental results, and section 4 concludes future research directions.

2 General approach and related work

Hook and Regal [8] present a survey on false negative estimation in epidemiology using two or more detection methods (classifiers) and the capture-recapture method [4]. Goldberg and Wittes [6] present a generalized approach to false estimation for the multi-class classification problem, which is illustrated using the 2-class case. Consider a labeled dataset which is classified by a $\{True, False\}$-class classifier, whose confusion matrix for the classifier is shown in the Table 1.

		Actual class		
		True	False	Total
Predicted	True	TP	FP	PP
class	False	FN	TN	PN
	Total	AP	AN	N

Table 1: Confusion matrix for a classifier

Here, TP, FP, FN and TN represent the numbers of *true positives*, *false positives*, *false negatives* and *true negatives* respectively. Also, AP, AN, PP and PN are the numbers of *actual positives*, *actual negatives*, *predicted positives* and *predicted negatives* instances, while N is the total number of instances in the dataset. Actual positives are the instances in the dataset whose actual (real) class is *True*. The performance of the classifier can be determined using this confusion matrix.

However, for a skewed-class distribution classifier with a very high data volume, e.g. network intrusion detection, for a given unlabeled dataset only the predicted positive instances are manually classified into true positives and false positives. The predicted negative instances, being very large in number, are not analyzed further by the human expert. Thus, the confusion table for the classifier for the dataset will look as shown in Table 2.

		Actual class	
		True	False
Predicted	True	TP	FP
class	False	FN + TN	

Table 2: Confusion matrix for a rare-class, large-dataset classifier.

The notation used in Table 2 is identical to that in Table 1. Here, only the total (TP+FN) can be obtained. Now, if AP in the dataset is known, then, from the Table 1, FN can be determined. (This is because TP+FN=AP) Thus, the method for estimation of FN is based on the estimation of AP in the dataset.

The main idea behind the method for estimating actual positives using the capture-recapture method can be explained using the following example problem.

Problem: Estimate the number of fish in a pond.
Estimation Method: A two step method, called the 'capture' and 'recapture' steps, is used for this. In step one (capture), let f_1 be the number of fish caught, which are then marked (presumably with an indelible ink) and released in the lake. In the second step (recapture), let f_2 be the number of fish that are caught (presumably after sufficient time to allow the fishes to mix, but not mate and produce more fishes, or even die). Let f_{12} be the number of fish caught in second step, which are found to be marked. Under the stated assumptions, f_{12} will follow a hyper-geometric distribution, since the process is equivalent to 'selection with replacement'. Thus, the estimate for the total number of the fish in the lake is $\left(\frac{f_1 * f_2}{f_{12}}\right)$. Now, if the actual positive instances in the dataset are compared to fish in the lake, then the capture-recapture methodology can be used to estimate the number of actual positives in the dataset, given that the two steps (samplings) are independent of each other. Thus, for applying this technique, there is a need for at least two independent classifiers (detection methods). It should be noted that this method can be extended to the case where more than two independent samplings are available. ∎

We now explain the method for estimating the number of actual positives using the capture-recapture method and the classifiers in detail.

		APs detected by classifier 1		
		Yes	No	Total
APs detected	Yes	n_{11}	n_{12}	n_2
by classifier 2	No	n_{21}	n_{22}	n_4
	Total	n_1	n_3	n

Table 3: Contingency table of actual positives for the case of two classifiers

Suppose that two independent classifiers classify the two-class dataset. Let n_1 and n_2 be the number of true positive instances detected by the first and second classifiers, respectively. Let n_{11} be the number of true positives detected by both classifiers. Also, as shown in Table 3, let n_{12} be the actual positive instances classified as *True* by only the first classifier and let n_{21} be the actual positive instances classified as *True* by only the second classifier. The value n_{22}, the number of actual positive instances not detected (i.e. classified *False*) by both classifiers, is unknown and needs to be estimated. The sum n of the values in all the cells of the Table 3 is equal to the number of actual positives in the dataset. If the two classifiers are independent, then the ML-estimate for the unknown value n_{22}, as shown by Goldberg and Wittes [6], is : $n_{22} = \left(\frac{n_{12} * n_{21}}{n_{11}}\right)$.

Wittes et al. [14, 13] discuss the problems arising from decision making in the capture and recapture steps being dependent. If so, i.e. when independence does not hold between the variables in the contingency table, log-linear models (Knoke and Burke [9]) must be used for the contingency table. Fienberg [5] describes a method for constructing log-linear models for the contingency table in such cases and obtaining the best-fitting model. In this approach, the conditional relationship between two or more discrete categorical variables (here, the class labels assigned by the classifiers are discrete categorical variables) is analyzed by taking the natural logarithm of the cell frequencies within a contingency table. For example, for the contingency Table 3, the following model is used to represent the expected frequency of each cell (i,j) in the table –

$$\text{Ln}(F_{ij}) = \mu + \lambda_i^A + \lambda_j^B + \lambda_{ij}^{AB}$$

where, $\text{Ln}(F_{ij})$ is the log of the expected cell frequency of the instances in the cell (i,j) in the contingency table; μ is the overall mean of the natural log of the expected frequencies; A and B are the variables (APs detected by each classifier); i,j refer to the categories within the variables; λ_i^A is the main effect of the variable A on the cell frequency; λ_i^B is the main effect of the variable B on the cell frequency; and λ_{ij}^{AB} is the interaction effect of variables A and B on cell frequency.

The basic strategy involves fitting a set of such models to the observed frequencies in all cells of the table. In fitting these models, no distinction is made between independent and dependent variables, i.e. log-linear models demonstrate the general association between variables. Different sets of models depending upon various possible dependencies among the variables are fitted to the table. A log-linear model for the entire table can thus be represented as a set of expected frequencies (which may or may not represent the observed frequencies). Such a model is described in terms of the marginals it fits and the dependencies that are assumed to be present in the data. Iterative computation methods for fitting such a model to a table are described in Christensen [2]. Using deviance measures, e.g. the likelihood ratio or χ^2 measure, as a measure of the goodness-of-fit for a model, the best-fitting, parsimonious (least number of dependencies) model for the table is determined. This model is then used to estimate of the unknown value n_{22}. The purpose of log-linear modeling is thus to choose minimum dependencies in a model for the given cells, while achieving a good goodness-of-fit. This method requires is computationally intensive since models corresponding to all possible dependencies among the variables need to be computed. The disadvantage of this method is that a sufficiently large amount of data (cell values) is required for obtaining a good estimation of the contingency table model. Also, high degrees of association among the variables makes it difficult to comprehend the model. [2]

---

[2]The capture-recapture method for false estimation thus requires modeling of concepts for independent, quasi-independent and dependent con-

The Figure 1 illustrates the method of estimating actual positives (and hence false negatives) using m classifiers. Given m different classifiers and a dataset, the number of

Figure 1: Method for estimation of false negatives.

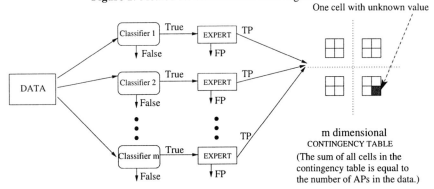

true positives detected by each of the m classifiers is determined and cross-tabulated in a contingency table. One cell in the contingency table will be unknown, which corresponds to the number of actual positives not detected by all m classifiers. Using ML-estimation technique or log-linear model (depending upon whether independence does or does not hold), an estimate for the unknown cell is obtained. Thus, the total number of actual positives is estimated. The assumption to be noted is that the classifiers used in the capture-recapture method do a good job of keeping the number of false positives low. This helps to keep the number of instances to be manually classified by experts low. Once an estimate of the number of actual positives, $\widehat{AP}$ in dataset has been obtained, the same dataset is classified using a classifier whose performance (accuracy) is to be evaluated. The instances predicted *True* by the classifier are analyzed manually to separate TP and FP. Next, the estimate $\widehat{AP}$ is used to estimate the false negatives ($\widehat{FN}$) and true negatives ($\widehat{TN}$) detected by the classifier. Using these estimates, the performance (accuracy) of the classifier is evaluated.

3 Experimental work

For experimental work, a two-class classification problem using the SPAM email dataset [1] was used. Goldberg and Wittes [6] defined independence of two classifiers as disjoint feature sets. Instead of using disjoint condition as the only criterion for independence, we quantified independence in terms of independence of feature sets, using mutual information [3]. Three disjoint subsets for the dataset were obtained and three different decision tree classifiers A, B and C were trained (using WEKA [12]). As all the features were continuous and due to the limited amount of

---

tingency tables which are summarized by Goodman [7].

Figure 2: Pair-wise mutual information given class 'True' for features used by the classifiers

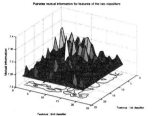 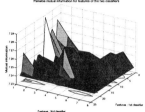

(a) Classifiers A and B   **(b)** Classifiers A and C

training data, it was not possible to decide the independence of two feature subsets (in terms of mutual information). In other words, it was not possible to estimate the exact mutual information between two feature subsets, each having sufficiently large number of continuous features. This is an effect of the curse of dimensionality. To overcome this, we instead computed the pair-wise mutual information (MI) [10] between the individual features pairs for each pair of classifiers. The plots of MI for two pairs of classifers, namely (A,B) and (A,C), are shown in Figure 2. [3] It was noted that the feature pairs for the classifiers A and B were on average more pair-wise dependent than feature pairs of classifiers A and C.

The classifiers A, B and C were used to classify the test dataset and the numbers of TPs detected by each classifier were determined. The TPs for each pair of classifiers were cross-tabulated into a contingency table and then the number of APs not detected by all classifiers was estimated using log-linear models. Since the test dataset used was labeled, the number of APs actually missed by all the classifiers was also determined. The results were summarized in the Table 4. The classifiers A, B and C had an approximate

Classifiers used	No. of APs not detected by both classifiers (Using labels for test data)	No. of APs not detected by both classifiers (Using log-linear modeling)
A and B	31	4
A and C	5	3
B and C	8	3

Table 4: Cross-tabulation of missed APs and estimated APs.

training accuracy of 95%, 93% and 74% respectively. Thus, it is noted that even though classifier B had higher accuracy than classifier C, the pair of classifiers A and C gave a better estimate of the total number of actual positives than the pair of classifiers A and B.

---

[3]Note: The range for Z-axis is different for two subfigures. Also light color represents more MI and vice versa. In subfigure (a), the features of the first classifier (A) were plotted along the X-axis and that of the second classifier (B) along the Y-axis. Likewise for subfigure(b).

4 Conclusions

In this paper, a capture-recapture based method for the estimation of false negatives has been presented. The need for having independent classifiers for the method of estimation of false negatives was illustrated using a real-world dataset. Furthermore, it was shown that if the pair-wise MI between the features of a pair of classifiers is low – even if that pair of classifiers has relatively lower accuracy than another pair of classifiers – it may be possible to obtain a better estimate of missed APs using the former pair. Thus, a better estimate for total number of APs, and hence for false negatives, is obtained using independent classifiers. Our current research will address the issues in obtaining *sufficiently accurate* and *independent classifiers* for a given dataset.

References

[1] C. Blake and C. Merz. UCI repository of machine learning databases, 1998.

[2] R. Christensen. *Log-Linear Models and Logistic Regression.* Springer-Verlag Inc, New York, USA, 1997.

[3] T. M. Cover and J. A. Thomas. *Elements of Information Theory.* New York: Wiley, 1991.

[4] J. N. Darroch. The multiple-recapture census: I. estimation of a closed population. *Biometrika*, 45(3/4), 1958.

[5] S. E. Fienberg. An iterative procedure for estimation in contingency tables. *Ann. Math. Stat.*, 41(3), 1970.

[6] J. Goldberg and J. Wittes. The estimation of false negatives in medical screening. *Biometrics*, 34(1):77–86, March 1978.

[7] L. A. Goodman. The analysis of cross-classified data: independence, quasi-independence and interactions in contingency tables with or without missing entries. *J. Amer. Stat. Assn.*, 63(324), 1968.

[8] E. B. Hook and R. R. Regal. Capture-recapture methods in epidemiology: methods and limitations. *Epid. Reviews*, 17(2), 1995.

[9] D. Knoke and P. Burke. *Log-Linear Models.* Sage Publications, Inc. USA, 1980.

[10] R. Moddemeijer. On estimation of entropy and mutual information of continuous distributions. *Sig. Proc.*, 16, 1989.

[11] J. Vayghan, J. Srivastava, S. Mane, P. Yu, and G. Adomavicius. Sales opportunity miner: Data mining for automatic evaluation of sales opportunity. *Book Chapter in New Generation of Data Mining Applications edited by Mehmed Kantardzic and Jozef Zurada*, 2004.

[12] I. H. Witten and E. Frank. *Data Mining: Practical machine learning tools with Java implementations.* Morgan Kaufmann, San Francisco, 2000.

[13] J. Wittes. Applications of a multinomial capture-recapture model to epidemiological data. *J. Amer. Stat. Assn.*, 69(345), 1974.

[14] J. Wittes, T. Colton, and V. Sidel. Capture-recapture methods for assessing the completeness of case ascertainment when using multiple information sources. *J. Chronic Diseases*, 27(1), 1974.

Correlation Preserving Discretization *

Sameep Mehta, Srinivasan Parthasarathy and Hui Yang

Department of Computer Science and Engineering, The Ohio State University

Contact: (mehtas,srini,yanghu)@cse.ohio-state.edu

Abstract

Discretization is a crucial preprocessing primitive for a variety of data warehousing and mining tasks. In this article we present a novel PCA-based unsupervised algorithm for the discretization of continuous attributes in multivariate datasets. The algorithm leverages the underlying correlation structure in the dataset to obtain the discrete intervals, and ensures that the inherent correlations are preserved. The approach also extends easily to datasets containing missing values. We demonstrate the efficacy of the approach on real datasets and as a preprocessing step for both classification and frequent itemset mining tasks. We also show that the intervals are meaningful and can uncover hidden patterns in data.

Keywords: Unsupervised Discretization, Missing Data

1 Introduction

Discretization is a widely used data preprocessing primitive. It has been frequently used for classification in the decision tree context, as well as for summarization in situations where one needs to transform a continuous attribute into a discrete one with minimum "loss of information". Dougherty *et al* [3] present an excellent classification of current methods in discretization. A majority of the discretization methods in the literature [2, 4, 6, 10, 13, 14] are supervised in nature and are geared towards minimizing error in classification algorithms. Such methods are not general-purpose and cannot, for instance, be used as a preprocessing step for frequent itemset algorithms.

In this article we propose a general-purpose unsupervised algorithm for discretization based on the *correlation structure* inherent in the dataset. Closely related to our work is the recent work by Bay[1] and Ludl and Widmer[9]. Bay proposed an approach for discretization that also considers the interactions among all attributes. The main limitation of this approach is that it can be computationally expensive, and impractically so for high dimensional and large datasets. Ludl and Widmer [9] propose a similar approach however the interactions amongst attributes considered in their work is only pair-wise and piecemeal.

In this work we present a PCA-based algorithm for discretization of continuous attributes in multivariate datasets. Our algorithm uses the distribution of *both* categorical and

*This work is funded by NSF grants ITR-NGS ACI-0326386, CAREER IIS-0347662 and SOFTWARE ACI-0234273.

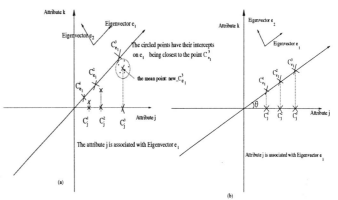

Figure 1. (a) K-NN (b)Direct Projection

continuous attributes and the underlying correlation structure in the dataset to obtain the discrete intervals. This approach also ensures that *all attributes are used simultaneously* for deciding the cut-points, rather than pairwise or one attribute at a time. An additional advantage is that the approach extends naturally to datasets with missing data.

We demonstrate the efficacy of the above algorithms as a preprocessing step for classical data mining algorithms such as frequent itemset mining and classification. Extensive experimental results on real and synthetic datasets demonstrate the discovery of meaningful intervals for continuous attributes and accuracy in prediction of missing values.

2 Algorithm

Our algorithm is composed of the following steps:

1. Normalization and Mean Centralization: The first step involves normalizing all the continuous attributes and mean centralizing the data.

Rationale: This is a standard preprocessing step [12].

2. Eigenvector Computation: We next compute the correlation matrix M from the data. We then compute the eigenvectors $\vec{e_1}, \ldots, \vec{e_d}$ from M. To find these eigenvectors, we rely on the popular Householder reduction to tridiagonal form and then apply the QL transform [5]. Once these eigenvectors have been determined, we retain only those that preserve 90% of the variance in the data.

Rationale: Retaining only those eigen vectors that are acounted for most of variance enables us to keep most of the correlations present among the continuous attributes in the dataset. Dimensionality reduction facilitates scalability.

3. Data Projection onto Eigen Space: Next, we project each data point in the original dataset D onto the eigen space formed by the vectors retained from the previous step. **Rationale:** To take advantage of dimensionality reduction.

4. Discretization in Eigen Space: We discretize each of the dimensions in the eigen space. Our approach to discretization depends on whether we have categorical attributes or not. If there are no categorical attributes, we apply a simple distance-based clustering along each dimension to derive a set of cut-points. If the dataset contains categorical attributes, our approach is as follows. First, we compute the frequent itemsets generated from all categorical attributes in the original dataset D (for a user-determined support value). Let us refer to this as set A. We then split the eigen dimension $\overrightarrow{e_i}$ into equal-frequency intervals and compute the frequent itemsets in each interval that are constrained to being a subset of A. Next, we compute the similarity between contiguous intervals B and C as follows:

For an element $x \in B$ (respectively in C), let $\sup_{d_1}(x)$ (respectively $\sup_{d_2}(x)$) be the frequency of x in d_1 (respectively in d_2). Our metric is defined as:

$$Sim(d_1, d_2) = \frac{\sum_{x \in B \cap C} \max\{0, 1 - \alpha| \sup_{d_1}(x) - \sup_{d_2}(x)|\}}{\|B \cup C\|}$$

where α is a scaling parameter. If the similarity exceeds a user defined threshold the contiguous intervals are merged. Again, we are left with a set of cut-points along each eigen dimension.

Rationale and Key Intuitions: First, there is no need to consider the influence of the other components in the eigen space since the second order correlations are zero after the PCA reduction, Second, the use of frequent itemsets (as a constraint measure) ensures that correlations w.r.t. the categorical attributes are captured effectively.

5. Correlating Original Dimensions with Eigenvectors: The next step is to determine which original dimensions correlate most with which eigenvectors. This can be computed by finding the contribution of dimension j on each of the eigenvectors ($\overrightarrow{e_1}, \ldots, \overrightarrow{e_n}$), scaled by the corresponding eigenvalue and picking the maximum [7].

Rationale: This step is analogous to computing factor loadings in factor analysis. This step ensures that the set of original dimensions associated with a single eigenvector have corresponding discrete intervals, which ensures that these original dimensions remain correlated with one another.

6. Reprojecting Eigen cutpoints to Original Dimensions: We consider two strategies which are explained below.

a. K-NN method: To project the cut-point $c_{e_i}^1$ onto the original dimension j, we first find the k nearest neighbor intercepts of $c_{e_i}^1$ on the eigenvector $\overrightarrow{e_i}$. The original points $p_1, \ldots, p_k$, representing each of the k nearest neighbors, as well as $c_{e_i}^1$, are obtained (as shown in Figure 1a). We then compute the mean (or median) value of of these points. This mean (or median) value represents the corresponding cut-point along the original dimension j.

b. Direct projection: In this approach, to project the cut points $c_{e_i}^1, \ldots, c_{e_i}^n$ onto the original dimension j, we need to find the angle θ_{ij} between eigenvector $\overrightarrow{e_i}$ and dimension j. The process is shown in Figure 1b. Now the cut-points $c_{e_i}^1 \ldots c_{e_i}^n$ can be projected to the original dimension j by multiplying it with $cos(\theta_{ij})$.

The re-projection will give us the intervals on the original dimensions. However, it is possible that we get some intervals that involves an insignificant number of real data points. In this case, we merge them with its adjacent intervals according to a user-defined threshold.

Key Intuition: If eigenvector $\overrightarrow{e_i}$ is associated with more than one original dimension (especially common in high dimensional datasets), the cut-points along that eigenvector $\overrightarrow{e_i}$ are projected back onto all associated original dimensions, *which enables the discretization method to preserve the inherent correlation in the data.*

Handling Missing Data: Incomplete datasets *seemingly* pose the following problems for our discretization method. First, if values for continuous attributes are missing, steps 1 through 3, of our algorithm will be affected. Fortunately, our PCA-based discretization approach enables us to handle missing values for continuous attributes effectively by adopting recent work by Parthasarathy and Aggarwal [12]. Second, if categorical attributes are missing they can affect step 4 of our algorithm. However, our premise is that, when entries are missing at random, the structure of the rest of the data, within a given interval, will enable us to identify the relevant frequent patterns; thus ensuring that the similarity metric computation is mostly unaffected. More details on the algorithms can be found in our technical report[11].

3 Experimental Results and Analysis

In Table 1 we describe the datasets[1] on which we evaluate the proposed algorithms. In terms of algorithmic settings, for our K-NN approach the value of K we select for all experiments is 4. Our default similarity metric threshold (for merging intervals) is 0.8 ($\alpha = 0$).

Dataset	Records	#Attributes	#Continuous
Adult	48844	14	6
Shuttle	43500	9	9
Musk (1)	476	164	164
Musk (2)	6598	164	164
Cancer	683	8	8
Bupa	345	6	6
Credit	690	14	6
Credit2	1000	20	7

Table 1. Datasets Used in Evaluation

Qualitative Results Based on Association Rules: In this section we focus on the discretization of the Adult dataset (containing both categorical and continuous attributes) as a preprocessing step for obtaining association rules and compare it with published work on multivariate discretization.

---

[1]All the datasets are obtained from UCI Data Repository

Specifically, we compare with ME-MDL (supervised) using salary as the class attribute and MVD (unsupervised), limiting ourselves only to those attributes discussed by Bay[1].

First, upon glancing at the results in Table 2 it is clear that KNN, MVD and Projection all outperform ME-MDL in terms of identifying meaningful intervals (also reported by Bay[1]). Moreover, ME-MDL seems to favor more number of cut-points many of which have little or no latent information. For the rest of the discussion we limit ourselves to comparing the first three methods.

Variable	Method	Cut-points
age	**Projection**	19, 23, 25, 29, 34, 37, 40, 63, 85
	KNN	19, 23, 24, 29, 33, 41, 44, 62
	MVD	19, 23, 25, 29, 33, 41, 62
	ME-MDL	21.5, 23.5, 24.5, 27.5, 29.5, 30.5, 35.5, 61.5, 67.5, 71.5
capital gain	**Projection**	12745
	KNN	7298, 9998
	MVD	5178
	ME-MDL	5119, 5316.5, 6389, 6667.5, 7055.5, 7436.5, 8296, 10041, 10585.5, 21045.5, 26532, 70654.5
capital loss	**Projection**	165
	KNN	450
	MVD	155
	ME-MDL	1820.5, 1859, 1881.5, 1894.5, 1927.5, 1975.5, 1978.5, 2168.5, 2203, 2218.5, 2310.5, 2364.5, 2384.5, 2450.5, 2581
hours/week	**Projection**	23, 28, 38, 40, 41, 48, 52
	KNN	19, 20, 25, 32, 40, 41, 50, 54
	MVD	30, 40, 41, 50
	ME-MDL	34.5, 41.5, 49.5, 61.5, 90.5

Table 2. Cut-points from different methods on *Adult*

For the *age* attribute, at a coarse-grained level, we would like to note that the cut-points obtained between the different methods are quite similar and quite intuitive. Similarly for the *capital loss* attribute, all methods return a single cutpoint, and the cutpoint returned by both Projection and MVD are almost identical. For the *capital gain* attribute, there is some difference in terms of the cutpoint values returned by all three methods. Using KNN we were able to get even better cut-points than the other two methods. It divides the entire range into three intervals, i.e., $(\$0, \$7298)$ low gain, which has 1981 people, $(\$7299, \$9998)$ moderate gain, having 920 people and $(\$9999, MAX)$ high gain, having 1134 people. For the above three attributes we get many of the same association rules that Bay reports in his paper. Details are provided in our technical report[11].

The *hours/week* attribute is one where we get significantly different cut-points from MVD. For example MVD's first cut-point is at 30 hours/week which implies anyone working less than 30 hours is similar. This includes people in the age group (5 to 27), which is a group of very different people with respect to working habits, education level etc. Yet all of these are grouped together in MVD. Using KNN we obtained the first cut-point at 19 hours/week. We are thus able to extract the rule $Hours/week \leq 19 \Rightarrow age \leq 20$, which makes sense as children and young adults typically work less than 20 hours a week while others (≥ 20 years) typically work longer hours. As another example, we obtain a rule that states that "people who work more than 54 hours a week typically earn less than 50K". Most likely this refers to blue-collar workers. More differences among the different methods is detailed in our technical report[11].

In terms of quantitative experiments, we could not really compare with the MVD method as the source/executable code was not available to us. We will point out that for the large datasets (both in terms of dimensionality and number of records), our approaches take on the order of a few seconds in running time. Our benefits over MVD in terms of execution time stem from the fact that we use PCA to reduce the dimensionality of the problem and the fact that we compute one set of cut-points on each principal component and project the resulting cut-points onto the original dimension(s) simultaneously.

Qualitative Results Using Classification: For both the direct projection and KNN algorithm, we bootstrap the results with the C4.5 decision tree classifier. We compare our approach against various classifiers supported by the Weka data mining toolkit[2]. We note that most of these classifiers use a supervised discretization algorithm whereas our approach is unsupervised. For evaluating our approaches, once the discretization has been performed, we append the class labels back to the discretized datasets and run C4.5. All results use 10-fold cross-validation.

Table 3 shows the mis-classification rates of our approaches (last two columns) as compared to seven other different classifiers (first seven columns). First, on viewing the results it is clear that our methods coupled with C4.5 often outperform the other approaches (including C4.5 itself) and especially so on high dimensional datasets (Musk(1) and Musk(2)). The Bupa dataset is the only one on which our methods perform marginally worse, and this may be attributed to the fact that the correlation structure of this dataset is weak[12].

Experiments with Missing Data: Our first experiment compares the impact of missing data on the classification results on three of the datasets. We randomly eliminated a certain percentage of the data and then adopted the approach described in Section 2. Table 4 documents these results. One can observe that the classification error is not affected much by the missing data, even if there is 30% of the data missing. This indicates that our discretization approach can tolerate missing data quite well.

In the second experiment, we randomly eliminated a percentage of the categorical components from the dataset and

---

[2]http://www.cs.waikato.ac.nz/ ml/

Dataset	C4.5	IBK	PART	Bayes	ONER	Kernel-based	SMO	Projection	KNN
Adult	**15.7**	20.35		15.8	16.8	19.54	17	**15.7**	**15.7**
Shuttle	0	0	0	5.1	0	0	0	0	0
Musk (1)	17.3	17.2	18.9	25.7	39.4	17.3	15.6	**14.1**	14.6
Musk (2)	4.7	4.7	4.1	16.2	9.2	5.1	N/A	**4.1**	**4.1**
Cancer	5.4	4.3	4.8	**4.1**	8.2	5.1	4.3	**4.1**	**4.1**
Bupa	**32**	40	35	45	45	36	43	33	34
Credit	15	14.9	17	23.3.	15.5	17.4	15	**14.8**	**14.9**

Table 3. Classification Results (error comparison - best results in bold)

Dataset	Original	10% Missing	20% Missing	30% Missing
Adult	15.7%	16%	17%	19%
Credit1	15%	17%	18.8%	18.9%
Credit2	25%	28%	30%	32%

Table 4. Classification Error on Missing Data

then predicted the missing values using the discretized intervals. For each interval, we identify frequent association rules. We next use these rules to predict the missing values [8, 15]. We compared this strategy, referred as PCA-based, against three strawman methods: **(1)Dominant Value:** Under this scheme, the missing value is predicted by the most dominant value for each attribute in an interval. **(2)Discretization w/o PCA:** Under this scheme we perform equi-width discretization, which is unsupervised and does not count the correlation as against our approach. **(3)Random:** Missing values are predicted by randomly picking a possible value of a specific attribute.

	Adult			Credit1			Credit2		
Missing(%)	10	20	30	10	20	30	10	20	30
PCA-based	75	63	62	58	53	55	65	60	60
Dominant	47	46	48	40	30	35	37	36	33
W/O PCA	22	15	29	15	10	10	20	18	11
Random	37	40	34	40	33	35	39	36	33

Table 5. Missing Value Prediction Accuracy (%)

Table 5 shows the accuracy of all four schemes on different datasets, in which all results are averaged over 10 different runs. It is clear that the PCA-based scheme has the highest accuracy among all four. Whereas the w/o PCA scheme has the lowest accuracy, which might be caused by not considering the inter-attribute correlation. Such a difference also validates the importance of preserving correlation when discretizing data of high dimensionality.

Compression of Datasets: In this section we evaluate the compressibility that can be achieved by discretization. Continuous attributes are usually floating numbers and thus require the minimum four bytes to represent. However, by discretizing them we can easily reduce the storage requirements for such attributes. Table 6 shows the results of compression on various datasets. As we can see from the results, on most datasets we achieve a compression factor around 3, and in some cases the results are even better.

Datasets	Original	Byte Compressed and Discretized	Compression Factor
Bupa	3795	1035	3.67
Adult	537350	195400	2.75
Musk1	85680	29693	2.89
Cancer	6830	3415	2.00
Musk2	1319800	422336	3.13
Credit1	28735	3450	8.33
Credit2	79793	16000	4.99
Shuttle	1153518	478500	2.4

Table 6. Compression Results

4 Conclusions and Future Work

In this article we propose correlation preserving discretization, an efficient method that can effectively discretize continuous attributes even in high dimensional datasets. The approach ensures that *all attributes are used simultaneously* for deciding the cut-points rather than one attribute at a time. We demonstrate the effectiveness of the approach on real datasets, including high dimensional datasets, as a preprocessing step for classification as well as for frequent association mining. We show that the resulting datasets can be easily used to store data in a compressed fashion ready to use for different data mining tasks. We also propose an extension to the algorithm so that it can deal with missing values effectively and validate this aspect as well.

References

[1] Stephen D. Bay. Multivariate discretization for set mining. *Knowledge and Information Systems*, 3(4):491–512, 2001.
[2] J. Catlett. Changing continuous attributes into ordered discrete attributes. In *Proceedings of European Working Session on Learning*, 1991.
[3] James Dougherty, Ron Kohavi, and Mehran Sahami. Supervised and unsupervised discretization of continuous features. In *ICML*, 1995.
[4] Usama. M. Fayyad and Keki B. Irani. Multi-interval discretization of continuous-valued attributes for classification learning. In *IJCAI*, 1993.
[5] I. T. Jolliffe. *Principal Component Analysis*. Springer-Verlag, 1986.
[6] Randy Kerber. Chimerge: Discretizaion of numeric attributes. In *National Conference on AI*, 1991.
[7] Jae-On Kim and Charles W. Mueller. *Factor Analysis : Statistical Methods and Practical Issues*. SAGE Publications, 1978.
[8] Bing Liu, Wynne Hsu, and Yiming Ma. Integrating classification and association rule mining. In *KDD*, pages 80–86, 1998.
[9] Marcus-Christopher Ludl and Gerhard Widmer. Relative unsupervised discretization for association rule mining. In *PKDD*, 2000.
[10] Wolfgang Maass. Efficient agnostic PAC-learning with simple hypotheses. In *COLT*, 1994.
[11] Sameep Mehta, Srinivasan Parthasarathy, and Hui Yang. Correlation preserving discretization. In *OSU-CISRC-12/03-TR69*, December 2003.
[12] Srinivasan Parthasarathy and Charu C. Aggarwal. On the use of conceptual reconstruction for mining massively incomplete data sets. In *TKDE*, 2003.
[13] J. R. Quinlan. *C4.5: Programs for Machine Learning*. Morgan Kaufmann, 1993.
[14] R. Subramonian, R. Venkata, and J. Chen. A visual interactive framework for attribute discretization. In *Proceedings of KDD'97*, 1997.
[15] Hui Yang and Srinivasan Parthasarathy. On the use of constrained association rules for web log mining. In *Proceedings of WEBKDD 2002*, 2002.

Active Feature-Value Acquisition for Classifier Induction

Prem Melville
Dept. of Computer Sciences
Univ. of Texas at Austin
melville@cs.utexas.edu

Maytal Saar-Tsechansky
Red McCombs School of Business
Univ. of Texas at Austin
maytal@mail.utexas.edu

Foster Provost
Stern School of Business
New York University
fprovost@stern.nyu.edu

Raymond Mooney
Dept. of Computer Sciences
Univ. of Texas at Austin
mooney@cs.utexas.edu

Abstract

Many induction problems include missing data that can be acquired at a cost. For building accurate predictive models, acquiring complete information for all instances is often expensive or unnecessary, while acquiring information for a random subset of instances may not be most effective. Active feature-value acquisition *tries to reduce the cost of achieving a desired model accuracy by identifying instances for which obtaining complete information is most informative. We present an approach in which instances are selected for acquisition based on the current model's accuracy and its confidence in the prediction. Experimental results demonstrate that our approach can induce accurate models using substantially fewer feature-value acquisitions as compared to alternative policies.*

1 Introduction

Many predictive modeling tasks include missing data that can be acquired at a cost, such as customers' buying preferences and lifestyle information that can be obtained through an intermediary. For building accurate models, ignoring instances with missing values leads to inferior model performance [7], while acquiring complete information for all instances often is prohibitively expensive or unnecessary. To reduce the cost of information acquisition, it is desirable to identify instances for which complete information is most informative to acquire.

In this paper we address this problem of *active feature-value acquisition* (AFA) for classifier induction: given a feature acquisition budget, identify the instances with missing values for which acquiring complete feature information will result in the most accurate model. Formally, assume m instances, each represented by n features $a_1, ..., a_n$. For all instances, the values of a subset of the features $a_1, ..., a_i$ are known, along with the class labels. The values of the remaining features $a_{i+1}, ..., a_n$ are unknown and can be acquired at a cost. The problem of feature-value acquisition is different from active learning [2] and optimum experi-

mental design [3], where the class labels rather than feature-values are missing and costly to obtain.

The approach we present for active feature acquisition is based on the following three observations: **(1)** Most classification models provide estimates of the confidence of classification, such as estimated probabilities of class membership. Therefore principles underlying existing active-learning methods like uncertainty sampling [2] can be applied. **(2)** For the data items subject to active feature-value acquisition, the correct classifications are known during training. Therefore, unlike with traditional active learning, it is possible to employ direct measures of the current model's accuracy for estimating the value of potential acquisitions. **(3)** Class labels are available for all complete and incomplete instances. Therefore, we can exploit all instances (including incomplete instances) to induce models, and to guide feature acquisition.

The approach we propose is simple-to-implement, computationally efficient and results in significant improvements compared to random sampling and a computationally-intensive method proposed earlier for this problem [11].

2 Task Definition and Algorithm

Pool-based Active Feature Acquisition: Assume a classifier induction problem, where each instance is represented with n feature values and a class label. For the set of complete instances G of the training set T, the values of all n features are known. For all other instances in T, only the values of a subset of the features $a_1, ..., a_i$ are known. The values of the remaining features $a_{i+1}, ..., a_n$ are missing and the set can be acquired at a fixed cost. We refer to these instances as incomplete instances, and the set is denoted as I. The class labels of all instances in T are known.

Unlike prior work [11], we assume that models are induced from the entire training set (rather than just from G). This is because models induced from all available data have been shown to be superior to models induced when instances with missing values are ignored [7]. [1] Beyond im-

---

[1] It was also noted in [11] that such a setting may result in better models.

proved accuracy, the choice of model induction setting also bears important implications for the acquisition mechanism, because the estimation of an acquisition's marginal utility is derived with respect to the model. Note that induction algorithms either include an internal mechanism for incorporating instances with missing feature-values [7] or require that missing values be imputed first. Henceforth, we assume that the induction algorithm includes some treatment for instances with missing values.

We study active feature-value acquisition policies within a generic iterative framework, shown in Algorithm 1. Each iteration estimates the utility of acquiring complete feature information for each incomplete example. The missing feature-values of a subset $S \in I$ of incomplete instances with the highest utility are acquired and added to T (these examples move from I to G). A new model is then induced from T, and the process is repeated. Different AFA policies correspond to different measures of utility. Our baseline policy, random sampling, selects acquisitions at random, which tends to select a representative set of examples [8].

Error Sampling: For a model trained on incomplete instances, acquiring missing feature-values is effective if it enables a learner to capture additional discriminative patterns that improve the model's prediction. Specifically, acquired feature-values are likely to have an impact on subsequent model induction when the acquired values pertain to a misclassified example and may embed predictive patterns that can be potentially captured by the model and improve the model. In contrast, acquiring feature-values of instances for which the current model already embeds correct discriminative patterns is not likely to impact model accuracy considerably. Motivated by this reasoning, our approach *Error Sampling* prefers to acquire feature-values for instances that the current model misclassifies. At each iteration, it randomly selects m incomplete instances that have been misclassified by the model. If there are fewer than m misclassified instances, then *Error Sampling* selects the remaining instances based on the *Uncertainty* score which we describe next. The uncertainty principle originated in work on optimum experimental design [3] and has been extensively applied in the active learning literature [2, 8]. The *Uncertainty* score captures the model's ability to distinguish between cases of different classes and prefers acquiring information regarding instances whose predictions are most uncertain. The acquisition of additional information for these cases is more likely to impact prediction, whereas information pertaining to strong discriminative patterns captured by the model is less likely to change the model. For a probabilistic model, the absence of discriminative patterns in the data results in the model assigning similar likelihoods for class membership of different classes. Hence, the *Uncertainty* score is calculated as the absolute difference between the estimated class probabilities of the two

most likely classes. Formally, for an instance x, let $P_y(x)$ be the estimated probability that x belongs to class y as predicted by the model. Then the *Uncertainty* score is given by $P_{y_1}(x) - P_{y_2}(x)$, where $P_{y_1}(x)$ and $P_{y_2}(x)$ are the first-highest and second-highest predicted probability estimates respectively. Formally, the *Error Sampling* score for a potential acquisition is set to -1 for misclassified instances; and for correctly classified instances we employ the *Uncertainty* score. At each iteration of the AFA algorithm, complete feature information is acquired for the m incomplete instances with the lowest scores.

Algorithm 1 Active Feature-Value Acquisition Framework

Given:
G - set of complete instances
I - set of incomplete instances
T - set of training instances, $G \cup I$
$\mathcal{L}$ - learning algorithm
m - size of each sample

1. Repeat until stopping criterion is met
2.   Generate a classifier, $C = \mathcal{L}(T)$
3. $\forall x_j \in I$, compute $Score(C, x_j)$ based on the current classifier
4.   Select a subset S of m instances with the highest utility based on the score
5.   Acquire values for missing features for each instance in S
6.   Remove instances in S from I and add to G
7.   Update training set, $T = G \cup I$
8. Return $\mathcal{L}(T)$

---

3 Experimental Evaluation

Methodology: We first compared *Error Sampling* to random feature acquisition. The performance of each system was averaged over 5 runs of 10-fold cross-validation. In each fold, the learner initially has access to all incomplete instances, and is given complete feature-values for a randomly selected subset of size m. For the active strategies, a sample of instances is then selected from the pool of incomplete instances based on the measure of utility. The missing values for these instances are acquired and the process is repeated until the pool of incomplete instances is exhausted. In the case of random sampling, the incomplete instances are selected uniformly at random. Each system is evaluated on the held-out test set after each iteration of feature acquisition. As in [11], the test data set contains only complete instances, since we want to estimate the true accuracy of the model given complete data. To maximize the gains of AFA, it is best to acquire features for a single instance in each iteration; however, to make our experiments computationally feasible, we selected instances in batches of 10 (i.e., sample size $m = 10$).

To compare the performance of any two schemes, A and B we compute the percentage reduction in error of A over B for a given number of acquisitions and report the average over all points on the learning curve. The reduction in error is considered to be *significant* if the average errors across the points on the learning curve of A is lower than that of B according to a paired t-test ($p < 0.05$).

All the experiments were run on 5 web-usage datasets (used in [6]) and 5 datasets from the UCI machine learning repository [1]. [2] The web-usage data contain information from popular on-line retailers about customer behavior and purchases. This data exhibit a natural dichotomy with a subset of features owned by a particular retailer and a set of features that the retailer may acquire at a cost. The learning task is to induce models to predict whether a customer will purchase an item during a visit to the store. Hence the pool of incomplete instances was initialized with the features privately owned by each retailer. For the UCI datasets, 30% of the features were randomly selected to be used in the incomplete instances. A different set of randomly selected features was used for each train-test split of the data.

The active framework we have proposed can be implemented using an arbitrary probabilistic classifier as a learner. For the results in this paper, we used J48, which is the Weka implementation of C4.5 decision-tree induction [10].

Results: The results comparing *Error Sampling* to random sampling are summarized in Table 1. All error reductions reported are statistically significant. As mentioned above, the main impact of AFA is lower on the learning curve. To capture this, we also report the percentage error reduction averaged over only the 20% of points on the learning curve where the largest improvements are produced. We refer to this as the *top-20% percentage error reduction*, which is similar to a measure reported in [8].

The results show that for all data sets using *Error Sampling* significantly improves on the model accuracy compared to random sampling. Figures 1 and 2 present learning curves that demonstrate the advantage of using an AFA scheme over random acquisition. Apart from average reduction in error, a good indicator of the effectiveness of an AFA scheme is the number of acquisitions required to obtain a desired accuracy. For example, on the *qvc* dataset once *Error Sampling* acquires approximately 400 complete instances, it induces a model with an accuracy of 87%; however, random sampling requires approximately 1200 complete instances to achieve the same accuracy. We also evaluated a policy that uses only the *Uncertainty* score for estimating the utility of potential acquisitions. This *Uncertainty Sampling* results in significantly better performance

compared to random sampling, but is inferior to *Error Sampling*. Detailed results comparing alternative AFA policies can be found in the extended version of this paper [5].

Table 1. Error reduction of *Error Sampling* **with respect to random sampling.**

Dataset	%Error Reduction	Top-20% %Err. Red.
bmg	10.67	17.77
etoys	10.34	23.88
expedia	19.83	29.12
priceline	24.45	34.49
qvc	15.44	24.75
anneal	22.65	49.27
soybean	8.03	14.79
autos	4.24	10.50
kr-vs-kr	36.82	53.23
hypo	16.79	40.48
Mean	16.93	29.83

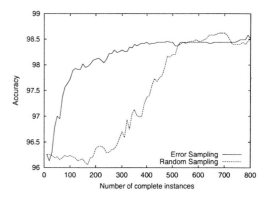

Figure 1. *Error Sampling* **vs.** *Random Sampling* **on** *anneal*.

Comparison with GODA: The most closely related work to this paper is the study by Zheng and Padmanabhan [11] of the active feature-value acquisition scheme GODA. GODA measures the utility of acquiring feature-values for a particular incomplete instance in the following way. It adds the instance to the training set, imputing the values that are missing and then induces a new model. The instance that leads to the model with the best performance on the complete training data is selected for acquisition. GODA has two important differences from *Error Sampling*: it employs a different utility measure and it induces its models from only the complete instances. To compare to our approach, we implemented GODA as described in [11], using J48 tree induction as the learner and *multiple imputation* for missing value imputation. Experiments comparing *Error Sampling* to GODA were run as before; however, due to GODA's tremendous computational requirements, we only ran one run of 10-fold cross-validation on 5 of the datasets. Some

[2] The details of the datasets used can be found in [5].

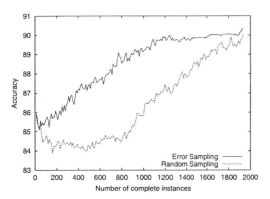

Figure 2. *Error Sampling* **vs.** *Random Sampling* **on** *qvc*.

datasets were also reduced in size. A summary of the results, along with the reduced dataset sizes, is presented in Table 2. The results show that in spite of the high computational complexity of GODA, it results in inferior performance compared to *Error Sampling* for all 5 domains. All improvements obtained by *Error Sampling* with respect to GODA are statistically significant. These results suggest that the ability of *Error Sampling* to capitalize on information from incomplete instances, and to utilize this knowledge in feature acquisition, allows it to capture better predictive patterns compared to those captured by GODA.

Table 2. Error reduction of *Error Sampling* **with respect to** GODA.

Dataset	Size	% Error Reduction
etoys	270	37.58
priceline	447	14.19
bmg	200	19.48
expedia	200	22.96
qvc	100	20.03

4 Related Work and Conclusions

Recent work on *budgeted learning* [4] also addresses the issue of active feature-value acquisition. However, the policies developed in [4] assume feature-values are discrete, and consider the acquisition of individual feature-values for randomly selected instances of a given class, rather than for specific incomplete instances. Some work on *cost sensitive* learning [9] has addressed the issue of inducing economical classifiers but it assumes that the *training* data are complete and focuses on learning classifiers that minimize the cost of classifying incomplete *test* instances. Traditional *active learning* [2] assumes access to unlabeled instances with complete feature-values and attempts to select the most use-

ful examples for which to acquire class labels. Active feature acquisition is a complementary problem that assumes labeled data and attempts to acquire the most useful feature-values.

We have presented a general framework for active feature acquisition that can be applied to different learners and can use alternate measures of utility for ranking acquisitions. Within this framework, we propose an effective and simple-to-implement policy that results in superior accuracy and is also significantly more efficient computationally compared to an existing approach.

Acknowledgments

We would like to thank Balaji Padmanabhan and Zhiqiang Zheng for providing us with the web usage datasets. Prem Melville and Raymond Mooney were supported by DARPA grant HR0011-04-1-007.

References

[1] C. L. Blake and C. J. Merz. UCI repository of machine learning databases. http://www.ics.uci.edu/~mlearn/MLRepository.html, 1998.

[2] D. Cohn, L. Atlas, and R. Ladner. Improving generalization with active learning. *Machine Learning*, 15(2):201–221, 1994.

[3] V. Federov. *Theory of optimal experiments*. Academic Press, 1972.

[4] D. Lizotte, O. Madani, and R. Greiner. Budgeted learning of naive-bayes classifiers. In *Proc. of 19th Conf. on Uncertainty in Artificial Intelligence (UAI-03)*, Acapulco, Mexico, 2003.

[5] P. Melville, M. Saar-Tsechansky, F. Provost, and R. Mooney. Active feature acquisition for classifier induction. Technical Report UT-AI-TR-04-311, University of Texas at Austin, 2004.

[6] B. Padmanabhan, Z. Zheng, and S. O. Kimbrough. Personalization from incomplete data: what you don't know can hurt. In *Proc. of 7th ACM SIGKDD Intl. Conf. on Knowledge Discovery and Data Mining (KDD-2001)*, pages 154–163, 2001.

[7] J. R. Quinlan. Unknown attribute values in induction. In *Proc. of 6th Intl. Workshop on Machine Learning*, pages 164–168, Ithaca, NY, June 1989.

[8] M. Saar-Tsechansky and F. Provost. Active sampling for class probability estimation and ranking. *Machine Learning*, 54:153–178, 2004.

[9] P. D. Turney. Types of cost in inductive concept learning. In *Proc. of the Workshop on Cost-Sensitive Learning at the 17th Intl. Conf. on Machine Learning*, Palo Alto, CA, 2000.

[10] I. H. Witten and E. Frank. *Data Mining: Practical Machine Learning Tools and Techniques with Java Implementations*. Morgan Kaufmann, San Francisco, 1999.

[11] Z. Zheng and B. Padmanabhan. On active learning for data acquisition. In *Proc. of IEEE Intl. Conf. on Data Mining*, 2002.

Privacy-Sensitive Bayesian Network Parameter Learning

D. Meng and K. Sivakumar
School of EECS, Washington State University
Pullman, WA 99164-2752, USA
{dmeng, siva}@eecs.wsu.edu

H. Kargupta*
Department of CSEE, UMBC
Baltimore, MD 21250, USA
hillol@cs.umbc.edu

Abstract

This paper considers the problem of learning the parameters of a Bayesian Network, assuming the structure of the network is given, from a privacy-sensitive dataset that is distributed between multiple parties. For a binary-valued dataset, we show that the count information required to estimate the conditional probabilities in a Bayesian network can be obtained as a solution to a set of linear equations involving some inner product between the relevant different feature vectors. We consider a random projection-based method that was proposed elsewhere to securely compute the inner product (with a modified implementation of that method).

1. Introduction

Advances in networking, storage, and computing technologies have resulted in an unprecedented increase in the amount of data collected and made available to the public. This explosive growth in digital data has brought increased concerns about the privacy of personal information [1]. Privacy is also an important issue in applications related to counter-terrorism and homeland security. For example, mining healthcare data for the detection of bio-terrorism may require mining clinical records and pharmaceutical purchases of certain specific drugs. However, combining such diverse datasets belonging to different parties may violate privacy laws. Therefore, it is important to be able to extract desired data mining models from the data, without accessing the raw data in its original form.

Privacy-sensitive data mining is an evolving area within the broad field of data mining [2, 3, 8]. In the following, we briefly review some of the important approaches proposed in the literature. Due to space constraints, we cite only a few important works.

1.1. Related Work

There exists a growing body of literature on privacy-sensitive data mining. These algorithms can be divided into two broad groups: (a) approaches based on randomization and (b) approaches based on secure multi-party computation (SMC).

The first approach to privacy-sensitive data mining starts by first perturbing the data using randomized techniques. The perturbed data is then used to extract the patterns and models. The randomized value distortion technique for learning decision trees [2] is an example of this approach. See [7] for a possible privacy breach using this approach. Evfimievski et al. [5] have also considered the approach in [2] in the context of association rule mining and suggest techniques for limiting privacy breaches.

SMC is the problem of evaluating a function of two or more parties' secret inputs, such that each party finally learns their specified function output and nothing else is revealed, except what is implied by the party's own inputs and outputs. SMC problem was first introduced by Yao [11]. Du and Atallah have presented a collection of new secure multi-party computation applications such as privacy-sensitive statistical analysis [4]. Clifton [3] has described several secure multi-party computation based algorithms that can support privacy-sensitive data mining. Feigenbaum et al. have addressed the problem of computing approximations using SMC [6]. More recently, Wright and Yang [10] have proposed a privacy-sensitive Bayesian Network structure learning algorithm.

1.2. Our Contribution

In this paper, we consider the problem of learning the parameters of a Bayesian Network (BN), assuming the structure of the network is given, from a privacy-sensitive dataset that is distributed between multiple parties. For a binary-valued dataset, we show that the

---

*Also affiliated with AGNIK, LLC, USA.

count information required to estimate the conditional probabilities (model parameters) in a Bayesian network can be obtained as a solution to a set of linear equations involving some inner product between the relevant different feature vectors. Therefore, any privacy-sensitive method for computing inner product between vectors can be used to solve the Bayesian network parameter learning problem. Specifically, we consider a random projection-based method (to compute the inner product) that was proposed elsewhere [9].

The rest of the paper is organized as follows. Section 2 provides a brief overview of Bayesian Networks (BN) followed by a description of the problem statement. In Section 3, we describe our proposed algorithm. Experimental results are presented in Section 4. Section 5 concludes the paper.

2. Problem Description

A BN is a probabilistic graph model, which is an important tool in data mining. It can be defined as a pair $(\mathcal{G}, p)$, where $\mathcal{G} = (\mathcal{V}, \mathcal{E})$ is a directed acyclic graph (DAG). For a variable $X \in \mathcal{V}$, a parent of X is a node from which there exists a directed link to X. Figure 1 is a BN called the ASIA model. Let $pa(X)$ denote the set of parents of X, then the conditional independence property can be used to factor the joint probability as follows: $P(\mathcal{V}) = \prod_{X \in \mathcal{V}} P(X \mid pa(X))$. The set of conditional distributions $\{P(X \mid pa(X)), X \in \mathcal{V}\}$ are called the parameters of a Bayesian network. Learning a BN involves learning the structure of the network and obtaining the conditional probabilities associated with the network.

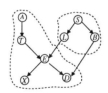

Figure 1. ASIA Model

We consider a set-up where the data corresponding to the different nodes are distributed among two or more parties. For example, in the ASIA model of Figure 1, party I contains observations for features (nodes) A, T, E, X, and D, whereas party II contains observations for features S, L, and B. This is usually referred to vertical partitioning of the data or a heterogeneous data distribution. The dataset is privacy-sensitive in the sense that each party does not wish to share its raw data with the other parties. However, they wish to mine the combined dataset to obtain a global BN. We

assume that the structure of the global BN is known to all the parties and focus on the problem of estimating the parameters of the network. Our proposed solution to this problem is presented in the following section.

3. Algorithm

In the following, we assume that the features of the BN are binary, taking values in the set $\{-1, 1\}$. Extensions to multi-variate (discrete) case is conceptually similar, except for the algebra. In Section 3.1, we describe a system of linear equations, whose solution yields the desired conditional probabilities. The coefficient matrix for the linear equations can be obtained from the BN structure, which is assumed to be known. The inner product between certain feature vectors are needed to obtain the "right-hand-side vector" of the linear equations. Any secure inner product computation module can be used for this purpose. This is discussed in Section 3.2. Finally, Section 3.3 provides a privacy analysis of the proposed method.

3.1. Equations for BN parameter learning

In this section we build a set of linear equations whose solution yields all the conditional probabilities for a BN. We assume that all the data are binary with values 1 or −1 and the structure of BN is given.

For simplicity, first consider a node z with two parent nodes x and y. We need to obtain the values of all the conditional probabilities for z, given the values of nodes x and y. As shown in Table 1, there are eight ($2^3 = 8$) different count values — $\{a, b, \dots, h\}$ — to be determined. For example, b represents the number of observations with $x = -1$, $y = 1$ and $z = -1$. The corresponding probabilities can be obtained simply by normalizing the count values with respect to the total number of observations N.

Let $N_{ijk}{}^{xyz}$ denote the number of observations for which $x = i$, $y = j$, and $z = k$, for $i, j, k \in \{-1, 1\}$. We then have $P(z = k \mid x = i, y = j) = \frac{N_{ijk}{}^{xyz}}{N_{ij}{}^{xy}}$, $i, j, k \in \{-1, 1\}$, where $N_{ij}{}^{xy}$ denotes the number of observations for which $x = i$, and $y = j$.

Definition 3.1 *(Pseudo inner product) Given $n \geq 1$ vectors $x_1, x_2, \dots, x_n$, each of dimension k, we define their pseudo-inner product (pip) $pip(x_1, x_2, \dots, x_n) = \sum_{j=1}^{k} \prod_{i=1}^{n} x_{ij}$, where $x_i = [x_{i1}, x_{i2}, \dots, x_{ik}]$, $i = 1, 2, \dots, n$ are the components of vector x_i.*

Let N be the total number of observations and X, Y, Z denote the data vector (column vector) for nodes x, y, z, respectively. Since there are three data

Table 1. Three-node example

	\multicolumn{4}{c}{x, y}			
	$-1, -1$	$-1, 1$	$1, -1$	$1, 1$
$z = -1$	a	b	c	d
$z = 1$	e	f	g	h

vectors, we can compute $2^3 - 1 = 7$ different pseudo inner products. Observe that each pseudo inner product can be expressed uniquely by count variables $a, b, \ldots, h$. For example, $pip(Z)$ equals the sum of the entries in vector Z, which is precisely the number of observations with $z = 1$ minus the number of observations with $z = -1$. Indeed, we can write $(e + f + g + h) - (a + b + c + d) = pip(Z)$. Another obvious condition is: $(e+f+g+h)+(a+b+c+d) = N$. Indeed, we can write eight linear equations as follows: $Ax = b$, where

$$
A = \begin{pmatrix}
-1 & -1 & -1 & -1 & 1 & 1 & 1 & 1 \\
-1 & -1 & 1 & 1 & -1 & -1 & 1 & 1 \\
-1 & 1 & -1 & 1 & -1 & 1 & -1 & 1 \\
1 & 1 & -1 & -1 & -1 & -1 & 1 & 1 \\
1 & -1 & 1 & -1 & -1 & 1 & -1 & 1 \\
-1 & 1 & 1 & -1 & 1 & -1 & -1 & 1 \\
1 & -1 & -1 & 1 & 1 & -1 & -1 & 1 \\
1 & 1 & 1 & 1 & 1 & 1 & 1 & 1
\end{pmatrix},
$$

$x = [a, b, c, d, e, f, g, h]^T$, and $b = [pip(Z), \ pip(X), \ pip(Y), \ pip(Z, X), \ pip(Z, Y), \ pip(Z, X, Y), \ pip(X, Y), \ N]^T$. It is easy to verify that matrix A is nonsingular. So we can solve the linear equations to get all the required conditional probabilities.

This simple idea can be easily generalized to the case of arbitrary number of parent nodes. The proof is by induction and has been omitted due to page limitations (see http://www.eecs.wsu.edu/~siva/icdm_04_longversion.pdf for details).

3.2. Secure Inner Product Computation

From the previous subsection, we know if a BN structure is given, the coefficient matrix A is uniquely determined. Therefore, if we can compute the pseudo inner products, the BN parameters can be obtained by solving the linear equations. If the variables corresponding to the parent node(s) of a given node belong to a different party than the variable of the node itself, then computing the pseudo inner product would require exchange of raw data between the parties. Therefore, we need a privacy-sensitive method to compute inner products in order to accomplish this step.

In our experiments, we used a random projection based method proposed in [9]. The important equa-

tions are reproduced below: Let U be an $m \times n$ data matrix, with m observations and n features. Suppose R is an $m \times m$ orthogonal matrix; i.e., $R^T R = RR^T = I$. Consider the (multiplicatively) perturbed matrix $U_1 = RU$. Note that we use a single projection as opposed to the proposed double projection in [9]. It is easy to see that $U_1^T U_1 = (U^T R^T)(RU) = U^T (R^T R)U = U^T U$. Therefore the inner products between the columns of U can be computed using the perturbed matrix U_1. So the owner of the data set U computes U_1 and hands over that to the other party (or a third party who does the data mining), who can then compute the required pseudo inner products. In practice, perturbation matrix R is chosen to be a random orthogonal matrix. This can be accomplished by starting with a random matrix with independent identically distributed (i.i.d.) entries W and orthogonalizing it.

3.3. Communication, Error, and Privacy Analysis

We now present a brief analysis of the communication cost and privacy of the proposed scheme.

First observe that for those nodes, all of whose parents are in the same site, there is no privacy or communication problem and those parameters (conditional probabilities) can be locally estimated and communicated to the other parties.

Suppose, node i has $n_a - 1$ parents at the same site and n_b parents at a different site. Therefore, roughly $2^{n_a} 2^{n_b} = 2^{n_a + n_b}$ pseudo inner products have to be computed securely. This would require communication of $O(m2^{n_i})$ bits, where $n_i = n_a + n_b$ is one more than the number of parents of node i. Therefore, the total communication cost is $O(m \sum_i 2^{n_i})$. Note that in typical BN applications $n_i << n$.

The pseudo inner product computation is the only step that requires some exchange of data between the parties. Therefore, any privacy breach would have to occur in that step. Theorem 1 in [9] discusses the privacy preserving properties of the random projection method. In particular, the $m \times m$ random orthogonal matrix R has $m(m-1)/2$ independent random entries (the rest of the $m(m+1)/2$ entries being determined by orthogonality constraints). As such, there are infinitely many solutions U, in general, to $U_1 = RU$, if R is unknown. By using a single random orthogonal matrix R in the projection instead of two random matrices R_1, R_2 as in [9], we do not have to "average" over results over multiple trials. Moreover, inner products computed using a single random orthogonal matrix R are virtually error-free as opposed to the case with double projection using random matrices, where the error goes to zero as the number of independent trials goes to infinity. More details about the privacy preserving properties of single and double projection methods can be found in [9].

4. Experimental Results

In this section, we present results of our experiments with the proposed privacy-sensitive BN parameter learning for the ASIA model (see Figure 1). The true conditional probabilities (parameters) of the ASIA model for nodes E and D (nodes with parents from different sites) are given in Table 2. A data set with 2000 samples was generated from this model.

Table 2. True conditional probabilities

E	0.9	0.1	0.1	0.01	0.1	0.9	0.9	0.99
D	0.9	0.2	0.8	0.9	0.1	0.8	0.2	0.1

We generated a random matrix R_1 whose entries were i.i.d. Gaussian with zero mean and unit variance. This matrix was then orthogonalized using a QR decomposition to obtain a random orthogonal matrix R. The estimated parameters using our proposed algorithm in Section 3 are tabulated in Table 3. As expected, the estimated parameters are almost identical to the true values.

Table 3. Estimated conditional probabilities

E	0.9	0.1	0.1	0.01	0.1	0.9	0.9	0.99
D	0.89	0.21	0.81	0.84	0.11	0.79	0.19	0.16

5. Discussion and Conclusions

We considered the problem of learning the parameters of a Bayesian Network, assuming the structure of the network is given, from a privacy-sensitive dataset that is distributed between multiple parties. We considered the case of vertical (or heterogeneous) partitioning, where different parties hold values corresponding to a different subset of the variables. For a binary-valued dataset, we showed that the count information required to estimate the conditional probabilities of a Bayesian network can be obtained as a solution to a set of linear equations involving some inner product between the relevant different feature vectors. In our experiments, we considered a random projection-based method with a single projection using a random orthogonal matrix. This implementation requires considerably less exchange of perturbed data and produces almost error-free results

as compared with that using double projection using random matrices.

Acknowledgements

The authors acknowledge supports from the United States National Science Foundation grants IIS-0329143 and IIS-0350533.

References

[1] The end of privacy. The Economist, May 1999.

[2] R. Agrawal and S. Ramakrishnan. Privacy-preserving data mining. In *Proceedings of SIGMOD Conference*, pages 439–450, 2000.

[3] C. Clifton, M. Kantarcioglu, J. Vaidya, X. Lin, and M. Zhu. Tools for Privacy Preserving Distributed Data Mining. *ACM SIGKDD Explorations*, 4(2):28–34, 2003.

[4] W. Du, Y. S. Han, and S. Chen. Privacy-preserving multivariate statistical analysis: Linear regression and classification. In *Proceedings of 2004 SIAM International Conference on Data Mining (SDM04)*, pages 222–233, Lake Buena Vista, FL, April 2004.

[5] A. Evfimevski, J. Gehrke, and R. Srikant. Limiting privacy breaches in privacy preserving data mining. In *Proceedings of the ACM SIGMOD/PODS Conference*, pages 211–222, San Diego, CA, June 2003.

[6] J. Feigenbaum, Y. Ishai, T. Malkin, K. Nissim, M. Strauss, and R. Wright. Secure multiparty computation of approximations. In *Proceedings of the 28th International Colloquium on Automata, Languages, and Programming (ICALP)*, volume 2076 of *Lecture Notes in Computer Science*, pages 927–938, Berlin, 2001. Springer.

[7] H. Kargupta, S. Datta, Q. Wang, and K. Sivakumar. On the Privacy Preserving Properties of Random Data Perturbation Techniques. In *Proceedings of the IEEE International Conference on Data Mining*, pages 99–106, Melbourne, FL, November 2003.

[8] Y. Lindell and B. Pinkas. Privacy preserving data mining. In *Advances in Cryptology - CRYPTO*, pages 36–54, 2000.

[9] K. Liu, H. Kargupta, and J. Ryan. Multiplicative noise, random projection, and privacy preserving data mining from distributed multi-party data. Technical Report TR-CS-03-24, Computer Science and Electrical Engineering Department, University of Maryland, Baltimore County, 2003.

[10] R. Wright and Z. Yang. Privacy-preserving Bayesian network structure computation on distributed heterogeneous data. In *Proceedings of the tenth ACM SIGKDD Conference*, Seattle, WA, August 2004.

[11] A. C. Yao. How to generate and exchange secrets. In *Proceedings 27th IEEE Symposium on Foundations of Computer Science*, pages 162–167, 1986.

MMSS: Multi-modal Story-oriented Video Summarization*

Jia-Yu Pan, Hyungjeong Yang,† Christos Faloutsos
Computer Science Department
Carnegie Mellon University
{jypan, hjyang, christos}@cs.cmu.edu

Abstract

We propose multi-modal story-oriented video summarization (MMSS) which, unlike previous works that use fine-tuned, domain-specific heuristics, provides a domain-independent, graph-based framework. MMSS uncovers correlation between information of different modalities which gives meaningful story-oriented news video summaries. MMSS can also be applied for video retrieval, giving performance that matches the best traditional retrieval techniques (OKAPI and LSI), with no fine-tuned heuristics such as tf/idf.

1. Introduction and related works

As more and more video libraries [9] become available, video summarization is in great demands for enabling users to efficiently access these video collections. Most previous work focuses on summarizing an *entire* video clip into a more compact movie to facilitate browsing and content-based retrieval [8, 4]. For story-oriented summarization, research has been done mainly under the context of multi-document summarization [3] in the textual domain. Little work has been done on story-oriented video summarization using the multi-modal information.

Identifying footages of the same evolving story is difficult. Broadcast news production commonly shows a small icon beside an anchorperson to represent the story on which the anchorperson is reporting at the time [1]. The same icon is usually reused later in the shots about the follow-up development of the story, as an aid for the viewers to link current coverage to past coverage. We call these icons *"news-logos"*, and the associated stories *logo stories*. The property of logos makes them a robust feature for linking separated footages of a story.

In this paper, we propose a method, *MMSS*, to generate multi-modal summary of a logo story. *MMSS* integrates multi-modal (visual/textual) information, treating it in a uniform, modality-independent fashion, with no need of parameter tuning. In fact, *MMSS* uncovers cross-modal correlation which, not only gives good story summaries, but also video retrieval performance matches the best finely tuned traditional information retrieval techniques.

The paper is organized as follows. Section 2 introduces the proposed method, *MMSS*. Sections 3 presents our experimental results on two applications, namely, story-oriented video summarization and video retrieval. Section 4 concludes the paper.

2. Proposed method: Video mining with *MMSS*

MMSS introduces a general framework for mining the cross-modal correlations among data of different modalities (frames/terms/logos) in video clips. The found cross-modal correlations are then used for story-oriented summarization and video retrieval.

The data set we used in this work is the TRECVID 2003 [7] data set. The data set is a collection of news programs. Each news program is broken into shots, each of which is associated with a keyframe and transcript words. For the words, we keep only the nouns and filter out the stop words.

In our experiments, logos are identified and extracted from the shot keyframes, using off the shelf algorithms for iconic matching [1, 2]. Figure 1 shows the keyframes and the associated words of three logos in the CNN news from the TRECVID 2003 data set.

Observation 1 *Logos provide robust visual hints and help alleviate the problems of tracking shots of a same story.*

Our goal is to exploit the logos, to facilitate video mining tasks. Particularly, we focus on the following two applications:

---

*Supported by the NSF under Grants No. IIS-0121641, IIS-0083148, IIS-0113089, IIS-0209107, IIS-0205224, INT-0318547, SENSOR-0329549, EF-0331657, IIS-0326322, and by the Pennsylvania Infrastructure Technology Alliance (PITA) Grant No. 22-901-0001.

†Supported by the Post-doctoral Fellowship Program of Korea Science and Engineering Foundation (KOSEF).

491

winter olympics nagano ceremony night round compe- tition result headline news superticker medal watch headline news superticker result	money trie source lawyer house intern monica informa- tion counsel starr immunity learned starr	arab league secre- tarygeneral strike iraq reaction arab brent sadler report iraqi president saddam hus- sein kind sentiment attack
(a) "Winter Olympics"	(b) "Lewinsky"	(c) "Iraq"

Figure 1. News logos

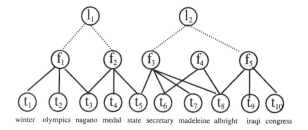

winter olympics nagano medal state secretary madeleine albright iraqi congress

Figure 2. (The MMSS graph G_{MMSS}) Three types of nodes, and two types of edges: logo-nodes l_i's, frame-nodes f_i's and term-nodes t_i's; "same-logo" edges (dotted) and the term-occurrence edges (solid).

- (Story summarization) How do we generate high-quality textual and visual summaries of a story?

- (Video retrieval) How can we exploit the logos, to re-trieve the video clips that are relevant to a text query?

In addition, we want to perform the above two tasks in a principled way, that is, using the same framework for both tasks, integrating all multi-modal sources easily, with no pa-rameter tuning.

Graph G_{MMSS} We integrate the information of shot-word co-occurrence with the logo information into a graph G_{MMSS}. The graph G_{MMSS} is a three-layer graph with 3 types of nodes and 2 types of edges. The 3 types of nodes are *logo-node*, *frame-node* and *term-node*, corresponding to the logos, keyframes (each representing a shot), and terms, respectively. The 2 types of edges are the *term-occurrence edge* and the *"same-logo"* edge. Figure 2 shows an example graph G_{MMSS} with 2 logo-nodes $\{l_1, l_2\}$, 5 frame-nodes $\{f_1, \ldots, f_5\}$, and 10 term-nodes $\{t_1, \ldots, t_{10}\}$. The term-occurrence edges are the solid lines, and the "same-logo" edges are the dotted lines.

A logo-node l_i is connected to a frame-node f_j by a "same-logo" edge, if the logo $O(l_i)$ appears in the frame $O(f_j)$. A frame-node f_j is connected to a term-node t_k by a term-occurrence edge, if the term $O(t_k)$ occurs in the shot whose keyframe is $O(f_j)$.

For logo story summarization and video retrieval, the essential part they share is to select objects pertaining to a query object. In logo story summarization, frames and terms forming the summary are selected based on their "rel-evance" to the query object, the logo(-node) of the story. As for video retrieval, we rank and select video shots by their "relevance" to the set of query terms. With the graph G_{MMSS}, we can turn the problem of computing "rele-vance" with respect to the query objects, into a random walk on the graph G_{MMSS}, as we show next.

Random walk with restarts (RWR) In this work, we propose to use *random walk with restarts* ("*RWR*") for esti-mating the *relevance* of node "v" with respect to the restart node "s". The "random walk with restarts" operates as fol-lows: to compute the relevance of node "v" for node "s", consider a random walker that starts from node "s". At every time-tick, the walker chooses randomly among the available edges, with one modification: before he makes a choice, he goes back to node "s" with probability c. Let $u_s(v)$ denote the stationary probability that our random walker will find himself at node "v". Then, $u_s(v)$ is what we want, the relevance of "v" with respect to "s", and we call it the *RWR score* of "v" (with respect to "s"). The intu-ition is that if the random walker who restarts from s (with probability c) has high chance of finding himself at node v, then node v is close and relevant to s. Details about RWR can be found in [5].

To use RWR to summarize a logo story $O(l_i)$, we set the restart node s be the logo-node $s=l_i$. The frame(-node)s and term(-node)s with the highest RWR scores are then se-lected as the story summary. Similarly, for video retrieval, the restart nodes are set to the term-nodes corresponding to the query terms. The query result is the shots (frame-nodes) with the highest RWR scores.

3. Experimental Results

The experiments are designed to answer the following questions: (a) For visual story summarization, how good are the shots that *MMSS* chooses? (b) For text story summariza-tion, how good are the terms that *MMSS* chooses? (c) For video retrieval by text query, how well does *MMSS* compare to successful existing text retrieval methods, like OKAPI and LSI?

We should emphasize that OKAPI and LSI can only an-swer queries of the form "given a query word, find relevant video shots". Our *MMSS* method, being modality-independent, can answer any type of query, like "given a shot (without a logo), find the best logo for it"; or "given a logo, find the best shots and/or terms for it".

In our experiments, we follow the guidelines from [6] and set the restart probability $c=0.65$ for our 3-layer G_{MMSS} graph.

3.1 Story summarization

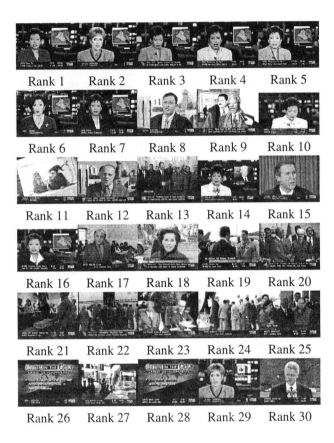

Rank 1   Rank 2   Rank 3   Rank 4   Rank 5

Rank 6   Rank 7   Rank 8   Rank 9   Rank 10

Rank 11   Rank 12   Rank 13   Rank 14   Rank 15

Rank 16   Rank 17   Rank 18   Rank 19   Rank 20

Rank 21   Rank 22   Rank 23   Rank 24   Rank 25

Rank 26   Rank 27   Rank 28   Rank 29   Rank 30

**Figure 3. (Visual summary of logo "Iraq")
Frames are sorted (highest score first).**

MMSS summarizes news-logo stories using the frames and texts which have high RWR score. Figures 3 shows the top 30 frames selected by *MMSS* for the logo "Iraq". The top 7 frames are the frames of logo "Iraq" detected by the iconic matching. These frames are ranked high, simply because they are connected directly to the restart logo-node. Interestingly, *MMSS* found extra logo frames (e.g. the logo frame ranked 16) missed by the iconic matching. *MMSS* selects informative frames about the logo story, where faces of the major players are easily seen. For example, Kofi Annan appears in the rank 9 frame. Frames which contain important information in the form of *overlaid text* are also

selected, as shown in the frames ranked 26-th and 28-th - the "Crisis in the Gulf"- on which current developments are summarized. We emphasize that the information of overlaid text is important and may not be available to the textual retrieval methods, for they are rarely fully mentioned by the anchorperson and are not in the transcript. Other logos pertaining to the logo "Iraq" are also detected and selected, for example, the "Yeltsin" logo at rank 14 and the "Canada-Iraq" logo at rank 29.

Observation 2 *(Visual summary by MMSS) MMSS summarizes logo stories by selecting relevant frames from the news video collections. Specifically, MMSS selects frames (a) of persons, objects, activities which are significant to the story; (b) of meaningful overlaid text; (c) which contain the "seed" logos but are missed by the "iconic matching" technique; (d) of other relevant logos.*

Table 1 shows the terms selected by *MMSS* for summarizing three logo stories in Figure 1, namely "Winter Olympics", "Lewinsky" and "Iraq". Together with the selected frames in Figure 3, we found that *MMSS* successfully select meaningful frames and terms for the logo stories. *MMSS* also picks meaningful frames for the logo stories "Winter Olympics" and "Lewinsky", but the selected frames are not shown due to the page limit. Detail results can be found in [5].

Story	Summarizing terms
"Winter Olympics"	winter medal gold state skier headline news result superticker olympics competition nagano ceremony watch night round game team sport weather photo woman that today canada bronze year home storm coverage
"Lewinsky"	house lawyer intern ginsburg starr bill whitewater counsel immunity president clinton monica source information money trie learned iraq today state agreement country client weapon force nation inspection courthouse germany support
"Iraq"	iraq minister annan kofi effort baghdad report president arab strike defense sudan iraqi today weapon secretary talk school window problem there desk peter student system damage apart arnett albright secretarygeneral

**Table 1. (Textual summary by *MMSS*) Terms
are sorted (highest score first).**

3.2 Video retrieval

In the task of video retrieval, we are given a query (a set of terms), the goal is to retrieve shots which are most relevant to the query. In other words, we want to rank all shots according to their "closeness" to the set of query words. The queries used in our experiments are: {``lewinsky''},

493

Figure 4. Keyframes of the top 5 shots retrieved by *MMSS* **(top row), OKAPI (middle row) and LSI (bottom row) on query** {``lewinsky'', ``clinton''}. **Frames are ranked (highest score first).**

{``clinton''}, {``lewinsky'', ``clinton''}, {``annan''}, {``iraq''}, {``annan'', ``iraq''}, {``olympics''}, {``white'', ``house'',``scandal''}.

Since the data set we use does not have ground truth for any query, we do not report the standard precision and recall measures. Instead, we inspect the result by human judgment. We leave the precision/recall experiments to the future works.

We notice that a shot which contains keywords to a query is not necessarily a shot with meaningful content about the query. For example, a "teaser" in the beginning of a news broadcast introduces all headline news and is full of keywords. However, a teaser is usually accompanied with the anchor shots and does not have meaningful scene shots. Traditional textual retrieval methods are likely to retrieve teaser-style shots. On the other hand, *MMSS* is unbiased to the teasers, as we show next.

MMSS successfully ranks relevant shots to the top of the list, as shown in Figure 4. The frontal view of the major players related to the query is at the top of the list, for example, Starr at rank 1 and Monica at rank 4. In addition, *MMSS* avoids the news "teasers" while OKAPI and LSI rank the teaser shots with high scores. For example, in Figure 4, the rank 1 shot chosen by OKAPI (middle row) and the rank 5 shot chosen by LSI (bottom row) are both teaser shots.

Observation 3 *(OKAPI and LSI are biased to teaser shots) Textual retrieval methods such as OKAPI and LSI prefer teaser shots, for example, the "headlines preview" at the beginning of news programs, due to the many keywords*

the news anchors mentioned in those shots. Unfortunately, these teasers are not major shots of story content.

4. Conclusions

We propose *MMSS* for story-oriented multi-modal video summarization and cross-modality correlation discovery. *MMSS* encodes both the textual and scene information, as well as logos which link shots of a story, as a graph. The random work with restarts (RWR) stationary probability is used to obtain a story-specific relevance ranking among the terms and shot keyframes. We report experiments on the TRECVID 2003 data set, for two applications, namely, story-oriented summarization and video retrieval. Our experiments show that *MMSS* is effective and gives meaningful summaries. Moreover, *MMSS* matches the best textual information retrieval methods on video retrieval; in fact, it sometimes does better, because it avoids the news "teasers" (Observation 3). Unlike the textual retrieval methods, *MMSS* achieves these with no sophisticated parameter tuning, and no domain knowledge.

References

[1] P. Duygulu, J.-Y. Pan, and D. A. Forsyth. Towards auto-documentary: Tracking the evolution of news stories. In *Proceedings of the ACM Multimedia Conference*, October 2004.

[2] J. Edwards, R. White, and D. Forsyth. Words and pictures in the news. In *HLT-NAACL03 Workshop on Learning Word Meaning from Non-Linguistic Data*, May 2003.

[3] J. Goldstein, V. O. Mittal, J. Carbonell, and J. Callan. Creating and evaluating multi-document sentence extract summaries. In *Proceedings of the Ninth International Conference on Information Knowledge Management (CIKM-00)*, November 2000.

[4] C.-W. Ngo, Y.-F. Ma, and H.-J. Zhang. Automatic video summarization by graph modeling. In *Proceedings of the Ninth IEEE International Conference on Computer Vision (ICCV 2003)*, 2003.

[5] J.-Y. Pan, H.-J. Yang, and C. Faloutsos. MMSS: Graph-based multi-modal story-oriented video summarization and retrieval. Technical report, CMU-CS-04-114, Carnegie Mellon University, 2004.

[6] J.-Y. Pan, H.-J. Yang, C. Faloutsos, and P. Duygulu. Automatic multimedia cross-modal correlation discovery. In *Proceedings of the 10th ACM SIGKDD Conference*, August 2004.

[7] A. F. Smeaton, W. Kraaij, and P. Over. TRECVID 2003 - an introduction. In *Proceedings of TREC 2003*, 2003.

[8] M. A. Smith and T. Kanade. Video skimming and characterization through the combination of image and language understanding techniques. In *Proceedings of CVPR 1997*, pages 775–781, June 17-19 1997.

[9] H. Wactlar, M. Christel, Y. Gong, and A. Hauptmann. Lessons learned from the creation and deployment of a terabyte digital video library. *IEEE Computer*, 32(2):66–73, February 1999.

A Comparative Study of
Linear and Nonlinear Feature Extraction Methods

Cheong Hee Park   Haesun Park *
Dept. of Computer Science and Engineering
University of Minnesota
Minneapolis, MN 55455
{chpark, hpark}@cs.umn.edu

Panos Pardalos[†]
Dept. of Industrial and Systems Engineering
University of Florida
Gainesville, FL 32611
pardalos@ise.ufl.edu

Abstract

This paper presents theoretical relationships among several generalized LDA algorithms and proposes computationally efficient approaches for them utilizing the relationships. Generalized LDA algorithms are extended nonlinearly by kernel methods resulting in nonlinear discriminant analysis. Performances and computational complexities of these linear and nonlinear discriminant analysis algorithms are compared.

1. Introduction

Linear Discriminant Analysis (LDA) finds a linear transformation that maximizes the between-class scatter and minimizes the within-class scatter so that the class separability is maximized in the reduced dimensional space. For a data matrix $A = [a_1, \cdots, a_n] = [A_1, A_2, \cdots, A_r] \in \mathbb{R}^{m \times n}$ where each class A_i $(1 \le i \le r)$ has n_i elements and N_i is the index set of data items in the class A_i, the between-class scatter matrix S_b, within-class scatter matrix S_w and total scatter matrix S_t are defined as

$$S_b = \sum_{i=1}^{r} n_i (c_i - c)(c_i - c)^T,$$
$$S_w = \sum_{i=1}^{r} \sum_{j \in N_i} (a_j - c_i)(a_j - c_i)^T, \qquad (1)$$
$$S_t = \sum_{i=1}^{n} (a_i - c)(a_i - c)^T,$$

using the class centroid $c_i = \frac{1}{n_i} \sum_{j \in N_i} a_j$ and the global centroid $c = \frac{1}{n} \sum_{j=1}^{n} a_j$. An optimization criterion in LDA is to find a linear transformation G^T which maximizes $\text{trace}((G^T S_w G)^{-1}(G^T S_b G))$ where $G^T S_i G$ for $i = b, w$

are the scatter matrices in the transformed space by G^T. It is well known [4] that this criterion is maximized when the columns of $G \in \mathbb{R}^{m \times (r-1)}$ are the eigenvectors corresponding to the $r - 1$ largest eigenvalues of $S_b g = \lambda S_w g$. In the classical LDA, S_w is assumed to be nonsingular and the problem becomes computing eigenvectors of $S_w^{-1} S_b$. However, when the number of data items is smaller than the dimension of data space, all of the scatter matrices become singular and the classical LDA is difficult to apply. In order to make LDA applicable for undersampled problems, several methods have been proposed [3, 5, 1, 8, 7]. In this paper, we study theoretical and algorithmic relationships among these generalized LDA algorithms and propose computationally efficient approaches to them by utilizing the relationships (Section 2). Nonlinear extensions of generalized LDA algorithms based on kernel methods are proposed (Section 3). Performances and computational complexities of these linear and nonlinear discriminant analysis algorithms are compared (Section 4). Due to the space limitation, we refer readers to the paper [6] for detailed discussions, proofs and pseudocodes of these algorithms.

2. A Comparison of Generalized LDA Algorithms for Undersampled Problems

Regularized LDA [RLDA] When S_w is singular or ill-conditioned, a diagonal matrix αI with $\alpha > 0$ is added to S_w. Since S_w is symmetric positive semidefinite, $S_w + \alpha I$ is nonsingular with any $\alpha > 0$. Therefore we can apply the classical LDA to solve the eigenvalue problem $S_b g = \lambda(S_w + \alpha I)g$.

LDA based on the Generalized Singular Value Decomposition [LDA/GSVD] Howland et al. [5] applied the Generalized Singular Value Decomposition (GSVD) to overcome the limitation of the classical LDA. Note that the scatter matrices defined in (1) can be computed as

$$S_b = H_b H_b^T, \quad S_w = H_w H_w^T, \quad S_t = H_t H_t^T,$$

*This work was supported in part by the National Science Foundation grants CCR-0204109 and ACI-0305543. Any opinions, findings and conclusions or recommendations expressed in this material are those of the authors and do not necessarily reflect the views of the National Science Foundation (NSF). The work of Haesun park has been performed while at the NSF and was partly supported by IR/D from the NSF.

[†]The work was partially supported by NSF and NATO grants.

$$H_b = [\sqrt{n_1}(c_1 - c), \cdots, \sqrt{n_r}(c_r - c)] \in \mathbb{R}^{m \times r},$$
$$H_w = [A_1 - c_1 e_1, \cdots, A_r - c_r e_r] \in \mathbb{R}^{m \times n}, \quad (2)$$
$$H_t = [a_1 - c, \cdots, a_n - c] \in \mathbb{R}^{m \times n},$$

where $e_i = [1, \cdots, 1] \in \mathbb{R}^{1 \times n_i}$. When the GSVD is applied to the pair $\{H_b^T, H_w^T\}$, we obtain

$$X^T S_b X = \begin{bmatrix} \Gamma_b^T \Gamma_b & \\ & 0_{m-s} \end{bmatrix}, X^T S_w X = \begin{bmatrix} \Gamma_w^T \Gamma_w & \\ & 0_{m-s} \end{bmatrix} (3)$$

where $s = \text{rank}([H_b \ H_w])$ and $\Gamma_b^T \Gamma_b$ and $\Gamma_w^T \Gamma_w$ are diagonal matrices with nonincreasing and nondecreasing diagonal components respectively. The $r - 1$ leftmost columns of X which correspond to the largest diagonal components in $\Gamma_b^T \Gamma_b$ and the smallest ones in $\Gamma_w^T \Gamma_w$ give a transformation matrix G_h for this method LDA/GSVD.

Now we show an efficient algorithm which computes the same solution as that by LDA/GSVD but saves computational complexity greatly. The proof can be found in [6].

1. Compute EVD of S_t: $S_t = Q_1 R^2 Q_1^T$ where $s = \text{rank}(S_t)$, $Q_1 \in \mathbb{R}^{m \times s}$ and the diagonal matrix R has positive nonincreasing diagonal components.

2. Compute W from the EVD of $\tilde{S}_b \equiv R^{-1} Q_1^T S_b Q_1 R^{-1}$: $\tilde{S}_b = W \Gamma_b^T \Gamma_b W^T$.

3. Assign the first $r - 1$ columns of $Q_1 R^{-1} W$ to G_h.
The matrices Q_1 and R in the EVD of $S_t \in \mathbb{R}^{m \times m}$ can be obtained by the EVD of $H_t^T H_t \in \mathbb{R}^{n \times n}$ instead of $H_t H_t^T \in \mathbb{R}^{m \times m}$ [4]. Hence, we just need to compute the EVD of a much smaller $n \times n$ matrix $H_t^T H_t$ instead of $m \times m$ matrix $S_t = H_t H_t^T$ when $m >> n$.

A Method based on Projection onto null(S_w) [To-N(S_w)] Chen et al. [1] proposed a generalized method for LDA and applied it for face recognition. Consider the SVD of S_w, $S_w = U_w \Sigma_w U_w^T$. Partitioning U_w as $U_w = [U_{w1} U_{w2}]$ where $s_1 = \text{rank}(S_w)$ and $U_{w1} \in \mathbb{R}^{m \times s_1}$, we have null($S_w$) = span($U_{w2}$). First, the transformation by $U_{w2} U_{w2}^T$ projects the original data to null(S_w). Then, the eigenvectors corresponding to the nonzero eigenvalues of the between-class scatter matrix $\tilde{S}_b \equiv U_{w2} U_{w2}^T S_b U_{w2} U_{w2}^T$ are found by the EVD of $\tilde{S}_b = \tilde{U}_{b1} \tilde{\Sigma}_{b1} \tilde{U}_{b1}^T$ where $s_2 = \text{rank}(\tilde{S}_b)$ and $\tilde{U}_{b1} \in \mathbb{R}^{m \times s_2}$. The transformation matrix G_e is obtained by $G_e = U_{w2} U_{w2}^T \tilde{U}_{b1}$. Let us call this method as To-N(S_w) for simplicity.

Denote X in (3) as $X = [\underbrace{X_1}_{\mu} \ \underbrace{X_2}_{\tau} \ \underbrace{X_3}_{s-\mu-\tau} \ \underbrace{X_4}_{m-s}]$, where the columns of X_1 correspond to nonzero diagonal components in $\Gamma_b^T \Gamma_b$ and zeros in $\Gamma_w^T \Gamma_w$, i.e., they belong to null(S_w) $\cap$ null(S_b)^c. Referring to the paper [6] for detailed discussions, a relationship between LDA/GSVD and the method To-N(S_w) can be found as $G_e = U_{w2} U_{w2}^T \tilde{U}_{b1} = X_1 H + X_4 K$ for some matrices $H \in \mathbb{R}^{\mu \times s_2}$, $K \in \mathbb{R}^{(m-s) \times s_2}$ and each column of H is nonzero. Since all data items are transformed to the constant point by x^T for $x \in$ null(S_w) $\cap$ null(S_b), the transformation by $X_4 K$ corresponds to the translation

which does not affect the classification performance. More discussions about relationships between two methods can be found in [6].

A Method based on the Transformation by a Basis of range(S_b) [To-R(S_b)] Contrary to the method To-N(S_w), the method by Yu and Yang [8] first transforms the original space by using a basis of range(S_b). Let the EVD of S_b be $U_{b1} \Sigma_{b1} U_{b1}^T$ where the diagonals in Σ_{b1} are nonzero. Then range(S_b) = span(U_{b1}). The original data is transformed to the range space of S_b by $V_y \equiv U_{b1} \Sigma_{b1}^{-1/2}$ and the between-class scatter matrix $\tilde{S}_b$ in the transformed space becomes $\tilde{S}_b = V_y^T S_b V_y = I$. Now consider the EVD of $\tilde{S}_w \equiv V_y^T S_w V_y = \tilde{U}_w \tilde{\Sigma}_w \tilde{U}_w^T$. Then $\tilde{U}_w^T V_y^T S_b V_y \tilde{U}_w = I$ and $\tilde{U}_w^T V_y^T S_w V_y \tilde{U}_w = \tilde{\Sigma}_w$. Scaling by $\tilde{\Sigma}_w^{-1/2}$, the transformation matrix is given as $G_y = V_y \tilde{U}_w \tilde{\Sigma}_w^{-1/2}$ where each column of G_y belongs to null(S_w)^c $\cap$ null(S_b)^c. Let us call this method To-R(S_b). An experiment demonstrating the effects of scaling by $\tilde{\Sigma}_w^{-1/2}$ can be found in [6].

A Method based on PCA plus Transformations to range(S_w) and null(S_w) [To-NR(S_w)] While the methods discussed search for discriminative vectors either in null(S_w) $\cap$ null(S_b)^c or in null(S_w)^c $\cap$ null(S_b)^c, recently Yang et al. [7] have proposed a method which try searching in both spaces, which we call To-NR(S_w). In the method by Yang et al., first, the transformation by the orthonormal basis of range(S_t), as in PCA, is performed. Let the SVD of S_t be $U_{t1} \Sigma_{t1} U_{t1}^T$ where $s = \text{rank}(S_t)$ and $\Sigma_{t1} \in \mathbb{R}^{m \times s}$. In the transformed space by U_{t1}, let the within-scatter matrix be $\tilde{S}_w \equiv U_{t1}^T S_w U_{t1}$. Then the basis of null($\tilde{S}_w$) and range($\tilde{S}_w$) can be obtained by the EVD of $\tilde{S}_w$

$$\tilde{S}_w = \tilde{U}_w \tilde{\Sigma}_w \tilde{U}_w^T = [\tilde{U}_{w1} \ \tilde{U}_{w2}] \begin{bmatrix} \tilde{\Sigma}_{w1} & 0 \\ 0 & 0 \end{bmatrix} \begin{bmatrix} \tilde{U}_{w1}^T \\ \tilde{U}_{w2}^T \end{bmatrix}.$$

In the transformed space by the basis $\tilde{U}_{w2}$ of null($\tilde{S}_w$), let Y be a matrix whose columns are the eigenvectors corresponding to nonzero eigenvalues of $\bar{S}_b \equiv \tilde{U}_{w2}^T U_{t1}^T S_b U_{t1} \tilde{U}_{w2}$. On the other hand, in the transformed space by the basis $\tilde{U}_{w1}$ of range($\tilde{S}_w$), let Z be a matrix whose columns are the eigenvectors with the largest nonzero eigenvalues of $\hat{S}_t^{-1} \hat{S}_b$ where $\hat{S}_b \equiv \tilde{U}_{w1}^T U_{t1}^T S_b U_{t1} \tilde{U}_{w1}$ and $\hat{S}_t \equiv \tilde{U}_{w1}^T U_{t1}^T S_t U_{t1} \tilde{U}_{w1}$. Then the transformation matrix is constructed as $G_d = [U_{t1} \tilde{U}_{w2} Y \ U_{t1} \tilde{U}_{w1} Z]$. The first part in G_d comes from null(S_w) $\cap$ null(S_b)^c, while the second part belongs to null(S_w)^c $\cap$ null(S_b)^c. When two parts $U_{t1} \tilde{U}_{w2} Y$ and $U_{t1} \tilde{U}_{w1} Z$ are used for transformation matrix G_d, it will be better to normalize the columns in $U_{t1} \tilde{U}_{w1} Z$ so that effects of both parts can be balanced. An efficient approach to compute Z was proposed in [6] which does not need to compute $\hat{S}_t^{-1}$ explicitly. We also showed that the transformation matrix G_e by the method To-N(S_w) is exactly same as $U_{t1} \tilde{U}_{w2} Y$ in G_d [6].

3. Nonlinear Discriminant Analysis based on Kernel Methods

In this section, we present nonlinear extensions of the generalized LDA algorithms by kernel methods. Kernel methods are based on that for any kernel function κ satisfying Mercer's condition, there exists a feature map Φ satisfying $<\Phi(a), \Phi(b)> = \kappa(a, b)$ where $<,>$ is an inner product in the mapped feature space [2]. We apply the kernel method to perform LDA in the feature space instead of the original input space. Given a kernel function κ, let $\mathcal{S}_b$ and $\mathcal{S}_w$ be the between-class and within-class scatter matrices in the feature space $\mathcal{F} \subset \mathbb{R}^N$ which has been transformed by a mapping Φ. Then the LDA in $\mathcal{F}$ finds a linear transformation $\mathcal{G} = [\varphi_1, \cdots, \varphi_l] \in \mathbb{R}^{N \times l}$, where the columns of $\mathcal{G}$ are the generalized eigenvectors corresponding to the largest eigenvalues of $\mathcal{S}_b \varphi = \lambda \mathcal{S}_w \varphi$.

Let us represent φ by a linear combination of $\Phi(a_i)$ as $\varphi = \sum_{i=1}^n u_i \Phi(a_i)$ where $u = [u_1, \cdots, u_n]^T$, and define

$$\mathcal{K}_b = [b_{ij}]_{(1 \leq i \leq n, 1 \leq j \leq r)}, \mathcal{K}_w = [w_{ij}]_{(1 \leq i \leq n, 1 \leq j \leq n)} \quad (4)$$

$$b_{ij} = \sqrt{n_j}(\frac{1}{n_j}\sum_{p \in N_j} \kappa(a_i, a_p) - \frac{1}{n}\sum_{p=1}^n \kappa(a_i, a_p)),$$

$$w_{ij} = \kappa(a_i, a_j) - \frac{1}{n_\delta}\sum_{p \in N_\delta} \kappa(a_i, a_p) \text{ when } a_j \in \text{class } \delta.$$

Then we can show that the generalized eigenvalue problem $\mathcal{S}_b \varphi = \lambda \mathcal{S}_w \varphi$ is equivalent to $\mathcal{K}_b \mathcal{K}_b^T u = \lambda \mathcal{K}_w \mathcal{K}_w^T u$. The proof can be found in [6]. Note that $\mathcal{K}_b \mathcal{K}_b^T$ and $\mathcal{K}_w \mathcal{K}_w^T$ can be viewed as the between-class scatter matrix and within-class scatter matrix of the kernel matrix $K = [\kappa(a_i, a_j)]_{(1 \leq i \leq n, 1 \leq j \leq n)}$ when each column in K is considered as a data point in the n-dimensional space. It can be observed by comparing the structures of $\mathcal{K}_b$ and $\mathcal{K}_w$ in (4) with those of H_b and H_w in (2). Since $\mathcal{K}_w \mathcal{K}_w^T$ is always singular, the classical LDA can not be applied. Now we apply the generalized LDA algorithm discussed in Section 2 for the between-class scatter, within-class scatter and total scatter matrices as $\mathcal{K}_b \mathcal{K}_b^T$, $\mathcal{K}_w \mathcal{K}_w^T$ and $\mathcal{K}_t \mathcal{K}_t^T$. Let

$$\mathcal{G} = [u^{(1)}, \cdots, u^{(l)}] \in \mathbb{R}^{n \times l} \quad (5)$$

be the transformation matrix obtained by applying the generalized LDA algorithm, where $u^{(i)} = [u_{1i}, \cdots, u_{ni}]^T$ $(1 \leq i \leq l)$. Defining $\varphi_i = \sum_{j=1}^n u_{ji} \Phi(a_j)$, $1 \leq i \leq l$, for any input vector $a \in \mathbb{R}^{m \times 1}$ the dimension reduced representation of a is given by

$$\begin{bmatrix} \varphi_1^T \\ \vdots \\ \varphi_l^T \end{bmatrix} \Phi(a) = \mathcal{G}^T \begin{bmatrix} \kappa(a_1, a) \\ \vdots \\ \kappa(a_n, a) \end{bmatrix}. \quad (6)$$

This nonlinear discriminant analysis is summarized as
1. Compute the scatter matrices of the kernel matrix $K = [\kappa(a_i, a_j)]_{(1 \leq i \leq n, 1 \leq j \leq n)}$.
2. Compute the transformation matrix $\mathcal{G}$ in (5) by applyig the generalized LDA algorithm discussed in Section 2.
3. For any input vector $a \in \mathbb{R}^{m \times 1}$, a dimension reduced representation is computed by Eq. (6).

Data	RLDA	LDA/GSVD	To-$N(S_w)$	To-$R(S_b)$	To-$NR(S_w)$
Re	**95.8**	95.1	94.5	94.2	94.7
Tr1	95.7	**98.3**	98.1	96.7	97.6
Tr2	87.9	90.3	91.5	88.2	**91.8**
Tr3	98.6	98.4	98.6	97.7	**98.7**
Tr4	**98.0**	97.3	97.0	96.3	97.1
Tr5	93.6	93.3	94.2	94.1	**94.4**
AT&T	98.0	93.5	98.0	**99.0**	98.8
Yale	97.6	**98.8**	97.6	89.7	98.2

		In the feature space			
Data	LDA	RLDA	LDA/GSVD	To-$N(S_w)$	To-$R(S_b)$ To-$NR(S_w)$
Musk	91.2	97.6	**99.4**	**99.4**	89.2 99.3
Isolet	93.9	95.8	96.8	97.0	89.7 **97.1**
Car	88.2	94.7	94.1	94.9	84.5 **95.2**
Mfeature	–	94.4	98.1	**98.3**	94.0 **98.3**
Bcancer	95.3	95.2	**96.4**	93.5	92.8 94.3
Bscale	87.0	**94.1**	86.5	86.5	86.5 86.1

Table 1. Prediction accuracies (%).

4 Experimental Comparisons and Computational Complexities

In order to compare the discussed generalized LDA algorithms, we conducted experiments using two types of undersampled problems, text classification and face recognition. Text datasets were downloaded from http://www-users.cs.umn.edu/~karypis/cluto/ download.html and preprocessed. Each dataset was randomly split to the training and test sets with the ratio of 4 : 1 and experiments were repeated 10 times. In face recognition, two face databases, AT&T (formerly ORL) and Yale face database were used and prediction accuracies were obtained by leave-one-out method. After computing a transformation matrix using training data, both training and test data are represented in the reduced dimensional space and the nearest neighbor classifier is applied for classification. The first table in Table 1 reports the prediction accuracies. For RLDA, the best accuracy among $\alpha = 0.5, 1, 1.5$ is reported. As shown in the table, no single method works the best in all situations, implying that the performances may depend on the characteristics of datasets.

For the comparison of performances of nonlinear discriminant analysis algorithms, six datasets were collected from UCI machine learning repository. By randomly splitting the data to the training set and test set of equal size and repeating it 10 times, ten pairs of training and test sets were created for each data. Using the training set of the first one among ten pairs and the nearest-neighbor classifier, 5 cross-validation was used in order to determine the optimal value for σ in Gaussian kernel function $\kappa(x, y) = \exp\left(-\frac{\|x-y\|^2}{2\sigma^2}\right)$. Using the optimal σ values

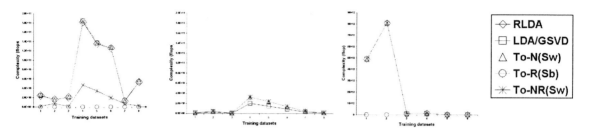

Figure 1. Comparison of computational complexities.

found, mean prediction accuracies by ten pairs of training and test sets in each dataset are reported in the second table of Table 1. It shows nonlinear discriminant analysis can improve the prediction accuracies of the classical LDA in the original data space. Experimental results of nonlinear discriminant analysis on undersampled problems can be found in [6]. Unlike in datasets from UCI database, classification performances on undersampled problems were not much improved by nonlinear discriminant analysis. It might indicate the linear separability in very high dimensional data such as text and face data.

Now we analyze computational complexities. For $S \in \mathbb{R}^{p \times q}$ and $p >> q$, when only eigenvectors corresponding to the nonzero eigenvalues of $SS^T \in \mathbb{R}^{p \times p}$ are needed, we utilized the approach of computing the EVD of $S^T S \in \mathbb{R}^{q \times q}$ instead of $SS^T \in \mathbb{R}^{p \times p}$. Please refer to [6] for more detailed discussions about computational complexities of the SVD, matrix multiplications and main decompositions which are needed to compute the transformation matrices for each algorithm. The left figure in Figure 1 illustrates the total computational complexities of five algorithms discussed in Section 2 by using specific sizes of training datasets used in the experiment. Training data sets on the horizontal axis follow the order of the datasets presented in Table 1. The second figure shows complexities of the proposed efficient algorithms for LDA/GSVD, To-$N(S_w)$ and To-$NR(S_w)$ which reduced the complexities of the original algorithms greatly. Recall that the transformation matrix G_e by the method To-$N(S_w)$ is exactly same as the first part $U_{t1}\tilde{U}_{w2}Y$ in the transformation matrix G_d by To-$NR(S_w)$, therefore the complexity of To-$N(S_w)$ should be less than the one of To-$NR(S_w)$. The third figure compares the computational complexities of nonlinear discriminant analysis algorithms using the datasets in the second table of Table 1.

RLDA, LDA/GSVD and the method To-$N(S_w)$ have high computational complexities overall, while To-$R(S_b)$ obtained the lowest computational costs. Compared with the dramatic differences in computational complexities, classification performances for undersampled problems do not show big difference. However, combining To-$R(S_b)$ with kernel methods does not make effective nonlinear dimension reduction method, indicating that the null space of

$\mathcal{K}_w \mathcal{K}_w^T$ contains discriminative information. The regularized LDA obtained good performances both in the original space and the feature space, while the computational complexity on the undersampled problems can be very demanding. And also the regularization parameter should be determined experimentally. The method To-$NR(S_w)$ showed favorable computational complexities and performances. In the transformed feature space, the generalized eigenvalue problem $\mathcal{K}_b \mathcal{K}_b^T u = \lambda \mathcal{K}_w \mathcal{K}_w^T u$ is formulated under the condition that the number of data and the data dimension become equal. Hence the PCA step in the transformed feature space is not so effective since the dimension reduction by the PCA is not great unlike in undersampled problems. We note that nonlinear discriminant analysis of To-$NR(S_w)$ was implemented disregarding the PCA step and therefore reducing computational complexity. We also confirmed the PCA step does not make any difference in the classification performance.

References

[1] L. Chen, H. Liao, M. Ko, J. Lin, and G. Yu. A new LDA-based face recognition system which can solve the small sample size problem. *pattern recognition*, 33:1713–1726, 2000.

[2] N. Cristianini and J. Shawe-Taylor. *An Introduction to Support Vector Machines and other kernel-based learning methods*. Cambridge, 2000.

[3] J. Friedman. Regularized discriminant analysis. *Journal of the American statistical association*, 84(405):165–175, 1989.

[4] K. Fukunaga. *Introduction to Statistical Pattern Recognition*. Acadamic Press, second edition, 1990.

[5] P. Howland, M. Jeon, and H. Park. Structure preserving dimension reduction for clustered text data based on the generalized singular value decomposition. *SIAM Journal on Matrix Analysis and Applications*, 25(1):165–179, 2003.

[6] C.H. Park, H. Park and P. Pardalos. A comparative study of linear and nonlinear feature extraction methods. Technical Reports 04-032, Department of Computer Science and Engineering, University of Minnesota, Twin Cities, 2004.

[7] J. Yang and J.-Y. Yang. Why can LDA be performed in PCA transformed space? *Pattern Recognition*, 36:563–566, 2003.

[8] H. Yu and J. Yang. A direct LDA algorithm for high-dimensional data- with application to face recognition. *Pattern Recognition*, 34:2067–2070, 2001.

SVM and Graphical Algorithms: a Cooperative Approach

François Poulet
ESIEA – Pôle ECD
BP 0339
53003 Laval Cedex - France
poulet@esiea-ouest.fr

Abstract

We present a cooperative approach using both Support Vector Machine (SVM) algorithms and visualization methods. SVM are widely used today and often give high quality results, but they are used as "black-box" (it is very difficult to explain the obtained results) and cannot treat easily very large datasets. We have developed graphical methods to help the user to evaluate and explain the SVM results. The first method is a graphical representation of the separating frontier quality, it is then linked with other visualization tools to help the user explaining SVM results. The information provided by these graphical methods is also used for SVM parameter tuning, they are then used together with automatic algorithms to deal with very large datasets on standard computers. We present an evaluation of our approach with the UCI and the Kent Ridge Bio-medical data sets.

1. Introduction

The size of data stored in the world is constantly increasing but data do not become useful until some of the information they carry is extracted. Knowledge Discovery in Databases (KDD) can be defined as the non-trivial process of identifying valid, novel, potentially useful, and ultimately understandable patterns in data [5]. In usual KDD approaches, visualization tools are only used in two particular steps: in one of the first steps to visualize the data or data distribution and in one of the last steps to visualize the results of the data mining algorithm. Between these two steps, automatic data mining algorithms are carried out. Some new methods have recently appeared [14], trying to involve more significantly the user in the data mining process and using more intensively the visualization, this new kind of approach is called visual data mining. We present some graphical methods we have developed to increase the visualization part in the data mining process and more precisely in supervised classification tasks.

The first method is used to evaluate the quality and interpret or explain the results of Support Vector Machine

(SVM) algorithms in supervised classification. Very few papers have addressed this topic [2], [10]. The graphical method is used to give the user an evaluation of the quality of the obtained separating surface. This graphical method is then linked with another one to try to explain what are the attributes having an important part in the classification. Then we also use the same representation to help the user in parameters tuning (a very important part of the data mining task, with SVM algorithms and with many other ones), but here again the process is nearly never described. We do not pretend to solve the whole problem but only avoid parsing all the possibilities and when we are dealing with very large datasets this can be really time saving. One restriction of the data visualization methods is well known: they usually cannot treat very large data sets. At last, we present a cooperative approach using both the previous graphical method and automatic algorithms to efficiently deal with very large datasets.

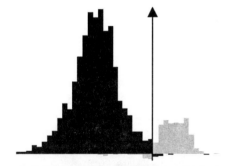

Figure 1. Distribution of the Segment data points

2. Graphical interpretation of SVM results

SVM algorithms [13] are kernel-based methods, they can be used for supervised classification, regression or novelty detection and have been successfully applied to a large number of applications. However, most of existing SVM algorithms have two disadvantages: it may be difficult to explain the results obtained and they need an important parameter tuning stage before to give the expected accuracy. We have developed a graphical method to try to explain the SVM results and evaluate their quality. We compute the data distribution according to the distance to the separating surface (while the classification task is performed). For each class, the positive distribution is the set of correctly classified data points, and the negative distribution is the set of misclassified data points. Then we display this distribution with a simple histogram. We can use this single tool to evaluate the quality of the separating frontier (for SVM separating boundary or any other separating feature: a cut in a decision tree algorithm or a regression line). Figure 1 shows an example of such a distribution with the class 5 of the Segment data from the UCI Machine Learning Repository. The separating frontier is a good one: there are only some misclassified data points (negative distribution) near the separating hyperplane (because we used a linear kernel). We can also use this tool linked with other data representations, for example a set of two-dimensional scatter plot matrices [1] (figure 2) or parallel coordinates [8].

When the user selects a bar in the graphical distribution, the corresponding data points are selected in the other graphical tools too. If we select the bars nearest from the separating plane, this allow the user to have some interesting information about the boundary between the two classes: what are the important attributes for the classification, is it a straight frontier or is it a complex one, etc. Figure 2 shows an example of a straight frontier between the class 2 and the other ones (Segment dataset): there is no data point near the boundary. In figure 3, we select the nearest points from the boundary (in the distribution), and they are automatically selected in the scatter plot matrices in the right part of Figure 3 (in bold white). We find the same information as in the distribution display: there is no point near the boundary (there is a wide empty space between the class 7 and the other ones).

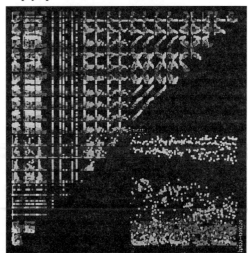

Figure 2. Scatter-plot matrices (Segment dataset)

We can also see that the boundary between the class 7 and the other ones is a straight line. And we can infer from the visualization that the attribute corresponding to the y axis in the bottom right part of the visualization is the one

deciding the membership of class 7. This simple graphical tool allows us to explain the results obtained by a SVM algorithm.

Linked with another graphical data representation (for example the scatter-plot matrices or the parallel coordinates), the distribution can help the user in interpreting the frontier: he is able to explain what are the attributes that make a point belonging to a given class. One must not forget nearly all SVM algorithms only give as results the accuracy and the support vectors. The comprehensibility and confidence in the result are never used in algorithm evaluation but an end user will not use a model if he has not a minimum comprehension and confidence in it.

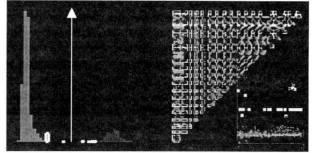

Figure 3. Visualization of the separating hyper-plane between class 7 and the other ones (Segment dataset)

4. Graphical SVM parameter tuning

Parameter tuning is a very important part of the SVM algorithms even if very few papers explain how to perform this task. We call parameter either the tuning of the algorithm input parameter, either the choice of the kernel function. One paper [6] explains how to perform this task. This is an exact citation from this paper:

"... A random tuning set of the size of 10% of the training data was chosen and separated from the training set. Several SVM were trained on the remaining 90% of the training data using values of v equal to 2^i with i=-12,...,0,...,12. Values of v and δ that gave the best SVM correctness on the tuning set were chosen.".

We can use the information obtained by the visualization tools described in the previous section to help the user. A first possibility is to use the results of the data distribution according to their distance to the separating frontier. In the example shown in Figure 3 (left part), we can see there is no data point near the frontier. This gives the user the following information: at least one parameter has not to be tuned finely. This simple information can really reduce the time needed for the classification task. Another possibility is to use the data visualization to help the user choosing the kernel function. In the examples shown in figure 2 and figure 3, we can see a linear boundary for the elements of the class 2 and class 7. So a linear kernel function will be sufficient to get good results, and if the visualization of the data distribution according to their distance to the separating froniter shows several misclassified data points near the boundary, another kernel function may be more suitable.

Another interesting feature is to use these tools for the multi-class case. SVM algorithms are only able to deal with two classes. When the dataset has more than two classes the most used approaches are the one-against-all and the one-against-one. We can use the visualization methods to help the user to tune parameters and to choose a kernel function for each class and so use sophisticated (with often high computational cost) kernel function only when needed. The visualization is used to guide the user in his choices and reduce the number of classification algorithms to run.

We have seen how simple visualization methods can help the user to evaluate the quality of the result obtained by an automatic SVM algorithm and interpret or understand this result on one hand, and to help him to choose the parameters or kernel functions to use to get high quality results without having to execute several times the classification algorithm on the other hand.

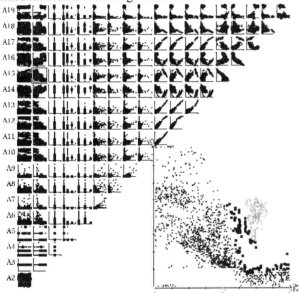

Figure 4. Interactive support vector selection

5. Cooperative methods

Scatter-plot matrices and parallel-coordinates are only useful if the the dataset size is limited to some dozens of dimensions and some thousands of items. In order to be able to deal with larger datasets [11], we combine automatic algorithms and visualization tools to get a cooperative method able to deal with large datasets.

5.1. Dimensionality reduction

Most of existing classification algorithms cannot deal with datasets having very large number of dimensions and use a pre-processing step to reduce the dataset dimensionality. We use a feature selection method with the 1-norm linear SVM proposed by [7] as data preprocessing. This algorithm maximizes the margin by minimizing the 1-norm (instead of 2-norm with standard SVM) of the plane coefficients. This algorithm provides results having many null coefficients. The corresponding dimensions are removed without losing too much information. We have evaluated the performances of the algorithm on the bio-medical datasets from the Kent Ridge Bio-medical Data Set Repository.

After a feature selection task with the 1-norm linear SVM, we have used LibSVM to classify these datasets. The results concerning accuracy (table 1) show it is equal or increased for four datasets and reduced in only one case. And then, visualization tools are able to work on these datasets, to help the user to interpret and explain the obtained results even with large number of attributes.

Table 1. Accuracy with and without feature selection

dataset (# dim. used / # dim)	Accuracy (%)	
	Feature selection	No selection
AML-ALL Leukemia (5 / 7129)	**94.12**	**94.12**
Breast Cancer (10 / 24481)	**78.95**	73.68
Colon Tumor (19 / 2000)	**96.77**	90.32
Lung Cancer (9 / 12533)	96.64	**98.66**
Ovarian Cancer (13 / 15154)	**100**	**100**

5.2. Data reduction

In order to deal with datasets having large number of items we use the same kind of approach as the RSVM algorithm [9]. First, we use a k-means algorithm to create clusters and then we sample data from the clusters. The resulting small dataset is then displayed with scatter-plot matrices and the user interactively selects the subset S of points (used as support vectors in input of the RSVM algorithm) closest to the separating boundary between the two classes. We illustrate our approach with the UCI Forest cover type dataset (581,012 data points, 54 dimensions and 7 classes), known as a difficult classification problem for SVM. Collobert and his colleagues [3] trained the models (2-against-all) with SVMTorch and a RBF kernel, the learning task needed more than 2 days and 5 hours with an accuracy being 83.24 %. We have also classified the class 2 against all. With our cooperative approach, about one hour was needed to create clusters and sampling points. Then, we interactively select support vectors from the reduced dataset as shown in figure 4. A rectangular RBF kernel is created and the learning task needed about 8 hours to construct the model (with an accuracy equal to 84.32%). This cooperative approach using both automatic algorithms and an interactive selection of the vector supports, allows us to deal with datasets having a very large number of items.

5.3. A graphical data-mining environment

All the algorithms described in this paper have been implemented in a graphical data-mining environment containing both automatic and graphical, interactive tools [12]. We use simultaneously in the same window several linked graphical tools. To display them together, we have chosen the same metaphor as in existing Virtual Reality environments: a large wall (with *n* displays along it), a cube with (up to six) displays on the different faces of the cube and a third user-defined possibility. Once the way the tools will be displayed has been chosen, the user will have to choose the tools used. Several graphical or automatic tools are available today in our environment and it is possible to add others easily.

Figure 5. Linked visualizations of the same dataset

6. Conclusion and future work

We have presented new graphical or cooperative methods useful for classification tasks in data mining. The first method is a graphical evaluation of the quality of the SVM result with a histogram displaying the data distribution according to the distance to the separating surface. The user can evaluate the quality of the frontier and it can be used for any other type of frontier (a cut in a decision tree, a regression line, etc). Then this tool is linked with scatter-plot matrices or parallel coordinates to try to explain the results of the SVM. The same linked views can help the user in the parameter tuning step (for example by avoiding fine tuning when the margin is very large). Here the accuracy will not be increased, it is only the time needed to perform the classification that is reduced. And last cooperative algorithms are used to deal with very large datasets. This allows us to increase the accuracy and the comprehensibility of the obtained models and to reduce the time needed to perform the classification. All the methods we have presented are only dedicated to the supervised classifications tasks. We have started to use the same kind of approach for the

unsupervised classification (clustering) and outlier detection tasks in high-dimensional datasets.

7. References

[1] Becker R., Cleveland W. and Wilks A., "Dynamics Graphics for Data Analysis", *Statistical Science*, 2:355-395, 1987.

[2] Caragea, D., Cook, D. and Honavar, V., "Towards Simple, Easy-to-Understand, yet Accurate Classifiers", in proc. of ICDM'03, Melbourne, USA, 2003, pp. 497-500.

[3] Collobert, R., Bengio, S. and Bengio, Y., "A parallel Mixture of SVMs for Very Large Scale Problems", in proc. of NIPS'02, Vol. 14, MIT Press, 2002, pp. 633-640.

[4] Cristianini, N. and Shawe-Taylor, J., *An Introduction to Support Vector Machines and Other Kernel-based Learning Methods*, Cambridge University Press, 2000.

[5] Fayyad U., Piatetsky-Shapiro G., Smyth P., Uthurusamy R., *Advances in Knowledge Discovery and Data Mining*, AAAI Press, 1996.

[6] Fung G. and Mangasarian O., "Finite Newton Method for Lagrangian Support Vector Machine Classification", *Neurocomputing* 55, 39-55, Sept.2003.

[7] Fung G. and Mangasarian O., "A Feature Selection Newton Method for Support Vector Machine Classification", *Computational Optimization and Applications*, 28(2):185-202, 2004.

[8] Inselberg A. and Avidan T., "The Automated Multidimensional Detective", in proc. IEEE Infoviz'99, 112-119.

[9] Lee, Y-J. and Mangasarian, O., "RSVM, Reduced Support Vector Machines", Data Mining Institute Technical Report 00-07, Comp. Sc. Dpt, Univ. of Wisconsin, Madison, USA, 2000.

[10] Poulet F., "Cooperation between Automatic Algorithms, Interactive Algorithms and Visualization Tools for Visual Data Mining", in proc. VDM@ECML/PKDD'2002, the 2nd Int. Workshop on Visual Data Mining, Helsinki, Finland, 2002.

[11] Poulet, F. and Do, T-N. "Mining Very Large Datasets with Support Vector Machine Algorithms", to appear *in Enterprise Information Systems V*, Camp O., Piattini M. and Hammoudi S. Eds, Kluwer, 2003.

[12] Poulet F., "FullView: A Visual Data Mining Environment", in *International Journal of Image and Graphics*, 2(1):127-143, Jan.2002.

[13] Vapnik V., 1995, "The Nature of Statistical Learning Theory", Springer-Verlag, New York.

[14] Wong P., "Visual Data Mining", in *IEEE Computer Graphics and Applications*, 19(5), 20-21, 1999.

RDF: A Density-based Outlier Detection Method using Vertical Data Representation

Dongmei Ren, Baoying Wang, William Perrizo
Computer Science Department
North Dakota State University
Fargo, ND 58105, USA
dongmei.ren@ndsu.nodak.edu

Abstract

Outlier detection can lead to discovering unexpected and interesting knowledge, which is critical important to some areas such as monitoring of criminal activities in electronic commerce, credit card fraud, etc. In this paper, we developed an efficient density-based outlier detection method for large datasets. Our contributions are: a) We introduce a relative density factor (RDF); b) Based on RDF, we propose an RDF-based outlier detection method which can efficiently prune the data points which are deep in clusters, and detect outliers only within the remaining small subset of the data; c) The performance of our method is further improved by means of a vertical data representation, P-trees. We tested our method with NHL and NBA data. Our method shows an order of magnitude speed improvement compared to the contemporary approaches.

1. Introduction

The problem of mining rare event, deviant objects, and exceptions is critically important in many domains, such as electronic commerce, network, surveillance, and health monitoring. Outlier mining is drawing more and more attentions. The current outlier mining approaches can be classified as five categories: statistic-based [1], distance-based[2][3][4],density-based[5][6], clustering-based [7], deviation-based [8][9]. Density-based outlier detection approaches are attracting most attentions for KDD in large database.

Breunig et al. proposed a **density-based approach** to mining outliers over datasets with different densities and arbitrary shapes [5]. Their notion of outliers is local in the sense that the outlier degree of an object is determined by taking into account the clustering structure in a bounded neighborhood of the object. The method does not suffer from local density problem, so it can mine outliers over non-uniform distributed datasets. However, the method needs three scans and the computation of neighborhood search costs highly, which makes the

method inefficient. Another density-based approach was introduced by Papadimitriou & Kiragawa [6] using local correlation integral (LOCI). This method selects a point as an outlier if its multi-granularity deviation factor (MDEF) deviates three times from the standard deviation of MDEF in a neighborhood. However, the cost of computing of the standard deviation is high.

In this paper, we propose an efficient density-based outlier detection method using a vertical data model P-Trees[1]. We introduce a novel local density measurement, relative density factor (RDF). RDF indicates the degree at which the density of the point P contrasts to those of its neighbors. We take RDF as an outlierness measurement. Based on RDF, our method prunes the data points that are deep in clusters, and detect outliers only within the remaining small subset of the data, which makes our method efficient. Also, the performance of our algorithm is enhanced significantly by means of P-Trees. Our method was tested over NHL and NBA datasets. Experiments show that our method has an order of magnitude of speed improvement with comparable accuracy over the current state-of-the-art density-based outlier detection approaches.

2. Review of P-trees

In previous work, we proposed a novel vertical data structure, the P-Trees. In the P-Trees approach, we decompose attributes of relational tables into separate files by bit position and compress the vertical bit files using a data-mining-ready structure called the P-trees. Instead of processing horizontal data vertically, we process these vertical P-trees horizontally through fast logical operations. Since P-trees remarkably compress the data and the P-trees logical operations scale extremely well, this vertical data structure has the potential to address the non-scalability with respect to size. In this section, we briefly review some useful features, which will

---

[1] Patents are pending on the P-tree technology. This work is partially supported by GSA Grant ACT#: K96130308.

be used in this paper, of P-Tree, including its optimized logical operations.

Given a data set with d attributes, $X = (A_1, A_2 \dots A_d)$, and the binary representation of the jth attribute A_j as $b_{j,m}$, $b_{j,m-1}, \dots, b_{j,i}, \dots, b_{j,1}, b_{j,0}$, we decompose each attribute into bit files, one file for each bit position [10]. Each bit file is converted into a P-tree. Logical AND, OR and NOT are the most frequently used operations of the P-trees, which facilitate efficient neighborhood search, pruning and computation of RDF.

Calculation of Inequality P-trees $P_{x \geq v}$ and $P_{x < v}$: Let x be a data point within a data set X, x be an m-bit data, and $P_m, P_{m-1}, \dots, P_0$ be P-trees for vertical bit files of X and $P'_m, P'_{m-1}, \dots P'_0$ be the complement set for the vertical bit files of X. Let $v = b_m \dots b_i \dots b_0$, where b_i is i^{th} binary bit value of v, then

$P_{x \geq v} = P_m \, op_m \dots P_i \, op_i \, P_{i-1} \dots op_1 \, P_0, \, i = 0, 1 \dots m$ (a)
$P_{x < v} = P'_m \, op_m \dots P'_i \, op_i \, P'_{i-1} \dots op_{k+1} P'_k, \, k \leq i \leq m$ (b)

In (a), op_i is $\cap$ if $b_i = 1$, op_i is $\cap$ otherwise; In (b) op_i is $\cap$ if $b_i = 0$, op_i is $\cup$ otherwise; In both (a) and (b), $\cup$ stands for OR and $\cap$ for AND; the operators are right binding, which means operators are associated from right to left, e.g., $P_2 \, op_2 \, P_1 \, op_1 \, P_0$ is equivalent to ($P_2 \, op_2 \, (P_1 \, op_1 \, P_0)$).

High Order Bit Metric (HOBit): The HOBit metric [12] is a bitwise distance function. It measures distance based on the most significant consecutive matching bit positions starting from the left. Assume A_i is an attribute in tabular data sets, $R(A_1, A_2, \dots, A_n)$ and its values are represented as binary numbers, x, i.e., $x = x(m)x(m-1) \dots x(1)x(0).x(-1) \dots x(-n)$. Let X and Y are A_i of two tuples/samples, the **HOBit similarity** between X and Y is defined by

$$m(X,Y) = \max \{i \mid x_i \oplus y_i\},$$

where x_i and y_i are the ith bits of X and Y respectively, and $\oplus$ denotes the XOR (exclusive OR) operation. Correspondingly, the **HOBit dissimilarity** is defined by

$$dm(X,Y) = 1 - \max\{i \mid x_i \oplus y_i\}.$$

3. RDF-based Outlier Detection Using P-trees

In this section, we first introduce some definitions related to outlier detection. Then propose a RDF-based outlier detection method. The performance of the algorithm is enhanced significantly by means of the bitwise vertical data structure, P-trees, and its optimized logical operations.

3.1. Outlier Definitions

From the density view, a point P is an outlier if it has much lower density than those of its neighbors. Based on

this intuition, we propose some definitions related to outliers.

Definition 1 (neighborhood)
The **neighborhood** of a data point P with the radius r is defined as a set Nbr $(P, r) = \{x \in X \mid |P-x| \leq r\}$, where $|P-x|$ is the distance between P and x. It is also called r-neighborhood. The points in this neighborhood are called neighbors of P, or direct r-neighbors of P. The number of neighbors of P is defined as N (Nbr (P, r)); **Indirect neighbors** of P are those points that are within the r-neighborhood of the direct neighbors of P but not include direct neighbors of P.

Definition 2 (density factor)
Given a data point P and the neighborhood radius r, **Density factor** (DF) of P is a measurement for local density around P, denoted as DF (P,r). It is defined as the number of neighbors of P divided by the radius r.

$$DF(P,r) = N(Nbr(P,r))/r. \tag{1}$$

Neighborhood density factor of the point P, denoted as $DF_{nbr}(P, r)$, is the average density factor of the neighbors of P.

$$DF_{nbr}(P,r) = \sum_{i=1}^{N(Nbr(P,r))} DF(q_i,r)/N(Nbr(P,r)),$$

where q_i is the neighbors of P, $i = 1, 2, \dots, N(Nbr(P,r))$.

Relative Density Factor (RDF) of the point P, denoted as RDF (P, r), is the ratio of neighborhood density factor of P over its density factor (DF).

$$RDF(P,r) = DF_{nbr}(P,r)/DF(P,r) \tag{2}$$

RDF indicates the degree at which the density of the point P contrasts to those of its neighbors. We take RDF as an outlierness measurement, which indicates the degree to which a point can be an outlier in the view of the whole dataset.

Definition 3 (outliers)
Based on RDF, we define **outliers** as a subset of the dataset X with RDF > t, where t is a RDF threshold defined by case. The outlier set is denoted as Ols(X, t) = $\{x \in X \mid RDF(x) > t\}$.

3.2. RDF-based Outlier Detection with Pruning

Given a dataset X and a RDF threshold t, the RDF-based outlier detection is processed in two phases: "zoom-out" procedure and "zoom-in" procedure. The detection process starts with the "zoom-out" procedure, which calls "zoom-in" procedure when necessary. On the other hand the "zoom-in" procedure also calls "zoom-out" procedure by case.

"Zoom-out" process: The procedure starts with an arbitrary point P and a small neighborhood radius r, and calculates RDF of the point. There are three possible local data distributions with regard to the value of RDF, which are shown in figure 1, where α is a small value number, while β is a large value number. In our experiments, we choose $\alpha < 0.3$ and $\beta > 12$, which leads to a good balance between accuracy and pruning speed.

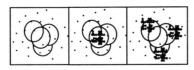

(a) RDF = 1 ± α   (b) RDF ≤ 1/β   (c) RDF ≥ β

Figure 1. Three different local data distributions

In case (a), it is observed that neither the point P is an outlier, nor the direct and indirect neighbors of P are. The local neighbors are distributed uniformly. The "zoom-in" procedure will be called to quickly reach points located on the boundary or outlier points.

In case (b), the point P is highly likely to be a center point of a cluster. We prune all neighbors of P, while calculating RDF for each of the indirect r-neighbors. In case RDF of one point larger than the threshold t, the point can be inserted into the outlier set together with its RDF value.

In case (c), RDF is large, P is inserted into the outlier set. We prune all the indirect neighbors of P.

"Zoom-in" process: The "zoom-in" procedure is a pruning process based on neighborhood expanding. We calculate DF and observe change of DF values. First we increase radius from r to 2r, compute DF (P, 2r) and compare DF (P, 2r) with DF (P, r). If DF (P, r) is close to DF (P, 2r), it indicates that the whole 2r-neighbohood has uniform density. Therefore, increase (e.g. double or 4 times) the radius until significant change is observed. As for significant decrease of DF is observed, cluster boundary and potential outliers are reached. Therefore, "zoom-out" procedure is called to detect outliers at a fine scale. Figure 2 shows this case. All the 4*r-neighbors are pruned off and "zoom-out" procedure detect outliers over points in 4*r-6*r ring. As for significant increase of DF is observed, we pick up a point with high DF value, likely to be in a denser cluster, and call "zoom-in" procedure further to prune off all points in the dense cluster.

As we can see, our method detects outliers using "zoom-out" process for small candidate outlier sets, the boundary points and the outliers. This subset of data as a whole is much smaller than the original dataset. This is where the performance of our algorithm lies in.

Both the "zoom-in" and "zoom-out" procedures can be further improved by using the P-trees data structure and its optimal logical operations. The speed

improvement lies in: a) P-trees make the "zoom-in" process on fly using HOBit metric; b) P-trees are very efficient for neighborhood search by its logical operations; c) P-tree can be used as a self-index for unprocessed dataset, clustered dataset and outlier set. Because of it, pruning is efficiently executed by logical operations of P-trees.

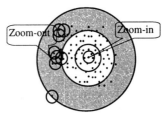

Figure 2. "Zoom-in" Process followed by "Zoom-out"

"Zoom-in" using HOBit metric: Given a point P, we define the neighbors of P hierarchically based on the HOBit dissimilarity between P and its neighbors, denoted as ξ-neighbors. ξ-neighbors represents the neighbors with ξ bits of dissimilarity, where $\xi = 0, 1 \ldots 7$ if P is an 8-bit value. The basic calculations in the procedure are computing DF (P, ξ) for each ξ-neighborhood and pruning neighborhood. HOBit dissimilarity is calculated by means of P-tree AND. For any data point, P, let $P = b_{11}b_{12} \ldots b_{nm}$, where $b_{i,j}$ is the ith bit value in the jth attribute column of P. The attribute P-trees for P with ξ-HOBit dissimilarity are then defined by

$$Pv_{i,\xi} = Pp_{i,1} \cap Pp_{i,2} \cap \ldots \cap Pp_{i,m-\xi}$$

The ξ-neighborhood P-tree for P are then calculated by

$$PNp,\xi = Pv_{1,m-\xi} \cap Pv_{2,m-\xi} \cap Pv_{3,m-\xi} \cap \ldots \cap Pv_{n,m-\xi}$$

Density factor, DF (P,r) of the ξ-neighborhood is simply the root counts of PNp,r divided by r.

The neighborhood pruning is accomplished by:

$$PU = PU \cap PN'p,\xi$$

where PU is a P-tree represents the unprocessed points of the dataset. PN'p,ξ represents the complement set of PNp,ξ.

"Zoom-out" using Inequality P-trees: In the "Zoom-out" procedure, we use inequality P-trees to search for neighborhood, upon which the RDF is calculated.

The direct neighborhood P-tree of a given point P within r, denoted as $PDN_{p,r}$ is P-tree representation of its direct neighbors. $PDN_{p,r}$ is calculated by $PDN_{p,r} = P_{x>p-r} \cap P_{x \leq p+r}$. The root count of $PDN_{p,r}$ is equal to N(Nbr(p,r)). Accordingly, DF (P,r) and RDF (P,r) are calculated based on equation (1) and (2) respectively.

Using P-Trees AND operations, the pruning is calculated as: In case of RDF (p,r)=1±α, we prune non-outlier points by $PU = PU \cap PDN'_{p,r} \cap PIN'_{p,r}$. In case RDF<1/ β, dataset is pruned by $PU = PU \cap PDN'_{p,r}$; If RDF > β the dataset is pruned by $PU = PU \cap PDN'_{p,r} \cap PIN'_{p,r}$.

4. Experimental Study

In this section, we experimentally compare our method (RDF) with current approaches: LOF (local outlier factor) and aLOCI (approximate local correlation integral). LOF is the first approach to density-based outlier detection. aLOCI is the fastest approach in the density-based area so far. We compare these three methods in terms of run time and scalability to data size. We will show our approach is efficient and has high scalability.

We ran the methods on a 1400-MHZ AMD machine with 1GB main memory and Debian Linux version 4.0. The datasets we used are the National Hockey League (NHL, 96) dataset and NBA dataset. Due to space limitation, we only show our result on NHL dataset in this paper. The result on NBA dataset also leads to our conclusion in terms of speed and scalability.

Figure 3 shows that our method has an order of magnitude improvements in speed compared to aLOCI method. Figure 4 shows our method is the most scalable among the three. When data size is large, e.g. 16384, our method starts to outperform these two methods.

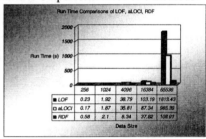

Figure 3. Run Time Comparison

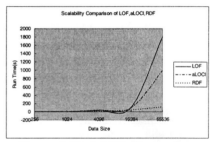

Figure 4. Scalability Comparison

5. Conclusion

In this paper, we propose a density based outlier detection method based on a novel local density measurement RDF. The method can efficiently mining outliers over large datasets and scales well with increase of data size. A vertical data representation, P-Trees, is used to speed up the process further. Our method was tested over NHL and NBA datasets. Experiments show that our method has an order of magnitude of speed improvements with comparable accuracy over the current state-of-art density-based outlier detection approaches.

6. Reference

[1] V.Barnett, T.Lewis, Outliers in Statistic Data, John Wiley's Publisher, NY,1994

[2] Knorr, Edwin M. and Raymond T. Ng. "A Unified Notion of Outliers: Properties and Computation", 3rd International Conference on Knowledge Discovery and Data Mining Proceedings, 1997, pp. 219-222.

[3] Knorr, Edwin M. and Raymond T. Ng., "Algorithms for Mining Distance-Based Outliers in Large Datasets", Very Large Data Bases Conference Proceedings, 1998, pp. 24-27.

[4] Sridhar Ramaswamy, Rajeev Rastogi, and Kyuseok Shim, "Efficient algorithms for mining outliers from large datasets", International Conference on Management of Data and Symposium on Principles of Database Systems, Proceedings of the 2000 ACM SIGMOD international conference on Management of data,2000, ISSN:0163-5808

[5] Markus M. Breunig, Hans-Peter Kriegel, Raymond T. Ng, Jörg Sander, "LOF: Identifying Density-based Local Outliers", Proc. ACM SIGMOD 2000 Int. Conf. On Management of Data, TX, 2000

[6] Spiros Papadimitriou, Hiroyuki Kitagawa, Phillip B. Gibbons, Christos Faloutsos, "LOCI: Fast Outlier Detection Using the Local Correlation Integral", 19th International Conference on Data Engineering, 2003, Bangalore, India

[7] A.K.Jain, M.N.Murty, and P.J.Flynn. "Data clustering: A review", ACM Comp. Surveys, 31(3):264-323, 1999

[8] Arning, Andreas, Rakesh Agrawal, and Prabhakar Raghavan. "A Linear Method for Deviation Detection in Large Databases", 2nd International Conference on Knowledge Discovery and Data Mining Proceedings, 1996, pp. 164-169.

[9] S. Sarawagi, R. Agrawal, and N. Megiddo. "Discovery-Driven Exploration of OLAP Data Cubes", EDBT'98.

[10] Q. Ding, M. Khan, A. Roy, and W. Perrizo, "The P-tree algebra". Proceedings of the ACM SAC, Symposium on Applied Computing, 2002.

[11] W. Perrizo, "Peano Count Tree Technology," Technical Report NDSU-CSOR-TR-01-1, 2001.

[12] Pan, F., Wang, B., Zhang, Y., Ren, D., Hu, X. and Perrizo, W., "Efficient Density Clustering for Spatial Data", PKDD 2003

Quantitative Association Rules Based on Half-Spaces:
An Optimization Approach

Ulrich Rückert, Lothar Richter, and Stefan Kramer
Technische Universität München
Institut für Informatik/I12
Boltzmannstr. 3,
D-85748 Garching b. München, Germany
{rueckert, richter, kramer}@in.tum.de

Abstract

We tackle the problem of finding association rules for quantitative data. Whereas most of the previous approaches operate on hyperrectangles, we propose a representation based on half-spaces. Consequently, the left-hand side and right-hand side of an association rule does not contain a conjunction of items or intervals, but a weighted sum of variables tested against a threshold. Since the downward closure property does not hold for such rules, we propose an optimization setting for finding locally optimal rules. A simple gradient descent algorithm optimizes a parameterized score function, where iterations optimizing the first separating hyperplane alternate with iterations optimizing the second. Experiments with two real-world data sets show that the approach finds non-random patterns and scales up well. We therefore propose quantitative association rules based on half-spaces as an interesting new class of patterns with a high potential for applications.

1 Introduction

Soon after the introduction of association rules for itemsets, researchers began to realize that association rules would also be useful for quantitative data [5]. Most of the generalizations and extensions of association rules to quantitative data either require a discretization of the numerical attributes [5, 7] or a characterization of the numerical attributes in the right-hand side by their means and standard deviations [1, 6].

The discretization process, however, leads to a loss of information in the data set. In the following we present a novel approach that works directly on the continuous data, without the need for any discretization or the calculation of statistical moments. It derives quantitative association rules of the form "if the weighted sum of some variables is greater than a threshold, then a different weighted sum of variables is with high probability greater than a second threshold". For instance, consider a table with wind strength, temperature and the wind chill index. Approaches so far applied to this data would approximate the relationship among the variables by a bundle of quantitative association rules. In contrast, the approach proposed here would find a weighted sum of wind strength and temperature on the left-hand side and the wind-chill index on the right-hand side. Thus, it allows for the discovery of *non-axis-parallel regularities* and can account for *cumulative effects* of several variables. Since the downward closure property frequently used in conventional association rule mining does not hold for this type of rule, we cast the problem of finding such rules as an optimization problem. The aim is to find rules that are locally optimal with respect to a parameterized score function. Consequently, the user can adjust the parameters of the presented algorithm to obtain association rules that match her individual interests. For instance, it is possible to specify target values for certain parameters, such that the algorithm attempts to find rules near the target (penalizing rules that are too far off), while simultaneously optimizing the rules' confidence. The whole framework is very flexible in several directions and can easily be adapted to incorporate user constraints. In summary, the paper has two main contributions: firstly, the *representation* of quantitative association rules based on half spaces, and secondly, the *optimization setting* for finding such rules.

2 Quantitative Association Rules Based on Half-Spaces

As outlined above, the aim of this paper is to extend the association rule framework to quantitative data. In general, an association rule is an implication of the form "if the left-

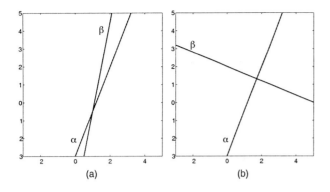

Figure 1. Two non-perpendicular hyperplanes α and β (a), and two perpendicular hyperplanes α and β (b).

hand side condition is true for an instance, then, with high probability, a right-hand side condition is also true". In the traditional setting, the conditions on the right-hand side and left-hand side are based on hyperrectangles of discrete attributes. To extend association rules to continuous data, we therefore need to decide which kind of "conditions" the quantitative association rules should be based on.

Of course, there are lots of different ways to impose conditions on numerical data. At the core we would expect from a useful condition that it separates the instance space in two subspaces, the space of instances that meets the condition, and the one that does not. The border between those two subspaces can then be conveniently expressed by some *separation function*. For numerical data, it makes sense to select a smooth separation function to minimize the error that is caused by random noise or measurement errors in the data. In this paper we will focus on *hyperplanes*, a particularly simple, but powerful class of separation functions. From a geometrical perspective, a hyperplane α is given by a vector $\bar{\alpha}$ and an intercept α_0. An instance x is then assigned to one half-space, if the dot product $\bar{\alpha} \cdot x + \alpha_0$ is positive and to the other half-space, if it is negative. In figure 1 (b), the one-dimensional hyperplane α (i.e. a line) separates the two-dimensional space into two half-spaces, one left of α, the other right of α.

In the case of association rules, the use of hyperplanes as conditions boils down to testing a weighted sum of variables against a threshold; i.e. an instance x in an n-dimensional space meets the condition $\alpha \in \mathbb{R}^{n+1}$, if $\alpha_1 x_1 + \alpha_2 x_2 + \cdots + \alpha_n x_n \geq -\alpha_0$ With this, one could build an association rule such as $x_1 \geq 31 \to 0.9x_5 + 1.2x_6 \geq 250$. In a particular medical application this association rule might be interpreted as "if the body mass index is greater than or equal to 31, then the weighted sum of the systolic and diastolic blood pressure is greater than or equal to 250".

Of course, it is quite easy to generate a large number of trivial association rules with high confidence. For example,

the association rule $1.5x_1 \geq 5 \to 2x_1 \geq 4$ has confidence 100%, but does not give any new insight. More generally, situations like the one in figure 1 (a) are problematic: we have two hyperplanes α and β in a two-dimensional space, that define an association rule $\alpha_1 x_1 + \alpha_2 x_2 \geq -\alpha_0 \to \beta_1 x_1 + \beta_2 x_2 \geq -\beta_0$. The problem is that α and β are highly correlated. If an instance is left of the α hyperplane, it is very likely to be left of the β hyperplane as well, simply because the space that is right of β, but left of α is much smaller than the space left of α and left of β[1]. For our purposes it is therefore essential, that α and β are uncorrelated, i.e. they have to be perpendicular as in figure 1 (b).

3 Quantitative Association Rule Mining

The main problem with finding good quantitative association rules is that the space of rules is uncountably infinite and therefore not suited to an enumeration strategy. In particular, the downward closure property does not hold for such rules, and thus we have to abandon the idea of generating the complete set of solutions. However, we can adopt an optimization approach, where the user can specify clearly the sort of rules she is looking for, and the algorithm returns locally optimal solutions. While this may seem unusual for association rule mining, it is common practice in other areas, for instance clustering (e.g, K-means clustering) and Bayesian learning (e.g., the EM algorithm).

In the following we describe one particular algorithm for mining quantitative association rules in this setting. First, we define a score function to assess the "interestingness" of an association rule. Then, we sketch a simple optimization algorithm searching for association rules with a low score. Before we go into further detail, however, we need to introduce the basic setting and some notational conventions.

For mining quantitative association rules we are given a *data set* X containing m *instances*. Each instance is given as a vector of n real values, i.e. $x \in \mathbb{R}^n$, so that $X \subset \mathbb{R}^n$. We are now looking for association rules that are defined by two hyperplanes $\alpha := (\alpha_0, \alpha_1, \ldots, \alpha_n)^T$ and $\beta := (\beta_0, \beta_1, \ldots, \beta_n)^T$. The α hyperplane specifies the condition on the left-hand side of the association rule, the β hyperplane specifies the right-hand side. Both hyperplanes are given in Hessian normal form: the α_0 value of a hyperplane α is the *intercept*, i.e. the hyperplane's distance to the origin. The *direction vector* $\bar{\alpha} := (\alpha_1, \ldots, \alpha_n)^T$ specifies the slope of the hyperplane. The hyperplanes α and β are perpendicular, if $\bar{\alpha}^T \bar{\beta} = 0$.

Due to space constraints we are not able to give the exact scoring function and the algorithm here and have to refer to

---

[1]Of course, in a strict mathematical sense it does not make sense to compare the "sizes" of subspaces, because all subspaces are infinite anyway. A more formal justification would demand that the resulting probability distributions are independent for uniform data.

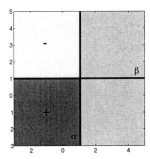

Figure 2. Confidence is optimal if the distribution is uneven left of α, while contrast is optimal if it is even right of α.

the long version of the paper [4] for details.

First of all, we are mainly interested in association rules with high *confidence*, i.e. the fraction of instances in X, that fulfill both conditions α and β divided by the fraction of instances that fulfill only the α condition should be as high as possible. Figure 2 illustrates this idea: If an instance x is located left of α and below β, it contributes to a high confidence score. If it is located left of α, but above β, it decreases the confidence measure. The following function is minimal for high confidence:

$$l(\alpha, \beta, X) := - \sum_{x \in X} \sigma(\delta(\alpha, x)) \cdot (2\sigma(\delta(\beta, x)) - 1)$$

where $\sigma(x) := \frac{1}{1+e^{-x}}$ is the well-known *sigmoid* function and $\delta(\xi, x)$ is the signed distance of instance x to the hyperplane ξ. Since we use the sigmoid function instead of the sharp step function, l is differentiable and puts lower weights to instances in the vicinity of the hyperplane, therewith compensating for noise in the data.

A second criterion for the interestingness of an association rule is its *coverage*. The coverage is simply the fraction of instances in the data set that satisfy the left-hand side condition. Unfortunately, the coverage of interesting rules is not clear a priori. If the coverage of an association rule is very large, the rule is true for almost the whole data set. Such rules often express trivial dependencies in the data. On the other hand, if the coverage of a rule is very small, the pattern describes a very local phenomenon that might just be a random fluctuation instead of a structural property of the underlying data. Thus, the coverage values for interesting association rules are somewhere in between, depending on the data at hand and the knowledge about the data. In practice, the desired coverage (or equivalently, the support) is often determined empirically. Similarly to the confidence score, we design a function $c(\alpha, g, t, X)$ that is minimal if the coverage of α is near to the user-specified target value t. The g parameter determines how coverage should be weighted relative to confidence.

The confidence and coverage scores determine what the

optimization algorithm is looking for on the left side of α in figure 2. Just like in traditional association rule mining, there is no constraint regulating the distribution of instances on the right side of α. For quantitative association rule mining, this can be a problem: one can simply move the β hyperplane upwards until it is located above all instances. While this achieves maximal confidence, the resulting association rule is not very interesting, because the right-hand side condition is true for all instances anyway. One way to overcome this problem is to regulate the distribution of instances that are right of α with regard to β. We call this criterion *contrast*. The rationale is that the "contrast" between the instance above and below β should be as low as possible on the right side of α in figure 2. Again, we formalize this criterion using a function $r(\alpha, \beta, X)$, that is minimal for low contrast settings.

For humans who have to interpret the resulting association rules, there is one more pragmatic criterion: the components of the α and β vectors are usually not zero. This means that the resulting association rule contains n addends on both sides of the implication. Usually, the user prefers finding *sparse* association rules, i.e. rules where most coefficients are zero and only the relevant coefficients are given. Those rules are shorter and thus easier to interpret and validate. To account for these pragmatic considerations, one can add a term $a(\alpha, h)$ to penalize non-sparse association rules. The user can adjust the importance of sparsity relative to the other scores using the parameter h.

The final interestingness scoring function simply calculates the sum of those scores:

$$L(\alpha, \beta, g, t, h, X) := l(\alpha, \beta, X) + c(\alpha, g, t, X) \\ + r(\alpha, \beta, X) + a(\alpha, h) + a(\beta, h)$$

A high score indicates that the association rule is uninteresting with regard to the selected parameter settings, a low score means we found an interesting rule. As the scoring function is continuous, there usually is a whole subspace of "good" rules and it is easy to modify a rule with a low score to some small extent and obtain a rule with an even lower score. We are therefore aiming at finding association rules with optimally low score, that is, the local optima of the scoring function, subject to the constraint that $\bar{\alpha}^T \bar{\beta} = 0$. This constrained optimization problem can be tackled using established methods from optimization theory. We take an approach that alternatingly keeps α fixed while optimizing β and vice versa. Empirical results in section 4 indicate that only a few iterations are sufficient to find such an optimum.

As any other optimization procedure, this algorithm can get stuck in local optima with comparably high scores. For the sake of simplicity we use random restarts to obtain association rules with low score. Of course, one can utilize simulated annealing or any other global optimization strategy as well. A high sparseness parameter leads to rules that

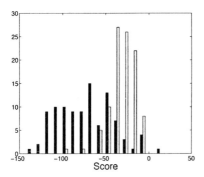

Figure 3. Distribution of scores on the original (black) and the permuted (grey) data sets.

Data Set Size	Overall Runtime	Number of Line Searches	Runtime per Line Search
100	2.6 s	19	0.14 s
1,000	7.4 s	27	0.28 s
5,000	23 s	22	1.0 s
10,000	46.9 s	17	2.7 s
50,000	264 s	18	14.7 s
100,000	623 s	23	27.1 s
300,000	2004 s	23	87.2 s
500,000	3529 s	20	176.5 s

Table 1. Runtimes of the optimization algorithm as a function of data set size.

have a few large and many small (but non-zero) coefficients. A post-processing step is required to set the small coefficients to zero while retaining the perpendicularity of α and β.

4 Experimental Results

To assess the applicability and feasibility of the described algorithm, we implemented a version in MATLAB.

For our first experiment, we chose the gene expression data set of Hughes *et al.* [3]. The data set contains the expression levels of 6316 genes in the yeast genome measured for 300 diverse mutations and chemical treatments of yeast cells. We selected the 50 genes with the largest standard deviation for our experiments. The parameters were set as follows: $g = 1.0$, $t = 0.5$, and the sparseness parameter h was set to 0.1, 0.3 and 0.5, respectively.

As expected, contrast and coverage were centered around the target value of 0.5 in the experiments. In the long version of the paper [4], a biological interpretation of five of the best rules is given. To assess the robustness and statistical significance of the rules, we performed a randomization test, where the values of the columns are permutated randomly to generate a new data set with the same distribution, but no structural relations between the columns. We then ran the algorithm ten times on the permuted data set and noted the best score found. This process was repeated one hundred times to get an estimate of the distribution of scores, that can be expected on random, but similar data. Figure 3 gives the resulting histograms for the original and the permuted data. The scores for the permuted data are peaked around -30, while the original data features a large number of association rules in the range between -50 and -150. Thus, we can be highly confident that the induced rules describe indeed structural properties of the yeast data set. In practical applications, we would recommend this randomization approach to focus on significant findings.

In order to investigate the scalability of the optimization algorithm with respect to the size of the data set, we exper-

imented with the "Cover Type" data set containing 581,012 instances from the UCI repository [2]. We removed the discrete attributes, leaving ten continuous attributes describing cartographic properties of 30 x 30 meter land cells. We normalized the data set, so that each column has a mean of zero and a standard deviation of one. We then applied the optimization algorithm on subsets of different size, with the t parameter set to 0.5, g set to 1, and h set to 0.5. The experiments were performed on a Pentium IV 2.8GHz machine. As the runtime of the optimization algorithm depends on the number of line search steps and the runtime per line search, the actual runtime varies for different random restarts.

We therefore give the total runtime, the number of line searches that were performed, and the runtime per line search for the various data set sizes in table 1. The table shows that the number of line search steps remains below thirty for all data set sizes and that the runtime per search step scales favorably with the data set size.

References

[1] Y. Aumann and Y. Lindell. A statistical theory for quantitative association rules. *Journal of Intelligent Information Systems*, 20(3):255–283, 2003.

[2] C. Blake and C. Merz. UCI repository of machine learning databases, 1998.

[3] T. Hughes et al. Functional discovery via a compendium of expression profiles. *Cell*, 102:109–126, July 2000.

[4] U. Rückert, L. Richter, and S. Kramer. Quantitative association rules based on half-spaces: An optimization approach. Technical Report TUM-I0412, Institut für Informatik, TU München, 2004.

[5] R. Srikant and R. Agrawal. Mining quantitative association rules in large relational tables. In H. V. Jagadish and I. S. Mumick, editors, *Proc. of the 1996 ACM SIGMOD International Conference on Management of Data*, pages 1–12, 1996.

[6] G. I. Webb. Discovering associations with numeric variables. In *Proc. of the 7th ACM SIGKDD International Conference on Knowledge Discovery and Data Mining*, pages 383–388. ACM Press, 2001.

[7] J. Wijsen and R. Meersman. On the complexity of mining quantitative association rules. *Data Mining and Knowledge Discovery*, 2(3):263–281, 1998.

Evaluating Attraction in Spatial Point Patterns with an Application in the Field of Cultural History

Marko Salmenkivi

Helsinki Institute for Information Technology, Basic Research Unit

P.O.Box 68, FIN–University of Helsinki, Finland

marko.salmenkivi@cs.helsinki.fi

Abstract

Spatial collocation rules are often useful for describing dependencies between spatial features. Still, the commonly used criteria for the interestingness of the rules and the selected neighbourhood constraints for spatial objects may be too rough for capturing the essentials of such dependencies. We demonstrate the difficulties with concrete examples on a large place-name data set. We propose a technique based on simple density estimation for assessing the interestingness with different neighbouring constraints.

1. Introduction

Spatial collocation rules describe how often sets of spatial features are associated with other sets of features in the neighbourhood. A collocation rule R is of the form $\mathcal{X} \xrightarrow{\mathcal{D}} \mathcal{Y}$, where $\mathcal{X}$ and $\mathcal{Y}$ are feature sets, and $\mathcal{D}$ is a neighbourhood relation. The interestingness of R is typically characterized by its confidence $\theta = \frac{\#\mathcal{D}(\mathcal{X} \cup \mathcal{Y})}{\#\mathcal{D}(\mathcal{X})}$, where $\mathcal{D}(\mathcal{X} \cup \mathcal{Y})$, and $\mathcal{D}(\mathcal{X})$ are *collocation patterns*.

A collocation pattern can be defined as an undirected graph (Fig. 1), where each node corresponds to a feature and an edge indicates a neighbourhood relationship between the features [7, 8]. The confidence of a rule R can be computed by finding and counting the instances of the collocation patterns $\mathcal{D}(\mathcal{X} \cup \mathcal{Y})$, and $\mathcal{D}(\mathcal{X})$.

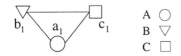

Figure 1. Instance $\{a_1, b_1, c_1\}$ **of collocation pattern** $\mathcal{D}(\mathcal{X})$. **Set** $\mathcal{X} = \{A, B, C\}$, **and** A, B, **and** C **are spatial features.**

Methods for mining collocation rules usually assume the neighbourhood constraint as given. For instance, if the Euclidean distance is used as $\mathcal{D}$, the maximum distance allowed for two objects to be neighbours is fixed [3, 5, 8].

In this paper the neighbourhood relation and interestingness measure are bound together; we ask whether there is a distance ϵ such that rule R is statistically significant. Below the notation $\xrightarrow{\epsilon}$ is always used to mean that the neighbouring constraint is the Euclidean distance of at most ϵ.

We study a large corpus of place-names, and consider terms occurring in the names as spatial features. We investigate collocation rules for pairs of terms with obvious semantic linkage, e.g., black/white, and show that significant attraction takes place between the features at small distances. Still, the confidences of the corresponding rules are low, and, thus, they are likely to be missed by rule mining algorithms (Sec. 2–3).

We propose a method for evaluating the interestingness of collocation rules that not only investigates the spatial features present in a specific rule but also takes into account the overall distribution of *all* features (Sec. 4). A case-study on the place-name data is briefly described (Sec. 5) before conclusion (Sec. 6).

2. Attraction between name elements

In this paper we investigate a data set of 717,746 Finnish place-names, their coordinates and types of locations [1]. Each object is represented by a pair of coordinates. The representation is unrealistic in case of large lakes, long rivers etc., but it is unlikely to cause significant distortion since the number of very large entities is small.

The corpus was earlier studied by [4] who also model the expected numbers of name instances, and apply hypothesis testing for finding attraction (or repulsion) patterns. The

---

[1] National Place Name Register maintained by the National Land Survey of Finland.

Table 1. Confidences of collocation rules. See explanation in text.

ϵ (km)	$A \to B$	$B \to A$	$C \to D$	$D \to C$
0.5	0.02 (0.03)	0.04 (0.06)	0.02	0.04
1	0.04 (0.05)	0.07 (0.09)	0.06	0.13
2	0.08 (0.11)	0.14 (0.22)	0.13	0.29
4	0.17 (0.24)	0.30 (0.44)	0.31	0.61
10	0.55 (0.75)	0.72 (0.89)	0.76	0.98

main advantage of our approach is that we allow the probability of occurrence of a specific name to vary in different regions.

We analyzed dependencies between several pairs of name elements such that the semantic connection between them is obvious. Here two examples are discussed: *ukko* (meaning 'old man') vs. *akka* (meaning 'old woman'), and *musta* ('black') vs. *valkoinen* ('white'). In both cases the meanings of the terms are very closely related, and the terms form a "natural" pair. Since the pairs consist of kinds of opposites they are good separators between locations.

There are 1385 instances of *ukko* (feature A), 693 instances of *akka* (B), 5233 instances of *musta* (C), and 2213 instances of *valkoinen* (D) in the corpus. The confidences of collocation rules between the pairs for different ϵ shown in Table 1 seem reasonably large, at least for $\epsilon \geq 2$ km. For instance, given an occurrence of B, an occurrence of A resides within 4 km in 30 % of the cases. The confidences in parentheses are computed based on the instances of the largest cluster only (more than half of the total) after a preliminary clustering step. It was conducted to zoom the analysis to the area where both the terms really occur. In a cluster for each instance at least one instance of the other type resides within 15 km. (An algorithm for this task was introduced in [2]).

In the following we show that in these cases significant attraction actually takes place at small distances, less than 1.5 km. Intuitively, this is easy to understand; if a place was given a name using the word meaning 'old man', it is likely that significantly often a nearby location within approx. 100–800 m is named with the word meaning 'old woman', not 4–5 km, for instance.

3. Testing hypothesis of attraction

In spatial statistics attraction in point patterns have been studied intensively (see [1] for further references). While the methods in spatial statistics are theoretically well-founded they may suffer from invalid model assumptions.

More importantly, they are often too slow for mining attraction patterns in large data sets.

Typically, the instances of a feature are considered as a realization of a stochastic process, which produces points in a plane. For the number of occurrences Y in area $\mathcal{A}$, $EY(\mathcal{A}) = \int_{\mathcal{A}} \lambda(\mathbf{s}) ds$, where λ is the *intensity* of the process.

Hypothesis testing typically sets a null hypothesis which explains the observed attraction by chance. Test statistics used for evaluating attraction include, e.g., nearest neighbour distances, or the *cross k-function*. Tests are usually based on Monte Carlo simulation of the process under the null hypothesis. The simplest version is the Poisson process with a constant intensity, which assumes *complete spatial randomness* (CSR) of each point of a realization.

Consider again the rule $A \xrightarrow{\epsilon} B$, and the clustered instances discussed above. The CSR hypothesis can be tested, e.g., by generating points uniformly randomly to fictive data sets B' of size $|B|$ within the area of investigation and counting for each set the number of instances of A within ϵ from the closest $b \in B'$.

As we have a large data set available, we utilize it to model the randomness in a more realistic way. Assuming that the distribution of all the place-names provides a better estimate for the intensity of B than the CSR hypothesis we choose randomly any of the 240,308 occurrences within less than 15 km from the closest A. Instead of fixing ϵ we first observe the numbers of instances of A such that the distance to the closest generated point is less than 0.5 km, 0.5–1 km, etc. Denote the random variables by $T_{d \leq 0.5}, T_{0.5 < d \leq 1}, \ldots$, and their values for the real B by $t_{d \leq 0.5}, t_{0.5 < d \leq 1}, \ldots$

In Fig. 2 the points indicate the values t. The errorbars with the label 'no kde' show the average and the range of values where 95 % of the corresponding values of T settled. The results suggest that 22 co-occurrences found within 0.5 km cannot be explained by chance. At distances longer than 2 km no significant differences between the real and fictive occurrences can be detected.

In the case of features C and D (Fig. 2, right) the attraction is even stronger. The most extreme values are yielded between 250–750 m. No attraction can be observed at distances more than 1.25 km.

4. Weighting based on density estimation

Next, let us consider the approach more formally. Denote the set of all place-names, ignoring the types, by $S = \{X_1, \ldots X_n\}$. The kernel density estimation inserts a density function, e.g., a Gaussian-shaped function, around each data point [1]. The kernel density estimate for the intensity of occurrence in location $\mathbf{x}$ is obtained by summing up the densities of the individual kernel functions $g_i, 1 \leq i \leq n$, i.e., $\hat{\lambda}(\mathbf{x}) = \sum_{i=1}^{n} g_i\left(\frac{d(\mathbf{x}, X_i)}{h}\right)$, where d is the Euclidean

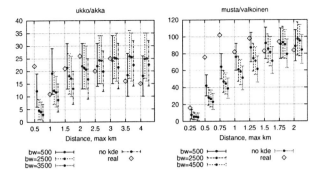

Figure 2. Summary of closeness of A and B (*ukko*, 'old man' and *akka*, 'old woman'), and C and D (*musta*, 'black' and *valkoinen*, 'white').

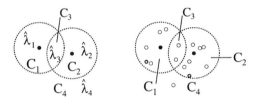

Figure 3. Kernel density estimate of intensity with constant kernels (left), and weighting the occurrences with the kernel densities (right).

distance. The parameter h controlling the degree of smoothing is called the *bandwidth*. When $h \to \infty$, $\hat{\lambda}(\mathbf{x}) \to \frac{n}{|\mathcal{A}|}$, where $\mathcal{A}$ is the area being investigated. Thus, the intensity is constant, and the situation is exactly that of the CSR hypothesis. Further, when $h \to 0$, $\hat{\lambda}(\mathbf{x}) \to \infty$, if $\mathbf{x} \in S$, and zero otherwise. Hence, a non-zero intensity is assigned only to the exact locations of the points. This is identical to the intensity we used in the example.

Above we assumed that the intensity of the randomized feature was proportional to that of all place-names. In the following we relax this assumption. Instead of sampling the points uniformly we assign weights to them, the weight of a location depending on its distance(s) from the instances of the feature B being randomized.

Let us estimate the intensity of B with the kernel density methods. For illustration purposes, let us first consider constant kernel functions, that is, $g_i(\mathbf{x}) = \frac{1}{\pi h^2}$, if $d(\mathbf{x}, B_i) \leq h$, and $g_i(\mathbf{x}) = 0$ otherwise. Fig. 3 illustrates the situation. The black points indicate the locations of two instances of type B. The radius of the circle is h. The kernel density estimated intensities are $\hat{\lambda}_1 = \hat{\lambda}_2 = \frac{1}{\pi h^2}$ (regions C_1, C_2), $\hat{\lambda}_3 = \frac{2}{\pi h^2}$ (C_3), and $\hat{\lambda}_4 = 0$ (C_4).

The instances of the features other than B are indicated by the white circles. Now, instead of continuous intensities

inside the areas C_i, we assign a non-zero intensity to the occurrence points only, so that $\hat{\lambda}(\mathbf{y}) = 0$ if $\mathbf{y} \notin S$, and $\hat{\lambda}(\mathbf{x}) = \hat{\lambda}(\mathbf{y})$ for $\mathbf{x}$ and $\mathbf{y}$ with an equal number of instances of B within h. Further, we normalize the values so that the expected numbers of occurrences in the areas C_i are equal to those in the continuous case.

Similarly, we can weight X_i by using more complex kernel functions around the instances of B. An important note is that when $h \to \infty$ we obtain equal weights for any point resulting in the method with no weighting. Further, $h \to 0$ leads to the original set B. In this case, we have $ET = t$ for all ranges of distances. Hence, it is interesting to conduct several trials, and observe the changes in the values of T as a function of h (that is, with different weightings).

Fig. 2 displays the results in the case of our running examples with three different bandwidths. Even if the points residing close to the real instances of B are strongly weighted ($h = 500$ m), the values of $T_{d \leq 0.5}$ are far from $t_{d \leq 0.5}$. The weighting causes the instances to shift slightly, resulting in a lot of randomized occurrences in the range 0.5–1 km. Further, the observed values $t_{1 < d \leq 1.5}$, and $t_{1.5 < d \leq 2}$, which seemed significantly high when no weighting was employed, are fairly close to the expected values with all the bandwidths used. As to the terms meaning black/white, Fig. 2 nicely shows how the most extreme values remain extreme even with strong weighting of the simulated values.

The values of $t_{d \leq c}$ continue to be significantly high to the distance of $c = 3$ km for A and B, and even up to 7 km for C and D (figures not shown). Thus, the corresponding rules $A \xrightarrow{\epsilon} B, \epsilon = 3$ km, and $C \xrightarrow{\epsilon} D, \epsilon = 7$ km are still statistically significant. As noted, this is due to the very large values at small distances, and, hence, the rules miss the geographical scale of the phenomenon.

More generally, the approach can be applied to collocation rules of type $\mathcal{X} \xrightarrow{\epsilon} Y$, where $\mathcal{X}$ is a set of features, and Y is a single feature. Then the instances of collocation pattern P of $\mathcal{X}$ correspond to the instances of A above. The distance between an instance y of Y and an instance p of P can be defined, e.g., as $dist(y, p) = \sum_1^k d(y, x_k)/k$, where $x_1, \dots, x_k$ are the instances of the features of P.

An open problem concerns autocorrelation. Since we are interested in testing the attraction between different features, we should maintain the amount of autocorrelation of the single feature Y in randomized data.

4.1. Computing the significance without simulation

It is not always necessary to actually generate the fictive data sets for the significance tests. Consider again the rule $A \xrightarrow{\epsilon} B$, and instead of B, let us treat A as the randomized feature. Denote by $w_A(X)$ the weight of point X. Further denote by $S^* \subset S$ the set of points such that for each $X \in$

$S^*, d(X, b) \leq \epsilon$ for some $b \in B$. Now the probability of generating a point a' such that $d(a', b) \leq \epsilon$ is given by

$$p = \frac{\sum_{X \in S^*} w_A(X)}{\sum_{Y \in S} w_A(Y)}.$$

Note that in practice, to approximate the sums for Gaussian kernels, we only need to find the points Y such that $d(Y, a) < \sim 3h$ for some $a \in A$.

Thus, for the number of points $T_{d \leq \epsilon}$ it holds that $T_{d \leq \epsilon} \sim$ Binomial$(|A|, p)$, and the test can be carried out by computing the probability $P(T \leq t)$ without simulation.

5. Semantic linkage between *hiisi* and death

Next we give an example of a research problem that can be approached by utilizing the developed techniques and the place-name data. This case-study is discussed in [6].

Hiisi was a cult place of ancient Finns. It is commonly interpreted as the centre of the Iron Age Finnish cultic community, a village or a clan, where the cult of the dead was practiced. If *hiisi* really was connected to the cult of the dead, it is plausible that signs of attraction could be found between the name element *hiisi* and names referring to death (e.g. *kalma, kuolema*). We found 662 occurrences of *hiisi* (feature H), and 542 names referring to death (feature K) in the sense that we considered relevant for our study.

We first clustered the occurrences similarly to the example in Sec. 2 to prevent large-scale differences in the distributions to distort the analysis. The largest cluster included 235 occurrences. After excluding the points of the largest cluster, we extended the allowed maximum distance of the cluster members to 25 km, and conducted another clustering round. This resulted in a cluster with 616 occurrences that covered large parts of the country.

We tested the rules $H \overset{\epsilon}{\to} K$, and $K \overset{\epsilon}{\to} H$ for different ϵ. Fig. 4 displays the cumulative values $t_{d \leq 0.5}, t_{d \leq 1}, \dots, t_{d \leq 4}$, and the corresponding randomized values for the first rule, separating the two clusters. The data set does not seem to give significant support to the hypothesis of the association of *hiisi* and death. Of course, the analysis, though providing a unique viewpoint, can only be a supplementary tool in the study of the problem

6. Conclusion and future work

Spatial collocation rules are often useful for describing dependencies between spatial features. Still, the commonly used criteria for the interestingness of the rules and the selected neighbourhood constraints for spatial objects may be too rough for capturing the essentials of such dependencies. We demonstrated the difficulties with concrete examples on a large place-name data set.

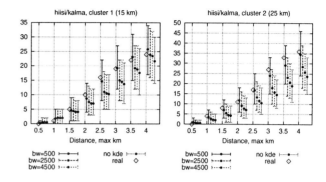

Figure 4. Summary of closeness of *hiisi* and death, cluster 1 (left), and cluster 2 (right).

We proposed a technique for evaluating the interestingness based on hypothesis testing and simple density estimation. The future plan aims at finding efficient methods for mining collocation rules based on the proposed interestingness measure. Another goal is to take the possible effect of autocorrelation into account.

References

[1] N. A. C. Cressie. *Statistics for Spatial Data.* Wiley, New York, 1993.

[2] M. Ester, H. Kriegel, J. Sander, and X. Xu. A density-based algorithm for discovering clusters in large spatial databases with noise. In *Proc. 2nd International Conf. on Knowledge Discovery and Data Mining*, pages 226–231, Portland, Oregon, 1996.

[3] Y. Huang, H. Xiong, S. Shekhar, and J. Pei. Mining confident co-location rules without a support threshold. In *Proc. 2003 ACM Symposium on Applied computing*, pages 497–501, Melbourne, Florida, 2003.

[4] A. Leino, H. Mannila, R. Pitkänen. Rule discovery and probabilistic modeling of onomastic data. In *Proc. 7th European Conf. on Principles and Practice of Knowledge Discovery in Databases*, pages 291–302. Cavtat-Dubrovnic, Croatia, 2003.

[5] Y. Morimoto. Mining frequent neighboring class sets in spatial databases. In *Proc. 7th ACM SIGKDD Conf. on Knowledge and Discovery and Data Mining*, pages 353–358, San Francisco, CA, 2001.

[6] R. Pulkkinen, M. Salmenkivi, A. Leino, and H. Mannila. What was the Finnish *hiisi*? Applying computational methods to the study of folk religion. *Temenos*, 2004 (to appear).

[7] S. Shekhar, Y. Huang, Discovering spatial co-location patterns: a summary of results. In *Proc.of 7th International Symposium on Advances in Spatial and Temporal Databases*, Redondo Beach, CA, USA, 2001.

[8] X. Zhang, N. Mamoulis, D. Cheung, Y. Shou. Fast mining of spatial collocations. In *Proc.10th ACM SIGKDD Conference on Knowledge Discovery and Data Mining*, Seattle, Washington, 2004.

Efficient Relationship Pattern Mining using Multi-relational Iceberg-cubes

Dawit Yimam Seid, Sharad Mehrotra
Department of Computer Science
University of California, Irvine
{dseid,sharad}@ics.uci.edu

Abstract

Multi-relational data mining(MRDM) is concerned with data that contains heterogeneous and semantically rich relationships among various entity types. In this paper, we introduce multi-relational iceberg-cubes (MRI-Cubes) as a scalable approach to efficiently compute data cubes (aggregations) over multiple database relations and, in particular, as mechanisms to compute frequent multi-relational patterns ("itemsets"). We also present a summary of performance results of our algorithm.

1 Introduction

Numerous analysis and data mining tasks in a wide variety of applications including intelligence analysis, social network analysis, business data analysis, web data mining and bioinformatics are based as much on the links among heterogeneous entities and events as the properties of individual entities. Hence, the databases in these applications contain both attribute and semantic relationship data. This data is stored in multi-relational (multi-table) form in relational database systems as a set of linked tables each corresponding to some conceptual entity or relationship. *Multi-relational data mining* (MRDM) is concerned with the discovery of models and patterns from such databases. However, applying most MRDM algorithms to realistically large databases is fraught with several challenges including scalability and lack of integration with database systems [6].

The two predominant approaches to MRDM are transformation of multi-relational data to a single table (and then applying conventional single-table algorithms) and direct mining of multi-relational databases. A transformation approach that simply converts multiple tables into one joined relation ("universal relation") has been shown by a number of studies to suffer from several disadvantages including extreme horizontal and vertical data blow-up [13], loss of important semantic entity-relationship information carried by the join links [14], and increased data redundancy

(duplication) that may introduce statistical skew [7]. *Propositionalization* is a more systematic transformation (albeit limited to classification tasks) that reduces the data explosion by summarizing relationship information using aggregation functions. However, propositionalization also results in exponentially large attribute-value problems especially for non-numeric data sets [13]. Moreover, propositionalization algorithms like Polka [9] and RELAGS [10] are based on inefficient data aggregation techniques (i.e. rely on multiple SQL group-bys which are known to scale poorly as compared to data cube operators).

This paper deals with the MRDM task of multi-relational association rule (pattern) mining that directly operates on multi-relational databases. We propose a scalable algorithm for frequent multi-relational pattern discovery that is efficiently integrated with database systems.

Multi-relational Patterns. A *multi-relational association rule(pattern)* [5], henceforth abbreviated as MRP, is given as:

$$\bigwedge_{i=1}^{p}(T_1.A_i, v_i) \wedge \bigwedge_{j=2,i=1}^{q,r}(T_j.A_l, v_l)$$

where T_1 is the *target table* corresponding to a particular real-world entity[1]) and T_j is another table in the database which is joined to table T_{j-1} through a foreign key constraint (i.e. T_j and T_{j-1} are part of a legal join path). Patterns over these tables are represented as conjunctions of atomic predicates which have the form $A_i = v_i$ where A_i is a categorical or numerical attribute and v_i is a value from a certain domain. p and r are the number of predicates and q is the number of tables over which this MRP is defined. Each MRP has an associated *support* and *confidence*. *Support* of a pattern is the number of tuples in T_1 that satisfy it while *confidence* is the probability of satisfying a certain subset of the pattern given the whole MRP.

Two streams of previous work has dealt with the discovery of association rules over multiple relations. For

---

[1] The support count is done on tuples in the target table

prolog databases and datalog queries, WARMR [5] extends the Apriori algorithm to discover a limited class of MRPs. There is also an optimization of WARMR called FARMER [12]. Our approach differs from these algorithms in the following ways: (1) It runs directly on relational databases and does not require the specification of any pattern structure; instead we directly use the links (i.e. foreign key constraints) among tables. (2) It is based on a much more efficient Iceberg-cube computation algorithms. (3) It does not require the key of the target table to appear in all tables as in WARMR.

The work [11, 8] has considered relational association rule mining on a star-schema where the target table is the fact table and joins are of length one. Unlike this body of work, we consider association rules over tables with arbitrary structure and depth of joins.

2 Multi-relational Iceberg-cubes

We propose a novel approach based on Iceberg-cube computation [3] that supports the critical component of MRP mining, namely frequent "itemset" (conjunction) discovery. Iceberg-cubes are a type of data cube computed over attributes (dimensions) of a table where each aggregated value (*measure*) is above a given user specified threshold (also called *iceberg condition*). When the aggregation function is COUNT, Iceberg-cubes are equivalent to *frequent conjunctions* (the threshold being the minimum support value). Iceberg-cube computation algorithms have two attractive features with respect to MRP mining: (1) they are based on depth-first traversal of the pattern lattice [2] which is much more efficient than breadth-first approaches employed by past work, (2) they can be implemented inside database systems with relative ease.

Below we present an algorithm called multi-relational Iceberg-cubes (MRI-Cubes) that extends an Iceberg-cube computation algorithm called BUC (Bottom-up computation) to compute MRPs. The MRI-Cube algorithm (1) efficiently interleaves cubing (predicate set enumeration) with join path traversal while retaining the scalability of BUC by ensuring that only one partition of a single table is read to memory at a time, (2) minimizes the number of tuples involved in the join paths reachable from the target table.

The Multi-Relational Iceberg-cube Trie. Our algorithm utilizes a prefix trees (trie) referred to as *multi-relational iceberg-cube trie* or simply *MRI-Cube trie*) to integrate cubing with join path traversal. Populated as the cubing algorithm progresses, the MRI-Cube trie also stores counts and link structures of MRPs. Each node in an MRI-Cube trie

---

[2]for single table association rule mining as well, the most efficient techniques like Eclat and FP-growth are based on depth-first approach (see [4] for comparison).

---

procedure MRI-Cube (input,CloneJoinNodes)
```
 1: // Cubing Phase
 2: CubingAttributes ← find next attributes to group by
 3: for each attribute attr_i of the input do
 4:     CellCounts[] ← Partition input by attr_i
 5:     j ← 0
 6:     for each partition p_j do
 7:         if CellCounts[j] ≥ min_supp then
 8:             insert count to current MRI-Cube trie LeafNode of attr_i (if
                absent, create a new one and append to the current leaf node)
 9:             // stop recursion at join attributes
10:             if attr_i is a data attribute then
11:                 for k = 1 … size of CloneJoinNodes do
12:                     //test for expansion pruning
13:                     if CloneJoinNodes[k − 1]'s expansion with p_j was ∅
                        then
14:                         break
15:                     else
16:                         expand CloneJoinNodes[k] using p_j
17:                 MRI-Cube (p_j, CloneJoinNodes)
18:         j + 1
19: //Expansion Phase
20: repeat
21:     currJoinNode ← pick the LM-LD node
22:     Joinedtable ← expand currJoinNode
23:     CloneJoinNodes[] ← insert currJoinNode (corres. to
        currJoinAttr)
24:     CloneJoinNodes[] ← traverse all leaves and add all other clone
        nodes of the current join node.
25:     //use join of ⟨tid, count⟩ pair in currJoinNode with the table
26:     MRI-Cube (Joinedtable, CloneJoinNodes)
27: until no more expansion is possible
```

Figure 4. The MRI-cube algorithm

corresponds to an attribute. The target table's key serves as the root node. A node at depth k (see figure 3 for an example) compactly stores all information pertaining to the cuboid resulting from grouping by the attributes in the path from the root to itself.

In order to interlink group-bys over attributes from multiple tables in the MRI-Cube trie, we distinguish between two types of attributes: *data* attributes and *join* attributes. Join attributes consist of foreign and primary keys of tables while all the other attributes are considered to be data attributes. We make the reasonable assumption that join attributes store relationship information only. The MRI-Cube trie consists of two types of nodes, namely *data nodes* and *join nodes* (designated by a boxed node in figure 2), that correspond to the two types of attributes.

Preprocessing. In a preprocessing step, we determine the *join graph*[3] rooted at the target table as well as the *cubing order* of attributes for each table using information in the database schema (catalog). Like BUC, we order the group-by attributes based on decreasing cardinality. The exception to this is the requirement that all join attributes be placed at the end of the cubing order.

The MRI-Cube Algorithm. The algorithm is shown

---

[3]Due to limited space, we only consider patterns over acyclic join paths in this paper.

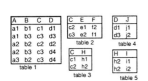

Figure 1. Example Tables

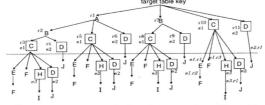

Figure 2. An MRI-Cube trie for the example tables with table1 as the target table

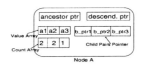

Figure 3. An MRI-Cube trie Node

in figure 4. It iterates between two phases, namely *cubing* phase and *expansion* phase. The inputs are a data partition (initially the whole target table) and a queue of join nodes (which is initially empty) on which the partition is to be joined as expansion.

The Cubing Phase. The cubing phase (lines 1-18 of figure 4) starts with the target table and recursively performs cubing on each attribute using BUC (i.e. applying *min_supp* pruning) *until* a join attribute is encountered or no more group-by is possible. When a join attribute is reached, group-by is performed on it like the other data nodes. But, the recursion stops and returns towards the root. As such, join nodes delineate the boundary of the cubing phase. Every time the recursion returns to the root, all the leaves in the MRI-Cube trie will have either join nodes or a data node with the finest granularity.

The Expansion Phase. The expansion phase is launched when the cubing recursion returns to the root. Expansion extends cubing to the next table on the join path. The expansion phase involves three steps:

Step 1. Pick the left-most leaf join node with the least-depth (henceforth referred to as the LM-LD node) from the MRI-Cube trie and join the set of keys in this node with the referenced table (lines 21-22 of figure 4). The join can be done using a hash based or sort merge technique. Since only foreign keys that meet the *min_supp* condition are kept in the join node, no redundant join is performed. More importantly, since the LM-LD node is the least aggregated node, the result of this join is sufficient to expand *all* the nodes in the MRI-Cube trie corresponding to the same join attribute as the LM-LD node (see [15] for a formal proof).

Step 2. Find all other leaf join nodes (called "*clones*") that correspond to the *same* attribute as the LM-LD node by traversing the MRI-Cube trie horizontally backward from *right-to-left*. Lines 23-24 in figure 4 perform this traversal and store the clone nodes in a queue called *CloneJoinNodes*.

Step 3. Recursively cube the joined table from step 1 while concurrently expanding the LM-LD node as well as all its clones (in the right-to-left order) with group-bys computed on the joined table's data attributes. Specifically, all clone join nodes found in the leaves of the MRI-Cube trie are simultaneously grown using only one scan (loading) of a partition from the new joined table. This can be performed

by applying intersection (e.g. hash set intersection) of the keys in the join node and the corresponding key in a partition. In figure 4, the *CloneJoinNodes* queue is passed in the recursive call to MRI-Cube (line 26) so that subsequent cubing based on each partition of the joined table is applied on all clones. Finally, once the expansion of the current LM-LD node and all its clones is completed, (i.e. the referenced table is cubed on all its data attributes), we pick the next LM-LD node and repeat the above process. This continues until no more cubing or expansion is possible (i.e. until all leaf nodes are data nodes with no right-brother).

In addition to ensuring correctness, the right-to-left expansion of clones allows us to prune expansion of join nodes when a partition can not result in cells that meet the *min_sup* (lines 13-14 in figure 4). As the clone nodes are traversed from right to left (i.e. from the least aggregated granule to the finer granule), we can prune the expansion of clone nodes using the Apriori property. This is because if a partition fails to produce qualifying cells when expanding a join node, then it will not produce any qualifying cells in *all* clones on its left (see [15] for a formal proof).

In summary, the MRI-Cube algorithm offers: (i) *CPU efficiency*: a data partition is scanned only once, (ii) *Space efficiency*: at a time, only one partition needs to reside in memory; hence if a table does not fit in memory, it can be partitioned until it does, (iii) Two types of pruning performed during the recursive cubing phase (*min_supp* pruning) and the expansion phase (clone expansion pruning).

Example 1 *The cubing and expansion operations described above are illustrated in the MRI-Cube trie shown in figure 2 whose construction also mirrors the MRI-Cube algorithm. The order in which the recursive cubing phase is executed is shown by the labels r1, r2, etc. The order in which the join nodes are expanded is shown by the labels e1, e2, etc. The horizontal line across the trie shows the point where the algorithm entered into the first expansion phase. After the first expansion phase, labels are shown only for the cubing done on the LM-LD nodes; the same processing is done simultaneously for all clones.*

3 Performance Analysis

In this section, we validate the performance of the MRI-Cube algorithm. We implemented our algorithm using C++.

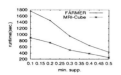

Figure 5. Comparison w.r.t. min. supp.

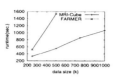

Figure 6. Comparison w.r.t. data size

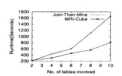

Figure 7. Comparison based on number of tables (avg. dim = 4, avg. attr. cardinality=3000)

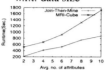

Figure 8. Comparison based on average number of dimensions (with 10 tables, avg. attr. cardinality=3000)

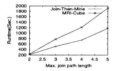

Figure 9. Comparison based on maximum join path length (with 10 tables, avg. dim = 4, avg. attr. cardinality=3000)

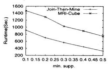

Figure 10. Comparison based on min_supp (with 10 tables, avg. dim = 4, avg. attr. cardinality=3000)

The test databases were stored in DB2 and accessed using efficient table scan calls. The experiments were conducted on a Sun Ultra Enterprise 450 with 3GB of RAM.

Real dataset. This is a bibliographic dataset drawn from CiteSeer [1] and HPSearch [2]. It consisted of tables on papers, authors, their institutes, citation and co-authorship links. The paper table contained 200K tuples, the authors table contained 126,024 tuples. Figures 5 and 6 compares MRI-Cube with the state-of-the-art MRP mining system FARMER [12] which we downloaded from the author's web site. For this comparison we used the *paper* table as a target table for MRI-Cube. For FARMER, we had to convert the dataset to a predicate-based representation and specify the required patterns (similar to the schema of the database) as well as other required parameters and biases. The figures show that, as both *min_supp* and data size increases, MRI-Cube achieves greater performance. In fact for data size above 500k, FARMER could not stop after an hour (see figure 6).

Synthetic dataset. This dataset was generated using the following parameters: number of records per table, number of attributes, average number of distinct values for each attribute, and average join cardinality for a pair of tables. Zipf distribution was used to generate attribute values. Since FARMER requires setting complex parameters and biases which make it difficult to run over complex schemas, we do not compare MRI-Cube with it on the synthetic data. Instead we compare MRI-Cube with a naive approach (called "Join-then-mine") that first performs joins and then applies single table cubing. The joined tables are found by a series of outer joins starting from the target table. Although the resulting cubes do not possess the useful structure found in MRI-Cube patterns, we believe this approach's performance as compared to MRI-Cube shades light on the effect of MRI-Cube's ability to avoid redundant joins.

Figure 7 and 8 show that while the run time of Join-then-mine explodes fast with increase in number of tables and average number of attributes per table, MRI-Cube achieves a much slower rate of increase. Figure 9 compares run time as the maximum join path length increases. Again MRI-Cube showed lower rate of rum-time increase. Finally, figure 10 shows performance against increase in min_supp. In this case, the rate of run time growth for Join-then-mine was close to that of MRI-Cube. This may be due to the common pruning technique (i.e. Iceberg cubing) used by both.

Acknowledgments. This research is supported by the National Science Foundation under Grant No. IIS-0331707 and IIS-0083489 and by the Knowledge Discovery and Dissemination (KD-D) Program.

References

[1] Citeseer. http://citeseer.nj.nec.com/cs.
[2] Homepagesearch. http://hpsearch.uni-trier.de.
[3] K. Beyer and R. Ramakrishnan. Bottom-up computation of sparse and iceberg cubes. In *SIGMOD*, pages 359–370, 1999.
[4] C. Borgelt. Efficient implementations of apriori and eclat. In *Workshop of Frequent Item Set Mining Implementations (FIMI 2003, Melbourne, FL, USA)*, 2003.
[5] L. Dehaspe and H. Toivonen. Discovery of relational association rules. In *Dzeroski, S. and Lavrac, N., ed. Relational Data Mining*, pages 189–212. Springer-Verlag, 2001.
[6] P. Domingos. Prospects and challenges for multi-relational data mining. *SIGKDD Explorations*, 5(1):80 – 83, 2003.
[7] L. Getoor. Multi-relational data mining using probabilistic relational models: research summary. In *Proceedings of the First Workshop in Multi-relational Data Mining*, 2001.
[8] V. C. Jensen and N. Soparkar. Frequent itemset counting across multiple tables. In *PAKDD*, pages 49–61, 2000.
[9] A. Knobbe, M. de Haas, and A. Siebes. Propositionalisation and aggregates. In *PAKDD*, pages 277–288, 2001.
[10] M. A. Krogel and S. Wrobel. Transformation-based learning using multirelational aggregation. In *Proc. of ILP*, pages 142–155, 2001.
[11] E. K. K. Ng, A. W.-C. Fu, and K. Wang. Mining association rules from stars. In *ICDM*, pages 322–329, 2002.
[12] S. Nijssen and J. Kok. Efficient frequent query discovery in farmer. In *PAKDD*, pages 350–362, 2003.
[13] L. D. Raedt. Attribute-value learning versus inductive logic programming: the missing links (extended abstract). In *Proc. of the 8th Intl. Conf.on ILP*, 1998.
[14] L. D. Raedt et al. Three companions for data mining in first order logic. In *Dzeroski, S. and Lavrac, N., ed. Relational Data Mining*, pages 105–139. Springer-Verlag, 2001.
[15] D. Y. Seid and S. Mehrotra. Efficient relationship pattern mining using multi-relational data cubes. Technical Report UCI-DB 04-05, Univ. of Calif., Irvine, 2004.

Cluster Cores-based Clustering for High Dimensional Data

Yi-Dong Shen, Zhi-Yong Shen and Shi-Ming Zhang
Laboratory of Computer Science
Institute of Software, Chinese Academy of Sciences
Beijing 100080, China
{ydshen, zyshen, zhangsm}@ios.ac.cn

Qiang Yang
Department of Computer Science
Hong Kong Univ. of Sci. & Technology
Clearwater Bay, Kowloon, Hong Kong
qyang@cs.ust.hk

Abstract

We propose a new approach to clustering high dimensional data based on a novel notion of cluster cores, instead of on nearest neighbors. A cluster core is a fairly dense group with a maximal number of pairwise similar objects. It represents the core of a cluster, as all objects in a cluster are with a great degree attracted to it. As a result, building clusters from cluster cores achieves high accuracy. Other major characteristics of the approach include: (1) It uses a semantics-based similarity measure. (2) It does not incur the curse of dimensionality and is scalable linearly with the dimensionality of data. (3) It outperforms the well-known clustering algorithm, ROCK, with both lower time complexity and higher accuracy.

1 Introduction

A number of clustering algorithms have been developed over the last decade in the data base/data mining community (e.g., DBSCAN, CURE, CHAMELEON, CLARANS, STING, and BIRCH). Most of these algorithms rely on a distance function (such as the Euclidean distance or the Jaccard distance that measures the similarity between two objects) such that objects are in the same cluster if they are nearest neighbors. However, recent research shows that clustering by distance similarity is not scalable with the dimensionality of data because it suffers from the so-called *curse of dimensionality*, which says that for moderate-to-high dimensional spaces, a full-dimensional distance is often irrelevant since the farthest neighbor of a data point is expected to be almost as close as its nearest neighbor. As a result, the effectiveness/accuracy of a distance-based clustering method would decrease significantly with increase of dimensionality. This suggests that "shortest distances/nearest neighbors" are not a robust criterion in clustering high dimensional data.

Our contributions: To resolve the curse of dimensionality, we propose a new definition of clusters that is based on a novel concept of *cluster cores*, instead of on nearest neighbors. A cluster core is a fairly dense group with a maximal number of pairwise similar objects (neighbors). It represents the core of a cluster so that all objects in a cluster are with a great degree attracted to it. This allows us to define a cluster as a direct expansion of a cluster core such that every object in the cluster is similar to most of the objects in the core. Moreover, instead of using Euclidean or Jaccard distances, we define the similarity of objects by taking into account the meaning (semantics) of individual attributes. In particular, two objects are *similar* (or *neighbors*) if a certain number of their attributes take on similar values. Whether two values of an attribute are similar is semantically dependent on applications and is defined by the user. Note that since any two objects are either similar or not, the concept of nearest neighbors does not apply in our approach.

Our definition of clusters shows several advantages. Firstly, since the similarity of objects is measured semantically w.r.t. the user's application purposes, the resulting clusters would be more easily understandable by the user. Secondly, a cluster core represents the core of a cluster, with the property that a unique cluster is defined given a cluster core and that all objects in a cluster are with a great degree attracted to the core. Due to this, the cluster cores-based method achieves high accuracy. Thirdly, since clusters are not defined in terms of nearest neighbors, our method does not incur the curse of dimensionality and is scalable linearly with the dimensionality of data. Fourthly, clustering results are not sensitive to the order of input data. Finally, outliers are effectively eliminated, as an outlier would be similar to no or just a very few objects in a core.

Related work: Closely related work on resolving the dimensionality curse with high dimensional data includes shared nearest neighbor methods, such as the Jarvis-Patrick method [4], SNN [1], and ROCK [2]. Like our cluster cores-based method, they do not rely on the shortest distance/nearest neighbor criterion. Instead, objects are clustered in terms of how many neighbors they share. A major operation of these methods is to merge small clusters into bigger ones. The key idea behind the Jarvis-Patrick method is that if any two objects share more than T (specified by the user) neighbors, then the two objects and any cluster they are part of can be merged. SNN extends the Jarvis-Patrick method by posing one stronger constraint: two clusters C_i and C_j could be merged if there are two *representative* objects, $o_i \in C_i$ and $o_j \in C_j$, which share more than T neighbors. An object A is a representative object if there are more than T_1 objects each of which shares more than T neighbors with A. To apply SNN, the user has to specify several thresholds including T and T_1. ROCK is a sophisticated agglomerative (i.e. bottom-up) hierarchical clustering approach. It tries to maximize links (common neighbors) within a cluster while minimizing links between clusters by applying a criterion function such that any two clusters C_i and C_j could be merged if their goodness value $g(C_i, C_j) = \frac{link[C_i, C_j]}{(|C_i|+|C_j|)^{1+2f(\theta)} - |C_i|^{1+2f(\theta)} - |C_j|^{1+2f(\theta)}}$ is the largest, where $link[C_i, C_j]$ is the number of common neighbors between C_i and C_j, θ is a threshold for two objects to be similar under the Jaccard distance measure, and $f(\theta)$ is a function with the property that for any cluster C_i, each object in it has approximately $|C_i|^{f(\theta)}$ neighbors. To apply ROCK, the user needs to provide a threshold θ and define a function $f(\theta)$. However, as the authors admit [2], it may not be easy to decide on an appropriate function $f(\theta)$ for different applications. Unlike the above mentioned shared nearest neighbor approaches, our cluster cores-based method does not perform any merge operations. It requires the user to specify only one threshold: the minimum size of a cluster core. We will show that our method outperforms ROCK, with both lower time complexity and higher accuracy.

Our approach is also closely related to HCS [3], a graph-based algorithm, which defines clusters as *highly connected subgraphs*. A highly connected subgraph is a subgraph whose edge connectivity exceeds half the number of nodes.

2 Semantics-based similarity

Let $A_1, ..., A_d$ be d attributes (dimensions) and $V_1, ..., V_d$ be their respective domains. Each V_i can be finite or infinite, and the values in V_i can be either numerical or categorical. A dataset (or database) DB is a finite set of objects (or data points), each o of which is of the form $(id_o, a_1, ..., a_d)$ where id_o is a natural number representing the unique identity of object o, and $a_i \in V_i$ or $a_i = nil$. nil is a special symbol not appearing in any V_i, and $a_i = nil$ represents that the value of A_i is not present in this object.

We introduce a non-distance similarity measure that relies on the semantics of individual attributes. We begin by defining the similarity of two values of an attribute. Informally, for a numerical attribute, two values are considered similar w.r.t. a specific application if their difference is within a scope specified by the user, and for a categorical attribute, two values are viewed similar if they are in the same class/partition of the domain. The domain is partitioned by the user based on his application purposes.

Definition 2.1 (Similarity of two numerical values) Let A be an attribute and V be its domain with numerical values. Let $\omega \geq 0$ be a scope specified by the user. $a_1 \in V$ and $a_2 \in V$ are *similar* if $|a_1 - a_2| \leq \omega$.

Definition 2.2 (Similarity of two categorical values) Let A be an attribute and $V = V_1 \cup V_2 \cup ... \cup V_m$ be its domain of categorical values, with each V_i being a partition w.r.t the user's application purposes. $a_1 \in V$ and $a_2 \in V$ are *similar* if both are in some V_i.

For instance, we may say that two people are similar in *age* if the difference of their ages is below 10 years, and similar in *salary* if the difference is not over \$500. We may also view two people similar in *profession* if both of their jobs belong to the group {soldier, police, guard} or the group {teacher, researcher, doctor}. The similarity of attribute values may vary from application to application.

With the similarity measure of attribute values defined above, the user can then measure the similarity of two objects by counting their similar attribute values. If the number of similar attribute values is above a threshold δ, the two objects can be considered similar w.r.t. the user's application purposes.

Definition 2.3 (Similarity of two objects) Let o_1 and o_2 be two d-dimensional objects and $\mathcal{K}$ be a set of key attributes w.r.t. the user's application purposes. Let δ be a *similarity threshold* with $0 < \delta \leq |\mathcal{K}| \leq d$. o_1 and o_2 are *similar* (or *neighbors*) if they have at least δ attributes in $\mathcal{K}$ that take on similar values.

Whether an attribute is selected as a key attribute depends on whether it is relevant to the user's application purposes. In case that the user has difficulty specifying key attributes, all attributes are taken as key attributes. The similarity threshold δ is expected to be specified by the user. It can also be learned from a dataset.

3 Cluster cores and disjoint clusters

The intuition behind our clustering method is that every cluster is believed to have its own distinct characteristics, which are implicitly present in some objects in a dataset. This suggests that the principal characteristics of a cluster may be represented by a certain number of pairwise similar objects.

Definition 3.1 (Cluster cores) $C^r \subseteq DB$ is a *cluster core* if it satisfies the following three conditions. (1) $|C^r| \geq \alpha$, where α is a threshold specifying the minimum size of a cluster core. (2) Any two objects in C^r are similar w.r.t. the user's application purposes. (3) There exists no C', with $C^r \subset C' \subseteq DB$, that satisfies condition (2). C^r is a *maximum cluster core* if it is a cluster core with the maximum cardinality.

Note that a cluster core C^r is a fairly dense group with a maximal number of pairwise similar objects. Due to this, it may well be treated as the core/center of a cluster, as other objects of the cluster not in C^r must be attracted with a great degree to C^r.

Definition 3.2 (Clusters) Let $C^r \subseteq DB$ be a cluster core and let θ be a *cluster threshold* with $0 \leq \theta \leq 1$. C is a *cluster* if $C = \{v \in DB | v \in C^r$ or C^r contains at least $\theta * |C^r|$ objects that are similar to $v\}$.

The threshold θ is the support (degree) of an object being attracted to a cluster core. Such a parameter can be learned from a dataset by experiments. Note that a unique cluster is defined given a cluster core. However, a cluster may be derived from different cluster cores, as the core/center of a cluster can be described with different sets of objects that satisfy the three conditions of Definition 3.1.

The above definition of cluster cores/clusters allows us to apply existing graph theory to compute them. We first define a similarity graph over a dataset.

Definition 3.3 (Similarity graphs) A *similarity graph*, $SG_{DB} = (V, E)$, of DB is an undirected graph where $V = DB$ is the set of nodes, and E is the set of edges such that $\{o_1, o_2\} \in E$ if objects o_1 and o_2 are similar.

An undirected graph $G = (V, E)$ is *complete* if its nodes are pairwise adjacent. In this case, V is called a *clique*. A *maximal clique* is a clique that is not a proper subset of any other clique. A *maximum clique* is a maximal clique that has the maximum cardinality. It is easy to show that a cluster core in DB corresponds to a maximal clique in SG_{DB}.

Example 3.1 Let us consider a sample dataset, DB_1, as shown in Table 1, where nil is replaced by a blank. For simplicity, assume all attributes have a domain $\{1\}$ with a single partition $\{1\}$. Thus, two values, v_1 and v_2, of an attribute are similar if $v_1 = v_2 = 1$. Let us assume all attributes are key attributes, and choose the similarity threshold $\delta \geq 2$. The similarity relationship between objects of DB_1 is depicted by a similarity graph SG_{DB_1} shown in Figure 1. We have four maximal cliques: $C_1 = \{1, 2, 3, 4\}$, $C_2 = \{4, 5\}$, $C_3 = \{5, 6, 7\}$ and $C_4 = \{5, 6, 8\}$. Let us choose $\alpha = 3$ and the cluster threshold $\theta = 0.6$. C_1, C_3 and C_4 are cluster cores. C_1 is also a cluster and $\{5, 6, 7, 8\}$ is a cluster which can be obtained by expanding either C_3 or C_4.

Table 1. A sample dataset DB_1.

id	A₁	A₂	A₃	A₄	A₅	A₆	A₇	A₈	A₉	A₁₀	A₁₁
1	1	1	1								
2		1	1	1							
3	1		1	1							
4	1	1			1	1	1	1			
5				1	1	1	1	1		1	1
6								1	1	1	
7									1	1	1
8								1		1	

Figure 1. A similarity graph SG_{DB_1}.

There may be overlaps among cluster cores and/or clusters. Like most graph-based clustering approaches, in this paper we are devoted to building disjoint clusters.

Definition 3.4 (Disjoint clusters) $DC(DB) = \langle C_1, ..., C_m \rangle$ is a list of *disjoint clusters* of DB if C_1 is a cluster in DB and for any $i > 1$, C_i is a cluster in $DB - \bigcup_{j=1}^{j=i-1} C_j$. $DC(DB)$ is a list of *maximum disjoint clusters* if each C_i is a cluster with a maximum cluster core in $DB - \bigcup_{j=1}^{j=i-1} C_j$.

4 Approximating maximum clusters

Ideally, we would like to have maximum disjoint clusters. However, this appears to be infeasible for a massive dataset DB, as computing a maximum cluster core over DB amounts to computing a maximum clique over its corresponding similarity graph SG_{DB} (a NP-complete problem). Therefore, we appeal to approximating maximum disjoint clusters. Here is a sketch of the algorithm, where $maximal\_clique(.)$ is a procedure for randomly building a maximal clique, and i starts from 1.

Step 1. Iterate $maximal\_clique(SG_{DB})$ for $maxitr$ times to build a large cluster core C^r, and then build a cluster C_i based on C^r.

Step 2. Remove from SG_{DB} all nodes in C_i.

Step 3. Repeat Steps 1 and 2 until SG_{DB} contains less than α nodes.

Let $<C_1, ..., C_m>$ be the list of disjoint clusters produced above. It can be shown that the time complexity is $O(m * maxitr * \overline{D}_G^2)$, where $\overline{D}_G$ is the maximum degree of nodes in SG_{DB}. Since it costs $O(|DB|^2)$ in time to construct a similarity graph SG_{DB} from a dataset DB, the overall time complexity of our cluster cores-based clustering is $O(|DB|^2 + m * maxitr * \overline{D}_G^2)$.

In a massive high dimensional dataset DB, data points would be rather sparse so that $\overline{D}_G \ll |DB|$. Our experiments show that most of the time is spent in constructing SG_{DB} because $|DB|^2 \gg m * maxitr * \overline{D}_G^2$. Note that the complexity of our method is lower than that of ROCK, which is $O(|DB|^2 * log|DB| + |DB| * \overline{D}_G * M)$, where M is the average number of neighbors for an object.

5   Preliminary experimental results

We report our experiments over the widely-used Mushroom data from the UCI Machine Learning Repository. This dataset consists of 8124 objects with 22 attributes each with a categorical domain. Each object has a class of either edible or poisonous. One major reason for us to choose this dataset is that ROCK [2] has achieved very high accuracy over it, so we can make a comparison with ROCK. Here, clustering accuracy is measured using the formula $accuracy = \frac{N}{|DB|}$, where N is the number of objects sitting in right clusters.

Our experiments go through two steps. First, we learn a similarity threshold δ. In many cases, the user cannot provide a precise similarity threshold used for measuring the similarity of objects. This requires us to be able to learn it directly from $|DB|$. Second, we learn a cluster threshold θ. The evaluation criterion on different thresholds is their clustering accuracy. Through the learning process, we observed that the highest accuracy was obtained at $\delta = 15$ and $\theta = 0.88$. The sizes of clusters that were produced with $\delta = 15$ and $\theta = 0.88$ are shown in Table 2 (C# stands for the cluster number and the results of ROCK were copied from [2]). Clearly, our method achieves higher accuracy than ROCK.

As one can see, our experimental evaluation is quite preliminary. More experimental results over large real life datasets and more comparison with closely related existing approaches will be reported in a short period of time.

Acknowledgement

We thank the three anonymous reviewers for helpful comments. Yi-Dong Shen is supported in part by Chinese National Natural Science Foundation and Foundation from the Chinese Ministry of Education.

Table 2. Clustering results (Mushroom data).

Cluster Cores-based Clustering					
C#	Edible	Poisonous	C#	Edible	Poisonous
1	1704	0	12	192	0
2	0	1280	13	0	172
3	0	1556	14	32	72
4	762	0	15	96	0
5	0	288	16	96	0
6	288	0	17	48	0
7	509	0	18	48	0
8	192	0	19	0	36
9	0	256	20	0	32
10	0	192	21	24	0
11	192	0			
$accuracy = 8035/8124 = 98.9\%$					

ROCK					
C#	Edible	Poisonous	C#	Edible	Poisonous
1	96	0	12	48	0
2	0	256	13	0	288
3	704	0	14	192	0
4	96	0	15	32	72
5	768	0	16	0	1728
6	0	192	17	288	0
7	1728	0	18	0	8
8	0	32	19	192	0
9	0	1296	20	16	0
10	0	8	21	0	36
11	48	0			
$accuracy = 7804/8124 = 96.1\%$					

References

[1] L. Ertoz, M. Steinbach and V. Kumar, Finding clusters of different sizes, shapes, and densities in noisy, high dimensional data, in: *Proc. 3rd SIAM International Conference on Data Mining* San Francisco, CA, USA, 2003

[2] S. Guha, R. Rastogi and K. Shim, ROCK: A robust clustering algorithm for categorical attributes, in: *Proc. IEEE Intl. Conf. on Data Engineering*, pp. 512-521, 1999.

[3] E. Hartuv and R. Shamir, A clustering algorithm based on graph connectivity, *Information Processing Letters* 76:175-181 (2000).

[4] R. A. Jarvis and E. A. Patrick, Clustering using a similarity measure based on shared nearest neighbors, *IEEE Transactions on Computers* C-22(11): 264-323 (1973).

Metric Incremental Clustering of Nominal Data

Dan Simovici
University of Massachusetts at Boston,
Department of Computer Science,
Boston, Massachusetts 02125, USA,
dsim@cs.umb.edu

Namita Singla
University of Massachusetts at Boston,
Department of Computer Science,
Boston, Massachusetts 02125, USA,
namita@cs.umb.edu

Michael Kuperberg
Karlsruhe University,
Department of Computer Science,
Karlsruhe, Germany,
Michael.Kuperberg@informatik.uni-karlsruhe.de

Abstract

We present an algorithm for clustering nominal data that is based on a metric on the set of partitions of a finite set of objects; this metric is defined starting from a lower valuation of the lattice of partitions. The proposed algorithm seeks to determine a clustering partition such that the total distance between this partition and the partitions determined by the attributes of the objects has a local minimum. The resulting clustering is quite stable relative to the ordering of the objects.

1 Introduction

Clustering is an unsupervised learning process that partitions data such that similar data items are grouped together in sets referred to as clusters. This activity is important for condensing and identifying patterns in data. Despite the substantial effort invested in researching clustering algorithms by the data mining community, there are still many difficulties to overcome in building clustering algorithms. Indeed, as pointed in [12] "there is no clustering technique that is universally applicable in uncovering the variety of structures present in multidimensional data sets".

In this paper we focus on an incremental clustering algorithm that can be applied to nominal data, that is, to data whose attributes have no particular natural ordering. In general clustering, objects to be clustered are represented as points in an n-dimensional space $\mathbb{R}^n$ and standard distances, such as the Euclidean distance is used to evaluate similarity between objects. For objects whose attributes are

nominal (e.g., color, shape, diagnostic, etc.), no such natural representation of objects is possible, which leaves only the Hamming distance as a dissimilarity measure, a poor choice for discriminating among multi-valued attributes of objects.

Incremental clustering has attracted a substantial amount of attention starting with Hartigan's algorithm [11] implemented in [6]. A seminal paper by D. Fisher [10] contained COBWEB, an incremental clustering algorithm that involved restructurings of the clusters in addition to the incremental additions of objects. Incremental clustering related to dynamic aspects of databases were discussed in [4, 5]. It is also notable that incremental clustering has been used in a variety of applications [13, 14, 7, 9]. The interest in incremental clustering stems from the fact that the main memory usage is minimal since there is no need to keep in memory the mutual distances between objects and the algorithms are scalable with respect to the size of the set of objects and the number of attributes.

An *object system* is a pair $\mathcal{S} = (S, H)$, where S is set called the set of objects of $\mathcal{S}$, $H = \{A_1, \ldots, A_m\}$ is a set of mappings defined on S. We assume that for each mapping A_i (referred to as an attribute of $\mathcal{S}$) there exists a nonempty set E_i called the domain of A_i such that $A_i : S \longrightarrow E_i$ for $1 \leq i \leq m$. The value of an attribute A_i on an object t is denoted by $t[A_i]$. Our terminology is consistent with the terminology used in relational databases, where a table can be regarded as an object system; however, the notion of object system is more general because objects have an identity as members of the set S, instead of being regarded as just m-tuples of values. In this spirit, we shall refer to $t[A_i]$ as *projection of t on A_i*.

Let S be a set. A partition on S is a non-empty collection of subsets of S indexed by a set I, $\pi = \{B_i \mid i \in I\}$ such that $\bigcup_{i \in I} B_i = S$ and $i \neq j$ implies $B_i \cap B_j = \emptyset$. The sets B_i are commonly referred to as the *blocks of the partition* π. The set of partitions on S is denoted by $\mathsf{PART}(S)$.

$\mathsf{PART}(S)$ can be naturally equipped with a partial order. For $\pi, \sigma \in \mathsf{PART}(S)$ we write $\pi \leq \sigma$ if every block B of π is included in a block of σ, or equivalently, if every block of σ is an exact union of blocks of π. This partial order generates a lattice structure; this means that for every $\pi, \pi' \in \mathsf{PART}(S)$ there is a least partition π_1 such that $\pi \leq \pi_1$ and $\pi' \leq \pi_1$ and there is a largest partition π_2 such that $\pi_2 \leq \pi$ and $\pi_2 \leq \pi'$. The first partition is denoted by $\pi \vee \pi'$, while the second is denoted by $\pi \wedge \pi'$.

An attribute A of an object system $\mathcal{S} = (S, H)$ generates a partition π^A of the set of objects S, where two objects belong to the same block of π^A if they have the same projection on A. We denote by B_a^A the block of π^A that consists of all tuples of S whose A-component is a. Note that for relational databases, π^A is the partition of the set of rows of a table that is obtained by using the **group by** A option of **select** in standard SQL.

A clustering of an object system $\mathcal{S} = (S, H)$ is defined as a partition κ of S. We seek to find clusterings starting from their relationships with partitions induced by attributes. As we shall see, this is a natural approach for nominal data.

The mapping $v : \mathsf{PART}(S) \longrightarrow \mathbb{R}$ by $v(\pi) = \sum_{i=1}^{n} |B_i|^2$, where $\pi = \{B_1, \ldots, B_n\}$ is a lower valuation on $\mathsf{PART}(S)$, that is,

$$v(\pi \vee \sigma) + v(\pi \wedge \sigma) \geq v(\pi) + v(\sigma) \qquad (1)$$

for $\pi, \sigma \in \mathsf{PART}(S)$. For every lower valuation v the mapping $d : (\mathsf{PART}(S))^2 \longrightarrow \mathbb{R}$ defined by $d(\pi, \sigma) = v(\pi) + v(\sigma) - 2v(\pi \wedge \sigma)$ is a metric on $\mathsf{PART}(S)$ (see [2, 1, 15]). A special property of this metric allows the formulation of an incremental clustering algorithm.

2 AMICA - A Metric Incremental Clustering Algorithm

Let $\mathcal{S} = (S, H)$ be an object system. We seek a clustering $\kappa = \{C_1, \ldots, C_n\} \in \mathsf{PART}(S)$ such that the total distance from κ to the partitions of the attributes: $D(\kappa) = \sum_{i=1}^{n} d(\kappa, \pi^{A_i})$ is minimal. The definition of d allows us to write:

$$d(\kappa, \pi^A) = \sum_{i=1}^{n} |C_i|^2 + \sum_{j=1}^{m_A} |B_{a_j}^A|^2 - 2 \sum_{i=1}^{n} \sum_{j=1}^{m_A} |C_i \cap B_{a_j}^A|^2,$$

Suppose now that t is a new object, $t \notin S$, and let $Z = S \cup \{t\}$. The following cases may occur:

1. the object t is added to an existing cluster C_k;

2. a new cluster, C_{n+1} is created that consists only of t.

Also, from the point of view of partition π^A, t is added to the block $B_{t[A]}^A$, which corresponds to the value $t[A]$ of the A-component of t.

In the first case let:

$$\begin{aligned} \kappa_{(k)} &= \{C_1, \ldots, C_{k-1}, C_k \cup \{t\}, C_{k+1}, \ldots, C_n\} \\ \pi^{A'} &= \{B_{a_1}^A, \ldots, B_{t[A]}^A \cup \{t\}, \ldots, B_{a_{m_A}}^A\} \end{aligned}$$

be the partitions of Z. Now, we have:

$$\begin{aligned} & d(\kappa_{(k)}, \pi^{A'}) - d(\kappa, \pi^A) \\ &= (|C_k| + 1)^2 - |C_k|^2 + (|B_{t[A]}^A| + 1)^2 \\ &\quad - |B_{t[A]}^A|^2 - 2(2|C_k \cap B_{t[A]}^A| + 1) \\ &= 2|C_k| + 1 + 2|B_{t[A]}^A| + 1 - 4|C_k \cap B_{t[A]}^A| - 2 \\ &= 2|C_k \oplus B_{t[A]}^A|. \end{aligned}$$

The minimal increase of $d(\kappa_{(k)}, \pi^{A'})$ is given by:

$$\min_k \sum_A 2|C_k \oplus B_{t[A]}^A|.$$

In the second case we deal with the partitions:

$$\begin{aligned} \kappa' &= \{C_1, \ldots, \ldots, C_n, \{t\}\} \\ \pi^{A'} &= \{B_{a_1}^A, \ldots, B_{t[A]}^A \cup \{t\}, \ldots, B_{a_{m_A}}^A\} \end{aligned}$$

and we have $d(\kappa', \pi^{A'}) - d(\kappa, \pi^A) - 2|B_{t[A]}^A|$. Consequently,

$$D(\kappa') - D(\kappa) = \begin{cases} 2 \cdot \sum_A |C_k \oplus B_{t[A]}^A| & \text{in Case 1} \\ 2 \cdot \sum_A |B_{t[A]}^A| & \text{in Case 2.} \end{cases}$$

Thus, if $\min_k \sum_A |C_k \oplus B_{t[A]}^A| < \sum_A |B_{t[A]}^A|$ we add t to a cluster C_k for which $\sum_A |C_k \oplus B_{t[A]}^A|$ is minimal; otherwise, we create a new one-object cluster.

Incremental clustering algorithms are affected, in general, by the order in which objects are processed by the clustering algorithm. Moreover, as pointed in [8], each such algorithm proceeds typically in a hill-climbing fashion that yields local minima rather than global ones. For some incremental clustering algorithms certain object orderings may result in rather poor clusterings. To diminish the ordering effect problem we expand the initial algorithm by adopting the "not-yet" technique introduced by Roure and Talavera in [16]. The basic idea is that a new cluster is created only when the inequality:

$$r(t) = \frac{\sum_A |B_{t[A]}^A|}{\min_k \sum_A |C_k \oplus B_{t[A]}^A|} < \alpha,$$

is satisfied, that is, only when the effect $r(t)$ of adding the object t on the total distance is significant enough. Here α

is a parameter provided by the user, such that $\alpha <= 1$. Note that if $\alpha = 1$, we make no use of the NOT-YET buffer.

We formulate now a metric incremental clustering algorithm (referred to as AMICA – an acronym of the previous five words) that is using the properties of distance d. The variable nc denotes the current number of clusters. If $\alpha < r(t) \leq 1$, then we place the object t in a NOT-YET buffer. If $r(t) \leq \alpha$ a new cluster that consists of the object $\{t\}$ is created. Otherwise, that is if $r(t) > 1$, the object t is placed in an existing cluster C_k that minimizes $\sum_A |C_k \oplus B^A_{t[A]}|$; this limits the number of new singleton clusters that would be otherwise created. After all objects of the set S have been examined, the objects contained by the NOT-YET buffer are processed with $\alpha = 1$. This prevents new insertions in the buffer and results in either placing these objects in existing clusters or in creating new clusters. The pseudocode of the algorithm is given next:

```
Input:   data set S and threshold α
Output:  clustering C₁,...,C_nc
Method:
nc = 0;
ℓ = 1;
while S ≠ ∅ do
        select an object t;
        S = S - {t};
        if  ∑_A |B^A_{t[A]}| ≤ α min_{1≤k≤nc} ∑_A |C_k ⊕ B^A_{t[A]}|
            then
                nc ++;
                create a new single-object
                cluster C_nc = {t};
            else
```
$$r(t) = \frac{\sum_A |B^A_{t[A]}|}{\min_{1\leq k\leq nc} \sum_A |C_k \oplus B^A_{t[A]}|}$$
```
        if r(t) > 1
            then
                k = arg min_k ∑_A |C_k ⊕ B^A_{t[A]}|
                add t to cluster C_k;
            else /* this means α < r(t) ≤ 1 */
                place t in NOT-YET buffer;
        end if;
endwhile;
process objects in the NOT-YET buffer
as above with α = 1;
```

3 Experimental Results

We applied AMICA to synthetic data sets produced by an algorithm that generates clusters of objects having real-numbered components grouped around a specified number of centroids. The resulting tuples were discretized using a specified number of discretization intervals which allowed

us to treat the data as nominal. The experiments were applied to several data sets with an increasing number of tuples and increased dimensionality and using several permutations of the set of objects. All experiments describe in this paper used $\alpha = 0.95$.

The stability of the obtained clusterings is quite remarkable. For example, in an experiment applied to a set that consists of 10,000 objects (grouped by the synthetic data algorithm around 6 centroids) a first pass of the algorithm produced 11 clusters; however, most objects (9895) are concentrated in the top 6 clusters, which approximate very well the "natural" clusters produced by the synthetic algorithm.

The next table compares the clusters produced by the first run of the algorithm with the cluster produced from a data set obtained by applying a random permutation.

Initial Run		Random Permutation		
Cluster	Size	Cluster	Size	Distribution (Original cluster)
1	1548	1	1692	1692 (2)
2	1693	2	1552	1548 (1), 3 (3), 1 (2)
3	1655	3	1672	1672 (5)
4	1711	4	1711	1711 (4)
5	1672	5	1652	1652 (3)
6	1616	6	1616	1616 (6)
7	1	7	85	85 (8)
8	85	8	10	10 (9)
9	10	9	8	8 (10)
10	8	10	1	1 (11)
11	1	11	1	1 (7)

Note that the clusters are stable; they remain almost invariant with the exception of their numbering. Similar results were obtained for other random permutations and collections of objects.

As expected with incremental clustering algorithms, the time requirements scale up very well with the number of tuples. On an IBM T20 system equipped with a 700 MHz Pentium III and with a 256 MB RAM, we obtained the following results for three randomly chosen permutations of each set of objects.

Number of objects	Time for 3 permutations (ms)			Average time (ms)
2000	131	140	154	141.7
5000	410	381	432	407.7
10000	782	761	831	794.7
20000	1103	1148	1061	1104

Another series of experiments involved the application of the algorithm to databases that contain nominal data. We applied AMICA to the mushroom data set from the standard UCI data mining collection (see [3]). The data set contains 8124 mushroom records and is typically used as test set for classification algorithms. In classification experiments the task is to construct a classifier that is able to predict the poisonous/edible character of the mushrooms based on the values of the attributes of the mushrooms. We discarded the class attribute (poisonous/edible) and applied AMICA to the remaining data set. Then, we identified the edible/poisonous character of mushrooms that are grouped together in the same cluster. This yields the clusters $C_1, \ldots, C_9$:

Cl. num.	Poisonous/Edible	Total	Percentage of dominant group
1	825/2752	3577	76.9%
2	8/1050	1058	99.2%
3	1304/0	1304	100%
4	0/163	163	100%
5	1735/28	1763	98.4%
6	0/7	7	100%
7	0/192	192	100%
8	36/16	52	69%
9	8/0	8	100%

Note that in almost all resulting clusters there is a dominant character, and for five out of the total of nine clusters there is complete homogeneity.

A study of the stability of the clusters similar to the one performed for synthetic data shows the same stability relative to input orderings as follows from the next table that describe a clustering obtained under a randomly chosen permutation of the set of objects:

C_i	Computed Clusters First Random Permutation									
	C'_1	C'_2	C'_3	C'_4	C'_5	C'_6	C'_7	C'_8	C'_9	C'_{10}
	3540	1797	1095	192	1296	8	36	7	137	16
3577	3540	0	37	0	0	0	0	0	0	0
1058	0	0	1058	0	0	0	0	0	0	0
1304	0	8	0	0	1296	0	0	0	0	0
163	0	26	0	0	0	0	0	0	137	0
1763	0	1763	0	0	0	0	0	0	0	0
7	0	0	0	0	0	0	0	7	0	0
192	0	0	0	192	0	0	0	0	0	0
52	0	0	0	0	0	0	36	0	0	16
8	0	0	0	0	0	8	0	0	0	0

Note that the previous table contains mostly zeros. This shows that the clusters remain essentially stable under input data permutations (with the exception of the order in which they are created).

4   Conclusion and Future Work

AMICA provides good quality, stable clusterings for nominal data, an area of clustering that is less explored than the standard clustering algorithms that act on ordinal data. Clusterings produced by the algorithm show a rather low sensitivity to input orderings.

Further investigations in the behavior of the algorithm are warranted. For example, we ran AMICA with a rather high value of the threshold $\alpha = 0.95$. Future work will

include an examination of the dependency of the maximal size of the NOT-YET buffer for various values of α.

AMICA could be combined with special discretization algorithms such as metric discretization [17] to obtain a more general incremental clustering algorithm applicable to mixed data, that is, to data having both nominal and ordinal attributes. This is currently work in progress.

References

[1] J. Barthélemy. Remarques sur les propriétés metriques des ensembles ordonnés. *Math. Sci. hum.*, 61:39–60, 1978.

[2] J. Barthélemy and B. Leclerc. The median procedure for partitions. In *Partitioning Data Sets*, pages 3–34, Providence, 1995. American Mathematical Society.

[3] C. L. Blake and C. J. Merz. *UCI Repository of machine learning databases.* University of California, Irvine, Dept. of Information and Computer Sciences, http://www.ics.uci.edu/~mlearn/MLRepository.html, 1998.

[4] F. Can. Incremental clustering for dynamic information processing. *ACM Transaction for Information Systems*, 11:143–164, 1993.

[5] F. Can, E. A. Fox, C. D. Snavely, and R. K. France. Incremental clustering for very large document databases: Initial MARIAN experience. *Inf. Sci.*, 84:101–114, 1995.

[6] G. Carpenter and S. Grossberg. Art3: Hierachical search using chemical transmitters in self-organizing pattern recognition architectures. *Neural Networks*, 3:129–152, 1990.

[7] M. Charikar, C. Chekuri, T. Feder, and R. Motwani. Incremental clustering and dynamic information retrieval. In *STOC*, pages 626–635, 1997.

[8] A. Cornuéjols. Getting order independence in incremental learning. In *European Conference on Machine Learning*, pages 196–212, 1993.

[9] M. Ester, H. P. Kriegel, J. Sander, M. Wimmer, and X. Xu. Incremental clustering for mining in a data warehousing environment. In *VLDB*, pages 323–333, 1998.

[10] D. Fisher. Knowledge acquisition via incremental conceptual clustering. *Machine Learning*, 2:139–172, 1987.

[11] J. A. Hartigan. *Clustering Algorithms*. John Wiley, New York, 1975.

[12] A. K. Jain, M. N. Murty, and P. J. Flynn. Data clustering: A review. *ACM Computing Surveys*, 31:264–323, 1999.

[13] T. Langford, C. G. Giraud-Carrier, and J. Magee:. Detection of infectious outbreaks in hospitals through incremental clustering. In *Proceedings of the 8th Conference on AI in Medicine (AIME)*, pages 30–39. Springer, 2001.

[14] J. Lin, M. Vlachos, E. J. Keogh, and D. Gunopulos. Iterative incremental clustering of time series. In *EDBT*, pages 106–122, 2004.

[15] B. Monjardet. Metrics on parially ordered sets – a survey. *Discrete Mathematics*, 35:173–184, 1981.

[16] J. Roure and L. Talavera. Robust incremental clustering with bad instance orderings: A new strategy. In *IBERAMIA*, pages 136–147, 1998.

[17] D. Simovici and R. Butterworth. A metric approach to supervised discretization. In *Extraction et Gestion des Connaisances (EGC'2004)*, pages 197–202, Toulouse, France, 2004. Cépaduès-Éditions.

On Ranking Refinements in the Step-by-step Searching through a Product Catalogue

Nenad Stojanovic

Institute AIFB, University of Karlsruhe, Germany
nst@aifb.uni-karlsruhe.de

Abstract

In our previous work we have developed a logic-based approach for the refinement of ontology-based queries that enables a user to search through a repository in a step-by-step fashion. Since the set of refinements in a step can be large, they should be ranked according to their relevance for fulfilling a user's need. In this paper we present such a ranking model, which takes into account the information content (informativeness) of a refinement as well as the preferences of the user.

1. Introduction

In our previous work [1] we present an approach for refining ontology-based, so called logic-based query refinement, that enables a user to navigate through the information content incrementally and interactively. In each refinement step a user is provided with a complete but minimal set of refinements, which enables him to develop/express his information need in a step-by-step fashion. The approach is based on the model-theoretic interpretation of the refinement problem, so that the query refinement process can be considered as the process of inferring all queries which are subsumed by a given query. Due to the complexity of subsumption reasoning, we use an alternative, more tractable generality order, θ-subsumption, frequently used for efficient implementation of inductive logic programming tasks. Since the θ-subsumption is a partial order relation, it generates a lattice of refinements, which serves as the basic structure for the step-by-step query refinement.

Although the logic-based query refinement generates the minimal number of refinements, it is possible that the entire set of refinements is too large for the searching habits of an average user. Indeed, by using an analogy to the browsing results of a query, one can expect that an average user will consider only several top-ranked refinements. Therefore, the set of refinements should be ranked according to their importance for fulfilling a user's need and in this paper we present such a ranking model. In Section 2 we first explain the basic terminology, whereas in Section 3 we present the ranking model. In Section 4 we give some concluding remarks.

2. Background

In this section we give the basic assumption/terminology we use in this paper.

Definition 1: Ontology
An ontology is a structure $O := (C, \leq_c, R, \sigma)$ consisting of:

- two disjoint sets C and R whose elements are called concept identifiers and relation identifiers, resp.,
- a partial order $\leq_c$ on C, called concept hierarchy or taxonomy (without cycles)
- a function $\sigma : R \to C^+$, called signature.

Definition 2: Knowledge Base
A Knowledge Base is a structure $KB := (C_{KB}, R_{KB}, I, l_c, l_r)$ consisting of:

- two disjoint sets C_{KB} and R_{KB}
- a set I whose elements are called instance identifiers (or instances or objects shortly)
- a function $l_C : C_{KB} \to I$ called concept instantiation
- a function $l_r : R_{KB} \to I^+$ called relation instantiation

A relation instance can be depicted as $r(I_1, I_2, ..., I_n)$, where $r \in R_{KB}, I_i \in I$. Similarly, $c(I_i)$, where $c \in C_{KB}$, represents the concept the instance I_i belongs to. r is called a predicate and I_i is called a term.

Definition 3: Query
A conjunctive query is of the form or can be rewritten into the form: $Q(\overline{X}) \equiv forall \ \overline{X} \ \overline{P}(\overline{X}, \overline{k})$, with $\overline{X}$ being a vector of variables $(X_1, ..., X_n)$, $\overline{k}$ being a vector of constants (concept instances), $\overline{P}$ being a vector of conjoined predicates (relations).

For example, for the query "forall x,y worksIn(x, KM) and researchIn(x, y)" (1)
we have: $\overline{X} := (x, y)$, $k := (KM)$, $\overline{P} := (P_1, P_2)$, $P_1(a,b,c) :=$ worksIn(a,b), $P_2(a,b,c) :=$ researchIn(a,c).

Since a predicate constrains the interpretation of a variable in a query, in the rest of the text we will use the term *query constraint* as the description of a predicate. For example, researchIn(x, y) is a constraint for the interpretation of the variable x.

3. Ranking model

In order to determine the relevance of a refinement for a user's need, we use two sources of information: (a) user's preferences for such a refinement and (b) informativeness (information content) of a refinement.

3.1. User's preferences

Since the users are reluctant to provide an explicit information about the relevance of a result, the ranking has to be based on the implicit information that are captured by observing user's behaviour, so-called implicit relevance feedback [2]. In the query refinement a user interacts subsequently with the system so that, by discovering user's preferences, we have to take into account not only the last query a user made, but rather the whole process of creating a query (query session). We define three types of such an implicit relevance feedback: *Actuality*, *ImplicitRelevance* and *ImplicitIrrelevance*.

Actuality. The *Actuality* parameter reflects the phenomena, accounted in the IR research, that a user may change the criteria about the relevance of a query term, when encountering newly retrieved results. In other words, the constraints most recently introduced in a user's query are more indicative of what the user currently finds relevant for his need. We model it using the analogy to the ostensive relevance proposed in [3]:

$$Actuality(c, Qs) = \frac{1}{num\_session(c, Qs) + 1},$$ where c is a query

constraint , Qs is the current query session and $num\_session(c, Qs)$ is the number of refinement steps, which the constraint c is involved in.

ImplicitRelevance. The theory about the implicit relevance feedback postulates that if a user selects a resource from the list of retrieved results, then this resource corresponds, to some extent, to his information need. However, a click on a particular resource in the resulted list cannot be treated as an absolute relevance judgement, since users typically scan only the top l ranked ($l \approx 10$) resources. For example, maybe a document ranked much lower in the list was much more relevant, but the user newer saw it. It appears that users click on the (relatively) most promising resources in the top l, independent of their absolute relevance. However, if we assume that a user scans the list of results from top to bottom, the relative relevance is evident: all non-clicked-on resources placed above a clicked-on resource are less relevant than the clicked-on resource. Obviously, the relevance is related to some feature that are contained in the clicked-on resource and not contained in non-clicked-on resources. It means that by analysing the commonalities in the attributes of results a user clicked/not clicked, we can infer more information about the intension of the user in the current query session. In order to achieve this, we define the relation *preferred ranking* as $R_i <_{rQ*} R_j$ for all pairs $1 <= j < i$, with $i \in C$ and $j \notin C$, where $(R_1, R_2, R_3, \ldots)$ is a ranked list of resources, set C contains the ranks of the clicked-on resources and Q is the posted query.

By analysing the difference between the features (attributes, constraints) of the clicked-on and non-clicked-on resources we get a set of so called *Preferred* constraints for a query Q in the following manner:
$Preferred(Q) = \{con \mid con \in \cup_j Preferred_j(Q)\}$, where
$Preferred_j(Q) = \{el \mid el \in Attr(R_j) \setminus \cup_i Attr(R_i), \forall R_i <_{rQ*} R_j\}$,
$Attr(R_x)$ is the set of constraints (attributes) that are defined for the resource R_x.

Therefore, the set of constraints that seems to be relevant for a user in a query Q_s can be calculated as: (1)

$$Im\,pl\,Rel(c, Qs) = \begin{cases} 0, & c \notin Preferred(Qs) \\ \dfrac{1}{n} \sum_{i=1,n} \dfrac{1}{num\_sessions(c, Q_s, i)}, & c \in Preferred(Qs) \end{cases}$$

, where $num\_sessions(c, Qs, i)$ is the number of refinement steps which the constraint c is involved as a preferred constraint in, whereas n is the total number of times the constraint c is treated as a preferred constraint in the current session Qs.

ImplicitIrrelevance. Since the recommended refinements are presented to a user in the decreasing order of relevance, one can assume that if a user has selected n-th ranked results, then the first n-1 ranked results (constraints) are wrongly ranked on the top of the list of the refinements. We call these constraint *implicit irrelevant*. They are calculated in similar manner as implicit relevant constraints: (2)

$$Im\,plIrrel(c, Qs) = \begin{cases} 0, & c \notin Nonpreferred(Qs) \\ \displaystyle\sum_{i=1,n} \dfrac{1}{num\_sessions(c, Q_s, i)}, & c \in Nonpreferred(Qs) \end{cases}$$

, where $NonPreferred(Q) = \{con \mid con \in \cup_j NonPreferred(Q)_j\}$
$NonPreferred_j(Q) = \{el \mid el \in \cup_i Attr(R_i) \setminus Attr(R_j), \forall R_i <_{rQ*} R_j\}$.
The definition of $num\_sessions(c, Qs, i)$ is analogue to (2), but regarding implicit irrelevance.

Similar to (1), formula (2) enables the correction of false assumptions (regarding the preferences of the current user) made in the ranking process.

Formulas (1) and (2) ensures the self-adaptivity of the ranking system, e.g. they do not allow that the system repeatedly ranks a non-interesting refinement highly. Finally, the calculated implicit relevance of a refinement c looks like:

$$Relevance(c, Qs) = \frac{Im\,pl\,Rel(c, Qs) + 1}{Im\,plIrrel(c, Qs) + 1}$$

3.2. Informativeness

Another source to define relevance of a refinement is

its informativeness or information content. From the machine learning research it is known that usefulness of an attribute (i.e. constraint) for traversing the searching space is proportional to its information content, that is frequently measured using entropy [4]. Indeed, the entropy shows the interestingness of a constraint regarding its relevance for the user's need.

In order to illustrate the relevance model let us consider the knowledge base represented in Figure 1.

car	Type	GPS	Automatic
c1	familyCar	g1	a1
c2	sportsCar	g2	a1
c3	sportsCar	g3	a2
c4	sportsCar	g4	a3
c5	familyCar	g3	a3
c6	familyCar	g1	a2

GPS	GPSType	Language	Automatic	AutomaticType	Level
g1	auto	eng	a1	type1	low
g2	semi	ger	a2	type2	high
g3	semi	fra	a3	type1	high
g4	auto	fra			

Figure 1. The knowledge base used for illustrating relevance model

However, there are two problems in direct applying the information theory for selecting the most informative attribute in the ontology-based querying:

1. Since in an ontology-based query an attribute is assigned to a concept (i.e. variable), before determining the informativeness of an attribute (using the entropy), the informativeness of a concept has to be determined. For example, in the query (3)
Q = "forall x,y,z Car(x) and GPS(y) and Automatic(z) and hasType(sportsCar, x) and hasLuxury(y, x) and hasLuxury(z, x)", the question is which of the variables x, y, z is the most suitable for the further refinement.

We define the suitability of each of these variables in the following manner:

$Suitability(X, Q) = VariableAmbiguity(X, Q)/Gain(X, Q).$ (4)

$$VariableAmbiguity(X,Q) = \frac{|Relation(Type(X))| + 1}{|AssignedRelations(Type(X),Q)| + 1},$$

where $Relation(C)$ is the set of all relations defined for the concept C in the ontology, $AssignedRelations(C,Q)$ is the set of all relations defined in the set $Relation(C)$ and which appear in the query Q.

If we assume that there two relations are defined for the concept GPS, then regarding (3):

$VariableAmbiguity(y, Q) = (2+1)/1 = 3.$

$Gain(X, Q) = Info(T) - Info(X, T)$ is the standard measure of the informativeness [4], i.e. for the probability distribution of the values (instances) that belongs to the variable X, X = (x1, ..., xn)

$$Info(X,T) = \sum_{i=1,n} \frac{|x_i|}{|T|} E(x_i)$$ (5)

where T is the set of all examples relevant for the query Q and E is the standard measure for the entropy:

$$E(w) = -\sum_{i \in Category} w_i * log(w_i)$$ (6)

where *Category* is the set of all categories for the classification and wi is the distribution of instances that belong to the category i (w = (w_1, ..., w_c)).

In order to compensate the effect of multivalued attributes the *SplitInfo* factor is introduced:

$Gain(X, T) = Gain(X, T)/SplitInfo(X, T)$ (7)

$$SplitInfo(X,T) = -\sum_{i=1,n} \frac{x_i}{T_i} * log(\frac{x_i}{T}).$$

For the given problem domain we define only two classes an example (instance) can belong to: *Relevant* and *Irrelevant*, representing the set of relevant and irrelevant examples regarding a users need (i.e. query). The set of relevant examples for the query (3) is depicted by the rectangle in the first table in Figure 1 (all sportsCars). Further, for the set T of examples given in Figure 1,

$Info(T) = E(3/6, 3/6)$
$Info(y, T) = ((2/6)*E(0,1) + (1/6)*E(1,0) +$
$\qquad (2/6)*E(1/2,1/2) + (1/6)*E(1,0))$
$SplitInfo(y, T) = ((2/6)*log(2/6) + (1/6)*log(1/6) +$
$\qquad (2/6)*log(2/6) + (1/6)*log(1/6))$

By applying (4) on variable x, y, z from query (3) we get that the variable y (GPS) is most suitable for the further refinement.

2. The second problem is the determination of the informativeness of an attribute of a variable from the query, since the relevance categories are defined on the level of the concepts. For example, by considering left-bottom table it is difficult to say if the example g3 is relevant or irrelevant since according to the query (3) it can be treated as both of them.

Therefore, we need a notation of fuzzy entropy, which we introduced in the following manner:

For each example x_i (instance) we introduce a partial membership to a category p(x_i) that is calculated from the set T. For example p(g1)=0, p(g3)=0.5.
Further the calculation of Entropy includes this fuzzy probability

$$E(w) = -\sum_{i \in Category} \frac{\sum_{j=1,k} p(w_j)}{k} * log(\frac{\sum_{j=1,k} p(w_j)}{k}),$$

where k is the number of examples that belong to a category.

For example, regarding attribute GPSType from Figure 1:
$E(semi) = -((1+1/2)/2)*log(1+1/2)/2) +$
$\qquad (0+1/2)/2)*log(0+1/2)/2).$

Formulas (5) and (7) are used to determine the informativeness of an attribute.

Finally, for a constraint e the *Informativeness* is calculated as: $Informativeness(e,Q)=$
$\qquad Suitability(Variable(e),Q))*Gain(Predicate(e), Q),$
where *Variable* retrieves the variable from a constraint

For example, a possible refinement of the query (3) can be e = " and GPSType(var, y)".

$Informativeness(e,Q)=Suitability(y,Q))*$
$$Gain(GPSType, Q),$$

Note that for numeric features, the values have to be discretized, for instance in equi-depth buckets [4].

3.3. The model

We assume that with every decision taken by the user more information is gained about the user's intensions and background. Each transition (refinement) from the query e to query d involves a conscious choice by the user by preferring the constraints contained in d to the other options in the constraint e. The probability of a constraint d being the target of the navigation process is related to the distance fluctuations while travelling the navigation path. Recent fluctuations have more impact then past fluctuations. For this purpose we will transform the search space into a transition network, allowing the use of Markov chains theory. First, the set of states is defined as the set of *query constraints* augmented with a special state called *stop*. This state represents the termination of the search process. The transition between states are defined as follows: if constraints x and y are connected regarding the ontology structure, then they are connected in the transition network.

We assume for each transaction e a probability $q_e > 0$ of occurring. In a transition network, for each state a: $\sum_{b:a \to b} q_{a \to b} = 1$. The transition matrix T is defined as

$$T(x,y) = \{ \begin{matrix} q_s & if & x \in Related(y) \\ 0 & & otherwise \end{matrix} ,$$

where q_s is uniformly distributed over all related constraints and $Related(c)$ is a function that retrieves constraints that are related to c regarding the underlying ontology.

Further, $T'(x,y)$ is the probability of reaching y starting from x in i transitions. $T^0 = I$, the identity matrix. Thus, the sum $\sum_{i=0}^{\infty} T^i(e,d)$ is the probability of reaching d from e in any number of steps. Next we focus on the probability $Pr(d \mid e)$ of a constraint d being the search target of a navigation path. The destination probability for d after traversing a path from e is defined as follows: $Pr(d \mid e) = \sum_{i=0}^{\infty} T^i(e,d) \cdot T(d, stop)$.

The infinite sum converges to $(I-T)-1(e,d)$. This requires the calculation of the inverse matrix of an $|\Omega(O)|$ x $|\Omega(O)|$ matrix, where $\Omega(O)$ is the set of elementary constraints regarding given ontology O. Note that this operation can be calculated off-line.

However, in a step-by-step refinement a user is navigating through queries Q_x that contain several constraints. In that case we expand the probability to include this information as follows:

$$Pr(Q_d \mid Q_e) = \frac{1}{|Q_d|} \cdot \sum_{d \in Q_d} \frac{1}{|Q_e|} \cdot \sum_{e \in Q_e} Pr(d \mid e),$$

where d and e are constraints from queries Q_d and Q_e respectively. $|Q_d|$ depicts the number of constraints in Q_d.

We use this destination probability function as a starting point for computing which neighbours bring the user most direct towards the highest probable destination constraint. Indeed, as we mentioned above the refinement process depends on the searching history (parameters *Actuality* and *Relevance*) and the content of the repository (parameters *Informativeness*).

This is formalized by assigning the coefficient *Rank* to each query Q_d that belongs to the lattice of the refinement for the query Q_e:

$$Rank(Q_d \mid Q_e) = \frac{1}{|Q_d|} \cdot \sum_{d \in Q_d} \frac{1}{|Q_e|} \cdot$$

$$(\sum_{e \in Q_e} Pr(d \mid e) \cdot (\frac{\lambda \cdot Relevance(d) \cdot Actuality(e) + Informativeness(e,Q_e)}{\lambda + 1})),$$

where λ is a forgetfulness coefficient that model the impact on the past user's behaviour on the ranking process: $\lambda = 0$ - the past is forgotten, $\lambda < 1$ - the past carries less weight then the present, usually $\lambda = 1/2$.

4. Conclusion

In this paper we have presented a comprehensive model for ranking refinements in a query refinement process. It uses two sources of information: a user's preferences for such a refinement and informativeness of a refinement. In that way the approach prioritises highly relevant refinements, i.e. the refinements that are related to the very characteristic (regarding a query) constraints and tailored to the user's need. Moreover, by using a user's implicit relevance feedback, the approach learns from its failures and successes, i.e. it has a self-improvement nature.

Acknowledgement. Research for this paper was partially financed by BMBF in the project "SemIPort" (08C5939).

5. References

[1] N. Stojanovic, "A Logic-based Approach for Query Refinement", WI 2004, IEEE, in press

[2] G. Salton, and C. Buckley, "Improving retrieval performance by relevance feedback", *Journal of the American Society for Information Science*, 41(4): 288-297, 1990.

[3] I. Ruthven, M. Lalmas, and C.J. van Rijsbergen, "Incorporating user search behaviour into relevance feedback", *Journal of the American Society for Information Science and Technology*, 54. 6. pp.528-548. 2003.

[Wit00] I.H. Witten, E. Frank, Data Mining, Morgan Kaufmann Publisher, 2000

Learning Conditional Independence Tree for Ranking

Jiang Su and Harry Zhang

Faculty of Computer Science, University of New Brunswick

P.O. Box 4400, Fredericton, NB, Canada E3B 5A3

hzhang@unb.ca

Abstract

Accurate ranking is desired in many real-world data mining applications. Traditional learning algorithms, however, aim only at high classification accuracy. It has been observed that both traditional decision trees and naive Bayes produce good classification accuracy but poor probability estimates. In this paper, we use a new model, conditional independence tree (CITree), which is a combination of decision tree and naive Bayes and more suitable for ranking and more learnable in practice. We propose a novel algorithm for learning CITree for ranking, and the experiments show that the CITree algorithm outperforms the state-of-the-art decision tree learning algorithm C4.4 and naive Bayes significantly in yielding accurate rankings. Our work provides an effective data mining algorithm for applications in which an accurate ranking is required.

1 Introduction

In data mining, a classifier is built from a set of training examples with class labels and its performance is measured by its predictive accuracy (or error rate, $1 -$ accuracy). Some classifiers can also produce the class probability estimates $p(c|E)$ that is the probability of an example E in the class c. This information is largely ignored, since the error rate considers only the class with the largest probability estimate. In some data mining applications, however, classification and error rate are not enough. For example, in direct marketing, we often need a ranking of customers in terms of their likelihood of buying.

If we are aiming at an accurate ranking based on the class probability, the area under the ROC (Receiver Operating Characteristics) curve [9, 6], or simply AUC, has been recently used as the performance measure. AUC compares the classifiers' performance cross the entire range of class distributions and error costs, and provides a good "summary" for comparing two classifiers. Hand and Till [1] show that,

for binary classification, AUC is equivalent to the probability that a randomly chosen example of class $-$ will have a smaller estimated probability of belonging to class $+$ than a randomly chosen example of class $+$. They present a simple approach to calculating the AUC of a classifier G below.

$$\hat{A} = \frac{S_0 - n_0(n_0 + 1)/2}{n_0 n_1}, \qquad (1)$$

where n_0 and n_1 are the numbers of negative and positive examples respectively, and $S_0 = \sum r_i$, where r_i is the rank of i_{th} positive example in the ranking.

From Equation 1, it is clear that AUC is essentially a measure of the quality of a ranking. For example, the AUC of a ranking is 1 (the maximum value of AUC) if there is no positive example preceding a negative example.

If we are aiming at the accurate probability-based ranking, what is the performance of the traditional learning algorithms, such as decision trees and naive Bayes? In a decision tree, the class probability $p(c|E)$ is the fraction of the examples of class c in the leaf that E falls into. While decision trees perform quite well in classification, it is also found that their probability estimates are poor [5, 7]. Building decision trees with accurate probability estimates, called probability estimation trees (PETs), has received a great deal of attention recently [8]. Some researchers ascribe the poor probability estimates of decision trees to the decision tree learning algorithms. Thus, many techniques have been proposed to improve the learning algorithms in producing accurate probability estimates [8]. Provost and Domingos propose propose the following techniques to improve the AUC of C4.5 [8].

1. Smooth probability estimates by Laplace correction. Assume that there are p examples of the class at a leaf, N total examples, and C total classes. The frequency-based estimation calculates the estimated probability as $\frac{p}{N}$. The Laplace estimation calculates the estimated probability as $\frac{p+1}{N+C}$.

2. Turn off pruning. Provost and Domingos [8] show that pruning a large tree damages the probability estima-

tion. Thus, a simple strategy to improve the probability estimation is to build a large tree without pruning.

Provost and Domingos call the resulting algorithm C4.4. They compared C4.4 to C4.5 by empirical experiments, and found that C4.4 is a significant improvement over C4.5 with regard to AUC.

Ling and Yan also propose a method to improve the AUC of a decision tree [3]. They present a novel probability estimation algorithm, in which the class probability of an example is an average of the probability estimates from all leaves of the tree, instead of only using the leaf into which it falls. In other word, each leaf contributes to the class probability estimate of an example.

To our observation, however, the representation of decision trees also plays an important role. In a decision tree, the class probabilities of all the examples in the same leaf are equal. However, an accurate ranking needs that different examples have different probability. This is an obstacle in building an accurate PET, because two contradictory factors are in play at the same time. On one hand, traditional decision tree algorithms, such as C4.5, prefer a small tree. Thus, a leaf has more examples and the class probability estimates are more reliable. A small tree, however, has a small number of leaves, thus more examples will have the same class probability. That prevents the learning algorithm from building an accurate PET. On the other hand, if the tree is large, not only may the tree overfitting the training data, but the number of examples in each leaf is also small, and thus the probability estimates would not be accurate and reliable. Such a contradiction does exist in traditional decision trees.

A CITree [11] (Conditional Independence Tree) is a novel representation model, which uses a traditional decision tree to explicitly represent conditional independences among attributes and a naive Bayes on each leaf to represent the local distribution. Thus, a CITree represents a joint distribution among all attributes. CITree is different from NBTree [2] in that the structure of a CITree represents conditional independence; that is, given the attributes (path attributes) that occur on the path from the root to a leaf, all the other attributes (leaf attributes) are independent. Since conditional dependence can be relaxed by the tree structure, so the probability estimates given by leaf naive Bayes will be accurate. In the mean while, naive Bayes can assign different probability to each example, which could lead to an accurate ranking. In other words, its AUC should be high.

2 A Novel Algorithm for Learning CITree

We believe that CITree is a suitable model for building an accurate PET, and thus yields an accurate ranking. But in practice, learning the structure of an accurate CITree is intractable, just as learning an optimal decision tree. However, a good approximation of a CITree, which gives good

estimates of class probabilities, is satisfiable in many data mining applications. If the structure of a CITree is sufficiently well, the probability estimates given by its leaf naive Bayes is also accurate, since the conditional dependences among attributes are relaxed by the structure of the CITree.

In building a CITree, we are looking for an attribute, given which all other attributes have the maximum independence. Thus, the key is to find such an attribute. The process of building a CITree could be also a greedy and recursive process, similar to building a decision tree. At each step, choose the "best" attribute as the root of the (sub)tree, split the associated data into disjoint subsets corresponding to the values of the attribute, and then recur this process for each subset until certain criteria are satisfied.

Notice as well, however, the difference between learning a CITree and learning a decision tree. The process of building a decision tree is guided by the purity of the (sub)dataset, measured by information gain. That is, we are looking for a sequence of attributes that leads to the maximum purity in all leaves of the tree. However, the process of building a CITree is guided by relaxing the conditional dependences among attributes. More precisely, we wish that, by choosing a sequences of attributes, all other attributes are independent. In practice, we intend to choose a set of attributes that make the local conditional independence among the rest of attributes true as much as possible. Thus, even though the impurity of a (sub)dataset is high, it could still be desired, as long as the conditional dependence is minimum. Thus, traditional decision tree learning algorithms are not directly suitable for learning CITrees.

One problem in learning a CITree is how to find the attribute (if it exists), given which all other attributes have the maximum conditional independence. We adopt a heuristic search process, in which we choose an attribute with the greatest improvement on the performance of the resulting CITree. Another reason for using this strategy is that, not all the conditional dependences will influence naive Bayes. Naive Bayes works well even when strong dependences exist. Thus a heuristic search guided by the performance of the CITree is suitable. More precisely, we try each possible attribute as the root at each step, evaluate the resulting tree, and choose the attribute that achieves the highest AUC. To avoid overfitting, the AUC of a leaf naive Bayes is conducted by a 5-fold cross validation.

Similar to C4.5, our learning algorithm has two separate steps: growing a tree and post-pruning. In growing a tree, each possible attribute is evaluated at each step, and the attribute that gives the most improvement in AUC is selected. The algorithm is depicted below.

Algorithm AUC-CITree (**T**, **S**, **A**)

Input : CITree **T**, a set **S** of labeled examples, a set of attributes **A**

Output : a CITree.

1. For all attributes A in $\mathbf{A}$
   - Partition $\mathbf{S}$ into $\mathbf{S_1}, \cdots, \mathbf{S_k}$, each of which corresponds to a value of A.
   - Create a leaf naive Bayes for each $\mathbf{S_i}$.
   - Evaluate the resulting CITree in terms of AUC.

2. Choose the attribute A_{opt} with the highest AUC.

3. For all values a of A_{opt}
   CITree($\mathbf{T}_a, \mathbf{S}_a, \mathbf{A} - \{A_{opt}\}$).
   Add $\mathbf{T}_a$ as a child of $\mathbf{T}$.

4. Return $\mathbf{T}$.

Notice that in the AUC-CITree algorithm described above, we grow a tree as large as possible until we are out of data or attributes, and then start a post-pruning process as following:

Apply pruning based on the AUC of leaf naive Bayes, in which the children of a node are removed only if the resulting pruned tree (making it a leaf node and deploying a naive Bayes at it) performs no worse than the original tree. Notice the AUC for the children of a node is computed using instances from all the children.

Our AUC-CITree algorithm is different from the NBTree algorithm [2] in several aspects:

1. Our AUC-CITree algorithm is based on AUC, instead of accuracy.

2. Our algorithm is less greedy than the NBTree algorithm, in which if the accuracy improvement is less than 5%, stop growing the tree. We always choose the best attribute at each step, even no improvement has been achieved.

3. The AUC-CITree algorithm adopts the post-pruning strategy, rather than early stop.

3 Experiments

We conduct experiments to compare our algorithm CITree with C4.4 and naive Bayes. Notice that the implementation of naive Bayes and C4.4 is from Weka [10], C4.4 is J48 in Weka with Laplace correction and turning off pruning. All algorithms are evaluated by using 29 datasets from the UCI repository [4]. Considering that large data sets seem more important in data mining, we also choose large data sets to show CITree's advantage in practical environment. In our experiment, multi-class AUC has been calculated by M-measure [1], and the average AUC on each data set is obtained by using 10-fold stratified cross validation 10 times. Some details in our implementation are summarized below.

1. In Step 1 of the AUC-CITree algorithm, we adopt an inner 5-fold cross-validation on the training data S which fall into a leaf to evaluate the AUC for a leaf naive Bayes, and choose the best one. For example, if a attribute has 4 attribute value which will result four leaf naive Bayes, the inner 5-fold cross-validations will be run in four leafs. Note that, we compute AUC by putting the instances from all the leaves together rather than computing the AUC for each leaf separately.

2. In Step 1, when the instances falling into a leaf are less than 5, all the instances will be assigned the random probability. This is a strategy to avoid overfitting.

3. Numeric attributes are discretized using ten-bin discretization implemented in Weka [10]. Missing value are also replaced by ReplaceMissingValues class in Weka.

Table 1 shows the average AUC obtained by the three algorithms. The comparison of the three algorithms on these datasets, in which a paired t-test with a confidence of 95% has been used, are summarized in Table 2. Our observations are summarized below.

1. The AUC-CITree algorithm outperforms naive Bayes significantly in terms of AUC: It wins in 10 datasets, ties in 19 datasets and loses in 0 dataset. The average AUC for CITree is 92.66%, higher than the average AUC 90.91% of naive Bayes.

2. The CITree algorithm also outperforms C4.4 significantly in terms of AUC: It wins in 16 datasets, ties in 11 datasets and loses in 2 datasets. The average AUC for decision trees is 89.02%, lower than CITree's.

3. The sizes of CITrees (not shown in Table 1) are significantly smaller than the sizes of decision trees over most of these datasets. Here the size of a tree is the number of nodes. The average tree size for CITrees is 64, and for C4.4 it is 610.

4 Conclusions

In this paper, we study using an extended decision tree model CITree for ranking, and present and implement a novel algorithm AUC-CITree which is based on AUC to build a CITree for ranking by exploring the conditional independence among attributes, different from traditional decision tree learning algorithms. Our experiments show that the AUC-CITree algorithm performs better than C4.4 and naive Bayes significantly in terms of ranking, measured by AUC. Our work provides an effective data mining algorithm for applications in which an accurate ranking is required.

Table 1. Experimental results on AUC.

Dataset	AUC-CITree	NB	C4.4
Abalone	79.25 ± 1.6	78.73 ± 1.58	77.86 ± 1.8
Adult	90.44 ± 0.3	90.1 ± 0.33	86.64 ± 0.42
Anneal	96.33 ± 0.61	95.9 ± 1.3	93.8 ± 2.9
B.-scale	84.46 ± 4.1	84.46 ± 4.1	59.4 ± 5.53
Wis.-breast	99.18 ± 1	99.26 ± 0.82	97.83 ± 1.54
Car	98.41 ± 1.47	92.06 ± 2.55	95.83 ± 1.74
Horse-colic	85.04 ± 7.59	84.04 ± 5.38	82.01 ± 5.25
Crd-rating	91.7 ± 3.85	92.05 ± 3.46	87.46 ± 3.46
G.-credit	78.25 ± 5.27	79.27 ± 4.74	68.59 ± 4.81
Pima	82.31 ± 5.17	82.31 ± 5.17	73.27 ± 4.84
Hypothy.	87.35 ± 7.04	87.37 ± 8.52	82.88 ± 8.95
Ionosphere	96.33 ± 2.7	93.61 ± 3.36	91.95 ± 4.31
Iris	98.58 ± 2.67	98.58 ± 2.67	97.42 ± 2.1
Kr-vs-kp	99.8 ± 0.16	95.17 ± 1.29	99.96 ± 0.05
Letter	98.57 ± 0.14	96.86 ± 0.24	95.27 ± 0.41
Mushroom	100 ± 0	99.79 ± 0.04	100 ± 0
Nursery	98.68 ± 3.27	98.91 ± 1.02	96.89 ± 6.04
Pendigits	99.77 ± 0.07	98.7 ± 0.19	98.23 ± 0.28
Satellite	66.44 ± 27.02	66.61 ± 17.63	83.31 ± 14.08
Segment	99.06 ± 0.34	98.51 ± 0.46	98.95 ± 0.27
Sick	98.53 ± 1.25	95.91 ± 2.35	99.07 ± 0.42
Soybean	99.55 ± 0.64	99.53 ± 0.6	91.35 ± 2.7
Splice	99.36 ± 0.32	99.41 ± 0.22	97.81 ± 0.55
Tic-tac-toe	90.33 ± 1.31	73.91 ± 2.18	93.99 ± 2.88
Vehicle	87.06 ± 2.58	80.81 ± 3.51	86.5 ± 2.61
Vote	98.64 ± 1.15	96.56 ± 2.09	97.46 ± 2.46
Vowel	99.29 ± 0.5	95.81 ± 0.84	91.01 ± 2.3
Waveform	95.27 ± 0.58	95.27 ± 0.58	80.44 ± 1.18
Yeast	89.2 ± 1.53	86.91 ± 1.91	76.35 ± 5.3
Average	92.66	90.91	89.02

Table 2. Summary of the experimental results. An entry w-t-l means that the algorithm at the corresponding row wins in w datasets, ties in t datasets, and loses in l datasets, compared to the algorithm at the corresponding column.

	NB	C4.4
AUC-CITree	10-19-0	16-11-2
NB		14-8-7

CITree can be viewed as a bridge between probabilistic models, such as Bayesian networks, and non-parametric models, such as decision trees [11]. However, a more effective CITree learning algorithm is desired. Currently, our learning algorithm is based on heuristics, similar to the NBTree algorithm [2]. We believe that if a better learning algorithm is found, a CITree will benefit much from its structure, and thus will be a good model for many data mining applications.

References

[1] D. J. Hand and R. J. Till. A simple generalisation of the area under the ROC curve for multiple class classification problems. *Machine Learning*, 45:171–186, 2001.

[2] R. Kohavi. Scaling up the accuracy of naive-bayes classifiers: A decision-tree hybrid. In *Proceedings of the Second International Conference on Knowledge Discovery and Data Mining*, pages 202–207. AAAI Press, 1996.

[3] C. X. Ling and R. J. Yan. Decision tree with better ranking. In *Proceedings of the 20th International Conference on Machine Learning*, pages 480–487. Morgan Kaufmann, 2003.

[4] C. Merz, P. Murphy, and D. Aha. UCI repository of machine learning databases. In *Dept of ICS, University of California, Irvine*. http://www.ics.uci.edu/ mlearn/MLRepository.html, 1997.

[5] M. Pazzani, C. Merz, P. Murphy, K. Ali, T. Hume, and C. Brunk. Reducing misclassification costs. In *Proceedings of the 11th International conference on Machine Learning*, pages 217–225. Morgan Kaufmann, 1994.

[6] F. Provost and T. Fawcett. Analysis and visualization of classifier performance: comparison under imprecise class and cost distribution. In *Proceedings of the Third International Conference on Knowledge Discovery and Data Mining*, pages 43–48. AAAI Press, 1997.

[7] F. Provost, T. Fawcett, and R. Kohavi. The case against accuracy estimation for comparing induction algorithms. In *Proceedings of the Fifteenth International Conference on Machine Learning*, pages 445–453. Morgan Kaufmann, 1998.

[8] F. J. Provost and P. Domingos. Tree induction for probability-based ranking. *Machine Learning*, 52(3):199–215, 2003.

[9] J. Swets. Measuring the accuracy of diagnostic systems. *Science*, 240:1285–1293, 1988.

[10] I. H. Witten and E. Frank. *Data Mining –Practical Machine Learning Tools and Techniques with Java Implementation*. Morgan Kaufmann, 2000.

[11] H. Zhang and J. Su. Conditional independence trees. In *to appear in Proceedings of the 15th European Conference on Machine Learning*. Springer, 2004.

Supervised Latent Semantic Indexing for Document Categorization

Jian-Tao Sun[1], Zheng Chen[2], Hua-Jun Zeng[2], Yu-Chang Lu[1], Chun-Yi Shi[1], Wei-Ying Ma[2]

[1]Department of Computer Science
TsingHua University, Beijing 100084, P.R.China
sjt@mails.tsinghua.edu.cn {lyc,scy}@tsinghua.edu.cn

[2]Microsoft Research Asia
5F, Sigma Center, 49 Zhichun Road, Beijing 100080, P.R.China
{zhengc,hjzeng,wyma}@microsoft.com

Abstract

Latent Semantic Indexing (LSI) is a successful technology in information retrieval (IR) which attempts to explore the latent semantics implied by a query or a document through representing them in a dimension-reduced space. However, LSI is not optimal for document categorization tasks because it aims to find the most representative features for document representation rather than the most discriminative ones. In this paper, we propose Supervised LSI (SLSI) which selects the most discriminative basis vectors using the training data iteratively. The extracted vectors are then used to project the documents into a reduced dimensional space for better classification. Experimental evaluations show that the SLSI approach leads to dramatic dimension reduction while achieving good classification results.

1. Introduction

Latent Semantic Indexing(LSI) is a promising approach for information retrieval problems [2, 3]. The main idea is to map queries and documents into a low dimensional space (LSI space) which captures the latent semantics of words present in the documents. The truncated Singular Value Decomposition (SVD) technique is used to calculate a set of basis vectors which span the LSI space. However, LSI does not produce an optimal representation for document categorization tasks. As an unsupervised approach, it does not take the categories of the documents into consideration [9]. That is, it aims to find the most representative features for document representation rather than the most discriminative ones, which are exactly the most important for classification tasks. At the same time, the high computational cost

of large scale LSI problems also limits its applicability.

Some researchers have applied LSI for document categorization tasks [6, 10, 8, 13]. The results reported show that the LSI-based classifier does not achieve significant improvements. While LSI is unsupervised, several supervised approaches are also proposed. Hull [6] applied local LSI to classification tasks. Just recently, Karypis et al. proposed concept indexing (CI) and Torkkola [9] used linear discriminative analysis (LDA) to represent documents for classification. At the same time, the theoretical study of LSI is still an ongoing research. Some variants of LSI are proposed recently, such as probabilistic LSI (PLSI) [5], iterative residual rescaling (IRR) [1] and Locality Preserving Indexing (LPI) [4].

In this paper, we propose an iterative approach called Supervised Latent Semantic Indexing (SLSI). Based on a set of training data, we first represent the documents of each category by the vector space model. Then in each iteration, a traditional SVD is performed on each category specific term-document matrix. From each category, we select the eigenvector corresponding to the largest eigenvalue. All the eigenvectors are used to construct a candidate set. The most discriminative candidate is selected as the basis vector in the current iteration. Then the effect of the selected basis vector is subtracted from each original term-document matrix. The iteration continues until the dimension of the resulted transform space reaches a pre-defined threshold. In this paper, we call the final transform space SLSI space.

It is worthwhile to highlight several aspects of our proposed approach here:

1. In each iteration, the selected basis vector is the most discriminative one in discriminating different categories, which ensures the overall discriminative capability when documents are represented in the final SLSI space.

2. We found that the dimension of the resulted SLSI

space can be reduced to very low, while maintaining the classification accuracy. That is, just a small number of iterations are enough. Thus our algorithm is also competitive in term of computational complexity.

3. Since each basis vector of the SLSI space corresponds to a specific concept, similarities between documents projected into this space are measured in semantic level. Thus the advantage of LSI representation is preserved.

The remainder of this paper is organized as follows. Section 2 provides an introduction to LSI. Section 3 describes our proposed SLSI algorithm. Section 4 presents the experimental results. Finally, Section 5 offers some concluding remarks and directions for future research.

2. Latent Semantic Indexing (LSI)

In this section, we give a brief review of LSI. Suppose there are m distinct terms in an n documents collection. The corpus can be represented as a term-document ($m \times n$) matrix X, whose component x_{ij} is the weight of term t_i in document d_j. The singular value decomposition (SVD) of the matrix X is given by:

$$X = U\Sigma V^T \qquad (1)$$

In equation (1), U and V are the matrices of the left and right singular vectors. Σ is the diagonal matrix of singular values. LSI approximates X with a rank-k matrix

$$X_k = U_k \Sigma V_k^T \qquad (2)$$

by setting the smallest $r - k$ singular values to zero (r is the rank of X). That is, the documents are represented in the k dimensional LSI space spanned by the basis vectors.

3. The SLSI Algorithm

In this section, we introduce the SLSI algorithm and give the comparisons between SLSI and LSI.

3.1. Description of SLSI

The input of the SLSI algorithm is the c categories of documents. For each category, the term-document matrix $X_s, s = 1, \cdots, c$ is constructed. The element x_{ij} of X_s is the weight of term t_i in document d_j. In this paper, the column vector of X_s is called document vector and the row vector is called term vector. The output of the algorithm is a set of basis vectors which span the resulted SLSI space.

What our algorithm differs from LSI is the process of basis vector construction. For LSI, a global term-document matrix D is constructed using all the training documents. The first eigenvector of DD' is selected as the first basis vector. Then the effect of this basis vector is removed from

the original document vectors. The next basis vector is chosen based on the new term-document matrix and the process is repeated t times. As a result, the t basis vectors span the LSI space. In each iteration, because the eigenvector with the largest eigenvalue is selected, the resulted basis vectors are optimal to approximate D in the sense of minimizing the reconstruction error [2].

In the SLSI algorithm, we employ the class informa-

Input: c categories of documents.
Output: t basis vectors of the SLSI space: $b_1, b_2, \cdots, b_t$
Algorithm:
X_s = term-document matrix of the documents in category s, $s = 1, \cdots, c$.
$R_s = X_s, s = 1, \cdots, c$.
$p = 1$
While ($p <= t$)
    g_s = the first eigenvector of $R_s R_s^T$, $s = 1, \cdots, c$.
    $G = \{g_1, g_2, \cdots, g_c\}$/* candidate eigenvector set */
    b_p = the most discriminative eigenvector of G.
    $R_s = b_p b_p^T R_s$/* subtract the influence of b_p from the category specific term-document matrix */
    $p = p + 1$
End

Figure 1: The pseudo-code of the SLSI algorithm

tion to guide the basis vector construction process. The basis vectors are also created iteratively. For each category, an SVD is performed on the corresponding matrix X_s and the eigenvector g_s associated with the largest eigenvalue is selected as a candidate basis vector. The set of eigenvectors of the c categories construct the candidate set $G = \{g_1, g_2, \cdots, g_c\}$. The most discriminative candidate vector is selected as a new basis vector. After that, each category-specific term-document matrix is updated by removing the effect of the newly computed basis vector in the same way as traditional SVD algorithm does. This process performs iteratively until t basis vectors are constructed. The pseudo-code of the SLSI algorithm is shown in Figure 1.

3.2. Basis Vector Selection

The basis vector selection step plays an important role in the SLSI algorithm. The general objective is to select a vector for which the projected documents are well separated. We use the class centroid distance to measure the distance between two classes. Here, v_s^p denotes the centroid of documents in category p when they are projected on vector g_s:

$$v_s^p = \frac{1}{|C_p|} \sum_{d \in C_p} g_s^T d \qquad (3)$$

where $|C_p|$ denotes the number of documents belonging to category p. If we employ $f_s^{pq} = |v_s^p - v_s^q|$ to denote the distance between the centroid of category p and q, the basis vector b is selected according to equation:

$$b = \arg_{b_i \in G}\{\max f_i^{pq}\} \qquad (4)$$

That is, the candidate which results in the largest distance between two class centroids is selected as the basis vector.

3.3. Advantages of SLSI

As for LSI space, each basis vector corresponds to a latent concept (or topic, latent semantic structure, etc) [3, 10]. In each iteration of the LSI algorithm, the eigenvector corresponding with the most significant concept is selected as a new basis of the resulted space. However, for document categorization tasks, the most significant concept may be unsuitable for discriminating document categories. In contrast, as for SLSI, each g_s corresponds to the most significant concept in category s. Since the most discriminative vectors are selected as basis vectors, the SLSI representation is more suitable for document categorization than LSI.

As shown in Figure 2, consider two categories of documents sharing a common concept in the concept space. A, B and C denotes some specific concept respectively. The area of the ellipse indicates the proportion of documents containing the corresponding concept. If we apply LSI on the global term-document matrix, the first eigenvector selected corresponds to concept A. On the contrary, if we use SLSI, the candidate B is first selected instead of A, which leads to better classification result.

Another difference between SLSI and LSI is that the

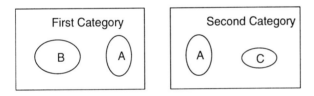

Figure 2: An example (two categories share concept A).

SLSI basis vectors are not orthogonal. Intuitively, these basis vectors better reflect the latent semantics. Two vectors are orthogonal if the dot product between them is zero. In general, it is unreasonable to assume two basis vectors are orthogonal, since the latent concepts corresponding with them are usually semantically related (similarity between them is not zero). Thus we expect documents projected into the SLSI space result in better representations than in the LSI space for document categorization tasks.

4. Experiments and Analysis

We present experiments in this section to demonstrate the effectiveness of the SLSI algorithm. The experiments

were performed on the benchmark dataset Reuters-21578. We use the "ModApte" split of the database into training and testing data. Documents without labels or with multiple labels are discarded. The top 8 largest categories are used(earn, acq, money-fx, grain, crude, trade, interest and ship). The training set has 5343 documents and the test set has 2315 documents. After the pre-processing step, 6260 terms are kept as features. The LSI analysis was done using SVDPACK/las2 software package[1].

We applied kNN and SVM to train classifiers. K is set to 45 according to Yang's conclusion [11]. For SVM, the SVM^{light} package is used[2]. In our experiments, the linear kernel is used because of its high accuracy for text categorization [11, 7]. The trade-off parameter C is fixed to 1 for comparison purpose and the one-against-all approach is used for the multi-class case. The macro-averaging and micro-averaging F1 measures are used for evaluation[12].

Classification results are shown in figure 3 and 4. The horizontal lines represent the classification results using VSM representations with all 6260 features. For almost all dimensions and both algorithms, the SLSI representation outperforms LSI. For both algorithms, the SLSI representation with dimension 11 leads to optimal classification result, which is much lower than the 32 dimensions of the LSI representation. Furthermore, with the SLSI representation of 11 dimensions, the kNN classifier achieves improved classification than with VSM representation.

According to the results, we find that SLSI is more ef-

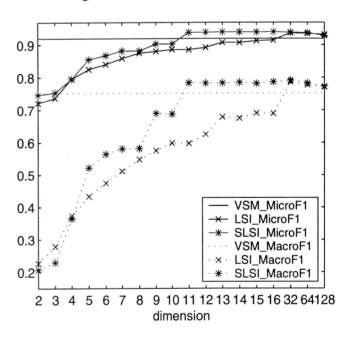

Figure 3: Performance curves for kNN (k=45).

---

1   Avaliable at http://www.netlib.org/svdpack.
2   Available at http://svmlight.joachims.org/

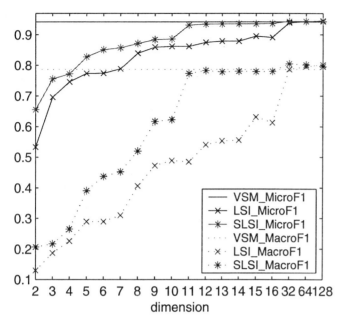

Figure 4: Performance curves for SVM.

fective than LSI in reducing the dimension of document representation. SLSI leads to a much lower dimensional representation than LSI when their classification results are comparable. Furthermore, SLSI representation at a very low dimension (slightly larger than category number) even improves the classification accuracy of kNN over VSM with all features. When SVM is used, neither LSI nor SLSI can outperform the original VSM representation. But the classification result based on the original representation can be approximated by a very low dimensional SLSI representation, which leads to cheaper computation cost.

5. Conclusions and Future Work

In this paper, we proposed Supervised Latent Semantic Indexing (SLSI) for document categorization tasks. Our evaluation with two classification algorithms shows that SLSI can drastically reduce the dimension of document representation without sacrificing the classification accuracy. In future, we will study how to optimize the dimension of the SLSI space automatically. And the theoretical analysis of SLSI is also under investigated.

Acknowledgements

We thank Xin-Jing Wang, Dou Shen and Guang-Chao Liu for comments on the paper and helpful discussions.

References

[1] R. K. Ando. Latent semantic space: iterative scaling improves precision of inter-document similarity measurement. In *Proceedings of the 23rd annual international ACM SIGIR conference on Research and development in information retrieval*, pages 216–223. ACM Press, 2000.

[2] M. W. Berry, S. T. Dumais, and G. W. O'Brien. Using linear algebra for intelligent information retrieval. *SIAM Rev.*, 37(4):573–595, 1995.

[3] S. C. Deerwester, S. T. Dumais, T. K. Landauer, G. W. Furnas, and R. A. Harshman. Indexing by latent semantic analysis. *Journal of the American Society of Information Science*, 41(6):391–407, 1990.

[4] X. He, D. Cai, H. Liu, and W.-Y. Ma. Locality preserving indexing for document representation. In *Proceedings of the 27th annual international conference on Research and development in information retrieval*, pages 96–103. ACM Press, 2004.

[5] T. Hofmann. Probabilistic latent semantic indexing. In *Proceedings of the 22nd annual international ACM SIGIR conference on Research and development in information retrieval*, pages 50–57. ACM Press, 1999.

[6] D. Hull. Improving text retrieval for the routing problem using latent semantic indexing. In *Proceedings of the 17th annual international ACM SIGIR conference on Research and development in information retrieval*, pages 282–291. Springer-Verlag New York, Inc., 1994.

[7] T. Joachims. Text categorization with support vector machines: learning with many relevant features. In C. Nédellec and C. Rouveirol, editors, *Proceedings of ECML-98, 10th European Conference on Machine Learning*, number 1398, pages 137–142, Chemnitz, DE, 1998. Springer Verlag, Heidelberg, DE.

[8] G. Karypis and E.-H. S. Han. Fast supervised dimensionality reduction algorithm with applications to document categorization & retrieval. In *Proceedings of the ninth international conference on Information and knowledge management*, pages 12–19. ACM Press, 2000.

[9] K. Torkkola. Linear discriminant analysis in document classification. In *IEEE Workshop on Text Mining*, 2001.

[10] Y. Yang. Noise reduction in a statistical approach to text categorization. In *Proceedings of the 18th annual international ACM SIGIR conference on Research and development in information retrieval*, pages 256–263. ACM Press, 1995.

[11] Y. Yang and X. Liu. A re-examination of text categorization methods. In *Proceedings of the 22nd annual international ACM SIGIR conference on Research and development in information retrieval*, pages 42–49. ACM Press, 1999.

[12] Y. Yang, S. Slattery, and R. Ghani. A study of approaches to hypertext categorization. *Journal of Intelligent Information Systems*, 18(2-3):219–241, 2002.

[13] S. Zelikovitz and H. Hirsh. Using lsi for text classification in the presence of background text. In *Proceedings of the tenth international conference on Information and knowledge management*, pages 113–118. ACM Press, 2001.

Sparse Kernel Least Squares Classifier

Ping Sun
School of Computer Science
The University of Birmingham
Birmingham, B15 2TT, U.K.
P.Sun@cs.bham.ac.uk

Abstract

In this paper, we propose a new learning algorithm for constructing kernel least squares classifier. The new algorithm adopts a recursive learning way and a novel two-step sparsification procedure is incorporated into learning phase. These two most important features not only provide a feasible approach for large-scale problems as it is not necessary to store the entire kernel matrix, but also produce a very sparse model with fast training and testing time. Experimental results on a number of data classification problems are presented to demonstrate the competitiveness of new proposed algorithm.

1. Introduction

Kernel-based methods such as support vector machines (SVMs)[11] and kernel fisher discriminant (KFD)[8] have been studied extensively in the last few years. The idea behind this new class of learning algorithms, usually known as "kernel trick", is a general technique which can produce nonlinear versions of conventional supervised and unsupervised learning algorithms. In particular, some authors obtained a nonlinear formulation of traditional linear least square algorithms (we name it as Kernel Least Squares or KLS) [2, 6] through this idea and very promising results were reported. Further, it can be easily proved that many existing methods inculding KFD, least squares support vector machines(LS-SVMs) and RBF neural networks are equivalant to KLS with some minor differences.

KLS was originally formulated as a problem of solving a system of linear equations and two obvious drawbacks may occur in practice.

1. In KLS, the size of coefficient matrix (i.e. kernel matrix) equals to $N \times N$, where N is training data size. For large data set, simply maintaining this matrix, estimating the corresponding parameter vector and evaluating new data points during prediction phase could prove prohibitive both in terms of space and time.

2. The order of the model produced by KLS would be equal to the number of training samples N, easily causing severe overfitting problem.

The potential solution to above-mentioned problems is to build a sparse model, which has drawn much attention in the literatures [1, 12, 9, 3]. In this paper, we propose a different algorithm to achieve sparse KLS model for classification tasks. Here, we refer to this approach as sparse kernel least squares classifier (SKLSC). The new algorithm includes a two-step sparsification procedure which not only decreases training and testing time but also produces an extremely sparse model. In addition, the present approach is not required to maintain all the columns of the kernel matrix in memory and just needs to compute the required column at runtime.

SKLSC is somewhat similar to OLS algorithm [5] which was used for training RBF networks in the past and was recently employed to learn KLS for classification problem [1]. The main difference between them is that SKLSC visits the columns of the kernel matrix only once but OLS had to visit each column far more than one time. Consequently, our method has the obvious advantage on training time while having almost the same model size and generalization performance as OLS algorithm.

The rest of this paper is organized as follows. Section II introduces KLS and provides a detailed description of the proposed SKLSC algorithm. Section III demonstrates the validity of our present algorithm and gives some comparisons with OLS algorithm in terms of training time, model size and prediction error using some classification benchmarks. Section IV concludes with a summary of the algorithm developed in this paper and future work.

2. SKLSC algorithm

2.1 Kernel least squares (KLS)

Consider a binary classification problem

$$D = \{(\mathbf{x}_1, y_1), \cdots, (\mathbf{x}_N, y_N)\}, \mathbf{x}_i \in \mathbb{R}^d, y_i \in \{\pm 1\},$$

and assume that the first N_1 examples are in '+' class (i.e. $y_i = +1$) and the next $N_2 = N - N_1$ examples are in '-' class (i.e. $y_i = -1$).

There have a number of papers [13, 1, 2] described how to derive KLS algorithm by simply applying well-known "kernel trick" to traditional linear least squares. So, here we omit the detailed derivation. According to previous results [1, 13], in the absence of regularization, KLS algorithm can be formulated to find optimal parameter vector $\Theta = [b \quad \alpha_1 \quad \alpha_2 \quad \cdots \quad \alpha_N]^\top$ by minimizing

$$L(\Theta) = \|Y - P\Theta\|^2, \tag{1}$$

where $Y = [y_1 \quad y_2 \quad \cdots \quad y_N]^\top$ and

$$P = \begin{bmatrix} 1 & k(\mathbf{x}_1, \mathbf{x}_1) & \cdots & k(\mathbf{x}_1, \mathbf{x}_N) \\ \vdots & \vdots & \vdots & \vdots \\ 1 & k(\mathbf{x}_N, \mathbf{x}_1) & \cdots & k(\mathbf{x}_N, \mathbf{x}_N) \end{bmatrix}.$$

The function $k(\cdot, \cdot)$ is called the kernel function and a typical one is gaussian kernel

$$k(\mathbf{x}_i, \mathbf{x}_j) = \exp(-\frac{\|\mathbf{x}_i - \mathbf{x}_j\|^2}{\sigma^2}), \tag{2}$$

The corresponding decision function can be expressed as

$$f(\mathbf{x}) = \sum_{i=1}^{N} \alpha_i k(\mathbf{x}_i, \mathbf{x}) + b. \tag{3}$$

In the prediction phase, if the new example $\mathbf{x}$ is closer to '+' class than '-' class, the corresponding value of $f(\mathbf{x})$ would be greater than 0. Therefore the decision rule can be obtained.

Various methods have been proposed in the literatures to achieve sparse solution for equation (1). In particular, Billings and Lee (2002) employed OLS algorithm in [1] and got a great success in the aspect of sparsity. However, this algorithm suffers from the expensive computational cost. In this paper, we shall develop a new algorithm which can remarkably decrease the training time but maintaining good generalization ability and can be seen as an improved version of OLS algorithm.

2.2 Algorithm Description

Similar to OLS algorithm, our present method SKLSC is also an iterative procedure of selecting some "important" columns (refers to basis vectors) from the matrix P progressively. But the selection criteria is different from the former one. During the whole training phase, SKLSC goes through all the columns of the matrix P one time. In each step, it visits one column and checks whether this column is qualified as a basis vector based on two sparsification principles which involve (a) pruning approximately linearly dependent basis vectors and (b) further omiting those basis vectors which can't give an enough contribution to decreasing Mean Squared Error (MSE) of training examples. After the algorithm visited all the columns, it will stop and a very sparsimious model will be created.

In implementing the second sparsification principle, we shall resort to the result from OLS algorithm which employs an orthogonal decomposition scheme and makes it easy to calculate the contribution of basis vector. Now we give the overall descriptions of the proposed algorithm.

Assume that at the p-th step, we have collected an orthogonal basis vector subset $\mathcal{BV}s = \{\mathbf{w}_j\}_{j=1}^n$ with satisfying $\mathbf{w}_i^\top \mathbf{w}_j \neq 0$, if $i \neq j$, where n is the number of basis vectors. Now we are presented with a new column $\mathbf{k}_{p+1}$, the working procedure of two sparsification steps in SKLSC from the p-th step to the $(p+1)$-th step can be summarized as follows.

(1) First sparsification step:

Check whether $\mathbf{k}_{p+1}$ can be expressed approximately by the linear combination of selected $\mathcal{BV}s$, i.e.

$$\delta_{p+1} = \min_{b_i} \left\| \mathbf{k}_{p+1} - \sum_{k=1}^{n} b_{p+1,k} \mathbf{w}_k \right\|_2 \overset{?}{<} \epsilon_1, \tag{4}$$

where ϵ_1 is a small constant which determines the sparsity degree. Solving (4) we can get the $\mathbf{b}_{p+1} = (b_{p+1,1} \quad b_{p+1,2} \quad \cdots \quad b_{p+1,n})^\top$ and δ_{p+1}:

$$\mathbf{b}_{p+1} = (W^\top W)^{-1} W^\top \mathbf{k}_{p+1}, \tag{5}$$

and

$$\delta_{p+1} = \|e_{p+1}\|_2 = \|\mathbf{k}_{p+1} \quad W\mathbf{b}_{p+1}\|_2, \tag{6}$$

where the matrix $W = [\mathbf{w}_1 \quad \mathbf{w}_2 \quad \cdots \quad \mathbf{w}_n]^\top$. If $\delta_{p+1} < \epsilon_1$, the column vector $\mathbf{k}_{p+1}$ will be pruned due to its approximate dependence on $\mathcal{BV}s$. Otherwise, i.e. $\delta_{p+1} > \epsilon_1$, the column vector $\mathbf{k}_{p+1}$ will enter into second sparsification step.

(2) Second sparsification step:

This step aims to test whether there is an enough decrease in the MSE of training examples. Here we adopt an orthogonal decompostion scheme — $\mathbf{k}_{p+1}$ is orthogonalized into $\mathbf{w}_{p+1}$ w.r.t the matrix W. We can easily know

$$\mathbf{w}_{p+1} = \mathbf{e}_{p+1} = \mathbf{k}_{p+1} - W\mathbf{b}_{p+1}. \qquad (7)$$

The corresponding contribution is then obtained, i.e.

$$Contri(\mathbf{w}_{p+1}) = \frac{g_{p+1}^2 \mathbf{w}_{p+1}^\top \mathbf{w}_{p+1}}{Y^\top Y}, \qquad (8)$$

where

$$g_{p+1} = \frac{\mathbf{w}_{p+1}^\top Y}{\mathbf{w}_{p+1}^\top \mathbf{w}_{p+1}} \qquad (9)$$

The result (8) directly comes from the OLS algorithm [1]. Now we can further eliminate some "unimportant" basis vectors by controlling

$$Contri(\mathbf{w}_{p+1}) > \epsilon_2, \qquad (10)$$

where ϵ_2 is another user-specified sparsity parameter.

We employ $I = \{i_1, ..., i_n\}$ to denote the selected column index and let $\mathbf{g} = (g_{i_1} \quad g_{i_2} \quad \cdots \quad g_{i_n})^\top$, $W = [\mathbf{w}_{i_1} \quad \mathbf{w}_{i_2} \quad \cdots \quad \mathbf{w}_{i_n}]^\top$ and

$$A = \begin{bmatrix} 1 & b_{i_1,1} & \cdots & b_{i_n,1} \\ 0 & 1 & \ddots & \vdots \\ \vdots & \cdots & \ddots & b_{i_n,n} \\ 0 & \cdots & \cdots & 1 \end{bmatrix} \qquad (11)$$

The vector $\Theta' = (\theta_1' \quad \theta_2' \quad \cdots \quad \theta_n')^\top$ is used to represent the final sparse solution for the problem (1), which can be obtained through solving the upper unit triangular system of equations

$$A\Theta' = \mathbf{g}. \qquad (12)$$

Correspondingly, the desicion function (3) becomes

$$f(\mathbf{x}) = \sum_{k=1}^{n} \theta_{i_k}' k(\mathbf{x}_{i_k}, \mathbf{x}). \qquad (13)$$

The algorithm in pseudo-code form and computational cost are described in Table 1. Here, we let $\mathbf{u} = (1 \quad 1 \quad \cdots \quad 1)^\top$ and $\kappa_i = \mathbf{w}_i^\top \mathbf{w}_i$.

Remarks: Compared with OLS algorithm, SKLSC algorithm introduces another sparsification step and changes the original procedure of selecting basis vectors. These improvements greatly accelerate the computation while having similar model size and generalization ability in practice. In

Parameters: σ, ϵ_1 and ϵ_2;	Cost
Initialize: $W = \mathbf{u}, A = 1, \mathbf{g} = \mathbf{u}^\top Y/N,$	$O(N)$
$\quad Z = W/N, \tau = Y^\top Y, n = 1$	$O(2N)$
for $p = 1, ..., N$	
$\quad$ 1. Get a new column: $\mathbf{k}_p$	$O(N)$
$\quad$ 2. Compute $\mathbf{b}_p = Z\mathbf{k}_p$ (5)	$O(nN)$
$\quad\quad \mathbf{e}_p$ and δ_p (6)	$O(nN)$
$\quad\quad$ and let $\mathbf{w}_p = \mathbf{e}_p$ (7)	
$\quad$ 3. Two sparsification steps:	
$\quad\quad$ if $\delta_p > \epsilon_1$	
$\quad\quad\quad$ Compute g_p(9), $Contri(\mathbf{w}_p)$(8)	$O(2N)$
$\quad\quad\quad$ if $Contri(\mathbf{w}_p) > \epsilon_2$	
$\quad\quad\quad\quad W = [W \quad \mathbf{w}_p], \mathbf{g} = [\mathbf{g} \quad g_p]$	
$\quad\quad\quad\quad A = \begin{bmatrix} A & \mathbf{b}_p \\ \mathbf{0}^\top & 1 \end{bmatrix}, Z = [Z^\top \frac{\mathbf{w}^\top}{\kappa_p}]^\top$	$O(N)$
$\quad\quad\quad\quad n = n + 1$	
$\quad\quad\quad$ end if	
$\quad\quad$ end if	
end for	
Output: A, $\mathbf{g}$ and Θ'(12)	
overall computation cost : $\simeq$	$O(nN^2)$

Table 1. Pseudo-code for SKLSC algorithm

addition, the present algorithm only maintain one column of the matrix P and a matrix W with fewer columns at running time. Instead, OLS algorithm must always store all the columns of the matrix P and the matrix W in memory.

Finally, SKLSC can be refined at least in two aspects which include: (a) Develop the regularized SKLSC just like generalizing OLS to regularized OLS in [4], which is expected to improve the generalization performance; (b) Introduce a parameter to stop the main loop (i.e. $p = 1, ..., N$ in Table 1) in advance, which will further reduce the training time.

3 Experiments

The two-class spiral benchmark and 5 artificial and real world datasets are used to evaluate empirically the performance of proposed SKLSC algorithm compared to OLS algorithm. All the programs developed by Matlab 6.0 were run on the machine with PIV 2.0G and 512M memory.

The two-spiral problem[7] is a well-known benchmark for testing the quality of classifers. Here a gaussian kernel function was employed with $\sigma^2 = 0.02$ in both SKLSC and OLS algorithms. The two sparsity degree parameters in SKLSC were set as $\epsilon_1 = 0.4$ and $\epsilon_2 = 10^{-4}$. The results obtained from SKLSC and OLS are shown in Figure 1. It can be seen that both of them produce the central and smooth separation hyperplanes which implies good generalization capability. The resulting model sizes are also sim-

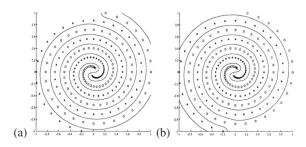

Figure 1. Two-class spiral problem with 196 training samples. The kernel used is gaussian function with $\sigma^2 = 0.02$. (a) SKLSC model with $n = 135$; (b) OLS model with $n = 133$.

Table 2. Comparison of the results from SKLSC and OLS algorithms on five benchmark problems in term of prediction error, model size and training time

DATASETS	ERROS(%)		MODEL SIZE		TRAIN TIME(S)	
	SKLSC	OLS	SKLSC	OLS	SKLSC	OLS
BANANA	11.1	11.0	25	23	0.06	4.04
CANCER	26.0	26.0	6	7	0.03	0.21
DIABETIS	22.3	22.7	6	5	0.06	0.35
GERMAN	21.3	21.0	12	12	0.13	2.6
HEART	18.0	18.0	5	10	0.02	0.33

ilar: SKLSC was 135 and OLS was 133. But the training time are obviously different: the former one is 0.22s and the later one is 29.2s.

In order to extensively test the performance of SKLSC algorithm, we implement our algorithm and OLS algorithm on other 5 classification benchmarks which are a part of data sets used in [10]. The original data file include 100 realizations for each data set. We just choose the first one as our employed data sets. In all cases, the gaussian kernel was used. The unknown parameters (σ, ϵ_1, ϵ_2) were selected based on the minimum classification error using 5-fold cross-validation on the training data. Table 2 compares the results of two algorithms in term of classification error, model size and training time.

From Table 2, the results obtained using SKLSC algorithm are quite competitive compared to OLS algorithm in the aspects of classification errors and model sizes. But our present algorithm have obvious advantage on the training time on all the data sets. Note that the TRAIN TIME in Table 2 only records the time spent on selecting basis vectors which doesn't include the evaluation of kernel matrix.

4 Conclusions

An efficient learning algorithm for constructing sparse KLS model, SKLSC, has been proposed. It includes two sparsification steps and learns the training data in a recursive manner. These characteristics bring two obvious advantages over the state-of-art OLS algorithm, i.e. small memory requirement and few computational costs. Experimental results on some classification benchmarks have demonstrated that SKLSC do produce a parsimious model with fast training time while having similar generalization performance compared to OLS algorithm. The future work will focus on efficiently selecting the optimal parameters (σ, ϵ_1, ϵ_2) and applying SKLSC algorithm to large data sets.

References

[1] S. Billings and K.-L.Lee. Nonlinear fisher discriminant analysis using a minimum squared error cost function and the orthogonal least squares algorithm. *Neural Networks*, 15(2):263–270, 2002.

[2] V. V. C. Saunders, A. Gammermann. Ridge regression learning algorithm in dual variables. In J. Shavlik, editor, *Machine Learning Proceedings of the Fifteenth International Conference(ICML '98)*, pages 515–521, San Francisco, CA, 1998. Morgan Kaufmann.

[3] G. C. Cawley and N. L. C. Tlabot. Reduced rank kernel ridge regression. *Neural Processing Letters*, 16(3):293–302, December 2002.

[4] S. Chen, E. S. Chng, and K. Alkadhimi. Regularized orthogonal least squares algorithm for constructing radial basis function networks. *International Journal of Control*, 64(5):829–837, 1996.

[5] S. Chen, C. F. N. Cowan, and P. M. Grant. Orthogonal least squares learning algorithm for radial basis function networks. *IEEE Transactions on Neural Networks*, 2(2):302–309, Mar 1991.

[6] Y. Engel, S. Mannor, and R. Meir. The kernel recusrive least squares algorithm. Technical Report 446, Technion CCIT, October 2003.

[7] K. Lang and M. Witbrock. Learning to tell two spiral apart. In *Proceedings of the 1988 Connectionist Summer Schools*. Morgan Kaufmann, 1988.

[8] S. Mika. *Kernel Fisher Discriminant*. PhD thesis, University of Technology, Berlin, October 2002.

[9] P. B. Nair, A. Choudhury, and A. J. Keane. Some greedy learning algorithms for sparse regression and classification with mercer kernels. *Journal of Machine Learning Research*, 3:781–801, December 2002.

[10] G. Rätsch, T. Onoda, and K.-R. Müller. Soft margins for adaboost. *Machine Learning*, 42(3):287–320, 2001.

[11] B. Schölkopf and A. Smola. *Learning with Kernels*. MIT Press, Cambridge, MA, 2002.

[12] J. A. K. Suykens, L. Lukas, and J. Vandewalle. Sparse least squares support vector machine classifiers. In *ESANN'2000 European Symposium on Artificial Neural Networks*, pages 37–42, 2000.

[13] J. Xu, X. Zhang, and Y. Li. Kernel MSE algorithm: a unified framework for KFD, LS-SVM and KRR. In *Proc. of IJCNN2001*, pages 1486–1491, 2001.

DRYADE: a new approach for discovering closed frequent trees in heterogeneous tree databases

Alexandre Termier,* Marie-Christine Rousset & Michèle Sebag
CNRS & Université Paris-Sud (LRI) - INRIA (Futurs)
Building 490, Université Paris-Sud, 91405 Orsay Cedex, France.
{termier, mcr, sebag}@lri.fr

Abstract

In this paper we present a novel algorithm for discovering tree patterns in a tree database. This algorithm uses a relaxed tree inclusion definition, making the problem more complex (checking tree inclusion is NP-complete), but allowing to mine highly heterogeneous databases. To obtain good performances, our DRYADE algorithm discovers only closed frequent tree patterns.

1. Introduction

With the rapid growth of structured documents (eg., XML documents) available online, discovering frequent tree structures in huge collections of tree data becomes a crucial issue for information extraction. In this paper, we propose a novel algorithm for discovering frequent trees. It has two main distinguishing features. First, it handles a tree inclusion definition which is more general than all those considered in the existing tree mining literature, thus leading to the discovery of non trivial pattern trees even in highly heterogeneous collections of tree data. Second, it computes *closed* frequent trees, which has the advantage to provide a compact representation of frequent trees without loss of information. The paper is structured as follows: in section 2, we give the formal background for tree mining. The state of the art is briefly reviewed in section 3. In section 4 we describe the DRYADE algorithm, and in section 5 we give some experimental results. The section 6 concludes this paper and provides some research perspectives.

2. Formal Background

Let $L = \{l_1, ..., l_n\}$ be a set of labels. A *labelled tree* $T = (N, A, root(T), \varphi)$ is an acyclic connected graph,

where N is the set of nodes, $A \subset N \times N$ is a binary relation over N defining the set of edges, $root(T)$ is a distinguished node called the *root*, and φ is a labelling function $\varphi : N \mapsto L$ assigning a label to each node of the tree.

Let $u \in N$ and $v \in N$. If there exists an edge $(u, v) \in A$, then v is a *child* of u, and u is the *parent* of v. If there exists a path from u to v in the tree $((u, v) \in A^+)$, then v is a *descendant* of u, and u is an *ancestor* of v.

Ancestor tree inclusion : Let $T_1 = (N_1, A_1, root(T_1), \varphi_1)$ and $T_2 = (N_2, A_2, root(T_2), \varphi_2)$ be two trees. T_1 is *included* into T_2 (noted $T_1 \sqsubseteq T_2$) if there exists an injective mapping $\mu : N_1 \mapsto N_2$ such that: **1.** μ preserves the labels : $\forall u \in N_1 \quad \varphi_1(u) = \varphi_2(\mu(u))$ and **2.** μ preserves the ancestor relationship : $\forall u, v \in N_1$ if $(u, v) \in A_1$ then $(\mu(u), \mu(v)) \in A_2^+$.

The set of mappings supporting the ancestor tree inclusion (or tree inclusion when no confusion is possible) is denoted $\mathcal{EM}_\sqsubseteq(T_1, T_2)$. The set of *occurrences* of T_1 in T_2, denoted $Locc_\sqsubseteq(T_1, T_2)$, is defined as the set of nodes $\mu(root(T_1))$, where μ ranges over $\mathcal{EM}_\sqsubseteq(T_1, T_2)$. Similarly, the set of *images* of T_1 in T_2 is the set of trees $\mu(T_1)$ where μ ranges over $\mathcal{EM}_\sqsubseteq(T_1, T_2)$.

Frequent trees : Let $TD = \{T_1, ..., T_m\}$ be a tree database. The *datatree* $\mathcal{D}$ is the tree whose root is an unlabelled node, and whose subtrees are the trees $\{T_1, ..., T_m\}$. Our goal is to find *frequent trees* in this datatree. Let ε be an absolute frequency threshold. P is a frequent tree of $\mathcal{D}$ if P has at least ε occurrences in $\mathcal{D}$ i.e. $| Locc_\sqsubseteq(P, \mathcal{D}) | \geq \varepsilon$.

A frequent tree T is *closed* if either i) T it is not included in any other frequent tree, or ii) for any frequent tree T' such that $T \sqsubseteq T'$, there exists at least one node in $Locc_\sqsubseteq(T, \mathcal{D})$ which is not contained in the image of T' in $\mathcal{D}$.

Testing the ancestor tree inclusion is a NP-complete problem [9]. In order to reduce the combinatorial explosion, we impose a second order restriction on the trees to be found by our algorithm DRYADE: from now on we restrict the discovery task to trees that do not contain two siblings with the same label. We call such trees *patterns*.

---

*Present address : ISIR, Osaka University, Japan

3. Related work

The first tree mining algorithms were proposed in 2002 by Asai et al. [1] and Zaki [13]. Both of these algorithms are based on efficient enumeration techniques, but handle simple tree inclusion definitions where the *sibling order* must be preserved by mapping μ. Asai's approach adds another constraint : μ must preserve the parent relationship instead of the ancestor relationship, further restraining the admissible solutions.

In 2003, several attempts were done to extend the above approaches and get rid of the constraint on the sibling order [2, 5], using canonical representations of the unordered trees to perform an efficient candidate enumeration.

In [12], we first introduced the general tree inclusion considered in this paper and presented the (incomplete) TreeFinder algorithm.

The most recent frequent tree algorithm to our best knowledge was proposed by Chi et al. [6]. In this *CMTreeMiner* algorithm, the search is restricted to closed trees, entailing significant savings with respect to both memory and computational resources. However, *CMTreeMiner* is based on a tree inclusion definition where the mapping preserves the parent relationship. Thus, as in [1, 2, 5, 13], the complexity of testing the considered tree inclusion is polynomial.

For truly heterogeneous databases, imposing either constraint (preserving the parent relationship or the sibling order) puts severe restrictions on the target solutions: not handling the variations in the order and nesting of the node labels result in finding many equivalent subtrees, and ultimately missing worthy subtrees.

4 The DRYADE algorithm

The DRYADE algorithm presented in this section makes use of the most general tree inclusion proposed in section 2.

The basic principle in DRYADE is to discover the closed frequent patterns of depth 1, and then to hook them together in order to build the higher depth closed frequent patterns in a levelwise fashion. The specificity of the DRYADE approach is to intensively use task decomposition and reformulation in order to perform all the frequency tests *using propositional algorithms*, focusing on the different depth levels of the closed frequent patterns to discover.

DRYADE is presented step-by-step in the following subsections. The results of each step are illustrated on the example datatree of figure 1, with $\varepsilon = 2$.

4.1 Discovering patterns of depth 1

The first step is to compute the closed frequent patterns of depth 1. This task is delegated to a closed Frequent Item

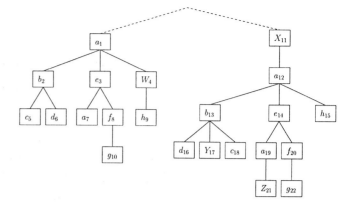

Figure 1. Datatree example *Legend a_i denotes a node with label a and identifier i (unique). The target frequent tree includes all labels with lowercase letters; capital letters corresponding to additional nodes.*

Set algorithm, by reformulating the data as follows: for each label $l \in L$, create a matrix M_l with as many lines as nodes of label l and as many columns as existing distinct labels in the datatree such that the boolean sign in the cell corresponding to the node u and the label l' indicate that the node u (of label l) has a descendant of label l'. Then a closed Frequent Item Set algorithm applied to M_l with threshold ε will provide all the closed frequent sets of descendants for nodes of label l in the datatree. The patterns whose roots are labelled by l and whose children are the nodes belonging to the closed frequent itemsets found previously are all the closed frequent patterns of depth 1 whose root has label l. The tid-list for each closed frequent pattern of depth 1 provides the set of occurrences of the corresponding closed frequent patterns of depth 1.

Here is the matrix of the labels of descendants of nodes of label a in our example:

a	a	b	c	d	e	f	g	h	W	X	Y	Z
1	X	X	X	X	X	X	X	X	X			
7												
12	X	X	X	X	X	X	X	X			X	X
19												X

With threshold $\varepsilon = 2$, the closed frequent itemsets are $\{a, b, c, d, e, f, g, h\}$ for occurrences $\{1, 12\}$, and $\{Z\}$ for occurrences $\{12, 19\}$. The closed frequent patterns of depth 1 are shown in figure 2.

We call $\mathcal{F}^1$ the set of closed frequent patterns of depth 1.

4.2 Pattern hooking

Let $\mathcal{F}$ denote the current set of closed frequent patterns, initialized to $\mathcal{F}^1$. DRYADE proceeds by hooking frequent patterns of $\mathcal{F}^1$ onto the patterns in $\mathcal{F}$, to gradually obtain deeper frequent trees.

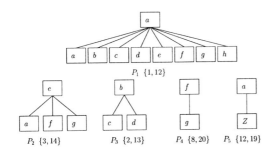

$P_1 \{1, 12\}$

$P_2 \{3, 14\}$ $P_3 \{2, 13\}$ $P_4 \{8, 20\}$ $P_5 \{12, 19\}$

Figure 2. The closed frequent patterns of depth 1 and their occurrences list

The challenge here is to prevent redundant hookings (e.g. resulting in non closed frequent patterns). To this aim, we first define the set of candidate hookable patterns, and use a propositional reformulation to determine which candidate patterns can be hooked simultaneously.

Candidate hooking patterns. A binary relation on the closed patterns is defined as follows. Pattern Q is hookable on pattern P iff i) the root label of Q is one of the leaf labels in P; ii) there exists at least one occurrence u of P and one occurrence v of Q such that u is an ancestor of v.

This binary relation induces a stratification on the current closed patterns (which is updated at each level). As formally proved in [11], the search can be restricted with no loss of information by hooking patterns Q on P, where i) P is maximal wrt the stratification order, we thus call P a *root pattern*; ii) Q is immediately below P (e.g. there is no R such that R is hookable on P and Q is hookable on R). In our example (Fig. 4.1), the root pattern is P_1, and only patterns P_2 and P_3 are candidates to be hooked on P_1.

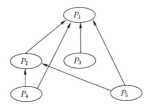

Figure 3. Stratification of $\mathcal{F}^1$

Closed hooking. Let P be a root pattern, and let $\mathcal{Q}_P = \{Q_1, .. Q_n\}$ the candidate patterns to be hooked on pattern P. In order to save redundant computations, we extract all closed subsets of $\mathcal{Q}_P$ which can be simultaneously hooked on P. As in section 4.1, this step is achieved using a propositional reformulation. To pattern P is associated the transaction matrix M_P; to each occurrence u of P in the data is associated a transaction; the items in transaction u are the patterns Q_j such that Q_j admits an occurrence v and u is an ancestor of v. As in section 4.1, a propositional (vertical) Frequent Item Set algorithm can be used to construct all

closed subsets of $\mathcal{Q}_P$ which can be simultaneously hooked on P. To each such closed subset $T = \{Q_{i_1}, .. Q_{i_K}\}$ is associated a novel closed pattern, obtained by hooking every Q_{i_j} on P. Due to space limitations, the interested reader is referred to [11] for more detail. In our example, the patterns $\{P_2, P_3\}$ are hooked together on P_1.

Pruning redundant leaves. From our example hooking $\{P_2, P_3\}$ on P_1 results in the pattern of figure 4.

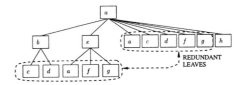

Figure 4. Hooking $\{P_2, P_3\}$ on P_1

The leaves of the root with label a, c, d, f, g represent descendant relations between nodes of label a and nodes of label a, c, d, f, g. This information is actually redundant with the existance of the leaves of depth 2 having the same labels. Hence the leaves of the root are redundant and must be pruned.

To detect the closed frequent combinations of redundant leaves, once again DRYADE uses a propositional closed Frequent Item Set algorithm. The input is a matrix M having as many lines there are occurrences of the pattern P whose redundant leaves we want to discover, and as many columns as potentially redundant leaves. The boolean sign in the cell corresponding to the occurrence o and the leaf lv indicate that the leaf lv is redundant for this occurrence. The closed frequent itemsets of M are the redundant leaves that must be pruned.

In our example after pruning the redundant leaves we obtain the pattern P_6 of figure 5 a). The next iteration of DRYADE will produce the final pattern P_7 shown in figure 5 b).

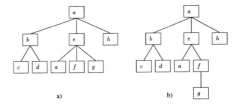

Figure 5. a) P_6, occurrences $\{1, 12\}$ b) P_7, occurrences $\{1, 12\}$

5 Experiments

This section briefly reports on the experimental validation of DRYADE, considering artificial and real-world datasets.

Experimental setting. A stochastic problem generator was implemented to test the scalabitily of DRYADE. More details on this generator can be found in [11]. For each order parameter values, 1,000 problems are independently generated. The frequency threshold ε is 15.

Comparison with WARMR. To our best knowledge, the only frequent pattern algorithm that accommodates a fully relational inclusion definition is WARMR [7]. With courtesy of L. Dehaspe, we could experiment WARMR on the artificial datasets. As could have been expected, these experiments show that WARMR is limited with respect to the size and number of labels of the trees. Comparatively, DRYADE scales up well, with computational cost lower by several orders of magnitude. The performance gain is explained from two specificities of DRYADE. First of all, DRYADE exploits the specific tree-structure of the data, while WARMR aims at the general extraction of relational patterns. Secondly, the closure restriction severely reduces the computational and memory resources needed.

Real world data. A corpus of XML documents from the AFP press agency, kindly given by the Xyleme company, was considered. This corpus includes 3396 documents, with depth in $[2, 3]$, and branching factor in $[4, 5]$, involving 32 different labels. Most of these documents share a complex structure (28 parent/child edges, average depth 2.15). Finding this common structure took 19.3 hours (Athlon 1 GHz, 1 Gb memory). The analysis of the computational time, omitted due to lack of space, shows that over 80% of the effort was spent to computing the closed frequent patterns of depth 1. It must be noted that DRYADE was implemented on the top of the propositional ECLAT algorithm [3]. Indeed, the cost of this first step could be trimmed up to an order of magnitude, using instead the closed CHARM algorithm [14]. This way, DRYADE will hopefully make it feasible to mine a few thousands of real-world XML documents and find worthy patterns in a couple of hours.

6 Conclusion and perspectives

A new algorithm for discovering closed frequent trees in a datatree was presented in this paper. The main motivation for this DRYADE algorithm is to face with highly heterogeneous data, involving many variations in their structures. The challenge was therefore to tackle efficiently a very general, fully relational definition of tree inclusion. This challenge was addressed using two different strategies. The first one is to restrict the search to closed solutions, as in [10, 14, 6]. The second one is based on the reformulation of several search operations in a propositional language. This way, DRYADE can benefit from any progress made in the rapidly evolving field of propositional Frequent Itemt Set algorithms.

This work opens several perspectives for further research. First of all, along the phase transition paradigm [4], ongoing studies are performed to determine the critical values for the order parameters, especially the number of labels. Another promising perspective is to extend the same approach to other types of structured data, e.g. DAGs and graphs, along the same lines as [8].

Acknowledgments

We acknowledge Luc Dehaspe and Chris Borgelt, who kindly made available their WARMR and ECLAT algorithms to us. Thanks also go to Jérôme Azé, Jérôme Maloberti and Mary Felkin, for their help on this work.

References

[1] T. Asai, K. Abe, S. Kawasoe, H. Arimura, H. Sakamoto, and S. Arikawa. Efficient substructure discovery from large semi-structured data. In *SDM2002, Arlington*, 2002.

[2] T. Asai, H. Arimura, T. Uno, and S. ichi Nakano. Discovering frequent substructures in large unordered trees. In *Discovery Sciences'03, Sapporo*, 2003.

[3] C. Borgelt. Efficient implementations of apriori and eclat. In *FIMI 2003, Melbourne, FL, USA*, 2003.

[4] M. Botta, A. Giordana, L. Saitta, and M. Sebag. Relational learning as search in a critical region. *Journal of Machine Learning Research*, 4:431–463, 2003.

[5] Y. Chi, Y. Yang, and R. R. Muntz. Mining frequent rooted trees and free trees using canonical forms. Technical report, UCLA, 2004.

[6] Y. Chi, Y. Yang, Y. Xia, and R. R. Muntz. Cmtreeminer: Mining both closed and maximal frequent subtrees. In *PAKDD'04, Sidney*, 2004.

[7] L. Dehaspe. *Frequent pattern discovery in first-order logic*. Phd, K.U.Leuven, Leuven, Belgium, dec 1998.

[8] A. Inokuchi, T. Washio, and H. Motoda. An apriori-based algorithm for mining frequent substructures from graph data. In *PKDD'00, Lyon*, 2000.

[9] P. Kilpeläinen. *Tree Matching Problems with Applications to Structured Text Databases*. PhD thesis, University of Helsinki, Novembre 1992. TR A-1992-6.

[10] N. Pasquier, Y. Bastide, R. Taouil, and L. Lakhal. Discovering frequent closed itemsets for association rules. In *ICDT '99, Jerusalem, Israel*.

[11] A. Termier. Phd. Technical Report 1388, LRI, May 2004. http://www.lri.fr/~termier/publis/phdTermierEN.ps.gz.

[12] A. Termier, M.-C. Rousset, and M. Sebag. Treefinder: a first step towards xml data mining. In *ICDM'02, Maebashi*.

[13] M. J. Zaki. Efficiently mining frequent trees in a forest. In *8th ACM SIGKDD*, 2002.

[14] M. J. Zaki and C.-J. Hsiao. Charm: An efficient algorithm for closed itemset mining. In *Proc. 2nd SIAM ICDM, Arlington*, Avril 2002.

A Greedy Algorithm for Selecting Models in Ensembles

Andrei L. Turinsky
University of Calgary, Canada
aturinsk@ucalgary.ca

Robert L. Grossman
University of Illinois at Chicago, USA
and Open Data Partners, USA
grossman@uic.edu

Abstract

We are interested in ensembles of models built over k data sets. Common approaches are either to combine models by vote averaging, or to build a meta-model on the outputs of the local models. In this paper, we consider the model assignment approach, in which a meta-model selects one of the local statistical models for scoring. We introduce an algorithm called Greedy Data Labeling (GDL) that improves the initial data partition by reallocating some data, so that when each model is built on its local data subset, the resulting hierarchical system has minimal error. We present evidence that model assignment may in certain situations be more natural than traditional ensemble learning, and if enhanced by GDL, it often outperforms traditional ensembles.

1. Introduction

In a standard approach to data mining, a learning algorithm F is applied to a single data set D, where D consists of instances of the form (x,y), with x a vector of data attributes and y a class label. The choice of the algorithm defines a parametric family of predictive models. Given the algorithm F and the dataset D, a predictive model $f: x \rightarrow y$ is built to predict the class value of unlabeled data instances.

Ensembles of models arise in several different ways. First, they can be built by taking a single data set and using sampling with replacement to produce k separate data sets [1]. Second, ensembles arise naturally in distributed data mining, where the data may be naturally distributed over k geographical sites. While it may be possible to move all data to a central site and build a single model there, it is often too costly or otherwise impractical. The alternative is to mine all data in-place and thus build k predictive models (base-models) locally. Third, ensembles of models arise naturally in hierarchical modeling. Here the outputs of one or more models are used as the inputs to another model [2]. Hierarchical modeling arises naturally when data comes from different underlying distributions, in which case a collection of specialized models is desirable. Consider an (idealized) application where a separate model predicts the risk of a heart disease for each age group. When a new patient arrives, the *meta-model* will invoke the predictive model that corresponds to the patient's age.

There are several ways to produce a single score from an ensemble of models. The simplest is a voting/averaging ensemble [3], in which case the meta-model is just an averaging function. A more complex one is meta-learning, where individual base-models make predictions, after which the meta-model reads their scores and makes the overall prediction [4].

A third technique is *model assignment*, or *model selection*, where the meta-model delegates the scoring of an unlabeled data instance to one of the base-models, as in the example with the heart disease prediction above.

Consider k data sets $D_1,..., D_k$, each represented by a different color. Denote by D their union as a bag (i.e. points may occur with multiplicity). A model assignment system is created as follows. A base-model f_i is built on each data subset D_i using a learning algorithm F. Then a sample of data from each color is used to train a meta-model that can predict colors.

In this paper, we assume that we are given the k data sets $D_1,..., D_k$, but have the flexibility to move data between them. This assumption is natural for the cases of distributed data mining and hierarchical modeling mentioned above. We introduce a novel algorithm, called Greedy Data Labeling (GDL), for learning base-models on $D_1,..., D_k$ and a meta-learner for model selection. The algorithm relies on moving small amounts of data between the various data sets D_i.

We give some preliminary experimental studies showing that in interesting cases involving heterogeneous data it outperforms traditional ensemble learning based upon voting. Since one of our interests is in exploring distributed data partitions, in this paper, we consider the special case in which data instances belong to only one color at a time. Naturally, the GDL algorithm depends on the initial distribution of data into the subsets $\{D_i\}$. This reflects the underlying structure of both distributed data mining and hierarchical modeling of heterogeneous data.

2. Related work

The GDL method is broadly related to unsupervised clustering, but uses a more general measure of tightness based on the choice of the learning algorithm F. It also employs an idea related to boosting [5], in which previously misclassified data is re-sampled more frequently to give the predictive model more chances to learn it. Bagging [1] is one of the main methods for building a collection of classifiers, where each classifier is trained on a subset of data drawn from the same distribution. In practice, the data subsets are usually created by re-sampling the original dataset with replacement and hence may share some data.

A system where classifiers may specialize and/or abstain from voting is considered in [6]. A method of selecting classifiers based on local accuracy is presented in [7]. A Behavior-Knowledge Space method considers each possible output combination in the space of combined outputs of multiple classifiers [8]. In [9], conceptual clustering creates a classification hierarchy based on how well objects fit descriptive concepts. For related results, see also [10]. There are various techniques to recover individual data distributions from a mixture of distributions, such as the popular EM algorithm [11]. Other related methods are described in [12].

The novelty of the GDL approach is in the fact that, unlike the above methods, it is geared towards applications and situations, such as distributed data mining with high bandwidth networks, in which moving some of the data between local data sets is practical. In particular, it uses data reallocation to improve the structure of local data distributions before the distributed learning process begins. The resulting system deploys local classifiers in a way that reflects the realities of the current data partition.

Finally, the GDL algorithm uses simulated annealing to escape local minima, which allows suboptimal exploration steps in greedy descend [13].

3. The Greedy Data Labeling algorithm

The GDL algorithm is concerned with the scenario in which we move some amount of data between the various D_i to improve the data partition. We are not interested in the two extreme cases in which we either combine all the data to produce a single data set D or leave all the data in separate partitions. We also assume that the attributes are discrete (or discretized by binning), an assumption that is required for several types of classifiers commonly used in practice, such as the naïve Bayesian classifiers.

Once the data partition $\{D_i\}$ is found by the GDL algorithm, we take a μ percent sample of the data from all subsets (a *meta-sample*) and train a meta-model to learn the k colors, as defined by the current data partition.

Given a data partition $\{D_i\}$, we define the color η as *native* for a data instance (x,y) if

$$\eta(x,y) = \arg \min_{1 \le i \le k} \| y - f_i(x) \|$$

i.e. if the base-model $f_\eta(x)$ built on the subset D_η predicts the true class of that instance better than base-models of other colors. Here, $\|y-f_i(x)\|$ is the appropriately defined prediction error. In case of a tie, the native color is chosen randomly among the candidates.

The GDL algorithm performs the following greedy iteration until all data points are in their native subsets:

- Initialize a batch size parameter T.
- For all data points (x,y) in D:
    - Find the prediction error $\varepsilon(i) = \|y-f_i(x)\|$ on this data point for each base-model.
    - Identify the native color η of the point.
    - Compute the greedy step $\delta = \varepsilon(c) - \varepsilon(\eta)$, where c is the current color.
    - Using simulated annealing, reallocate the data point with probability p=exp(-1/(δt)).
    - Stop when T data points are reallocated.
- Update all base-models.
- Reduce batch size T in half for the next iteration.

Here, t is a control parameter tied to the batch size T. When δ=0, p=0 and the data instance is never chosen. Alternatively, p=exp(-1/((δ+1)t)) would allow to select instances with δ=0 with non-zero probability and escape local minima better at the expense of a larger number of iterations. GDL moves data in batch to minimize base-model rebuilding after each reallocation, and thus requires only a few base-model updates before convergence. We have not noticed any problems related to overfitting.

There are noticeable similarities between the GDL method and clustering techniques. For example, the k-means clustering is initially seeded with k centroids. New data is placed into the cluster with the nearest centroid, after which the centroid is recomputed. In the GDL, the algorithm is seeded by the initial data partition. New data is placed into the subset whose model gives the least prediction error, after which the model is recomputed. In both cases, instances are moved between data subsets to improve a certain measure of tightness within subsets.

4. Experimental datasets and partitions

The goal of our experiments was two-fold: (a) to show that a model assignment approach may in certain situations outperform traditional voting methods which use all base-models for prediction; (b) to explore the quality of data partitions produced by the GLD algorithm.

We selected several datasets from the UCI Machine Learning Repository [14] that satisfy three criteria: (a) all attributes are discrete, (b) the number of data instances is at least 500, sufficiently large to understand the behavior of the GDL algorithm on well studied data, (c) random data partitions results in at least 1% classification error, i.e. the domain is sufficiently complex. The UCI datasets we used in our experiments are:

- Balance Scale data: 625 instances, 4 attributes
- Tic-Tac-Toe data: 958 instances, 9 attributes
- Car Evaluation data: 1728 instances, 6 attributes
- Chess data: 3196 instances, 36 attributes
- Nursery data: 12960 instances, 8 attributes

To examine the quality of data partitions produced by the GDL method, we compared three types of partitions.

First, we were interested in modeling the situations for the initial partitions where data comes from either a single source or different sources. Because we used real data and could not control its source, we modeled these two situations as follows. For a *homogeneous* initial split, the training data was divided into k equal parts randomly. To model a *heterogeneous* partition, we sorted the training data by its most informative attribute (found by building a C4.5 tree) and split it sequentially into k subsets.

Second, random mixture partitions (RM) were produced by making each initial subset D_i exchange a λ percent of its randomly selected data with other subsets, divided equally among the receiving subsets.

Third, the GDL partitions were made by exchanging data instances selected by the GDL algorithm between initial subsets. We initialized the batch size parameter T to $(\lambda/2)|D|$ for each value of λ, using the same values as in random mixture (RM). Because GDL reduces T in half after each iteration, this choice ensures that the total data traffic does not exceed $\lambda/2+\lambda/4+... < \lambda$ percent. Our goal was to demonstrate that with GDL, we get superior colorings moving less data than with the RM approach.

5. Test results and discussion

The models were built using the WEKA package [15], with C4.5 decision trees as the base-models [16] and three different types of meta-models: C4.5, naïve Bayesian, and one-nearest neighbor models. Three 5-fold cross-validations were used to test model assignment systems, as well as voting ensembles for non-GDL partitions. We set k=3 or k=10, the meta-sample percentage μ = 100, 50, 25 and 10%, and the data mixing parameter λ = 10, 20, 40, 60, 80, and 90%. With zero-or-one classification error, annealing parameter $\delta(x,y)$ takes values 0 or 1 (native or non-native current color), which can be shown to reduce annealing to a random selection of T currently misclassified data points.

We observed that the nearest neighbor meta-model was the best choice. Table 1 shows classification errors for a voting ensemble of C4.5 base-models (ENS) vs. a

model assignment system with the same base-models and a nearest neighbor meta-model (NN μ) built for different values of μ. The results are shown for each type of data partition for both homogeneous (same) and heterogeneous (different) data, averaged over the five UCI datasets.

Table 1. Classification errors (%) of voting ensembles v. NN-based model assignment systems with different meta-sample sizes (%), on different type of data partitions, average for 5 UCI datasets

Data source	Data part.	ENS	NN 100	NN 50	NN 25	NN 10
Same k=3	Init	13.5	14.1	14.8	15.3	15.7
	RM	13.6	14.3	14.9	15.4	15.8
	GDL	n/a	11.3	12.5	13.7	14.7
Same k=10	Init	16.0	17.3	18.2	19.0	19.8
	RM	16.1	17.0	18.1	18.9	19.8
	GDL	n/a	12.1	14.3	16.1	18.0
Diff k=3	Init	28.4	10.7	11.6	13.9	16.6
	RM	15.7	12.3	13.3	14.5	15.7
	GDL	n/a	9.6	10.5	12.8	16.1
Diff k=10	Init	30.5	12.3	14.5	18.3	22.0
	RM	17.9	14.1	16.1	18.1	19.7
	GDL	n/a	10.8	13.1	17.1	21.0

The tests confirm that combining data into fewer subsets results in better predictive systems of either type, and that the quality of the model assignment system drops as the size μ of the meta-sample decreases. Given the same collection of base models, care must be taken to build a sufficiently accurate meta-model.

For the homogeneous data (same-source), ensembles built on initial partitions are generally superior, and exchanging random samples of already homogeneous data has no effect. However, model assignment systems enhanced by GDL consistently outperform ensembles, sometimes even with meta-samples as small as 10%.

For the heterogeneous data (different-sources), ensembles perform poorly on the initial partitions. Their accuracy can be improved dramatically by exchanging random samples of data, which creates a more homogeneous data distribution across the k datasets. On the other hand, model assignment systems appear to be far superior to ensembles, and with GDL their accuracy improves even further. In effect, ensembles are "penalized" if their base-models are over-specialized, whereas model assignment systems are "rewarded"', and the GDL makes this effect even more pronounced.

In Table 2, we compare ensemble systems to model assignment under their respective optimal conditions: ensembles are built on random mixture partitions, and the model assignment systems are built on GDL partitions with meta-sample size μ =100%. We make several observations. The choice of a meta-model algorithm affects the performance significantly, with nearest neighbor being the best meta-models. GDL moves only a small percentage of data, especially when the initial partition already represents different data sources (5.0% vs. 10.3% for k=10). In contrast, the amount of traffic in random mixture approach is fixed, potentially large, and not reflecting the internal structure of data. In terms of efficiency, an average of about four greedy GDL iterations is required for convergence.

Table 2. Classification errors, data traffic in GDL (% of total data size), and the number of greedy iterations, average for 5 UCI datasets

Data source	k	ENS %	NN %	C45 %	NB %	Traf %	Iter
Same	3	13.6	11.3	13.5	15.2	6.7	3.8
Same	10	16.1	12.1	15.7	18.5	10.3	4.9
Diff	3	15.7	9.6	11.4	14.5	4.2	3.2
Diff	10	17.9	10.8	11.7	17.3	5.0	4.3

6. Conclusion

We compared several scenarios for selecting models out of an ensemble of k models. It appears that in the case of a homogeneous data distribution, traditional voting or averaging ensembles outperform model selection approaches. On the other hand, when the base models reflect a natural heterogeneity in the data, delegating the prediction to one model out of an ensemble outperforms voting/averaging. We also introduced an algorithm called Greedy Data Labeling (GDL) that enhances data partitions in model assignment problems by moving small portions of data between the different datasets before the learning algorithms are applied. The resulting model assignment system outperforms traditional ensembles for both homogeneous and heterogeneous datasets. Future work on GDL includes developing data weighting schemas and randomization mechanisms for distributed applications.

10. References

[1] L. Breiman, "Bagging predictors". *Machine Learning*, 1996, Vol.24, No. 2, pp.123-140.

[2] Draper, D., *Bayesian Hierarchical Modeling*, Springer-Verlag, New York, 2001.

[3] T.G. Dietterich, "An experimental comparison of three methods for constructing ensembles of decision trees: bagging, boosting, and randomization", *Machine Learning*, 2000, Vol. 40, No.2, pp. 139-157.

[4] P.K. Chan and S.J. Stolfo, "Learning arbiter and combiner trees from partitioned data for scaling machine learning", *Proc. 1st Int. Conf. Knowledge Discovery and Data Mining*, AAAI Press, Menlo Park, CA, 1995, pp. 39--44

[5] Y. Freund, "Boosting a weak learning algorithm by majority", *Information and Computation*, 1995, Vol. 121, No. 2, pp. 256--285.

[6] Y. Freund, R.E. Schapire, Y. Singer, and M.K. Warmuth, "Using and combining predictors that specialize", *Proc. of the 29th Annual ACM Symposium on the Theory of Computing*, 1997, pp.334--343.

[7] K. Woods, W.P. Kegelmeyer, and K. Bowyer, "Combination of Multiple Classifiers using Local Accuracy Estimates", *IEEE Trans. on Pattern Analysis and Machine Intelligence*, 1997, Vol. 19, No. 4, pp. 405-410.

[8] Y.S. Huang and C.Y. Suen, "Combination of multiple experts for the recognition of unconstrained handwritten numerals", *IEEE Trans. on Pattern Analysis and Machine Intelligence*, 1995, Vol. 17, pp. 90-94.

[9] R.S. Michalski and R.E. Stepp, "Automated construction of classifications: conceptual clustering versus numerical taxonomy", *IEEE Trans. Pattern Analysis and Machine Intelligence*, 1983, Vol. 5, pp. 396-410.

[10] U. Fayyad, C. Reina, and P.S. Bradley, "Initialization of iterative refinement clustering algorithms", *Proc. 4th Int. Conf. Knowledge Discovery and Data Mining*, AAAI Press, Menlo Park, CA, 1998, pp. 194-198

[11] M.I. Jordan and R.A. Jacobs, "Hierarchical mixtures of experts and the EM algorithm", *Neural Computation*, 1994, Vol. 6, No. 2, pp. 181-214.

[12] Kuncheva, L.I., *Combining Pattern Classifiers: Methods and Algorithms*, Wiley-InterScience, 2004.

[13] Van Laarhoven, P.J.M. and E.H.L. Aarts, *Simulated Annealing: Theory and Applications*, D.Reidel, Norwell, 1987.

[14] C.L. Blake and C.J. Merz, *UCI Repository of machine learning databases*, University of California, Department of Information and Computer Science, Irvine, CA, 1998. Avail. at http://www.ics.uci.edu/~mlearn/MLRepository.html.

[15] Witten, I.H. and E. Frank, *Data Mining: Practical Machine Learning Tools and Techniques with Java Implementations*, Morgan Kaufmann, San Mateo, CA, 1999. WEKA software avail. at http://www.cs.waikato.ac.nz/ml/weka/.

[16] Quinlan, J.R. *C4.5: Programs for Machine Learning*, Morgan Kaufmann, San Mateo, CA, 1993.

Mining web data to create online navigation recommendations

Juan D. Velásquez[1,3], Alejandro Bassi[2,4], Hiroshi Yasuda[1] and Terumasa Aoki[1]
[1]Research Center for Advanced Science and Technology,
University of Tokyo, {jvelasqu,yasuda,aoki}@mpeg.rcast.u-tokyo.ac.jp
[2]Center for Collaborative Research, University of Tokyo
abassi@vp.ccr.u-tokyo.ac.jp
[3]Department of Industrial Engineering, University of Chile
[4]Department of Computer Sciences, University of Chile

Abstract

A system to provide online navigation recommendation for web visitors is introduced. We call visitor the anonymous user, i.e., when only data about her/his browsing behavior (web logs) are available.

We first apply clustering techniques over a large sample of web data. Next, from the significant patterns that are discovered, a set of rules about how to use them is created. Finally, comparing the current web visitor session with the patterns, online navigation recommendations are proposed using the mentioned rules.

The system was tested using data from a real web site, showing its effectiveness.

1 Introduction

From the beginning of the Web, web site designers have always strived to create sites whose structure and content facilitate to find the information that a user is looking for [5]. However, they often fail to attain this goal. In many cases, the chosen structure hides the desired information, even though it is contained in the web site. In fact, some web sites incorporate too much content in a same page, which, aggravated by a bad structure, make users feel "lost in the hyperspace" where they cannot find the specific information they want.

In order to improve the compatibility between users and web sites, some sites have incorporated auxiliary systems to provide online navigation recommendations. It is the case of amazon[1], where the user receives recommendations about others items related with her/his query.

This paper introduces online navigation recommendations for web site visitors, based on their past navigation browsing behavior. Here the word visitor refers to the occasional user of a web site, when no personal information is available about her/him.

This paper is organized as follows. In section 2 the related work is presented. Section 3 describes the knowledge base proposed to create online navigation recommendations. The method to create and validate the recommendations is explained in section 4. A real world application is shown in section 5, and the conclusions are presented in section 6.

2 Related work

Some research initiatives are oriented to understand the visitor browsing behavior [3, 4, 6, 10] in order to create more attractive web sites, personalizing its structure and content. These efforts aim at facilitating Web site navigation, and in the case of commercial sites, at increasing market shares, transforming visitors into customers, increasing customers' loyalty and predicting their preferences.

2.1 Web personalization

It is a process in which the web server and its related applications, mainly CGI-Bin[2], dynamically customize the content (pages, items, browsing recommendations, etc.) shown to the user, based on information about his/her behavior in a web site [3].

The key of web personalization for occasional visitors is to understand their desires and needs from their interaction. This allows to design and construct information repositories using the data of the visitors' transactions, in order to predict the correct supply of products and services [4].

---

[1]http://www.amazon.com

[2]Common Gateway Interface http://www.msg.net/tutorial/cgi/

2.2 Web recommendations

These can be grouped in two categories: Online and Offline [9]. Online consist principally of navigation recommendations shown at the bottom of web pages [1]. It is a non invasive scheme which gives the user the possibility of following the suggestion or not.

Offline recommendations are targeted to the web master. They give advice on the addition or elimination of links, and changes in the web content. It is a non invasive scheme, because the web master can accept or reject the recommendations.

In this work, we focus on the online navigation recommendations.

2.3 Modeling the visitor browsing behavior

Our model of the visitor behavior uses three variables: the sequence of visited pages, their content and the time spent on each page [10]. The model is based on a n-dimensional visitor behavior vector which is defined as follows.

Definition 1 (Visitor Behavior Vector)
$v = [(p_1, t_1) \ldots (p_n, t_n)]$, where the pair (p_i, t_i) represent the ith page viewed (p_i) and the percentage of time spent on it within a session (t_i), respectively.

Let α and β be two visitor behavior vectors of dimension C^α and C^β, respectively. A similarity measure has been proposed elsewhere to compare visitor sessions as follows [10]:

$$sm(\alpha, \beta) = sg(G_\alpha, G_\beta) \frac{1}{\eta} \sum_{k=1}^{\eta} st(t_{\alpha,k}, t_{\beta,k}) * sp(p_{\alpha,k}, p_{\beta,k})$$
(1)

where $\eta = \min\{C^\alpha, C^\beta\}$, and $sp(p_{\alpha,k}, p_{\beta,k})$ is the similarity between the text content of the kth page of vector α and the kth page of vector β (see **vector space model** in [7]).

Finally, the term $st(t_{\alpha,k}, t_{\beta,k}) = \min\{\frac{t_{\alpha,k}}{t_{\beta,k}}, \frac{t_{\beta,k}}{t_{\alpha,k}}\}$ is the similarity between the time spent on the kth page by each of the two visitors. The term sg is the similarity between the sequences of pages viewed by the two visitors [6].

3 A knowledge base for navigation recommendations

A web mining tool developed for a particular web site allows to discover significant patterns about the visitor behavior and her/his preferences. However, the collaboration of an expert is required to validate the patterns and provide a short description about how to use them.

In this sense, we need a **Knowledge Base** (KB) as a repository of the discovered patterns and the information on how to use them.

The KB [2] contains wisdom represented by "if-then-else" rules derived from the discovered patterns. Figure 1 shows the general structure of the proposed KB. It is composed of a Pattern Repository that contains the discovered patterns, and a Rule Repository where the general rules about how to use the patterns are stored.

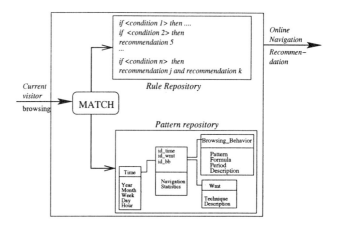

Figure 1. A Knowledge Base for visitor browsing behavior

In order to use the KB, when a pattern is presented, a matching process is performed to find the most similar patterns in the Pattern Repository. With this information, the set of rules that will create the suggestion of the KB is selected from the Rule Repository.

4 Creating the navigation recommendation

A online navigation recommendation is a set of web pages belonging to the web site, shown to the visitor as a suggestion, based on her/his browsing behavior [1].

4.1 Using clustering to extract significant patterns

The cluster identification is sometimes a difficult process, because it depends on a subjective definition, i.e., what we understand by cluster [8]. While for some persons a given cluster doesn't make sense, for others it allows to discover new knowledge. Then it is appropriate to rely on the assistance of a business expert for a relative good interpretation.

4.2 How to use the patterns?

We can classify the visitor browsing behavior in one of the clusters discovered by the web mining process, comparing the cluster centroid with the current session, using the similarity measure introduced in (1).

Let $\alpha = [(p_1, t_1), \ldots, (p_m, t_m)]$ be the current visitor session and $C_\alpha = [(p_1^\alpha, t_1^\alpha), \ldots, (p_H^\alpha, t_H^\alpha)]$ the centroid such as $\max\{sm(\alpha, C_i)\}$ whith C_i the set of centroid discovered. The recommendations are created as a set of pages whose text content is related with p_{m+1}^α. These pages are selected with the expert collaboration.

Let $R_{m+1}(\alpha)$ be the online navigation recommendation for the $(m+1)^{th}$ page to be visited by visitor α, and δ the minimum number of pages visited to prepare the suggestion, with $\delta < m < H$. Then, we can write $R_{m+1}(\alpha) = \{l_{m+1,0}^\alpha, \ldots, l_{m+1,j}^\alpha, \ldots, l_{m+1,k}^\alpha\}$, with $l_{m+1,j}^\alpha$ the jth link page suggested for the $(m+1)^{th}$ page to be visited by visitor α and k the maximum number of pages for each suggestion.

In this notation, $l_{i+1,0}^\alpha$ represents the "no suggestion" case.

4.3 Recommendation effectiveness

We use a percentage of the complete web data (the training set) to extract significant patterns and define the set of rules for them. Then we test the effectiveness of our method with the remaining percentage (the test set).

Let $ws = \{p_1, \ldots, p_n\}$ be the web site and the pages that compose it. Comparing the page text content and with the collaboration of a web site content expert, we can define an equivalence relation for the pages, so that pages belonging to the same equivalence class contain similar information. The classes generate a partition of the web site in disjoint subsets of pages.

Let Cl_x be the xth equivalence class for the web site. It is such as $\forall p_z \in Cl_x, p_z \notin Cl_y, x \neq y \bigcup_{x=1}^{w} Cl_x = ws$ where w is the number of equivalence classes.

Let $\alpha = [(p_1, t_1), \ldots, (p_H, t_H)]$ be a visitor behavior vector from the test set. Based on the first m pages actually visited, the proposed system recommends for the following page $m+1$ several possibilities, i.e., possible pages to be visited. We test the effectiveness of the suggestions made for the $(m+1)^{th}$ page for a visitor α following this procedure. Let Cl_q be the equivalence class for p_{m+1}, if $\exists l_{m+1,j}^\alpha \in R_{m+1}^\alpha / l_{m+1,j}^\alpha \in Cl_q, j > 0$ then we assume the suggestion is successful.

Owing to the way the recommendations are constructed, the number of selected pages could be very big, producing a confusion in the visitor about which page to follow. We set a maximum number k of pages per recommendation. Comparing the page text content, we can choose the k pages closer to p_{m+1}.

$$E_{m+1}^k(\alpha) = \{l_{m+1,j}^\alpha \in sort_k(sp(p_{m+1}, l_{m+1,j}^\alpha))\}, \quad (2)$$

with sp being a distance to compare text content between web pages. The "$sort_k$" function sorts the result of sp in descendent order and extracts the "k" links pages whose distance to p_{m+1} are the largest.

A particular case is when $E_{m+1}(\alpha) = \{l_{m+1,0}^\alpha\}$, i.e., no suggestion is proposed.

5 A practical application

We applied our methodology over web data from a real web site belonging to a financial institution, the first Chilean virtual bank **Tbanc**[3] (Technological Bank). The site is written in Spanish. It has 217 static web pages and approximately eight million web log registers corresponding to the period January to March, 2003.

5.1 Significant patterns extraction

We applied a Self-Organizing Feature Map (SOFM) assuming that the maximum number of components of a visitor behavior vector is $H = 6$. Vectors with three components are completed with zero values. The SOFM receives 6 variables as input and has 32x32 output neurons.

In the training task a 80% of the total visitor behavior vectors was used, approximately 220,000.

The clusters discover are presented in table 1. The second and third columns of this table contain the center neurons (winner neuron) of each of the clusters, representing the visited pages and the time spent in each one of them.

Table 1. Visitor behavior clusters

Cluster	Pages Visited	Time spent in seconds
A	(78,81,150,193,138,81)	(7,61,43,18,82,93)
B	(157,178,187,102,115,1)	(12,87,98,105,42,3)
C	(4,18,29,41,141,205)	(8,39,113,138,149,58)
D	(127,116,129,130,47,65)	(37,51,41,63,105,23)

The pages in the web site were labeled with a number to facilitate the respective analysis.

5.2 Creating rules for navigation suggestions

First, we need to identify the current visitor session. Since the selected web site uses cookies, we can use them for online session identification.

In order to prepare the online suggestion for the $(m+1)^{th}$ page to be visited, we compare the current session

---

[3]http://www.tbanc.cl/

553

with the patterns in the Patterns Repository. The comparison needs a minimum of three pages visited ($\delta = 3$) to determine the cluster centroid most similar to the current visit, allowing to prepare the suggestion for the fourth page visited. This process can be repeated after the visitor has visited more than three pages, i.e., in the suggestions for the fifth page, we use the four pages visited in the current session.

The final online suggestion is made using the rule base developed with the help of the domain expert. For the four clusters we found, sixteen rules were created. We suggest at most three candidate pages for the fourth, fifth, and sixth page to be visited, i.e. $k = 3$.

5.3 Testing the online navigation effectiveness

From the 20% of the visitor behavior vectors that belong to the test set, we selected only those with six real components, i.e., it was not necessary to complete the visitor vectors with zero values to get the six components. Given this selection, we have 9,751 vectors to test the effectiveness of the online navigation suggestions.

Figure 2 shows a histogram with the percentage of the accepted suggestions using our validation method.

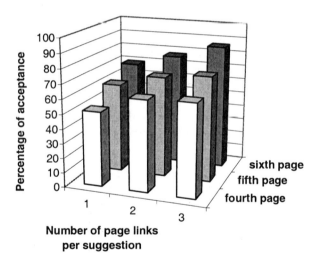

Figure 2. Percentage of acceptance of online navigation recommendations

If using the proposed methodology just one page is suggested it would have been accepted in slightly more than 60% of the cases. This has been considered a very successful suggestion by the business expert, since we are dealing with a complex web site with many pages, many links between pages, and a high rate of visitors that leave the site after a few clicks.

Furthermore, it should be mentioned that the percentage

of acceptance would probably have been even higher if we have actually suggested the respective page during the session. Since we are comparing past visits stored in log files, we could only analyze the behavior of visitors that did not actually receive any of the suggestions we propose.

6 Conclusions and future work

In this work a method to create online navigation recommendations was introduced. It considers the extraction of significant navigation patterns from web data and the creation of rules on how to use them in the creation of the recommendations.

Using the KB, online navigation recommendations were created and tested with real web logs data.

Since the KB contains the knowledge discovered using 80% of the complete web data, it was possible to test its effectiveness in the remaining 20%. The results show that the visitor would follow the recommendations in a high percentage of the cases.

As future work, we want to apply the online recommendations in the normal operation of a web site.

References

[1] P. Brusilovsky. Adaptive web-based system: Technologies and examples. Tutorial, IEEE Web Intelligence Int. Conference, October 2003.

[2] M. Cadoli and F. M. Donini. A survey on knowledge compilation. *AI Communications*, 10(3-4):137–150, 1997.

[3] Z. Lu, Y. Yao, and N. Zhong. *Web Intelligence*. Springer-Verlag, Berlin, 2003.

[4] B. Mobasher, R. Cooley, and J. Srivastava. Creating adaptive web sites through usage-based clustering of urls. In *Procs. IEEE Knowledge and Data Engineering Exchange*, November 1999.

[5] J. Nielsen. User interface directions for the web. *Communications of ACM*, 42(1):65–72, 1999.

[6] T. A. Runkler and J. Bezdek. Web mining with relational clustering. *International Journal of Approximate Reasoning*, 32(2-3):217–236, Feb 2003.

[7] G. Salton, A. Wong, and C. S. Yang. A vector space model for automatic indexing. *Communications of the ACM archive*, 18(11):613–620, November 1975.

[8] S. Theodoridis and K. Koutroumbas. *Pattern Recognition*. Academic Press, 1999.

[9] J. D. Velásquez, H. Yasuda, and T. Aoki. Web site structure and content recommendations. In *Procs. 3th IEEE/WIC Int. Conf. on Web Intelligence*, page to appear, Beijing, China, September 2004.

[10] J. D. Velásquez, H. Yasuda, T. Aoki, and R. Weber. A new similarity measure to understand visitor behavior in a web site. *IEICE Transactions on Information and Systems, Special Issues in Information Processing Technology for web utilization*, E87-D(2):389–396, February 2004.

Alpha Galois Lattices

Véronique Ventos

L.R.I., UMR-CNRS 8623, Université Paris-Sud, 91405 Orsay, France

Henry Soldano

L.I.P.N, UMR-CNRS 7030, Université Paris-Nord, 93430 Villetaneuse, France

Thibaut Lamadon

L.R.I., UMR-CNRS 8623, Université Paris-Sud, 91405 Orsay, France

Abstract

In many applications there is a need to represent a large number of data by clustering them in a hierarchy of classes. Our basic representation is a Galois lattice, a structure that exhaustively represents the whole set of concepts that are distinguishable given the instance set and the representation language. What we propose here is a method to reduce the size of the lattice, and thus simplify our view of the data, while conserving its formal structure and exhaustivity. For that purpose we use a preliminary partition of the instance set, representing the association of a "type" to each instance. By redefining the notion of extent of a term in order to cope, to a certain degree (denoted as α), with this partition, we define a particular family of Galois lattices denoted as Alpha Galois lattices. We also discuss the related implication rules defined as inclusion of such α-extents.

1 Introduction

One way to cluster instances in classes organized in a hierarchy is to build a concept lattice [4], a structure in which each node corresponds to a class represented as its *extent* (the set of the instances of the class) and its *intent* (the common properties of these instances expressed as a term of a given language). Concept lattices express all the subsets of instances distinguishable when using the language. Various techniques have been proposed to reduce the size of concept lattices by eliminating part of the nodes. In particular, frequent concept lattices [11, 10] represent the topmost part of a concept lattice, i.e. the nodes which *extent* cardinality exceeds a given threshold. In our approach, we reduce the number of nodes of the concept lattice by accounting in a flexible manner a prior partition of data. The partition is a set of *basic classes* which are clusters of instances sharing the same basic type. Basic classes are then used in order to add a local criterion of frequency to the notion of *extent* as follows: an instance i now belongs to the α-*extent* of a term T of the language, when it belongs to $ext(T)$, the extent of T, (i.e. i has every T's property), and when at least α % of the instances of the basic class of i also belong to $ext(T)$. Defining α-*extents* results in a family of flexible concept lattices that we call *Alpha Galois lattices*. For instance, in an Alpha Galois lattice representing the C/net electronic catalog, with $\alpha= 92$, the "support" property will appear since in the $HardDrives$ basic class, 92 % instances were sold with support. Actually, this property is not frequent (13 products out of 2274, i.e. 0.5 %) and so would not apppear in a frequent concept lattice.

We show that the set of nodes of an *Alpha Galois Lattices* is a subset of the set of nodes of the corresponding concept lattice and that the values of α define a total order on *Alpha Galois lattices*. Finally, the inclusion of α-extents corresponds to particular implication rules, representing some kind of approximation of usual implication rules (i.e. association rules with confidence 1), that depends on the *a priori* partition of the data. Such α-implication rules can be extracted in the same way that ordinary implication (and association) rules are extracted from concept lattices.

The general framework of Galois lattices is given in section 2. In section 3, we present Alpha Galois lattices. Section 4 presents experimental results on the C/net data set and discuss the ability of such a representation to deal with exceptional data (α near 0 or near 100). Finally, discussion and conclusion are given in section 5.

2 Preliminaries and definitions

Detailed definitions, results and proofs regarding Galois connections and lattices may be found in [1], and, in the framework of Formal Concept Analysis in [4] . However we need for our purpose a more general presentation than the one in [4] as our *extents* are different from those used in *concept lattices* .

Definition 1 (Galois connection and Galois lattice) *Let m1: P → Q and m2: Q → P be maps between two lattices $(P, \leq_P)$ and $(Q, \leq_Q)$. (m1, m2) s called a Galois connection if for all p, p1, p2 in P and for all q, q1, q2 in Q:*

C1- $p1 \leq_P p2 \Rightarrow m1(p2) \leq_Q m1(p1)$
C2- $q1 \leq_Q q2 \Rightarrow m2(q2) \leq_P m2(q1)$
C3- $p \leq_P m2(m1(p))$ and $q \leq_Q m1(m2(q))$

Let G={ (p,q) with p an element of P and q an element of Q such that p=m2(q) and q = m1(p)}. Let $\leq$ be defined by: $(p1,q1) \leq (p2,q2)$ iff $q1 \leq_Q q2$, then:

(G,$\leq$) is a lattice called a Galois lattice. When necessary it will be denoted as G(P, m1, Q, m2)

Example 1 *The two ordered sets are $(\mathcal{L}, \preceq)$ and $(\mathcal{P}(I), \subseteq)$. $\mathcal{L}$ is a language a term of which is a subset of a set of attributes $\mathcal{A} = \{t1, t2, t3, a3, a4, a5, a6, a7, a8\}$. Here $c1 \preceq c2$ means that c1 is less specific than c2 (e.g. $\{a3, a4\} \preceq \{a3, a4, a6\}$), I is a set of individuals = $\{i1, i2, i3, i4, i5, i6, i7, i8\}$. Let int and ext be two maps int: $\mathcal{P}(I) \to \mathcal{L}$ and ext: $\mathcal{L} \to \mathcal{P}(I)$ such that int(e1) is the subset of attributes common to all the individuals in e1 and ext(c1) is the subset of instances of I that belongs to the term c1, i.e. the set of individuals which have all the attributes of c1.*

The example is represented in Figure 1 where each line is an individual and each column is an attribute. Together with $\mathcal{L}$ and $\mathcal{P}(I)$, int and ext define a Galois connection. We also have G={(c,e) where c belongs to $\mathcal{L}$, and e belongs to $\mathcal{P}(\mathcal{I})$ and are such that e=ext(c) and c=int(e)}. Then (G, $\leq$) is a Galois lattice denoted as a concept lattice.

	t1	t2	t3	a3	a4	a5	a6	a7	a8
i1	1			1	1		1		1
i2	1			1		1	1		
i3		1			1		1		1
i4		1			1		1	1	
i5		1		1			1		1
i6			1	1			1		1
i7			1	1			1		1
i8			1		1		1	1	1

Figure 1. Example 1. $Tab(i, j) = 1$ if the jth attribute belongs to the ith individual.

In concept lattices, a node (c, e) is a concept, c is the *intent* and e is the *extent* of the concept. A characteristic property of Galois lattices is that each node (c, e) is a pair of closed terms, so we have in particular $int(ext(c)) = c$,

and c is the greatest term whose extent is $e = ext(c)$. So the intent c is a representative of the equivalence class of terms whose extent is e. We refer to the corresponding equivalence relation as $\equiv_{\mathcal{L}}$.

Example: In example 1, $ext(\{a4\}) = \{i1, i3, i4\}$, $int(\{i1, i2, i3, i4\}) = \{a4, a6\}$. The term $\{a4, a6\}$ is therefore a closed term as $int(ext(\{a4\})) = \{a4, a6\}$

3 Alpha Galois lattices

In this section we start with the concept lattice $G(\mathcal{L}, ext, \mathcal{P}(I), int)$ as previously examplified. Then we modify *ext* to obtain an equivalence relation $\equiv_{\mathcal{L}}'$ coarser than the original one. This results in larger equivalence classes on $\mathcal{L}$ and therefore in less nodes in the corresponding Galois lattice.

The new *ext* function relies on the association of a predefined type to each individual of I. The corresponding clusters of instances are denoted as *basic classes*. The first idea is then to gather such clusters rather than individuals (see [9]). For instance, let us assume that the attributes $t1, t2, t3$ express the types of the individuals of example 1. These types corresponds to three basic classes $BC1, BC2, BC3$ whose descriptions are the following: BC1={i1,i2}, int(BC1)= {t1,a3,a6}; BC2={i3,i4,i5}, int(BC2)= {t2,a6}; BC3={i6,i7,i8}, int(BC3)= {t3,a3,a6,a8}.

Let us consider the concept lattice built on a new set of individuals: {bc1,bc2,bc3} (let us call them the *prototypes* of their respective basic classes) such that, for any index i, $int(BCi) = int(\{bci\})$. This concept lattice is represented in Figure 2 as a particular case of Alpha Galois lattice, and is much smaller than the original concept lattice (6 *vs* 19 nodes).

Now, by relaxing the constraint that enforces to consider only whole basic classes we define *Alpha Galois lattices*.

Definition 2 (Alpha satisfaction) *Let α belong to [0,100]. Let e=$\{i_1, \ldots, i_n\}$ be a set of individuals and T be a term of $\mathcal{L}$. Then,*

$$e \; \alpha - satisfies \; T \; (e \; sat_\alpha \; T) \; iff \mid ext(T) \cap e \mid \; \geq \frac{|e| \cdot \alpha}{100}$$

We check now whether at least α % of a basic class satisfies a term of $\mathcal{L}$ and add this constraint to *isa*, the membership relation between individuals and terms:

Definition 3 (Alpha membership and Alpha extent) *Let $\mathcal{BC}$ be a partition of the set of individuals I as a set of basic classes. Let us denote as $BCl(i)$ the basic class to which belongs i, and let T be a term of $\mathcal{L}$, then:*

$i \; isa_\alpha \; T$ iff $i \; isa \; T$ and $BCl(i) \; sat_\alpha \; T$
The α-extent of T in I w.r.t. $\mathcal{BC}$ is then:

$ext_\alpha(T) = \{i \in I \mid i \; isa_\alpha \; T\}$

Example. *Let T={a6,a8}, ext(T) = {i1,i3,i5,i6,i7,i8}. BC2*

sat_{60} T since $\mid ext(T) \cap BC2 \mid \geq \frac{\mid BC2 \mid .60}{100}$. So we have $i3$ and $i5$ isa_{60} T. We also have $BC3$ sat_{100} T, as 100 % of $BC3$ belong to the extent of T, and so $BC3$ sat_{60} T. So we have $i6$, $i7$, and $i8$ isa_{60} T and isa_{100} T. As a result, $ext_0(T)= ext(T) = \{i1, i3,i5, i6,i7,i8\}$, $ext_{60}(T)=\{i3,i5,i6,i7,i8\}$ and $ext_{100}(T)= \{i6,i7,i8\}$

We now define the corresponding *Alpha Galois lattices*:

Proposition 1 (Alpha Galois lattices) *Let* $E_\alpha = \{e \in \mathcal{P}(I) \mid \forall i \in e, \mid e \cap BCl(i) \mid \geq \frac{\mid BCl(i) \mid .\alpha}{100}\}$.
Then, int and ext_α *define a Galois connection on* $\mathcal{L}$ *and* E_α *and the corresponding Galois lattice* $G_\alpha= G(\mathcal{L}, ext_\alpha, E_\alpha, int)$ *is called an Alpha Galois lattice.*

When α is equal to 0, $E_\alpha = \mathcal{P}(I)$ and $ext_\alpha = ext$. Therefore, G_0 simply is is the corresponding concept lattice. The extents of the nodes of G_{100} are whole basic classes gathered and here the Alpha Galois lattice is the concept lattice obtained by considering as instances the *prototypes* of the basic classes (Figure 2).

Figure 3 presents the topmost part of G_{60}. Note that *intents* of the nodes of G_{100} are also intents of nodes of G_{60} that in turn are all intents of nodes of the original concept lattice G_0

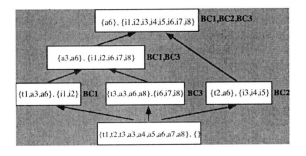

Figure 2. The G_{100} Alpha Galois lattice of example 1

Figure 3. $\alpha = 60$: The topmost part of G_{60} of example 1. New nodes, w.r.t. G_{100} are the lighter ones.

In [3] the authors extend formal concept analysis to more sophisticated languages of terms and use the notion of *projection* as a way to obtain smaller lattices by reducing the language. [9] also introduces *extensional* projections that reduces the concept lattice by modifying the notion of *extent*. It is easy to show that there exists an extensional projection $proj_\alpha$ such that $E_\alpha = proj_\alpha(\mathcal{P}(\mathcal{I}))$ and that then $ext_\alpha=proj_\alpha \circ ext$. Applying a theorem presented in [9] allows then to prove Proposition 1. By changing *ext*, an extensional projection changes a Galois lattice to a smaller one corresponding to larger equivalence classes on $\mathcal{L}$.

An interesting case is the one of the partition $\{I\}$ in which we consider only one basic class, i.e. the case in which all individuals share the same type. The corresponding Alpha Galois lattice is the topmost part of the concept lattice defined by the same language $\mathcal{L}$ and the same set I of individuals. The lattice then only contains nodes whose extents have a size greater than $\frac{\alpha}{100}\mid I \mid$ (plus the bottom node whose extent is empty). This structure has been previously investigated and is denoted as an *Iceberg* (or *frequent*) *Concept lattice* [10, 11] where $\frac{\alpha}{100}$ corresponds to the value of the support threshold *minsupp*.

4 Experiments

The program ALPHA that computes Alpha Galois lattices relies on a straightforward top-down procedure in which nodes are generated as follows: a current node intent c is specialized by adding a new attribute a, then $int° ext_\alpha$ is applied to $c \cup \{a\}$ in order to obtain a closed term; the corresponding node has then to be compared to previous nodes in order to avoid duplicates. We have experimented ALPHA on a real dataset composed of 2274 computer products extracted from the C/Net catalog. Each product is described using a subset of 234 attributes. There are 59 types of products and each product is labelled by one and only one type.

In our first experiment we have built G_{100} using the whole data set (so practically restricted to 59 prototypical instances), Then we smoothly lowered the value of α and recomputed the corresponding G_α lattice. As we can see hereunder the number of nodes (and so the CPU time) exponentially grows from 211 concepts to 107734 as α varies from 100% to 92%. This means that it is here impossible to have a complete view of the data at the level of instances (α=0):

Alpha	100	98	96	94	92
Nodes	211	664	8198	44021	107734

We are first interested in what happens with high values of α. Starting from G_{100}, new nodes appear as α slowly decreases. For instance at $\alpha = 99\%$, a new node appears under the G_{100} node standing for the basic class *Laptop*. The intent of the new node now contains the attribute "network-card". This is due to the fact that most instances of the class *Laptop* do possess a network card. So by relaxing the basic class constraint we get rid of the few, exceptional, instances of *Laptop* found in the catalog and that were hiding this "default" property of *Laptop* in G_{100}. So, by slowly decreasing α from 100 % we have a more accurate view of our data by revealing properties that are relevant to at least some basic class.

A second experiment with 24 basic classes and 1187 objects (some large basic classes are removed thus resulting in a more homogenous class size distribution) shows that the size of Alpha Galois lattices can be really different from the one of frequent lattices:

Alpha Values	100	80	50	30	0
Alpha Nodes	158	842	1493	1900	2202
Frequent Nodes	2	18	18	50	2202

Here as α slowly grows from 0 to small values (say 10%), some instances, which behavior is *exceptional* within their basic class w.r.t. some term t of $\mathcal{L}$, will disappear from the corresponding α-extent. These instances are exceptional as they belong to the extent of the term t whereas very few instances of the same basic class do belong to this extent. As a result some properties that are very unfrequent within some basic class will no more be allowed to discriminate concepts. For example, only few *Laptops* have the property "Digital-Signal-Protocol", and so when $\alpha = 6\%$, nodes which intent contains the "Digital Signal Protocol" property no more include instances of *Laptop* in their extent. As a result terms including" Digital-Signal-Protocol" become equivalent whenever their extent only differed because of Laptop instances, thus resulting on a smaller (and so simpler) lattice.

5 Related work and conclusion

Recent work in Knowledge Representation and Machine Learning investigates Galois connections and lattices based on languages of terms more complex than those used in concept lattices, so modifying the notion of intent of a concept [4, 2, 6, 3]. We have shown here that by restricting the notion of extent of a term with respect to a *a priori* partition of the instance set I, we also modifies the lattice of extents which is no longer $\mathcal{P}(I)$ and we obtain a new family of Galois lattices. As mentioned above Iceberg (or frequent) concept lattices [11, 10] formally are Alpha Galois lattices in which all individuals belong to the same basic class. Besides, the implication rules related to Alpha-Galois lattices simply correspond to inclusion of α-extents and a canonical basis of such $\alpha - implication$ rules can be extracted from the Alpha-Galois lattices in the same way as from frequent concept lattices (the *intents* of the nodes are usually denoted as *closed frequent itemsets*. Association rules are then built using closed frequent itemsets [7, 12]). Note that $\alpha - implication$ rules inherit from the Galois lattice structure interesting properties (as transitivity) unusual when dealing with "approximate" rules.

About construction of Alpha Galois lattices, it should be interesting to adapt efficient algorithms aimed at the construction of concept lattices (e.g. [5]). Now there is another particular set theory view of *a priori* partitioned data referred to as *rough sets* theory ([8]). As the partitioning on rough sets expresses some indiscernibility between individuals of the same basic class, the rough sets view results in some degree of membership of i to an extent e, even if the individual i does not belong to e. At the contrary in the Alpha Galois lattice view, membership of i to an extent e is a prerequisite for α-membership. A fortunate consequence of the latter view is the opportunity to construct Galois lattices.

As a conclusion there is still much work to experiment and to investigate theoretical issues and practical use of Alpha Galois lattices and corresponding α-implication rules. However we do believe that they represent a flexible tool to investigate data and handle exceptions that are relative to a preliminary view of the data.

Acknowledgments Many thanks to Nathalie Pernelle for its valuable contribution to the work presented here, and to Philippe Dague for its patient reading of an earlier draft of this paper.

References

[1] G. Birkhoff. *Lattice Theory*. American Mathematical Society Colloquium Publications, Rhode Island, 1973.

[2] J. Ganascia. Tdis: an algebraic formalization. In *Int. Joint Conf. on Art. Int.*, volume 2, pages 1008–1013, 1993.

[3] B. Ganter and S. O. Kuznetsov. Pattern structures and their projections. *ICCS-01, LNCS*, 2120:129–142, 2001.

[4] B. Ganter and R. Wille. *Formal Concept Analysis: Logical Foundations*. Springer Verlag., 1999.

[5] S. Kuznetsov and S. Obiedkov. Comparing performance of algorithms for generating concept lattices. *J. of Experimental and Theoritical Art. Int.*, 2/3(14):189 216, 2002.

[6] M. Liquiere and J. Sallantin. Structural machine learning with galois lattice and graphs. In *ICML98, Morgan Kaufmann*, 1998.

[7] N. Pasquier, Y. Bastide, R. Taouil, and L. Lakhal. Efficient mining of association rules using closed itemset lattices. *Information Systems*, 24(1):25?46, 1999.

[8] Z. Pawlak. Rough sets, rough relations and rough functions. *Fundamenta Informaticae*, 27(2/3):103–108, 1996.

[9] N. Pernelle, M.-C. Rousset, H. Soldano, and V. Ventos. Zoom: a nested galois lattices-based system for conceptual clustering. *J. of Experimental and Theoretical Artificial Intelligence*, 2/3(14):157–187, 2002.

[10] G. Stumme, R. Taouil, Y. Bastide, N. Pasquier, and L. Lakhal. Computing iceberg concept lattices with titanic. *Data and Knowledge Engineering*, 42(2):189–222, 2002.

[11] K. Waiyamai and L. Lakhal. Knowledge discovery from very large databases using frequent concept lattices. In *11th Eur. Conf. on Machine Learning, ECML'2000*, pages 437–445, 2000.

[12] M. J. Zaki. Generating non-redundant association rules. *Intl. Conf. on Knowledge Discovery and DataMining (KDD 2000)*, 2000.

AGILE: A General Approach to Detect Transitions in Evolving Data Streams

Jiong Yang
Department of EECS
Case Western Reserve University
jiong@eecs.cwru.edu

Wei Wang
Department of Computer Science
University of North Carolina at Chapel Hill
weiwang@cs.unc.edu

Abstract

In many applications such as e-commerce, system diagnosis and telecommunication services, data arrives in streams at a high speed. It is common that the underlying process generating the stream may change over time, either as a result of the fundamental evolution or in response to some external stimulus. Detecting these changes is a very challenging problem of great practical importance. The overall volume of the stream usually far exceeds the available main memory and access to the data stream is typically performed via a linear scan in ascending order of the indices of the records. In this paper, we propose a novel approach, AGILE, to monitor streaming data and to detect distinguishable transitions of the underlying processes. AGILE has many advantages over the traditional Hidden Markov Model, e.g., AGILE only requires one scan of the data.

Keywords: Stream processing, Transition detection, Variable memory Markov model, Emission tree

1 Introduction

Analyzing stream data has drawn increasing interests recently. A data stream is a long ordered sequence of records that do not support efficient random access. Access to the data stream is typically performed via a linear scan in ascending order of the indices of the records. The overall data volume usually far exceeds the available memory. Only a summary of the past data and/or a recently observed portion of the stream may be able to be stored in the memory. This poses an exceptional challenge to many existing data mining techniques that require multiple scans and/or random access of the data. This, in part, makes many previous algorithms assume that (1) the data was generated from a stationary distribution and (2) any portion of the stream can serve as a good representative of the entire stream. These assumptions, in general, do not hold in many of today's applications because the underlying process that generates the stream may change over time, either as a result of the fundamental evolution or in response to some external stimulus. Applying algorithms designed for stationary process to an evolving stream may lead to invalid conclusions.

Our focus in this paper is on detecting transitions of underlying processes of a data stream, which has great importance in many applications, e.g., web page recommendation, intrusion detection, network traffic analysis, etc. Many of these applications build their models upon some statistics (e.g., count, conditional dependency, etc.) of the data assuming a stationary process. Successful transition detection provides an opportunity to apply many existing techniques directly to streaming data without the concern of deriving invalid models. A model is always valid before a transition of the underlying process occurs. The detection of a transition can be regarded as a signal to trigger verification and/or revision of the existing model. We shall show later in the experimental result that our proposed method can successfully support, for example, the maintenance of a decision tree on an evolving stream.

The most common statistical approach to model an evolving sequence is the Hidden Markov Model (HMM). The learning of a Hidden Markov Model involves constructing the structure (e.g., the set of states and their connections) and estimating the parameters (e.g. transition and emission probabilities). In practice, the structure and topology of the HMM and the transition path are often predetermined, and, the memory length is limited to the first order to make the learning process a feasible task, which make the success of HMM vulnerable to erroneous settings. Furthermore, this learning process typically requires multiple scans of the entire sequence before the transition points can be determined, which makes it not practical for monitoring streaming data. Mining massive stream data has been an active topic in recent years. Much work was developed. Due to the space limitations, we omit the related work discussion, interested readers please refer to [5].

In this paper, we devise a novel approach, AGILE, as an alternative to the HMM. AGILE employs the variable memory Markov (VMM) model [2] to represent each underlying process, which has been proven to be very powerful in capturing longer dependencies and higher order statistics [1, 3] and can be learned with a single scan of the sequence. These advantages make the VMM model an ideal choice for modelling each underlying process of the stream. Moreover, with the VMM model on hand, the potential change can be detected easily by checking whether the most recent observations in the stream still *comply with* the current VMM model. One way to perform the compliance check is to estimate the probability of generating the (recently observed portion of the) sequence using the VMM model. If this probability is significantly higher than the probability under a memoryless random process, we may think that the underlying process remains static. Otherwise, it may signal a potential transition of the underlying processes. When the underlying process remains static, the recent observations will be used to perfect the VMM model; while a new VMM model will be built to reflect the current state if the underlying process changes. This new VMM model will be continuously refined until the next transition point. To facilitate the learning and maintenance of each VMM model, a novel variation of suffix tree, **emission tree**, is utilized to organize the emission probabilities. The emission tree is succinct, highly adaptable, and easy to retrieve and update.

559

When monitoring a data stream, AGILE uses a buffer to hold the most recently observed portion of the stream and employs an emission tree to maintain the emission probabilities of the current underlying process, which is continuously enriched as AGILE scans through the stream until a transition is detected. Comparing to the traditional HMM approach, AGILE has many important advantages that are crucial to monitoring high speed data streams. (1) The state path, topology, and complexity of each underlying process do not need to be predetermined and can be automatically learned from the data stream. (2) The transition points can be identified promptly without tracing back the history of the stream. (3) The computational complexity to process each record is linearly proportional to the memory length of the underlying process and all computations are performed in memory.

The remainder of this paper is organized as follows. Section 2 describes the problem definition while the basic algorithm is discussed in Section 3. We present the empirical results in Section 4. Finally, we draw conclusions in Section 5.

2 Problem Definition

We now formalize the problem studied in this paper. A stream is an ordered sequence of records $r_1, r_2, \ldots$. For the sake of brevity, we assume that each record r_i is represented by a symbol in a finite alphabet $\Im = \{s_1, s_2, \ldots, s_n\}$. The stream is assumed to be generated from a number of *distinguishable* (but unknown) stationary stochastic processes with some upperbound on the transition rate. That is, the stream can be viewed as the concatenation of an (unknown) number of continuous fragments, each of which is generated by a single process with an (unknown) duration greater than some (unknown) constant ℓ. The concept of distinguishability is introduced to ensure the stability of each underlying process and to enable reliable discrimination between different processes.

The emission probabilities of a general stationary stochastic process specify the conditional probability distribution of the next record given the preceding segments. The probability of generating a segment $r_1 r_2 \ldots r_l$ from a stochastic process π can be calculated as $P^\pi(r_1 r_2 \ldots r_l) = P^\pi(r_1) \times P^\pi(r_2|r_1) \times \cdots \times P^\pi(r_l|r_1 \ldots r_{l-1})$, where $P^\pi(r_i|r_1 \ldots r_{i-1})$ is the probability of generating r_i right after the segment $r_1 \ldots r_{i-1}$. This probability can be used to infer whether an observed segment was generated from a particular underlying process. If the probability $P^\pi(r_1 r_2 \ldots r_l)$ is considerably higher than the probability $P^r(r_1 r_2 \ldots r_l)$ of generating the same segment from a memoryless random process, we may conclude with fairly high confidence that π is the underlying process. In this case, we also say that the segment $r_1 r_2 \ldots r_l$ *complies* with π.

Definition 2.1 *A segment $r_1 r_2 \ldots r_l$* **complies** *with a stationary stochastic process π iff $\frac{P^\pi(r_1 r_2 \ldots r_l)}{P^r(r_1 r_2 \ldots r_l)} > c$ where $c > 1$ is a constant real number*[1].

Under the variable memory Markov (VMM) model, the conditional probability $P^\pi(r_i|r_1 \ldots r_{i-1})$ is equal to (or can be well approximated by) $P^\pi(r_i|r_{i-j} \ldots r_{i-1})$ where j $(0 < j < i)$ is called the *memory length* of the segment $r_1 \ldots r_{i-1}$. In general, the memory length is short (comparing to the length of the segment) and may vary for different segments. The probability

$P^\pi(r_1 r_2 \ldots r_l)$ becomes $\Pi_{i=1}^l P^\pi(r_i|r_{i-j_i} \ldots r_{i-1})$ where j_i is the memory length of $r_1 \ldots r_{i-1}$. It has been demonstrated [1, 2, 3] that the VMM model is a very powerful model to capture stationary stochastic process.

Two VMM models are said to be **distinguishable** if there exists a segment longer than a certain threshold ℓ such that it complies to only one of these two VMM models. A transition between two VMM models is called a **distinguishable transition** if these two models are distinguishable. Given a stream, our goal is to detect each distinguishable transition of the underlying processes at the earliest possible moment as the stream is parsed.

3 AGILE

In this paper, we propose a novel algorithm, AGILE, to promptly detect the transition of the underlying processes. The emission tree is employed to capture and organize the emission probabilities of each underlying VMM model. The emission tree is similar as the probabilistic tree presented in [4] with one difference. Since the data stream arrives continuously, the emission tree needs to grow with new data. There are two types of nodes in an emission tree. One is the matured nodes where a large amount of evidences are collected so the probability distribution captured in these matured nodes is stable and will not be updated. When new data arrives, the unmatured nodes will be updated to include more evidences for the probability distribution. Figure 2 shows an example of emission tree. Readers may refer to [5] for the detailed description of the emission tree.

3.1 Overview

Figure 1 is the flowchart of major steps taken by AGILE as the data stream is being parsed. At the beginning, a buffer is allocated to track the recently observed portion of the stream and a VMM model is initialized. Since only *mature* node(s) in the emission tree will be used for compliance verification, AGILE first goes through a short *warm-up* stage until the root node matures. In this warm-up stage, every time a new record arrives, it will be put in the buffer and will be used to train the VMM model. Once the root node matures, AGILE proceeds to the *verification and training* stage where, in addition to training the VMM model, the buffered segment will also be used to check for potential transition. Every time a new record arrives, it will be put in the buffer and the most obsolete record will be replaced if the buffer is full. (Records in the buffer are stored in the chronological order.) For example, after the 41st record is read in, the buffer content becomes *babbaabbba* as shown in Figure 2 where the most obsolete record (the 31st record, a, in the example) is discarded. The buffered stream is then examined to see whether it still complies with the current VMM model. If so, it will be used to further train the current VMM model. Otherwise, the conflict may signal a transition of the underlying process. The buffer is purged by removing previous records that show compliance to the obsolete VMM model. A new VMM model is then initiated based on the remaining records in the buffer. AGILE will then enters the warm-up stage again.

---

[1]In theory, c can be any real number greater than 1. We choose c to be 2 in this paper. A study on the optimal range of c is in Section 5.2.2.

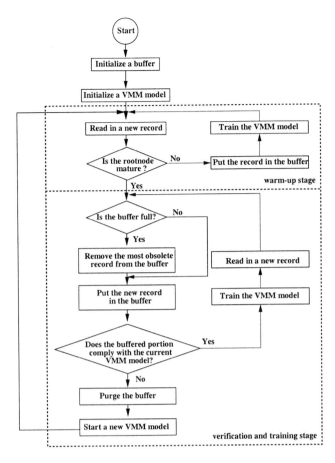

Figure 1. The Flowchart of AGILE

3.2 Compliance Verification

Without loss of generality, let's assume that the buffer size is much larger than the memory length of the underlying process of the stream and the buffer currently holds records $r_1 \ldots r_l$. By definition, the compliance of $r_1 \ldots r_l$ with the current VMM model, say π, is

$$\frac{P^\pi(r_1 \ldots r_l)}{P^r(r_1 \ldots r_l)} = \frac{\Pi_{i=1}^l P^\pi(r_i | r_{i-j_i} \ldots r_{i-1})}{P^r(r_1 \ldots r_l)}$$

where j_i $(1 \le j_i < i)$ is the memory length of the segment $r_1 \ldots r_{i-1}$ in the VMM model π, for $i = 1, \ldots, l$. In fact, $r_{i-j_i} \ldots r_{i-1}$ should be the longest suffix of $r_1 \ldots r_{i-1}$ which labels a mature node in the emission tree. This node can be located by, starting from the root of the emission tree, traversing along the path $root \rightsquigarrow r_{i-1} \rightsquigarrow r_{i-2} \rightsquigarrow \cdots \rightsquigarrow r_1$ to the furthest mature node. The emission probability of r_i in the emission probability table at this node is the value of $P^\pi(r_i | r_{i-j_i} \ldots r_{i-1})$.

The computational complexity is $O(l \times \min\{l, h\})$ where l and h are the buffer size and the memory length of the VMM model (i.e., the height of the emission tree), respectively.

3.3 Purging the Buffer

Once a transition is detected, the buffer needs to be purged to ensure that records generated by the previous underlying process will not interfere the learning of the new model. All records except the most recent record are discarded.

3.4 Initializing a VMM model

This step is invoked in one of the two following conditions: when we start to monitor a new stream and when a transition of the underlying process is detected. Before any information is injected, the initial status of a VMM model is represented by a degenerate emission tree with a single root node. In the case when a new stream starts to be monitored, the user may also choose to construct an emission tree to reflect the *a priori* knowledge of the emission probabilities as an alternative initial VMM model.

3.5 Training the VMM Model

Again, let's assume that the buffer holds records $r_1 \ldots r_l$ where r_l is the most recently observed symbol. We need to update the information related to r_l at the following nodes: the root, node r_{l-1}, node $r_{l-2}r_{l-1}$, ..., and node $r_{l-j} \ldots r_{l-1}$, where j is the memory length of $r_1 \ldots r_{l-1}$. These nodes all locate on a single path, referred to as the **updating path**, in the emission tree and can be accessed by traversing down along the branch $root \rightsquigarrow r_{l-1} \rightsquigarrow r_{l-2} \rightsquigarrow \cdots \rightsquigarrow r_{l-j}$. For each node $r_{l-k} \ldots r_{l-2}r_{l-1}$ $(k = 1, 2, \ldots, j)$, the counter $N(r_{l-k} \ldots r_{l-2}r_{l-1}r_l)$ is incremented by 1 and the emission probability entries (if immature) are also updated accordingly.

$$N_{new}(r_{l-k} \ldots r_{l-2}r_{l-1}r_l) = N_{old}(r_{l-k} \ldots r_{l-2}r_{l-1}r_l) + 1$$

$$P_{new}(r_l | r_{l-k} \ldots r_{l-2}r_{l-1}) = P_{old}(r_l | r_{l-k} \ldots r_{l-2}r_{l-1})$$
$$\times \frac{N_{new}(r_{l-k} \ldots r_{l-2}r_{l-1}r_l)}{N_{new}(r_{l-k} \ldots r_{l-2}r_{l-1}r_l) - 1}$$

$$\forall y \ne r_l \quad N_{new}(r_{l-k} \ldots r_{l-2}r_{l-1}y) = N_{old}(r_{l-k} \ldots r_{l-2}r_{l-1}y)$$

$$P_{new}(y | r_{l-k} \ldots r_{l-2}r_{l-1}) =$$
$$\frac{N_{new}(r_{l-k} \ldots r_{l-2}r_{l-1}y) \times P_{old}(y | r_{l-k} \ldots r_{l-2}r_{l-1})}{N_{new}(r_{l-k} \ldots r_{l-2}r_{l-1}y) + P_{old}(y | r_{l-k} \ldots r_{l-2}r_{l-1})}$$

If the updated value of $N(r_{l-k} \ldots r_{l-2}r_{l-1}r_l)$ is equal to α (i.e., the segment $r_{l-k} \ldots r_{l-2} \ r_{l-1}r_l$ just becomes significant), then a new node $r_{l-k} \ldots r_{l-2}r_{l-1}r_l$ needs to be initiated (to monitor the emission probabilities given $r_{l-k} \ldots r_{l-2} \ r_{l-1}r_l$ as the preceding segment). Assume that there is still space available in main memory[2]. This new node is inserted as a child of node $r_{l-k+1} \ldots r_{l-2}r_{l-1}r_l$ in the emission tree, which may reside on a different branch other than the one we just visited. The parent node of the new node can be located by traversing along the updating path $root \rightsquigarrow r_l \rightsquigarrow r_{l-1} \rightsquigarrow \cdots \rightsquigarrow r_{l-k+1}$ to reach the furthest node.

Due to space limitations, we do not present the formal proof of correctness and several additional improvements on the basic algorithm of AGILE. Interested readers please refer to [5].

---

[2]If the main memory is full, AGILE needs to adjust the significance threshold α. This scenario is investigated in [5].

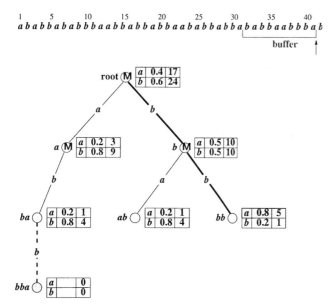

```
 1    5    10    15    20    25    30    35    40
a b a b b a b a b b b a a b b a b b a b b a a b a b b a b b a b a b b a a b b b a b
                                              └─────────────────┘
                                                   buffer ↑
```

Figure 2. The Emission Tree After Examining the 41st Record

4 Experimental Results

We implement the AGILE algorithm in C. The experiments are performed on a SUN Ultra-Sparc 10 workstation with 1GB main memory and a 500 MHz CPU. In all tests, the initial significance threshold α is set to 25.

We experimented the AGILE system on both real and synthetic data sets. Due to the space limitations, we only show the results on the real data set here. Interested readers please refer to [5] for more detailed empirical results. The real data stream is constructed from a web page access log of an online merchant[3]. This trace log consists of the merchandize web pages that were accessed by users between March 15, 2003 to July 31, 2003. Each user is identified by the IP address. A user session is a list of web pages that accessed by a single user (IP address) within a certain time period, e.g., 1 hour. A stream is generated by concatenating all sessions in chronological order of their starting time, separated by a special symbol, $. There are over 20 million sessions in the trace and the overall length of the stream is over 400 million merchandize visits. The overall distinct number of merchandizes is 1678. When constructing the emission tree and verifying the compliance of the VMM model, we do not consider any segments that cross the session boundary. This is achieved by purging the buffer every time $ is reached. Roughly 500MB space is used to store the emission tree.

Three transitions are detected by AGILE. One transition corresponds to a major renovation of the web site, e.g., merchandize re-categorization. The second transition is due to a major revision of recommendation list for each merchandize when it is browsed by a user. We can observe that the recommendation system influences the user's browsing behavior significantly. The last transition reported by AGILE does not correspond to any important "mechanical" change of the web site. After further investigation, we found that the transition is a

consequence of some recommendation list becoming obsolete when the NBA season ends. The probability that a user would follow a NBA-related recommendation declines dramatically after the NBA season is over. It is interesting to know that the merchant was not aware of this transition before AGILE detects it. From this test, we can see that AGILE can be very useful to detect unknown yet important changes in a stream. Last but not least, it takes less than 4ms to process each symbol on average.

To further demonstrate the usefulness of AGILE, we compare three alternative methods of online classification based on the web access trace. The objective is to build a decision tree to predict user's purchasing behavior in the immediate future. (1) The decision tree is rebuilt once a month. (2) A sliding window is employed and the decision tree is (partially) rebuilt after every session. (3) AGILE is employed and the decision tree is rebuilt once a transition is detected be AGILE. We found that the third method can produce equally good result[4] as the second method during the entire course of the trace. This suggests that AGILE is powerful to capture every transition that may result in a different decision tree. Further, AGILE can successfully avoid the expensive computation required by the second method. In our experiment, AGILE manages to save more than 70% of the computational cost consumed by the second method. Even though the first method requires less computational effort than the second method, it fails to respond to the transition promptly.

5 Conclusions and Future Work

In this paper, we develop a framework, AGILE, for online detection of changes of streaming data in the form of transitions of the underlying processes. The variable memory Markov model is used to characterize each stationary underlying process and is represented via a compact data structure — emission tree. The potential transition can be promptly detected by checking whether the recently observed records still well comply with the current emission tree. It has been shown that AGILE is very effective and efficient in terms of high accuracy and low storage requirement and computation cost. AGILE guarantees to report any distinguishable transition with an incubation period no longer than ℓ.

References

[1] G. Bejerano and G. Yona. Modeling protein families using probabilistic suffix trees. *Proc. of ACM RECOMB*, pp. 15-24, 1999.

[2] D. Ron, Y. Singer, N. Tishby. The power of amnesia: learning probabilistic automata with variable memory length. *Machine Learning*, vol. 25, no. 2-3, pp. 117-149, 1996.

[3] Y. Seldin, G. Bejerano, and N. Tishby. Unsupervised sequence segmentation by a mixture of switch variable memory Markov sources. *Proc. of ICML*, 2001.

[4] J. Yang and W. Wang. CLUSEQ: efficient and effective sequence clustering. Proceedings of the 19th IEEE International Conference on Data Engineering (ICDE), 2003.

[5] J. Yang and W. Wang. A general approach to detect transitions in in evolving data streams. *UNC Technical Report TR03-023*, 2003.

---

[3]Due to confidential agreement, we are not able to disclose the identity of the web site.

---

[4]The quality of the result is assessed by the accuracy of the classification model.

Scalable Construction of Topic Directory with Nonparametric Closed Termset Mining

Hwanjo Yu, Duane Searsmith, Xiaolei Li, Jiawei Han
Department of Computer Science
University of Illinois at Urbana-Champaign
Urbana, IL 61801
hwanjoyu@uiuc.edu, dsears@ncsa.uiuc.edu, xli10@uiuc.edu, hanj@cs.uiuc.edu

ABSTRACT

A topic directory, *e.g.*, Yahoo directory, provides a view of a document set at different levels of abstraction and is ideal for the interactive exploration and visualization of the document set. We present a method that dynamically generates a topic directory from a document set using a frequent closed termset mining algorithm. Our method shows experimental results of equal quality to recent document clustering methods and has additional benefits such as automatic generation of topic labels and determination of a clustering parameter.

Keywords

topic directory, document clustering, hierarchical clustering

1. INTRODUCTION

A topic directory is a hierarchical document tree or graph structure in which each node has a *topic label* (or a cluster description) and corresponding *documents*. The topic of a higher node conceptually covers its children nodes. For a *static* topic directory, *e.g.*, Yahoo Web directory, the taxonomy is static and manually constructed by the domain experts, and documents are classified into the taxonomy by (non-)automatic classifiers. Such static directories are usually used for organizing and searching targeted documents. On the other hand, *dynamic* topic directories are constructed automatically given a fixed document set or a temporal interest across document sets, *e.g.*, browsing the main news of year 2000 from the AP news data. The directory and topic labels are constructed dynamically (*i.e.*, no preset taxonomy) based on the contents of the document set.

Construction of a dynamic topic directory requires the techniques of *hierarchical document soft-clustering* and *cluster summarization* for constructing topic labels. Recent studies in document clustering show that UPGMA [4] and bisecting k-means [7, 3] are the most accurate algorithms in the categories of agglomerative and partitioning clustering algorithms respectively and outperform other recent hierarchical clustering methods in terms of the clustering quality [7, 4, 3]. However, such clustering methods (1) do not provide cluster descriptions, (2) are not scalable to large document sets (for UPGMA), (3) require the user to decide the number of clusters a priori which is usually unknown in real applications, and (4) focus on hard-clustering (whereas in the real world a document could belong to multiple categories).

Another recent approach is to use frequent itemset mining to construct clusters with corresponding topic labels [2, 5]. This approach first run a frequent itemset mining algorithm, *e.g.*, Apriori [1], to mine frequent termsets from a document set. (An itemset corresponds to a termset, *i.e.*, a set of terms, in this case.) Then they cluster documents based on only the low-dimensional frequent termsets. Each frequent termset serves as the topic label of a cluster. The corresponding cluster consists of the set of documents containing the termset. This method indeed turns out to be as accurate as the other leading document clustering algorithms (*e.g.*, bisecting k-means and UPGMA) in terms of clustering quality [5], and is more efficient since it substantially reduces the dimensions when constructing clusters.

However, this approach introduces another critical issue – *determination of the support threshold*. Since clusters are constructed by frequent termsets and cluster size is the support of termset, the number of clusters (*i.e.*, previously a user parameter) is now determined by the support threshold (*i.e.*, a new user parameter). The support threshold affects the entire cluster processing in terms of the quality and scalability: An over-set threshold could delay the mining time exponentially and also generate too many frequent terms. An under-set threshold could generate a too abstract directory to cover every document in the set. The seemingly best way to adjust the support threshold is to run the mining algorithm multiple times with different support thresholds from small to large, and probe the information about the abstraction level of the directory or the *cluster coverage, i.e., what portion of documents is covered by the clusters*. However, then we would end up losing the benefit of using mining algorithm for document clustering. The entire clustering process becomes unscalable and need tedious manual optimization.

We propose a *nonparametric closed* termset mining method for efficient topic directory construction, which (1) adjusts the support threshold before running the mining algorithm by introducing an FT-tree (See Section 2.1), and (2) run the most efficient frequent closed termset mining algorithm – CLOSET+ [8]. While the previous clustering methods [5, 2] use all the frequent termsets to construct hierarchical clusters, only *closed* termsets are meaningful in hierarchical clustering (discussed in Section *2.1.3*). We finally present an efficient way to build the soft-clusters from the initial clusters. Soft-clustering is necessary for many applications because a document can belong to multiple clusters. Empirically, our method shows clustering quality as high as most recent document clustering methods but is more efficient. It also naturally produces topic labels for the clusters using frequent closed termsets.

2. SCALABLE CONSTRUCTION OF TOPIC DIRECTORY WITH NONPARAMETRIC CLOSED TERMSET MINING

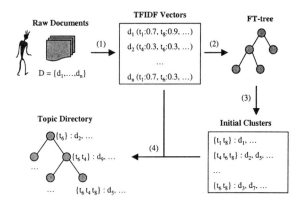

Figure 1: Framework

Every text clustering method preprocesses documents in several steps, such as removing stopwords (*i.e.*, "I", "am", "and") and word-stemming (*i.e.*, merging the same words of different forms like "term" and "terms"). After we preprocess the raw documents (Step (1) in Figure 2), each document can be represented as a vector of the weighted term frequencies, i.e., *term frequency × inverse document frequency (TFIDF)*, which the information retrieval community calls a *vector space model*. Our algorithm applies TFIDF. However, in our running examples, we will simply use TF for better understanding.

Starting from this vector space model, we construct FT-tree to mine closed termsets and then construct the initial clusters (Step (2)). Note that termsets are found based on word presence not on the TFIDF. After that, we construct the initial clusters from the FT-tree (Step (3)), which can be done without scanning the TFIDF vectors. The initial clusters are a list of a frequent closed termset with the documents that contain the termset. So, the documents are duplicated in multiple clusters within the initial clusters. When we construct the final topic directory with maximally *max_dup* number of document duplications (Step (4)), we use the original TFIDF vectors to trim the duplication from the initial clusters.

2.1 Nonparametric Closed Termset Mining for Document Clustering

2.1.1 FT-tree Construction

The *FP-tree* published in [6] is a prefix tree with sorted items in which each node contains an item and the support of the itemset from root to path. The FP-tree has proven to be an efficient structure for mining frequent (closed) itemsets [8]. The *FT-tree* is similar to the FP-tree except that the FT-tree includes document IDs in addition. For instance, Figure 2(a) shows the FT-tree constructed from document set D of the table in Fig. 2. The FT-tree can be defined as the FP-tree including document ID at the last node of the corresponding path. Constructing a FT-tree is also similar to constructing a FP-tree except that when we insert a termset representing a document (i.e., a pattern in the FP-tree) into the tree, we insert the document ID at the last node. Note that each document ID will show only once the FT-tree because each document or termset is represented by only one path in the FT-tree, so multiple paths cannot have the same document ID.

2.1.2 Probing Support Threshold

How can we efficiently identify the maximal sup_thr without running a mining algorithm, such that the clusters (i.e., the mined termsets) generated from the sup_thr cover every document in the document set (or cluster coverage = 1.0*)?* To illustrate, consider the FT-tree of Figure 2(a) that is constructed from the table in Fig. 2. We start pruning the tree from the bottom. (Since a FT-tree is a prefix tree with sorted items, as is a FP-tree, the lower nodes contain the items of lower supports.) The item f of *support* = 2, i.e., the two nodes of thick lines in Figure 2(a), will be pruned first. If the pruned nodes contain any document IDs, we pass the IDs to their parents nodes. Thus, the FT-tree after pruning f becomes the tree of Figure 2(b). As you see, the parent nodes a and b now in Figure 2(b) contain the IDs d_1 and d_4 respectively. This means that after we prune a term f, documents d_1 and d_4 – previously covered by termsets $\{e, b, a, f\}$ and $\{b, f\}$ respectively – are now covered by termsets $\{e, b, a\}$ and $\{b\}$. Next, we prune the term a of *support* = 3, i.e., the three nodes of thick lines in Figure 2(b). Then, the tree of Figure 2(b) becomes the tree of Figure 2(c). In other words, documents d_1, d_5 and d_2 – previously covered by termsets $\{e, b, a\}$, $\{e, c, d, a\}$ and $\{c, d, a\}$ respectively – are now covered by termsets $\{e, b\}$, $\{e, c, d\}$ and $\{c, d\}$. When we start pruning the terms b and d of the next higher *support* = 4, i.e., the four nodes of thick lines in Figure 2(c), we find that d_4 will not be covered by any node since its parent is *Null*. Thus, we stop the pruning procedure here, and the maximal *sup_thr* that covers every document is 4.

Note that we can compute this maximal *sup_thr* without actually pruning the tree but not by searching over the tree from the bottom to find the first node whose parent is *Null*. However, showing the "flow" of document IDs in the tree as *sup_thr* increases helps users understand the relations among the *sup_thr*, the covered documents, and the length of the termset that covers the documents. In addition to the shown example, there are certain subtleties. For instance, suppose that a document set contains very few "outlier" documents that do not share any terms with other documents in the set, then the maximal *sup_thr* becomes very low for mined termsets to cover such outlier documents. In such cases, the document coverage information of Table *2.1.2* becomes very useful in determining the proper *sup_thr*. Col-

ID	termset	ordered
d_1	a, b, e, f	e, b, a, f
d_2	a, c, d	c, d, a
d_3	e	e
d_4	b, f	b, f
d_5	a, c, d, e	e, c, d, a
d_6	c, d	c, d
d_7	c, d	c, d
d_8	c, e	e, c
d_9	b, e	e, b
d_{10}	b, e	e, b

Document set D

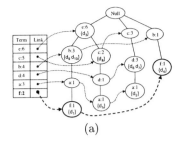

(a)

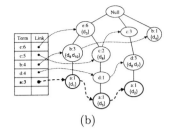

(b)

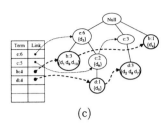

(c)

Figure 2: Determining Support

sup	Cov	Not Covered Doc.
4	1.0	
5	0.9	d_4
6	0.6	d_2 d_6 d_7
7	0.0	d_1 d_3 d_5 d_8 d_9 d_{10}

Table 1: Coverage table

Cluster	Doc. IDs
$< e >$	$\{d_1 d_3 d_5 d_8 d_9 d_{10}\}$
$< c >$	$\{d_2 d_5 d_6 d_7 d_8\}$
$< b >$	$\{d_1 d_4 d_9 d_{10}\}$
$< cd >$	$\{d_2 d_5 d_6 d_7\}$

Table 2: Initial clusters

umn "Coverage" in the table denotes the portion of documents that is covered by the corresponding *sup_thr*. Column "Not Covered Doc. IDs" denotes the actual document IDs that are not covered by the *sup_thr*. This coverage table can be efficiently generated from the FT-tree before mining frequent terms.

2.1.3 Mining Closed Termsets from FT-tree

As noted in [8], mining frequent *closed* termsets can lead to orders of magnitude smaller result termsets than mining frequent termsets while retaining the completeness, i.e., from the concise result set, it is straightforward to generate all the frequent termsets with accurate support counts. Closed termsets are meaningful for constructing a topic directory since non-closed termsets are always covered by closed sets.

Since FT-tree subsumes FP-tree, we can simply apply the most recent closed itemset mining algorithm CLOSET+ [8] on an FT-tree. Running CLOSET+ on the FT-tree of Figure 2(c) with *sup_thr* = 4 generates closed termsets: $< e >$, $< c >$, $< b >$, $< cd >$.

2.2 Constructing Initial Clusters

For each frequent closed termset, we construct an initial cluster to contain all the documents that contain the itemset. Initial clusters are not disjoint because one document may contain several termsets. We will restrain the maximal number of duplications of each document in the clusters in Section 2.3. The termset of each cluster is the *cluster label* – identity of each cluster. Cluster labels also specify the set-containment relationship of the hierarchical structure in topic directory.

Using FT-tree, we do not need to scan the documents to construct the initial clusters while the previous methods [5] do. Document IDs are included in a FT-tree. To retrieve all the documents containing a closed termset, we need to find all the paths containing the termset; the document IDs below the paths are all the documents containing the termset. Figure 2.2 describes the method and rationale for retrieving the document IDs for each closed termset to construct initial clusters. Table *2.1.2* shows the initial clusters constructed from the FT-tree of our running example (Figure 2(c)).

2.3 Topic Directory Construction

- Input: frequent closed termsets
- Output: initial clusters (pairs of termset and document IDs)

Method:
- for each closed termset T
  - for each node t in the sidelink of the last term of T from the header table
    * if the path from the root to t contains the termset T, assign to the termset with the document IDs in and below t

Figure 3: Constructing initial clusters from FT-tree

After initial clusters are constructed, Step (4) builds a topic directory from the initial clusters and the TFIDF vectors. Before building the topic directory, we prune the directory by (1) removing "inner termsets" (Section *2.3.1*) and (2) constraining the maximal number of document duplication (Section *2.3.2*). After that, a topic directory is constructed (Section *2.3.3*) and the first level nodes are finally merged (Section *2.3.4*).

2.3.1 Removing Inner Termsets

Doc	Cluster Labels
d_1	$< e >, < b >$
d_2	$(< c >), < cd >$
d_3	$< e >$
d_4	$< b >$
d_5	$< e >, (< c >), < cd >$
d_6	$(< c >), < cd >$
d_7	$(< c >), < cd >$
d_8	$< e >, < c >$
d_9	$< e >, < b >$
d_{10}	$< e >, < b >$

Table 3: Clusters for each document. termsets within parentheses are inner termsets

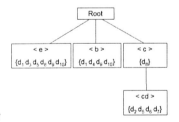

Table 4: Topic directory

If multiple nodes in the same path in a directory contain the same documents, to minimize the document redundancy, we only leave the one in the lowest node and remove the others. This is done by removing "inner termsets" – among frequent closed termsets, the termsets whose superset exists in the same document, e.g., in Table *2.3.1*, termset $< c >$ in document d_2 is an *inner termset* as its superset $< cd >$ also exists in d_2. Removing inner termsets will not cause an empty node in the directory and will not affect the clustering quality.

2.3.2 Constraining Document Duplication

We allow the user to set the maximal number of duplication max_dup of each document in the directory. By allowing the directory to be a graph and $max\_dup \geq 1$, our method naturally supports soft clustering, which is necessary for many applications (*e.g.*, Yahoo directory) because a document can belong to multiple clusters. We refer to the original TFIDF vectors to exclude inferior nodes for each document by applying a heuristic score function such as $score(d, T) = \sum_{t \in T} d \times t$ where $d \times t$ denotes the vector of term t in document d.

2.3.3 Constructing Topic Directory

Constructing a topic directory from the document-cluster list, e.g., Table *2.3.1* with $max\_dup = 2$, can be done in a top-down way.

- Input: nodes (termsets), document-cluster list
- Output: topic directory

Main:

- for m = 1 to maximal length of nodes
  - for node of length = m
    - * link(node, m)
- connect document IDs to corresponding nodes using the document-cluster list

link(node, m):

- if $m = 0$, then link node to root, else:
  - if there exist inner nodes of length $m - 1$, then link the node to them as a child, else link(node, m-1)

Figure 4: Constructing topic directory

We start building a directory from the root: link the nodes of length one at the first level, and link the nodes of larger length to their inner nodes as children nodes. Figure *2.3.3* describes the method of constructing a topic directory. The topic directory from Table *2.3.1*, i.e., $max\_dup = 2$, is shown in Figure *2.3.1*.

2.3.4 Merging the First Level Nodes

Common mining algorithms usually generate a large number of frequent termsets of length one. Thus, a clustering method based on frequent termset mining tends to generate a lot of first level nodes, in which merging the first level nodes helps to provide users with more comprehensible interface. We merge the nodes of high similarity by creating a higher level node between the root and the similar nodes until the total number of the first level nodes becomes less than or equal to a user-specified number. We use a heuristic similarity function as follows:

$$sim(n_1, n_2) = \frac{\# \ of \ common \ documents \ in \ n1 \ and \ n2}{\# \ of \ documents \ in \ n1 \ and \ n2}$$

3. EXPERIMENT

We compare our method with other recent document clustering methods – agglomerative UPGMA [4], bisecting k-means [7, 3], and those using frequent itemset mining –

FIHC [5], HFTC [2]. We used the same evaluation method and the same datasets as used in [5] except that, for Reuters, we do not exclude the articles assigned to multiple categories. Due to space limitations, we report the main results and leave the details to a technical report.

3.0.5 Performance comparison

Dataset	# of clus	TDC	FIHC	Bi k-means	UPGMA
Hitech	3	**0.57**	0.45	0.54	0.33
	15	**0.52**	0.42	0.44	0.33
	30	**0.48**	0.41	0.29	0.47
	60	**0.44**	0.41	0.21	0.40
	Ave.	**0.50**	0.42	0.37	0.38
ReO	3	**0.57**	0.53	0.34	0.36
	15	**0.51**	0.45	0.38	0.47
	30	**0.47**	0.43	0.38	0.42
	60	**0.41**	0.38	0.28	0.34
	Ave.	**0.49**	0.45	0.34	0.40
Wap	3	**0.47**	0.40	0.40	0.39
	15	0.45	0.56	**0.57**	0.49
	30	0.43	0.57	0.44	**0.58**
	60	0.41	0.55	0.37	**0.59**
	Ave.	0.44	0.52	0.45	**0.51**
Classic4	3	0.61	**0.62**	0.59	×
	15	**0.53**	0.52	0.46	×
	30	0.48	**0.52**	0.43	×
	60	0.41	**0.51**	0.27	×
	Ave.	0.50	**0.54**	0.44	×
Reuters	3	**0.46**	0.37	0.40	×
	15	**0.45**	0.40	0.34	×
	30	**0.42**	0.40	0.31	×
	60	**0.40**	0.39	0.26	×
	Ave.	**0.43**	0.39	0.33	×

Table 5: F-measure comparison. # of clus: # of clusters; ×: not scalable to run

Table *3.0.5* shows the overall performance of the four methods on the five data sets. TDC outperforms the other methods on data sets *Hitech*, *ReO*, and *Reuters*, and shows similar performance to FIHC for others. Table *3.0.5* shows the sup_thr of $coverage = 1.0$ determined for each data set.

	Hitech	ReO	Wap	Classic4	Reuters
sup_thr	363/2301	138/1504	333/1560	70/7094	174/10802

Table 6: sup_thr of $coverage = 1.0$ # of total document in each data set is within the parentheses.

4. REFERENCES

[1] R. Agrawal and R. Srikant. Fast algorithms for mining association rules. In *Proc. Int. Conf. Very Large Databases (VLDB'94)*, pages 487–499, 1994.

[2] F. Beil, M. Ester, and X. Xu. Frequent term-based text clustering. In *Proc. ACM SIGKDD Int. Conf. Knowledge Discovery and Data Mining (KDD'02)*, pages 436–442, 2002.

[3] D. R. Cutting, D. R. Karger, J. O. Pedersen, and J. W. Tukey. Scatter/gather: A cluster-based approach to browsing large document collections. In *Proc. ACM SIGIR Int. Conf. Information Retrieval (SIGIR'92)*, pages 318–329, 1992.

[4] R. C. Dubes and A. K. Jain, editors. *Algorithms for clustering data*. Prentice Hall, 1998.

[5] B. C. M. Fung, K. Wang, and M. Ester. Herarchical document clustering using frequent itemsets. In *SIAM Int. Conf. Data Mining*, 2003.

[6] J. Han, J. Pei, and Y. Yin. Mining frequent patterns without candidate generations. In *Proc. ACM SIGMOD Int. Conf. Management of Data (SIGMOD'00)*, 2000.

[7] M. Steinbach, G. Karypis, and V. Kumar. A comparison of document clustering techiniques. In *KDD Workshop on Text Mining*, 2000.

[8] J. Wang, J. Han, and J. Pei. CLOSET+: Searching for the best strategies for mining frequent closed itemsets. In *Proc. ACM SIGKDD Int. Conf. Knowledge Discovery and Data Mining (KDD'03)*, pages 236–245, 2003.

Learning Weighted Naive Bayes with Accurate Ranking

Harry Zhang
Faculty of Computer Science
University of New Brunswick
Fredericton, NB, Canada E3B 5A3
hzhang@unb.ca

Shengli Sheng
Department of Computer Science
University of Western Ontario
London, Ontario, Canada N6A 5B7
ssheng@uwo.ca

Abstract

Naive Bayes is one of most effective classification algorithms. In many applications, however, a ranking of examples are more desirable than just classification. How to extend naive Bayes to improve its ranking performance is an interesting and useful question in practice. Weighted naive Bayes is an extension of naive Bayes, in which attributes have different weights. This paper investigates how to learn a weighted naive Bayes with accurate ranking from data, or more precisely, how to learn the weights of a weighted naive Bayes to produce accurate ranking. We explore various methods: the gain ratio method, the hill climbing method, and the Markov Chain Monte Carlo method, the hill climbing method combined with the gain ratio method, and the Markov Chain Monte Carlo method combined with the gain ratio method. Our experiments show that a weighted naive Bayes trained to produce accurate ranking outperforms naive Bayes.

1 Introduction

Naive Bayesian Classifier, or simply naive Bayes, is one of the most effective and efficient classification algorithms. In classification, a classifier, which assigns a class label to an example, is built from a set of training examples with class labels. Assume that A_1, A_2, $\cdots$, A_n are n attributes. An example E is represented by a vector $(a_1, a_2, \cdots, a_n)$, where a_i is the value of A_i. Let C represent the class variable that corresponds to the class, and c represent the value that C takes. In naive Bayes, all attributes are assumed independent given the value of the class variable (conditional independence assumption):

$$p(a_1, a_2, \cdots, a_n|c) = \prod_{i=1}^{n} p(a_i|c).$$

An example E is classified to the class with the maximum posterior probability. More precise, the classification on E given by naive Bayes, denoted by $V_{nb}(E)$, is defined as below:

$$V_{nb}(E) = \arg\max_{c} p(c) \prod_{i=1}^{n} p(a_i|c). \quad (1)$$

Since the conditional independence assumption is rarely true in reality, it is natural to extend naive Bayes to relax the conditional independence assumption. There are two major ways to do it: (1) The structure of naive Bayes is extended to represent explicitly the dependences among attributes, and the resulting model is called augmented naive Bayes (ANB) [3]. (2)Attributes are weighted differently, and the resulting model is called weighted naive Bayes (WNB). A WNB is formally defined as below.

$$V_{wnb}(E) = \arg\max_{c} p(c) \prod_{i=1}^{n} p(a_i|c)^{w_i}, \quad (2)$$

where $V_{wnb}(E)$ denotes the classification give by the WNB, and w_i is the weight of attribute A_i.

In recent years, AUC has been noticed by machine learning and data mining community, and some researchers believe [4] that AUC is a more discriminant evaluation method than error rate for learning algorithms that also produce class probability estimates. Since naive Bayes performances well in terms of accuracy [1], a natural question is: What is the performance of naive Bayes, in terms of ranking, or AUC? Can we improve its AUC by using some sort of extended naive Bayes, such as WNBs?

The remainder of this paper is organized as follows: In Section 2, we present several algorithms for learning a WNB with high AUC. We implemented these learning algorithms and the related experimental results are presented in Section 3.

2 Learning Weighted Naive Bayes with High AUC

As we discussed in Section 1, a WNB is an extension of naive Bayes in which attributes are assigned different weights. How to learn the weight vector in a WNB is the key in learning a WNB. In this section, we investigate various methods for learning the weight vector in a WNB.

2.1 Gain Ratio

Gain ratio was originally used to choose an attribute that classifies best among a set of attributes in the decision tree algorithm [7]. We argue that an attribute of higher gain ratio deserves higher weight in a WNB. Thus, we propose a gain ratio based method that calculate the weight of an attribute from a dataset as follows:

$$w_i = \frac{GainRatio(Tr, A_i) \times n}{\sum_{i=1}^{n} GainRatio(Tr, A_i)}, \qquad (3)$$

where n is the number of attributes, and Tr is the dataset. The gain ratio of attribute A_i is defined as [7].
The WNB based on gain ratio is denoted by WNB-G.

2.2 Hill Climbing

This method has been widely used in many areas. In a WNB, the weight w_i of attribute A_i is found by a search process consisting of a sequence of steps. In each step, the weight is revised to achieve higher AUC, according to the rule below:

$$w_i(n) \leftarrow w_i(n-1) + \Delta w(n), \qquad (4)$$

where $w_i(n)$ and $w_i(n-1)$ are the weights at step n and step $n-1$ respectively, and $\Delta w(n)$ is the weight update performed at step n. In our implementation, $\Delta w(n)$ is defined as follows:

$$\Delta w(n) = \eta O(auc)(1 - O(auc))^2, \qquad (5)$$

where η is the learning rate, auc is the current value of AUC, and $O(auc)$ is defined as:

$$O(auc) = \frac{1}{1 + e^{-auc}}.$$

The initial weight of an attribute is assigned to 1. We adjust the weight of each attribute separately. For each attribute A_i, the weight w_i is repeatedly revised until the increase between the current AUC and the previous AUC is less than a small value ϵ.
The WNB based on hill climbing is denoted by WNB-HC.

2.3 Markov Chain Monte Carlo

The weights vector of a WNB can be also learned through a random walk. First, we initialize the weight vector as $< 1, 1, \cdots, 1 >$. Then we revise the weights by randomly choosing adding or subtracting a constant value Δw or unchanging it in each step. More precisely, we randomly choose one from the three equations below:

$$w_i(n) \leftarrow w_i(n-1) + \Delta w,$$
$$w_i(n) \leftarrow w_i(n-1) - \Delta w,$$
$$w_i(n) \leftarrow w_i(n-1).$$

The constant value Δw can be adjusted manually until it achieves the best performance in AUC in most datasets. In experiments, we find an appropriate Δw value manually for each dataset.

Like the hill climbing method, we stop adjusting the weights when the increase between the current AUC and the previous AUC is less than a very small value ϵ. However, we adjust all the weights in a WNB simultaneously, unlike the hill climbing method, in which we adjust each weight individually.

We investigate both Monte Carlo and Markov Chain Monte Carlo in a random walk. In the Monte Carlo method, we can try to achieve a higher AUC by adjusting the direction randomly in each step. However, in the Markov Chain Monte Carlo method, we only randomly choose the direction at the beginning. We then adjust the weights in the same direction, as long as the current direction causes the AUC to increase. We readjust the direction only when it does not achieve a higher AUC. Our experiments show that the Markov Chain Monte Carlo method outperforms the Monte Carlo method.

A WNB with Markov Chain Monte Carlo is denoted by WNB-MCMC.

2.4 Combined Methods

In the hill climbing method and the Markov Chain Monte Carlo method, the initial weight vector is $< 1, 1, \cdots, 1 >$. Since the weight vector can be calculated directly by the gain ratio method, we can use it as the initial value, and apply hill climbing or Markov Chain Monte Carlo to search for a better weight vector. Thus, we have two corresponding combined methods: hill climbing with gain ratio, denoted by WNB-G-HC, and Markov Chain Monte Carlo with gain ratio, denoted by WNB-G-MCMC.

3 Experiment

The process of learning a WNB consists of two steps: (1)learning $p(a_i|c)$; (2)learning the weight vector. The first

Table 1. Description of the datasets used in the experiments.

Dataset	# Attributes	# Classes	# examples
Abalone	8	7	4177
Australia	11	2	690
Breast	9	10	683
Cars	6	2	446
Dermatology	33	6	366
Ecolidis	6	2	332
Hepatitis	3	2	320
Importdis	23	2	205
Iris	4	3	150
Lungcancer	56	2	32
Pima	6	2	392
Segment	18	9	2310
Vehicle	18	3	846
Vote	16	2	232

Table 2. Experimental results on the variants of weighted naive Bayes in AUC. In this table, G, HC, MCMC, G-HC and G-MCMC stand for WNB-G, WNB-HC, W-MCMC, WNB-G-HC and WNB-G-MCMC, respectively.

Dataset	G	HC	MCMC	G-HC	G-MCMC
Abalone	98.1±0.04	98.3±0.04	98.0±0.26	98.3±0.05	98.1±0.24
Australia	77.4±0.32	76.9±0.28	76.6±0.42	77.9±0.24	76.7±0.17
Breast	81.9±1.48	80.6±1.70	80.8±1.64	80.7±1.89	81.4±1.69
Cars	91.0±0.48	91.1±0.53	91.1±0.48	91.1±0.59	91.0±0.52
Dermatology	100.0±0.05	99.9±0.04	99.9±0.05	99.9±0.0	100.0±0.05
Ecolidis	99.5±0.12	99.4±0.08	99.4±0.08	99.4±0.08	99.4±0.09
Hepatitis	62.7±0.77	62.7±0.77	62.4±0.92	62.4±0.92	62.3±0.84
Importdis	99.9±0.08	99.9±0.08	100.0±0.05	100.0±0.04	100.0±0.05
Iris	90.9±1.22	90.9±1.22	90.9±1.22	90.9±1.22	90.9±1.22
Lungcancer	71.9±8.41	84.9±3.09	84.9±3.09	84.7±7.34	76.1±4.27
Pima	77.1±0.29	77.1±0.39	76.8±0.44	77.4±0.21	76.9±0.56
Segment	89.4±1.10	91.0±1.03	90.6±1.21	91.1±0.89	90.4±1.19
Vehicle	95.2±0.40	95.5±0.50	96.1±0.30	95.8±0.40	95.9±0.30
Vote	87.9±0.84	87.2±0.44	86.9±0.53	87.7±0.91	87.7±0.46

step is straightforward just as in naive Bayes. In this section, we conduct experiments to investigate the methods for learning the weight vector of a WNB described in Section 2, and each of them corresponds to a variant of WNBs. We also compare them with naive Bayes and the decision tree learning algorithm C4.4 [6], the revised version of the decision tree learning algorithm C4.5 [7] for accurate probability estimation.

All the experiments are based on eight datasets from the UCI repository [5]. Table 1 shows the properties of the datasets. In these datasets, all continuous attributes are discretized using the entropy-based method [2].

Since the Laplace correction used in C4.4 significantly increases the AUC value, we use it in naive Bayes and the five variants of WNBs. Instead of simply estimating $p(a_i|c)$ by the percentage of the number of examples with $A_i = a_i$ among the number of examples in class c, the Laplace correction used in our experiments is:

$$p(a_i|c) = \frac{N_{a_i} + 1}{N_c + k},$$

where N_c is the number of examples in class c, N_{a_i} is the number of examples in class c and with $A_i = a_i$, and k is the number of classes.

For each dataset, we ran all of the five variants of WNBs, naive Bayes (NB in short), and C4.4 with the 5-fold cross-validation 6 times. Our experiments follow the procedure below:

1. For each dataset, discretize the continuous values of the attributes by the entropy-based method [2].

Table 3. Experimental results on naive Bayes and C4.4 in AUC .

Dataset	C4.4	NB
Abalone	75.3±3.43	97.9±0.0
Australia	72.3±0.33	75.7±0.30
Breast	59.0±3.17	80.4±1.66
Cars	86.1±0.99	91.1±0.48
Dermatology	99.6±0.13	99.9±0.0
Ecolidis	97.2±0.48	99.2±0.12
Hepatitis	61.6±1.17	62.7±0.7
Importdis	100.0±0.0	99.5±0.18
Iris	86.2±2.80	90.9±1.22
Lungcancer	78.4±2.28	70.9±4.5
Pima	74.2±0.69	76.8±0.32
Segment	80.7±3.11	88.9±1.19
Vehicle	92.4±0.48	92.0±0.51
Vote	82.8±2.04	86.6±0.34

2. Run each variant of WNBs, naive Bayes, and C4.4 with 5-fold cross-validation, and obtain the accuracy and AUC on the test sets.

3. Repeat step 2 above 6 times and obtain an average accuracy and AUC on the test sets for each variant of WNBs, naive Bayes, and C4.4.

After the experiments, we analyzed the results with ANOVA contrasts by using 90% as the confidence level. We compared the five variants of WNBs with naive Bayes and C4.4 separately. Further more, we also compared the five variants of WNBs each other. The experimental results are shown in Table 2 and 3 (we use two tables due to the space limitation.) The comparisons among all the methods are summarized in Table 4.

Table 4. Summary of the experimental results in AUC. An entry w-t-l means that the algorithm at the corresponding row wins in w datasets, ties in t datasets, and loses in l datasets, compared to the algorithm at the corresponding column.

Variant	C4.4	NB	G	HC	MCMC	G-HC
NB	11-1-2					
G	12-0-2	7-7-0				
HC	13-1-0	7-7-0	3-9-2			
MCMC	12-2-0	6-8-0	3-8-3	1-12-1		
G-HC	12-2-0	9-5-0	5-8-1	1-13-0	4-10-0	
G-MCMC	11-3-0	8-6-0	1-12-1	0-12-2	1-12-1	1-9-4

From Table 4, we can observe four interesting facts. Firstly, all variants of WNBs outperform naive Bayes in terms of AUC. More precisely, all of WNB-G, WNB-HC and WNB-MCMC outperform naive Bayes in 7 datasets and does not lose in any dataset; WNB-G-HC outperforms naive Bayes in 9 datasets and loses in 0 dataset; WNB-G-MCMC outperforms naive Bayes in 8 datasets and lose in 0 dataset.

The second observation is that the combined methods WNB-G-HC and G-MCMC outperform slightly the original methods WNB-G, WNB-HC and WNB-MCMC. We can see that WNB-G-HC performs better than WNB-G (5 wins, 8 ties, 1 loss). It is also slightly better than WNB-HC (1 wins, 13 ties, 0 loss). In addition, compared with naive Bayes, it outperforms naive Bayes (9 wins, 5 ties, 0 loss) in more datasets than WNB-HC (7 wins, 7 ties, 0 loss). If just looking at the values of AUC, WNB-G-HC has higher values of AUC than WNB-HC in 7 datasets. WNB-G-MCMC also performs slightly better than WNB-MCMC. Compared with naive Bayes, it also outperforms naive Bayes (8 wins, 6 ties, 0 loss) in more datasets than WNB-MCMC (6 wins, 8 ties, 0 loss).

Another interesting fact is that both the five variants of WNBs and naive Bayes outperform C4.4 in terms of AUC. All WNBs outperform C4.4 on Most of 14 datasets. Besides WNB-G loses to C4.4 in two datasets, other variants of WNBs don't lose to C4.4. Naive Bayes outperforms C4.4 on 11 out of 14 datasets, ties with C4.4 in one dataset Vehicle, and loses to C4.4 in two datasets. This observation indicates that naive Bayes and its extensions may have better performance than the decision tree algorithm in accurate ranking.

Lastly, WNB-G-HC is the best WNB among the five variants of WNBs, according to the experimental results, although the differences among them are not that big. This observation suggests us that WNB-G-HC is the first choice in practice.

4 Conclusions and Discussions

In this paper, we studied various methods for learning the weight vector in a WNB for accurate ranking. Our experiments show us a few interesting facts illustrated below.

1. WNBs outperform naive Bayes in terms of accurate ranking. Hence it should be used if the goal is to achieve good ranking.

2. Among the WNBs studied in this paper, the hill climbing method with gain ratio is the best one.

3. WNBs and naive Bayes have better performance than the decision tree learning algorithm C4.4 in ranking.

To our knowledge, this paper has two major contributions:

1. Although there are some recent works addressing the issue of learning a WNB in term of accuracy, none of them directly addresses learning a WNB with accurate ranking, measured by AUC. This paper studied systematically various methods for learning a WNB with high AUC.

2. We proposed using gain ratio to calculate the weight of an attribute, which can be combined with other search based methods to achieve better performance. Our experiments show that gain ratio based method (WNB-G-HC) achieves the best performance among the methods studied in this paper.

References

[1] P. Domingos and M. Pazzani. Beyond independence: Conditions for the optimality of the simple Bayesian classifier. *Machine Learning*, 29:103–130, 1997.

[2] U. Fayyad and K. Irani. *Multi-interval discretization of continuous-valued attributes for classification learning.* Proceedings of Thirteenth International Joint Conference on Artificial Intelligence. Morgan Kaufmann, 1993.

[3] N. Friedman, D. Geiger, and M. Goldszmidt. Bayesian network classifiers. *Machine Learning*, 29:131–163, 1997.

[4] C. X. Ling, J. Huang, and H. Zhang. *AUC: a statistically consistent and more discriminating measure than accuracy.* Proceedings of the International Joint Conference on Artificial Intelligence IJCAI03. Morgan Kaufmann, 2003.

[5] C. Merz, P. Murphy, and D. Aha. UCI repository of machine learning databases. 1997.

[6] F. J. Provost and P. Domingos. Tree induction for probability-based ranking. *Machine Learning*, 52(3):199–215, 2003.

[7] J. R. Quinlan. *C4.5: Programs for Machine Learning.* Morgan Kaufmann, San Mateo, CA, 1993.

Learning Rules from Highly Unbalanced Data Sets

Jianping Zhang [1]
AOL, Inc.
44900 Prentice Drive
Dulles, VA 20166
jianpingz032@aol.com

Eric Bloedorn   Lowell Rosen   Daniel Venese
MITRE Corporation
7515 Colshire Drive
McLean, Virginia 22102-750
{bloedorn, lrosen, venese}@mitre.org

Abstract

This paper presents a simple and effective rule learning algorithm for highly unbalanced data sets. By using the small size of the minority class to its advantage this algorithm can conduct an almost exhaustive search for patterns within the known fraudulent cases. This algorithm was designed for and successfully applied to a law enforcement problem, which involves discovering common patterns of fraudulent transactions.

1. Introduction

Most of the standard classification algorithms usually assume that training examples are evenly distributed among different classes. However, as indicated in [1], unbalanced data sets often appear in many practical applications. Studies show that unbalanced class distributions in many applications cause poor performances from standard classification algorithms.

There have been many attempts at dealing with classification of unbalanced data sets. Methods include resizing training sets, adjusting misclassification costs, and recognition-based learning. Resizing training sets is a simple strategy that includes over-sampling minority class examples [2] and down-sizing the majority class [3]. Cost-sensitive classifiers [4] have been developed to handle the problems with different misclassification error costs, but may also be used for unbalanced data sets. Recognition-based learning approaches learn rules from the minority class examples with or without using the examples of the majority class [5].

In this paper, we describe a simple and effective recognition-based rule learning algorithm, RLSD (Rule Learning for Skewed Data), for highly unbalanced data sets. RLSD was developed for a law enforcement problem and achieved encouraging results in a field test. It is currently being transferred for a routine use. The goal of this project is neither to replace human inspectors nor to automate the fraudulent transaction detection process. Instead, it is intended to assists inspectors in identifying potential fraudulent transactions in an operational environment.

2. The Data Mining Task

Application of this algorithm is presented in terms of a hypothetical application for fraud detection. Each transaction in the database has a time stamp and is associated with a person. A person is often involved in more than one transaction. In addition to time and person, each transaction has six other features. One of the six features indicates if the transaction is fraudulent.

While fraud is defined over individual transactions, the aggregation of a person's transactions plays a vital role in identifying him. To prepare the data for mining, we create an example for each transaction. Each example is a vector of 70 attribute values that are mostly numeric. Most attributes are computed from the person's historical transactions during a prior period.

An example is marked as *bad*, if the corresponding transaction was found to be fraudulent. Otherwise, it is marked as *good*. The distribution of examples among these two classes, *bad* and *good*, is highly unbalanced with about 0.01% to 0.05% of all examples belonging to class *bad*.

Unlike many other classification tasks, the discovery of highly accurate rules is improbable due to the insufficient information. Human inspectors may have to pull out thousands of transactions before actually finding a fraudulent one. Human inspectors and the fraudulent detection system complement each other. Rules with 1% classification accuracy can help human inspectors focus on a small set of highly suspicious transactions.

Because of resource limits, the number of transactions that could be pulled out for detailed inspection is restricted by a maximum inspection rate, called inspection budget, for example 2% of all transactions. Under the constraint of the maximum inspection rate, the rules generated cannot be overly general.

3. RLSD Rule Learning Algorithm for Skewed Datasets

We assume that the learning task involves two classes: the minority class P and the majority class N. The goal of RLSD is to learn rules for the minority class. RLSD consists of three

---

[1] The work was done when the author was with MITRE Coporation

571

phases: feature discretization, rule generation, and rule evaluation and selection.

3.1 Feature Discretization

Most of the attributes in our application are numeric. Therefore it is critical to develop an effective and efficient feature discretization algorithm in RLSD. We modified the ChiMerge algorithm [6] for unbalanced data sets. For each numeric attribute, ChiMerge first sorts all training examples according to their values of the attribute. Each pair of neighboring values forms an initial interval. Then, ChiMerge repeatedly merges adjacent intervals with the most similar class distributions until no adjacent intervals have similar class distributions.

ChiMerge does not scale well for a large number of training examples, because it must sort all training examples for every numeric attribute and the number of initial intervals is often very large. We developed a new version of ChiMerge, ChiMerge-RLSD, for unbalanced data sets. In ChiMerge-RLSD, initial intervals are formed based on values of all minority class examples, so it sorts only minority class examples and the number of initial intervals is significantly smaller. Majority class examples are then assigned to one of the initial intervals according to their values. ChiMerge-RLSD scales very well and is thousands of times faster than ChiMerge in our application. ChiMerge-RLSD serves also as a feature selection algorithm, because it ignores the attributes in which class distributions are not significantly different.

3.2 Rule Generation

Rule generation in RLSD is a frequent pattern discovery task and it discovers all frequent patterns of the minority class examples. Each frequent pattern constitutes a minority class rule that covers some minority class examples. The algorithm of rule generation is given in Table 1.

This algorithm conducts a specific-to-general search. For each positive example, an initial rule is created as the example itself. This rule is the most specific rule covering the example. If this rule has already been generated, then it is discarded. Otherwise, the algorithm tries to merge this rule with each of the existing rules to generate more general rules covering this example. This process repeats for each of the positive examples. After all rules are generated, rules with recall less than the minimum recall are removed.

Two rules may be merged to form a new rule if they share some common conditions. The merged rule, which includes all shared conditions, is more general than both rules and covers the examples covered by either of them. It can be shown that the merged rule is the most specific rule covering these examples.

When the number of rules exceeds the maximum number of rules allowed, an existing rule is removed. In the current implementation, a randomly selected rule is removed. The random method works well because many similar rules are generated.

Table 1. Rule Generation Algorithm

P: the set of all positive examples
M: the maximum number of rules allowed
RuleGeneration(P, M)
Rules = empty
For each positive example *p* in *P*
CurrentRule = *p* and mark *CurrentRule* as initial rule
If *CurrentRule* is in *Rules*
For each rule *r* in *Rules*
If *r* is more general than *CurrentRule*
increase #positive-examples covered by *r* by 1
Else
MergeRules(*CurrentRule, Rules, M*)
AddRule(*CurrentRule, Rules, M*)
For each rule *r* in *Rules*
If recall(*r*) < minimum_recall Remove *r*
MergeRules(*cr, Rules, M*)
For each rule *r* in *Rules*
If *r* is more general than *cr*
increase # of positive examples covered by *r* by 1
Else If *r* is more specific than *cr*
If *r* is marked as initial rule
increase # of positive examples covered by *cr* by 1
Else if *r* and *cr* share common conditions
generate a new rule *nr* with all common conditions
AddRule(*nr, Rules, M*)
AddRule(r, Rules, M)
If r is not in *Rules*
Add *r* to *Rules*
If # of rules in *Rules* is larger than *M*
Randomly remove a non-initial rule from *Rules*

3.3 Rule Evaluation And Selection

Rules generated in the rule generation phase are matched against all negative examples in this phase. This algorithm consists of two steps: rule evaluation and rule selection. The rule evaluation step repeatedly matches each rule with each negative example. The rule is removed, should its precision fall below minimum precision. By the end of the process, a subset of rules whose precision are larger than or equal to the minimum precision survives.

The rule selection algorithm is simple and selects rules with the largest F-measure scores. F-measure of a rule r is defined below.

$$F-measure(r) = \frac{\beta^2 + 1}{\dfrac{\beta^2}{recall(r)} + \dfrac{1}{precision(r)}}$$

It selects the rule with the largest F-measure score and then removes the positive examples covered by the selected rule. F-measure scores of the remaining rules are recomputed with the remaining positive examples. It repeats this process until there are no remaining positive examples or no rule that satisfies both minimum precision and recall covers any remaining positive examples.

4. Experiments

We ran experiments on four data sets from the law enforcement application discussed in Section 2. Each of the four data sets consists of the data of three consecutive months for training and the fourth month data for testing. Each of the four training data set contains more than 6 millions transactions which involve more than 600,000 people and each test data set contains more than 2 million transactions with more than 200,000 people. To run experiments in a controlled environment, all training and test examples were generated from transactions that were inspected. This made the distributions of the data sets less skewed than deployment environments. Table 2 shows the summary of the four data sets.

RLSD has three important parameters: β, *minimum recall*, and *minimum precision*. With different values of β, rules are ranked differently. With a high minimum recall, specific rules are pruned to avoid generating rules that overfit the training data. With a high minimum

precision, only accurate rules survive. We ran RLSD with different values of minimum recall and minimum precision. β was set to 2. For comparison, we conducted experiments using a popular decision tree learning system C5.0 with two different strategies for unbalanced data distributions, resizing training data sets and adjusting misclassification costs.

Table 2. Summary of the four experimental data sets

		#bad Exas	#good Exas
Data Set 1	Training	273	68988
	Test	59	24317
Data Set 2	Training	220	73421
	Test	84	26169
Data Set 3	Training	237	67350
	Test	74	25924
Data Set 4	Training	232	68333
	Test	266	38630

Table 3 shows the results with varying values of the minimum recall and precision. The purpose of this experiment is to understand the role of the minimum recall and minimum precision and how recall may be traded for precision. It provides us a base line performance. Results reported in Table 3 are the average on the four data sets. Results in the last four columns are the results on the test sets.

Table 3. RLSD's experimental results with varying minimum recall and precision values

Minimum Recall	Minimum Precision	# of Rules Selected	Recall on Training Set	All Selected Rules		Best Rule	
				Recall	Precision	Recall	Precision
0.01	0.005	48.75	1	0.65	0.0076	0.062	0.048
	0.01	49.75	0.97	0.59	0.0087	0.095	0.041
	0.02	50	0.85	0.38	0.0115	0.057	0.042
	0.03	56.25	0.72	0.26	0.0122	0.050	0.040
	0.04	51.25	0.65	0.19	0.0131	0.035	0.046
0.05	0.005	41.75	1	0.72	0.0072	0.077	0.029
	0.01	43	0.96	0.62	0.0093	0.092	0.037
	0.02	39.75	0.79	0.40	0.0102	0.074	0.042
	0.03	29.25	0.57	0.27	0.0126	0.062	0.041
	0.04	17	0.37	0.15	0.0180	0.048	0.043
0.1	0.005	25.5	1	0.80	0.0068	0.128	0.029
	0.01	28	0.94	0.72	0.0077	0.089	0.025
	0.02	17.75	0.57	0.35	0.0124	0.135	0.030
	0.03	5.75	0.27	0.12	0.0148	0.058	0.024
0.2	0.005	14.5	1	0.91	0.0062	0.236	0.018
	0.01	19.25	0.82	0.70	0.0076	0.238	0.018

When the minimum precision was low (0.005), RLSD was able to find some rule for every fraudulent transaction. With the increase of the minimum precision, the recall on training set decreases quickly. The recall on training set also decreases as the minimum recall increases. No rule was found when the minimum recall and precision were respectively set to 0.1 and 0.04 or 0.2 recall and 0.02. The number of rules selected decreases with the increase of the minimum recall. RLSD may

generate rules that overfit the training data with low minimum recalls and precisions.

When the minimum recall increases, the number of selected rules decreases. This is because when the minimum recall is high, rules with low recalls and high precisions were pruned and RLSD had to select more general rules with a lower precision. The number of selected rules increases with the increase of the minimum precision until a point and then decreases with the increase of the minimum precision. This is due to the fact that when the minimum precision increases, the selected rules become more and more specific and therefore more rules have to be selected to cover fraudulent transactions. When the minimum precision gets too large, only a small number of rules satisfy it so that the number of selected rules starts to drop.

As expected, with the increase of the minimum precision, the recall on test data decreases and the precision increases. The precision increases with the minimum precision because rules with low precision were pruned when the minimum precision was high. When the minimum precision is small, the recall increases and precision decreases with the increase of the minimum recall. When the minimum precision becomes large, the recall starts decreasing and the precision starts increasing with the increase of the minimum recall. The highest precision (0.018) is achieved when the minimum recall is 0.05 and the minimum precision is 0.04 and is 4.5 times better than the random selection (0.0042). When both the minimum recall and precision were small, RLSD selected a large number of highly specific rules and many of these rules overfit the training data and did not cover any fraudulent transactions on test data.

The best rule is the rule with the highest F-measure score on test data. The recall of the best rule increases with the minimum recall with some exceptions and the precision decreases while the minimum recall increases. It seems that the minimum precision itself has little impact on the precision of the best rule. This is not surprising because when the minimum recall is fixed, the best rule is always the rule with the highest precision. The highest precision of the best rule is 0.048, which is about 12 times better than the random selection.

We conducted experiments with C5.0 on the same four data sets using two methods adjusting misclassification cost of minority class examples and downsizing majority class examples.

In our experiment, we set the misclassification cost of minority class examples to 100, 200, 300, and 400 respectively. When the cost was set to 100, no rule was generated for the minority class, so the recall is 0. When the cost was set to 400, all examples were classified as minority class examples, so the recall is 1. When the cost was set to 200 and 300, C5.0 generated a few highly specific rules for the minority class, each of which covers only one minority class example. A default rule was also generated for the minority class. When applying these rules to test data, only the default rule covered some minority class examples.

In downsizing majority class examples, we randomly selected 5%, 3%, 1%, 0.5%, 0.3%, and 0.1% majority class examples. The recall increases and the precision decreases when the percentage of randomly selected majority class examples decreases. With downsizing, C5.0 performed reasonably well. The curves shown in Figure 1 compare C5.0 results with RLSD results. RLSD-

1 represents the results in Table 4 with the minimum recall = 0.01 while RLSD-2 is for the minimum recall = 0.05 in Table 4.

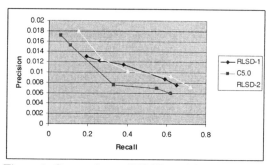

Figure 1. Comparison of RLSD and C5.0

5. Conclusion

We described a novel recognition-based rule learning algorithm, RLSD, for data sets with highly unbalanced class distributions and a law enforcement data mining application. The law enforcement application posed several challenges such as highly unbalanced class distributions, high uncertainty, and inspection budget for exiting data mining tools. RLSD was designed for these challenges and achieved reasonably well results in this application. Despite this application inspiration, RLSD is generic enough to be applied to other applications with similar challenges.

6. References

[1] Japkowicz N. and Stephen, S. (2002). The class imbalance problem: A systematic study. *Intelligent Data Analysis.* 6(5).

[2] Ling, C.X., and Li, C. (1998). Data mining for direct marketing: Problems and solutions. *Proceedings of The Forth ACM SIGKDD International Conference on Knowledge Discovery and Data Mining*, pp. 73-79, New York, NY, AAAI Press.

[3] Kubat, M. & Matwin, S. (1997). Addressing the curse of imbalanced data sets: One-sided sampling. *Proceedings of the Fourteenth International Conference on Machine Learning*, pp. 179-186. Morgan Kaufmann.

[4] Domingos, P. (1999). MetaCost: A general method for making classifiers cost-sensitive. *Proceedings of the fifth ACM SIGKDD International Conference on Knowledge Discovery and Data Mining,* pp. 155-164, San Diego, CA.

[5] Kubat, M., Holte, R., and Matwin, S. (1998). Machine learning for the detection of oil spills in satellite radar images. *Machine Learning* 30, pp.195-215.

[6] Kerber, R. (1992). ChiMerge: Discretization of Numeric Attributes. *Proceedings of the Tenth National Conference on Artificial Interlligence*, pp. 123-128, San Jose, CA.

Relational Peculiarity Oriented Data Mining

Ning Zhong[1], Chunnian Liu[2], Y.Y. Yao[3], Muneaki Ohshima[1], Mingxin Huang[2], Jiajin Huang[2]

[1] Department of Information Engineering, Maebashi Institute of Technology
460-1 Kamisadori-Cho, Maebashi 371-0816, Japan
[2] The Computer Science College, Beijing University of Technology
Multimedia and Intelligent Software Technology Beijing Municipal Key Laboratory
Beijing 100022, China
[3] Department of Computer Science, University of Regina
Regina, Saskatchewan, Canada S4S 0A2

Abstract

Peculiarity rules are a new type of interesting rules which can be discovered by searching the relevance among peculiar data. A main task of mining peculiarity rules is the identification of peculiarity. Traditional methods of finding peculiar data are attribute-based approaches. This paper extends peculiarity oriented mining to relational peculiarity oriented mining. Peculiar data are identified on record level, and peculiar rules are mined and explained in a relational mining framework. The results from preliminary experiments show that relational peculiarity oriented mining is very effective.

1 Introduction

Peculiarity represents a new interpretation of interestingness, an important notion long identified in data mining. Peculiarity may be hidden in a relatively small number of records. Peculiarity oriented mining focuses on some interesting data (peculiar data) in order to find novel and interesting rules (peculiarity rules). Peculiarity rules are new, surprising, interesting patterns, which can be discovered from peculiar data by searching the relevance among peculiar data [11, 12].

Roughly speaking, data are peculiar if they represent cases described by a relatively small number of objects and are very different from other objects in a dataset. Data are usually stored in a relational database. A relational database may consist of many relations/tables. It is a challenge to discover peculiarity rules from multi-relations/tables. Zhong *et al.* used RVER (Reverse Variant Entity-Relationship) model to represent peculiar data and the conceptual relationships among peculiar data discovered from multi-database [12]. The RVER model has been used to mine peculiarity rules in many databases, such as Japan-survey, amino-acid, weather, supermarket, hep-

atitis, fMRI, brain waves and multi-people tracking images [3, 10, 11, 12, 13]. The method to learn peculiarity rules is in fact attribute-value learning. Another type of inductive learning is relational learning, called inductive logic programming (ILP) [6]. ILP is one of the main technologies used in relational data mining. Compared with attribute-value learning methods, ILP has some advantages. ILP can learn knowledge which is more expressive than that of attribute-value learning methods. The former is in predicate logic, whereas the latter is usually in propositional logic. ILP can use background knowledge naturally and effectively. In ILP, examples, background knowledge, learned knowledge are all expressed within the same logic framework. It is natural to use ILP to learn peculiarity rules. Huang and Liu applied relational data mining to peculiarity oriented mining and implemented the PR_MINE system for finding peculiarity rules from multiple relations [2].

A main task of mining peculiarity rules is the identification of peculiar data. Peculiarity can be observed at two levels, the attribute value level, and record level. From the view of database, the world consists of entities and the relations on entities. An entity is a collection of distinguishable real-world objects with common properties. An attribute describes a property of an entity or a relationship. Entities have attributes that describe the entity's characteristics. The attribute-oriented methods focuses on finding peculiar attribute rules. In contrast, record-oriented methods look for surprising, interesting patterns by analyzing the relationship among peculiarity entities. Both levels of peculiarity are useful. A complete model of peculiarity must consider those two levels.

The main objective of this paper is to propose a framework for record-oriented peculiarity analysis. By drawing results from relational mining, we present a model for mining relational peculiarity rules (RPR). The relational peculiarity oriented mining deals with two tasks, namely, description and explanation. A RPR summarizes relationships between peculiarity entities. By mining RPR from multi-database, one also provides explanations of peculiarity in one database from information in other databases. The explanation facility makes the relational peculiarity oriented mining more useful.

2 Peculiarity Oriented Relational Mining Based on ILP

Relational peculiarity rules are discovered from peculiar records. One task of mining relational peculiarity rules is the identification of peculiar records. Peculiar records represent a relatively small number of records and, furthermore, those records are very different from other records in the database.

Relational peculiarity rules mining is multi-database mining. Multi-database mining involves many related topics including interestingness and relevance checking, granular computing, and distributed data mining. Those topics have been considered by many researchers [5, 7]. A key to multi-database mining is to find/build the relevance among different databases. Different databases may use different terminology and conceptual level to define their schemes. Explicit foreign key relationships may not exist among different databases. Granular computing techniques provide a useful tool for solving this problem [8].

2.1 Peculiar Attribute Values and Peculiarity Rules

Zhong *et al.* described an attribute-oriented method that analyzes the peculiarity of data by the *Peculiarity Factor*, $PF(x_{ji})$ [12]. Let a relation A be with attributes a_1, a_2, ..., a_m, and x_{ji} be the value of a_i of the jth record and n be the number of records. The peculiarity of x_{ji} is:

$$PF(x_{ji}) = \sum_{r=1}^{n} D(x_{ji}, x_{jr})^{\beta} \qquad (1)$$

where D denotes the conceptual distance, β is a parameter which can be adjusted by a user, and $\beta = 0.5$ is used as default. Equation (1) evaluates whether x_{ji} has a low frequency and is very different from other value x_{jr}.

According to the PF, we can label the peculiar data in tables and select an attribute as a target attribute to learn why the data is peculiar in the dataset, then we can get peculiarity rules by analyzing the relevance of peculiar data.

The peculiarity factor defined by Eq. (1) focuses on attribute values. It enables us to select one of the attributes of a table as the target attribute, and explain why the data is peculiar in the dataset of the target attribute.

2.2 Peculiar Records and Relational Peculiarity Rules

Peculiarity rules only reflect the peculiarity of attribute of the entity and not show the peculiarity of the entity. The peculiarity of single attribute of an entity does not always represent the peculiarity of the entity. It is necessary to analyze the peculiarity of an entity.

Records are peculiar if they represent a relatively small number of objects and, furthermore, those objects are very different from other objects in a dataset. Relational peculiarity rules are discovered by searching the relevance among peculiar records.

The main task of mining relational peculiarity rules is the identification of peculiar records. There are many ways of finding peculiar records. We describe a method that computes record peculiarity based on the attribute-oriented method.

Let X denote a record set in a relation A, that is, $X = \{X_1, X_2, \ldots, X_n\}$. A record X_j is represented by $\{x_{j1}, x_{j2}, \ldots, x_{ji}, \ldots, x_{jm}\}$, where x_{ji} denotes the value of the X_j on attribute a_i. The peculiarity of X_j can be evaluated by the *Record Peculiarity Factor*, $RPF(X_j)$:

$$RPF(X_j) = \sum_{k=1}^{n} \sqrt{\sum_{i=1}^{m} \alpha_i \times (PF(x_{ji}) - PF(x_{ki}))^2} \qquad (2)$$

where α_i is the weight of attribute a_i which depends on the knowledge provided by a user. $\alpha_i = 1$ is used as default.

Let prior knowledge denote the knowledge provided by a user. In Eq. (2), $D(x_{ri}, x_{ji})$ can be calculated as follows:

(1) a_i is a non-key attribute

- a_i is a numerical attribute and no prior knowledge is available:

$$D(x_{ri}, x_{ji}) = |x_{ri} - x_{ji}|. \qquad (3)$$

It is obvious that the measurement unit of attribute a_i will affect the result of Eq. (3). In turn, the result of Eq. (3) will affect the result of Eq. (2). To avoid the problem, the data can be standardized. Standardizing measurements attempts to make all variables to have equal contribution. To standardize measurements, one choice is to convert the original measurements to unitless variables [1]. Let $a_{1i}, \ldots, a_{ti}$ be t values of a_i, and m_i be that the mean value of a_i. $s_i = \frac{1}{t}(|a_{1i} - m_i| + \cdots + |a_{ti} - m_i|)$, x_{ri} and x_{ji} can be standardized respectively as follows:

$$x'_{ri} = \frac{x_{ri} - m_i}{s_i}, \quad x'_{ji} = \frac{x_{ji} - m_i}{s_i}. \qquad (4)$$

Eq. (3) is transformed into:
$$D(x_{ri}, x_{ji}) = |x'_{ri} - x'_{ji}|. \qquad (5)$$

This method is valid to standardize interval-scaled variables. For other kinds of variables, such as ratio-scaled variables, a new method is needed for standardization.

A difficulty with variable standardization is that we may not have the information of the variable's type. Instead of standardizing variables, we can normalize the peculiarity factor as follow:

$$PF'(x_{ji}) = PF(x_{ji})/ \max_{r=1..n}(PF(x_{jr})). \quad (6)$$

Thus, peculiarity factors of an attribute are normalized to the unit interval [0,1], which are divided by the maximum.

- a_i is a symbolic or continuous attribute and prior knowledge is available. $D(x_{ri}, x_{ji})$ is defined by the prior knowledge.

- a_i is a symbolic attribute (or other type of attribute) and no prior knowledge is available.

$$D(x_{ri}, x_{ji}) = 1. \quad (7)$$

- a_i is a date attribute. $D(x_{ri}, x_{ji})$ denotes the interval between x_{ri} and x_{ji}

(2) a_i is a key attribute

- a_i is a main key of relation A. In this case, a_i is not a factor for the distance because the main key is the identification of a record.

- a_i is a foreign key of relation A. Relation A and relation B are linked by both attribute a_i in A and attribute b_k in B. Let $Y_j = \{y_{j1}, y_{j2}, \ldots, y_{jn}\}$ be the jth record in relation B, where y_{jk} denotes the value of the jth record on attribute b_k in relation B. We have $x_{ji} = y_{jk}$. Thus, we first obtain x'_{ri} by:

$$x'_{ri} = RPF(Y_r) \quad (8)$$

and then the peculiarity of x_{ri} can be computed by:

$$PF(x_{ri}) = PF(x'_{ri}) \quad (9)$$

after replacing the values of a_i by x'_{ri}.

Furthermore, we can set a threshold value to test if peculiar data exist or not:

$$threshold = mean\ of\ RPF(X) +$$
$$\gamma \times standard\ deviation\ of\ RPF(X) \quad (10)$$

where γ can be adjusted by a user and $RPF(X)$ denotes the standard deviation of $RPF(X)$. The threshold indicates that a record is a peculiar one if its RPF value is much larger than the mean of the record peculiar factors. In other words, if $RPF(X_j)$ is over the threshold value, X_j is a peculiar record. By adjusting γ, we can define a suitable threshold value, and $\gamma = 1$ is used as default.

The proposed method can handle both numerical and symbolic attributes based on a unified semantic interpretation. Background knowledge represented by binary neighborhoods can be used to evaluate the peculiarity if such background knowledge is provided by a user. The method can also handle the foreign key attribute, where the attribute is described by another table. A future work is to extend a foreign key attribute into a foreign link so that various related tables can be handled naturally [7].

2.3 Algorithms of Relational Peculiarity Oriented Mining

There are two key steps for relational peculiarity rule mining. One is to find peculiar records and the other is to discover rules. The following Algorithm 1 is first employed to find peculiar records and Algorithm 2 is then employed to generate rules.

Algorithm 1 Finding Peculiar Records

Step 1. Calculate $RPF(X_j)$ for all records in a relation.

Step 2. Calculate the threshold value based on the result obtained in *step 1*.

Step 3. Select the records which is over the threshold value as peculiar records.

Step 4. If the current peculiarity level is enough, then go to *Step 6*.

Step 5. Remove peculiar records from the current records and, thus, we get a new records set. Then, go back to *Step 1*.

Step 6. End.

Algorithm 2 Generating Peculiarity Rules

Step 1. Select a main relation/table as a targeted relation/table and identify other relation/tables related to the main relation/table in a database.

Step 2. Find peculiar records in main relation/table and other relation/tables.

Step 3. Identify the relations/tables related to the main relation/table in a database.

Step 4. Obtain the input document for FOIL through the target predicate and background knowledge.

Step 5. Get the study result by using FOIL.

Step 6. Evaluate the result.

In Steps 4 and 5 of Algorithm 2, we simple use a well-known relational learning algorithm called FOIL [4]. Our main purpose is to apply the relational learning method for relational peculiarity oriented mining.

3 Experimental Results

The relational peculiarity mining algorithms are applied to analyze the China Statistics Yearbook database (www.efair.gov.cn). More specifically, we want to answer the question why sale price of house in Beijing and Shanghai, etc. is different from that in other areas. Since the number of these areas is small, the house price of these areas is peculiar and the entities that describe the sales price of these areas are peculiar entities. It is known that the income of these areas is different from that in other areas and consumption of these areas is also different. Intuitively, it is believed that income determines sales price of house and if the income of one area is high then the price of house is high. If the proposed framework is effective, it should reveal such relational peculiarity rule. Hence, we employ the proposed algorithms to test if the relational peculiarity rule can be found in the Statistics Yearbook database.

In the database, there are 46 relations/tables. Relation *EstatePrice* and *income* are two examples. Relation *EstatePrice* reflects the sale prices of residence, villa, apartment, economic house, office building and business building, and so on, in cities of China. Relation *income* is related to relation *EstatePrice* in aspect of economics. Relation *income* gives the annual income per head of families in various areas. In relation *income*, attribute *disposable* is the disposable income, attribute *nationalcorp* is the income of the state-owned unit employee, etc.

We choose relation *EstatePrice* as the main table and information in relation *income* as background knowledge. According to Eqs. (2) and (10), we can identify peculiar records by Algorithm 1. The discretization and attribute selection are also carried out as steps of preprocessing, respectively [9]. Furthermore, the following rule can be obtained by using Algorithm 2:

$$estateprice\_building(A, B) : -$$
$$income\_nationalcorp(A, B),$$
$$income\_disposal(A, B).$$

We also analyzed the target attribute and peculiarity in related tables respectively. The result is that several interesting rules are obtained. We omit the details on the rules since the space limitation.

The rules indicate that

- If both disposable-income and income of the state-owned unit employee are high in certain area, the price of building of this area is high.

- If fact-income and income of the state-owned unit employee are high in certain area, the price of building of this area is high.

- If income of state-owned unit employee and other income are high, the price of building of this area is high.

We can see that disposable-income, fact-income, and other income are symbols of family income of certain area. The rules verify the notion that if the income of one area is high then the price of house is high.

As expected, the proposed method found relational peculiarity rules. The results, although inconclusive, demonstrate that relational peculiarity oriented mining is potentially useful and effective.

4 Conclusions

There are at least two levels of peculiarity in a database. The attribute value level peculiarity reveals the local characteristics of a record. The record level peculiarity reflects the overall characteristics of a record. Both levels of peculiarity are potentially useful for the understanding of knowledge embedded in a database. Existing methods of peculiarity oriented mining concentrate on the attribute value level. By extending the existing studies, this paper addresses the record level peculiarity mining. A framework of relational peculiarity oriented data mining is proposed, studied and experimentally evaluated. The preliminary results are very encouraging.

Acknowledgements

This work is supported by the NSF of China (69883001), Beijing Municipal NSF (4022003) and Multimedia & Intelligent Software Tech. Beijing Municipal Key Lab Open Foundation.

References

[1] J.W. Han, M. Kamber: *Data Mining Concepts and Techniques*, Morgan Kaufmann (2001).

[2] M.X. Huang, C.N. Liu: Peculiarity Rules Mining using Inductive Logic Programming, *J. Beijing University of Technology*, 29 (2003) 495-499.

[3] M. Ohshima, N. Zhong, Y.Y. Yao, S. Murata: Peculiarity Oriented Analysis in Multi-people Tracking Images, *Proc. PAKDD'04*, LNAI 3056, Springer (2004) 508-518.

[4] J.R. Quinlan, R.M. Cameron-Jones: Induction of Logic Programs: FOIL and Related Systems, *New Generation Computing*, 13 (1995) 287-312.

[5] J.S. Ribeiro, K.A. Kaufman, L. Kerschberg: Knowledge Discovery from Multiple Databases, *Proc. KDD'95* (1995) 240-245.

[6] S. Dzeroski, N. Lavrac (Eds.): *Relational Data Mining*, Springer (2001).

[7] S. Wrobel: An Algorithm for Multi-relational Discovery of Subgroups, *Proc. PKDD'97*, LNAI 1263, Springer (1997) 367-375.

[8] Y.Y. Yao: Granular Computing using Neighborhood Systems, R. Roy et al (Eds.) *Advances in Soft Computing: Eng. Design and Manufacturing* (1999) 539-553.

[9] N. Zhong, A. Skowron: A Rough Sets Based Knowledge Discovery Process, *Inter. J. Applied Mathematics and Computer Science*, 11 (3) (2001) 101-117.

[10] N. Zhong, M. Ohshima, S. Ohsuga: Peculiarity Oriented Mining and Its Application for Knowledge Discovery in Amino-acid Data, *Proc. PAKDD'01*, LNAI 2035, Springer (2001) 260-269.

[11] N. Zhong, Y.Y. Yao, M. Ohshima, S. Ohsuga: Interestingness, Peculiarity, and Multi-Database Mining, *Proc. ICDM'01*, IEEE CS Press (2001) 566-573.

[12] N. Zhong, Y.Y. Yao, M. Ohshima: Peculiarity Oriented Multidatabase Mining, *IEEE TKDE*, 15(4) (2003) 952-960.

[13] N. Zhong, J.L. Wu, A. Nakamaru, M. Ohshima, H. Mizuhara: Peculiarity Oriented fMRI Brain Data Analysis for Studying Human Multi-Perception Mechanism, *Cognitive Systems Research*, 5(3) Elsevier (2004) 241-256.

Invited Talks

Open-Source Search Engines: A Data Mining Platform
  Wray Buntine, Helsinki Institute of Information Technology, Finland

Deception, Distortion, and Discovery: Data Quality in Data Mining
  David Hand, Imperial College, London, UK

Learning to Predict Complex Objects
  Thorsten Joachims, Cornell University, USA

Faster and More Sensitive Homology Search
  Ming Li, University of Waterloo, Canada

Tutorials

10 Data Mining Mistakes—and How to Avoid Them
  John F. Elder IV, Chief Scientist, Elder Research, Inc.

Data Mining in Time Series Databases
  Eamonn Keogh, University of California, Riverside

Algorithmic Excursions in Data Streams
  Sudipto Guha, University of Pennsylvania

Data Grid Management Systems (DGMS)
  Arun swaran Jagatheesan, University of California, San Diego

Workshops

Alternative Techniques for Data Mining and Knowledge Discovery
Organizers: Juan Carlos Cubero, Daniel Sanchez, Z. Ras, and Thomas Sudkamp

Data Mining and the Grid
Organizers: Assaf Schuster and Ran Wolff

Data Mining in Bioinformatics
Organizers: Jiong Yang, Sun Kim, Mehmet M. Dalkilic, and Wei Wang

Foundations of Data Mining
Organizers: T. Y. Lin, Stephen Smale, and Tomaso Poggio

Foundations of Urban Security
Organizer: Paul Cohen

Frequent Itemsets Mining Implementations
Organizers: Roberto Bayardo, Bart Goethals, and Mohammed J. Zaki

Life Sciences Data Mining
Organizers: Chung-Sheng Li and Stephen Wong

Privacy and Security Aspects of Data Mining
Organizers: LiWu Chang, Carlisle Adams, Stan Matwin, and Justin Zhan

Temporal Data Mining: Algorithms, Theory and Applications
Organizers: Sheng Ma, Tao Li, and Charles Perng

Notes

Author Index